NAVIGATOR
BRITAIN
EASY-USE FORMAT

T0304796

www.philips-maps.co.uk

First published in 1994 by Philip's,
a division of Octopus Publishing Group Ltd
www.octopusbooks.co.uk
Carmelite House, 50 Victoria Embankment
London EC4Y 0DZ
An Hachette UK Company
www.hachette.co.uk

Sixth edition 2021
First impression 2021

ISBN 978-1-84907-569-5

Cartography by Philip's
Copyright © 2021 Philip's

This product includes mapping data licensed from Ordnance Survey®, with the permission of the Controller of Her Majesty's Stationery Office. © Crown copyright 2021. All rights reserved. Licence number 100011710

Data for the caravan sites provided by The Camping and Caravanning Club.

Information for the selection of Wildlife Trust nature reserves provided by The Wildlife Trusts.

Information for National Parks, Areas of Outstanding Natural Beauty, National Trails and Country Parks in Wales supplied by the Countryside Council for Wales.

Information for National Parks, Areas of Outstanding Natural Beauty, National Trails and Country Parks in England supplied by Natural England. Data for Regional Parks, Long Distance Footpaths and Country Parks in Scotland provided by Scottish Natural Heritage.

Information for Forest Parks supplied by the Forestry Commission.

Information for the RSPB reserves provided by the RSPB

Gaelic name forms used in the Western Isles provided by Comhairle nan Eilean.

Data for the National Nature Reserves in England provided by Natural England. Data for the National Nature Reserves in Wales provided by Countryside Council for Wales. Darparwyd data'n ymwneud â Gwarchodfeydd Natur Cenedlaethol Cymru gan Gyngor Cefn Gwlad Cymru.

Information on the location of National Nature Reserves in Scotland was provided by Scottish Natural Heritage.

Data for National Scenic Areas in Scotland provided by the Scottish Executive Office. Crown copyright material is reproduced with the permission of the Controller of HMSO and the Queen's Printer for Scotland. Licence number C02W0003960.

Printed in China

*The Daily Telegraph

CONTENTS

II Key to map symbols

III Motorway service areas

IV Restricted motorway junctions

VI Route planning maps

XII Distances and journey times

1 Road maps of Britain

315 Urban approach maps

315 Bristol *approaches*   **320** Glasgow *approaches*   **327** Manchester *approaches*
316 Birmingham *approaches*   **321** Leeds *approaches*   **328** Newcastle *approaches*
318 Cardiff *approaches*   **322** London *approaches*   **329** Nottingham *approaches*
319 Edinburgh *approaches*   **326** Liverpool *approaches*   **330** Sheffield *approaches*

331 Town plans

331 Aberdeen, Aberystwyth, Ashford, Ayr, Bangor
332 Barrow-in-Furness, Bath, Berwick-upon-Tweed, Birmingham, Blackpool
333 Bournemouth, Bradford, Brighton, Bristol, Bury St Edmunds
334 Cambridge, Canterbury, Cardiff, Carlisle, Chelmsford, Cheltenham
335 Chester, Chichester, Colchester, Coventry, Derby, Dorchester
336 Dumfries, Dundee, Durham, Edinburgh, Exeter
337 Fort William, Glasgow, Gloucester, Grimsby, Hanley
338 Harrogate, Holyhead, Hull, Inverness, Ipswich, Kendal
339 King's Lynn, Leeds, Lancaster, Leicester, Lewes
340 London
342 Lincoln, Liverpool, Llandudno, Llanelli, Luton
343 Macclesfield, Manchester, Maidstone, Merthyr Tydfil, Middlesbrough
344 Milton Keynes, Newcastle, Newport, Newquay, Newtown, Northampton
345 Norwich, Nottingham, Oban, Oxford, Perth, Peterborough
346 Plymouth, Poole, Portsmouth, Preston, Reading, St Andrews
347 Salisbury, Scarborough, Shrewsbury, Sheffield, Southampton
348 Southend-on-Sea, Stirling, Stoke, Stratford-upon-Avon, Sunderland, Swansea
349 Swindon, Taunton, Telford, Torquay, Truro, Wick
350 Winchester, Windsor, Wolverhampton, Worcester, Wrexham, York

351 Index to town plans

367 Index to road maps of Britain

Inside back cover: County and unitary authority boundaries

Road map symbols

M25	Motorway
16 17	Motorway junctions – full access, restricted access
	Toll motorway
Pease Pottage Services	Motorway service area
	Motorway under construction
S	Primary route – dual, single carriageway, services – under construction, narrow
Cardiff	Primary destination
25 26	Numbered junctions – full, restricted access
	A road – dual, single carriageway – under construction, narrow
	B road – dual, single carriageway – under construction, narrow
	Minor road – dual, single carriageway
	Drive or track
	Urban side roads
	Roundabout, multi-level junction
2	Distance in miles
	Tunnel
Toll	Toll, steep gradient – points downhill
CLEVELAND WAY	National trail – England and Wales
GREAT GLEN WAY	Long distance footpath – Scotland
YATTON ROPLEY	Railway with station, level crossing, tunnel / Preserved railway with level crossing, station, tunnel / Tramway
	National boundary
	County or unitary authority boundary
	Car ferry, catamaran
	Passenger ferry, catamaran
CALAIS	Ferry destination
	Hovercraft
V P	Internal ferry – car, passenger
✈ ✈	Principal airport, other airport or airfield
MENDIP HILLS	Area of outstanding natural beauty, National Forest – England and Wales, Forest park, National park, National scenic area – Scotland, Regional park
	Woodland
	Beach – sand, shingle
KENNET AND AVON CANAL 6	Navigable river or canal / Lock, flight of locks, canal bridge number
CC CF CS LS	Caravan or camping sites – CCC* Club Site, Ready Camp Site, Camping in the Forest Site – CCC Certificated Site, Listed Site *Categories defined by the Camping and Caravanning Club of Great Britain
☼ P&R ▲965	Viewpoint, park and ride, spot height – in metres / Linear antiquity
29	Adjoining page number
SY 70 / 80	Ordnance Survey National Grid reference – see inside back cover

Road map scale 1: 112 903 • 1cm = 1.13km • 1 inch = 1.78 miles

0 1 2 3 4 5 km
0 1 2 3 miles

Road map scale – Isle of Man and parts of Scotland
1: 225 806 • 1cm = 2.25km • 1 inch = 3.56 miles

0 1 2 3 4 5 6 7 8 9 10 km
0 1 2 3 4 5 6 miles

Tourist information

BYLAND ABBEY	✠	Abbey or priory
WOODHENGE		Ancient monument
SEALIFE CENTRE		Aquarium or dolphinarium
CITY MUSEUM AND ART GALLERY		Art collection or museum
TATE ST IVES		Art gallery
1644	⚔	Battle site and date
ABBOTSBURY SWANNERY		Bird sanctuary or aviary
BAMBURGH CASTLE		Castle
YORK MINSTER	✝	Cathedral
SANDHAM MEMORIAL CHAPEL		Church of interest
SEVEN SISTERS		Country park – England and Wales
LOCHORE MEADOWS		– Scotland
ROYAL BATH & WEST SHOWGROUND		County show ground
MONK PARK FARM		Farm park
HILLIER GARDENS AND ARBORETUM	✿	Garden, arboretum
ST ANDREWS		Golf course – 18-hole
TYNTESFIELD		Historic house
SS GREAT BRITAIN		Historic ship
HATFIELD HOUSE		House and garden
CUMBERLAND PENCIL MUSEUM		Museum
MUSEUM OF DARTMOOR LIFE		– Local
NAT MARITIME MUSEUM	◇	– Maritime or military

Place	Symbol	Description
	⚓	Marina
SILVERSTONE		Motor racing circuit
		Nature reserves
HOLTON HEATH		– National nature reserve
BOYTON MARSHES		– RSPB reserve
DRAYCOTT SLEIGHTS		– Wildlife Trust reserve
	Ⓟ	Picnic area
WEST SOMERSET RAILWAY		Preserved railway
THIRSK		Racecourse
LEAHILL TURRET		Roman antiquity
THRIGBY HALL		Safari park
FREEPORT BRAINTREE		Shopping village
PRINCIPALITY STADIUM		Sports venue
ALTON TOWERS		Theme park
	i	Tourist information
NATIONAL RAILWAY MUSEUM		Transport collection
LEVANT MINE		World heritage site
HELMSLEY	△	Youth hostel
MARWELL		Zoo
SUTTON BANK VISITOR CENTRE	•	Other place
GLENFIDDICH DISTILLERY	✦	of interest

Approach map symbols

M6	Motorway
	Toll motorway
6 5	Motorway junction – full, restricted access
S	Service area
	Under construction
A6	Primary route – dual, single carriageway
S	Service area
	Multi-level junction
	Roundabout
	Under construction
A195	A road – dual, single carriageway
B1288	B road – dual, single carriageway
	Minor road – dual, single carriageway
	Ring road
3	Distance in miles
COSELEY	Railway with station
LOXDALE	Tramway with station
M ⊖ ⊖ ●	Underground or metro station
	Congestion charge area

Motorway service area

Kinross
M9   M90
Stirling
M80   Old Inns   M9
Bothwell   M8   Heart of Scotland
Hamilton
M74
Happendon
Abington
A74(M)
Annandale Water
Gretna Green
Todhills   Washington
Southwaite   Durham
M6   A1(M)
Tebay
Killington Lake   Scotch Corner
Burton-in-Kendal
A1(M)
Lancaster   Wetherby
M55   M6
M65   Hartshead   Leeds Skelton Lake
Blackburn with Darwen   Moor   Ferrybridge
Charnock Richard   M62
Birch   Doncaster North
Rivington   Woolley Edge   M62
Burtonwood   M1   M180
Knutsford   Blyth
M56
Chester   Woodall
Sandbach
Tibshelf
Keele   M1
Stafford Trowell
M6
Telford   Donington Park
M54   Norton Canes   Leicester
Hilton Park   Leicester Forest East   Peterborough
Frankley Tamworth   A1(M)
Corley   M1
M6
Hopwood Park   Watford Gap
Warwick   Northampton
Strensham
M5   Newport Pagnell
M50   M40   M1   Baldock
Ross Spur   Cherwell Valley   M11
Gloucester   Toddington   A1(M)   Birchanger Green
M5   Oxford   M25
Pont Abraham   Michaelwood   South Mimms
Swansea   Beaconsfield   London Gateway
M4   Cardiff   Magor   M4   M25
Sarn Park   Gate   Severn   Membury   M4   Heston   Thurrock
View   Reading
Cardiff West   Gordano   Leigh   Chieveley   Medway
M5   Delamere   Cobham   M2
Sedgemoor   M3   Clacket Lane   Maidstone
Fleet   M25   M20
Bridgwater   Winchester   M23   Stop 24
M5   Taunton Deane   Pease Pottage
Tiverton   M27   Rownhams
Cullompton   M27
Exeter

Restricted motorway junctions

M1 Junction 34

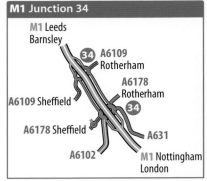

M1 Leeds Barnsley
34 A6109 Rotherham
A6178 Rotherham
A6109 Sheffield
A6178 Sheffield
34
A631
A6102
M1 Nottingham London

M1 Junctions 6, 6A
M25 Junctions 21, 21A

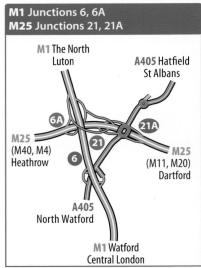

M1 The North Luton
A405 Hatfield St Albans
6A
21A
M25 (M40, M4) Heathrow
21
M25 (M11, M20) Dartford
6
A405 North Watford
M1 Watford Central London

M4 Junctions 25, 25A, 26

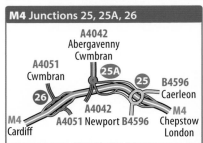

A4042 Abergavenny Cwmbran
A4051 Cwmbran
25A
25
B4596 Caerleon
26
A4042
A4051 Newport B4596
M4 Cardiff
M4 Chepstow London

M5 Junction 11A

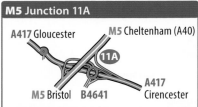

A417 Gloucester
M5 Cheltenham (A40)
11A
M5 Bristol B4641
A417 Cirencester

M8 Junctions 8, 9 · M73 Junctions 1, 2 · M74 Junctions 2A, 3, 3A, 4

M8 9 Glasgow
M73 Stirling
8
A89 Coatbridge
2
A8 M8 Edinburgh
A74 B765 B7058
A74
M73
1/4 B7001
M74 Glasgow
2A 3
M74 3A
A763 B758
A721
M74 Carlisle
B7071

M1	Northbound	Southbound
2	No exit	No access
4	No exit	No access
6A	No exit. Access from M25 only	No access. Exit to M25 only
7	No exit. Access from A414 only	No access. Exit to A414 only
17	No access. Exit to M45 only	No exit. Access from M45 only
19	No exit to A14	No access from A14
21A	No access	No exit
23A		Exit to A42 only
24A	No exit	No access
35A	No access	No exit
43	No access. Exit to M621 only	No exit. Access from M621 only
48	No exit to A1(M) southbound	

M3	Eastbound	Westbound
8	No exit	No access
10	No access	No exit
13	No access to M27 eastbound	
14	No exit	No access

M4	Eastbound	Westbound
1	Exit to A4 eastbound only	Access from A4 westbound only
2	Access from A4 eastbound only	Access to A4 westbound only
21	No exit	No access
23	No access	No exit
25	No exit	No access
25A	No exit	No access
29	No exit	No access
38		No access
39	No exit or access	No exit
41	No access	No exit
41A	No exit	No access
42	Access from A483 only	Exit to A483 only

M5	Northbound	Southbound
10	No exit	No access
11A	No access from A417 eastbound	No exit to A417 westbound

M6	Northbound	Southbound
3A	No access.	No exit. Access from M6 eastbound only
4A	No exit. Access from M42 southbound only	No access. Exit to M42 only
5	No access	No exit
10A	No access. Exit to M54 only	No exit. Access from M54 only
11A	No exit. Access from M6 Toll only	No access. Exit to M6 Toll only
20	No exit to M56 eastbound	No access from M56 westbound
24	No exit	No access
25	No access	No exit
30	No exit. Access from M61 northbound only	No access. Exit to M61 southbound only
31A	No access	No exit
45	No access	No access

M6 Toll	Northbound	Southbound
T1		No exit
T2	No exit, no access	No access
T5	No exit	No access
T7	No access	No exit
T8	No access	No exit

M8	Eastbound	Westbound
6	No exit	No access
6A	No access	No exit
7	No Access	
7A	No exit. Access from A725 northbound only	No access. Exit to A725 southbound only
8	No exit to M73 northbound	No access from M73 southbound
9	No access	No exit
13	No exit southbound	Access from M73 southbound only
14	No access	No exit
16	No exit	No access
17	No exit	
18		No exit
19	No exit to A814 eastbound	No access from A814 westbound
20	No exit	No access
21	No access from M74	No exit
22	No exit. Access from M77 only	No access. Exit to M77 only
23	No exit	No access
25	Exit to A739 northbound only. Access from A739 southbound only	
25A	No exit	No access
28	No exit	No access
28A	No exit	No access
29A	No exit	No access

M9	Eastbound	Westbound
2	No access	No exit
3	No exit	No access
6	No access	No exit
8	No exit	No access

M11	Northbound	Southbound
4	No exit	No access
5	No access	No exit
8A	No access	No exit
9	No access	No exit
13	No access	No exit
14	No exit to A428 westbound	No exit. Access from A14 westbound only

M20	Eastbound	Westbound
2	No access	No access
3	No exit. Access from M26 eastbound only	No access. Exit to M26 westbound only
10	No access	No exit
11A	No access	No exit

M23	Northbound	Southbound
7	No exit to A23 southbound	No access from A23 northbound
10A	No exit	No access

M25	Clockwise	Anticlockwise
5	No exit to M26 eastbound	No access from M26 westbound
19	No access	No exit
21	No exit to M1 southbound. Access from M1 southbound only	No exit to M1 southbound. Access from M1 southbound only
31	No exit	No access

M27	Eastbound	Westbound
10	No exit	No access
12	No access	No exit

M40	Eastbound	Westbound
3	No exit	No access
7	No exit	No access
8	No exit	No access
13	No exit	No access
14	No access	No exit
16	No access	No exit

M42	Northbound	Southbound
1	No exit	No access
7	No access. Exit to M6 northbound only	No exit. Access from M6 northbound only
7A	No access. Exit to M6 southbound only	No exit
8	No exit. Access from M6 southbound only	Exit to M6 northbound only. Access from M6 southbound only

M45	Eastbound	Westbound
M1 J17	Access to M1 southbound only	No access from M1 southbound
With A45	No access	No exit

M48	Eastbound	Westbound
M4 J21	No exit to M4 westbound	No access from M4 eastbound
M4 J23	No access from M4 westbound	No exit to M4 eastbound

M49	Southbound	Northbound
18A	No exit to M5 northbound	No access from M5 southbound

M53	Northbound	Southbound
11	Exit to M56 eastbound only. Access from M56 westbound only	Exit to M56 eastbnd only. Access from M56 westbound only

M56	Eastbound	Westbound
2	No exit	No access
3	No access	No exit
4	No exit	No access
7		No access
8	No exit or access	No exit
9	No access from M6 northbound	No access to M6 southbound
15	No exit to M53	No access from M53 northbound

M57	Northbound	Southbound
3	No exit	No access
5	No exit	No access

M58	Eastbound	Westbound
1	No exit	No access

M60	Clockwise	Anticlockwise
2	No exit	No access
3	No exit to A34 northbound	No exit to A34 northbound
4	No access from M56	No exit to M56
5	No exit to A5103 southbound	No exit to A5103 northbound
14	No exit	No access
16	No exit	No access
20	No access	No exit
22		No access
25	No access	
26		No exit or access
27	No exit	No access

M61	Northbound	Southbound
2	No access from A580 eastbound	No exit to A580 westbound
3	No access from A580 eastbound. No access from A666 southbound	No exit to A580 westbound
M6 J30	No exit to M6 southbound	No access from M6 northbound

M62	Eastbound	Westbound
23	No access	No exit

M65	Eastbound	Westbound
9	No access	No exit
11	No access	No exit

M66	Northbound	Southbound
1	No access	No exit

M67	Eastbound	Westbound
1A	No access	No exit
2	No exit	No access

M69	Northbound	Southbound
2	No exit	No access

M73	Northbound	Southbound
2	No access from M8 eastbound	No exit to M8 westbound

M74	Northbound	Southbound
3	No access	No exit
3A	No exit	No access
7	No exit	No access
9	No exit or access	
10		No exit
11	No exit	No access
12	No access	No access

M77	Northbound	Southbound
4	No exit	No access
6	No exit	No access
7	No exit	
8	No access	No access

M80	Northbound	Southbound
4A	No access	No exit
6A	No exit	No access
8	Exit to M876 northbound only. No access	Access from M876 southbound only. No exit

M90	Northbound	Southbound
1	Access from A90 northbound only	No access. Exit to A90 southbound only
2A	No access	No exit
7	No exit	No access
8	No access	No exit
10	No access from A912	No exit to A912

M180	Eastbound	Westbound
1	No access	No exit

M621	Eastbound	Westbound
2A	No exit	No access
4	No exit	
5	No exit	No access
6	No access	No exit

M876	Northbound	Southbound
2	No access	No exit

A1(M)	Northbound	Southbound
2	No access	No exit
3		No access
5	No exit	No exit, no access
14	No exit	No access
40	No access	No access
43	No exit. Access from M1 only	No access. Exit to M1 only
57	No access	No access
65	No access	No access

A3(M)	Northbound	Southbound
1	No exit	No access
4	No access	No exit

A38(M) with Victoria Rd, (Park Circus) Birmingham	
Northbound	No exit
Southbound	No access

A48(M)	Northbound	Southbound
M4 Junc 29	Exit to M4 eastbound only	Access from M4 westbound only
29A	Access from A48 eastbound only	Exit to A48 westbound only

A57(M)	Eastbound	Westbound
With A5103	No access	No exit
With A34	No access	No exit

A58(M)		Southbound
With Park Lane and Westgate, Leeds		No access

A64(M)	Eastbound	Westbound
With A58 Clay Pit Lane, Leeds	No access from A58	No exit to A58

A74(M)	Northbound	Southbound
18	No access	No exit
22		No exit to A75

A194(M)	Northbound	Southbound
A1(M) J65 Gateshead Western Bypass	Access from A1(M) northbound only	Exit to A1(M) southbound only

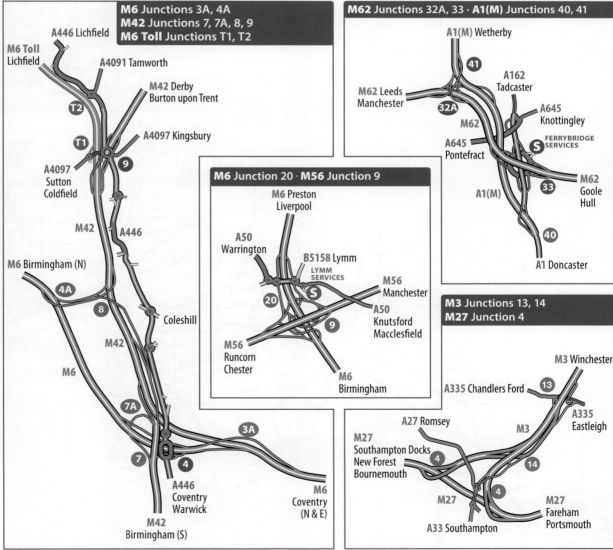

M6 Junctions 3A, 4A
M42 Junctions 7, 7A, 8, 9
M6 Toll Junctions T1, T2

M6 Toll Lichfield
A446 Lichfield
A4091 Tamworth
M42 Derby Burton upon Trent
A4097 Kingsbury
T2
9
A4097 Sutton Coldfield
T1
M42
A446
M6 Birmingham (N)
4A
8
Coleshill
M42
7A
M6
3A
7
4
A446 Coventry Warwick
M6 Coventry (N & E)
M42 Birmingham (S)

M62 Junctions 32A, 33 · A1(M) Junctions 40, 41

A1(M) Wetherby
41
A162 Tadcaster
M62 Leeds Manchester
32A
M62
A645 Knottingley
A645 Pontefract
FERRYBRIDGE SERVICES
S
A1(M)
33
M62 Goole Hull
40
A1 Doncaster

M6 Junction 20 · M56 Junction 9

M6 Preston Liverpool
A50 Warrington
B5158 Lymm
LYMM SERVICES
S
20
M56 Manchester
A50 Knutsford Macclesfield
9
M56 Runcorn Chester
M6 Birmingham

M3 Junctions 13, 14
M27 Junction 4

M3 Winchester
A335 Chandlers Ford
13
A335 Eastleigh
A27 Romsey
M3
M27 Southampton Docks New Forest Bournemouth
4
14
4
M27
A33 Southampton
M27 Fareham Portsmouth

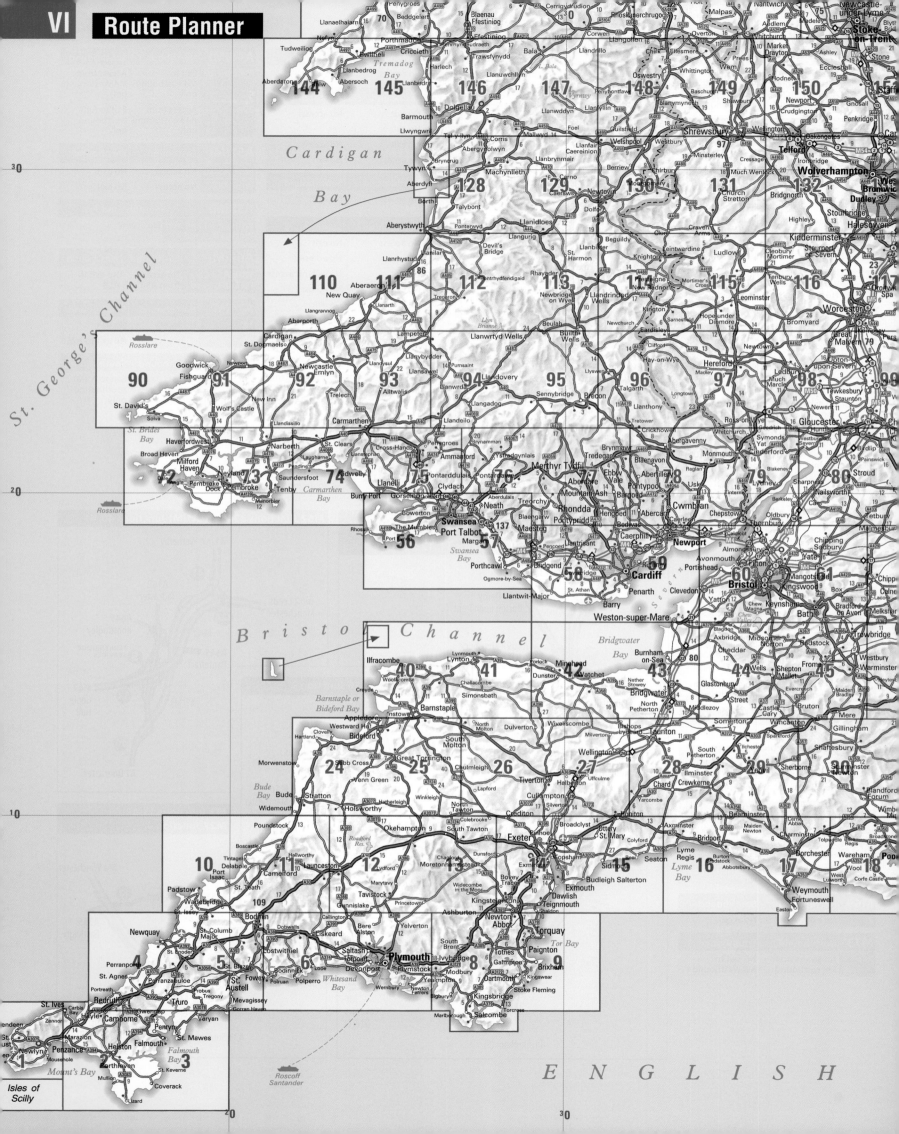

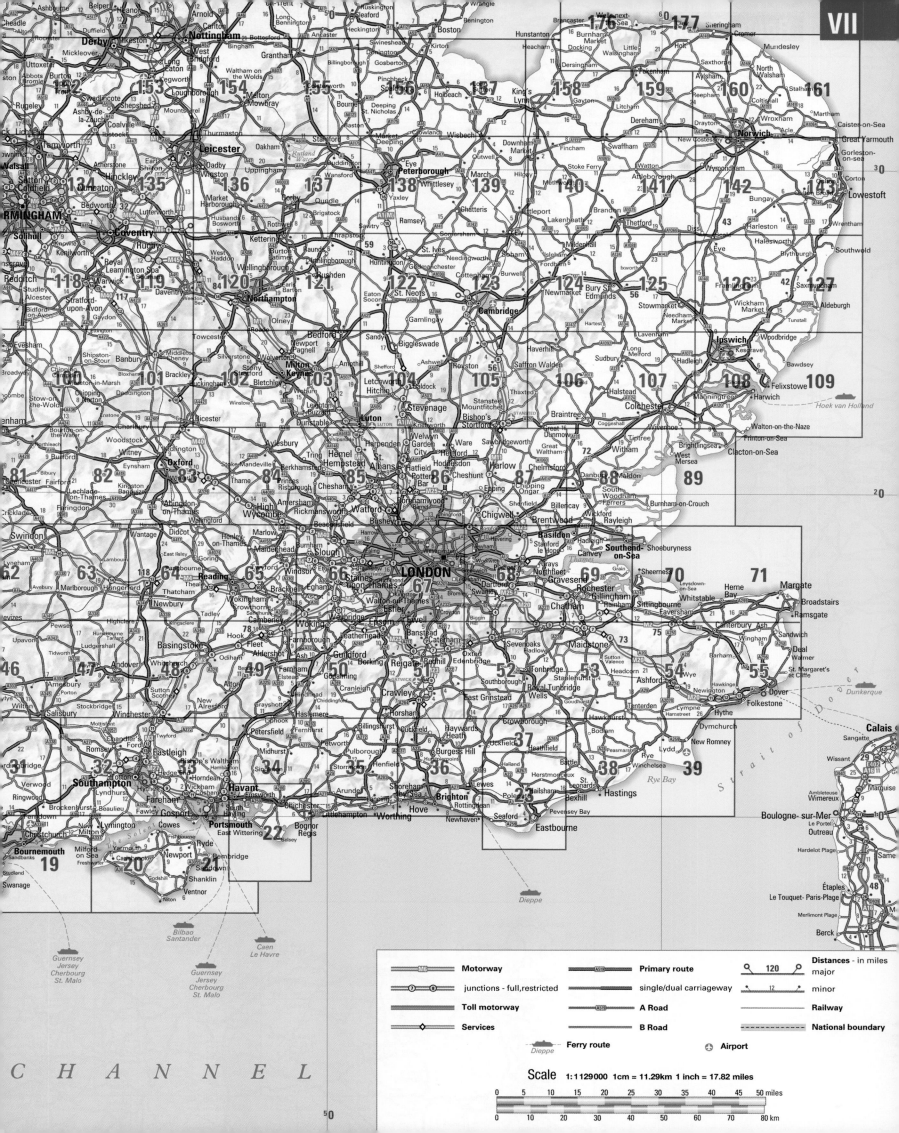

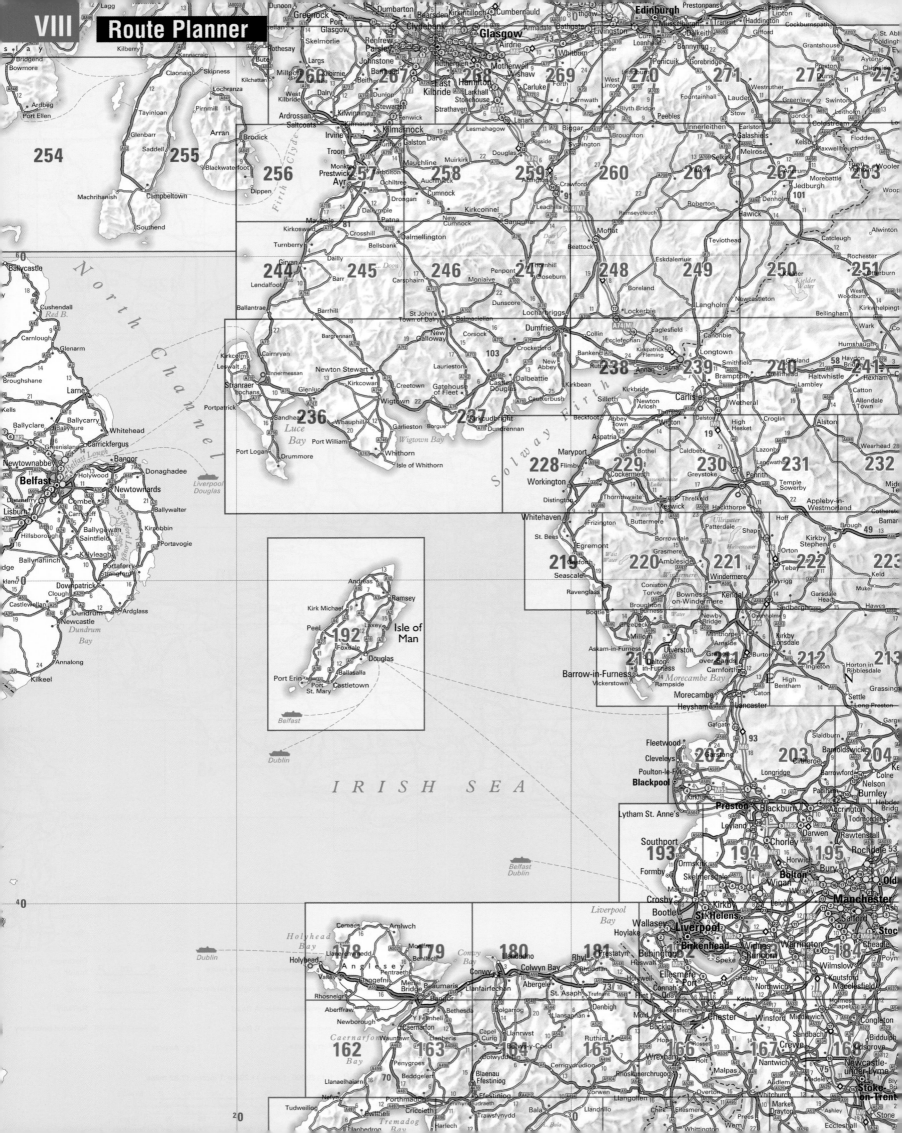

Distances and journey times

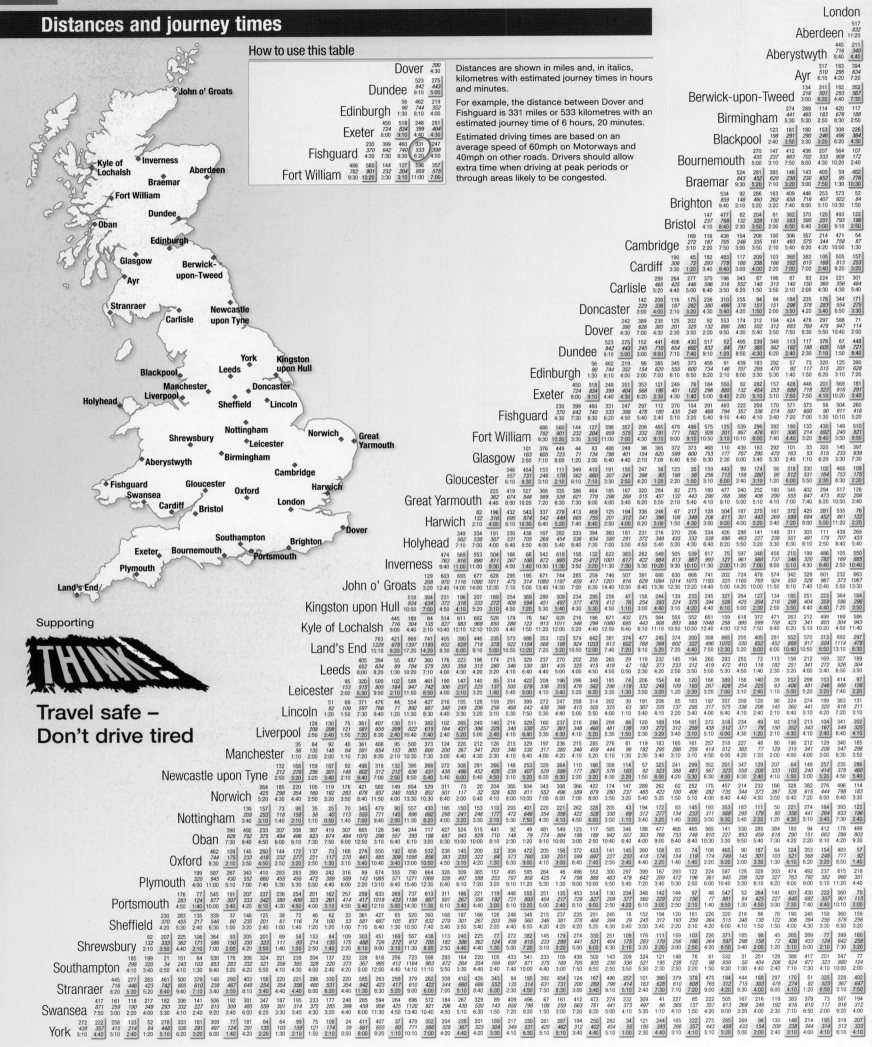

How to use this table

Distances are shown in miles and, in italics, kilometres with estimated journey times in hours and minutes.

For example, the distance between Dover and Fishguard is 331 miles or 533 kilometres with an estimated journey time of 6 hours, 20 minutes.

Estimated driving times are based on an average speed of 60mph on Motorways and 40mph on other roads. Drivers should allow extra time when driving at peak periods or through areas likely to be congested.

Supporting

THINK!

Travel safe – Don't drive tired

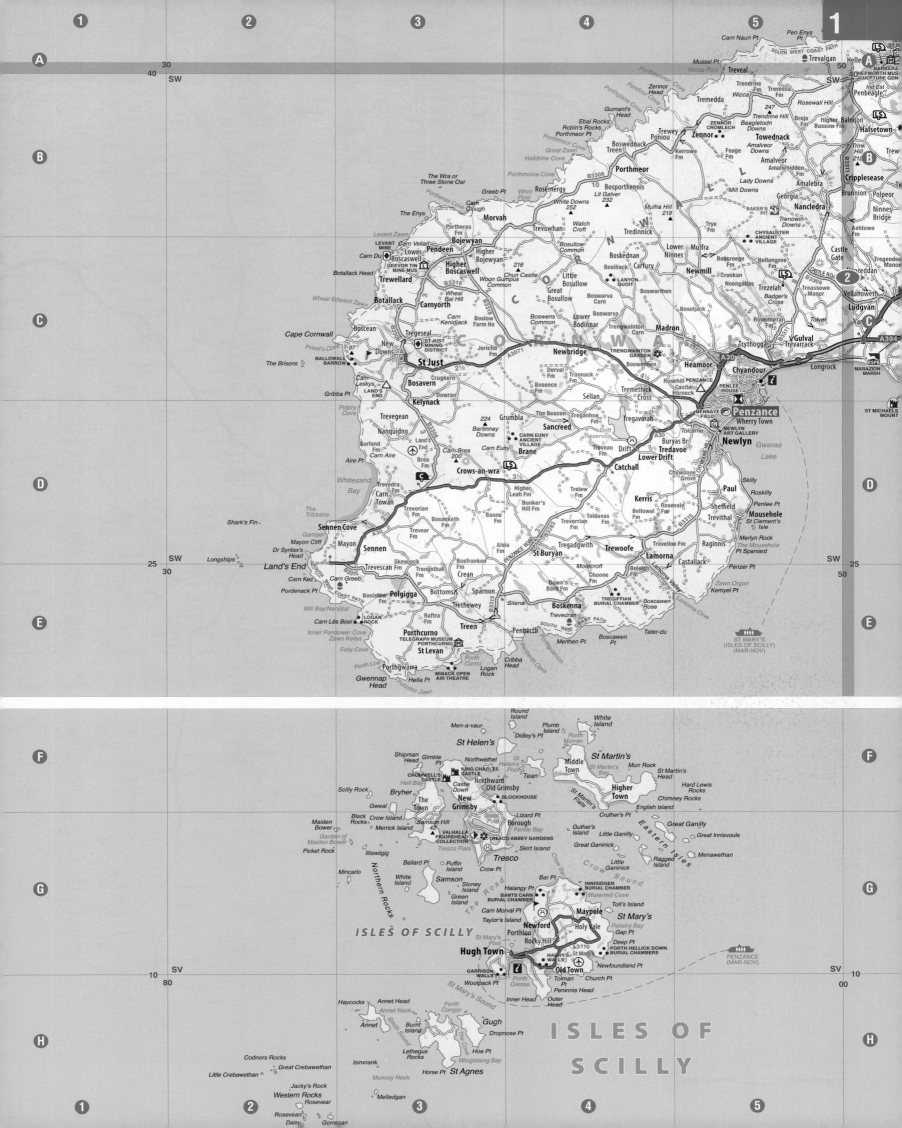

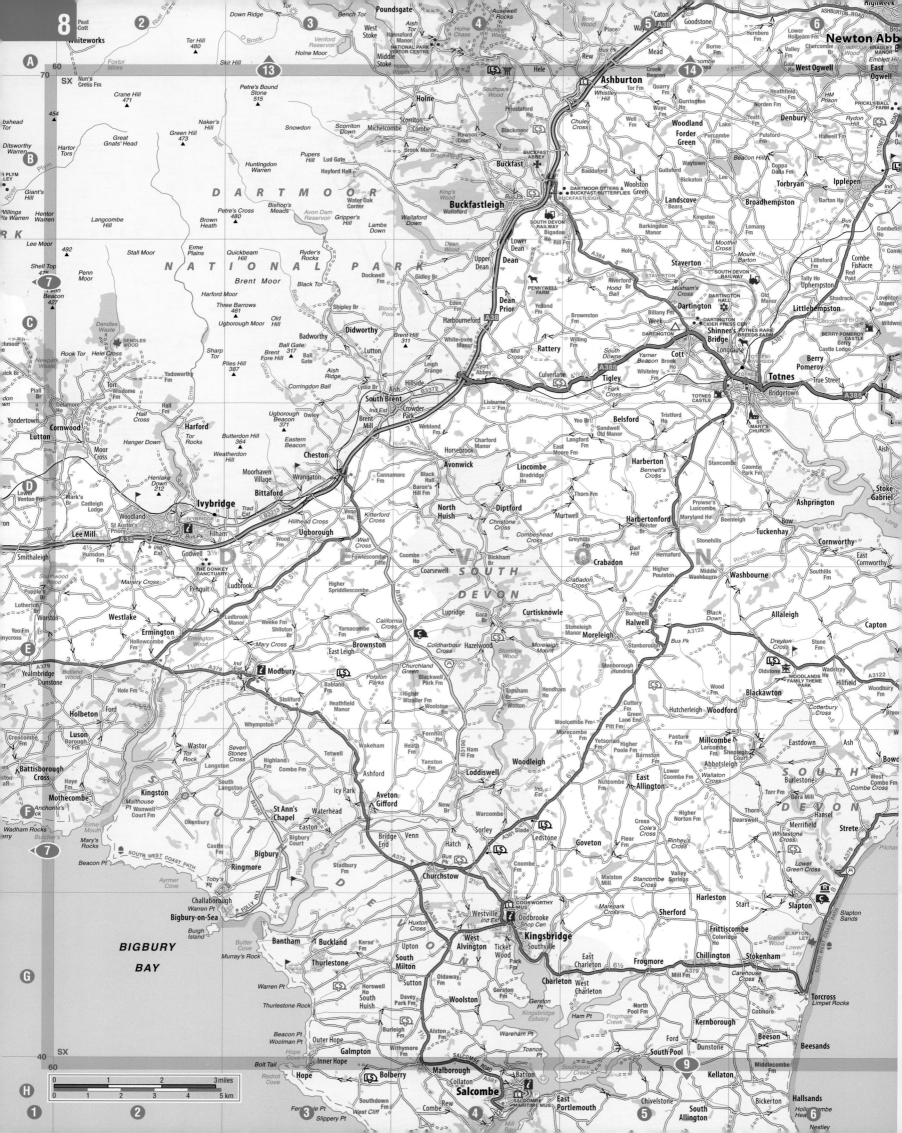

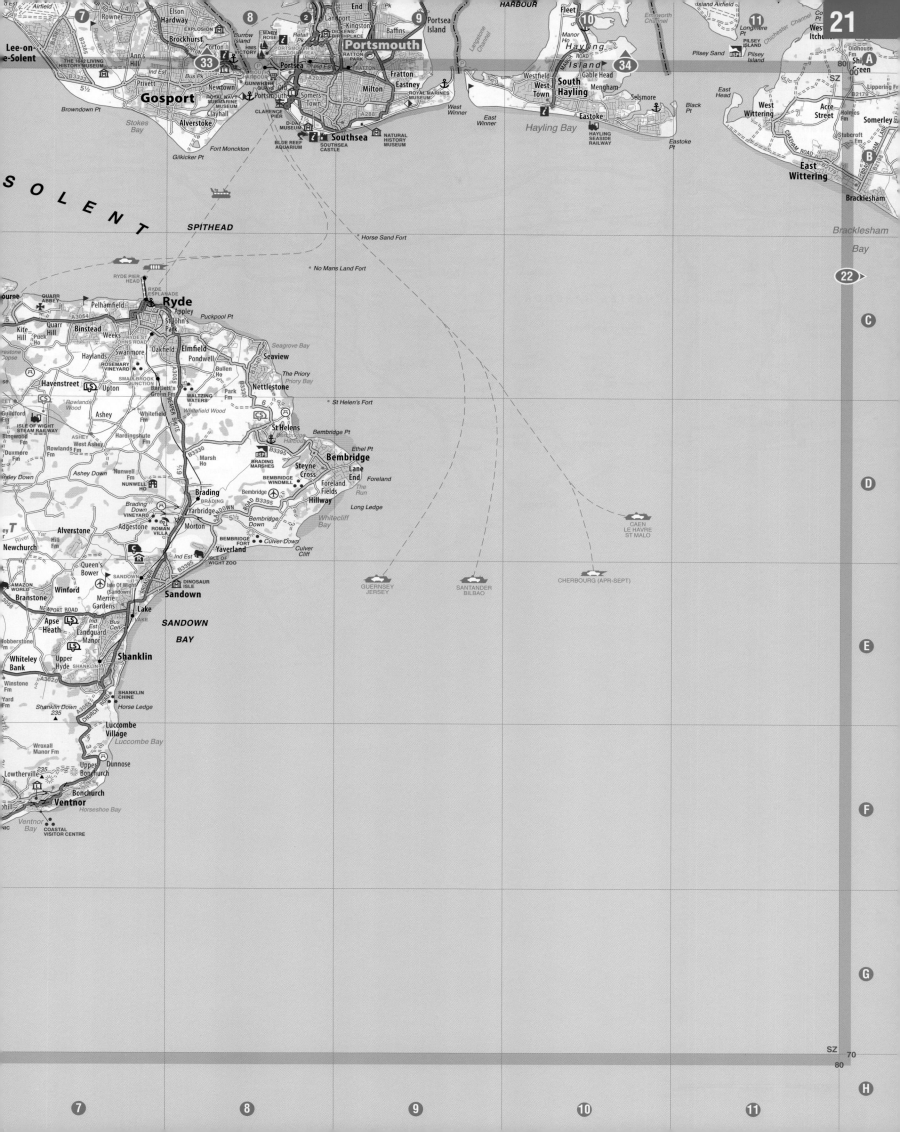

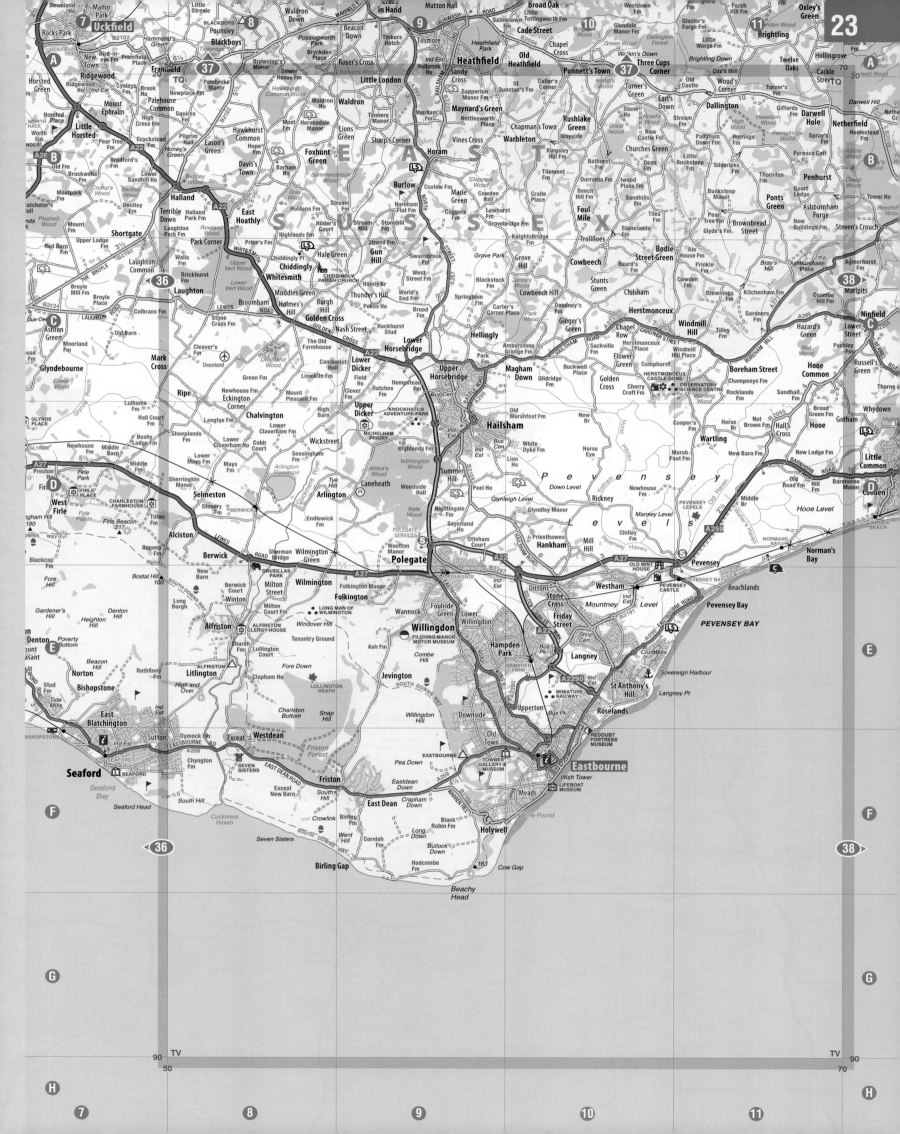

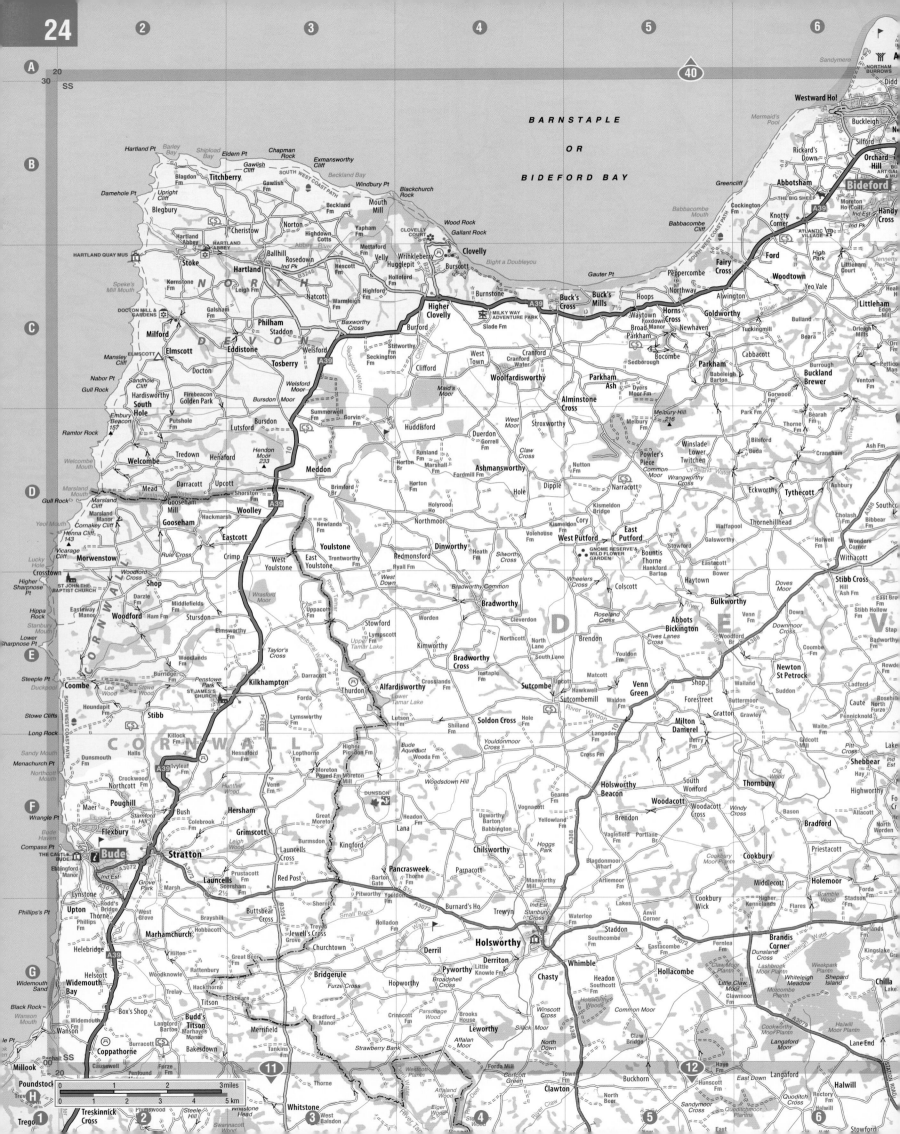

Lundy

Hen &
Chickens
Seals' Rock
North
West Pt
North
East Pt
Gannets' Rock
Gannets' Bay

St James's
Stone
Tibbetts
Hill
138
LUNDY MARINE
NATURE
RESERVE
Tibbett's Pt
Jenny's
Cove

Dead Cow
Pt
Ackland's
Moor
142
Lundy
Roads
BIDEFORD
(APRIL-OCT)
ILFRACOMBE
(APRIL-OCT)

Halftide
Rock
Beacon
Hill
Rat Island
Castle
Hill
Surf Pt

South West
Pt

LUNDY
(ARPIL-OCT)
Capstone Pt
Samson's Bay
Water
Mouth
WATERMOUTH
CASTLE
Rawn's Rocks
Blackstone
Elwill Bay
Trentishoe
High

Ilfracombe
Hele Bay
Hele
HELE
CORN MILL
Hole Fm
Hole
Goosewell
Hangman Pt
Little
Hangman
218
Gt Hangman
318
SOUTH WEST COAST PATH
South
Dean Fm
Holdstone
Down
349

Bull Pt
Pensport
Rock
Shag Pt
Flat Pt
MUSEUM
Chambercombe
CHAMBERCOMBE
MANOR
Berrynarbor
Lee
Lester Cliff
Girt Fm
Girt Down
Trentishoe
Down
Holdstone
Fm
Trentishoe
Manor
Walner
Fm
Tattiscombe

Lee
Lincombe
Higher
Slade
Kitstone
Hill
Warmscombe
Fm
NORTH DEVON
Sterridge
Combe Martin
Knap Down
Verwill
Fm
Stony
Corner
Dean

Rockham Bay
North
Merle Fm
Higher
Warcombe
Whitestone
Lower
Slade
Slade
Resrvr
Oakridge
Fm
Two
Pots
Ruggaton
Fm
Bowden
Fm
Smythen
Fm
Stoneditch
Hill
Henstridge
Nutcombe
Fm
WESTLEIGH
Truckham
Fm
Cowley
Wood

Morte Pt
Mortehoe
Mill Rock
Borough
Cross
Little
Shelfin Fm
B3343
Ind
Est
A3123
Hore Down
Stapleton
Fm
Berry
Down
WILDLIFE &
DINOSAUR PARK
LONG
South
Ley
LANE
Kentisbury

Grunta Pool
Higher
Warcombe
Manor Fm
Trimstone
Willingcott
Cheglinch
Dean
Berry Down
Cross
Outer Narracott
Fm
Cleave Fm
Highlands
Fm
Bugford
Stonecombe
Higher
Week Fm
Preston
Ho
Kentisbury
Down

Woolacombe
Ossaborough
Ivycott
Bradwell
Dean
Cross
Higher
Aylescott
Fullabrook
Bittadon
Hillcrest
Fm
Century
Fm
Collacott
Fm
Dingles
Fm
Wigmore
Fm
Clifton
Patchole
Northcote Fm
Kentisbury
Ford
Halls
Cross
Hallsdown
Bridwick

Morte
Bay
Black Rock
Putsborough
Sand
Pickwell
Down
Spreacombe
Manor
North
Downs
West
Down
Fullabrook
Burland
Fm
Little
Silver
Hewish
Fm
Bowden
Corner
Ford
Fm
East Down
Arlington
Beccott
Huckaby
Fm
Besshill

Baggy Pt
SOUTH WEST COAST PATH
Vention
Putsborough
Pickwell
Castle
Street Fm
Buckland
Down
Stoneyard
Wood
Fullabrook Down
Metcombe
Down
Whitefield
Down
Okewill
Cross
Garman's
Fm
Churchill
Churchill
Down
Arlington
ARLINGTON
COURT
Arlington
Court
White
Cawsey
Tidicombe
Rye
Park

Croyde Bay
Ora Hill
Fm
Georgeham
North
Buckland
Winsham
Down Ho
Halsinger
Down
Beara
Down
Patsford
Swindon
Down
Milltown
Viveham
Fm
Woolley
Fm
South
Woolley Fm
Deerpark
Wood
Huckaby
Fm

Croyde Bay
Croyde
Forda
Cross
Darracott
Upcott
Incledon
Fm
Halsinger
Winsham
Beara
Middle
Marwood
Gipsy
Corner
Whiddon
Crockers
Plaistow
Barton
The
Warren
Chilbridge
Loxhore
Loxhore
Cott

Saunton
Sands
CROYDE ROAD
SAUNTON
ROAD 4½
B3231
Lobb
Buckland
Manor
Knowle
Boode
Beara
Marwood
Higher
Muddiford
Plaistow
Mill
Muddiford
Guineaford
Shirwell
Cross
Shirwell
Lower
Loxhore

Saunton
Sandy Lane
Fm
Shop Cen
Braunton
Pippacott
Luscott
Barton
Whitehall
MARWOOD
HILL
Marwood
Kingsheanton
Prixford
BROOMHILL
SCULPTURE
GARDENS
Varley
Fm
South Hill
Waytown
Sepscott
Fm
Youlston
Wood
Bratton
Fleming

NORTH
DEVON
SOUTH WEST COAST PATH
Braunton
Down
Knowl
Water
Heanton
Punchardon
West
Ashford
Mainstone
Springfield
Cross
Brightlycott
Chelfham
Horridge
Bratton
Cross
Birch

Braunton
Burrows
Braunton
Marsh
Velator
Wrafton
Ashford
A361
Burridge
Kingdom's
Gardens
Hakeford
Stoke Rivers

Horsey
Island
Chivenor
Chivenor
Penhill Pt
Allen's
Rock
Penhill
SOUTH WEST COAST PATH
River Taw
Bradiford
Pilton
Pottington
Ind Est
Raleigh
Pitt
Fm
Snapper
Northleigh
Goodleigh
Middle
Dean Fm
Hutcherton
Down
Stone
Cross

Airy Pt
Danger area
Saltpill
Duck Pond
Penhill
CHAPEL & MUSEUM
ST ANNE'S
Barnstaple
MUSEUM OF BARNSTAPLE &
NORTH DEVON
Derby
Bus
Sta
Youlden
Fm
Coombe Willesleigh
Fm
Dean
Head
Gunn

LUNDY
(APRIL-OCT)
Broad Sands
Lower
Yelland
BICKINGTON ROAD
Muddlebridge
Sticklepath
BARNSTAPLE
Ind Est
Newport
P&R
Portmor
Westacott
East Acland
Birch
Accott

Crow
Rock
Instow
Sands
Yelland
B3233
Fremington
Combrew
Bickington
Ind Est
Lake
A361
Landkey
Landkey
Newland
Swimbridge
Newland
Harford
Sandick
Cross
Hurscott

Sandymere
NORTHAM
BURROWS
N DEVON
MARITIME MUSEUM
Appledore
The Quay
Worlington
Bickleton
Brynsworthy
Roundswell
A39
Rumsam
Swimbridge
Yeoland
Riverton
Yarnacott
High
Down

Diddywell
24
Instow
Fullingford
Fm
Collacott
Fm
Hollamoor
Clump
Eastacombe
Bishops
Tawton
Bydown
Ho
Lane
End Fm

Westleigh
Northam
Silford
Huish
St John's
Chapel
Stonyland
Prospect
Corner
Tawstock
25
Downrew
Ho
Horswell
Hannaford
Swimbridge
Kerscott

Rickard's
Horwood
Holmacott
Eastleigh
Manor
Harepie
Uppacott
Summer

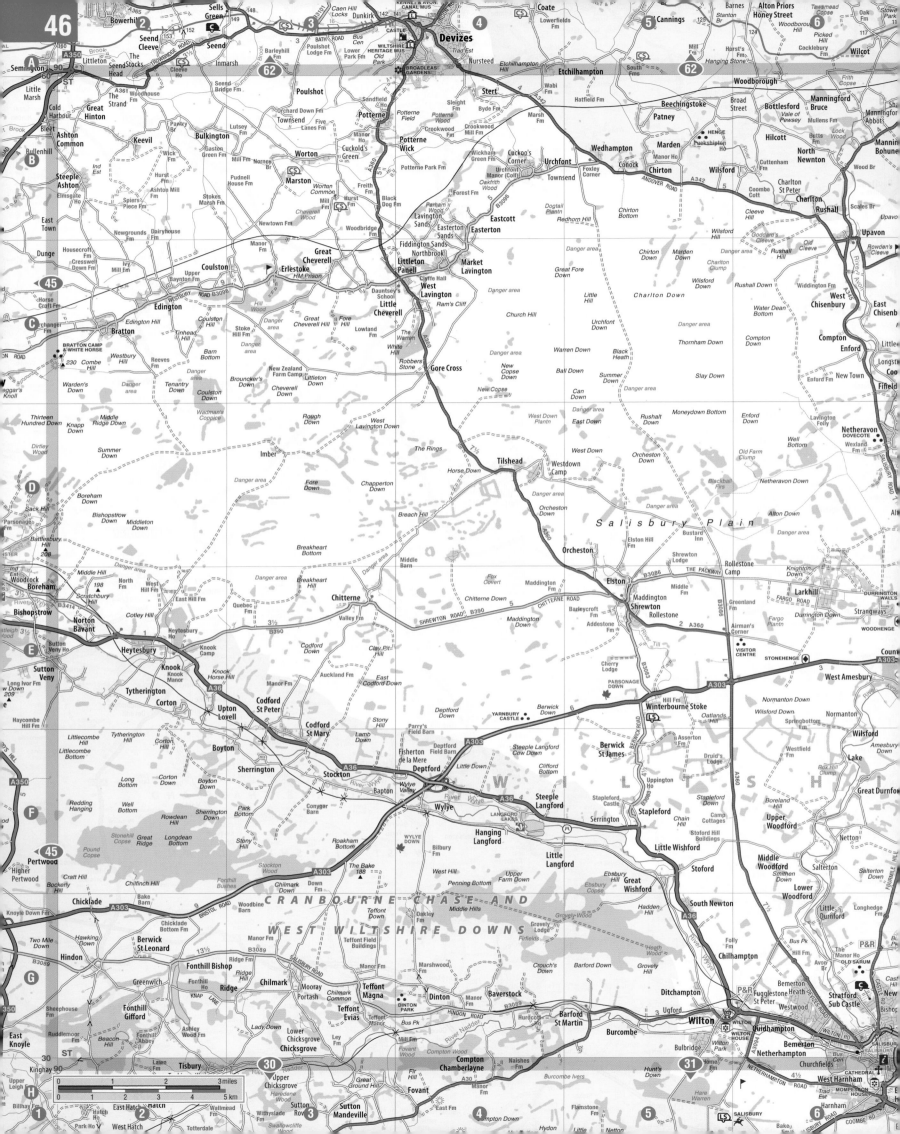

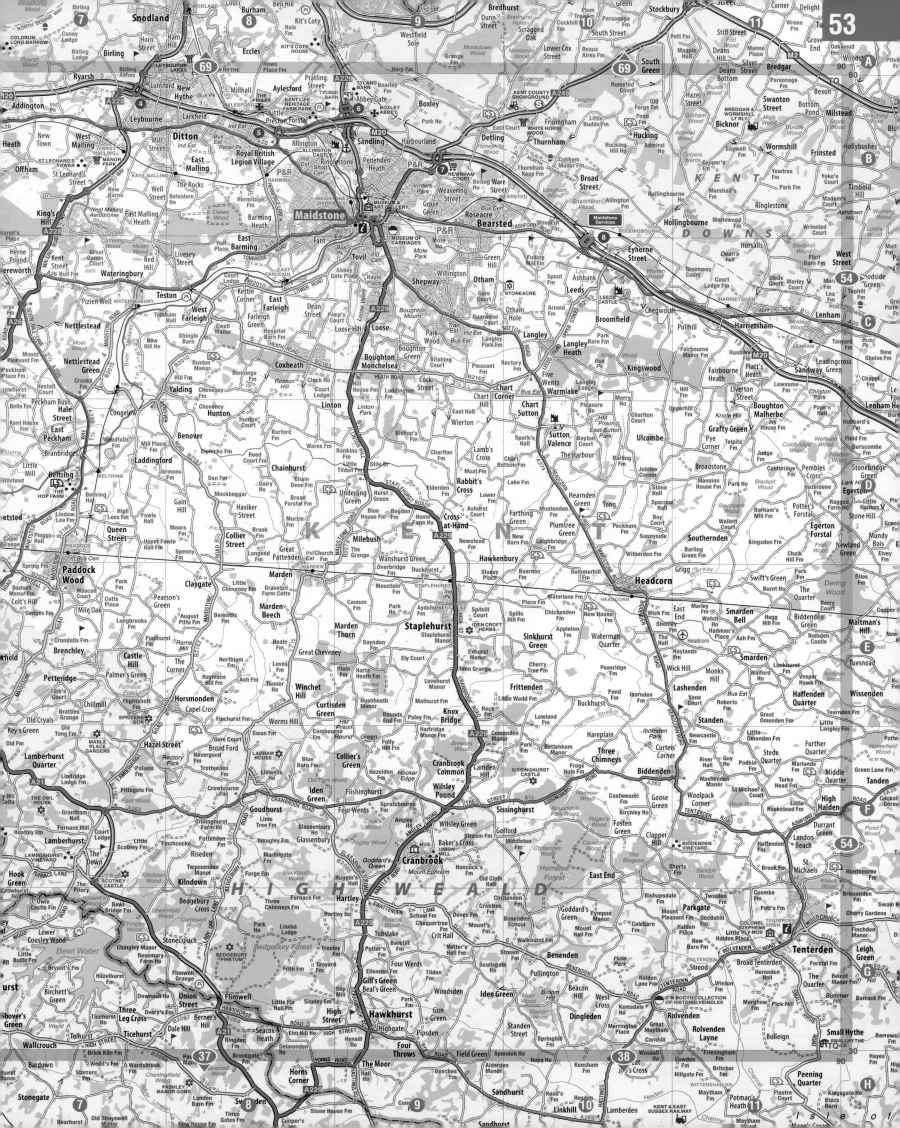

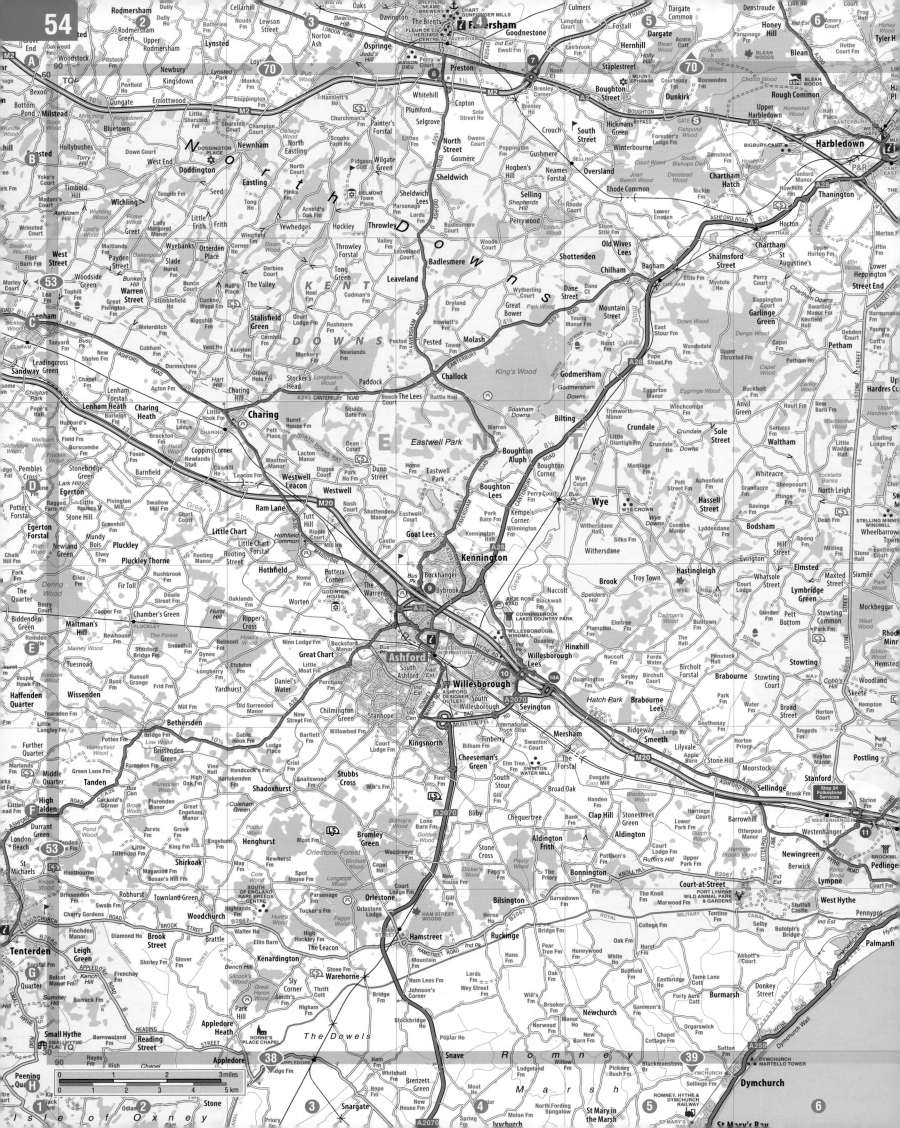

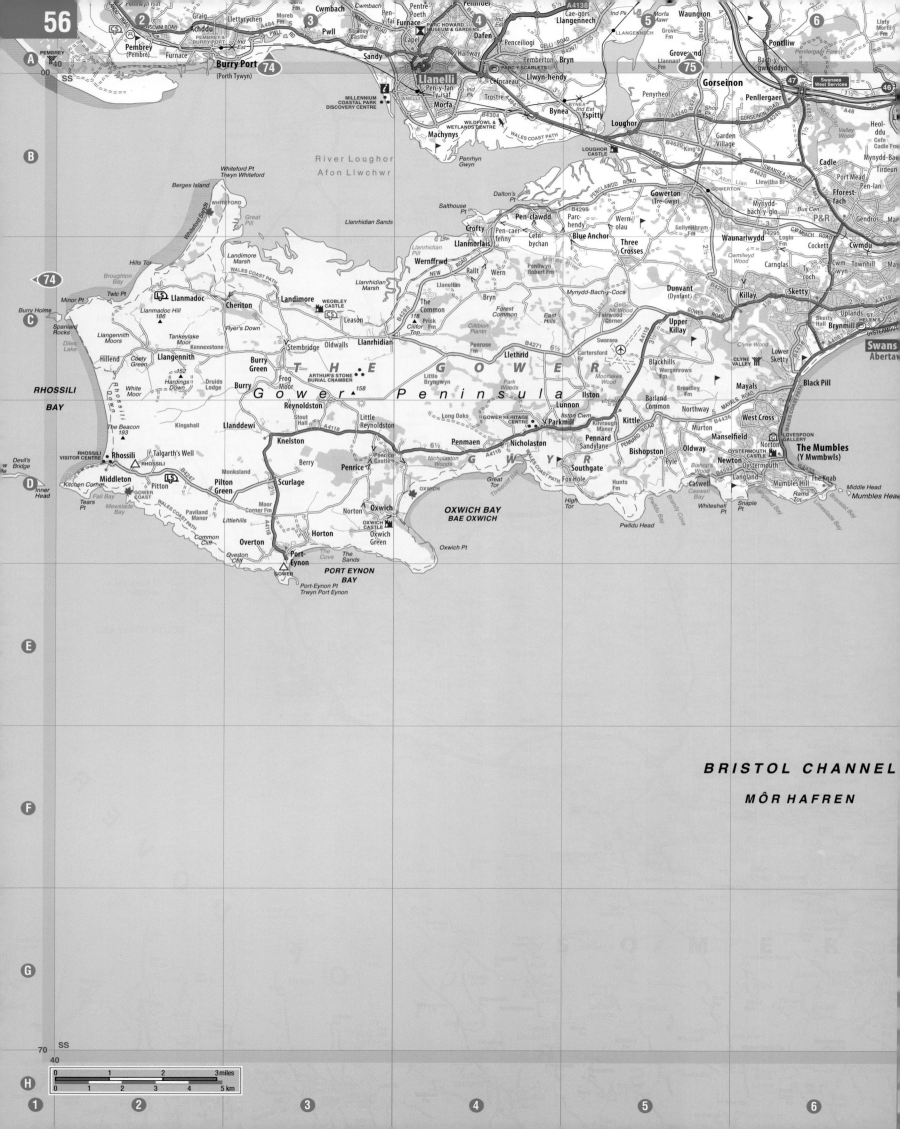

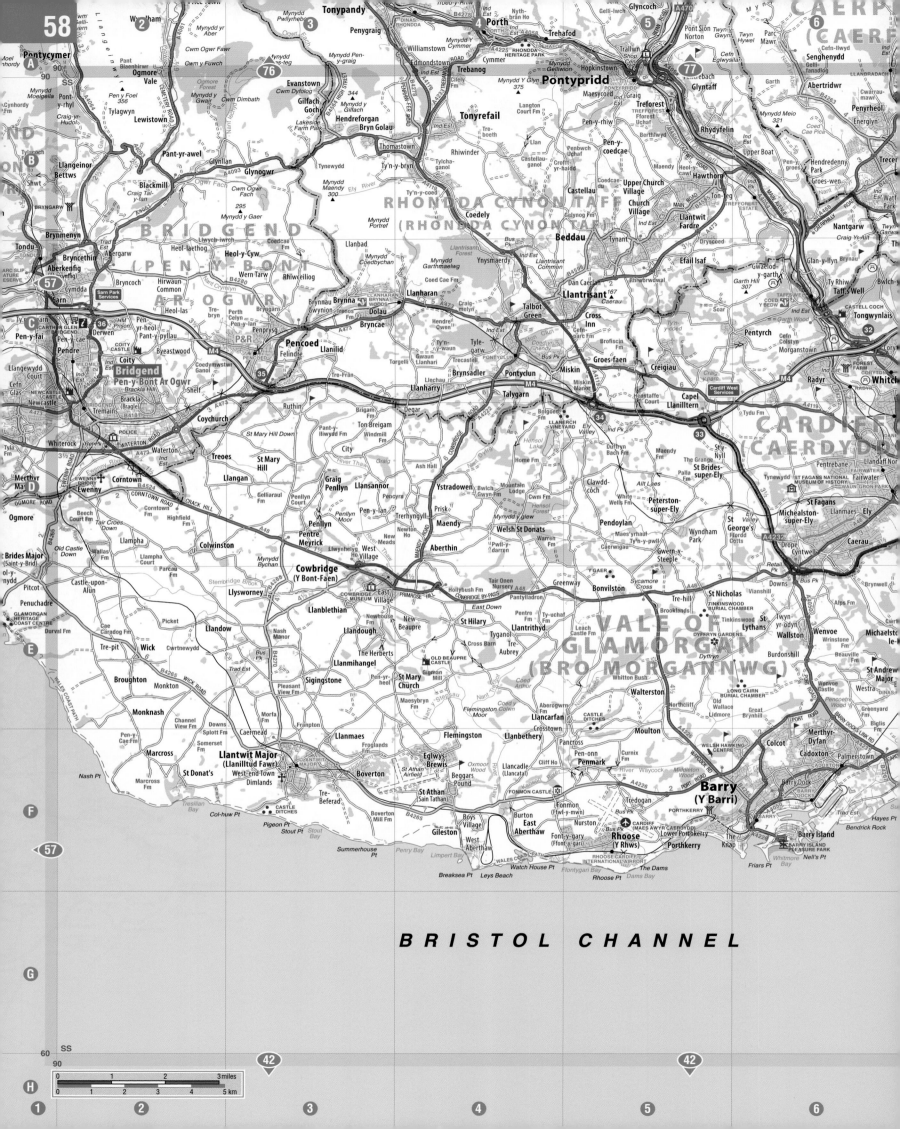

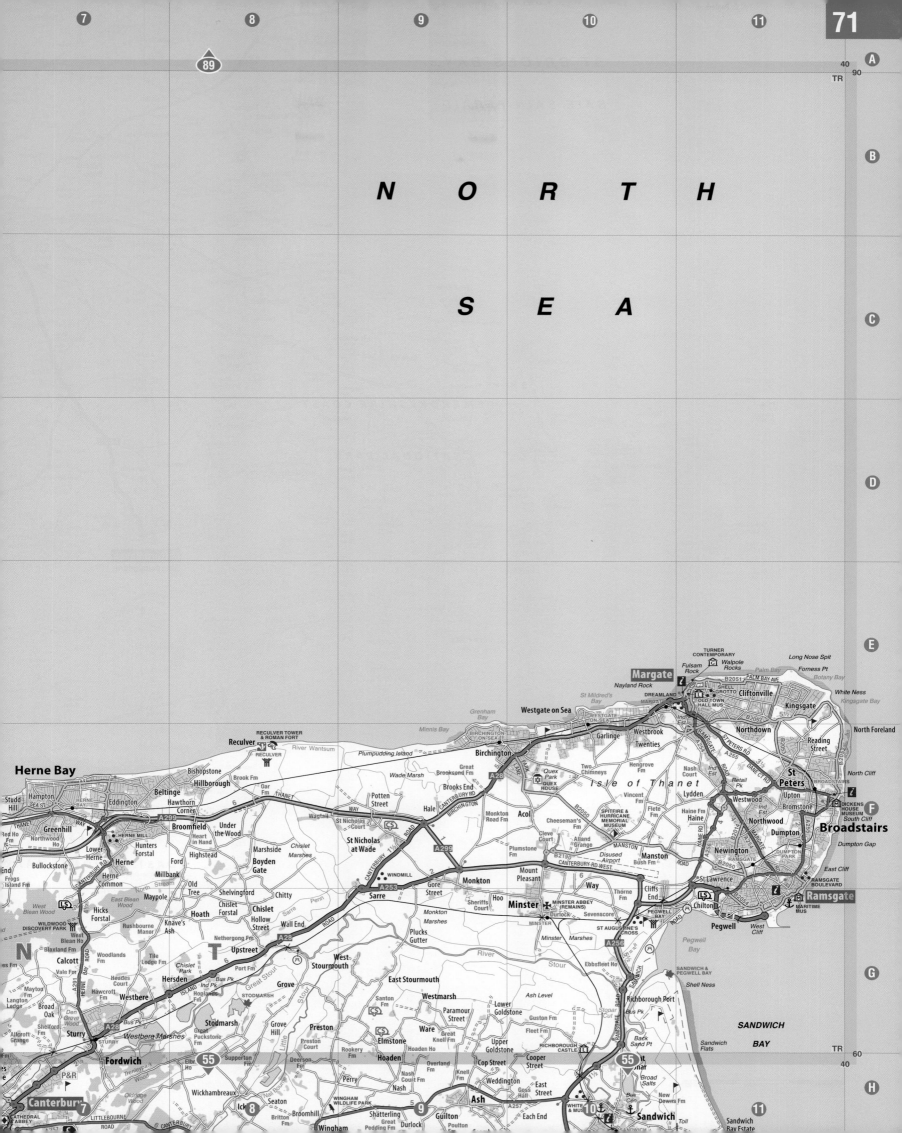

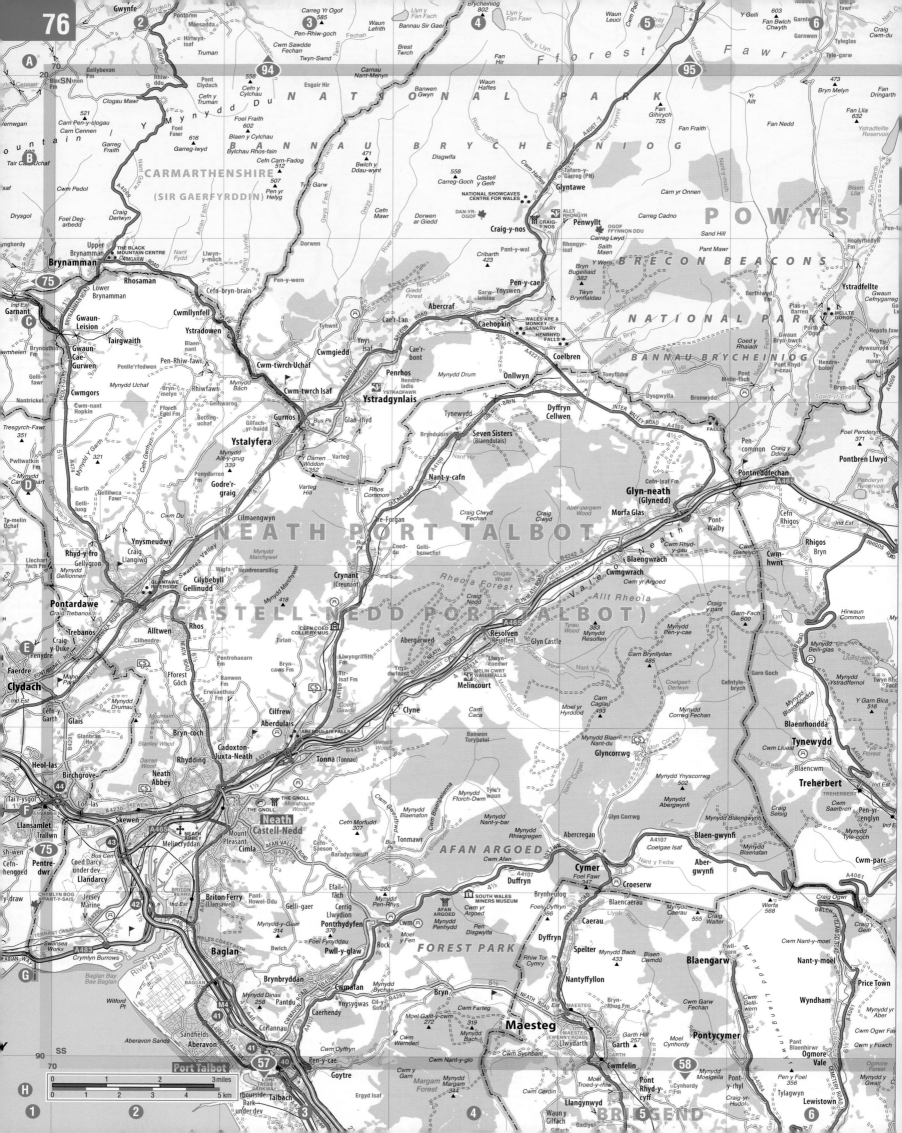

IRISH SEA

MÔR IWERDDON

Ynys Deullyn

CARREG SAMPSO

Pwll Whiting
Pwll Llong
Pwll Olfa
Trwyn Llwyd

Trefin
(Trevine)

Penclegyr

Porth-gain

Aber Draw

Porth Dwfn
Porth Egr

Porthgain

Trwyncastell

Barry Island Fm

Felindre Ho

Binchurn Fm

Pe

Abereiddi Bay

Abereiddy
Portheiddy

Cwmwdig Water

Llanrhian

Llanon

Mesur-y-dorth

Penyso

Aberdinas

Bank Ho

A487

Croes-goch

Porth Tre-wen

Berea

LLWYBR ARFORDIR PENFR

Tremynydd Fawr

Trefochlyd Fm

Trevigan

Trenewydd Fawr

Dduallt

Treffynnon

Penllechwen

PEMBROKESHIRE COAST PATH

Waun Beddau

Tretio
Tretio Common

Spite Moor

Waun Fawr

Llechenhinen

Treglemais

Carn Trelwyd

Carnhedryn Uchaf

Carn Treglemaes

WALES COAST PATH

Carn Llidi
181

ST DAVID'S

PEMBROKESHIRE COAST

Carnhedryn

Abernant

St David's Head
Penmaen Dewi

Carn Hen

Porthmelgan

Carnhedryn

Llanhowel
Skyfog

Llanddinog

Trenoch
Loc

North Bishop

Treleddyd fawr

Hendre

Rhodiad

Porth Lleuog

B 45

Dowrog Common

Caerfarchell

Caer Noriog

Paran

Whitesands Bay
Porth-mawr

Mynydd du

NATIONAL PARK

Tremaenhir

Porthsel

Treswny Moor

Point St John

Middle Mill

Rickeston Hall

Carreg Rhoson

Rhosson

River Alun

Penarthur

BISHOP'S PALACE

CATHEDRAL

St David's
(Tyddewi)

Vachelich

Whitchurch

Bishops and Clerks

Trwyn-Siôn-Owen

St Justinian

i

Nine Wells

Trwyn-drain-du

Carnysgubor

ST NON'S CHAPEL

Llandruidion

St Non's Bay

Morfa Common

Prendergast

Solva (Solfach)

Mount Fm

Brawdy Airfield (disused

Daufraich

Aber Mawr
RAMSEY ISLAND

RSPB
RAMSEY ISLAND

Ramsey Island
Ynys Dewi

Rhod Isaf
136

Aberfelin

Treginnis

Caer Bwdy Bay

Upper Solva

Lower Solva

PEMBROKESHIRE

Bus Pk

Porthlisky

A487

Pointz Castle

South Bishop/Em-sger

Trwynmynachdy

Penrhyn Twll

Porthclais

Carreg Fran

Green Scar

Dinas Fawr

PENFRO

COAST PATH LLWYBR ARFORDIR

Bay Dinny

Black Scar

Dinas Fach

Pwll March

Newgale

Meini Duon

Newgale San

Maidenh

Rickets

0   1   2   3 miles
0 1 2 3 4 5 km

60
50
SM

SM
20
60

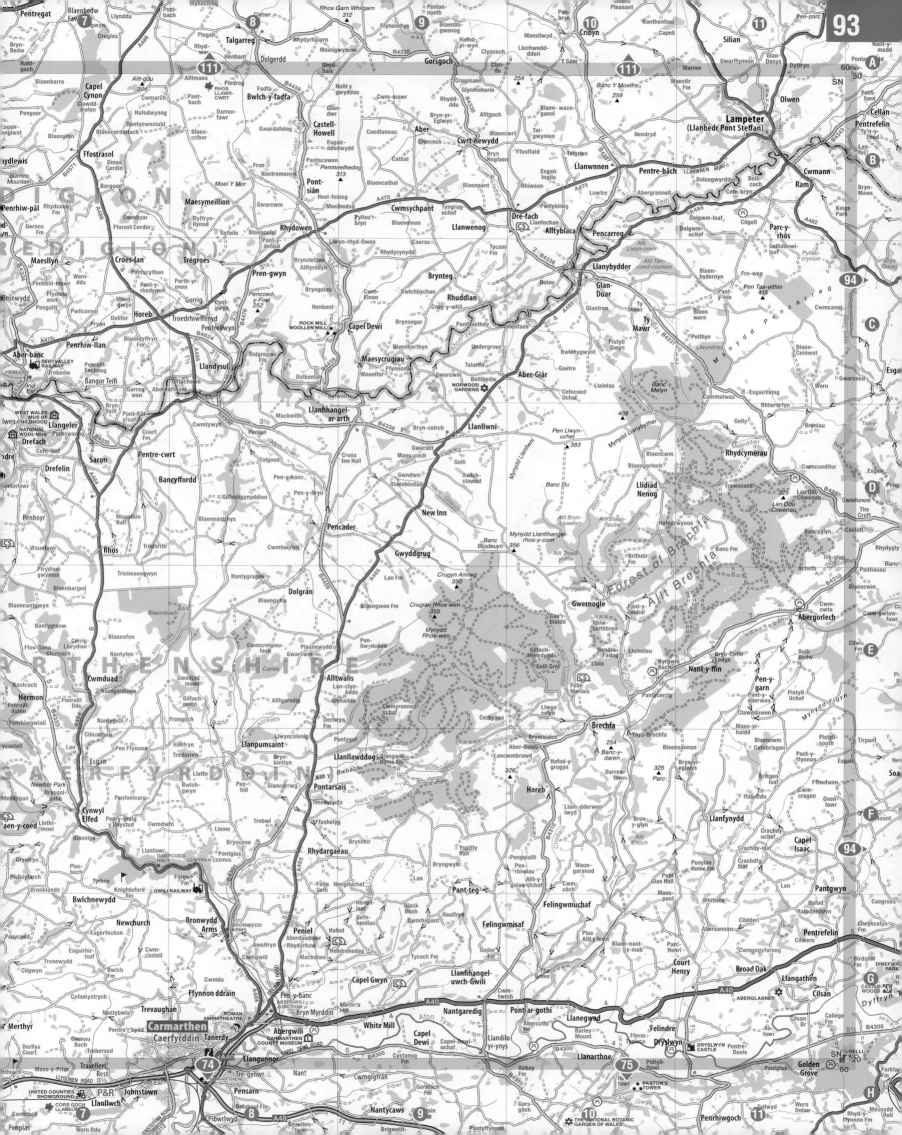

NORTH

SEA

CARDIGAN BAY

BAE CEREDIGION

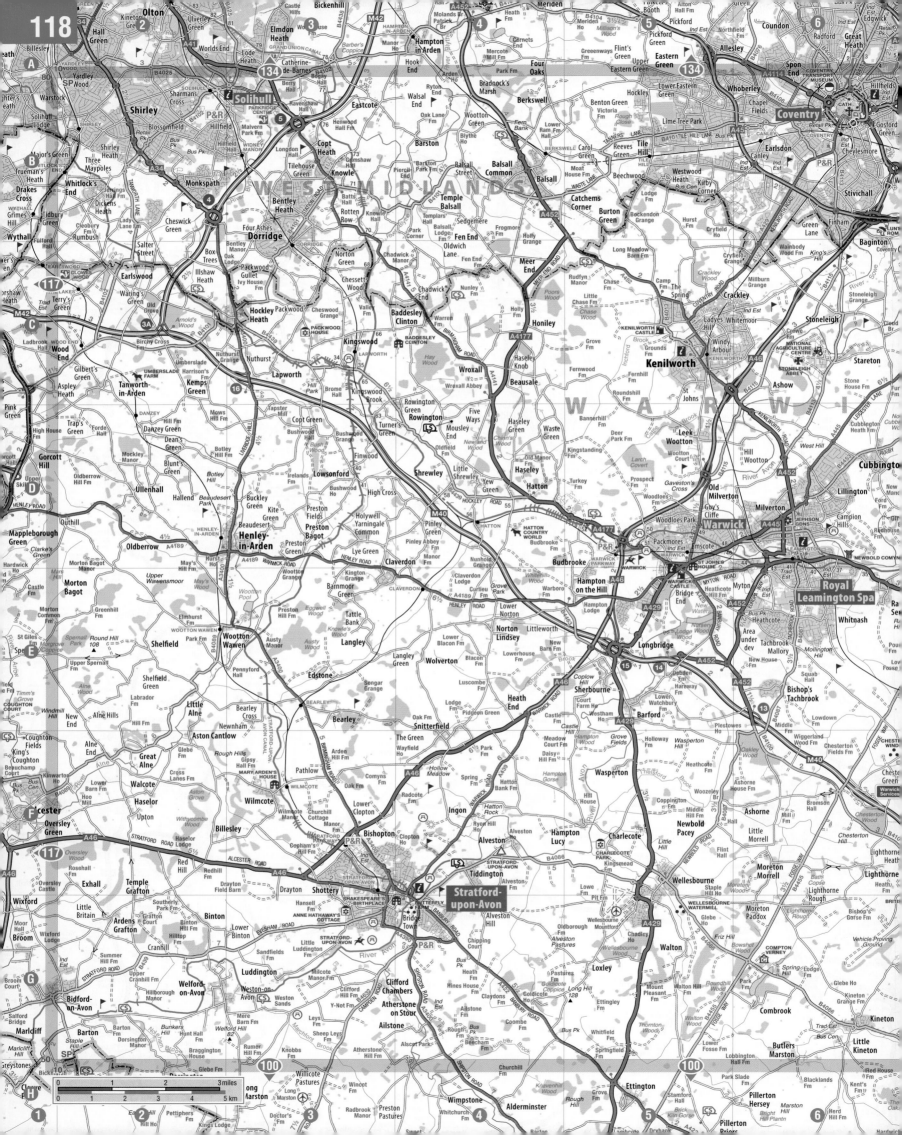

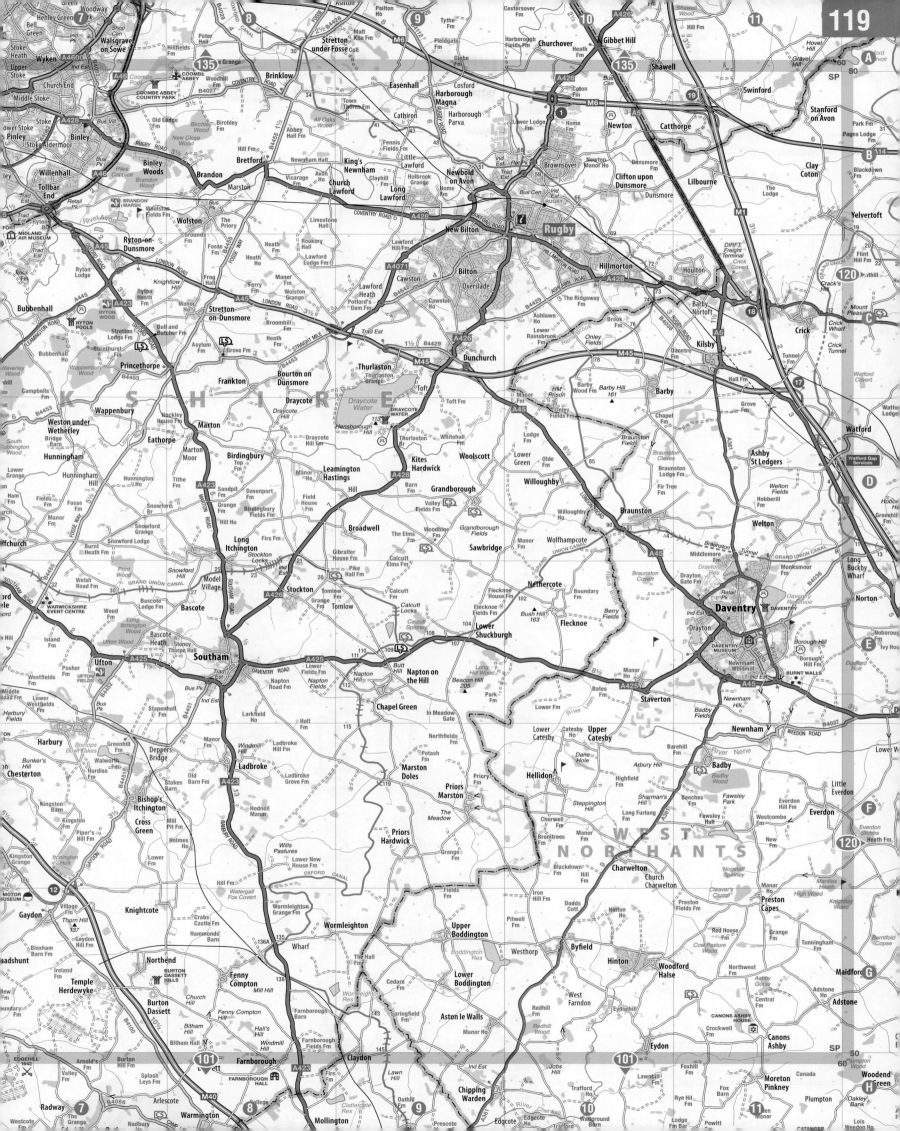

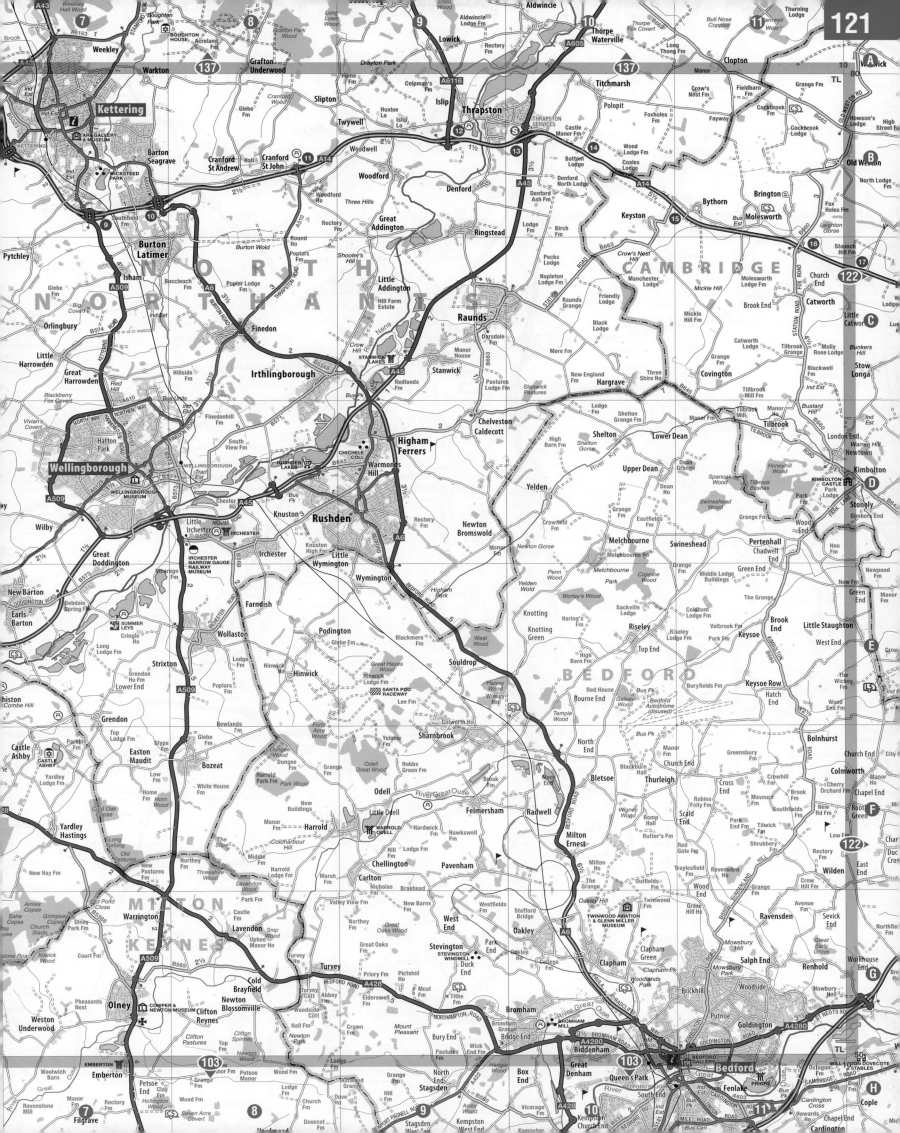

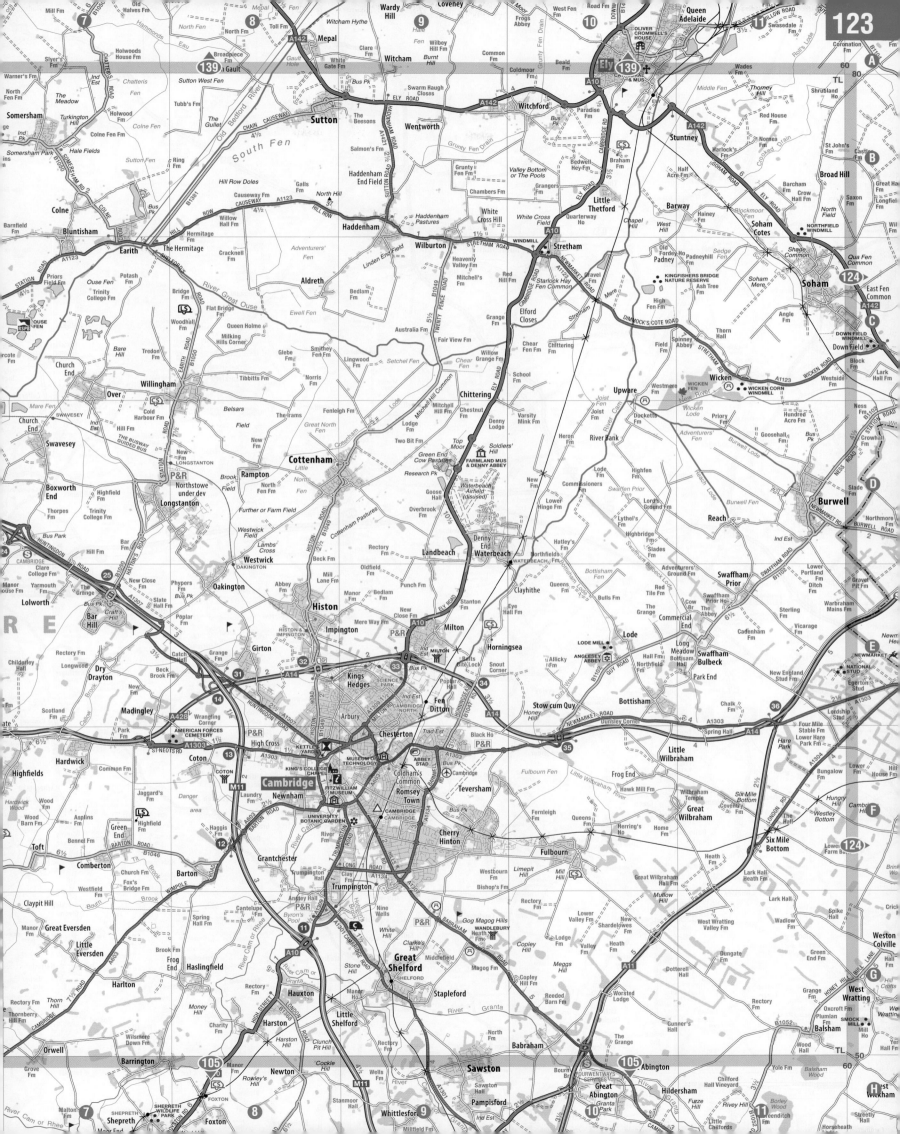

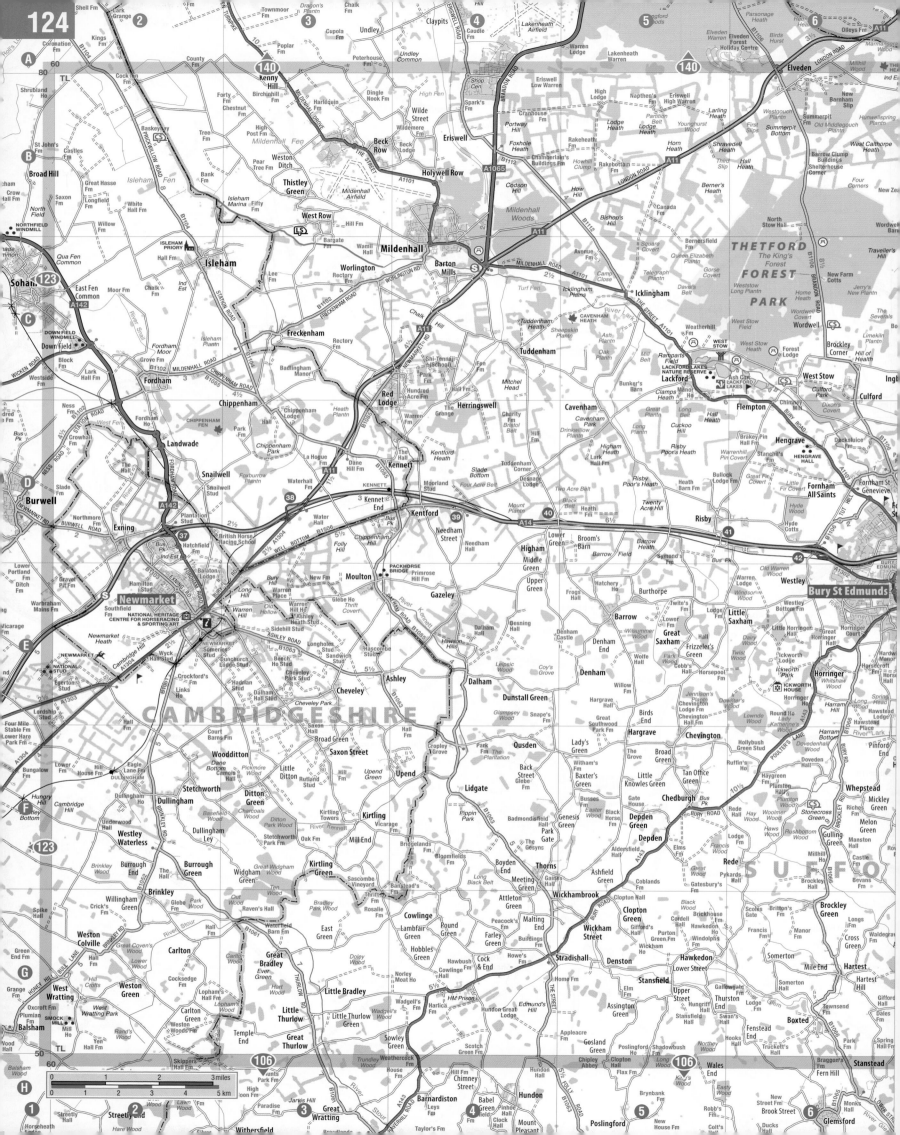

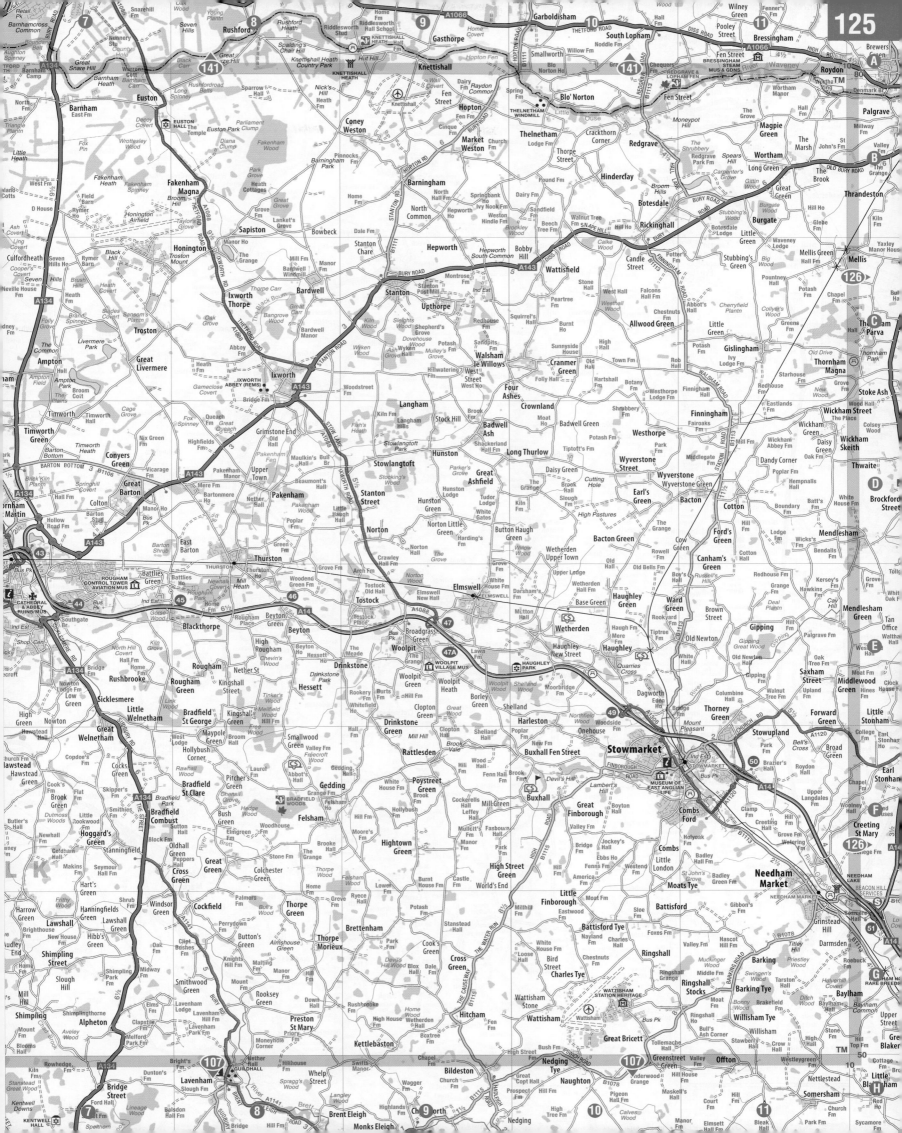

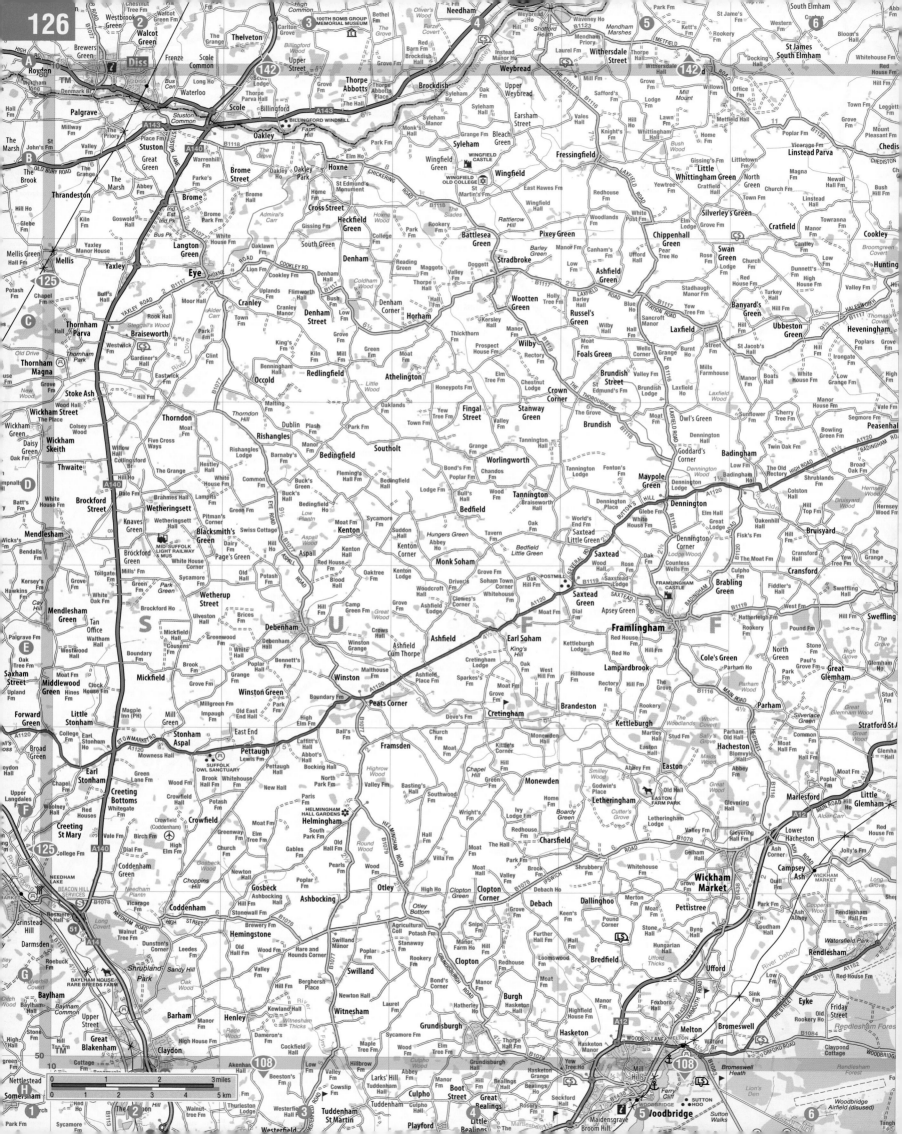

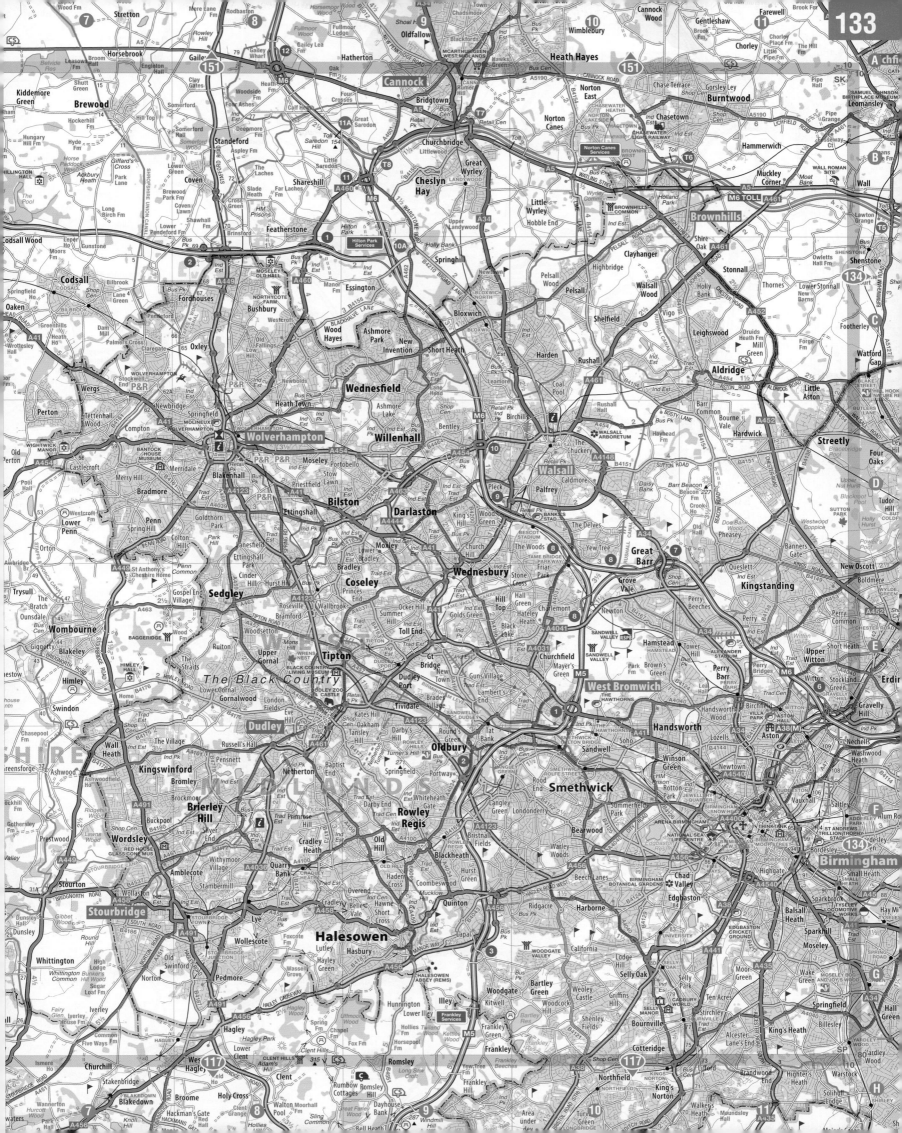

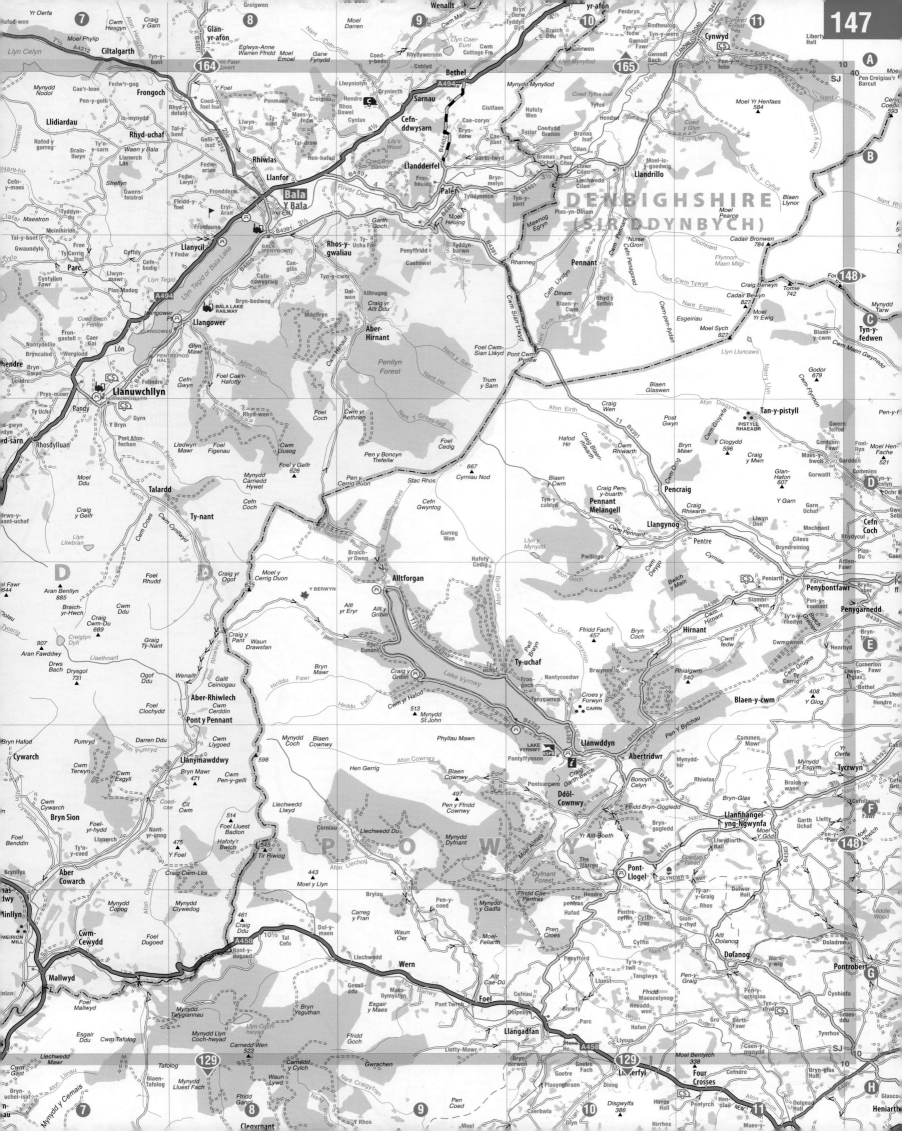

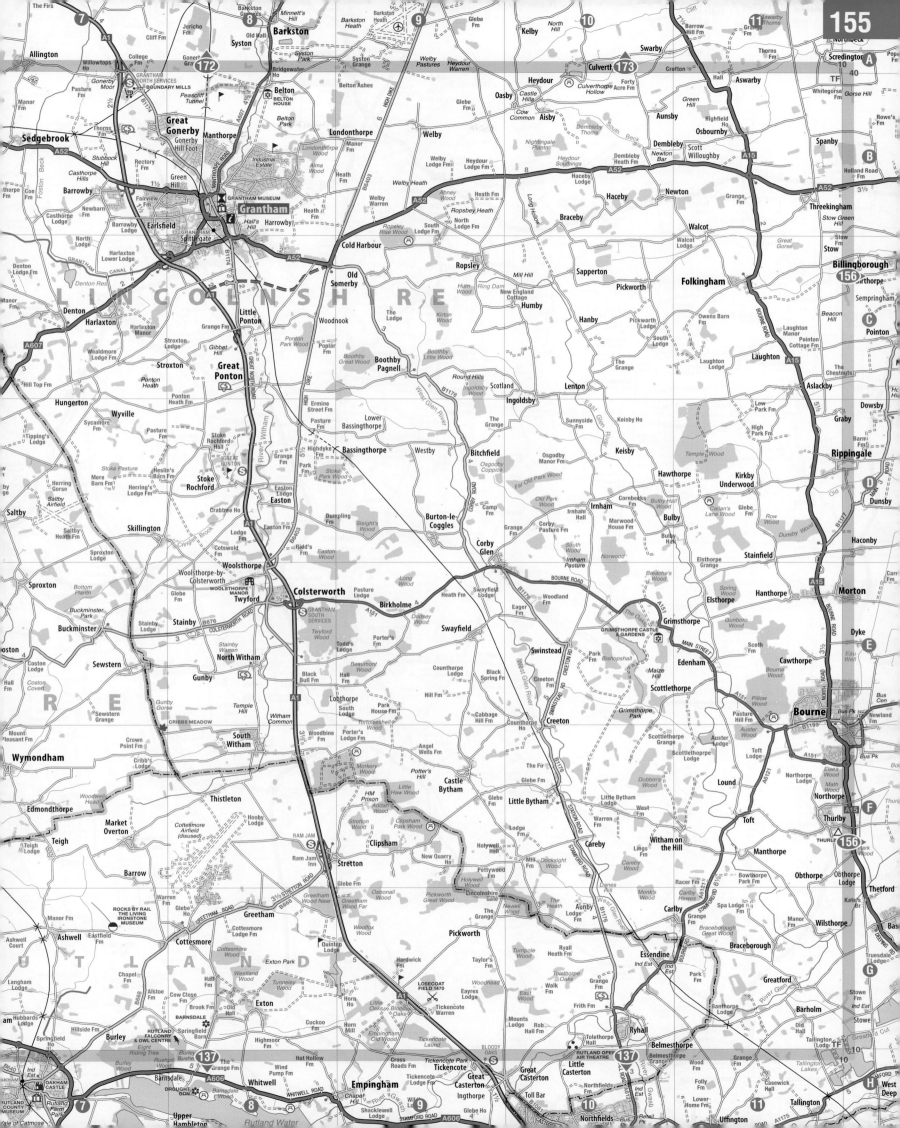

THE WASH

NORFOLK

CAMBRIDGE

Holbeach

Wisbech

Long Sutton

Sutton Bridge

Terrington St Clement

Clenchwarton

NORTH

SEA

NORFOLK COAST

ENGLAND COAST PATH

THE BROADS

Keswick
Walcott
Rookery Fm
Ostend
Happisburgh
Whimpwell Green
Eccles on Sea
Fox Hill
East Ruston Hall
Mill Fm
Bush Estate
Manor Ho
Castle Fm
Grove Ho
Silcock's Fm
Happisburgh Common
EAST RUSTON OLD VICARAGE GDN
Lessingham
Hempstead
Manor Ho
High Hill
Brunstead Grange
New Hall
Ingham Corner
Heath Fm
Hampstead Marshes
Sea Palling
Brumstead Hall
The Grove
The Hall
Great Moss Fen
WAXHAM GREAT BARN
Brumstead Common
Old Hall
Manor Ho
Randall's Mill
CALTHORPE BROAD
Waxham
Ingham
Stalham
Lound Fm
Brograve Fm
Manor Ho
Chapel Field
Stalham Green
Whinmere Fm
Hickling
Walnut Fm
Warren Fm
Berry Hall
Sutton Hall
Eastfield Fm
Lambrigg Mill
Horsey Corner
Middle Marsh
Sutton Broad
Longmoor Fm
Sutton
Hickling Green
Brayden Marshes
The Hall
HORSEY WINDMILL
Horsey
ENGLAND COAST PATH
Bray Fm
Stubb
Barton Turf
Hickling Heath
Hill Common
HICKLING BROAD NR
Stubb Mill
Horsey Mere
WINTERTON DUNES
Wood Fm
Wood Street
Catfield
Heath Fm
HICKLING BROAD
Rush Hill
Swim Coots
Blackfleet Broad
Winterton Holmes
Barton Broad
ANT BROADS & MARSHES
Catfield Hall
Catfield Common
Hill Slea
MARTHAM BROAD
Somerton Holmes
Workhouse Common
Hall Fen
Sound Plantn
Heigham Sound
Somerton Holmes
Irstead
Sharp Street
Walton Hall
Rookery Fm
Hall Fm
MARTHAM BROAD
Burnley Hall
East Somerton
Crome's Broad
HOW HILL
How Hill
Ludham
Damgate
West Somerton
Neatishead
Turf Fen
Potter Heigham
Winterton-on-Sea
RAF AIR DEFENCE RADAR MUSEUM
River Ant
Fritton
River Thurne
Mustard Hyrn
Mill Fm
Ludham
Ludham Hall
LUDHAM & POTTER HEIGHAM MARSHES
White Gate Fm
Thunder Hill
High Barn Fm
Blood Hills
Johnson Street
Cold Harbour
Bastwick
Grange Fm
Cess
Martham
Upper Street
Hundred Dike
Repps
Thurne
Ashby Hall
Hemsby
Newport
ST BENET'S ABBEY (REMS)
Thurne Mouth
Rollesby
Ranworth
Ranworth Marshes
Ward Marsh
Clippesby
Clippesby Ho
Ormesby Broad
Decoy Fm
Dowe Hill
Scratby Hall
Sand Cliffs
NORTH BROAD
SOUTH WALSHAM BROAD
Boundary Ho
Manor Fm
Narrowgate Corner
Ormesby St.Michael
Scratby
FAIRHAVEN WOODLAND & WATER GARDEN
Pilson Green
Burgh St Margaret (Fleggburgh)
Lily Broad
Ormesby St Margaret
California
Tyegate Green
South Walsham
Low Fm
Filby Broad
Nova Scotia Fm
Town Green
Highfield
Upton
Newgate Corner
Filby
Filby Heath
Mill Hill Fm
Upton Green
Charity Fm
Billockby
Burgh Common
ROMAN TOWN
Watt's Hall Fm
Thrigby
THRIGBY HALL WILDLIFE GARDENS
Mautby Lodge
Mautby
Caister Hall
CAISTER CASTLE & MOTOR MUSEUM
Caister-on-Sea
Long Plantn
Fishley
Whitegate
Winsford Hall
Barn Fm
Lower Caister Wood Fm
West End
West Caister
Caister Pt
Muck Fleet
Woodlands
Runham
Decoy Fm
North Denes
North Burlingham
Stokesby
Manor Fm
Gt Yarmouth North Denes
Burlingham Green
Acle
Damgate
Mautby Marsh Fm
North Beach
Lingwood
Lingwood Lodge
ACLE
The Hall
NEW ROAD
Ashtree Fm
NEW ROAD
Newtown
Great Yarmouth
Beighton
Moulton St Mary
Tunstall
Britannia
Runham Vauxhall
Runham
The Beach

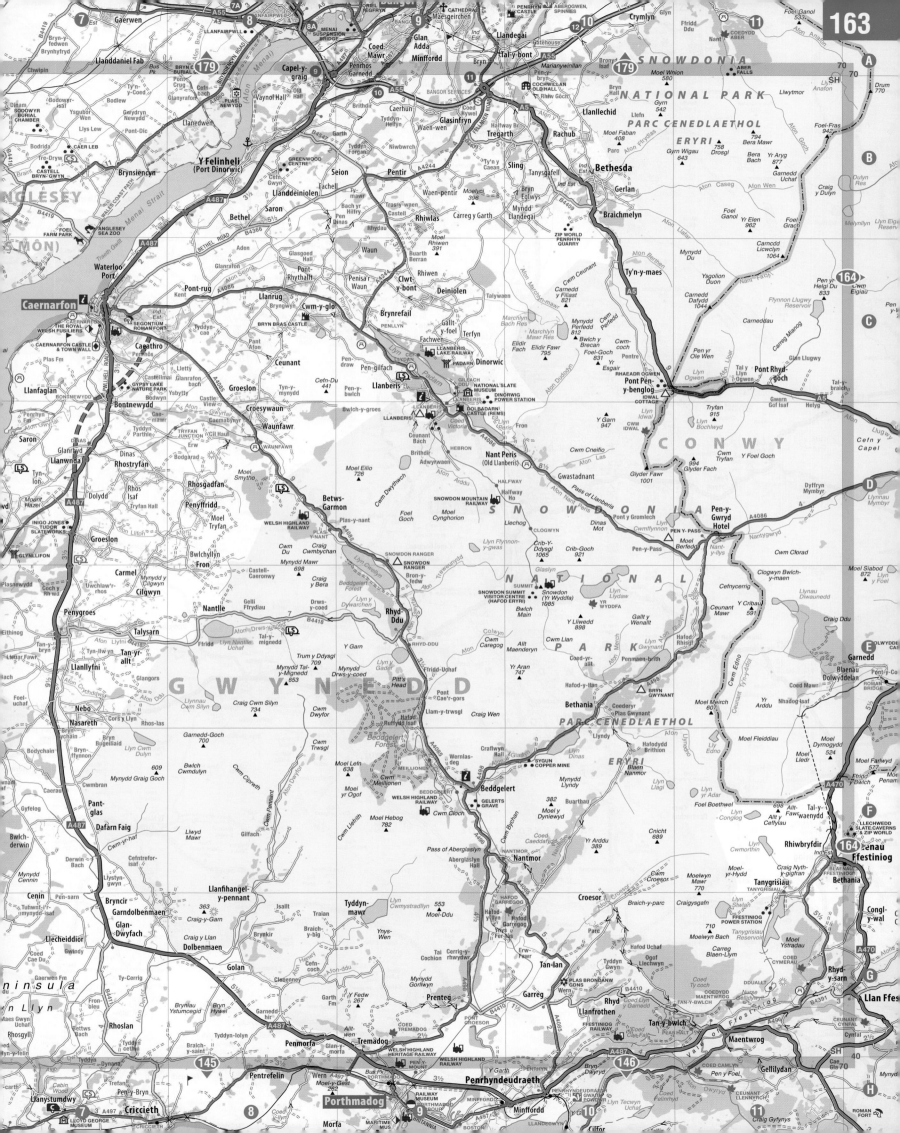

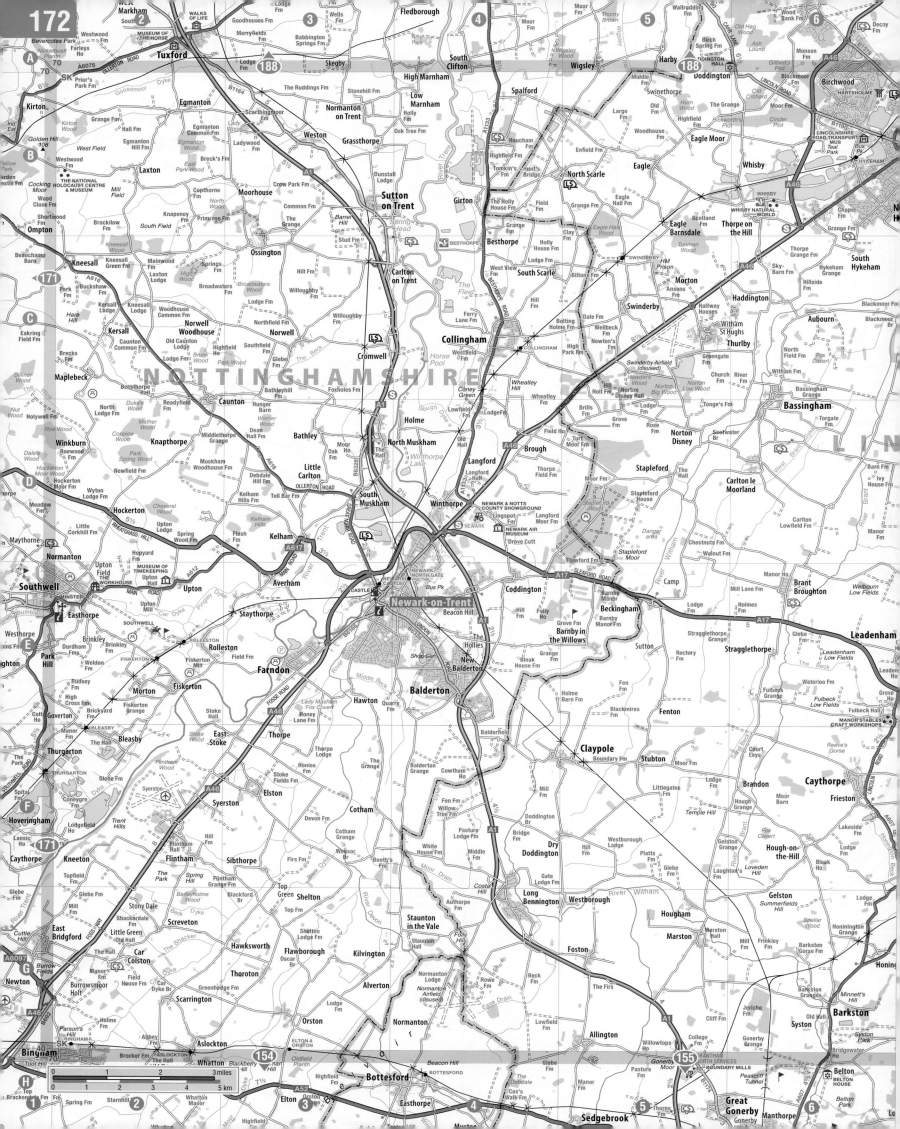

THE WASH

Willoughby
Maxby
Sloothby
Welton le Marsh
Candlesby
Orby
Burgh le Marsh
Bratoft
Firsby
Irby in the Marsh
Thorpe Culvert
Thorpe St Peter
Wainfleet Common
Wainfleet Bank
Wainfleet All Saints
Wainfleet St Mary
Wainfleet Tofts
Friskney Eaudyke
Friskney
Fold Hill
Friskney Tofts

Hogsthorpe
Slackholme End
Addlethorpe
Ashington End
Seathorne Winthorpe
Ingoldmells
Ingoldmells Pt

Skegness
NATURELAND SEAL SANCTUARY
THE LIFEBOAT STATION MUSEUM
AQUARIUM

Croft
Croft Marsh
Seacroft
Croft Grange
Havenhouse
New England

GIBRALTAR POINT
GIBRALTAR POINT NNR
Gibraltar Point
Inner Knock

Wainfleet Harbour
Wainfleet Sand

Friskney Flats
The Horseshoe
Wrangle Flats

Holme next the Sea
HOLME BIRD OBSERVATORY
Gore Pt
HOLME DUNES
Old Hunstanton
St Edmund's Pt
Hunstanton
SEA LIFE SANCTUARY
Ringstead
Ringstead Downs
NORFOLK LAVENDER

HARDY'S ANIMAL FARM
FANTASY ISLAND
BUTLIN'S SKEGNESS

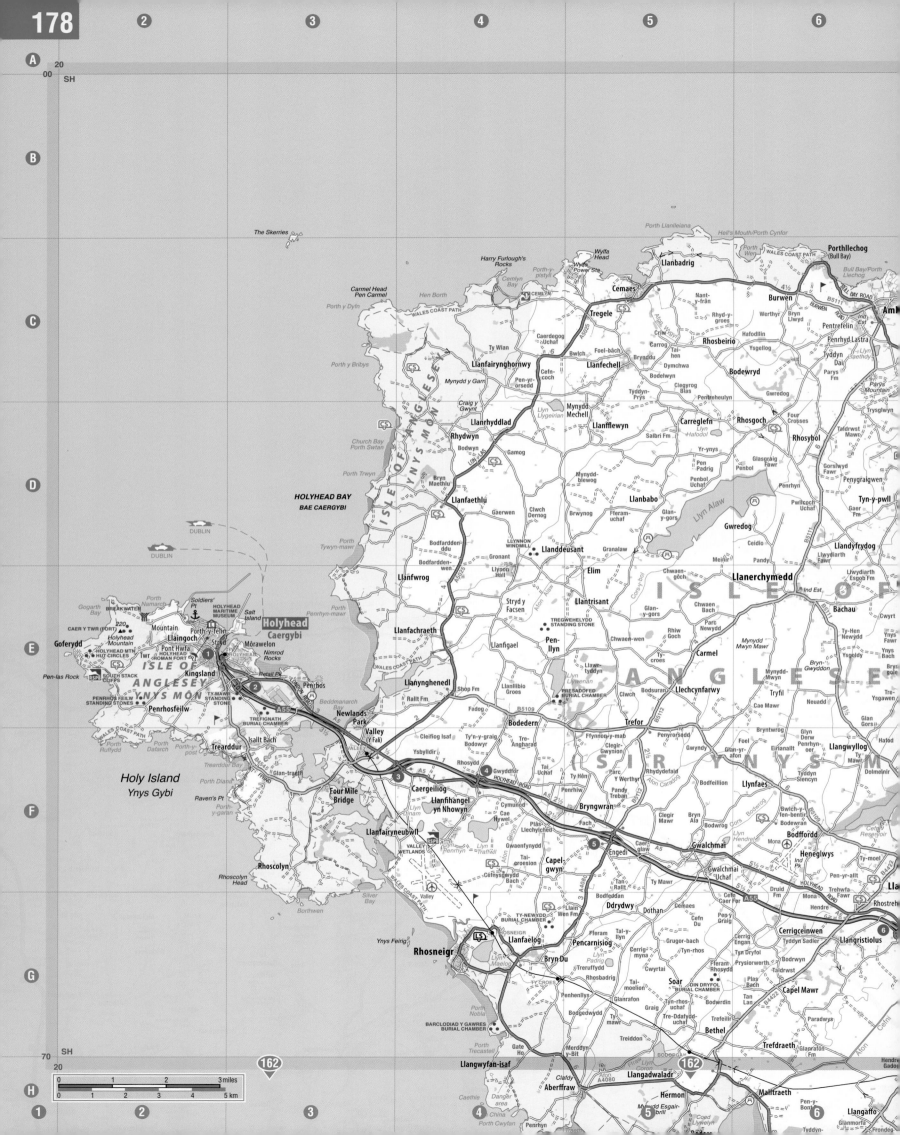

IRISH SEA

MÔR IWERDDON

SNOWDONIA
NATIONAL PARK
PARC CENEDLAETHOL
ERYRI

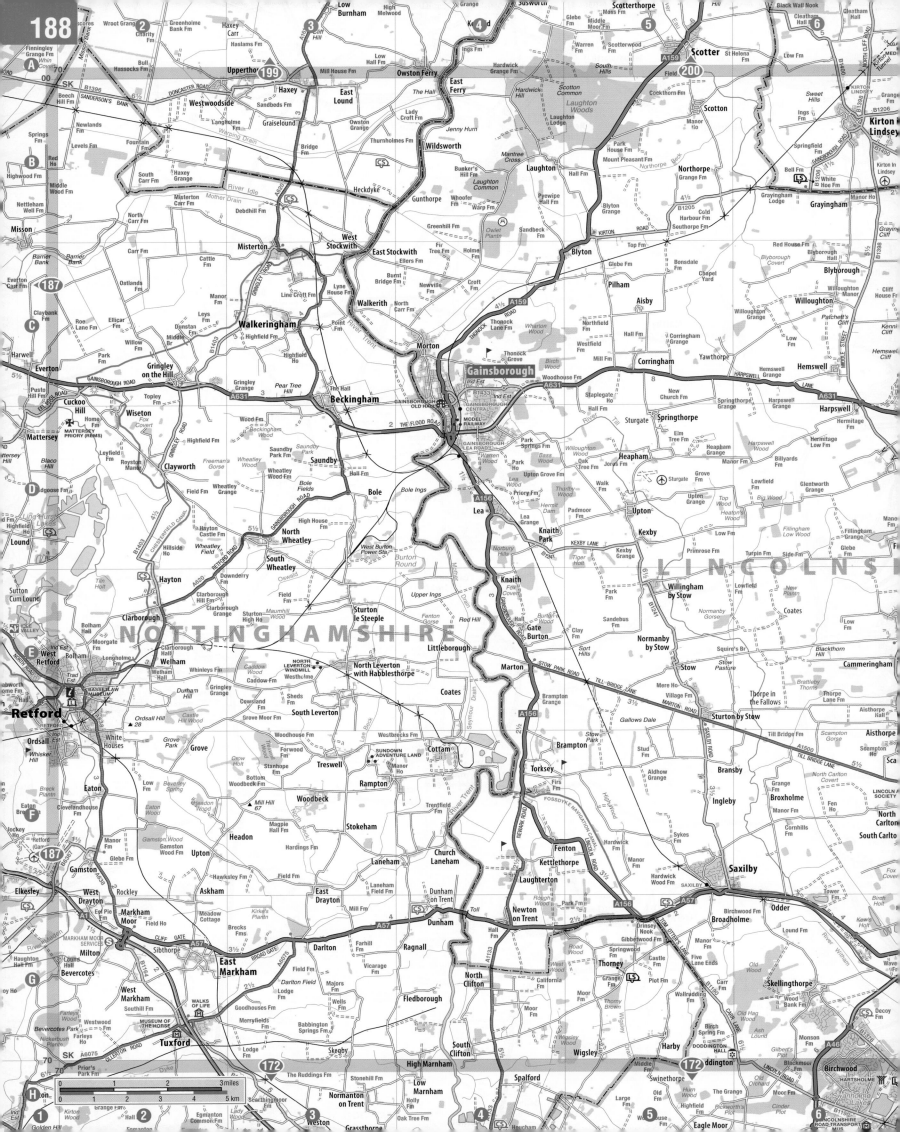

NORTH

SEA

Saltfleet
Saltfleet Haven
Sea View Fm
Rimac
SALTFLEETBY THEDDLETHORPE DUNES
Saltfleetby All Saints
Lodge Fm
Theddlethorpe St Helen
Manor Ho
Hall Fm
Gayton Engine
Theddlethorpe All Saints
Great
High Gate
Will Row
Gas Terminal
North End
THE SEAL SANCTUARY & WILDLIFE CENTRE
Meers Bridge
Westfield Fm
Stain Hill
Meers Bank
Mablethorpe Hall
FUN FAIR
Mablethorpe
Strubby Grange
Poplar Fm
Earl's Br
Grange Fm
Trusthorpe
Willow Fm
Bamber's Br
Strubby
Thorpe
Trusthorpe Hall
Sutton on Sea
Maltby le Marsh
Manor Ho
Sandilands
Mill Hill
Poplar Lodge Fm
Beesby
Abbey Fm
Beesby Grange
Manor Fm
Hagnaby
Sea Bank Fm
Saleby
Washdyke Br
Hannah
America Fm
Cob Hill
Markby
Glebe Fm
Priory Fm
Saleby Manor
The Grange
College Fm
Asserby
Willow Fm
Black House Fm
Thoresthorpe
Asserby Turn
Bilsby
Dryby Fm
Wold Sea Fm
Moat Ho
Huttoft
Manor Fm
Anderby Creek
Alford
The Grange
The Manor
Bilsby Field
Thurlby
Anderby
Farlesthorpe
ON YOUR MARQUES
Wolla Bank
Mumby
Manor Ho
Langham Fm
Chapel Six Marshes
Manor Fm
School Fm
Mill Hill
Cumberworth
Cherry Fm
Mickleberry Hill
Authorpe Row
Chapman's Fm
Chapel Pt
Mawthorpe
Elsom Fm
Bonthorpe
Helsey
Croft Fm
Manor Fm
Listoft
Chapel St Leonards
Willoughby
Poplar Fm
Hogsthorpe
Willoughby High Drain
Willoughby Wood
Hogsbeck Ho
Sloothby
Burlands Beck
Howlet Ho
Slackholme End
Hope Fm
Beeches Fm
Welton Low Wood
Hasthorpe
Welbourne Fm
HARDY'S ANIMAL FARM
Welton High Wood
175
175
Thwaite Hall
Highfield Fm
Habertoft
Drain
Ingoldmells
Candlesby Hill
Boothby Hall
FANTASY ISLAND
Rookery
Welton Marsh
Addlethorpe
Ingoldmells Pt
Boothby Grange
Whitehouse

A
B
C
D
E
F
G
H

7
8
9
10
11

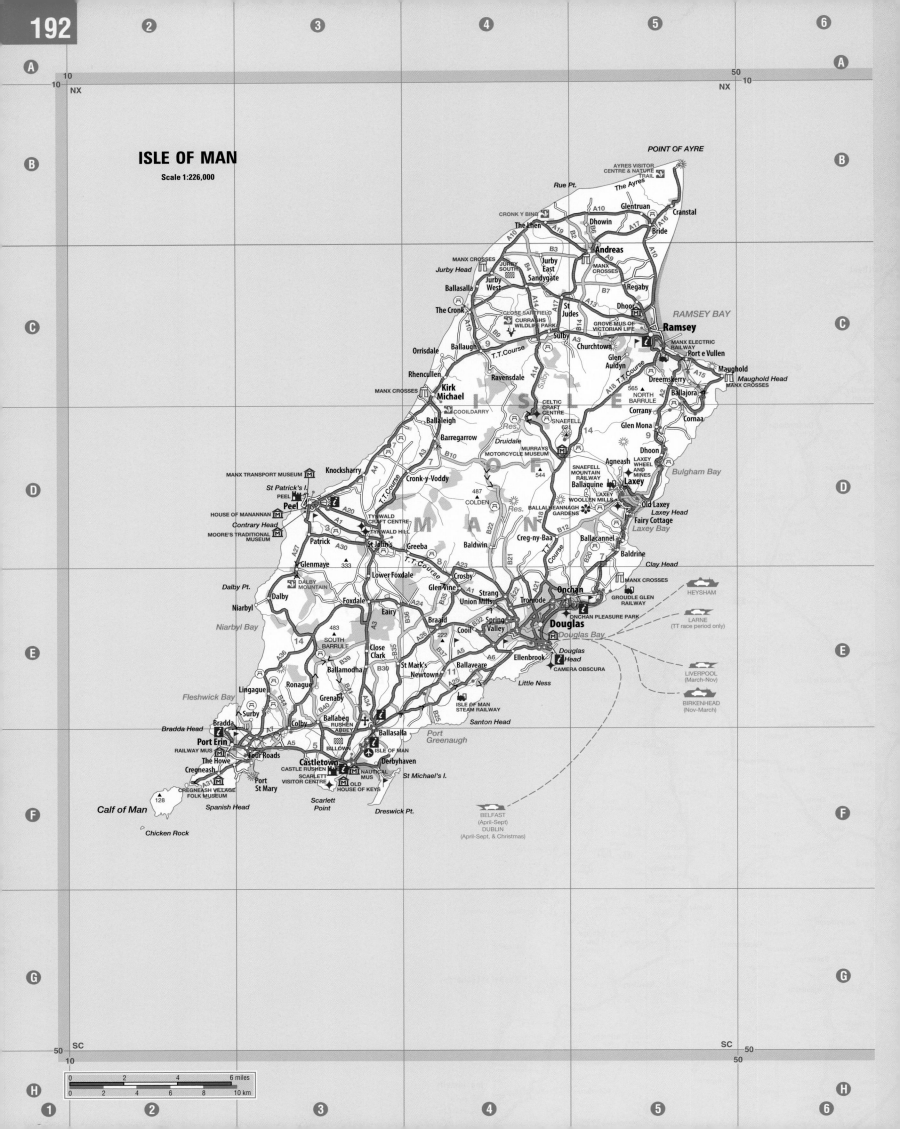

Westby

Peel

Blackpool

Great
Marton Moss

Higher
Ballam

Lower
Ballam

Moss
Side

Aspect
Fm

New
House Fm

SD

Dryning
Kellamergh

Brynin
Hall Fm

Windy
Harbo.

North Hollow

St Annes

Salter's Bank

Lytham St Anne's

Fairhaven

Fairhaven
Lake

Church Scar

LYTHAM
WINDMILL MUSEUM

WEST BEACH

Crusader Bank

North Houses

Hey
Houses

Ansdell

Lytham

Moss
Hall Fm

Birks
Fm

Eastham
Hall

Saltcotes

Little Carr
Side Fm

Warton

Warton
Bank

River Ribble

Hesketh
Sands

Long Bank

Great Bank

Foulnaze

Marshside Sands

Crossens Marsh

Horse Bank

Angry Brow

Southport Sands

Birkdale Sands

RIBBLE ESTUARY

Banks Sands

George's Brow

Banks
Marsh

Old
Hollow Fm

Taylor's
Fm

Far
Banks

Goose
Dub Fm

Fiddler's
Ferry

Banks

Holmes
Moss

MARSHSIDE

Crossens

Marshside

BOTANIC
GARDEN

Churchtown

Meol's Hall

Hollywood
Fm

High
Park

Wyke
Hey Fm

Winacre
Fm

Wyke
House Fm

Leisure
Lakes

ECO VISITOR
CENTRE

Marine
Lake

SOUTHPORT MODEL
RAILWAY VILLAGE

Southport

Bus Cen
SOUTHPORT

Shop
Cen

Blowick

Wyke Thorn
Fm

Midge
Hall Fm

Whams
Fm

Mere
Hall

Birkdale

Hillside

Birkdale Hills

Brown
Edge

Pool Hey

Shaw's
Fm

Carr Cross

Snape
Green

Wyke Road
Fm

BESCAR
LANE

Greenings

Ainsdale-
on-Sea

Ainsdale

Ainsdale Sands

Ainsdale Hills

Woodvale

White
Otter Fm

Shirdley
Hill

Scarisbrick

Manor
House Fm

Olverston House
Fm

Hooton's
Fm

Bescar

Scarisbrick
Hall (Coll)

Drummersdale
Smithy
Lane Ends

Pinfold

AINSDALE
SAND DUNES

Woodvale

Halsall Moss

Heather
Fm

Green
Kettle Ho

Hurlston
Green

L A N C S

Gettern
Fm

Park House
Fm

Halsall

Primrose
Hill

Hurlston

Mad
Wharf

FRESHFIELD

Freshfield

Formby
Hall

Barton

Bangor's
Green

Asmall
Ho

Ormskirk

Formby

Little Altcar

Downholland Brook

Downholland Moss

Haskayne

Downholland
Cross

Clieves
Hills

Holly
Ho

Gaw Hill

AUGHTON
PARK

Aughton
Park

Formby Pt

Great
Altcar

Alt
Bridge

Worrall House
Fm

Downholland
Fm

Walsh
Hall

Hollands
Fm

Hollin
House Fm

Aughton

Holt
Green

Aughton
Chase

Mickering
Fm

Bowker's
Green

Gerard
Hall

CABIN
HILL

The
Withins

Town
Green

Taylor's Bank

North End
Whitedge
Fm

Lady
Green

Carr
Houses

Gore
House Fm

Rose
Hill Fm

Scaffold Lane

Hightown

Ince Blundell

Carr
Side Fm

Homer
Green

Mercer
Court

Lydiate

Formby Bank

Moss
Fm

Crosby
Hall

Lunt

Maghull

Cunscar
Hall

Moss Side
HM
Prison

Crosby Channel

Little Crosby

Sefton

Thornton

Netherton

Melling

Melling
Mount

Moorfield
Ho

SD

Blundellsands

Brighton le Sands

Great
Crosby

Buckley Hill

Waddicar

ANTONY GORMLEY
SCULPTURES

Crosby

Waterloo
Park

Waterloo

Ford

Aintree

Aintree

Westvale

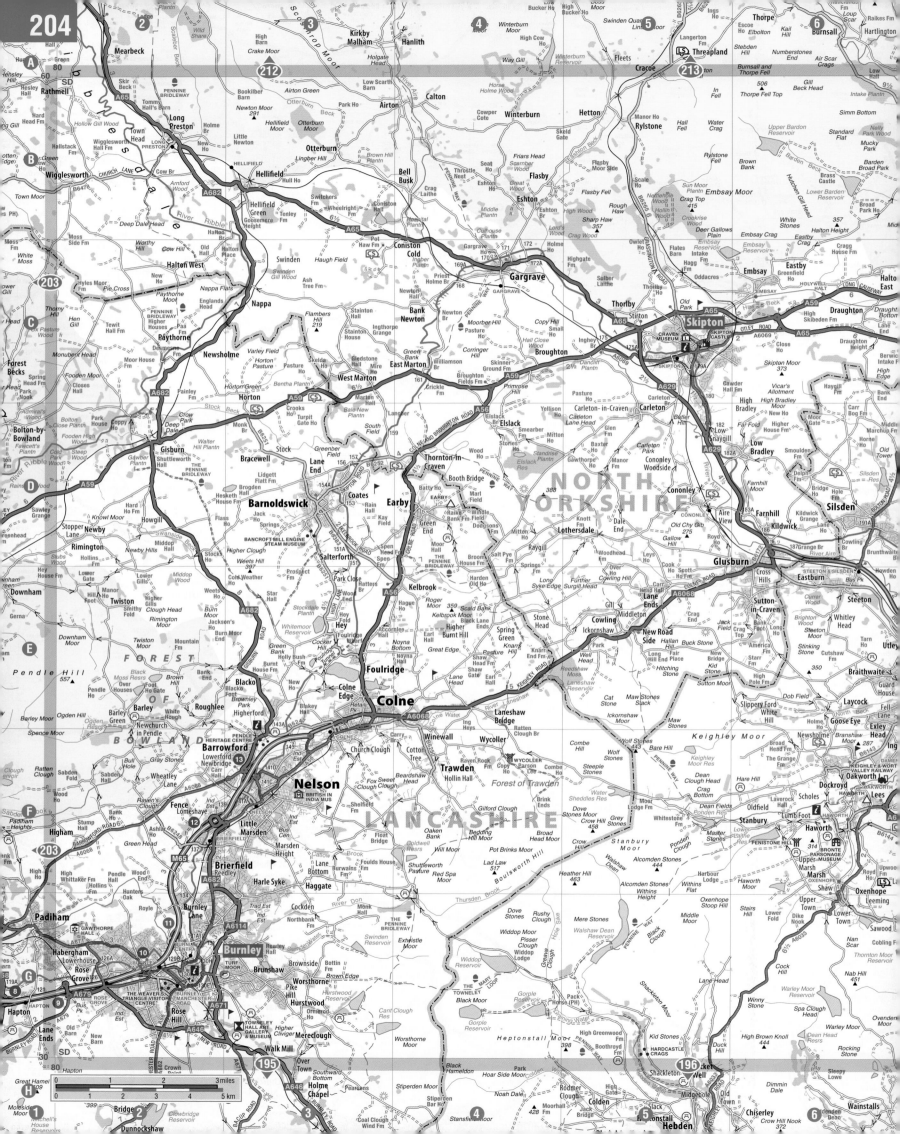

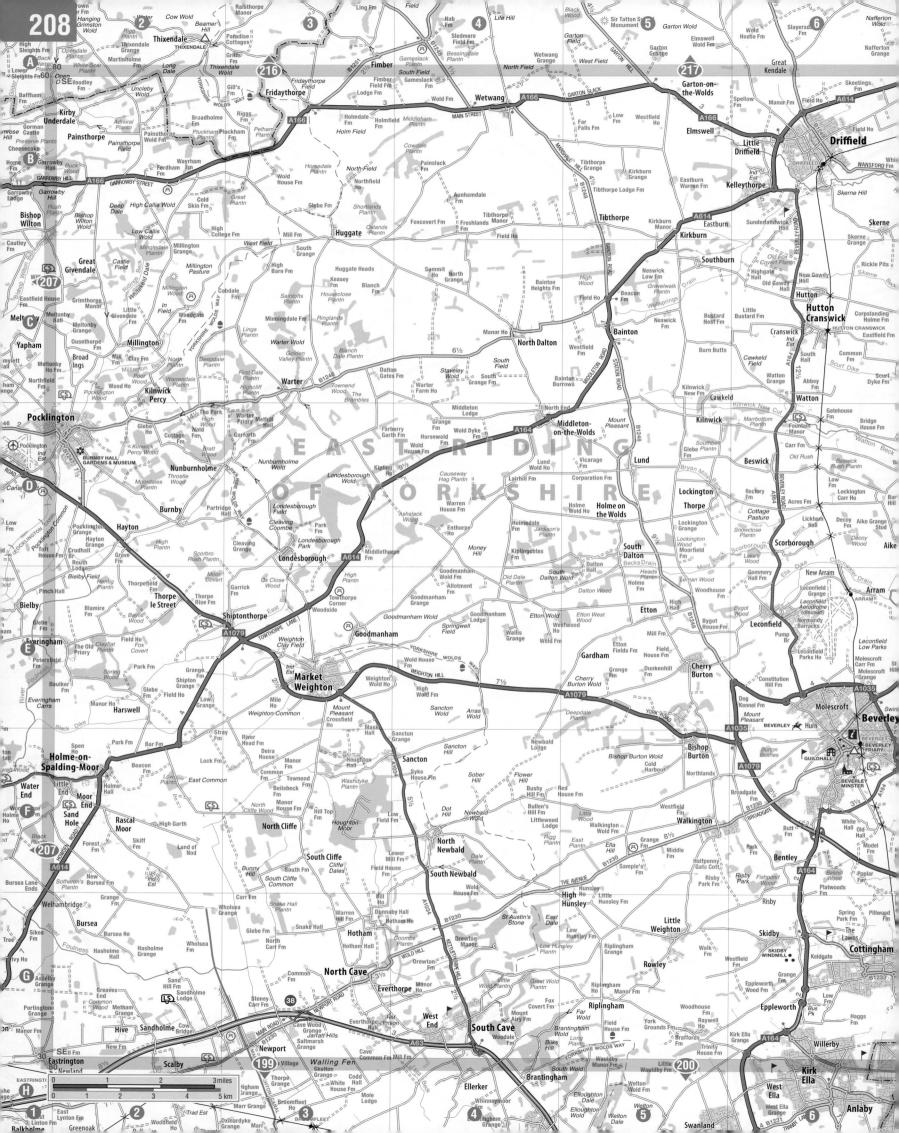

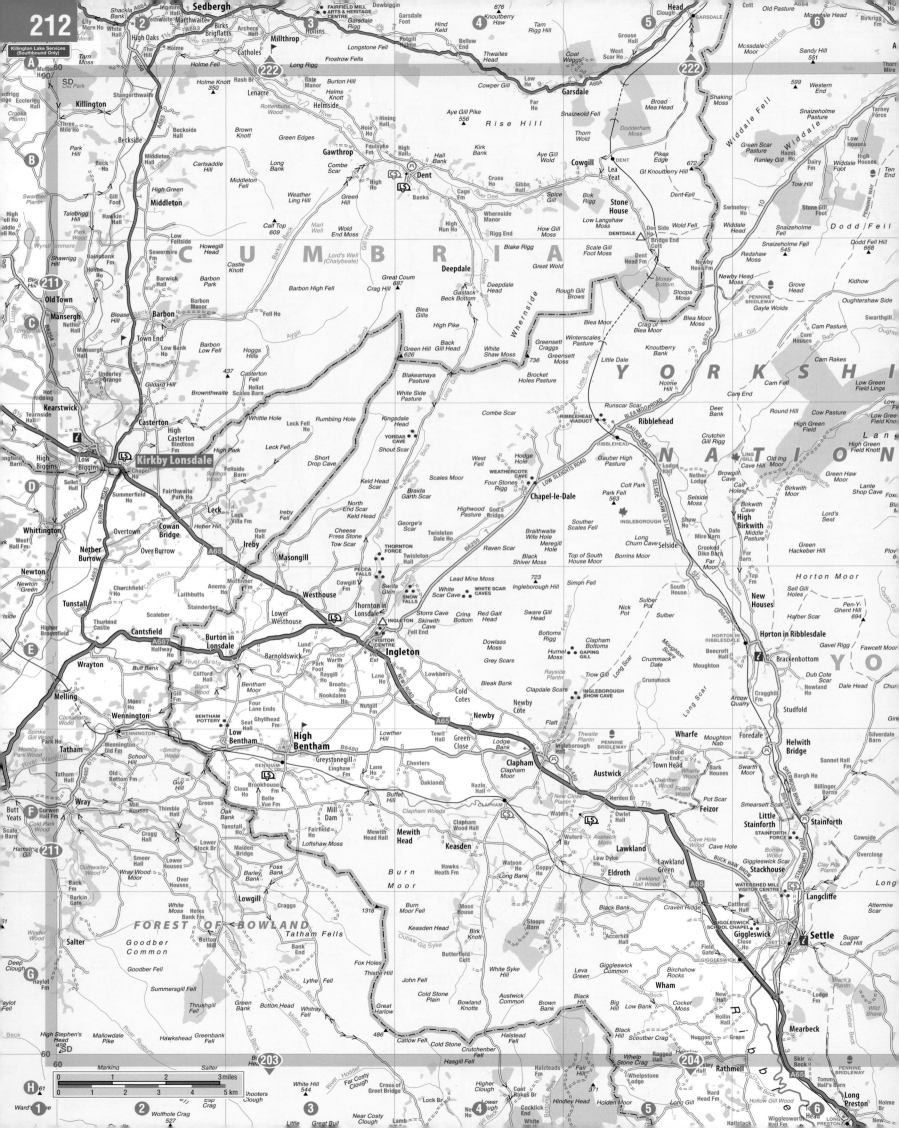

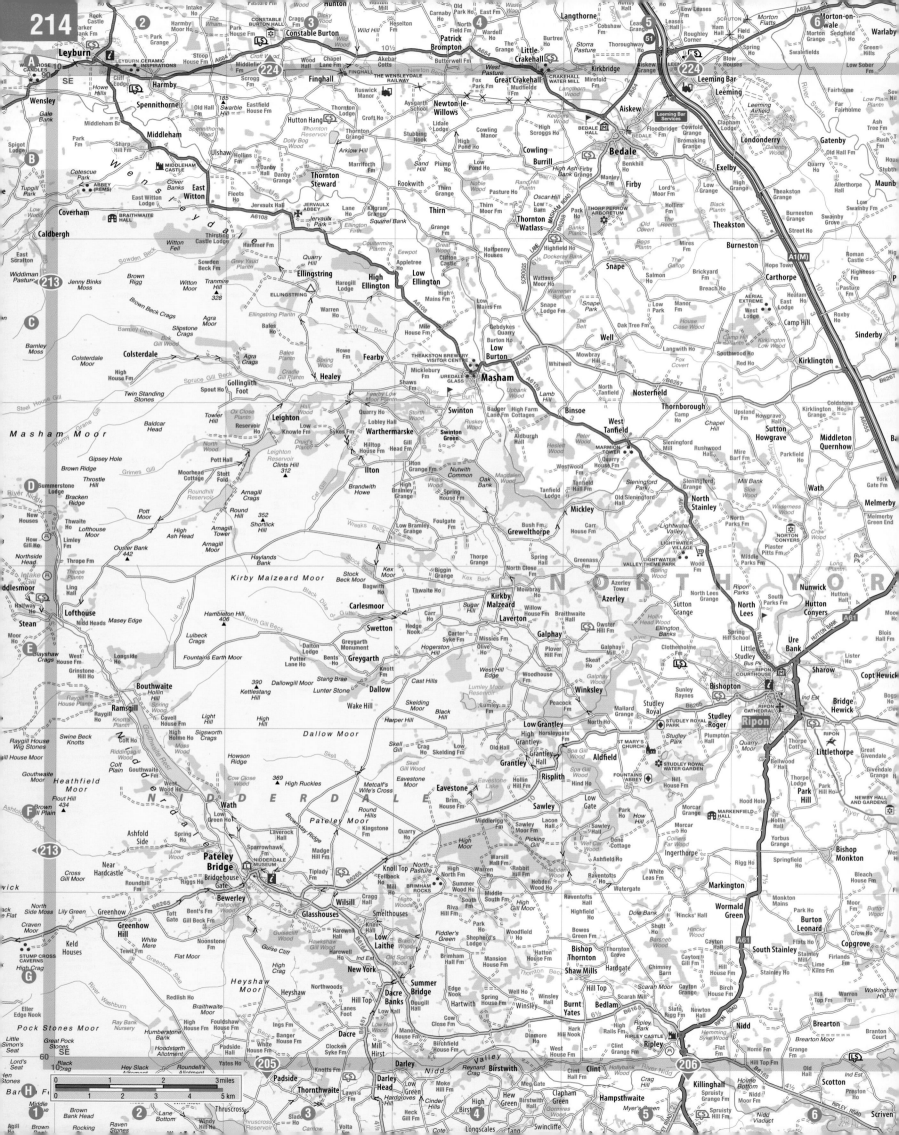

NORTH YORK MOORS NATIONAL PARK

HOWARDIAN HILLS

Thirsk
Sowerby
New Thirsk
Old Thirsk
Norby
Carlton Miniott
Sandhutton
Newsham
North Otterington
South Otterington
Thornton-le-Moor
Thornton-le-Street
Thornton-le-Beans
North Kilvington
South Kilvington
Knayton
Borrowby
Leake
Cowesby
Kepwick
Upsall
Kirby Knowle
Boltby
Felixkirk
Thirlby
Old Byland
Cold Kirby
Rievaulx
Scawton
Sutton-under-Whitestonecliffe
Bagby
Balk
Great Thirkleby
Little Thirkleby
Kilburn
High Kilburn
Oldstead
Wass
Byland Abbey
Coxwold
Ampleforth
Kilburn Mouseman Visitor Centre
Newburgh Priory
Husthwaite
Oulston
Yearsley
Brandsby
Stearsby
Crayke
Easingwold
Stillington
Marton-in-the-Forest
Sutton-on-the-Forest
Huby
Tollerton
Alne
Flawith
Youlton
Aldwark
Tholthorpe
Myton-on-Swale
Brafferton
Helperby
Raskelf
Sessay
Birdforth
Thormanby
Hutton Sessay
Carlton Husthwaite
Little Sessay
Dalton
Topcliffe
Asenby
Rainton
Skipton-on-Swale
Baldersby St James
Skelton-on-Ure
Boroughbridge
Aldborough
Roecliffe
Minskip
Langthorpe
Kirby Hill
Dishforth
Cundall
Norton-le-Clay
Crakehill
Fawdington
Marton-le-Moor
Lower Dunsforth
Upper Dunsforth
Grafton
Marton
Branton Green
Great Ouseburn
Little Ouseburn
Arkendale
Staveley
Ferrensby
Linton-on-Ouse
Newton on Ouse
Shipton
Beningbrough
Thorpe Underwood
Aldwark
Wigginton
Haxby
Knaresborough
Kirby Wiske
Kirby Grange
Sowber Gate
Newby Wiske
Hawnby
Rievaulx Abbey
Helmsley Castle
Duncombe Park
Carlton
Ampleforth Abbey and College
Aldborough Roman Town
World of James Herriot
Sutton Bank National Park Centre
White Horse
Hood Hill
Gormire Lake

A1(M)
A19
A61
A168
A167
A170
B1257
B1363
B6265

NORTH

SEA

FILEY

BAY

BRIDLINGTON

BAY

EAST RIDING

OF YORKSHIRE

Bridlington

Flamborough

Filey

North Landing

Flamborough Head

Sewerby

Yons Nab
Lebberston Cliff
Cunstone Nab
The Wyke
Cliff Fm
Newbiggin
Club Pt
North Cliff
WOLDS WAY
Gristhorpe
Filey Brigg
Filey Field
Filey Sands
Brigg End
Filey
Beacon Hill
Muston
Muston Grange
Muston Sands
Lowfield Fm
Royal Oak
Hunmanby Sands
Primrose Valley
Hunmanby Gap
Pilmoor Fm
Foxhill Fm
Airy Hill Fm
Hunmanby Moor
Moor Fm
Reighton Sands
Rosedale Fm
Moor Ho
Reighton Gap
Graffitoe Fm
Bart Fm
Moor Fm
Vicarage Fm
Speeton Sands
Reighton
Speeton Hills
Speeton
Speeton Cliffs
Buckton Cliffs
Dale Fm
Reighton Field
Speeton Moor
Hill Fm
Speeton Grange
Buckton Hall
Howe Fm
Wasters Plantn
Bartindale Fm
Field Greenlands Fm
High Huntow Fm
Buckton
Bempton Cliffs
Standard Hill
Scale Nab
Cat Nab
Bempton Grange
Wandale Fm
Gull Nook
Burton Fleming
Grindale Field
North Dale
Bempton
Dane's Dyke
Dykes Plantn
Thornwick Bay
North Cliff
North Landing
FLAMBOROUGH CLIFFS NATURE RESERVE
Maidensgrave Fm
Grindale
East Fm
North Mount
Newsham Field
Butterwicks Fm
North Moor
Cradle Head
Stottle Bank Nook
Finley Hill
Fox Covert Plantn
East Leys Fm
High Barn
Lynhams Fm
The Crofts
Flatmere Plantn
Selwicks Bay
Flamborough Head
Charlestone Fm
Field Ho
Highcliffe Manor
FLAMBOROUGH HEAD LIGHTHOUSE
High Stacks
North Wood
High Easton Fm
Danes Dyke Fm
Flamborough
Old Fall Plantn
Springdale Fm
East Crags Wood
Eastfield Fm
Beacon Fm
Beacon Hill
Binsdale Fm
Boynton
Sewerby
SEWERBY HALL & GARDEN
South Landing
West Law Wood
Fish Ponds Wood
Wandale Fm
PRIORY
BAYLE MUS
Old Town
Sewerby Rocks
BONDVILLE MODEL VILLAGE
Ruds
Thorpe Hall
Carr Plantn
Sands Wood
Temple Fm
Carnaby Temple
High Wood
BRIDLINGTON
Bridlington
i
OLD PENNY MEMORIES
South Side Mount
Hallowkiln Wood
West Hill
The Spa
Wold Gate
Carnaby
Bessingby
Hilderthorpe
Tufthill Fm
Haisthorpe Field
Ind Est
P&R
Thornholme Field
Haisthorpe
Carnaby Moor
Wilstorpe
South Sands
Burton Agnes Field
Thornholme
BRIDLINGTON BIRDS OF PREY & ANIMAL PARK
Brackendale Fm
Auburn Fm
Harpham Grange
BURTON AGNES HALL
BURTON AGNES MANOR HOUSE
Burton Agnes
Oak Wood Fm
Demming Fm
Fraisthorpe
Fraisthorpe Sands
Hords Covert
Burton Agnes Stud Fm
Harpham
Little Kelk Fm
Thornholme Moor
Gransmoor Wood
Woodside Fm
Low Stonehills
High Stonehills
Hamiltonhill Fm
Turtle Hill Fm
Gransmoor Low Ho
Gransmoor Lodge
Barmston Sands
Great Kelk
Park Ho
Lissett
Allison Lane End
Barmston
Barmston Main Drain
Ulrome

A165
A614
A1039
B1229
B1253
B1255
B1259

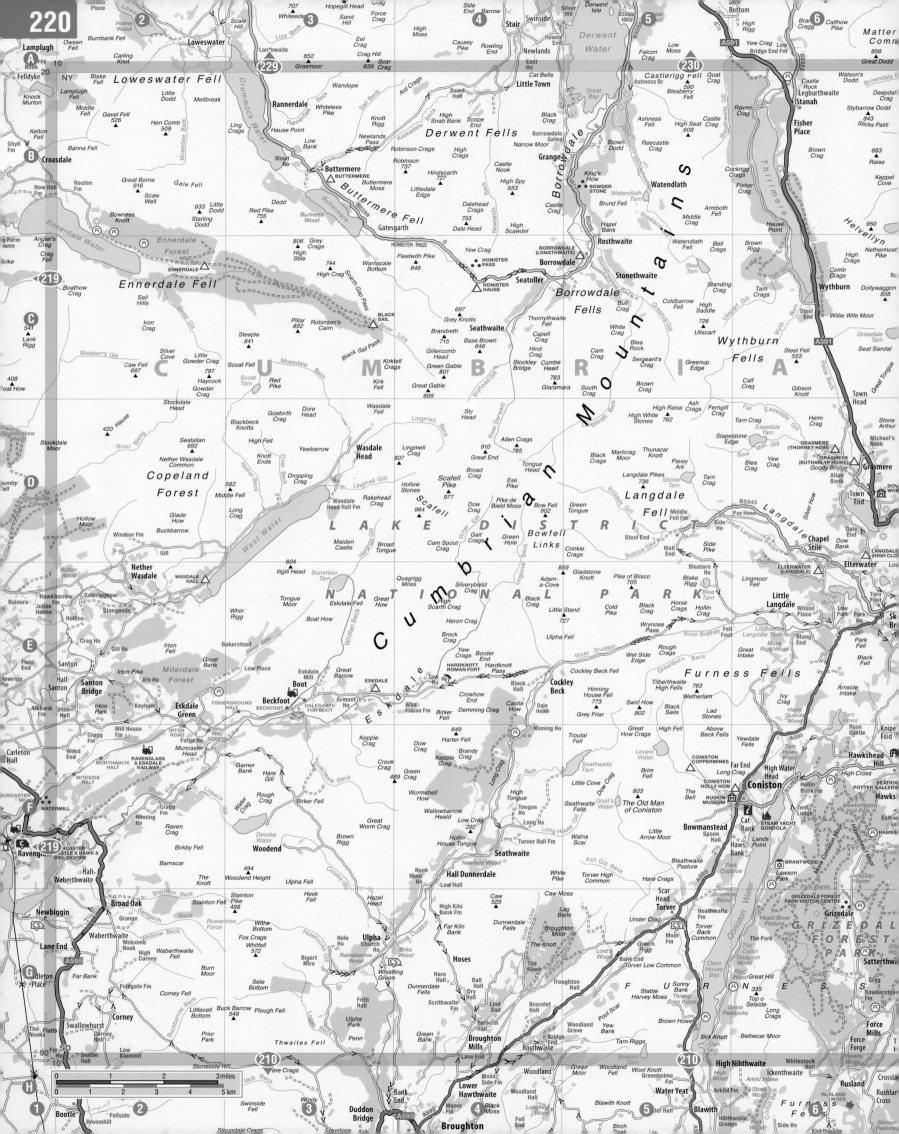

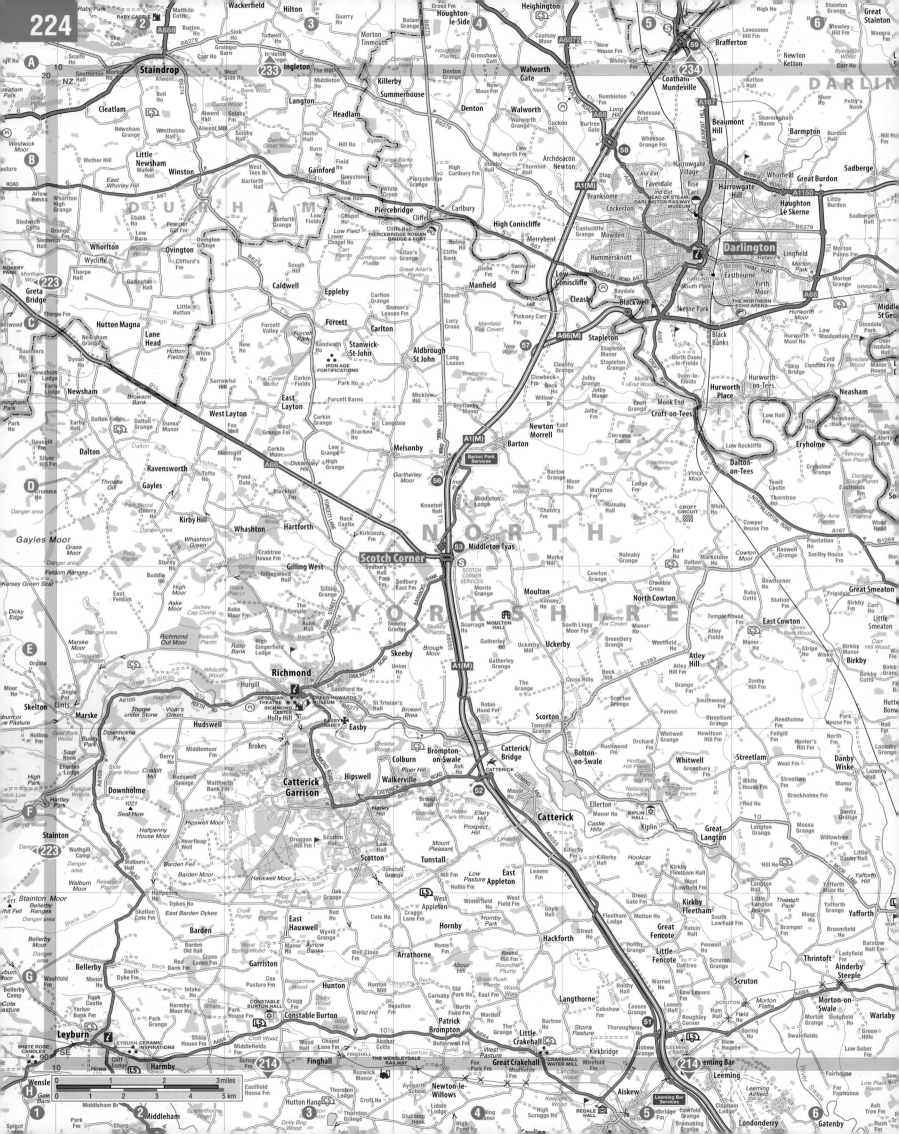

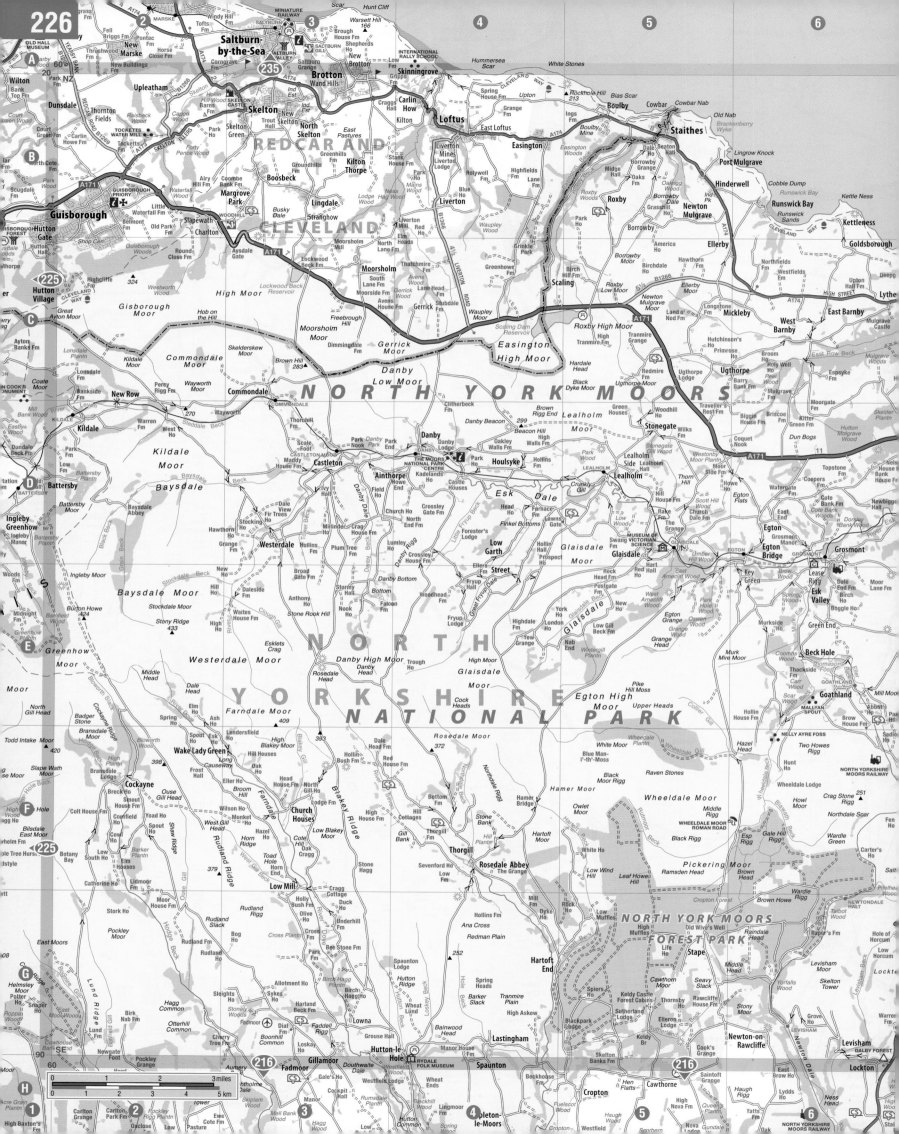

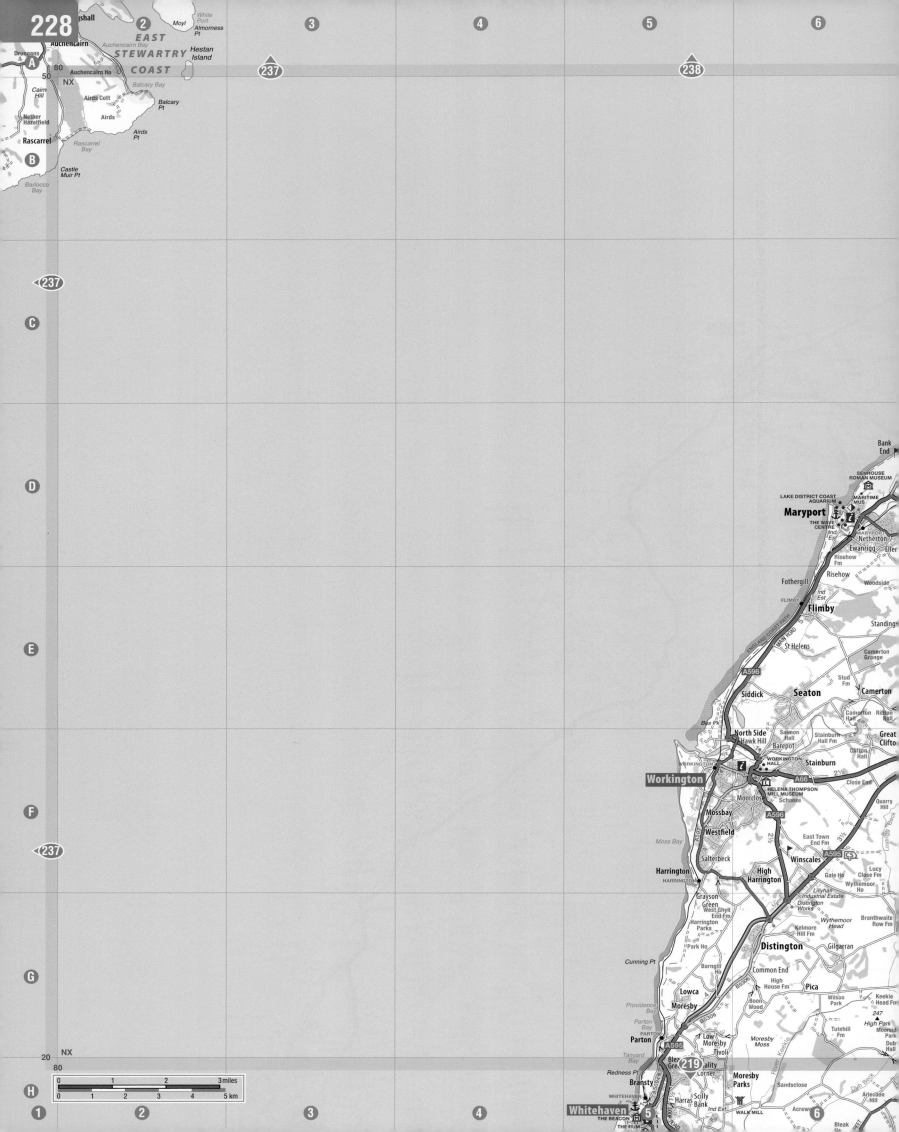

EAST
STEWARTRY
COAST

A
B
C
D
E
F
G
H

1 2 3 4 5 6

Drungans
Auchencairn
Auchencairn Ho
NX
Cairn Hill
Nether Hazelfield
Airds Cott
Airds
Rascarrel
Rascarrel Bay
Castle Muir Pt
Barlocco Bay

shall
Moyl
White Port
Almorness Pt
Auchencairn Bay
Hestan Island
Balcary Bay
Balcary Pt
Airds Pt

237
237
237
238
219
NX

Bank End
SENHOUSE ROMAN MUSEUM
LAKE DISTRICT COAST AQUARIUM
MARITIME MUS
Maryport
THE WAVE CENTRE
MARYPORT Ind Est
Netherton
Ewanrigg
Eller
Risehow Fm
Risehow
Fothergill
Risehow
Woodside
Ind Est
FLIMBY
Flimby
Standing
ENGLAND COAST PATH
MAIN ROAD
St Helens
Camerton Grange
A596
Siddick
Seaton
Camerton
Camerton Hall
Ribton Hall
North Side
Hawk Hill
Salmon Hall
Barepot
Stainburn Hall Fm
Clifton Hall
Great Clifto
Bus Pk
WORKINGTON
WORKINGTON HALL
Stainburn
Workington
HELENA THOMPSON MILL MUSEUM
Schoose
A66
Close End
Moorclose
Mossbay
A596
Quarry Hill
Westfield
East Town End Fm
A595
Moss Bay
Salterbeck
Winscales
Lucy Close Fm
Harrington
High Harrington
Gale Ho
Wythemoor Ho
HARRINGTON
Lillyhall Industrial Estate
Distington Works
Grayson Green
West Ghyll End Fm
Harrington Parks
Kelmore Hill Fm
Wythemoor Head
Branthwaite Row Fm
Park Ho
Distington
Gilgarran
Cunning Pt
Barngill
Common End
High House Fm
Pica
Wilson Park
Keekle Head Fm
Lowca
Boon Wood
247
High Park Fm
Providence Bay
Moresby
BS300
Tutehill Fm
Dub Hall
Parton Bay
Low Moresby
Tivoli
Moresby Moss
NX
PARTON
A595
Parton
Bleach Green
219
Quality
Moresby Parks
Sandsclose
Tanyard Bay
Redness Pt
Corner
River Keekle
Dub Beck
Bransty
Scilly Bank
Arlecdon Hill
Bleak
WHITEHAVEN
Whitehaven
Harras
WALK MILL
Acrewa
THE BEACON
THE RUM

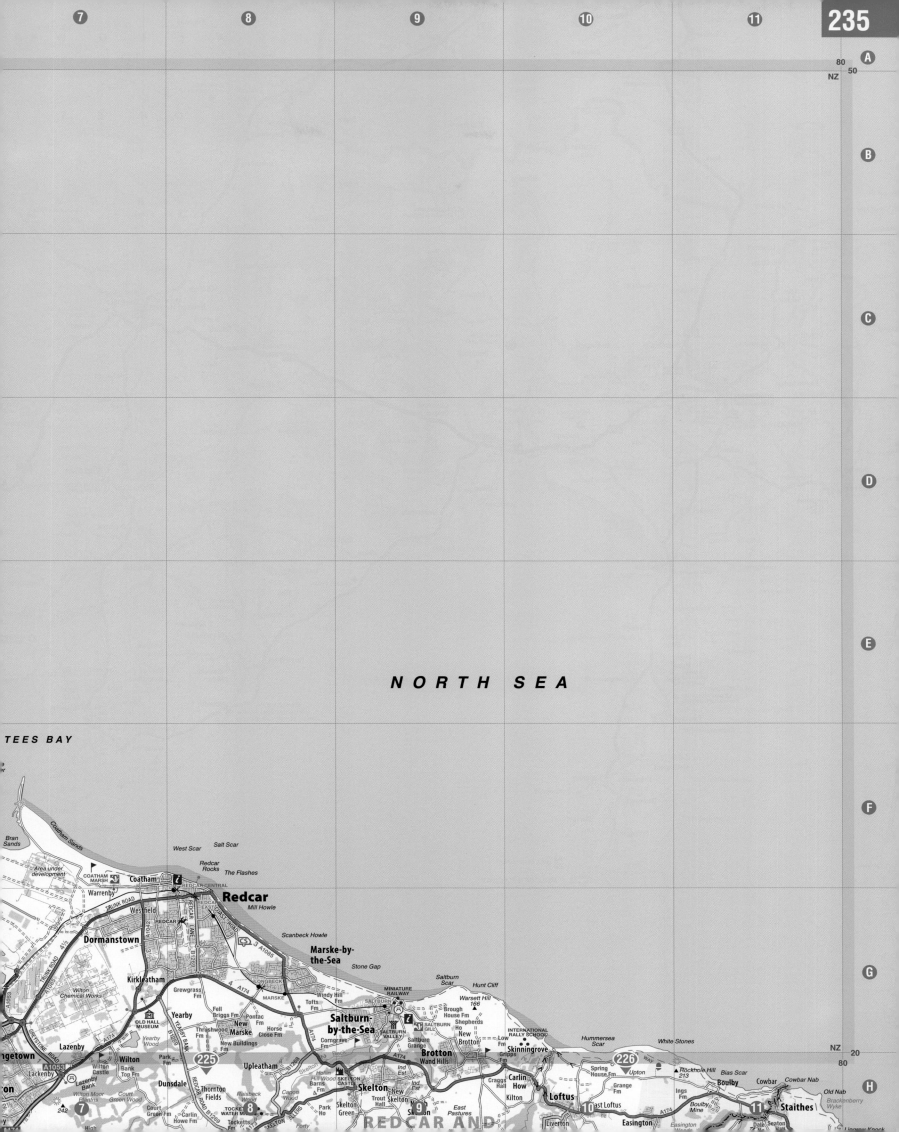

7 **8** **9** **10** **11**

A
B
C
D
E
F
G
H

NZ
80
50
NZ
20
80

NORTH SEA

TEES BAY

Bran
Sands

Coatham Sands

Area under
development

COATHAM MARSH

Coatham

West Scar   Salt Scar

Redcar
Rocks   The Flashes

REDCAR CENTRAL

Redcar
Mill Howle

Warrenby

Westfield

REDCAR EAST
REDCAR

Dormanstown

TRUNK ROAD

Scanbeck Howle

**Marske-by-
the-Sea**
Stone Gap

Kirkleatham

Wilton
Chemical Works

Grewgrass
Fm

Fell
Briggs Fm

Pontac
Fm

LONGBECK
MARSKE

Windy Hill
Fm

Tofts
Fm

MINIATURE
RAILWAY

Saltburn
Scar   Hunt Cliff

Warsett Hill
166

Yearby

Thrushwood
Fm

New
Marske

Horse
Close Fm

Yearby
Bank

New Buildings
Fm

Corngrave
Fm

**Saltburn-
by-the-Sea**

SALTBURN
VALLEY

Saltburn
Grange

Brough
House Fm

Shepherds

New
Brotton

INTERNATIONAL
RALLY SCHOOL

Lazenby

Wilton
Castle

Lazenby
Bank

Park
Fm

Dunsdale

Bank
Top Fm

Upleatham

225

Thornton
Fields

TOCKETTS
WATER MILL

Raisbeck
Wood

Capon
Wood

Holling
Hill Wood
Barns

SKELTON
CASTLE

Ind
Est

Ind
Est

Brotton
Wand Hills

Low
Fm

Gripps

Hummersea
Scar

Skinningrove

White Stones

226

Spring
House Fm   Upton

Boulby
Cowbar   Cowbar Nab

A1053

getown

Lackenby

242

7

High

Greystone Road

A174

Court Green Wood

Wilton Moor
Plantns

OLD HALL
MUSEUM

Carlin
Howe Fm

Park
Ho

Forty

Skelton

Skelton
Green

New
Skelton

Trout
Hall

East
Pastures

Kilton

Craggs
Hall

**Carlin
How**

Loftus

East Loftus

Liverton

Grange
Fm

Boulby
Mine

Rockhole Hill
213

Ings
Fm

Easington
Fm

Bias Scar

Old Nab

Brackenberry
Wyke

Staithes

Dale
Ho

Seaton
Hall

8   **9**   **10**   **11**

REDCAR AND

FIRTH

OF

CLYDE

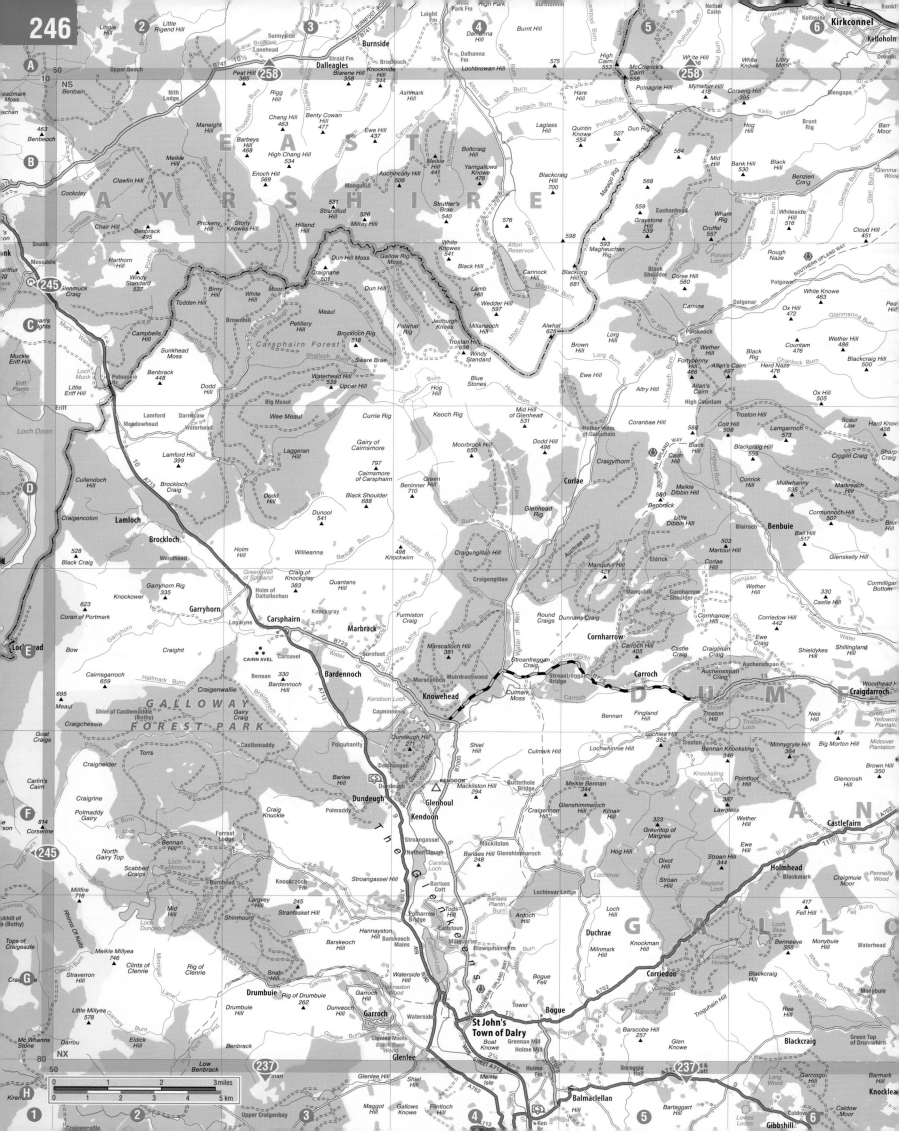

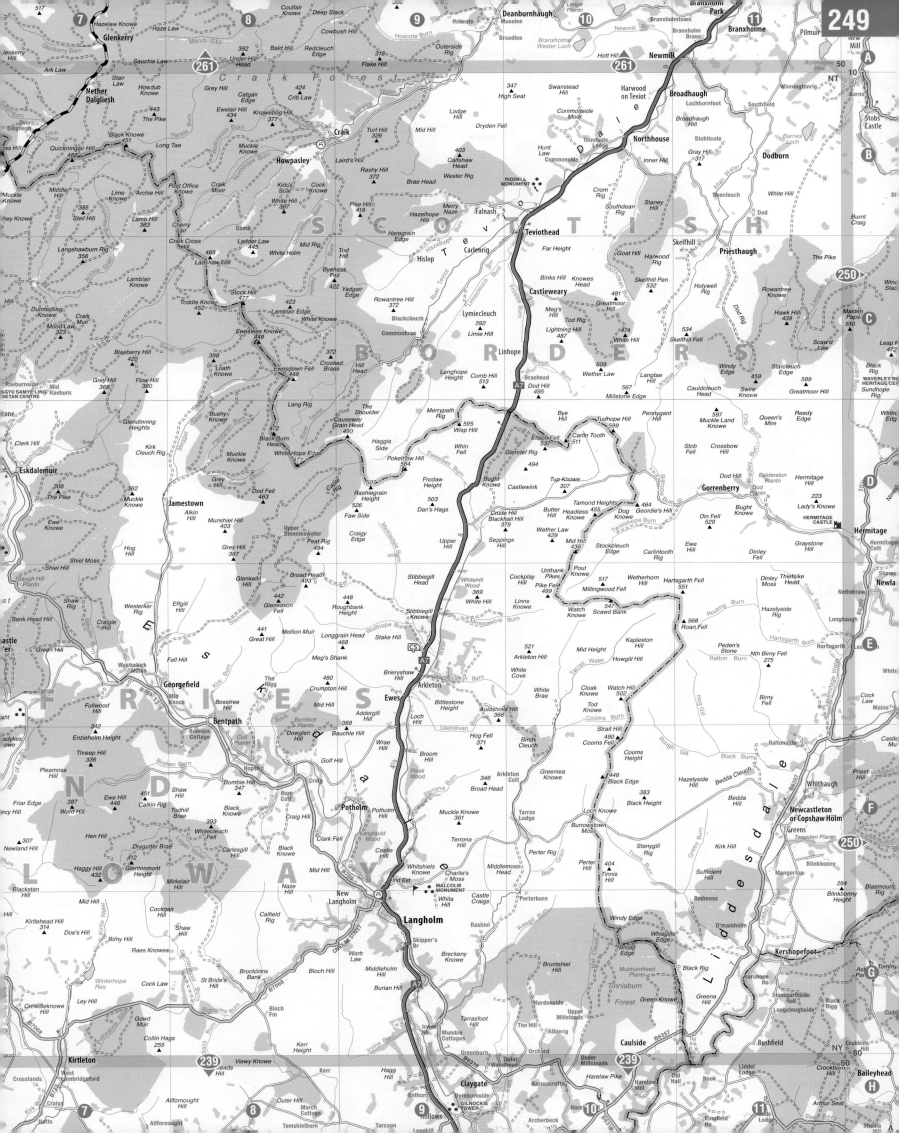

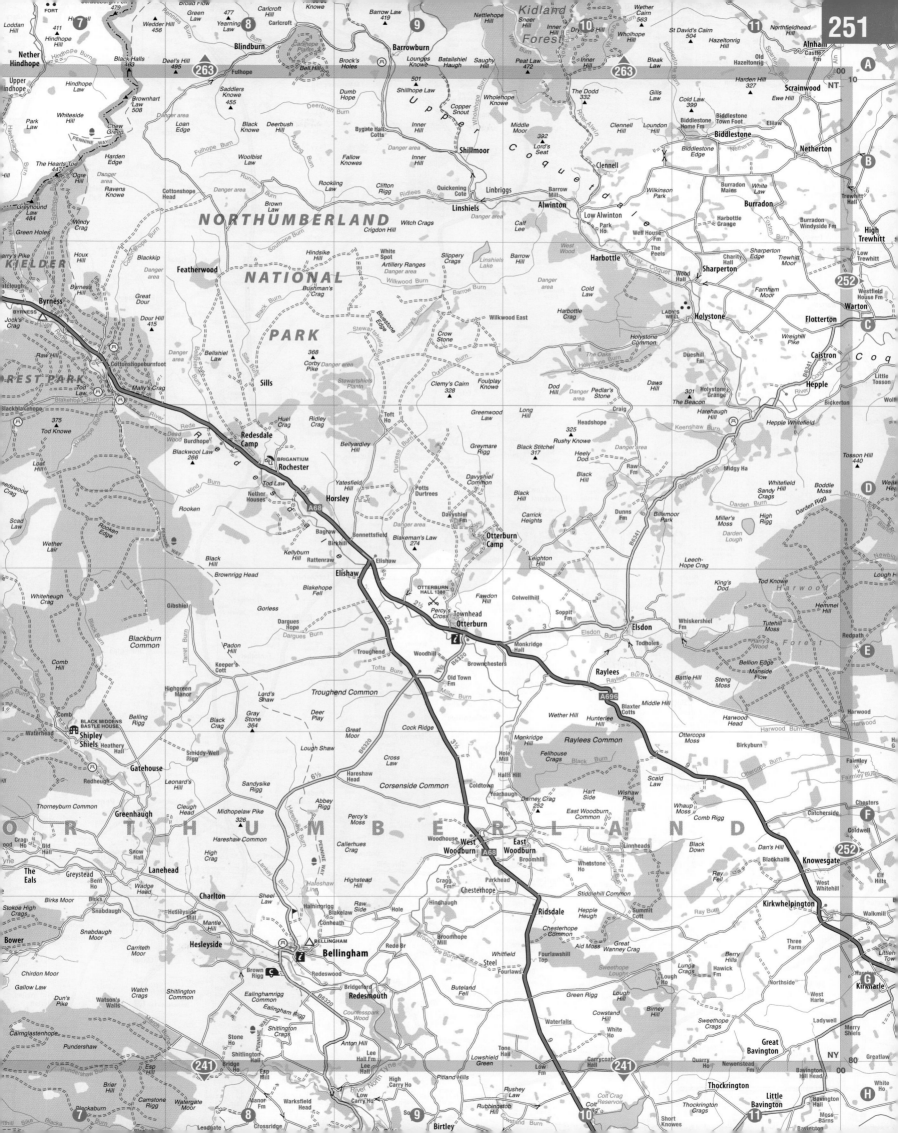

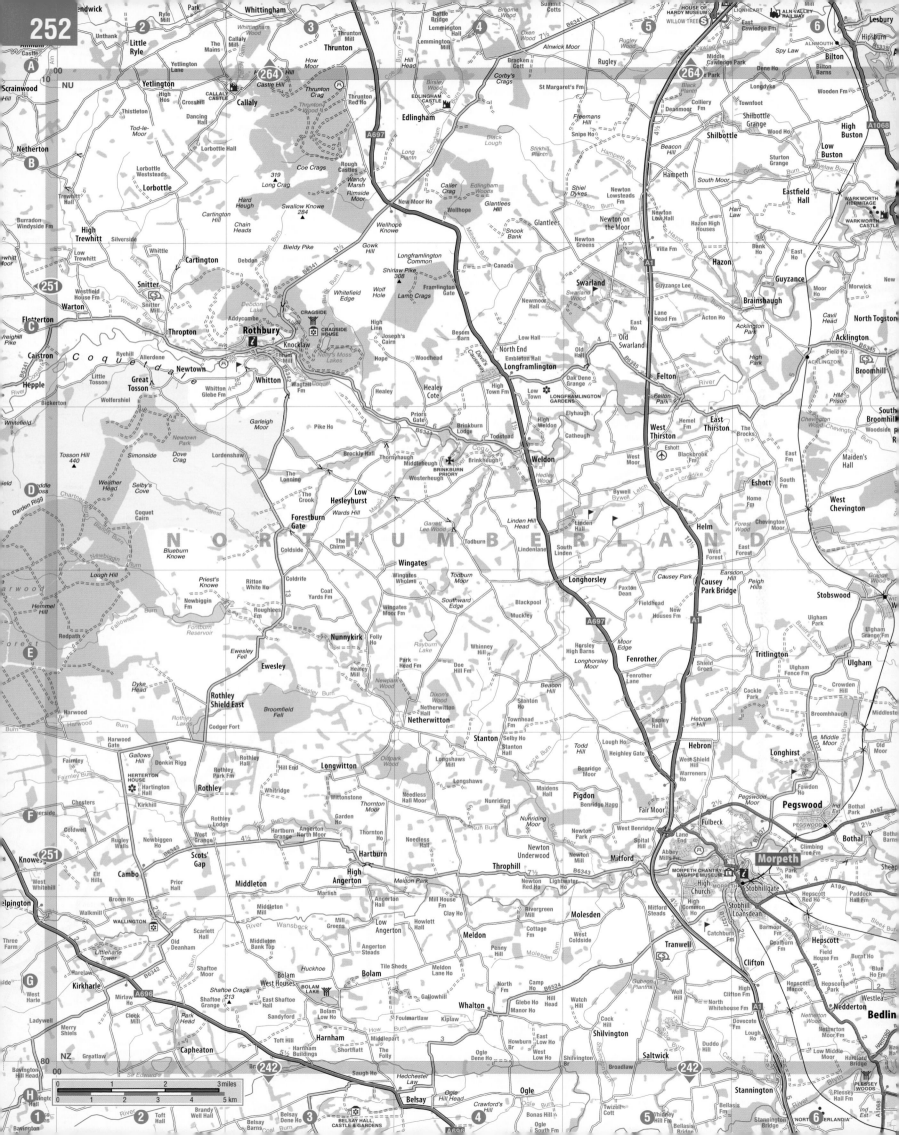

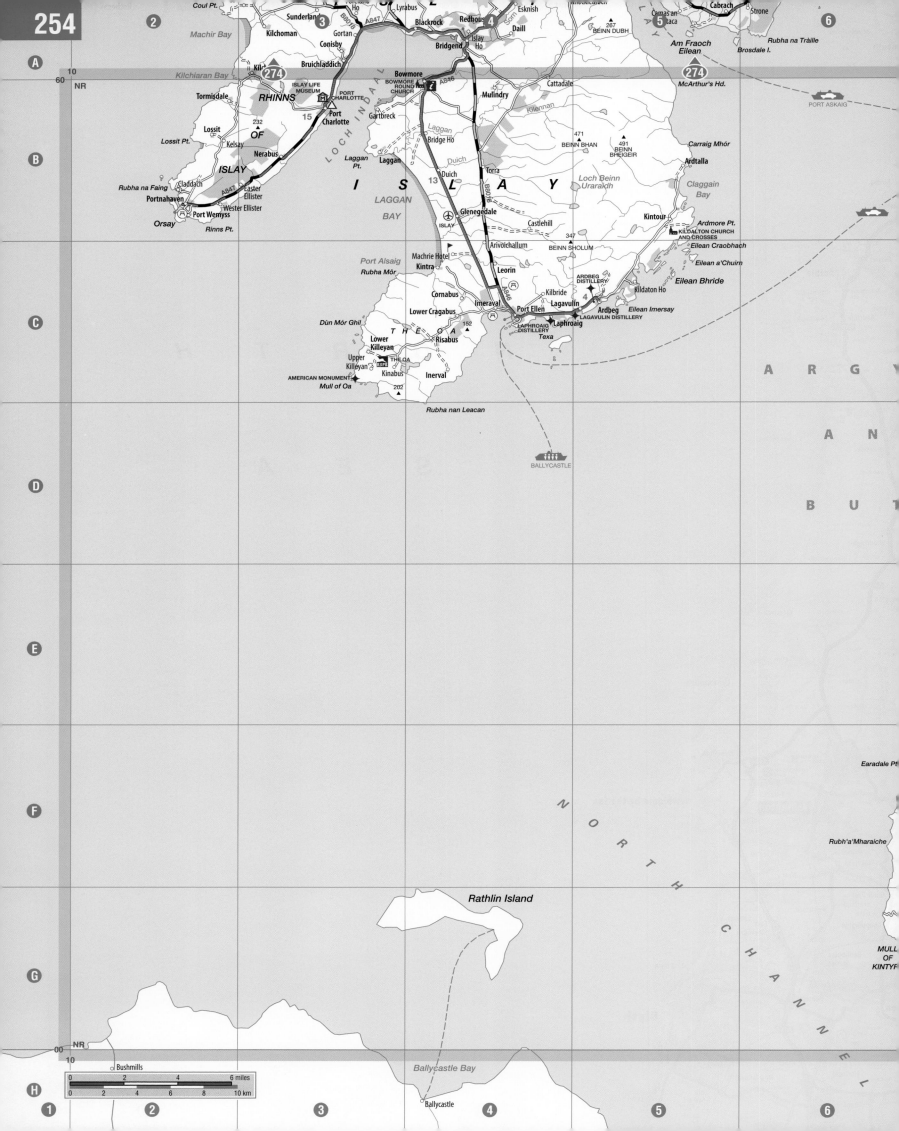

A

B

C

D

E

F

G

H

1 2 3 4 5 6

10
60
NR

Coul Pt.
Lyrabus
Esknish
Cabrach
Strone

Sunderland
Blackrock
Redhouse
Camas an
taca

Kilchoman
Gortan
Daill
Am Fraoch
Eilean
Rubha na Tràille
Machir Bay
Conisby
Islay
Ho
Brosdale I.

Bridgend
267
BEINN DUBH
McArthur's Hd.
PORT ASKAIG

Kilchiaran Bay
Bowmore
274
A846
Cattadale

Port
Charlotte
BOWMORE
ROUND
CHURCH
Mulindry
Killennan

Tormisdale
ISLAY LIFE
MUSEUM
Gartbreck
471
BEINN BHAN
491
BEINN
BHEIGEIR
Carraig Mhór

RHINNS
Port Charlotte
15
Laggan
Bridge Ho
Ardtalla

Lossit
232
OF
Laggan
Pt.
Laggan
Duich
Loch Beinn
Uraraidh
Claggain
Bay

Lossit Pt.
Kelsay
Duich
Torra

Nerabus
ISLAY
I S L A Y
Kintour

Rubha na Faing
Claddach
LAGGAN
Kildaton Ho
Ardmore Pt.

Portnahaven
Easter
Ellister
BAY
Glenegedale
Castlehill
KILDALTON CHURCH
AND CROSSES

Port Wemyss
Wester Ellister
ISLAY
347
Eilean Craobhach

Orsay
Rinns Pt.
Arivoichallum
BEINN SHOLUM
Eilean a'Chuirn

Port Alsaig
Machrie Hotel
Leorin
ARDBEG
DISTILLERY
Eilean Bhride

Rubha Mòr
Kintra
Kilbride
Kildaton Ho

Cornabus
Imeraval
Lagavulin
Ardbeg
LAGAVULIN DISTILLERY
Eilean Imersay

Dùn Mór Ghil
Lower Cragabus
Port Ellen
Laphroaig
LAPHROAIG
DISTILLERY
152

Lower
Killeyan
Risabus
Texa

Upper
Killeyan
THE OA
RSPB
Kinabus
Inerval

AMERICAN MONUMENT
Mull of Oa
202

Rubha nan Leacan

BALLYCASTLE

A R G Y

A N

B U T

Earadale Pt

Rubh'a'Mharaiche

N
O
R
T
H
Rathlin Island
C
H
A
N
N
E
L
MULL
OF
KINTYF

Bushmills
0 2 4 6 miles
0 2 4 6 8 10 km

Ballycastle Bay
Ballycastle

F I R T H

O F

C L Y D E

Isle

of

Arran

N O R T H

A Y R S H I R E

Merkland
Merkland Wood
Merkland Pt
Wine Port
BRODICK CASTLE
Cladach
Old Quay
ISLE OF ARRAN HERITAGE MUSEUM
Brodick
Strathwhillan
North Corriegills
South Corriegills
Dun Dubh
Fairy Glen
Clauchland Hills
Clauchlands Fm
Clauchlands Pt
Margnaheglish
Clauchlands
Kerr's Port
Hamilton Isle
Blairbeg
Lamlash
The Ross
▲ 311
Monamore Br
Cordon
Gortonallister
White Pt
Mullach Beag
Holy Island
314 ▲ Mullach Mor
Pillar Rock Pt
Monamore Glen
The Knowe Fm
Auchencairn
Kingscross Pt
Kingscross
Knockenkelly
Sandbraes
Urie Loch
Borrach
North Kiscadale
Glas Choirein
South Kiscadale
Whiting Bay
Cnoc an Fheidh
GLENASHDALE FALLS
Largymore
Auchareoch
Largymeanoch
Cnoc na Garbad
Cnoc na Comhairle
Largybeg
Largybeg Pt
Port na Gaillin
Cnoc Craobhach
Torr Dubh Mor
Dippin Head
Margenaish Fm
Levencorroch Hill
Dippin
Southbank
East Bennan
Levencorroch
Auchenhew
Drumla
Porta Leacach
West Bennan
STRUEY ROCKS
Port a'Ghillie Ghlais
Porta Buidhe
Port Deang
Kildonan
Bennan Head

Sound of Pladda

Pladda

Glen Rosa
Glenshant Hill
Creag Rosa
Maol Donn 368 ▲
Torr Breac
Glenrosa
Glen Shurig
THE STRING
Glen Gaoithe
Glen Ormidale
Sgiath Bhan
Cnoc Breac
Cnoc Dubh
Meall Buidhe
Benlister Glen
Benlister Burn
Cnoc Dubh
hvein
Cnoc Donn

Port nam Balach

CAMPBELTOWN (May-Sept only)
BRODICK
ARDROSSAN HARBOUR
South Bay
NORTH AYRSHIRE HERITAGE CENTRE
Saltcoats
Outer Nebbock

ARDROSSAN

CAMPBELTOWN (May-Sept Sat only)

CULZEAN CASTLE
CULZEAN
Culzean Bay
Broad Craig
Glasson Rock
Barwhin Pt
Maidenhead Bay
Morriston
Balvaird
Birniehi
Port Murray
Thom
Swan Pond

NS
40
00
NS
10
00

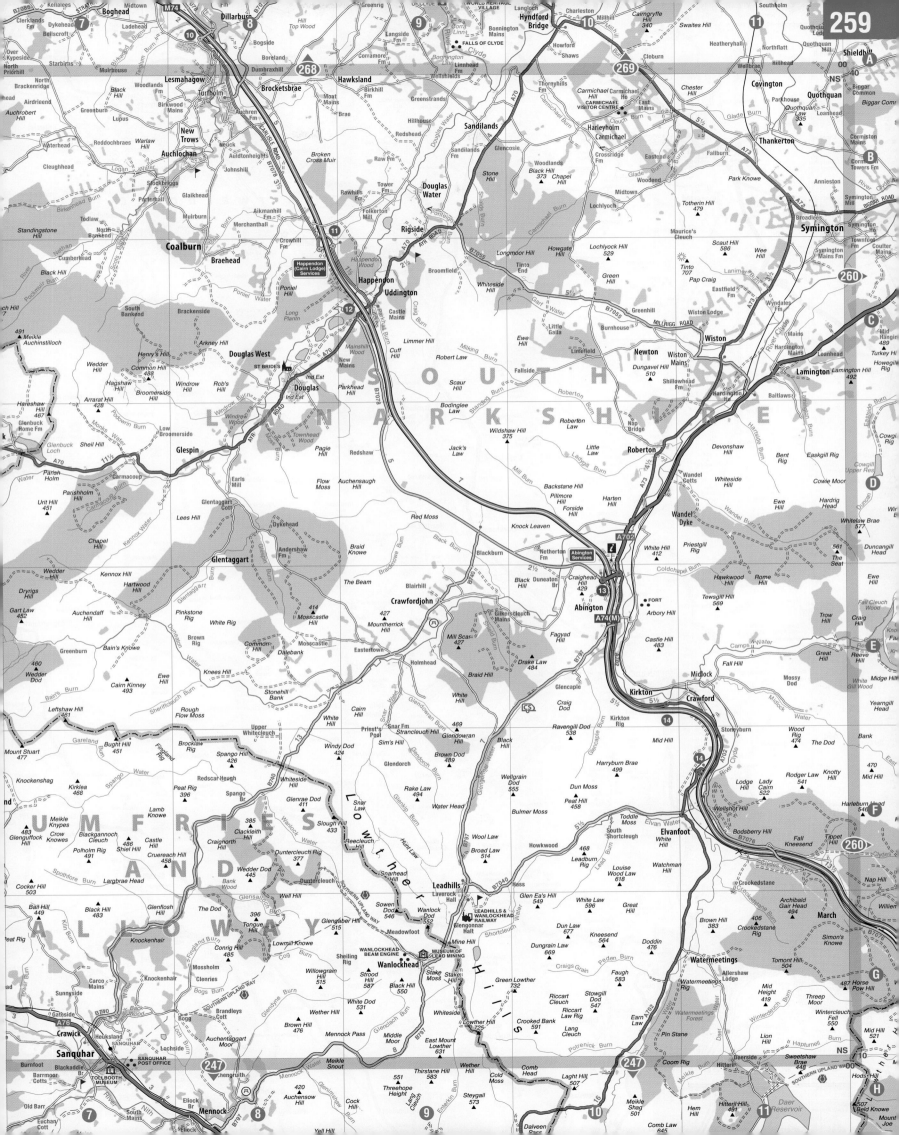

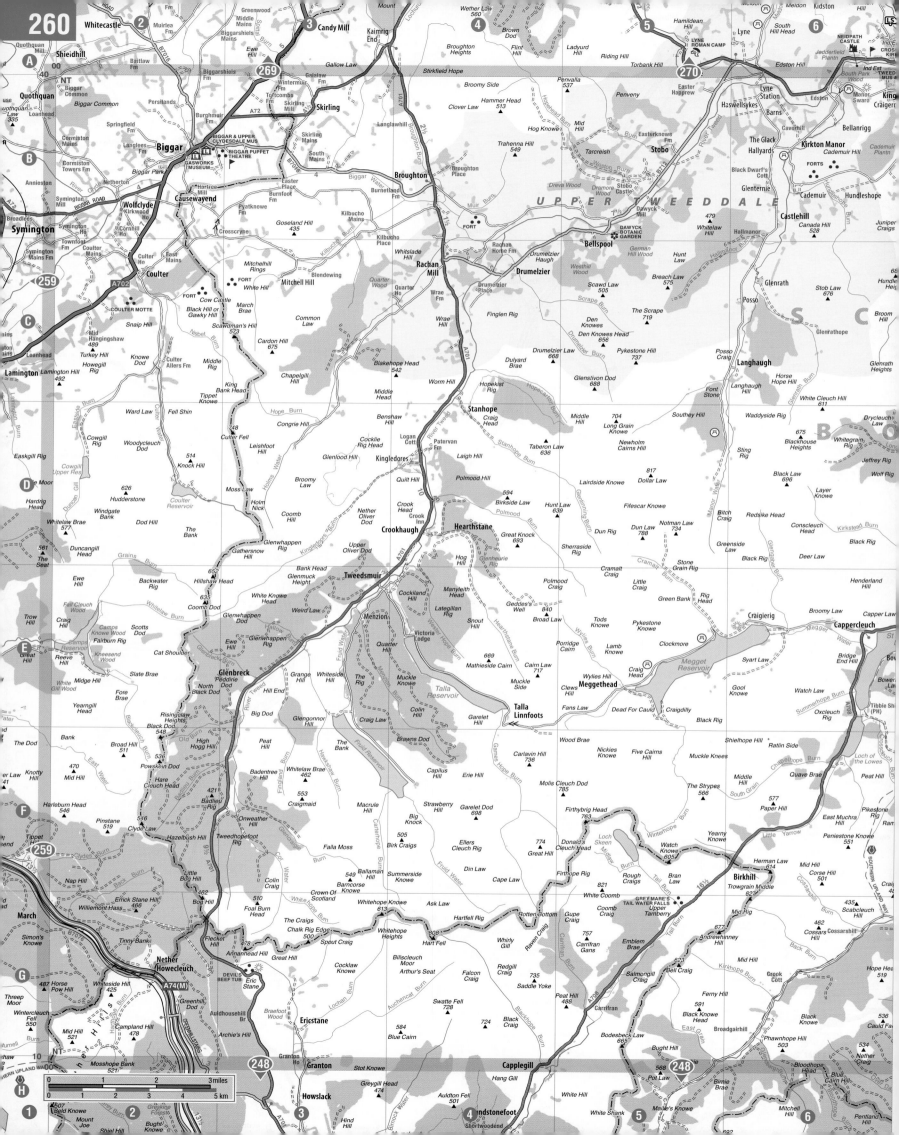

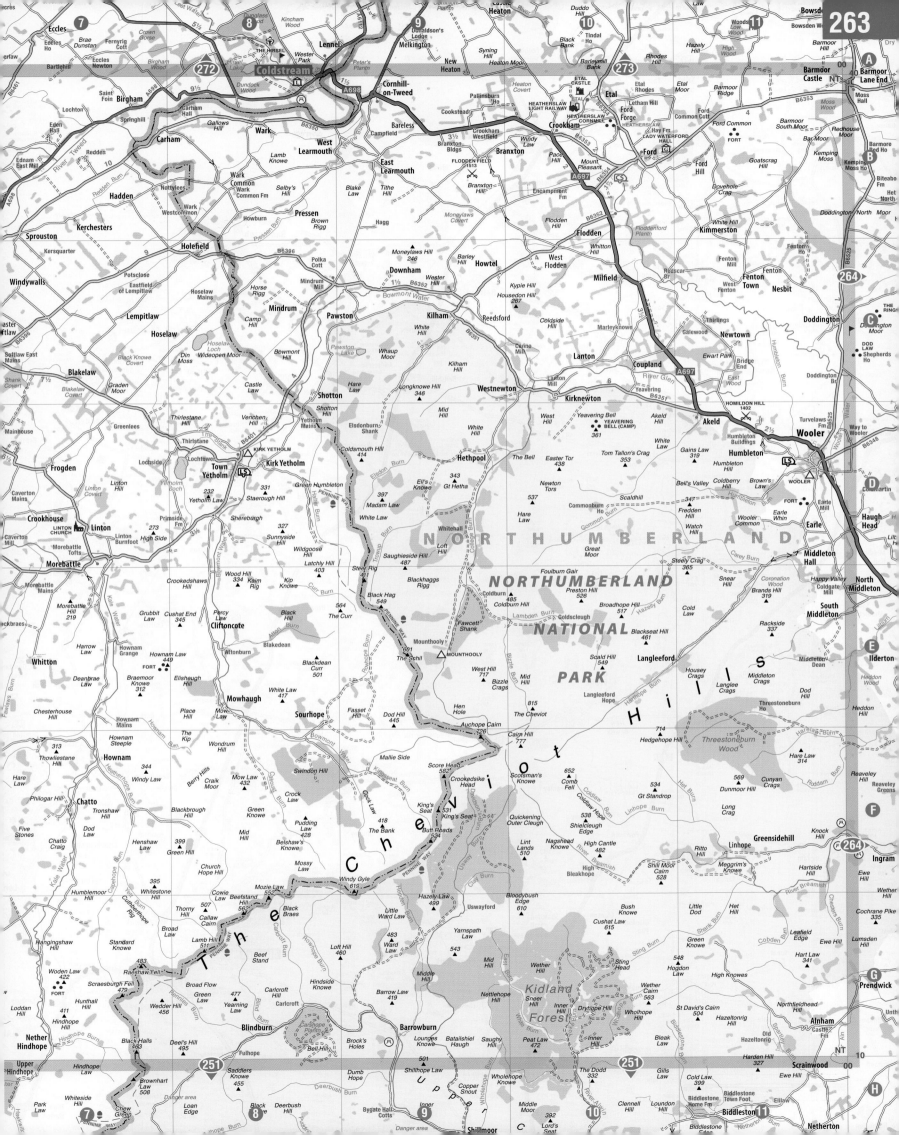

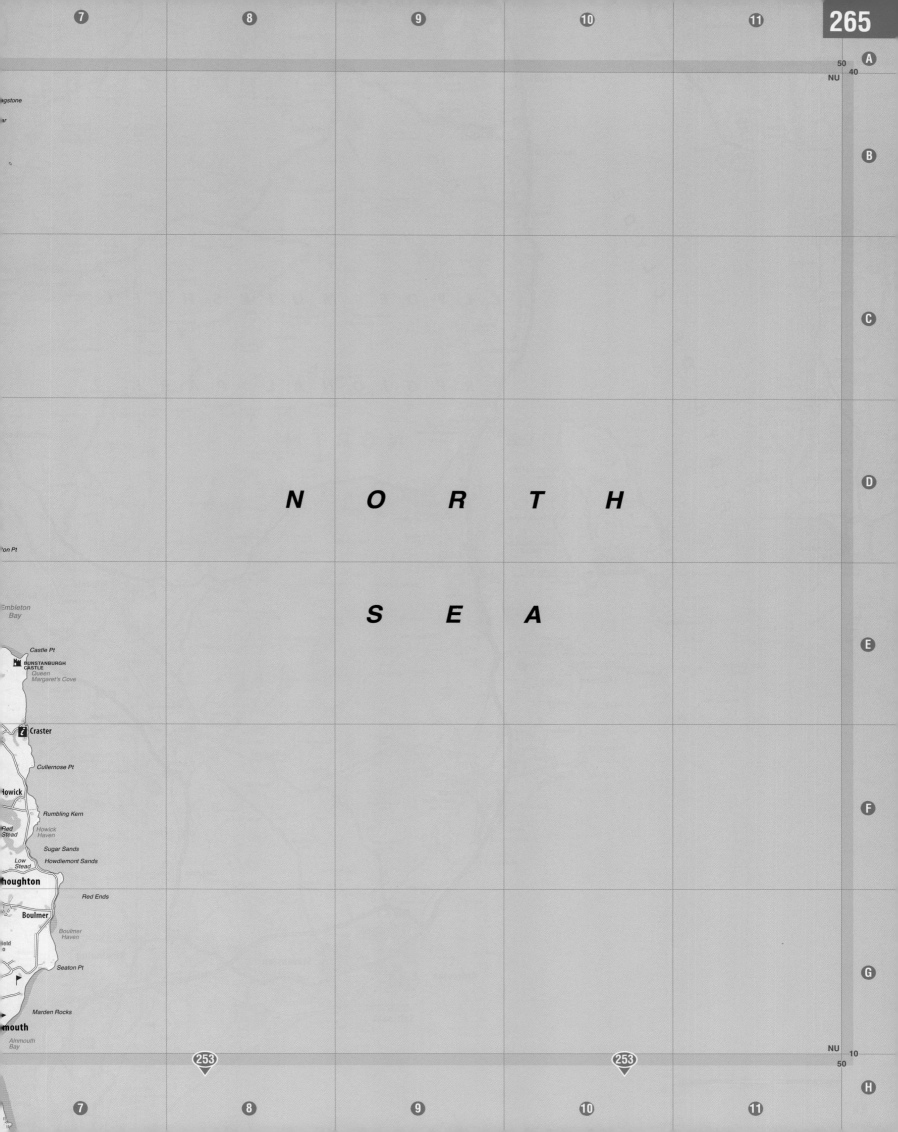

N O R T H

S E A

253

253

EAST LOTHIAN

SCOTTISH BORDERS

Major places: Cockburnspath, Cove, Oldhamstocks, Ecclaw, Grantshouse, Abbey St Bathans, Cranshaws, Ellemford, Longformacus, Duns, Preston, Cumledge, Edrom, Lintlaw, Blanerne, Buxley, Manderston, Clockmill, Cheeklaw, Blackadder West, Wedderlie, Westruther, Choicelee, Gavinton, Polwarth, Sisterpath, Fogo, Fogorig, Bogend, Swinton, Swinton Kirk, Merse, Swintonmill, Leitholm, Orange Lane, Eccles, Halliburton, Thornydykes, Houndslow, Whiteburn, Greenlaw, Gordon, Huntlywood, Middlethird, Easter Howlaws, Lambden, Hume, Stichill, Legerwood, West Morriston, Fans, Coldstream, Birgham, Carham

Hills / features: Nunraw Abbey, White Castle (Fort), Dunbar Common, Clints Dod 399, Rangely Kip 400, Bleak Law, Lammermuir Hills, Nine Stones, Spartleton, Kingside Hill, Summer Hill, Bothwell Hill, Crichness Law, Heart Law, Ewelairs Hill, Corse Law, Dunglass Common, Black Law, Nether Monynut, Peat Law, Dunter Law, Laughing Law, Barnside Hill, Whiteadder Reservoir, Priestlaw Hill, Penshiel Hill, Dod Hill, Collar Law, Herd's Hill, Hareshaw Knowe, Killpallet Heights, Meikle Law, Byrecleugh Ridge, Mutiny Stones, Black Hill, Lamb Hill, Wrunk Law, Wedder Lairs, Upper Knowe, Dunside Hill, Philips Knowe, Scar Law, Whinrig Hill, Pulpit Law 450, Twin Law 447, Sting Law, Dirrington Hill, Dirrington Gt Law 398, Dirrington Lit Law 363, White Knowe, Eve Law 311, Inch Moor, Sale Moss, Shiningpool Moss, Lees Hill, Racecleugh Head, Camp Moor, Hardens Hill, Knock Hill 272, Duns Law 218, Dronshiel Hill, Blacksmill Hill, Hurd Law, Harelaw Moor, Dogden Moss, Hule Moss, Greenlaw Moor, Kyles Hill, Backlea Moss, Polwarth Moss, Bedshiel, The Kaims, Foulshot Law, Crumrig, Ploughlands, Knock Hill, Corsbie

Roads: A1, A1107, A1087, A6105, A697, A6089, A6112, A6464, A6460, A6405, A6355, A6438, A6365, A6456, B6355, B6456, B6460, B6461, B6364, B6369, 282, 271, 262, 263

Whiteadder Water, Dye Water, Watch Water, Watch Water Reservoir, Blackadder Water, Monynut Water, Faseny Water, Bothwell Water, Kell Burn, Southern Upland Way

JIM CLARKE MOTORSPORT MUS, Edinshall Broch, Edrom Church, Dunglass Collegiate Church, Belvidere Wood, Pease Dean, Green Knowe Tower, Hume Castle

Iona
St Columba Exhibition & Welcome Centre
Baile Mor
IONA HERITAGE CENTRE
Stac an Aoineidh
Slignach
Fionnphort
Kintra
Aridhglas
A849
Fidden
Tiraghoil
Bunessan
Loch Assapol
Knockvologan
Erraid
Soa I.
ROSS OF MULL
Ardalanish
Ardchiavaig
Uisken
Scoor
Eilean a'Chalmain
Rubh Ardalanish

Achnahard
Eorabus
Knokan
Lower Ardtun
Lee
18
CRUACHAN MIN
BROLASS
Leidle
Carsaig
376
376
CARSAIG ARCHES
Malcolm's Pt.
Rubha nam Braithrean
Carsaig Bay
Rubha Dubh

288
289

10
20
NM

Torran Rocks

OBAN

Dubh Artach

Rubh'a'Geadha
Kiloran Bay
Balnahard
Uragaig
KILORAN GARDENS
Kiloran
Kilchattan
136
Scalasaig
COLONSAY
Ardskenish
Garvard
Loch Staosnaig
Rubha Dubh
Balerominhor

Corpach Bay
BEINN
453
RAINBERG MOR
Shian Bay
Loch Righ Mor
318
Shian

PRIORY
Dubh Eilean
Oronsay
Eilean nan Ron

Rubh'an t-Sàilein
Loch Tarbert

Rubha Lang-aoinidh

JURA

Rubha Bholsa
Rubha a'Mhail
439
Loch an Aircill
Lagg

Nave Island
Ardnave Pt.
364
SGARBH BREAC
Loch a Chnuic Bhric
785
755
PAPS OF JURA
JURA FOREST
Loch Lesgamaill

Carraig Bhan
Ardnave
Kilnave
Gortantaoid
316
Bunnahabhain
BUNNAHABHAIN DISTILLERY
Cnocbreac
Gleann Astaile
Ardmenish
An Dùna

An Clachan
Sanaigmore
Leckgruinart
Killinallan
SOUND OF ISLAY
Caol Ila
Corran
Leargybreck
Knockrome
Lowlandman Bay
Ardfernal
Loch na Mile

Braigo
Smaull
Ballinaby
Carnduncan
LOCH GRUINART
Loch Gruinart
RSPB
LOCH GRUINART NATURE RESERVE VISITORS CENTRE
Craigens
CAOL ILA DISTILLERY
FINLAGGAN CENTRE
Port Askaig
Feolin Ferry
Keills
Craighouse
ISLE OF JURA DISTILLERY
Small Isles
561

Saligo Bay
Saligo
Aoradh
Tighnacachla
Balole
Ballygrant
Lossit Lodge
8
Kilmeny
Knocklearoch
Keills
342
BRAT BHEINN
Crackaig

Coul Pt.
Coull
Loch Gorm
Foreland Ho
Lyrabus
ISLAY
Esknish
8
Strone
Cabrach
Stone

Machir Bay
Sunderland
B8018
A847
Blackrock
Redhouses
Daill
267
BEINN DUBH
Camas an Staca
8
Rubha na Tràille
Brosdale I.

Kilchoman
Gortan
Conisby
Bridgend
Islay Ho
Am Fraoch Eilean

Kilchiaran
Bruichladdich
Bowmore
BOWMORE ROUND CHURCH
A846
Mulindry
Cattadale
's Hd.

Kilchiaran Bay
254
ISLAY LIFE MUSEUM
PORT CHARLOTTE
Tormisdale
RHINNS
Port Charlotte
Gartbreck
471
BEINN BHAN
Kilennan
254

NR
60
10

Lossit
Kelsay
Nerabus
OF
Lossit Pt.
LOCHINDAAL
Bridge Ho
Laggan
491
BEINN
Carraig Mhór

A   B   C   D   E   F   G   H

1   2   3   4   5   6

A

10
00
NT

B

C

D

E

F

G

Fast Castle
Head　Wheat Stack

Telegraph
Hill　FAST
CASTLE

NT
70
10

Dowlaw Burn　Oatlee Hill

273　St Abb's Head

Lumsdaine　ST ABB'S HEAD
Horsecastle Bay

SETTLEMENT　Mire
Loch
Coldingham Loch
dingham
ommon　Lumsdaine
Moor

7　Cross
Law　Bell
Hill
Moorside
Plant'n　Starney Bay

273

9　　　10　　　11

H

Map labels

Grid reference markers (top): 2, 3, 4, 5, 6

Grid reference markers (side): A, B, C, D, E, F, G, H

00
80 NM

294

294

Gallanach
Port Mor
Muck
137

Eilean nan Each

SOUND OF EIGG

N'SGURR
393
Galmis

Sanna Point
Sanna Bay
Sanna
Achnaha
Portuairk
Achosnich
Point of
Ardnamurchan
ARDNAMURCHAN LIGHTHOUSE
An Acairseid
Ormsaigmore
Ormsaigbeg
Kilch
Kilchoan Bay
B8007

Cairns of Coll
Eilean Mor
Rubha Mor
Sorisdale
Bousd
Cornaigmore
Cliad Bay
B8072
Gallanach
B807
73
COLL
Arnabost
Grishipoll
Clabhach
B8071
Loch Cliad
Ballyhaugh
104
Hogh Bay
Loch Eatharna
COLL RSPB
Totronald
Acha
Arinagour
OBAN
B8070
Arileod
Uig
Eilean Ornsay
Feall Bay
Breachacha Castle
Friesland

Ardmore Bay
Ardmore Pt.
Bloody
Glengorm Castle
MULL MUSEUM
Tobermory
Quinish Pt.
Rubha an Aird
Mishnish
S'AIRDE-BEINN
292
B8073
Caliach Pt.
Sunipol
Croig
Penmore Mill
Cuin
MULL THEATRE
7
Achnadrish
Dervaig
West Ardhu
THE OLD BYRE HERITAGE CENTRE
Druimnacroish
Calgary
Caliach
Mornish
Calgary Bay
Ensay
342
CARN MOR
Kengharair
Achnacraig
Treshnish Pt.
Haunn
B8073
Burg
Kilninian
Achleck
23
Fanmore
390
EAS FORS WATERFALL
Ballygown
LOCH TUATH
424
BEINN NA DRISE
Lagganulva
Oskamull
Sound of Ulva

Calgary Pt.
Gunna
Crossapol Bay
Soa
Loch Breachacha

TIREE
Vaul Bay
Salum
Caolas
Vaul
Rubha Dubh
Kirkapol
B8069
Ruaig
Cornaigmore
Balephetrish Bay
Cornaigbeg
Kenovay
Gott
Gott Bay
Scarinish
Soa
TIREE
Baugh
B8068
Heanish
B8065
Rubha Traigh an Duin
Hynish Bay
Moss
Heylipol
B8065
Balinoe
B8067
rapol
141
Balemartine
Mannal
West Hynish
Hynish
noig

Rubh a'Chaoil
Eilean Dioghlum
Baligortan
Bearnus
313
Ardalum Ho
Gometra
Gometra Ho
Ulva
Ardalum Ho
Ulva House
LOCH NA KEAL

Treshnish Isles
Fladda
Lunga
Bac Mor

Little Colonsay
Staffa
STAFFA
FINGAL'S CAVE
Eorsa
INCH KENNETH CHAPEL
Inch Kenneth
ISLE OF
17
De
Balnahard
561
MACKINNON'S CAVE
Balmeanach
519
Glen Seilisdeir
BEINN NA SREINE
ARDMEANACH
Tiroran
THE BURG
Burg
Kilfin Bay
LOCH SCRIDAIN

Erisgeir

Eilean Annraidh
MACLEAN'S CROSS
Rubha nan Cearc
100
IONA ABBEY AND CATHEDRAL
IONA HERITAGE CENTRE
Kintra
ST COLUMBA EXHIBITION & WELCOME CENTRE
Iona
Baile Mor
Aridhglas
Achnahard
Knokan
Stac an Aoineidh
Slugneach
Fionnphort
A849
Eorabus
18
Fidden
Tiraghoil
Bunessan
Lower Ardtun
Lee
376
CRUACHAN MIN
Erraid
20 NM
20
Knockvologan
ROSS OF MULL
274
Soa I.
Ardalanish
Uisken
Scoor
Eilean a'Chalmain
Ardchiavaig
125
Rubha nam Braithrean
Rubh Ardalanish
Malcolm's Pt

Scale

0   2   4   6 miles
0 2 4 6 8 10 km

1   2   3

Inset map (Tiree)

Gunna
TIREE
Vaul Bay
Salum
Caolas
Balephetrish Bay
Vaul
Rubha Dub
Sraid Ruadh
Cornaigmore
Kirkapol
B8069
Ruaig
Balevullin
Cornaigbeg
Kenovay
Gott
Gott Bay
Hough
Kilmoluaig
Gott
Soa
E
Kilkenneth
Moss
TIREE
Scarinish
Middleton
Heylipol
Baugh
B8068
Crossapol
Heanish
t Mor
Barrapol
B8065
Balinoe
Rubha Traigh an Duin
Loch a'Phuill
B8067
Hynish Bay
Balephuil
141
Balemartine
Mannal
Rinn ais
F
West Hynish
Balephuil Bay
Hynish
Port Snoig

E, F, G, H

1   2   3   4   5   6

40
10
20

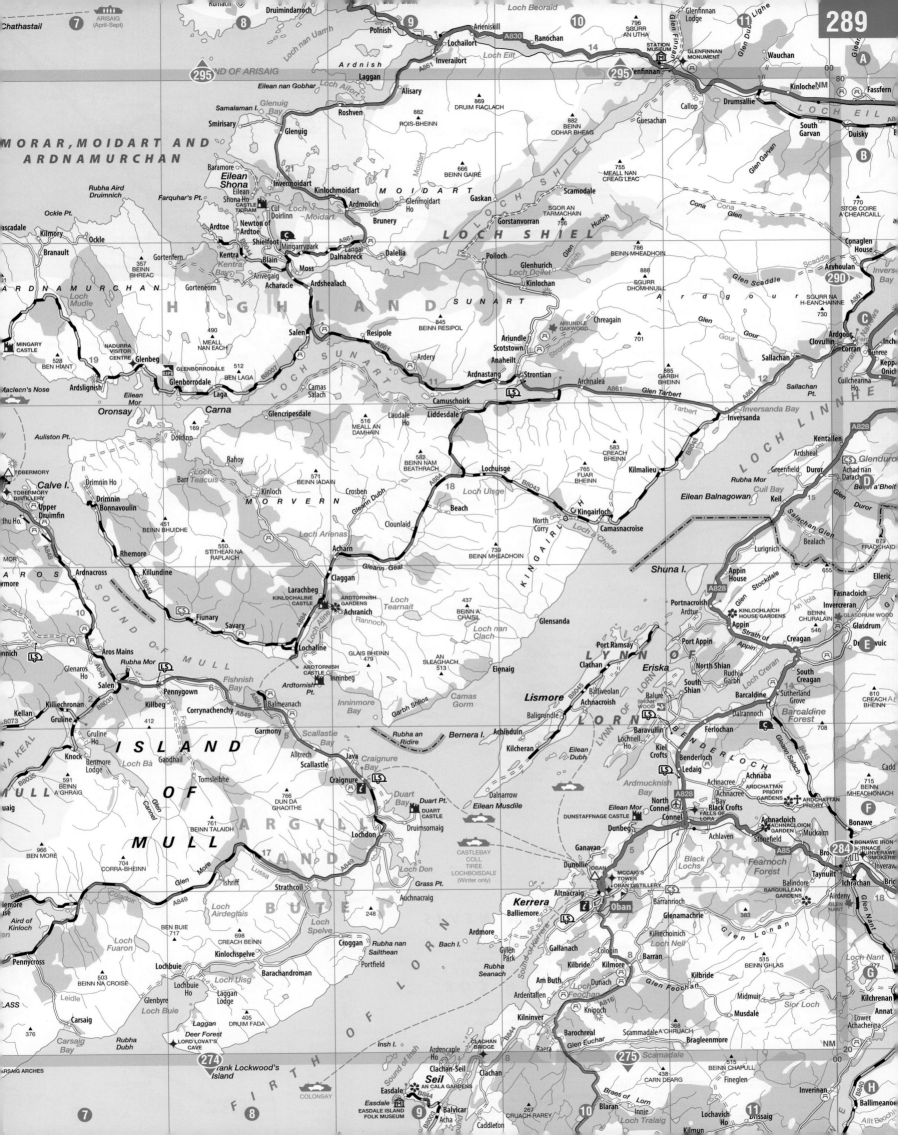

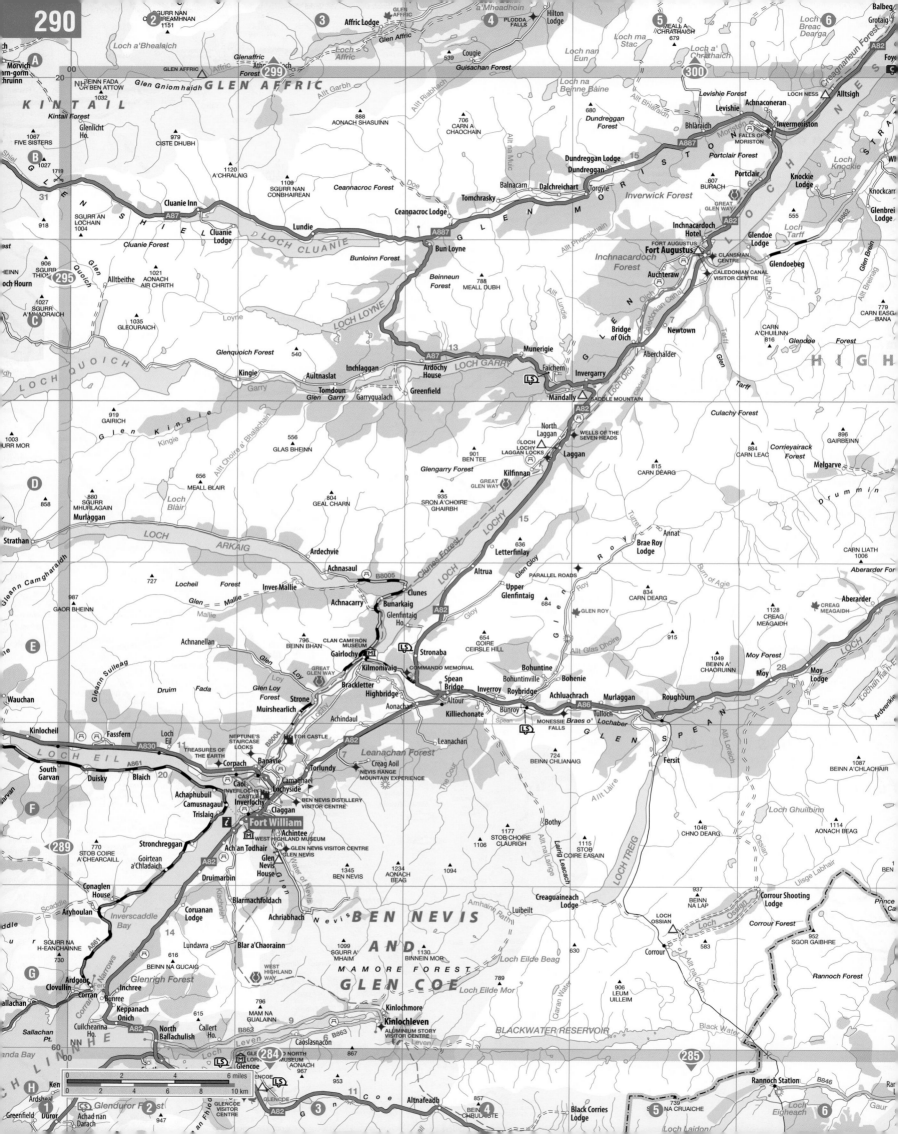

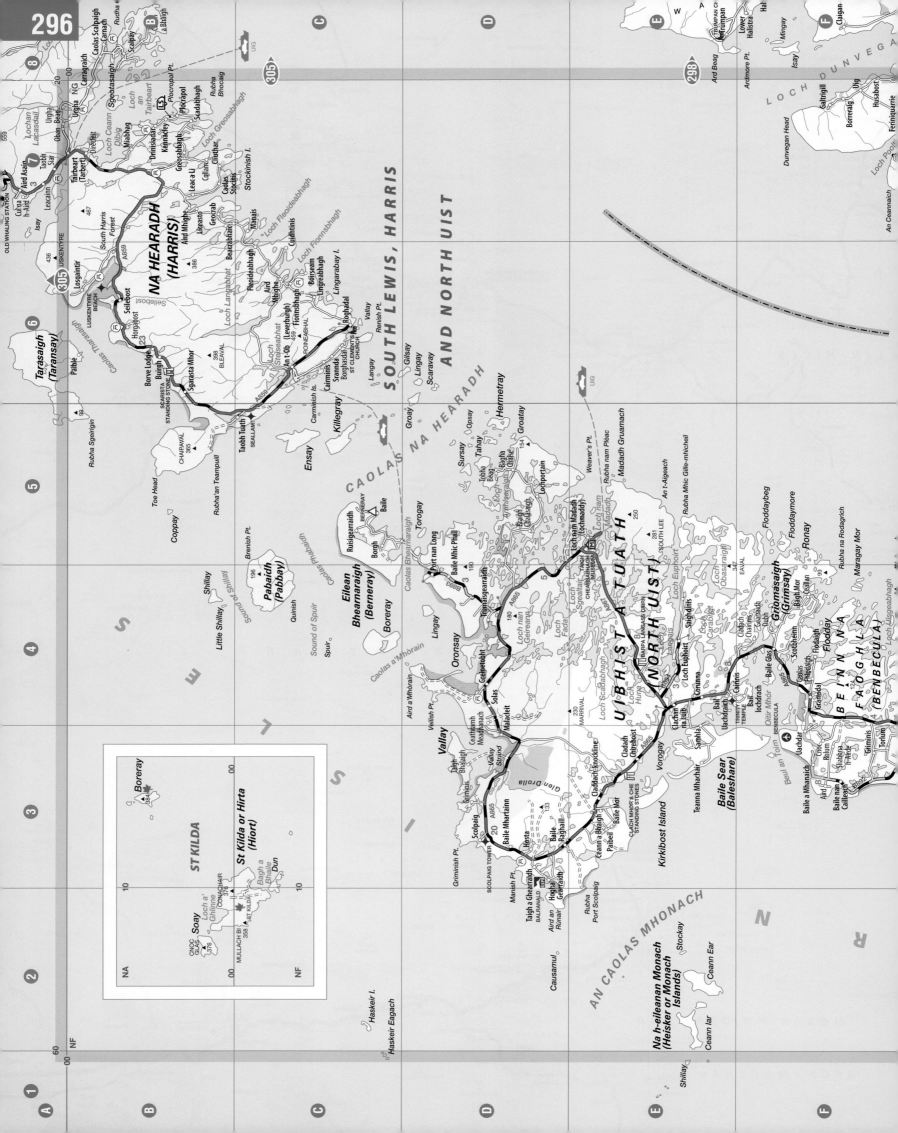

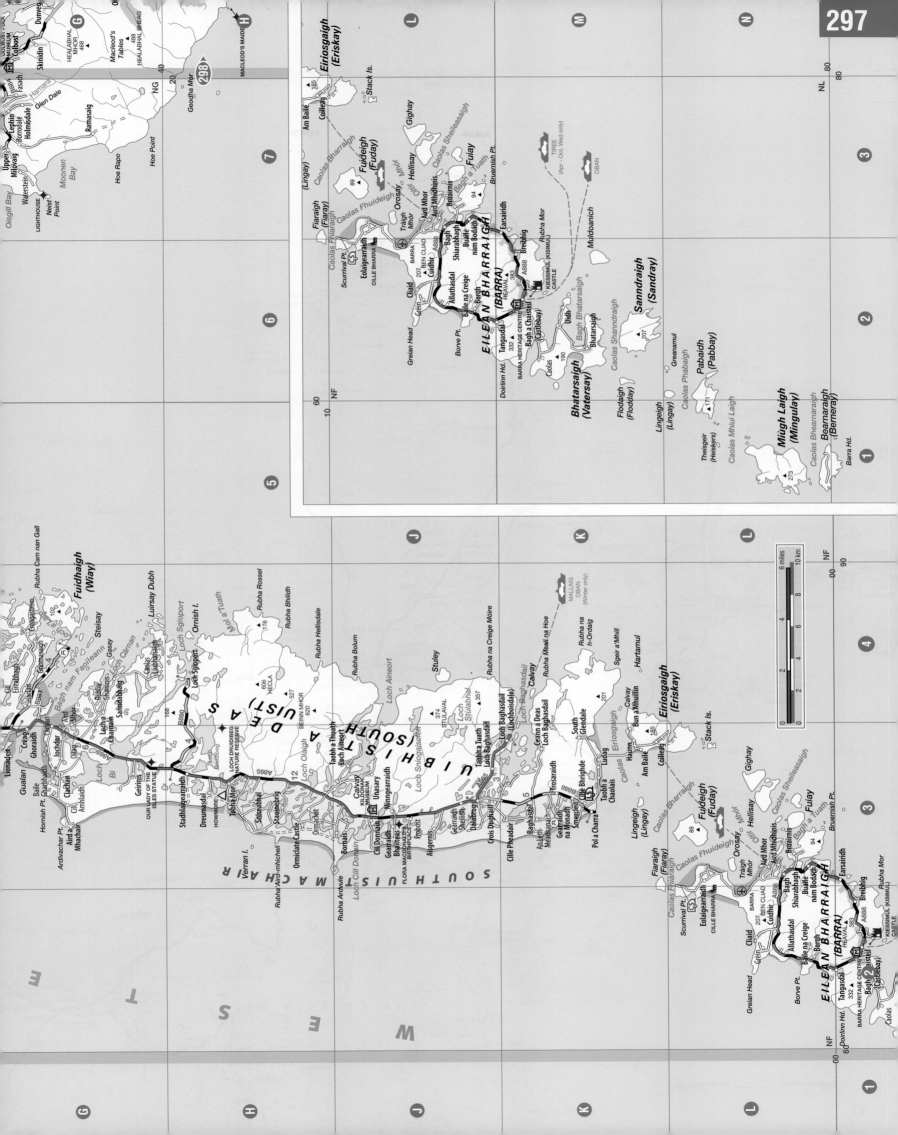

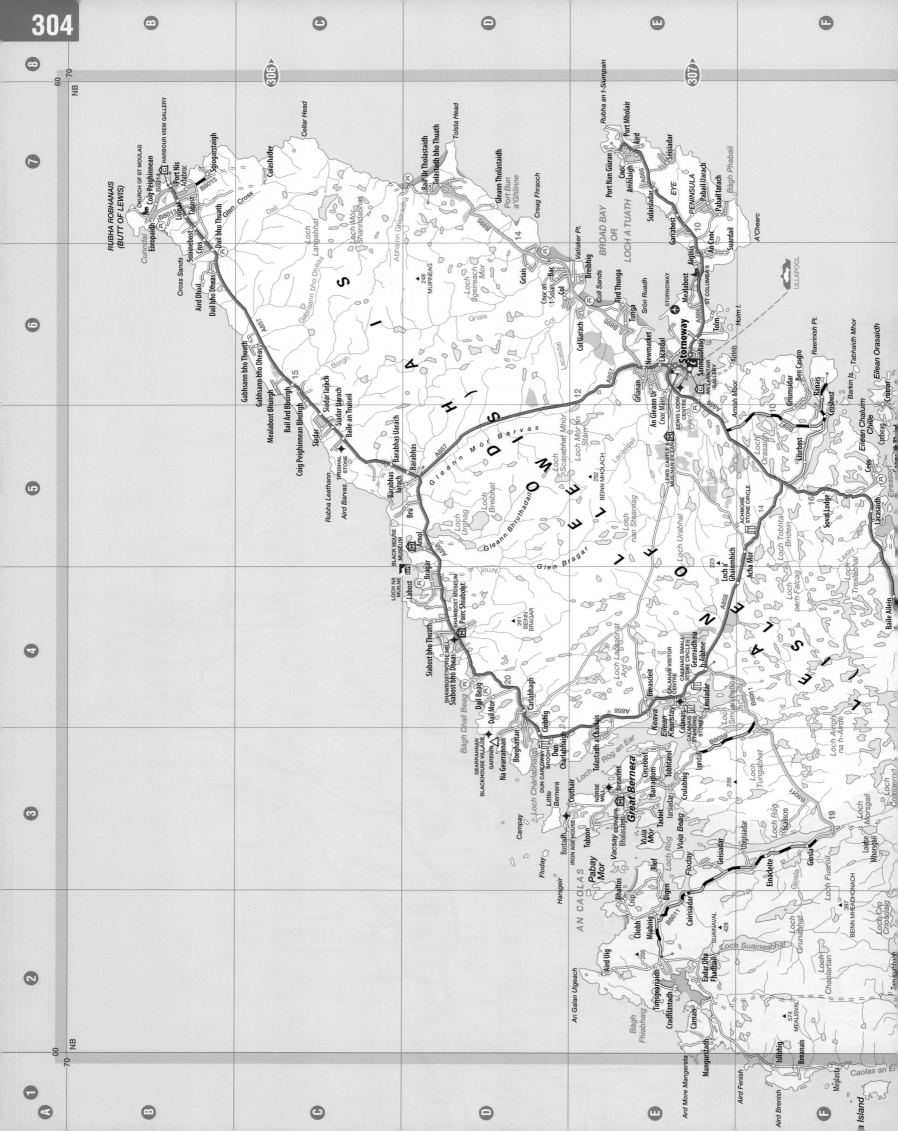

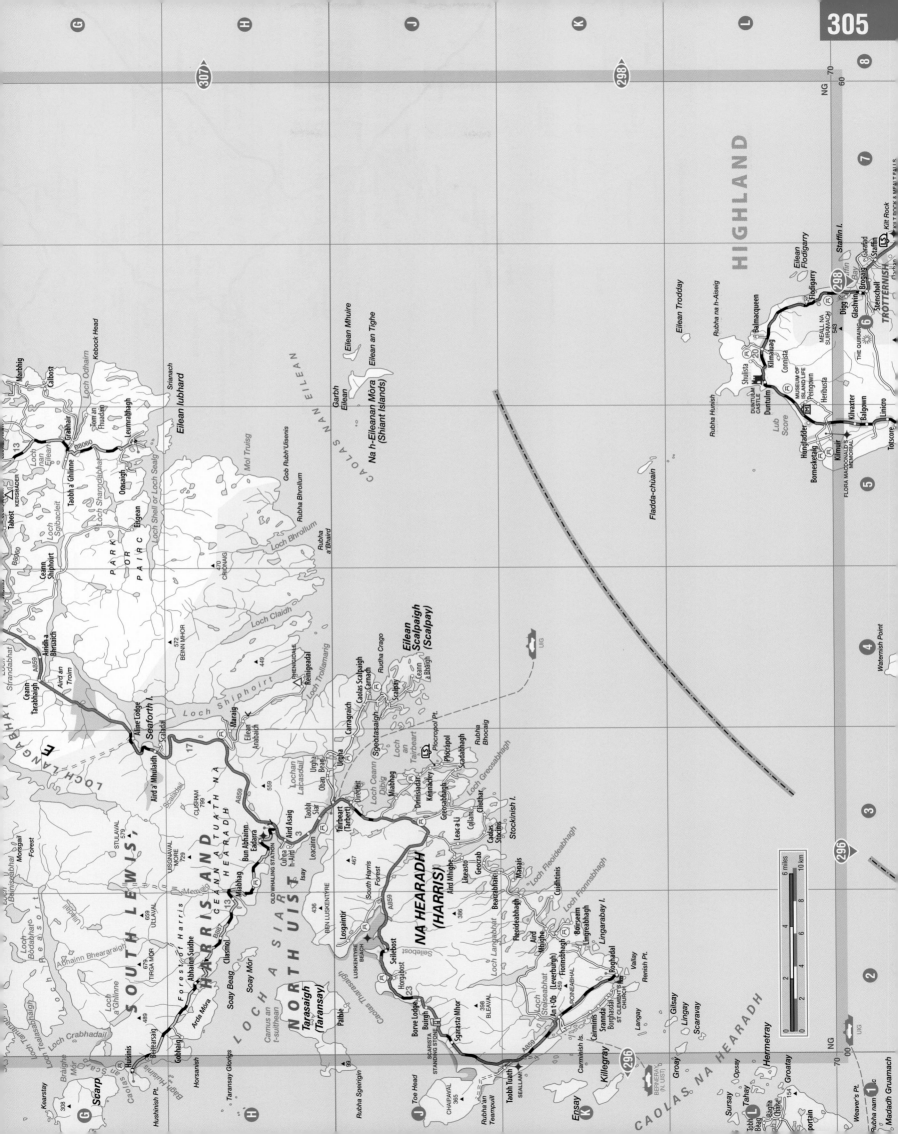

NG 70 60

8

7

6

5

4

3

2

1

HIGHLAND

TROTTERNISH

Staffin I.
Kilt Rock
Staffin
Brogaig
Flodigarry
Eilean Flodigarry
Eilean Troddday
Rubha na h-Aiseig
Balmacqueen
Digg
Bay
Glashvin
Stenscholl
Connista
Duntulm
DUNTULM CASTLE
MUSEUM OF ISLAND LIFE
Kilmaluag
MEALL NA SUIRAMACH
543
THE QUIRAING
Shulista
Kilvaxter
Balgown
Linicro
Totscore
Kilmuir
FLORA MACDONALD'S MEMORIAL
Hungladder
Bornesketaig
Peingown
Herbusta

Rubha Hunish

Lub
Score

Rubha na h-Aiseig

Eilean Mhuire
Garbh Eilean
Na h-Eileanan Mòra
(Shiant Islands)
Eilean an Tighe

CAOLAS NAN EILEAN

Waternish Point
Fladda-chùain

UIG

UIG

296

6 miles
10 km

298

307

298

Kebock Head
Loch Odhairn
Calbost
Marbhig
Iom an Fhuadain
Grabhair
Leumrabhagh
Oasaigh
Taobh a' Ghlinne
Srianach
Eilean Iubhard

B8060
Loch nan Eilean
Tabost
Kershader
Ceann Shiphoirt
Eitgean
Loch Sgibacleit
Loch Shell or Loch Sealg

PARK OR PAIRC

Mol Truisg

Gob Rubh'Uisenis
Rubha Bhrollum
Loch Bhrollum

470
CRIONAIG

Loch Claidh

Rubha a'Bhaird

572
BEINN MHOR
449

Loch Shiphoirt

Eilean Scalpaigh
(Scalpay)
Rudha Crago
Caolas Scalpaigh
Camach
Scalpay
Ceann à Bhàigh

Rhenigidale
Reinigeadal
Loch Trollamarig

Rubha Bhocaig

Stockinish I.

STULAVAL
579
UISGNAVAL MORE
729

Aird an Troim
Abhainn Bhearararaigh

SOUTH LEWIS, HARRIS AND NORTH UIST

CEANN A TUATH NA HEARADH

Aline Lodge
Seaforth I.
Scaladal
Maraig
Eilean Anabaich

CLISHAM
799
Urgha
Lochan Lacasdail
559

Urgha
Uigha
Carragraich
Sgeotasaigh
Loch an Tairbeart
Tarbert (Tairbert)
Plocropol Pt.
Plocrapol
Kadabhagh
Greosabhagh
Loch Greosabhagh
Drinisiadar
Kennach
Loch Ceann Dibig
Miabhag
Leac a Li
Collam
Caolas Stocinis

Ardhasaig
Bun Abhainn Eadarrà
Cùthar
Taobh Siar
Leacalin
Direcleit
Crageo
Urgha
Miabhag
Geocrab
Manais
Loch Fleoideabhagh

A859
OLD WHALING STATION
Isay
467
Geocrab

SOUTH HARRIS FOREST

NA HEARADH (HARRIS)

Beacrabhaic
Cuidhtinis
Loch Fionnsbhagh

LOCH A SIAR

Meavaig
436
BEN LUSKENTYRE
386
BLEAVAL
398

NORTH UIST

Tarasaigh
(Taransay)
Camas an t-suithean

LUSKENTYRE BEACH
Losgaintir
An t-Ob (Leverburgh)
Fleoideabhagh
Aird Mhighe
Lingreabhagh
Boirseam
Lingarabay I.
Loch Langabhat

Horgabost
Sellebost
Seilebost
Fionnsbhagh
Strannda
Borghadal
Valley
Renish Pt.

HARRIS AND CEANN A TUATH NA HEARADH

Forest of Harris
ULLAVAL
659
Abhainn Suidhe
Clasnol
TIRGA MOR
679
Soay Mor
Soay Beag
ARDA MHOR
489

Borve Lodge
Buirgh
Sgarasta Mhor
An t-Ob
SCARISTA STANDING STONE
23
RONEABHAL
459
St Clement's Church
Borghadal
Manish

Bràighe
BEINISEABHAL
Beasort
Loch Bodabhat
Loch a'Ghlinne
Horsanish
Rubha Speirigin
Pable
Toe Head
Rubha'an Teampull
SEALLAM
CHAIPAVAL
365
Taobh Tuath

Scarp
Hushinish
Kearstay
Caolas an Scarp
Loch Teatabhagh
Loch Crabhadail
308
Hushinish Pt.
Gobhaig
Taransay Glorigs

Ensay
Killegray
Carminish Is.
Bernera (N. Uist)
Groay
Lingay
Gilsay
Scaravay

Sursay
Opsay
Tahay
Bagha Chaise
Berneray
Groatay
154
MADADH GRUAMACH

CAOLAS NA HEARADH

Hermetray

Weaver's Pt.

Loch Langabhaig

G   H   J   K   L

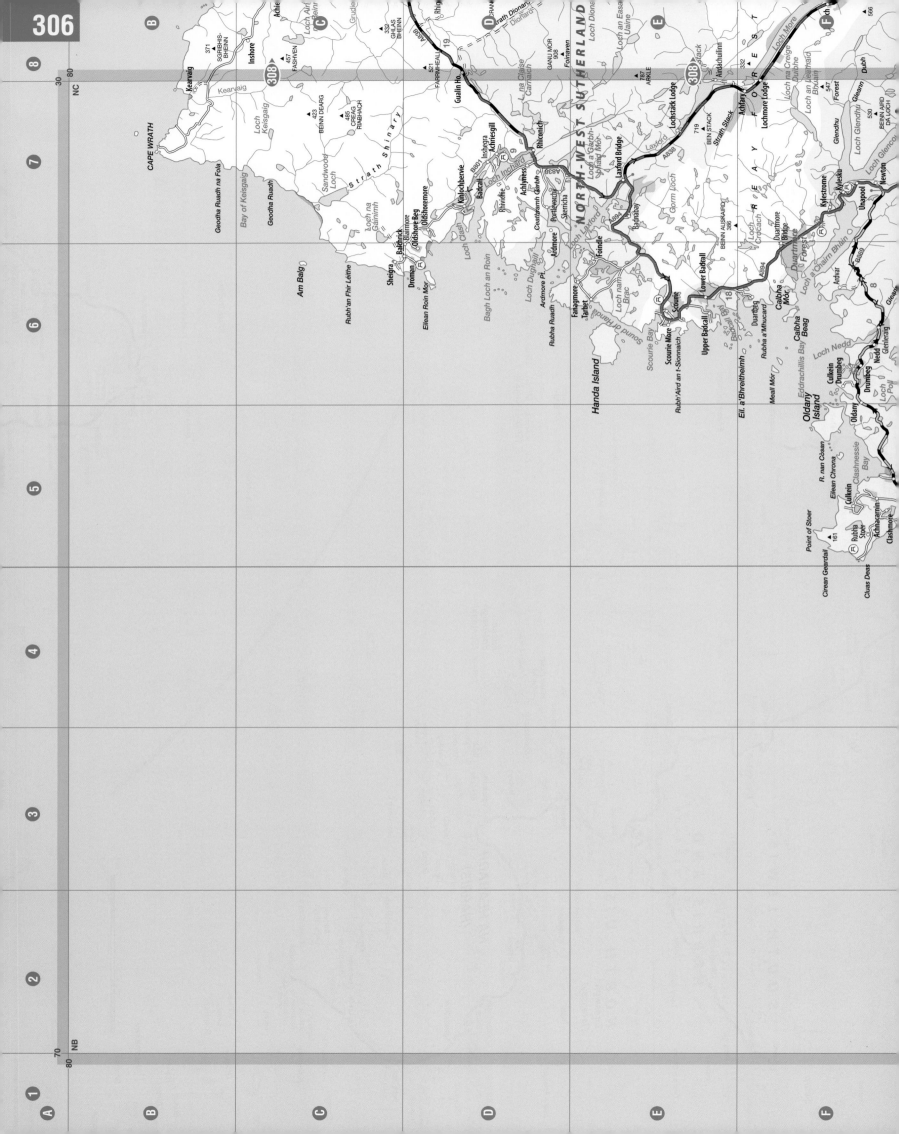

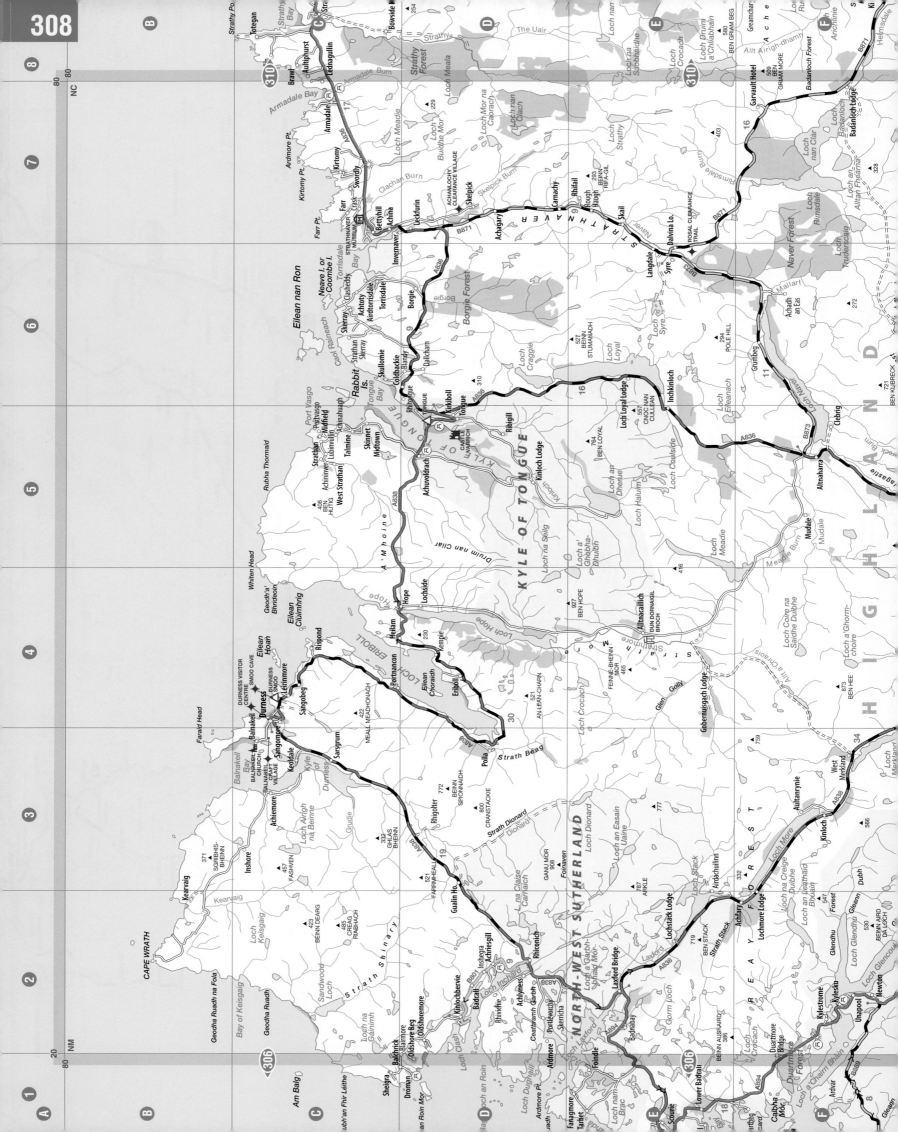

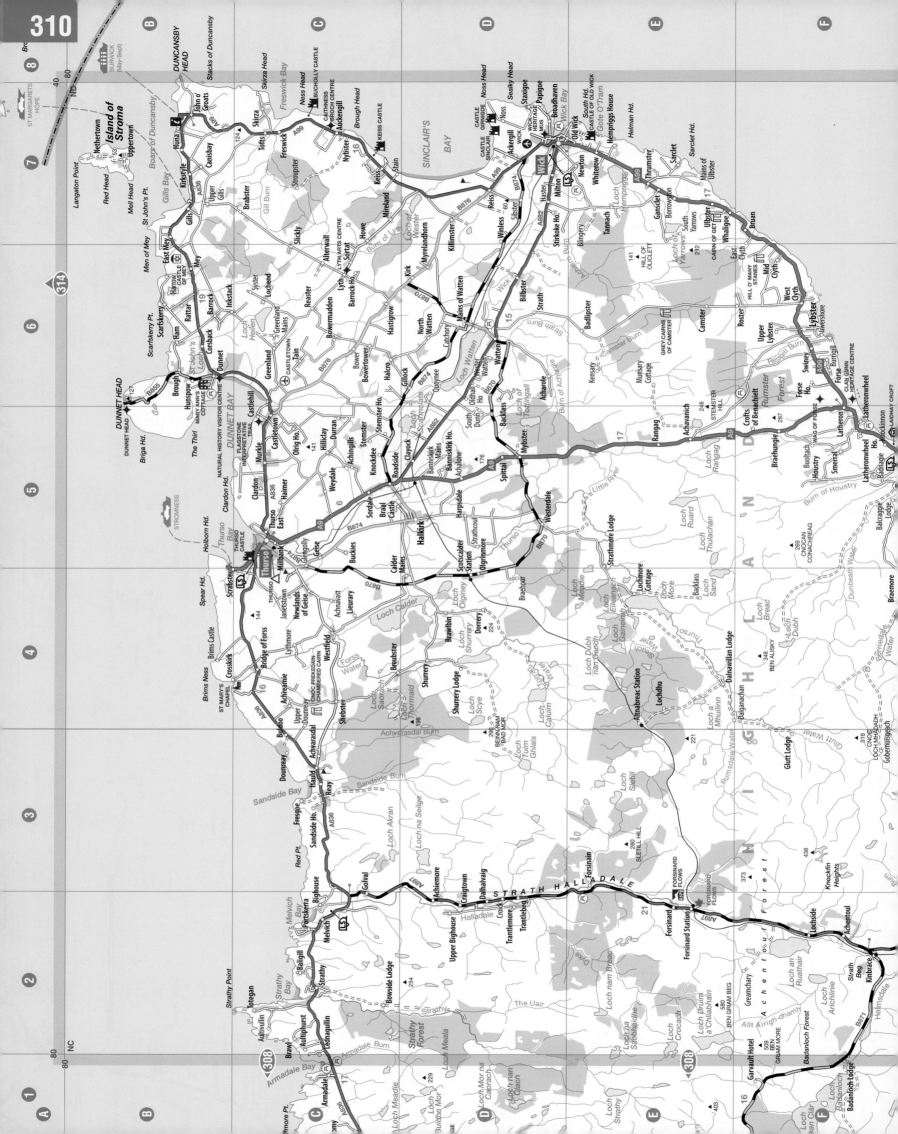

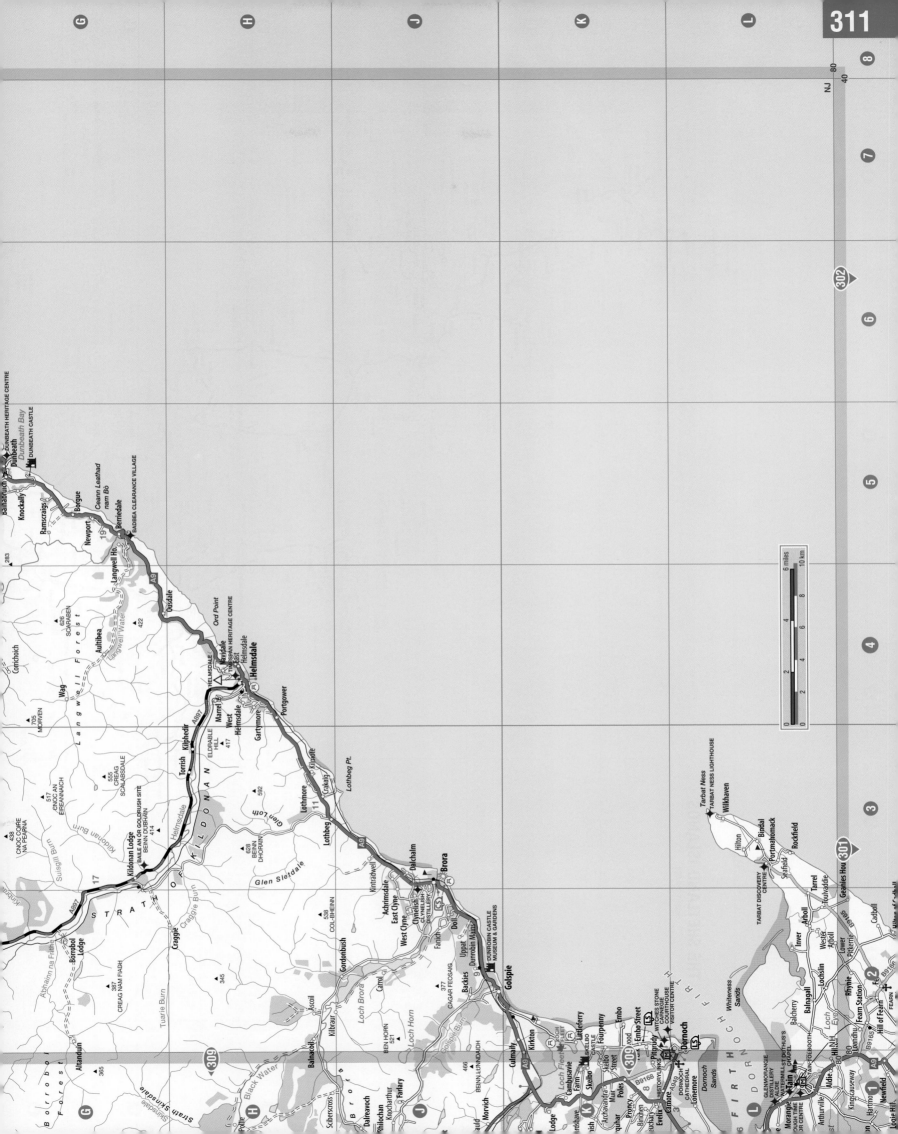

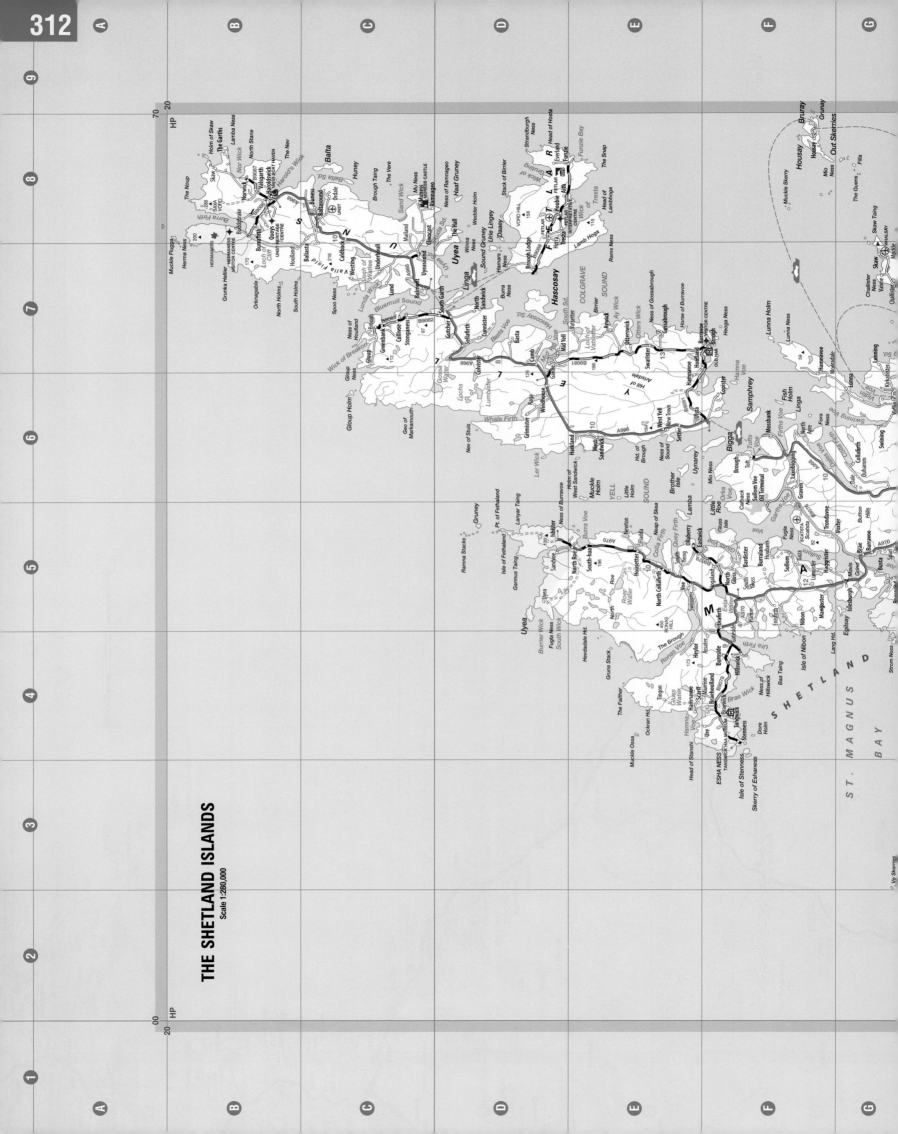

THE SHETLAND ISLANDS

Scale 1:280,000

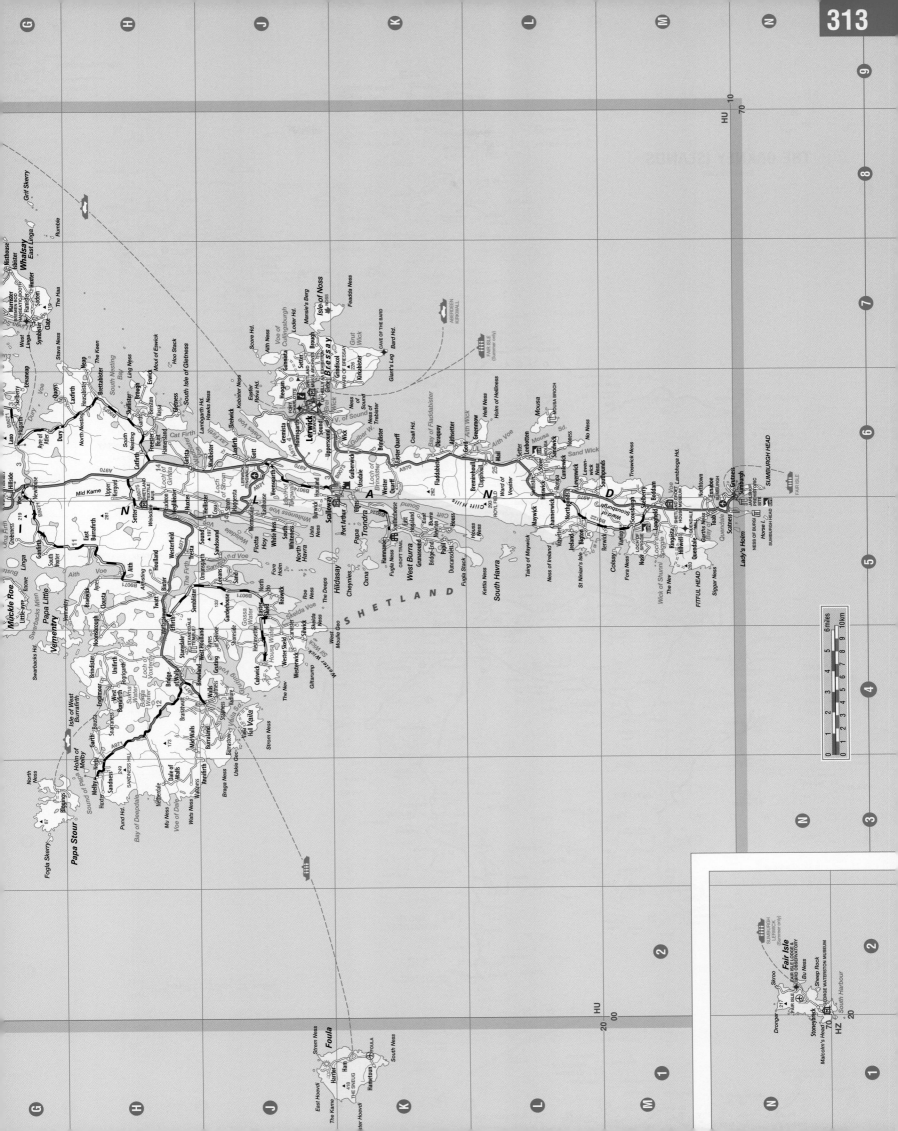

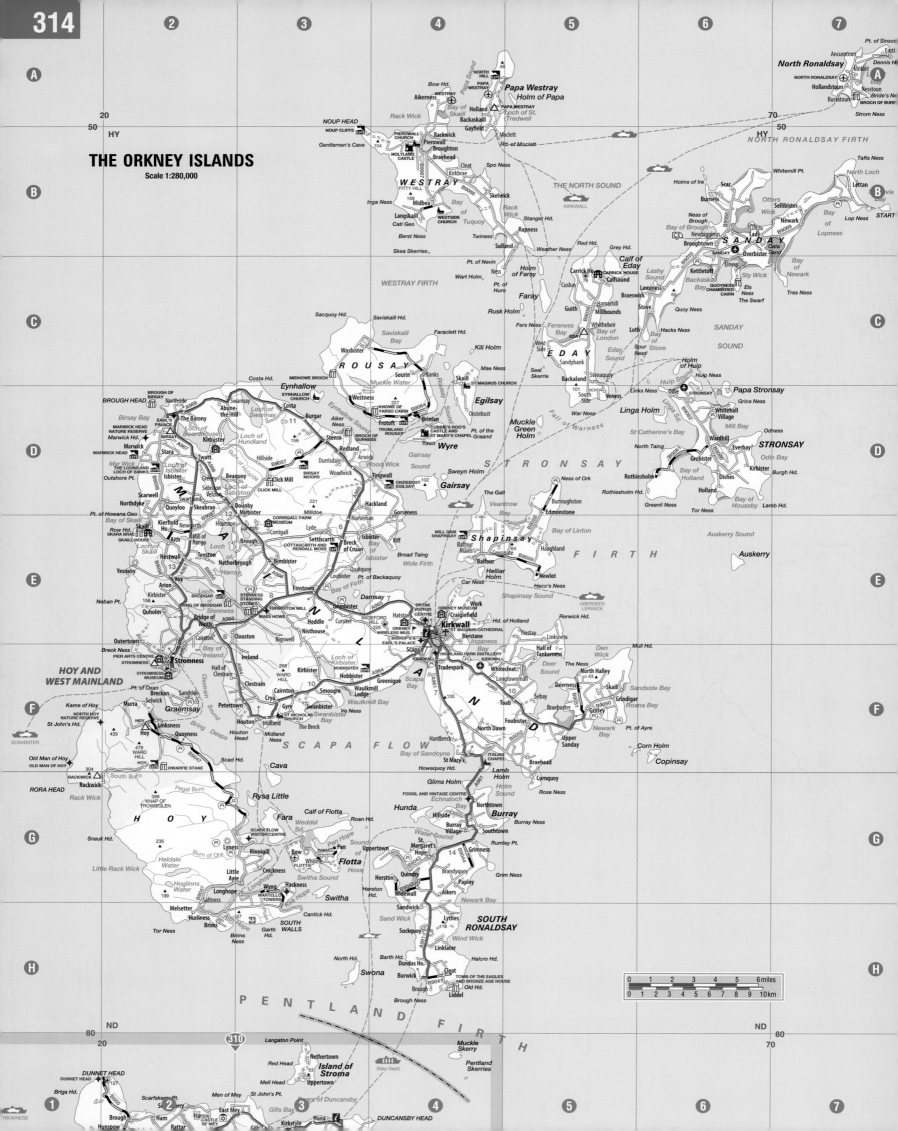

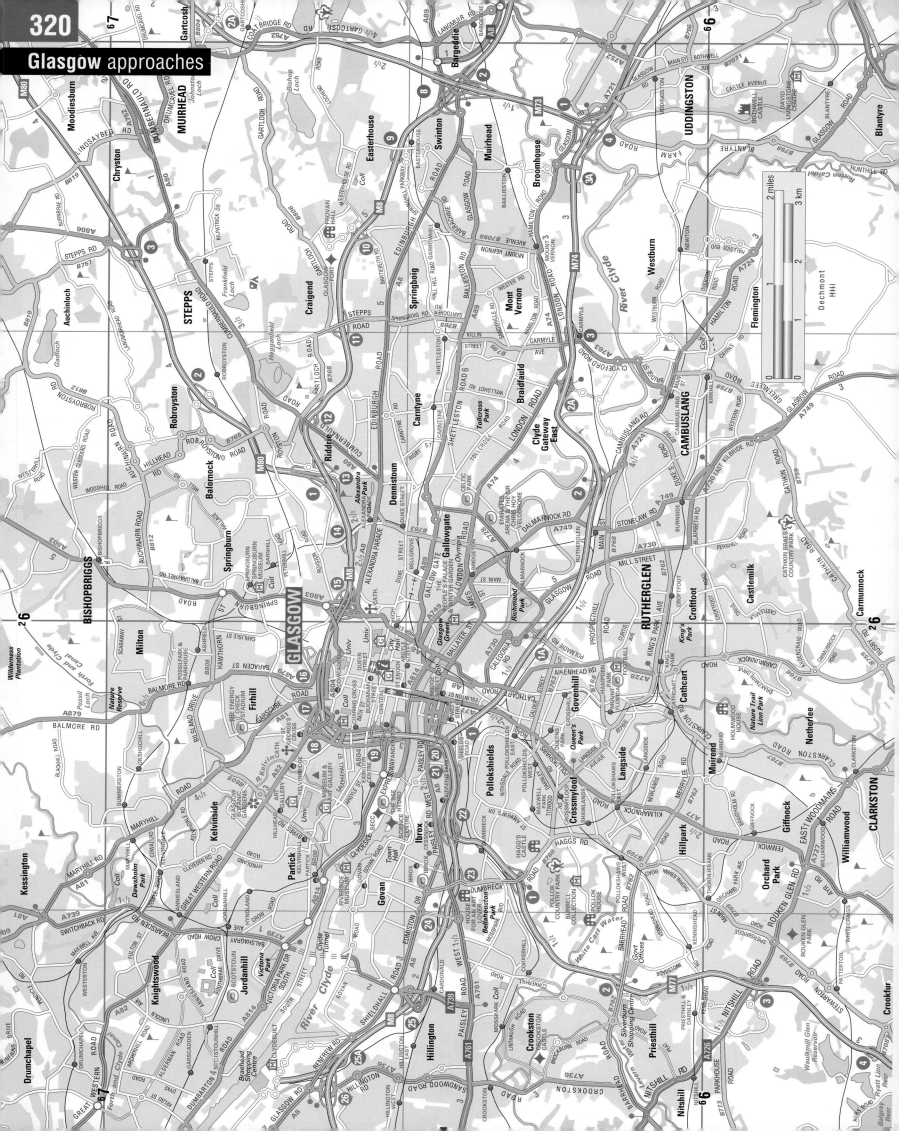

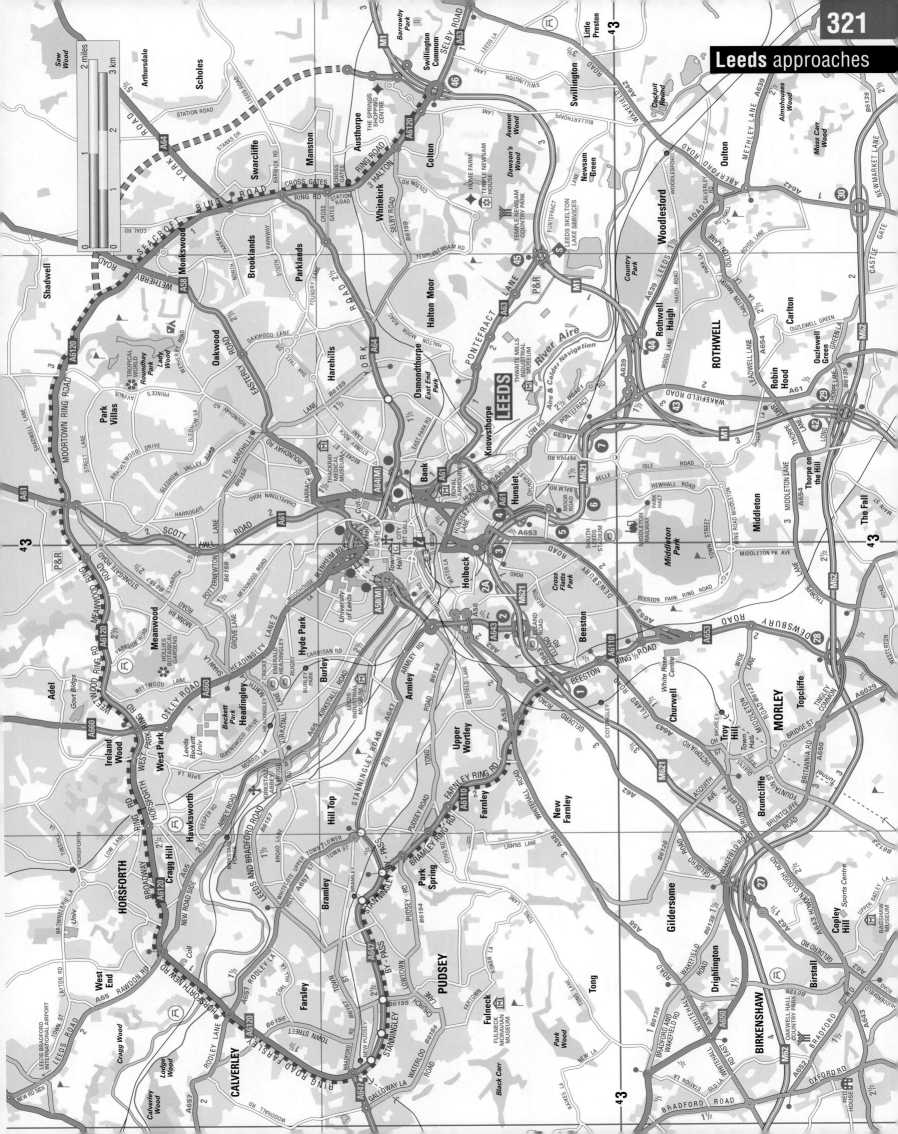

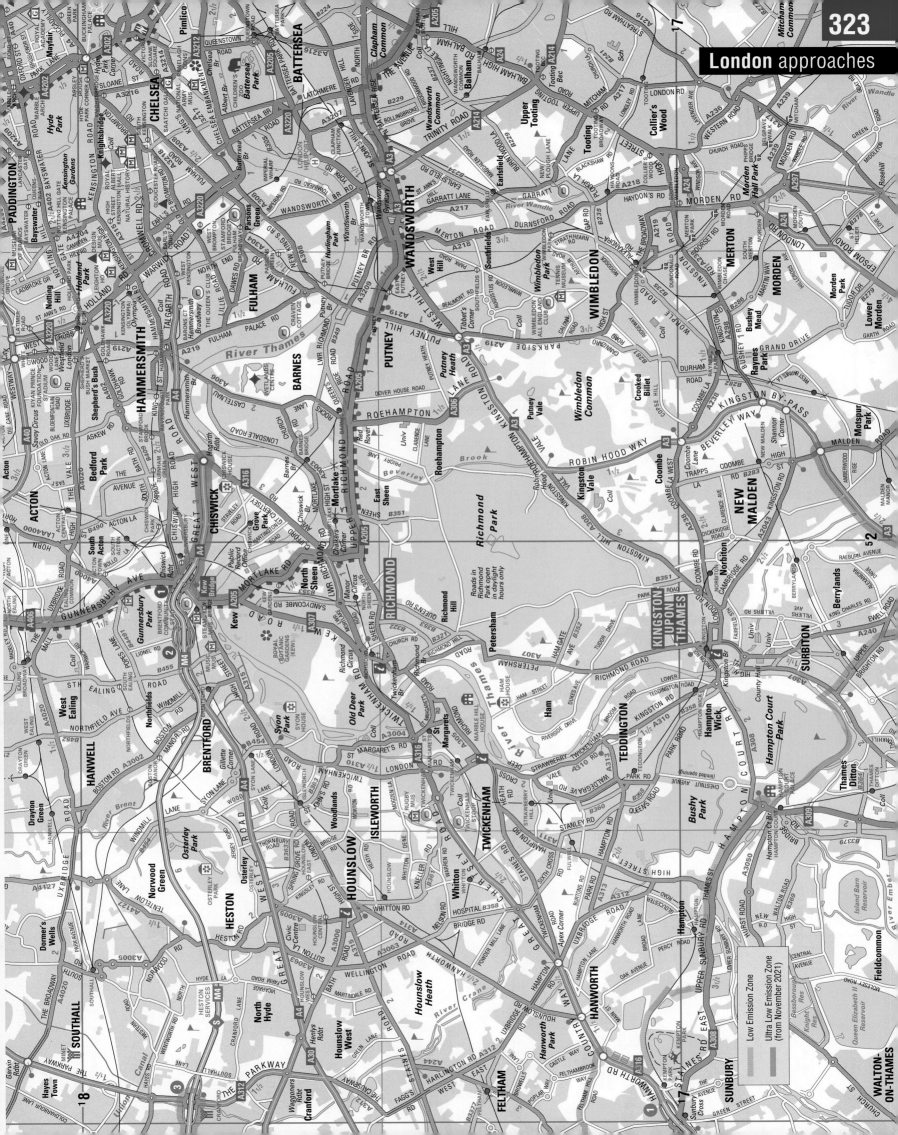

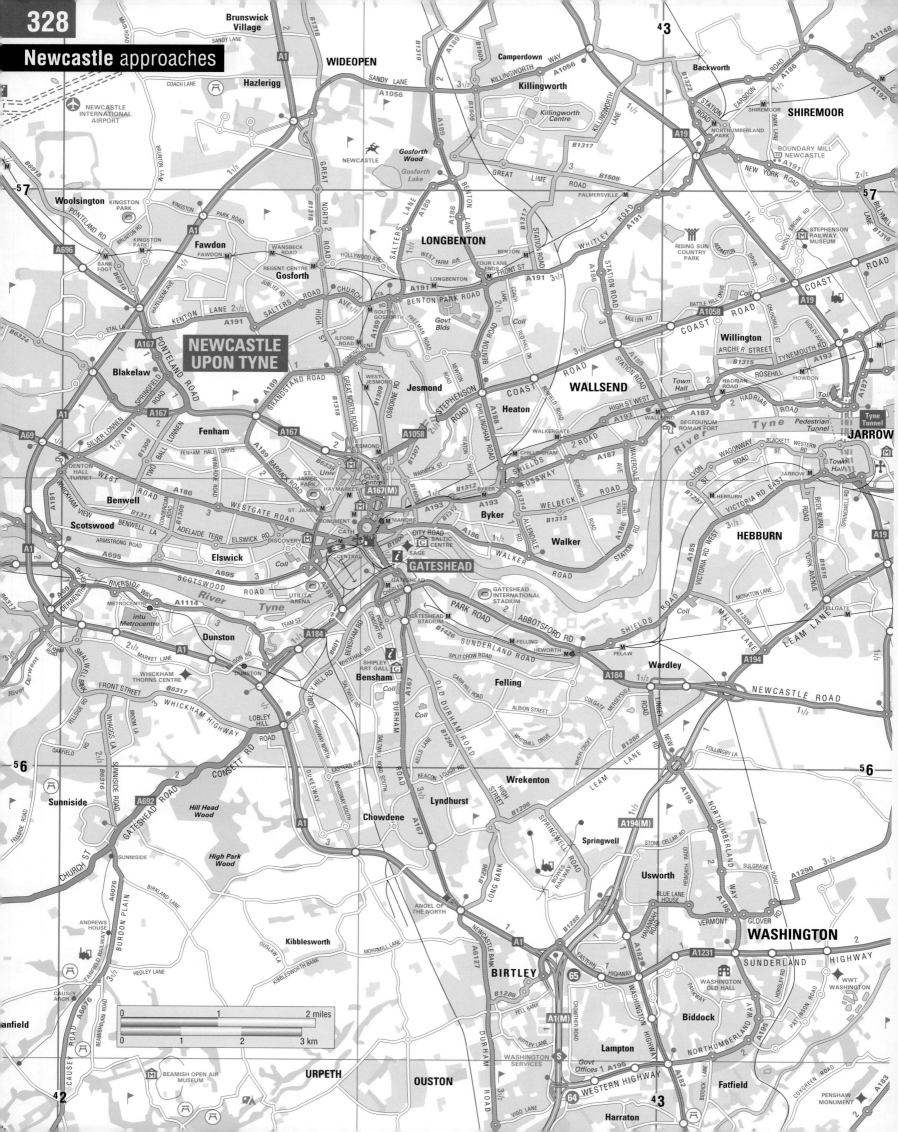

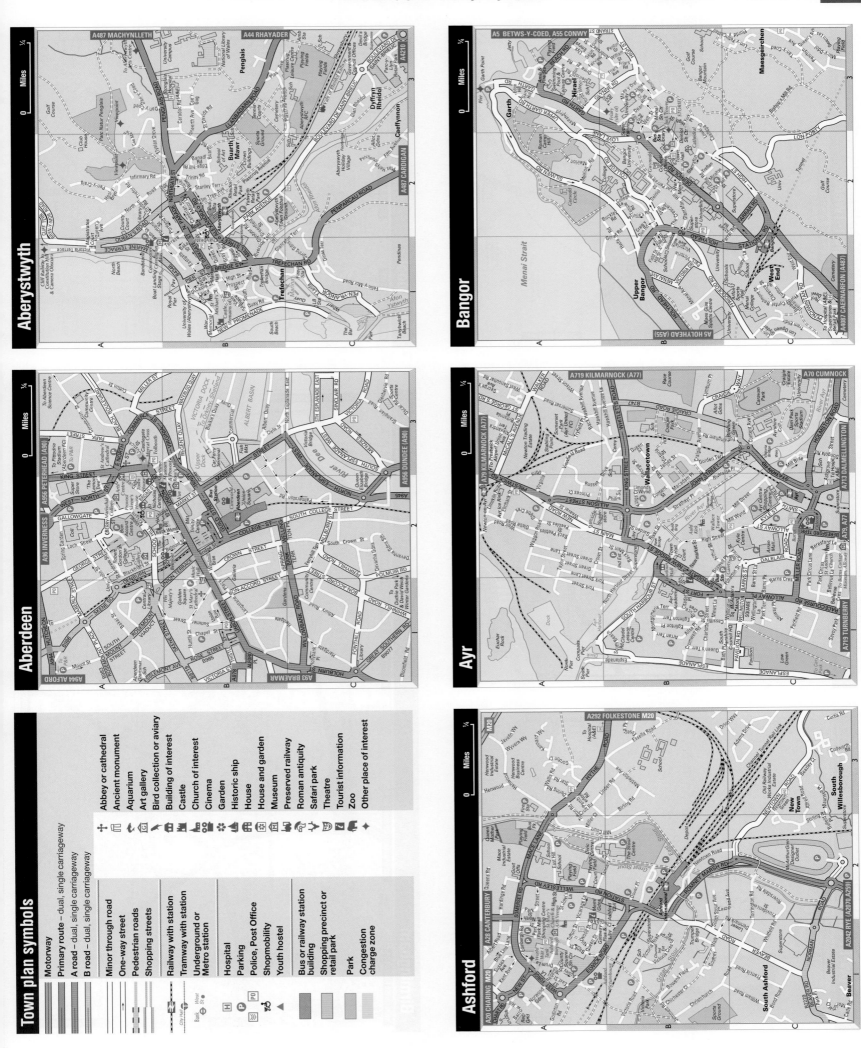

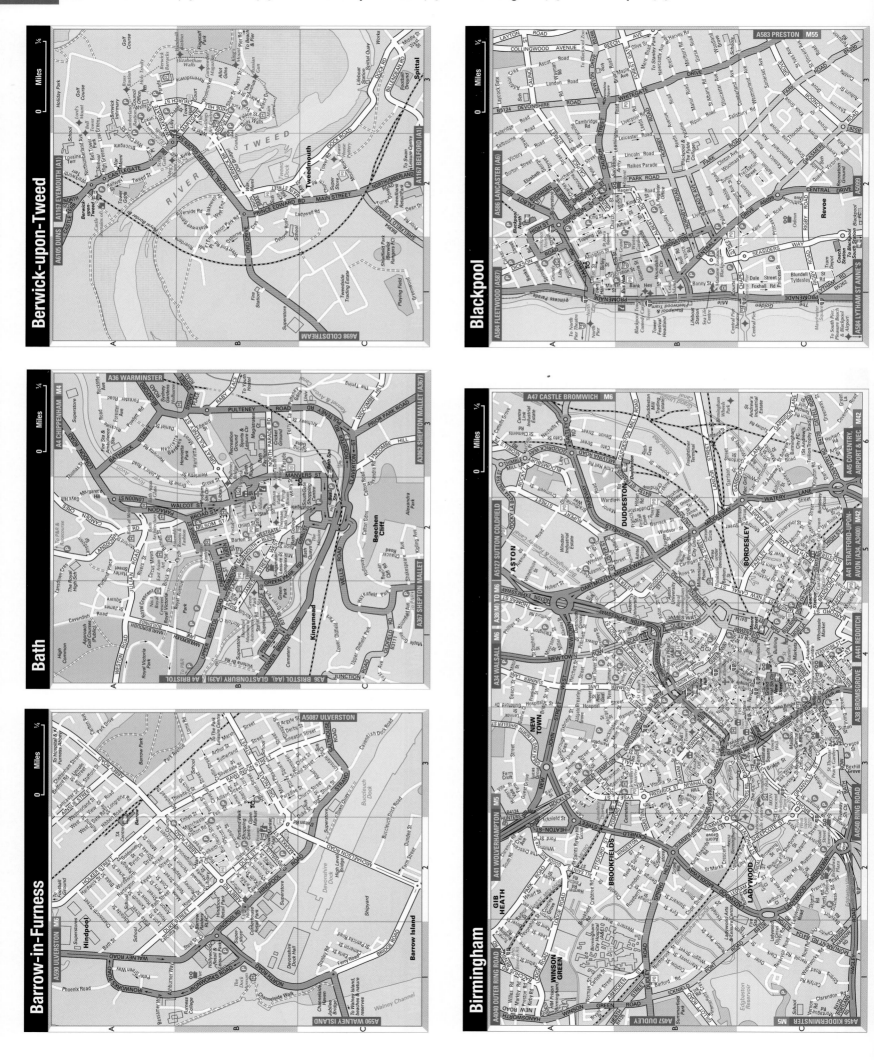

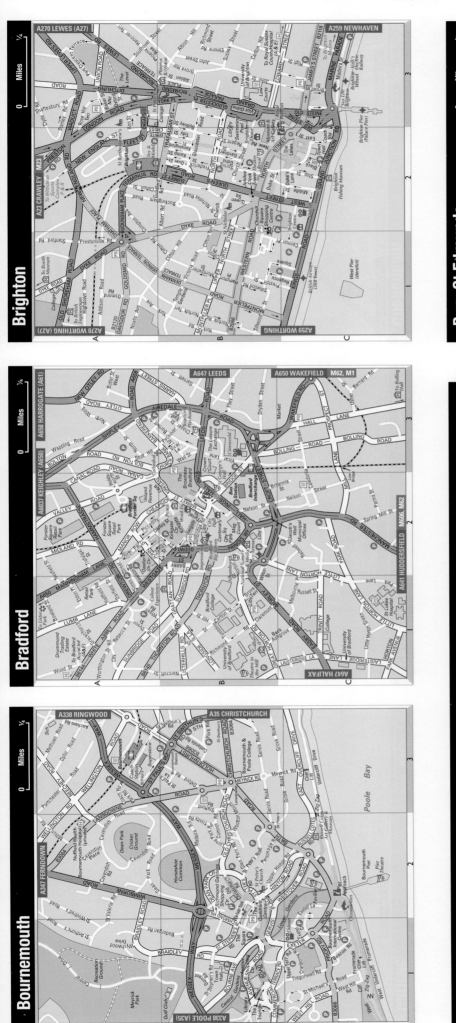

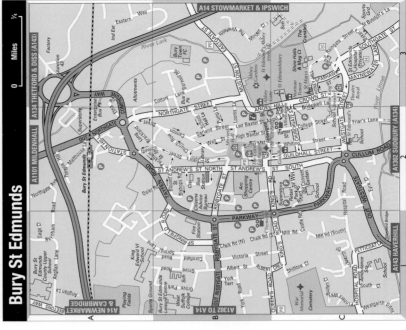

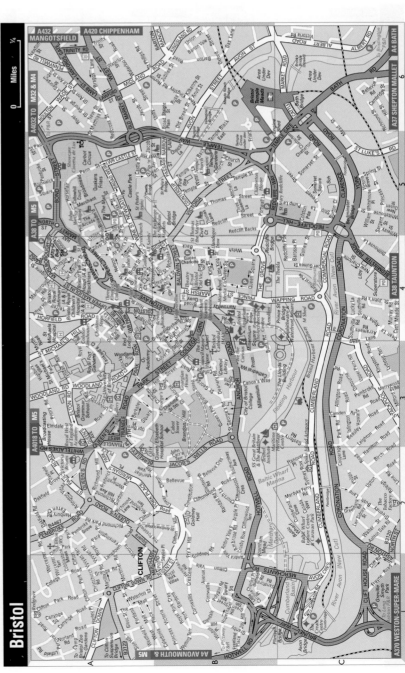

Cardiff / Caerdydd

Cheltenham

Canterbury

Chelmsford

Cambridge

Carlisle

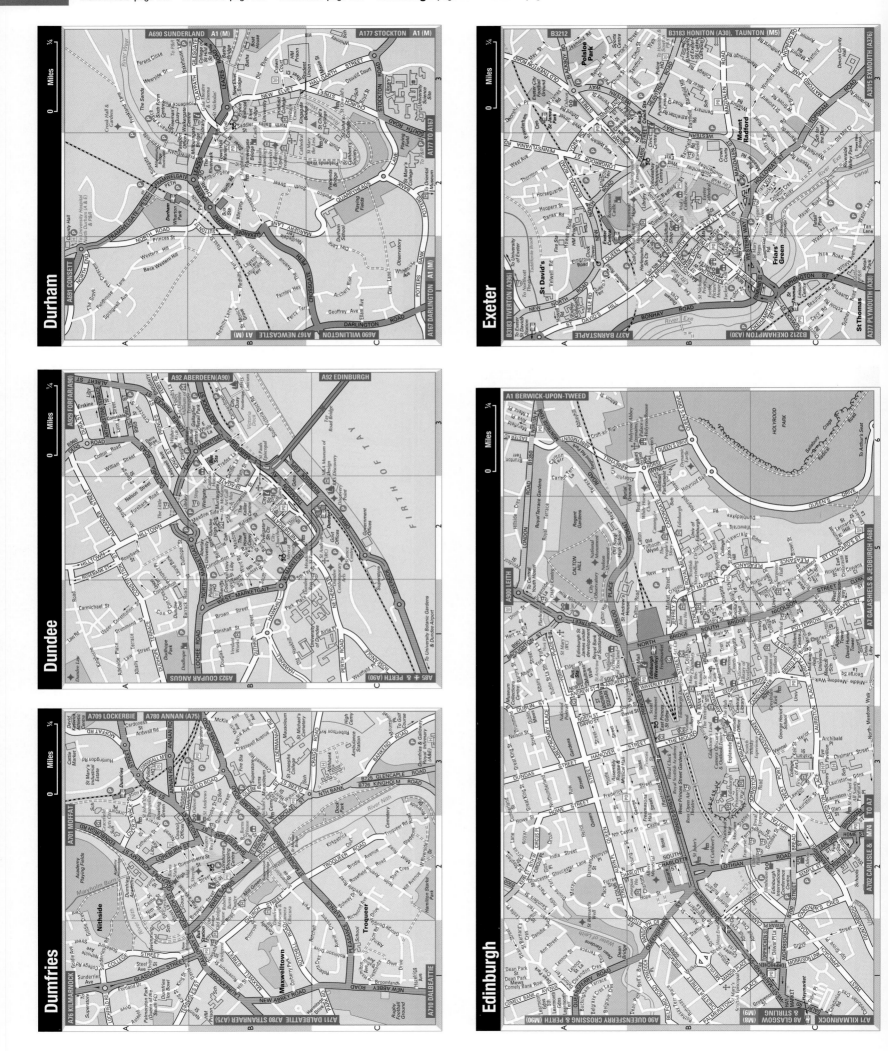

Fort William page 290 • **Glasgow** page 267 • **Gloucester** page 80 • **Grimsby** page 201 • **Hanley (Stoke-on-Trent)** page 168

337

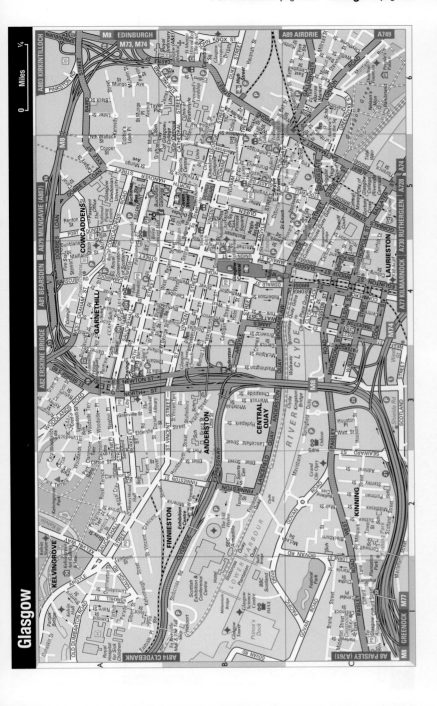

Glasgow

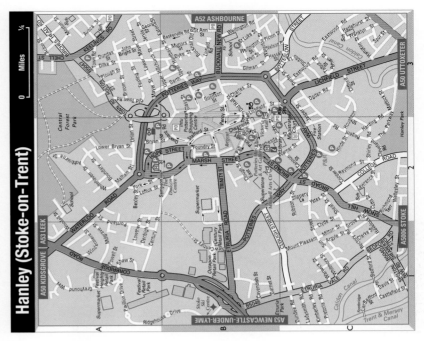

Hanley (Stoke-on-Trent)

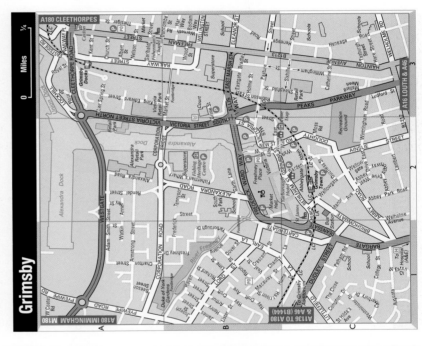

Grimsby

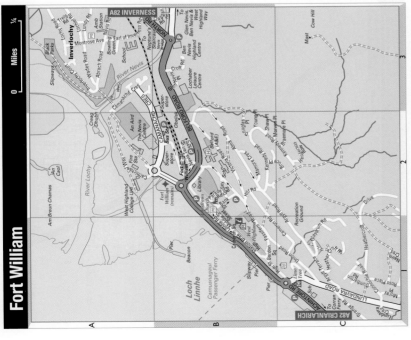

Fort William

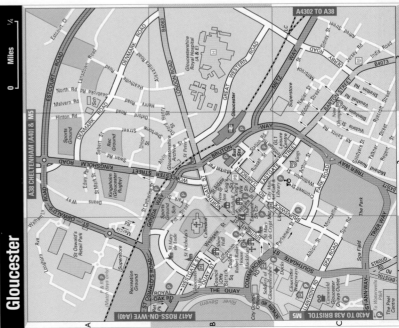

Gloucester

338

Harrogate page 206 • **Holyhead** page 178 • **Hull** page 200 • **Inverness** page 300 • **Ipswich** page 108 • **Kendal** page 221

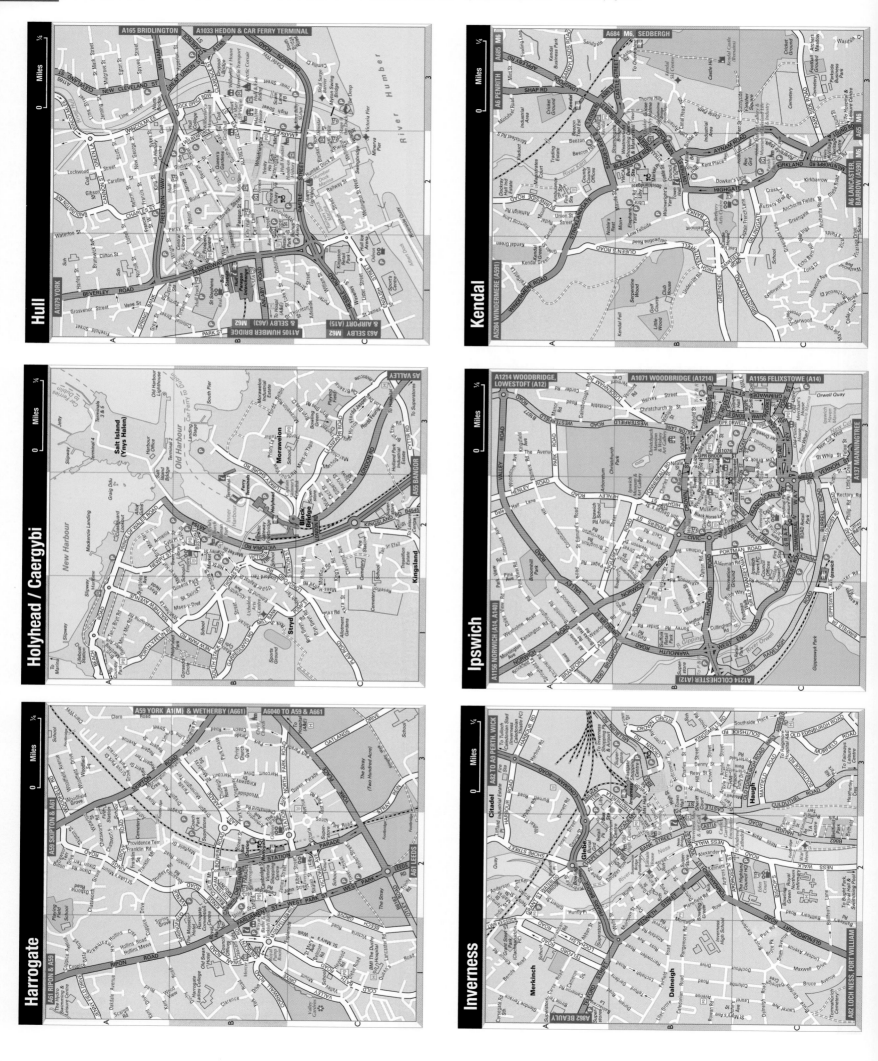

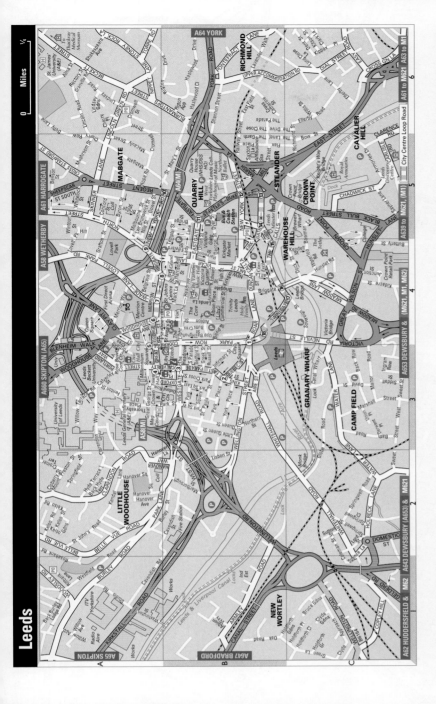

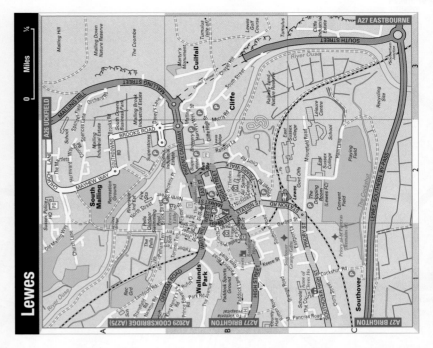

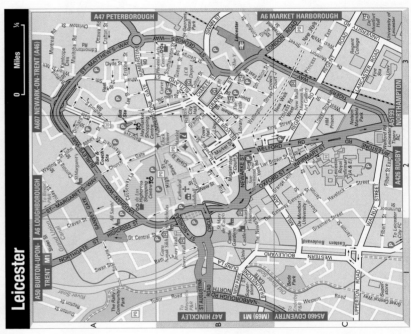

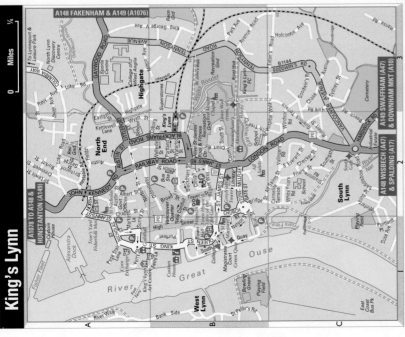

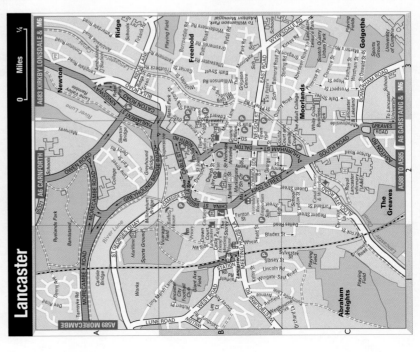

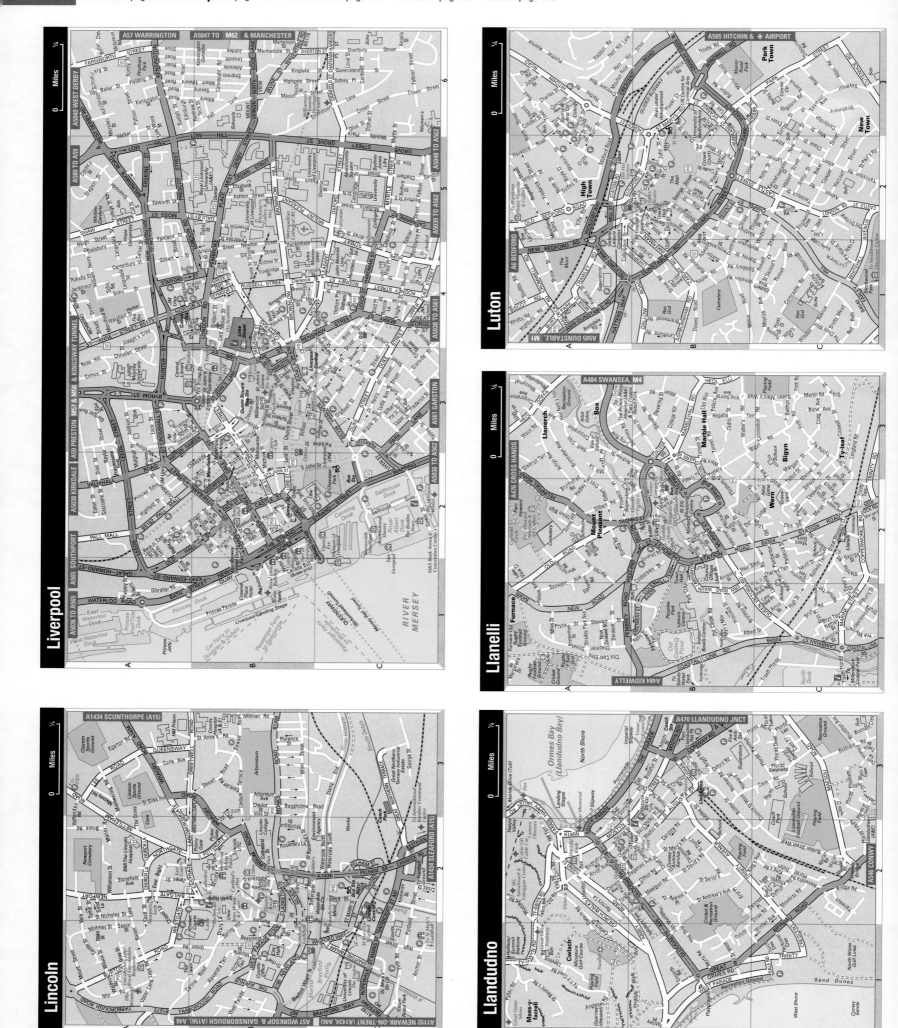

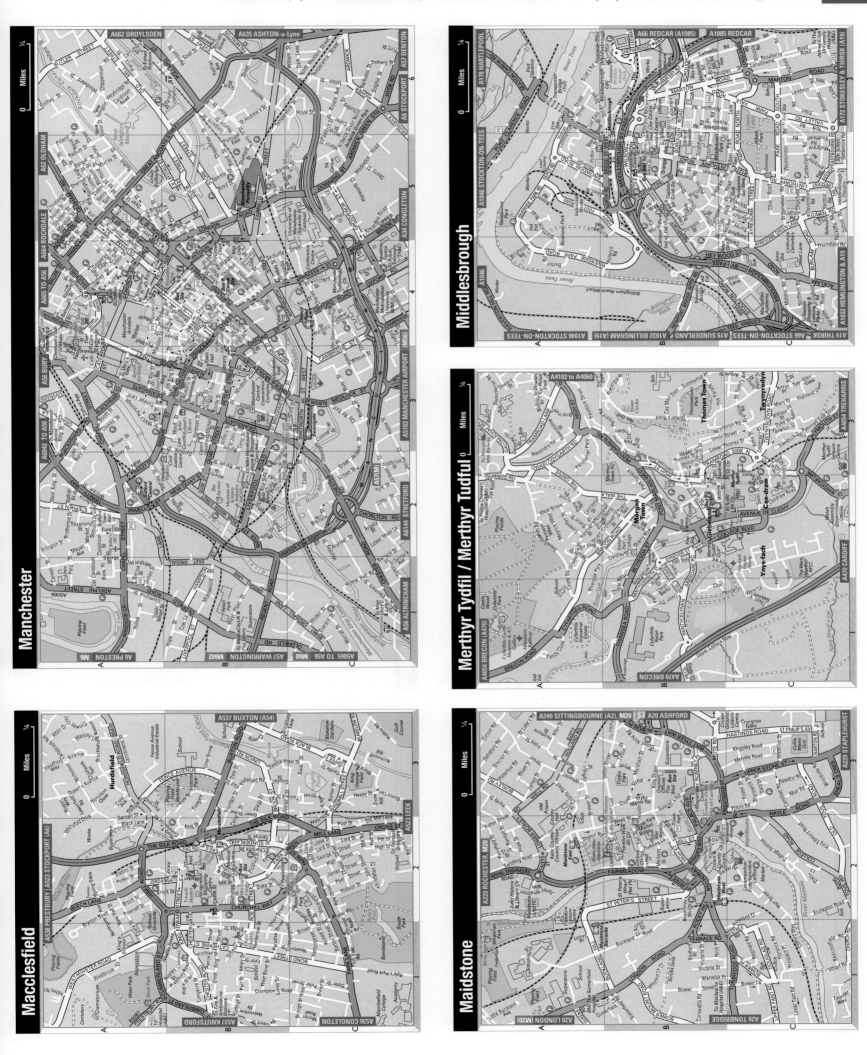

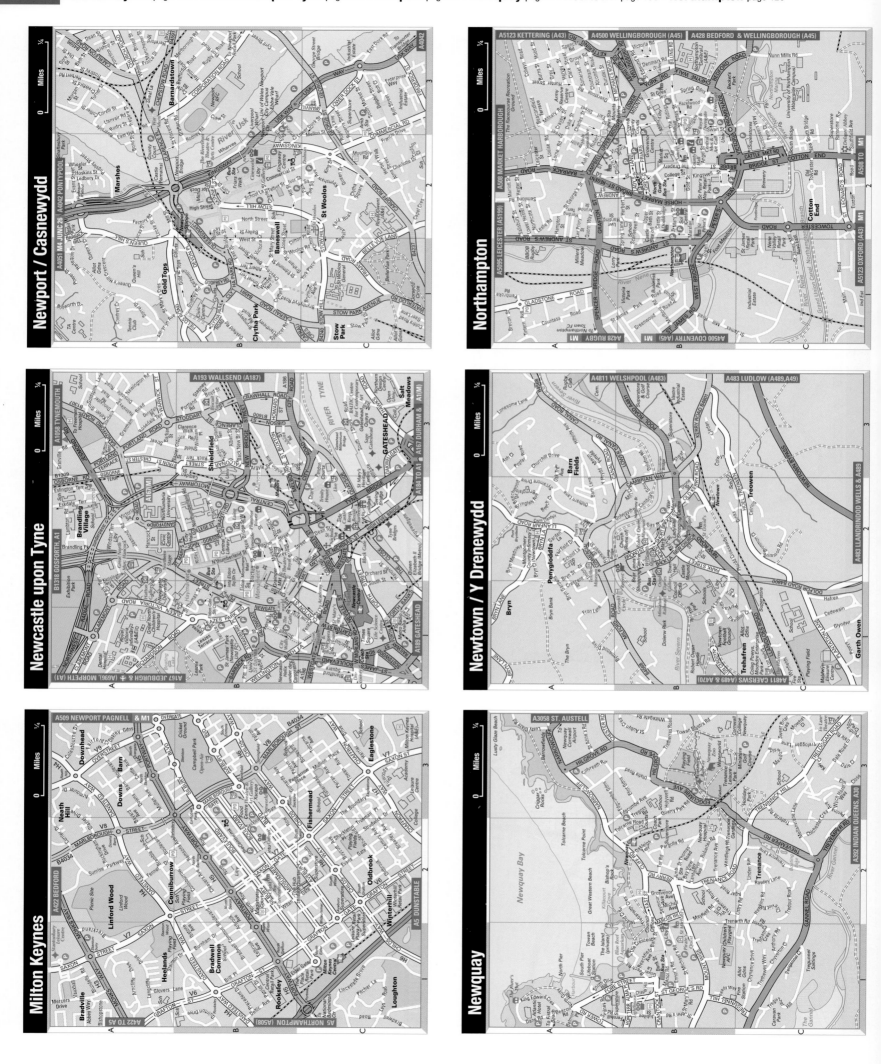

Oban

Peterborough

Nottingham

Perth

Norwich

Oxford

346

Plymouth page 7 • **Poole** page 18 • **Portsmouth** page 21 • **Preston** page 194 • **Reading** page 65 • **St Andrews** page 287

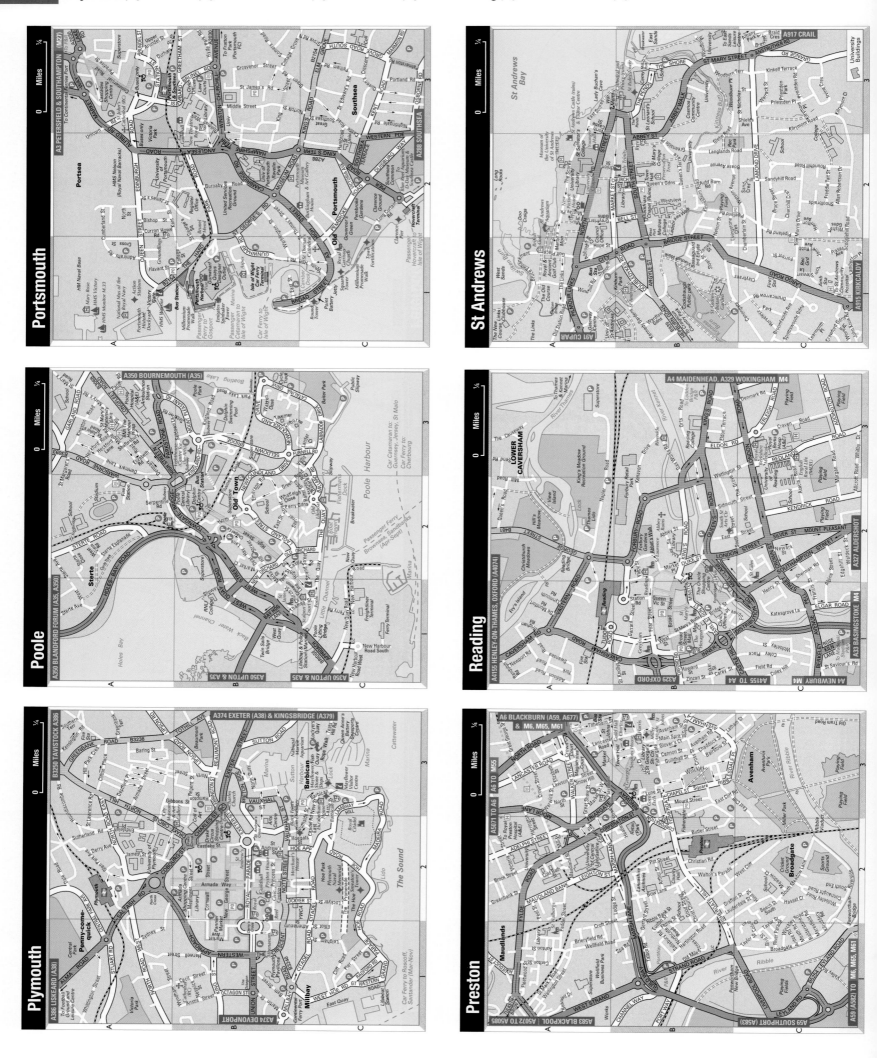

Shrewsbury

Southampton

Scarborough

Sheffield

Salisbury

348

Southend page 69 • **Stirling** page 278 • **Stoke** page 168 • **Stratford-upon-Avon** page 118 • **Sunderland** page 243 • **Swansea** page 56

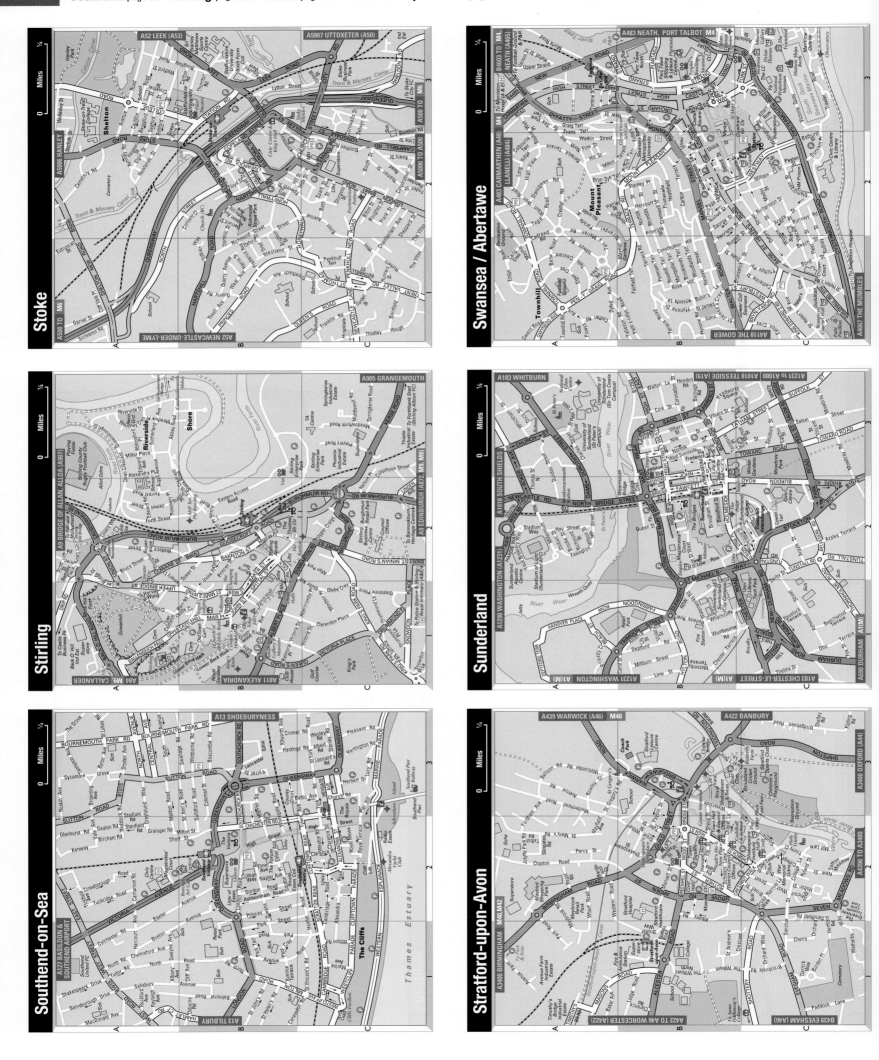

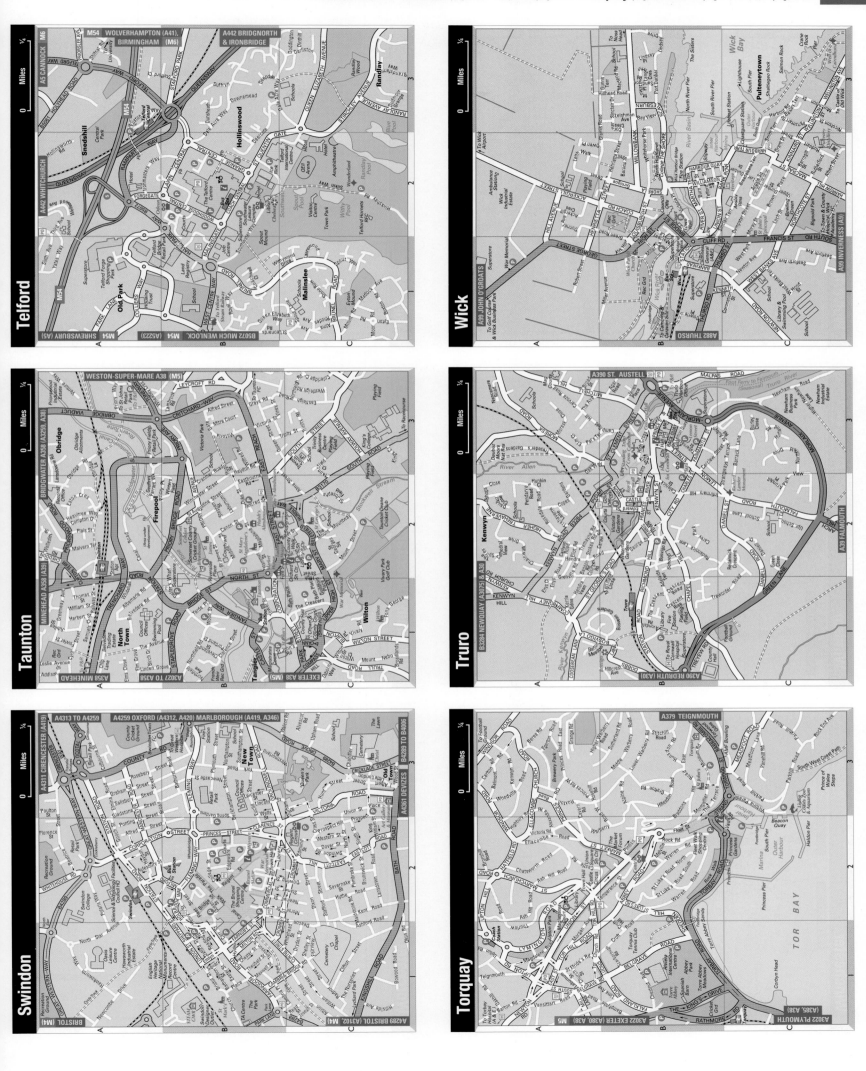

Aberdeen • Aberystwyth • Ashford • Ayr • Bangor • Barrow-in-Furness • Bath • Berwick-upon-Tweed • Birmingham 351

Town plan indexes

Aberdeen 331

Aberdeen ≋ B2
Aberdeen Grammar School A1
Academy, The B2
Albert Basin B3
Albert Quay B3
Albury Rd C1
Alford Pl B1
Art Gallery A2
Arts Centre A2
Back Wynd A2
Baker St A1
Beach Blvd A3
Belmont B2
Belmont St B2
Berry St A2
Blackfriars St A2
Blaikie's Quay B3
Bloomfield Rd C1
Bon Accord Centre A2
Bon-Accord St B1/C1
Bridge St B2
Broad St A2
Bus Station B2
Car Ferry Terminal B3
Castlegate A3
Central Library A1
Chapel St B1
Cineworld B2
Clyde St B3
College A2
College St B2
Commerce St A3
Commercial Quay B3
Community Ctr A3/C1
Constitution St A3
Cotton St A3
Crown St B2
Denburn Rd A2
Devanha Gdns C2
Devanha Gdns South C2
East North St A3
Esslemont Ave A1
Ferryhill Rd C2
Ferryhill Terr C2
Fish Market B3
Fonthill Rd C1
Galleria B1
Gallowgate A2
George St A2
Glenbervie Rd C3
Golden Sq B1
Grampian Rd C3
Great Southern Rd C1
Guild St B2
Hardgate B1/C1
His Majesty's Theatre A1
Holburn St C1
Hollybank Pl C1
Huntly St B1
Hutcheon St A1
Information Ctr B2
John St A2
Justice St A3
King St A2
Langstane Pl B1
Lemon Tree, The A2
Library C1
Loch St A2
Maberly St A1
Marischal College A2
Maritime Mus & Provost Ross's House B2
Market B2
Market St B2/B3
Menzies Rd C3
Mercat Cross ✦ A3
Millburn St C2
Miller St A3
Mount St A1
Music Hall B1
North Esp East C3
North Esp West C2
Oscar Rd C3
Palmerston Rd C2
Park St A3
Police Station A2
Polmuir Rd C2
Post Office A1/A2/A3/B1/C3
Provost Skene's Ho A2
Queen Elizabeth Br C2
Queen St A2
Regent Quay B3
Regent Road B3
Robert Gordon's Coll. A2
Rose St B1
Rosemount Pl A1
Rosemount Viaduct A1
St Andrew St A2
St Andrew's Cath ✝ A3
St Mary's Cathedral ✝ B1
St Nicholas Centre A2
St Nicholas St A2
School Hill A2
Sinclair Rd C3
Skene Sq A1
Skene St B1
South College St C2
South Crown St C2
South Esp East C3
South Esp West C3
South Mount St A1
Sports Centre C3
Spring Garden A2
Springbank Terr C2
Summer St B1
Superstore A2
Thistle St B1
Tolbooth A3
Town House A2
Trinity Centre B2
Union Row B1
Union Square B2
Union St B1/B2
University A2
Upper Dock B3
Upper Kirkgate A2
Victoria Bridge C3
Victoria Dock B3
Victoria Rd C3
Victoria St B2
Virginia St A3
Vue B2
Waterloo Quay B3
Wellington Pl B2
West North St A2
Whinhill Rd C1
Willowbank Rd C1
Windmill Brae B2

Aberystwyth 331

Aberystwyth Holiday Village C2
Aberystwyth Library and Ceredigion Archives A2
Aberystwyth RFC C3
Aberystwyth Sta ≋ B2
Aberystwyth Town Football Ground B2
Alexandra Rd B2
Ambulance Station C3
Baker St B1
Banadl Rd B2
Bandstand A1
Bar, The C1
Bath St A2
Boat Landing Stage A1
Bvd de Saint-Brieuc C3
Bridge St B1
Bronglais Hospital B3
Bryn-y-Mor Rd A2
Buarth Rd B2
Bus Station B2
Cae Melyn A2
Cae'r-Gog B3
Cambrian St B2
Caradoc Rd B3
Caravan Site C2
Castle (Remains of) B1
Castle St B1
Cemetery B3
Ceredigion Mus A1
Chalybeate St B1
Cliff Terr A2
Club House A2
Commodore A2
County Court A2
Crown Buildings B2
Dan-y-Coed A3
Dinas Terr C1
Eastgate B1
Edge-hill Rd B2
Elm Tree Ave B2
Elysian Gr A2
Felin-y-Mor Rd C1
Fifth Ave C2
Fire Station C1
Glanrafon Terr B1
Glan Rheidol C3
Glyndwr Rd B2
Golf Course A3
Government & Council Offices C3
Gray's Inn Rd B1
Great Darkgate St B1
Greenfield St B2
Heol-y-Bryn A2
High St B1
Infirmary Rd A2
Information Ctr B1
Iorwerth Ave B3
King St B1
Lauraplace B1
Lifeboat Station C1
Llanbadarn Rd B3
Loveden Rd A2
Magistrates Court A1
Marina C1
Marine Terr A1
Market Hall B1
Mill St B1
Moor La B2
National Library of Wales B3
New Promenade B1
New St B1
North Beach A1
North Parade B2
North Rd A2
Northgate St B2
Parc Natur Penglais A3
Parc-y-Llyn Retail Park C3
Park Ave B2
Pavillion B1
Pen-y-Craig A2
Pen-yr-angor C1
Pendinas C1
Penglais Rd B3
Penrheidol C2
Pier St B1
Plas Ave B3
Plas Helyg C2
Plascrug Ave B2/C3
Plascrug Leisure Ctr C3
Police Station C2
Poplar Row B2
Portland Rd B2
Portland St A2
Powell St B1
Prospect St B1
Quay Rd B1
Queen St B1
Queen's Ave A2
Queen's Rd A2
Rheidol Retail Park B2
Riverside Terr B1
St Davids Rd B3
St Michael's B1
School of Art B2
Seaview Pl B1
Shopmobility B2
South Beach B1
South Rd B1
Sports Ground B2
Spring Gdns C1
Stanley Terr B2
Superstore B1/B2
Superstore B2/C3
Swimming Pool & Leisure Centre C3
Tanybwlch Beach C1
Tennis Courts B3
Terrace Rd B1
Trefechan Bridge B1
Trefechan Rd C2
Trefor Rd A2
Trinity Rd B2
University Campus B3
University of Wales (Aberystwyth) B1
Vale of Rheidol Railway C3
Vaynor St B2
Victoria Terr A1
Viewpoint ✦ A2
Viewpoint ✦ A3
War Memorial B1
Wharf Quay C1
Y Lanfa C1
Ystwyth Retail Park B2

Ashford 331

Adams Drive C3
Albert Rd A1
Alfred Rd C3
Apsley St A1
Ashford Borough Museum A1
Ashford College B2
Ashford International Station ≋ B2
Ashford Picturehouse A1
Bank St A1
Barrowhill Gdns A1
Beaver Industrial Est C1
Beaver Rd C1
Beazley Ct C3
Birling Rd B3
Blue Line La A1
Bond Rd C1
Bowens Field B1
Bulleid Pl C2
Business Park A2
Cade Rd C1
Chart Rd A1
Chichester Cl B1
Christchurch Rd B1
Chunnel Industrial Est B1
Church Rd A1
Civic Centre A2
County Square Shopping Centre A1
Croft Rd A3
Cudworth Rd C3
Curtis Rd C3
Dering Rd A3
Dover Pl B2
Drum La A1
East Hill A2
East St A1
Eastmead Ave B2
Edinburgh Rd A1
Elwick Rd A1
Essella Pk B3
Essella Rd B3
Fire Sta A3
Forge La A1
Francis Rd C1
Gateway Plus and Liby A1
George St B1
Godfrey Walk B1
Gordon Cl A3
Government Offices A2
Hardinge Rd A2
Henwood A3
Henwood Bsns Centre A3
Henwood Ind Est A3
High St A2
Hythe Rd A3
Information Ctr A1
Javelin Way A3
Jemmett Rd B1
Kennard Way A3
Kent Ave A1
Linden Rd B3
Lower Denmark Rd C1
Mabledon Ave B3
Mace Industrial Est A2
Mace La A2
Maunsell Pl C3
McArthurGlen Designer Outlet C2
Memorial Gdns A2
Mill Ct A2
Miller Cl A2
Mortimer Cl C1
New St A1
Newtown Green C3
Newtown Rd B2/C3
Norman Rd C1
North St A2
Norwood Gdns A1
Norwood St A1
Old Railway Works Industrial Estate C3
Orion Way C3
Pk Mall Shopping Ctr A1
Park Pl A1
Park St A1/A2
Pemberton Rd A3
Police Station A1
Post Office A1
Providence St C2
Queen St A1
Queens Rd A2
Regents Pl A1
Riversdale Rd C2
Romney Marsh Rd B2
St John's La A2
St Mary's Church & Arts Venue A1
Somerset Rd A2
South Stour Ave B2
Star Rd A3
Station Rd B2
Stirling Rd C2
Stour Centre, The B2
Sussex Ave A1
Tannery La A2
Torrington Rd C2
Trumper Bridge B1
Tufton Rd A3
Tufton St A1
Vicarage La A2
Victoria Cres B1
Victoria Park B1
Victoria Rd B1
Wallis Rd A3
Wellesley Rd A2
West St A1
Whitfeld Rd C1
William Rd C1
World War I Tank ✦ A1
Wyvern Way A3

Ayr 331

Ailsa Pl B1
Alexandra Terr A3
Allison St B2
Alloway Pk C1
Alloway Pl C1
Alloway St C2
Arran Mall C2
Arran Terr B1
Arthur St B2
Ashgrove St C2
Auld Brig B2
Auld Kirk B2
Ayr ≋ C2
Ayr Academy B1
Ayr Central Shopping Centre C2
Ayr Harbour A1
Ayr Ice Rink A2
Ayrshire Coll C3
Back Hawkhill Ave A3
Back Main St B2
Back Peebles St A2
Barns Cres C1
Barns Pk C1
Barns St C1
Barns Street La C1
Bath Pl B1
Bellevue Cres C1
Bellevue La C1
Beresford La C2
Beresford Terr C2
Boswell Pk B2
Britannia Pl A3
Bruce Cres B1
Burns Statue ✦ C2
Bus Sta B1
Carrick St C2
Cassillis St B1
Cathcart St B1
Charlotte St B1
Citadel Leisure Ctr B1
Citadel Pl B1
Compass Pier A1
Content Ave C3
Content St B2
Craigie Ave B3
Craigie Rd B3
Craigie Way B3
Cromwell Rd B1
Crown St A2
Dalblair Rd C2
Dam Park Sports Stadium C3
Damside A2
Dongola Rd C3
Eglinton Pl B1
Eglinton Terr B1
Elba St B2
Elmbank St A2
Esplanade B1
Euchar Rock A1
Farifield Rd C1
Fort St B1
Fothringham Rd C3
Fullarton St C1
Gaiety C2
Garden St B2
George St B2
George's Ave A3
Glebe Cres A2
Glebe Rd A2
Gorden Terr B3
Green St A2
Green Street La A2
Hawkhill Ave A3
Hawkhill Avenue La B3
High St B2
Holmston Rd C3
Information Ctr B1
James St B3
John St B2
King St B2
Kings Ct B2
Kyle Centre C2
Kyle St C2
Library B2
Limekiln Rd A2
Limonds Wynd B2
Loudoun Hall B2
Lymburn Pl B3
Macadam Pl B2
Main St B2
Mcadam's Monument C1
Mccall's Ave A3
Mews La B1
Mill Brae C3
Mill St C2
Mill Wynd C2
Miller Rd C1
Montgomerie Terr B1
New Bridge B2
New Bridge St B2
New Rd A2
Newmarket St B2
Newton-on-Ayr Station ≋ A2
North Harbour St B1
North Pier A1
Odeon C2
Park Circus C1
Park Circus La C1
Park Terr C1
Pavilion Rd C1
Peebles St A2
Philip Sq B2
Police Station B2
Prestwick Rd B1
Princes Ct A2
Queen St B3
Queen's Terr B1
Racecourse Rd C1
River St B2
Riverside Pl B2
Russell Dr A2
St Andrews Church C2
St George's Rd A3
Sandgate B1
Savoy Park C1
Smith St C2
Somerset Park (Ayr United FC) A3
Somerset Rd A3
South Beach Rd B1
South Harbour St B1
South Pier A1
Station Rd C2
Strathayr Pl B2
Superstore A2/B2
Taylor St A2
Town Hall B2
Tryfield Pl A3
Turner's Bridge B2
Union Ave A3
Victoria Bridge C3
Victoria St B3
Viewfield Rd A3
Virginia Gdns A2
Waggon Rd A2
Walker Rd A3
Wallace Tower ✦ B2
Weaver St A2
Weir Rd A2
Wellington La C1
Wellington Sq C1
West Sanouhar Rd A3
Whitletts Rd B3
Wilson St A3
York St A1
York Street La B1

Bangor 331

Abbey Rd C2
Albert St B1
Ambrose St A3
Ambulance Station A3
Arfon Sports Hall C1
Ashley Rd B3
Bangor Mountain B3
Bangor Station ≋ C1
Bangor University B2
Beach Rd A3
Belmont St C1
Bishop's Mill Rd C3
Brick St B3
Buckley Rd B2
Bus Station B3
Caellepa B2
Caernarfon Rd C1
Cathedral ✝ B2
Cemetery C1
Clarence St C1
Clock Tower ✦ B3
College B2
College La B2
College Rd B2
Convent La C1
Council Offices B2
Craig y Don Rd B2
Crescent, The B2
Dean St B3
Deiniol Rd B2
Deiniol Shopping Ctr B2
Deiniol St B2
Edge Hill A3
Euston Rd C1
Fairview Rd A3
Farrar Rd C2
Ffordd Cynfal C1
Ffordd Islwyn A3
Ffordd y Castell C3
Ffriddoedd Rd B1
Field St B1
Fountain St A3
Friars Ave B3
Friars Rd B3
Friary (Site of) ✦ B3
Gardd Deman C1
Garth Hill A3
Garth Point A3
Garth Rd A3
Glanrafon B2
Glanrafon Hill B2
Glynne Rd B3
Golf Course B3
Golf Course C2
Gorad Rd B1
Gorsedd Circle A2
Gwern Las C3
Heol Dewi C1
High St B3/C2
Hill St B1
Holyhead Rd B1
Hwfa Rd B1
James St B3
Library B2
Llys Emrys A3
Lon Ogwen C1
Lon-Pobty C2
Lon-y-Felin C3
Lon-y-Glyder C1
Love La B2
Lower Penrallt Rd B2
Lower St B2
Maes Glas Sports Ctr B1
Maes-y-Dref B3
Maeshyfryd A3
Meirion La A2
Meirion Rd A2
Menai Ave B1
Menai College C1
Menai Shopping Ctr B3
Min-y-Ddol C3
Minafon B2
Mount St B3
Orme Rd A3
Parc Victoria B1
Penchwintan Rd C1
Penlon Gr B3
Penrhyn Ave C3
Pier ✦ A3
Police Station B2
Post Office B2/B3/C3
Prince's Rd B2
Queen's Ave C3
Sackville Rd B2
St Paul's St B2
Seion Rd A3
Seiriol Rd A3
Siliwen Rd A2
Snowdon View B1
Station Rd C1
STORIEL B2
Strand St B3
Superstore B3/C2
Swimming Pool and Leisure Centre A3
Tan-y-Coed C3
Tegid Rd B3
Temple Rd B2
Theatr Gwynedd B2
Totton Rd A3
Town Hall B2
Treflan B2
Trem Elidir C1
University A2
Upper Garth Rd A3
Victoria Ave B1
Victoria Dr B1
Victoria St B1
Vron St B2
Well St B3
West End C1
William St B3
York Pl B3

Barrow-in-Furness 332

Abbey Rd A3/B2
Adelaide St A2
Ainslie St A3
Albert St C3
Allison St B3
Anson St A2
Argyle St B3
Arthur St B3
Ashburner Way A1
Barrow Park A3
Barrow Raiders RLFC B1
Barrow Station ≋ A2
Bath St A1/B2
Bedford Rd A3
Bessamer Way A1
Blake St A1/A2
Bridge Rd C1
Buccleuch Dock C3
Buccleuch Dock Rd C2/C3
Buccleuch St B2/B3
Byron St A2
Calcutta St A1
Cameron St C1
Carlton Ave A3
Cavendish Dock Rd C3
Cavendish St B2/B3
Channelside Haven C1
Channelside Walk B1
Chatsworth St A2
Cheltenham St A3
Church St C3
Clifford St B2
Clive St B1
Collingwood St B2
Cook St A2
Cornerhouse Retail Park B2
Cornwallis St B2
Courts A2
Crellin St B3
Cross St C3
Custom House ✦ B2
Dalkeith St B2
Dalton Rd B2/C2
Derby St B3
Devonshire Dock C2
Devonshire Dock Hall B1
Dock Museum, The B1
Drake St A2
Dryden St A2
Duke St A1/B2/C3
Duncan St B2
Dundee St C2
Dundonald St B2
Earle St C1
Emlyn St B2
Exmouth St A2
Farm St C2
Fell St B3
Fenton St B3
Ferry Rd C1
Forum, The B2
Furness College B1
Glasgow St B3
Goldsmith St A2
Greengate St B3
Hardwick St A2
Harrison St B3
Hartington St A2
Hawke St B2
Hibbert Rd A2
High Level Bridge C2
High St B2
Hindpool Rd B2
Hindpool Retail Park B2
Holker St A2
Hollywood Retail & Leisure Park B1
Hood St A2
Howard St B2
Howe St A2
Information Ctr B2
Ironworks Rd A1/B1
James St B3
Jubliee Bridge C1
Keith St B2
Keyes St A2
Lancaster St A3
Lawson St B2
Library B2
Lincoln St A3
Longreins Rd A3
Lonsdale St C3
Lord St B3
Lorne Rd B3
Lyon St A2
Manchester St B2
Market B2
Market St B2
Marsh St B3
Michaelson Rd C2
Milton St A2
Monk St B2
Mount Pleasant B3
Nan Tait Centre B2
Napier St B2
Nelson St B2
North Rd B1
Open Market B2
Parade St B2
Paradise St B3
Park Ave A3
Park Dr A3
Parker St A2
Parry St A2
Peter Green Way A1
Phoenix Rd A1
Police Station B2
Portland Walk Shopping Centre B2
Raleigh St A2
Ramsden St B3
Rawlinson St B3
Robert St B3
Rodney St B2
Rutland St A2
St Patricks Rd C1
Salthouse Rd C3
School St B2
Scott St B2
Settle St A3
Shore St C3
Sidney St B2
Silverdale St B3
Slater St B2
Smeaton St B3
Stafford St A3
Stanley Rd C1
Stark St C3
Steel St B1
Storey Sq B3
Strand C3
Superstore A1/B1/C3
Sutherland St B3
TA Centre A2
Thwaite St B3
Town Hall B2
Town Quay C3
Vernon St B2
Vincent St B2
Vue Cinema B2
Walney Rd A1
West Gate Rd A2
West View Rd A3
Westmorland St A3
Whitehead St A3
Wordsworth St A2

Bath 332

Alexandra Park C2
Alexandra Rd C2
Ambulance Station A3
Approach Golf Courses (Public) A1
Archway St C3
Assembly Rooms & Fashion Museum A2
Avon St B2
Barton St B2
Bath Abbey ✝ B2
Bath Aqua Glass A2
Bath at Work Mus A2
Bath College B2
Bath Rugby (The Rec) B3
Bath Spa Station ≋ C3
Bathwick St A3
Beckford Road A3
Beechen Cliff Rd C2
Bennett St A2
Bloomfield Ave C1
Broad Quay C2
Broad St B2
Brock St A1
Bus Station C2
Calton Gdns C2
Calton Rd C2
Camden Cr A2
Cavendish Rd A1
Cemetery B1
Charlotte St B2
Chaucer Rd C2
Cheap St B2
Circus Mews A2
Claverton St C2
Corn St C2
Cricket Ground B3
Daniel St A3
East Asian Art Mus A2
Edward St B3
Ferry La B3
Fire Station A3
First Ave C1
Forester Ave A3
Forester Rd A3
Gays Hill A2
George St B2
Great Pulteney St B3
Green Park B1
Green Park Rd B2
Green Park Station ✦ B1
Grove St B2
Guildhall B2
Harley St A2
Hayesfield Park C1
Henrietta Gdns A3
Henrietta Mews B3
Henrietta Park B3
Henrietta Rd A3
Henrietta St B3
Henry St B2
Herschel Museum of Astronomy B1
High Common A1
Holburne Museum B3
Holloway C2
Information Ctr B2
James St West B1/B2
Jane Austen Centre B2
Julian Rd A1
Junction Rd C1
Kingsmead Leisure Complex B2
Kipling Ave C2
Lansdown Cr A1
Lansdown Gr A2
Lansdown Rd A2
Library B2
London Rd A3
London St A2
Lower Bristol Rd B1
Lower Oldfield Park C1
Lyncombe Hill C3
Magistrates' Court B3
Manvers St B3
Maple Gr C1
Margaret's Hill A2
Marlborough Bldgs A1
Marlborough La B1
Midland Bridge Rd B1
Milk St B2
Milsom St B2
Mission The B2
Monmouth St B2
Morford St A2
Museum of Bath Architecture, The A2
New King St B1
No 1 Royal Cres A1
Norfolk Bldgs B1
Norfolk Cr B1
North Parade Rd B3
Oldfield Rd C1
Paragon A2
Pines Way B1
Podium Shopping Ctr B2
Police Station B3
Portland Pl A2
Post Office B2/C2
Postal Museum B2
Powlett Rd A3
Prior Park Rd C3
Pulteney Bridge ✦ B2
Pulteney Gdns B3
Pulteney Rd B3/C3
Queen Sq B2
Raby Pl B3
Recreation Ground B3
Rivers St A2
Rockliffe Ave A3
Rockliffe Rd A3
Roman Baths & Pump Room B2
Rossiter Rd C3
Royal Ave A1
Royal Crescent A1
Royal High School, The A2
Royal Victoria Park A1
St James Sq A1
St John's Rd A3
Sally Lunn's House ✦ B2
Shakespeare Ave C2
Shopmobility B2
South Pde B3
SouthGate Shopping Centre C2
Sports & Leisure Ctr B3
Spring Gdns C3
Stall St B2
Stanier Rd B1
Superstore A3/B1
Sydney Gdns A3
Sydney Pl B3
Sydney Rd B3
Theatre Royal B2
Thermae Bath Spa ✦ B2
Thomas St A3
Tyning, The C3
Union St B2
University C3
Upper Bristol Rd B1
Upper Oldfield Park C1
Victoria Art Gallery B2
Victoria Bridge Rd B1
Walcot St B2
Wells Rd C1
Westgate Buildings B2
Westgate St B2
Weston Rd A1
Widcombe Hill C3

Berwick-upon-Tweed 332

Avenue, The B3
Bank Hill B2
Bell Tower ✦ A3
Bell Tower Pk A2
Berwick Barracks A3
Berwick Br B2
Berwick Infirmary A3
Berwick-upon-Tweed ≋ A2
Billendean Rd C3
Blakewell Gdns B2
Blakewell St B2
Brass Bastion ✦ A3
Bridge St B3
Brucegate St A2
Castle (Remains of) A2
Castle Terr A2
Castlegate A2
Chapel St A3
Church Rd C2
Church St B3
Council Office A3
Court B3
Coxon's La A3
Cumberland Bastion ✦ A3
Dean Dr C2
Dock Rd C2/C3
Elizabethan Walls A2/B3
Fire Station B1
Flagstaff Park B3
Football Ground C3
Foul Ford B3
Golden Sq B2
Golf Course A3
Granary ✦ B3
Greenwood C1
Gunpowder Magazine ✦ B3
Hide Hill B3
High Greens A2
Holy Trinity A3
Information Ctr A2
Kiln Hill B2
King's Mount ✦ B3
Ladywell Rd C2
Library A2
Lifeboat Station C3
Lord's Mount ✦ A3
Lovaine Terr A2
Low Greens A3
Main Guard B3
Main St B2/C2
Maltings Art Centre, The ✦ B3
Marygate B3
Meg's Mount ✦ A2
Middle St C3
Mill St C2
Mount Rd C2
Museum B3
Ness St B3
North Rd A2
Northumberland Ave A2
Northumberland Rd C2
Ord Dr B1
Osborne Cr B2
Osborne Rd B1
Palace Gr B3
Palace St B3
Palace St East B3
Parade A3
Pier Rd B3
Playing Field C1
Police Station B3
Post Office B2/B3/C2
Prince Edward Rd B2
Prior Rd C2
Quay Walls B3
Railway St A2
Ravensdowne B3
Riverdene B1
Riverside Rd B2
Royal Border Br A2
Royal Tweed Br B2
Russian Gun ✦ B3
Scots Gate ✦ A2
Scott's Pl A2
Shielfield Park (Berwick Rangers FC) C1
Shielfield Terr C2
Silver St B3
Spittal Quay C3
Superstore B1/C1/C2
Tower Gdns A2
Tower Ho Pottery ✦ C2
Tower Rd C2
Town Hall B3
Turret Gdns C2
Tweedbank Retail Pk C2
Tweed Dock B2
Tweed St A2
Tweedside Trading Est C1
Union Brae B2
Union Park Rd B2
Walkergate A3
Wallace Gr A3
War Memorial A2
War Memorial B2
Warkworth Terr A2
Well Close Sq A2
West End B2
West End Pl B1
West End Rd B1
West St B3
West St C3
Windmill Bastion ✦ B3
Woolmarket B3
Works C3

Birmingham 332

Abbey St A2
Aberdeen St A1
Acorn Gr B2
Adams St A5
Adderley St C5
Albert St B4
Albion St B2
Alcester St C5
Aldgate Gr A3
All Saint's St A2
All Saints Rd A2
Allcock St C5
Allesley St A4
Allison St C4
Alma Crescent B6

352 Blackpool • Bournemouth • Bradford • Brighton • Bristol

Alston Rd C1
Arcadian Centre C4
Arena Birmingham ✦ C2
Arthur St C6
Assay Office B3
Ashted Circus B5
Aston Expressway A5
Aston St B4
Aston University B4/B5
Avenue Rd A5
Bacchus Rd A1
Bagot St B4
Banbury St B5
Barford Rd B1
Barford St C4
Barn St C5
Barnwell Rd C6
Barr St A3
Barrack St B5
Barwick St B4
Bath Row C3
Beaufort Rd C1
Belmont Row B5
Benson Rd A1
Berkley St C3
Bexhill Gr C3
Birchall St C5
Birmingham City FC C6
Birmingham City Hospital (A&E) A1
Birmingham City University B3
Birmingham Wheels Park ✦ B6
Bishopsgate St C3
Blews St A4
Bloomsbury St A6
Blucher St C3
Bordesley St C4
Bowyer St C5
Bradburne Way A5
Bradford St C5
Branston St A3
Brearley St A4
Brewery St A4
Bridge St C3
Bridge St West A4
Brindley Dr B3
Brindley Place C3
Broad St C3
Broad St Cineworld C2
Broadway Plaza ✦ C2
Bromley St C5
Bromsgrove St C4
Brookfield Rd A2
Browning St C2
Bryant St A1
BT Tower ✦ B3
Buckingham St A3
Bull St B4
Bull St B4
Bullring C4
Cambridge St C3
Camden Dr B3
Camden St B2
Cannon St C4
Cardigan St B5
Carlisle St A1
Carlyle Rd C1
Caroline St B3
Carver St B2
Cato St A6
Cattell Rd C6
Cattells Gr A6
Cawdor Cr C1
Cecil St B4
Cemetery A2/B2
Cemetery La A2
Centenary Square C3
Centre Link Industrial Estate A6
Charlotte St B3
Cheapside C4
Chester St A5
Children's Hospital (A&E) B4
Church St B4
Claremont Rd A2
Clarendon Rd C1
Clark St C1
Clement St B3
Clissold St B2
Cliveland St B4
Coach Station C5
College St B2
Colmore Circus B4
Colmore Row B4
Commercial St C3
Constitution Hill B3
Convention Ctr, The C3
Cope St B2
Coplow St B1
Corporation St C4
Council House B3
County Court B4
Coveley Gr A2
Coventry Rd C6
Coventry St C5
Cox St B3
Crabtree Rd A2
Cregoe St C3
Crescent Ave A2
Crescent Theatre C3
Crescent, The A2
Cromwell St A6
Cromwell St B3
Cube, The C3
Curzon Circle B5
Curzon St B5
Custard Factory ✦ C5
Cuthbert Rd B1
Dale End B4
Dart St C6
Dartmouth Circus A4
Dartmouth Middleway A5
Dental Hospital B4
Deritend C5
Devon St A6
Devonshire St A1
Digbeth High St C4
Dolman St B6
Dover St A1
Duchess Rd C2
Duddeston B6
Duddeston Manor Rd B5
Duddeston Mill Rd B6
Duddeston Mill Trading Estate B6
Dudley Rd B1
Edgbaston Village C2
Edmund St B3
Edward St B3
Elkington St A4
Ellen St B2
Ellis St C3
Erskine St B6
Essex St C4
Everyman C3
Eyre St B2
Farm Croft A3
Farm St A3
Fazeley St B4/C5
Felstead Way B5
Finstall Cl B5
Five Ways C2
Five Ways C2
Fiveway Shopping Ctr C2
Fleet St B3
Floodgate St C5
Ford St A2
Fore St C4
Forster St B5
Francis Rd C2
Francis St B5
Frankfort St A4
Frederick St B3
Freeth St C1
Freightliner Terminal B6
Garrison Circus C5
Garrison La C6
Garrison St B6
Gas St C3
Geach St A4
George St B3
George St West B2
Gibb St C5
Gilby Rd C2
Gillott Rd B1
Glover St C5
Goode Ave A2
Goodrick Way A6
Gordon St B6
Graham St B3
Grand Central Shopping Centre C4
Granville St C3
Gray St C6
Great Barr St C5
Great Charles St Queensway B3
Great Francis St B6
Great Hampton Row A3
Great Hampton St A3
Great King St A3
Great King St North A3
Great Lister St A5
Great Tindal St C2
Green La C6
Green St C5
Greenway St C6
Grosvenor St West C2
Guest Gr A3
Guild Cl C2
Guildford Dr A4
Guthrie Cl A3
Hagley Rd C1
Hall St B3
Hampton St A3
Handsworth New Rd A1
Hanley St B4
Harford St A3
Harmer Rd A2
Harold Rd C1
Hatchett St A4
Heath Mill La C5
Heath St B1
Heaton St A2
Heneage St B5
Henrietta St B4
Herbert Rd C6
High St C4
High St C5
Hilden Rd B5
Hill St C3/C4
Hindlow Cl B6
Hingeston St B2
Hippodrome Theatre C4
HM Prison A1
Hockley Circus A2
Hockley Hill A3
Hockley St A3
Holliday St C3
Holloway Circus C4
Holloway Head C3
Holt St B5
Horse Fair C4
Hospital St A4
Howard St B3
Howe St B5
Hubert St A5
Hunters Rd A2
Hunters Vale A3
Huntly Rd C2
Hurst St C4
Icknield Port Rd B1
Icknield Sq B2
Icknield St A2/B2
IKON C3
Information Ctr C3
Inge St C4
Irving St C3
James Watt Queensway B4
Jennens Rd B5
Jewellery Quarter A3
Jewellery Quarter A3
Jewellery Quarter Museum B3
John Bright St C4
Keeley St C6
Kellett Rd B5
Kent St C4
Kenyon St B3
Key Hill A3
Key Hill Circus A2
Kilby Ave C2
King Edwards Rd B2
King Edwards Rd C3
Kingston Rd C6
Kirby Rd A1
Ladywood Arts & Leisure Centre B1
Ladywood Circus C1
Ladywood Middleway C2/C3
Ladywood Rd C1
Lancaster St B4
Landor St B6
Law Courts B4
Lawley Middleway B5
Ledbury Cl C2
Ledsam St B2
Lees St A1
Legge La B3
Lennox St A3
Library A6/C3
Library C3
Lighthorne Ave B2
Link Rd B1
Lionel St B3
Lister St B5
Little Ann St C5
Little Hall Rd A6
Liverpool St C5
Livery St B3/B4
Lodge Rd A1
Lord St A5
Love La A5
Loveday St B4
Lower Dartmouth St C6
Lower Loveday St B4
Lower Tower St A4
Lower Trinity St C5
Lucus Circus A3
Ludgate Hill B3
Mailbox Centre & BBC C3
Margaret St B3
Markby Rd A1
Marroway St B1
Maxstoke St C6
Melvina Rd A6
Meriden St C4
Midland St B6
Milk St C5
Mill St A5
Millennium Point B5
Miller St A4
Milton St A4
Moat La C4
Montague Rd C1
Montague St C5
Monument Rd C1
Moor St Queensway C4
Moor Street C4
Moorsom St A4
Morville St C2
Mosborough Cr A3
Moseley St C4
Mott St B3
Mus & Art Gallery B3
Musgrave Rd A1
National Sea Life Centre C3
Navigation St C3
Nechell's Park Rd A6
Nechells Parkway B5
Nechells Pl A6
New Alexandra C3
New Bartholomew St C4
New Canal St C5
New John St West A3
New Spring St B2
New St C4
New Street C4
New Summer St A4
New Town Row A4
Newhall Hill B3
Newhall St B3
Newton St B4
Newtown A4
Noel Rd C1
Norman St A1
Northbrook St B1
Northwood St B3
Norton St A2
Odeon C2
Old Crown House C5
Old Rep Theatre, The C4
Old Snow Hill B4
Oliver Rd C1
Oliver St A5
Osler St C1
Oxford St C5
Palmer St C5
Paradise Circus Queensway C3
Paradise St C3
Park Rd A2
Park St C4
Pavilions C4
Paxton Rd A2
Peel St A1
Pershore St C4
Phillips St A4
Pickford St C5
Pinfold St C4
Pitsford St A2
Plough & Harrow Rd C1
Police Station A4/B4/C2/C4
Pope St B2
Portland Rd C1
Post Office A5/B1/B3/B5/C3/C5
Preston Rd A1
Price St B4
Princip St B4
Printing House St B4
Priory Queensway B4
Pritchett St A4
Proctor St A5
Radnor St A2
Rea St C4
Regent Pl B3
Register Office C3
Repertory Theatre C3
Reservoir Rd C1
Richard St A5
River St C5
Rocky La A5/A6
Rodney Cl C2
Roseberry St B2
Rotton Park St B1
Royal Birmingham Conservatoire ✦ B5
Rupert St A5
Ruston St C2
Ryland St C2
St Andrew's Ind Est C6
St Andrew's Rd C6
St Andrew's St C6
St Bolton St C6
St Chads A4
St Chad's Cath (RC) ✝ B4
St Chads Queensway B4
St Clements Rd A6
St George's St A3
St James Pl B5
St Marks Cr B2
St Martin's C4
St Paul's B3
St Paul's B3
St Paul's Sq B3
St Philip's ✝ B4
St Stephen's St A4
St Thomas' Peace Garden C3
St Vincent St C2
Saltley Rd A6
Sand Pits Pde B3
Severn St C3
Shadwell St B4
Sheepcote St C2
Shefford Rd A4
Sherborne St C2
Shylton's Croft C2
Skipton Rd C2
Smallbrook Queensway C4
Smith St A3
Snow Hill B4
Snow Hill Queensway B4
Soho, Benson Rd A1
South Rd A2
Spencer St B3
Spring Hill B2
Staniforth St B4
Station St C4
Steelhouse La B4
Stephenson St C4
Steward St B2
Stirling Rd C1
Stour St B2
Suffolk St Queensway C3
Summer Hill Rd B2
Summer Hill St B2
Summer Hill Terr B2
Summer La A4
Summer Row B3
Summerfield Cr B1
Summerfield Park B1
Superstore B2
Sutton St C3
Swallow St C3
Sydney Rd C6
Symphony Hall C3
Talbot St A1
Temple Row C4
Temple St C4
Templefield St C6
Tenby St B3
Tenby St North B2
Tennant St C2/C3
Thimble Mill La A6
Thinktank (Science & Discovery) B5
Thomas St A4
Thorpe St C4
Tilton Rd C6
Tower St A4
Town Hall C3
Town Hall C3
Trent St C5
Turner's Buildings A1
Unett St A3
Union Terr B5
Upper Trinity St C5
Uxbridge St A3
Vauxhall Gr B5
Vauxhall Rd B5
Vernon Rd C1
Vesey St B4
Viaduct St B5
Victoria Sq C3
Villa St A3
Vittoria St B3
Vyse St B3
Walter St A6
Wardlow Rd A5
Warstone La B2
Washington St C3
Water St B3
Waterworks Rd C1
Watery La C5
Western Rd B1
Wharf St A2
Wheeler St A3
Whitehouse St A5
Whitmore St A2
Whittall St B4
Wholesale Market C4
Wiggin St B1
Willes Rd A1
Windsor Industrial Estate A5
Windsor St A5
Windsor St B5
Winson Green Rd A1
Witton St C6
Wolseley St C6
Woodcock St B5

Blackpool 332

Abingdon St A1
Addison Cr A3
Adelaide St B1
Albert Rd B2
Alfred St B2
Ascot Rd A3
Ashton Rd C2
Auburn Gr C3
Bank Hey St B1
Banks St A1
Beech Ave A3
Bela Gr C2
Belmont Ave B2
Birley St A1
Blackpool & Fleetwood Tram B1
Blackpool & the Fylde College B2
Blackpool FC C2
Blackpool North A2
Blackpool North A2
Blackpool Tower ✦ B1
Blundell St C1
Bonny St B1
Breck Rd B3
Bryan Rd A3
Buchanan St A2
Bus Hub B1
Cambridge Rd A3
Caunce St A2/A3
Central Dr B1/C2
Central Pier ✦ C1
Central Pier C1
Central Pier Theatre C1
Chapel St C1
Charles St A2
Charnley Rd B2
Church St A1/A2
Clinton Ave B2
Coach Station A2/C1
Cocker St A1
Coleridge Rd A3
Collingwood Ave A3
Comedy Carpet ✦ B1
Condor Gr C3
Cookson St A2
Coronation St B1
Corporation St A1
Courts B1
Cumberland Ave B3
Cunliffe Rd C3
Dale St C1
Devonshire Rd A3
Devonshire Sq A3
Dickson Rd A1
Elizabeth St A2
Ferguson Rd C3
Forest Gate B3
Foxhall Rd C1
Freckleton St C2
George St A2
Gloucester Ave B3
Golden Mile, The C1
Gorse Rd B3
Gorton St A2
Grand Theatre, The B1
Granville Rd A2
Grasmere Rd C2
Grosvenor St A2
Grundy Art Gallery A1
Harvey Rd B3
Hornby Rd B2
Houndshill Shopping Centre B1
Hull Rd B1
Ibbison Ct C2
Kent Rd C2
Keswick Rd C2
King St A2
Knox Gr C3
Laycock Gate A3
Layton Rd A3
Leamington Rd B2
Leeds Rd B3
Leicester Rd B2
Levens Gr C2
Library A1
Lifeboat Station B1
Lincoln Rd B2
Liverpool Rd B3
Livingstone Rd B2
London Rd A3
Lune Gr C2
Lytham Rd C1
Madame Tussaud's Blackpool B1
Manchester Sq C1
Manor Rd B3
Maple Ave B3
Market St A1
Marlboro Rd B3
Mere Rd B3
Milbourne St A2
Newcastle Ave B3
Newton Dr A3
North Pier ✦ A1
North Pier A1
North Pier Theatre A1
Odeon C2
Olive Gr B3
Palatine Rd B2
Park Rd B2/C3
Peter St A2
Post Office A1/B1/B2/B3
Princess Pde A1
Princess St C1/C2
Promenade A1/C1
Queen St A1
Queen Victoria Rd C2
Raikes Pde B2
Reads Ave B2
Regent Cinema B2
Regent Rd B2
Register Office B2
Ribble Rd B2
Rigby Rd C1/C2
Ripon Rd B3
St Albans Rd B3
St Ives Ave C3
St John's Square A1
St Vincent Ave C3
Salisbury Rd B3
Salthouse Ave C2
Salvation Army Ctr A2
Sands Way C2
Sea Life Centre B1
Seasiders Way C1
Selbourne Rd A2
Sharrow Gr C3
Somerset Ave C3
South King St B2
Springfield Rd A1
Sutton Pl B2
Talbot Rd A1/A2
Thornber Gr C2
Topping St A1
Tower B1
Town Hall A1
Tram Depot C1
Tyldesley Rd C1
Vance Rd B1
Victoria St B1
Victory Rd A2
Wayman Rd A3
Westmorland Ave C2/C3
Whitegate Dr B3
Winter Gardens Theatre B1
Woodland Gr B3
Woolman Rd B2

Bournemouth 333

Ascham Rd A3
Avenue Rd B1
Ave Shopping Centre B1
Bath Rd C2
Beacon Rd C1
Beechey Rd A3
Bodorgan Rd B1
Bourne Ave B1
Bournemouth A3
Bournemouth & Poole College B3
Bournemouth Int Ctr C1
Bournemouth Pier C2
Bournemouth Sta B3
Braidley Rd A1
Cavendish Place A2
Cavendish Rd A2
Central Drive A1
Central Gdns B1
Christchurch Rd B3
Cliff Lift C1/C3
Coach House Pl A3
Coach Station A3
Commercial Rd B1
Cotlands Rd B3
Cranborne Rd C1
Cricket Ground A2
Cumnor Rd B2
Dean Park A2
Dean Park Cr B2
Dean Park Rd A2
Durrant Rd B1
East Overcliff Dr C3
Exeter Cr C1
Exeter La C2
Exeter Rd C1
Gervis Place B1
Gervis Rd B3
Glen Fern Rd B2
Golf Club B1
Grove Rd B3
Hinton Rd C2
Holdenhurst Rd B3
Horseshoe Common B2
Information Ctr C2
Lansdowne B3
Lansdowne Rd A2
Lorne Park Rd B2
Lower Gdns B1/C2
Madeira Rd B2
Methuen Rd A3
Meyrick Park A1
Meyrick Rd B3
Milton Rd A2
Nuffield Health Bournemouth Hospital (private) A2
Oceanarium C2
Odeon Cinema C1
Old Christchurch Rd B2
Ophir Rd A3
Oxford Rd B3
Park Rd A3
Parsonage Rd B2
Pavilion C2
Pier Approach C2
Pier Theatre C2
Police Station A3/B3
Portchester Rd A3
Post Office B1/B3
Priory Rd C1
Quadrant, The B2
Recreation Ground A1
Richmond Gardens Shopping Centre B2
Richmond Hill Rd B1
Russell-Cotes Art Gallery & Museum C2
Russell Cotes Rd C2
St Anthony's Rd A1
St Michael's Rd C1
St Paul's A3
St Paul's La B3
St Paul's Rd A3
St Peter's B2
St Peter's B2
St Peter's Rd B2
St Stephen's Rd B1/B2
St Swithun's B3
St Swithun's Rd B3
St Swithun's Rd South B3
St Valerie Rd A2
St Winifred's Rd A2
Square, The B1
Stafford Rd B3
Terrace Rd B1
Town Hall B1
Tregonwell Rd C1
Triangle, The B1
Trinity Rd B2
Undercliff Drive C3
Upper Hinton Rd B2
Upper Terr Rd C1
Wellington Rd A2/A3
Wessex Way A3/B1/B2
West Cliff Promenade C1
West Hill Rd C1
West Undercliff Promenade C1
Westover Rd B2
Wimborne Rd A2
Wootton Mount B2
Wychwood Dr A1
Yelverton Rd B2
York Rd B3
Zig-Zag Walks C1/C3

Bradford 333

Alhambra B2
Back Ashgrove B1
Barkerend Rd A3
Barnard Rd C3
Barry St B2
Bolling Rd C3
Bolton Rd A3
Bowland St A1
Bradford Big Screen ✦ B2
Bradford College B1
Bradford Forster Sq A2
Bradford Interchange B3
Bradford Playhouse B3
Bridge St B2
Britannia St B2
Broadway Bradford, The B2
Burnett St B3
Bus Station B2
Butler St West A3
Caledonia St C2
Canal Rd A2
Carlton St B1
Cathedral ✝ A3
Centenary Sq B2
Chapel St B3
Cheapside A2
Church Bank B3
Cineworld B3
City Hall B2
City Rd A1
Claremont B1
Colour Experience B1
Croft St B2
Crown Court B3
Darfield St A1
Darley St A2
Drewton Rd A1
Drummond Trading Estate A1
Dryden St B3
Dyson St A1
Easby Rd C1
East Parade B3
Eldon Pl A1
Filey St B3
Forster Square Retail Park A2
Gallery II B1
Garnett St B3
Godwin St B2
Gracechurch St A1
Grattan Rd B1
Great Horton Rd B1/B2
Grove Terr B1
Hall Ings B2
Hall La C3
Hallfield Rd A1
Hammstrasse A2
Harris St B3
Holdsworth St A2
Ice Arena ✦ B2
Impressions B2
Information Ctr B2
Inland Revenue A2
Ivegate B2
Jacob's Well Municipal Offices B2
James St A2
John St A2
Kirkgate B2
Kirkgate Centre B2
Laisteridge La C1
Leeds Rd B3
Leisure Exchange, The B3
Library B1/B2
Listerhills Rd B1
Little Horton Gn C1
Little Horton La C1
Longside La B1
Lower Kirkgate B2
Lumb La A1
Magistrates Court B2
Manchester Rd C2
Manningham La A1
Manor Row A2
Market C3
Market St B2
Melbourne Place C1
Midland Rd A2
Mill La C2
Morley St B1
National Science and Media Museum B2
Nelson St B2/C2
Nesfield St A2
New Otley Rd A3
Norcroft St B1
North Parade A2
North St A3
North Wing A3
Oastler Shopping Ctr A2
Otley Rd A3
Park Ave C1
Park La C1
Park Rd C2
Parma St C2
Peace Museum B2
Peckover St B3
Piccadilly A2
Police Station C2
Post Office B1/B2/B3/C3
Princes Way B2
Prospect St C3
Radwell Drive C2
Rawson Rd A1
Rebecca St A1
Richmond Rd B1
Russell St C1
St George's Hall B2
St Lukes Hospital C1
Shipley Airedale Rd A3/B3
Shopmobility A2
Simes St A1
Smith St B1
Spring Mill St C2
Stott Hill A3
Sunbridge Rd A1/B1/B2
Theatre in the Mill B1
Thornton Rd A1/B1
Trafalgar St A2
Trinity Rd C1
Tumbling Hill St B1
Tyrrel St B2
Univ of Bradford B1/C1
Usher St C3
Valley Rd A2
Vicar La B3
Wakefield Rd C3
Wapping Rd A3
Well St B3
Westgate A1
White Abbey Rd A1
Wigan Rd A1
Wilton St B1
Wood St A1
Wool Exchange B2
Worthington St A1

Brighton 333

Addison Rd A1
Albert Rd B2
Albion Hill B3
Albion St B3
Ann St A3
Baker St A3
Black Lion St C2
Brighton A2
Brighton Centre C2
Brighton Fishing Museum C2
Brighton Pier (Palace Pier) ✦ C3
Brighton Wheel ✦ C3
British Airways i360 Tower ✦ C1
Broad St C3
Buckingham Pl A2
Buckingham Rd B2
Cannon Pl C1
Carlton Hill B3
Chatham Pl A1
Cheapside A3
Church St B2
Churchill Square Shopping Centre B2
Clifton Hill B1
Clifton Pl B1
Clifton Rd B1
Clifton St A2
Clifton Terr B1
Clyde Rd A3
Coach Station C3
Compton Ave A2
Davigdor Rd A1
Denmark Terr B1
Ditchling Rd A3
Dome B2
Duke St B2
Duke's La C2
Dyke Rd A1/B2
East St C2
Edward St B3
Elmore Rd B3
Fleet St A2
Frederick St B2
Gardner St B2
Gloucester Pl B3
Gloucester Rd B2
Goldsmid Rd A1
Grand Junction Rd C2
Grand Pde B3
Grove Hill B3
Guildford St A2
Hampton Pl B1
Hanover Terr A3
High St C3
Highdown Rd A1
Information Ctr C2
John St B3
Jubilee Clock Tower B2
Kemp St B2
Kensington Pl B2
Kings Rd C1
Lanes, The C2
Law Courts B3
Lewes Rd A3
Library C2
London Rd A3
Madeira Dr C3
Marine Pde C3
Middle St C2
Montpelier Pl B1
Montpelier Rd B1
Montpelier St B1
Mus & Art Gallery B3
New England Rd A2
New England St A2
New Rd B2
Nizells Ave A1
Norfolk Rd B1
Norfolk Terr B1
North Rd B2
North St B2
Odeon C2
Old Shoreham Rd A1
Old Steine C3
Osmond Rd A1
Over St B2
Oxford St A3
Park Crescent Terr A3
Phoenix Brighton B3
Phoenix Rise A3
Police Station B3
Post Office A1/A3/C3
Preston Rd A2
Preston St B1
Prestonville Rd A1
Queen's Rd B2
Queen Sq B2
Regency Sq C1
Regent St B2
Richmond Pl B3
Richmond St B3
Richmond Terr A3
Rose Hill Terr A3
Royal Pavilion B2
St Bartholomew's A3
St James's St C3
St Nicholas Rd B2
St Nicholas' B2
St Peter's A3
Sea Life Brighton C3
Shaftesbury Rd A3
Ship St C2
Sillwood Rd B1
Sillwood St B1
Southover St A3
Spring Gdns B2
Stanford Rd A1
Stanley Rd A3
Surrey St B2
Sussex St B3
Swimming Pool B3
Sydney St B3
Temple Gdns B1
Terminus Rd A2
Theatre Royal B2
Tidy St B2
Town Hall C2
Toy & Model Mus A2
Trafalgar St B2
Union Rd A3
University of Brighton B3
Upper Lewes Rd A3
Upper North St B1
Viaduct Rd A3
Victoria Gdns B3
Victoria Rd B1
Volk's Electric Railway ✦ C3
West Pier (derelict) C1
West St C2
Western Rd B1
Whitecross St B2
YHA ▲ C3
London B1
York Pl B3
York Rd B1

Bristol 333

Acramans Rd C4
Albert Rd C6
Alfred Hill A4
All Saint's St A4
All Saints' B4
Allington Rd C3
Alpha Rd C4
Ambra Vale B1
Ambra Vale East B2
Ambrose Rd B2
Amphitheatre & Waterfront Sq ✦ C4
Anchor Rd B3
Anvil St B6
Arcade, The A5
Architecture Centre, The ✦ B4
Argyle Pl B2
Arlington Villas A2
Arnolfini ✦ B4
Art Gallery A3
Ashton Gate Rd C2
Ashton Rd C1
Avon Bridge C1
Avon Cr C1
Avon St B6
Baldwin St B4
Baltic Wharf C2
Baltic Wharf Leisure Ctr & Caravan Pk ✦ C2
Baltic Wharf Marina C2
Barossa Pl C4
Barton Manor B6
Barton Rd B6
Barton Vale B6
Bath Rd C6
Bathurst Basin C4
Bathurst Parade C4
Beauley Rd C3
Bedminster Bridge C5
Bedminster Parade C4
Bellevue B2
Bellevue Cr B2
Bellevue Rd C6
Berkeley Pl A2
Berkeley Sq A3
Birch Rd C2
Blackfriars A4
Bond St A5
Braggs La A6
Brandon Hill B3
Brandon Steep B3
Bristol Aquarium B4
Bristol Beacon B4
Bristol Bridge B5
Bristol Cath (CE) ✝ B3
Bristol Eye Hospital (A&E) A4
Bristol Grammar Sch A3

Bristol Harbour Railway C3
Bristol Royal Children's Hospital H A4
Bristol Royal Infirmary (A&E) H A4
Bristol Temple Meads Station ≥ B6
Broad Plain B6
Broad Quay B4
Broad St A4
Broad Weir A5
Broadcasting House A3
Broadmead A5
Brunel Institute ✦ B3
Brunel Way C1
Brunswick Sq A5
Burton Cl C5
Bus Station A4
Butts Rd B3
Cabot Circus A5
Cabot Tower ✦ B3
Caledonia Pl B1
Callowhill Ct A5
Cambridge St C6
Camden Rd C3
Camp Rd A1
Canada Way C2
Cannon St A4
Canon's Way B3
Cantock's Cl A3
Canynge Rd A1
Canynge Sq A1
Castle Park A5
Castle St A5
Cathedral Walk B3
Catherine Meade St C4
Cattle Market Rd C6
Central Library B3
Charles Pl B1
Charlotte St B3
Charlotte St South B3
Chatterton House B5
Chatterton Sq C5
Chatterton St C5
Cheese La B5
Christchurch A4
Christchurch Rd A1
Christmas Steps ✦ A4
Church La B2/B5
Church St B5
City Museum A3
City of Bristol College B3
Civil and Family Justice Centre B5
Clare St B4
Clarence Rd C5
Cliff Rd C1
Clift House Rd C1
Clifton Cath (RC) ✝ A2
Clifton Down A1
Clifton Down Rd A1
Clifton Hill B2
Clifton Park A1/A2
Clifton Park Rd A1
Clifton Rd A2
Clifton Vale B1
Cliftonwood Cr B2
Cliftonwood Rd B2
Cliftonwood Terr B2
Cobblestone Mews A1
College Green B3
College Rd A1
College St B3
Colston Almshouses A4
Colston Ave B4
Colston Parade C5
Colston St A4
Commercial Rd C4
Constitution Hill B2
Cooperage La C2
Corn St B4
Cornwallis Ave B1
Cornwallis Cr B1
Coronation Rd C2/C4
Council House B3
Counterslip B5
Create Centre, The ✦ C1
Crosby Row B2
Crown Court A4
Culver St B3
Cumberland Basin C1
Cumberland Cl C2
Cumberland Rd C2/C3
Dean La C4
Deanery Rd B3
Denmark St B4
Dowry Sq B1
Eaton Cr A2
Elmdale Rd A3
Elton Rd A3
Eugene St A4/A6
Exchange and St Nicholas' Mkts, The B4
Fairfax St A4
Fire Station B5
Floating Harbour C3
Fosseway, The A2
Foster Almshouses A4
Frayne Rd C1
Frederick Pl A2
Freeland Pl B1
Friary B5
Frogmore St B3
Fry's Hill B2
Gas La B6
Gasferry Rd C3
Georgian House B3
Glendale B1
Glentworth Rd B2
Gloucester St A1
Goldney Hall B2
Goldney Rd B1
Gordon Rd A2
Granby Hill B1
Grange Rd A1
Great Ann St A6
Great George Rd B3
Great George St A6/B3
Green St North B1
Green St South B1
Greenay Bush La C2
Greenbank Rd C2
Greville Smyth Park C1
Grove, The B4
Guinea St C4
Guildhall A4
Hamilton Rd C3
Hanbury Rd A2
Hanover Pl C2
Harley Pl A1
Haymarket A5
Hensman's Hill B1
High St B4
Highbury Villas A3
Hill St B3
Hill St C6
Hippodrome B4
Hopechapel Hill B1
Horfield Rd A4
Horsefair, The A5
Horton St B6
Host St A4
Hotwell Rd B1/B2
Houlton St A6
Howard Rd C3
IMAX Cinema B4
Information Ctr B4
Islington Rd C3
Jacob St A5/A6
Jacob's Wells Rd B2
John Carr's Terr B2
John Wesley's Chapel A5
Joy Hill B1
Jubilee St B6
Kensington Pl A2
Kilkenny St B6
King St B4
Kingsland Rd B6
Kingston Rd C3
Lamb St A6
Lansdown Rd A2
Lawford St A6
Lawfords Gate A6
Leighton Rd C3
Lewins Mead A4
Lime Rd C2
Litfield Rd A1
Little Ann St A6
Little Caroline Pl B1
Little George St A6
Little King St B4
Llandoger Trow B4
Lloyds' Building, The C3
Lodge St A4
Lord Mayor's Chapel, The B4
Lower Castle St A5
Lower Church La A4
Lower Clifton Hill B2
Lower Guinea St C4
Lower Lamb St B3
Lower Maudlin St A4
Lower Park Rd A4
Lower Sidney St C2
Lucky La C4
Lydstep Terr C3
M Shed C4
Magistrates' Court A4
Mall (Galleries Shopping Centre), The A5
Mall, The A1
Manilla Rd A1
Mardyke Ferry Rd C2
Maritime Heritage Centre B3
Marlborough Hill A4
Marlborough St A4
Marsh St B4
Mead St C5
Merchant Dock B2
Merchant Seamen's Almshouses B4
Merchant St A5
Merchants Rd A1
Merchants Rd C1
Meridian Pl A2
Meridian Vale A2
Merrywood Rd C3
Midland Rd A6
Milford St C3
Millennium Prom B3
Millennium Sq B3
Mitchell La B5
Mortimer Rd A1
Murray Rd C4
Myrtle Rd A3
Narrow Plain B5
Narrow Quay B4
Nelson St A4
New Charlotte St C4
New Kingsley Rd B6
New Queen St C5
New St A6
Newgate A5
Newton St A6
Norland Rd A1
North St C2
O2 Academy B3
Oakfield Gr A2
Oakfield Pl A2
Oakfield Rd A2
Old Bread St B6
Old Market St A6
Old Park Hill A4
Oldfield Rd B1
Orchard Ave B4
Orchard La B4
Orchard St B4
Osbourne Rd C3
Oxford St B6
Park Pl A2
Park Rd C3
Park Row A3
Park St A3
Passage St B5
Pembroke Gr A2
Pembroke Rd A2
Pembroke Rd C3
Pembroke St A5
Penn St A5
Pennywell Rd A6
Percival Rd A1
Pero's Bridge B4
Perry Rd A4
Phipps St C2
Pip 'n' Jay B5
Plimsoll Bridge B1
Police Sta A6
Polygon Rd B1
Portland St A1
Portwall La B5
Post Office A1/A3/A5/B1/B4/C4/C5
Prewett St C5
Prince St B4
Prince St Bridge C4
Princess St C5
Princess Victoria St B1
Priory Rd A3
Pump La C5
QEH Theatre A2
Quakers Friars A5
Quay St A4
Queen Charlotte St B4
Queen Elizabeth Hospital School B2
Queen Sq B4
Queen St A5
Queen's Ave A3
Queen's Parade B3
Queen's Rd A2/A3
Raleigh Rd C2
Randall Rd B2
Red Lodge A4
Redcliffe Backs B5
Redcliffe Bridge B4
Redcliffe Hill C5
Redcliffe Parade C4
Redcliffe St B5
Redcliffe Way C5
Redcross St A6
Redgrave Theatre A1
Regent St B1
Richmond Hill A2
Richmond Hill Ave A2
Richmond La A2
Richmond Park Rd A2
Richmond St C6
Richmond Terr A2
River St A6
Rownham Mead B2
Royal Fort Rd A3
Royal Park A2
Royal West of England Academy A3
Royal York Cr B1
Royal York Villas B1
Rupert St A4
Russ St B6
St Andrew's Walk B2
St George's B3
St George's Rd B3
St James A4
St John's A4
St John's Rd C4
St Luke's Rd C5
St Mary Redcliffe C5
St Matthias Park A6
St Michael's Hill A3
St Michael's Hosp H A3
St Michael's Park A3
St Nicholas St B4
St Paul St A5
St Paul's Rd A2
St Peter's (ruin) A5
St Philip's Bridge B5
St Philips Rd A6
St Stephen's B4
St Stephen's St B4
St Thomas St B5
St Thomas the Martyr B5
Sandford Rd B1
Sargent St C5
Saville Pl B1
Ship La C5
Shopmobility A5
Showcase Cinema de Lux A5
Silver St A4
Sion Hill A1
Small St A4
Smeaton Rd C1
Somerset Sq C5
Somerset St C5
Southernhay Ave B2
Southville Rd C4
Spike Island Artspace C2
Spring St C5
Superstore C4
SS Great Britain and the Matthew B2
Stackpool Rd C3
Staight St B6
Stillhouse La C4
Sydney Row C2
Tankard's Cl A3
Temple Back B5
Temple Back East B5
Temple Bridge B5
Temple Church B5
Temple Circus B5
Temple Gate C5
Temple St B5
Temple Way B5
Terrell St A4
Theatre Royal (Bristol Old Vic) B4
Thekla B4
Thomas La B5
Three Kings of Cologne A4
Three Queens La B5
Tobacco Factory, The C2
Tower Hill B5
Tower La A4
Trenchard St A4
Triangle South A3
Triangle West A3
Trinity Rd A6
Trinity St A6
Tyndall Ave A3
Union St A5
Union St B6
Unity St A6
Unity St B3
University of Bristol A3
University Rd A3
Upper Byron Pl A3
Upper Maudlin St A4
Upper Perry Hill C3
Upton Rd C2
Valentine Bridge B6
Victoria Gr C5
Victoria Rd C6
Victoria Rooms A2
Victoria Sq A2
Victoria St B5
Vyvyan Rd A1
Vyvyan Terr A1
Wade St A6
Walter St C2
Wapping Rd C4
Water La B5
Waterloo Rd A6
Waterloo St A1
Waterloo St A6
Watershed Media Centre ✦ B4
We the Curious ✦ B3
Welling Terr B1
Welsh Back B4
West Mall A1
West St A6
Westfield Pl A1
Wetherell Pl A2
Whitehouse Pl C5
Whitehouse St C5
Whiteladies Rd A2
Whitson St A4
William St C5
Willway St C5
Windsor Pl B1
Wine St A4
Woodland Rd A3
Woodland Rise A3
Worcester Rd A1
Worcester Terr A1
YHA B4
York Gdns B1
York Pl A2
York Rd C5

Bury St Edmunds 333

Abbey Gardens B3
Abbey Gate B3
Abbeygate St B2
Albert Cr B1
Albert St B1
Ambulance Sta C1
Angel Hill B2
Angel La B2
Anglian Lane A1
Arc Shopping Centre B2
Athenaeum C2
Baker's La C3
Barwell Rd B3
Beetons Way A1
Bishops Rd B2
Bloomfield St B2
Bridewell La C2
Bullen Cl C1
Bury St Edmunds ≥ A2
Bury St Edmunds County Upper Sch A1
Bury St Edmunds Leisure Centre B1
Bury Town FC B3
Bus Station B2
Business Park B3
Butter Mkt B2
Cannon St B2
Castle Rd C1
Cemetery C1
Chalk Rd (N) B1
Chalk Rd (S) B1
Church Row B2
Churchgate St C2
Cineworld B1
Citizens Advice Bureau B2
College St C2
Compiegne Way A3
Corn Exchange, The B2
Cornfield Rd B1
Cotton Lane B3
Courts B2
Covent Garden C2
Crown St C3
Cullum Rd C2
Eastern Way A3
Eastgate St B3
Enterprise Bsns Park A2
Etna Rd A2
Eyre Cl C2
Fire Station B1
Friar's Lane C2
Gage Cl A1
Garland St B2
Greene King Brewery C3
Grove Park B1
Grove Rd B1
Guildhall C2
Guildhall St C2
Hatter St C2
High Baxter St B2
Honey Hill C2
Hospital Rd C1/C2
Ickworth Dr C1
Industrial Estate A3
Information Ctr B2
Ipswich St A2
King Edward VI School A1
King's Rd C1/B2
Library B2
Long Brackland A2
Looms La B2
Lower Baxter St B2
Malthouse La A2
Maynewater La C3
Mill Rd C1
Mill Rd (South) C1
Minden Close B3
Moyses Hall B2
Mustow St B3
Norman Tower C3
Northgate Ave A2
Northgate St B2
Nutshell, The B2
Osier Rd A2
Out Northgate A2
Out Risbygate B1
Out Westgate C2
Parkway B1/C2
Peckham St B2
Petticoat La C1
Phoenix Day Hosp H C1
Pinners Way C1
Police Station C3
Post Office B2/B3
Pump La B2
Queen's Rd B1
Raingate St C3
Raynham Rd A1
Retail Park C2
Risbygate St B1/B2
Robert Boby Way C2
St Andrew's St North B2
St Andrew's St South B2
St Botolph's La C3
St Edmund's C2
St Edmund's Abbey (Remains) ✦ B3
St Edmunds Hospital (private) H C3
St Edmundsbury ✝ C3
St John's St B2
St Marys C3
School Hall La B2
Shillitoe Cl C1
Shire Halls & Magistrates Ct C3
South Cl C1
Southgate St C3
Sparhawk St C3
Spring Lane B1
Springfield Rd B1
Station Hill A2
Swan La C3
Tayfen Rd B2
Theatre Royal C3
Thingoe Hill A2
Victoria St B1
Vinefields, The B3
War Memorial ✦ C1
Well St B2
West Suffolk College B1
Westgarth Gdns C1
Westgate St C2
Whiting St C2
York Rd B1
York Terr B1

Cambridge 334

Abbey Rd A3
ADC A2
Anglia Ruskin Univ B3
Archaeology & Anthropology B2
Arts Picture House B2
Arts Theatre B1
Auckland Rd A3
Backs, The B1
Bateman St C2
Benet St B1
Bradmore St B3
Bridge St A1
Broad St B3
Brookside C2
Brunswick Terr A3
Burleigh St B3
Bus Station B2
Butt Green A2
Cambridge Contemporary Art Gallery B1
Castle Mound A1
Castle St A1
Cemetery B3
Chesterton La A1
Christ's (Coll) B2
Christ's Lane B2
Christ's Pieces B2
City Rd B3
Clare (Coll) B1
Clarendon St B2
Coe Fen C2
Coronation St C2
Corpus Christi (Coll) B1
Court A3
Cross St C3
Crusoe Bridge C1
Darwin (Coll) C1
Devonshire Rd C3
Downing (Coll) C2
Downing St B2
Earl St B2
East Rd B3
Eden St B3
Elizabeth Way A3
Elm St B2
Emery St B3
Emmanuel (Coll) B2
Emmanuel Rd B2
Emmanuel St B2
Fair St A3
Fen Causeway, The C1
Fenner's Cricket Gd C3
Fire Station B3
Fitzroy St A3
Fitzwilliam Mus C2
Fitzwilliam St C2
Garrett Hostel Bridge B1
Glisson Rd C3
Gonville & Caius (Coll) B1
Gonville Place C2
Grafton Centre, The A3
Grand Arcade B2
Green St B1
Gresham Rd C3
Guest Rd B3
Guildhall B2
Harvey Rd C3
Hills Rd C3
Hobson St B2
Hughes Hall (Coll) B3
Information Ctr B2
James St A3
Jesus (Coll) A2
Jesus Green A2
Jesus La A2
Jesus Terr B3
John St B3
Kelsey Kerridge Sports Centre B3
Kettle's Yard A1
King's Bridge B1
King St A2
King's (Coll) B1
King's Coll Chapel B1
King's Parade B1
Lammas Land Recreation Ground C1
Lensfield Rd C2
Library B2
Lion Yard B2
Little St Mary's La B1
Lyndewod Rd C3
Magdalene (Coll) A1
Magdalene St A1
Maid's Causeway A3
Malcolm St A2
Market Hill B1
Market St B1
Mathematical Bridge B1
Mawson Rd C3
Midsummer Common A3
Mill La B1
Mill Rd B3
Mill St C3
Mumford B3
Museum of Cambridge A1
Museum of Classical Archeology C1
Napier St A3
New Square A3
Newmarket Rd A3
Newnham Rd C1
Norfolk St B3
Northampton St A1
Norwich St C2
Orchard St B2
Panton St C2
Paradise Nature Reserve C1
Paradise St B3
Park Parade A1
Park St A2
Park Terr B2
Parker St B2
Parker's Piece B2
Parkside B3
Parkside Pools B3
Parsonage St A3
Pemberton Terr C2
Pembroke (Coll) B2
Pembroke St B1
Perowne St B3
Peterhouse (Coll) C1
Petty Cury B2
Polar Museum, The C2
Police Station B3
Post Office A1/A3/B2/B3/C1/C2/C3
Queen's La B1
Queen's Rd B1
Queens' (Coll) B1
Regent St B2
Regent Terr B2
Ridley Hall (Coll) C1
Riverside A3
Round Church, The A1
Russell St C2
St Andrew's St B2
St Benet's B1
St Catharine's (Coll) B1
St Eligius St C2
St John's (Coll) A1
St Mary's B1
St Paul's Rd C3
Saxon St C2
Sedgwick Museum B2
Sheep's Green C1
Shire Hall A1
Sidgwick Ave C1
Sidney St A2
Sidney Sussex (Coll) A2
Silver St B1
Station Rd C3
Tenison Ave C3
Tenison Rd C3
Tennis Court Rd B2
Thompson's La A1
Trinity (Coll) A1
Trinity Hall (Coll) B1
Trinity St B1
Trumpington Rd C2
Trumpington St B1
Union Rd C2
University Botanic Gardens C2
Victoria Ave A2
Victoria St B2
Warkworth St B3
Warkworth Terr B3
Wesley House (Coll) A2
West Rd B1
Westcott House (Coll) A2
Westminster (Coll) A1
Whipple B2
Willis Rd B3
Willow Walk A2
YMCA C3

Canterbury 334

Artillery St B2
Barton Mill Rd A3
Beaconsfield Rd A1
Beaney, The B2
Beverley Rd A1
Bingley's Island B1
Black Griffin La B1
Broad Oak Rd A2
Broad St B2
Brymore Rd A3
Burgate B2
Bus Station C2
Canterbury College C3
Canterbury East ≥ C1
Canterbury Tales, The ✦ B2
Canterbury West ≥ A1
Castle C1
Castle Row C1
Castle St C1
Cathedral ✝ B2
Causeway, The A2
Chaucer Rd A3
Christ Church University B3
Christchurch Gate ✦ B2
City Council Offices A3
City Wall B2
Coach Park A2
College Rd B3
Cossington Rd C2
Court B2
Craddock Rd A3
Crown & County Courts B3
Dane John Gdns C2
Dane John Mound ✦ C1
Deanery B2
Dover St C2
Duck La B2
Eastbridge Hosp B1
Edgar Rd B3
Ersham Rd C3
Ethelbert Rd C3
Fire Station C2
Forty Acres Rd A1
Friars, The B2
Gordon Rd C1
Greyfriars ✦ B1
Guildford Rd C1
Havelock St B2
Heaton Rd C1
High St B2
Information Ctr A2/B2
Ivy La B2
Ivy Pl C1
King St B2
King's School B2/B3
King's School Rec Ctr, The A2
Kingsmead Leisure Ctr A2
Kingsmead Rd A2
Kirby's La B1
Lansdown Rd C2
Lime Kiln Rd C1
Longport B3
Lower Chantry La C3
Mandeville Rd A1
Market Way A2
Marlowe Arcade B2
Marlowe Ave C2
Marlowe Theatre B2
Martyrs Field Rd C1
Mead Way B1
Military Rd B2
Monastery St B2
Mus of Canterbury (Rupert Bear Mus) B1
New Dover Rd C3
Norman Rd C2
North Holmes Rd B3
North La B1
Northgate A2
Nunnery Fields C2
Nunnery Rd C2
Oaten Hill C2
Odeon Cinema C2
Old Dover Rd C2
Old Palace B2
Old Ruttington La B2
Old Weavers B2
Orchard St B1
Oxford Rd C1
Palace St B2
Pilgrims Way C3
Pin Hill C1
Pine Tree Ave A1
Police Station C2
Post Office B2
Pound La B1
Puckle La C2
Raymond Ave C2
Recreation Ground A2
Registry Office A2
Rheims Way B1
Rhodaus Cl C2
Rhodaus Town C2
Roman Museum B2
Roper Gateway A1
Roper Rd A1
Rose La B2
Shopmobility B2
St Augustine's Abbey (remains) ✝ B3
St Augustine's Rd C3
St Dunstan's A1
St Dunstan's St A1
St George's Pl C2
St George's St B2
St George's Tower ✦ B2
St Gregory's Rd B3
St John's Hospital A2
St Margaret's St B2
St Martin's B3
St Martin's Ave B3
St Martin's Rd B3
St Michael's Rd A1
St Mildred's C1
St Peter's Gr B1
St Peter's La B2
St Peter's Pl B1
St Peter's St B1
St Radigunds St B2
St Stephen's Ct A1
St Stephen's Path A1
St Stephen's Rd A2
Salisbury Rd A1
Simmonds Rd C1
Spring La C3
Station Rd West B1
Stour St B1
Sturry Rd A3
Tourtel Rd A3
Tudor Rd C1
Union St B2
University for the Creative Arts C3
Vernon Pl C2
Victoria Rd C1
Watling St B2
Westgate Gdns B1
Westgate Towers B1
Whitefriars B2
Whitehall Gdns B1
Whitehall Rd B1
Wincheap C1
York Rd C1
Zealand Rd C2

Cardiff Caerdydd 334

Adam St B3
Alexandra Gdns A2
Allerton St C1
Arran St A3
ATRiuM (Univ of Glamorgan) C3
Beauchamp St C1
Bedford St A3
Blackfriars Priory (rems) ✝ B1
Boulevard De Nantes B2
Brains Brewery C2
Brook St B1
Bute Park A1
Bute St C2
Bute Terr C3
Callaghan Sq C2/C3
Capitol Shopping Centre, The B3
Cardiff Arms Park (Cardiff Blues) B1
Cardiff Bridge B1
Cardiff Castle B2
Cardiff Central Station ≥ C2
Cardiff Story, The B2
Cardiff University A1/A2/B3
Cardiff University Student's Union A2
Caroline St C2
Castle Green B2
Castle Mews A1
Castle St (Heol y Castell) B1
Cathays Station ≥ A2
Celerity Drive C3
Central Library C2
Charles St (Heol Siarl) B3
Churchill Way B3
City Hall A2
City Rd A3
Clare Rd C1
Clare St C1
Coburn St A3
Coldstream Terr B1
College Rd A1
Colum Rd A1
Court C2
Court Rd C1
Craiglee Drive C3
Cranbrook St A3
Customhouse St C2
Cyfartha St A3
David's B2/C2
Despenser Place C1
Despenser St C1
Dinas St C1
Duke St (Heol y Dug) B2
Dumfries Place B3
East Grove A3
Ellen St C3
Fire Station B3
Fitzalan Place B3
Fitzhamon Emb C1
Fitzhamon La C1
Friary, The B2
g39 B2
Gloucester St C1
Glynrhondda St A2
Gordon Rd A3
Gorsedd Gdns B2
Green St B1
Greyfriars Rd B2
Hafod St C1
Hayes, The B2
Herbert St C3
High St B2
HM Prison B3
Industrial Estate C3
John St C3
Jubilee St C1
King Edward VII Ave A1
Kingsway (Ffordd y Brenin) B2
Knox Rd B3
Law Courts B2
Llanbleddian Gdns A2
Llantwit St A2
Lloyd George Ave C3
Lower Cathedral Rd B1
Lowther Rd A3
Magistrates Court B3
Mansion House A3
Mardy St C1
Mark St B1
Market B2
Mary Ann St C3
Merches Gdns C1
Mill La C2
Millennium Bridge B1
Miskin St A2
Monmouth St C1
Motorpoint Arena Cardiff ✦ C3
Museum Ave A2
Museum Place A2
National Museum Cardiff A2
National War Memorial ✦ A2
Neville Place C1
New Theatre B2
Newport Rd B3
Northcote La A3
Northcote St A3
Parade, The A3
Park Grove A4
Park Place A2
Park St C2
Penarth Rd C2
Pendyris St C1
Plantaganet St C1
Post Office B2
Principality Stadium C1
Principality Stadium Tours (Gate 3) ✦ B2
Quay St B2
Queen's Arcade B2
Queen Anne Sq A1
Queen St (Heol y Frenhines) B2
Queen St Station ≥ B3
Regimental Museums B2
Rhymney St A3
Richmond Rd A3
Royal Welsh College of Music and Drama A1
Russell St A3
Ruthin Gdns A2
St Andrews Place A2
St David's ✝ B2
St David's Hall ✦ B2
St John the Baptist B2
St Mary St (Heol Eglwys Fair) B2
St Peter's St A3
Salisbury Rd A3
Sandon St B3
Schooner Way C3
Scott Rd C2
Scott St C2
Senghennydd Rd A2
Sherman Theatre A2
Sophia Gardens A1
Sophia Gardens Stadium ✦ A1
South Wales Baptist College A3
Sport Wales National Ctr ✦ A1
Stafford Rd C1
Stadium Plaza C1
Station Terr B3
Stuttgarter Strasse B2
Sussex St C1
Taffs Mead Emb C1
Talworth St A3
Temple of Peace & Health ✦ A1
Treharris St A3
Trinity St B2
Tudor La C1
Tudor St C1
Tyndall St C3
Vue C2
Walk, The A3
Welsh Government A1
West Grove A3
Westgate St (Heol y Porth) B2
Windsor Place B3
Womanby St B2
Wood St C2
Working St B2
Wyeverne Rd A2

Carlisle 334

Abbey St A1
Aglionby St B3
Albion St C3
Alexander St C3
AMF Bowl ✦ C2
Annetwell St A1
Bank St B2
Bitts Park A1
Blackfriars St B2
Blencome St C1
Blunt St C1
Botchergate B2
Boustead's Grassing C2
Bowman St B3
Bridge St A1
Broad St B3
Brook St C3
Brunswick St B2
Bus Station B2
Caldew Bridge A1
Caldew St C1
Carlisle (Citadel) Station ≥ B2
Carlisle College A2
Castle A1
Castle St A1
Castle Way A1
Cathedral ✝ A1
Cecil St B2
Chapel St A2
Charles St B3
Charlotte St B1
Chatsworth Square A2
Chiswick St B2
Citadel, The ✦ B2
City Walls A1

Civic Centre A2
Clifton St C1
Close St B3
Collingwood St C1
Colville St C1
Colville Terr C1
Council Offices B3
Court B2
Court St Brow C2
Crosby St B2
Crown St C2
Currock Rd C2
Dacre Rd A1
Dale St C1
Denton St C1
Devonshire Walk A1
Duke's Rd A2
East Dale St C1
East Norfolk St C1
Eden Bridge A2
Edward St B3
Elm St B1
English St B2
Fire Station A2
Fisher St A1
Flower St B3
Freer St C1
Fusehill St B3
Georgian Way A2
Gloucester Rd C3
Golf Course A2
Graham St C1
Grey St B3
Guildhall Museum A2
Halfey's La B3
Hardwicke Circus A2
Hart St B3
Hewson St C2
Howard Pl A3
Howe St B3
Information Ctr A2
James St B2
Junction St B1
King St B2
Lancaster St B2
Lanes Shopping Centre, The B2
Laser Quest ✦ B2
Library A2
Lime St B1
Lindisfarne St C3
Linton St B3
Lismore Pl A3
Lismore St B3
London Rd C3
Lonsdale Rd B2
Lord St C3
Lorne Cres B1
Lorne St B1
Lowther St B2
Madford Retail Park B1
Magistrates' Ct A2
Market Hall A2
Mary St B2
Memorial Bridge A3
Metcalfe St C1
Milbourne St B1
Myddleton St B3
Nelson St C1
Norfolk St C1
Old Fire Sta, The A2
Old Town Hall A2
Oswald St C3
Peter St A2
Petteril St B3
Pools B2
Portland Pl B2
Portland Sq B2
Post Office A2/B2/C1/C3
Princess St C2
Pugin St B1
Red Bank Terr C2
Regent St C3
Richardson St C1
Rickerby Park A3
Rickergate A2
River St B3
Rome St C2
Rydal St B3
St Cuthbert's B2
St Cuthbert's La B2
St James' Park C1
St James' Rd C1
St Nicholas Gate Retail Park C3
St Nicholas St C3
Sands Centre, The A2
Scotch St A2
Shaddongate B1
Sheffield St B1
Shopmobility A2
South Henry St B3
South John St C2
South St B3
Spencer St B2
Station Retail Park B2
Strand Rd A2
Superstore B1
Sybil St B3
Tait St B2
Thomas St B1
Thomson St C3
Trafalgar St C1
Trinity Leisure Centre A2
Tullie Mus & Art Gallery A1
Tyne St C3
University of Cumbria B3
Viaduct Estate Rd B1
Victoria Pl A2
Victoria Viaduct B2
Vue B2
Warwick Rd B2
Warwick Sq B3
Water St B2
West Walls B1
Westmorland St C1

Chelmsford 334

Anchor St C1
Anglia Ruskin Univ A2
Arbour La A3
Baddow Rd B2/C3
Baker St C1
Barrack Sq B2
Bellmead B2
Bishop Hall La A2
Bishop Rd A2
Bond St B2
Boswells Dr B3
Bouverie Rd C2
Bradford St C1
Braemar Ave C1
Brook St A2
Broomfield Rd A1
Burgess Springs B1
Burns Cres C2
Bus Station B1/B2
Cedar Ave A1
Cedar Ave West A1
Cemetery A1
Cemetery A2
Cemetery C1
Central Park B1
Chelmsford ✝ B2
Chelmsford ⇌ A1
Chichester Dr A3
Chinery Cl A3
City Council A1
Civic Centre A1
Civic Theatre B1
Cloudfm County Cricket Ground, The B2
College C1
Cottage Pl A2
County Hall B2
Coval Ave B1
Coval La B1
Coval Wells B1
Crown Court B2
Duke St B2
Elm Rd C1
Elms Dr A1
Essex Record Office, The B3
Fairfield Rd B1
Falcons Mead B1
George St C2
Glebe Rd A1
Godfrey's Mews C2
Goldlay Ave C3
Goldlay Rd C2
Grove Rd C2
Hall St C2
Hamlet Rd C2
Hart St C1
Henry Rd A2
High Bridge Rd B2
High Chelmer Shopping Centre B2
High St B2
Hill Cres B3
Hill Rd B3
Hill Rd Sth B3
Hillview Rd A3
HM Prison A3
Hoffmans Way A2
Hospital B2
Lady La C2
Langdale Gdns C3
Legg St B2
Library B2
Lionfield Terr A3
Lower Anchor St C1
Lynmouth Ave C2
Lynmouth Gdns C3
Magistrates Court B2
Maltese Rd A1
Manor Rd C2
Marconi Rd A2
Market B2
Market Rd B2
Marlborough Rd C1
Meadows Shopping Centre, The B2
Meadowside A3
Mews Ct C2
Mildmay Rd C2
Moulsham Dr C2
Moulsham Mill ✦ C3
Moulsham St C1/C2
Navigation Rd B3
New London Rd B2/C1
New St A2/B2
New Writtle St C1
Nursery Rd C2
Orchard St C2
Odeon B2
Parker Rd C2
Parklands Dr A3
Parkway A1/B1/B2
Police Station A2
Post Office B2/C2
Primrose Hill A1
Prykes Dr B1
Queen St C1
Queen's Rd B3
Railway St A1
Rainsford Rd A1
Ransomes Way A2
Rectory La A2
Regina Rd A2
Riverside Ice & Leisure Centre B2
Riverside Retail Park A3
Rosebery Rd C2
Rothesay Ave C1
St John's Rd C2
Sandringham Pl B3
Seymour St B1
Shopmobility B2
Shrublands Cl B3
Southborough Rd C1
Springfield Rd A3/B2/B3
Stapleford Cl C1
Superstore B2/C3
Swiss Ave A1
Telford Pl A3
Tindal St B2
Townfield St A1
Trinity Rd B3
University B1
Upper Bridge Rd C1
Upper Roman Rd C2
Van Dieman's Rd C3
Viaduct Rd B1
Vicarage Rd C1
Victoria Rd A2
Victoria Rd South B2
Vincents Rd C2
Waterloo La B2
Weight Rd B3
Westfield Ave A1
Wharf Rd B3
Writtle Rd C1
YMCA A2
York Rd C1

Cheltenham 334

Albert Rd A3
Albion St B3
All Saints Rd B3
Ambrose St B2
Andover Rd C1
Back Montpellier Terr C2
Bandstand ✦ C2
Bath Pde B2
Bath Rd C2
Bays Hill Rd C1
Bennington St B2
Berkeley St B3
Brewery Quarter, The A2
Brunswick St South A2
Bus Station B2
Carlton St B3
Central Cross Road A3
Cheltenham College C2
Cheltenham FC A3
Cheltenham General (A&E) C3
Cheltenham Ladies' College B2
Christchurch Rd B1
Cineworld A2
Clarence Rd A2
Clarence Sq A2
Clarence St B2
Cleeveland St A1
College Baths Road C3
College Rd C2
Colletts Dr A1
Corpus St C3
Devonshire St A2
Douro Rd B1
Duke St B3
Dunalley Pde A2
Dunalley St A2
Everyman B2
Evesham Rd A3
Fairview Rd B3
Fairview St B3
Fire Station C3
Folly La A2
Gloucester Rd A1
Grosvenor St B3
Grove St A1
Hanover St A2
Hatherley St C1
Henrietta St A2
Hewlett Rd B3
High St B2/B3
Holst Birthplace Museum A3
Hudson St A2
Imperial Gdns C2
Imperial La B2
Imperial Sq C2
Information Centre B2
Keynsham Rd C3
King St A2
Knapp Rd B2
Lansdown Cr C1
Lansdown Rd C1
Leighton Rd B3
Library B2
London Rd C3
Lypiatt Rd C1
Magistrates' Court & Register Office B1
Malvern Rd B1
Manser St A2
Market St A1
Marle Hill Pde A2
Marle Hill Rd A2
Millbrook St A1
Milsom St A2
Montpellier Gdns C2
Montpellier Gr C2
Montpellier Pde C2
Montpellier Spa Rd C2
Montpellier St C1
Montpellier Terr C2
Montpellier Walk C2
New St B2
North Pl B2
Old Bath Rd C3
Oriel Rd B2
Overton Park Rd B1
Overton Rd B1
Oxford St C3
Parabola Rd B1
Park Pl C1
Park St A1
Pittville Circus A3
Pittville Crescent A3
Pittville Lawn A3
Pittville Park A2
Playhouse B2
Portland St B3
Prestbury Rd A3
Prince's Rd C1
Priory St B3
Promenade B2
Queen St A1
Recreation Ground A2
Regent Arcade B2
Regent St B2
Rodney Rd B2
Royal Crescent B2
Royal Well Pl B2
Royal Wells Rd B2
St George's Pl B2
St Georges Rd B1
St Gregory's B2
St James St B3
St John's Ave B3
St Luke's Rd C2
St Margarets Rd A2
St Mary's B2
St Matthew's B2
St Paul's La A2
St Paul's Rd A2
St Paul's St A2
St Stephen's Rd C1
Sandford Parks Lido C3
Sandford Mill Road C3
Sandford Park C3
Sandford Rd C2
Selkirk St A3
Sherborne Pl B3
Sherborne St B3
Suffolk Pde C2
Suffolk Rd C1
Suffolk Sq C1
Sun St A1
Swindon Rd B2
Sydenham Villas Rd C3
Tewkesbury Rd A1
The Courtyard B1
Thirlstaine Rd C2
Tivoli Rd C1
Tivoli St C1
Town Hall & Theatre B2
Townsend St A1
Trafalgar St C2
Union St B3
Univ of Gloucestershire (Francis Cl Hall) A2
Univ of Gloucestershire (Hardwick) A1
Victoria Pl B3
Victoria St A2
Vittoria Walk C2
Wellesley Rd A2
Wellington Rd A3
Wellington Sq A3
Wellington St B2
West Drive A3
Western Rd B1
Wilson The B2
Winchcombe St B3
Winston Churchill Memorial Gardens A1

Chester 335

Abbey Gateway A2
Appleyards La C3
Bars, The B3
Bedward Row B1
Beeston View C3
Bishop Lloyd's Pal B2
Black Diamond St A2
Bottoms La C3
Boughton B3
Bouverie St A1
Bus Interchange A2
Bridge St B2
Bridgegate C2
Brook St A3
Brown's La C2
Cambrian Rd A1
Canal St A2
Carrick Rd C1
Castle C2
Castle Dr C2
Cathedral ✝ B2
Catherine St A1
Chester ⇌ A3
Cheyney Rd A1
Chichester St A1
City Rd A3
City Walls B1/B2
City Walls Rd B1
Cornwall St A2
Cross Hey C3
Cross, The ✦ B2
Crown Ct C2
Cuppin St B2
Curzon Park North C1
Curzon Park South C1
Dee Basin A1
Dee La B3
Delamere St A2
Dewa Roman Experience B2
Duke St B2
Eastgate B2
Eastgate St B2
Eaton Rd C2
Edinburgh Way C3
Elizabeth Cr B3
Fire Station A2
Foregate St B2
Forum, The B2
Frodsham St B2
Gamul House B2
Garden La A1
George St A2
Gladstone Ave A1
God's Providence House B2
Gorse Stacks A2
Greenway St C2
Grosvenor Bridge C1
Grosvenor Museum B2
Grosvenor Park B3
Grosvenor Park Terr C1
Grosvenor Shopping Ctr B2
Grosvenor St B2
Groves Rd B3
Groves, The B3
Guildhall Museum B1
Handbridge C2
Hartington St C3
Hoole Way A2
Hunter St B2
Information Ctr B2
King Charles' Tower ✦ A2
King St A2
Leisure Centre A2
Library B2
Lightfoot St A3
Little Roodee C2
Liverpool Rd A2
Love St B3
Lower Bridge St B2
Lower Park Rd B3
Lyon St A2
Magistrates Court B2
Meadows La C3
Meadows, The B3
Military Museum C2
Milton St A3
New Crane St B1
Nicholas St B2
Northgate A2
Northgate St A2
Nun's Rd B1
Old Dee Bridge ✦ C2
Overleigh Rd C2
Park St B2
Police Station B2
Post Office A2/A3/B2
Princess St B2
Queen St B2
Queen's Park Rd C3
Queen's Rd A3
Race Course B1
Raymond St A1
River La C2
Roman Amphitheatre & Gardens B2
Roodee (Chester Racecourse), The B1
Russell St A3
St Anne St A2
St George's Cr C3
St Martin's Gate A1
St Martin's Way B1
St Mary's Priory ✦ B2
St Oswalds Way A2
Saughall Rd A1
Sealand Rd A1
South View Rd A1
Stanley Palace B1
Station Rd A3
Steven St A3
Storyhouse B2
Superstore B2
Tower Rd B1
Town Hall B2
Union St B3
University of Chester C2
Vicar's La B2
Victoria Cr C3
Victoria Rd A2
Walpole St A1
Water Tower St A1
Water Tower, The ✦ B1
Watergate B1
Watergate St B2
Whipcord La A1
White Friars B2
York St B3

Chichester 335

Adelaide Rd A3
Alexandra Rd A3
Arts Centre B2
Ave de Chartres B1/B2
Barlow Rd A1
Basin Rd C2
Beech Ave B1
Bishops Pal Gardens B2
Bishopsgate Walk A3
Bramber Rd C3
Broyle Rd A2
Bus Station B2
Caledonian Rd B3
Cambrai Ave B3
Canal Pl C2
Canal Wharf C2
Canon La B2
Cathedral ✝ B2
Cavendish St A1
Cawley Rd B2
Cedar Dr A1
Chapel St A2
Cherry Orchard Rd C3
Chichester ⇌ B2
Chichester By-Pass C2/C3
Chichester Coll B1
Chichester Cinema B3
Chichester Festival B2
Chichester Gate Leisure Pk C1
Churchside A2
Cineworld C1
City Walls B2
Cleveland Rd B3
College La A2
Cory Cl C2
Council Offices B2
County Hall B2
District B2
Duncan Rd A1
Durnford Cl A1
East Pallant B2
East Row B2
East St B2
East Walls B3
Eastland Rd C3
Ettrick Cl B1
Ettrick Rd B1
Exton Rd C3
Fire Station A2
Football Ground A2
Franklin Pl A2
Friary (Rems of) A2
Garland Cl C3
Green La A3
Grove Rd C3
Guilden Rd B3
Guildhall A2
Hawthorn Cl A1
Hay Rd C3
Henty Gdns B1
Herald Dr C3
Hornet, The B3
Information Ctr B2
John's St B2
Joys Croft A3
Jubilee Pk A3
Jubilee Rd A3
Juxon Cl B1
Kent Rd A3
King George Gdns A2
King's Ave C2
Kingsham Ave C3
Kingsham Rd C2
Laburnum Gr B2
Leigh Rd C1
Lennox Rd A3
Lewis Rd A3
Library B2
Lion St B2
Litten Terr A3
Litten, The A3
Little London B2
Lyndhurst Rd B3
Market B3
Market Ave B2
Market Cross B2
Market Rd B3
Melbourne Rd A3
Minerva B2
Mount La B1
New Park Rd A3
Newlands La A1
North Pallant B2
North St A2
North Walls A2
Northgate A2
Novium, The B2
Oak Ave A1
Oak Cl A1
Oaklands Park A2
Oaklands Way A2
Orchard Ave A1
Orchard St A1
Ormonde Ave B3
Pallant House B2
Parchment St A1
Parklands Rd A1/B1
Peter Weston Pl B3
Police Station C2
Post Office A1/B2/C3
Priory La A2
Priory Park A2
Priory Rd A2
Queen's Ave C1
Riverside A3
Roman Amphitheatre B3
St Cyriacs A2
St Martins' St B2
St Pancras A3
St Paul's Rd A2
St Richard's Hospital (A&E) A3
Shamrock Cl A3
Sherbourne Rd A1
Somerstown A2
South Bank C2
South Downs Planetarium ✦ C2
South Pallant B2
South St B2
Southgate B2
Spitalfield La A3
Stirling Rd B3
Stockbridge Rd C1/C2
Swanfield Dr A3
Terminus Ind Est C1
Tower St A2
Tozer Way A3
Turnbull Rd A3
Upton Rd C1
Velyn Ave B3
Via Ravenna B1
Walnut Ave A1
West St B2
Westgate B1
Westgate Fields B1
Westgate Leisure Ctr B1
Weston Ave C1
Whyke Cl C3
Whyke La B3
Whyke Rd C3
Winden Ave B3

Colchester 335

Abbey Gateway ✝ C2
Albert St A1
Albion Grove C2
Alexandra Rd C1
Artillery St C3
Arts Centre B1
Balkerne Hill B1
Barrack St C3
Beaconsfield Rd C1
Beche Rd C3
Bergholt Rd A1
Bourne Rd C3
Brick Kiln Rd A1
Brigade Gr C2
Bristol Rd B2
Broadlands Way A3
Brook St B3
Bury Cl B2
Bus Sta C2
Butt Rd C1
Campion Rd C2
Cannon St C3
Canterbury Rd C2
Captain Gardens C2
Castle B2
Castle Park B2
Castle Rd B2
Catchpool Rd A1
Causton Rd B1
Chandlers Row C3
Circular Rd East C2
Circular Rd North C1
Circular Rd West C1
Clarendon Way A1
Claudius Rd C2
Colchester ⇌ A1
Colchester Camp Abbey Field C1
Colchester Retail Pk B1
Colchester Town ⇌ C2
Colne Bank Ave A1
Colne View Retail Pk A2
Compton Rd A3
Cowdray Ave A1/A2
Cowdray Centre, The A2
Crouch St B1
Crowhurst Rd B1
Culver Square Shopping Centre B1
Culver St East B2
Culver St West B1
Dilbridge Rd A3
East Hill B2
East St B3
East Stockwell St B1
Eld La B1
Essex Hall Rd A1
Exeter Dr B2
Fairfax Rd C2
Fire Station A2
Firstsite B2
Flagstaff Rd C1
Garrison Parade C2
George St B2
Gladstone Rd C2
Golden Noble Hill C2
Goring Rd A3
Granville Rd C3
Greenstead Rd B3
Guildford Rd B2
Harsnett Rd C3
Harwich Rd B3
Head St B1
High St B1/B2
High Woods Ctry Park A2
Hollytrees B2
Hyderabad Cl C2
Hythe Hill C3
Information Ctr B2
Jarmin Rd A2
Kendall Rd C3
Kimberley Rd C3
King Stephen Rd C3
Leisure World A2
Library B1
Lincoln Way B2
Lion Wlk Shopping Ctr B1
Lisle Rd C2
Lucas Rd C2
Magdalen Green C3
Magdalen St C2
Maidenburgh St B2
Maldon Rd C1
Manor Rd B1
Margaret Rd A1
Mason Rd A2
Mercers Way A1
Mercury B1
Mersea Rd C2
Meyrick Cr C2
Mile End Rd A1
Military Rd C2
Mill St C2
Minories B2
Moorside B3
Morant Rd C3
Napier Rd C2
Natural History B2
New Town Rd C2
Norfolk Cr A3
North Hill B1
North Station Rd A1
Northgate St B1
Nunns Rd B1
Odeon B1
Old Coach Rd B3
Old Heath Rd C3
Osborne St B2
Petrolea Cl A1
Police Station C1
Popes La B1
Port La C3
Post Office B2/C1
Priory St B2
Queen St B2
Rawstorn Rd B1
Rebon St C3
Recreation Rd C3
Ripple Way A3
Roberts Rd C2
Roman Rd B2
Roman Wall B2
Romford Cl A3
Rosebery Ave B2
St Andrews Ave B3
St Andrews Gdns B3
St Botolph St B2
St Botolphs B2
St John's Abbey (site of) ✝ C2
St John's St B1
St Johns Walk Shopping Centre B1
St Leonards Rd C3
St Marys Fields B1
St Peter's St B1
St Peters B1
Salisbury Ave C1
Saw Mill Rd C3
Sergeant St C2
Serpentine Walk A1
Sheepen Pl B1
Sheepen Rd B1
Sir Isaac's Walk B1
Smythies Ave B2
South St C1
South Way C1
Sports Way A2
Suffolk Cl A3
Superstore A1
Town Hall B1
Valentine Dr A3
Victor Rd C3
Wakefield Cl B2
Wellesley Rd C1
Wells Rd B2/B3
West St C1
West Stockwell St B1
Weston Rd C3
Westway A1
Wickham Rd C1
Wimpole Rd C3
Winchester Rd C2
Winnock Rd C2
Worcester Rd B2

Coventry 335

Abbots La A1
Albany B1
Albany Rd B1
Alma St B3
Ambulance Sta A2
Art Faculty B3
Asthill Grove C2
Bablake School A1
Barras La A1/B1
Barr's Hill School A1
Belgrade B2
Bishop St A2
Bond's Hospital B1
Broad Gate B2
Broadway C1
Burges, The B2
Bus Station A3
Butts Radial B1
Byron St A3
Canal Basin ✦ A2
Canterbury St A3
Cathedral ✝ B3
Central Six Retail Pk C1
Chester St A1
Cheylesmore Manor House B2
Christ Church Spire ✦ B2
City Coll A3
City Walls & Gates ✦ A2
Corporation St B2
Council House B2
Coundon Rd A1
Coventry Station ⇌ C2
Coventry Transport Museum A2
Coventry University Technology Park C3
Cox St A3
Croft Rd B1
Dalton Rd C1
Deasy Rd C3
Earl St B2
Eaton Rd C2
Fairfax St B2
Foleshill Rd A2
Ford's Hospital B2
Fowler Rd A1
Friars Rd C2
Gordon St C1
Gosford St B3
Greyfriars Green ✦ B2
Greyfriars Rd B2
Gulson Rd B3
Hales St A2
Harnall Lane East A3
Harnall Lane West A2
Herbert Art Gallery & Museum B3
Hertford St B2
Hewitt Ave A1
High St B2
Hill St B1
Holy Trinity B2
Holyhead Rd A1
Howard St A3
Huntingdon Rd C1
Information Ctr B2
Jordan Well B3
King Henry VIII School C1
Lady Godiva Statue ✦ B2
Lamb St A2
Leicester Row A2
Library B2
Lincoln St A2
Little Park St B2
London Rd C3
Lower Ford St B3
Lower Precinct Shopping Centre B2
Magistrates & Crown Courts B2
Manor House Drive B2
Manor Rd C2
Market B2
Martyrs Memorial ✦ C2
Meadow St B1
Meriden St A1
Michaelmas Rd C2
Middleborough Rd A1
Mile La C3
Millennium Place ✦ A2
Much Park St B3
Naul's Mill Park A1
New Union B2
Odeon B1
Park Rd C2
Parkside C3
Planet Ice Arena B1
Post Office B2
Primrose Hill St A3
Priory Gardens & Visitor Centre B2
Priory St B3
Puma Way C3
Quarryfield La C3
Queen's Rd B1
Quinton Rd C2
Radford Rd A1
Raglan St B3
Ringway (Hill Cross) A1
Ringway (Queens) B1
Ringway (Rudge) B1
Ringway (St Johns) B3
Ringway (St Nicholas) A2
Ringway (St Patricks) C2
Ringway (Swanswell) A2
Ringway (Whitefriars) B3
St John St B2
St John the Baptist B2
St Nicholas St A2
Sidney Stringer Acad A3
Skydome B1
Spencer Ave C1
Spencer Rec Gnd C1
Spencer Rd C1
Spon St B1
Sports Centre B3
Stoney Rd C2
Stoney Stanton Rd A3
Superstore B2
Swanswell Pool A3
Technocentre C3
Thomas Landsdail St C2
Tomson Ave A1
Top Green C1
Trinity St B2
University B3
University Sports Ctr B3
Upper Hill St A1
Upper Well St A2
Victoria St A3
Vine St A3
Warwick Rd C2
Waveley Rd B1
West Orchards Shopping Ctr B2
Westminster Rd C1
White St A3
Windsor St B1

Derby 335

Abbey St C1
Agard St B1
Albert St B2
Albion St B2
Ambulance Station B1
Arthur St A1
Ashlyn Rd B3
Assembly Rooms B2
Babington La C2
Becket St B1
Belper Rd A1
Bold La B1
Bradshaw Way C2
Bradshaw Way Retail Park C2
Bridge St B1
Brook St B1
Burton Rd C1
Bus Station B2
Business Park A3
Caesar St A2
Canal St C3
Carrington St C3
Cathedral ✝ B2
Cathedral Rd B1
Charnwood St C2
Chester Green Rd A2
City Rd A2
Clarke St A3
Cock Pitt B3
Council House B2
Courts B1
Cranmer Rd B3
Crompton St C1
Crown & County Courts B2
Curzon St B1
Darley Grove A1
Derby ⇌ C3
Derby C2
Derwent Bsns Centre A2
Derwent St B2
Drewry La C1
Duffield Rd A1
Duke St A2
Dunton Cl B3
Eagle Market C2
East St B2
Eastgate B3
Exeter St B2
Farm St C1
Ford St B1
Forester St C1
Fox St A2
Friar Gate B1
Friary St B1
Full St B2
Gerard St C1
Gower St C2
Green La C2
Grey St C1
Guildhall B2
Harcourt St C1
Highfield Rd A1
Hill La C2
Incora County Ground (Derbyshire CCC), The B3
Information Ctr B2
intu Derby C2
Iron Gate B2
John St C3
Joseph Wright Centre B1
Kedleston Rd A1
Key St B2
King Alfred St C1
King St A1
Kingston St A1
Lara Croft Way C2
Leopold St C2
Library B1
Liversage St C3
Lodge La B1
London Rd C2
London Rd Community Hospital C2
Macklin St C1
Mansfield Rd A2
Market B2
Market Pl B2
May St C1
Meadow La B3
Melbourne St C2
Mercian Way C1
Midland Rd C3
Monk St C1
Morledge B2
Mount St C1

Mus & Art Gallery 🏛 . .B1
Noble St C3
North Parade A1
North St A1
Nottingham Rd B3
Osmaston Rd C2
Otter St A1
Park St C3
Parker St A1
Pickfords House 🏛 B1
Police HQ A2
Police Station 🗛 B2
Post Office
🖃 A1/A2/B1/C2/C3
Pride Parkway C3
Prime Enterprise Park A2
Prime Parkway A2
QUAD B2
Queens Leisure
  Centre B1
Racecourse Park A3
Railway Terr C3
Register Office B2
Sadler Gate B1
St Alkmund's Way . .B1/B2
St Helens House ✦ A1
St Mary's 🏛 A1
St Mary's Bridge A1
St Mary's Bridge
  Chapel 🏛 B1
St Mary's Gate B1
St Paul's Rd A1
St Peter's 🏛 C2
St Peter's St C2
Showcase De Lux 🎦 C2
Siddals St C3
Sir Frank Whittle Rd . . .A3
Spa La C1
Spring St C1
Stafford St B1
Station Approach C3
Stockbrook St C1
Stores Rd A3
Traffic St C2
Wardwick B1
Werburgh St A1
West Ave A1
West Meadows Ind Est B3
Wharf Rd A2
Wilmot St C2
Wilson St C1
Wood's La C1

Dorchester 335
Ackerman Rd B3
Acland St A1
Albert Rd A1
Alexandra Rd A1
Alfred Place B3
Alfred Rd A2
Alington Ave B3
Alington Rd B2
Ambulance Station B3
Ashley Rd A2
Balmoral Cres C3
Barnes Way B2/C2
Borough Gdns B1
Brewery Sq B1
Bridport Rd A1
Buckingham Way C3
Caters Place A1
Cemetery A3/C1
Charles St B2
Coburg Rd A1
Colliton St B2
Cornwall Rd B1
Cromwell Rd B1
Culliford Rd B3
Culliford Rd North B2
Dagmar Rd B1
Damer's Rd B1
Diggory Cres C2
Dinosaur Museum 🏛 . . .A2
Dorchester Bypass C1
Dorchester South
  Station ⊇ B1
Dorchester West
  Station ⊇ B1
Dorset County (A&E)
  🏥 A3
Dorset County Council
  Offices B2
Dorset County Mus 🏛 . .B2
Duchy Close A3
Duke's Ave B2
Durngate St B2
Durnover Court A3
Eddison Ave B1
Edward Rd B1
Egdon Rd C2
Elizabeth Frink
  Statue ✦ B2
Farfrae Cres B3
Forum Centre, The B1
Friary Hill A2
Friary Lane A2
Frome Terr A2
Garland Cres C3
Glyde Path Rd A1
Government Offices B3
Grosvenor Cres C1
Grosvenor Rd C1
Grove, The A2
Gt Western Rd B1
Herrington Rd C1
High St East A2
High St Fordington A2
High Street West A1
Holloway Rd A2
Icen Way A2
Keep Military Museum,
  The A1
Kings Rd A3/B3
Kingsbere Cres C2
Lancaster Rd B2
Library C1
Lime Cl C1
Linden Ave B1
London Cl A3
London Rd A2/A3

Lubbecke Way A3
Lucetta La B2
Maiden Castle Rd C1
Manor Rd C2
Market B1
Marshwood Pl B2
Maumbury Rd C1
Maumbury Rings 🏛 B1
Mellstock Ave C2
Mill St A3
Miller's Cl A1
Mistover Cl C1
Monmouth Rd B1/B2
Moynton Rd C1
Nature Reserve A2
North Sq A2
Northernhay A1
Odeon 🎦 B1
Old Crown Court &
  Cells 🏛 A1
Olga Rd B1
Orchard St A2
Police Station 🗛 B1
Post Office 🖃 B1
Pound Lane A2
Poundbury Rd A1
Prince of Wales Rd B2
Prince's St B1
Queen's Ave B1
Roman Town House 🏛 . .A1
Roman Wall 🏛 A2
Rothesay Rd C2
St George's Rd B2
Salisbury Field A2
Sandringham Sports
  Centre B3
Shaston Cres C3
Smokey Hole La B3
South Court Ave C1
South St B1
South Walks Rd B2
Superstore B2
Teddy Bear House 🏛 . . .A1
Temple Cl C1
Terracotta Warriors &
  Teddy Bear Mus 🏛 A2
Town Hall 🏛 A1
Town Pump ✦ A2
Trinity St A1
Tutankhamun Ex 🏛 A1
Victoria Rd B1
Weatherbury Way C1
Wellbridge Cl C1
West Mills Rd A1
West Walks Rd A1
Weymouth Ave C1
Williams Ave A1
Winterbourne (BMI)
  🏥 A1
Wollaston Rd A2
York Rd B2

Dumfries 336
Academy St A2
Aldermanhill Rd C3
Ambulance Station C3
Annan Rd A3
Ardwall Rd A3
Ashfield Dr A1
Atkinson Rd A1
Averill Cres C1
Balliol Ave C1
Bank St B2
Bankend Rd C3
Barn Slaps B3
Barrie Ave C2
Beech Ave A1
Bowling Green B2
Brewery St B2
Bridgend Theatre 🎭 . . .B1
Brodie Ave C2
Brooke St B2
Broomlands Dr C1
Brooms Rd B3
Buccleuch St B2
Burns House 🏛 B2
Burns Mausoleum B3
Burns St B2
Burns Statue ✦ A2
Bus Station B2
Cardoness St A3
Castle St A2
Catherine St A2
Cattle Market B3
Cemetery B3
Cemetery C2
Church Cres A3
Church St B2
College Rd A1
College St B1
Corbelly Hill B1
Corberry Park B1
Cornwall Mt C2
Council Offices A2
Court B2
Craigs Rd C3
Cresswell Ave B3
Cresswell Hill B3
Cumberland St B3
David Keswick
  Athletic Centre A3
David St B1
Dock Park B3
Dockhead B2
Dumfries 🗛 B2
Dumfries Academy A2
Dumfries Ice Bowl A1
Dumfries Museum &
  Camera Obscura 🏛 B2
Dumfries & Galloway
  Royal Infirmary
  (A&E) 🏥 C3
East Riverside Dr C3
Edinburgh Rd A3
English St B2
Fire Station B3
Friar's Vennel B2
Galloway St B1
George Douglas Dr B1
George St A2

Gladstone Rd C2
Glasgow St A1
Glebe St B2
Glencaple Rd C3
Goldie Ave A1
Goldie Cres A1
Golf Course A1
Gracefield Arts Ctr 🏛 . .C2
Greyfriars 🏛 A2
Grierson Ave C3
Hamilton Ave C1
Hamilton Starke Park . . .C1
Hazelrigg Ave C1
Henry St A2
Hermitage Dr C1
High Cemetery C3
High St A2
Hill Ave C1
Hill St B1
HM Prison A3
Holm Ave C1
Hoods Loaning A3
Howgate St B1
Huntingdon Rd A3
Information Ctr 🛈 B2
Irish St B2
Irving St A2
King St A2
Kingholm Rd C3
Kirkpatrick Ct C2
Laurieknowe B1
Leafield Rd B3
Library B2
Lochfield Rd A1
Loreburn Pk A3
Loreburn St A2
Loreburne Shopping
  Centre B2
Lover's Walk A2
Martin Ave B3
Mausoleum B3
Maxwell St B1
McKie Ave A3
Mews La A3
Mid Steeple ✦ B2
Mill Green B2
Mill Rd B2
Moat Rd C2
Moffat Rd A3
Mountainhall Pk C3
Nelson St B1
New Abbey Rd B1/C1
New Bridge B1
Newall Terr A2
Nith Ave A1
Nith Bank C2
Nithbank Hospital 🏥 . . .C2
Nithsdale Ave C1
Odeon 🎦 B2
Old Bridge B1
Old Bridge House 🏛 B1
Palmerston Park (Queen
  of the South FC) A1
Park Rd C1
Pleasance Ave C1
Police HQ C1
Police Station 🗛 A2/A3
Portland Dr A1
Post Office 🖃 B1/B2/B2
Priestlands Dr C1
Primrose St B1
Queen St B3
Queensberry St B2
Rae St A2
Richmond Ave C2
Robert Burns Ctr 🏛 B2
Roberts Cres C2
Robertson Ave A1
Robinson Dr C1
Rosefield Rd C2
Rosemount St B1
Rotchell Park C1
Rotchell Rd C1
Rugby Football Gd A1
Ryedale Rd C1
St Andrews 🏛 B2
St John the
  Evangelist 🏛 B2
St Josephs College C1
St Mary's Ind Est A3
St Mary's St A2
St Michael's 🏛 B3
St Michael's Bridge B2
St Michael's Bridge
  Rd B2
St Michael's
  Cemetery B3
Shakespeare St B2
Solway Dr C1
Stakeford St A1
Stark Cres C2
Station Rd B3
Steel Ave C2
Sunderries Ave A2
Sunderries Rd A1
Superstore B3
Suspension Brae B2
Swimming Pool A1
Terregles St B1
Theatre Royal 🎭 B2
Troqueer Rd C2
Union St B1
Wallace St A2
Welldale B2
West Riverside Dr C2
White Sands B2

Dundee 336
Abertay University B2
Adelaide Pl A1
Airlie Pl C1
Albany Terr A1
Albert St A3
Alexander St A2
Ann St A2
Arthurstone Terr A3
Bank St B2
Barrack Rd A1
Barrack St B2

Bell St B2
Blinshall St B1
Broughty Ferry Rd A3
Brown St B1
Bus Station B3
Caird Hall 🏛 B2
Camperdown St B3
Candle La B3
Carmichael St A1
City Churches 🏛 B2
City Quay B3
City Sq B2
Commercial St B2
Constable St A3
Constitution Cres A1
Constitution Ct A1
Constitution St A1/B2
Cotton Rd A3
Courthouse Sq B1
Cowgate B3
Crescent St A3
Crichton St B2
Dens Brae A3
Dens Rd A3
Discovery Point ✦ C2
Douglas St B1
Drummond St A1
Dudhope Castle 🏛 A1
Dudhope St A2
Dudhope Terr A1
Dundee ⊇ C2
Dundee Contemporary
  Arts ✦ C2
Dundee High School . . .B2
Dundee Law ✦ A1
Dundee Rep 🎭 C2
Dunhope Park A1
Dura St A3
East Dock St B3
East Marketgait B3
East Whale La B3
Erskine St A3
Euclid Cr B2
Forebank Rd A2
Foundry La A3
Gallagher Retail Park . . .B3
Gellatly St B3
Government Offices B1
Guthrie St B1
Hawkhill B1
Hilltown A2
HMS Unicorn ✦ B3
Howff Cemetery, The . . .B2
Information Ctr 🛈 B2
Keiller Shopping Ctr B2
Keiller Ctr, The B2
King St A3
Kinghorne Rd A1
Ladywell Ave A3
Laurel Bank A2
Law Rd A1
Law St A2
Library A2/A3
Library and Steps
  Theatre 🎭 A2
Little Theatre, The 🎭 . . .A2
Lochee Rd B1
Lower Princes St A3
Lyon St A3
McManus Art Gallery &
  Museum, The 🏛 B2
Meadow Side B2
Meadowside
  St Pauls 🏛 B2
Mercat Cross ✦ B2
Murraygate B2
Nelson St A2
Nethergate B2/C1
North Lindsay St B2
North Marketgait B1
Old Hawkhill B1
Olympia Leisure
  Centre B3
Overgate Shopping
  Centre B2
Park Pl B1
Perth Rd C1
Police Station 🗛 B1
Post Office 🖃 B2
Princes St A3
Prospect Pl A2
Reform St B2
Riverside Dr C2
Riverside Esplanade . . .C2
Roseangle C1
Rosebank St A2
RRS Discovery ⚓ C2
St Andrew's † B3
St Pauls Episcopal † . . .B3
Science Centre ✦ C2
Seagate B3
Sheriffs Court B1
Shopmobility B2
South George St A2
South Marketgait B2
South Tay St B2
South Victoria Dock
  Road B3
South Ward Rd B2
Tay Road Bridge ✦ C3
Thomson Ave B2
Trades La B3
Union St B2
Union Terr A1
University Library B2
University of
  Dundee B1
Upper Constitution St . .A1
Verdant Works ♦ B1
V&A Museum of
  Design C2
Victoria Dock B3
Victoria Rd A2
Victoria St A3
Ward Rd B1
Wellgate B2
West Bell St B1
West Marketgait B1/B2
Westfield Pl C1
William St A3
Wishart Arch ✦ A3

Durham 336
Alexander Cr B1
Allergate B2
Archery Rise C1
Avenue, The A1
Back Western Hill A1
Bakehouse La A3
Baths B3
Baths Bridge B3
Boat House B3
Bowling A2
Boyd St C3
Bus Station B2
Castle 🏛 B2
Castle Chare B2
Cathedral † B2
Church St C3
Clay La C3
Claypath B3
College of St Hild &
  St Bede B3
County Hall A1
County Hospital 🏥 B1
Crescent, The A1
Crook Hall &
  Gardens ✦ A3
Crossgate B2
Crossgate Peth C1
Crown Court B3
Darlington Rd C1
Durham ⊇ A2
Durham School C2
Durham University
  Science Site C3
Ellam Ave C1
Elvet Bridge B3
Elvet Court B3
Farnley Hey B1
Ferens Cl A3
Fieldhouse La A1
Flass St B1
Framwelgate Bridge B2
Framwelgate A2
Framwelgate Peth A2
Framwelgate
  Waterside B2
Frankland La A3
Freeman's Pl A3
Freeman's Quay
  Leisure Centre A3
Gala Theatre &
  Cinema 🎭 B3
Geoffrey Ave C1
Gilesgate B3
Grey College C3
Grove, The A1
Hallgarth St C3
Hatfield College B3
Hawthorn Terr B1
Heritage Centre 🏛 B3
HM Prison B3
Information Ctr 🛈 B1
John St B1
Kingsgate Bridge B3
Laburnum Terr B1
Lawson Terr B1
Leazes Rd B2/B3
Library B1
Library B2
Margery La B2
Market B2
Mavin St C3
Millburngate B2
Millburngate Bridge B2
Millennium Bridge
  (foot/cycle) A2
Mountjoy Research
  Centre C3
Museum of
  Archaeology 🏛 B2
Nevilledale Terr B1
New Elvet B3
New Elvet Bridge B3
North Bailey B3
North End A1
North Rd A1/B2
Observatory C1
Old Elvet B3
Open Treasure 🏛 B2
Oriental Museum 🏛 C3
Oswald Court C3
Parkside B2
Passport Office A2
Percy Terr B1
Pimlico C2
Police Station 🗛 B2
Post Office 🖃 B1/B2
Potters Bank C1/C2
Prebends Bridge C2
Prebends Walk C2
Prince Bishops
  Shopping Centre B3
Princes St B1
Providence Row A3
Quarryheads La C2
Redhills La B1
Redhills Terr B1
Riverwalk, The B2
Saddler St B3
St Chad's College C3
St Cuthbert's Society . . .C2
St John's College B3
St Margaret's 🏛 B2
St Mary the Less 🏛 C3
St Mary's College C2
St Monica Grove C1
St Nicholas' 🏛 B3
St Oswald's 🏛 C3
Sands, The A3
Shopmobility B3
Sidegate A2
Silver St B2
Sixth Form College A1
South Bailey C2
South Rd C2
South St B2
Springwell Ave A1
Stockton Rd C3
Student Union B3
Sutton St B1

Town Hall B2
University Arts Block . . .B3
University College B2
Walkergate Centre A3
Wearside Dr A1
Western Hill A1
Wharton Park A1
Whinney Hill C3
Whitehouse Ave C1
YHA ▲ C3

Edinburgh 336
Abbey Strand B6
Abbeyhill A6
Abbeyhill Cr B6
Abbeymount A6
Abercromby Pl A3
Adam St C5
Albany La A4
Albany St A4
Albert Memorial ✦ B2
Albyn Pl A3
Alva Pl A6
Alva St B1
Ann St A1
Appleton Tower C4
Archibald Pl C3
Assembly Rooms &
  Musical Hall A3
Atholl Cr B1
Atholl Crescent La B1
Bank St B4
Barony St A4
Beaumont Pl C5
Belford St A1
Belgrave Cr A1
Belgrave Crescent La . . .A1
Bell's Brae A1
Blackfriars St B4
Blair St B4
Bread St C2
Bristo Pl C4
Bristo St C4
Brougham St C3
Broughton St A4
Brown St C5
Brunton Terr A6
Buckingham Terr A1
Burial Ground A6
Bus Station A4
Caledonian Cr C1
Caledonian Rd C1
Calton Hill A4
Calton Hill A5
Calton Rd B4
Camera Obscura &
  Outlook Tower ✦ B3
Candlemaker Row C4
Canning St B1
Canongate B5
Canongate 🏛 B5
Carlton St A1
Carlton Terr A5
Carlton Terrace La A6
Castle St B3
Castle Terr B2
Castlehill B3
Central Library B4
Chalmers Hospital 🏥 . . .C3
Chalmers St C3
Chambers St C4
Chapel St C4
Charles St C4
Charlotte Sq B2
Chester St B1
Circus La A2
Circus Pl A2
City Art Centre 🏛 B4
City Chambers 🏛 B4
City Observatory ✦ A5
Clarendon Cr A1
Clerk St C5
Coates Cr B1
Cockburn St B4
College of Art C3
Comely Bank Ave A1
Comely Bank Row A1
Cornwall St C2
Cowans Cl C5
Cowgate B4
Cranston St B5
Crichton St C4
Croft-An-Righ A6
Cumberland St A3
Dalry Pl C1
Dalry Rd C1
Danube St A1
Darnaway St A2
David Hume Tower C4
Davie St C5
Dean Bridge A1
Dean Gdns A1
Dean Park Cr A1
Dean Park Mews A1
Dean Path B1
Dean St A1
Dean Terr A2
Dewar Pl B1
Dewar Place La C1
Doune Terr A2
Drummond Pl A3
Drummond St C5
Drumsheugh Gdns B1
Dublin Mews A3
Dublin St A4
Dublin Street Lane
  South A4
Dumbiedykes Rd B5
Dundas St A3
Dynamic Earth ✦ B6
Earl Grey St C2
East Crosscauseway . . .C5
East Market St B4
East Norton Pl A6
East Princes St Gdns . . .B3
Easter Rd A6
Edinburgh
  (Waverley) ⊇ B4
Edinburgh Castle 🏛 B3

Edinburgh
  Dungeon ✦ B4
Edinburgh International
  Conference Ctr C2
Elder St A4
Esplanade B3
Eton Terr A1
Eye Pavilion 🏥 C3
Festival Office B3
Festival Theatre
  Edinburgh 🎭 C4
Filmhouse 🎦 C2
Fire Station C2
Floral Clock ✦ B3
Forres St A2
Forth St A4
Fountainbridge C2
Frederick St A3
Freemasons' Hall 🏛 B3
Fruitmarket 🏛 B4
Gardner's Cr C2
George Heriot's
  School C3
George IV Bridge B4
George Sq C4
George Sq La C4
George St B3
Georgian House 🏛 B2
Gladstone's Land 🏛 B3
Glen St C3
Gloucester La A2
Gloucester Pl A2
Gloucester St A2
Graham St C3
Grassmarket B3
Great King St A3
Great Stuart A2
Greenside La A5
Greenside Row A5
Greyfriars Kirk 🏛 C4
Grindlay St C2
Grosvenor St C1
Grove St C1
Gullan's Cl B5
Guthrie St B4
Hanover St A3
Hart St A4
Haymarket C1
Haymarket Station ⊇ . . .C1
Heriot Pl C3
Heriot Row A2
High School Yard B5
High St B4
Hill Pl C5
Hill St A2
Hillside Cr A5
Holyrood Abbey
  (Remains) † A6
Holyrood Gait B6
Holyrood Park C6
Holyrood Rd B5
Home St C2
Hope St B2
Horse Wynd B6
Howden St C5
Howe St A2
Hub, The ✦ B3
India Pl A2
India St A2
Infirmary St C4
Information Ctr 🛈 B3
Jeffrey St B4
John Knox House 🏛 B5
Johnston Terr C3
Keir St C3
Kerr St A2
King's Stables Rd B2
Lady Lawson St C3
Lauriston Gdns C3
Lauriston Park C3
Lauriston Pl C3
Lauriston St C3
Lawnmarket B3
Learmonth Gdns A1
Learmonth Terr A1
Leith St A4
Lennox St A1
Lennox St La A1
Leslie Pl A1
London Rd A5
Lothian Rd B2
Lothian St C4
Lower Menz Pl A6
Lynedoch Pl B1
Manor Pl B1
Market St B4
Marshall St C4
Maryfield A6
McEwan Hall C4
Medical School C4
Melville St B1
Meuse La B4
Middle Meadow Walk . . .C4
Milton St A6
Montrose Terr A6
Moray Place A2
Morrison Link C1
Morrison St C1
Mound Pl B3
Mound, The B3
Multrees Walk A4
Mus Collections Ctr A4
Mus of Childhood 🏛 . . .B5
Mus of Edinburgh 🏛 . . .B5
Museum of Fire 🏛 C3
Mus on the Mound 🏛 . .B3
National Archives of
  Scotland 🏛 A4
National Museum of
  Scotland 🏛 C4
National Gallery 🏛 B3
National Library of
  Scotland B4
National Monument ✦ . .A5
National Portrait
  Gallery 🏛 A4
National War
  Museum 🏛 B3
Nelson Monument ✦ . . .A5
Nelson St A3
New St B5

Nicolson Sq C4
Nicolson St C4
Niddry St B4
North Bank St B4
North Bridge B4
North Castle St A2
North Charlotte St A2
North Meadow Walk C4
North St Andrew St A4
North St David St A3
North West Circus Pl . . .A2
Northumberland St A3
Odeon 🎦 C5
Old Royal High School . .A5
Old Tolbooth Wynd B5
OMNi Centre ✦ A4
Oxford Terr A1
Palace of
  Holyroodhouse 🏛 B6
Palmerston Pl B1
Panmure Pl C3
Parliament Sq B4
People's Story, The 🏛 . .B5
Playhouse Theatre 🎭 . . .A4
Pleasance C5
Police Station 🗛 A4
Ponton St C2
Post Office
  🖃 A3/B4/B5/C1/C2/C4
Potterrow C4
Princes Mall B4
Princes St B2
Princes St ⊇ B3
Prisoners of War 🏛 B3
Queen's Gallery 🏛 B6
Queen St A2
Queen Street Gdns A3
Queen's Dr B6/C6
Queensferry Rd A1
Queensferry St B2
Queensferry Street La . .B2
Radical Rd C6
Randolph Cr B2
Regent Gdns A5
Regent Rd A5
Regent Rd Park A5
Regent Terr A5
Richmond La C5
Richmond Pl C5
Rose St B2
Ross Open Air
  Theatre B3
Rothesay Pl B1
Rothesay Terr B1
Roxburgh Pl C5
Roxburgh St C5
Royal Bank of
  Scotland A4
Royal Circus A2
Royal Lyceum 🎭 C2
Royal Mile, The B5
Royal Scottish Acad 🏛 .B3
Royal Terr A5
Royal Terrace Gdns A5
Rutland Sq B2
Rutland St B2
St Andrew Sq A4
St Andrew Sq ⊇ A4
St Andrew's House A4
St Bernard's Cr A1
St Bernard's Well ✦ A1
St Cecilia's Hall B4
St Colme St A2
St Cuthbert's 🏛 B2
St Giles' † B4
St John St B5
St John's 🏛 B2
St John's Hill C5
St Leonard's Hill C5
St Leonard's La C5
St Leonard's St C5
St Mary's 🏛 B4
St Mary's Scottish
  Episcopal † B1
St Mary's St B5
St Michael &
  All Saints 🏛 C3
St Stephen St A2
Salisbury Crags C6
Saunders St A2
Scotch Whisky
  Experience ✦ B3
Scott Monument ✦ B4
Scottish Parliament B6
Scottish Storytelling
  Centre ✦ B5
Semple St C2
Shandwick Pl B2
South Bridge B4
South Charlotte St B2
South College St C4
South Learmonth
  Gdns A1
South St Andrew St A4
South St David St A3
Spittal St C2
Stafford St B1
Student Centre C4
Surgeons' Hall 🏛 C5
Supreme Courts 🏛 B4
Teviot Pl C4
Thistle St A3
Torphichen Pl C1
Torphichen St C1
Traverse Theatre 🎭 B2
Tron, The ✦ B4
Union St A4
University C4
University Library C4
Univ of Edinburgh B5
Upper Grove Pl C1
Usher Hall ✦ C2
Vennel C3
Victoria St B3
Viewcraig Gdns B5
Viewcraig St B5
Vue 🎦 A4
Walker St B1
Waterloo Pl A4
Waverley Bridge B4

Wemyss Pl A2
West Approach Rd C1
West Crosscauseway . . .C5
West End ⊇ B1
West Maitland St C1
West of Nicholson St . . .C4
West Port C3
West Princes St Gdns . .B3
West Richmond St C5
West Tollcross C2
White Horse Cl ✦ B6
William St B1
Windsor St A5
Writer's Mus, The 🏛 . . .B4
York La A4
York Pl A4
York Pl ⊇ A4
Young St B2

Exeter 336
Alphington St C1
Athelstan Rd B3
Bampfylde St B2
Barnardo Rd C2
Barnfield Hill B3
Barnfield Rd B2/B3
Barnfield Theatre 🎭 B2
Bartholomew St East . . .B1
Bartholomew St West . .B1
Bear St B2
Beaufort Rd C1
Bedford St B2
Belgrave Rd A3
Belmont Rd A3
Blackall Rd A2
Blackboy Rd A3
Bonhay Rd B1
Bull Meadow Rd C2
Bus & Coach Sta B2
Castle St B2
Cecil Rd C1
Cheeke St A3
Church Rd C1
Chute St A3
City Wall B1/B2
Civic Centre B2
Clifton Rd B3
Clifton St B3
Clock Tower A1
College Rd B3
Colleton Cr C2
Commercial Rd C1
Coombe St B2
Cowick St C1
Crown Courts B2
Custom House ✦ C2
Cygnet
  New Theatre 🎭 C2
Danes' Rd A2
Denmark Rd B3
Devon County Hall C3
Devonshire Pl A3
Dinham Cres B1
East Grove Rd C3
Edmund St C1
Elmgrove Rd A3
Exe St B1
Exeter Cathedral † B2
Exeter Central Sta ⊇ . . .A1
Exeter City Football
  Ground A3
Exeter College A2
Exeter Picture Ho 🎦 . . .B1
Fire Station B1
Fore St B1
Friars Walk C2
Guildhall 🏛 B2
Guildhall Shopping
  Centre B2
Harlequins Shopping
  Centre B1
Haven Rd C2
Heavitree Rd B3
Hele Rd A1
High St B2
HM Prison A2
Holloway St C2
Hoopern St A2
Horseguards A2
Howell Rd A1
Information Ctr 🛈 B3
Iron Bridge B1
Isca Rd C1
Jesmond Rd A3
King St B1
King William St A2
Larkbeare Rd C2
Leisure Centre B2
Library B2
Longbrook Rd A2
Longbrook Terr A2
Lower North St B1
Lucky La C2
Lyndhurst Rd C3
Magdalen Rd C3
Magdalen St C2
Market B2
Market St B2
Marlborough Rd C3
Mary Arches St B2
Matford Ave C2
Matford La C3
Matford Rd C3
May St A3
Mol's Coffee House 🏛 . .B2
New Bridge St B1
New North Rd A1/A2
North St B2
Northernhay St B1
Norwood Ave C3
Odeon 🎦 B3
Okehampton St C1
Old Mill Cl C2
Old Tiverton Rd A3
Oxford Rd A3
Paris St B2
Parr St A3
Paul St B2
Pennsylvania Rd A2
Police HQ B3

Portland Street A3
Post Office A3/B2/B3/C1
Powderham Cr A3
Preston St B1
Princesshay Shopping Centre B2
Pyramids Leisure Ctr B3
Quay, The C2
Queen St A1
Queen's Terr A1
Queens Rd C1
Radford Rd C2
Richmond Rd A1
Roberts Rd C2
Rougemont Castle A2
Rougemont House ✦ B2
Royal Albert Memorial Museum B2
St David's Hill A1
St James' Pk Sta A3
St James' Rd A3
St Leonard's Rd C3
St Mary Steps C1
St Nicholas Priory B1
St Thomas Station C1
Sandford Walk B3
School for the Deaf C2
School Rd C1
Sidwell St A2
Smythen St B1
South St B2
Southernhay East B2
Southernhay West B2
Spacex Gallery B1
Spicer Rd B3
Sports Centre A3
Summerland St A3
Sydney Rd C1
Tan La C2
Thornton Hill A2
Topsham Rd C3
Tucker's Hall B1
Tudor St B1
Underground Passages ✦ B2
University of Exeter (St Luke's Campus) B3
Velwell Rd A1
Verney St A3
Water La C1/C2
Weirfield Rd C2
Well St A3
West Ave A2
West Grove Rd C3
Western Way A3/B1/B2
Willeys Ave C1
Wonford Rd B3/C3
York Rd A2

Fort William 337

Abrach Rd A3
Achintore Rd C1
Alma Rd B2
Am Breun Chamas A2
Ambulance Station A3
An Aird A2
Argyll Rd C1
Argyll Terr C1
Bank St B2
Belford Hospital B2
Ben Nevis Highland Centre B3
Black Parks A3
Braemore Pl C2
Bruce Pl C2
Bus Station B2
Camanachd Cr A3/B2
Cameron Rd C1
Cameron Sq B1
Carmichael Way A2
Claggan Rd B3
Connochie Rd C1
Cow Hill C3
Creag Dhubh A2
Croft Rd B3
Douglas Pl B2
Dudley Rd B2
Dumbarton Rd C1
Earl of Inverness Rd A3
Fassifern Rd B1
Fire Station A2
Fort William B2
Fort William (Remains) ✦ B2
Glasdrum Rd C1
Glen Nevis Pl B3
Gordon Sq B1
Grange Rd C1
Heathercroft Dr C1
Heather Croft Rd C1
Henderson Row C2
High St B1
Hill Rd B2
Information Ctr A3
Inverlochy Ct A3
Kennedy Rd B2/C2
Library B2
Lime Tree Gallery ✦ C1
Linnhe Rd B1
Lochaber Leisure Ctr B3
Lochiel Rd A3
Lochy Rd A3
Lundavra Cres C1
Lundavra Rd C1
Lundy Rd A3
Mamore Cr B2
Mary St B2
Middle St B1
Montrose Ave A3
Moray Pl C1
Morven Pl C2
Nairn Cres C1
Nevis Bridge B3
Nevis Centre, The A2
Nevis Rd A3
Nevis Terr B2
North Rd B3
Obelisk B2
Parade Rd B2
Police Station C1
Post Office A3/B2
Ross Pl C1
St Andrews B2
Shaw Pl B2
Station Brae B1
Superstore B3
Treig Rd A3
Union Rd C1
Victoria Rd B2
Wades Rd A3
West Highland B1
West Highland College UHI A2
Young Pl B2

Glasgow 337

Admiral St C2
Albert Bridge C5
Albion St B5
Anderston B3
Anderston Quay B3
Argyle Arcade B5
Argyle St A1/A2/B3/B4/B5
Argyle Street B5
Arlington St A3
Arts Centre B3
Ashley St A3
Bain St C6
Baird St A6
Baliol St A3
Ballater St C5
Barras (Market), The C6
Bath St A3
BBC Scotland B1
Bell St C6
Bell's Bridge B1
Bentinck St A2
Berkeley St A3
Bishop La B3
Black St A6
Blackburn St C2
Blackfriars St B6
Blantyre St A1
Blythswood Sq A4
Blythswood St B4
Bothwell St B4
Brand St C1
Breadalbane St A2
Bridge St C4
Bridge St C4
Bridgegate C5
Briggait C5
Broomielaw B4
Broomielaw Quay Gdns B3
Brown St B4
Brunswick St B5
Buccleuch St A3
Buchanan Bus Station A5
Buchanan Galleries A5
Buchanan St B5
Buchanan St B5
Cadogan St B4
Caledonian University A5
Calgary St A5
Cambridge St A4
Canal St A5
Candleriggs B5
Carlton Pl C4
Carnarvon St A3
Carrick St B4
Castle St B6
Cathedral Sq B6
Cathedral St B5
Central Mosque C5
Ctr for Contemporary Arts A4
Centre St C4
Cessnock C1
Cessnock St C1
Charing Cross A3
Charlotte St C6
Cheapside St B3
Cineworld A5
Citizens' Theatre C5
City Chambers Complex B5
City Halls B5
City of Glasgow Coll (City Campus) B5
City of Glasgow Coll (Riverside Campus) C5
Clairmont Gdns A2
Claremont St A2
Claremont Terr A2
Claythorne St C6
Cleveland St A3
Clifford La C1
Clifford St C1
Clifton Pl A2
Clifton St A2
Clutha St C1
Clyde Arc B2
Clyde Pl C4
Clyde Place Quay C4
Clyde St C5
Clyde Walkway C3
Clydeside Expressway B2
Coburg St C4
Cochrane St B5
College St B6
Collins St B6
Commerce St C4
Cook St C4
Cornwall St C2
Couper St A5
Cowcaddens A4
Cowcaddens Rd A4
Crimea St B3
Custom Ho Quay Gdns C4
Dalhousie St A4
Dental Hospital A4
Derby St A2
Dobbie's Loan A4/A5
Dobbie's Loan Pl A5
Dorset St A3
Douglas St B4
Doulton Fountain ✦ C6
Dover St A2
Drury St B4
Drygate B6
Duke St B6
Dunaskin St A1
Dunblane St A4
Dundas St B5
Dunlop St C5
East Campbell St C6
Eastvale Pl A1
Eglinton St C4
Elderslie St A3
Elliot St B2
Elmbank St A3
Esmond St A1
Exhibition Centre B2
Festival Park C1
Film Theatre A4
Finnieston Quay B2
Finnieston St B2
Fire Station C6
Florence St C5
Fox St C5
Gallowgate C6
Garnet St A3
Garnethill St A4
Garscube Rd A4
George Sq B5
George St B5
George V Bridge C4
Gilbert St A1
Glasgow Bridge C4
Glasgow Cathedral B6
Glasgow Central B4
Glasgow City Free Church B4
Glasgow Green C6
Glasgow Necropolis ✦ B6
Glasgow Royal Concert Hall A5
Glasgow Science Centre ✦ B1
Glasgow Tower ✦ B1
Glassford St B5
Glebe St A6
Gorbals Cross C5
Gorbals St C5
Gordon St B4
Govan Rd B1/C1/C2
Grace St B3
Grafton Pl A5
Grand Ole Opry ✦ C2
Grant St A3
Granville St A3
Gray St A2
Greendyke St C6
Grey Eagle St B7
Harley St C1
Harvie St C1
Haugh Rd A1
Havanah St B6
Heliport B1
Henry Wood Hall A2
High Court C5
High St B6
High Street B6
Hill St A3
Holland St A3
Holm St B4
Hope St A5
Houldsworth St B2
Houston Pl C3
Houston St C3
Howard St C5
Hunter St C6
Hutcheson St B5
Hydepark St B3
Imax Cinema B1
India St A3
Information Ctr B5
Ingram St B5
Jamaica St B4
James Watt St B4
John Knox St B6
John St B5
Kelvin Hall ✦ A1
Kelvin Statue ✦ A2
Kelvin Way A2
Kelvingrove Art Gallery & Museum A1
Kelvingrove Park A2
Kelvingrove St A2
Kelvinhaugh St A1
Kennedy St A6
Kent Rd A2
Killermont St A5
King St B5
King's, The A3
Kingston Bridge C3
Kingston St C4
Kinning Park C2
Kyle St A5
Lancefield Quay B2
Lancefield St B3
Langshot St C1
Lendel Pl C1
Lighthouse, The ✦ B4
Lister St A6
Little St B3
London Rd C6
Lorne St C1
Lower Harbour B1
Lumsden St A1
Lymburn St A1
Lyndoch Cr A3
Lynedoch Pl A3
Lynedoch St A3
Maclellan St C1
Mair St C2
Maitland St A4
Mansell St C7
Mavisbank Gdns C2
Mcalpine St B3
Mcaslin St A6
McLean Sq C2
McLellan Gallery A4
McPhater St A4
Merchants' House B5
Middlesex St C2
Middleton St C1
Midland St B4
Miller St B5
Millennium Bridge B1
Millroad St C6
Milnpark St C2
Milton St A4
Minerva St B2
Mitchell St West B4
Mitchell Liby, The ✦ A3
Modern Art Gallery B5
Moir St C6
Molendinar St C6
Moncur St C6
Montieth Row C6
Montrose St B5
Morrison St C3
Nairn St A1
National Piping Centre, The ✦ A5
Nelson Mandela Sq B5
Nelson St C4
Nelson's Monument C6
Newton Pl A3
Newton St A3
Nicholson St C4
Nile St B5
Norfolk Court C4
Norfolk St C4
North Frederick St B5
North Hanover St B5
North Portland St B6
North St A3
North Wallace St A5
O2 ABC A4
O2 Academy ✦ C4
Odeon C3
Old Dumbarton Rd A1
Osborne St B5/C5
Oswald St B4
Overnewton St A1
Oxford St C4
Pacific Dr B1
Paisley Rd C3
Paisley Rd West C1
Park Circus A2
Park Gdns A2
Park St South A2
Park Terr A2
Parkgrove Terr A2
Parnie St C5
Parson St A6
Partick Bridge A1
Passport Office A5
Pavilion Theatre A4
Pembroke St A3
People's Palace C6
Pinkston Rd A6
Pitt St A4/B4
Plantation Park C1
Plantation Quay B1
Police Mus B5
Police Station A4/A6
Port Dundas Rd A5
Port St B2
Portman St C2
Prince's Dock B1
Princes Sq B5
Provand's Lordship B6
Queen St B5
Queen Street B5
Ramshorn B5
Renfrew St A3/A4
Renton St A5
Richmond St B5
Robertson St B4
Rose St A4
Rottenrow B5
Royal Concert Hall A5
Royal Conservatoire of Scotland A4
Royal Cr A2
Royal Exchange Sq B5
Royal Highland Fusiliers Museum A3
West Glasgow Ambulatory Care A1
Royal Infirmary B6
Royal Terr A2
Rutland Cres C2
St Andrew's in the Square C6
St Andrew's (RC) C5
St Andrew's St C5
St Enoch B5
St Enoch Shopping Ctr B5
St Enoch Sq B4
St George's Rd A3
St James Rd B6
St Kent St C6
St Mungo Ave A5/A6
St Mungo Museum of Religious Life & Art B6
St Mungo Pl A6
St Vincent Cr A2
St Vincent Pl B5
St Vincent St B3/B4
St Vincent Terr B3
Saltmarket C5
Sandyford Pl A3
Sauchiehall St A2/A4
SEC Armadillo B2
School of Art A4
Sclater St B7
Scotland St C2
Scott St A4
Scottish Exhibition & Conference Centre B1
Seaward St C2
Shaftesbury St B3
Sheriff Court C5
Shields Rd C3
Shopmobility A5
Shuttle St B6
Somerset Pl A2
South Portland St C4
Springburn Rd A6
Springfield Quay C3
SSE Hydro The B2
Stanley St C2
Stevenson St C6
Stewart St A4
Stirling Rd B6
Stobcross Quay B1
Stobcross Rd B1
Stock Exchange B5
Stockwell Pl C5
Stockwell St B5
Stow College A4
Sussex St C2
Synagogue A3
Taylor Pl A6
Tenement House A3
Teviot St A1
Theatre Royal A4
Tolbooth Steeple & Mercat Cross ✦ C6
Tower St C2
Trades House B5
Tradeston St C4
Transport Mus A1
Tron C5
Trongate B5
Tunnel St B2
Turnbull St C5
Union St B4
Univ of Strathclyde B6
Victoria Bridge C5
Virginia St B5
Wallace St C3
Walls St B6
Walmer Cr C1
Warrock St B3
Washington St B3
Waterloo St B4
Watson St B6
Watt St C3
Wellington St B4
West Campbell St B4
West George St B4
West Graham St A4
West Greenhill Pl B2
West Regent St A4
West Regent St B4
West St C4
West St C4
Whitehall St B3
Wilkes St C7
Wilson St B5
Woodlands Gate A3
Woodlands Rd A3
Woodlands Terr A2
Woodside Pl A3
Woodside Terr A3
York St B4
Yorkhill Pde A1
Yorkhill St A1

Gloucester 337

Albion St C1
Alexandra Rd B3
Alfred St C3
All Saints Rd C2
Alvin St B2
Arthur St C2
Barrack Square B1
Barton St C2
Blackfriars B1
Blenheim Rd C2
Bristol Rd C1
Brunswick Rd C2
Bruton Way B2
Bus Station B2
Cineworld C1
City Council Offices B1
City Mus, Art Gall & Library B2
Clarence St B2
Commercial Rd B1
Council Offices B1
Courts B1
Cromwell St C2
Deans Way A2
Denmark Rd A3
Derby Rd C3
Docks ✦ C1
Eastgate St B2
Eastgate, The B1
Edwy Pde A2
Estcourt Cl A3
Estcourt Rd A3
Falkner St C2
GL1 Leisure Centre C2
Gloucester Cath B1
Gloucester Life B1
Gloucester Quays Outlet C1
Gloucester Station B2
Gloucester Waterways C1
Gloucestershire Archive B2
Gloucestershire Royal Hospital (A&E) B3
Goodyere St C2
Gouda Way A1
Great Western Rd B3
Guildhall B2
Heathville Rd A3
Henry Rd B3
Henry St B2
Hinton Rd A2
India Rd C3
Information Ctr B1
Jersey Rd C3
King's C2
King's Walk Shopping Centre B2
Kingsholm (Gloucester Rugby) A2
Kingsholm Rd A2
Lansdown Rd A3
Library C2
Llanthony Rd C1
London Rd B3
Longhorn Ave A1
Longsmith St B1
Malvern Rd A3
Market B2
Market Pde B2
Mercia Rd A1
Metz Way C3
Midland Rd C2
Millbrook St C3
Montpellier C1
Napier St C3
Nettleton Rd C2
New Inn B2
New Olympus C3
North Rd A3
Northgate St B2
Oxford Rd A2
Oxford St B2
Pk & Ride Gloucester A1
Park Rd C2
Park St B2
Park, The C2
Parliament St C1
Peel Centre, The C1
Pitt St B1
Police Station C3
Post Office B2
Quay St B1
Quay, The B1
Recreation Gd A1/A2
Regent St C2
Robert Raikes Ho B1
Royal Oak Rd B1
Russell St B2
Ryecroft St C2
St Aldate St B2
St Ann Way C1
St Catherine St A2
St Mark St A2
St Mary de Crypt B1
St Mary de Lode B1
St Nicholas's B1
St Oswald's Rd A1
St Oswald's Retail Pk A1
St Peter's B2
Seabroke Rd A3
Sebert St A2
Severn Rd C1
Sherborne St B2
Shire Hall B1
Sidney St C3
Soldiers of Gloucestershire B1
Southgate St B1/C1
Spa Field C1
Spa Rd C1
Sports Ground A2/B2
Station Rd B2
Stratton Rd C3
Stroud Rd C1
Superstore A1
Swan Rd A2
Trier Way C1/C2
Union St A2
Vauxhall Rd C3
Victoria St C2
Walham Lane A1
Wellington St C2
Westgate Retail Park B1
Westgate St B1
Widden St C2
Worcester St B2

Grimsby 337

Abbey Drive East C2
Abbey Drive West C2
Abbey Park Rd C2
Abbey Rd C2
Abbey Walk C2
Abbeygate Shopping Centre C2
Abbotsway C2
Adam Smith St A1/A2
Ainslie St C2
Albert St A3
Alexandra Dock A2/B2
Alexandra Rd A2/B2
Alexandra Retail Park A2
Annesley St A2
Armstrong St A1
Arthur St B1
Augusta St C1
Bargate C1
Beeson St A1
Bethlehem St C2
Bodiam Way B3
Bradley St B3
Brighowgate C1/C2
Bus Station C2
Canterbury Dr C1
Cartergate B1/C1
Catherine St C3
Caxton A3
Chantry La B1
Charlton St A1
Church La C2
Church St A3
Cleethorpe Rd A3
Close, The C1
College St C1
Compton Dr C1
Corporation Bridge A2
Corporation Rd A1
Court B3
Crescent St B1
Deansgate C1
Doughty Rd C2
Dover St B1
Duchess St C2
Dudley St C1
Duke of York Gardens B1
Duncombe St B3
Earl La B1
East Marsh St B3
East St B2
Eastgate B3
Eastside Rd A3
Eaton Ct C1
Eleanor St B3
Ellis Way B3
Fisherman's Chapel A3
Fisherman's Wharf B2
Fishing Heritage Centre B2
Flour Sq A3
Frederick St B1
Frederick Ward Way B2
Freeman St A3/B3
Freshney Dr B1
Freshney Pl B2
Garden St C2
Garibaldi St A3
Garth La B2
Grime St B3
Grimsby Docks Sta A3
Grimsby Town Sta C2
Hainton Ave C3
Har Way B3
Hare St C3
Harrison St B1
Haven Ave B1
Hay Croft Ave B1
Hay Croft St B1
Heneage Rd B3/C3
Henry St B1
Holme St B3
Hume St C1
James St B1
Joseph St B1
Kent St A3
King Edward St A3
Lambert Rd C2
Library B2
Lime St B1
Lister St B1
Littlefield La C1
Lockhill A3
Lord St B1
Lower Spring St A3
Ludford St C3
Macaulay St B1
Mallard Mews C3
Manor Ave C2
Market A3
Market Hall B2
Market St B3
Moss Rd C2
Nelson St A3
New St B2
Osbourne St B2
Pasture St B3
Peaks Parkway C3
Pelham Rd C1
Police Station B3
Post Office B1/B2
Pyewipe Rd A1
Railway Pl A3
Railway St A3
Recreation Ground C2
Rendel St A2
Retail Park A2/B3
Richard St B1
Ripon St B1
Robinson St East B3
Royal St A3
St Hilda's Ave C1
St James C2
Sheepfold St B3/C3
Shopmobility B2
Sixhills St C3
South Park B2
Superstore B3/B2
Tasburgh St C3
Tennyson St B2
Thesiger St A3
Time Trap C2
Town Hall B2
Veal St B1
Victoria Retail Park A3
Victoria St North A2
Victoria St South B2
Victoria St West B2
Watkin St A1
Welholme Ave C2
Welholme Rd C3
Wellington St B3
Wellowgate C2
Werneth Rd B3
West Coates Rd A1
Westgate A2
Westminster Dr C1
Willingham St C3
Wintringham Rd C2
Wood St B3
Yarborough Dr B1
Yarborough Hotel C2

Hanley 337

Acton St A3
Albion St B2
Argyle St C1
Ashbourne Gr A2
Avoca St A3
Baskerville Rd B3
Bedford Rd C1
Bedford St C1
Bethesda St B2
Bexley St A2
Birches Head Rd A3
Botteslow St C3
Boundary St A2
Broad St C2
Broom St A3
Bryan St A2
Bucknall New Rd B3
Bucknall Old Rd B3
Bus Station C3
Cannon St C2
Castlefield St C1
Cavendish St B1
Central Forest Pk A2
Century Retail Park B1
Charles St B3
Cheapside B2
Chell St A3
Cinema A2
Clarke St C1
Cleveland Rd C2
Clifford St C3
Clough St B1
Clough St East B2
Clyde St C1
College Rd C2
Cooper St C2
Corbridge Rd A1
Cutts St C2
Davis St C1
Denbigh St A1
Derby St C3
Dilke St A3
Dudson Ctr, The A2
Dundas St A3
Dundee Rd C1
Dyke St B3
Eastwood Rd C3
Eaton St A3
Etruria Park B1
Etruria Rd B1
Etruria Vale Rd C1
Festing St A3
Festival Heights Retail Park A1
Festival Retail Park A1
Fire Station C2
Foundry St B2
Franklyn St C3
Garnet St B1
Garth St B3
George St A3
Gilman St B3
Glass St B3
Goodson St B3
Greyhound Way A1
Grove Pl C1
Hampton St C3
Hanley Park C2
Hanley Park C2
Harding Rd C2
Hassall St B3
Havelock Pl C1
Hazlehurst St C3
Hinde St C2
Hope St B2
Houghton St C2
Hulton St A3
Information Ctr B2
intu Potteries Shopping Centre B2
Jasper St C2
Jervis St A3
John Bright St A3
John St B2
Keelings Rd A3
Kimberley Rd C1
Ladysmith Rd C1
Lawrence St C2
Leek Rd C3
Library C2
Lichfield St C3
Linfield Rd B3
Loftus St A2
Lower Bedford St C1
Lower Bryan St A2
Lower Mayer St A3
Lowther St A1
Magistrates Court C2
Malham St A2
Marsh St B2
Matlock St C3
Mayer St A3
Milton St C1
Mitchell Arts Centre B2
Moston St A3
Mount Pleasant C1
Mulgrave St A1
Mynors St B3
Nelson Pl B3
New Century St B1
Octagon Retail Park B1
Ogden Rd C3
Old Hall St B3
Old Town Rd A3
Pall Mall B2
Palmerston St C3
Park and Ride C2
Parkway, The C2
Pavilion Dr A1
Pelham St C3
Percy St B2
Piccadilly B2
Picton St B3
Plough St A3
Police Station C2
Portland St A1
Post Office A3/B2
Potteries Museum & Art Gallery B2
Potteries Way B1
Powell St A1
Pretoria Rd C1
Quadrant Rd B2
Ranelagh St C2
Raymond St C2
Rectory Rd C1
Regent Rd C2
Regent Theatre B2
Richmond Terr C2
Ridgehouse Dr A1
Robson St C2
St Ann St B3
St Luke St B3
Sampson St B2
Shaw St A1
Sheaf St C2
Shearer St C1
Shelton New Rd C1
Shirley Rd C2
Slippery La C2
Shopmobility B3
Snow Hill C2
Spur St C3
Stafford St B2
Stubbs La C3
Sun St C1
Supermarket A1/B2
Superstore B2
Talbot St C3
Town Hall B2
Town Rd A3
Trinity St B2
Union St A2
Upper Hillchurch St A3
Upper Huntbach St B3
Victoria Hall B3
Warner St C2
Warwick St C1
Waterloo Rd A1
Waterloo St B3
Well St B3
Wellesley St C2
Wellington Rd B3
Wellington St B3
Whitehaven Dr A2
Whitmore St C1
Windermere St A1
Woodall St A1
Yates St C2
York St A2

Harrogate 338

Albert St C2
Alexandra Rd B2
Arthington Ave B2
Ashfield Rd A2
Back Cheltenham Mount B2
Beech Grove C1
Belmont Rd C1
Bilton Dr A2
BMI The Duchy Hospital C1
Bower Rd B2
Bower St B2
Bus Station B2
Cambridge Rd B2
Cambridge St B2
Cemetery A2
Chatsworth Grove A2
Chatsworth Pl A2
Chatsworth Rd A2
Chelmsford Rd B3
Cheltenham Cr B2
Cheltenham Mt B2
Cheltenham Pde B2
Christ Church B3
Christ Church Oval B3
Chudleigh Rd B3
Clarence Dr B1
Claro Rd A3
Claro Way A3
Coach Park B2
Coach Rd B3
Cold Bath Rd C1
Commercial St B2
Coppice Ave A1
Coppice Dr A1
Coppice Gate A1
Cornwall Rd B1
Council Offices B1
Crescent Gdns B1
Crescent Rd B1
Dawson Terr A2
Devonshire Pl B3
Dixon Rd A2
Dixon Terr A2
Dragon Ave B3
Dragon Parade B2
Dragon Rd B2
Duchy Rd B1
East Parade B2
East Park Rd C3
Esplanade B1
Everyman B2
Fire Station A2
Franklin Mount A2
Franklin Rd B2
Franklin Square A2
Glebe Rd C1
Grove Park Ct A3
Grove Park Terr A3
Grove Rd A2
Hampsthwaite Rd A1
Harcourt Dr B3
Harcourt Rd B3
Harrogate B2
Harrogate Convention Centre B1
Harrogate Justice Centre (Magistrates' and County Courts) C2
Harrogate Ladies Coll B1
Harrogate Theatre B2
Heywood Rd C1
Hollins Cr A1
Hollins Mews A1
Hollins Rd A1
Hydro Leisure Ctr, The A1
Information Ctr B1
James St B2
Jenny Field Dr A1
John St B2
Kent Dr A1
Kent Rd A1
Kings Rd A2
Kingsway B3
Kingsway Dr B3
Lancaster Rd C1
Leeds Rd C2
Lime Grove B3
Lime St A3
Mayfield Grove B2
Mercer B1
Montpellier Hill B1
Mornington Cr A3
Mornington Terr B3
Mowbray Sq B3
North Park Rd B3
Oakdale Ave A1
Oatlands Dr C3
Odeon B2
Osborne Rd A2
Otley Rd C2
Oxford St B2
Parade, The B2
Park Chase B3
Park Parade B3
Park View B2
Parliament St B1
Police Station C3
Post Office B2/C1
Providence Terr A2
Queen Parade C3
Queen's Rd C1
Raglan St C2
Regent Ave A3

Regent Grove A3
Regent Parade A3
Regent St A3
Regent Terr A3
Ripon Rd A1
Robert St C2
Royal Baths & Turkish Baths 🏛 B1
Royal Pump Room 🏛 B1
St Luke's Mount A2
St Mary's Ave C1
St Mary's Walk C1
Scargill Rd A1
Skipton Rd A3
Skipton St A2
Slingsby Walk C3
South Park Rd C2
Spring Grove A1
Springfield Ave B1
Station Ave B2
Station Parade B2
Stray Rein C3
Stray, The C2/C3
Studley Rd A2
Superstore B2/C1
Swan Rd B1
Tower St C2
Trinity Rd C2
Union St B2
Valley Dr C1
Valley Gardens ✿ C1
Valley Mount C1
Victoria Ave C2
Victoria Rd C1
Victoria Shopping Ctr B2
Waterloo St A2
West Park C2
West Park St C2
Wood View A1
Woodfield Ave A3
Woodfield Dr A3
Woodfield Grove A3
Woodfield Rd A3
Woodfield Square A3
Woodside B3
York Pl C3
York Rd B1

Holyhead Caergybi 338

Armenia St A2
Arthur St C2
Beach Rd A1
Boston St B2
Bowling Green C3
Bryn Erw Rd C3
Bryn Glas Cl C3
Bryn Glas Rd C3
Bryn Gwyn Rd C1
Bryn Marchog A1
Bryn Mor Terr A2
Bryngoleu Ave A1
Cae Braenar C3
Cambria St B1
Captain Skinner's Obelisk ✦ B2
Cecil St C2
Celtic Gateway Footbridge B2
Cemetery C1/C2
Cleveland Ave C2
Coastguard Lookout A2
Court B2
Cybi Pl A2
Cyttir Rd C3
Edmund St B1
Empire 🎦 B2
Ferry Terminals B2
Ffordd Beibio B3
Ffordd Feurig C3
Ffordd Hirnos C3
Ffordd Jasper C3
Ffordd Tudur B3
Fire Station C2
Garreglwyd Rd B1
Gilbert St C2
Gorsedd Circle B1
Gwelfor Ave A1
Harbour Office A3
Harbour View B3
Henry St C2
High Terr C1
Hill St B2
Holborn Rd C2
Holland Park Ind Est C3
Holyhead Park B1
Holyhead Station ≋ B2
Information Ctr ℹ B2
King's Rd C2
Kingsland Rd C2
Lewascote C3
Library B2
Lifeboat Station A1
Llanfawr Cl C3
Llanfawr Rd C3
Lligwy St C2
Lon Deg C3
London Rd C3
Longford Rd B1
Longford Terr B1
Maes Cybi B1
Maes Hedd A1
Maes-Hyfryd Rd C1
Maes-y-Dref B1
Maes-yr-Haf A2/B1
Maes-yr-Ysgol C3
Marchog C3
Marina A1
Maritime Museum 🏛 A1
Market B2
Market St B2
Mill Bank B1
Min-y-Mor Rd A1
Morawelon Ind Est B3
Morawelon Rd B3
Moreton Rd C1
New Park Rd B1
Newry St A2
Old Harbour Lighthouse A3
Plas Rd C1
Police Station ⊠ B2
Porth-y-Felin Rd A1
Post Office ✉ A1/B2/B3
Prince of Wales Rd A2
Priory La B3
Pump St C1
Queens Park B1
Reseifion Rd C1
Rock St B1
Roman Fort ♜ B2
St Cybi St B2
St Cybi's Church ⛪ B2
St Seiriol's Close B1
Salt Island Bridge A2
Seabourne Rd A1
South Stack Rd B1
Sports Ground B1
Stanley St B2
Station St B2
Superstore C2
Tan-y-Bryn Rd A1
Tan-yr-Efail C2
Tara St C1
Thomas St B1
Town Hall A2
Treseifion Estate C2
Turkey Shore Rd B2
Ucheldre Arts Ctr ✦ B1
Ucheldre Ave B1
Upper Baptist St B1
Victoria Rd B2
Victoria Terr B2
Vulcan St B1
Walthew Ave A1
Walthew La A1
Wian St C2

Hull 338

Adelaide St C1
Albert Dock C1
Albion St B2
Alfred Gelder St B2
Anlaby Rd B1
Arctic Corsair ✦ B3
Beverley Rd A1
Blanket Row C2
Bond St B2
Bonus Arena B2
Bridlington Ave A2
Brook St B1
Brunswick Ave A1
Bus Station B1
Camilla Cl C3
Cannon St A2
Caroline St A2
Carr La B2
Castle St C2
Central Library B1
Charles St A2
Citadel Way B3
Clarence St B3
Cleveland St A3
Clifton St A1
Colonial St B1
Court B2
Deep, The ✦ C3
Dinostar 🏛 C2
Dock Office Row B3
Dock St B2
Drypool Bridge B3
Egton St A3
English St C1
Ferens Gallery 🏛 B2
Ferensway B1
Fire Sta A1
Francis St A2
Francis St West A2
Freehold St A1
Freetown Way A2
Früit Theatre 🎭 C2
Garrison Rd B3
George St B2
Gibson St A2
Great Thornton St B1
Great Union St A3
Green La A2
Grey St A1
Grimston St B2
Grosvenor St A1
Guildhall 🏛 B2
Guildhall Rd B2
Hands-on History 🏛 B2
Harley St A1
Hessle Rd C1
High St B3
Hull Minster ⛪ B2
Hull Paragon Interchange Sta ≋ B1
Hull & East Riding Museum 🏛 B3
Hull Ice Arena C1
Hull City Hall 🎭 B2
Hull College B3
Hull History Centre A2
Hull New Theatre 🎭 A2
Hull Truck Theatre 🎭 B1
Humber Dock Marina C2
Humber Dock St C2
Humber St C2
Hyperion St A3
Information Ctr ℹ B2
Jameson St B1
Jarratt St B2
Jenning St A3
King Billy Statue ✦ C2
King Edward St B2
King St A2
Kingston Retail Park C1
Kingston St C2
Liddell St A1
Lime St A3
Lister St C1
Lockwood St A2
Maister House 🏛 B3
Maritime Museum 🏛 B2
Market B2
Market Place B2
Minerva Pier C2
Mulgrave St A3
Myton Swing Bridge C3
Myton St B1
NAPA (Northern Acad of Performing Arts) 🎭 B1
Nelson St C2
New Cleveland St A3
New George St A2
Norfolk St A1
North Bridge A3
North St B1
Odeon 🎦 C1
Old Harbour C3
Osborne St B1
Paragon St B2
Park St B1
Percy St A2
Pier St C2
Police Station ⊠ B1
Porter St C1
Portland St B1
Post Office ✉ B1/B2
Posterngate B2
Prince's Quay B2
Prospect Centre B1
Prospect St B1
Queen's Gdns B2
Railway Dock Marina C2
Railway St C2
Real 🎦 B1
Red Gallery 🏛 B1
Reform St A2
Retail Park B1
Riverside Quay C2
Roper St B2
St James St C1
St Luke's St B1
St Mark St A3
St Mary the Virgin ⛪ B3
St Stephens Shopping Centre B1
Scale Lane Footbridge B3
Scott St A2
South Bridge Rd B3
Sport's Centre C1
Spring Bank A1
Spring St B1
Spurn Lightship ⛴ C2
Spyvee St A3
Stage @TheDock 🎭 C3
Streetlife Transport Museum 🏛 B3
Sykes St A2
Tidal Surge Barrier ✦ C3
Tower St B3
Trinity House B2
Vane St A1
Victoria Pier ✦ C2
Waterhouse La B2
Waterloo St A1
Waverley St C1
Wellington St C2
Wellington St West C2
West St B1
Whitefriargate B2
Wilberforce Dr B2
Wilberforce House 🏛 B3
Wilberforce Monument ✦ B3
William St C1
Wincolmlee A3
Witham A3
Wright St A1

Inverness 338

Abban St A1
Academy St B2
Alexander Pl B2
Anderson St A2
Annfield Rd C3
Ardconnel St B3
Ardconnel Terr B3
Ardross Pl B2
Ardross St B2
Argyle St B3
Argyle Terr B3
Attadale Rd B1
Ballifeary La C2
Ballifeary Rd C1/C2
Balnacraig La A1
Balnain House ✦ B2
Balnain St B2
Bank St B2
Bellfield Park C2
Bellfield Terr C3
Benula Rd A1
Birnie Terr A1
Bishop's Rd C2
Bowling Green B2
Bridge St B2
Brown St A2
Bruce Ave C1
Bruce Gdns C1
Bruce Pk C1
Burial Ground A2
Burnett Rd A3
Bus Station B3
Caledonian Rd B1
Cameron Rd A1
Cameron Sq A1
Carse Rd A1
Carsegate Rd Sth A1
Castle Garrison Encounter ✦ B2
Castle Rd B2
Castle St B3
Celt St B2
Chapel St A2
Charles St B3
Church St B2
Columba Rd B1/C1
Crown Ave B3
Crown Circus B3
Crown Dr B3
Crown Rd B3
Crown St B3
Culduthel Rd C3
Dalneigh Cres C1
Dalneigh Rd C1
Denny St B3
Dochfour Dr B1/C1
Douglas Row B2
Duffy Dr C3
Dunabban Rd A1
Dunain Rd B1
Duncraig St B2
Eastgate Shopping Centre B3
Eden Court 🎭🎦 C2
Fairfield Rd B1
Falcon Sq B3
Fire Station A3
Fraser St B2
Fraser St C2
Friars' Bridge A2
Friars' La B2
Friars' St A2
George St A2
Gilbert St A2
Glebe St A2
Glendoe Terr A1
Glenurquhart Rd C1
Gordon Terr B3
Gordonville Rd C2
Grant St A2
Grant Street Park (Clachnacuddin FC) A1
Greig St B2
Harbour Rd A3
Harrowden Rd B1
Haugh Rd C2
Heatherley Cres C3
High St B3
Highland Council HQ, The C2
Hill Park C3
Hill St B3
HM Prison B3
Huntly Pl A2
Huntly St B2
India St A2
Industrial Estate A3
Information Ctr ℹ B2
Innes St A2
Inverness ≋ B3
Inverness High Sch B1
Inverness Museum & Art Gallery 🏛 B2
Jamaica St A2
Kenneth St B2
Kilmuir Rd A1
King St B2
Kingsmills Rd B3
Laurel Ave B1/C1
Library A3
Lilac Gr B1
Lindsay Ave C1
Lochalsh Rd A1/B1
Longman Rd A3
Lotland Pl A2
Lower Kessock St A1
Madras St A2
Maxwell Dr C1
Mayfield Rd C3
Millburn Rd B3
Mitchell's La C3
Montague Row B2
Muirfield Rd C3
Muirtown St B1
Nelson St A2
Ness Bank C2
Ness Bridge B2
Ness Walk B2/C2
Old Edinburgh Rd C3
Old High Church ⛪ B2
Park Rd C1
Paton St C2
Perceval Rd B1
Planefield Rd B2
Police Station ⊠ A3
Porterfield Bank C3
Porterfield Rd C3
Portland Pl A2
Post Office ✉ A2/B1/B2
Queen St B2
Queensgate B2
Railway Terr A3
Rangemore Rd B1
Reay St B3
Riverside St A2
Rose St A2
Ross Ave B1
Rowan Rd B1
Royal Northern Infirmary Ⓗ C2
St Andrew's Cath ✝ C2
St Columba ⛪ B2
St John's Ave C1
St Mary's Ave C1
Sheriff Court B3
Shore St A2
Smith Ave C1
Southside Pl C3
Southside Rd C3
Spectrum Centre B2
Strothers La B3
Superstore A1/B2
TA Centre C2
Telford Gdns B1
Telford Rd A1
Telford St A1
Tomnahurich Cemetery C1
Tomnahurich St B2
Town Hall B3
Union Rd B3
Union St B3
Victorian Market B3
Walker Pl A2
Walker Rd A3
War Memorial ✦ C2
Waterloo Bridge A2
Wells St B1
Young St B2

Ipswich 338

Alderman Rd B2
All Saints' Rd A1
Alpe St B2
Ancaster Rd C1
Ancient House 🏛 B3
Anglesea Rd B2
Ann St B2
Arboretum A2
Austin St C2
Avenue, The A3
Belstead Rd C2
Berners St B2
Bibb Way B1
Birkfield Dr C1
Black Horse La B2
Bolton La B3
Bond St C3
Bowthorpe Cl B2
Bramford La A1
Bramford Rd A1
Bridge St C2
Brookfield Rd A1
Brooks Hall Rd A1
Broomhill A2
Broomhill Park A2
Broomhill Rd A1
Broughton Rd A2
Bulwer Rd B1
Burrell Rd C2
Bus Station B3
Butter Market B2
Buttermarket Shopping Centre, The B3
Cardinal Park Leisure Park C2
Carr St B3
Cecil Rd B2
Cecilia St C2
Chancery Rd C2
Charles St B2
Chevallier St A1
Christchurch Mansion & Wolsey Art Gallery 🏛 B3
Christchurch Park A3
Christchurch St B3
Cineworld 🎦 C2
Civic Centre B2
Civic Dr B2
Clarkson St B1
Cobbold St B3
Commercial Rd C2
Constable Rd A3
Constantine Rd C1
Constitution Hill A2
Corder Rd A3
Corn Exchange B2
Cotswold Ave A2
Council Offices C2
County Hall B3
Crown Court C2
Crown St B2
Cullingham Rd B1
Cumberland St B2
Curriers La B2
Dale Hall La A2
Dales View Rd A1
Dalton Rd B2
Dillwyn St B1
Elliot St B1
Elm St B2
Elsmere Rd A3
Falcon St C2
Felaw St C3
Fire Station C2
Flint Wharf C3
Fonnereau Rd B2
Fore St C3
Foundation St C3
Franciscan Way C2
Friars St C2
Gainsborough Rd A3
Gatacre Rd B1
Geneva Rd B2
Gippeswyk Ave C1
Gippeswyk Park C1
Grafton Way C2
Graham Rd A1
Great Whip St C3
Grimwade St C3
Handford Cut B1
Handford Rd B1
Henley Rd A2
Hervey St B3
High St B2
Holly Rd A2
Information Ctr ℹ B3
Ipswich Haven Marina ✦ C3
Ipswich Museum & Art Gallery 🏛 B2
Ipswich School A2
Ipswich Station ≋ C2
Ipswich Town FC (Portman Road) C2
Ivry St A2
Kensington Rd A1
Kesteven Rd C1
Key St C3
Kingsfield Ave A3
Kitchener Rd A1
Little's Cr C2
London Rd B1
Low Brook St C3
Lower Orwell St C3
Luther Rd C2
Magistrates Court B2
Manor Rd A3
Mornington Ave A1
Museum St B2
Neale St B3
New Cardinal St C2
New Cut East C3
New Cut West C3
New Wolsey 🎭 B2
Newson St B2
Norwich Rd A1/B1
Oban St B2
Old Custom House 🏛 C3
Old Foundry Rd B3
Old Merchant's Ho 🏛 C3
Orford St B2
Paget Rd A2
Park Rd A3
Park View Rd A2
Peter's St C2
Philip Rd C2
Pine Ave A2
Pine View Rd A2
Police Station ⊠ A2
Portman Rd B2
Portman Walk C1
Post Office ✉ B2
Princes St C2
Prospect St B1
Queen St B2
Ranelagh Rd C1
Recreation Ground B1
Rectory Rd C2
Regent Theatre 🎭 B3
Retail Park C1
Retail Park C2
Richmond Rd A1
Rope Walk C3
Rose La C2
Russell Rd C2
St Edmund's Rd A2
St George's St B2
St Helen's St B3
Sherrington Rd A1
Shopmobility B2
Silent St C2
Sir Alf Ramsey Way C1
Sirdar Rd B1
Soane St B3
Springfield La A1
Star La C3
Stevenson Rd B1
Suffolk College C3
Suffolk Retail Park B1
Superstore B1
Surrey Rd B1
Tacket St C3
Tavern St B3
Tower Ramparts B2
Tower Ramparts Shopping Centre B2
Tower St B3
Town Hall 🏛 B2
Tuddenham Rd A3
University C3
Upper Brook St B3
Upper Orwell St B3
Valley Rd A2
Vermont Cr B3
Vermont Rd B3
Vernon St C3
Warrington Rd A2
Waterloo Rd A1
Waterworks St C3
Wellington St B1
West End Rd B1
Westerfield Rd A3
Westgate St B2
Westholme Rd A1
Westwood Ave A1
Willoughby Rd C2
Withipoll St B3
Woodbridge Rd B3
Woodstone Ave A3
Yarmouth Rd B1

Kendal 338

Abbot Hall Art Gallery & Museum of Lakeland Life & Industry 🏛 C2
Ambulance Station A2
Anchorite Fields C2
Anchorite Rd C2
Ann St A3
Appleby Rd A3
Archers Meadow C3
Ashleigh Rd A2
Aynam Rd B2
Bankfield Rd B1
Beast Banks B2
Beezon Fields A2
Beezon Rd A2
Beezon Trad Est A3
Belmont B2
Birchwood Cl C1
Blackhall Rd B2
Brewery Arts Ctr 🎭🎦 B2
Bridge St B2
Brigsteer Rd C1
Burneside Rd A2
Bus Station B2
Buttery Well Rd C2
Canal Head North B3
Captain French La C2
Caroline St A2
Castle Hill B3
Castle Howe B2
Castle Rd B3
Castle St A3/B3
Cedar Gr C1
Council Offices B2
County Council Offices A2
Cricket Ground A3
Cricket Ground C3
Cross La C2
Dockray Hall Ind Est A2
Dowker's La B2
East View B1
Echo Barn Hill C1
Elephant Yard B2
Fairfield La A1
Finkle St B2
Fire Station A2
Fletcher Square C3
Football Ground C3
Fowling La A3
Gillinggate C2
Glebe Rd C2
Golf Course B1
Goose Holme B3
Gooseholme Bridge B3
Green St A1
Greengate C2
Greengate La C1/C2
Greenside B1
Greenwood C1
Gulfs Rd B2
High Tenterfell B1
Highgate B2
Hillswood Ave C1
Horncop La A2
Information Ctr ℹ B2
Kendal 🏛 A3
Kendal Business Park A3
Kendal Castle (Remains) ♜ B3
Kendal Fell B1
Kendal Green A1
Kendal Ski Centre ✦ B3
Kendal Station ≋ A3
Kent Pl B2
Kirkbarrow C2
Kirkland C2
Library B2
Library Rd B2
Little Aynam B3
Little Wood B1
Long Cl C1
Longpool A3
Lound Rd C3
Lound St C3
Low Fellside B2
Lowther St B2
Magistrates Court A2
Maple Dr C1
Market Pl B2
Maude St B2
Miller Bridge B2
Milnthorpe Rd C2
Mint St A3
Mintsfeet Rd A3
Mintsfeet Rd South A2
New Rd B2
Noble's Rest B2
Parish Church ⛪ C2
Park Side Rd C3
Parkside Bsns Park C3
Parr St B3
Police Station ⊠ A2
Post Office ✉ A3/B2
Quaker Tapestry ✦ B2
Queen's Rd B1
Riverside Walk C2
Rydal Mount A2
Sandes Ave A2
Sandgate A3
Sandylands Rd A3
Serpentine Rd B1
Serpentine Wood B1
Shap Rd A3
South Rd C2
Stainbank Rd C1
Station Rd A3
Stramongate B2
Stramongate Bridge B2
Stricklandgate A2/B2
Sunnyside C3
Thorny Hills B3
Town Hall B2
Undercliff Rd B1
Underwood C1
Union St A2
Vicar's Fields C2
Vicarage Dr C1/C2
Wainwright's Yard B2
Wasdale Cl C3
Well Ings C2
Westmorland Shopping Centre & Market Hall B2
Westwood Ave C1
Wildman St A3
Windermere Rd A1
YHA ▲ B2
YWCA B2

King's Lynn 339

Albert St A2
Albion St B2
Alive St James' Swimming Pool B2
All Saints ⛪ B2
All Saints St B2
Austin Fields A2
Austin St A2
Avenue Rd B3
Bank Side B1
Beech Rd C2
Birch Tree Cl B2
Birchwood St A2
Blackfriars Rd B2
Blackfriars St B2
Boal St B1
Bridge St B2
Broad St B2
Broad Walk B3
Burkitt St A2
Bus Station A2
Carmelite Terr C2
Chapel St A2
Chase Ave C3
Checker St C2
Church St B2
Clough La B2
Coburg St B2
College of West Anglia A3
Columbia Way A3
Corn Exchange 🎭 A1
County Court Rd B2
Cresswell St A2
Custom House 🏛 A1
East Coast Bsns Park C1
Eastgate St A2
Edma St A2
Exton's Rd C3
Ferry La B1
Ferry St A1
Framingham's Almshouses 🏛 B2
Friars St C2
Friars Walk C2
Gaywood Rd A3
George St A2
Gladstone Rd C2
Goodwin's Rd C3
Green Quay ✦ B1
Greyfriars' Tower ✦ B2
Guanock Terr C2
Guildhall 🏛 A1
Hansa Rd C3
Hardwick Rd C2
Hextable Rd A2
High St B1
Holcombe Ave C3
Hospital Walk C2
Information Ctr ℹ B1
John Kennedy Rd A2
Kettlewell Lane A2
King George V Ave B3
King St B1
King's Lynn Art Ctr 🏛 A1
King's Lynn FC B3
King's Lynn Station ≋ B2
Library B2
Littleport St A2
Loke Rd A2
London Rd B2
Lynn Museum B2
Magistrates Court B1
Majestic 🎦 B2
Market La A1
Millfleet B2
Milton Ave A3
Nar Valley Walk C2
Nelson St B1
New Conduit St B2
Norfolk St A2
North Lynn Discovery Centre ✦ A3
North St A2
Oldsunway B2
Ouse Ave C1
Page Stair Lane A1
Park Ave B3
Police Station ⊠ B2
Portland Pl C1
Portland St B2
Purfleet B1
Queen St B1
Raby Ave A3
Railway Rd A2
Red Mount Chapel ⛪ B3
Regent Way B2
River Walk A1
Robert St C2
Saddlebow Rd C2
Shopmobility B2
St Ann's St A1
St James St B2
St James' Rd B2
St John's Walk B3
St Margaret's ⛪ B1
St Nicholas ⛪ A2
St Nicholas St A1
St Peter's Rd B1
Sir Lewis St A2
Smith Ave A3
South Everard St C2
South Gate ✦ C2
South Quay B1
South St B2
Southgate St C2
Stonegate St B2
Surrey St A1
Sydney St C3
Tennyson Ave B3
Tennyson Rd B3
Tower St B2
Town Hall B1
Town Ho & Tales of the Old Gaol Ho 🏛 B1
Town Wall (Remains) ✦ B3
True's Yard Fisherfolk Museum 🏛 A2
Valingers Rd C2
Vancouver Ave C2
Vancouver Quarter B2
Waterloo St B2
Wellesley St B2
White Friars Rd C2
Windsor Rd C2
Winfarthing St C2
Wyatt St A2
York Rd C3

Lancaster 339

Aberdeen Rd C3
Adult College, The C3
Aldcliffe Rd C2
Alfred St B3
Ambleside Rd A3
Ambulance Sta A3
Ashfield Ave B1
Ashton Rd C2
Assembly Rooms Emporium 🏛 B2
Balmoral Rd B3
Bath House ♜ B2
Bath Mill La B3
Bath St B3
Blades St B1
Borrowdale Rd B3
Bowerham Rd C3
Brewery La B2
Bridge La B2
Brook St C1
Bulk Rd A3
Bulk St B2
Bus Station B2
Cable St B2
Canal Cruises & Waterbus ✦ C2
Carlisle Bridge A1
Carr House La C2
Castle ♜ B1
Castle Park B1
Caton Rd A3
China St B2
Church St B2
City Museum 🏛 B2
Clarence St C3
Common Gdn St B2
Coniston Rd A3
Cottage Museum 🏛 B2
Council Offices B2
County Court & Family Court B2
Cromwell Rd C1
Crown Court B1
Dale St C3
Dallas Rd B1/C1
Dalton Rd B3
Dalton Sq B2
Damside St B2
De Vitre St B3
Dee Rd A1
Denny Ave A1
Derby Rd A2
Dukes, The B2
Earl St A2
East Rd B3
Eastham St C3
Edward St B3
Fairfield Rd B1
Fenton St B2
Firbank Rd A3
Fire Station B2
Friend's Meeting House 🏛 B1
Garnet St B3
George St B2
Giant Axe Field B1
Grand 🎭 B2
Grasmere Rd B3
Greaves Rd C2
Green St A3
Gregson Centre, The B3
Gregson Rd C3
Greyhound Bridge A2
Greyhound Bridge Rd A2
High St B2
Hill Side B1
Hope St C3
Hubert Pl B1
Information Ctr ℹ B2
Kelsy St B1
Kentmere Rd B3
King St B2
Kingsway A3
Kirkes Rd C3
Lancaster & Lakeland Ⓗ C3
Lancaster City Football Club B1
Lancaster Station ≋ B1
Langdale Rd A3
Ley Ct B1
Library B2
Lincoln Rd B1
Lindow St C2
Lodge St B2
Long Marsh La B1
Lune Rd A1
Lune St A2
Lune Valley Ramble A3
Mainway A2
Maritime Museum 🏛 A1
Marketgate Shopping Centre B2
Market St B2
Meadowside C2
Meeting House La B1
Millennium Bridge A2
Moor La B2
Moorgate B3
Morecambe Rd A1/A2
Nelson St B2
North Rd B2
Orchard La C1
Owen Rd A2
Park Rd B3
Parliament St A3
Patterdale Rd A3
Penny St B2
Police Station ⊠ B2
Portland St C2
Post Office ✉ B2
Primrose St C3
Priory ⛪ B1
Prospect St C3
Quarry Rd B3
Queen St C2
Regent St C2
Ridge La A3
Ridge St A3
Royal Lancaster Infirmary (A&E) Ⓗ C2
Rydal Rd B3
Ryelands Park A1
St Georges Quay A1
St John's ⛪ B2
St Leonard's Gate B2
St Martin's Rd C3
St Nicholas Arcades Shopping Centre B2
St Oswald St C3
St Peter's ✝ B3
St Peter's Rd B3
Salisbury Rd B1
Scotch Quarry Urban Park C3
Sibsey St B1
Skerton Bridge A2
South Rd C2
Station Rd B1
Stirling Rd C3
Storey Ave B1
Sunnyside La C1
Sylvester St C1
Tarnsyke Rd A1
Thurnham St C2
Town Hall B2
Troutbeck Rd B3
Ulleswater Rd B3
University of Cumbria C3
Vicarage Field B1
Vue 🎦 B2
West Rd B1
Westbourne Dr C1
Westbourne Rd B1
Westham St C3
Wheatfield St B1
White Cross Business Park C2
Williamson Rd B3
Willow La B1
Windermere Rd B3
Wingate-Saul Rd B1
Wolseley St B3
Woodville St B3
Wyresdale Rd C3

Leeds 339

Aire St....B3
Albion Pl....B4
Albion St....B4
Albion Way....B1
Alma St....A6
Ambulance Sta....B5
Arcades....B4
Armley Rd....B1
Armories Dr....C5
Back Burley Lodge Rd....A1
Back Hyde Terr....A2
Back Row....C3
Bath Rd....C3
Beckett St....A6
Bedford St....B3
Belgrave St....A4
Belle Vue Rd....A2
Benson St....A5
Black Bull St....C5
Blenheim Walk....A3
Boar La....B4
Bond St....B4
Bow St....C5
Bowman La....C4
Brewery....C4
Brewery Wharf....C5
Bridge St....A5/B5
Briggate....B4
Bruce Gdns....C1
Burley Rd....A1
Burley St....B1
Burmantofts St....B6
Bus & Coach Station....C4
Butterly St....C4
Butts Cr....B5
Byron St....A5
Call La....B4
Calls, The....B5
Calverley St....A3/B3
Canal St....B1
Canal Wharf....C3
Carlisle Rd....C5
Cavendish Rd....A1
Cavendish St....A2
Chadwick St....C5
Cherry Pl....A6
Cherry Row....A5
City Museum....A4
City Varieties
  Music Hall....B4
City Sq....B3
Civic Hall....A3
Clarence Road....C5
Clarendon Rd....A2
Clarendon Way....A3
Clark La....C6
Clay Pit La....A4
Cloberry St....A2
Close, The....B6
Clyde Approach....C1
Clyde Gdns....C1
Coleman St....C2
Commercial St....B4
Concord St....A5
Cookridge St....A4
Copley Hill....C1
Core, The....B4
Corn Exchange....B4
Cromer Terr....A2
Cromwell St....A5
Cross Catherine St....B6
Cross Green La....C6
Cross Stamford St....A5
Crown & County
  Courts....A3
Crown Point Bridge....C5
Crown Point Rd....C4
Crown Point Retail Pk....C4
David St....C3
Dent St....C6
Derwent Pl....C3
Dial St....C6
Dock St....C4
Dolly La....A6
Domestic St....C2
Drive, The....B6
Duke St....B5
Duncan St....B4
Dyer St....B5
East Field St....B6
East Pde....B3
East St....C5
Eastgate....B5
Easy Rd....C6
Edward St....B4
Ellerby La....C6
Ellerby Rd....C6
Fenton St....A3
Fire Station....B2
First Direct Arena....A4
Fish St....B4
Flax Pl....B5
Garth, The....B5
Gelderd Rd....C1
George St....B4
Globe Rd....C2
Gower St....A5
Grafton St....A5
Grand Theatre....B4
Granville Rd....A6
Great George St....A3
Great Wilson St....C3
Greek St....B3
Green La....C1
Hanover Ave....A2
Hanover La....A2
Hanover Sq....A2
Hanover Way....A2
Harewood St....B4
Harrison St....B4
Haslewood Cl....B6
Haslewood Drive....B6
Headrow, The....B3/B4
High Court....B5
Holbeck La....C2
Holdforth Cl....C1
Holdforth Gdns....C1
Holdforth Gr....C1
Holdforth Pl....C1

Holy Trinity....B4
Hope Rd....A5
Hunslet La....C4
Hunslet Rd....C4
Hyde Terr....A2
Infirmary St....B3
Information Ctr....B3
Ingram Row....C3
ITV Yorkshire....A1
Junction St....C4
Kelso Gdns....A2
Kelso Rd....A2
Kelso St....A2
Kendal La....A2
Kendell St....C4
Kidacre St....C4
King Edward St....B4
King St....B3
Kippax Pl....C6
Kirkgate....B4
Kirkgate Market....B4
Kirkstall Rd....B1
Kitson St....C6
Knight's Way Bridge....C5
Lady La....B4
Lands La....B4
Lane, The....B5
Lavender Walk....B6
Leeds Art Gallery....B3
Leeds Beckett Univ....A3
Leeds Bridge....C4
Leeds Coll of Music....B5
Leeds Discovery Ctr....C5
Leeds General
  Infirmary (A&E)....B3
Leeds Minster....B5
Leeds Station....B3/B4
Library....B3/B4
Light, The....B3
Lincoln Green Rd....A6
Lincoln Rd....A6
Lindsey Gdns....A6
Lindsey Rd....A6
Lisbon St....B2
Little Queen St....B3
Long Close La....C2
Lord St....C1
Lovell Park....A4
Lovell Park Hill....A4
Lovell Park Rd....A4
Lower Brunswick St....A5
Mabgate....A5
Macauley St....A5
Magistrates Court....A3
Manor Rd....C3
Mark La....A4
Marlborough St....B2
Marsh La....B5
Marshall St....C3
Meadow La....C4
Meadow Rd....C4
Melbourne St....A4
Merrion Centre....A4
Merrion St....A4
Merrion Way....A4
Mill St....B5
Millennium Sq....A3
Monk Bridge....C2
Mount Preston St....A2
Mushroom St....A5
Neville St....C3
New Briggate....A4/B4
New Market St....B4
New York Rd....A5
New York St....B5
Nile St....A5
Nippet La....A6
North St....A4
Northern Ballet....B4
Northern St....B3
Oak Rd....B1
Oxford Pl....B3
Oxford Row....A3
Parade, The....B6
Park Cross St....B3
Park La....A2
Park Pl....B3
Park Row....B4
Park Sq....B3
Park Sq East....B3
Park Sq West....B3
Police Station....A3
Pontefract La....B6
Portland Cr....A3
Portland Way....A3
Post Office....B4/B5
Quarry House (NHS/DSS
  Headquarters)....A5
Quebec St....B3
Queen St....B3
Radio Aire....A1
Railway St....B5
Rectory St....A6
Regent St....A5
Richmond St....C5
Rigton Approach....B6
Rigton Dr....B6
Rillbank La....A1
Rosebank Rd....A1
Rose Bowl
  Conference Centre....A3
Royal Armouries....B6
Russell St....B3
St Anne's Cath (RC)....B4
St Anne's St....B4
St James' Hospital....A6
St John's Rd....A2
St Johns Centre....B4
St Mary's St....B5
St Pauls St....B3
Saxton La....B5
Sayner La....C4
Shakespeare Ave....A6
Sheepscar St South....A5
Siddall St....C3
Skinner La....A5
South Pde....B3
Sovereign St....C4
Spence La....C2

Springfield Mount....A2
Springwell Ct....C2
Springwell Rd....C2
Springwell St....C2
Stoney Rock La....A6
Studio Rd....A1
Sutton St....C3
Sweet St....C3
Sweet St West....C3
Swinegate....B4
Templar St....B5
Thoresby Pl....A3
Torre Rd....A6
Town Hall....B3
Trinity Leeds....B4
Union Pl....C4
Union St....B5
University of Leeds....A3
Upper Accommodation
  Rd....B6
Upper Basinghall St....B4
Vicar La....B4
Victoria Bridge....C4
Victoria Gate....B4
Victoria Quarter....B4
Victoria Rd....C3
Vue....B4
Wade La....A4
Washington St....A1
Water La....C3
Waterloo Rd....B2/C1
Wellington Rd....B2/C1
Wellington St....B3
West St....B2
West Yorkshire
  Playhouse....B5
Westfield Rd....A1
Westgate....B3
Whitehall Rd....B3/C2
Whitelock St....A5
Willis St....C6
Willow Approach....A1
Willow Ave....A1
Willow Terrace Rd....A3
Wintoun St....A5
Woodhouse La....A3/A4
Woodsley Rd....A1
York Pl....B3
York Rd....B6

Leicester 339

Abbey St....A1
All Saints'....A1
Aylestone Rd....C2
Bath La....A1
Bede Park....C1
Bedford St....A3
Bedford St South....A3
Belgrave Gate....A2
Belvoir St....B2
Braunstone Gate....B1
Burleys Way....A2
Burnmoor St....C2
Bus & Coach Station....A2
Canning St....A2
Carlton St....B1
Castle....B1
Castle Gardens....B1
Cathedral....B2
Causeway La....A2
Charles St....B3
Chatham St....B2
Christow St....A3
Church Gate....A2
City Gallery....B3
City Hall....B2
Clank St....B2
Clock Tower....B2
Clyde St....A3
Colton St....B3
Conduit St....B3
Crafton St....B3
Craven St....A1
Crown Courts....B3
Curve....B3
De Lux....B3
De Montfort Hall....C3
De Montfort
  University....C1
Deacon St....C2
Dover St....B3
Duns La....B1
Dunton St....A1
East St....B3
Eastern Boulevard....C1
Edmonton St....A3
Erskine St....A3
Filbert St....C1
Filbert St East....C2
Fire Station....C2
Fleet St....A3
Friar La....B2
Friday St....A1
Gateway St....C2
Gateway, The....C2
Glebe St....B3
Granby St....B3
Grange La....C2
Grasmere St....C1
Great Central St....A1
Guildhall....B2
Guru Nanak Sikh
  Museum....B1
Halford St....B2
Havelock St....C2
Haymarket
  Shopping Centre....A2
High St....B2
Highcross
  Shopping Centre....A2
Highcross St....A1
HM Prison....C2
Horsefair St....B2
Humberstone Gate....B2
Humberstone Rd....A3
Infirmary St....C2
Information Ctr....B2
Jarrom St....C1

Jewry Wall....B1
Kamloops Cr....A3
King St....B2
Lancaster Rd....C3
LCB Depot....B3
Lee St....A2
Leicester Royal
  Infirmary (A&E)....C2
Leicester Station....B3
Library....B2
London Rd....B3
Lower Brown St....B2
Magistrates' Court....B2
Manitoba Rd....A3
Mansfield St....A2
Market....B2
Market St....B2
Mill La....C2
Montreal Rd....A3
Narborough Rd North....B1
Nelson Mandela Park....C1
New Park St....B1
New St....B2
New Walk....C3
New Walk Museum &
  Art Gallery....C3
Newarke Houses....B2
Newarke St....B2
Newarke, The....B1
Northgate St....A1
Orchard St....A2
Ottawa Rd....A3
Oxford St....C2
Phoenix Arts Centre....B3
Police Station....B2
Post Office....A1/B1/B2
Prebend St....C3
Princess Rd East....C3
Princess Rd West....C3
Queen St....B3
Rally Com Park, The....A2
Regent College....C3
Regent Rd....C2/C3
Repton St....A1
Rutland St....B3
St Augustine Rd....B1
St Georges
  Retail Park....B3
St George St....B3
St Georges Way....B3
St John St....A2
St Margaret's....A2
St Margaret's Way....A2
St Martins....B2
St Matthew's Way....A3
St Nicholas Circle....B1
Sanvey Gate....A2
Silver St....B2
Slater St....A1
Soar La....A1
South Albion St....B3
Southampton St....B3
Sue Townsend
  Theatre....B2
Swain St....B3
Swan St....A1
Tigers Way....C3
Tower St....B3
Town Hall....B2
Tudor Rd....B1
University of
  Leicester....C3
University Rd....C3
Upperton Rd....C1
Vaughan Way....A2
Walnut St....C1
Watling St....A2
Welford Rd....B2
Welford Rd Leicester
  Tigers RC....C2
Wellington St....B2
West St....C2
West Walk....C3
Western Boulevard....C1
Western Rd....C1
Wharf St North....A3
Wharf St South....A3
Y Theatre, The....B3
Yeoman St....B2
York Rd....B2

Lewes 339

Abinger Place....B1
All Saints Centre....B2
Anne of Cleves
  House....C1
Avenue, The....B1
Barbican Ho Mus....C1
Brewery....B2
Brook St....A2
Brooks Rd....A2
Bus Station....B2
Castle Ditch La....B1
Castle Precincts....B1
Chapel Hill....B2
Church La....A1/A2
Cliffe High St....B2
Cliffe Industrial Est....C3
Cluny St....C2
Cockshut Rd....C1
Convent Field....C1
Coombe Rd....A2
County Hall....A2
Course, The....C1
Court Rd....A1
Crown Court....B2
Cuilfail Tunnel....B3
Davey's La....A3
Dripping Room, The
  (Lewes FC)....C2
East St....B2
East Sussex College....B2
Eastport La....C1
Fire Station....B2
Fisher St....B2
Friars Walk....B2
Garden St....B1

Grange Rd....B1
Ham La....C2
Harveys Way....B2
Hereward Way....A3
High St....B1/B2
Hop Gallery....B2
Information Ctr....B1
Keere St....B1
King Henry's Rd....B1
Landport Rd....A1
Leisure Centre....A2
Lewes Bridge....B2
Lewes Castle....B1
Lewes Golf Course....B3
Lewes Southern
  By-Pass....C2
Lewes Station....B2
Library....B2
Malling Brook Ind Est....A3
Malling Down Nature
  Reserve....A3
Malling Hill....A3
Malling Ind Est....A2
Malling St....A3/B3
Market St....B1
Martlets, The....B2
Martyr's Monument....B3
Mayhew Way....A2
Morris Rd....B3
Mountfield Rd....C2
Needlemakers, The....B2
New Rd....B1
Newton Rd....A1
North St....A2/B2
Offham Rd....A1
Old Malling Way....A1
Orchard Rd....A3
Paddock La....B1
Paddock Rd....B1
Paddock Sports Gd....B1
Park Rd....B1
Pelham Terr....A1
Pells Outdoor
  Swimming Pool....A1
Pells, The....A1
Phoenix Causeway....B2
Phoenix Ind Est....B2
Phoenix Pl....B2
Pinwell Rd....B2
Police Station....B2
Post Office....B2
Prince Edward's Rd....B1
Priory of St Pancras
  (remains of)....C1
Priory St....C1
Railway La....B2
Railway Land Nature
  Reserve....B3
Rotten Row....B1
Riverside Ind Est....A2
Rufus Cl....B1
St John St....B1
St John's Terr....B1
St Nicholas La....B1
St Pancras Rd....C1
Sewage Works....C3
South Downs Bsns Pk....A3
South St....B3/C3
Southdowns Rd....A2
Southerham Junction....C3
Southover Grange
  Gdns....B1
Southover High St....B1
Southover Rd....B1
Spences Field....A3
Spences La....A3
Stansfield Rd....A1
Station Rd....B2
Station St....B2
Sun St....B1
Superstore....A2/B2
Sussex Police HQ....A1
Talbot Terr....B1
Thebes Gallery....B2
Toronto Terr....B1
Town Hall....B2
West St....B2
White Hill....B1
Willeys Bridge....A1

Lincoln 342

Alexandra Terr....B1
Anchor St....C1
Arboretum....B3
Arboretum Ave....B3
Avenue, The....B1
Baggholme Rd....B3
Bailgate....A2
Beaumont Fee....B1
BMI The Lincoln
  Hospital....A2
Brayford Way....A1
Brayford Wharf East....C1
Brayford Wharf North....B1
Bruce Rd....A2
Burton Rd....A1
Bus Station (City)....C2
Canwick Rd....C2
Cardinal's Hat....B2
Castle....B1
Castle St....A1
Cathedral....B2
Cecil St....A2
Chapel La....A2
Cheviot St....B3
Church La....A2
City Hall....A1
Clasketgate....B2
Clayton Sports Gd....A3
Coach Park....A1
Collection, The....B2
County Hosp (A&E)....B3
County Office....B1
Courts....C1
Cross St....A2
Crown Courts....B2
Curle Ave....A3

Danesgate....B2
Drill Hall....B2
Drury La....B1
East Bight....A2
East Gate....A2
Eastcliff Rd....B3
Eastgate....A2
Egerton Rd....A3
Ellis Windmill....A1
Engine Shed, The....C1
Environment Agency....B2
Exchequer Gate....B2
Firth Rd....C1
Flaxengate....B2
Florence St....B3
George St....C1
Good La....A2
Gray St....A1
Great Northern
  Terrace....C3
Great Northern Terrace
  Industrial Estate....C3
Greetwell Rd....B3
Greetwellgate....B3
Grove, The....A3
Haffenden Rd....A2
High St....B2/C1
HM Prison....A1
Hungate....B2
James St....A2
Jews House & Ct....B2
Kesteven St....C2
Langworthgate....A2
Lawn, The....B1
Lee Rd....A3
Library....B2
Lincoln Central Sta....C2
Lincoln College....B2
Lincolnshire Life/Royal
  Lincolnshire Regiment
  Museum....A1
Lincoln Univ Technical
  Coll (UTC)....B2
Lindum Rd....B2
Lindum Sports
  Ground....A3
Lindum Terr....B3
Mainwaring Rd....A3
Manor Rd....A2
Market....B2
Massey Rd....A3
Medieval Bishop's
  Palace....B2
Mildmay St....A1
Mill Rd....A1
Millman Rd....A3
Minster Yard....B2
Monks Rd....B3
Montague St....B2
Mount St....A1
Nettleham Rd....A2
Newland....B1
Newport....A2
Newport Arch....A2
Newport Cemetery....A2
Northgate....A2
Odeon....C1
Orchard St....B1
Oxford St....B1
Park St....B1
Pelham Bridge....C2
Pelham St....C2
Police Station....B1
Portland St....C1
Post Office....A1/B3/C2
Potter Gate....B2
Priory Gate....B2
Queensway....A3
Rasen La....A1
Ropewalk....C1
Rosemary La....B2
St Anne's Rd....B3
St Benedict's....B1
St Giles Ave....A3
St Mark's
  Shopping Centre....C1
St Marks St....C1
St Mary's St....C2
St Nicholas St....A2
St Rumbold's St....B2
St Swithin's....B2
Saltergate....C1
Saxon St....A1
Sewell Rd....B3
Silver St....B2
Sincil St....C2
Spital St....A2
Spring Hill....B1
Stamp End....C3
Steep Hill....B2
Stonebow &
  Guildhall....C2
Stonefield Ave....A2
Tentercroft St....C1
Theatre Royal....B2
Tritton Rd....C1
Tritton Retail Park....C1
Union Rd....A1
University of Lincoln....C1
Upper Lindum St....B3
Upper Long Leys Rd....A1
Usher....B2
Vere St....A2
Victoria St....B1
Victoria Terr....B1
Vine St....A3
Wake St....A1
Waldeck St....A1
Waterside North....C2
Waterside Shopping
  Centre....C2
Waterside South....C2
West Pde....B1
Westgate....A2
Wigford Way....C1
Williamson St....A2
Wilson St....A1
Winn St....B3
Wragby Rd....A3
Yarborough Rd....A1

Liverpool 342

Abercromby Sq....C5
Addison St....A3
Adelaide Rd....B6
Ainsworth St....B4
Albany Rd....B6
Albert Edward Rd....B6
Angela St....C6
Anson St....A4
Argyle St....C3
Arrad St....C5
Ashton St....B5
Audley St....A4
Back Leeds St....A2
Basnett St....B3
Bath St....A1
Beacon, The....B2
Beatles Story, The....C2
Beckwith St....C3
Bedford Close....C6
Bedford St North....C5
Bedford St South....C5
Benson St....B4
Berry St....C4
Birkett St....A4
Bixteth St....B2
Blackburne Place....C4
Bluecoat....B3
Bold Place....C4
Bold St....C4
Bolton St....B3
Bridport St....B4
Bronte St....B4
Brook St....A1
Brownlow Hill....B4/B5
Brownlow St....B5
Brunswick Rd....B5
Brunswick St....B1
Bus Station....B3
Butler Cr....A6
Byrom St....A3
Caledonia St....C4
Cambridge St....C5
Camden St....A4
Canada Blvd....B1
Canning Dock....C2
Canterbury St....A4
Cardwell St....C6
Carver St....A4
Cases St....B3
Castle St....B2
Catherine St....C4
Cavern Club....B3
Central Library....B3
Chapel St....B1
Charlotte St....B3
Chatham Place....C6
Chatham St....C5
Cheapside....B2
Chestnut St....C5
Christian St....A3
Church St....B3
Clarence St....C4
Clayton Square
  Shopping Centre....C1
Coach Station....A5
Cobden St....A6
Cockspur St....B2
College St....A4
College St North....A5
College St South....A5
Colquitt St....C4
Comus St....A3
Concert St....C4
Connaught Rd....B6
Cook St....B2
Copperas Hill....B4
Cornwallis St....C3
Covent Garden....B2
Craven St....A4
Cropper St....B3
Crown St....B5/C6
Cumberland St....B2
Cunard Building....B1
Dale St....B2
Dansie St....B4
Daulby St....B5
Dawson St....B3
Dental Hospital....B5
Derby Sq....B2
Drury La....B2
Duckinfield St....C4
Duke St....C3
Earle St....A2
East St....A2
Eaton St....A2
Edgar St....A3
Edge La....B6
Edinburgh Rd....B6
Edmund St....B2
Elizabeth St....B5
Elliot St....B3
Empire Theatre....B4
Empress Rd....B6
Epstein Theatre....B3
Epworth St....A5
Erskine St....A5
Everyman Theatre....C5
Exchange St East....B2
FACT....C4
Falkland St....A4
Falkner St....C5/C6
Farnworth St....A6
Fenwick St....B2
Fielding St....A6
Fire Station....A4
Fleet St....C3
Fraser St....A4
Freemasons Row....A2
Gardner Rd....A6
Gascoyne St....A2
Gibraltar Road....A1
Gilbert St....C3
Gildart St....A4
Gill St....B4
Goree....B2
Gower St....C2
Gradwell St....C3

Great Crosshall St....A3
Great George St....C4
Great Howard St....A1
Great Newton St....B4
Greek St....B4
Green La....A5
Greenside....A5
Greetham St....C3
Gregson St....A5
Grenville St....C3
Grinfield St....C6
Grove St....C5
Guelph St....A6
Hackins Hey....B2
Haigh St....A4
Hall La....A5
Hanover St....B3
Harbord St....C6
Hardman St....C4
Harker St....A4
Hart St....B4
Hatton Garden....B2
Hawke St....B4
Helsby St....B6
Henry St....C3
Highfield St....A2
Highgate St....B6
Hilbre St....B4
Hope Place....C4
Hope St....C4
Hope University....B5
Houghton St....B3
Hunter St....A4
Hutchinson St....A6
Information Ctr....B4/C2
Institute for the
  Performing Arts....C4
Int Slavery Mus....C2
Irvine St....B6
Irwell St....B1
Islington....A4
James St....B2
James St Station....B2
Jenkinson St....A4
John Moores
  Univ....A2/A3/A4/B4/C4
Johnson St....A2
Jubilee Drive....B6
Kempston St....A4
Kensington....B6
Kensington Gdns....B6
Kent St....C3
King Edward St....B1
Kinglake St....B6
Knight St....C4
Lace St....A3
Langsdale St....A4
Law Courts....B2
Leece St....C4
Leeds St....A2
Leopold Rd....B6
Lime St....B3
Lime St Station....B4
Liver St....C2
Liverpool Central
  Station....B3
Liverpool Landing
  Stage....B1
Liverpool Institute for
  Performing Arts
  (LIPA)....C4
Liverpool ONE....C2
Liverpool Wheel, The....C2
London Rd....A4/B4
Lord Nelson St....B4
Lord St....B2
Lovat St....B6
Low Hill....A5
Low Wood St....A6
Lydia Ann St....C3
M&S Bank Arena....C2
Mansfield St....A4
Marmaduke St....B6
Marsden St....A6
Martensen St....B6
Marybone....A3
Maryland St....C4
Mason St....B5
Mathew St....B3
May St....C4
Melville Place....C5
Merseyside Maritime
  Museum....C2
Metquarter....B3
Metropolitan
  Cathedral (RC)....B5
Midghall St....A2
Molyneux Rd....A6
Moor Place....B4
Moorfields....B2
Moorfields Station....B2
Moss St....A5
Mount Pleasant....B4/B5
Mount St....C4
Mount Vernon....B6
Mulberry St....C5
Municipal Buildings....B2
Mus of Liverpool....C2
Myrtle St....C5
Naylor St....A3
Nelson St....C3
New Islington....A4
New Quay....B1
Newington St....C3
North John St....B2
North St....A3
North View....B6
Norton St....A4
O2 Academy....C3
Oakes St....B5
Odeon....C1
Old Hall St....A1
Old Leeds St....A2
Oldham Place....C4
Oldham St....C4
Olive St....C5
Open Eye Gallery....C2
Oriel St....A2
Ormond St....B2
Orphan St....C6

Overbury St....C6
Overton St....B6
Oxford St....C5
Paisley St....A1
Pall Mall....A2
Paradise St....C3
Park La....C3
Parker St....B3
Parr St....C3
Peach St....B5
Pembroke Place....B4
Pembroke St....B5
Philharmonic Hall....C4
Phythian Park....A6
Pickop St....A2
Pilgrim St....C4
Pitt St....C3
Playhouse Theatre....B3
Pleasant St....B4
Police HQ....B2
Police Sta....A4/A6/B4
Pomona St....B4
Port of Liverpool
  Building....B2
Post Office....B2/B3/B4/C4
Pownall St....C2
Prescot St....A5
Preston St....B3
Princes Dock....A1
Princes Gdns....A2
Princes Jetty....A1
Princes Pde....A1
Princes St....B2
Pythian St....A6
Queen Square Bus Sta....B3
Queensland St....C6
Queensway Tunnel
  (Docks exit)....B1
Queensway Tunnel
  (Entrance)....B3
Radio City....B2
Ranelagh St....B3
Redcross St....B2
Renfrew St....B6
Renshaw St....B4
Richmond Row....A4
Richmond St....B3
Rigby St....A2
Roberts St....A1
Rock St....B4
Rodney St....C4
Rokeby St....A4
Romily St....A4
Roscoe La....C4
Roscoe St....C4
Rose Hill....A3
Royal Albert Dock....C2
Royal Court
  Theatre....B3
Royal Liver
  Building....B1
Royal Liverpool
  Hospital (A&E)....B5
Royal Mail St....B4
Rumford Place....B2
Rumford St....B2
Russell St....B4
St Andrew St....B4
St Anne St....A4
St Georges Hall....B3
St John's Centre....B3
St John's Gdns....B3
St John's La....B3
St Joseph's Cr....A4
St Minishull St....B5
St Nicholas Place....A1
St Paul's Sq....A2
Salisbury St....A4
Salthouse Dock....C2
Salthouse Quay....C2
Sandon St....C5
Saxony Rd....B6
Schomberg St....A6
School La....B3
Seel St....C3
Seymour St....B4
Shaw St....A5
Shopmobility....C2
Sidney Place....C6
Sir Thomas St....B3
Skelhorne St....B4
Slater St....C3
Smithdown La....B6
Soho Sq....A4
Soho St....A4
South John St....B2
Springfield....A4
Stafford St....A4
Standish St....A3
Stanley St....B2
Strand St....C2
Strand, The....B2
Suffolk St....C3
Sydney Jones Liby....C5
Tabley St....C3
Tarleton St....B3
Tate Liverpool
  Gallery....C2
Teck St....B6
Temple St....B2
Titanic Memorial....B1
Tithebarn St....B2
Town Hall....B2
Trowbridge St....B4
Trueman St....A3
Union St....B2
Unity Theatre....C4
University....C5
University of
  Liverpool....C5
Upper Baker St....A6
Upper Duke St....C4
Upper Frederick St....C3
Vauxhall Rd....A2
Vernon St....B2
Victoria Gallery &
  Museum....B5
Victoria St....B2
Vine St....C5
Wakefield St....A4

Walker Art Gallery ⌂ . . .A3
Walker St A6
Wapping C2
Water St B1/B2
Waterloo Rd A1
Wavertree Rd B6
West Derby Rd A6
West Derby St B5
Western Approaches
  War Museum ⌂ B2
Whitechapel B3
Whitley Gdns A5
William Brown St B3
William Henry St A4
Williamson St B3
Williamson's Tunnels
  Heritage Centre ✦ . . .C6
Women's Hospital H . . .B3
Wood St B3
World Museum,
  Liverpool ⌂ A3
York St C3

Llandudno 342
Abbey Pl B1
Abbey Rd B1
Adelphi St C2
Alexandra Rd C2
Anglesey Rd A1
Argyll Rd C2
Arvon Ave C2
Atlee Cl C3
Augusta St C2
Back Madoc St B2
Bodafon St B2
Bodhyfryd Rd A2
Bodnant Cr C3
Bodnant Rd C3
Bridge Rd C2
Bryniau St B2
Builder St B3
Builder St West B3
Cabin Lift Cable Car ✦ .B2
Camera Obscura ✦ A3
Caroline Rd B2
Chapel St B2
Charlton St B3
Church Cr C1
Church Walks B2
Claremont Rd B1/B2
Clement Ave C2
Clifton Rd B2
Clonmel St B3
Coach Station B3
Conway Rd B3
Conwy Archive
  Service B2
Council St West C3
Cricket and Rec Gd A2
Cwlach Rd A2
Cwlach St A1
Cwm Pl C3
Cwm Rd C3
Dale Rd C2
Deganwy Ave C2
Denness Pl C2
Dinas Rd C2
Dolydd B1
Erol Pl C3
Ewloe Dr C3
Fairways C3
Fordd Dewi C3
Fordd Dulyn C2
Fordd Dwyfor C3
Fordd Elisabeth C3
Fordd Gwynedd C3
Fordd Las C3
Fordd Morfa C3
Fordd Penrhyn C3
Fordd Tudno C3
Fordd yr Orsedd C2
Fordd Ysbyty C3
Fire & Ambulance Sta .B3
Garage St A2
George St B2
Gloddaeth Ave B2
Gloddaeth St B1
Gogarth Rd B1
Great Orme Mines ✦ . .A1
Great Orme
  Tramway ✦ A2
Happy Valley A2
Happy Valley Rd A2
Haulfre Gardens ❀ A1
Herkomer Cr C1
Hill Terr A2
Home Front Mus ⌂ B1
Hospice B1
Howard Rd B3
Information Ctr i B1
Invalids' Walk B1
James St B3
Jubilee St B3
King's Ave C2
King's Rd C2
Knowles Rd C2
Lees Rd C2
Library B2
Llandudno ⌂ B2
Llandudno (A&E) H C2
Llandudno Station ≷ . . .B3
Llandudno Football
  Ground A2
Llewelyn Ave A2
Lloyd St B2
Lloyd St West B1
Llwynon Rd A1
Llys Maelgwn C1
Madoc St B2
Maelgwn Rd C2
Maes-y-Cwm C3
Maes-y-Orsedd C3
Maesdu Bridge C2
Maesdu Rd C2/C3
Marian Pl C2
Marian Rd C2
Marine Drive (Toll) A3

Market St A2
Miniature Golf Course .A1
Morfa Rd B1
Mostyn B3
Mostyn Broadway B3
Mostyn St B2
Mowbray Rd C2
New St B2
Norman St B3
North Parade A2
North Wales
  Golf Links C1
Old Bank, The ⌂ B3
Old Rd A2
Oval, The B1
Oxford Rd B3
Parade, The B3
Parc Llandudno
  Retail Park B3
Pier ✦ A3
Plas Rd A2
Police Station ◼ B3
Post Office ◼ A2/B3
Promenade A2
Pyllau Rd A1
Rectory La A2
Rhuddlan Ave C3
St Andrew's Ave B1
St Andrew's Pl B2
St Beuno's Rd A1
St David's Pl B2
St David's Rd B2
St George's Pl A3
St Mary's Rd B2
St Seriol's Rd B2
Salisbury Pass B3
Salisbury Rd B2
Somerset St B2
South Parade A2
Stephen St B2
Tabor Hill A2
Town Hall B2
Trinity Ave B1
Trinity Cres C1
Trinity Sq B2
Tudno St A2
Ty-Coch Rd B3
Ty-Gwyn Rd A1/A2
Ty'n-y-Coed Rd A1
Vaughan St B3
Victoria Shopping Ctr .B3
Victoria ◼ A2
War Memorial ✦ A2
Werny Wylan C3
West Parade B1
Whiston Pass A2
Winllan Ave C2
Wyddfyd Rd A2
York Rd A2

Llanelli 342
Alban Rd A3
Albert St B1
Als St A1
Amos St C1
Andrew St A3
Ann St B2
Annesley St B2
Arfryn Ave A2
Avenue Cilfig, The A2
Belvedere Rd A1
Bigyn Park Terr C3
Bigyn Rd C2
Bond Ave C2
Brettenham St A1
Bridge St B2
Bryn Pl C1
Bryn Rd C1
Bryn Terr C1
Bryn-More Rd C1
Brynhyfryd Rd A2
Brynmelyn Ave A3
Brynmor Rd B1
Burry St A2
Bus Station B2
Caersalem Terr C1
Cambrian St B1
Caswell St C3
Cedric St B3
Cemetery A1
Chapman St A2
Charles Terr C1
Church St B2
Clos Caer Elms A1
Clos Sant Paul C2
Coastal Link Rd B1/C1
Coldstream St B2
Coleshill Terr B1
College Hill B2
College Sq B3
Copperworks Rd C2
Coronation Rd C3
Corporation Ave A3
Council Offices B2
Court B2
Cowell St B2
Cradock St C2
Craig Ave C3
Cricket Ground A1
Derwent St B2
Dillwyn St C2
Druce St C2
Eastgate Leisure
  Complex ✦ B2
Elizabeth St B2
Emma St B1
Erw Rd B1
Felinfoel Rd A2
Fire Station A3
Firth Rd B1
Fron Terr C1
Furnace United Rugby
  Football Ground B1
Gelli-On B2
George St A2
Gilbert Cres A2
Gilbert Rd A2
Glanmor Rd C2
Glanmor Terr A3
Glasfryn Terr A1

Glenalla Rd B3
Glevering St B3
Goring Rd A2
Gorsedd Circle ⌂ A2
Grant St B1
Graveyard B1
Great Western Cl C2
Greenway St B1
Hall St B2
Harries Ave A2
Hedley Terr B1
Heol Elli B3
Heol Goffa A3
Heol Nant-y-Felin A3
Heol Siloh B2
Hick St C1
High St C1
Indoor Bowls Centre . . .B1
Inkerman St B2
Island Pl B2
James St B2
John St B2
King George Ave B3
Lake View Cl A1
Lakefield Pl C1
Lakefield Rd C1
Langland St C3
Leisure Centre B2
Library B2
Llanelli House ⌂ C2
Llanelli Parish
  Church B2
Llanelli Station ≷ C2
Llewellyn St A3
Lliedi Cres A3
Lloyd St B2
Llys Alys A3
Llys Fran A3
Llysnewedd C1
Long Row A3
Maes Gors C2
Maesyrhaf A3
Mansel St B2
Marble Hall Rd B3
Margam St C2
Marged St C2
Marine St C2
Mariners, The C1
Market B2
Market St B2
Marsh St C2
Martin Rd C3
Miles St A1
Mill La A3/B2
Mincing La C2
Murray St B2
Myn y Mor B1
Nathan St C1
Nelson Terr C2
Nevill St C2
New Dock Rd C2
New Rd A1
New Zealand St A1
Odeon ⌂ B2
Old Lodge C2
Old Rd A2
Paddock St C2
Palace Ave B3
Parc Howard A2
Parc Howard Museum &
  Art Gallery ⌂ A2
Park Cres B1
Park St B2
Parkview Terr B1
Pemberton St C3
Pembrey Rd A1
Peoples Park B1
Police Station ◼ B2
Post Office ◼ B2/C2
Pottery Pl B3
Pottery St B3
Princess St B2
Prospect Pl A2
Pryce St A1
Queen Mary's Walk C3
Queen Victoria Rd C1
Raby St B1
Railway Terr C2
Ralph St B2
Ralph Terr C1
Regalia Terr B1
Rhydyrafon A3
Richard St B2
Robinson St B2
Roland Ave B1
Russell St C3
St David's Cl C1
St Elli Shopping Ctr B2
St Margaret's Dr A1
Spowart Ave A1
Station Rd B2/C2
Stepney Pl B2
Stepney St B2
Stewart St A1
Stradey Park Ave A1
Sunny Hill A2
Superstore A2
Swansea Rd A3
Talbot St C2
Temple St B3
Thomas St A2
Tinopolis
  TV Studios ✦ B2
Toft Pl A3
Town Hall B2
Traeth Ffordd C1
Trinity Rd C3
Trinity Terr C1
Tunnel Rd B1
Tyisha Rd B1
Union Blgs B2
Upper Robinson St B2
Vauxhall Rd B2
Walter's Rd B3
Waun Lanyrafon B2
Waun Rd A2
Wern Rd B2
West End C1
Y Bwthyn A1
Zion Row B2

London 340
Abbey Orchard St E4
Abbey St E8
Abchurch La D7
Abingdon St E5
Achilles Way D3
Acton St B5
Addington St E5
Addle St C7
Air St D4
Albany St A3
Albemarle St D4
Albert Embankment . . .F5
Alberta St F6
Aldenham St A4
Alderney St F3
Aldersgate St C7
Aldford St D3
Aldgate ◉ C8
Aldgate High St C8
Aldwych C5
Allsop Pl B2
Alscot Rd E8
Amwell St B6
Angel ◉ A6
Appold St C8
Argyle Sq B5
Argyle St B5
Argyll St C4
Arnold Circus B8
Artillery La C8
Artillery Row E4
Ashbridge St B2
Association of
  Photographers
  Gallery B7
Baker St ◉ B2
Baker St B2
Balaclava Rd F8
Balcombe St B2
Baldwin's Gdns C6
Balfour St F7
Baltic St B7
Bank ◉ C7
Bank Museum ⌂ C7
Bank of England ⌂ C7
Bankside D7
Bankside Gallery ⌂ D6
Banner St B7
Barbican ◉ C7
Barbican Centre
  for Arts, The C7
Barbican Gallery ⌂ C7
Basil St E2
Bastwick St B7
Bateman's Row B8
Bath St B7
Bath Terr E7
Bayley St C4
Baylis Rd E6
Bayswater Rd D2
Beak St D4
Beauchamp Pl E2
Bedford Row C5
Bedford Sq C4
Bedford St D5
Bedford Way B4
Beech St C7
Belgrave Pl E3
Belgrave Rd F4
Belgrave Sq E3
Bell La C8
Belvedere Rd E5
Berkeley Sq D3
Berkeley St D3
Bermondsey St E8
Bernard St B5
Berners Pl C4
Berners St C4
Berwick St C4
Bessborough St F4
Bethnal Green Rd B8
Bevenden St B7
Bevis Marks C8
BFI (British Film
  Institute) ⌂ D5
BFI London IMAX
  Cinema ⌂ D6
Bidborough St B5
Binney St C3
Birdcage Walk E4
Bishopsgate C8
Black Prince Rd F5
Blackfriars ◉ D6
Blackfriars Bridge D6
Blackfriars Rd D6
Blackfriars Passage D6
Blandford St C3
Blomfield St C7
Bloomsbury St C4
Bloomsbury Way C5
Bolton St D3
Bond St ◉ C3
Borough ◉ E7
Borough High St E7
Borough Rd E6
Boswell St C5
Bourne St F3
Bow St C5
Bowling Green La B6
Brad St D6
Brandon St F7
Bressenden Pl E4
Brewer St D4
Brick St D3
Bridge St E5
Britannia Walk B7
British Film Institute
  (BFI) ⌂ D5
British Library ⌂ B4
British Museum ⌂ C5
Britton St B6
Broad Sanctuary E4
Broadley St B2
Broadway E4
Brompton Rd E2
Brompton Sq E2
Brook Dr F6
Brook St C3
Brown St C2
Brunswick Pl B7

Brunswick Shopping
  Centre, The B5
Brunswick Sq B5
Brushfield St C8
Bruton St D3
Bryanston St C2
BT Centre C7
Buckingham Gate E4
Buckingham Palace ⌂ .E4
Buckingham Palace Rd F3
Bunhill Row B7
Byward St D8
Cabinet War Rooms &
  Churchill Museum ⌂ .E4
Cadogan La E3
Cadogan Pl E3
Cadogan Sq F2
Cadogan St F2
Cale St F2
Caledonian Rd A5
Calshot St A5
Calthorpe St B6
Calvert Ave B8
Cambridge Circus C4
Cambridge Sq C2
Cambridge St F3
Camomile St C8
Cannon St D7
Cannon St ◉ D7
Capland St B2
Carey St C6
Carlisle La E5
Carlisle Pl E4
Carlton House Terr D4
Carmelite St D6
Carnaby St C4
Carter La C6
Carthusian St C7
Cartwright Gdns B5
Castle Baynard St D6
Cavendish Pl C3
Cavendish Sq C3
Caxton Hall E4
Caxton St E4
Central St B7
Chalton St A4
Chancery Lane ◉ C6
Chapel St E3
Chapel St B2
Charing Cross ◉ D5
Charing Cross Rd C4
Charles II St D4
Charles Dickens
  Museum, The ⌂ B5
Charles St D3
Charles St D3
Charlotte Rd B8
Charlotte St C4
Chart St B7
Charterhouse Sq C6
Charterhouse St C6
Chatham St F7
Cheapside C7
Chenies St C4
Chesham St E3
Chester Sq F3
Chester Way F6
Chesterfield Hill D3
Cheval Pl E2
Chiltern St C3
Chiswell St C7
Church St B2
City Garden Row A6
City Rd B7
City Thameslink ≷ C6
City University, The B6
Claremont Sq A6
Clarendon St F3
Clarges St D3
Clerkenwell Cl B6
Clerkenwell Green B6
Clerkenwell Rd C6
Cleveland St C4
Clifford St D4
Clink Prison Mus ⌂ D7
Cliveden Pl F3
Clock Museum ⌂ C7
Club Row B8
Cockspur St D4
Coleman St C7
Columbia Rd B8
Commercial Rd C9
Commercial St B8
Compton St B6
Conduit St D4
Congreve St F8
Connaught Sq C2
Connaught St C2
Constitution Hill E3
Copperfield St E6
Coptic St C5
Cornhill C7
Cornwall Rd D6
Coronet St B8
County St E7
Courtauld Gallery ⌂ D5
Courtenay St F6
Covent Garden ◉ D5
Covent Garden ✦ D5
Cowcross St C6
Cowper St B7
Crampton St F6
Cranbourn St D4
Craven St D5
Crawford Pl C2
Crawford St C2
Creechurch La C8
Cricket Museum ⌂ B1
Cromer St B5
Cromwell Rd F1
Crosby Row E7
Crucifix La E8
Cumberland Gate D2
Cumberland Mkt A3
Cumberland Terr A3
Cuming Mus ⌂ F7
Curtain Rd B8
Curzon St D3
Cut, The E6
D'arblay St C4
Dante Rd F6

Davies St C3
Dean St C4
Deluxe Gallery ⌂ B8
Denbigh St F4
Denmark St C4
Dering St C3
Devonshire St C3
Diana, Princess of Wales
  Memorial Garden ✦ .D1
Diana, Princess of Wales
  Memorial Walk E4
Dingley Rd B7
Dorset St C3
Doughty St B5
Douglas St F4
Dover St D3
Downing St E5
Draycott Ave F2
Draycott Pl F2
Druid St E8
Drummond St B4
Drury La C5
Drysdale St B8
Duchess St C3
Dufferin St B7
Duke of Wellington
  Place E3
Duke St C3/D3
Duke St Hill D7
Duke's Pl C8
Duncannon St D5
Dunton Rd F8
East Rd B7
East St F7
Eastcastle St C4
Eastcheap D8
Eaton Gate F3
Eaton Pl E3
Eaton Sq E3
Eaton Terr F3
Ebury Bridge F3
Ebury Bridge Rd F3
Eccleston Bridge F3
Eccleston Pl F3
Eccleston St E3
Edgware Rd C2
Edgware Rd ◉ C2
Egerton Gdns E2
Eldon St C7
Elephant & Castle ◉ . . .F7
Elephant and
  Castle ≷ ◉ E6
Elephant Rd F7
Elizabeth Bridge F3
Elizabeth St F3
Elm Tree Rd B1
Elystan Pl F2
Elystan St F2
Embankment ◉ D5
Endell St C5
Endsleigh Pl B4
Enid St E8
Ennismore Gdns E2
Erasmus St F4
Euston ≷ ◉ B4
Euston Rd B4
Euston Square ◉ B4
Evelina Children's
  Hospital E5
Eversholt St A4
Exhibition Rd E1
Exmouth Market B6
Fair St E8
Falmouth Rd E7
Fann St B7
Farringdon ≷ ◉ C6
Farringdon Rd C6
Farringdon St C6
Featherstone St B7
Fenchurch St D8
Fenchurch St ≷ D8
Fetter La C6
Finsbury Circus C7
Finsbury Pavement C7
Finsbury Sq B7
Fitzalan St F6
Fitzmaurice Pl D3
Fleet St C6
Fleming Lab. Mus ⌂ . . .C1
Floral St C5
Florence Nightingale
  Museum ⌂ E5
Folgate St C8
Fore St C7
Foster La C7
Foundling Mus, The ⌂ .B5
Francis St F4
Frazier St E6
Freemason's Hall C5
Friday St C7
Fulham Rd F1
Gainsford St E8
Garden Row E6
Gee St B7
Geological Mus ⌂ E1
George Row E9
George St C2
Gerrard St D4
Gibson Rd F5
Giltspur St C6
Glasshouse St D4
Glasshouse Walk F5
Gloucester Pl C2
Gloucester Sq C1
Gloucester St F4
Godliman St C6
Golden Hinde ⚓ D7
Golden La B7
Golden Sq D4
Goodge St ◉ C4
Goodge St C4
Gordon Hospital H F4
Gordon Sq B4
Goswell Rd B6
Gough St B6
Goulston St C8
Gower St B4
Gracechurch St D7
Grafton Way B4
Graham Terr F3

Grange Rd E8
Grange Walk E8
Gray's Inn Rd B5
Great College St E4
Great Cumberland Pl . . .C2
Great Dover St E7
Great Eastern St B8
Great Guildford St D7
Great Marlborough St .C4
Great Ormond Street
  Children's Hospital H .B5
Great Percy St B6
Great Peter St E4
Great Portland St ◉ C4
Great Portland St C3
Great Queen St C5
Great Russell St C4
Great Scotland Yd D5
Great Smith St E4
Great Suffolk St D6/E6
Great Titchfield St C4
Great Tower St D8
Great Windmill St D4
Greek St C4
Green Park ◉ D3
Green St D3
Greencoat Pl F4
Gresham St C7
Greville St C6
Greycoat Hosp Sch. . . .E4
Greycoat St E4
Grosvenor Cres E3
Grosvenor Gdns E3
Grosvenor Pl E3
Grosvenor Sq D3
Grosvenor St D3
Grove End Rd B1
Guards Museum
  and Chapel ⌂ E4
Guildhall Art
  Gallery ⌂ C7
Guilford St B5
Guy's Hospital H D7
Haberdasher St B7
Hackney Rd B8
Half Moon St D3
Halkin St E3
Hall Pl B1
Hall St B6
Hallam St C3
Hamilton Pl D3
Hampstead Rd B4
Hanover Sq C3
Hans Cres E2
Hans Rd E2
Hanway St C4
Hardwick St B6
Harewood Ave B2
Harper Rd E7
Harrington Rd F1
Harrison St B5
Harrowby St C2
Hasker St F2
Hastings St B5
Hatfields D6
Hay's Galleria D8
Hay's Mews D3
Hayles St F6
Haymarket D4
Hayward Gallery ⌂ D5
Helmet Row B7
Herbrand St B5
Hercules Rd E5
Hertford St D3
Heygate St F7
High Holborn C5
Hill St D3
HMS Belfast ⚓ D8
Hobart Pl E3
Holborn ◉ C5
Holborn C6
Holborn Viaduct C6
Holland St D6
Holmes Mus ⌂ B2
Holywell La B8
Horse Guards' Rd D4
Horseferry Rd F4
Houndsditch C8
Houses of
  Parliament ⌂ E5
Howland St C4
Hoxton Sq B8
Hoxton St B8
Hugh St F3
Hunter St B5
Hunterian Mus ⌂ C5
Hyde Park D2
Hyde Park Corner ◉ E3
Hyde Park Cres C2
Hyde Park St C2
Imperial Coll London . .E1
Imperial College Rd . . .E1
Imperial War Mus ⌂ . .E6
Inner Circle B3
Institute of Archaeology
  (London Univ) B3
Ironmonger Row B7
Jacob St E9
Jamaica Rd E8
James St C3
James St D5
Jermyn St D4
Jockey's Fields C5
John Carpenter St D6
John Fisher St D9
John Islip St F4
John St B5
Johnathan St F5
Judd St B5
Kennings Way F6
Kennington ◉ F6
Kennington La F5
Kennington Park Rd F6
Kensington Gardens D1
Kensington Gore E1
Kensington Rd E1
Keyworth St E6
King Charles St E5

King St D5
King William St C7
King's College
  London D5
King's Cross ◉ A5
King's Cross Rd B5
King's Cross
  St Pancras ◉ A5
King's Rd F2
Kingley St C4
Kingsland Rd B8
Kingsway C5
Kinnerton St E3
Kipling St E7
Knightsbridge ◉ E2
Lamb St C8
Lamb's Conduit St C5
Lambeth Bridge F5
Lambeth High St F5
Lambeth North ◉ E6
Lambeth Palace ⌂ E5
Lambeth Palace Rd E5
Lambeth Rd E6
Lambeth Walk F5
Lancaster Gate ◉ D1
Lancaster Pl D5
Lancaster Terr D1
Langham Pl C3
Lant St E7
Leadenhall St C8
Leake St E5
Leather La C6
Leathermarket St E8
Leicester Sq ◉ D4
Leicester Sq D4
Leonard St B7
Leroy St E8
Lever St B7
Lexington St D4
Lidlington Pl A4
Lime St D8
Lincoln's Inn Fields C5
Lindsey St C6
Lisle St D4
Lisson Gr B1
Lisson St B2
Liverpool St C8
Liverpool St ≷ ◉ C8
Lloyd Baker St B6
Lloyd Sq B6
Lodge Rd B2
Lollard St F6
Lombard St C7
London Aquarium ✦ E5
London Bridge ◉ D7
London Bridge
  Hospital H D7
London City Hall ⌂ D8
London Dungeon ✦ E5
London Guildhall
  University C8
London Rd E6
London Transport
  Museum ⌂ D5
London Wall C7
London Eye ✦ E5
Long Acre D5
Long La C6
Long La E7
Longford St B3
Lord's Cricket Gd
  (MCC & Middlesex CCC) .B1
Lower Belgrave St E3
Lower Grosvenor Pl E3
Lower Marsh E5
Lower Sloane St F3
Lower Thames St D7
Lowndes St E3
Ludgate Circus C6
Ludgate Hill C6
Lupus St F4
Luxborough St C3
Lyall St E3
Macclesfield Rd B7
Maddox St D3
Madame Tussaud's ✦ . .B3
Maltby St E8
Mall, The E4
Manchester Sq C3
Manchester St C3
Manciple St E7
Mandela Way F8
Mandeville Pl C3
Mansell St D8
Mansion House ◉ D7
Mansion House ⌂ D7
Maple St C4
Marble Arch ◉ C2
Marble Arch C2
Marchmont St B5
Margaret St C4
Margery St B6
Mark La D8
Marlborough Rd D4
Marshall St C4
Marshalsea Rd E7
Marsham St E4
Marylebone ≷ ◉ B2
Marylebone High St . . .C3
Marylebone La C3
Marylebone Rd B3/C2
Marylebone St C3
Mecklenburgh Sq B5
Middle Temple La D6
Middlesex St
  (Petticoat La) C8
Midland Rd A4
Migration Mus ⌂ F7
Millbank F5
Minories D8
Monck St E4
Monkton St F6
Monmouth St C5
Montagu Pl C2
Montagu Sq C2
Montagu St C2
Montague Pl C4

Montpelier St E2
Montpelier Walk E2
Monument ◉ D7
Monument St D7
Monument, The ✦ D7
Moor La C7
Moorfields C7
Moorfields
  Eye Hospital H B7
Moorgate ◉ C7
Moorgate C7
Moreland St B6
Morley St E6
Mortimer St C4
Mossop St F2
Mount Pleasant B6
Mount St D3
Murray Gr A7
Mus of Gdn History ⌂ .E5
Museum of London ⌂ .C7
Museum St C5
Myddelton Sq B6
Myddelton St B6
National Gallery ⌂ D4
National Hospital H . . .B5
National Portrait
  Gallery ⌂ D4
Natural History
  Museum ⌂ E1
Neal St C5
Nelson's Column ✦ . . .D5
Neville St F1
New Bond St C3/D3
New Bridge St C6
New Cavendish St C3
New Change C7
New Fetter La C6
New Inn Yard B8
New Kent Rd F7
New North Rd A7
New Oxford St C4
New Scotland Yard E4
New Sq C5
Newburn St F5
Newgate St C6
Newington Butts F6
Newington Causeway . .E7
Newton St C5
Nile St B7
Noble St C7
Noel St C4
Norfolk Cres C2
Norfolk Sq C1
North Audley St D3
North Carriage Dr D2
North Cres C4
North Ride D2
North Row D3
North Wharf Rd C1
Northampton Sq B6
Northington St B5
Northumberland Ave . . .D5
Norton Folgate C8
Nottingham Pl C3
Old Bailey C6
Old Broad St C7
Old Brompton Rd F1
Old Compton St C4
Old County Hall E5
Old Gloucester St C5
Old Jamaica Rd E9
Old Kent Rd F8
Old King Edward St . . .C7
Old Marylebone Rd . . .C2
Old Montague St C9
Old Nichol St B8
Old Paradise St F5
Old Spitalfields Mkt. . .C8
Old St B7
Old St ◉ B7
Old Vic ✦ E6
Onslow Gdns F1
Onslow Sq F1
Ontario St E6
Open Air Theatre ✦ . . .B3
Operating Theatre
  Museum ⌂ D7
Orange St D4
Orchard St C3
Ossulston St A4
Outer Circle B2
Ovington Sq E2
Oxford Circus ◉ C4
Oxford St C3/C4
Paddington ≷ ◉ C1
Paddington St C3
Page's Walk E8
Palace St E4
Pall Mall D4
Pall Mall East D4
Pancras Rd A5
Panton St D4
Paris Gdn D6
Park Cres B3
Park La D2
Park Rd B2
Park St D3
Park St D7
Parker St C5
Parliament Sq E5
Parliament St E5
Paternoster Sq C6
Paul St B7
Pear Tree St B6
Pelham Cres F2
Pelham St F1
Penfold St B2
Penton Pl F6
Penton Rise B5
Penton St A6
Pentonville Rd A5/B6
Percival St B6
Petticoat La
  (Middlesex St) C8
Petty France E4
Phoenix Pl B5
Phoenix Rd A4
Photo Gallery ⌂ D4
Piccadilly D3
Piccadilly Circus ◉ D4
Pilgrimage St E7

Pimlico ⊖ F4
Pimlico Rd F3
Pitfield St B8
Pollock's Toy Mus . . .C4
Polygon Rd A4
Pont St E2
Porchester Pl C2
Portland Pl C3
Portman Mews C3
Portman St C2
Portugal St C5
Postal Mus, The 🏛 . . .B5
Poultry C7
Praed St C1
Primrose St C8
Prince Consort Rd . . .E1
Prince's Gdns E1
Princes St C7
Procter St C5
Provost St B7
Quaker St B8
Queen Anne St C3
Queen Elizabeth
  Hall 🎵 D5
Queen Elizabeth St . .E8
Queen Sq B5
Queen St D7
Queen Street Pl D7
Queen Victoria St . . .D6
Queens Gallery 🏛 E4
Queensberry Pl F1
Quilter St B9
Radnor St B7
Rathbone Pl C4
Rawlings St F2
Rawstorne St B6
Red Lion Sq C5
Red Lion St C5
Redchurch St B8
Redcross Way D7
Reedworth St F6
Regency St F4
Regent Sq B5
Regent St C4
Regent's Park B3
Richmond Terr E5
Ridgmount St C4
Riley Rd E8
Rivington St B8
Robert St C4
Rochester Row F4
Rockingham St E7
Rodney Rd F7
Rolls Rd F8
Ropemaker St C7
Rosebery Ave B6
Rossmore Rd B2
Rothsay St E8
Rotten Row E2
Roupell St D6
Royal Acad of Arts 🏛 . D4
Royal Academy of
  Dramatic Art B4
Royal Acad of Music . .B3
Royal Albert Hall 🎵 . .E1
Royal Artillery
  Memorial ✦ E2
Royal Brompton
  Hosp Ⓗ F1/F2
Royal College of
  Nursing C3
Royal College of
  Surgeons C5
Royal Festival Hall 🎵 .D5
Royal London Hospital
  for Integrated
  Medicine Ⓗ C5
Royal Marsden Hosp Ⓗ F1
Royal National
  Theatre 🎭 D6
Royal National Throat,
  Nose and Ear Hosp Ⓗ B5
Royal Opera House 🎵 .D5
Rushworth St E6
Russell Sq B4
Russell Square ⊖ B5
Rutland Gate E2
Saatchi Gall 🏛 F2
Sackville St D4
Sadlers Wells 🎭 B6
Saffron Hill C6
St Alban's St D4
St Andrew St C6
St Barnabas St F3
St Bartholomew's
  Hospital Ⓗ C6
St Botolph St C8
St Bride St C6
St George's Circus . . .E6
St George's Dr F4
St George's Rd E6
St Giles High St C4
St James's Palace 🏛 . .D4
St James's Park ⊖ E4
St James's St D4
St John St B6
St John's Wood Rd . . .B1
St Margaret St E5
St Mark's Hosp Ⓗ B6
St Martin's La D5
St Martin's Le Grand . .C7
St Mary Axe C8
St Mary's Hosp Ⓗ C1
St Pancras Int ≥ A5
St Paul's ⊖ C7
St Paul's Cath † C7
St Paul's Churchyard . .C6
St Thomas St E7
St Thomas' Hosp Ⓗ . . .E5
Sale Pl C1
Sancroft St F5
Savile Row D4
Savoy Pl D5
Savoy St D5
School of Hygiene &
  Tropical Medicine . .C4
Science Mus 🏛 E1
Scrutton St B8
Sekforde St B6

Serpentine Gallery .E1
Serpentine Rd D2
Seven Dials C5
Seward St B6
Seymour Pl C2
Seymour St C2
Shad Thames D8/E8
Shaftesbury Ave D4
Shakespeare's Globe
  Theatre 🎭 D7
Shepherd Market D3
Sherwood St D4
Shoe La C6
Shoreditch High St . . .B8
Shoreditch High St ≥ .B8
Shorts Gdns C5
Shouldham St C2
Shrek's Adventure ✦ .E5
Sidmouth St B5
Silk St C7
Sir John Soane's
  Museum 🏛 C5
Skinner St B6
Sloane Ave F2
Sloane Sq F2
Sloane Square ⊖ F2
Sloane St E2
Snow Hill C6
Soho Sq C4
Somerset House 🏛 . . .D5
South Audley St D3
South Carriage Dr E2
South Eaton Pl F3
South Kensington ⊖ . .F1
South Molton St C3
South Parade F1
South Pl C7
South St D3
South Terr F1
South Wharf Rd C1
Southampton Row . . .C5
Southampton St D5
Southwark ⊖ D6
Southwark Bridge D7
Southwark Bridge Rd .D7
Southwark Cath † D7
Southwark Park Rd . . .D7
Southwark St D7
Spa Rd E8
Speakers' Corner D2
Spencer St B6
Spital Sq C8
Spring St C1
Stamford St D6
Stanhope Pl B4
Stanhope Terr D1
Stephenson Way B4
Stock Exchange C6
Stoney St D7
Stratford Pl D2
Stratton St D3
Sumner St D6
Sussex Gdns C1
Sussex Pl C1
Sussex Sq D1
Sussex St F3
Sutton's Way B7
Swan St E7
Swanfield St B8
Swinton St B5
Sydney Pl F1
Sydney St F2
Tabard St E7
Tabernacle St B7
Tachbrook St F4
Tanner St E8
Tate Britain 🏛 F5
Tate Modern 🏛 D7
Tavistock Pl B5
Tavistock Sq B4
Tea & Coffee Mus 🏛 . .D7
Temple ⊖ D6
Temple Ave D6
Temple Pl D5
Terminus Pl E3
Thayer St C3
Theobald's Rd C5
Thorney St F5
Threadneedle St C7
Throgmorton St C7
Thurloe Pl F1
Thurloe Sq F2
Tonbridge St B5
Tooley St D8
Torrington Pl B4
Tothill St E4
Tottenham Court Rd . .B4
Tottenham Ct Rd ⊖ . . .C4
Tottenham St C4
Tower Bridge ✦ D8
Tower Bridge App. D8
Tower Bridge Rd E8
Tower Hill ⊖ D8
Tower Hill D8
Tower of London,
  The 🏰 D8
Toynbee St C8
Trafalgar Square D4
Trinity Sq D8
Trinity St E7
Trocadero Centre D4
Tudor St D6
Turin St B8
Turnmill St C6
Tyers St F5
Ufford St E6
Union St D6
University Coll
  Hospital Ⓗ B4
University of London . .C4
Univ of Westminster . .C3
Upper Belgrave St E3
Upper Berkeley St C2
Upper Brook St D3
Upper Grosvenor St . .D3
Upper Ground D6
Upper Montague St . . .C2
Upper St Martin's La . .D5
Upper Thames St D7

Upper Wimpole St C3
Upper Woburn Pl B4
Vauxhall Bridge Rd. . .F4
Vauxhall St F5
Vere St C3
Vernon Pl C5
Vestry St B7
Victoria ⊖ F3
Victoria and Albert
  Museum 🏛 E1
Victoria Coach Station F3
Victoria Embankment . .D5
Victoria Place
  Shopping Centre F3
Victoria St E4
Villiers St D5
Vincent Sq F4
Vinopolis City of
  Wine D7
Virginia Rd B8
Wakley St B6
Walbrook C7
Walcot Sq F6
Wallace Collection . . .C3
Walnut Tree Walk F6
Walton St F2
Walworth Rd F7
Wardour St C4/D4
Warner St B6
Warren St ⊖ B4
Warren St B4
Warwick Sq F4
Warwick Way F3
Waterloo ⊖ E6
Waterloo Bridge D5
Waterloo East ≥ D6
Waterloo Rd E6
Watling St C7
Webber St E6
Welbeck St C3
Wellington Arch ✦ . . .E3
Wellington Mus 🏛 E3
Wellington Rd B2
Wellington Row B9
Wells St C4
Wenlock St A7
Wentworth St C8
West Carriage Dr D2
West Smithfield C6
West Sq F6
Westbourne St D1
Westbourne Terr C1
Westminster ⊖ E5
Westminster Abbey † .E5
Westminster Bridge . .E5
Westminster Bridge
  Rd E6
Westminster
  Cathedral (RC) † E4
Westminster City Hall . E4
Westminster Hall 🏛 . . .E5
Weymouth St C3
Wharf Rd A7
Wharton St B5
Whitcomb St D4
White Cube 🏛 B8
White Lion Hill D7
White Lion St A6
Whitechapel Rd C9
Whitecross St B7
Whitefriars St D6
Whitehall D5
Whitehall Pl D5
Wigmore Hall C3
Wigmore St C3
William IV St D5
Willow Walk E8
Wilmington Sq B6
Wilson St C7
Wilton Cres E3
Wilton Rd F4
Wimpole St C3
Winchester St F3
Wincott St F6
Windmill Walk D6
Woburn Pl B5
Woburn Sq B4
Wood St C7
Woodbridge St B6
Wootton St D6
Wormwood St C8
Worship St B7
Wren St B5
Wynyatt St B6
York Rd E5
York St C2
York Terrace East B3
York Terrace West B3
York Way A5

Luton 342

Adelaide St C1
Albert Rd C2
Alma St B2
Alton Rd C3
Anthony Gdns C1
Arthur St C2
Ashburnham Rd B1
Ashton Rd C2
Avondale Rd A1
Back St A2
Bailey St C2
Baker St C2
Biscot Rd A1
Bolton Rd B3
Boyle Cl B1
Brantwood Rd B1
Bretts Mead C1
Bridge St B2
Brook St A1
Brunswick St A3
Bury Park Rd A1
Bute St B2
Buxton Rd B2
Cambridge St C3
Cardiff Grove B1
Cardiff Rd B1
Cardigan St A2
Castle St B2/C2

Chapel St C2
Charles St A3
Chase St C2
Cheapside B2
Chequer St C2
Chiltern Rise C3
Church St B2/B3
Cinema 🎬 A2
Cobden St A3
College C3
Collingdon St A2
Community Centre . . .A3
Concorde Ave C3
Corncastle Rd C1
Cowper St C2
Crawley Green Rd. . . .B3
Crawley Rd A2
Crescent Rd C3
Crescent Rise C3
Cromwell Rd A1
Cross St A2
Cross Way, The C1
Crown Court B2
Cumberland St B2
Cutenhoe Rd C3
Dallow Rd B1
Downs Rd C1
Dudley St A2
Duke St A2
Dumfries St C2
Dunstable Place B2
Dunstable Rd A1/B1
Edward St A3
Elizabeth St C2
Essex Cl C3
Farley Hill C1
Farley Lodge C1
Flowers Way B2
Francis St A1
Frederick St A2
Galaxy Leisure
  Complex A2
George St B2
George St West B2
Gordon St B2
Grove Rd B1
Guildford St A2
Haddon Rd A3
Harcourt St C1
Hart Hill Drive A3
Hart Hill Lane A3
Hartley Rd A3
Hastings St B2
Hat Factory, The 🎭 . . .B2
Hatters Way. A1
Havelock Rd A2
Hibbert St C2
High Town Rd A3
Highbury Rd A1
Hightown Community
  Sports & Arts Centre .A3
Hillary Cres C1
Hillborough Rd C1
Hitchin Rd A3
Holly St C3
Holm C1
Hucklesby Way A2
Hunts Cl C1
Inkerman St A2
John St B2
Jubilee St A3
Kelvin Cl C2
King St B2
Kingsland Rd C2
Larches, The A2
Latimer Rd C2
Lawn Gdns C1
Lea Rd B3
Library B2
Library Rd B2
Library Theatre 🎭 B2
Liverpool Rd B1
London Rd C2
Luton Station ≥ A2
Lyndhurst Rd B1
Magistrates Court A2
Mall, The B2
Manchester St B2
Manor Rd B3
Manor Road Park B3
May St A2
Meyrick Ave C1
Midland Rd A2
Mill St A2
Milton Rd B1
Moor St A1
Moor, The A1
Moorland Gdns A2
Moulton Rise A3
Napier Rd B1
New Bedford Rd A1
New Town St C2
North St A2
Old Bedford Rd A2
Old Orchard C2
Osbourne Rd C3
Oxen Rd A3
Park Sq B2
Park St B3/C3
Park St West C2
Park Viaduct C2
Parkland Drive C1
Police Station 🚓 B1
Pomfret Ave A3
Pondwicks Rd B3
Post Office 🏤 A1/B2
Power Court B3
Princess St B1
Red Rails C1
Regent St B1
Reginald St A2
Rothesay Rd B1
Russell Rise C1
Russell St C1
St Ann's Rd B3
St George's Square . . .B2
St Mary's 🏛 B3
St Marys Rd C3
St Paul's Rd C2
St Saviour's Cres C1
Salisbury Rd B1

Seymour Ave C3
Seymour Rd C3
Silver St B2
South Rd C1
Stanley St B1
Station Rd A2
Stockwood Cres C2
Stockwood Park C1
Strathmore Ave C2
Stuart St B2
Studley Rd A1
Surrey St C3
Sutherland Place C1
Tavistock St C2
Taylor St A3
Telford Way A1
Tennyson Rd C2
Tenzing Grove C1
Thistle Rd B3
Town Hall B2
Townsley Cl C2
UK Centre for
  Carnival Arts ✦ B3
Union St B2
Univ of Bedfordshire . .B3
Upper George St. B2
Vicarage St B3
Villa Rd A2
Waldeck Rd A1
Wardown House
  Mus & Gallery 🏛 . .A1/B2
Wellington St B1/B2
Wenlock St C2
Whitby Rd A1
Whitehill Ave. C1
William St A2
Wilsden Ave. C1
Windmill Rd B3
Windsor St C2
Winsdon Rd B1
York St A3

Macclesfield 343

108 Steps B2
Abbey Rd A1
Alton Dr A3
Armett St C1
Athey St B1
Bank St C3
Barber St C3
Barton St C2
Beech La A2
Beswick St B3
Black La A2
Black Rd C2
Blakelow Gardens C3
Blakelow Rd C3
Bond St B1/C1
Bread St B1
Bridge St B1
Brock St C2
Brocklehurst Ave A3
Brook St B3
Brookfield La B3
Brough St West C1
Brown St C2
Brynton Rd A2
Buckley St C2
Bus Station C2
Buxton Rd B3
Byrons St B2
Canal St C2
Carlsbrook Ave A2
Castle St B2
Catherine St B2
Cemetery A1
Chadwick Terr A1
Chapel St C1
Charlotte St B2
Chester Rd A1
Chestergate B1
Christ Church 🏛 B2
Churchill Way B2
Coare St A1
Commercial Rd C1
Conway Cres A3
Copper St C3
Cottage St B2
Crematorium A1
Crew Ave A3
Crompton Rd B1/C1
Cross St C2
Crossall St C1
Cumberland St A1/B1
Dale St B3
Duke St B2
Eastgate C3
Exchange St B2
Fence Ave A3
Fence Ave Ind Est A3
Flint St B3
Foden St C1
Fountain St B3
Garden St A2
Gas Rd B2
Gateway Gallery ✦ . . .B1
George St B2
Glegg St C3
Golf Course A3
Goodall St C3
Grange Rd C1
Great King St B3
Green St B3
Grosvenor
  Shopping Centre B2
Gunco La C3
Half St B2
Hallefield Rd B3
Hatton St C1
Hawthorn Way A3
Heapy St C3
Henderson St B1
Heritage Centre 🏛 B2
Hibel Rd A2
High St C2
Hobson St C2
Hollins Rd C1
Hope St West B1
Horseshoe Dr A1
Hurdsfield Rd A3

Information Ctr ℹ B2
James St C2
Jodrell St B3
John St C2
Jordangate A2
King Edward St B2
King George's Field . .C3
King St B2
King's School A1
Knight Pool C1
Knight St C3
Lansdowne St A3
Library B2
Lime Gr. B3
Loney St B1
Longacre St C2
Lord St C2
Lowe St C2
Lowerfield Rd A3
Lyon St B3
Macclesfield College. .C2
Macclesfield Sta ≥ . . .B2
MADS Little
  Theatre 🎭 C2
Marina B3
Market B2
Market Pl B2
Masons La A3
Mill La C1
Mill Rd B2
Mill St B2
Moran Rd C1
New Hall St C1
Newton St C1
Nicholson Ave. A3
Nicholson Cl A3
Northgate Ave. A2
Old Mill La C2
Paradise Mill 🏛 B1
Paradise St B1
Park Green B2
Park La C2
Park Rd C1
Park St C2
Park Vale Rd C1
Parr St B1
Peel St C2
Percyvale St A3
Peter St C1
Pickford St B2
Pierce St B1
Pinfold St B1
Pitt St C2
Police Station 🚓 C2
Pool St C2
Poplar Rd C2
Post Office 🏤 B2
Pownall St A2
Prestbury Rd A1/B1
Queen Victoria St B2
Queen's Ave. A3
Registrar B2
Retail Park C2
Richmond Hill C3
Riseley St B1
Roan Ct. B3
Roe St B2
Rowan Way A3
Ryle St C1
Ryle's Park Rd C1
St George's St C2
St Michael's 🏛 B2
Samuel St B2
Saville St C3
Shaw St C1
Silk Rd, The A2/B2
Slater St C1
Snow Hill C3
South Park C1
Spring Gdns A2
Statham St C2
Station St A2
Steeple St A3
Sunderland St B2
Superstore A1/A2/C2
Swettenham St B3
Thistleton Cl A3
Thorp St B3
Town Hall B2
Townley St B2
Treacle Market ✦ B2
Turnock St C2
Union Rd B3
Union St B2
Victoria Park B3
Vincent St C1
Waters Green B2
Waterside B2
West Bond St B1
West Park A1
West Park Museum 🏛 .A1
Westbrook Dr A1
Westminster Rd A1
Whalley Hayes B1
Windmill St B3
Withyfold Dr A2

Maidstone 343

Albion Pl B3
All Saints 🏛 B2
Allen St A3
Amphitheatre ✦ C2
Archbishop's Pal 🏰🏛 . .B2
Bank St B2
Barker Rd C2
Barton Rd C3
Beaconsfield Rd C1
Bedford Pl B1
Bishops Way B2
Bluett St A3
BMI The Somerfield
  Hospital Ⓗ C3
Bower La C1
Bower Mount Rd B1
Bower Pl C1
Bower St A1
Boxley Rd A2
Brenchley Gardens . . .A2
Brewer St A3

Broadway B2
Broadway
  Shopping Centre B2
Brunswick St C3
Buckland Hill A1
Buckland Rd B1
Bus Station B1
Campbell Rd C3
Church Rd C1
Church St B3
Clifford Way C1/C2
College Ave C2
College Rd C2
Collis Memorial Gdn . .B2
Cornwallis Rd B1
Corpus Christi Hall . . .B3
Council Offices. B3
County Hall A3
County Rd A3
Crompton Gdns C1
Crown & County
  Courts A3
Curzon Rd A3
Dixon Cl C2
Douglas Rd A1
Earl St B2
Eccleston Rd C3
Fairmeadow B2
Fisher St A2
Florence Rd C1
Foley St A3
Foster St C3
Freedom Leisure
  Centre A1/A2
Fremlin Walk
  Shopping Centre B2
Gabriel's Hill B2
George St C3
Grecian St A3
Hardy St A3
Hart St B2
Hastings Rd C3
Hayle Rd C2
Heathorn St A3
Hedley St A3
High St B2
HM Prison A2
Holland Rd A3
Hope St A2
Information Ctr ℹ B2
James St A3
James Whatman Way .A2
Jeffrey St A3
Kent County Council
  Offices A2
Kent History & Liby Ctr A2
King Edward Rd C3
King St B3
Kingsley Rd C3
Knightrider St C2
Launder Way C1
Lesley Pl A1
Library B2
Little Buckland Ave . . .A1
Lockmeadow Leisure
  Complex C2
London Rd B1
Lower Boxley Rd A2
Lower Fant Rd C1
Magistrates Court B3
Maidstone Barracks
  Station ≥ A1
Maidstone East Sta ≥ .A2
Maidstone Museum &
  Bentlif Art Gall 🏛 . . .B2
Maidstone Utd FC. . . .A2
Maidstone West Sta ≥ .B2
Mall, The A3
Market B2
Market Buildings B2
Marsham St B3
Medway St B2
Melville Rd C3
Mill St B2
Millennium Bridge B2
Mote Rd B3
Muir Rd C3
Old Tovil Rd C2
Palace Ave B3
Perryfield St A2
Police Station 🚓 B1
Post Office 🏤 B2/C3
Priory Rd C2
Prospect Pl C1
Pudding La B2
Queen Anne Rd B3
Queens Rd A1
Randall St A2
Rawdon Rd C3
Reginald Rd C1
Riverstage 🎭 A1
Rock Pl B1
Rocky Hill B1
Romney Pl B3
Rose Yard B2
Rowland Cl C1
Royal Engineers' Rd . .A2
Royal Star Arcade B2
St Annes St B2
St Faith's St B2
St Luke's Rd A3
St Peter St B2
St Peter's Bridge B2
St Peter's Wharf B2
St Philip's Ave C3
Salisbury Rd A3
Sandling Rd A2
Scott St A2
Scrubs La B3
Sheal's Cres B3
Somerfield La B1
Somerfield Rd B1
Staceys St A2
Station Rd A2
Superstore A1/B2/B3
Terrace Rd B1
Tonbridge Rd C1
Tovil Rd A3

Town Hall B2
Trinity Park B3
Tufton St B3
Tyrwhitt-Drake Museum
  of Carriages 🏛 A2
Union St B3
Upper Fant Rd C1
Upper Stone St C3
Victoria St B1
Warwick Pl C1
Wat Tyler Way B3
Waterloo St C3
Waterlow Rd A3
Week St B2
Well Rd A3
Westree Rd C1
Wharf Rd C1
Whatman Park A2
Wheeler St A3
Whitchurch Cl. B1
Woodville Rd C1
Wyatt St B3
Wyke Manor Rd B3

Manchester 343

Adair St B6
Addington St A4
Adelphi St A1
Albert Sq B3
Albion St C3
Ancoats Gr. B6
Ancoats Gr North A6
Angela St C2
Aquatics Centre C4
Ardwick Green North .C5
Ardwick Green Park . .C5
Ardwick Green South .C5
Arlington St A2
Artillery St B3
Arundel St C2
Atherton St B2
Atkinson St B3
Aytoun St B4
Back Piccadilly A4
Baird St B5
Balloon St A4
Bank Pl A1
Baring St B5
Barrack St C1
Barrow St A1
Bendix St A5
Bengal St A5
Berry St C5
Blackfriars Rd A3
Blackfriars St A3
Blantyre St C2
Bloom St B4
Blossom St A5
Boad St B5
Bombay St C4
Booth St B3
Booth St B4
Bootle St B3
Brazennose St B3
Brewer St A5
Bridge St B3
Bridgewater Hall B3
Bridgewater Pl A4
Bridgewater St C2
Brook St C4
Brotherton Dr C1
Brown St A3
Brown St B3
Brunswick St C6
Brydon Ave C6
Buddhist Centre A4
Bury St A2
Bus & Coach Station . .B4
Bus Station A4
Butler St A6
Buxton St C5
Byrom St B2
Cable St A5
Cambridge St C3/C4
Camp St B3
Canal St B4
Cannon St A3
Cardroom Rd A6
Carruthers St A6
Castle St C2
Castlefield Arena B2
Cateaton St A3
Cathedral † A3
Cathedral St A3
Cavendish St C3
Chapel St A1/A3
Chapeltown St B5
Charles St C4
Charlotte St B4
Chatham St B4
Chepstow St B3
Chester Rd C1/C2
Chester St C3
Chetham's School
  of Music A3
China La B4
Chippenham Rd A6
Chorlton Rd C2
Chorlton St B4
Church St A4
Church St A5
City Park A4
City Rd East C3
Civil Justice Centre . . .B2
Cleminson St A1
Clowes St A3
College Land A3
Collier St B2
Commercial St C3
Conference Centre . . .C4
Cooper St B4
Copperas St A4
Corn Exchange, The . .A3
Cornbrook 🚋 C1
Cornell St A5
Corporation St A4
Cotter St C6
Cotton St A5
Cow La B1
Cross St B3

Crown Court B4
Crown St C2
Dalberg St C6
Dale St A4/B5
Dancehouse, The 🎭 . .C4
Dantzic St A4
Dark La C6
Dawson St C2
Dean St A5
Deansgate A3/B3/C2
Deansgate
  Castlefield 🚋 C2
Deansgate Station ≥ . .C3
Dolphin St C6
Downing St C5
Ducie St B5
Duke Pl C2
Duke St B2
Durling St C6
East Ordsall La A2/B1
Edge St A4
Egerton St C2
Ellesmere St C1
Everard St C1
Every St B6
Exchange Sq 🚋 A4
Factory, The 🎭 B2
Fairfield St B5
Faulkner St B4
Fennel St A3
Ford St A2
Ford St C6
Fountain St B4
Frederick St A2
Gartside St B2
Gaythorne St A1
George Leigh St A5
George St B4
Gore St A2
Goulden St A5
Granby Row B4
Gravel La A3
Great St B6
Great Ancoats St A5
Great Bridgewater St .B3
Great George St A1
Great Jackson St C2
Great Marlborough St.C4
Great Northern
  Warehouse Leisure &
  Shopping Complex . .B3
Greengate A3
Grosvenor St C5
Gun St A5
Hadrian Ave B6
Hall St B3
Hampson St B1
Hanover St A4
Hanworth Cl C5
Hardman St B3
Harkness St C6
Harrison St B6
Hart St B4
Helmet St B6
Henry St A5
Heyrod St B6
High St A4
Higher Ardwick C6
Hilton St A4/A5
Holland St A6
HOME ✦ C3
Hood St A5
Hope St B1
Hope St B4
Houldsworth St A5
Hoyle St C6
Hulme Hall Rd C1
Hulme St A3
Hulme St C3
Hyde Rd C6
Islington Way A1
Information Ctr ℹ B4
Irwell St A2
Jackson Cr. C2
Jackson's Row B3
James St A1
Jenner Cl C2
Jersey St A5
John Dalton St B3
John Ryland's Liby 🏛 . .B3
John St A2
Kennedy St B3
Kincardine Rd C5
King St A3
King St West A3
Law Courts B3
Laystall St B5
Lever St A4
Library A5
Linby St C2
Little Lever St A4
Liverpool Rd B2
Liverpool St B1
Lloyd St B3
Lockton Cl C5
London Rd B4
Long Millgate A3
Longacre St B6
Loom St A5
Lower Byrom St B2
Lower Mosley St B3
Lower Moss La C1
Lower Ormond St C4
Loxford St C3
Luna St A5
Major St B4
Manchester Arndale . .A4
Manchester
  Art Gallery 🏛 B4
Manchester Central
  Convention Complex .B3
Manchester
  Metropolitan University
  (MMU) B4/C4
Manchester Piccadilly
  Station ≥ B5
Manchester
  Technology Centre . .C4
Mancunian Way C4
Manor St C5
Marble St A4

Market St A2
Market St A4
Market St A4
Marsden St A3
Marshall St A5
Mayan Ave A2
Medlock St C3
Middlewood St B1
Miller St A4
Minshull St B4
Mosley St A4
Mount St B3
Mulberry St B3
Murray St A5
Museum of Science & Industry (MOSI) B2
Nathan Dr A2
National Football Museum A4
Naval St A5
New Bailey St A2
New Elm Rd B2
New Islington A6
New Islington Sta B6
New Quay St B2
New Union St A6
Newgate St A4
Newton St A5
Nicholas St B4
North Western St C6
Oak St A4
Odeon A4/B3
Old Mill St A6
Oldfield Rd A1/C1
Oldham Rd A5
Oldham St A4
Opera House B3
Ordsall La C1
Oxford Rd C4
Oxford Rd C4
Oxford St B4
Paddock St C6
Palace Theatre B4
Pall Mall A3
Palmerston St B6
Parker St B4
Peak St B5
Penfield Cl C5
Peoples' History Museum B2
Peru St A1
Peter St B3
Piccadilly A4
Piccadilly B5
Piccadilly Gdns B4
Piercy St A6
Poland St A5
Police Station B3/B5
Pollard St B6
Port St A5
Portland St B4
Portugal St East B5
Post Office A1/A2/A4/A5/B3/B4
Potato Wharf B2
Princess St B3/C4
Pritchard St C4
Quay St A2
Quay St B2
Queen St B3
Radium St A5
Redhill St A5
Regent Rd B1
Retail Park A5
Rice St B2
Richmond St B4
River St C3
Roby St B5
Rodney St A6
Roman Fort B2
Rosamond St A2
Royal Exchange A3
Sackville St B4
St Andrew's St B6
St Ann St A3
St Ann's A3
St George's Ave C1
St James St B4
St John St B3
St John's Cath (RC) A2
St Mary's B3
St Mary's Gate A3
St Mary's Parsonage A3
St Peter's Sq B3
St Stephen St A2
Salford Approach A3
Salford Central A2
Sheffield St B5
Sherratt St A5
Shopmobility A4
Shudehill A4
Shudehill A4
Sidney St C4
Silk St A5
Silver St B4
Skerry Cl C5
Snell St B6
South King St B3
Sparkle St B5
Spear St A4
Spring Gdns A4
Stanley St A2/B2
Store St B5
Superstore B1
Swan St A4
Tariff St B5
Tatton St C1
Temperance St B6/C6
Thirsk St C6
Thomas St A4
Thompson St A5
Tib La B3
Tib St A4
Town Hall (Manchester) B3
Town Hall (Salford) A2
Trafford St C3
Travis St B5
Trinity Way A2
Turner St A4
Union St C6
University of Manchester (Sackville Street Campus) C5
University of Salford A1
Upper Brook St C5
Upper Cleminson St A1
Upper Wharf St A1
Urban Exchange A5
Vesta St B6
Victoria A4
Victoria Station A4
Wadesdon Rd C5
Water St B2
Watson St B3
West Fleet St B1
West King St A2
West Mosley St B4
Weybridge Rd A6
Whitworth St B4
Whitworth St West C3
William St A2
William St C6
Wilmott St C3
Windmill St B3
Windsor Cr A1
Withy Gr A4
Woden St C1
Wood St B3
Woodward St A6
Worrall St C1
Worsley St C2
York St B4
York St C2
York St C4

Merthyr Tydfil
Merthyr Tudful 343

Aberdare Rd B2
Abermorlais Terr B2
Alexandra Rd A3
Alma St C3
Arfryn Pl C3
Argyle St C3
Avenue De Clichy C2
Beacons Place Shopping Centre C2
Bethesda St B2
Bishops Gr A3
Brecon Rd A1/B2
Briarmead A3
Bryn St C3
Bryntirion Rd B3/C3
Bus Station B2
Cae Mari Dwn B3
Caedraw Rd C2
Castle Sq A1
Castle St B2
Chapel C2
Chapel Bank A1
Church St B3
Civic Centre B2
Clos Penderyn B1
Coedcae'r Ct C3
College Blvd C2
County and Crown Courts B2
Court St C3
Cromwell St B2
Cyfarthfa Castle, Mus and Art Gallery A1
Cyfarthfa Ind Est A1
Cyfarthfa Park A1
Cyfarthfa Retail Park B1
Cyfarthfa Rd A1
Dane St A2
Dane Terr A2
Danyparc B3
Darren View A3
Dixon St B2
Dyke St C3
Dynevor St B2
Elwyn Dr C3
Fire Station B2
Fothergill St B3
Galonuchaf Rd A3
Garth St B2
Georgetown B2
Grawen Terr A2
Grove Pk A2
Grove, The A2
Gurnos Rd A2
Gwaelodygarth Rd A2/A3
Gwaunfarren Gr A3
Gwaunfarren Rd A3
Gwendoline St A3
Hampton St C3
Hanover St A2
Heol S O Davies B1
Heol-Gerrig B1
High St A3/B2/B3/C2
Highland View C3
Howell Cl B1
Information Ctr B2
Jackson's Bridge B2
James St C3
John St B3
Joseph Parry's Cott B2
Lancaster St A2
Library B2
Llewellyn St A2
Llwyfen St B2
Llwyn Berry B1
Llwyn Dic Penderyn B1
Llwyn-y-Gelynen C1
Lower Thomas St B3
Market C2
Mary St C3
Masonic St C2
Merthyr Tydfil College B2
Merthyr Town FC B3
Merthyr Tydfil Leisure Centre C3
Merthyr Tydfil Sta C3
Meyrick Villas A2
Miniature Railway A1
Mount St A2
Nantygwenith St B1
Norman Terr B2
Oak Rd A2
Old Cemetery B3
Pandy Cl A1
Pantycelynen B1
Parade, The B3
Park Terr B2
Penlan View C2
Penry St B2
Pentwyn Villas A2
Penyard Rd B3
Penydarren Park A3
Penydarren Rd B3
Plymouth St C3
Police Station C2
Pont Marlais West B2
Post Office B2
Quarry Row B2
Queen's Rd B3
Rees St C3
Rhydycar Link C2
Riverside Park A1
St David's B3
St Tydfil's C2
St Tydfil's Ave C3
St Tydfil's Square Shopping Centre C2
Saxon St A2
School of Nursing A2
Seward St A3
Shiloh La B3
Stone Circles B3
Stuart St A2
Summerhill Pl B3
Superstore B3
Swan St C2
Swansea Rd B1
Taff Glen View C3
Taff Vale Ct B3
Theatre Soar B2
Thomastown Park B3
Tramroad La A3
Tramroad Side B2
Tramroad Side North B3
Tramroad Side South C3
Trevithick Gdns C3
Trevithick St A3
Tudor Terr B2
Twynyrodyn Rd C3
Union St B3
Upper Colliers Row B1
Upper Thomas St B3
Victoria St B2
Vue C3
Vulcan Rd B2
Walk, The B2
Warlow St C3
Well St A2
Welsh Assembly Government Offices C2
Wern La C1
Wern, The (Merthyr RFC) C2
West Gr A2
William St C3
Yew St C3
Ynysfach Engine Ho C2
Ynysfach Rd C2

Middlesbrough 343

Abingdon Rd C3
Acklam Rd C1
Albert Park C2
Albert Rd B2
Albert Terr C2
Ambulance Station C1
Aubrey St C3
Avenue, The C2
Ayresome Gdns C2
Ayresome Green La C1
Ayresome St C2
Barton Rd A1
Bilsdale Rd C3
Bishopton Rd C3
Borough Rd B2/B3
Bowes Rd A2
Breckon Hill Rd B3
Bridge St West B2
Brighouse Rd A1
Burlam Rd C1
Bus Station B2
Cannon Park B1
Cannon Park Way B2
Cannon St B1
Captain Cook Sq B2
Carlow St C1
Castle Way C3
Chipchase Rd C2
Cineworld B3
Cleveland Centre B2
Clive Rd C2
Commercial St A2
Corporation Rd B2
Costa St C2
Council Offices B3
Crescent Rd C2
Crescent, The C2
Cumberland Rd C2
Depot Rd A2
Derwent St B2
Devonshire Rd C2
Diamond Rd B2
Dock St B3
Dorman Museum C2
Douglas St B3
Eastbourne Rd C2
Eden Rd C3
Fire Sta A3
Forty Foot Rd A2
Gilkes St B2
Gosford St A2
Grange Rd B2
Gresham Rd B2
Harehills Rd C1
Harford St C2
Hartington Rd B2
Haverton Hill Rd A1
Hey Wood St B1
Highfield Rd C3
Hillstreet Centre B2
Holwick Rd B1
Hutton Rd C3
Ironmasters Way B1
Lambton Rd C3
Lancaster Rd C2
Lansdowne Rd C3
Latham Rd C2
Law Courts B2/B3
Lees Rd B2
Leeway B3
Library B2/C2
Linthorpe Cemetery C1
Linthorpe Rd B2
Lloyd St B2
Longford St C2
Longlands Rd C3
Lower East St A3
Lower Lake C3
Macmillan Academy C1
Maldon Rd C1
Manor St B2
Marsh St B2
Marton Rd B3
Middlesbrough By-Pass B2/C1
Middlesbrough Coll B3
Middlesbrough Dock B3
Middlesbrough Leisure Park B3
Middlesbrough Sta B2
Middletown Park C2
MIMA B3
Mulgrave Rd C2
Newport Bridge B1
Newport Bridge Approach Rd B1
Newport Rd B2
North Ormesby Rd B3
North Rd B2
Northern Rd C1
Outram St B2
Oxford Rd C2
Park La C2
Park Rd North C2
Park Rd South C2
Park Vale Rd C3
Parliament Rd B1
Police Station A2
Port Clarence Rd A3
Portman St B2
Post Office B3/C1/C2
Princes Rd B2
Python A2
Riverside Park Rd A1
Riverside Stadium (Middlesbrough FC) B3
Rockliffe Rd C2
Romaldkirk Rd B1
Roman Rd C2
Roseberry Rd C3
St Barnabas' Rd C2
St Paul's Rd B2
Saltwells Rd B3
Scott's Rd A3
Seaton Carew Rd A3
Shepherdson Way B3
Shopmobility B2
Snowdon Rd A2
South West Ironmasters Park B1
Southfield Rd B2
Southwell Rd C2
Springfield Rd C1
Startforth Rd A2
Stockton Rd C1
Stockton St A2
Superstore B2
Surrey St C2
Sycamore Rd C2
Tax Offices B3
Tees Viaduct C1
Teessaurus Park A2
Teesside Tertiary Coll C3
Temenos B3
Thornfield Rd C1
Town Hall B2
Transporter Bridge (Toll) A3
Union St B2
University of Teesside B2
Upper Lake C2
Valley Rd C3
Ventnor Rd C2
Victoria Rd B2
Vulcan St A2
Warwick St C2
Wellesley Rd B3
West La C1
West Lane Hospital C1
Westminster Rd C2
Wilson St B2
Windward Way B3
Woodlands Rd B2
York Rd C3

Milton Keynes 344

Abbey Way A1
Arbrook Ave B1
Armourer Dr A3
Arncliffe Dr A1
Avebury C2
Avebury Blvd C2
Bankfield B3
Bayard Ave A2
Belvedere A2
Bishopstone A1
Blundells Rd A1
Boundary, The C3
Boycott Ave C2
Bradwell Comm Blvd B1
Bradwell Rd C1
Bramble Ave A2
Brearley Ave C2
Breckland A1
Brill Place B1
Burnham Dr B1
Campbell Park B3
Cantle Ave A3
Central Retail Park C1
Century Ave C2
Chaffron Way C3
Childs Way C1
Christ the Cornerstone B2
Cineworld B2
Civic Offices B2
Cleavers Ave B2
Colesbourne Dr A3
Conniburrow Blvd B2
Currier Dr A2
Dansteed Way A2/A3/B1
Deltic Ave B1
Downs Barn A2
Downs Barn Blvd A3
Eaglestone C3
Eelbrook Ave B1
Elder Gate B1
Evans Gate C2
Fairford Cr A3
Falcon Ave B3
Fennel Dr A2
Fishermead Blvd C3
Food Centre B3
Fulwoods Dr C3
Glazier Dr A2
Glovers La A1
Grafton Gate C1
Grafton St A1/C2
Gurnards Ave B3
Harrier Dr C3
The Hub Leisure Quarter B2/C2
Ibstone Ave B1
intu Milton Keynes B2
Langcliffe Dr A1
Leisure Centre C3
Leisure Plaza C1
Leys Rd C1
Library B2
Linceslade Grove C1
Linford Wood A2
Magistrates Court B2
Marlborough Gate B3
Marlborough St A2/B3
Mercers Dr A1
Midsummer C2
Midsummer Blvd B2
Milton Keynes Central C1
Milton Keynes Hospital (A&E) C3
Monks Way A1
Mullen Ave A3
Mullion Pl C3
Neath Hill A3
North Elder C1
North Grafton B1
North Overgate A3
North Row B2
North Saxon B2
North Secklow B2
North Skeldon A3
North Witan B1
Oakley Gdns A3
Odeon B2
Oldbrook Blvd C2
Open-Air Theatre B3
Overgate A3
Overstreet A3
Patriot Dr B1
Pencarrow Pl B3
Penryn Ave B3
Perran Ave C3
Pitcher La C1
Place Retail Park, The C1
Police Station B2
Portway B2
Post Office A2/B2/B3
Precedent Dr B1
Quinton Dr B1
Ramsons Ave B2
Retail Park C2
Rockingham Dr A2
Rooksley B1
Saxon Gate B2
Saxon St A1/C3
Secklow Gate B2
Shackleton Pl C2
Shopmobility B2
Silbury Blvd B2
Skeldon A3
South Enmore B3
South Grafton C2
South Row C2
South Saxon C2
South Secklow B3
South Witan C2
Springfield B3
Stainton Dr A1/B1
Stanton Wood A1
Stantonbury A1
Stantonbury Leisure Centre A1
Strudwick Dr C2
Sunrise Parkway A2
Superstore C1/C2
Theatre & Art Gallery B3
theCentre:mk B2
Tolcarne Ave C3
Towan Ave C3
Trueman Pl C2
Vauxhall A1
Winterhill Retail Park C2
Witan Gate B2
Xscape B3

Newcastle upon Tyne 344

Albert St B3
Argyle St B3
Back New Bridge St B3
BALTIC Centre for Contemporary Art C3
Barker St A3
Barrack Rd B1
Bath La B1
Bessie Surtees Ho C2
Bigg Market C2
Biscuit Factory B3
Black Gate C2
Blackett St B2
Blandford Sq C1
Boating Lake A1
Boyd St B3
Brandling Park A2
Bus Station B2
Buxton St B3
Byron St A3
Camden St B2
Castle Keep C2
Central C1
Central Library B2
Central Motorway B2
Chester St A3
Cineworld B1
City Hall B2
City Rd B3/C3
City Walls C1
Civic Centre A2
Claremont Rd A1
Clarence St B3
Clarence Walk B3
Clayton St C1/B1
Clayton St West C1
Close, The C2
Coach Station C1
College St B2
Collingwood St C2
Copland Terr B3
Coppice Way B3
Corporation St B1
Courts C3
Crawhall Rd B3
Dean St C2
Dental Hospital A1
Dinsdale Pl A3
Dinsdale Rd A3
Discovery C1
Doncaster Rd A3
Durant Rd B2
Eldon Sq B1
Ellison Pl B2
Eskdale Terr A2
Eslington Terr A2
Exhibition Park A1
Falconar St B3
Fenkle St C1
Forth Banks C1
Forth St C1
Gallowgate B1
Gate, The B1
Gateshead Millennium Bridge C3
Gateshead Quays C3
Gibson St B3
Goldspink La A3
Grainger Market B2
Grainger St B2
Grantham Rd A3
Granville Rd A3
Great North Children's Hospital A1
Great North Mus:Hancock A2
Grey St B2
Groat Market C2
Guildhall C2
Hancock St A2
Hanover St C2
Hatton Gallery A1
Hawks Rd C3
Haymarket B2
Heber St B1
Helmsley Rd A3
High Bridge B2
High Level Bridge C2
Hillgate C3
Howard St B3
Hutton Terr A3
intu Eldon Square Shopping Centre B2
Jesmond A2
Jesmond Rd A2/A3
John Dobson St B2
Jubilee Rd B3
Kelvin Gr A3
Kensington Terr A2
Laing Gallery B2
Lambton Rd A2
Leazes Cr B1
Leazes La B1
Leazes Park B1
Leazes Park Rd B1
Leazes Terr B1
Library A2
Life Science Centre C1
Live C2
Low Friar St C1
Manor Chare C2
Manors B2
Manors Station B2
Market St B2
Melbourne St B2
Mill Rd C3
Monument B2
Monument Mall Shopping Centre B2
Morpeth St A2
Mosley St C2
Napier St A3
New Bridge St West B2/B3
Newcastle Central Station C1
Newcastle University A1
Newgate St B1
Newington Rd A3
Northern Design Ctr C3
Northern Stage Theatre A2
Northumberland Rd B2
Northumberland St B2
Northumbria University A2
Northwest Radial Rd A1
O2 Academy C1
Oakwellgate C3
Open Univ C3
Orchard St C2
Osborne Rd A2
Osborne Terr A3
Pandon C3
Pandon Bank B3
Park Terr A1
Percy St B1
Pilgrim St B2
Pipewellgate C2
Pitt St B1
Plummer Tower A2
Police Station C1
Portland Rd A3/B3
Portland Terr A3
Post Office B1/B2
Pottery La C1
Prudhoe Pl B1
Prudhoe St B1
Quayside C2
Queen Elizabeth II Bridge C2
Queen Victoria Rd A1
Richardson Rd A1
Ridley Pl B2
Rock Terr B3
Rosedale Terr A3
Royal Victoria Infirmary A1
Sage Gateshead C3
St Andrew's St B1
St James B1
St James' Blvd C1
St James' Park (Newcastle Utd FC) B1
St Mary's Heritage Centre C3
St Mary's (RC) C1
St Mary's Place B2
St Nicholas C2
St Nicholas St C2
St Thomas' St B1
Sandyford Rd A2/A3
Shield St B3
Shieldfield B3
Shopmobility B1
Side, The C2
Simpson Terr B3
South Shore Rd C3
South St C1
Starbeck Ave A3
Stepney Rd B3
Stoddart St B3
Stowell St B1
Strawberry Pl B1
Swing Bridge C2
Temple St C1
Terrace Pl B1
Theatre Royal B2
Times Sq C1
Tower St B3
Trinity House C2
Tyne Bridge C2
Tyne Bridges C2
Tyne Theatre & Opera House C1
Tyneside B2
Victoria Sq A2
Warwick St A3
Waterloo St C1
Wellington St B1
Westgate Rd C1/C2
Windsor Terr A2
Worswick St B2
Wretham Pl B3

Newport
Casnewydd 344

Albert Terr B1
Allt-yr-Yn Ave A1
Alma St C2
Ambulance Station C3
Bailey St B2
Barrack Hill A2
Bath St A3
Bedford Rd B3
Belle Vue La C1
Belle Vue Park C1
Bishop St A3
Blewitt St B1
Bolt Cl C3
Bolt St C3
Bond St A2
Bosworth Dr A1
Bridge St B1
Bristol St A3
Bryngwyn Rd B1
Brynhyfryd Ave C1
Brynhyfryd Rd C1
Bus Station B2
Caerau Cres C1
Caerau Rd B1
Caerleon Rd A3
Capel Cres C2
Cardiff Rd C2
Caroline St B3
Castle (Remains) A2
Cedar Rd B3
Charles St B2
Charlotte Dr C2
Chepstow Rd A3
Church Rd A3
Cineworld B2
Civic Centre B1
Clarence Pl A2
Clifton Pl B1
Clifton Rd C1
Clyffard Cres B1
Clytha Park Rd B1
Clytha Sq C2
Coldra Rd C1
Collier St A3
Colne St B3
Comfrey Cl A1
Commercial Rd C3
Commercial St B2
Corelli St A3
Corn St B2
Corporation Rd B3
Coulson Cl C2
County Court A1
Courts A1
Courts B1
Crawford St A3
Cyril St B3
Dean St A3
Devon Pl B1
Dewsland Park Rd C2
Dolman B2
Dolphin St C3
East Dock Rd C3
East St B1
East Usk Rd A3
Ebbw Vale Wharf B3
Emlyn St B2
Enterprise Way C3
Eton Rd B3
Evans St A2
Factory Rd A2
Fields Rd B1
Francis Dr C2
Frederick St C3
Friars Rd C1
Friars Walk B2
Gaer La C1
George St C3
George Street Bridge C3
Godfrey Rd B1
Gold Tops B1
Gore St A3
Gorsedd Circle C1
Grafton Rd A3
Graham St B1
Granville St C3
Harlequin Dr A1
Harrow Rd B3
Herbert Rd A3
Herbert Walk C2
Hereford St A3
High St B2
Hill St B2
Hoskins St A2
Information Ctr B2
Ivor St B2
Jones St B1
Junction Rd A3
Keynshaw Ave C2
King St C2
Kingsway B2
Kingsway Centre B2
Ledbury Dr A2
Library A3
Library, Museum & Art Gallery B2
Liverpool Wharf B3
Llanthewy Rd B1
Llanvair Rd A3
Locke St A2
Lower Dock St C3
Lucas St A2
Manchester St A3
Market B2
Marlborough Rd B3
Mellon St C3
Mill St A2
Morgan St A3
Mountjoy Rd C2
Newport Bridge A2
Newport Ctr B2
Newport RFC B3
Newport Station B2
North St B2
Oakfield Rd B1
Park Sq C2
Police Station A3/C2
Post Office B2/C3
Power St A1
Prince St A3
Pugsley St A2
Queen St C2
Queen's Cl A1
Queen's Hill A1
Queen's Hill Cres A1
Queensway B2
Railway St B2
Riverfront Theatre & Arts Centre, The B2
Riverside A3
Rodney Rd B2
Royal Gwent (A&E) C2
Rudry St A3
Rugby Rd B3
Ruperra La C3
Ruperra St C3
St Edmund St B1
St Mark's Cres A1
St Mary St B1
St Vincent Rd A3
St Woolos B2
St Woolos General (no A&E) C1
St Woolos Rd B1
School La B2
Serpentine Rd B1
Shaftesbury Park A2
Sheaf La A3
Skinner St B2
Sorrel Dr A1
South Market St C3
Spencer Rd B1
Stow Hill B2/C1/C2
Stow Park Ave C1
Stow Park Dr C1
TA Centre A1
Talbot St B2
Tennis Club A1
Tregare St A3
Trostrey St A3
Tunnel Terr B1
Turner St A3
Univ of Wales Newport City Campus B3
Upper Dock St B2
Usk St A3
Usk Way B3/C3
Victoria Cr B1
War Memorial A3
Waterloo Rd C1
West St B1
Wharves B2
Wheeler St A2
Whitby Pl A3
Windsor Terr B1
York Pl C1

Newquay 344

Agar Rd B2
Alma Pl B1
Ambulance Station B2
Anthony Rd C1
Atlantic Hotel A1
Bank St B1
Barrowfields A3
Bay View Terr B2
Beach Rd B1
Beachfield Ave B1
Beacon Rd A1
Belmont Pl A1
Berry Rd B2
Blue Reef Aquarium B1
Boating Lake C2
Bus Station B1
Chapel Hill B1
Chester Rd A3
Cheviot Rd C1/C2
Chichester Cres C2
Chynance Dr C1
Chyverton Cl C1
Cliff Rd B2
Coach Park B2
Colvreath Rd A3
Cornwall College Newquay B3
Council Offices B1
Crantock St B1
Crescent, The B1
Criggar Rocks A3
Dale Cl C3
Dale Rd C3
Dane Rd A1
East St B2
Edgcumbe Ave B3
Edgcumbe Gdns B3
Eliot Gdns B3
Elm Cl C3
Ennor's Rd B1
Fernhill Rd B1
Fire Station B1
Fore St B1
Gannel Rd C2
Golf Driving Range B3
Gover La B1
Great Western Beach A2
Grosvenor Ave B2
Harbour A1
Hawkins Rd C2
Headleigh Rd B2
Hilgrove Rd A3/B3
Holywell Rd B3
Hope Terr B1
Huer's Hut, The A1
Information Ctr B1
Island Cres B2
Jubilee St B1
Kew Cl C3
Killacourt Cove A2
King Edward Cres A1
Lanhenvor Ave B2
Library B1
Lifeboat Station A1
Lighthouse B1
Linden Ave C2
Listry Rd C2
Lusty Glaze Beach A3
Lusty Glaze Rd A3
Manor Rd B1
Marcus Hill B2
Mayfield Rd B2
Meadowside C3
Mellanvrane La C2
Michell Ave B2
Miniature Golf Course C3
Miniature Railway B3
Mount Wise B1
Mowhay Cl C3
Narrowcliff A3
Newquay B2
Newquay Hospital B2
Newquay Town Football Ground B1
Newquay Zoo B3
North Pier A1
North Quay Hill A1
Oakleigh Terr B2
Pargolla Rd B2
Pendragon Cres C3
Pengannel Cl C1
Penina Ave C3
Pirate's Quest B1
Police Sta & Courts B2
Post Office B1/B2
Quarry Park Rd B3
Rawley La C2
Reeds Way B1
Robartes Rd B2
St Anne's Rd A3
St Aubyn Cres B3
St George's Rd B1
St John's Rd B1
St Mary's Rd B1
St Michael's B1
St Michael's Rd B1
St Thomas' Rd B2
Seymour Ave B2
South Pier A1
South Quay Hill A1
Superstore B2
Sweet Briar Cres C3
Sydney Rd A1
Tolcarne Beach A2
Tolcarne Point A2
Tolcarne Rd B2
Tor Rd B2
Towan Beach A1
Towan Blystra Rd B3
Tower Rd A1
Trebarwith Cres B2
Tredour Rd C2
Treforda Rd C3
Tregoss Rd B3
Tregunnel Hill B1/C1
Tregunnel Saltings C1
Trelawney Rd B2
Treloggan La C3

Treloggan Rd. ...C3
Trembath Cres ...C1
Trenance Ave ...B2
Trenance Gardens .C1
Trenance La. ...B2
Trenance Leisure
  Park ...B3
Trenance Rd ...B2
Trenarth Rd. ...B2
Treninnick Hill ...B3
Tretherras Rd ...B3
Trethewey Way ...C1
Trevemper Rd ...C2
Ulalia Rd. ...B2
Vivian Cl. ...B2
Waterworld ...B3
Whitegate Rd ...B3
Wych Hazel Way ...C3

Newtown
Y Drenewydd   344
Ash Cl. ...A3
Back La. ...B2
Baptist Chapel ...B2
Barn La. ...A2
Bear Lanes
  Shopping Centre ..B2
Beech Cl ...A2
Beechwood Dr ...A2
Brimmon Cl ...C2
Brimmon Rd ...C2
Broad St. ...B2
Bryn Bank ...A1
Bryn Cl ...A1
Bryn Gdns ...A1
Bryn La. ...A1/A2
Bryn Meadows ...A2
Bryn St ...A2
Bryn, The ...A1
Brynglais Ave ...A2
Brynglais Cl. ...A2
Bus Station ...B2
Byrnmodd Dr ...A1
Cambrian Bridge ...B3
Cambrian Gdns. ...B2
Cambrian Way. ...B2
Canal Rd. ...A3
Castle Mound ...B2
Cedewain. ...C1
Ceiriog ...C2
Cemetery. ...A2
Church (Remains of) .B2
Churchill Dr. ...B3
Cledan ...B3
Colwyn. ...B2
Commercial St ...B2
Council Offices. ...B1
Crescent St ...A1
Cwm Llanfair. ...A2
Dinas ...B2
Dolafon Rd. ...B3
Dolerw Park ...C1
Dolfor Rd ...C2
Fairfield Dr ...A2
Fford Croesawdy. ...B2
Fire Station ...C1
Frankwell St ...B2
Frolic St ...B2
Fron La. ...A1
Garden La ...A2
Gas St ...B2
Glyndwr ...C1
Golwydre La ...B2
Gorsedd Circle ...B1
Hafren ...C1
Halfpenny Bridge. ...B2
High St. ...B2
Hillside Ave ...A3
Hoel Treowen ...C2
Kerry Rd. ...B3
Ladywell Shopping Ctr B2
Library ...B2
Llanfair Rd. ...C2
Llanidloes Rd ...C1
Llys Ifor ...C2
Lon Cerddyn ...B1
Lon Helyg. ...C1
Lonesome La. ...A3
Long Bridge. ...B2
Lower Canal Rd. ...B3
Maldwyn Leisure Ctr ..C1
Market ...B2
Market St. ...B2
Milford Rd ...C2
Mill Cl ...B2
Miniature Railway ...B1
Montgomery
  County Infirmary
  (Newtown) ...A2
Mwyn Fynydd ...A3
New Church St ...B2
New Rd. ...B2
Newtown Bypass ...C3
Newtown Football Gd .B1
Newtown Station ...B2
Oak Tree Ave ...A3
Old Kerry Rd ...A3
Oldbarn La. ...C2
Oriel Davies Gallery ..B2
Park Cl ...B2
Park La. ...A1
Park St ...B2
Park, The ...B2
Parklands ...C2
Pavillion Ct ...C1
Plantation La. ...A2
Police Station ...B1
Pont Brynfedw ...B1
Pool Rd. ...A3
Poplar Rd. ...A3
Post Office ...A2
Powys ...B1
Powys Theatre ...B2
Regent ...B2
Robert Owen House. ...B2
Robert Owen Mus ...B2
Rugby Club ...A3
St David's ...B2
School La. ...A3
Sheaf St ...B2

Short Bridge St ...B2
Stone St. ...B2
Superstore ...B3/C1
Sycamore St ...A2
Textile Museum ...B1
Town Hall ...B2
Union St ...A2
Vastre Industrial Est ..B3
War Memorial. ...B2
WHSmith Museum ...B2
Wynfields ...C1
Y Ffrydd ...A3

Northampton   344
78 Derngate ...B3
Abington Sq ...B3
Abington St ...B3
Alcombe St ...A3
All Saints' ...B2
Ambush St ...B1
Angel St ...B2
Army Reserve Centre. .A3
Arundel St ...A2
Ash St ...A2
Auctioneers Way ...C2
Bailiff St. ...A2
Barrack Rd. ...A2
BBOB Rugby FC. ...A1
Beaconsfield Terr ...A3
Becket's Park ...C3
Bedford Rd ...B3
Billing Rd. ...B3
Brecon St ...A1
Brewery ...C2
Bridge St ...C2
Broad St. ...B2
Burns St ...A3
Bus Station ...B2
Campbell St ...A2
Castle (Site of) ...B2
Castle St. ...B2
Cattle Market Rd ...C2
Central Museum &
  Art Gallery ...B2
Charles St ...A3
Cheyne Walk ...C2
Church La ...A3
Clare St ...A3
Cloutsham St. ...A3
College St. ...B2
Colwyn Rd ...A3
Cotton End. ...C2
Countess Rd ...A1
Court ...A2
Craven St ...A3
Crown & County
  Courts ...B3
Denmark Rd. ...B3
Derngate ...B3
Doddridge Church ...B2
Drapery, The. ...B2
Duke St. ...A3
Dunster St ...A3
Earl St. ...A3
Euston Rd. ...C2
Fire Station ...A3
Foot Meadow ...C2
Gladstone Rd. ...A1
Gold St. ...B2
Grafton St ...A2
Gray St. ...A3
Green St. ...B1
Greenwood Rd ...A1
Greyfriars ...B2
Grosvenor Centre ...B2
Grove Rd ...A3
Guildhall ...B2
Hampton St. ...A2
Harding Terr ...A2
Hazelwood Rd ...B3
Herbert St. ...B2
Hervey St ...A3
Hester St ...A2
Holy Sepulchre ...B2
Hood St ...A3
Horse Market ...B2
Hunter St. ...A3
Information Ctr ...A3
Kettering Rd. ...A3
Kingswell St ...B2
Lady's La ...B2
Leicester St. ...A2
Leslie Rd ...A2
Library ...B3
Lorne Rd ...A2
Lorry Park ...A1
Louise Rd. ...A2
Lower Harding St ...A2
Lower Hester St ...A2
Lower Mounts. ...B3
Lower Priory St. ...A2
Main Rd. ...C1
Marefair. ...B2
Market Sq ...B2
Marlboro Rd ...B1
Marriott St ...A1
Millers Meadow ...C1
Military Rd. ...A3
Mounts Baths
  Leisure Centre ...A3
Nene Valley Retail Pk. .C1
New South Bridge St. .C2
Northampton General
  Hospital (A&E) ...A2
Northampton Marina .C3
Northampton Sta ...A2
Northcote St ...A2
Nunn Mills Rd ...C3
Old Towcester Rd. ...C2
Overstone Rd ...B3
Pembroke Rd ...A1
Penn Court ...C1
Police Station ...B3
Post Office ...A1/B3
Quorn Way ...A2
Ransome Rd ...C3
Regent Sq ...A2
Ridings, The ...B3
Robert St ...A2

Royal & Derngate
  Theatres ...B2
St Andrew's Rd ...B1
St Andrew's St. ...A2
St Edmund's Rd. ...B3
St George's St ...A2
St Giles ...B2
St Giles St ...B3
St Giles' Terr ...B3
St James Park Rd ...B1
St James Rd. ...B1
St James Retail Park ..C1
St James' Mill Rd ...C1
St James' Mill Rd East .C1
St Leonard's Rd ...C2
St Mary's St ...B2
St Michael's Rd ...A3
St Peter's
  Shopping Precinct. ..B2
St Peter's Way ...B2
Salisbury St ...A2
Scarletwell St ...B2
Semilong Rd ...A2
Sheep St. ...B2
Sol Central
  (Leisure Centre) ...B2
Somerset St ...A3
South Bridge ...C2
Southfield Ave ...A3
Spencer Bridge Rd. ...A1
Spencer Rd ...A2
Spring Gdns. ...B3
Spring La ...A2
Superstore ...C2
Swan St. ...A3
Tintern Ave ...A1
Towcester Rd ...C2
Univ of Northampton
  (Waterside Campus).C3
Upper Bath St ...B2
Upper Mounts ...A2
Victoria Park. ...A2
Victoria Promenade ..B2
Victoria Rd. ...B3
Victoria St. ...A2
Wellingborough Rd ..B3
West Bridge ...B2
York Rd. ...B3

Norwich   345
Albion Way ...C3
All Saints Green ...C2
Anchor St. ...A3
Anglia Sq ...A2
Argyle St ...C3
Arts Centre ...B1
Ashby St ...C2
Assembly House ...B1
Bank Plain ...B2
Barker St. ...A1
Barn Rd ...A1
Barrack St ...A3
Ber St ...C2
Bethel St ...B1
Bishop Bridge ...A3
Bishopbridge Rd. ...A3
Bishopgate ...A2
Blackfriars St ...A2
Botolph St. ...A2
Bracondale ...C3
Brazen Gate. ...C2
Bridewell Museum ...B2
Brunswick Rd ...C1
Bull Close Rd. ...A3
Bus Station ...C2
Calvert St. ...A2
Cannell Green. ...A3
Carrow Rd ...C3
Castle & Museum ...B2
Castle Mall. ...B2
Castle Meadow. ...B2
Cathedral ...B2
Cathedral (RC) ...B1
Cathedral Retail Park .A1
Cattlemarket St ...B2
Chantry Rd. ...C1
Chapel Loke ...C2
Chapelfield East. ...B1
Chapelfield Gdns ...B1
Chapelfield North ...B1
Chapelfield Rd ...B1
Cinema City ...B2
City Hall ...B1
City Rd ...C2
City Wall ...C1/C3
Close, The. ...B2/B3
Colegate ...A2
Coslany St ...B1
Cow Hill ...B1
Cow Tower. ...A3
Cowgate. ...A2
Crown & Magistrates'
  Courts ...B2
Dragon Hall Heritage
  Centre ...C3
Duke St. ...B1
Edward St ...A2
Elm Hill. ...B2
Erpingham Gate ...B2
Fishergate. ...A2
Forum, The ...B1
Foundry Bridge ...B3
Fye Bridge ...A2
Garden St. ...C2
Gas Hill. ...B3
Gentlemans Walk. ...B2
Grapes Hill. ...B1
Great Hosp Halls, The .A3
Grove Ave. ...C1
Grove Rd ...C1
Guildhall ...B2
Gurney Rd ...A3
Hall Rd ...C2
Heathgate. ...A3
Heigham St ...A1
Hollywood ...C2
Horn's La ...C2
Hungate
  Medieval Art ...B2

Information Ctr ...B1
intu Chapelfield ...C1
Ipswich Rd. ...C1
ITV Anglia ...C3
James Stuart Gdns. ...B3
King St ...B2
King St ...C3
Koblenz Ave ...C3
Leisure Centre ...A3
Library ...B2
London St ...B2
Lower Clarence Rd. ...B3
Maddermarket ...B1
Magdalen St ...A2
Mariners La ...C2
Market ...B2
Market Ave ...B2
Mountergate. ...B2
Mousehold St ...A3
Newmarket Rd ...C1
Norfolk St ...C1
Norwich City FC ...C3
Norwich Gallery ...B2
Norwich School ...B2
Norwich Station ...B3
Oak St. ...A1
Odeon ...C3
Palace St ...B2
Pitt St ...A2
Playhouse ...B2
Police Station ...A3
Post Office
  ...A2/B2/B3/C1
Pottergate. ...B1
Prince of Wales Rd. ...B2
Princes St. ...B2
Pull's Ferry ...B3
Puppet Theatre ...A2
Queen St ...B2
Queens Rd ...C2
Recorder Rd ...B3
Riverside Entertainment
  Centre ...B3
Riverside Leisure Ctr. .B3
Riverside Rd ...B3
Riverside Retail Park. .B3
Rosary Rd. ...B3
Rose La. ...B2
Rouen Rd. ...C2
St Andrews St ...B2
St Augustines St. ...A1
St Benedicts St. ...B1
St Crispins Road ...A1
St Ethelbert's Gate ...B2
St Faiths La ...B2
St Georges St ...A2
St Giles St ...B1
St James Cl ...A2
St Julians ...C2
St Leonards Rd ...B3
St Martin's La ...A1
St Peter Mancroft ...B1
St Peters St ...B2
St Stephens Rd ...C1
St Stephens St. ...C1
Shopmobility ...B2
Silver Rd. ...A2
Silver St ...A2
Southwell Rd. ...C2
St. Andrew's &
  Blackfriars' Hall ...B2
Strangers' Hall ...B1
Superstore ...C2
Surrey St ...C2
Sussex St ...A1
Theatre Royal ...B1
Theatre St ...B1
Thorn La. ...B2
Thorpe Rd ...B3
Tombland ...B2
Union St ...C1
Vauxhall St ...B1
Victoria St. ...C1
Vue ...B2
Walpole St ...B1
Waterfront, The ...C3
Wensum St ...B2
Wessex St ...C1
Westwick St ...A1
Wherry Rd. ...C3
Whitefriars ...A2
Willow La. ...B1

Nottingham   345
Abbotsford Dr. ...A3
Addison St. ...A1
Albert Hall ...B1
Alfred St Central ...A3
Alfreton Rd ...A1
All Saints St. ...A1
Annesley Gr. ...A1
Arboretum ...A1
Arboretum St ...A1
Arthur St ...A1
Arts Theatre ...B3
Ashforth St ...A3
Balmoral Rd ...A1
Barker Gate. ...B3
Bath St ...B3
BBC Nottingham. ...C3
Beacon Hill Rise ...B3
Belgrave Rooms. ...B1
Bellar Gate ...B3
Belward St. ...B3
Brewhouse Yard ...C2
Broad Marsh Bus Sta. .C2
Broad St. ...B3
Brook St. ...B3
Burns St. ...A1
Burton St. ...B2
Bus Station ...C2
Canal St ...C2
Carlton St. ...B3
Carrington St ...C2
Castle ...C1
Castle Blvd. ...C1
Castle Gate ...C2
Castle Meadow Rd ...C1
Castle Meadow
  Retail Park ...C1

Castle Rd ...C2
Castle Wharf. ...C2
Cavendish Rd East ...C1
Cemetery. ...A1/B1
Chaucer St. ...B1
Cheapside ...B2
Church Rd ...A3
City Link ...C3
City of Caves ...C2
Clarendon St. ...B1
Cliff Rd ...C3
Clumber Rd East. ...C1
Clumber St ...B2
College St. ...B1
Collin St ...C2
Contemporary ...C3
Conway St ...C3
Cornerhouse, The ...B2
Council House ...B2
Cranbrook St ...B3
Cranmer St. ...A2
Cromwell St. ...B1
Curzon St. ...B2
Derby Rd ...B1
Dryden St. ...A2
Exchange Ctr, The. ...B2
Fishpond Dr. ...C1
Fletcher Gate ...B3
Forest Rd East. ...A1
Forest Rd West. ...A1
Friar La. ...C2
Gedling Gr. ...A1
Gedling St ...B3
George St. ...B2
Gill St ...A2
Glasshouse St ...B2
Goldsmith St. ...B2
Goose Gate. ...B3
Great Freeman St. ...A2
Guildhall ...B2
Hamilton Dr. ...C1
Hampden St. ...A1
Heathcote St. ...B3
High Pavement. ...C3
High School ...A1
HM Revenue &
  Customs. ...C2
Holles Cr. ...C1
Hope Dr ...C1
Hungerhill Rd. ...A3
Huntingdon Dr ...C1
Huntingdon St. ...A2
Information Ctr ...B2
Instow Rise ...A3
International Com Ctr .A2
intu Broadmarsh ...C2
intu Victoria Centre. ..B2
Kent St ...B3
King St ...B2
Lace Market ...B3
Lace Mkt Theatre ...B3
Lamartine St. ...B3
Leisure Ctr. ...C1
Lenton Rd ...C1
Lewis Cl ...A3
Lincoln St. ...B2
London Rd ...C3
Long Row ...B2
Low Pavement ...C2
Lower Parliament St .B3
Magistrates' Court. ...C2
Maid Marian Way ...B2
Mansfield Rd. ...A2/B2
Middle Hill ...C2
Milton St ...B2
Mount St ...C2
National Ice Centre &
  Motorpoint Arena ..C3
National Justice
  Museum ...C2
Newcastle Dr. ...B1
Newstead Gr. ...A1
North Sherwood St ..A2
Nottingham Arena ...C3
Nottingham Cath ...B1
Nottingham College ..C3
Nottingham Station ..C2
Nottingham Trent
  University ...A2/B2
Old Market Square ...B2
Oliver St. ...A1
Park Dr. ...C1
Park Row ...C1
Park Terr. ...C1
Park Valley ...C1
Park, The ...C1
Peas Hill Rd ...A3
Peel St ...A1
Pelham St ...B2
Peveril Dr. ...C1
Plantagenet St. ...A3
Playhouse Theatre ...B1
Plumptre St. ...C3
Police Station ...B1/B2
Poplar St ...C3
Portland Rd. ...C1
Queen's Rd ...C2
Raleigh St ...A1
Regent St. ...B1
Rick St ...B3
Robin Hood St. ...B3
Robin Hood Statue ...C2
Ropewalk, The ...B1
Royal Centre ...B2
Royal Children Inn ...C2
Royal Concert Hall ...B2
St Ann's Hill Rd ...A2
St Ann's Way ...A3
St Ann's Well Rd ...A3
St James' St. ...B2
St Mark's St. ...A3
St Mary's Rest Garden .B3
St Mary's Gate. ...B3
St Nicholas ...C2
St Peter's ...B2
St Peter's Gate. ...B2
Salutation Inn ...C2
Shakespeare St ...B2
Shelton St. ...A2
Shopmobility ...B2

South Pde ...B2
South Rd. ...C1
South Sherwood St ...B2
Station Street ...C2
Stoney St ...B3
Talbot St. ...B1
Tattershall Dr ...C1
Tennis Dr ...B1
Tennyson St ...A1
Theatre Royal ...B2
Trent St ...C3
Trent University ...B2
Union Rd ...B3
Upper Parliament St ..B2
Victoria Leisure Ctr ..B3
Victoria Park. ...B3
Victoria St. ...B2
Walter St ...A1
Warser Gate ...B3
Watkin St ...A2
Wilford Rd. ...C2
Wilford St ...C2
Wollaton St ...B1
Woodborough Rd. ...A2
Woolpack La ...B3
Ye Old Trip to
  Jerusalem ...C2
York St ...A2

Oban   345
Aird's Cres. ...A2
Albany St ...B2
Albert La ...B2
Albert St. ...A2
Alma Cres ...A2
Ambulance Station ...C2
Angus Terr. ...C3
Ardconnel Rd ...B2
Ardconnel Terr. ...B2
Argyll Sq ...B2
Argyll St ...B2
Atlantis Leisure Ctr ..A2
Bayview Rd. ...A1
Benvoulin Rd. ...C2
Bowling Green ...A1
Breadalbane St. ...B2
Bus Station ...B2
Campbell St. ...B2
Catte St ...B2
Cemetery. ...A3
Combie St ...B2
Corran Brae. ...A2
Corran Esplanade ...A1/A2
Corran Halls, The ...B2
Court ...B2
Crannaig-a-Mhinistir ..B1
Crannog La ...B2
Croft Ave ...C2
Dalintart Dr ...C3
Dalriach Rd ...A1
Distillery ...B2
Drummore Rd. ...A2
Dunollie Rd ...A2
Dunuaran Rd. ...B1
Feochan Gr ...C3
Ferry Terminal ...B1
Gallanach Rd. ...C1
George St. ...A2
Glencruitten Dr ...C3
Glencruitten Rd ...B3
Glenmore Rd ...C1
Glenshellach Rd ...C1
Glenshellach Terr ...B2
Hazeldean Cres ...C3
High St ...B2
Hill St ...B2
Industrial Estate. ...C2
Information Ctr ...B2
Islay St ...B2
Jacob's Ladder ...B2
Jura Rd. ...C3
Knipoch Pl ...C3
Laurel Cres ...A2
Laurel Rd ...A2/A3
Library ...B1
Lifeboat Station ...B1
Lighthouse Pier ...B1
Lismore Cres. ...A2
Lochavullin Dr ...B2
Lochavullin Rd ...C2
Lochside St ...B2
Longsdale Cres. ...A2
Longsdale Rd ...A2/A3
Longsdale Terr. ...A3
Lunga Rd. ...C2
Lynn Rd. ...C2
McCaig Rd ...C3
McCaig's Tower ...B2
Mill La. ...A2
Miller Rd ...B2
Millpark Ave ...C2
Millpark Rd ...C2
Mossfield Ave. ...B3
Mossfield Dr. ...B3
Mossfield Stadium. ...B3
Nant Dr. ...C3
Nelson Rd ...A2
North Pier ...B1
Nursery La. ...A2
Oban ...B2
Oban Phoenix ...B2
Police Station ...B2
Post Office ...A2/B2
Polvinister Rd. ...B2
Pulpit Dr. ...C1
Pulpit Hill ...C1
Pulpit Hill
  Viewpoint ...B1
Quarry Rd. ...C2
Queen's Park Pl ...B2
Railway Quay. ...B1
Retail Park. ...B2
Rockfield Rd. ...B2
St Columba's ...A1
St John's ...A2
Scalpay Terr. ...C3

Shore St. ...B1
Shuna Terr. ...C3
Sinclair Dr ...C3
Soroba Rd ...B2/C2
South Pier ...B1
Stevenson St ...B2
Tweedale St. ...B2
Ulva Rd. ...C2
Villa Rd. ...B1
War & Peace ...A2

Oxford   345
Adelaide St ...A1
Albert St. ...A1
All Souls (Coll) ...B2
Ashmolean Mus ...B2
Balliol (Coll) ...B2
Banbury Rd ...A1
Bate Collection of
  Musical Instruments .C1
Beaumont St ...B1
Becket St. ...B1
Blackhall Rd ...A2
Blue Boar St ...B2
Bodleian Library ...B2
Botanic Garden ...B3
Brasenose (Coll) ...B2
Brewer St ...C2
Broad St. ...B2
Burton-Taylor
  Theatre ...B2
Bus Station ...B1
Canal St. ...A1
Carfax Tower. ...B2
Castle ...B1
Castle St. ...B1
Catte St ...B2
Christ Church (Coll) ..C2
Christ Church Cath ...C2
Christ Church Mdw ...C2
Clarendon Centre ...B2
Coach & Lorry Park ..A1
College. ...C2
Coll of Further Ed. ...C1
Cornmarket St ...B2
County Hall ...B1
Covered Market ...B2
Cowley Pl. ...C3
Cranham St. ...A1
Cranham Terr. ...A1
Cricket Ground. ...B1
Crown & County
  Courts ...C2
Deer Park. ...B3
Exeter (Coll) ...B2
Folly Bridge. ...C2
George St. ...B1
Great Clarendon St ...A1
Hart St ...A1
Hertford (Coll) ...B2
High St ...B2
Hollybush Row ...B1
Holywell St ...B2
Hythe Bridge St ...B1
Ice Rink ...B1
Information Ctr ...B2
Jericho St ...A1
Jesus (Coll) ...B2
Jowett Walk ...B3
Juxon St ...A1
Keble (Coll) ...A2
Keble Rd. ...A2
Library ...B2
Linacre (Coll) ...A3
Lincoln (Coll) ...B2
Little Clarendon St. ...A1
Longwall St. ...B3
Magdalen (Coll) ...B3
Magdalen Bridge ...B3
Magdalen St ...B2
Magistrate's Court. ...C2
Manchester (Coll) ...B2
Manor Rd ...A3
Mansfield (Coll) ...A3
Mansfield Rd ...A3
Market ...B2
Marlborough Rd ...C2
Martyrs' Memorial ...B2
Merton (Coll) ...B2
Merton Field ...B3
Merton St ...B2
Mus of Modern Art ...B2
Museum of Oxford ...B2
Museum Rd ...A2
New College (Coll) ...B3
New Inn Hall St ...B2
New Rd ...B1
New Theatre ...B2
Norfolk St ...C1
Nuffield (Coll) ...B1
Observatory ...A1
Observatory St ...A1
Odeon ...B1/B2
Old Fire Station ...B1
Old Greyfriars St ...C2
Oriel (Coll) ...B2
Oxford Station ...B1
Oxford University
  Research Centres ...A1
Oxpens Rd ...C1
Paradise Sq ...C1
Paradise St ...B1
Park End St ...B1
Parks Rd ...A2/B2
Pembroke (Coll) ...C2
Phoenix ...A1
Picture Gallery ...C2
Plantation Rd ...A1
Playhouse ...B2
Police Station ...B2
Post Office ...A1/B2
Pusey St. ...B2
Queen's (Coll). ...B2
Queen's La. ...B2
Radcliffe Camera ...B2
Rewley Rd ...B1

Richmond Rd. ...A1
Rose La. ...B3
Ruskin (Coll) ...B1
Said Business School ..A1
St Aldates ...C2
St Anne's (Coll) ...A1
St Antony's (Coll) ...A1
St Bernard's St ...A1
St Catherine's (Coll) ..B3
St Cross Building ...A3
St Cross Rd ...A3
St Edmund Hall (Coll) .B3
St Giles ...B2
St Hilda's (Coll) ...C3
St John St ...B2
St John's (Coll). ...B2
St Mary the Virgin ...B2
St Michael at the
  Northgate ...B2
St Peter's (Coll) ...B2
St Thomas St ...B1
Science Area. ...A2
Science Museum ...B2
Sheldonian
  Theatre ...B2
Somerville (Coll) ...A1
South Parks Rd ...A2
Speedwell St ...C2
Sports Ground ...C2
Thames St ...C1
Town Hall ...B2
Trinity (Coll) ...B2
Turl St. ...B2
University Coll (Coll). .B2
University Mus &
  Pitt Rivers Mus ...A2
University Parks. ...A2
Wadham (Coll) ...B2
Walton Cr. ...A1
Walton St. ...A1
Western Rd ...C2
Westgate ...C2
Woodstock Rd. ...A1
Worcester (Coll) ...B1

Perth   345
AK Bell Library ...B2
Abbot Cres. ...C1
Abbot St. ...C1
Albany Terr. ...A1
Albert Monument. ...A2
Alexandra St ...B2
Atholl St ...A2
Balhousie St ...A2
Ballantine Pl ...B1
Barossa Pl ...A2
Barossa St ...A2
Barrack St ...A2
Bell's Sports Centre. ..A1
Bellwood ...C3
Blair St. ...B1
Burn Park. ...C1
Bus Station ...B2
Caledonian Rd ...B1
Canal Cres. ...B2
Canal St. ...B2
Cavendish Ave. ...C1
Charles St ...B2
Charlotte Pl. ...A2
Charlotte St ...A2
Church St. ...A1
City Hall ...B2
City Mills ...B2
Club House ...C3
Clyde Pl ...C1
Coach Park ...C2
Commercial St ...A3
Concert Hall ...B2
Council Chambers ...B3
County Pl ...B2
Court ...A2
Craigie Pl ...C2
Crieff Rd. ...A1
Croft Park ...A1
Cross St ...A2
Darnhall Cres ...C1
Darnhall Dr ...C1
Dewars Centre ...B1
Dundee Rd. ...B3
Dunkeld Rd ...A1
Earl's Dykes. ...B1
Edinburgh Rd ...C2
Elibank St ...C1
Fair Maid's House ...A3
Fergusson ...B2
Feus Rd ...A1
Fire Station ...A1
Foundary La ...B1
Friar St. ...C1
George St. ...B3
Glamis Pl ...C2
Glasgow Rd ...C1
Glenearn Rd ...C2
Glover St ...B1/C1
Golf Course ...A3
Gowrie St. ...A3
Gray St. ...B1
Graybank Rd ...B1
Greyfriars Burial Gd ..A2
Hay St ...A2
High St. ...B2/B3
Inchaffray St ...A1
Industrial/Retail Park. .C1
Information Ctr ...B2
Isla Rd. ...A3
James St ...B3
Keir St. ...A1
King Edward St ...B2
King James VI
  Golf Course ...C3
King St. ...B2
Kings Pl ...C1
Kinnoull Causeway. ...B1
Kinnoull St. ...A2
Knowelea Pl ...C1
Knowelea Terr ...C1
Ladeside Bsns Centre ..C1
Leisure Pool ...B1

Leonard St. ...B2
Lickley St. ...A2
Lochie Brae. ...A3
Long Causeway. ...A1
Low St. ...A2
Main St. ...A2
Marshall Pl ...C2
Melville St. ...A1
Mill St. ...A2
Milne St. ...B2
Murray Cres. ...C1
Murray St. ...B2
Needless Rd ...C1
New Rd. ...B2
North Inch ...A2
North Methven St. ...A2
Park Pl ...C2
Perth ...B2
Perth Bridge ...A3
Perth Business Park ...B1
Perth Museum &
  Art Gallery ...B3
Perth Station ...B2
Pickletullum Rd. ...B1
Pitheavlis Cres ...C1
Playhouse ...B2
Police Station ...A2
Pomarium St. ...B1
Post Office ...B2/C2
Princes St ...B2
Priory Pl. ...C1
Queen St. ...C1
Queen's Bridge. ...B3
Riggs Rd. ...B1
Riverside ...B3
Riverside Park ...A3
Rodney Gdns. ...C3
Rose Terr. ...A2
St Catherine's Rd ...A1/A2
St Catherine's
  Retail Park. ...A1
St John St. ...B2
St John's Kirk ...B3
St John's Shopping Ctr .B2
St Leonards Bridge ...C2
St Ninians Cathedral ..A2
Scott Monument. ...C2
Scott St ...B2
Sheriff Court. ...B3
Shore Rd ...C3
Skate Park. ...C3
South Inch. ...C2
South Inch Bsns Ctr. ..C3
South Inch Park ...C2
South Inch View. ...C2
South Methven St. ...B2
South St. ...B3
South William St. ...C2
Stables, The. ...A1
Stanners, The. ...A3
Stormont St. ...A2
Strathmore St. ...A3
Stuart Ave ...C1
Superstore ...B1/B2
Tay St. ...B3
Union La. ...A2
Victoria St. ...B2
Watergate. ...B3
Wellshill Cemetery ...A1
West Bridge St ...A3
West Mill St. ...B2
Whitefriars Cres. ...B1
Whitefriars St. ...B1
Wilson St. ...C1
Windsor Terr. ...C1
Woodside Cres ...C1
York Pl ...B2
Young St. ...C1

Peterborough   345
Athletics Arena. ...B2
Bishop's Palace ...B2
Bishop's Rd ...B2/B3
Boongate. ...A3
Bourges Boulevard ...A1
Bourges Retail Pk ...B1/B2
Bridge House
  (Council Offices) ...C2
Bridge St ...B2
Bright St. ...A1
Broadway. ...A2
Brook St. ...A2
Burghley Rd. ...A2
Bus Station ...B2
Cavendish St. ...A3
Charles St ...A3
Church St. ...B2
Church Walk ...A2
Cobden Ave ...A1
Cobden St ...A1
Cowgate. ...B2
Craig St ...A2
Crawthorne Rd ...A2
Cromwell Rd ...A1
Dickens St ...A2
Eastfield Rd. ...A3
Eastgate. ...B2
East Station Road. ...C2
Fire Station ...A2
Fletton Ave ...C2
Frank Perkins
  Parkway ...C3
Geneva St. ...A2
George St. ...C1
Gladstone St ...A1
Glebe Rd ...C2
Gloucester Rd ...A3
Granby St. ...B3
Grove St ...C1
Guildhall ...B2
Hadrians Ct ...C3
Hawksbill Way ...C2
Henry St ...A1
Hereward Cross
  (shopping) ...B2
Hereward Rd. ...B3
Information Ctr ...B2
Jubilee St ...C1
Kent Rd. ...A2

Key Theatre ♦ C2
Kirkwood Cl. B1
Lea Gdns B1
Library A2
Lincoln Rd A2
London Rd B2
Long Causeway B2
Lower Bridge St C2
Magistrates Court B2
Manor House St A1
Mayor's Walk A1
Midland St A2
Monument St A2
Morris St A2
Mus & Art Gallery ♦ B2
Nene Valley Railway ♦ C1
New Rd A2
New Rd C1
Northminster A2
Old Customs House ♦ C1
Oundle Rd C1
Padholme Rd A3
Palmerston Rd C1
Park Rd C1
Passport Office A2
Peterborough Cath † B2
Peterborough Nene
Valley ♦ B1
Peterborough Sta ≋ B1
Police Station ◙ B1
Post Office ◙ A3/B2
Priestgate B2
Queen's Walk C2
Queensgate Centre B2
Railworld Wildlife
Haven ♦ C1
Regional Fitness &
Swimming Centre B2
River La B1
Rivergate Shopping
Centre B2
Riverside Mead. C1
Russell St. A1
St John's ♦ B2
St John's St. A3
St Marks St A2
St Peter's Rd A2
Saxon Rd A1
Spital Bridge A1
Stagshaw Dr C3
Star Rd B1
Superstore B1
Thorpe Lea Rd. B1
Thorpe Rd B1
Thorpe's Lea Rd B1
Tower St. A2
Town Hall B2
Viersen Platz. B2
Vineyard Rd. B3
Wake Rd. A3
Wellington St A3
Wentworth St B2
Westgate B2
Weston Homes Stadium
(Peterborough United
FC) The. C1
Whalley St A1
Wharf Rd C1
Whitsed St. A3
YMCA A3

Plymouth 346
Alma Rd A1
Anstis St. A2
Armada Shopping Ctr B2
Armada St. A3
Armada Way B2
Arts Centre B2
Athenaeum ♦ B1
Athenaeum St. B2
Barbican ♦ C3
Barbican ♦ C3
Baring St A3
Bath St B1
Beaumont Park. B3
Beaumont Rd. B3
Black Friars Gin
Distillery ♦ C2
Breton Side. B3
Castle St. C3
Cathedral (RC) † B1
Cecil St. A1
Central Park A1
Central Park Ave. A1
Charles Church ♦ B3
Charles Cross ♦ B3
Charles St B2
Citadel Rd C2
Citadel Rd East C2
City Museum &
Art Gallery ♦ A2
Civic Centre ♦ B2
Cliff Rd C2
Clifton Pl A3
Cobourg St B2
College of Art B2
Continental
Ferry Port B1
Cornwall St. B1
Crescent, The. B1
Dale Rd. A3
Deptford Pl. A3
Derry Ave. A2
Derry's Cross ♦ B1
Drake Circus B2
Drake Circus
Shopping Centre B2
Eastlake St. B2
Elizabethan House ♦ C3
Elliot St. C1
Endsleigh Pl A3
Exeter St B3
Fire Station A2
Fish Quay. C3
Gibbons St. A3
Glen Park Ave A1
Grand Parade C2
Great Western Rd. C1
Greenbank Rd. A3

Greenbank Terr A3
Guildhall B2
Hampton St B2
Harwell St B1
Hill Park Cr A3
Hoe Approach B2
Hoe Rd C2
Hoe, The C2
Hoegate St C2
Houndiscombe Rd A2
Information Ctr ⓘ C3
James St A2
Kensington Rd A3
King St B1
Lambhay Hill C3
Leigham St C1
Library B2
Lipson Rd A3/B3
Lockyer St C2
Lockyers Quay C3
Madeira Rd C2
Marina B3
Market Ave B1
Martin St B1
Mayflower St. B2
Mayflower Stone &
Steps C2
Mayflower Visitor
Centre ♦ C2
Merchant's House ♦ B2
Millbay Rd B1
National Marine
Aquarium ♦ C3
Neswick St. B1
New George St B2
New St C3
North Cross ⊙ A2
North Hill. A3
North Quay. B3
North Rd East A2
North Rd West. A1
North St. B3
Notte St C2
Octagon, The ⊙ B1
Octagon St. B1
Pannier Market. B2
Pennycomequick ⊙ A1
Pier St. C1
Plymouth Naval
Memorial ♦ C2
Plymouth Pavilions B1
Plymouth Station ≋ B3
Police Station ◙ B3
Post Office ◙ B2
Princess St C2
Promenade, The. C2
Prysten House ♦ B2
Queen Anne's Battery
Seasports Centre C3
Radford Rd C1
Reel ♦ B2
Regent St. A3
Rope Walk C3
Royal Citadel ♦ C3
Royal Pde. B2
Royal Theatre ♦ B2
St Andrew's ♦ B2
St Andrew's Cross ⊙ B2
St Andrew's St B2
St Lawrence Rd. A2
Saltash Rd A2
Shopmobility B2
Smeaton's Tower ♦ C2
Southern Terr. A3
Southside St C2
Stuart Rd. A1
Sutherland Rd. A2
Sutton Rd. B3
Sydney St. A1
Teats Hill Rd C3
Tothill Ave B3
Union St. B1
Univ of Plymouth A2
Vauxhall St B2/3
Victoria Park. A1
West Hoe Rd C1
Western Approach. B1
Whittington St A1
Wyndham St A1
YMCA B1
YWCA C2

Poole 346
Ambulance Station A3
Baiater Gdns C2
Baiter Park C3
Ballard Cl. B3
Ballard Rd B3
Bay Hog La. B1
BMI The Harbour
Hospital Ⓗ A3
Bridge Approach C1
Bus Station B1
Castle St. B2
Catalina Dr C3
Chapel La. B2
Church St. B2
Cinnamon La. B1
Colborne Cl A3
Dear Hay La. B1
Denmark La. A2
Denmark Rd A2
Dolphin Ctr B2
East St. B2
Elizabeth Rd A3
Emerson Rd B2
Ferry Rd. C1
Ferry Terminal. C1
Fire Station A3
Freightliner Terminal C1
Furnell Rd A3
Garland Rd. A3
Green Rd B2
Heckford La A3
Heckford Rd A3
High St B2
High St North A2
Hill St B2
Holes Bay Rd A1
Hospital (A&E) Ⓗ A3

Information Ctr ⓘ C2
Kingland Rd A3
Kingston Rd. C3
Labrador Dr. C3
Lagland St B2
Lander St C2
Lighthouse, Poole
Centre for the Arts ♦ B3
Longfleet Rd A3
Maple Rd A3
Market Cl. B2
Market St. B2
Mount Pleasant Rd. A3
New Harbour Rd C1
New Harbour Rd South C1
New Harbour Rd West C1
New Orchard. B1
New Quay Rd C1
New St B2
Newfoundland Dr. B2
North St. B2
Old Lifeboat ♦ B2
Old Orchard. B2
Parish Rd A3
Park Lake Rd C3
Parkstone Rd A3
Perry Gdns. C2
Pitwines Cl B2
Police Station ◙ B2
Poole Central Library B2
Poole Lifting Bridge C1
Poole Park. C2
Poole Station ≋ B2
Poole Museum ♦ B2
Post Office ◙ B2
Quay, The. C2
RNLI College C2
St John's Rd. A3
St Margaret's Rd A2
St Mary's Maternity
Unit. A3
St Mary's Rd. A3
Seldown Bridge B3
Seldown La B3
Seldown Rd B3
Serpentine Rd. A2
Skinner St B2
Slipway. C2
Stanley Rd. B3
Sterte Ave A2
Sterte Ave West A1
Sterte Cl. A2
Sterte Esplanade A2
Sterte Rd A2
Strand St C2
Superstore B3
Swimming Pool B3
Taverner Cl B3
Thames St. B1
Towngate Bridge B2
Twin Sails Bridge B1
Vallis Cl. C3
Waldren Cl. B3
West Quay B1
West Quay Rd. B1
West St. B1
West View Rd A2
Whatleigh Cl B2
Wimborne Rd A3

Portsmouth 346
Action Stations ♦ C1
Admiralty Rd A1
Alfred Rd A2
Anglesea Rd B2
Arundel St B3
Aspex ♦ C1
Bishop St. A2
Broad St. C1
Buckingham
House ♦ B2
Burnaby Rd. B2
Bus Station B3
Camber Dock C1
Cambridge Rd. B2
Car Ferry to Isle of
Wight. B1
Cascades Shopping
Centre A3
Castle Rd. C3
Civic Offices B3
Clarence Pier. C2
College St. A3
Commercial Rd. A3
Cottage Gr. C3
Cross St. A2
Cumberland St A2
Duisburg Way C2
Durham St. A3
East St. C1
Edinburgh Rd A2
Elm Gr. C3
Emirates Spinnaker
Tower ♦ B1
Governor's Grn. C1
Great Southsea St C3
Green Rd B3
Greetham St B3
Grosvenor St. B3
Groundlings ♦ A2
Grove Rd North. C3
Grove Rd South. C3
Guildhall ♦ B3
Guildhall Walk B3
Gunwharf Quays
Designer Outlet B1
Gunwharf Rd. B1
Hambrook St. C2
Hampshire Terr B2
Hanover St. A1
Hard, The. A1
High St C2
HM Naval Base A1
HMS Nelson (Royal
Naval Barracks) A1
HMS Monitor M.33 ♦ A1
HMS Victory ♦ A1
HMS Warrior ♦ A1

Hovercraft Terminal C2
Hyde Park Rd. B3
Information Ctr ⓘ A1/B3
Isambard Brunel Rd. B3
Isle of Wight
Car Ferry Terminal. B1
Kent Rd C2
Kent St A2
King St B3
King's Rd C2
King's Terr. C2
Lake Rd A3
Law Courts B3
Library B3
Long Curtain Rd C2
Marina B1
Market Way. A3
Marmion Rd. C3
Mary Rose ♦ A1
Middle St. B3
Millennium Promenade
Walk B1/C1
Museum Rd. B2
National Museum of
the Royal Navy ♦ A1
Naval Recreation Gd C2
Nightingale Rd C3
Norfolk St. B3
North St. A2
Osborne Rd C3
Paradise St A3
Park Rd. B2
Passenger Catamaran
to Isle of Wight B1
Passenger Ferry to
Gosport B1
Pelham Rd. C3
Pembroke Gdns. C2
Pier Rd. C2
Point Battery. C1
Police Station ◙ B3
Portsmouth & Southsea
Station ≋ A3
Portsmouth Harbour
Station ≋ A1
Portsmouth Historic
Dockyard ♦ A1
Portsmouth Museum &
Art Gallery ♦ B2
Post Office ◙ A1/A3/B3
Queen St A1
Queen's Cr. C3
Ravelin Park B2
Register Office. B2
Round Tower ♦ C1
Royal Garrison
Church ♦ C1
St Edward's Rd. C3
St George's Rd. B3
St George's Sq. B1
St George's Way. C2
St James's Rd B3
St James's St C2
St John's Cath (RC) † A3
St Thomas's Cath † C1
Shopmobility A3/B1
Somers Rd. B3
Southsea Common C2
Southsea Terr. C2
Square Tower ♦ C1
Station St. A3
Town Fortifications ♦ C1
Unicorn Rd. A2
United Services
Recreation Ground B2
University of
Portsmouth. A2/B2
Univ of Portsmouth A3
Upper Arundel St A3
Victoria Ave. C2
Victoria Park. A2
Victory Gate A1
Vue ♦ B1
Warblington St B1
Western Parade. C2
White Hart Rd. C1
Winston Churchill Ave. B3

Preston 346
Adelphi St A2
Anchor Ct. A2
Aqueduct St. A1
Ardee Rd. C1
Arthur St B1
Ashton St. A1
Avenham La. B3
Avenham Park. B3
Avenham Rd. B3
Bairstow St. B3
Balderstone Rd. C1
Beamont Dr. A1
Beech St South. C2
Bird St. C1
Bow La. B2
Brierfield Rd C1
Broadgate C1
Brook St. A2
Bus Station B2
Butler St. B2
Cannon St. B2
Carlton St. A3
Chaddock St. B3
Channel Way. B1
Chapel St. B2
Christ Church St. B2
Christian Rd. B2
Cold Bath St. A2
Coleman St. C1
Connaught Rd. A1
Corn Exchange ♦ B2
Corporation St. A2/B2
County Hall B2
Cricket Ground A1
Croft St. C1
Cross St. A2
Crown Court B3
Crown St. A2
East Cliff B3

East Cliff Rd. B3
Edward St. A2
Elizabeth St. A3
Euston St. C1
Fishergate B2/3
Fishergate Hill B2
Fishergate
Shopping Centre B2
Fitzroy St. B3
Fleetwood St. A1
Fylde Rd A1/A2
Gerrard St. B3
Glover's Ct. B3
Good St. A1
Grafton St. B2
Great George St. B3
Great Shaw St. A2
Greenbank St. A2
Guild Way. B1
Guild Hall & Charter ♦ B3
Guildhall St B2
Harrington St. A2
Harris Museum ♦ B3
Hartington Rd. B3
Hasset Cl. C2
Heatley St. A2
Hind St. C2
Information Ctr ⓘ B3
Kilruddery Rd A3
Lancashire Archives B2
Lancaster Rd A3/B3
Latham St C2
Lauderdale St. C2
Lawson St. A3
Leighton St. A2
Leyland Rd A1
Library B3
Liverpool Rd C1
Lodge St. B2
Lune St. B2
Magistrate's Court. A3
Main Sprit West B3
Maresfield Rd. C1
Market St West A2
Marsh La B1/2
Maudland Bank. A2
Maudland Rd. A2
Meadow Ct. C2
Meath Rd. C2
Mill Hill. A2
Miller Arcade ♦ B3
Miller Park. C3
Moor La. A3
Mount St. B3
North Rd. A3
North St. A2
Northcote Rd. B1
Old Milestones. B1
Old Tram Rd. C3
Pedder St. A1/A2
Peel St A2
Penwortham Bridge C2
Penwortham
New Bridge C1
Pitt St B2
Playhouse ♦ B2
Police Station ◙ B2
Port Way. B1
Post Office ◙ B3
Preston Station ≋ B2
Retail Park. B2
Ribble Bank St B2
Ribble Viaduct C2
Ribblesdale Pl. B3
Ringway. B3
River Parade. B2
Riverside C2
St George's
Shopping Centre B3
St Georges B3
St Johns B3
St Johns Shopping Ctr A3
St Mark's Rd. A1
St Walburges ♦ A1
Salisbury Rd. B1
Sessions House ♦ B3
Snow Hill A3
South End C2
South Meadow La. C1
Spa Rd. B1
Sports Ground A1
Strand Rd. B1
Syke St. B3
Talbot Rd. A2
Taylor St. C1
Tithebarn St. A3
Town Hall B2
Tulketh Brow. A1
University of Central
Lancashire A2
Valley Rd. C1
Victoria Rd. C1
Walker St. A3
Walton's Parade. B2
Warwick St. A3
Wellfield Bsns Park A1
Wellfield Rd. A1
Wellington St. A1
West Cliff. B3
West Strand. A1
Whitby Dr. C3
Winckley St. B3
Winckley Square B3
Wolseley Rd. C2

Reading 346
Abbey Ruins † B2
Abbey Sq. B2
Abbey St. B2
Abbot's Walk. B2
Acacia Rd. C3
Addington Rd. C3
Addison Rd. A1
Allcroft Rd. C3
Alpine St. C3
Auld Burn Rd. B2
Baker St. B1
Berkeley Ave. C1
Bridge St. B2
Brigham Rd. A1

Broad St. B1
Broad Street Mall. B1
Carey St. B1
Castle Hill. C1
Castle St. B1
Causeway, The A3
Caversham Rd. A1
Christchurch
Meadows A2
Civic Offices C1
Coley Hill C1
Coley Pl. C1
Craven Rd. C3
Crown St C2
De Montfort Rd. A1
Denmark Rd. C3
Duke St. B2
East St. B2
Edgehill St. C2
Eldon Rd. B3
Eldon Terr. B3
Elgar Rd. C1
Erleigh Rd C3
Field Rd. C1
Fire Station A1
Fobney St. C1
Forbury Gdns. B2
Forbury Rd. B2
Forbury Retail Park. B2
Francis St. C1
Friar St. B1
Garrard St. B1
Gas Works Rd B3
George St. A2
Great Knollys St. B1
Greyfriars ♦ B1
Grove, The. B2
Gun St. B1
Henry St. C1
Hexagon Theatre,
The ♦ B1
Hill's Meadow A2
Howard St. C1
Inner Distribution Rd. B1
Katesgrove La. C2
Kenavon Dr. B2
Kendrick Rd. C2
King's Meadow
Recreation Ground A2
King's Rd. B2
Library B2
London Rd. C3
London Rd. C2
London St. C2
Lynmouth Rd. A1
Magistrate's Court. B1
Market Pl. B2
Mill La. C2
Mill Rd. A3
Minster St. B1
Morgan Rd. C3
Mount Pleasant C2
Museum of English
Rural Life (MERL) ♦ C3
Napier Rd. A2
Newark St. C2
Newport Rd. A1
Oracle Shopping
Centre, The. B1
Orts Rd. B3
Oxford Road B1
Pell St. C1
Post Office ◙ B1
Queen Victoria St. B1
Queen's Rd. B2
Queen's Rd. B3
Randolph Rd. A1
Reading Bridge. A2
Reading College. B3
Reading Station ≋ A1
Redlands Rd. C3
Riverside Museum ♦ B3
Rose Kiln La. C1
Royal Berkshire Medical
Museum ♦ C3
Royal Berks Hospital
(A&E) Ⓗ C3
St Giles ♦ C2
St Laurence ♦ B2
St Mary's ♦ B1
St Saviour's Rd C1
Send Rd A3
Sherman Rd. C1
Sidmouth St. B2
Silver St. C2
South St. B2
South St Arts Ctr ♦ B2
Southampton St. C2
Station Rd. A1
Superstore A3
Swansea Rd. A1
Thames Lido A2
Tudor Rd. A1
University of Reading C3
Valpy St. B2
Vastern Rd. A1
Vue ♦ B1
Waldeck St. C2
Watlington St B3
West St. B1
Whitley St. C2
Wolseley St. C1
York Rd. A1
Zinzan St. B1

St Andrews 346
Abbey St. B2
Abbey Walk. B3
Abbotsford Cres. A1
Albany Pk. C3
Allan Robertson Dr C2
Ambulance Station C1
Anstruther Rd. C2
Argyle St. B1
Auld Burn Rd. B2
Bassaguard Ind Est A1
Bell St. B2
Blackfriars Chapel
(Ruins) ♦ B2
Boase Ave A1

Braid Cres C3
Brewster Pl C3
Bridge St B2
British Golf Mus ♦ B2
Broomfaulds Ave C1
Bruce Embankment A1
Bruce St B2
Byre Theatre ♦ B2
Canongate C2
Cathedral and Priory
(Ruins) † B3
Cemetery B3
Chamberlain St. B2
Church St. B2
Churchill Cres. C3
City Rd B1
Claybraes. C1
Cockshaugh
Public Park B2
Cosmos Community
Centre A2
Council Office. A2
Crawford Gdns C2
Doubledykes Rd B1
Drumcarrow Rd C1
East Sands. C2
East Scores B3
Fire Station C1
Forrest St B2
Fraser Ave C1
Freddie Tait St C2
Gateway Centre ♦ A1
Glebe Rd C2
Golf Pl. A1
Grange Rd C3
Greenside Pl. B2
Greyfriars Gdns B2
Hamilton Ave. B1
Hepburn Gdns. B1
Holy Trinity ♦ B2
Horseleys Park C1
Information Ctr ⓘ B2
Irvine Cres. C3
James Robb Ave C2
James St B1
John Knox Rd C2
Kennedy Gdns. B1
Kilrymont Cl C3
Kilrymont Pl C3
Kilrymont Rd C3
Kinburn Park. B1
Kinkell Terr. C3
Kinnesburn Rd B2
Ladebraes Walk B2
Lady Buchan's Cave A3
Lamberton Pl C3
Lamond Dr. C2
Langlands Rd C2
Largo Rd C1
Learmonth Pl C1
Library B2
Links Clubhouse. A1
Links, The A1
Livingstone Cres C3
Long Rocks. A2
Madras College C2
Market St B2
Martyr's Monument. A1
Murray Pk A2
Murray Pl. A2
Mus of the Univ of St
Andrews (MUSA) ♦ B2
Nelson St. B2
New Course, The A1
New Picture House ♦ A2
North Castle St B2
North St B2
Old Course, The A1
Old Station Rd. A1
Pends, The. B3
Pilmour Links A1
Pipeland Rd. B2/C2
Police Station ◙ C2/C1
Post Office ◙ B2
Preservation Trust ♦ B2
Priestden Pk C3
Priestden Pl C3
Priestden Rd C3
Queen's Gdns. B2
Queen's Terr. B2
Roundhill Rd. C2
Royal & Ancient
Golf Club A1
St Andrews ≋ B1
St Andrews Aquarium A1
St Andrews Botanic
Garden ❀ C1
St Andrews Castle
(Ruins) & Visitor
Centre ♦ B3
St Leonard's School. B3
St Mary St B2
St Mary's College B2
St Nicholas St. C3
St Rules Tower ♦ B3
St Salvator's College. A2
Sandyhill Cres. C2
Sandyhill Rd C2
Sconiehill Rd C3
Scores, The. A2
Shields Ave C3
Shoolbraids. C3
Shore, The. B3
Sloan St. B1
South St. B2
Spottiswoode Gdns. C1
Station Rd. A1
Swilcen Bridge A1
Tom Morris Dr. C2
Tom Stewart La. C1
Town Hall B2
Union St. B2
University Chapel ♦ A2
University Library A2
Univ of St Andrews. A1
Viaduct Walk. B1
War Memorial. A3
Wardlaw Gdns. C1
Warrack St. C2

Watson Ave B2
West Port. B2
West Sands. A1
Westview B2
Windmill Rd. B1
Winram Pl C1
Wishart Gdns C2
Woodburn Pk B3
Woodburn Terr. B3
Younger Hall ♦ A2

Salisbury 347
Albany Rd. A3
Arts Centre ♦ A3
Ashley Rd. A1
Avon Approach. A2
Ayleswade Rd C2
Bedwin St. A2
Belle Vue A1
Bishops Walk B2
Blue Boar Row B2
Bourne Ave. A3
Bourne Hill A2
Britford La. C2
Broad Walk. C2
Brown St B2
Castle St. A2
Catherine St B2
Chapter House ♦ B2
Church House ♦ B2
Churchfields Rd B1
Churchill Gdns C3
Churchill Way East. B3
Churchill Way North A3
Churchill Way South C2
Churchill Way West A1
City Hall B2
Close Wall B2
Coldharbour La. A1
College St A2
Council and Registry
Offices A3
Court A1
Crane Bridge Rd B2
Crane St. B2
Cricket Ground C1
Culver St South. B3
De Vaux Pl C2
Devizes Rd. A1
Dews Rd. B1
Elm Grove B3
Elm Grove Rd. A3
Endless St. A2
Estcourt Rd. A3
Exeter St. C2
Fairview Rd. A3
Fire Station A1
Fisherton St A1
Folkestone Rd. C1
Fowlers Hill B3
Fowlers Rd. B3
Friary La. B2
Friary, The. B3
Gas La. A1
Gigant St B2
Greencroft B3
Greencroft St A3
Guildhall ♦ B2
Hall of John Halle ♦ B2
Hamilton Rd A2
Harnham Mill C1
Harnham Rd C1/C2
High St B2
House of
John A'Port ♦ B2
Information Ctr ⓘ B2
Kelsey Rd. A3
King's Rd A2
Laverstock Rd. B3
Library B2
London Rd A3
Lower St. C1
Maltings, The B2
Manor Rd. A3
Marsh La B1
Medieval Hall ♦ B2
Milford Hill B3
Milford St. B2
Mill Rd. B1
Mill Stream Approach A2
Mompesson House ♦ B2
New Bridge Rd C2
New Canal B2
New Harnham Rd C2
New St B2
North Canonry ♦ B2
North Gate. B2
North Walk B2
Old Blandford Rd. C1
Old Deanery ♦ B2
Old George Hall ♦ B2
Park St. A3
Parsonage Green C1
Playhouse Theatre ♦ A2
Police Station ◙ B3
Post Office ◙ A2/B2
Poultry Cross ♦ B2
Queen Elizabeth Gdns. B1
Queen's Rd B3
Rampart Rd. B3
Rifles, The ♦ B2
St Ann St B2
St Ann's Gate. B2
St Marks Rd. A3
St Martins ♦ B2
St Mary's College B2
St Nicholas St. C3
St Rules Tower ♦ B3
St Salvator's College. A2

South Gate. C2
Southampton Rd A3
Spire View A1
Sports Ground A3
Tollgate Rd. C3
Town Path C1
Wain-a-Long Rd. A3
Wessex Rd A1
West Walk C2
Wilton Rd. A1
Wiltshire College B3
Winchester St. B3
Windsor Rd B1
Wyndham Rd. A2
YHA ▲ B3
York Rd. A1

Scarborough 347
Aberdeen Walk. B2
Albert Rd. B2
Albion Rd. C2
Auborough St. B2
Balmoral Ctr B2
Belle Vue St. C1
Belmont Rd. C2
Blenheim Terrace. A2
Brunswick
Shopping Ctr. B2
Castle Dykes. B3
Castle Hill. A3
Castle Rd. B3
Castle Walls. A3
Cemetery. C1
Central Tramway ♦ B2
Coach Park. B2
Columbus Ravine A1
Court B2
Crescent, The. C2
Cricket Ground. A1
Cross St. C2
Crown Terr. C2
Dean Rd. B1
Devonshire Dr. A1
East Harbour. B3
East Pier. B3
Eastborough B2
Elmville Ave. B1
Esplanade C2
Falconers Rd. B2
Falsgrave Rd. C1
Fire Station C1
Foreshore Rd. B3
Friargate. B2
Gladstone Rd. B1
Gladstone St. B1
Hollywood Plaza ♦ A1
Holms, The. A1
Hoxton Rd. B1
King St B2
Library B2
Lifeboat Station ♦ B3
Londesborough Rd C1
Longwestgate. B3
Marine Dr. A3
Luna Park. B3
Miniature Railway ♦ C1
Nelson St. B1
Newborough B2
Nicolas St. C2
North Marine Rd. A1
North St. B2
Northway. B1
Old Harbour B3
Olympia Leisure ♦ C2
Peasholm Park A1
Peasholm Rd. A1
Police Station ◙ B1
Post Office ◙ B1
Princess St. B2
Prospect Rd. B1
Queen St. B2
Queen's Parade. A2
Queen's Tower
(Remains). A3
Ramshill Rd. C2
Roman Signal Sta ♦ A3
Roscoe St. C1
Rotunda Museum ♦ C2
Royal Albert Dr. A2
Royal Albert Park. A2
St Martin-
on-the-Hill ♦ C2
St Martin's Ave. C2
St Mary's ♦ B3
St Thomas St. B2
Sandside B3
Scarborough ≋ B2
Scarborough
Art Gallery ♦ C2
Scarborough Bowls
Centre A1
Scarborough Castle ♦ A3
Shopmobility C2
Somerset Terr. C2
South Cliff Lift C2
Spa Theatre, The ♦ C2
Spa, The ♦ C2
Stephen Joseph
Theatre ♦ C1
Tennyson Ave. B1
Tollergate B2
Town Hall B1
Trafalgar Rd. B1
Trafalgar Square A1
Trafalgar St West A1
Valley Bridge Parade. B1
Valley Rd. C1
Vernon Rd. B1
Victoria Park Mount A1
Victoria Rd. B1
West Pier. B2
Westborough B2
Westover Rd. B2
Westwood C1
Woodall Ave. A1
YMCA Theatre ♦ B2
York Pl. B2
Yorkshire Coast College
(Westwood Campus). C1

Sheffield 347

Addy Dr A2
Addy St A2
Adelphi St A3
Albert Terrace Rd A3
Albion St A2
Aldred Rd A1
Allen St A4
Alma St A4
Angel St B5
Arundel Gate B5
Arundel St C4
Ashberry Rd A2
Ashdell Rd C1
Ashgate Rd C1
Athletics Centre B2
Attercliffe Rd A6
Bailey St B4
Ball St A4
Balm Green B4
Bank St B4
Barber Rd A2
Bard St B5
Barker's Pool B4
Bates St A1
Beech Hill Rd C1
Beet St B3
Bellefield St A3
Bernard Rd A6
Bernard St B6
Birkendale A2
Birkendale Rd A2
Birkendale View A1
Bishop St C4
Blackwell Pl B6
Blake St A2
Blonk St A5
Bolsover St B2
Botanical Gdns C1
Bower Rd A1
Bradley St A1
Bramall La C4
Bramwell St A3
Bridge St A4/A5
Brighton Terrace Rd A1
Broad La B3
Broad St B6
Brocco St A3
Brook Hill B3
Broomfield Rd C1
Broomgrove Rd C2
Broomhall Pl C3
Broomhall Rd C2
Broomhall St C3
Broomspring La C2
Brown St C5
Brunswick St B3
Burgess St B4
Burlington St A2
Burns Rd A2
Cadman St A6
Cambridge St B4
Campo La B4
Carver St B4
Castle Square B5
Castlegate A5
Cathedral B4
Cathedral (RC) B4
Cavendish St B3
Charles St C4
Charter Row C4
Children's Hospital B2
Church St B4
City Hall B4
City Hall B4
City Rd C6
Claremont Cr B2
Claremont Pl B2
Clarke St C3
Clarkegrove Rd C2
Clarkehouse Rd C1
Clarkson St B2
Cobden View Rd A1
Collegiate Cr C2
Commercial St B5
Commonside A1
Conduit Rd B1
Cornish St A3
Corporation St A4
Cricket Inn Rd B6
Cromwell St A1
Crookes Rd B1
Crookes Valley Park B2
Crookes Valley Rd B2
Crookesmoor Rd A2
Crown Court A4
Crucible Theatre B5
Cutlers' Hall B4
Cutlers Gate A6
Daniel Hill A2
Dental Hospital B2
Derek Dooley Way A5
Devonshire Green B3
Devonshire St B3
Division St B4
Dorset St C2
Dover St A3
Duchess Rd C5
Duke St B5
Duncombe St A1
Durham Rd B2
Earl St C4
Earl Way C4
Ecclesall Rd C3
Edward St B3
Effingham Rd A6
Effingham St A6
Egerton St C3
Eldon St B3
Elmore Rd B1
Exchange St B5
Eyre St C4
Fargate B4
Farm Rd C5
Fawcett St A3
Filey St B3
Fir St A1
Fire Station C4
Fitzalan Sq/ Ponds Forge B5
Fitzwater Rd C6
Fitzwilliam Gate C4
Fitzwilliam St B3
Flat St B5
Foley St A6
Foundry Climbing Ctr A4
Fulton Rd A1
Furnace Hill A4
Furnival Rd A5
Furnival Sq C4
Furnival St C4
Garden St B3
Gell St B3
Gibraltar St A4
Glebe Rd B1
Glencoe Rd C6
Glossop Rd B2/B3/C1
Gloucester St C2
Government Offices C4
Granville Rd C6
Granville Rd / The Sheffield College C5
Graves Gallery B5
Green La A4
Hadfield St A1
Hanover St C3
Hanover Way C3
Harcourt Rd B1
Harmer La B5
Havelock St C2
Hawley St B4
Haymarket B5
Headford St C3
Heavygate Rd A1
Henry St A3
High St B4
Hodgson St C3
Holberry Gdns C2
Hollis Croft B4
Holly St B4
Hounsfield Rd B3
Howard Rd A1
Hoyle St A3
Hyde Park A6
Infirmary Rd A3
Infirmary Rd A3
Jericho St A3
Johnson St A5
Kelham Island Industrial Museum A4
Lawson Rd C1
Leadmill Rd C5
Leadmill St C5
Leadmill, The C5
Leamington St A1
Leavygreave Rd B3
Lee Croft B4
Leopold St B4
Leveson St A6
Library A2/B5/C1
Light, The C4
Lyceum Theatre B5
Malinda St A3
Maltravers St A5
Manor Oaks Rd B6
Mappin St B3
Marlborough Rd B1
Mary St C4
Matilda St C4
Matlock Rd A1
Meadow St A3
Melbourn Rd A1
Melbourne Ave C1
Millennium Galleries B5
Milton St C3
Mitchell St B3
Mona Ave A1
Mona Rd A1
Montgomery Terr Rd A3
Montgomery Theatre B4
Monument Grounds C6
Moor Oaks Rd B1
Moor, The C4
Moor Market C4
Moore St C3
Mowbray St A4
Mushroom La B2
National Emergency Service A4
National Videogame B5
Netherthorpe Rd B3
Netherthorpe Rd B3
Newbould La C1
Nile St C1
Norfolk Park Rd C6
Norfolk Rd C6
Norfolk St B4
North Church St B4
Northfield Rd A1
Northumberland Rd B1
Nursery St A5
O2 Academy B5
Oakholme Rd C1
Octagon B2
Odeon B5
Old St B6
Orchard Square Shopping Centre B4
Oxford St A2
Paradise St B4
Park La C2
Park Sq B5
Parker's Rd B1
Pearson Building (University) C2
Penistone Rd A3
Pinstone St B4
Pitt St B3
Police Station B5
Pond Hill B5
Pond St B5
Pondorosa, The A2
Ponds Forge Int Sports Ctr B5
Portobello St B3
Post Office A2/B3/B5/C1/C3/C4/C6
Powell St A2
Queen St B4
Queen's Rd C5
Ramsey Rd B1
Red Hill B3
Redcar Rd B1
Regent St B3
Rockingham St B4
Roebuck Rd A2
Royal Hallamshire Hospital C2
Russell St A4
Rutland Park C1
St George's Cl B3
St Mary's Gate C3
St Mary's Rd C4/C5
St Philip's Rd A3
Savile St A5
School Rd B1
Scotland St A4
Severn Rd B1
Shalesmoor A4
Shalesmoor A3
Sheaf St B5
Sheffield Cathedral B4
Sheffield Hallam Univ B5
Sheffield Ice Sports Ctr – Skate Central C5
Sheffield Institute of Arts B5
Sheffield Interchange B5
Sheffield Parkway A6
Sheffield Station C6
Sheffield Sta/ Sheffield Hallam Univ B5
Sheffield University B2
Shepherd St A3
Shipton St A2
Shopmobility B3
Shoreham St C4
Showroom C5
Shrewsbury Rd C5
Sidney St C4
Site Gallery C5
Slinn St A1
Smithfield A4
Snig Hill A5
Snow La A4
Solly St B3
South La C4
South Street Park B5
Southbourne Rd C1
Spital Hill A5
Spital St A5
Spring Hill B1
Spring Hill Rd B1
Springvale Rd A1
Stafford Rd C6
Stafford St B6
Suffolk Rd C5
Summer St B2
Sunny Bank C3
Superstore A3/C3
Surrey St B4
Sussex St A6
Sutton St B3
Sydney Rd A2
Sylvester St C4
Talbot St B5
Taptonville Rd B1
Tenter St B4
Town Hall B4
Townend St A1
Townhead St B4
Trafalgar St B4
Tree Root Walk B1
Trinity St A4
Trippet La B4
Turner Mus of Glass B3
Union St B4
Univ Drama Studio B2
Univ of Sheffield B3
Upper Allen St A3
Upper Hanover St B3
Upperthorpe Rd A2/A3
Verdon St A5
Victoria Rd C2
Victoria St B3
Waingate B5
Watery St A3
Watson Rd C1
Wellesley Rd B2
Wellington St C3
West Bar A4
West Bar Green A4
West One Plaza B3
West St B3
West St B3
Westbourne Rd C1
Western Bank B2
Western Rd A1
Weston Park B2
Weston Park Hosp B2
Weston Park Mus B2
Weston St B2
Wharncliffe Rd C3
Whitham Rd B1
Wicker A5
Wilkinson St B2
William St C3
Winter Garden B4
Winter St B2
York St B4
Yorkshire Artspace C5
Young St C4

Shrewsbury 347

Abbey Foregate B3
Abbey Gardens B2
Abbey Lawn Bsns Park B3
Abbots House B2
Albert St B2
Alma St B1
Ashley St A3
Ashton Rd C1
Avondale Dr A3
Bage Way C3
Barker St B1
Beacall's La A2
Beeches La C2
Beehive La C1
Belle Vue Gdns C2
Belle Vue Rd C2
Belmont Bank C1
Berwick Ave A1
Berwick Rd A1
Betton St C2
Bishop St B3
Bradford St B3
Bridge St B1
Burton St A3
Bus Station B2
Butcher Row B2
Butler Rd C1
Bynner St C2
Canon St B3
Canonbury C1
Castle Bsns Park, The A2
Castle Foregate A2
Castle Gates B2
Castle Walk B3
Castle St B2
Cathedral (RC) C1
Chester St A2
Cineworld C3
Claremont Bank B1
Claremont Hill B1
Cleveland St B3
Coleham Head B2
Coleham Pumping Station C2
College Hill B1
Corporation La A1
Coton Cres A1
Coton Hill A2
Coton Mount A1
Crescent La C1
Crewe St A2
Cross Hill B1
Dana, The B2
Darwin Centre B2
Dingle, The B1
Dogpole B2
English Bridge B2
Fish St B2
Frankwell B1
Gateway Ctr, The A2
Gravel Hill La A1
Greenhous West Mid Showground A1
Greyfriars Rd C2
Hampton Rd A3
Haycock Way C3
High St B1
Hills La B1
Holywell St B3
Hunter St A1
Information Ctr B1
Ireland's Mansion & Bear Steps B1
John St A3
Kennedy Rd C1
King St B3
Kingsland Bridge C1
Kingsland Bridge (toll) C1
Kingsland Rd C1
Library B2
Lime St C2
Longden Coleham C2
Longden Rd C1
Longner St B1
Luciefelde Rd C1
Mardol B1
Marine Terr C2
Market B1
Monkmoor Rd B3
Moreton Cr C2
Mount St A1
New Park Cl A3
New Park Rd A2
New Park St A3
North St A2
Oakley St C1
Old Coleham C2
Old Market Hall B1
Old Potts Way C3
Par Shopping Ctr, The B2
Police Station B2
Post Office B1/B2/B3
Pride Hill B1
Pride Hill Centre B1
Priory Rd B1
Pritchard Way C3
Quarry Swimming & Fitness Centre, The B1
Queen St A3
Raby Cr C2
Rad Brook C1
Rea Brook C3
Rea Brook Valley Country Park & Local Nature Reserve C3
Riverside B1
Roundhill La A1
St Alkmund's B2
St Chad's B1
St Chad's Terr B1
St John's Hill B1
St Julians Friars C2
St Mary's B2
St Mary's St B2
Salters La C2
Scott St C3
Severn Theatre B1
Severn Bank A3
Severn St A2
Shrewsbury B2
Shrewsbury Abbey B3
Shrewsbury High School C1
Shrewsbury Museum & Art Gallery B1
Shrewsbury Prison Tours B2
Shrewsbury School C1
Shropshire Regimental Museum B2
Shropshire Wildlife Trust B3
Smithfield Rd B1
South Hermitage C1
Square, The B1
Superstore C3
Swan Hill B1
Sydney Ave A3
Tankerville St B3
Tilbrook Dr A3
Town Walls C1
Trinity St C2
Underdale Rd B3
Univ Ctr Shrewsbury (Guildhall) B1
Victoria Ave B1
Victoria Quay B1
Victoria St B2
Welsh Bridge B1
Whitehall St B3
Wood St A2
Wyle Cop B2

Southampton 347

Above Bar St A2
Albert Rd North B3
Albert Rd South C3
Andersons Rd B3
Argyle Rd A2
Arundel Tower B1
Bargate, The B2
BBC Regional Centre A1
Bedford Pl A1
Belvidere Rd A3
Bernard St C2
Blechynden Terr A1
Brinton's Rd A2
Britannia Rd A3
Briton St C2
Brunswick Pl A2
Bugle St C1
Canute Rd C3
Castle Way C2
Catchcold Tower B1
Central Bridge C3
Central Rd C2
Channel Way C3
Chapel Rd B3
City Art Gallery A1
City College B3
City Cruise Terminal C1
Civic Centre A1
Civic Centre Rd A1
Coach Station B1
Commercial Rd A1
Cumberland Pl A1
Cunard Rd C2
Derby Rd A3
Devonshire Rd A1
Dock Gate 4 C2
Dock Gate 8 B1
East Pk (Andrew's Pk) A2
East Park Terr A2
East St B2
Endle St B3
European Way C2
Fire Station A2
Floating Bridge Rd C3
God's House Tower C2
Golden Grove A3
Graham Rd A2
Guildhall A1
Hanover Bldgs B2
Harbour Lights C3
Harbour Pde B1
Hartington Rd A3
Havelock Rd A1
Henstead Rd A1
Herbert Walker Ave B1
High St B2
Hoglands Park B2
Holy Rood (Rems), Merchant Navy Memorial B2
Houndwell Park B2
Houndwell Pl B2
Hythe Ferry C2
Information Ctr A1
Isle of Wight Ferry Terminal C1
James St B3
Kingsway A2
Leisure World B1
Library A1
Lime St B2
London Rd A2
Marine Pde B3
Marlands Shopping Ctr, The A1
Marsh La B2
Mayflower Meml C1
Mayflower Park C1
Mayflower Theatre, The A1
Medieval Merchant's House C1
Melbourne St B3
Millais A2
Morris Rd A1
National Oceanography Centre C3
Neptune Way C3
New Rd A2
Nichols Rd A3
North Front A2
Northam Rd A3
Ocean Dock C2
Ocean Village Marina C3
Ocean Way C3
Odeon B1
Ogle Rd B1
Old Northam Rd A2
Orchard La B2
Oxford Ave A2
Oxford St C2
Palmerston Park A2
Palmerston Rd A2
Parsonage Rd A3
Peel St A3
Platform Rd C2
Polygon, The A1
Portland Terr B1
Post Office A2/A3/B2
Pound Tree Rd B2
Quays Swimming & Diving Complex, The B1
Queen's Park C2
Queen's Peace Fountain A2
Queen's Terr C2
Queensway B2
Radcliffe Rd A3
Rochester St A3
Royal Pier C1
Royal South Hants Hospital A2
St Andrew's Rd A2
St Mary's B3
St Mary St A2
St Mary's Leisure Ctr A2
St Mary's Pl B2
St Mary's Rd A2
St Mary's Stadium (Southampton FC) A3
St Michael's C1
Sea City Mus A1
Showcase Cinema de Lux B1
Solent Sky C3
South Front B2
Southampton Central Station A1
Southampton Solent University A2
SS Shieldhall C2
Terminus Terr C2
Threefield La B2
Titanic Engineers' Memorial A2
Town Quay C1
Town Walls B2
Tudor House C1
Vincent's Walk B2
Westgate Hall C1
West Marlands Rd A1
West Park A1
West Park Rd A1
West Quay Rd B1
West Quay Retail Park B1
Western Esplanade B1
Westquay Shopping Ctr B1
Westquay Watermark B1
White Star Way C2
Winton St A2

Southend-on-Sea 348

Adventure Island C3
Albany Ave A1
Albert Rd C3
Alexandra Rd C2
Alexandra St C2
Alexandra Yacht Club C2
Ashburnham Rd B2
Ave Rd B1
Avenue Terr B1
Balmoral Rd B1
Baltic Ave B3
Baxter Ave A2/B2
Beecroft Art Gallery B2
Bircham Rd A2
Boscombe Rd B3
Boston Ave A1/B2
Bournemouth Park Rd A3
Browning Ave A3
Bus Station C3
Byron Ave A3
Cambridge Rd C1/C2
Canewdon Rd B1
Carnarvon Rd A2
Central Ave A3
Central Museum B2
Chelmsford Ave A1
Chichester Rd B2
Church Rd C3
Civic Centre A2
Clarence Rd C2
Clarence St C2
Cliff Ave B1
Cliffs Pavilion C1
Clifftown Parade C2
Clifftown Rd C2
Colchester Rd A1
Coleman St B3
College Way B2
County Court B3
Cromer Rd B3
Crowborough Rd A2
Dryden Ave A3
East St A2
Elmer App B2
Elmer Ave B2
Forum, The B2
Gainsborough Dr A1
Gayton Rd A2
Glenhurst Rd A2
Gordon Pl B2
Gordon Rd B2
Grainger Rd A2
Greyhound Way A3
Grove, The A3
Guildford Rd B3
Hamlet Ct Rd B1
Hamlet Rd C1
Harcourt Ave A1
Hartington Rd C3
Hastings Rd B3
Herbert Gr C3
Heygate Ave C3
High St B2/C2
Information Ctr C3
Kenway A2
Kilworth Ave B3
Lancaster Gdns B3
London Rd B1
Lucy Rd C3
MacDonald Ave A1
Magistrates' Court A2
Maldon Rd A2
Marine Ave C1
Marine Parade C3
Marine Rd C1
Milton Rd B1
Milton St B2
Napier Ave B2
North Ave A3
North Rd A1/B1
Odeon B2
Osborne Rd B1
Park Cres B1
Park Rd B1
Park St B1
Park Terr B1
Pier Hill C3
Pleasant Rd C3
Police Station A2
Post Office B2/B3
Princes St B2
Queens Rd B2
Queensway B2/B3/C3
Radio Essex C2
Rayleigh Ave A1
Redstock Rd A2
Rochford Ave A1
Royal Mews C2
Royal Terr C2
Royals Shopping Centre, The C3
Ruskin Ave A3
St Ann's Rd B3
St Helen's Rd B1
St John's Rd B1
St Leonard's Rd C3
St Lukes Rd A3
St Vincent's Rd C1
Salisbury Ave A1/B1
Scratton Rd C2
Shakespeare Dr A1
Shopmobility B2
Short St A2
South Ave A3
Southchurch Rd B3
Southend Central B2
Southend Pier Railway C3
Southend United FC A1
Southend Victoria B2
Stanfield Rd A2
Stanley Rd C3
Sutton Rd A3/B3
Swanage Rd B3
Sweyne Ave A1
Sycamore Gr A3
Tennyson Ave A3
Tickfield Ave A2
Tudor Rd A1
Tunbridge Rd A2
Tylers Ave B3
Tyrrel Dr B3
Univ of Essex B2/C2
Vale Ave A2
Victoria Ave A2
Victoria Shopping Centre, The B2
Warrior Sq B3
Wesley Rd C3
West Rd A1
West St A1
Westcliff Ave C1
Westcliff Parade C1
Western Esplanade C1
Weston Rd C2
Whitegate Rd B3
Wilson Rd C1
Wimborne Rd B3
York Rd C3

Stirling 348

Abbey Rd A3
Abbotsford Pl A3
Abercromby Pl C1
Albert Halls B1
Albert Pl B1
Alexandra Pl A3
Allan Park C2
Ambulance Station A2
AMF Ten Pin Bowling B2
Argyll Ave A3
Argyll's Lodging B1
Back O' Hill Ind Est A1
Back O' Hill Rd A1
Baker St B2
Ballengeich Pass A1
Balmoral Pl B1
Barn Rd B1
Barnton St B2
Bastion, The C2
Bow St B1
Bruce St A2
Burghmuir Retail Park C2
Burghmuir Rd A2/B2/C2
Bus Station B2
Cambuskenneth Bridge A3
Castle Ct B1
Causewayhead Rd A2
Cemetery A1
Changing Room, The B1
Church of the Holy Rude B1
Clarendon Pl C1
Club House B1
Colquhoun St C3
Corn Exchange B2
Council Offices C2
Court B2
Cowane Ctr A2
Cowane St A2
Cowane's Hospital B1
Crofthead Rd A1
Dean Cres A3
Douglas St A2
Drip Rd A1
Drummond La C1
Drummond Pl C1
Drummond Pl La C1
Dumbarton Rd C2
Eastern Access Rd B2
Edward Ave A3
Edward Rd A2
Forrest Rd A2
Fort A1
Forth Cres B2
Forth St A2
Gladstone Pl C1
Glebe Ave C1
Glebe Cres C1
Golf Course C1
Goosecroft Rd B2
Gowanhill A1
Greenwood Ave B1
Harvey Wynd A1
Information Ctr B1
Irvine Pl B2
James St A2
John St B1
Kerse Rd C3
King's Knot B1
King's Park C1
King's Park Rd C1
Laurencecroft Rd A2
Leisure Pool B2
Library B2
Linden Ave C2
Lovers Wk A2
Lower Back Walk B1
Lower Bridge St A2
Lower Castlehill A1
Mar Pl B1
Meadow Pl A3
Meadowforth Rd C3
Middlemuir Rd C3
Millar Pl A3
Morris Terr B2
Mote Hill A1
Murray Pl B2
Nelson Pl C2
Old Town Cemetery B1
Old Town Jail B1
Park Terr C1
Phoenix Industrial Est C3
Players Rd C3
Port St C2
Post Office A3
Princes St B2
Queen St B2
Queen's Rd B1
Queenshaugh Dr A3
Ramsay Pl A2
Riverside Dr A3
Ronald Pl A1
Rosebery Pl A2
Royal Gardens B1
Royal Gdns B1
St Mary's Wynd B1
St Ninian's Rd C2
Scott St A2
Seaforth Pl B2
Shore Rd B2
Smith Art Gallery & Museum B1
Snowdon Pl C1
Snowdon Pl La C1
Spittal St B2
Springkerse Ind Est C3
Springkerse Rd C3
Stirling Arcade B2
Stirling Bsns Centre C2
Stirling Castle A1
Stirling County Rugby Football Club A3
Stirling Enterprise Pk B3
Stirling Old Bridge A2
Stirling Station B2
Superstore A1/A2
Sutherland Ave A3
TA Centre C3
Tannery La A2
Thistle Industrial Est C3
Thistles Shopping Centre, The B2
Tolbooth B1
Town Wall B1
Union St A2
Upper Back Walk B1
Upper Bridge St A1
Upper Castlehill B1
Upper Craigs C2
Victoria Pl C1
Victoria Rd B1
Victoria Sq B1/C1
Vue B2
Wallace St A2
Waverley Cres A3
Wellgreen Rd C2
Windsor Pl C1
YHA B1

Stoke 348

Ashford St A3
Avenue Rd A3
Aynsley Rd A2
Barnfield C1
Bath St C2
Beresford St A3
Bilton St C2
Boon Ave C2
Booth St C2
Boothen Rd C2/C3
Boughey St C2
Boughey Rd B3
Brighton St B1
Campbell Rd C2
Carlton Rd B3
Cauldon Rd A3
Cemetery A2
Cemetery Rd A2
Chamberlain Ave C1
Church (RC) B2
Church St C2
City Rd C3
Civic Centre & King's Hall B3
Cliff Vale Pl A1
College Rd A3
Convent Cl B2
Copeland St B2
Cornwallis St C2
Corporation St C2
Crowther St A3
Dominic St B1
Elenora St B2
Elgin St B2
Epworth St A3
Etruscan St A1
Film Theatre B3
Fleming Rd C2
Fletcher Rd C2
Floyd St B2
Foden St C2
Frank St C2
Franklin Rd C1
Frederick Ave B1
Garden St C1
Garner St A1
Gerrard St B2
Glebe St B3
Greatbach Ave B1
Hanley Park A3
Harris St B1
Hartshill Rd B1
Hayward St A2
Hide St B2
Higson Ave B2
Hill St B2
Honeywall B2
Hunters Dr C1
Hunters Way C1
Keary St C2
Kingsway B2
Leek Rd B3
Library C2
Lime St C2
Liverpool Rd B2
London Rd C2
Lonsdale St C2
Lovatt St B2
Lytton St B3
Market C2
Newcastle La C1
Newlands St A2
Norfolk St A2
North St A1/B2
Northcote Ave B2
Oldmill St C3
Oriel St B1
Oxford St B1
Penkhull New Rd C1
Penkhull St C1
Portmeirion Pottery C2
Post Office A3
Princes Rd B1
Pump St B2
Quarry Ave B1
Quarry Rd B1
Queen Anne St A3
Queen's Rd C1
Queensway A1/B2/C3
Richmond St B1
Richmond St Park B1
Rothwell St C1
St Peter's B3
St Thomas Pl C1
Scrivenor Rd A1
Seaford St A3
Selwyn St C3
Shelton New Rd A1
Shelton Old Rd B2
Sheppard St C2
Sir Stanley Matthews Sports Centre B3
Spark St C2
Spencer Rd B3
Spode St C2
Squires View B3
Staffordshire Univ B3
Station Rd B3
Stoke Business Park C3
Stoke Rd A2
Stoke-on-Trent Coll A3
Stoke-on-Trent Sta B3
Sturgess St C2
Thistley Hough C1
Thornton Rd B3
Tolkien Way B1
Trent Valley Rd C1
Vale St B2
Villas, The C1
Watford St A3
Wellesley St A3
West Ave B1
Westland St B1
Yeaman St C2
Yoxall Ave B1

Stratford-upon-Avon 348

Albany Rd B1
Alcester Rd B1
Ambulance Station B1
Arden St B2
Avenue Farm A1
Ave Farm Ind Est A1
Avenue Rd A3
Baker Ave A1
Bandstand C3
Benson Rd A3
Birmingham Rd A2
Boat Club B3
Borden Pl C1
Bridge St B2
Bridgetown Rd C3
Bridgeway B3
Broad St C2
Broad Walk C2
Brookvale Rd C1
Brunel Way B1
Bull St C2
Butterfly Farm C3
Cemetery C1
Chapel La B2
Cherry Orchard C1
Chestnut Walk B2
Children's Playground C3
Church St C2
Civic Hall B2
Clarence Rd B1
Clopton Bridge B3

Clopton Rd A2
College C1
College La C2
College St B2
Com Sports Centre . . .B1
Council Offices
 (District) B2
Courtyard, The ♥ C2
Cox's Yard ♦ C2
Cricket Ground C3
Ely Gdns A3
Ely St B2
Evesham Rd C1
Fire Station B1
Foot Ferry C2
Fordham Ave A2
Garrick Way C2
Gower Memorial ♦ . . .B3
Great William St B2
Greenhill St B2
Greenway, The C2
Grove Rd B2
Guild St B2
Guildhall & School ♦ . . .B2
Hall's Croft ♦ B2
Harvard House ♦ B2
Henley St C1
Hertford Rd C1
High St B2
Holton St C2
Holy Trinity ♦ C2
Information Ctr ℹ B2
Jolyffe Park Rd A2
Kipling Rd C3
Library B1
Lodge Rd C1
Maidenhead Rd A3
Mansell St B3
Masons Court B2
Masons Rd A1
Maybird Shopping Pk . . .A2
Maybrook Retail Park . .A1
Maybrook St A1
Mayfield Ave B2
Meer St B2
Mill La C2
Moat House Hotel C2
Narrow La C2
Nash's Ho & New Pl ♦ . .B2
New St C2
Old Town C1
Orchard Way C1
Other Place, The ♥ . . .C1
Paddock La C1
Park Rd B1
Payton St B2
Percy St B1
Police Station ▣ B2
Post Office ⊠ B2
Recreation Ground . . .C2
Regal Road B2
Rother St B2
Rowley Cr A3
Royal Shakespeare
 Theatre ♥ B3
Ryland St B3
Saffron Meadow C2
St Andrew's Cr B1
St Gregory's A3
St Gregory's Rd A3
St Mary's Rd A2
Sanctus Dr C1
Sanctus St C1
Sandfield Rd B2
Scholars La B2
Seven Meadows Rd . . .C2
Shakespeare Institute . .C2
Shakespeare St B2
Shakespeare's
 Birthplace ♦ B2
Sheep St B2
Shelley Rd C3
Shipston Rd C3
Shottery Rd C1
Slingates Rd B1
Southern La B2
Station Rd B1
Stratford
 Healthcare ℍ B2
Stratford Hospital ℍ . . .B2
Stratford Leisure Ctr . . .B2
Stratford Sports Club . . .B1
Stratford-upon-Avon
 Station ≷ B3
Swan Theatre ♥ B3
Swan's Nest La B3
Talbot Rd A2
Tiddington Rd C3
Timothy's Bridge
 Industrial Estate A1
Timothy's Bridge Rd . . .A1
Town Hall & Council
 Offices B2
Town Sq B2
Trinity Cl B2
Tyler St B2
War Memorial Gdns . . .B3
Warwick Rd B3
Waterside B3
Welcombe Rd A3
West St B2
Western Rd A2
Wharf Rd B2
Willows North, The . . .B1
Willows, The B1
Wood St B2

Sunderland 348
Albion Pl C2
Alliance Pl B1
Argyle St C2
Ashwood St C1
Athenaeum St B2
Azalea Terr C1
Beach St A1
Bedford St B2
Beechwood Terr. C1
Belvedere Rd. C2
Blandford St B2
Borough Rd B3

Bridge Cr B2
Bridge St B2
Bridges, The B2
Brooke St A2
Brougham St B2
Burdon Rd C2
Burn Park. C1
Burn Park Rd C1
Burn Park Tech Park . . .C1
Carol St B1
Charles St A3
Chester Rd C1
Chester Terr B1
Church St A3
Civic Centre. C2
Cork St B3
Coronation St C3
Cowan Terr C2
Dame Dorothy St A2
Deptford Rd B1
Deptford Terr A1
Derby St C2
Derwent St C2
Dock St A2
Dundas St A2
Durham Rd C1
Easington St A1
Egerton St C3
Empire 🎭 B3
Empire Theatre 🎭 B2
Farringdon Row B1
Fawcett St B2
Fire Station B1
Fox St C1
Foyle St B2
Frederick St B2
Hanover Pl. A1
Havelock Terr C1
Hay St A1
Headworth Sq. B3
Hendon Rd C3
High St East B3
High St West B2/B3
Holmeside B2
Hylton Rd B1
Information Ctr ℹ B2
John St B2
Kier Hardie Way A2
Lambton St B3
Laura St C1
Lawrence St B3
Library & Arts Centre . . .B2
Lily St B1
Lime St B1
Livingstone Rd B2
Low Row. B2
Magistrates' Court. B1
Matamba Terr B1
Millburn St B1
Millennium Way A2
Minster ♦ B2
Monkwearmouth
 Station Museum ⋒ . . .A2
Mowbray Park. C2
Mowbray Rd C3
Murton St C2
National Glass Ctr ♦ . . .A3
New Durham Rd C1
Newcastle Rd A2
Nile St B3
Norfolk St B2
North Bridge St A2
Northern Gallery for
 Contemporary Art
 (NGCA) ⋒ B3
Otto Terr C1
Park La C2
Park Lane Ⓜ C2
Park Rd C2
Paul's Rd B1
Peel St C1
Point, The ♦ B2
Police Station ▣ B2
Priestly Cr A1
Queen St B2
Railway Row B1
Retail Park. C1
Richmond St A2
Roker Ave. A2
Royalty Theatre 🎭 C1
Royalty, The C1
Ryhope Rd C2
St Mary's Way B2
St Michael's Way B3
St Peter's ♦ A3
St Peter's Ⓜ A3
St Peter's Way A3
St Vincent St C3
Salem Rd C3
Salem St C3
Salisbury St C3
Sans St B3
Shopmobility B2
Silkworth Row B1
Southwick Rd A2
Stadium of Light
 (Sunderland AFC) . . .A2
Stadium Way A2
Stobart St A2
Stockton Rd C2
Suffolk St. C3
Sunderland ≷ B2
Sunderland Aquatic
 Centre B1
Sunderland College. . .B1
Sunderland Mus ⋒ . . .B3
Sunderland St B3
Sunderland
 Station ≷ B2
Tatham St C3
Tavistock Pl. B3
Thelma St C1
Thomas St North A1
Thornholme Rd. C1
Toward Rd C3
Transport
 Interchange C2
Trimdon St Way B1
Tunstall Rd C1
University Ⓜ C1
University Library C1

University of Sunderland
 (City Campus). B1
University of Sunderland
 (St Peter's Campus) . . .A3
Univ of Sunderland (Sir
 Tom Cowie Campus) .A3
Vaux Brewery Way A2
Villiers St B3
Villiers St South B3
Vine Pl C2
Violet St B1
Walton La B3
Waterworks Rd. C1
Wearmouth Bridge A2
West Sunniside. B3
West Wear St B3
Westbourne Rd C3
Western Hill C1
Wharncliffe. B1
Whickham St. A3
White House Rd C3
Wilson St North B1
Winter Gdns B2
Wreath Quay. A1

Swansea Abertawe 348
Adelaide St C3
Albert Row. C3
Alexandra Rd. B2
Argyle St C1
Baptist Well Pl A2
Beach St C1
Belle Vue Way B3
Berw Rd A1
Berwick Terr A1
Bond St C1
Brangwyn
 Concert Hall 🎭 C1
Bridge St A3
Brooklands Terr B1
Brunswick St C1
Bryn-Syfi Terr A1
Bryn-y-Mor Rd C1
Bullins La C1
Burrows Rd C1
Bus Station B2
Cadfan Rd A1
Cadrawd Rd A1
Caer St B2
Carig Cr A1
Carlton Terr. B1
Carmarthen Rd A2
Castle Square B3
Castle St B2
Catherine St C1
Cinema 🎬 C3
Civic Centre & Library . . .C2
Clarence Terr C2
Colbourne Terr A2
Constitution Hill. B1
Court B3
Creidiol Rd. A2
Cromwell St B2
Crown Courts C1
Duke St B1
Dunvant Pl. C2
Dyfatty Park A3
Dyfatty St A3
Dyfed Ave. A1
Dylan Thomas Ctr ♦ . . .B3
Dylan Thomas
 Theatre 🎭 C3
Eaton Cr C1
Eigen Cr A1
Elfed Rd A1
Emlyn Rd A1
Evans Terr A3
Fairfield Terr. B1
Ffynone Dr. C1
Ffynone Rd B1
Fire Station B3
Firm St A2
Fleet St C1
Francis St. C1
Fullers Row B2
George St B2
Glamorgan St C2
Glynn Vivian Art Gall . . .B2
Gower Coll Swansea . . .C1
Graig Terr A3
Grand Theatre 🎭 C1
Granogwen Rd A2
Guildhall C1
Guildhall Rd South. C1
Gwent Rd A1
Gwynedd Ave A1
Hafod St A3
Hanover St B1
Harcourt St B2
Harries St A2
Heathfield B2
Henrietta St B1
Hewson St B2
High St A3/B3
High View A2
Hill St A2
Historic Ships Berth
 ⚓ C3
HM Prison A2
Information Ctr ℹ C2
Islwyn Rd A1
King Edward's Rd. C1
Kingsway, The B2
LC, The C3
Long Ridge A2
Madoc St C2
Mansel St B2
Maritime Quarter C3
Market B2
Mayhill Gdns A1
Mayhill Rd A1
Milton Terr A2
Mission Gallery ⋒ C3
Montpelier Terr B1
Morfa Rd A3
Mount Pleasant B2
National Waterfront
 Museum ⋒ C3

New Cut Rd A3
New St A3
Nicander Pde A2
Nicander Pl A2
Nicholl St B2
Norfolk St A2
North Hill Rd A2
Northampton La B2
Observatory ♦ C3
Orchard St B3
Oxford St B2
Oystermouth Rd C1
Page St B2
Pant-y-Celyn Rd. B1
Parc Tawe North B3
Parc Tawe Shopping &
 Leisure Centre B3
Patti Pavilion 🎭 C1
Paxton St C2
Pen-y-Graig Rd A1
Penmaen Terr. C1
Phillips Pde. C1
Picton Terr B2
Plantasia ✿ B3
Plantasia ✿ B3
Police Station ▣ B2
Post Office ⊠
 . . . . . .A1/A2/C1/C2
Powys Ave A1
Primrose St A1
Princess Way. B3
Promenade C2
Pryder Gdns A1
Quadrant Shopping
 Centre C2
Quay Park B3
Rhianfa La B1
Rhondda St. B1
Richardson St C2
Rodney St. C1
Rose Hill B1
Rosehill Terr. B1
Russell St B1
St Helen's Ave C1
St Helen's Cr C1
St Helen's Rd. C1
St James Gdns B1
St James's Cr B1
St Mary's ♦ B3
Sea View Terr A3
Singleton St C2
South Dock C3
Stanley Pl. B2
Strand B3
Swansea Castle ♦ B3
Swansea Metropolitan
 University C1
Swansea Museum ⋒ . . .C3
Swansea Station ≷ A3
Taliesyn Rd A2
Tan y Marian Rd A1
Tegid Rd A1
Teilo Cr A1
Tenpin Bowling ♦🎳 B3
Terrace Rd B1/B2
Tontine St B3
Townhill Rd A1
Tramshed, The ⋒ C3
Trawler Rd C3
Union St B2
Upper Strand A3
Vernon St A3
Victoria Quay C3
Victoria Rd. B3
Vincent St C1
Walter Rd. B1
Watkin St A2
Waun-Wen Rd. A2
Wellington St C2
Westbury St C1
Western St. C1
Westway C2
William St C2
Wind St B3
Woodlands Terr B1
YMCA B1
York St C3

Swindon 349
Albert St C2
Albion St C1
Alfred St A2
Alvescot Rd C3
Ashford Rd. C1
Aylesbury St A2
Bath Rd. C2
Bathampton St B1
Bathurst Rd B3
Beatrice St A3
Beckhampton St B2
Bowood Rd C1
Bristol St B1
Broad St A3
Brunel Shopping Centre,
 The B2
Brunel Statue ♦ B2
Brunswick St C2
Bus Station B2
Cambria Bridge Rd. . . .B1
Cambria Place B1
Canal Walk. B2
Carr St A3
Cemetery C1/C3
Chandler Cl C1
Chapel B1
Chester St B1
Christ Church ♦ C3
Church Place. B1
Cirencester Way A3
Clarence St B2
Clifton St C2
Cockleberry ♦ A3
Colbourne ♦ A3
Colbourne St A3
College St B2
Commercial Rd. B2
Corporation St A2
Council Offices B1
County Cricket Gd A3

County Rd A3
Courts B2
Cricklade Street. A3
Crombey St B1/C2
Cross St C2
Curtis St. B2
Deacon St C1
Designer Outlet (Great
 Western) A1
Dixon St C2
Dover St C1
Dowling St B2
Drove Rd C3
Dryden St C1
Durham St C3
East St B3
Eastcott Hill C2
Eastcott Rd C2
Edgeware Rd. B2
Edmund St B2
Elmina Rd. A3
Emlyn Square B1
English Heritage
 National Monuments
 Record Centre B1
Euclid St B2
Exeter St C2
Fairview. C1
Faringdon Rd B1
Farnsby St B1
Fire Station B3
Fleet St B2
Fleming Way B2/B3
Florence St A3
Gladstone St A3
Gooch St A3
Graham St A3
Great Western
 Way A1/A2
Groundwell Rd B3
Hawksworth Way A1
Haydon St A2
Henry St. B2
Hillside Ave C1
Holbrook Way B2
Hunt St C1
Hydro B1
Hythe Rd C2
Information Ctr ℹ B2
Joseph St C1
Kent Rd. C2
King William St C2
Kingshill Rd C1
Lansdown Rd C2
Lawn, The C3
Leicester St B3
Library B2
Lincoln St B3
Little London. C3
London St B1
Magic ♦ B3
Maidstone Rd B2
Manchester Rd. A3
Maxwell St B1
Milford St B2
Milton Rd B2
Morse St C2
Newcastle St B3
Newcombe Drive A1
Hawsworth Ind Est. A1
Newhall St C2
North St C2
North Star ♦ A1
North Star Ave A1
Northampton St B3
Nurseries, The C2
Oasis Leisure Centre . . .A1
Ocotal Way A3
Okus Rd C1
Old Town C3
Oxford St B3
Parade, The B2
Park Lane B1
Park Lane ♦ B1
Park, The B1
Pembroke St C2
Plymouth St B3
Polaris Way A2
Police Station ▣ B2
Ponting St A3
Post Office ⊠ B1/B2/C3
Poulton St B3
Princes St B3
Prospect Hill. C3
Prospect Place C2
Queen St B2
Queen's Park C3
Radnor St C1
Read St C2
Reading St B1
Regent Circus ♦ C2
Regent St B2
Retail Park. A2/A3/B2
Rosebery St A3
St Mark's ♦ A3
Salisbury St A3
Savernake St C2
Science & Technology
 Facilities Council HQ . . .A2
Shelley St. C1
Sheppard St. B1
Shopmobility B2
South St C2
Southampton St B3
Spring Gardens B3
Stafford Street C2
Stanier St C2
Station Road A2
STEAM GWR ⋒ B1
Swindon College B2
Swindon Rd C2
Swindon Station ≷ A2
Swindon Town
 Football Club. A3
TA Centre. B3
Tennyson St. B1
Theobald St B1
Town Hall B2
Transfer Bridges ♦ C3
Union St. C2
Upham Rd C3

Victoria Rd. C3
Walcot Rd B3
War Memorial ♦ B2
Wells St B3
Western St C2
Westmorland Rd. B3
Whalebridge ♦. B2
Whitehead St C1
Whitehouse Rd A2
William St C1
Wood St C3
Wyvern Theatre & Arts
 Centre ♥. B3
York Rd B3

Taunton 349
Addison Gr. A1
Albemarle Rd A1
Alfred St B3
Alma St B3
Avenue, The A1
Bath Pl B2
Belvedere Rd. A1
Billet St B2
Billetfield C2
Birch Gr A1
Brewhouse Theatre ♥ . .B2
Bridge St B1
Bridgwater & Taunton
 Canal A2
Broadlands Rd C1
Burton Pl. C1
Bus Station B1
Canal Rd A2
Cann St C1
Canon St B3
Castle St B1
Cheddon Rd A2
Chip Lane. A1
Clarence St B3
Cleveland St B1
Clifton Terr A2
Coleridge Cres C3
Compass Hill C1
Compton Cl A2
Corporation St B1
Council Offices. A2
County Walk Shopping
 Centre C2
Courtyard B2
Cranmer Rd. B2
Crescent, The C1
Critchard Way. B3
Cyril St A1
Deller's Wharf B1
Duke St. B2
East Reach. B3
East St B3
Eastbourne Rd B3
Eastleigh Rd C3
Eaton Cres A2
Elm Gr. A1
Elms Cl A1
Fons George C1
Fore St B2
Fowler St A1
French Weir Rec Grd . . .B1
Geoffrey Farrant Wk . . .A2
Gray's Almshouses B2
Grays Rd B3
Greenway Ave A1
Guildford Pl. C1
Hammet St B2
Haydon Rd B3
Heavitree Way A1
Herbert St A1
High St C2
Holway Ave C3
Hugo St B3
Huish's Almshouses
 ♦. C2
Hurdle Way C2
Information Ctr ℹ B2
Jubilee St A3
King's College. C3
Kings Cl C3
Laburnum St B3
Lambrook Rd. B3
Lansdowne Rd A3
Leslie Ave. A3
Leycroft Rd B3
Library C2
Linden Gr A1
Magdalene St B2
Magistrates Court A1
Malvern Terr A1
Market House ⋒ B2
Mary St. C2
Middle St B2
Mitre Court B3
Mount Nebo. B1
Mount St C2
Mount, The C2
Mountway C1
Mus of Somerset ⋒ B1
North St B2
Northfield Ave B1
Northfield Rd B1
Northleigh Rd C3
Obridge Allotments A3
Obridge Lane A3
Obridge Rd A3
Obridge Viaduct A3
Orchard Shopping Ctr . .C2
Osborne Way. C1
Park St C1
Paul St C2
Plais St B1
Playing Field B3
Portland St B1
Priorswood Ind Est A3
Priorswood Rd. A3
Priory Ave A2
Priory Bridge Rd. A2
Priory Fields Retail Pk . . .A3
Priory Park A2
Priory Way A3
Queen St B3

Railway St A1
Records Office A2
Recreation Grd C1
Riverside Place. B2
St Augustine St B2
St George's 🎭 B2
St Georges Sq B2
St James ♦ B2
St James St B2
St John's ♦ C1
St John's Rd. C1
St Josephs Field C1
St Mary Magdalene's
 ♦. B2
Samuels Ct A1
Shire Hall & Law
 Courts. C1
Somerset County
 Cricket Ground B3
Somerset County Hall . . .C1
Somerset Cricket ⋒ B3
South Rd C2
South St C2
Staplegrove Rd B1
Station Approach. A1
Station Rd A1
Stephen St B2
Superstore C2
Tancred St. B2
Tangier Way A1
Tauntfield Cl C3
Taunton Castle ♦ B1
Taunton Dean
 Cricket Club C2
Taunton Station ≷ A2
Thomas St A1
Toneway B3
Tower St B1
Trenchard Way A1
Trevor Smith Pl. C3
Trinity Bsns Centre C3
Trinity Rd C3
Trinity St C3
Trull Rd C1
Tudor House ♦ B2
Upper High St C1
Venture Rd B3
Victoria Gate B3
Victoria Park B3
Victoria St B3
Viney St B3
Vivary Park Golf Club. . .C2
Vivary Rd C2
War Memorial ♦ A2
Wellesley St A2
Wheatley Cres A3
Whitehall A1
Wilfred Rd B3
William St A1
Wilton Church ♦ C1
Wilton Cl C1
Wilton Gr C1
Wilton St C1
Winchester St B3
Winters Field B2
Wood St B1
Yarde Pl B1

Telford 349
Alma Ave. C1
Amphitheatre C2
Bowling Alley B2
Brandsfarm Way. C3
Brunel Rd B1
Bus Station B2
Buxton Rd C1
Central Park A2
Chelsea Gardens ✿ B2
Coach Central B2
Coachwell Cl B1
Colliers Way A1
Courts B2
Dale Acre Way B3
Darliston C3
Deepdale A3
Deercote. B3
Dinthill C1
Doddington C3
Dodmoor Grange C3
Downemead B3
Duffryn. B3
Dunsheath B3
Euston Way A3
Eyton Mound C1
Eyton Rd. C1
Forgegate A2
Grange Central B2
Hall Park Way B1
Hinkshay Rd C2
Hollinsworth Rd A2
Holyhead Rd B1
Housing Trust A1
Ice Rink B2
Information Ctr ℹ B2
Ironmasters Way A2
Job Centre. B1
Land Registry B1
Lawn Central. B2
Lawnswood C3
Library B2
Malinslee. C2
Matlock Ave. C1
Moor Rd A1
Mount Rd C1
Odeon 🎬 B2
Park Lane A1
Police Station ▣ B1
Post Office ⊠ A2/B2/C1
Priorslee Ave A3
Queen Elizabeth Ave . .A2/B3
Queen Elizabeth Way. . .B1
QEII Arena A3
Rampart Way A2
Randlay Ave C3
Randlay Wood C3
Rhodes Ave C2
Royal Way B1
St Leonards Rd. B2

St Quentin Gate B2
Shifnal Rd A3
Silkin Way C2
Southwater Leisure
 Complex 🎭. B2
Southwater Way B1
Spout Lane B1
Spout Mound. B1
Spout Way B1
Stafford Court C2
Stafford Park C3
Stirchley Ave. C2
Stone Row C1
Superstore C1
Telford Bridge
 Retail Park. A1
Telford Central Sta ≷ . . .A3
Telford Centre, The B2
Telford Forge
 Shopping Park A1
Telford Hornets RFC . . .C2
Telford Int Ctr C2
Telford Way. A3
Third Ave. A3
Town Park C2
Town Park Visitor Ctr . . .B2
Wellswood Ave B2
West Centre Way B1
Withywood Drive C1
Woodhouse Central. . . .B2
Yates Way A1

Torquay 349
Abbey Rd B2
Alexandra Rd A2
Alpine Rd B3
AMF Bowling C3
Ash Hill Rd A2
Babbacombe Rd A3
Bampfylde Rd B1
Barton Rd. A1
Beacon Quay C2
Belgrave Rd A1/B1
Belmont Rd A3
Berea Rd A3
Braddons Hill Rd East . .B3
Brewery Park A3
Bronshill Rd A2
Carlton Rd A2
Castle Circus A2
Castle Rd A2
Cavern Rd A3
Central 🎭 B2
Chatsworth Rd A2
Chestnut Ave B1
Church St. A1
Coach Station A1
Corbyn Head C1
Croft Hill B1
Croft Rd B1
East St A1
Egerton Rd A3
Ellacombe Church Rd . .A3
Ellacombe Rd A2
Falkland Rd B1
Fleet St. B2
Fleet Walk
 Shopping Centre B2
Grafton Rd B3
Grange Rd A3
Haldon Pier C2
Hatfield Rd A2
Highbury Rd A1
Higher Warberry Rd. . . .A3
Hillesdon Rd B3
Hoxton Rd A3
Hunsdon Rd. B3
Information Ctr ℹ B2
Inner Harbour C2
Kenwyn Rd A3
King's Drive, The A1
Laburnum St A1
Law Courts A2
Library A2
Lime Ave A1
Living Coasts ♦ C3
Lower Warberry Rd B3
Lucius St B1
Lymington Rd A1
Magdalene Rd A1
Marina C2
Market Forum, The A2
Market St. A2
Meadfoot Lane C3
Meadfoot Rd C3
Melville St B2
Middle Warberry Rd . . .A3
Mill Lane A1
Montpellier Rd B3
Morgan Ave A1
Museum Rd B3
Newton Rd A1
Oakhill Rd A1
Outer Harbour C2
Parkhill Rd C3
Pimlico B2
Police Station ▣ A1
Post Office ⊠ A1/B2
Prince of Wales Steps . .C3
Princes Rd A3
Princes Rd East A3
Princes Rd West A3
Princess Gdns C2
Princess Pier. C2
Princess Theatre ♥ C2
Rathmore Rd C1
Recreation Grd C1
Riviera Int Ctr C1
Rock End Ave C3
Rock Rd B2
Rock Walk B2
Rosehill Rd A3
South West
 Coast Path ♦ C3
St Efride's Rd A1
St John's ♦. B3
St Luke's Rd B2
St Luke's Rd North B2

St Luke's Rd South B2
St Marychurch Rd A2
Scarborough Rd. B1
Shedden Hill B2
South Pier C2
South St. A1
Spanish Barn ♦ C1
Stitchill Rd. B3
Strand B2
Sutherland Rd A3
Teignmouth Rd A1
Temperance St B2
Terrace, The B3
Thurlow Rd A1
Tor Bay C2
Tor Church Rd A1
Tor Hill Rd A1
Torbay Rd B2
Torquay Museum ⋒ B3
Torquay Station ≷ B1
Torquay Tennis Club . . .A1
Torre Abbey ♦ B1
Torre Abbey Meadows. .B1
Torre Abbey Sands. . . .C1
Torwood Gdns. C3
Torwood St C3
Town Hall A2
Union Square
 Shopping Centre A2
Union St A1
Upton Hill. A1
Upton Park A1
Upton Rd A1
Vanehill Rd C3
Vansittart Rd. A1
Vaughan Parade C2
Victoria Parade C3
Victoria Rd. A2
Warberry Rd West B2
Warren Rd B2
Windsor Rd A2/A3
Woodville Rd A3

Truro 349
Adelaide Ter B1
Agar Rd A3
Arch Hill C2
Arundell Pl C2
Avenue, The A3
Avondale Rd B1
Back Quay B3
Barrack La C2
Barton Meadow A1
Benson Rd C2
Bishops Cl A2
Bosvean Gdns. B1
Bosvigo Gardens ✿ ♦ . .B1
Bosvigo La A1
Bosvigo Rd B1
Broad St A3
Burley Cl A3
Bus Station B3
Calenick St C2
Campfield Hill. B3
Carclew St B3
Carew Rd A2
Carey Park C2
Carlyon Rd A2
Carvoza Rd A3
Castle St. B2
Cathedral View. B1
Chainwalk Dr A2
Chapel Hill B1
Charles St B2
City Hall B2
City Rd A3
Coinage Hall ♦ B3
Comprigney Hill A1
Coosebean La A1
Copes Gdns. A3
County Hall C1
Courtney Rd A2
Crescent Rd. B1
Crescent Rise B1
Crescent, The B1
Daniell Court. C1
Daniell Rd C1
Daniell St C2
Daubuz Cl A3
Daubuz Moors
 Nature Reserve. A3
Dobbs La A1
Edward St B2
Eliot Rd A2
Elm Court. A3
Enys Cl A1
Enys Rd A1
Fairmantle St B3
Falmouth Rd C2
Ferris Town B2
Fire Station B2
Frances St. B2
George St B2
Green Cl C2
Green La B2
Grenville Rd C2
Hall For Cornwall ♥ B3
Hendra Rd A2
Hendra Vean A1
High Cross B3
Higher Newham La. C3
Higher Trehaverne A2
Hillcrest Ave B1
Hospital ℍ B2
Hunkin Cl A2
Hurland Rd C3
Infirmary Hill. B2
James Pl B2
Kenwyn Church Rd A1
Kenwyn Hill A1
Kenwyn Rd B2
Kenwyn St B2
Kerris Gdns A1
King St B2
Leats, The B2
Lemon Quay B3
Lemon St Gallery ♦ C2
Library B1/B3
Malpas Rd A3
Magistrates Court. A3

Market B3
Merrifield Close B1
Mitchell Hill A3
Moresk Cl A3
Moresk Rd A3
Morlaix Rd A3
Nancemere Rd A3
Newham Bsns Park C3
Newham Industrial Est C3
Newham Rd C3
Northfield Dr C3
Oak Way A3
Pal's Terr C2
Park View C2
Pendarves Rd A2
Plaza Cinema ♦ B3
Police Station A2/B3
Post Office B3
Prince's St B3
Pydar St A2
Quay St B3
Redannick Cres C2
Redannick La B2
Richard Lander Monument ♦ B2
Richmond Hill B1
River St B2
Rosedale Rd A2
Royal Cornwall Museum B2
St Aubyn Rd C3
St Clement St C3
St George's Rd C3
Standing Cross ♦ B3
School La C2
Spires, The A2
Station Rd B1
Stokes Rd A2
Strangways Terr B3
Tabernacle St B3
Trehaverne La A2
Tremayne Rd A2
Treseder's Gdns A3
Treworder Rd B1
Treyew Rd B1
Truro Cathedral † B3
Truro Harbour Office B3
Truro Station ≋ B3
Union St B2
Upper School La C2
Victoria Gdns B2
Waterfall Gdns B1

Wick 349

Ackergill Cres A2
Ackergill St A2
Albert St A2
Ambulance Station A2
Argyle Sq C2
Assembly Rooms C2
Bank Row C2
Bankhead B1
Barons Well B2
Barrogill St C2
Bay View B3
Bexley Terr C3
Bignold Park C2
Bowling Green C2
Breadalbane Terr C2
Bridge of Wick B1
Bridge St B2
Brown Pl C2
Burn St B2
Bus Station B2
Caithness General Hospital (A&E) Ⓗ B1
Cliff Rd B1
Coach Rd C2
Coastguard Station A3
Corner Cres B3
Coronation St C1
Council Offices B2
Court A2
Crane Rock C3
Dempster St B2
Dunnet Ave A3
Fire Station B2
Francis St C1
George St A1
Girnigoe St C2
Glamis Rd C2
Gowrie Pl C2
Grant St C2
Green Rd B2
Gunns Terr B1
Harbour Quay C2
Harbour Rd C2
Harbour Terr C2
Harrow Hill C2
Henrietta St A2/B2
Heritage Museum B2
High St B2
Hill Ave A2
Hillhead Rd A3
Hood St C1
Huddart St B2
Kenneth St B1
Kinnaird St B1
Kirk Hill C2
Langwell Cres B3
Leishman Ave B3
Leith Walk A2
Library B2
Liby & Swimming Pool C1
Lifeboat Station C3
Lighthouse C3
Lindsay Dr B3
Lindsay Pl B3
Loch St B2
Louisburgh St B2
Lower Dunbar St B2
Macleay La B1
Macleod Rd B2
MacRae St C2
Martha Terr C1
Miller Ave B1
Miller La B1
Moray St C2
Mowat Pl B3
Murchison St C3
Newton Ave C1
Newton St C1
Nicolson St C1
North Highland Coll B2
North River Pier C1
Northcote St C2
Owen Pl B2
Police Station B1
Port Dunbar C2
Post Office B2/C2
Pulteney Distillery ♦ C2
River St B2
Robert St A1
St John's Episcopal C2
Sandigoe Rd B3
Scalesburn B3
Seaforth Ave C1
Shore La B2
Shore, The B2
Sinclair Dr B3
Sinclair Terr C3
Smith Terr C3
South Pier C2
South Quay C3
South Rd B2
South River Pier B3
Station Rd B1
Superstore A1/B1
Telford St B2
Thurso Rd B1
Thurso St B1
Town Hall B2
Union St B2
Upper Dunbar St C2
Vansittart St C3
Victoria Pl B2
War Memorial A1
Well of Cairndhuna ♦ C3
Wellington Ave C3
Wellington St C2
West Banks Ave C1
West Banks Terr C1
West Park C1
Whitehorse Park B2
Wick Harbour Bridge B2
Wick Industrial Estate B1
Wick Parish Church B1
Wick Station ≋ B2
Williamson St B2
Willowbank B2

Winchester 350

Andover Rd A2
Andover Rd Retail Pk A2
Archery La C2
Arthur Rd A2
Bar End Rd C3
Beaufort Rd C2
Beggar's La B3
Bereweeke Ave A1
Bereweeke Rd A1
Boscobel Rd A2
Brassey Rd A2
Broadway B3
Brooks Shopping Centre, The B3
Bus Station B3
Butter Cross ♦ B3
Canon St C2
Castle Wall C2/C3
Cathedral † C2
Cheriton Rd A1
Chesil St C3
Chesil Theatre 🎭 C3
Christchurch Rd C1
City Mill B3
City Museum B2
City Rd B2
Clifton Rd B1
Clifton Terr B2
Close Wall C2/C3
Coach Park A2
Colebrook St C3
College St C3
College Walk C3
Compton Rd C2
Council Offices B2
County Council Offices B2
Cranworth Rd A2
Cromwell Rd C2
Culver Rd C2
Discovery Centre ♦ B2
Domum Rd C3
Durngate Pl B3
Eastgate St B3
East Hill C3
Edgar Rd C2
Egbert Rd A2
Elm Rd B1
Everyman 🎬 C2
Fairfield Rd A1
Fire Station A3
Fordington Ave A2
Fordington Rd A1
Friarsgate B3
Gordon Rd B3
Great Hall & Round Table, The B2
Greenhill Rd B1
Guildhall B3
Hatherley Rd A1
High St B2
Hillier Way A3
HM Prison B1
Hyde Abbey (Remains) † B2
Hyde Abbey Rd B2
Hyde Cl B2
Hyde St A2
Information Ctr B2
Jane Austen's Ho B2
Jewry St B2
King Alfred Pl A2
Kingsgate Arch C2
Kingsgate Park C2
Kingsgate Rd C2
Kingsgate St C2
Lankhills Rd A2
Law Courts B2
Library B2
Lower Brook St B3
Magdalen Hill B3
Market La B2
Mews La B1
Middle Brook St B3
Middle Rd B1
Military Museums B2
Milland Rd C3
Milverton Rd A1
Monks Rd A3
North Hill Cl A2
North Walls A2
North Walls Rec Gnd A3
Nuns Rd A3
Oram's Arbour A2
Owens Rd A2
Parchment St B2
Park & Ride B3
Park Ave B3
Playing Field A1
Police HQ B2
Portal Rd C3
Post Office B2/C1
Ranelagh Rd C1
Regimental Mus B2
River Park Leisure Ctr B3
Romans' Rd C2
Romsey Rd B1
Royal Hampshire County Hospital (A&E) B1
St Cross Rd C2
St George's St B2
St Giles Hill C3
St James Villas C2
St James' La C2
St James' Terr C2
St John's St B3
St John's St B3
St Michael's Rd C2
St Paul's Hill B1
St Peter St B2
St Swithun St C2
St Thomas St C2
Saxon Rd A2
School of Art B3
Sleepers Hill Rd C1
Southgate St C2
Sparkford St C1
Square, The B2
Staple Gdns B2
Station Rd B2
Step Terr A1
Stockbridge Rd A1
Stuart Cres C1
Sussex St B2
Swan Lane B2
Tanner St B3
Theatre Royal 🎭 B3
Trinity Pl A2
Vansittart Rd B1/C1
Victoria Barracks B1
Victoria St C1
Westmead C1
White Lilies Island A1
William St B3
Winchester Sta ≋ A2
Winnall Moors Wildlife Reserve C3
Wolvesey Castle C3
Worthy Lane A2
Worthy Rd A2

Windsor 350

Adelaide Sq C3
Albany Rd C3
Albert St B2
Alexandra Gdns B2
Alexandra Rd C2
Alma Rd C2
Arthur Rd B2
Bachelors Acre B3
Barry Ave B2
Beaumont Rd C2
Bexley St C1
Boat House B2
Brocas St B2
Brocas, The A2
Brook St C3
Bulkeley Ave C1
Castle Hill B3
Charles St C2
Claremont Rd C2
Clarence Cr B1
Clarence Rd B1
Clewer Court Rd B1
Coach Park B2
College Cr C1
Cricket Ground A3
Dagmar Rd C2
Datchet Rd A3
Devereux Rd C2
Dorset Rd C2
Duke St B1
Elm Rd C1
Eton College ♦ A3
Eton College Natural History Museum A3
Eton Ct A2
Eton Sq A2
Eton Wick Rd A1
Farm Yard A3
Fire Station B1
Frances Rd C2
Frogmore Dr C3
Gloucester Pl C2
Goslar Way C1
Goswell Hill B2
Goswell Rd B2
Green La C1
Grove Rd C2
Guildhall B3
Helena Rd C3
Helston La A1
High St A2/B3
Holy Trinity C2
Home Park, The A3/B3
Household Cavalry B2 C1
Imperial Rd B2
Information Ctr B2
Keats La B1
King Edward VII Ave B3
King Edward VII Hospital C2
King George V Memorial ♦ B3
King Stable St A2
King's Rd C2
Library A2/B2
Long Walk, The C2
Maidenhead Rd B1
Meadow La A1
Municipal Offices C2
Nell Gwynne's Ho C3
Osborne Rd C2
Oxford Rd B1
Park St B3
Peascod St B2
Police Station B2
Portal Rd C1
Post Office B2/C1
Princess Margaret Hospital (private) C2
Old Court Art Space, The B2
Queen Elizabeth Bridge
Queen Victoria's Walk B3
Queen's Rd C2
River St C2
Romney Island A3
Romney Lock A3
Romney Lock Rd A3
Russell St C1
St George's Chapel B3
St John's C2
St John's Chapel A2
St Leonards Rd C1
St Mark's Rd C1
Sheet St C2
Shopmobility B2
South Meadow A2
South Meadow La A2
Springfield Rd C1
Stovell Rd B1
Sunbury Rd A2
Tangier La C2
Temple Rd C2
Thames St B2
Theatre Royal 🎭 B3
Trinity Pl A2
Vansittart Rd B1/C1
Victoria Barracks B1
Victoria St C1
Westmead C1
White Lilies Island A1
William St B3
Windsor & Eton Central ≋ B2
Windsor & Eton Riverside ≋ A3
Windsor Bridge B3
Windsor Castle B2
Windsor Leisure Ctr B1
Windsor Relief Rd A1
Windsor Royal Station Shopping Centre B2
Windsor Yards B2
York Ave C1
York Rd C1

Wolverhampton 350

Albion St B2
Arena 🎭 B2
Art Gallery B2
Ashland St C1
Austin St A1
Badger Dr A3
Bailey St B2
Bath Ave B1
Bath Rd B1
Bell St C2
Berry St B2
Bilston Rd C3
Bilston St C3
Birmingham Canal A3
Bone Mill La A2
Brewery Rd B1
Bright St A1
Burton Cres B3
Bus Station B3
Cambridge Rd A3
Camp St B2
Cannock Rd A3
Castle St C2
Chapel Ash C1
Cherry St C1
Chester St A1
Church La C2
Church St C2
Civic Centre B2
Civic Hall B2
Clarence Rd B2
Cleveland St C2
Clifton St C1
Coach Station B3
Compton Rd B1
Corn Hill B3
Coven St A2
Craddock St A1
Cross St North A1
Crown & County Courts B2
Crown St A2
Culwell St A3
Dale St C1
Darlington St B1
Devon Rd A1
Drummond St B3
Dudley Rd C2
Dudley St B2
Duke St C3
Dunkley St B1
Dunstall Ave A2
Dunstall Hill A2
Dunstall Rd A1/A2
Evans St A2
Fawdry St A1
Field St B3
Fire Station C1
Fiveways ↺ A2
Fowler Playing Fields A3
Fox's La A2
Francis St A2
Fryer St B3
Gloucester St A1
Gordon St C3
Graiseley St C1
Grand 🎭 B3
Grand Station C3
Granville St C3
Great Brickkiln St C1
Great Hampton St A1
Great Western St A2
Grimstone St B3
Harrow St A1
Hilton St A3
Hive Liby The B2
Horseley Fields C3
Humber Rd C1
Information Centre B2
Jack Hayward Way A2
Jameson St A1
Jenner St C3
Kennedy Rd B3
Kimberley St C1
King St B2
Laburnum St C1
Lansdowne Rd B1
Leicester St A1
Lever St C3
Library C2
Lichfield St B2
Light House 🎬 B3
Little's La B3
Lock St B3
Lord St C1
Lowe St A2
Maltings, The C1
Mander Centre B2
Mander St C1
Market B3
Market St B2
Maxwell Rd C3
Merridale St C1
Middlecross C3
Molineux St A2
Mostyn St A1
Newhampton Arts Ctr B1
New Hampton Rd East A1
Nine Elms La A3
North Rd A2
Oaks Cres C1
Oxley St A1
Paget St A1
Park Ave C1
Park Road East C1
Park Road West B1
Paul St C2
Pelham St C1
Penn Rd C2
Piper's Row B3
Piper's Row 🚉 B3
Pitt St C2
Police Station C3
Pool St C2
Poole St A3
Powlett St C3
Queen St B3
Raby St C2
Railway Dr B3
Red Hill St A2
Red Lion St B2
Retreat St C1
Ring Rd C2
Royal, The 🚉 C3
Rugby St A1
Russell St C1
St Andrew's A1
St David's B2
St George's C2
St George's Pde C2
St James St C3
St John's C2
St John's 🚉 C2
St John's Retail Park C2
St John's Square C2
St Mark's C1
St Marks Rd C1
St Marks St C1
St Patrick's B2
St Peter's B2
St Peter's B2
Salisbury St A1
Salop St C2
School St C2
Sherwood St A2
Smestow St A3
Snow Hill C2
Springfield Rd A3
Stafford St A2/B2
Staveley Rd A1
Steelhouse La C3
Stephenson St C1
Stewart St C2
Sun St B3
Tempest St C2
Temple St C2
Tettenhall Rd B1
Thomas St C2
Thornley St B3
Tower St C2
University C3
Upper Zoar St C1
Vicarage Rd C3
Victoria St B2
Walpole St A1
Walsall St C3
Ward St C1
Warwick St C3
Water St A3
Waterloo Rd B3
Wednesfield Rd B3
West Pk (not A&E) B1
West Park Swimming Pool B1
Wharf St C3
Whitmore Hill B2
Wolverhampton 🚉 B3
Wolverhampton 🚍 B3
Wolverhampton St George's 🚋 C2
Wolverhampton Wanderers Football Gnd (Molineux) B2
Worcester St C2
Wulfrun Centre C2
Yarwell Cl C3
York St C3
Zoar St C1

Worcester 350

Albany Terr A1
Angel Pl B2
Angel St B2
Ashcroft Rd A2
Athelstan Rd C3
Avenue, The C1
Back Lane North A1
Back Lane South A1
Barbourne Rd A2
Bath Rd C2
Battenhall Rd C3
Bridge St B2
Britannia Sq A1
Broad St B2
Bromwich La C1
Bromwich Rd C1
Bromyard Rd C1
Bus Station B2
Butts, The B2
Carden St B3
Castle St A2
Cathedral † B2
Cathedral Plaza B2
Charles St B3
Chequers La B1
Chestnut St A2
Chestnut Walk A2
Citizens' Advice Bureau B2
City Walls Rd B2
Cole Hill C3
College St C2
Commandery, The C3
Cripplegate Park B1
Croft Rd B1
Cromwell St B3
Cross, The B2
Crowngate Ctr B2
Deansway B2
Diglis Pde C2
Diglis Rd C2
Edgar Tower ♦ C2
Farrier St B2
Foregate St B2
Fort Royal Hill C3
Fort Royal Park C3
Foundry St B2
Friar St C2
George St B3
Grand Stand Rd B1
Greenhill C3
Greyfriars B2
Guildhall B2
Henwick Rd B1
High St B2
Hill St C2
Hive, The B2
Huntingdon Hall B2
Hylton Rd B1
Information Ctr B2
King Charles Place Shopping Centre B2
King's School C2
King's School Playing Field C2
Kleve Walk B2
Lansdowne Cr A3
Lansdowne Rd A3
Lansdowne Walk A3
Laslett St B3
Little Chestnut St A2
Little London B2
London Rd C3
Lowell St A3
Lowesmoor B2
Lowesmoor Terr A3
Lowesmoor Wharf A3
Magistrates Court A2
Midland Rd B3
Mill St C2
Moors Severn Terrace, The A1
Mus & Art Gallery A2
Museum of Royal Worcester C1
New Rd C1
New St B2
Northfield St A2
Odeon 🎬 A2
Old Palace, The B2
Padmore St B3
Park St B3
Pheasant St B3
Pitchcroft A1
Police Station C3
Portland St B2
Post Office A2/C1
Quay St B2
Queen St B2
Rainbow Hill A3
Recreation Ground B2
Reindeer Court B2
Rogers Hill A3
Sabrina Terr A1
St Dunstan's Cr C3
St John's C1
St Martin's Gate B3
St Martin's Quarter B3
St Oswald's Rd A2
St Paul's St B3
St Swithin's Church B2
St Wulstans Cres C3
Sansome Walk A2
Severn St C2
Shambles, The B2
Shaw St A2
Shire Hall Crown Ct A2
Shrub Hill Rd B3
Shrub Hill Retail Park B3
Slingpool Walk C1
South Parade B2
Southfield St A2
Sports Centre A3
Stanley Rd C3
Swan, The A2
Swimming Pool B1
Tallow Hill B3
Tennis Walk A2
Tolladine Rd B3
Tudor House B2
Tybridge St B1
Tything, The A2
Univ of Worcester B2
Vincent Rd C3
Vue B2
Washington St A3
Woolhope Rd C1
Worcester Bridge B2
Worcester County Cricket Club C1
Worcester Foregate Street ≋ B2
Worcester Shrub Hill ≋ B3
Worcester Royal Grammar School A2
Wylds La C3

Wrexham Wrecsam 350

Abbot St A2
Acton Rd A3
Albert St B2
Alexandra Rd B2
Aran Rd A3
Barnfield C2
Bath Rd B2
Beeches, The C3
Beechley Rd C3
Belgrave Rd C3
Bellevue Park C2
Bellevue Rd C2
Belvedere Dr A1
Bennion's Rd C3
Berse Rd A1
Bersham Rd C1
Birch St C2
Bodhyfryd B3
Border Retail Park B2
Bradley Rd C2
Bright St C1
Bron-y-Nant C1
Bryn-y-Cabanau Rd C3
Bury St B2
Bus Station B2
Butchers Market B2
Caia Rd C3
Cambrian Ind Est C3
Caxton Pl B2
Cemetery C1
Centenary Rd C1
Central Retail Park C2
Chapel St B2
Charles St B3
Chester Rd A2
Chester St B2
Cilcen Gr A3
Citizens Advice Bureau B2
Cobden Rd C1
Council Offices B2
County B3
Crescent Rd A3
Crispin La A2
Croesnewyth Rd B1
Cross St A2
Cunliffe St B3
Derby Rd C3
Dolydd Rd B1
Duke St B2
Eagles Meadow C3
Earle St C2
East Ave A2
Edward St C2
Egerton St B2
Empress Rd C1
Erddig Rd C2
Fairy Rd C2
Fire Station C2
Foster Rd A1
Foxwood Dr C1
Garden Rd A2
General Market B2
Gerald St B2
Gibson St C1
Glyndwr University Plas Coch Campus A1
Greenbank St C3
Greenfield B2
Grosvenor Rd B3
Grove Park Rd B3
Grove Rd B3
Guildhall B2
Haig Rd C3
Hampden Rd C3
Hazel Gr A3
Henblas St B2
High St B2
Hightown Rd C3
Hill St C2
Holt Rd A3
Holt St B3
Hope St B2
Huntroyde Ave C3
Information Ctr B2
Island Green Shopping Centre B2
Jobcentre Plus C2
Jubilee Rd B2
King St B2
Kingsmills Rd C3
Lambpit St B2
Law Courts B2
Lawson Cl A2
Lawson Rd A2
Lea Rd A2
Library & Arts Centre B2
Lilac Way A2
Llys David Lord B1
Lorne St A2
Maesgwyn Rd B1
Maesydre Rd A3
Manley Rd C3
Market St B2
Mawddy Ave A2
Mayville Ave A2
Memorial Gallery B2
Memorial Hall B2
Mold Rd A1
Mount St C1
Neville Cres A3
New Rd B2
North Wales Regional Tennis Centre A1
Oak Dr A3
Park Ave A2
Park St C1
Peel St C1
Pen y Bryn C1
Pentre Felin C1
Penymaes Ave A3
Peoples Market B3
Percy St B3
Pines, The A1
Plas Coch Rd A1
Plas Coch Retail Park A1
Police Station B2
Poplar Rd C3
Post Office A2/B3/B2
Powell Rd B2
Poyser St C3
Price's La C1
Primose Way A1
Princess St C1
Queen St B2
Queens Sq B2
Regent St B2
Rhosddu Rd A2/B2
Rhosnesni La A3
Rivulet Rd C2
Ruabon Rd C2
Ruthin Rd C1/C2
St Giles B1
St Giles Way B1
St James St A2
St Mary's † B2
Salisbury Rd A2
Salop Rd B3
Sontley Rd C1
Spring Rd A2
Stanley St B3
Stansty Rd A2
Station Approach B2
Studio 🎭 B2
Superstore B3/C1
Talbot Rd A2
Techniquest Glyndwr ♦ A1
Town Hill B2
Trevor St C1
Trinity St B2
Tuttle St C2
Vale Park A1
Vernon St C2
Vicarage Hill B2
Victoria Rd C2
Walnut St A2
War Memorial ♦ B2
Waterworld Leisure Centre ♦ B2
Watery Rd B1/B2
Wellington Rd C2
Westminster Dr C3
William Aston Hall A1
Windsor Rd C1
Wrecsam
Wrexham AFC A1
Wrexham Central ≋ B2
Wrexham General ≋ B2
Wrexham Maelor Hospital (A&E) B1
Wrexham Technology Park B1
Wynn Ave A2
Yale College A3
Yale Gr A3
York St C3

York 350

Aldwark B2
Barbican Rd C3
Bar Convent Living Heritage Ctr C1
Barley Hall B2
Bishopgate St C2
Bishophill Senior C2
Bishopthorpe Rd C1
Blossom St C1
Bootham A1
Bootham Cr A1
Bootham Terr A1
Bridge St B2
Brook St A2
Brownlow St A2
Burton Stone La A1
Castle Museum B2
Castlegate B2
Cemetery Rd C3
Cherry St C2
City Screen B2
City Wall A2/B1/C3
Clarence St A2
Clementhorpe C2
Clifford St B2
Clifford's Tower B2
Clifton A1
Coach park B2
Coney St B2
Coppergate Ctr B2
Cromwell Rd C2
Crown Court B2
Davygate B2
Deanery Gdns A2
DIG B2
Dodsworth Ave A3
Eboracum Way A3
Ebor Industrial Estate B3
Eldon St A3
Everyman 🎬 B2
Fairfax House B2
Fire Station C3
Fishergate C3
Foss Islands Rd B3
Foss Islands Retail Park B3
Fossbank A3
Garden St A2
George St C2
Gillygate A2
Goodramgate B2
Grand Opera House B2
Grosvenor Terr A1
Guildhall A3
Hallfield Rd A3
Heslington Rd C3
Heworth Green A3
Holy Trinity B2
Hope St C2
Huntington Rd A3
Information Ctr B2
James St B3
Jorvik Viking Ctr B2
Kent St C3
Lawrence St C3
Layerthorpe A3
Leeman Rd B1
Lendal B2
Lendal Bridge B1
Library A2/B1
Longfield Terrace A1
Lord Mayor's Walk A2
Lowther St A2
Mansion House B2
Margaret St C3
Marygate A1
Melbourne St C3
Merchant Adventurers' Hall B2
Merchant Taylors' Hall C1
Micklegate B1
Micklegate Bar C1
Monkgate A2
Moss St C1
Museum Gdns B1
Museum St B1
National Railway Museum B1
Navigation Rd B3
Newton Terr C1
North Pde A2
North St B2
Nunnery La C1
Nunthorpe Rd C1
Ouse Bridge B2
Paragon St C3
Park Gr A3
Park St C1
Parliament St B2
Peasholme Green B3
Penley's Grove St A2
Piccadilly B2/C3
Police Station B2
Post Office B1/B2/C2
Priory St B1
Queen Anne's Rd A1
Regimental Mus B2
Richard III Experience at Monk Bar A2
Roman Bath B2
Rowntree Park C2
St Andrewgate B2
St Benedict Rd C1
St John St A2
St Olave's Rd A1
St Peter's Gr A1
St Saviourgate B2
Scarcroft Hill C1
Scarcroft Rd C1
Shambles, The B2
Shopmobility C2
Skeldergate C2
Skeldergate Bridge C2
Station Rd B1
Stonebow, The B2
Stonegate B2
Superstore A3
Sycamore Terrace A1
Terry Ave C2
Theatre Royal 🎭 B2
Thorpe St C1
Toft Green B1
Tower St C2
Townend St A2
Treasurer's House A2
Trinity La B1
Undercroft Mus B2
Union Terr A2
Victor St C2
Vine St C2
Walmgate B3
War Memorial ♦ B1
Wellington St C3
York Art Gallery A1
York Barbican C3
York Brewery ♦ B1
York Dungeon, The B2
York Minster † B2
York St John University A2
York Station ≋ B1

Map of Britain (region labels)

W Isles · Moray · Aberds · Highland · Aberdeen · Perth and Kinross · Angus · Argyll and Bute · Stirling · Dundee · Glasgow · Edin · E Loth · N Ayrs · S Lanark · Midloth · Borders · E Ayrs · Dumfries and Galloway · Northumberland · Tyne and Wear · Hartlepool · Redcar and Cleveland · Middlesbrough · Darlington · Stockton-on-Tees · Cumbria · Durham · IoM · North Yorkshire · York · Blackpool · Lancs · W Yorks · E Yorks · N Lincs · Gtr Man · S Yorks · NE Lincs · Anglesey · Mers · Lincolnshire · Conwy · Flint · Denb · Ches · Derbys · Notts · Gwyn · Wrex · Telford · Staffs · Leics · Rutland · Norfolk · Ceredigion · Shrops · W Mid · N Nhants · Cambs · Powys · Worcs · Warks · Bedford · Suffolk · Pembs · Hereford · Mon · Glos · Bucks · Herts · Essex · C Beds · Swansea · Oxon · London · Southend · Medway · Cardiff · Bristol · W Berks · Wilts · Hants · Surrey · Kent · Somerset · Soton · IoW · W Sus · E Sus · Brighton · Devon · Dorset · BCP · Ptsmouth · Cornwall · Torbay · Plymouth · Scilly

Abbreviations used in the index

Abbr	Meaning
Aberdeen	Aberdeen City
Aberds	Aberdeenshire
Ald	Alderney
Anglesey	Isle of Anglesey
Angus	Angus
Argyll	Argyll and Bute
Bath	Bath and North East Somerset
BCP	Bournemouth, Christchurch and Poole
Bedford	Bedford
Blackburn	Blackburn with Darwen
Blackpool	Blackpool
Bl Gwent	Blaenau Gwent
Borders	Scottish Borders
Brack	Bracknell
Bridgend	Bridgend
Brighton	City of Brighton and Hove
Bristol	City and County of Bristol
Bucks	Buckinghamshire
Caerph	Caerphilly
Cambs	Cambridgeshire
Cardiff	Cardiff
Carms	Carmarthenshire
C Beds	Central Bedfordshire
Ceredig	Ceredigion
Ches E	Cheshire East
Ches W	Cheshire West and Chester
Clack	Clackmannanshire
Conwy	Conwy
Corn	Cornwall
Cumb	Cumbria
Darl	Darlington
Denb	Denbighshire
Derby	City of Derby
Derbys	Derbyshire
Devon	Devon
Dorset	Dorset
Dumfries	Dumfries and Galloway
Dundee	Dundee City
Durham	Durham
E Ayrs	East Ayrshire
Edin	City of Edinburgh
E Dunb	East Dunbartonshire
E Loth	East Lothian
E Renf	East Renfrewshire
Essex	Essex
E Sus	East Sussex
E Yorks	East Riding of Yorkshire
Falk	Falkirk
Fife	Fife
Flint	Flintshire
Glasgow	City of Glasgow
Glos	Gloucestershire
Gtr Man	Greater Manchester
Guern	Guernsey
Gwyn	Gwynedd
Halton	Halton
Hants	Hampshire
Hereford	Herefordshire
Herts	Hertfordshire
Highld	Highland
Hrtlpl	Hartlepool
Hull	Hull
Invclyd	Inverclyde
IoM	Isle of Man
IoW	Isle of Wight
Jersey	Jersey
Kent	Kent
Lancs	Lancashire
Leicester	City of Leicester
Leics	Leicestershire
Lincs	Lincolnshire
London	Greater London
Luton	Luton
Mbro	Middlesbrough
Medway	Medway
Mers	Merseyside
Midloth	Midlothian
M Keynes	Milton Keynes
Mon	Monmouthshire
Moray	Moray
M Tydf	Merthyr Tydfil
N Ayrs	North Ayrshire
Neath	Neath Port Talbot
Newport	City and County of Newport
N Lanark	North Lanarkshire
N Lincs	North Lincolnshire
N Nhants	North Northamptonshire
Norf	Norfolk
Northumb	Northumberland
Nottingham	City of Nottingham
Notts	Nottinghamshire
N Som	North Somerset
N Yorks	North Yorkshire
Orkney	Orkney
Oxon	Oxfordshire
Pboro	Peterborough
Pembs	Pembrokeshire
Perth	Perth and Kinross
Plym	Plymouth
Powys	Powys
Ptsmth	Portsmouth
Reading	Reading
Redcar	Redcar and Cleveland
Renfs	Renfrewshire
Rhondda	Rhondda Cynon Taff
Rutland	Rutland
S Ayrs	South Ayrshire
Scilly	Scilly
S Glos	South Gloucestershire
Shetland	Shetland
Shrops	Shropshire
S Lanark	South Lanarkshire
Slough	Slough
Som	Somerset
Soton	Southampton
Southend	Southend-on-Sea
Staffs	Staffordshire
Stirling	Stirling
Stockton	Stockton-on-Tees
Stoke	Stoke-on-Trent
Suff	Suffolk
Sur	Surrey
Swansea	Swansea
Swindon	Swindon
S Yorks	South Yorkshire
T&W	Tyne and Wear
Telford	Telford and Wrekin
Thurrock	Thurrock
Torbay	Torbay
Torf	Torfaen
V Glam	The Vale of Glamorgan
Warks	Warwickshire
Warr	Warrington
W Berks	West Berkshire
W Dunb	West Dunbartonshire
Wilts	Wiltshire
Windsor	Windsor and Maidenhead
W Isles	Western Isles
W Loth	West Lothian
W Mid	West Midlands
W Nhants	West Northamptonshire
Wokingham	Wokingham
Worcs	Worcestershire
Wrex	Wrexham
W Sus	West Sussex
W Yorks	West Yorkshire
York	City of York

Index to road maps of Britain

How to use the index

Example **Westonzoyland Som 43 G11**
- grid square
- page number
- county or unitary authority

A

Aaron's Hill Sur 50 E3
Aaron's Town Cumb. 240 E2
Abbas Combe Som. 30 C2
Abberley Worcs. 116 D5
Abberton Essex. 89 B8
  Worcs 117 G9
Abberwick Northumb 264 G4
Abbess End Essex. 87 C9
Abbess Roding Essex 87 C9
Abbey Devon 27 E10
Abbeycwmhir Powys 113 C11
Abbey-cwm-hir Powys 113 C11
Abbeydale Glos. 80 B5
  S Yorks 186 E4
Abbeydale Park S Yorks 186 E4
Abbey Dore Hereford. 97 E7
Abbey Field Essex 107 G9
Abbey Gate Kent 53 B9
Abbey Green Shrops 149 C10
  Staffs 169 D7
Abbey Hey Gtr Man 184 B5
Abbeyhill Edin 280 G5
Abbey Hulton Stoke 168 F6
Abbey Mead Sur 66 F4
Abbey St Bathans Borders 272 C5
Abbeystead Lancs. 203 C7
Abbey Town Cumb. 238 G5
Abbey Village Lancs. 194 C6
Abbey Wood London 68 D3
Abbots Bickington Devon 24 E5
Abbots Bromley Staffs 151 E11
Abbotsbury Dorset. 17 D7
Abbotsford W Sus 36 C4
Abbotsham Devon. 24 B6
Abbotskerswell Devon 9 B7
Abbots Langley Herts 85 E9
Abbotsleigh Devon. 8 E6
Abbots Leigh N Som 60 E4
Abbotsley Cambs 122 F4
Abbot's Meads Ches W 166 B5
Abbots Morton Worcs 117 F10
Abbots Ripton Cambs 122 B4
Abbots Salford Warks 117 G11
Abbotstone Hants. 48 G5
Abbotswood Hants 32 C5
  Sur 50 C4
Abbots Worthy Hants 48 G3
Abbotts Ann Hants 47 E10
Abcott Shrops 115 B7
Abdon Shrops 131 F11
Abdy S Yorks 186 B6
Aber Ceredig. 93 B9
Aberaeron Ceredig 111 E9
Aberaman Rhondda 77 E8
Aberangell Gwyn 146 G6
Aber-Arad Carms. 92 D6
Aberarder Highld 290 E6
Aberarder House Highld 300 G6
Aberarder Lodge Highld 291 E7

Aberargie Perth 286 F5
Aberarth Ceredig. 111 E9
Aberavon Neath 57 C8
Aber-banc Ceredig. 93 C7
Aberbargoed Caerph 77 E11
Aberbechan Powys 130 E2
Aberbeeg Bl Gwent 78 E2
Abercanaid M Tydf 77 E9
Abercarn Caerph. 78 G2
Abercastle Pembs. 91 E7
Abercegir Powys 128 C6
Aberchalder Highld 290 C5
Aberchirder Aberds 302 D6
Abercorn W Loth 279 F11
Aber Cowarch Gwyn 147 F2
Abercraf Powys 76 C4
Abercregan Neath 57 B11
Abercrombie Fife 287 G9
Abercwmboi Rhondda 77 F8
Abercych Pembs 92 C4
Abercynafon Powys 77 B9
Abercynffig = Aberkenfig Bridgend 57 E11
Abercynon Rhondda 77 F9
Aberdalgie Perth 286 E4
Aberdâr = Aberdare Rhondda 77 E7
Aberdare = Aberdâr Rhondda 77 E7
Aberdaron Gwyn 144 D3
Aberdeen Aberdeen. 293 C11
Aberdesach Gwyn 162 E6
Aberdour Fife 280 D3
Aberdovey = Aberdyfi Gwyn 128 D2
Aberdulais Neath 76 E3
Aberdyfi = Aberdovey Gwyn 128 D2
Aberedw Powys. 95 B11
Abereiddy Pembs. 90 E5
Abererch Gwyn 145 B7
Aberfan M Tydf 77 E9
Aberfeldy Perth. 286 C2
Aberffraw Anglesey 162 B5
Aberffrwd Ceredig 112 B3
  Mon 78 D5
Aberford W Yorks 206 F4
Aberfoyle Stirling 285 G9
Abergarw Bridgend. 58 C2
Abergarwed Neath. 76 E4
Abergavenny Mon 78 C3
Abergele Conwy 180 F6
Aber-Giâr Carms 93 C10
Abergorlech Carms 93 E11
Abergwaun = Fishguard Pembs. 91 D9
Abergwesyn Powys 113 G7
Abergwili Carms 93 G8
Abergwynant Gwyn 146 F3
Abergwynfi Neath. 57 B11
Aber-gwynfi Neath. 57 B11
Abergwyngregyn Gwyn 179 G11
Abergynolwyn Gwyn 128 B3
Aber-Hirnant Gwyn 147 C9
Aberkenfig = Abercynffig Bridgend 57 E11
Aberlady E Loth 281 E9
Aberlemno Angus 287 B9
Aberllefenni Gwyn 128 B5

Aberllydan = Broad Haven Pembs 72 C5
Aberllynfi = Three Cocks Powys 96 D3
Abermagwr Ceredig 112 C3
Abermaw = Barmouth Gwyn 146 F2
Abermeurig Ceredig 111 F11
Aber miwl = Abermule Powys 130 E3
Abermorddu Flint 166 D4
Abermule = Aber-miwl Powys 130 E3
Abernant Powys 148 E2
Aber-nant Rhondda 77 E8
Abernethy Perth 286 F5
Abernyte Perth 286 D6
Aber-oer Wrex 166 F3
Aberogwr = Ogmore by Sea V Glam 57 F11
Aberpennar = Mountain Ash Rhondda 77 F8
Aberporth Ceredig 110 G5
Aber-Rhiwlech Gwyn 147 E8
Aberriw = Berriew Powys 130 C3
Abersoch Gwyn 144 D6
Abersychan Torf 78 E3
Abertawe = Swansea Swansea 56 C6
Aberteifi = Cardigan Ceredig 92 B3
Aberthin V Glam 58 D4
Abertillery Bl Gwent 78 E2
Abertridwr Caerph 58 B6
  Powys 147 F10
Abertrinant Gwyn 128 B2
Abertysswg Caerph 77 D10
Aberuchill Castle Perth 285 E11
Aberuthven Perth 286 F3
Aber-Village Powys 96 G2
Aberyscir Powys 95 F9
Aberystwyth Ceredig 111 A11
Abhainn Suidhe W Isles 305 H2
Abingdon-on-Thames Oxon 83 F7
Abinger Common Sur 50 D6
Abinger Hammer Sur 50 D5
Abington S Lanark 259 E10
  W Nhants 120 E5
Abington Pigotts Cambs 104 C6
Abington Vale W Nhants 120 E5
Ab Kettleby Leics 154 E4
Ab Lench Worcs 117 G11
Ablington Glos 81 D10
  Wilts 47 D7
Abney Derbys 185 F11
Aboyne Aberds 293 D7
Abraham Heights Lancs 211 G9
Abram Gtr Man 194 G6
Abriachan Highld 300 F5
Abridge Essex 87 F7
Abronhill N Lanark 278 F5
Abshot Hants 33 F8

Abson S Glos 61 E8
Abthorpe W Nhants 102 B2
Abune-the-Hill Orkney 314 D2
Aby Lincs 190 F6
Acaster Malbis York 207 D7
Acaster Selby N Yorks 207 E7
Accrington Lancs 195 B9
Acha Argyll 275 B8
  Argyll 288 D3
Achabraid Argyll 275 E9
Achachork Highld 298 E4
Achadh an Eas Highld 308 F6
Achad nan Darach Highld 284 B4
Achadunan Argyll 284 F5
Achafolla Argyll 275 B8
Achagary Highld 308 D7
Achaglass Argyll 255 C8
Achahoish Argyll 275 D8
Achalader Perth 286 C5
Achallader Argyll 285 C7
Achalone Highld 310 D5
Acha Mor W Isles 304 F5
Achanalt Highld 300 C2
Achanamara Argyll 275 E8
Achandunie Highld 300 B6
Ach'an Todhair Highld 290 F2
Achany Highld 309 J5
Achaphubuil Highld 290 F2
Acharacle Highld 289 C8
Acharn Highld 289 D9
  Perth 285 C11
Acharole Highld 310 D6
Acharossan Argyll 275 F10
Acharry Muir Highld 309 K6
Achath Aberds 293 B9
Achavanich Highld 310 E5
Achavelgin Highld 301 D9
Achavraat Highld 301 E9
Achddu Carms 74 E6
Achdregnie Moray 302 G2
Achduart Highld 307 J5
Achentoul Highld 310 F2
Achfary Highld 306 F7
Achfrish Highld 309 H5
Achgarve Highld 307 K3
Achiemore Highld 308 C3
  Highld 310 D2
A'Chill Highld 294 E4
Achiltibuie Highld 307 J5
Achina Highld 308 C7
Achinahuagh Highld 308 C5
Achindaul Highld 290 E3
Achindown Highld 301 E8
Achinduich Highld 309 J5
Achinduin Argyll 289 F10
Achingills Highld 310 C5
Achininver Highld 308 C5
Achintee Highld 290 F3
  Highld 299 E9
Achintraid Highld 295 B10
Achlaven Argyll 289 F10
Achlean Highld 291 D10
Achleck Argyll 288 E6
Achlorachan Highld 300 D3
Achluachrach Highld 290 E4
Achlyness Highld 306 D7
Achmelvich Highld 307 G5
Achmore Highld 295 B10
  Stirling 285 D9

Achnaba Argyll 275 E10
  Argyll 289 F11
Achnabat Highld 300 F5
Achnabreck Argyll 275 D9
Achnacarnin Highld 306 F5
Achnacarry Highld 290 E3
Achnacloich Argyll 289 F11
  Highld 295 E7
Achnaconeran Highld 290 B6
Achnacraig Argyll 288 E6
Achnacree Argyll 289 F11
Achnacree Bay Argyll 289 F11
Achnacroish Argyll 289 E10
Achnadrish Argyll 288 D6
Achnafalnich Argyll 284 E6
Achnagarron Highld 300 C6
Achnaha Highld 288 C6
Achnahanat Highld 309 K5
Achnahannet Highld 301 G9
Achnahard Argyll 288 G5
Achnairn Highld 309 H5
Achnaluachrach Highld 309 J6
Achnandarach Highld 295 B10
Achnanellan Highld 290 E3
  Highld 290 E3
Achnasaul Highld 290 E3
Achnasheen Highld 299 D11
Achnashelloch Argyll 275 D9
Achnavast Highld 310 C5
Achneigie Highld 299 B10
Achormlarie Highld 309 K6
Achorn Highld 310 F5
Achosnich Highld 288 C6
  Highld 301 D9
Achranich Highld 289 E9
Achreamie Highld 310 C4
Achriabhach Highld 290 G3
Achriesgill Highld 306 D7
Achrimsdale Highld 311 J3
Achtoty Highld 308 C7
Achurch N Nhants 137 G10
Achuvoldrach Highld 308 D5
Achvaich Highld 309 K7
Achvarasdal Highld 310 C3
Ackenthwaite Cumb 211 C10
Ackergill Highld 310 D7
Acklam Mbro 225 B9
  N Yorks 216 A5
Ackleton Shrops 132 D5
Acklington Northumb 252 C6
Ackton W Yorks 198 C2
Ackworth Moor Top W Yorks 198 D2
Acle Norf 161 G8
Acock's Green W Mid 134 G2
Acol Kent 71 F10
Acomb Northumb 241 D10
  York 207 C7
Acre Gtr Man 196 F2
  Lancs 195 C9
Acrefair Wrex 166 F3
Acres Nook Staffs 168 E4
Acre Street W Sus 21 B11
Acton Ches E 167 E10
  Dorset 18 F6
  London 67 C8
  Shrops 130 G6
  Staffs 168 G4
  Suff 107 C7

Acton continued
  Worcs 116 D6
  Wrex 166 E4
Acton Beauchamp Hereford 116 G3
Acton Bridge Ches W 183 F9
Acton Burnell Shrops 131 C10
Acton Green Hereford 116 G3
  London 67 D8
Acton Pigott Shrops 131 C10
Acton Place Suff 107 B7
Acton Reynald Shrops 149 E10
Acton Round Shrops 132 D2
Acton Scott Shrops 131 F9
Acton Trussell Staffs 151 F8
Acton Turville S Glos 61 C10
Adabroc W Isles 304 B7
Adambrae W Loth 269 A10
Adam's Green Dorset 29 E8
Adbaston Staffs 150 D5
Adber Dorset 29 C9
Adbolton Notts 154 B2
Adderbury Oxon 101 D9
Adderley Shrops 150 B3
Adderley Green Stoke 168 G6
Adderstone Northumb 264 C4
Addiewell W Loth 269 C9
Addingham W Yorks 205 D7
Addingham Moorside W Yorks 205 D7
Addington Bucks 102 F4
  Kent 53 B7
  London 67 G11
Addinston Borders 271 E10
Addiscombe London 67 G10
Addlestone Sur 66 G5
Addlestonemoor Sur 66 F4
Addlethorpe Lincs 175 B8
Adel W Yorks 205 F11
Adeney Telford 150 F4
Adeyfield Herts 85 D9
Adfa Powys 129 C11
Adforton Hereford 115 C8
Adgestone IoW 21 D7
Adisham Kent 55 C8
Adlestrop Glos 100 F4
Adlingfleet E Yorks 199 C10
Adlington Ches E 184 E6
  Lancs 194 E6
Adlington Park Lancs 194 E5
Admaston Staffs 151 E10
  Telford 150 G2
Admington Warks 100 B4
Adpar Ceredig 92 C6
Adsborough Som 28 B3
Adscombe Som 43 F7
Adstock Bucks 102 E4
Adstone W Nhants 119 G11
  Shrops 130 C6
Adswood Gtr Man 184 D5
Adversane W Sus 35 C9
Advie Highld 301 F11
Adwalton W Yorks 197 B8
Adwell Oxon 83 F11

Adwick le Street S Yorks 198 F4
Adwick upon Dearne S Yorks 198 G3
Adziel Aberds 303 D9
Ae Dumfries 247 F11
Ae Village Dumfries 247 F11
Affetside Gtr Man 195 E9
Affleck Aberds 303 G8
Affpuddle Dorset 18 C2
Afon Eitha Wrex 166 F3
Afon-wen Flint 181 G10
Afon Wen Gwyn 145 B8
Afton IoW 20 D2
Agar Nook Leics 153 G9
Agbrigg W Yorks 197 D10
Aggborough Worcs 116 B6
Agglethorpe N Yorks 213 B11
Aglionby Cumb 239 F10
Aigburth Mers 182 D5
Aiginis W Isles 304 E6
Aike E Yorks 209 D7
Aikerness Orkney 314 A4
Aikers Orkney 314 G4
Aiketgate Cumb 230 B5
Aikton Cumb 239 G2
Ailby Lincs 190 F6
Ailey Hereford 96 B6
Ailsworth Pboro 138 D2
Aimes Green Essex 86 E5
Ainderby Quernhow N Yorks 215 C7
Ainderby Steeple N Yorks 224 G6
Aingers Green Essex 108 G2
Ainley Top W Yorks 196 D6
Ainsdale Mers 193 E10
Ainsdale-on-Sea Mers 193 E9
Ainstable Cumb 230 B6
Ainsworth Gtr Man 195 E9
Ainthorpe N Yorks 226 D4
Aintree Mers 182 B5
Aird Argyll 275 C8
  Dumfries 236 C2
  Highld 299 B7
  W Isles 296 K3
  W Isles 304 E7
Aird a' Mhachair W Isles 297 G3
Aird a' Mhulaidh W Isles 305 G3
Aird Asaig W Isles 305 H3
Aird Dhail W Isles 304 B6
Airdens Highld 309 K6
Aird Mhidhinis W Isles 297 L3
Aird Mhighe W Isles 296 C6
  W Isles 305 J3
Aird Mhòr W Isles 297 G4
  W Isles 297 L3
Aird of Sleat Highld 295 E7
Airdrie N Lanark 268 B5
Airds of Kells Dumfries 237 B8

Aar–Alc

Aird Thunga W Isles 304 E6
Airdtorrisdale Highld 308 C6
Aird Uig W Isles 304 E2
Airedale W Yorks 198 B3
Aire View N Yorks 204 D5
Airidh a Bhruaich W Isles 305 G4
Airieland Dumfries 237 D9
Airinis W Isles 304 E6
Airlie Angus 287 B7
Airlies Dumfries 236 D5
Airmyn E Yorks 199 B8
Airntully Perth 286 D4
Airor Highld 295 E9
Airth Falk 279 D7
Airthrey Castle Stirling 278 B6
Airton N Yorks 204 B4
Airyhassen Dumfries 236 E5
Airy Hill N Yorks 227 D7
Airyligg Dumfries 236 C4
Aisby Lincs 155 B10
  Lincs 188 C5
Aisgernis W Isles 297 J3
Aish Devon 8 C3
  Devon 8 D6
Aisholt Som 43 F7
Aiskew N Yorks 214 B5
Aislaby N Yorks 216 B5
  N Yorks 227 D7
  Stockton 225 C8
Aisthorpe Lincs 188 E6
Aith Orkney 314 E2
  Shetland 312 D8
  Shetland 313 H5
Aithnen Powys 148 E4
Aithsetter Shetland 313 K6
Aitkenhead S Ayrs 245 B8
Aitnoch Highld 301 F9
Akeld Northumb 263 D11
Akeley Bucks 102 D4
Akenham Suff 108 B2
Albany T&W 243 F7
Albaston Corn 12 G4
Alberbury Shrops 149 G7
Albourne W Sus 36 D3
Albourne Green W Sus 36 D3
Albrighton Shrops 132 C6
  Shrops 149 F9
Albro Castle Ceredig 92 B3
Alburgh Norf 142 F5
Albury Herts 105 G8
  Sur 50 D5
Albury End Herts 105 G8
Albury Heath Sur 50 D5
Alby Hill Norf 160 C3
Alcaig Highld 300 D5
Alcaston Shrops 131 F9
Alcester Dorset 30 D5
  Warks 117 F11
Alcester Lane's End W Mid 133 G11
Alciston E Sus 23 D8
Alcombe Som 42 D3
  Wilts 61 F10
Alconbury Cambs 122 B3

Alconbury Weald Cambs 122 B4
Alconbury Weston Cambs 122 B3
Aldbar Castle Angus 287 B9
Aldborough Norf 160 C3
N Yorks 215 F8
Aldborough Hatch London 68 B3
Aldbourne Wilts 63 D9
Aldbrough E Yorks 209 F10
Aldbrough St John N Yorks 224 C4
Aldbury Herts 85 C7
Aldcliffe Lancs 211 C9
Aldclune Perth 291 G11
Aldeburgh Suff 127 F9
Aldeby Norf 143 E8
Aldenham Herts 85 F10
Alderbrook E Sus 37 B8
Alderbury Wilts 31 B11
Aldercar Derbys 170 F6
Alderford Norf 160 F2
Alder Forest Gtr Man 184 B3
Alderholt Dorset 31 E10
Alderley Glos 80 G3
Alderley Edge Ches E 184 F4
Alderman's Green W Mid 135 G7
Aldermaston W Berks 64 F5
Aldermaston Soke W Berks 64 G6
Aldermaston Wharf W Berks 64 F6
Alderminster Warks 100 B4
Aldermoor Soton 32 D5
Alder Moor Staffs 152 E4
Alderney BCP 18 C6
Alder Row Som 45 E9
Aldersbrook London 68 B2
Alder's End Hereford 98 C2
Aldersey Green Ches E 167 D7
Aldershawe Staffs 134 B2
Aldershot Hants 49 C11
Alderton Glos 99 E10
Shrops 149 E9
Suff 108 C6
Wilts 61 C10
W Nhants 102 B4
Alderton Fields Glos 99 E10
Alderwasley Derbys 170 E4
Aldfield N Yorks 214 F5
Aldford Ches W 166 D6
Aldgate Rutland 137 C9
Aldham Essex 107 F8
Suff 107 B10
Aldie Highld 309 L7
Aldingbourne W Sus 22 B6
Aldingham Cumb 210 E5
Aldington Kent 54 F5
Worcs 99 C11
Aldington Frith Kent 54 F4
Aldivalloch Moray 302 G3
Aldochlay Argyll 277 C7
Aldon Shrops 115 B8
Aldoth Cumb 229 B8
Aldourie Castle Highld 300 F6
Aldreth Cambs 123 C8
Aldridge W Mid 133 C11
Aldringham Suff 127 E8
Aldrington Brighton 36 F3
Aldsworth Glos 81 C11
Aldunie Moray 302 G3
Aldwark Derbys 170 D2
N Yorks 215 G9
Aldwarke S Yorks 186 C6
Aldwick W Sus 22 D6
Aldwincle N Nhants 137 G10
Aldworth S Berks 64 D5
Alehouseburn Aberds 302 C6
Alehousehill Aberds 303 G10
Ale Oak Shrops 130 G4
Alexandria W Dunb 277 F7
Aley Som 43 F7
Aley Green C Beds 85 B9
Alfardisworthy Devon 24 E3
Alfington Devon 15 B8
Alfold Sur 50 G4
Alfold Bars W Sus 50 G4
Alfold Crossways Sur 50 G4
Alford Aberds 293 B7
Lincs 191 F7
Som 44 G6
Alfred's Well Worcs 117 C8
Alfreton Derbys 170 D6
Alfrick Worcs 116 G4
Alfrick Pound Worcs 116 G4
Alfriston E Sus 23 E8
Algakirk Lincs 156 B5
Algaltraig Argyll 275 F11
Algarkirk Lincs 156 B5
Alhampton Som 44 G6
Aline Lodge W Isles 305 G3
Alisary Highld 289 B9
Alkborough N Lincs 199 C11
Alkerton Glos 80 D3
Oxon 101 C7
Alkham Kent 55 E9
Alkington Shrops 149 B10
Alkmonton Derbys 152 B3
Alkrington Garden Village Gtr Man 195 G11
Alladale Lodge Highld 309 L4
Allaleigh Devon 8 E6
Allanaquoich Aberds 292 D3
Allanbank Borders 271 F10

Allanbank continued N Lanark 268 D6
Allangrange Mains Highld 300 D6
Allanshaugh Borders 271 F8
Allanshaws Borders 271 G9
Allanton Borders 273 E7
N Lanark 269 D7
S Lanark 268 E4
Allaston Glos 79 E10
Allathasdal W Isles 297 L2
Allbrook Hants 33 C7
All Cannings Wilts 62 G5
Allendale Town Northumb 241 F8
Allen End Warks 134 D3
Allenheads Northumb 232 B3
Allensford Durham 242 G3
Allens Green Herts 87 B7
Allensmore Hereford 97 D9
Allenton Derby 153 C7
Allerby Cumb 229 C7
Aller Park Devon 9 B7
Allerston N Yorks 217 C7
Allerthorpe E Yorks 207 D11
Allerton Mers 182 D6
W Yorks 205 G8
Allerton Bywater W Yorks 198 B2
Allerton Mauleverer N Yorks 206 B4
Allesley W Mid 134 G6
Allestree Derby 152 B6
Allet Corn 4 F5
Allexton Leics 136 C6
Allgreave Ches E 169 B7
Allhallows Medway 69 D10
Allhallows-on-Sea Medway 69 D10
Allimore Green Staffs 151 F7
Allington Kent 53 B8
Lincs 172 G5
Wilts 47 F8
Wilts 61 D11
Wilts 62 G5
Allington Bar Wilts 61 E11
Allithwaite Cumb 211 D7
Alloa Clack 279 C7
Allonby Cumb 229 C7
Allostock Ches W 184 G2
Alloway S Ayrs 257 F8
Allowenshay Som 28 E5
All Saints Devon 9 D7
All Saints South Elmham Suff 142 G6
Allscot Shrops 132 D4
Allscott Telford 150 G2
All Stretton Shrops 131 D9
Allt Carms 75 E9
Alltami Flint 166 B3
Alltbeithe Highld 290 C2
Alltchaorunn Highld 284 B5
Alltforgan Powys 147 E9
Alltmawr Powys 95 B11
Alltnacaillich Highld 308 E4
Allt-na-giubhsaich Aberds 292 E4
Allt na h-Airbhe Highld 307 K6
Allt-nan-sùgh Highld 295 C11
Alltrech Argyll 289 F8
Alltsigh Highld 290 B6
Alltwalis Carms 93 E8
Alltwen Neath 76 E2
Alltyblaca Ceredig 93 B10
Allt-yr-yn Newport 59 B9
Allwood Green Suff 125 C10
Alma Notts 171 E7
Almagill Dumfries 238 B3
Almeley Hereford 114 G6
Almeley Wootton Hereford 114 G6
Almer Dorset 18 B4
Almholme S Yorks 198 F5
Almington Staffs 150 C4
Alminstone Cross Devon 24 C4
Almondbank Perth 286 E4
Almondbury W Yorks 197 D7
Almondsbury S Glos 60 C6
Almondvale W Loth 269 B11
Almshouse Green Essex 106 E5
Alne N Yorks 215 F9
Alne End N Yorks 118 F2
Alne Hills Warks 118 E2
Alness Highld 300 C6
Alnessferry Highld 300 C6
Alne Station N Yorks 215 F10
Alnham Northumb 263 G11
Alnmouth Northumb 264 G5
Alnwick Northumb 264 G5
Alperton London 67 C7
Alphamstone Essex 107 D7
Alpheton Suff 107 B7
Alphington Devon 14 C4
Alpington Norf 142 C5
Alport Derbys 170 C2
Powys 130 D5
Alpraham Ches E 167 D9
Alresford Essex 107 G11
Alrewas Staffs 152 F3
Alsager Ches E 168 D3
Alsagers Bank Staffs 168 F4

Alsop en le Dale Derbys 169 D11
Alston Cumb 231 B10
Devon 28 G4
Alstone Glos 99 E9
Glos 99 G8
Som 43 D10
Alstonefield Staffs 169 D10
Alston Sutton 44 C2
Alswear Devon 26 C2
Altandhu Highld 307 H4
Altanduin Highld 311 G2
Altarnun Corn 11 C10
Altass Highld 309 J4
Altbough Hereford 97 E10
Altdargue Aberds 293 C7
Alterwall Highld 310 C6
Altham Lancs 203 G11
Alt Hill Gtr Man 196 G2
Althorne Essex 88 F6
Althorpe N Lincs 199 F10
Alticane S Ayrs 244 F6
Alticry Dumfries 236 D4
Altmore Highld 65 D11
Altnabreac Station Highld 310 E4
Altnacealgach Hotel Highld 307 H7
Altnacraig Argyll 289 G10
Altnafeadh Highld 284 B6
Altnaharra Highld 308 F5
Altofts W Yorks 197 C11
Alton Derbys 170 C5
Hants 49 F8
Staffs 169 G9
Wilts 47 D7
Alton Barnes Wilts 62 G6
Altonhill E Ayrs 257 B10
Alton Pancras Dorset 30 G2
Alton Priors Wilts 62 G6
Altonside Moray 302 D2
Altour Highld 290 E4
Altrincham Gtr Man 184 D3
Altrua Highld 290 E4
Altskeith Stirling 285 G8
Altyre Ho Moray 301 D10
Alum Rock W Mid 134 F2
Alva Clack 279 B7
Alvanley Ches W 183 G7
Alvaston Derby 153 C7
Alvechurch Worcs 117 C10
Alvecote Warks 134 C4
Alvediston Wilts 31 C7
Alveley Shrops 132 G5
Alverdiscott Devon 25 B8
Alverstoke Hants 21 B8
Alverstone IoW 21 D7
Alverthorpe W Yorks 197 C10
Alverton Notts 172 G3
Alves Moray 301 C11
Alvescot Oxon 82 E3
Alveston S Glos 60 B6
Warks 118 F4
Alveston Down S Glos 60 B6
Alveston Hill Warks 118 G4
Alvie Highld 291 C10
Alvingham Lincs 190 C5
Alvington Glos 79 E10
Som 29 D8
Alwalton Cambs 138 D2
Alway Newport 59 B10
Alweston Dorset 29 E11
Alwington Devon 24 C6
Alwinton Northumb 251 B10
Alwoodley W Yorks 205 E11
Alwoodley Gates W Yorks 206 E2
Alwoodley Park W Yorks 205 E11
Alyth Perth 286 C6
Amalebra Corn 1 B5
Amalveor Corn 1 B5
Amatnatua Highld 309 K4
Am Baile W Isles 297 K3
Ambaston Derbys 153 C8
Ambergate Derbys 170 E4
Amber Hill Lincs 174 F2
Amberley Glos 80 E5
Hereford 97 B10
W Sus 35 E8
Amble Northumb 253 C7
Amblecote W Mid 133 F7
Ambler Thorn W Yorks 196 B5
Ambleside Cumb 221 E7
Ambleston Pembs 91 F10
Ambrosden Oxon 83 B10
Am Buth Argyll 289 G10
Amcotts N Lincs 199 E11
Amen Corner Brack 65 F10
Amersham Bucks 85 F7
Amersham Common Bucks 85 F7
Amersham Old Town Bucks 85 F7
Amersham on the Hill Bucks 85 F7
Amerton Staffs 151 D9
Amesbury Bath 45 B7
Wilts 47 E7
Ameysford Dorset 31 G9
Amington Staffs 134 C4
Amisfield Dumfries 247 G11
Amlwch Anglesey 178 C6
Amlwch Port Anglesey 179 C7
Ammanford = Rhydaman Carms 75 C10
Ammerham Som 28 F5
Amod Argyll 255 D8
Amotherby N Yorks 216 E4
Ampfield Hants 32 C6
Ampleforth N Yorks 215 D11
Ampney Crucis Glos 81 E9
Ampney St Mary Glos 81 E9
Ampney St Peter Glos 81 E9

Amport Hants 47 E9
Ampthill C Beds 103 D10
Ampton Suff 125 C7
Amroth Pembs 73 D11
Amulree Perth 286 D2
Amwell Herts 85 C11
Anagach Highld 301 G10
Anaheilt Highld 289 C10
Anancaun Highld 299 C10
An Caol Highld 298 D6
An Cnoc W Isles 304 E6
Ancaster Lincs 173 G7
Anchor Shrops 130 G3
Anchorage Park Ptsmth 33 G11
Anchor Corner Norf 141 D10
Anchorsholme Blackpool 202 E2
Anchor Street Norf 160 E6
Ancroft Northmoor Northumb 273 F9
Ancroft Northumb 273 F9
Ancrum Borders 262 E4
Ancton W Sus 35 G7
Ancumtoun Orkney 314 A7
Anderby Lincs 191 F9
Anderby Creek Lincs 191 F9
Andersea Som 43 G10
Andersfield Som 43 G8
Anderson Dorset 18 B5
Anderton Ches W 183 F10
Corn 7 E8
Lancs 194 E6
Andertons Mill Lancs 194 E4
Andover Hants 47 D11
Andover Down Hants 47 D11
Andoversford Glos 81 B8
Andreas IoM 192 C5
Andwell Hants 49 C7
An Gleann Ur W Isles 304 E6
Angmering W Sus 35 G9
Angram N Yorks 206 D6
N Yorks 223 F7
Anick Northumb 241 D11
Anie Stirling 285 F9
Ankerdine Hill Worcs 116 F4
Ankerville Highld 301 B8
Anlaby E Yorks 200 B4
Anlaby Park N Lincs 200 B5
Anmer Norf 158 D4
Anmore Hants 33 E11
Annan Dumfries 238 D5
Annaside Cumb 210 B1
Annat Highld 299 D8
Highld 284 G4
Anna Valley Hants 47 E10
Annbank S Ayrs 257 E10
Annesley Notts 171 E8
Annesley Woodhouse Notts 171 E7
Annfield Plain Durham 242 G5
Anniesland Glasgow 267 B10
Annifirth Shetland 313 J3
Annishader Highld 298 D4
Annis Hill Suff 143 F7
Annitsford T&W 243 C7
Annscroft Shrops 131 B9
Ann's Hill Hants 33 G9
Annwell Place Derbys 152 F6
Ansdell Lancs 193 B10
Ansells End Herts 85 B11
Ansford Som 44 G6
Ansley Warks 134 E5
Ansley Common Warks 134 E6
Anslow Staffs 152 D4
Anslow Gate Staffs 152 D3
Ansteadbrook Sur 50 G2
Anstey Herts 105 E8
Leics 135 B10
Anstruther Easter Fife 287 G9
Anstruther Wester Fife 287 G9
Ansty Hants 49 E8
Warks 135 G7
Wilts 31 B7
W Sus 36 C3
Ansty Coombe Wilts 31 B7
Ansty Cross Dorset 30 G3
Anthill Common Hants 33 E10
Anthony Corn 7 E7
Anthony's Cross Glos 98 G4
Anthorn Cumb 238 F5
Antingham Norf 160 C5
An t-Ob W Isles 296 C6
Anton's Gowt Lincs 174 F3
Antonshill Falk 279 E7
Antony Corn 7 E7
Antony Passage Corn 7 D8
Antrobus Ches W 183 F10
Anvil Green Kent 54 D6
Anvilles W Berks 63 F10
Anwick Lincs 173 E10
Anwoth Dumfries 237 D7
Aoradh Argyll 274 G3
Apedale Staffs 168 F4

Aperfield London 52 B2
Apes Dale Worcs 117 C9
Apes Hall Cambs 139 E11
Apethorpe N Nhants 137 D10
Apeton Staffs 151 F7
Apley Lincs 189 F10
Apley Forge Shrops 132 D4
Apperknowle Derbys 186 F5
Apperley Glos 99 F7
Apperley Bridge W Yorks 205 F9
Apperley Dene Northumb 242 F3
Appersett N Yorks 223 G7
Appin Argyll 289 E11
Appin House Argyll 289 E11
Appleby N Lincs 200 E3
Appleby Magna Leics 134 B6
Appleby Parva Leics 134 B6
Appleby-in-Westmorland Cumb 231 G9
Applecross Highld 299 E7
Applecross Ho Highld 299 E7
Appledore Devon 27 C6
Devon 40 G3
Kent 39 D7
Appledore Heath Kent 54 G3
Appleford Oxon 83 G8
Applegarthtown Dumfries 248 G4
Applehouse Hill Windsor 65 C10
Applemore Hants 32 F5
Appleshaw Hants 47 D10
Applethwaite Cumb 229 F11
Appleton Halton 183 D8
Oxon 82 E6
Appleton-le-Moors N Yorks 216 B4
Appleton-le-Street N Yorks 216 E4
Appleton Park Warr 183 E10
Appleton Roebuck N Yorks 207 E7
Appleton Thorn Warr 183 E10
Appleton Wiske N Yorks 225 E7
Appletreehall Borders 262 F2
Appletreewick N Yorks 213 G11
Appley IoW 21 C8
Appley Bridge Lancs 194 F4
Apse Heath IoW 21 E7
Apsey Green Suff 126 E5
Apsley Herts 85 D9
Apsley End C Beds 104 E2
Apuldram W Sus 22 C4
Aqueduct Telford 132 B3
Aquhythe Aberds 293 B9
Arabella Highld 301 B8
Arbeadie Aberds 293 D8
Arberth = Narberth Pembs 73 C10
Arbirlot Angus 287 C10
Arboll Highld 311 L2
Arborfield Wokingham 65 F9
Arborfield Cross Wokingham 65 F9
Arborfield Garrison Wokingham 65 F9
Arbourthorne S Yorks 186 D5
Arbroath Angus 287 C10
Arbury Cambs 123 E8
Arbuthnott Aberds 293 F9
Archavandra Muir Highld 309 K7
Archdeacon Newton Darl 224 B5
Archenfield Hereford 96 C5
Archiestown Moray 302 E2
Archnalea Highld 289 C10
Arclid Ches E 168 C3
Arclid Green Ches E 168 C3
Ardachu Highld 309 J6
Ardailly Argyll 255 C7
Ardalanish Argyll 274 B4
Ardallie Aberds 303 F10
Ardalum Ho Argyll 288 F6
Ardamaleish Argyll 275 G11
Ardanaiseig Argyll 284 E4
Ardaneaskan Highld 295 B10
Ardanstur Argyll 275 B9
Ardargie House Hotel Perth 286 F4
Ardarroch Highld 295 B10
Ardbeg Argyll 289 B9
Argyll 276 E3
Argyll 254 C5
Ardcharnick Highld 275 B10
Ardchiavaig Argyll 274 B4
Ardchonnell Argyll 275 B10
Ardchronie Highld 309 L6
Ardchullarie More Stirling 285 F9
Ardchyle Stirling 285 E9
Ard-dhubh Highld 299 E7
Arddleen Powys 148 F5
Ardechive Highld 290 D3
Ardeley Herts 104 F6
Ardelve Highld 295 C10
Arden Argyll 277 E7
E Renf 267 D10
Ardencaple Ho Argyll 275 B8
Arden Park Gtr Man 184 C6

Ardens Grafton Warks 118 G2
Ardentallen Argyll 289 G10
Ardentinny Argyll 276 D3
Ardentraive Argyll 275 F11
Ardeonaig Stirling 285 D10
Ardersier Highld 301 D7
Ardery Highld 289 C9
Ardessie Highld 307 L5
Ardfern Argyll 275 C9
Ardfernal Argyll 274 F6
Ardgartan Argyll 284 G6
Ardgay Highld 309 K5
Ardglassie Aberds 303 C9
Ardgour Highld 290 G2
Ardgye Moray 301 C11
Ardheslaig Highld 299 D7
Ardiecow Moray 302 C5
Ardinamir Argyll 275 B8
Ardindrean Highld 307 L6
Ardingly W Sus 36 B4
Ardington Oxon 64 B2
Ardington Wick Oxon 64 B2
Ardintoul Highld 295 C10
Ardlair Aberds 302 G5
Highld 299 B9
Ardlamey Argyll 255 C7
Ardlamont Ho Argyll 275 G10
Ardlawhill Aberds 303 C8
Ardleigh Essex 107 F11
Ardleigh Green London 68 B4
Ardleigh Heath Essex 107 E10
Ardler Perth 286 C6
Ardley Oxon 101 F10
Ardley End Essex 87 C8
Ardlui Argyll 285 E7
Ardlussa Argyll 275 E7
Ardmair Highld 307 K6
Ardmay Argyll 284 G6
Ardmenish Argyll 274 F6
Ardmolich Highld 289 B9
Ardmore Argyll 289 G9
Highld 306 D7
Highld 309 L7
Ardnacross Argyll 289 E7
Ardnadam Argyll 276 F3
Ardnagowan Argyll 284 G4
Ardnagrask Highld 300 E5
Ardnarff Highld 295 B10
Ardnastang Highld 289 C10
Ardnave Argyll 274 F3
Ardno Argyll 284 G5
Ardo Aberds 303 F8
Ardoch Perth 286 B4
Ardochy House Highld 290 C4
Ardo Ho Aberds 303 G9
Ardoyne Aberds 302 G6
Ardpatrick Argyll 275 G8
Ardpatrick Ho Argyll 255 B8
Ardpeaton Argyll 276 D4
Ardradnaig Perth 285 C11
Ardrishaig Argyll 275 E9
Ardross Fife 287 G9
Highld 300 B6
Ardross Castle Highld 300 B6
Ardrossan N Ayrs 266 G4
Ardshave Highld 309 K7
Ardsheal Highld 289 D11
Ardshealach Highld 289 C8
Ardskenish Argyll 274 D4
Ardslignish Highld 289 C7
Ardtalla Argyll 254 B5
Ardtalnaig Perth 285 D11
Ardtaraig Argyll 275 E11
Ardtoe Highld 289 B8
Ardtrostan Perth 285 E10
Ardtur Argyll 289 E11
Arduaine Argyll 275 B8
Ardullie Highld 300 C5
Ardvannie Highld 309 L6
Ardvar Highld 306 F6
Ardvasar Highld 295 E8
Ardveenish W Isles 297 L3
Ardverikie Highld 291 E7
Ardvorlich Perth 285 E10
Ardwell Dumfries 236 E3
Moray 302 F3
S Ayrs 244 G4
Ardwell Mains Dumfries 236 E3
Ardwick Gtr Man 184 B5
Areley Kings Worcs 116 C6
Arford Hants 49 F10
Argoed Caerph 77 F11
Powys 113 G9
Powys 130 E5
Shrops 130 G6
Shrops 148 E6
Argos Hill E Sus 37 B9
Arichamish Argyll 275 C10
Arichastlich Argyll 284 D6
Aridhglas Argyll 288 G5
Arieniskill Highld 295 G9
Arileod Argyll 288 D3
Arinacrinachd Highld 299 D7
Arinagour Argyll 288 D4
Arineckaig Highld 299 E9
Arion Orkney 314 E2
Arisaig Highld 295 G8
Arivegaig Highld 289 C8
Arivoichallum Argyll 254 C4
Arivruaich W Isles 305 G4
Arkendale N Yorks 215 G7
Arkesden Essex 105 E9
Arkholme Lancs 211 E11
Arkle Town N Yorks 223 E10
Arkleby Cumb 229 C8
Arkleside N Yorks 213 B8
Arkleton Dumfries 249 E9
Arkley London 86 F2

Arksey S Yorks 198 F5
Arle Glos 99 G8
Arlebrook Glos 80 D4
Arlecdon Cumb 219 B10
Arlescote Warks 101 B7
Arlesey C Beds 104 D3
Arleston Telford 150 G3
Arley Ches E 183 E11
Arley Green Ches E 183 E11
Arlingham Glos 80 C2
Arlington Devon 40 E6
E Sus 23 D8
Glos 81 D10
Arlington Beccott Devon 40 E6
Armadale Highld 308 C7
W Loth 269 B8
Armadale Castle Highld 295 E8
Armathwaite Cumb 230 B6
Armigers Essex 105 F11
Arminghall Norf 142 C5
Armitage Staffs 151 F11
Armitage Bridge W Yorks 196 E6
Armley W Yorks 205 G11
Carms 94 F3
Hants 32 D5
Hereford 97 G11
Shrops 148 G6
Stirling 285 G11
Suff 126 F4
Armscote Warks 100 C4
Armsdale Staffs 150 C5
Armshead Staffs 168 F6
Armston N Nhants 137 F11
Armthorpe S Yorks 198 F6
Arnabost Argyll 288 D4
Arnaby Cumb 210 C3
Arncliffe N Yorks 213 E8
Arncroach Fife 287 G9
Arnabost S Yorks 198 F5 → Ardilly Ho Moray 302 E2
Arne Dorset 18 D5
Arnesby Leics 136 E2
Arngask Perth 286 F5
Arnisdale Highld 295 D10
Arnish Highld 298 E5
Arniston Midloth 270 C6
Arnol W Isles 304 D5
Arnold E Yorks 209 E8
Notts 171 F9
Arno's Vale Bristol 60 E6
Arnprior Stirling 278 C2
Arnside Cumb 211 D9
Aros Mains Argyll 289 E7
Arowry Wrex 149 B9
Arpafeelie Highld 300 D6
Arpinge Kent 55 F7
Arrad Foot Cumb 210 C6
Arram E Yorks 208 E6
Arrathorne N Yorks 224 G4
Arreton IoW 20 D6
Arrington Cambs 122 G6
Arrivain Argyll 284 D6
Arrochar Argyll 284 G6
Arrow Warks 117 F11
Arrowe Hill Mers 182 D3
Arrowfield Top Worcs 117 C10
Arrow Green Hereford 115 F8
Arthington W Yorks 205 E11
Arthingworth W Nhants 136 G4
Arthog Gwyn 146 G2
Arthrath Aberds 303 F9
Arthursdale W Yorks 206 F3
Arthurstone Perth 286 C6
Arthurville Highld 309 L7
Artington Sur 50 D3
Artrochie Aberds 303 F10
Arundel W Sus 35 F8
Arwick Orkney 314 D3
Aryhoulan Highld 290 G2
Asby Cumb 229 G2
Ascog Argyll 266 C2
Ascoil Highld 311 H2
Ascot Windsor 66 F2
Ascott Warks 100 E6
Ascott d'Oyley Oxon 82 B4
Ascott Earl Oxon 82 B3
Ascott-under-Wychwood Oxon 82 B4
Asenby N Yorks 215 D7
Asfordby Leics 154 F4
Asfordby Hill Leics 154 F4
Asgarby Lincs 173 F10
Lincs 174 B4
Ash Devon 8 G6
Dorset 30 E5
Kent 55 D10
Kent 68 G5
Som 29 C7
Sur 49 C11
Ash Bank Staffs 168 F6
Ashbocking Suff 126 G3
Ashbourne Derbys 169 F11
Ashbrittle Som 27 C9
Ashbrook Shrops 131 E9
Ashburnham Forge E Sus 23 B11
Ashburton Devon 8 B5
Ashbury Devon 12 B6
Oxon 63 C9
Ashby N Lincs 200 F4
Ashby by Partney Lincs 174 B6
Ashby cum Fenby NE Lincs 201 G9

Ashby de la Launde Lincs 173 D9
Ashby-de-la-Zouch Leics 153 F7
Ashby Folville Leics 154 G4
Ashby Hill NE Lincs 201 G8
Ashby Magna Leics 135 E11
Ashby Parva Leics 135 F11
Ashby Puerorum Lincs 190 G4
Ashby St Ledgers W Nhants 119 D10
Ashby St Mary Norf 142 D6
Ashchurch Glos 99 E8
Ashcombe Devon 14 F4
Ashcombe Park N Som 59 G8
Ashcott Som 44 F2
Ashcott Corner Som 44 F2
Ashculme Devon 27 D10
Ashdon Essex 105 C11
Ashe Hants 48 D5
Asheldham Essex 89 E7
Ashen Essex 106 C4
Ashendon Bucks 84 C2
Asheridge Bucks 84 E6
Ashey IoW 21 D7
Ashfield Argyll 275 E8
Carms 94 F3
Hants 32 D5
Hereford 97 G11
Stirling 285 G11
Suff 126 E4
Ashfield Cum Thorpe Suff 126 E4
Ashfield Green Suff 124 C5
W Sus 36 C3
Ashfields Shrops 150 D4
Ashfold Crossways W Sus 36 C3
Ashfold Side N Yorks 214 G2
Ashford Devon 40 G4
Devon 8 F3
Hants 31 E11
Kent 54 E4
Sur 66 E5
Ashford Bowdler Shrops 115 C10
Ashford Carbonell Shrops 115 C10
Ashford Common Sur 66 E5
Ashford Hill Hants 64 G4
Ashford in the Water Derbys 185 G11
Ashgate Derbys 186 G5
Ashgill S Lanark 268 E5
Warks 134 F4
Ashgrove Bath 45 B8
Ash Green Sur 50 D2
Ash Grove Wrex 166 G5
Ash Hill Devon 14 G4
Ashiestiel Borders 261 B10
Ashill Devon 27 E9
Norf 141 C7
Som 28 D4
Ashingdon Essex 88 G5
Ashington BCP 18 B6
Northumb 253 F7
Som 29 C9
W Sus 35 D11
Ashington End Lincs 175 B8
Ashintully Castle Perth 292 G3
Ashkirk Borders 261 E11
Ashlett Hants 33 G7
Ashleworth Glos 98 F6
Ashley Cambs 124 E3
Ches E 184 D3
Dorset 31 G10
Glos 80 G6
Hants 19 B11
Hants 47 G11
Kent 55 D10
N Nhants 136 E5
Som 29 C9
Staffs 150 B5
Wilts 61 F10
Ashley Down Bristol 60 D5
Ashley Green Bucks 85 D7
Ashleyhay Derbys 170 E3
Ashley Heath Ches E 184 D3
Dorset 31 G10
Staffs 150 B4
Ashley Moor Hereford 115 D9
Ashley Park Sur 66 F5
Ash Magna Shrops 149 B11
Ashmanhaugh Norf 160 E6
Ashmansworth Hants 48 B2
Ashmansworthy Devon 24 D4
Ashmead Green Glos 80 F3
Ashmill Devon 12 B3
Ash Mill Devon 26 C3
Ashmore Devon 26 D3
Ashmore Green W Berks 64 F4
Ashmore Lake W Mid 133 D9
Ashmore Park W Mid 133 C9
Ashnashellach Lodge Highld 299 D10
Ashopton Derbys 185 D11
Ashorne Warks 118 F6
Ashover Derbys 170 C4
Ashover Hay Derbys 170 C5
Ashow Warks 118 C6
Ash Parva Shrops 149 B11
Ashperton Hereford 98 C2
Ashprington Devon 8 E6
Ash Priors Som 27 B11
Ashreigney Devon 25 E10
Ashridge Court Devon 25 G11
Ash Street Suff 107 B10

Ashtead Sur 51 B7
Ash Thomas Devon 27 E8
Ashton Corn 2 D4
Hants 33 D9
Hereford 115 E10
Invclyd 276 F4
N Nhants 137 F11
Pboro 138 B2
Som 44 D2
W Nhants 102 B5
Ashton Common
Wilts 45 B11
Ashton Gate Bristol 60 E5
Ashton Green E Sus 23 C7
Ashton Hayes
Ches W 167 B8
Ashton Heath
Halton 183 F9
Ashton-in-Makerfield
Gtr Man 183 B9
Ashton Keynes Wilts 81 G8
Ashton under Hill
Worcs 99 D9
Ashton-under-Lyne
Gtr Man 184 B6
Ashton upon Mersey
Gtr Man 184 C3
Ashton Vale Bristol 60 E5
Ashurst Hants 32 E4
Kent 52 F4
Lancs 194 F3
W Sus 35 D11
Ashurst Bridge Hants 32 E4
Ashurst Wood W Sus 52 F2
Ashvale Bl Gwent 77 C10
Ash Vale Sur 49 C11
Ashwater Devon 12 B3
Ashwell Devon 14 G3
Herts 104 D5
Rutland 155 F2
Som 28 D5
Ashwell End Herts 104 C5
Ashwellthorpe Norf 142 D2
Ashwick Som 44 D6
Ashwicken Norf 158 F4
Ashwood Staffs 133 F7
Ashybank Borders 262 F2
Askam in Furness
Cumb 210 D4
Askern S Yorks 198 E5
Askerswell Dorset 16 C6
Askerton Hill Lincs 172 F4
Askett Bucks 84 D4
Askham Cumb 230 G6
Notts 188 G2
Askham Bryan York 207 D7
Askham Richard
York 206 D6
Asknish Argyll 275 D10
Askrigg N Yorks 223 G8
Askwith N Yorks 205 D9
Aslackby Lincs 155 C11
Aslacton Norf 142 E3
Aslockton Notts 154 B4
Asloun Aberds 293 B7
Asney Som 44 F3
Aspall Suff 126 D3
Aspatria Cumb 229 C8
Aspenden Herts 105 F7
Asperton Lincs 156 B5
Aspley Nottingham 171 G8
Staffs 150 C6
Aspley Guise
C Beds 103 D8
Aspley Heath
C Beds 103 D8
Warks 117 C11
Aspull Gtr Man 194 F6
Aspult Common
Gtr Man 183 B10
Assater Shetland 312 F4
Asselby E Yorks 199 B8
Asserby Lincs 191 F7
Asserby Turn Lincs 191 F7
Assington Suff 107 D8
Assington Green
Suff 124 G5
Assynt Ho Highld 300 C5
Astbury Ches E 168 C4
Astcote W Nhants 120 G3
Asterby Lincs 190 F3
Asterley Shrops 131 B7
Asterton Shrops 131 F7
Asthall Oxon 82 C3
Asthall Leigh Oxon 82 C4
Astle Ches E 184 G4
Highld 309 K7
Astley Gtr Man 195 G8
Shrops 149 F10
Warks 134 F6
Worcs 116 D5
Astley Abbotts
Shrops 132 D4
Astley Bridge
Gtr Man 195 E8
Astley Cross Worcs 116 D6
Astley Green
Gtr Man 184 B2
Astmoor Halton 183 E8
Aston Ches E 167 F10
Ches W 183 F9
Derbys 152 C3
Derbys 185 E11
Flint 166 B4
Hereford 115 D10
Hereford 115 F9
Herts 104 G5
Oxon 82 E4
Powys 130 E5
Shrops 132 E6
Shrops 149 D10
Staffs 151 E7
Staffs 168 G3
S Yorks 187 D7
Telford 132 B2
W Mid 133 F11
Wokingham 65 C9
Aston Abbotts
Bucks 102 G6
Aston Bank Worcs 116 C4
Aston Botterell
Shrops 132 G2

Aston-by-Stone
Staffs 151 C8
Aston Cantlow
Warks 118 F2
Aston Clinton Bucks 84 C5
Aston Crews Hereford 98 G3
Aston Cross 99 E8
Aston End Herts 104 G5
Aston Eyre Shrops 132 E3
Aston Fields Worcs 117 D9
Aston Flamville
Leics 135 E9
Aston Ingham
Hereford 98 G3
Aston juxta Mondrum
Ches E 167 D11
Aston le Walls
W Nhants 119 G9
Aston Magna Glos 100 D3
Aston Munslow
Shrops 131 F10
Aston on Carrant
Glos 99 E8
Aston on Clun
Shrops 131 G7
Aston-on-Trent
Derbys 153 D8
Aston Pigott Shrops 130 B6
Aston Rogers
Shrops 130 B6
Aston Rowant Oxon 84 F2
Aston Sandford
Bucks 84 D3
Aston Somerville
Worcs 99 D10
Aston Square
Shrops 148 D6
Aston Subedge Glos 100 C2
Aston Tirrold Oxon 64 B5
Aston Upthorpe
Oxon 64 B5
Astrop W Nhants 101 D10
Astrope Herts 84 C5
Astwick C Beds 104 D4
Astwith Derbys 170 C6
Astwood M Keynes 103 B9
Worcs 117 D8
Worcs 117 F7
Astwood Bank
Worcs 117 D10
Aswarby Lincs 173 G9
Aswardby Lincs 190 G5
Atcham Shrops 131 B10
Atch Lench Worcs 117 G10
Athelhampton
Dorset 17 C11
Athelington Suff 126 C4
Athelney Som 28 B4
Athelstaneford
E Loth 281 F10
Atherfield Green IoW 20 F5
Atherington Devon 25 C9
W Sus 35 G8
Athersley North
S Yorks 197 F11
Athersley South
S Yorks 197 F11
Atherstone Som 28 D5
Warks 134 D6
Atherstone on Stour
Warks 118 G4
Atherton Gtr Man 195 G8
Athnamulloch
Highld 299 G11
Athron Hall Perth 286 G4
Atley Hill N Yorks 224 E5
Atlow Derbys 170 F2
Attadale Highld 295 B11
Attadale Ho Highld 295 B11
Attenborough
Notts 153 B10
Atterby Lincs 189 C7
Attercliffe S Yorks 186 D5
Atterley Shrops 132 E2
Atterton Leics 135 D7
Attleborough Norf 141 D10
Warks 135 E7
Attlebridge Norf 160 F2
Attleton Green Suff 124 G4
Atwick E Yorks 209 C9
Atworth Wilts 61 F11
Auberrow Hereford 97 B9
Aubourn Lincs 172 C6
Auch Argyll 285 D7
Auchagallon N Ayrs 255 D9
Auchallater Aberds 292 E3
Auchareoch
Argyll 255 E10
Aucharnie Aberds 302 E6
Auchattie Aberds 293 D8
Auchavan Angus 292 G3
Auchbreck Moray 302 G3
Auchenback
E Renf 267 D10
Auchenbainzie
Dumfries 247 D8
Auchenblae Aberds 293 F9
Auchenbrack
Dumfries 247 D7
Auchenbreck Argyll 255 C9
Argyll 275 G11
Auchencairn
Dumfries 237 D9
Dumfries 247 G11
N Ayrs 256 D2
Auchencairn Ho
Dumfries 237 D10
Auchencarroch
W Dunb 277 E8
Auchencrosh
S Ayrs 236 B3
Auchencrow
Borders 273 C7
Auchendinny
Midloth 270 C4
Auchengray
S Lanark 269 E9
Auchenhalrig Moray 302 C3
Auchenharvie
N Ayrs 266 G5

Auchenheath
S Lanark 268 G6
Auchenhew N Ayrs 256 E2
Auchenlaich
Stirling 285 G10
Auchenleck
Dumfries 237 D9
Auchenlochan
Argyll 275 F10
Auchenmalg
Dumfries 236 D4
Auchenreoch
E Dunb 278 F3
Auchensoul S Ayrs 245 E7
Auchentiber
N Ayrs 267 F7
Auchertyre Highld 295 C10
Auchessan Stirling 285 E8
Auchgourish
Highld 291 B11
Auchinairn E Dunb 268 B2
Auchindrain Argyll 284 G4
Auchindrean Highld 307 L6
Auchininna Aberds 302 E6
Auchinleck Dumfries 236 B6
E Ayrs 258 E3
Auchinloch
N Lanark 278 G3
Auchinner Perth 285 F10
Auchinraith
S Lanark 268 D3
Auchinroath Moray 302 D2
Auchinstarry
N Lanark 278 F4
Auchintoul Aberds 293 B7
Aberds 302 G6
Auchiries Aberds 303 F10
Auchlee Aberds 293 D10
Auchleeks Ho Perth 291 G9
Auchleven Aberds 302 G6
Auchlochan
S Lanark 259 B8
Auchlossan Aberds 293 C7
Auchlunachan
Highld 307 L6
Auchlunies Aberds 293 D10
Auchlyne Stirling 285 E9
Auchmacoy Aberds 303 F9
Auchmair Moray 302 G3
Auchmantle
Dumfries 236 C3
Auchmenzie Aberds 302 G5
Auchmillan E Ayrs 258 C2
Auchmithie Angus 287 C10
Auchmore Highld 300 D4
Auchmuirbridge
Fife 286 G6
Auchmull Angus 293 F7
Auchnacraig Argyll 289 G9
Auchnacree Angus 292 G6
Auchnafree Perth 286 D2
Auchnagallin
Highld 301 F10
Auchnagarron
Argyll 275 E11
Auchnagatt Aberds 303 E9
Auchnaha Argyll 275 E10
Auchnahillin Highld 301 F7
Auchnarrow Moray 302 G2
Auchnashelloch
Perth 285 F11
Auchnotteroch
Dumfries 236 C1
Aucholzie Aberds 292 D5
Auchrannie Angus 286 B6
Auchroisk Highld 301 G10
Auchronie Angus 292 E6
Auchterarder Perth 286 F3
Auchteraw Highld 290 C5
Auchterderran Fife 280 B4
Auchterhouse
Angus 287 D7
Auchtermuchty Fife 286 F6
Auchterneed Highld 300 D4
Auchtertool Fife 280 C4
Auchtertyre Stirling 285 E7
Moray 301 D11
Auchtubh Stirling 285 E9
Auckengill Highld 310 C7
Auckley S Yorks 199 G2
Audenshaw Gtr Man 184 B6
Audlem Ches E 167 G11
Audley Staffs 168 E3
Audley End Essex 105 D10
Essex 106 D4
Norf 142 G2
Suff 125 G7
Auds Aberds 302 C6
Aughertree Cumb 229 D11
Aughton E Yorks 207 F10
Lancs 193 F11
Lancs 211 F10
S Yorks 187 D7
Wilts 47 B8
Aughton Park Lancs 194 F2
Aukside Durham 232 F4
Auldearn Highld 301 D9
Aulden Hereford 115 G9
Auldgirth Dumfries 247 F10
Auldhame E Loth 281 E11
Auldhouse S Lanark 268 E2
Auldtown of Carnoustie
Aberds 302 E6
Ault a'chruinn
Highld 295 C11
Aultanrynie
Highld 308 F3
Aultbea Highld 307 L3
Aultdearg Highld 300 C2
Aultgrishan Highld 307 L2
Aultguish Inn Highld 300 B3
Ault Hucknall
Derbys 171 B7
Aultibea Highld 311 G4
Aultiphurst Highld 310 C2
Aultivullin Highld 310 C2
Aultmore Highld 301 G10
Moray 302 D4
Aultnagoire Highld 300 G5
Aultnamain Inn
Highld 309 L6

Aultnaslat Highld 290 C3
Aulton Aberds 302 G6
Aulton of Atherb
Aberds 303 E9
Aultvaich Highld 300 E5
Aunby Lincs 155 G10
Aundorach Highld 291 B11
Aunk Devon 27 G8
Aunsby Lincs 155 B10
Auquhorthies
Aberds 303 G8
Aust S Glos 60 B5
Austendike Lincs 156 E5
Austen Fen Lincs 190 C5
Austenwood Bucks 66 B3
Austerfield
S Yorks 187 C11
Austerlands
Gtr Man 196 F3
Austhorpe W Yorks 206 G3
Austrey Warks 134 B5
Austwick N Yorks 212 F5
Authorpe Lincs 190 E6
Authorpe Row Lincs 191 G8
Avebury Wilts 62 F6
Avebury Trusloe
Wilts 62 F5
Aveley Thurrock 68 C5
Avening Glos 80 F5
Avening Green
S Glos 80 G2
Averham Notts 172 E3
Avery Hill London 68 E2
Aveton Gifford Devon 8 F3
Avielochan Highld 291 B10
Aviemore Highld 291 B10
Avington Hants 48 G4
W Berks 63 F11
Avoch Highld 301 D7
Avon Hants 19 B8
Wilts 62 D3
Avonbridge Falk 279 G8
Avoncliff Wilts 45 B11
Avon Dassett Warks 101 B8
Avonmouth Bristol 60 D4
Avonwick Devon 8 D4
Awbridge Hants 32 C4
Awhirk Dumfries 236 D2
Awkley S Glos 60 B5
Awliscombe Devon 27 G10
Awre Glos 80 D2
Awsworth Notts 171 G7
Axbridge Som 44 C2
Axford Hants 48 E6
Wilts 63 F8
Axminster Devon 15 B11
Axmouth Devon 15 C11
Axton Flint 181 E10
Axtown Devon 7 B10
Axwell Park T&W 242 E5
Aycliff Kent 55 E10
Aycliffe Durham 233 G11
Aydon Northumb 242 D2
Aykley Heads
Durham 233 C11
Aylburton Glos 79 E10
Aylburton Common
Glos 79 E10
Ayle Northumb 231 B10
Aylesbeare Devon 14 C6
Aylesbury Bucks 84 C4
Aylesby NE Lincs 201 F8
Aylesford Kent 53 B8
Aylesham Kent 55 C8
Aylestone Leicester 135 C11
Aylestone Hill
Hereford 97 C10
Aylestone Park
Leicester 135 C11
Aylmerton Norf 160 B3
Aylsham Norf 160 D3
Aylton Hereford 98 D3
Aylworth Glos 100 G2
Aymestrey Hereford 115 D8
Aynho W Nhants 101 E10
Ayot Green Herts 86 C2
Ayot St Lawrence
Herts 85 B11
Ayot St Peter Herts 86 B2
Ayr S Ayrs 257 E8
Ayre of Atler
Shetland 313 G6
Ayres Shetland 313 H5
Ayres End Herts 85 C11
Ayres of Selivoe
Shetland 313 J4
Ayres Quay T&W 243 F9
Aysgarth N Yorks 213 B10
Ayshford Devon 27 D8
Ayside Cumb 211 C7
Ayston Rutland 137 C7
Aythorpe Roding
Essex 87 B9
Ayton Borders 273 C8
T&W 243 F7
Ayton Castle
Borders 273 C8
Aywick Shetland 312 E7
Azerley N Yorks 214 E5

B
Babbacombe Torbay 9 B8
Babbington Notts 171 G7
Babbinswood
Shrops 148 C6
Babbs Green Herts 86 B5
Babcary Som 29 B9
Babel Carms 94 D6
Babel Green Suff 106 B4
Babell Flint 181 G11
Babeny Devon 13 F9
Babingley Norf 158 D3
Babraham Cambs 123 G10
Babworth Notts 187 E11
Bac W Isles 304 D6
Bachau Anglesey 178 E6
Bache Shrops 131 G9
Bacheldre Powys 130 E4

Bachelor's Bump
E Sus 38 E4
Bache Mill Shrops 131 F10
Bach-y-gwreiddyn
Swansea 75 E10
Backaland Orkney 314 C5
Backaskaill Orkney 314 A4
Backbarrow Cumb 211 C7
Backbower Gtr Man 185 C7
Backburn Aberds 293 D10
Backe Carms 74 B3
Backfolds Aberds 303 D10
Backford Ches W 182 G6
Backford Cross
Ches W 182 G5
Backhill Aberds 303 F7
Aberds 303 F10
Backhill of Clackriach
Aberds 303 E9
Backhill of Fortree
Aberds 303 E9
Backhill of Trustach
Aberds 293 D8
Backies Highld 311 J2
Backlass Highld 310 D6
Highld 310 E4
Back Muir Fife 279 D11
Back of Keppoch
Highld 295 G8
Back o' th' Brook
Staffs 169 E9
Back Rogerton
E Ayrs 258 E3
Back Street Suff 124 F4
Backwell N Som 60 F3
Backwell Common
N Som 60 F3
Backwell Green
N Som 60 F3
Backworth T&W 243 C8
Bacon End Essex 87 B10
Baconend Green
Essex 87 B10
Bacon's End W Mid 134 F3
Baconsthorpe Norf 160 B2
Bacton Hereford 97 E7
Norf 160 C6
Suff 125 D11
Bacton Green Norf 160 C6
Suff 125 D10
Bacup Lancs 195 C11
Badachonacher
Highld 300 B6
Badachro Highld 299 B7
Badanloch Lodge
Highld 308 F7
Badarach Highld 309 K5
Badavanich Highld 299 D11
Badbea Highld 307 K5
Badbury Swindon 63 C7
Badbury Wick
Swindon 63 C7
Badby W Nhants 119 F11
Badcall Highld 306 D7
Badcall Highld 306 E7
Badcaul Highld 307 K5
Baddeley Edge
Stoke 168 E6
Baddeley Green
Stoke 168 E6
Baddesley Clinton
Warks 118 C4
Baddesley Ensor
Warks 134 D5
Baddidarach Highld 307 G5
Baddock Aberds 292 C3
Baddock Highld 301 D7
Baddow Park Essex 88 E2
Badeach Moray 302 F2
Badenscallie Highld 307 J5
Badenscoth Aberds 303 F7
Badentoy Park
Aberds 293 D11
Badenyon Aberds 292 B5
Badgall Corn 11 D10
Badgeney Cambs 139 D8
Badger Shrops 132 D5
Badgergate Shrops 132 D5
Badger's Hill Worcs 99 B10
Badger's Mount Kent 68 G3
Badger Street Som 28 D3
Badgeworth Glos 80 B6
Badgworth Som 43 D11
Badharlick Corn 11 D11
Badicaul Highld 295 C9
Badingham Suff 126 D6
Badintagairt Highld 309 H4
Badlesmere Kent 54 C4
Badlipster Highld 310 E6
Badluarach Highld 307 K4
Badminton S Glos 61 C10
Badnaban Highld 307 G5
Badnabay Highld 306 E7
Badnagie Highld 310 F5
Badninish Highld 309 K7
Badrallach Highld 307 K5
Badsey Worcs 99 C11
Badshalloch
W Dunb 277 D9
Badshot Lea Sur 49 D11
Badsworth W Yorks 198 E3
Badwell Ash Suff 125 D9
Badworthy Devon 8 D4
Bae Cinmel = Kinmel Bay
Conwy 181 E7
Bae Colwyn = Colwyn Bay
Conwy 180 F4
Bae Penrhyn = Penrhyn Bay
Conwy 180 E4
Baffins Ptsmth 33 G11
Bagber Dorset 30 E3
Bagby N Yorks 215 C9
Bag Enderby Lincs 190 G5
Bagendon Glos 81 D8
Bagginswood
Shrops 132 G3
Baggrow Cumb 229 C9
Bàgha Chàise
W Isles 296 D5

Bagh a Chaisteil
W Isles 297 M2
Bagham Kent 54 C5
Baghasdal W Isles 297 K3
Bagh Mor W Isles 296 F4
Bagh Shiarabhagh
W Isles 297 L3
Bagillt Flint 182 F2
Baginton Warks 118 C6
Baglan Neath 57 C8
Bagley Shrops 149 D8
Som 44 D3
Bagley Green Som 27 D10
Bagley Marsh
Shrops 149 D7
Bagmore Hants 49 E7
Bagnall Staffs 168 E6
Bagnor W Berks 64 F3
Bagpath Glos 80 E5
Glos 80 G4
Bagshaw Derbys 185 E9
Bagshot Sur 66 G2
Wilts 63 F10
Bagshot Heath Sur 66 G2
Bagslate Moor
Gtr Man 195 E11
Bagstone S Glos 61 B7
Bagthorpe Norf 158 C5
Notts 171 E7
Baguley Gtr Man 184 D4
Bagworth Leics 135 B8
Bagwyllydiart
Hereford 97 F8
Bagwy Llydiart
Hereford 97 F8
Bail Àrd Bhuirgh
W Isles 304 C6
Bailbrook Bath 61 F9
Baildon W Yorks 205 F9
Baildon Green
W Yorks 205 F9
Baile W Isles 296 C5
Baile Ailein W Isles 304 F4
Baile a Mhanaich
W Isles 296 F3
Baile an Truiseil
W Isles 304 C5
Bailebeag Highld 291 B9
Baile Boidheach
Argyll 275 F8
Baile Gharbhaidh
W Isles 297 G3
Baile Glas W Isles 296 F4
Baile Mhartainn
W Isles 296 D3
Baile Mhic Phail
W Isles 296 D4
Baile Mor Argyll 288 G4
W Isles 296 F3
Baile na Creige
W Isles 297 L2
Baile nan Cailleach
W Isles 296 F3
Baile Raghaill
W Isles 296 D3
Bailey Green Hants 33 B11
Baileyhead Cumb 240 B2
Bailiesward Aberds 302 F4
Bailiff Bridge
W Yorks 196 C6
Baillieston Glasgow 268 C3
Bail' lochdrach
W Isles 296 F4
Bailrigg Lancs 202 B5
Bail Uachdraich
W Isles 296 F4
Bail' Ur Tholastaidh
W Isles 304 D7
Bainbridge N Yorks 223 G8
Bainsford Falk 279 E7
Bainshole Aberds 302 F6
Bainton E Yorks 208 C5
Oxon 101 F11
Pboro 137 B11
Baintown Fife 287 G7
Bairnkine Borders 262 F5
Baker's Cross Kent 53 F9
Bakers End Herts 86 B5
Baker's Hill Glos 79 C9
Baker Street Thurrock 68 C6
Baker's Wood Bucks 66 B4
Bakesdown Corn 24 G2
Bakewell Derbys 170 B2
Bala = Y Bala Gwyn 147 B8
Balachroick Perth 291 C10
Balachuirn Highld 298 E5
Balavil Highld 291 C9
Balavoulin Perth 291 G10
Balbeg Highld 300 F4
Highld 300 G4
Balbeggie Perth 286 E5
Balbithan Aberds 293 B9
Balbithan Ho
Aberds 293 B10
Balblair Highld 300 E4
Highld 301 C7
Highld 309 K5
Balby S Yorks 198 G5
Balcherry Highld 311 L2
Balchladich Highld 306 F5
Balchraggan Highld 300 E5
Highld 300 F5
Balchrick Highld 306 D6
Balchrystie Fife 287 G8
Balcladaich Highld 300 G2
Balcombe W Sus 51 F5
Balcombe Lane
W Sus 51 F5
Balcomie Fife 287 F10
Balcraggie Lodge
Highld 310 F5
Balcurvie Fife 287 G7
Baldersby N Yorks 215 D6
Baldersby St James
N Yorks 215 D7

Balderstone
Gtr Man 196 E2
Lancs 203 E8
Balderton Ches W 166 C5
Notts 172 E4
Baldhu Corn 4 G5
Baldingstone
Gtr Man 195 E10
Baldinnie Fife 287 F8
Baldock Herts 104 E4
Baldon Row Oxon 83 E9
Baldovie Dundee 287 D8
Baldrine IoM 192 D5
Baldslow E Sus 38 E3
Baldwin IoM 192 D4
Baldwinholme
Cumb 239 G8
Baldwin's Gate
Staffs 168 G3
Baldwins Hill W Sus 51 F11
Bale Norf 159 B10
Balearn Aberds 303 D10
Balemartine Argyll 288 E1
Balephuil Argyll 288 E1
Balerno Edin 270 B3
Balerominor Argyll 274 D4
Balevulin Argyll 288 E1
Balfield Angus 293 G7
Balfour Orkney 314 E4
Balfour Mains
Orkney 314 E4
Balfron Stirling 277 D10
Balfron Station
Stirling 277 D10
Balgaveny Aberds 302 E6
Balgavies Angus 287 B9
Balgonar Fife 279 C10
Balgove Aberds 303 F8
Balgowan Highld 291 D8
Perth 286 E3
Balgown Highld 298 C3
Highld 300 C7
Balgrennie Aberds 292 B5
Balgrochan E Dunb 278 G2
Balgy Highld 299 D8
Balhaldie Stirling 286 G2
Balhalgardy Aberds 303 G7
Balham London 67 E9
Balhary Perth 286 C6
Baliasta Shetland 312 C8
Baligill Highld 310 C2
Baligortan Argyll 288 E5
Baligrundle Argyll 289 E10
Balindore Argyll 289 F11
Balinoe Argyll 288 E1
Balintore Angus 286 B6
Highld 301 B8
Balintraid Highld 301 B7
Balintuim Aberds 292 E3
Balk N Yorks 215 C9
Balkeerie Angus 287 C7
Balkemback Angus 287 D7
Balkholme E Yorks 199 B9
Balkissock S Ayrs 244 G4
Ball Corn 10 G4
Shrops 148 D6
Ballabeg IoM 192 E3
Ballacannel IoM 192 D5
Ballachraggan
Moray 301 E11
Ballachrochin
Highld 301 F8
Ballachulish Highld 284 B4
Balladen Lancs 195 C10
Balladoole IoM 192 F3
Ballafesson IoM 192 F3
Ballagawne IoM 192 E4
Ballajora IoM 192 C5
Ballakilpheric IoM 192 E3
Ballamodha IoM 192 E3
Ballantrae S Ayrs 244 G3
Ballaquine IoM 192 D5
Ballard's Gore Essex 88 G6
Ballards Green
Warks 134 E5
Ballasalla IoM 192 C4
IoM 192 E3
Ballater Aberds 292 D5
Ballaugh IoM 192 C4
Ballaveare IoM 192 E4
Ballcorach Moray 301 G11
Ballechin Perth 286 B3
Balleich Stirling 277 B10
Balleigh Highld 309 L7
Ballencrieff E Loth 281 F9
Ballencrieff Toll
W Loth 279 G9
Ballentoul Perth 291 G10
Ball Green Stoke 168 E5
Ball Haye Green
Staffs 169 D7
Ball Hill Hants 64 G2
Ballidon Derbys 170 E2
Balliekine N Ayrs 255 D9
Balliemore Argyll 275 E11
Argyll 289 G11
Ballikinrain Stirling 277 D11
Ballimeanoch Argyll 284 F4
Ballimore Argyll 275 E10
Stirling 285 F9
Ballinaby Argyll 274 G3
Ballindean Perth 286 E6
Ballingdon Suff 107 C7
Ballinger Bottom
Bucks 84 E5
Ballinger Bottom
(South) Bucks 84 E5
Ballinger Common
Bucks 84 E6
Ballingham Hereford 97 E11
Ballingham Hill
Hereford 97 E11
Ballingry Fife 280 B3
Ballinlick Perth 286 C3
Ballinluig Perth 286 B3
Ballintean Highld 291 C9
Ballintuim Perth 286 B5
Balliveolan Argyll 289 E10

Balloch Angus 287 B7
Highld 301 E7
N Lanark 278 G4
W Dunb 277 E7
Ballochan Aberds 293 D7
Ballochearn
Stirling 277 D11
Ballochford Moray 302 F3
Ballochmorrie
S Ayrs 244 G6
Ball o'Ditton Halton 183 D7
Balls Cross W Sus 35 B7
Balls Green Essex 107 G11
E Sus 52 F3
Essex 35 C10
Ball's Green Glos 80 F5
Balls Hill W Mid 133 E9
Ballygown Argyll 288 E6
Ballygrant Argyll 274 G4
Ballygroggan Argyll 255 F7
Ballyhaugh Argyll 288 D3
Balmacara Highld 295 C10
Balmacara Square
Highld 295 C10
Balmaclellan
Dumfries 237 B9
Balmacneil Perth 286 B3
Balmacqueen Highld 298 B4
Balmae Dumfries 237 E8
Balmaha Stirling 277 C8
Balmalcolm Fife 287 G7
Balmalloch
N Lanark 278 F4
Balmeanach Argyll 289 E8
Argyll 289 E8
Highld 295 B7
Highld 298 E5
Highld 298 E5
Balmedie Aberds 293 B11
Balmer Heath
Shrops 149 C8
Balmerino Fife 287 E7
Balmerlawn Hants 32 G4
Balmesh Dumfries 236 D3
Balmichael N Ayrs 255 D10
Balminnoch
Dumfries 236 C4
Balmirmer Angus 287 D9
Balmoral Borders 261 B11
Balmore E Dunb 278 G2
Highld 298 E2
Highld 300 E3
Highld 301 E8
Perth 286 B3
Balmule Fife 280 D4
Balmullo Fife 287 E8
Balmungie Highld 301 D7
Balmurrie Dumfries 236 C4
Balnaboth Angus 292 G5
Balnabruaich Highld 301 C7
Highld 311 G5
Balnabruich Highld 311 G5
Balnacarn Highld 290 B4
Balnacoil Highld 311 H2
Balnacra Highld 299 E9
Balnacruie Highld 301 G9
Balnafoich Highld 300 F6
Balnagall Highld 311 L2
Balnagrantach
Highld 300 F4
Balnaguard Perth 286 B3
Balnaguisich
Highld 300 B6
Balnahanaid Perth 285 C10
Balnahard Argyll 274 D4
Argyll 288 F5
Balnain Highld 300 F4
Balnakeil Highld 308 C3
Balnaknock Highld 298 C4
Balnamoon Aberds 303 D9
Angus 293 G7
Balnapaling Highld 301 C7
Balne N Yorks 198 D5
Balnoon Corn 2 B2
Balochroy Argyll 255 B8
Balole Argyll 274 G4
Balone Fife 287 F8
Balornock Glasgow 268 B2
Balquharn Perth 286 D4
Balquhidder Stirling 285 E9
Balquhidder Station
Stirling 285 E9
Balsall Common
W Mid 118 B4
Balsall Heath
W Mid 133 G11
Balsall Street
W Mid 118 B4
Balscote Oxon 101 C7
Balsham Cambs 123 G11
Balsporran Cottages
Highld 291 F8
Balstonia Thurrock 69 C7
Baltasound Shetland 312 C8
Balterley Staffs 168 E2
Balterley Green
Staffs 168 E3
Balterley Heath
Staffs 168 E2
Baltersan Dumfries 236 C6
Balthangie Aberds 303 D8
Balthayock Perth 286 E5
Baltonsborough
Som 44 G4
Balure Argyll 289 E11
Balvaird Highld 300 D5
Balvenie Moray 302 E3
Balvicar Argyll 275 B8
Balvraid Highld 295 D10
Highld 301 F8
Balwest Corn 2 C3

Bamber Bridge
Lancs 194 B5
Bamber's Green
Essex 105 G11
Bamburgh Northumb .264 C5
Bamff Perth 286 B6
Bamford Derbys 186 E2
Gtr Man 195 E11
Bamfurlong Glos 99 G8
Gtr Man 194 G5
Bampton Cumb 221 B10
Devon 27 C7
Oxon 82 E4
Bampton Grange
Cumb 221 B10
Banavie Highld 290 F3
Banbury Oxon 101 C9
Bancffosfelen Carms .75 C7
Banchor Highld 301 E9
Banchory Aberds 293 D8
Banchory-Devenick
Aberds 293 C11
Bancycapel Carms . . .74 B6
Banc-y-Darren
Ceredig 128 G3
Bancyfelin Carms 74 B4
Bancyffordd Carms . . .93 D6
Bandirran Perth 286 D6
Bandonhill London . . .67 G9
Bandrake Head
Cumb 210 B6
Banff Aberds 302 C6
Bangor Gwyn 179 G9
Bangor is y coed =
Bangor on Dee Wrex 166 F5
Bangor on Dee = Bangor-
is-y-coed Wrex . . .166 F5
Bangors Corn 11 B10
Bangor Teifi Ceredig . .93 C7
Banham Norf 141 F11
Bank Hants 32 F3
Bankend Dumfries . . .238 D2
Bank End Cumb 210 B3
Cumb 228 C6
Bank Fold Blackburn .195 C8
Bankfoot Perth 286 D4
Bankglen E Ayrs 258 G4
Bankhead
Aberdeen 293 B10
Aberds 293 C8
Dumfries 236 C2
Falk 278 E6
S Lanark 269 G7
Bank Hey Blackburn . .203 G9
Bank Houses Lancs .202 C4
Bankland Som 28 B4
Bank Lane Gtr Man . .195 D9
Bank Newton
N Yorks 204 C4
Banknock Falk 278 F5
Banks Cumb 240 E3
Lancs 193 C11
Orkney 314 C4
Bank's Green
Worcs 117 D9
Bankshead Shrops . .130 F6
Bankshill Dumfries . .248 G5
Bankside Falk 279 E7
Bank Street Worcs . .116 E2
Bank Top Gtr Man . . .195 E8
Lancs 194 F4
Stoke 168 E5
T&W 242 D4
W Yorks 196 C6
W Yorks 205 B10
Banners Gate
W Mid 133 D11
Banningham Norf . . .160 D4
Banniskirk Ho
Highld 310 D5
Banniskirk Mains
Highld 310 D5
Bannister Green
Essex 106 G3
Bannockburn
Stirling 278 C5
Banns Corn 4 F4
Banstead Sur 51 B8
Bantam Grove
W Yorks 197 B9
Bantaskin Falk 279 F7
Bantham Devon 8 G3
Banton N Lanark 278 F5
Banwell N Som 43 B11
Banyard's Green
Suff 126 C5
Bapchild Kent 70 G2
Baptist End W Mid . . .133 F8
Bapton Wilts 46 F3
Barabhas W Isles 304 D5
Barabhas Iarach
W Isles 304 C5
Barabhas Uarach
W Isles 304 C5
Barachandroman
Argyll 289 G8
Baramore Highld 289 B8
Barassie S Ayrs 257 C8
Baravullin = Barravullin
Argyll 289 F10
Barbadoes Stirling . .277 B11
Barbaraville Highld. . .301 B7
Barbauchlaw
W Loth 269 B8
Barber Booth
Derbys 185 E10
Barber Green Cumb . .211 C7
Barber's Moor
Lancs 194 D3
Barbican Plym 7 E9
Barbieston S Ayrs . . .257 F10
Barbon Cumb 212 C2
Barbourne Worcs . . .116 F6
Barbridge Ches E . . .167 D10
Barbrook Devon 41 D8
Barby W Nhants 119 C10
Barby Nortoft
W Nhants 119 C11
Barcaldine Argyll . .289 E11

Barcelona Corn 6 E4
Barcheston Warks . . .100 D5
Barclose Cumb 239 E10
Barcombe Cross
E Sus 36 D6
Barcroft W Yorks 204 F6
Barden N Yorks 224 G2
Bardennoch
Dumfries 246 E3
Barden Park Kent 52 C5
Barden Scale
N Yorks 205 B7
Bardfield End Green
Essex 106 E2
Bardfield Saling
Essex 106 F3
Bardister Shetland . .312 F5
Bardnabeinne
Highld 309 K7
Bardney Lincs 173 B10
Bardon Leics 153 G8
Bardon Mill
Northumb 241 E7
Bardowie E Dunb 277 G11
Bardown E Sus. 37 B11
Bardrainney Invclyd. .276 G6
Bardsea Cumb 210 E6
Bardsey W Yorks 206 E3
Bardsley Gtr Man 196 G2
Bardwell Suff 125 C8
Bare Lancs 211 G9
Bare Ash Som 43 F9
Bareless Northumb . . .263 B9
Bar End Hants 33 B7
Barepot Cumb 228 F6
Bareppa Corn. 3 D7
Barfad Argyll 275 G9
Dumfries 236 C5
Barford Norf 142 B2
Sur 49 F11
Warks 118 E5
Barford St John
Oxon 101 E8
Barford St Martin
Wilts 46 G5
Barford St Michael
Oxon 101 E8
Barfrestone Kent 55 C9
Bargaly Dumfries 236 C6
Bargarran Renfs 277 G9
Bargate Derbys 170 F5
Bargeddie N Lanark . .268 C4
Bargod = Bargoed Caerph .77 F10
Bargoed Caerph 77 F10
Bargrennan
Dumfries 236 B5
Barham Cambs 122 B2
Kent 55 C8
Suff 126 G2
Barharrow Dumfries. .237 D8
Barhill Dumfries 237 C10
Bar Hill Cambs 123 E7
Staffs 168 G3
Barholm Dumfries . . .237 D7
Lincs 155 G11
Barkby Leics 136 B2
Barkby Thorpe
Leics 136 B2
Barkers Green
Shrops 149 D10
Barkers Hill Wilts 30 B6
Barkestone-le-Vale
Leics 154 C5
Barkham Wokingham . .65 F9
Barking London 68 C2
Suff 125 G11
Barkingside London . .68 B2
Barking Tye Suff 125 G11
Barkisland W Yorks . .196 C5
Barkla Shop Corn 4 E4
Barkston Lincs 172 G6
N Yorks 206 F5
Barkston Ash
N Yorks 206 F5
Barkway Herts 105 D7
Barlake Som 45 D7
Barlanark Glasgow . .268 C3
Barland Powys 114 E5
Barland Common
Swansea 56 D5
Barlaston Staffs 151 B7
Barlavington W Sus . . .35 D7
Barlborough Derbys . .187 F7
Barlby N Yorks 207 G8
Barlestone Leics 135 B8
Barley Herts 105 D7
Lancs 204 E2
Barleycroft End
Herts 105 F8
Barley End Bucks 85 C7
Barley Green Lancs . .204 E2
Barley Mow T&W 243 G7
Barleythorpe
Rutland 136 B6
Barling Essex 70 B2
Barlings Lincs 189 G9
Barlow Derbys 186 G4
N Yorks 198 B6
T&W 242 E5
Barlow Moor
Gtr Man 184 C4
Barmby Moor
E Yorks 207 D11
Barmby on the Marsh
E Yorks 199 B7
Barmer Norf 158 C6
Barming Heath Kent . .53 B8
Barmolloch Argyll . . .275 D9
Bar Moor T&W 242 E4
Barmoor Castle
Northumb 263 B11
Barmoor Lane End
Northumb 264 B2
Barmouth = Abermaw
Gwyn 146 F2
Barmpton Darl 224 B6
Barmston E Yorks . . .209 B9
T&W 243 F8
Barmulloch Glasgow .268 B2
Barnaby Green Suff . .127 B9
Barnacabber Argyll . .276 D3

Barnack Pboro 137 B11
Barnacle Warks 135 G7
Barnaline Argyll 275 B10
Barnard Castle
Durham 223 B11
Barnard Gate Oxon . . .82 C6
Barnardiston Suff 106 B4
Barnard's Green
Worcs 98 B5
Barnardtown
Newport 59 B10
Barnbarroch
Dumfries 237 D10
Barnbow Carr
W Yorks 206 F3
Barnburgh S Yorks . .198 G3
Barnby Suff 143 F9
Barnby Dun S Yorks . .198 F6
Barnby in the Willows
Notts 172 E5
Barnby Moor Notts. . .187 E11
Barncluith S Lanark . .268 E4
Barndennoch
Dumfries 247 F9
Barne Barton Plym 7 D8
Barnehurst London. . . .68 D4
Barnes Cray London . .68 D4
Barnes Hall S Yorks . .186 B4
Barnes Street Kent. . . .52 C6
Barnet London 86 F2
Barnet Gate London . . .86 F2
Barnettbrook Worcs .117 B7
Barnett Brook
Ches E 167 G10
Barney Norf 159 C9
Barnfield Kent. 54 D2
Barnfields Hereford . . .97 C9
Shrops 169 D7
Barnham Suff 125 B7
W Sus 35 G7
Barnham Broom
Norf 141 B11
Barnhead Angus 287 B10
Barnhill Ches W 167 E7
Dundee 287 D8
Moray 301 D11
Barnhills Dumfries . .236 B1
Barthol Chapel
Aberds 303 F8
Bartholomew Green
Essex 106 G4
Barthomley Ches E . . .168 E3
Bartington Ches W . .183 F10
Barton Cambs 32 E4
Bartley Green
W Mid 133 G10
Bartlow Cambs 105 B11
Barton Cambs 123 F8
Ches W 166 E6
Glos 80 B4
Glos 99 F11
IoW 20 D6
Lancs 193 F11
Lancs 202 F6
N Som 43 B11
N Yorks 224 D4
Oxon 83 D9
Torbay 9 B8
Warks 118 G2
Barton Abbey Oxon . .101 G9
Barton Bendish
Norf 140 B4
Barton Court
Hereford 98 C4
Barton End Glos 80 F4
Barton Gate Devon . . .41 E7
Staffs 152 F3
Barton Green Staffs . .152 F3
Barton Hartshorn
Bucks 102 E2
Barton Hill Bristol 60 E6
N Yorks 216 G4
Barton in Fabis
Notts 153 C10
Barton in the Beans
Leics 135 B7
Barton-le-Clay
C Beds 103 E11
Barton-le-Street
N Yorks 216 E4
Barton-le-Willows
N Yorks 216 G4
Barton Mills Suff 124 C4
Barton on Sea
Hants 19 C10
Barton on the Heath
Warks 100 D4
Barton St David Som . .44 G4
Barton Seagrave
N Nhants 121 B7
Bartonsham
Hereford 97 D10
Barton Stacey Hants . .48 E2
Barton Town Devon . . .41 E7
Barton Turf Norf 161 E7
Barton Turn Staffs . . .152 F4
**Barton-under-
Needwood** Staffs . .152 F2
Barton-upon-Humber
N Lincs 200 C4
Barton Upon Irwell
Gtr Man 184 B4
Barton Waterside
N Lincs 200 C4
Barugh S Yorks 197 F10
Barugh Green
S Yorks 197 F10
Barway Cambs 123 B10
Barwell Leics 135 D8
Barwick Devon 25 F9
Herts 86 B5
Som 29 E9
Barwick in Elmet
W Yorks 206 F4
Barwinnock
Dumfries 236 E5
Baschurch Shrops . . .149 E8
Bascote Warks 119 E8
Bascote Heath
Warks 119 E7
Basford Shrops 131 F7

Basford continued
Staffs 168 F5
Basford Green
Staffs 169 E7
Bashall Eaves Lancs . .203 E9
Bashley Hants 19 B10
Bashley Park Hants . . .19 B10
Basildon Essex 69 B8
Basingstoke Hants . . .48 C6
Baslow Derbys 186 G3
Bason Bridge Som . . .43 D10
Bassaleg Newport 59 B9
Bassenthwaite
Cumb 229 E10
Bassett Soton 32 D6
Bassett Green Soton . .32 D6
Bassingbourn
Cambs 104 C6
Bassingfield Notts . . .154 B2
Bassingham Lincs . . .172 C6
Bassingthorpe Lincs . .155 D9
Bassus Green Herts . .104 F6
Basta Shetland 312 D7
Basted Kent 52 B6
Baston Lincs 156 G2
Bastonford Worcs . . .116 G6
Bastwick Norf 161 F8
Baswick Steer
E Yorks 209 D7
Batavaime Stirling . . .285 D8
Batch Som 43 B10
Batchcott Shrops 115 C9
Batchfields Hereford . .98 B3
Batchley Worcs 117 D10
Batchworth Herts. 85 G9
Batchworth Heath
Herts 85 G9
Batcombe Dorset 29 G10
Som 45 F7
Bate Heath Ches E . . .183 F11
Bateman's Green
Worcs 117 B11
Bateman's Hill Pembs 73 E8
Batemoor S Yorks 186 E5
Batford Herts 85 B10
Bath Bath 61 F8
Bathampton Bath 61 F9
Bathealton Som 27 C9
Batheaston Bath 61 F9
Bathford Bath 61 F9
Bathgate W Loth 269 B9
Bathley Notts 172 D3
Bathpool Corn. 11 G11
Som 28 B3
Bath Side Essex 108 E5
Bath Vale Ches E 168 C5
Bathville W Loth 269 B8
Bathway Som 44 C5
Bathwick Bath 61 F9
Batlers Green Herts . . .85 F11
Batley W Yorks 197 C8
Batley Carr W Yorks . .197 C8
Batsford Glos 100 E3
Batson Devon 9 G9
Batsworthy Devon 26 D4
Batten's Green Som . .28 D3
Battenton Green
Worcs 116 D6
Battersby N Yorks 225 D11
Battersea London 67 D9
Battisborough Cross
Devon 7 F11
Battisford Suff. 125 G11
Battisford Tye Suff. . . .125 G10
Battle E Sus 38 D2
Powys 95 E10
Battledown Cross
Devon 25 F7
Battlefield Shrops 149 F10
Battle Hill T&W 243 D8
Battlesbridge Essex . . .88 G3
Battlescombe Glos. . . .80 D6
Battlesden C Beds 103 F9
Battlesea Green
Suff 126 B4
Battleton Som 26 B6
Battlies Green Suff. . . .125 E7
Battram Leics 135 B7
Battramsley Hants . . .20 B2
Battramsley Cross
Hants 115 F7
Batt's Corner Hants . . .49 E10
Battyeford W Yorks. . . .197 C7
Batworthy Devon 13 D10
Bauds of Cullen
Moray 302 C4
Baugh Argyll 288 E2
Baughton Worcs 99 C7
Baughurst Hants 48 B5
Baulking Oxon 82 G4
Baumber Lincs 190 G2
Baunton Glos 81 E8
Baverstock Wilts. 46 G4
Bawburgh Norf 142 B3
Bawdeswell Norf 159 E10
Bawdrip Som 43 F10
Bawdsey Suff 108 C6
Bawsey Norf. 158 F3
Bawtry S Yorks 187 C11
Baxenden Lancs 195 B9
Baxterley Warks 134 D5
Baxter's Green Suff . .124 F5
Bay Dorset 30 B4
Highld 298 D2
Baybridge Hants. 33 C8
Baydon Wilts 63 D9
Bayford Herts 86 D4
Som 30 B2
Bay Gate Lancs 203 D11
Baydon W Isles 305 H3
Bayles Cumb 231 C10
Bayley's Hill Kent 52 C4
Baylham Suff 126 G2
Baylis Green
Worcs 117 C11
Baynard's Green
Oxon 101 F10

Baynhall Worcs 99 B7
Baysham Hereford 97 F11
Bayston Hill Shrops . .131 B9
Bayswater London. 67 C9
Baythorne End
Essex 106 C4
Baythorpe Lincs 174 G2
Bayton Worcs 116 C3
Bayton Common
Worcs 116 C4
Bayworth Oxon 83 E8
Beach Highld 289 D9
S Glos 61 E8
Beachampton Bucks 102 D5
Beachamwell Norf . . .140 B5
Beachans Moray 301 E10
Beacharr Argyll 255 C7
Beachborough Kent . . .55 F7
Beach Hay Worcs 116 C5
Beachley Glos 79 G9
Beacon Corn 2 B5
Devon 27 F11
Devon 28 F2
Beacon Down E Sus . . .37 C9
Beacon End Essex . . .107 G9
Beaconhill Northumb .243 B7
Beacon Hill Bath. 61 F9
Bucks 84 G6
Cumb 210 E4
Dorset 18 C5
Essex 88 C5
Kent 53 G10
Notts 172 E4
Suff 108 B4
Sur. 49 F11
Beacon Lough T&W . .243 F7
Beacon's Bottom
Bucks. 84 F3
Beaconsfield Bucks . . .66 B2
Beaconside Staffs 151 E8
Beacrabhaic
W Isles 305 J3
Beadlam N Yorks 216 C3
Beadlow C Beds 104 D2
Beadnell Northumb . . .264 C6
Beaford Devon 25 E9
Beal Northumb 273 G11
N Yorks 198 B4
Bealach Highld 289 D11
Bealach Maim
Argyll 275 E10
Bealbury Corn 7 B7
Beal's Green Kent. 53 G9
Bealsmill Corn. 12 F3
Beambridge
Shrops 131 F10
Beam Bridge Som 27 D10
Beam Hill Staffs 152 E4
Beamhurst Staffs 151 B11
Beamhurst Lane
Staffs 151 B11
Beaminster Dorset . . .29 G7
Beamish Durham 242 G6
Beamond End Bucks . .84 F6
Beamsley N Yorks 205 C7
Bean Kent. 68 E5
Beanacre Wilts 62 F2
Beancross Falk 279 F8
Beanhill M Keynes . . .103 D7
Beanley Northumb . . .264 F3
Beansburn E Ayrs 257 B10
Beanthwaite Cumb . .210 C4
Beaquoy Orkney 314 D3
Bear Cross BCP 19 B7
Beard Hill Som. 44 E6
Beardly Batch Som . . .44 E6
Beardwood
Blackburn 195 B7
Beare Devon 27 G7
Beare Green Sur. 51 E7
Bearley Warks 118 E3
Bearley Cross
Warks 118 E3
Bearnus Argyll 288 E5
Bearpark Durham 233 C10
Bearsbridge
Northumb 241 F7
Bearsden E Dunb 277 G10
Bearsted Kent 53 B9
Bearstone Shrops. 150 B4
Bearwood BCP. 18 B6
Hereford 115 F7
W Mid 133 F10
Beasley Staffs 168 F4
Beattock Dumfries . . .248 C3
Beauchamp Roding
Essex 87 C9
Beauchief S Yorks 186 E4
Beauclerc Northumb. .242 E2
Beaudesert Warks . . .118 D3
Beaufort Bl Gwent. 77 C11
Beaufort Castle
Highld 300 E5
Beaulieu Hants. 32 G5
Beaulieu Park Essex . .88 G2
Beaulieu Wood
Dorset 30 F2
Beauly Highld 300 E5
Beaumaris
Anglesey 179 F10
Beaumont Cumb 239 F8
Essex 108 G3
Windsor. 66 E3
Beaumont Hill Darl . . .224 B5
Beaumont Leys
Leicester 135 B11
Beausale Warks 118 C4
Beauvale Notts 171 F8
Beauworth Hants 33 B9
Beavan's Hill
Hereford 98 G3
Beaworthy Devon 12 B5
Beazley End Essex . . .106 F4
Bebington Mers 182 E4
Bebside Northumb. . . .253 G7
Beccles Suff 143 E8
Becconsall Lancs 194 C2
Beck Bottom Cumb . . .210 D4
W Yorks 197 C10
Beckbury Shrops 132 C5

Beckces Cumb 230 F4
Beckenham London. . . .67 F11
Beckermet Cumb 219 D10
Beckermonds
N Yorks 213 C7
Beckery Som 44 F3
Beckett End Norf 140 D5
Beckfoot Cumb 220 E3
Cumb 229 B7
Beck Foot Cumb 222 F2
Beckford Worcs 99 D9
Worcs 205 F8
Beckhampton Wilts. . . .62 F5
Beck Head Cumb 211 C8
Beck Hole N Yorks 226 E6
Beck Houses Cumb. . .221 F11
Beckingham Lincs . . .172 E5
Notts 188 E3
Beckington Som 45 C10
Beckjay Shrops 115 B7
Beckley E Sus. 38 C5
Hants 19 B10
Oxon 83 C9
Beckton London 68 C2
Beckwith N Yorks 205 C11
Beckwithshaw
N Yorks 205 C10
Becontree London . . .68 B3
Bedale N Yorks 214 B5
Bedburn Durham 233 E8
Bedchester Dorset 30 D5
Beddau Rhondda 58 B5
Beddgelert Gwyn 163 F9
Beddingham E Sus . . .36 F6
Beddington London . .67 G10
Beddington Corner
London 67 F9
Bedfield Suff 126 D4
Bedford Bedford 121 G11
Gtr Man 183 B11
Bedford Park London . .67 D8
Bedgebury Cross
Kent 53 G8
Bedgrove Bucks 84 C4
Bedham W Sus 35 C8
Bedhampton Hants . . .22 B2
Bedingfield Suff 126 D3
Bedingham Green
Norf 142 E5
Bedlam N Yorks 214 G5
Som 45 D9
Bedlam Street
W Sus 36 D3
Bedlar's Green
Essex 105 G10
Bedlington
Northumb 253 G7
Bedlington Station
Northumb 253 G7
Bedling M Tydf. 77 E8
Bedminster Bristol 60 E5
Bedminster Down
Bristol 60 F5
Bedmond Herts 85 E9
Bednall Staffs 151 F9
Bednall Head Staffs . .151 F9
Bedrule Borders 262 F4
Bedstone Shrops. 115 B7
Bedwas Caerph 59 B8
Bedwell Herts 104 G4
Wrex 166 F4
Bedwellty Caerph 77 E11
Bedwellty Pits
Bl Gwent 77 D11
Bedworth Warks 135 F7
Bedworth Heath
Warks 134 F6
Bedworth Woodlands
Warks 134 F6
Bed-y-coedwr
Gwyn 146 D4
Beeby Leics 136 B3
Beech Hants 49 F7
Staffs 151 B7
Beechcliff Staffs 151 B7
Beechcliffe
W Yorks 205 E7
Beechen Cliff Bath . . .61 G9
Beech Hill Gtr Man . . .194 F5
W Berks 65 G7
Beechingstoke
Wilts 46 B5
Beech Lanes
W Mid 133 F10
Beechwood Halton . .183 E8
Newport 59 B10
W Mid 118 B5
W Yorks 206 F2
Beecroft C Beds 103 G10
Beedon W Berks 64 D3
Beedon Hill W Berks. . .64 D3
Beeford E Yorks. 209 C8
Beeley Derbys 170 B3
Beelsby NE Lincs 201 G8
Beenham W Berks. 64 F5
Beenham's Heath
Windsor. 65 D10
Beenham Stocks
W Berks 64 F5
Beeny Devon 11 C8
Beer Devon 15 D10
Som 44 A3
Beercrocombe Som. . .28 C4
Beer Hackett Dorset . .29 E9
Beesands Devon 8 G6
Beesby Lincs 191 F7
Beeslack Midloth 270 C4
Beeson Devon 8 G6
Beeston C Beds 104 B3
Ches W 167 D8
Norf 159 F8
Notts 153 B10
W Yorks 205 G11
Beeston Hill
W Yorks 205 G11

Beeston Park Side
W Yorks 197 B9
Beeston Regis
Norf 177 E11
Beeston Royds
W Yorks 205 G11
Beeston St Lawrence
Norf 160 E6
Beeswing Dumfries. . .237 C10
Beetham Cumb 211 D9
Som 28 E3
Beetley Norf 159 F9
Beffcote Staffs 150 F6
Began Cardiff. 59 C8
Begbroke Oxon 83 C7
Begelly Pembs 73 D10
Beggarington Hill
W Yorks 197 C9
Beggar's Bush
Powys 114 E5
W Sus 35 F11
Beggar's Bush
Powys 114 E5
Beggars Ash Hereford .98 D4
Beggars Bush
W Sus 35 F11
Beggar's Bush
Powys 114 E5
Beggars Pound
V Glam 58 F4
Beggearn Huish Som . .42 F4
Beguildy Powys 114 B3
Beighton Norf 143 B7
S Yorks 186 E6
Beighton Hill
Derbys 170 E3
Beili-glas Mon. 78 C4
Beitearsaig W Isles . . .305 G1
Beith N Ayrs 266 E6
Bekesbourne Kent 55 C7
Bekesbourne Hill
Kent 55 C7
Belah Cumb 239 F9
Belan Powys 130 C4
Belaugh Norf 160 F5
Belbins Hants. 32 C5
Belbroughton
Worcs 117 B9
Belchalwell Dorset. . . .30 F3
Belchalwell Street
Dorset 30 F3
Belchamp Otten
Essex 106 C6
Belchamp St Paul
Essex 106 C5
Belchamp Walter
Essex 106 C6
Belcher's Bar Leics . .135 B8
Belchford Lincs 190 F3
Beleybridge Fife 287 F9
Belfield Gtr Man. 196 E2
Belford Northumb 264 C4
Belgrano Conwy 181 F7
Belgrave Ches W 166 C5
Leicester 135 B11
Staffs 134 C4
Belgravia London 67 D9
Belhaven E Loth 282 F7
Belhelvie Aberds 293 B11
Belhinnie Aberds 302 G4
Bellabeg Aberds 292 B5
Bellamore S Ayrs. 244 F6
Bellanoch Argyll 275 D8
Bellanrigg Borders . . .260 B6
Bellasize E Yorks. 199 B10
Bellaty Angus. 286 B6
Bell Bar Herts. 86 D3
Bell Busk N Yorks 204 B4
Bell Common Essex. . .86 E6
Belleau Lincs 190 F6
Belle Eau Park
Notts 171 D11
Belle Green
S Yorks 197 F11
Bellehiglash Moray .301 F11
Belle Isle W Yorks 197 B10
Bell End Worcs. 117 B8
Bellerby N Yorks 224 G2
Belle Vale Mers. 182 D6
W Mid 133 G9
Bellever Devon 13 F9
Bellevue Worcs 117 C9
Belle Vue Cumb 229 E8
Cumb 239 F9
Gtr Man 184 B5
Shrops 149 G9
S Yorks 198 G5
W Yorks 197 D10
Bellfield E Ayrs 257 B10
Bellfields Sur. 50 C3
Bell Green London 67 E11
W Mid 135 G7
Bell Heath Worcs 117 B9
Bell Hill Hants 34 C2
Belliehill Angus 293 G7
Bellingdon Bucks 84 D6
Bellingham London . . .67 E11
Northumb 251 G8
Bellmount Norf 157 F10
Belloch Argyll. 255 D7
Bellochantuy Argyll . .255 D7
Bell o' th' Hill
Ches W 167 F8
Bellsbank E Ayrs 245 C11
Bell's Close T&W 242 E5
Bell's Corner Suff 107 D9
Bellshill N Lanark 268 C4
Northumb 264 C4
Bellside N Lanark 268 D6
Bellsmyre W Dunb . . .277 F8
Bellspool Borders 260 B5
Bellsquarry
W Loth 269 C10
Bells Yew Green
E Sus 52 F6
Belluton Bath 60 G6
Bellyeoman Fife 280 D2
Belmaduthy Highld. . .300 D6
Belmesthorpe
Rutland 155 G10
Belmont Blackburn . .195 D7
Durham 234 C2
E Sus 38 C4
London 67 G9
London 85 G11

Belmont *continued*
Oxon 63 B11
S Ayrs 257 E8
Shetland 312 C7
Belnacraig Aberds . . 292 B5
Belnagarrow Moray . . 302 E3
Belnie Lincs 156 C5
Belowda Corn 5 C9
Belper Derbys 170 F4
Belper Lane End
Derbys 170 F4
Belph Derbys 187 F8
Belsay Northumb . . 242 B4
Belses Borders 262 D3
Belsford Devon 8 D5
Belsize Herts 85 E8
Belstead Suff 108 C2
Belston S Ayrs 257 E9
Belstone Devon 13 C8
Belstone Corner
Devon 13 B8
Belthorn Blackburn . . 195 C8
Beltinge Kent 71 F7
Beltingham
Northumb 241 E7
Beltoft N Lincs 199 F10
Belton Leics 153 E8
Lincs 155 B8
N Lincs 199 F9
Norf 143 C9
Belton in Rutland
Rutland 136 C6
Beltring Kent 53 D7
Belts of Collonach
Aberds 293 D8
Belvedere London . . . 68 D3
Belvoir Leics 154 C6
Bembridge IoW 21 D8
Bemersyde Borders . 262 C3
Bemerton Wilts 46 G6
Bemerton Heath
Wilts 46 G6
Bempton E Yorks . . . 218 E3
Benacre Suff 143 G10
Ben Alder Lodge
Highld 291 F7
Ben Armine Lodge
Highld 309 H7
Benbuie Dumfries . . 246 D6
Ben Casgro W Isles . 304 F6
Benchill Gtr Man . . 184 D4
Bencombe Glos 80 F3
Benderloch Argyll . 289 F11
Bendish Herts 104 G3
Bendronaig Lodge
Highld 299 F10
Benenden Kent 53 G10
Benfield Dumfries . . 236 C5
Benfieldside
Durham 242 G3
Bengal Pembs 91 E9
Bengate Norf 160 D6
Bengeo Herts 86 C4
Bengeworth Worcs . . 99 C10
Bengrove Glos 99 E9
Benhall Glos 99 G8
Benhall Green Suff . . 127 E7
Benhall Street Suff . . 127 E7
Benhilton London . . . 67 F9
Benholm Aberds . . . 293 G10
Beningbrough
N Yorks 206 B6
Benington Herts . . . 104 G5
Lincs 174 F5
Benington Sea End
Lincs 174 F6
Benllech Anglesey . . 179 E8
Benmore Argyll 276 E2
Stirling 285 E8
Benmore Lodge
Argyll 289 F7
Highld 309 H3
Bennacott Corn 11 C11
Bennah Devon 14 E2
Bennan N Ayrs 255 E10
Bennane Lea S Ayrs . 244 F3
Bennetland
E Yorks 199 B10
Bennetsfield Highld . 300 D6
Bennett End Bucks . . 84 F3
Bennetts End Herts . . 85 D9
Benniworth Lincs . . 190 E2
Benover Kent 53 D8
Ben Rhydding
W Yorks 205 D8
Bensham T&W 242 E6
Benslie N Ayrs 266 G6
Benson Oxon 83 G10
Benston Shetland . . 313 H6
Bent Aberds 293 F8
Benter Som 44 D6
Bentfield Bury
Essex 105 F9
Bentfield Green
Essex 105 F10
Bentgate Gtr Man . . 196 E2
Bent Gate Lancs . . . 195 C9
Benthall Northumb . . 264 D6
Shrops 132 C3
Bentham Glos 80 B6
Benthoul Aberdeen . 293 C10
Bentilee Stoke 168 F6
Bentlass Pembs 73 E7
Bentlawnt Shrops . . 130 C6
Bentley Essex 87 F9
E Yorks 208 F6
Hants 49 E9
Suff 108 D2
S Yorks 198 F5
Warks 134 D5
W Mid 133 D9
Worcs 117 D9
Bentley Common
Warks 134 D5
Bentley Heath Herts . 86 F2
W Mid 118 B3
Bentley Rise
S Yorks 198 G5
Benton Devon 41 F7
Benton Green
W Mid 118 B5

Bentpath Dumfries . 249 E8
Bents W Loth 269 C9
Bents Head W Yorks . 205 F7
Bentwichen Devon . . 41 G8
Bentworth Hants . . . 49 E7
Benvie Dundee 287 D7
Benville Dorset 29 G8
Benwell T&W 242 E6
Benwick Cambs . . . 138 E6
Beobridge Shrops . . 132 E5
Beoley Worcs 117 D11
Beoraidbeg Highld . . 295 F8
Bepton W Sus 34 D5
Berden Essex 105 F9
Bere Alston Devon . . 7 B8
Bere Ferrers Devon . . 7 C9
Berefold Aberds . . . 303 F9
Berepper Corn 2 E5
Bere Regis Dorset . . 18 C2
Bergh Apton Norf . . 142 C6
Berghers Hill Bucks . 66 B2
Berhill Som 44 F2
Berinsfield Oxon . . . 83 F9
Berkeley Glos 79 F11
Berkeley Heath Glos . 79 F11
Berkeley Road Glos . . 80 E2
Berkeley Towers
Ches E 167 E11
Berkhamsted Herts . . 85 D7
Berkley Som 45 D10
Berkley Down Som . . 45 D9
Berkley Marsh Som . . 45 D10
Berkswell W Mid . . 118 B4
Bermondsey London . 67 D10
Bermuda Warks . . . 135 F7
Bernards Heath
Herts 85 D11
Bernera Highld . . . 295 C10
Berner's Cross
Devon 25 F10
Berner's Hill E Sus . . 53 G8
Berners Roding
Essex 87 D10
Bernice Argyll 276 C2
Bernisdale Highld . . 298 D4
Berrick Salome
Oxon 83 G10
Berriedale Highld . . 311 G5
Berrier Cumb 230 F3
Berriew = *Aberriw*
Powys 130 C3
Berrington
Northumb 273 G10
Shrops 131 B10
Worcs 115 D11
Berrington Green
Worcs 115 D11
Berriowbridge Corn . 11 F11
Berrow Som 43 D10
Worcs 98 E5
Berrow Green
Worcs 116 F4
Berry Swansea 56 D3
Berry Brow W Yorks . 196 E6
Berry Cross Devon . . 25 E7
Berry Down Cross
Devon 40 E5
Berryfield Wilts . . . 61 G11
Berryfields Oxon . . . 84 B3
Berrygate Hill
E Yorks 201 C8
Berry Hill Glos 79 C9
Pembs 91 C11
Stoke 168 F6
Worcs 117 C7
Berryhillock Moray . 302 C5
Berrylands London . . 67 F7
Berry Moor S Yorks . 197 G9
Berrynarbor Devon . . 40 D5
Berry Pomeroy Devon . 8 E6
Berrysbridge Devon . 26 G6
Berry's Green London . 52 B2
Bersham Wrex 166 F4
Berstane Orkney . . . 314 E4
Berth-ddu Flint . . . 166 B2
Berthengam Flint . . 181 F10
Berwick E Sus 23 D8
Kent 54 F6
S Glos 60 C5
Berwick Bassett
Wilts 62 E6
Berwick Hill
Northumb 242 B5
Berwick Hills Mbro . 225 B10
Berwick St James
Wilts 46 F5
Berwick St John
Wilts 30 C6
Berwick St Leonard
Wilts 46 G2
Berwick-upon-Tweed
Northumb 273 E9
Berwick Wharf
Shrops 149 G10
Berwyn Denb 165 G11
Bescaby Leics 154 D6
Bescar Lancs 193 E11
Bescot W Mid 133 D10
Besford Shrops . . . 149 E11
Worcs 99 C8
Bessacarr S Yorks . . 198 G6
Bessels Green Kent . 52 B4
Bessels Leigh Oxon . 83 E7
Besses o' th' Barn
Gtr Man 195 F10
Bessingby E Yorks . . 218 F3
Bessingham Norf . . 160 B3
Best Beech Hill
E Sus 52 G6
Besthorpe Norf . . . 141 D11
Notts 172 C4
Bestwood
Nottingham 171 G9
Bestwood Village
Notts 171 F9
Beswick E Yorks . . . 208 D6
Betchcott Shrops . . 131 D8
Betchton Heath
Ches E 168 C3
Betchworth Sur . . . 51 D8

Bethania Ceredig . . 111 E11
Gwyn 163 E10
Gwyn 164 F2
Bethany Corn 6 D6
Bethel Anglesey . . . 178 G5
Corn 5 E10
Gwyn 147 B9
Gwyn 163 B8
Bethelnie Aberds . . 303 F7
Bethersden Kent . . . 54 E2
Bethesda Gwyn . . . 163 B10
Pembs 73 B9
Bethlehem Carms . . 94 F3
Bethnal Green
London 67 C10
Betley Staffs 168 F3
Betley Common
Staffs 168 F2
Betsham Kent 68 E6
Betteshanger Kent . . 55 C10
Bettiscombe Dorset . 16 B3
Bettisfield Wrex . . . 149 B9
Betton Shrops 130 C6
Shrops 150 B3
Betton Strange
Shrops 131 B10
Bettws Bridgend . . . 58 B2
Mon 78 B3
Newport 78 G3
Bettws Cedewain
Powys 130 D2
Bettws Gwerfil Goch
Denb 165 F8
Bettws Ifan Ceredig . 92 B6
Bettws Newydd
Mon 78 D5
Bettws-y-crwyn
Shrops 130 G4
Betws Bledrws
Ceredig 111 G11
Betws Bridgend . . . 57 D11
Carms 75 C11
Betws-Garmon
Gwyn 163 D9
Betws Ifan Ceredig . 92 B6
Betws-y-Coed
Conwy 164 D4
Betws-yn-Rhos
Conwy 180 G5
Beulah Ceredig . . . 92 B5
Powys 113 G8
Bevendean Brighton . 36 F4
Bevercotes Notts . . 187 G11
Beverley E Yorks . . . 208 F6
Beverston Glos 80 G5
Bevington Glos 79 F11
Bewaldeth Cumb . . 229 E10
Bewbush W Sus . . . 51 F8
Bewcastle Cumb . . 240 C3
Bewdley Worcs . . . 116 B5
Bewerley N Yorks . . 214 G3
Bewholme E Yorks . . 209 C9
Bewley Common
Wilts 62 F2
Bewsey Warr 183 D9
Bexfield Norf 159 D10
Bexhill E Sus 38 F2
Bexley London 68 E3
Bexleyheath London . 68 D3
Bexleyhill W Sus . . . 34 B6
Bexon Kent 53 B11
Bexwell Norf 140 C2
Beyton Suff 125 E8
Beyton Green Suff . . 125 E8
Bhalasaigh W Isles . 304 E3
Bhaltos W Isles . . . 304 E2
Bhatarsaigh
W Isles 297 M2
Bhlàraidh Highld . . 290 B5
Bibstone S Glos . . . 79 G11
Bibury Glos 81 D10
Bicester Oxon 101 G11
Bickenhall Som . . . 28 D3
Bickenhill W Mid . . 134 G3
Bicker Lincs 156 B4
Bicker Bar Lincs . . . 156 B4
Bicker Gauntlet
Lincs 156 B4
Bickershaw
Gtr Man 194 G6
Bickerstaffe Lancs . 194 G2
Bickerton Ches E . . 167 E8
Devon 9 G11
N Yorks 206 C5
Bickford Staffs . . . 151 G7
Bickham Som 42 E3
Bickingcott Devon . 26 B3
Bickington Devon . . 13 G11
Devon 40 G4
Bickleigh Devon . . . 7 C10
Devon 26 F6
Bickleton Devon . . . 40 G4
Bickley Ches W . . . 167 F8
London 68 F2
N Yorks 206 B2
Worcs 116 C2
Bickley Moss
Ches W 167 F8
Bickley Town
Ches W 167 F8
Bickleywood
Ches W 167 F8
Bicknacre Essex . . . 88 E3
Bicknoller Som . . . 42 F6
Bicknor Kent 53 B11
Bickton Hants 31 E11
Bicton Hereford . . . 115 E9
Pembs 72 D4
Shrops 130 D5
Shrops 149 F8
Bicton Heath
Shrops 149 G9
Bidborough Kent . . 52 E5
Bidden Hants 49 D8
Biddenden Kent . . . 53 F11
Biddenden Green
Kent 53 E11

Biddenham
Bedford 103 B10
Biddestone Wilts . . 61 E11
Biddick T&W 243 F8
Biddick Hall T&W . . 243 E9
Biddisham Som . . . 43 C11
Biddlesden Bucks . . 102 C2
Biddlestone
Northumb 251 B11
Biddulph Staffs . . . 168 D5
Biddulph Moor
Staffs 168 D6
Bideford Devon . . . 25 B7
Bidford-on-Avon
Warks 118 G2
Bidlake Devon 12 D5
Bidston Mers 182 C3
Bidston Hill Mers . . 182 D3
Bidwell C Beds . . . 103 G10
Bielby E Yorks . . . 207 E11
Bieldside Aberdeen . 293 C10
Bierley IoW 20 F6
W Yorks 205 G9
Bierton Bucks 84 B4
Bigbury Devon 8 F3
Bigbury-on-Sea
Devon 8 G3
Bigby Lincs 200 F5
Bigfrith Windsor . . 65 C11
Biggar Cumb 210 F3
S Lanark 260 B2
Biggar Road
N Lanark 268 C5
Biggin Derbys 169 D11
Derbys 170 F3
N Yorks 206 F6
Biggings Shetland . 313 G3
Biggin Hill London . 52 B2
Biggleswade
C Beds 104 C3
Bighouse Highld . . 310 C2
Bighton Hants 48 G6
Biglands Cumb . . . 239 G7
Big Mancot Flint . . 166 B4
Bignall End Staffs . 168 E4
Bignor W Sus 35 E7
Bigods Essex 106 G2
Bigram Stirling . . . 285 G10
Bigrigg Cumb 219 C10
Big Sand Highld . . . 299 B7
Bigswell Orkney . . . 314 E3
Bigton Shetland . . . 313 L5
Bilberry Corn 5 C10
Bilborough
Nottingham 171 G8
Bilbrook Som 42 E4
Staffs 133 C7
Bilbrough N Yorks . 206 D6
Bilbster Highld . . . 310 D6
Bilby Notts 187 E10
Bildershaw
Durham 233 G10
Bildeston Suff 107 B9
Billacombe Plym . . . 7 E10
Billacott Corn 11 C11
Billericay Essex . . . 87 G11
Billesdon Leics . . . 136 C4
Billesley Warks . . . 118 F2
Billesley Common
W Mid 133 G11
Billingborough
Lincs 156 C2
Billinge Mers 194 G4
Billingford Norf . . . 126 B3
Norf 159 E10
Billingham Stockton . 234 G5
Billinghay Lincs . . . 173 E11
Billingley S Yorks . . 198 G2
Billingshurst W Sus . 35 B9
Billingsley Shrops . . 132 F4
Billington C Beds . . 103 G8
Lancs 203 F10
Staffs 151 E7
Billockby Norf . . . 161 G8
Billy Mill T&W 243 D8
Billy Row Durham . . 233 D9
Bilmarsh Shrops . . . 149 D9
Bilsborrow Lancs . . 202 F6
Bilsby Lincs 191 F7
Bilsby Field Lincs . . 191 F7
Bilsdon Devon 14 C2
Bilsham W Sus 35 G7
Bilsington Kent . . . 54 G4
Bilson Green Glos . . 79 C11
Bilsthorpe Notts . . . 171 C10
Bilsthorpe Moor
Notts 171 D11
Bilston Midloth . . . 270 C5
W Mid 133 D9
Bilstone Leics 135 B7
Bilting Kent 54 D5
Bilton E Yorks 209 G9
Northumb 264 G6
N Yorks 206 B2
Warks 119 C9
Bilton Haggs
N Yorks 206 D5
Bilton in Ainsty
N Yorks 206 D5
Bimbister Orkney . . 314 E3
Binbrook Lincs . . . 190 C2
Binchester Blocks
Durham 233 E10
Bincombe Dorset . . 17 E9
Som 43 F7
Bindal Highld 311 L3
Bindon Som 27 C10
Binegar Som 44 D6
Bines Green W Sus . 35 D11
Binfield Brack 65 E10
Binfield Heath Oxon . 65 D8
Bingfield Northumb . 241 C11
Bingham Edin 280 G6
Notts 154 B4
Bingley W Yorks . . . 205 F8
Bings Heath
Shrops 149 F11
Binham Norf 159 B9
Binley Hants 48 C2

Binley *continued*
W Mid 119 B7
Binley Woods
Warks 119 B7
Binnegar Dorset . . . 18 D3
Binniehill Falk 279 G7
Binscombe Sur 50 D3
Binsey Oxon 83 D7
Binsoe N Yorks . . . 214 D4
Binstead IoW 21 C7
Binsted Hants 49 E9
IoW 21 C7
Binton Warks 118 G2
Bintree Norf 159 E10
Binweston Shrops . . 130 C6
Birch Essex 88 B6
Gtr Man 195 F11
Birch Acre Worcs . . 117 C11
Birchall Hereford . . 98 D3
Staffs 169 E7
Bircham Newton
Norf 158 C5
Bircham Tofts Norf . 158 C5
Birchan Coppice
Worcs 116 C6
Birchanger Essex . . 105 G10
Birchdale Hereford . 98 C3
Birchdale Staffs . . . 151 B11
Bircher Hereford . . 115 D9
Birches Green
W Mid 134 E2
Birches Head Stoke . 168 F5
Birchett's Green
E Sus 53 G7
Birchfield Highld . . 301 G9
W Mid 133 E11
Birch Green Essex . . 88 B6
Herts 86 C3
Lancs 194 F3
Worcs 99 B7
Birchgrove Cardiff . 59 D7
E Sus 36 B6
Swansea 57 B8
Birchhall Corner
Essex 107 E10
Birch Heath
Ches W 167 C8
Birch Hill Brack . . . 65 F11
Ches W 183 G8
Birchill Devon 28 G4
Birchills W Mid . . . 133 D10
Birchington Kent . . 71 F9
Birchley Heath
Warks 134 E5
Birchmoor Warks . . 134 C5
Birchmoor Green
C Beds 103 E8
Bircholt Forstal Kent . 54 E5
Birchover Derbys . . 170 C2
Birch Vale Derbys . . 185 D8
Birchwood Herts . . 86 D2
Lincs 172 B6
Som 29 E11
Warr 183 C10
Birchy Hill Hants . . 19 B11
Bircotes Notts 187 C10
Birdbrook Essex . . . 106 C4
Birdbush Wilts 30 C6
Birdfield Argyll . . . 275 D10
Birdforth N Yorks . . 215 D9
Birdham W Sus . . . 22 D4
Birdholme Derbys . . 170 B5
Birdingbury Warks . 119 D8
Birdlip Glos 80 C6
Birdsall N Yorks . . . 216 F6
Birds Edge W Yorks . 197 F8
Birds End Suff 124 E5
Birdsgreen Shrops . . 132 F5
Birds Green Essex . . 87 D9
Birdsmoorgate
Dorset 28 G5
Birdston E Dunb . . . 278 F3
Bird Street Suff . . . 125 G10
Birdwell S Yorks . . . 197 G10
Birdwood Glos 80 B2
Birgham Borders . . 263 B7
Birichen Highld . . . 309 K7
Birkacre Lancs 194 D5
Birkby Cumb 229 D7
N Yorks 224 E6
W Yorks 196 D6
Birkdale Mers 193 D10
Birkenbog Aberds . . 302 C5
Birkenhead Mers . . 182 D4
Birkenhills Aberds . 303 E7
Birkenshaw
N Lanark 268 C3
S Lanark 268 F5
W Yorks 197 B8
Birkenshaw Bottoms
W Yorks 197 B8
Birkenside Borders . 271 G11
Birkett Mire Cumb . 230 G2
Birkhall Aberds . . . 292 D5
Birkhill Angus 287 D7
Borders 260 F6
Borders 271 G11
Birkholme Lincs . . . 155 E9
Birkhouse W Yorks . 197 C7
Birkin N Yorks 198 B4
Birks Cumb 222 G3
W Yorks 197 B9
Birkshaw Northumb . 241 D7
Birley Hereford . . . 115 G9
Birley Carr S Yorks . 186 C4
Birley Edge S Yorks . 186 C4
Birleyhay Derbys . . 186 E5
Birling Kent 69 G7
Northumb 252 B6
Birling Gap E Sus . . 23 F9
Birlingham Worcs . . 99 C8
Birmingham
W Mid 133 F11
Birnam Perth 286 C4

Birse Aberds 293 D7
Birsemore Aberds . . 293 D7
Birstall Leics 135 B11
W Yorks 197 B8
Birstall Smithies
W Yorks 197 B8
Birstwith N Yorks . . 205 B10
Birthorpe Lincs . . . 156 C2
Birtle Gtr Man 195 E10
Birtley Hereford . . . 115 D7
Northumb 241 B9
Shrops 131 E9
T&W 243 F7
Birtley Green Sur . . 50 E4
Birts Street Worcs . . 98 D5
Bisbrooke Rutland . . 137 D7
Biscathorpe Lincs . . 190 D2
Biscombe Som 27 E11
Biscot Luton 103 G11
Biscovey Corn 5 E11
Bisham Windsor . . . 65 C10
Bishampton Worcs . . 117 G9
Bish Mill Devon . . . 26 B2
Bishon Common
Hereford 97 C8
Bishop Auckland
Durham 233 F10
Bishopbridge Lincs . 189 C8
Bishopbriggs
E Dunb 278 G2
Bishop Burton
E Yorks 208 F5
Bishopdown Wilts . . 47 G7
Bishop Kinkell
Highld 300 D5
Bishop Middleham
Durham 234 E2
Bishopmill Moray . . 302 C2
Bishop Monkton
N Yorks 214 F6
Bishop Norton Lincs . 189 C7
Bishopsbourne Kent . 55 C7
Bishops Cannings
Wilts 62 G4
Bishop's Castle
Shrops 130 F6
Bishop's Caundle
Dorset 29 E11
Bishop's Cleeve Glos . 99 F9
Bishop's Down
Dorset 29 E11
Bishops Frome
Hereford 98 B3
Bishopsgarth
Stockton 234 G4
Bishopsgate Sur . . . 66 E3
Bishops Green Essex . 87 B5
Bishop's Green
W Berks 64 G4
Bishop's Hull Som . . 28 C2
Bishop's Itchington
Warks 119 F7
Bishops Lydeard
Som 27 B11
Bishop's Norton Glos . 98 G6
Bishop's Nympton
Devon 26 C3
Bishop's Offley
Staffs 150 D5
Bishop's Quay Corn . 2 D6
Bishop's Stortford
Herts 105 G9
Bishop's Sutton
Hants 48 G6
Bishop's Tachbrook
Warks 118 D6
Bishops Tawton
Devon 40 G5
Bishopsteignton
Devon 14 G4
Bishopstoke Hants . . 33 D7
Bishopston Bristol . . 60 D5
Swansea 56 D5
Bishopstone Bucks . . 84 C4
E Sus 23 E7
Hereford 97 C8
Kent 71 F8
Swindon 63 C8
Wilts 31 B9
Bishopstrow Wilts . . 45 E11
Bishop Sutton Bath . 44 B5
Bishop's Waltham
Hants 33 D9
Bishopswood Som . . 28 E3
Bishop's Wood
Staffs 132 B6
Bishopsworth Bristol . 60 F5
Bishop Thornton
N Yorks 214 G5
Bishopthorpe York . 207 D7
Bishopton Darl . . . 234 G3
Dumfries 236 E6
N Yorks 214 E6
Renfs 277 G8
Warks 118 F3
Bishopwearmouth
T&W 243 F9
Bishop Wilton
E Yorks 207 B11
Bishpool Newport . . 59 B10
Bishton Newport . . 59 B11
Staffs 151 E11
Bisley Glos 80 D6
Sur 50 B3
Bisley Camp Sur . . . 50 B2
Bispham Blackpool . 202 E2
Bispham Green
Lancs 194 E3
Bissoe Corn 4 G5
Bissom Corn 3 C7
Bisterne Hants 31 G11
Bisterne Close Hants . 32 G3
Bitchet Green Kent . 52 C5
Bitchfield Lincs . . . 155 D9
Bittadon Devon . . . 40 E4
Bittaford Devon . . . 8 D2
Bittering Norf 159 F8
Bitterley Shrops . . . 115 B11
Bitterne Soton 33 E7
Bitterne Park Soton . 32 E6
Bitterscote Staffs . . 134 C4

Bitteswell Leics . . . 135 F10
Bittles Green Dorset . 30 C5
Bitton S Glos 61 E7
Bix Oxon 65 B8
Bixter Shetland . . . 313 H5
Blaby Leics 135 D11
Blackacre Dumfries . 248 E2
Blackadder West
Borders 272 E6
Blackawton Devon . . 8 E6
Black Bank Cambs . . 139 F10
Warks 135 F7
Black Banks Darl . . 224 C5
Black Barn Lincs . . . 157 D8
Blackbeck Cumb . . 219 D10
Blackbird Leys Oxon . 83 E9
Blackborough Devon . 27 F9
Norf 158 G3
Blackborough End
Norf 158 G3
Blackboys E Sus . . . 37 C8
Blackbraes Aberds . . 293 B10
Blackbrook Derbys . . 170 F4
Mers 183 B8
Staffs 150 B5
Sur 51 D7
Blackburn Aberds . . 293 B10
Aberds 302 F5
Blackburn 195 B7
S Yorks 186 C5
W Loth 269 B9
Black Callerton
T&W 242 D5
Black Carr Norf . . . 141 D11
Blackcastle Midloth . 271 D8
Blackchambers
Aberds 293 B9
Black Clauchrie
S Ayrs 245 G7
Black Corner W Sus . 51 F9
Black Corries Lodge
Highld 284 B6
Blackcraig Dumfries . 246 D6
Blackcraigs Angus . . 293 E7
Black Crofts Argyll . 289 F11
Black Cross Corn . . . 5 C8
Black Dam Hants . . 48 C6
Blackden Heath
Ches E 184 G3
Blackditch Oxon . . . 82 D6
Blackdog Aberds . . . 293 B11
Blackdown Devon . . 26 F4
Dorset 28 G5
Hants 33 D8
Warks 118 D6
Blackdyke Cumb . . 238 G4
Blackdykes E Loth . 281 E11
Blacker Hill
S Yorks 197 G11
Blacketts Kent 70 F2
Blackfell T&W 243 F7
Blackfen London . . . 68 E3
Blackfield Hants . . . 32 G6
Blackford Cumb . . . 239 E9
Dumfries 248 G4
Perth 286 G2
Shrops 131 G11
Som 29 B11
Som 42 D2
Som 44 D2
Blackford Bridge
Gtr Man 195 F10
Blackfordby Leics . . 152 F6
Blackfords Staffs . . 151 G9
Blackgang IoW . . . 20 F5
Blackgate Angus . . 287 B8
Blackhall Aberds . . 293 D8
Edin 280 G4
Renfs 267 C9
Blackhall Colliery
Durham 234 D5
Blackhall Mill T&W . 242 F4
Blackhall Rocks
Durham 234 D5
Blackham E Sus . . . 52 F3
Blackhaugh
Borders 261 B10
Blackheath Essex . . 107 G10
London 67 D11
Suff 127 C8
Sur 50 D4
W Mid 133 F9
Blackheath Park
London 67 D11
Black Heddon
Northumb 242 B3
Blackhill Aberds . . . 303 D10
Aberds 303 E10
Durham 242 G3
Hants 32 D4
Highld 298 D3
Black Hill W Yorks . 204 E6
Blackhillock Moray . 302 E4
Blackhills Highld . . 301 D9
Moray 302 D2
Blackhorse Devon . . 14 C5
S Glos 61 D7
Black Horse Drove
Cambs 139 E11
Blackjack Lincs . . . 156 B5
Black Lake W Mid . . 133 E9
Blackland Wilts . . . 62 F4
Blacklands E Sus . . 38 E4
Hereford 98 C2
Black Lane Gtr Man . 195 F9
Blacklaw Aberds . . 302 E6
Blackleach S Ayrs . . 202 G5
Blackley Gtr Man . . 195 G11
W Yorks 196 D6
Blacklunans Perth . 292 G3
Blackmarstone
Hereford 97 D10
Blackmill Bridgend . 58 B2
Blackminster Worcs . 99 C11
Blackmoor Bath . . . 60 G5
Hants 49 G9

Blackmoor *continued*
N Som 60 G3
Som 27 D11
Black Moor Lancs . . 194 E3
W Yorks 205 F11
Blackmoorfoot
W Yorks 196 E5
Blackmoor Gate
Devon 41 E7
Blackmore Essex . . 87 E10
Shrops 130 B6
Blackmore End
Essex 106 E4
Herts 85 B11
Black Mount Argyll . 284 C6
Blackness Aberds . . 293 D8
E Sus 52 G4
Falk 279 F11
Blacknest Hants . . . 49 E9
Windsor 66 F3
Blacknoll Dorset . . . 18 D2
Black Notley Essex . 106 G5
Blacko Lancs 204 E3
Blackpark Dumfries . 236 C5
Black Park Wrex . . . 166 G4
Black Pill Swansea . . 56 C6
Blackpole Worcs . . . 117 F7
Black Pole Lancs . . . 202 F5
Blackpool Blackpool . 202 F2
Devon 7 E11
Devon 9 F7
Devon 14 G2
Pembs 73 C9
Blackpool Gate
Cumb 240 B2
Blackridge W Loth . 269 B7
Blackrock Argyll . . 274 G4
Bath 60 F6
Mon 78 C2
Black Rock Brighton . 36 G4
Corn 2 C5
Blackrod Gtr Man . . 194 E6
Blackshaw Dumfries . 238 D2
Blackshaw Head
W Yorks 196 B3
Blackshaw Moor
Staffs 169 D8
Blacksmith's Corner
Suff 108 C2
Blacksmith's Green
Suff 126 D2
Blacksnape
Blackburn 195 C8
Blackstone Worcs . . 116 C5
W Sus 36 D2
Black Street Suff . . 143 F10
Black Tar Pembs . . . 73 D7
Blackthorn Oxon . . 83 B10
Blackthorpe Suff . . 125 E8
Blacktoft E Yorks . . 199 C10
Blacktop Aberdeen . 293 C10
Black Torrington
Devon 25 F7
Blacktown Newport . 59 C9
Black Vein Caerph . . 78 G2
Blackwall Derbys . . 170 F3
London 67 C11
Blackwall Tunnel
London 67 C11
Blackwater BCP . . . 19 B8
Corn 4 F4
Hants 49 B11
IoW 20 D6
Norf 159 E11
Som 28 D3
Blackwaterfoot
N Ayrs 255 E9
Blackwater Lodge
Moray 302 G3
Blackweir Cardiff . . 59 D7
Blackwell Cumb . . . 239 G10
Darl 224 C5
Derbys 170 C6
Derbys 185 G10
Devon 27 B8
Warks 100 C4
Worcs 117 C9
W Sus 51 F11
Blackwood Caerph . 77 E11
S Lanark 268 G5
Warr 183 C10
Blackwood Hill
Staffs 168 D6
Blacon Ches W . . . 166 B5
Bladbean Kent 55 D7
Blades N Yorks . . . 223 F9
Bladnoch Dumfries . 236 D6
Bladon Oxon 82 C6
Blaenannerch
Ceredig 92 B4
Blaenau Carms . . . 75 C10
Flint 166 D2
Blaenau Dolwyddelan
Conwy 164 E2
Blaenau Ffestiniog
Gwyn 164 F2
Blaenau-Gwent
Bl Gwent 78 E2
Blaenavon Torf . . . 78 D2
Blaenbedw Fawr
Ceredig 111 G7
Blaencaerau
Bridgend 57 C11
Blaencelyn Ceredig . 111 G7
Blaen-Cil-Llech
Ceredig 92 C6
Blaen Clydach
Rhondda 77 G7
Blaencwm Rhondda . 76 F6
Blaendulais = *Seven Sisters*
Neath 76 D4
Blaendyryn Powys . 95 D8
Blaenffos Pembs . . 92 D3
Blaengarw Bridgend . 76 F6
Blaengwrach Neath . 76 D5
Blaengwynfi Neath . 57 B11
Blaen-gwynfi Neath . 57 B11

Blaenllechau Rhondda. 77 F8
Blaen-pant Ceredig . 92 C5
Blaenpennal Ceredig 112 G2
Blaenplwyf Ceredig .111 B11
Blaenporth Ceredig . . 92 B5
Blaenrhondda
Rhondda 76 E6
Blaenwaun Carms . . . 92 F4
Blaen-y-coed Carms. 92 F6
Blaencwm Ceredig .112 B6
Blaen-y-cwm
Bl Gwent 77 C10
Denb 147 C10
Gwyn 146 E4
Powys 147 E11
Blagdon N Som 44 B4
Torbay 9 C7
Blagdon Hill Som . . 28 C2
Blagill Cumb. 231 B10
Blaguegate Lancs. . 194 F3
Blaich Highld 290 F2
Blain Highld 289 C8
Blaina Bl Gwent 78 D2
Blainacraig Ho
Aberds. 293 D7
Blair Fife. 280 C6
Blair Atholl Perth . 291 G10
Blairbeg N Ayrs 256 C2
Blairburn Fife 279 D9
Blairdaff Aberds 293 B8
Blair Drummond
Stirling. 278 B4
Blairdryne Aberds. . 293 D9
Blairglas Argyll 276 D6
Blairgorm Highld. . . 301 G10
Blairgowrie Perth. . . 286 C5
Blairhall Fife 279 D10
Blairhill N Lanark . . 268 B4
Blairingone Perth . . 279 B9
Blairland N Ayrs . . . 266 F6
Blairlinn N Lanark . . 278 G5
Blairlogie Stirling. . 278 B6
Blairlomond Argyll . 276 B3
Blairmore Argyll . . . 276 E3
Highld 306 D6
Blairnamarrow
Moray 292 B4
Blairquhosh
Stirling. 277 E10
Blair's Ferry Argyll . 275 G10
Blairskaith E Dunb. 277 F11
Blaisdon Glos. 80 B2
Blaise Hamlet Bristol. 60 D5
Blakebrook Worcs . 116 B6
Blakedown Worcs . . 117 B7
Blake End Essex 106 G4
Blakelands
M Keynes. 103 C7
Blakelaw Borders . . 263 C7
T&W 242 D6
Blakeley Staffs. 133 E7
Blakeley Lane Staffs 169 F7
Blakelow Ches E. . . . 167 E11
Blakemere Hereford. 97 C7
Blakemere Heath
W Mid 133 C10
Blakeney Glos. 79 D10
Norf. 177 E8
Blakenhall Ches E. . 168 F2
W Mid 133 D8
Blakeshall Worcs . . 132 G6
Blakesley W Nhants . 120 G2
Blanchland
Northumb 241 G11
Blandford Camp
Dorset 30 F6
Blandford Forum
Dorset 30 F5
Blandford St Mary
Dorset 30 F5
Bland Hill N Yorks . . 205 C10
Blandy Highld 308 D6
Blanefield Stirling. . 277 F11
Blanerne Borders . . 272 D6
Blank Bank Staffs . . 168 F4
Blankney Lincs 173 C9
Blantyre S Lanark. . 268 D3
Blar a'Chaorainn
Highld 290 G3
Blaran Argyll. 275 B9
Blarghour Argyll . . . 275 B10
Blarmachfoldach
Highld 290 G2
Blarnalearoch
Highld 307 K6
Blasford Hill Essex. . 88 C2
Blashford Hants . . . 31 F11
Blaston Leics 136 D6
Blatchbridge Som . . 45 D9
Blathwycke
N Nhants 137 D9
Blawith Cumb. 210 B5
Blaxhall Suff. 127 F7
Blaxton S Yorks . . . 199 G7
Blaydon T&W 242 E5
Blaydon Burn T&W . . 242 E5
Blaydon Haughs
T&W 242 E5
Bleach Green Cumb. 219 B9
Suff. 126 B4
Bleadney Som 44 D3
Bleadon N Som 43 B10
Bleak Acre Hereford. 98 B2
Bleak Hall
M Keynes. 103 D7
Bleak Hey Nook
Gtr Man 196 F4
Bleak Hill Hants. . . 31 F11
Blean Kent 70 G6
Bleasby Lincs 189 G10
Notts 172 F2
Bleasby Moor
Lincs 189 E10
Bleasdale Lancs . . . 203 D7
Bleatarn Cumb. 222 C4
Blebocraigs Fife. . . . 287 F8
Bleddfa Powys 114 D4

Bledington Glos. . . . 100 G4
Bledlow Bucks. 84 E3
Bledlow Ridge Bucks. 84 F3
Bleet Wilts. 45 B11
Blegbie E Loth 271 C9
Blegbury Devon. 24 B2
Blencarn Cumb. 231 E8
Blencogo Cumb 229 B9
Blendworth Hants . . 34 E2
Blenheim Oxon 83 D9
Oxon 83 E9
Blenheim Park Norf. 158 C6
Blenkinsopp Hall
Northumb 240 E5
Blennerhasset
Cumb. 229 C9
Blervie Castle
Moray 301 D10
Bletchingdon Oxon . 83 B8
Bletchingley Sur. . . . 51 C10
Bletchley M Keynes. 103 E7
Shrops. 150 C2
Bletherston Pembs . 91 G11
Bletsoe Bedford. . . . 121 F10
Blewbury Oxon 64 B4
Blickling Norf 160 D3
Blidworth Notts. . . . 171 D9
Blidworth Bottoms
Notts 171 E9
Blidworth Dale
Notts 171 E9
Blindburn Northumb. 263 G8
Blindcrake Cumb. . . 229 D8
Blindley Heath Sur. . 51 D11
Blindmoor Som. 28 E3
Blingery Highld 310 E7
Blisland Corn. 11 G8
Blissford Hants 31 E11
Bliss Gate Worcs . . 116 C4
Blisworth W Nhants . 120 G4
Blithbury Staffs. . . . 151 E11
Blitterlees Cumb. . . 238 C4
Blockley Glos. 100 D3
Blofield Norf 142 B6
Blofield Heath Norf. . 160 G6
Blo' Norton Norf. . . . 125 C10
Bloodman's Corner
Suff. 143 D10
Bloomfield Bath 45 B7
Bath. 61 G8
Borders 262 E3
W Mid 133 E9
Bloomsbury London. 67 C10
W Loth 269 B9
Blore Staffs 150 C4
Staffs. 169 F10
Blorenheath Staffs . 150 B4
Blossomfield
W Mid 118 B2
Blount's Green
Staffs 151 C11
Blowick Mers. 193 D11
Blowinghouse Corn. . 4 E4
Bloxham Oxon 101 D8
Bloxholm Lincs 173 D9
Bloxwich W Mid. . . . 133 C10
Bloxworth Dorset . . . 18 C3
Blubberhouses
N Yorks. 205 B9
Blue Anchor Corn. . . . 5 D8
Som 42 E4
Swansea 56 B4
Bluebell Telford. . . . 149 G11
Blue Bell Hill Kent. . 69 G8
Bluecairn Borders . . 271 G10
Blue Hill Herts 104 G5
Blue Row Essex. 89 C8
Bluetown Kent. 54 B4
Blue Town Kent. 70 D2
Blue Vein Wilts. 61 F10
Bluewater Kent. 68 E5
Blughasary Highld . . 307 J6
Blundellsands Mers. 182 B4
Blundeston Suff. . . . 143 D10
Blundies Staffs. 132 F5
Blunham C Beds . . . 122 G3
Blunsdon St Andrew
Swindon. 62 B6
Bluntington Worcs. . 117 C9
Bluntisham Cambs . 123 C7
Blunts Corn. 6 C5
Blunt's Green
Warks 118 D2
Blurton Stoke. 168 G5
Blyborough Lincs . . 188 C5
Blyford Suff. 127 B8
Blymhill Staffs. 150 G6
Blymhill Lawns
Staffs 150 G6
Blyth Borders 270 F2
Northumb 253 G8
Notts 187 D10
Blyth Bridge
Borders 270 F2
Blythburgh Suff. . . . 127 B9
Blythe Borders 271 F11
Blythe Bridge Staffs. 169 G7
Blythe Marsh Staffs. 169 G7
Blyth End Warks. . . . 134 E4
Blythswood Renfs. . . 267 B10
Blyton Lincs 188 C5
Boarhills Fife. 287 F9
Boarhunt Hants 33 F10
Boarsgreave Lancs . 195 C10
Boarshead E Sus. . . . 52 G4
Boars Hill Oxon 83 E7
Boarstall Bucks 83 C10
Boasley Cross Devon . 12 C5
Boath Highld. 300 B5
Boat of Garten
Highld 291 B11
Bobbing Kent. 69 F11
Bobbington Staffs. . . 132 E6
Bobbingworth Essex . 87 D8
Bobby Hill Suff 125 C10
Boblainy Highld. . . . 300 F4
Bocaddon Corn. 6 D3
Bochastle Stirling . . 285 G10
Bockhanger Kent. . . . 54 E4
Bocking Essex 106 G5
Bocking Churchstreet
Essex. 106 F5

Bocking's Elm Essex .89 B11
Bockleton Worcs . . . 115 E11
Bockmer End Bucks. .65 B10
Bocombe Devon 24 C5
Bodantionail Highld. .299 B7
Boddam Aberds. . . . 303 E11
Shetland 313 M5
Boddington Glos. 99 F7
Bodedern Anglesey . 178 E4
Bodellick Corn. 10 G5
Bodelwyddan Denb. .181 F8
Bodenham
Hereford 115 G10
Wilts 31 B10
Bodenham Bank
Hereford. 98 E2
Bodenham Moor
Hereford. 115 G10
Bodermid Gwyn 144 D3
Bodewryd Anglesey . 178 C5
Bodfari Denb. 181 G9
Bodffordd Anglesey . 178 F6
Bodham Norf 177 E10
Bodiam E Sus. 38 B3
Bodicote Oxon 101 D9
Bodieve Corn. 10 G5
Bodiggo Corn. 5 D10
Bodilly Corn 2 C5
Bodinnick Corn. 6 E2
Bodle Street Green
E Sus 23 C11
Bodley Devon 41 D7
Bodmin Corn. 5 B11
Bodmiscombe
Devon 27 F10
Bodney Norf. 140 D6
Bodorgan Anglesey . 162 B5
Bodsham Kent. 54 E6
Boduan Gwyn. 144 B6
Boduel Corn. 6 C4
Bodymoor Heath
Warks 134 D4
Bofarnel Corn. 6 C2
Bogallan Highld. . . . 300 D6
Bogbrae Aberds. . . . 303 F10
Bogend Borders 272 F5
Leics 135 B9
S Ayrs. 257 C9
Bogentory Aberds. . . 293 C9
Boghall Midloth 270 B4
W Loth 269 B9
Boghead Aberds 293 D8
S Lanark. 268 G5
Bogmoor Moray 302 C3
Bogniebrae Aberds . 302 E5
Aberds 302 E6
Bognor Regis W Sus. . 22 D6
Bograxie Aberds . . . 293 B9
Bogs Aberds 302 G5
Bogs Bank Borders . 270 E3
Bogside N Lanark. . . 268 E6
Bogthorn W Yorks . . 204 F6
Bogton Aberds 302 D6
Bogtown Aberds 302 C5
Bogue Dumfries 246 G4
Bohemia E Sus. 38 E4
Wilts 32 D2
Bohenie Highld. 290 E4
Bohetherick Corn. . . . 7 B8
Bohortha Corn 3 C9
Bohuntine Highld . . 290 E4
Bohuntinville
Highld 290 E4
Boirseam W Isles . . . 296 C6
Bojewyan Corn 1 C3
Bokiddick Corn. 5 C11
Bolahaul Fm Carms . 74 B6
Bolam Durham 233 G9
Northumb 252 G3
Bolam West Houses
Northumb 252 G3
Bolas Heath Telford. .150 E3
Bolberry Devon 9 G8
Bold Heath Mers. . . . 183 D8
Boldmere W Mid 134 E2
Boldon T&W. 243 E9
Boldre Hants 20 B2
Boldron Durham . . . 223 C10
Bole Notts 188 D3
Bolehall Staffs. 134 C4
Bolehill Derbys 170 E3
Derbys 186 G6
S Yorks 186 E5
Bole Hill Derbys . . . 186 G4
Bolenowe Corn 2 B5
Boleside Borders . . . 261 C11
Boley Park Staffs . . 134 B2
Bolham Devon 27 E7
Notts 188 E2
Bolham Water
Devon 27 E11
Bolholt Gtr Man 195 E9
Bolingey Corn 4 E5
Bolitho Corn 2 C5
Bollihope Durham. . . 232 E6
Bollington Ches E . . 184 F6
Bollington Cross
Ches E 184 F6
Bolney W Sus 36 C3
Bolnhurst Bedford. . 121 F11
Bolnore W Sus 36 C4
Bolshan Angus. 287 B10
Bolsover Derbys . . . 187 G7
Bolsterstone
S Yorks 186 B3
Bolstone Hereford. . . 97 E11
Boltby N Yorks 215 B9
Bolter End Bucks. . . . 84 G3
Bolton Cumb. 231 G8
E Loth 281 G10
E Yorks 207 C11
Gtr Man 195 F8
Northumb 264 C6
W Yorks 205 F9
Bolton Abbey
N Yorks 205 C7

Bolton Bridge
N Yorks 205 C7
Bolton-by-Bowland
Lancs 203 D11
Boltonfellend
Cumb 239 D11
Boltongate Cumb . . 229 C10
Bolton Green Lancs . 194 D5
Bolton Houses
Lancs 202 G4
Bolton-le-Sands
Lancs 211 F9
Bolton Low Houses
Cumb 229 C10
Bolton New Houses
Cumb 229 C10
Bolton-on-Swale
N Yorks 224 F5
Bolton Percy
N Yorks 206 E6
Bolton Town End
Lancs 211 F9
Bolton upon Dearne
S Yorks 198 G3
Bolton Wood Lane
Cumb 229 C11
Bolton Woods
W Yorks 205 F9
Boltshope Park
Durham 232 B4
Bolventor Corn 11 F9
Bomarsund
Northumb 253 G7
Bombie Dumfries . . . 237 D9
Bomby Cumb. 221 B10
Bomere Heath
Shrops. 149 F9
Bonaly Edin. 270 B4
Bonar Bridge Highld. 309 K6
Bonawe Argyll 284 D4
Bonby N Lincs 200 D4
Boncath Pembs 92 D4
Bonchester Bridge
Borders 262 G3
Bonchurch IoW 21 F7
Bondend Glos. 80 B5
Bond End Staffs. . . . 152 F2
Bondleigh Devon . . . 25 G11
Bondman Hays
Leics 135 B9
Bonds Lancs. 202 E5
Bondstones Devon . . 25 F9
Bonehill Devon 13 F10
Staffs. 134 C3
Bo'ness Falk. 279 E9
Bonhill W Dunb 277 F7
Boningale Shrops. . . 132 C6
Bonjedward Borders . 262 E5
Bonkle N Lanark. . . . 268 D6
Bonnavoulin Highld . 289 D7
Bonning Gate Cumb . 221 F9
Bonnington Borders . 261 B7
Edin 270 B2
Kent. 54 F5
Bonnybank Fife. . . . 287 G7
Bonnybridge Falk. . . 278 E6
Bonnykelly Aberds . . 303 D8
Bonnyrigg and Lasswade
Midloth 270 B6
Bonnyton Aberds . . . 302 F6
Angus 287 B10
Angus 287 D7
E Ayrs. 257 B10
Bonsall Derbys. 170 D3
Bonskeid House
Perth 291 G10
Bonson Som 43 B8
Bont Mon 78 B5
Bontddu Gwyn 146 F3
Bont-Dolgadfan
Powys 129 C7
Bont Fawr Carms . . . 94 F4
Bont goch = Elerch
Ceredig 128 E3
Bont-newydd
Ceredig 112 D2
Gwyn 163 D7
Bont-newydd
Conwy 181 G8
Bont Newydd Gwyn . 146 E5
Gwyn 164 G2
Bontuchel Denb 165 D9
Bonvilston = Tresimwn
V Glam. 58 E5
Bon-y-maen
Swansea 57 B7
Boode Devon 40 F4
Booker Bucks. 84 G4
Bookham Dorset 30 G2
Booleybank Shrops 149 D11
Boon Borders 271 F11
Boon Hill Staffs 168 E4
Boorley Green
Hants. 33 E8
Boosbeck Redcar . . . 226 B3
Boose's Green
Essex. 106 E6
Boosley Corn 11 D7
Booth Staffs 151 D10
W Yorks 196 B4
Booth Bank Ches E . 184 D2
Booth Bridge Lancs . 204 D4
Boothby Graffoe
Lincs 173 D7
Boothby Pagnell
Lincs 155 C9
Boothgate Derbys. . . 170 E5
Boothroyd W Yorks . . 197 C8
Boothsdale Ches W . . 167 B8
Boothstown
Gtr Man 195 G8
Boothtown W Yorks . 196 B5
Boothville W Nhants . 120 E5
Booth Wood
W Yorks 196 D4
Booton Norf. 160 E2
Bothal Northumb. . . 252 F6

Boots Green
Ches W 184 G3
Boot Street Suff. . . . 108 B4
Booze N Yorks 223 E10
Boquhan Stirling . . . 277 D10
Boquio Corn. 2 C5
Boraston Shrops . . . 116 D2
Boraston Dale
Shrops. 116 C2
Borden Kent. 69 G11
W Sus 34 C4
Border Cumb 238 G5
Bordesley W Mid. . . 133 F11
Bordesley Green
W Mid 134 F2
Bordlands Borders . 270 F3
Bordley N Yorks . . . 213 G8
Bordon Hants 49 F10
Bordon Camp Hants . 49 F9
Boreham Essex 88 D3
Wilts 45 E11
Boreham Street
E Sus 23 C11
Borehamwood
Herts 85 F11
Boreland Dumfries . 236 C5
Dumfries 248 E5
Fife 280 C6
Stirling. 285 D7
Boreland of Southwick
Dumfries 237 C11
Boreley Worcs 116 D6
Borestone Shrops. . . 278 C5
Borgh W Isles. 296 C5
W Isles. 297 L2
Borghasdal W Isles . 296 C6
Borghastan W Isles . 304 D4
Borgie Highld 308 D6
Borgue Dumfries . . . 237 E8
Highld 311 G5
Borley Essex 106 C6
Borley Green Essex . 106 C6
Suff 125 E9
Bornais W Isles 297 J3
Bornesketaig Highld . 298 B3
Borness Dumfries . . 237 E8
Borough Scilly 1 G3
Boroughbridge
N Yorks 215 F7
Borough Green Kent. . 52 B6
Borough Marsh
Wokingham 65 D9
Borough Park Staffs 134 B4
Borough Post Som . . 28 C4
Borras Wrex. 166 E4
Borras Head Wrex . . 166 E5
Borreraig Highld . . . 296 F7
Borrobol Lodge
Highld 311 G2
Borrodale Highld. . . 297 G7
Borrohill Aberds . . . 303 D9
Borrowash Derbys . . 153 C8
Borrowby N Yorks . . 215 B8
N Yorks. 226 B5
Borrowdale Cumb. . . 220 C5
Borrowfield
Aberds 293 D10
Borrowston Highld . . 310 E7
Borrowstoun Mains
Falk 279 E9
Borstal Medway 69 F8
Borth = Y Borth
Ceredig 128 E2
Borthwick Midloth . . 271 D7
Borthwickbrae
Borders 261 G10
Borthwickshiels
Borders 261 F10
Borth-y-Gest
Gwyn 145 B11
Borve Highld. 298 E4
Borve Lodge
W Isles 305 J2
Borwick Lancs 211 E10
Borwick Rails Cumb. 210 D3
Bosavern Corn. 1 C3
Bosbury Hereford . . . 98 C3
Boscadjack Corn. 2 C5
Boscastle Corn 11 C8
Boscean Corn 1 C3
Boscombe BCP 19 C8
Wilts 47 E8
Boscomoor Staffs . . 151 G8
Boscoppa Corn 5 E10
Boscreege Corn 2 C3
Bosham W Sus. 22 C4
Bosham Hoe W Sus . . 22 C4
Bosherston Pembs . . 73 F7
Boskednan Corn 1 C4
Boskenna Corn 1 E4
Bosleake Corn 4 G3
Bosley Ches E. 168 B6
Boslowick Corn 3 C7
Boslymon Corn 5 C11
Bosoughan Corn 5 C7
Bosporthennis Corn . . 1 B4
Bossall N Yorks 216 G4
Bossiney Corn 11 D7
Bossingham Kent. . . 54 D6
Bossington Hants . . 47 G10
Kent. 55 B8
Som 41 D11
Bostadh W Isles. . . . 304 D3
Bostock Green
Ches W 167 B11
Boston Lincs. 174 G4
Boston Long Hedges
Lincs 174 F5
Boston Spa
W Yorks 206 D4
Boston West Lincs . . 174 F3
Boswednack Corn . . . 1 B4
Boswin Corn. 2 C5
Boswinger Corn 5 G9
Boswyn Corn 2 B5
Botallack Corn 1 C3
Botany Bay London. . 86 F3
Mon 79 E8
Botcherby Cumb . . . 239 F10
Botcheston Leics . . . 135 B9
Botesdale Suff. 125 B10
Bothal Northumb. . . 252 F6

Bothampstead
W Berks. 64 D4
Bothamsall Notts . . 187 G11
Bothel Cumb. 229 D9
Bothenhampton
Dorset 16 C5
Bothwell S Lanark . . 268 D4
Bothy Highld. 290 F4
Botley Bucks. 85 E7
Hants. 33 E8
Oxon 83 D7
Botloe's Green Glos. . 98 F4
Botolph Claydon
Bucks. 102 G4
Botolphs W Sus 35 F11
Botolph's Bridge
Kent. 55 F6
Bottacks Highld . . . 300 C4
Botternell Corn. 11 G11
Bottesford Leics . . . 154 B6
N Lincs 199 F11
Bottisham Cambs . . 123 E10
Bottlesford Wilts . . . 46 B6
Bottom Boat
W Yorks 197 C11
Bottomcraig Fife. . . 287 E7
Bottom House
Staffs. 169 E8
Bottomley
W Yorks 196 D5
Bottom of Hutton
Lancs 194 B3
Bottom o' th' Moor
Gtr Man 195 E7
Bottom Pond Kent. . . 53 B11
Bottoms Corn 1 E3
Cumb. 238 G5
Bottreaux Mill Devon. 26 B4
Bottrells Close Bucks .85 G7
Botts Green Warks. . 134 E4
Botusfleming Corn. . . 7 C8
Botwnnog Gwyn . . . 144 C5
Bough Beech Kent . . 52 D3
Boughrood Powys . . 96 D2
Boughrood Brest
Powys 96 D2
Boughspring Glos . . . 79 F9
Boughton Ches W . . 166 B6
Lincs 173 F10
Norf. 140 C3
Notts 171 B11
W Nhants. 120 D5
Boughton Aluph
Kent. 54 D4
Boughton Corner
Kent. 54 D4
Boughton Green
Kent. 53 C9
Boughton Heath
Ches W 166 B6
Boughton Lees Kent. . 54 D4
Boughton Malherbe
Kent. 53 D11
Boughton Monchelsea
Kent. 53 C9
Boughton Street
Kent. 54 B5
Bougton End
C Beds 103 D9
Boulby Redcar 226 B5
Bouldon Shrops. . . . 131 F10
Boulder Clough
W Yorks 196 C4
Bouldnor IoW 20 D3
Bouldon Shrops. . . . 131 F10
Boulmer Northumb . 265 G7
Boulsdon Glos. 98 G4
Boulston Pembs 73 C7
Boultenstone
Aberds 292 B6
Boultham Lincs 173 B7
Boultham Moor
Lincs 173 B7
Boulton Derbys 153 C7
Boulton Moor
Derbys 153 C7
Boundary Leics 152 F6
Staffs. 169 G7
Boundstone Sur. . . . 49 E10
Bountis Thorne
Devon 24 D5
Bourn Cambs 122 F6
Bournbrook
W Mid 133 G10
Bourne Lincs 155 E11
N Som 44 B3
Bourne End
Bedford. 121 E10
Bucks. 65 B11
C Beds 103 C9
Herts 85 D8
Bournemouth BCP. . . 19 C7
Bournes Green Glos . 80 E6
Southend. 70 B2
Worcs 117 C8
Bourne Vale
W Mid 133 D11
Bourne Valley BCP. . . 19 C7
Bournheath Worcs . . 117 C9
Bournmoor Durham . 243 G8
Bournside Glos 99 G8
Bournstream
Glos. 80 G2
Bournville W Mid. . . 133 G10
Bourton Bucks. 102 E4
Dorset 45 G9
N Som 59 G11
Oxon 63 B8
Shrops. 131 D11
Wilts 62 G4
Bourton on Dunsmore
Warks 119 C9
Bourton-on-the-Hill
Glos 100 D3
Bourton-on-the-Water
Glos 100 G3
Bourtreehill N Ayrs . . 257 B8
Bousd Argyll 288 C4
Bousta Shetland . . . 313 H4
Boustaead Hill Cumb . 239 F7
Bouth Cumb 210 B6
Bouthwaite N Yorks . 214 E2
Bouts Worcs 117 F10
Bovain Stirling 285 D9
Boveney Bucks. 66 D2
Boveridge Dorset . . . 31 E9
Boverton V Glam 58 F3

Bovey Tracey Devon. . 14 F2
Bovingdon Herts. 85 E8
Bovingdon Green
Bucks. 65 B10
Herts. 85 E8
Bovinger Essex 87 D8
Bovington Camp
Dorset 18 D2
Bow Borders 271 G7
Devon. 8 F6
Devon. 26 G2
Oxon 82 G4
Bowbank Durham . . 232 G4
Bowbeck Suff. 125 B8
Bow Brickhill
M Keynes. 103 E8
Bowbridge Glos. 80 D5
Bowbrook Shrops. . . 149 G9
Bow Broom S Yorks . 187 B7
Bowburn Durham . . 234 D2
Bowcombe IoW 20 D5
Bow Common
London. 67 C11
Bowd Devon 15 C8
Bowden Borders 262 C3
Devon. 8 F6
Dorset 30 C3
Bowden Hill Wilts. . . 62 F2
Bowdens Som 28 B6
Bowderdale Cumb . . 222 E3
Bowdon Gtr Man . . . 184 D3
Bower Highld. 310 C6
Northumb 251 G7
Bower Ashton Bristol. 60 E5
Bowerchalke Wilts. . 31 C8
Bower Heath Herts . . 85 B10
Bowerhill Wilts 62 G2
Bower Hinton Som . . 29 D7
Bowerhope Borders . 261 E7
Bowermadden
Highld 310 C6
Bowers Staffs. 150 B6
Bowers Gifford Essex. 69 B9
Bowershall Fife. . . . 279 C11
Bowertower Highld . 310 C6
Bowes Durham 223 C9
Bowes Park London. . 86 G4
Bowgreave Lancs . . 202 E5
Bowgreen Gtr Man . . 184 D3
Bowhill Borders . . . 261 D10
Fife 280 B4
Bowhouse Dumfries . 238 D2
Bowhousebog or Liquo
N Lanark 269 D7
Bowhouse Dumfries . 238 D2
Bowing Park Mers. . 182 D6
Bowismiln Borders . 262 E2
Bowithick Corn. 11 E9
Bowker's Green
Lancs 194 G2
Bowland Bridge
Cumb. 211 B8
Bowldown Wilts 62 D2
Bowlee Gtr Man 195 F10
Bowlees Durham . . . 232 F4
Bowley Hereford . . . 115 G10
Bowley Town
Hereford 115 G10
Bowlhead Green Sur. 50 F2
Bowling W Dunb . . . 277 G9
W Yorks 205 G9
Bowling Alley Hants. . 49 D9
Bowling Bank Wrex. . 166 F5
Bowling Green Corn . 5 D10
Glos. 81 D8
Hants. 19 B11
Shrops. 150 D2
W Mid 133 D8
Worcs 116 G6
Bowlish Som 44 E6
Bowmans Kent 68 E4
Bowmanstead Cumb . 220 F6
Bowmore Argyll 254 B4
Bowness-on-Solway
Cumb. 238 E6
Bowness-on-
Windermere Cumb .221 F8
Bow of Fife Fife. . . . 287 F7
Bowridge Hill Dorset. 30 B4
Bowrie-fauld Angus .287 C9
Bowsden Northumb. 273 G9
Bowsey Hill Windsor .65 C10
Bowshank Borders . 271 G9
Bowside Lodge
Highld 310 C2
Bowston Cumb. 221 F9
Bow Street Ceredig . 128 G2
Norf. 141 D10
Bowthorpe Norf 142 B3
Bowyer's Common
Hants. 34 B3
Box Glos 80 E5
Wilts 61 F10
Boxbush Glos. 80 C2
Glos. 98 G3
Box End Bedford . . . 103 B10
Boxford Suff. 107 C9
W Berks 64 E2
Boxgrove W Sus. 22 B6
Box Hill Sur. 51 C7
Wilts 61 F10
Boxley Kent 53 B9
Boxmoor Herts 85 D9
Box's Shop Corn 24 G2
Boxted Essex 107 E10
Suff. 124 G6
Boxted Cross
Essex. 107 E10
Boxted Heath
Essex. 107 E10
Box Trees W Mid . . . 118 C2
Boxwell Glos. 80 G4
Boxworth Cambs . . . 122 E6
Boxworth End
Cambs 123 D7

Boyatt Wood Hants . . 32 C6
Boyden End Suff. . . . 124 F4
Boyden Gate Kent. . . . 71 F7
Boyland Common
Norf. 141 G11
Boylestone Derbys . .152 B3
Boylestonfield
Derbys. 152 B3
Boyndie Aberds 302 C6
Boyn Hill Windsor . . . 65 C11
Boynton E Yorks . . . 218 F2
Boysack Angus 287 C10
Angus 287 C10
Boys Hill Dorset. 29 E11
Boys Village V Glam . 58 F4
Boythorpe Derbys. . 186 G5
Boyton Corn 12 C2
Suff. 109 B7
Wilts 46 F3
Boyton Cross Essex. .87 D10
Boyton End Essex. . .106 E2
Suff. 106 C4
Bozeat N Nhants . . . 121 F9
Bozen Green Herts. . 105 F8
Braaid IoM 192 E4
Braal Castle Highld. .310 C5
Brabling Green Suff. .126 E5
Brabourne Kent. 54 E5
Brabourne Lees Kent . 54 E5
Brabster Highld 310 C7
Bracadale Highld. . . 294 B5
Bracara Highld. 295 F9
Braceborough
Lincs 155 G11
Bracebridge Lincs . . 173 B7
Bracebridge Heath
Lincs 173 B7
Bracebridge Low Fields
Lincs 173 B7
Braceby Lincs 155 B10
Bracewell Lancs . . . 204 D3
Bracken Bank
W Yorks 204 F6
Brackenber Cumb . . 222 B4
Brackenbottom
N Yorks 212 E6
Brackenfield Derbys 170 D5
Brackenhall
W Mid 197 D7
Bracken Hill
W Mid 197 C7
Brackenlands
Cumb. 229 B11
Bracken Park
W Yorks 206 E3
Brackenthwaite
Cumb 229 B11
Cumb. 229 G10
N Yorks. 205 C11
Brackla = Bragle
Bridgend 58 C2
Bracklamore Aberds 303 D8
Bracklesham W Sus . 22 D4
Brackletter Highld . . 290 E3
Brackley Argyll 255 C8
W Nhants 101 D11
Brackloch Highld. . . 307 G6
Bracknell Brack. 65 F11
Braco Perth 286 G2
Bracobrae Moray . . . 302 D5
Braco Castle Perth . . 286 F2
Bracon N Lincs 199 F9
Bracon Ash Norf . . . 142 D3
Braco Park Aberds . . 303 C9
Bracorina Highld. . . 295 F9
Bradaford Devon. 12 C3
Bradbourne Derbys . 170 E2
Bradbury Durham . . 234 F2
Bradda IoM 192 F2
Bradden W Nhants . . 102 B2
Braddock Corn 6 C3
Braddocks Hay
Staffs. 168 D5
Bradeley Stoke. 168 E5
Bradeley Green
Ches E 167 G8
Bradenham Bucks . . 84 F4
Norf. 141 B8
Bradenstoke Wilts . . 62 D4
Brades Village
W Mid 133 F9
Bradfield Devon 27 F9
Essex 108 E2
Norf. 160 C5
W Berks 64 E6
Bradfield Combust
Suff. 125 F7
Bradfield Green
Ches E 167 D11
Bradfield Heath
Essex. 108 F2
Bradfield St Clare
Suff. 125 F8
Bradfield St George
Suff. 125 E8
Bradford Corn. 11 F8
Derbys. 170 C2
Devon. 24 F6
Gtr Man 184 B5
Northumb 264 C5
W Yorks 205 G9
Bradford Abbas
Dorset. 29 E9
Bradford Leigh
Wilts 61 G10
Bradford-on-Avon
Wilts 61 G10
Bradford-on-Tone
Som 27 C11
Bradford Peverell
Dorset. 17 C9
Bradgate S Yorks . . 186 C6
Bradiford Devon . . . 40 G5
Brading IoW 21 D8
Bradley Derbys 170 F2
Glos 80 G3
Hants. 48 E6
NE Lincs. 201 F8
Staffs. 151 F7
W Mid 133 D8
Wrex 166 E4
W Yorks 197 C7

Bradley Cross Som... 44 C3
Bradley Fold
Gtr Man......195 F9
Bradley Green
Ches W......167 F8
Glos......80 G2
Som......43 F9
Warks......134 C5
Worcs......117 E9
Bradley in the Moors
Staffs......169 G9
Bradley Mills
W Yorks......197 D7
Bradley Mount
Ches E......184 F6
Bradley Stoke S Glos..60 C6
Bradlow Hereford..98 D4
Bradmore Notts 153 C11
W Mid......133 D7
Bradney Shrops..132 D5
Som......43 F10
Bradninch Devon...27 G8
Bradnock's Marsh
W Mid......118 B4
Bradnop Staffs 169 D8
Bradnor Green
Hereford......114 F5
Bradpole Dorset...16 C5
Bradshaw Gtr Man..195 E8
W Yorks......196 E5
W Yorks......205 G7
Bradstone Devon...12 E3
Bradville M Keynes..102 C6
Bradwall Green
Ches E......168 C3
Bradway S Yorks..186 E4
Bradwell Derbys..185 E11
Devon......40 E3
Essex......106 G6
M Keynes......102 D6
Norf......143 C10
Staffs......168 F4
Bradwell Common
M Keynes......102 D6
Bradwell Grove Oxon..82 D2
Bradwell Hills
Derbys......185 E11
Bradwell on Sea
Essex......89 D8
Bradwell Waterside
Essex......89 D7
Bradworthy Devon..24 E4
Bradworthy Cross
Devon......24 E4
Brae Dumfries...237 B10
Highld......307 L3
Highld......309 J4
Shetland......312 G5
Braeantra Highld...300 B5
Braebuster Orkney..314 F5
Braedownie Angus..292 F4
Braeface Falk......278 E5
Braefield Highld...300 F4
Braefindon Highld..300 D6
Braegrum Perth...286 E4
Braehead Dumfries..236 B6
Orkney......314 B4
Orkney......314 F5
S Ayrs......257 C8
S Lanark......259 C8
S Lanark......267 D11
S Lanark......269 E9
Stirling......278 C4
Braehead of Lunan
Angus......287 B10
Braehoulland
Shetland......312 F4
Braehour Highld...310 D4
Braehungie Highld..310 F5
Braeintra Highld...295 B10
Braelangwell Lodge
Highld......309 K5
Braemar Aberds...292 D3
Braemore Highld..299 B11
Highld......310 F4
Brae of Achnahaird
Highld......307 H5
Brae of Boquhapple
Stirling......285 G10
Braepark Perth...280 F3
Brae Roy Lodge
Highld......290 D5
Braeside Inverclyd..276 F4
Braes of Enzie
Moray......302 D3
Braes of Ullapool
Highld......307 K6
Braeswick Orkney..314 C6
Braevallich Argyll..275 C10
Braewick Shetland..312 F4
Shetland......313 H5
Brafferton Darl...233 G11
N Yorks......215 E8
Brafield-on-the-Green
W Nhants......120 F6
Bragar W Isles...304 D4
Bragbury End Herts..104 G5
Bragenham Bucks..103 F8
Bragle = Brackla
Bridgend......58 D2
Bragleenmore
Argyll......289 G11
Braichmelyn Gwyn..163 B10
Braichyfedw Powys..129 E7
Braid Edin......280 G4
Braides Lancs......202 C4
Braidfauld Glasgow..268 C2
Braidley N Yorks..213 C10
Braids Argyll......255 C8
Braidwood S Lanark..268 F6
Braigh Chalasaigh
W Isles......296 D5
Braigo Argyll......274 G3
Brailsford Derbys..170 G3
Brailsford Green
Derbys......170 G3
Braingortan Argyll..275 F11
Brain's Green S Glos..79 D11
Brainshaugh
Northumb......252 C6
Braintree Essex..106 G5

Braiseworth Suff..126 C2
Braishfield Hants...32 B5
Braiswick Essex..107 F9
Braithwaite Cumb..229 G10
S Yorks......198 E6
W Yorks......204 E6
Braithwell S Yorks..187 C8
Brakefield Green
Norf......141 B10
Brakenhill W Yorks..198 D2
Bramber W Sus...35 E11
Brambledown
Dorset......30 G3
Brambridge Hants..33 C7
Bramcote Notts..153 B10
Warks......135 H8
Bramcote Hills
Notts......153 B10
Bramcote Mains
Warks......135 H8
Bramdean Hants...33 B10
Bramerton Norf..142 C5
Bramfield Herts...86 B3
Suff......127 C7
Bramford Suff...108 B2
W Mid......133 D8
Bramhall Gtr Man..184 D5
Bramhall Moor
Gtr Man......184 D6
Bramhall Park
Gtr Man......184 D5
Bramham W Yorks..206 E4
Bramhope
W Yorks......205 E11
Bramley Derbys..186 F6
Hants......48 B6
Sur......50 D4
S Yorks......187 C7
W Yorks......205 F10
Bramley Corner
Hants......48 B6
Bramley Green Hants..49 B7
Bramley Head
N Yorks......205 B8
Bramley Vale
Derbys......171 B7
Bramling Kent......55 B8
Brampford Speke
Devon......14 B4
Brampton Cambs..122 C4
Cumb......231 G9
Cumb......240 E2
Derbys......186 G5
Hereford......97 D8
Lincs......188 F4
Norf......160 E4
Suff......143 G8
S Yorks......198 G2
Brampton Abbotts
Hereford......98 F2
Brampton Ash
N Nhants......136 F5
Brampton Bryan
Hereford......115 C7
Brampton en le Morthen
S Yorks......187 D7
Brampton Park
Cambs......122 C4
Brampton Street
Suff......143 G8
Bramshall Staffs 151 C11
Bramshaw Hants...32 D3
Bramshill Hants...65 G8
Bramshott Hants...49 G10
Bramwell Som......28 B6
Branatwatt Shetland..313 H4
Branault Highld...289 C7
Branbridges Kent...53 D7
Brancaster Norf..176 E3
Brancaster Staithe
Norf......176 E3
Brancepeth
Durham......233 D10
Branch End
Northumb......242 D4
Branchill Moray...301 D10
Branchton Inverclyd..276 F4
Brand End Lincs..174 F5
Branderburgh
Moray......302 B2
Brandesburton
E Yorks......209 D8
Brandeston Suff..126 E4
Brand Green Glos..98 F4
Hereford......98 C5
Brandhill Shrops..115 B8
Brandis Corner
Devon......24 G6
Brandish Street Som..42 D2
Brandiston Norf..160 E2
Brandlingill Cumb..229 F8
Brandon Durham..233 D10
Lincs......172 F6
Northumb......264 F2
Suff......140 F5
Warks......119 B8
Brandon Bank
Cambs......140 F2
Brandon Creek Norf..140 E2
Brandon Parva
Norf......141 B11
Brandsby N Yorks..215 E11
Brands Hill Windsor..66 D4
Brandwood Shrops..149 D9
Brandwood End
W Mid......117 B11
Brandy Carr
W Yorks......197 C10
Brandy Hole Essex..88 F4
Brandyquoy Orkney..314 G4
Brandy Wharf Lincs..189 B8
Brane Corn......1 D4
Bran End Essex..106 F3
Branksome BCP...18 C6
Branksome Park BCP..19 C7
Bransbury Hants...48 E3
Bransby Lincs......188 F5
Branscombe Devon..15 D9
Bransford Worcs..116 G5
Bransgore Hants..19 B9
Branshill Clack...279 C7

Bransholme Hull...209 G8
Branson's Cross
Worcs......117 C11
Branston Leics..154 D6
Lincs......173 B8
Staffs......152 E4
Branston Booths
Lincs......173 B9
Branstone IoW......21 E7
Bransty Cumb......219 B9
Brant Broughton
Lincs......172 E6
Brantham Suff...108 E2
Branthwaite Cumb..229 D11
Cumb......229 G7
Branthwaite Edge
Cumb......229 G7
Brantingham
E Yorks......200 B2
Branton Northumb..264 F2
S Yorks......198 G6
Branton Green
N Yorks......215 G6
Branxholme
Borders......261 G11
Branxholm Park
Borders......261 G11
Branxton Northumb..263 B9
Brascote Leics..135 C8
Brassey Green
Ches W......167 C8
Brassington Derbys..170 E2
Brasted Kent......52 C3
Brasted Chart Kent..52 C3
Brathens Aberds..293 D8
Bratoft Lincs......175 B7
Brattle Kent......54 G2
Brattleby Lincs..188 E6
Bratton Som......42 D2
Telford......150 G2
Wilts......46 C2
Bratton Clovelly
Devon......12 C5
Bratton Fleming
Devon......40 F6
Bratton Seymour
Som......29 B11
Braughing Herts..105 F7
Braughing Friars
Herts......105 G8
Braulen Lodge
Highld......300 F2
Braunston
W Nhants......119 D10
Braunstone Leics..135 C11
Braunstone Town
Leicester......135 C11
Braunston-in-Rutland
Rutland......136 B6
Braunton Devon...40 F3
Brawby N Yorks..216 D4
Brawith N Yorks..225 D10
Brawl Highld......310 C2
Brawlbin Highld..310 D4
Bray Windsor......66 D2
Braybrooke
N Nhants......136 G5
Braydon Side Wilts..62 B4
Brayford Devon...41 G7
Brayfordhill Devon..41 G7
Bray Shop Corn...12 G2
Braystones Cumb..219 D10
Brayswick Worcs..98 B6
Braythorn N Yorks..205 D10
Brayton N Yorks..207 G8
Braytown Dorset...18 D2
Bray Wick Windsor..65 D11
Braywoodside
Windsor......65 D11
Brazacott Corn...11 C11
Brazenhill Staffs..151 E7
Brea Corn......4 G3
Breach Bath......60 G6
Kent......69 F10
Som......22 B3
Breacacha Castle
Argyll......288 D3
Breachwood Green
Herts......104 G2
Breacleit W Isles..304 E3
Breaden Heath
Shrops......149 B8
Breadsall Derbys..153 B7
Breadsall Hilltop
Derby......153 B7
Breadstone Glos..80 E2
Bread Street Glos..80 D4
Breage Corn......2 D4
Breakachy Highld..300 E4
Brealeys Devon...25 D8
Bream Glos......79 D10
Breamore Hants..31 D11
Bream's Meend Glos..79 D9
Brean Som......43 B9
Breanais W Isles..304 F11
Brearley W Yorks..196 B4
Brearton N Yorks..214 G6
Breascleit W Isles..304 E4
Breaston Derbys..153 C9
Brechfa Carms..93 E10
Brechin Angus..293 G7
Breckan Orkney..314 F2
Breckles Norf..141 E9
Breck of Cruan
Orkney......314 E3
Breckrey Highld..298 C5
Brecks S Yorks..187 C7
Brecon Powys..95 F10
Bredbury Gtr Man..184 C6
Bredbury Green
Gtr Man......184 C6
Brede E Sus......38 D4
Bredenbury
Hereford......116 F2
Bredfield Suff...126 G5
Bredgar Kent......69 G11
Bredhurst Kent...69 G9
Bredicot Worcs..117 G8
Bredon Worcs......99 D8
Bredon's Hardwick
Worcs......99 D8

Bredon's Norton
Worcs......99 D8
Bredwardine
Hereford......96 C6
Breedon on the Hill
Leics......153 E8
Breeds Essex..87 C11
Breedy Butts Lancs..202 E2
Breibhig W Isles..297 M2
W Isles......304 E6
Breich W Loth..269 C8
Breightmet Gtr Man..195 F8
Breighton E Yorks..207 G10
Breinton Hereford..97 D9
Breinton Common
Hereford......97 C9
Brelston Green
Hereford......97 G11
Bremhill Wilts......62 E3
Bremhill Wick Wilts..62 E3
Bremirehoull
Shetland......313 L6
Brenachoile Lodge
Stirling......285 G8
Brenchley Kent...53 E7
Brenchoillie Argyll..284 G4
Brendon Devon...24 E5
Devon......24 F5
Devon......41 D9
Brenkley T&W..242 B6
Brent Corn......6 E4
Brent Cross London..67 B8
Brent Eleigh Suff..107 B8
Brentford London..67 D7
Brentford End
London......67 D7
Brentingby Leics..154 F5
Brent Knoll Som..43 C10
Brent Mill Devon...8 D3
Brent Pelham Herts..105 E8
Brentry Bristol......60 D5
Brentwood Essex..87 G9
Brenzett Kent......39 B8
Brenzett Green Kent..39 B8
Brereton Staffs..151 F11
Brereton Cross
Staffs......151 F11
Brereton Green
Ches E......168 C3
Brereton Heath
Ches E......168 C4
Breretonhill Staffs..151 F11
Bressingham Norf..141 G11
Bressingham Common
Norf......141 G11
Bretby Derbys..152 E5
Bretford Warks..119 B8
Bretforton Worcs..99 C11
Bretherdale Head
Cumb......221 E11
Bretherton Lancs..194 C3
Brettabister
Shetland......313 H6
Brettenham Norf..141 G8
Suff......125 G9
Bretton Derbys..186 F2
Flint......166 C5
Pboro......138 C3
Brewer's End
Essex......105 G11
Brewers Green Norf..142 G2
Brewer Street Sur..51 C11
Brewlands Bridge
Angus......292 G3
Brewood Staffs..133 B7
Briach Moray..301 D10
Briants Puddle
Dorset......18 C2
Briar Hill W Nhants..120 F4
Brick End Essex..105 F11
Brickendon Herts..86 D4
Bricket Wood Herts..85 E10
Brickfields Worcs..117 F7
Brickhill Bedford..121 G11
Brick Hill Sur......66 G3
Brick House End
Essex......105 F9
Brickhouses Ches E..168 C3
Brick Houses
S Yorks......186 E4
Brick-kiln End
Notts......171 D9
Brickkiln Green
Essex......106 E4
Bricklehampton
Worcs......99 C9
Bride IoM..192 B5
Bridekirk Cumb..229 E8
Bridell Pembs..92 C3
Bridestowe Devon..12 D6
Brideswell Aberds..302 F5
Bridford Devon...14 D2
Bridfordmills Devon..14 D2
Bridge Corn......2 D6
Corn......4 G3
Kent......55 C7
Som......28 F5
Bridge Ball Devon..41 D8
Bridge End
Bedford......121 G10
Cumb......230 B3
Devon......8 F3
Durham......232 D6
Essex......106 E3
Flint......166 D4
Hereford......98 B2
Lincs......156 B2
Northumb......241 D10
Northumb......241 E10
Oxon......83 G9
Bridge-End
Shetland......313 K5
Bridge End Sur..50 B5
Warks......118 E5
Worcs......98 E6
Bridgefoot Aberds..292 C6
Angus......287 D7
Cumb......229 F7
Bridge Green Essex..105 D9
Norf......142 G2
Bridgehampton Som..29 C9

Bridge Hewick
N Yorks......214 E6
Bridgehill Durham..242 E3
Bridge Ho Argyll..254 B4
Bridgeholm Green
Derbys......185 E8
Bridgehouse Gate
N Yorks......214 F3
Bridgelands
Borders......261 C11
Bridgemary Hants..33 G9
Bridgemere Ches E..168 F2
Bridgemont Derbys..185 E8
Bridgend Aberds..293 B7
Aberds......302 F5
Angus......293 G7
Argyll......255 D8
Argyll......274 G4
Argyll......275 D9
Corn......6 D2
Cumb......221 C7
Devon......7 F11
Fife......287 F7
Glos......80 E4
Highld......300 D3
Inverclyd......276 F5
Moray......302 F3
N Lanark......278 G3
Pembs......92 B3
W Loth......279 F10
Bridgend = Pen-y-Bont
ar-ogwr Bridgend..58 C2
Bridgend of Lintrathen
Angus......286 B6
Bridgeness Falk..279 E10
Bridge of Alford
Aberds......293 B7
Bridge of Allan
Stirling......278 B5
Bridge of Avon
Moray......301 F11
Moray......301 G11
Bridge of Awe
Argyll......284 E4
Bridge of Balgie
Perth......285 C9
Bridge of Cally
Perth......286 B5
Bridge of Canny
Aberds......293 D8
Bridge of Craigisla
Angus......286 B6
Bridge of Dee
Dumfries......237 D9
Bridge of Don
Aberdeen......293 B11
Bridge of Dun
Angus......287 B10
Bridge of Dye
Aberds......293 E8
Bridge of Earn
Perth......286 F5
Bridge of Ericht
Perth......285 B9
Bridge of Feugh
Aberds......293 D9
Bridge of Forss
Highld......310 C4
Bridge of Gairn
Aberds......292 D5
Bridge of Gaur
Perth......285 B9
Bridge of Lyon
Perth......285 C11
Bridge of Muchalls
Aberds......293 D10
Bridge of Muick
Aberds......292 D5
Bridge of Oich
Highld......290 C5
Bridge of Orchy
Argyll......284 D6
Bridge of Waith
Orkney......314 E2
Bridge of Walls
Shetland......313 H4
Bridge of Weir
Renfs......267 C7
Bridge Reeve Devon..25 E11
Bridgerule Devon...24 G3
Bridges Corn......5 D10
Shrops......131 D7
Bridge Sollers
Hereford......97 C8
Bridge Street Suff..107 B7
Bridgeton Glasgow..268 C2
Bridgetown Corn...12 D2
Devon......8 C6
Som......42 G2
Staffs......133 B9
Bridge Town Warks..118 G4
Bridge Trafford
Ches W......183 G7
Bridge Yate S Glos..61 E7
Bridgham Norf..141 F9
Bridgnorth Shrops..132 E4
Bridgtown Staffs..133 B9
Bridgwater Som...43 F10
Bridlington E Yorks..218 F3
Bridport Dorset...16 C5
Bridstow Hereford..97 G11
Brierfield Lancs..204 F2
Brierholme Carr
S Yorks......199 E7
Brierley Glos......79 C10
Hereford......115 F9
S Yorks......198 E2
Brierley Hill W Mid..133 F8
Brierton Hrtlpl..234 E5
Briery Cumb..229 G11
Briery Hill Bl Gwent..77 D11
Briestfield W Yorks..197 D8
Brigflatts Cumb..222 G2
Brigg N Lincs..200 F3
N Lincs......200 F4
Briggate Norf..160 D6
Briggswath N Yorks..227 D7
Brigham Cumb..229 E7
Cumb......229 F7
E Yorks......209 C7
Brighouse W Yorks..196 C6
Brighstone IoW...20 E4

Brightgate Derbys..170 D3
Brighthampton Oxon..82 E5
Brightholmlee
S Yorks......186 B3
Brightley Devon...13 B7
Brightling E Sus...37 C11
Brightlingsea Essex..89 B9
Brighton Brighton..36 G4
Corn......5 E8
Brighton Hill Hants..48 D6
Brighton le Sands
Mers......182 B4
Brightons Falk..279 F8
Brightside S Yorks..186 D5
Brightwalton
W Berks......64 D2
Brightwalton Green
W Berks......64 D2
Brightwalton Holt
W Berks......64 D2
Brightwell Suff..108 C4
Brightwell Baldwin
Oxon......83 F11
Brightwell cum Sotwell
Oxon......83 G9
Brigmerston Wilts..47 D7
Brignall Durham..223 C11
Brig o'Turk Stirling..285 G9
Brigsley NE Lincs..201 G9
Brigsteer Cumb..211 B9
Brigstock N Nhants..137 F8
Brill Bucks..83 C11
Corn......2 D6
Brilley Hereford..96 B5
Brilley Mountain
Powys......114 G5
Brimaston Pembs..91 G8
Brimfield Hereford..115 D7
Brimington Derbys..186 G6
Brimington Common
Derbys......186 G6
Brimley Devon...13 F11
Brimpsfield Glos..80 C6
Brimps Hill Glos..79 B11
Brimpton W Berks..64 G5
Brimpton Common
W Berks......64 G5
Brims Orkney..314 H2
Brims Castle Highld..310 B4
Brimscombe Glos..80 E5
Brimstage Mers..182 E4
Brinacory Highld..295 F9
Brincliffe S Yorks..186 E4
Brind E Yorks..207 G10
Brindham Som......44 E4
Brindister Shetland..313 H4
Shetland......313 K6
Brindle Lancs..194 C6
Brindle Heath
Gtr Man......195 G10
Brindley Ches E..167 E9
Brindley Ford Stoke..168 E5
Brindwoodgate
Derbys......186 F4
Brineton Staffs..150 G6
Bringewood Forge
Hereford......115 C9
Bringhurst Leics..136 E6
Bringsty Common
Hereford......116 F4
Brington Cambs..121 B11
Brinian Orkney..314 D4
Briningham Norf..159 C10
Brinkhill Lincs..190 G5
Brinkley Cambs..124 G2
Notts......172 E2
Brinkley Hill
Hereford......97 E11
Brinklow M Keynes..103 D8
Warks......119 B8
Brinkworth Wilts..62 C4
Brinmore Highld..300 G6
Brinnington
Gtr Man......184 C6
Brinscall Lancs..194 C6
Brinsea N Som..60 G2
Brinsford Staffs..133 B8
Brinsley Notts..171 F7
Brinsop Hereford..97 C8
Brinsop Common
Hereford......97 C8
Brinsworth S Yorks..186 D6
Brinsworthy Devon..41 G7
Brinton Norf..159 C10
Brisco Cumb..239 G10
Briscoe Cumb..219 C10
N Yorks......205 C11
Brisley Norf..159 E8
Brislington Bristol..60 E6
Brissenden Green
Kent......54 F2
Bristnall Fields
W Mid......133 F9
Bristol Bristol......60 E5
Briston Norf..159 C11
Britain Bottom
S Glos......61 B9
Britannia Lancs..195 C11
Britford Wilts..31 B11
Brithdir Caerph..77 E11
Ceredig......92 B6
Gwyn......146 F5
Brithem Bottom
Devon......27 E8
British Torf......78 E2
Briton Ferry = Llansawel
Neath......57 C7
Britten's Bath..45 B7
Britwell Slough..66 C3
Britwell Salome
Oxon......83 G11
Brixham Torbay...9 D8
Brixton Devon...7 E11
London......67 D10
Brixton Deverill
Wilts......45 F11
Brixworth W Nhants..120 C4
Brize Norton Oxon..82 D6
Broad Alley Worcs..117 D7

Broad Blunsdon
Swindon......81 G11
Broadbottom
Gtr Man......185 C7
Broadbridge W Sus..22 B6
Broadbridge Heath
W Sus......50 G6
Broadbury Devon..12 D5
Broadbush Swindon..81 G11
Broad Campden
Glos......100 D3
Broad Carr W Yorks..196 D5
Broad Chalke Wilts..31 B8
Broad Clough
Lancs......195 C11
Broadclyst Devon..14 B5
Broad Colney Herts..85 E11
Broad Common
Worcs......117 D7
Broadfield
Gtr Man......195 E10
Inverclyd......276 G6
Lancs......194 C4
Lancs......195 B8
Pembs......73 E10
W Sus......51 G9
Broadford Highld..295 C8
Sur......50 D3
Broad Ford Kent..53 F8
Broadford Bridge
W Sus......35 C9
Broadgate Hants..32 C6
Broadgrass Green
Suff......125 E9
Broad Green Cambs..124 F3
C Beds......103 C9
Essex......105 D8
Essex......107 G7
London......67 G10
Mers......182 C6
Suff......124 F5
Suff......125 F11
Worcs......116 F5
Worcs......117 C9
Broadgreen Wood
Herts......86 D4
Broadhalgh
Gtr Man......195 E11
Broadham Green
Sur......51 C11
Broadhaugh
Borders......249 B10
Broadhaven Highld..310 D7
Broad Haven = Aberllydan
Pembs......72 C5
Broadheath
Gtr Man......184 D3
Broad Heath Powys..114 E6
Worcs......116 C3
Broadheath
Worcs......116 F5
Broadhembury
Devon......27 G10
Broadhempston Devon..8 B6
Broad Hill Cambs..123 B11
Broad Hinton Wilts..62 D6
Broadholm Derbys..170 F4
Broadholme Derbys..170 F5
Lincs......188 G5
Broad Ings E Yorks..208 C2
Broadland Row
E Sus......38 D4
Broadlands Devon..14 G3
Broadlane Corn......2 C4
Broad Lane Corn......4 G3
Broad Lanes Shrops..132 F5
Broadlay Carms..74 C5
Broad Laying Hants..64 G2
Broadley Lancs..195 D11
Moray......302 C3
Broadley Common
Essex......86 D6
Broadleys Aberds..303 E11
Broad Marston
Worcs......100 B2
Broadmayne Dorset..17 D10
Broad Meadow
Staffs......168 F4
Broadmeadows
Borders......261 C10
Broadmere Hants..48 D6
Broadmoor Pembs..73 D9
Sur......50 D6
Broadmoor Common
Hereford......98 D2
Broadmoor Green
Worcs......116 C5
Broadoak Dorset...16 B4
Glos......80 C2
Hants......33 E8
Shrops......149 F9
Wrex......166 D5
Broad Oak Carms..93 G11
Cumb......220 G2
Dorset......30 E3
E Sus......37 C10
E Sus......38 D4
Hants......49 C9
Hereford......97 G9
Kent......71 G7
Mers......183 B8
Shrops......132 F5
Broadoak End Herts..86 C4
Broadoak Park
Gtr Man......195 G10
Broad Parkham
Devon......24 C5
Broadplat Oxon..65 C8
Broadrashes Moray..302 D4
Broadrock Glos..79 F8
Broadsands Torbay..9 D7
Broadsea Aberds..303 C9
Broad's Green
Essex......87 C11
Wilts......62 E3
Broadshard Som..28 E6
Broadstairs Kent..71 F11
Broadstone BCP...18 B6
Kent......53 D11
Mon......79 E8
Shrops......131 F10

Broad Street E Sus..38 D5
Kent......53 B10
Kent......54 E6
Kent......55 E7
Medway......69 E9
Suff......107 C9
Wilts......46 B6
Broadstreet Common
Newport......59 C11
Broad Street Green
Essex......88 D5
Broad Tenterden
Kent......53 G11
Broad Town Wilts..62 D5
Broadwas Worcs..116 B6
Broadwater Herts..104 G4
W Sus......35 G11
Broadwater Down
Kent......52 F5
Broadwaters Worcs..116 B6
Broadwath Cumb..239 F11
Broadway Carms..74 D3
Carms......74 D5
Pembs......72 C5
Som......28 D4
Suff......127 B7
Worcs......99 D11
Broadway Lands
Hereford......97 E11
Broadwell Glos..79 C9
Glos......100 F4
Oxon......82 E3
Warks......119 D9
Broadwey Dorset......17 E9
Broadwindsor Dorset..28 G6
Broadwood Kelly
Devon......25 F10
Broadwoodwidger
Devon......12 D4
Brobury Hereford..96 C6
Brochel Highld..298 E5
Brochroy Argyll..284 D4
Brock Lancs..202 E6
Brockamin Worcs..116 G5
Brockbridge Hants..33 D10
Brockdish Norf..126 B4
Brockencote Worcs..117 C7
Brockenhurst Hants..32 G4
Brocketsbrae
S Lanark......259 B8
Brockfield Devon..28 F4
Brockford Green
Suff......126 D2
Brockford Street
Suff......126 D2
Brockhall W Nhants..120 E2
Brockhall Village
Lancs......203 F10
Brockham Sur..51 D7
Brockham End Bath..61 F8
Brockham Park Sur..51 D8
Brockhampton Glos..99 F8
Glos......99 G10
Hants......22 B2
Hereford......97 E11
Brockhampton Green
Dorset......30 F2
Brockhill Borders..261 E9
Brock Hill Essex..88 F2
Brockholes W Yorks..197 E7
Brockhollands Glos..79 D10
Brockhurst Derbys..170 C4
Hants......33 G10
Warks......135 G9
Brocklebank Cumb..230 C2
Brockleyhirst
Dumfries......238 C3
Brockley Lincs..200 E6
Brockley London..67 E11
N Som......60 F3
Brockley Corner
Suff......124 C6
Brockley Green Suff..106 B4
Suff......124 G6
Brockleymoor
Cumb......230 D5
Brockloch Dumfries..246 D2
Brockmanton
Hereford......115 F10
Brockmoor W Mid..133 F8
Brockscombe Devon..12 C5
Brock's Green Hants..64 G4
Brock's Watering
Norf......142 E2
Brockton Shrops..130 C6
Shrops......130 F6
Shrops......131 E11
Shrops......132 C4
Shrops......150 C6
Staffs......150 F4
Telford......150 F4
Brockweir Glos..79 E8
Brockwell Som..42 E2
Brockwood Hants..33 B10
Brockworth Glos..80 B5
Brocton Corn......5 B10
Staffs......151 F9
Brodick N Ayrs..256 B2
Brodie Moray..301 D9
Brodiesord Aberds..302 C5
Brodsworth S Yorks..198 F4
Brogaig Highld..298 C4
Brogborough
C Beds......103 D9
Broke Hall Suff..108 C3
Brokenborough
Wilts......62 B2
Broken Cross
Ches E......184 G5
Ches W......183 G11
Broken Green Herts..105 G8
Brokerswood Wilts..45 C10
Brokes N Yorks..224 F3
Bromborough Mers..182 E4
Bromborough Pool
Mers......182 E4
Bromdon Shrops..132 G2
Brome Suff......126 B2
Bromesberrow Glos..98 E4

Bromesberrow Heath
Glos 98 E4
Brome Street Suff 126 B3
Bromeswell Suff 126 G6
Bromfield Cumb 229 B9
Shrops 115 B9
Bromford W Mid 134 E2
Bromham Bedford 121 G10
Wilts 62 F3
Bromley Herts 105 G8
London 67 C11
London 68 F2
Shrops 132 D4
Shrops 149 D8
S Yorks 186 B4
W Mid 133 F8
Bromley Common
London 68 F2
Bromley Cross
Essex 107 F11
Gtr Man 195 E8
Bromley Green Kent 54 F3
Bromley Hall Staffs 150 C5
Bromley Heath
S Glos 61 D7
Bromley Park
London 67 F11
Bromley Wood
Staffs 152 E2
Bromlow Shrops 130 C6
Brompton London 67 D9
Medway 69 F9
N Yorks 217 C8
N Yorks 225 F7
Shrops 131 B10
Brompton-by-Sawdon
N Yorks 217 C8
Brompton-on-Swale
N Yorks 224 F4
Brompton Ralph Som 42 G5
Brompton Regis Som 42 G3
Bromsash Hereford 98 G2
Bromsberrow Heath
Glos 98 E4
Bromsgrove Worcs 117 C9
Bromstead Common
Staffs 150 F6
Bromstead Heath
Staffs 150 F6
Bromstone Kent 71 F11
Bromyard Hereford 116 G3
Bromyard Downs
Hereford 116 F3
Bronaber Gwyn 146 C4
Broncroft Shrops 131 F10
Brondesbury London 67 C8
Brondesbury Park
London 67 C8
Broneirion Powys 129 F10
Brongest Ceredig 92 B6
Brongwyn Ceredig 92 C5
Bronington Wrex 149 B9
Bronllys Powys 96 D2
Bronnant Ceredig 112 D2
Bronwydd Ceredig 93 C7
Bronwydd Arms
Carms 93 G8
Bronydd Powys 96 B4
Bronygarth Shrops 148 B5
Brook Carms 74 D3
Devon 12 G5
Devon 14 C2
Hants 32 B4
Hants 32 E3
IoW 20 E3
Kent 54 E5
Sur 50 D5
Sur 50 F2
Brook Bottom
Gtr Man 185 D7
Gtr Man 196 G3
Lancs 202 E6
Brooke Norf 142 D5
Rutland 136 B6
Brookenby Lincs 190 B2
Brookend Glos 79 E11
Glos 79 F9
Oxon 100 G6
Brook End Bedford 121 E11
Cambs 121 C11
C Beds 104 B3
Herts 104 F6
M Keynes 103 C8
Wilts 61 C10
Worcs 99 B7
Brookfield Derbys 185 B8
Lancs 203 G7
Mbro 225 B9
Renfs 267 C8
Brookfoot W Yorks 196 C6
Brookgreen IoW 20 E3
Brook Green London 67 D8
Suff 125 F7
Brookhampton
Oxon 83 F10
Shrops 131 E11
Som 29 B10
Brook Hill Hants 32 E3
Notts 153 C11
Brookhouse
Blackburn 195 B7
Ches E 184 F6
Denb 165 B9
Lancs 211 G10
S Yorks 187 D8
W Yorks 196 B5
Brookhouse Green
Ches E 168 C4
Brookhouses
Derbys 185 D8
Staffs 169 G7
Brookhurst Mers 182 E4
Brookland Kent 39 B7
Brooklands
Dumfries 237 B10
Gtr Man 184 C3
Shrops 167 G8
Sur 66 G5
W Yorks 206 F2
Brookleigh Devon 14 B5
Brookmans Park
Herts 86 E2
Brookpits W Sus 35 G8
Brook Place Sur 66 G3
Brookrow Shrops 116 C2
Brooks Corn 6 C3
Powys 130 D2
Brooksbottoms
Gtr Man 195 D9
Brooksby Leics 154 F3
Brooks End Kent 71 F9
Brooks Green
W Sus 35 C10
Brookside Brack 66 E2
Derbys 186 G5
Telford 132 B3
Brook Street Essex 87 G9
Kent 52 D5
Kent 54 G2
Suff 106 B6
W Sus 36 B4
Brookthorpe Glos 80 C4
Brookvale Halton 183 E8
Brookville Norf 140 D4
Brook Waters Wilts 30 C6
Brookwood Sur 50 B2
Broom C Beds 104 C3
Cumb 231 G9
Devon 28 G4
E Renf 267 D10
Pembs 73 D10
S Yorks 186 C5
Warks 117 G11
Broombank Worcs 116 C3
Broome Norf 143 E7
Shrops 131 D10
Shrops 131 G8
Worcs 117 B8
Broomedge Warr 184 D2
Broome Park
Northumb 264 G4
Broomer's Corner
W Sus 35 C10
Broomershill W Sus 35 D9
Broomfield Aberds 303 F9
Cumb 230 B2
Essex 88 D2
Kent 53 C10
Kent 71 F7
Som 43 G8
Wilts 61 D11
Broomfields Shrops 149 F8
Broomfleet
E Yorks 199 B11
Broom Green Norf 159 E9
Broomhall Ches E 167 F10
Windsor 66 F3
Broomhall Green
Ches E 167 F10
Broomham E Sus 23 C8
Broomhaugh
Northumb 242 E2
Broomhill Borders 261 D11
Bristol 60 D6
Ches W 167 B7
Highld 301 G9
Kent 55 B8
Norf 140 C2
Northumb 252 C6
Notts 171 F8
S Yorks 198 G2
Broom Hill Bristol 60 E6
Dorset 31 G8
Durham 242 G4
London 68 F3
Suff 108 B5
Worcs 117 B8
Broomhill Bank Kent 52 E5
Broomholm Norf 160 C6
Broomhouse
Glasgow 268 C3
Broomlands N Ayrs 257 B8
Broomley Northumb 242 E2
Broompark
Durham 233 C10
Broomridge Stirling 278 C6
Broom's Barn Suff 124 D5
Broom's Green Glos 98 E4
Broomsgrove E Sus 38 E4
Broomsthorpe Norf 158 D6
Broom Street Kent 70 G4
Broomton Highld 301 B8
Broomy Hill Hereford 97 D9
Broomy Lodge Hants 32 E2
Broomyshaw Staffs 169 F9
Brora Highld 311 J3
Broseley Shrops 132 C3
Brotherhouse Bar
Lincs 156 G5
Brotheridge Green
Worcs 98 C6
Brotherlee Durham 232 D4
Brotherstone
Borders 262 B4
Brothertoft Lincs 174 F3
Brotherton N Yorks 198 B3
Brothybeck Cumb 230 C2
Brotton Redcar 226 B3
Broubster Highld 310 C4
Brough Cumb 222 C5
Derbys 185 E11
E Yorks 200 B2
Highld 310 B6
Notts 172 D4
Orkney 314 E3
Orkney 314 H4
Shetland 312 C7
Shetland 312 F6
Shetland 312 F7
Shetland 313 G7
Shetland 313 H6
Shetland 313 J7
Broughall Shrops 167 G9
Brough Lodge
Shetland 312 D7
Brough Sowerby
Cumb 222 C5
Broughton Borders 260 B4
Bucks 84 C4
Cambs 122 B5
Edin 280 F5
Broughton *continued*
Flint 166 C4
Hants 47 G10
Lancs 202 F6
M Keynes 103 C7
N Lincs 200 F3
N Nhants 120 B6
N Yorks 204 C4
N Yorks 216 E5
Orkney 314 B4
Oxon 101 D8
Shrops 132 E6
Staffs 150 C5
V Glam 58 E2
Broughton Astley
Leics 135 E10
Broughton Beck
Cumb 210 C5
Broughton Common
N Lincs 200 E3
Wilts 61 G11
Broughton Cross
Cumb 229 E7
Broughton Gifford
Wilts 61 G11
Broughton Green
Worcs 117 E9
Broughton Hackett
Worcs 117 G8
Broughton in Furness
Cumb 210 B4
Broughton Lodges
Leics 154 E4
Broughton Mills
Cumb 220 G4
Broughton Moor
Cumb 228 E6
Broughton Park
Gtr Man 195 G10
Broughton Poggs
Oxon 82 E2
Broughtown Orkney 314 B6
Broughty Ferry
Dundee 287 D8
Brow Edge Cumb 211 C7
Browhouses
Dumfries 239 D7
Browland Shetland 313 H4
Brown Bank
N Yorks 205 C10
Brownber Cumb 222 D4
Brownbread Street
E Sus 23 B11
Brown Candover
Hants 48 F5
Brownedge Ches E 168 C3
Brown Edge Lancs 193 E11
Mers 183 C8
Staffs 168 E6
Brownheath Devon 27 D10
Shrops 149 D9
Brown Heath
Ches W 167 B7
Hants 33 D8
Brownheath Common
Worcs 117 E7
Brownhill Aberds 302 E6
Aberds 303 E8
Blackburn 203 G9
Shrops 149 E8
Brownhills Fife 287 F9
Shrops 150 B3
W Mid 133 B10
Brownieside
Northumb 264 E5
Browninghill Green
Hants 48 B5
Brown Knowl
Ches W 167 E7
Brown Lees Staffs 168 D5
Brownlow Ches E 168 C4
Mers 194 G4
Brownlow Fold
Gtr Man 195 E8
Brownlow Heath
Ches E 168 C4
Brown Moor
W Yorks 206 G3
Brownmuir Aberds 293 F9
Brown's Bank
Ches E 167 G10
Brown's End Glos 98 E4
Brown's Green
W Mid 133 E10
Brownshill Glos 80 E5
Brownshill Green
W Mid 134 G6
Brownside Lancs 204 G3
Brownsover Warks 119 B10
Brownston Devon 8 E3
Brown Street Suff 125 E11
Browns Wood
M Keynes 103 D8
Browsburn
N Lanark 268 C5
Browston Green
Norf 143 C9
Browtop Cumb 229 G7
Broxa N Yorks 227 G8
Broxbourne Herts 86 D5
Broxburn E Loth 282 F3
W Loth 279 G11
Broxfield Northumb 264 F6
Broxholme Lincs 188 F6
Broxted Essex 105 F11
Broxton Ches W 167 E7
Broxtowe
Nottingham 171 G8
Broxwood Hereford 115 G7
Broyle Side E Sus 23 C7
Brù W Isles 304 D5
Bruairnis W Isles 297 L3
Bruan Highld 310 F7
Bruar Lodge Perth 291 F10
Brucefield Fife 280 D2
Brucehill W Dunb 277 F7
Bruche Warr 183 D10
Brucklebog Aberds 293 D9
Bruera Ches W 166 C6
Bruern Abbey Oxon 100 G5
Bruichladdich
Argyll 274 G3
Bruisyard Suff 126 D6
Brumby N Lincs 199 F11
Brunant Powys 130 B5
Brund Staffs 169 C10
Brundall Norf 142 B6
Brundish Norf 143 D7
Suff 126 D5
Brundish Street
Suff 126 C5
Brundon Suff 107 C7
Brunery Highld 289 B9
Brunnion Corn 2 B2
Brunshaw Lancs 204 G3
Brunstane Edin 280 G6
Brunstock Cumb 239 F10
Brunswick Gtr Man 184 B4
Brunswick Park
London 86 G3
Brunswick Village
T&W 242 C6
Bruntcliffe W Yorks 197 B9
Brunt Hamersland
Shetland 313 H6
Brunthwaite
W Yorks 205 D7
Bruntingthorpe
Leics 136 F2
Brunton Fife 287 E7
Northumb 264 E6
Wilts 47 B8
Brushes Gtr Man 185 B7
Brushfield Derbys 185 G11
Brushford Devon 25 F11
Som 26 B6
Bruton Som 45 G7
Bryans Midloth 270 C6
Bryan's Green
Worcs 117 D7
Bryanston Dorset 30 F5
Bryant's Bottom
Bucks 84 F5
Brydekirk Dumfries 238 C5
Bryher Scilly 1 G3
Brymbo Conwy 180 G4
Wrex 166 E3
Brympton Som 29 D8
Brympton D'Evercy
Som 29 D8
Bryn Caerph 77 F11
Carms 75 E8
Ches W 183 G10
Gtr Man 194 G5
Gwyn 179 G9
Neath 57 C10
Powys 130 C3
Rhondda 76 D6
Shrops 130 F5
Swansea 56 C4
Brynafan Ceredig 112 C4
Brynamman Carms 76 C2
Brynawel Caerph 77 G11
Brynberian Pembs 92 D2
Brynbryddan Neath 57 C9
Neath 57 C9
Bryn Bwbach Gwyn 146 B2
Bryncae Rhondda 58 C3
Rhondda 58 C3
Bryn Celyn
Anglesey 179 F10
Flint 181 F11
Bryncethin Bridgend 58 C2
Bridgend 58 C2
Bryncir Gwyn 163 G7
Bryncoch Bridgend 58 C2
Bryn-coch Neath 57 B8
Bryn Common Flint 166 D3
Bryncroes Gwyn 144 C4
Bryncrug Gwyn 128 C2
Brynderwen Powys 130 D3
Bryndu Carms 75 D8
Bryn Du Anglesey 178 G4
Bryn Dulas Conwy 180 F6
Bryneglwys Denb 165 F10
Bryn Eglwys Gwyn 163 B10
Brynford Flint 181 G11
Bryn Gates Gtr Man 194 G5
Brynglas Newport 59 B10
Bryn-glas Conwy 164 B4
Brynglas Sta Gwyn 128 C2
Bryn Golau Rhondda 58 B3
Bryngwran Anglesey 178 F4
Bryngwyn Ceredig 92 B5
Mon 78 D5
Powys 96 B3
Brynhenllan Pembs 91 D10
Bryn-henllan Pembs 91 D10
Brynheulog
Bridgend 57 C11
Brynhoffnant
Ceredig 110 G6
Bryniau Denb 181 E9
Bryning Lancs 194 B2
Brynithel Bl Gwent 78 E2
Bryn-Iwan Carms 92 E6
Brynllywarch Powys 130 F3
Brynmawr Bl Gwent 77 C11
Bryn-mawr Gwyn 144 C4
Bryn Mawr Powys 148 F5
Brynmenyn Bridgend 58 B2
Brynmill Swansea 56 C6
Brynmorfudd Conwy 164 C4
Bryn Myrddin Carms 93 G8
Brynna Rhondda 58 C3
Bryn-nantllech
Conwy 164 B6
Brynnau Gwynion
Rhondda 58 C3
Bryn-newydd
Denb 165 G11
Bryn Offa Wrex 166 F4
Brynore Shrops 149 B7
Bryn-penarth
Powys 130 C2
Bryn Pen-y-lan
Wrex 166 G4
Bryn Pydew Conwy 180 F4
Brynrefail Anglesey 179 D7
Gwyn 163 C9
Bryn Rhyd-yr-Arian
Conwy 165 B7
Bryn-rhys Conwy 180 F4
Brynsadler Rhondda 58 C4
Bryn Saith Marchog
Denb 165 E9
Brynsiencyn
Anglesey 163 B7
Bryn Sion Gwyn 147 F7
Brynsworthy Devon 40 G4
Bryn Tanat Powys 148 E4
Brynteg Anglesey 179 E7
Ceredig 93 C9
Wrex 166 E4
Bryntirion Bridgend 57 E11
Bryn-y-cochin
Shrops 149 B7
Bryn-y-gwenin Mon 78 B4
Bryn-y-maen Conwy 180 F4
Bryn-yr-Eos Wrex 166 G3
Bryn-yr-eryr Gwyn 162 F5
Bryn-yr-ogof
Denb 165 D11
Buaile nam Bodach
W Isles 297 L3
Bualintur Highld 294 C6
Bualnaluib Highld 307 K3
Buarthmeini Gwyn 146 C6
Bubbenhall Warks 119 C7
Bubblewell Glos 80 E5
Bubnell Derbys 186 G2
Bubwith E Yorks 207 F10
Buccleuch Borders 261 G8
Buchanan Smithy
Stirling 277 D9
Buchanhaven
Aberds 303 E11
Buchan Hill W Sus 51 G9
Buchanty Perth 286 E3
Buchley E Dunb 277 G11
Buchlyvie Stirling 277 C11
Buckabank Cumb 230 B3
Buckbury Worcs 98 E6
Buckden Cambs 122 D3
N Yorks 213 D8
Buckenham Norf 143 B7
Buckerell Devon 27 G10
Bucket Corner Hants 32 C6
Buckfast Devon 8 B4
Buckfastleigh Devon 8 B4
Buckham Dorset 29 G7
Buckhaven Fife 281 B7
Buck Hill Wilts 62 E3
Buckholm Borders 261 B11
Buckholt Mon 79 B8
Buckhorn Devon 12 B3
Buckhorn Weston
Dorset 30 C3
Buckhurst Kent 53 E10
Buckhurst Hill Essex 86 G6
Buckie Moray 302 C4
Buckies Highld 310 C5
Buckingham Bucks 102 E3
Buckland Bucks 84 C5
Devon 8 G3
Devon 14 G3
Glos 99 D11
Hants 20 B2
Herts 105 E7
Kent 55 E10
Oxon 82 F4
Sur 51 C8
Buckland Brewer
Devon 24 C6
Buckland Common
Bucks 84 D6
Buckland Dinham
Som 45 C9
Buckland Down Som 45 C8
Buckland End
W Mid 134 F2
Buckland Filleigh
Devon 25 F7
Buckland in the Moor
Devon 13 G10
Buckland Marsh
Oxon 82 F4
Buckland Monachorum
Devon 7 B9
Buckland Newton
Dorset 29 F11
Buckland Ripers
Dorset 17 E8
Bucklands Borders 262 F2
Buckland St Mary
Som 28 E3
Buckland Valley
Kent 55 E10
Bucklandwharf Bucks 84 C5
Bucklebury W Berks 64 E5
Bucklebury Alley
W Berks 64 E4
Bucklegate Lincs 156 B6
Buckleigh Devon 24 B6
Bucklerheads
Angus 287 D8
Bucklers Hard Hants 20 B4
Bucklesham Suff 108 C4
Buckley = *Bwcle*
Flint 166 C3
Buckley Green
Warks 118 D3
Buckley Hill Mers 182 B4
Bucklow Hill Ches E 184 E2
Buckminster Leics 155 E7
Buckmoorend Bucks 84 E4
Bucknall Lincs 173 B11
Stoke 168 F6
Bucknell Oxon 101 F11
Shrops 115 C7
Buckoak Ches W 183 G8
Buckover S Glos 79 G11
Buckpool Moray 302 C4
W Mid 133 F7
Buckridge Worcs 116 C4
Bucksburn
Aberdeen 293 C10
Buck's Cross Devon 24 C4
Bucks Green W Sus 50 G5
Buckshaw Village
Lancs 194 C5
Bucks Hill Herts 85 E9
Bucks Horn Oak
Hants 49 E10
Buckskin Hants 48 C6
Buck's Mills Devon 24 C5
Buckton E Yorks 218 E3
Hereford 115 C7
Northumb 264 B3
Buckton Vale
Gtr Man 196 G3
Buckworth Cambs 122 B2
Budbrooke Warks 118 D5
Budby Notts 171 B10
Buddgbrake
Shetland 312 B8
Buddileigh Staffs 168 F3
Budd's Titson Corn 24 G2
Bude Corn 24 F2
Budge's Shop Corn 6 D6
Budlake Devon 14 B5
Budle Northumb 264 B5
Budleigh Som 27 D11
Budleigh Salterton
Devon 15 E7
Budlett's Common
E Sus 37 C7
Budock Water Corn 3 C7
Budworth Heath
Ches W 183 F11
Buersil Head
Gtr Man 196 E2
Buerton Ches E 167 G11
Buffler's Holt Bucks 102 D3
Bufton Leics 135 B8
Bugbrooke
W Nhants 120 F3
Bugford Devon 40 E6
Bughtlin Edin 280 G3
Buglawton Ches E 168 C5
Bugle Corn 5 D10
Bugle Gate Worcs 116 D6
Bugley Dorset 30 C3
Wilts 45 E11
Bugthorpe E Yorks 207 B11
Building End Essex 105 D8
Buildwas Shrops 132 C2
Builth Road Powys 113 G10
Builth Wells Powys 113 G10
Buirgh W Isles 305 J2
Bulbourne Herts 84 C6
Bulbridge Wilts 46 G5
Bulby Lincs 155 D11
Bulcote Notts 171 G11
Buldoo Highld 310 C3
Bulford Wilts 47 E7
Bulford Camp Wilts 47 E7
Bulkeley Ches E 167 E8
Bulkeley Hall
Shrops 168 G2
Bulkington Warks 135 F7
Wilts 46 B2
Bulkworthy Devon 24 E5
Bullamoor N Yorks 225 G7
Bull Bay = *Porthllechog*
Anglesey 178 C6
Bullbridge Derbys 170 E5
Bullbrook Brack 65 F11
Bulleign Kent 53 G11
Bullenhill Wilts 45 B11
Bullen's Green Herts 86 D2
Bulley Glos 80 B3
Bullgill Cumb 229 D7
Bull Hill Hants 20 B2
Bullhurst Hill
Derbys 170 G3
Bullinghope
Hereford 97 D10
Bullington Hants 48 E3
Lincs 189 F9
Bullo Glos 79 D11
Bullock's Horn Wilts 81 G7
Bullockstone Kent 71 F7
Bulls Cross London 86 F4
Bulls Green Som 45 D8
Bull's Green Herts 86 B3
Norf 143 E8
Bull's Hill Hereford 97 G11
Bullwood Argyll 276 G3
Bullyhole Bottom
Mon 79 F7
Bulmer Essex 106 C6
N Yorks 216 F3
Bulmer Tye Essex 106 D6
Bulphan Thurrock 68 B6
Bulstrode Herts 85 E8
Bulthy Shrops 148 G6
Bulverhythe E Sus 38 F3
Bulwark Aberds 303 E9
Mon 79 G8
Bulwell Nottingham 171 F8
Bulwell Forest
Nottingham 171 F8
Bulwick Leics 136 E3
N Nhants 137 E9
Bumble's Green
Essex 86 D6
Bumwell Hill Norf 142 E2
Bun Abhainn Eadarra
W Isles 305 H3
Bunacaimb Highld 295 G8
Bun a'Mhuillin
W Isles 297 K3
Bunarkaig Highld 290 E3
Bunbury Ches E 167 D9
Bunbury Heath
Ches E 167 D9
Bunce Common Sur 51 D8
Bunchrew Highld 300 E6
Bundalloch Highld 295 C10
Buness Shetland 312 C8
Bunessan Argyll 288 G5
Bungay Suff 142 F6
Bunkers Hill
Gtr Man 184 D6
Oxon 83 B7
Bunker's Hill Cambs 139 B8
Lincs 174 E3
Lincs 189 G7
Norf 142 B3
Suff 143 C10
Bunloit Highld 300 G5
Bun Loyne Highld 290 C4
Bunnahabhain
Argyll 274 F5
Bunny Notts 153 D11
Bunny Hill Notts 153 D11
Bunree Highld 290 G2
Bunroy Highld 290 E4
Bunsley Bank
Ches E 167 G11
Bunstead Hants 32 C6
Buntait Highld 300 F3
Buntingford Herts 105 F7
Bunting's Green
Essex 106 E6
Bunwell Norf 142 E2
Bunwell Bottom
Norf 142 D2
Buoltach Highld 310 F5
Burbage Derbys 185 G8
Leics 135 E8
Wilts 63 G8
Burcher Hereford 114 E6
Burchett's Green
Windsor 65 C10
Burcombe Wilts 46 G5
Burcot Oxon 83 F9
Worcs 117 C9
Burcote Shrops 132 D4
Burcott Bucks 84 B4
Bucks 103 G7
Som 44 D4
Burdiehouse Edin 270 B5
Burdon T&W 243 G9
Burdonshill V Glam 58 E6
Burdrop Oxon 101 D7
Bures Suff 107 E8
Bures Green Suff 107 D8
Burford Ches E 167 E10
Devon 24 C4
Oxon 82 C3
Shrops 115 D11
Som 44 E5
Burg Argyll 288 E5
Argyll 288 G6
Burgar Orkney 314 D3
Burgate Hants 31 D11
Suff 125 B11
Burgates Hants 34 B3
Burgedin Powys 148 G4
Burge End Herts 104 E2
Burgess Hill W Sus 36 D4
Burgh Suff 126 G4
Burgh by Sands
Cumb 239 F8
Burgh Castle Norf 143 B9
Burghclere Hants 64 G3
Burghclere Common
Hants 64 G3
Burgh Common
Norf 141 E11
Burghead Moray 301 C11
Burghfield W Berks 65 F7
Burghfield Common
W Berks 64 F6
Burghfield Hill
W Berks 65 F7
Burgh Heath Sur 51 B8
Burgh Hill E Sus 23 C8
E Sus 38 B2
Burghill Hereford 97 C9
Burgh le Marsh
Lincs 175 B8
Burgh Muir Aberds 293 B9
Aberds 303 G7
Burgh next Aylsham
Norf 160 D4
Burgh on Bain Lincs 190 D2
Burgh St Margaret =
Fleggburgh Norf 161 G8
Burgh St Peter Norf 143 E9
Burgh Stubbs Norf 159 C10
Burghwallis S Yorks 198 E4
Burgois Corn 10 G4
Burham Kent 69 G8
Burham Court Kent 69 G8
Buriton Hants 34 C2
Burland Ches E 167 E10
Burlawn Corn 10 G5
Burleigh Brack 65 E11
Glos 80 E5
Burlescombe Devon 27 D9
Burleston Dorset 17 C11
Burlestone Devon 8 F6
Burley Hants 32 G2
Rutland 155 G7
Shrops 131 G9
W Yorks 205 G11
Burley Beacon
Hants 32 G2
Burleydam Ches E 167 G10
Burley Gate
Hereford 97 B11
Burley in Wharfedale
W Yorks 205 D9
Burley Lawn Hants 32 G2
Burley Lodge Hants 32 F2
Burley Street Hants 32 G2
Burley Woodhead
W Yorks 205 E9
Burlinch Som 28 B3
Burlingham Green
Norf 161 G7
Burlingjobb Powys 114 F5
Burlish Park Worcs 116 C6
Burlorne Tregoose
Corn 5 B10
Burlow E Sus 23 B9
Burlton Shrops 149 D9
Burmantofts
W Yorks 206 G2
Burmarsh Hereford 97 B10
Kent 54 G5
Burmington Warks 100 D5
Burn N Yorks 198 B5
Burnage Gtr Man 184 C5
Burnard's Ho Devon 24 G4
Burnaston Derbys 152 C5
Burnbank S Lanark 268 D4
Burn Bridge
N Yorks 206 C2
Burnby E Yorks 208 D2
Burncross S Yorks 186 B4
Burndell W Sus 35 G7
Burnden Gtr Man 195 F8
Burnedge Gtr Man 196 E2
Burnend Aberds 303 E8
Burneside Cumb 221 F10
Burness Orkney 314 B6
Burneston N Yorks 214 B6
Burnett Bath 61 F7
Burnfoot Borders 261 G10
Borders 262 F2
Dumfries 239 C7
Dumfries 247 E11
E Ayrs 245 B10
N Lanark 268 B5
Perth 286 G3
Burngreave S Yorks 186 D5
Burnham Bucks 66 C2
N Lincs 200 D5
Burnham Deepdale
Norf 176 E4
Burnham Green
Herts 86 B3
Burnham Market
Norf 176 E4
Burnham Norton
Norf 176 E4
Burnham-on-Crouch
Essex 88 F6
Burnham-on-Sea
Som 43 D10
Burnham Overy Staithe
Norf 176 E4
Burnham Overy Town
Norf 176 E4
Burnham Thorpe
Norf 176 E5
Burnhead Aberds 293 D10
Borders 262 F2
Dumfries 247 D9
Dumfries 247 G10
S Ayrs 244 C6
Burnhervie Aberds 293 B9
Burnhill Green
Staffs 132 C5
Burnhope Durham 233 B9
Burnhouse N Ayrs 267 E7
Burnhouse Mains
Borders 271 F8
Burniere Corn 10 G5
Burniestrype Moray 302 C3
Burniston N Yorks 227 G10
Burnlee W Yorks 196 F6
Burnley Lancs 204 G2
Burnley Lane Lancs 204 G2
Burnley Wood
Lancs 204 G2
Burnmouth Borders 273 C9
Burn Naze Lancs 202 E2
Burn of Cambus
Stirling 285 G11
Burnopfield
Durham 242 F5
Burnrigg Cumb 239 F11
Burnsall N Yorks 213 G10
Burn's Green Herts 104 G6
Burnside Aberds 303 E8
Angus 287 B9
E Ayrs 258 G3
Fife 286 G5
Perth 286 E4
Shetland 312 F4
S Lanark 268 C2
T&W 243 G8
W Loth 279 G11
Burnside of Duntrune
Angus 287 D8
Burnstone Devon 24 C4
Burnswark Dumfries 238 B5
Burnt Ash Glos 80 E5
Burntcommon Sur 50 C4
Burntheath Derbys 152 C4
Burnt Heath Derbys 186 F2
Essex 107 F11
Burnt Hill W Berks 64 E5
Burnthouse Corn 3 B7
Burnt Houses
Durham 233 G8
Burntisland Fife 280 D4
Burnt Mills Essex 88 G2
Burnt Oak E Sus 37 B8
London 86 G2
Burnton E Ayrs 245 B11
Burnt Tree W Mid 133 E9
Burnturk Fife 287 G7
Burntwood Staffs 133 B11
Burntwood Green
Staffs 133 B11
Burntwood Pentre
Flint 166 C3
Burnt Yates
N Yorks 214 G5
Burnworthy Som 27 D11
Burnwynd Edin 270 B2
Burpham Sur 50 C4
W Sus 35 F8
Burradon Northumb 251 B11
T&W 243 C7
Burrafirth Shetland 312 B8
Burraland Shetland 312 F5
Shetland 313 J4
Burras Corn 2 C5
Burrastow Shetland 313 J4
Burraton Corn 7 D8
Burraton Coombe
Corn 7 D8
Burravoe Shetland 312 F7
Shetland 312 G5
Burray Village
Orkney 314 G4
Burreldales Aberds 303 F7
Burrells Cumb 222 B3
Burrelton Perth 286 D6
Burridge Devon 28 F4
Devon 40 F5
Hants 33 E8
Burrigill Highld 310 F6
Burrill N Yorks 214 B4
Burringham
N Lincs 199 F10
Burrington Devon 25 D10
Hereford 115 C8
N Som 44 B3
Burrough End
Cambs 124 F2
Burrough Green
Cambs 124 F2
Burrough on the Hill
Leics 154 G5

Burroughs Grove
Bucks 65 B11
Burroughston
Orkney 314 D5
Burrow Devon 14 B5
Som 28 C6
Som 42 E2
Burrowbridge Som 43 G11
Burrow-bridge Som 28 B5
Burrowhill Sur 66 G3
Burrows Cross Sur 50 D5
Burrowsmoor Holt
Notts 172 G2
Burrsville Park
Essex 89 B11
Burrswood Kent 52 F4
Burry Swansea 56 C3
Burry Green Swansea 56 C3
Burry Port = *Porth Tywyn*
Carms 74 E6
Burscott Devon 24 C4
Burscough Lancs 194 E2
Burscough Bridge
Lancs 194 E2
Bursdon Devon 24 D3
Bursea E Yorks 208 G2
Burshill E Yorks 209 D7
Bursledon Hants 33 F7
Burslem Stoke 168 F5
Burstall Suff 107 C11
Burstallhill Suff 107 B11
Burstock Dorset 28 G6
Burston Devon 26 G2
Norf 142 G2
Staffs 151 C8
Burstow Sur 51 E10
Burstwick E Yorks 201 B8
Burtersett N Yorks 213 B7
Burtholme Cumb 240 E2
Burthorpe Suff 124 E5
Burthwaite Cumb 230 B4
Burtle Som 43 E11
Burtle Hill Som 43 E11
Burtoft Lincs 156 B5
Burton BCP 17 C9
BCP 19 C9
Ches W 167 C8
Ches W 182 G4
Lincs 189 G7
Northumb 264 C5
Pembs 73 D7
Som 29 E8
Som 43 E7
V Glam 58 F4
Wilts 45 G10
Wilts 61 D10
Wrex 166 D5
Burton Agnes
E Yorks 218 G2
Burton Bradstock
Dorset 16 D5
Burton Corner Lincs 174 F4
Burton Dassett
Warks 119 G7
Burton End Cambs 106 B2
Essex 105 G10
Burton Ferry Pembs 73 D7
Burton Fleming
E Yorks 217 E11
Burton Green Essex 106 F6
W Mid 118 B5
Wrex 166 D4
Burton Hastings
Warks 135 E8
Burton-in-Kendal
Cumb 211 D10
Burton in Lonsdale
N Yorks 212 E3
Burton Joyce
Notts 171 G10
Burton Latimer
N Nhants 121 C8
Burton Lazars Leics 154 F5
Burton-le-Coggles
Lincs 155 D9
Burton Leonard
N Yorks 214 G6
Burton Manor Staffs 151 E8
Burton on the Wolds
Leics 153 E11
Burton Overy Leics 136 D3
Burton Pedwardine
Lincs 173 G10
Burton Pidsea
E Yorks 209 G10
Burton Salmon
N Yorks 198 B3
Burton Stather
N Lincs 199 D11
Burton upon Stather
N Lincs 199 D11
Burton upon Trent
Staffs 152 E5
Burton Westwood
Shrops 132 D2
Burtonwood Warr 183 C9
Burwardsley
Ches W 167 D8
Burwarton Shrops 132 F2
Burwash E Sus 37 C11
Burwash Common
E Sus 37 C10
Burwash Weald
E Sus 37 C10
Burwell Cambs 123 D11
Lincs 190 F5
Burwen Anglesey 178 C6
Burwick Orkney 314 H4
Shetland 313 J5
Burwood Shrops 131 F9
Burwood Park Sur 66 G6
Bury Cambs 138 G5
Gtr Man 195 E10
Som 26 B6
W Sus 35 E8
Buryas Br Corn 1 D4
Burybank Staffs 151 B7
Bury End Bedford 121 G9
C Beds 104 E2
Worcs 99 D11
Bury Green Herts 86 E4
Herts 105 G8
Bury Hollow W Sus 35 E8
Bury Park Luton 103 G11
Bury St Edmunds
Suff 125 E7
Bury's Bank W Berks 64 F3
Burythorpe N Yorks 216 G5
Busbiehill N Ayrs 257 B9
Busbridge Sur 50 E3
Busby E Renf 267 D11
Buscot Oxon 82 F2
Buscott Som 44 F2
Bush Aberds 293 G9
Corn 24 F2
Bush Bank Hereford 115 G9
Bushbury Sur 51 D7
W Mid 133 C8
Bushby Leics 136 C3
Bush Crathie
Aberds 292 D4
Bush End Essex 87 B9
Bush Estate Norf 161 D8
Bushey Dorset 18 E5
Herts 85 G10
Bushey Ground Oxon 82 D4
Bushey Heath Herts 85 G11
Bushey Mead London 67 F8
Bushfield Cumb 249 G11
Bush Green Norf 141 D10
Norf 142 F4
Suff 125 F8
Bush Hill Park London 86 F4
Bushley Worcs 99 E7
Bushley Green Worcs 99 E7
Bushmead Bedford 122 E2
Bushmoor Shrops 131 F8
Bushton Wilts 62 D5
Bushy Common
Norf 159 G9
Bushy Hill Sur 50 C4
Busk Cumb 231 C8
Gtr Man 196 F2
Buslingthorpe Lincs 189 D9
Bussage Glos 80 E5
Bussex Som 43 F11
Busta Shetland 312 G5
Bustard Green
Essex 106 F2
Bustard's Green
Norf 142 E3
Bustatoun Orkney 314 A7
Busveal Corn 4 G4
Butcher's Common
Norf 160 E6
Butcher's Cross
E Sus 37 B9
Butcombe N Som 60 G4
Butetown Cardiff 59 D7
Bute Town Caerph 77 D10
Butlane Head
Shrops 149 G8
Butleigh Som 44 G4
Butleigh Wootton
Som 44 G4
Butlersbank
Shrops 149 E11
Butlers Cross Bucks 85 G7
Butler's Cross Bucks 84 D4
Butler's End Warks 134 G4
Butler's Hill Notts 171 F8
Butlers Marston
Warks 118 G6
Butley Suff 127 G7
Butley High Corner
Suff 109 B7
Butley Low Corner
Suff 109 B7
Butley Town Ches E 184 F6
Butlocks Heath Hants 33 F7
Butter Bank Staffs 151 E7
Butterburn Cumb 240 C5
Buttercrambe
N Yorks 207 B10
Butteriss Gate Corn 2 C6
Butterknowle
Durham 233 F8
Butterleigh Devon 27 F7
Butterley Derbys 170 C4
Derbys 170 E6
Buttermere Cumb 220 B3
Wilts 63 G10
Butterrow Glos 80 E5
Butters Green Staffs 168 E4
Buttershaw
W Yorks 196 B6
Butterstone Perth 286 C4
Butterton Staffs 168 G4
Staffs 169 D9
Butterwick Cumb 221 B10
Durham 234 F3
Lincs 174 G5
N Yorks 216 D4
N Yorks 217 E9
Butteryhaugh
Northumb 250 E4
Butt Green Ches E 167 E11
Buttington Powys 130 B5
Butt Lane Staffs 168 E4
Buttonbridge
Shrops 116 B4
Button Haugh Green
Suff 125 D9
Buttonoak Worcs 116 B5
Button's Green Suff 125 G8
Butts Devon 14 D2
Buttsash Hants 32 F6
Buttsbear Cross Corn 24 G3
Buttsbury Essex 87 F11
Butts Green Essex 105 E9
Butt's Green Essex 88 E3
Hants 32 B4
Buttsole Kent 55 C10
Butt Yeats Lancs 211 F11
Buxhall Suff 125 F10
Buxhall Fen Street
Suff 125 F10
Buxley Borders 272 E6
Buxted E Sus 37 C7
Buxton Derbys 185 G9
Norf 160 E4
Buxworth Derbys 185 E8
Bwcle = *Buckley*
Flint 166 C3
Bwlch Flint 181 G11
Powys 96 G2
Bwlch-derwin Gwyn 163 F7
Bwlchgwyn Wrex 166 E3
Bwlch-Llan Ceredig 111 F11
Bwlchnewydd Carms 93 G7
Bwlch-newydd
Carms 93 G7
Bwlchtocyn Gwyn 144 D6
Bwlch-y-cibau
Powys 148 F3
Bwlch-y-cwm Cardiff 58 C6
Bwlchyddar Powys 148 E3
Bwlch-y-fadfa
Ceredig 93 B8
Bwlch-y-ffridd
Powys 129 D11
Bwlchygroes Pembs 92 D4
Bwlchyllyn Gwyn 163 D8
Bwlch-y-Plain
Powys 114 B4
Bwlch-y-sarnau
Powys 113 C10
Bybrook Kent 54 E4
Bycross Hereford 97 C7
Byeastwood Bridgend 58 C2
Byebush Aberds 303 F7
Bye Green Bucks 84 C5
Byerhope Northumb 232 B3
Byermoor T&W 242 F5
Byers Green
Durham 233 E10
Byfield W Nhants 119 G10
Byfleet Sur 66 G5
Byford Hereford 97 C7
Byford Common
Hereford 97 C7
Bygrave Herts 104 D5
Byker T&W 243 E7
Byland Abbey
N Yorks 215 D10
Bylchau Conwy 165 C7
Byley Ches W 168 B2
Bynea Carms 56 B4
Byram N Yorks 198 B3
Byrness Northumb 251 C7
Bythorn Cambs 121 B11
Byton Hereford 115 E7
Byton Hand
Hereford 115 E7
Bywell Northumb 242 E2
Byworth W Sus 35 C7

C

Cabbacott Devon 24 C6
Cabbage Hill Brack 65 E11
Cabharstadh
W Isles 304 F5
Cabin Shrops 130 F6
Cablea Perth 286 D3
Cabourne Lincs 200 G6
Cabrach Argyll 274 G5
Moray 302 G3
Cabrich Highld 300 E5
Cabus Lancs 202 D5
Cackle Hill Lincs 157 D7
Cackleshaw
W Yorks 204 F6
Cackle Street E Sus 23 B11
E Sus 37 B7
E Sus 38 D4
Cadboll Highld 301 B8
Cadbury Devon 26 G6
Cadbury Barton
Devon 25 D11
Cadbury Heath
S Glos 61 E7
Cadder E Dunb 278 G2
Cadderlie Argyll 284 D4
Caddington C Beds 85 B9
Caddleton Argyll 275 B8
Caddonfoot
Borders 261 C10
Caddonlee
Borders 261 B10
Cadeby Leics 135 C8
S Yorks 198 G4
Cadeleigh Devon 26 F6
Cademuir Borders 260 B6
Cader Denb 165 C8
Cade Street E Sus 37 C10
Cadger Path Angus 287 B8
Cad Green Som 28 D4
Cadgwith Corn 2 G6
Cadham Fife 286 G6
Cadishead Gtr Man 184 C2
Cadle Swansea 56 B6
Cadley Lancs 202 G6
Wilts 47 C8
Wilts 63 F8
Cadmore End Bucks 84 G3
Cadnam Hants 32 E3
Cadney N Lincs 200 G4
Cadney Bank Wrex 149 C9
Cadole Flint 166 C2
Cadoxton V Glam 58 F6
Cadoxton-Juxta-Neath
Neath 57 B9
Cadshaw Blackburn 195 D8
Cadwell Herts 104 E3
Cadzow S Lanark 268 E4
Caeathro Gwyn 163 C7
Cae Clyd Gwyn 164 G2
Cae-gors Carms 75 E9
Caehopkin Powys 76 C4
Caemorgan Ceredig 92 B3
Caenby Lincs 189 D8
Caenby Corner
Lincs 189 D7
Caerau Bridgend 57 C11
Cardiff 58 D6
Caerau Park Newport 59 B9
Cae'r-bont Powys 76 C4
Cae'r-bryn Carms 75 C9
Caerdeon Gwyn 146 F2
Caer-Estyn Wrex 166 D4
Caerfarchell Pembs 90 F5
Caer-Farchell Pembs 90 F5
Caerffili = *Caerphilly*
Caerph 59 B7
Caerfyrddin = *Carmarthen*
Carms 93 G8
Caergeiliog
Anglesey 178 F4
Caergwrle Flint 166 D4
Caergybi = *Holyhead*
Anglesey 178 E2
Caerhendy Neath 57 C9
Caerhun Gwyn 163 B9
Cae'r-Lan Powys 76 C4
Caerleon Newport 78 G4
Caer Llan Mon 79 D7
Caermead V Glam 58 F3
Caermeini Pembs 92 E2
Caernarfon Gwyn 163 C7
Caerphilly = *Caerffili*
Caerph 59 B7
Caersws Powys 129 E10
Caerwedros Ceredig 111 F7
Caerwent Mon 79 G7
Caerwent Brook Mon 60 B3
Caerwych Gwyn 146 B2
Caerwys Flint 181 G10
Caethle Gwyn 128 D2
Cage Green Kent 52 D5
Caggan Highld 291 B10
Caggle Street Mon 78 B5
Cailness Stirling 285 G7
Caim Anglesey 179 E10
Cainscross Glos 80 D4
Caio Carms 94 D3
Cairinis W Isles 296 E4
Cairisiadar W Isles 304 E2
Cairminis W Isles 296 C6
Cairnbaan Argyll 275 D9
Cairnbanno Ho
Aberds 303 E8
Cairnborrow Aberds 302 E4
Cairnbrogie Aberds 303 G8
Cairnbulg Castle
Aberds 303 C10
Cairncross Angus 292 F6
Borders 273 C7
Cairnderry Dumfries 236 B5
Cairndow Argyll 284 F5
Cairness Aberds 303 C10
Cairneyhill Fife 279 D10
Cairnfield Ho
Moray 302 C4
Cairngaan Dumfries 236 F3
Cairngarroch
Dumfries 236 E2
Cairnhill Aberds 302 F6
Aberds 303 D7
N Lanark 268 C5
Cairnie Aberds 293 C10
Aberds 302 E4
Cairnlea S Ayrs 244 G6
Cairnleith Crofts
Aberds 303 F9
Cairnmuir Aberds 303 C9
Cairnorrie Aberds 303 E8
Cairnpark Aberds 293 B10
Dumfries 247 D9
Cairnryan Dumfries 236 C2
Cairnton Orkney 314 F3
Cairston Orkney 314 E2
Caister-on-Sea
Norf 161 G10
Caistor Lincs 200 G6
Caistor St Edmund
Norf 142 C4
Caistron Northumb 251 C11
Caitha Bowland
Borders 271 G9
Cakebole Worcs 117 C7
Calais Street Suff 107 D9
Calanais W Isles 304 E4
Calbost W Isles 305 G6
Calbourne IoW 20 D4
Calceby Lincs 190 F5
Calcoed Flint 181 G11
Calcot Glos 81 C9
W Berks 65 E7
Calcot Row W Berks 65 E7
Calcott Kent 71 G7
Shrops 149 G8
Calcott's Green Glos 80 B3
Calcutt N Yorks 206 B2
Wilts 81 G10
Caldback Shetland 312 C8
Caldbeck Cumb 230 D2
Caldbergh N Yorks 213 B11
Caldecote Cambs 122 F6
Cambs 138 F2
Herts 104 D4
Warks 135 E7
W Nhants 120 G3
Caldecote Hill
Herts 85 G11
Caldecott N Nhants 121 D9
Oxon 83 F7
Rutland 137 E7
Caldecotte
M Keynes 103 D7
Calder Cumb 219 E10
Calderbank
N Lanark 268 C5
Calder Bridge
Cumb 219 D10
Calderbrook
Gtr Man 196 D2
Caldercruix
N Lanark 268 B6
Calder Grove
W Yorks 197 D10
Calder Hall Cumb 219 E10
Calder Mains Highld 310 D4
Caldermill S Lanark 268 G3
Caldermoor
Gtr Man 196 D2
Calderstones Mers 182 D6
Calder Vale Lancs 202 D6
Calderwood
S Lanark 268 D2
Caldhame Angus 287 C8
Caldicot = *Cil-y-coed*
Mon 60 B3
Caldmore W Mid 133 D10
Caldwell Derbys 152 F5
N Yorks 224 C3
Caldy Mers 182 D2
Caledrhydiau
Ceredig 111 G9
Cale Green Gtr Man 184 D5
Calenick Corn 4 G6
Caleys Fields Worcs 100 C4
Calf Heath Staffs 133 B8
Calford Green Suff 106 B3
Calfsound Orkney 314 C5
Calgary Argyll 288 D5
Califer Moray 301 D10
California Cambs 139 G10
Falk 279 F8
Norf 161 G10
Suff 108 C3
W Mid 133 G10
Calke Derbys 153 E7
Callakille Highld 298 D6
Callaly Northumb 252 B3
Callander Stirling 285 G10
Callandrode
Stirling 285 G10
Callands Warr 183 C9
Callaughton Shrops 132 D2
Callendar Park Falk 279 F7
Callert Ho Highld 290 G2
Callerton T&W 242 D5
Callerton Lane End
T&W 242 D5
Callestick Corn 4 E5
Calligarry Highld 295 E8
Callington Corn 7 B7
Callingwood Staffs 152 E3
Calloose Corn 2 B3
Callop Highld 289 B11
Callow Derbys 170 E3
Hereford 97 E9
Callow End Worcs 98 B6
Callow Hill Mon 79 B8
Som 44 E3
Wilts 62 C4
Worcs 116 C4
Callow Marsh
Hereford 98 B3
Callows Grave
Worcs 115 D11
Calmore Hants 32 E4
Calmsden Glos 81 D8
Calne Wilts 62 E4
Calne Marsh Wilts 62 E4
Calow Derbys 186 G6
Calow Green Derbys 170 B6
Calrofold Ches E 184 G6
Calshot Hants 33 G7
Calstock Corn 7 B8
Calstone Wellington
Wilts 62 F4
Calthorpe Norf 160 C3
Oxon 101 D9
Calthwaite Cumb 230 C5
Calton Glasgow 268 C2
N Yorks 204 B4
Staffs 169 E10
Calton Lees Derbys 170 B3
Calvadnack Corn 2 B5
Calveley Ches E 167 D9
Calver Derbys 186 G2
Calverhall Shrops 150 B2
Calver Hill Hereford 97 B7
Calverleigh Devon 26 E6
Calverley W Yorks 205 F10
Calver Sough
Derbys 186 F2
Calvert Bucks 102 G3
Calverton M Keynes 102 D5
Notts 171 F10
Calvine Perth 291 G10
Calvo Cumb 238 G4
Cam Glos 80 F3
Camaghael Highld 290 F3
Camas an Staca
Argyll 274 G5
Camas-luinie
Highld 295 C11
Camasnacroise
Highld 289 D10
Camas Salach
Highld 289 C8
Camastianavaig
Highld 295 B7
Camasunary Highld 295 D7
Camault Muir Highld 300 E5
Camb Shetland 312 D7
Camber E Sus 39 D7
Camberley Sur 65 G11
Camberwell London 67 D10
Camblesforth
N Yorks 199 B7
Cambo Northumb 252 F2
Cambois Northumb 253 G8
Camborne Corn 4 G3
Cambourne Cambs 122 F6
Cambridge Borders 271 F11
Cambs 123 F9
Glos 80 E3
W Yorks 205 D10
Cambridge Batch
N Som 60 F4
Cambridge Town
Southend 70 C2
Cambrose Corn 4 F3
Cambus Clack 279 C7
Cambusavie Farm
Highld 309 K7
Cambusbarron
Stirling 278 C5
Cambusdrenny
Stirling 278 C5
Cambuskenneth
Stirling 278 C6
Cambuslang
S Lanark 268 D2
Cambusmore Lodge
Highld 309 K7
Cambusnethan
N Lanark 268 D6
Camden London 67 C9
Camden Hill Kent 53 F9
Camden Park Kent 52 F5
Cameley Bath 44 B6
Camelford Corn 11 E8
Camel Green Dorset 31 E10
Camelon Falk 279 E7
Camelsdale Sur 49 G11
Camer Kent 69 F7
Cameron Fife 280 B6
Cameron Bridge
Fife 280 B6
Camerory Highld 301 F10
Camer's Green
Worcs 98 D5
Camerton Bath 45 B7
Cumb 228 E6
E Yorks 201 B8
Camghouran Perth 285 B9
Cammachmore
Aberds 293 D11
Cammeringham
Lincs 188 E6
Camnant Powys 113 F11
Camoquhill Stirling 277 D10
Camore Highld 309 K7
Camp Lincs 172 E5
Campbeltown Argyll 255 E8
Camp Corner Oxon 83 E10
Camperdown T&W 243 C7
Camphill Derbys 185 F11
Camp Hill N Yorks 214 C6
Pembs 73 C10
Warks 134 E6
W Yorks 196 D5
Campion Hills
Warks 118 D6
Campions Essex 87 C7
Cample Dumfries 247 E9
Campmuir Perth 286 D6
Campsall S Yorks 198 E4
Campsea Ashe Suff 126 F6
Camps End Cambs 106 C2
Campsey Ash Suff 126 F6
Campsfield Oxon 83 B7
Camps Heath Suff 143 E10
Campton C Beds 104 D2
Camptoun E Loth 281 F10
Camptown Borders 262 G5
Camp Town
W Yorks 206 F2
Camquhart Argyll 275 E10
Camrose Pembs 91 G8
Camserney Perth 286 C2
Camster Highld 310 E6
Camuschoirk Highld 289 C9
Camuscross Highld 295 D8
Camusnagaul Highld 290 F2
Highld 307 L5
Camusrory Highld 295 F10
Camusteel Highld 299 E7
Camusterrach
Highld 299 E7
Camusvrachan
Perth 285 C10
Canada Hants 32 D3
Lincs 200 G6
Canadia E Sus 38 D2
Canal Foot Cumb 210 D6
Canal Side S Yorks 199 E7
Canbus Clack 279 C7
Candacraig Ho
Aberds 292 B5
Candlesby Lincs 175 B7
Candle Street Suff 125 C10
Candy Mill
S Lanark 269 G11
Cane End Oxon 65 D7
Caneheath E Sus 23 D9
Canewdon Essex 88 G5
Canford Bottom
Dorset 31 G8
Canford Cliffs BCP 19 D7
Canford Heath BCP 18 C6
Canford Magna BCP 18 B6
Cangate Norf 160 F6
Canham's Green
Suff 125 D11
Canholes Derbys 185 G8
Canisbay Highld 310 B7
Canklow S Yorks 186 C6
Canley W Mid 118 B6
Cann Dorset 30 C5
Cannalidgey Corn 5 B8
Cannard's Grave
Som 44 E6
Cann Common
Dorset 30 C5
Cannich Highld 300 F3
Cannington Som 43 F9
Canning Town
London 68 C2
Cannock Staffs 133 B9
Cannock Wood
Staffs 151 G10
Cannon's Green
Essex 87 D9
Cannop Glos 79 C10
Canonbie Dumfries 239 B9
Canon Bridge
Hereford 97 C8
Canonbury London 67 C10
Canon Frome
Hereford 98 C3
Canon Pyon Hereford 97 B9
Canons Ashby
W Nhants 119 G11
Canonsgrove Som 28 C2
Canons Park London 85 G11
Canon's Town Corn 2 B2
Canterbury Kent 54 B6
Cantley Norf 143 C7
S Yorks 198 G6
Cantlop Shrops 131 B10
Canton Cardiff 59 D7
Cantraybruich
Highld 301 E7
Cantraydoune
Highld 301 E7
Cantraywood Highld 301 E7
Cantsfield Lancs 212 E2
Canvey Island Essex 69 C9
Canwick Lincs 173 B7
Canworthy Water
Corn 11 C10
Caol Highld 290 F3
Caolas Argyll 288 E2
W Isles 297 M2
Caolas Fhlodaigh
W Isles 296 F4
Caolas Liubharsaigh
W Isles 297 G4
Caolas Scalpaigh
W Isles 305 J4
Caolas Stocinis
W Isles 305 J3
Caol Ila Argyll 274 F5
Caolslasnacon
Highld 290 G3
Capel Carms 75 E8
Kent 52 E6
Sur 51 E7
Capel Bangor
Ceredig 128 G3
Capel Betws Lleucu
Ceredig 112 F2
Capel Carmel Gwyn 144 D3
Capel Coch Anglesey 179 E7
Capel Cross Kent 53 E8
Capel Curig Conwy 164 D2
Capel Cynon Ceredig 93 B7
Capel Dewi Carms 93 G9
Ceredig 93 C9
Ceredig 128 G2
Capel Garmon
Conwy 164 D4
Capel Green Suff 109 B7
Capel-gwyn
Anglesey 178 F4
Capel Gwyn Carms 93 G9
Capel Gwynfe Carms 94 G4
Capel Hendre Carms 75 C9
Capel Hermon
Gwyn 146 D4
Capel Isaac Carms 93 F11
Capel Iwan Carms 92 D5
Capel-le-Ferne Kent 55 F8
Capel Llanilltern
Cardiff 58 C5
Capel Mawr
Anglesey 178 G6
Capel Newydd = *Newchapel*
Pembs 92 D4
Capel Parc Anglesey 178 D6
Capel St Andrew
Suff 109 B7
Capel St Mary Suff 107 D11
Capel Seion Carms 75 C8
Ceredig 112 B2
Capel Siloam Conwy 164 E4
Capel Tygwydd
Ceredig 92 C5
Capel Uchaf Gwyn 162 F6
Capelulo Conwy 180 F2
Capel-y-ffin Powys 96 E5
Capel-y-graig Gwyn 163 B8
Capenhurst Ches W 182 G5
Capernwray Lancs 211 E10
Capheaton
Northumb 252 G2
Capland Som 28 D4
Cappercleuch
Borders 260 E6
Capplegill Dumfries 248 B4
Capstone Medway 69 F9
Captain Fold
Gtr Man 195 E11
Capton Devon 8 E6
Som 42 F5
Caputh Perth 286 D4
Caradon Town Corn 11 G11
Carbis Corn 5 D10
Carbis Bay Corn 2 B2
Carbost Highld 294 B5
Highld 298 E4
Carbrain N Lanark 278 G5
Carbrook S Yorks 186 D5
Carbrooke Norf 141 C9
Carburton Notts 187 G10
Carcant Borders 271 E7
Carcary Angus 287 B10
Carclaze Corn 5 E10
Carclew Corn 3 B7
Car Colston Notts 172 G2
Carcroft S Yorks 198 E4
Cardenden Fife 280 C4
Cardeston Shrops 149 G7
Cardew Cumb 230 B2
Cardewlees Cumb 239 G8
Cardiff Cardiff 59 D7
Cardigan = *Aberteifi*
Ceredig 92 B3
Cardinal's Green
Cambs 106 B2
Cardington
Bedford 103 B11
Shrops 131 D10
Cardinham Corn 6 B2
Cardonald
Glasgow 267 C10
Cardow Moray 301 E11
Cardrona Borders 261 B8
Cardross Argyll 276 F6
Cardurnock Cumb 238 F5
Careby Lincs 155 F10
Careston Angus 293 G7
Careston Castle
Angus 287 B9
Care Village Leics 136 D4
Carew Pembs 73 E8
Carew Cheriton
Pembs 73 E8
Carew Newton
Pembs 73 E8
Carey Hereford 97 E11
Carey Park Corn 6 E4
Carfin N Lanark 268 D5
Carfrae E Loth 271 B11
Carfury Corn 1 C4
Cargate Common
Norf 142 E2
Cargenbridge
Dumfries 237 B11
Cargill Perth 286 D5
Cargo Cumb 239 F9
Cargo Fleet Mbro 234 G6
Cargreen Corn 7 C8
Carham Northumb 263 B8
Carhampton Som 42 E4
Carharrack Corn 4 G4
Carie Perth 285 B10
Perth 285 D10
Carines Corn 4 D5
Carisbrooke IoW 20 D5
Cark Cumb 211 D7
Carkeel Corn 7 C8
Carlabhagh W Isles 304 D4
Carland Cross Corn 5 E7
Carlbury N Yorks 224 B4
Carlby Lincs 155 G11
Carlecotes S Yorks 197 G7
Carleen Corn 2 C4
Carlenrig Borders 249 C9
Carlesmoor N Yorks 214 E3
Carleton Cumb 219 D10
Cumb 230 F6
Cumb 239 G10
Lancs 202 F2
N Yorks 204 D5
W Yorks 198 C3
Carleton Forehoe
Norf 141 B11
Carleton Hall
Cumb 219 F11
Carleton-in-Craven
N Yorks 204 D5
Carleton Rode Norf 142 E2
Carleton St Peter
Norf 142 C6
Carley Hill T&W 243 F9
Carlidnack Corn 3 D7
Carlincraig Aberds 302 E6
Carlingcott Bath 45 B7
Carlinghow
W Yorks 197 C8
Carlingwark Devon 27 E11
Carlin How Redcar 226 B4
Carlisle Cumb 239 F10
Carloggas Corn 5 B7
Corn 5 E9
Carloonan Argyll 284 F4
Carlops Borders 270 D3
Carlton Bedford 121 F9
Cambs 124 G2
Leics 135 C7
Notts 171 G10
N Yorks 198 C6
N Yorks 213 C11
N Yorks 216 B2
N Yorks 224 C3
Stockton 234 G3
Suff 127 E7
S Yorks 197 E11
W Yorks 197 B10
Carlton Colville
Suff 143 F10
Carlton Curlieu
Leics 136 D3
Carlton Green
Cambs 124 G2
Carlton Husthwaite
N Yorks 215 D9
Carlton in Cleveland
N Yorks 225 E10
Carlton in Lindrick
Notts 187 E9
Carlton le Moorland
Lincs 172 D6
Carlton Miniott
N Yorks 215 C7
Carlton on Trent
Notts 172 C3
Carlton Purlieus
N Nhants 136 F6
Carlton Scroop
Lincs 172 G6
Carluddon Corn 5 D10
Carluke S Lanark 268 E6
Carlyon Bay Corn 5 E11
Carmarthen = *Caerfyrddin*
Carms 93 G8
Carmel Anglesey 178 E5
Carms 75 B9
Flint 181 F11
Gwyn 163 E7
Powys 113 D11
Carmichael
S Lanark 259 B10
Carminow Cross Corn 5 B11
Carmont Aberds 293 E10
Carmunnock
Glasgow 268 D2
Carmyle Glasgow 268 C2
Carmyllie Angus 287 C9
Carnaby E Yorks 218 F2
Carnach Highld 299 G10
Highld 307 K5
W Isles 305 J4
Carnachy Highld 308 D7
Càrnais W Isles 304 E2
Càrnan W Isles 297 G3
Carn Arthen Corn 2 B5
Carnbahn Perth 285 C10
Carnbee Fife 287 G9
Carnbo Perth 286 G4
Carnbrea Corn 4 G3
Carn Brea Village
Corn 4 G3
Carnbroe N Lanark 268 C4
Carndu Highld 295 C10
Carnduff S Lanark 268 F3
Carnduncan Argyll 274 G3
Carne Corn 3 B10
Corn 3 E7
Corn 5 D9
Carnebone Corn 2 C6
Carnedd Powys 129 E10
Carnetown Rhondda 77 G9
Carnforth Lancs 211 E9
Lancs 211 E10
Carnglas Swansea 56 C6
Carn-gorm Highld 295 C11
Carnhedryn Pembs 90 F6
Carnhedryn Uchaf
Pembs 90 F5
Carnhell Green Corn 2 B4
Carnhot Corn 4 F4
Carnkie Corn 2 B5
Corn 2 C6

Carnkief Corn 4 E5
Carno Powys 129 D9
Carnoch Highld 300 D2
  Highld 300 F3
Carnock Fife 279 D10
Carnon Downs Corn 4 G5
Carn Towan Corn 1 D3
Carntyne Glasgow 268 B2
Carnwadric E Renf . . 267 D10
Carnwath S Lanark . . . 269 F9
Carnyorth Corn 1 C3
Caroe Corn 11 G9
Carol Green W Mid . . . 118 B5
Carpalla Corn 5 E9
Carpenders Park
  Herts 85 G10
Carpenter's Hill
  Worcs 117 C11
Carperby N Yorks . . . 213 B10
Carpley Green
  N Yorks 213 B8
Carr Gtr Man 195 D9
  S Yorks 187 C8
Carradale Argyll 255 D9
Carragraich W Isles . . 305 J3
Carr Bank Cumb 211 D9
Carrbridge Highld . . . 301 G9
Carrbrook Gtr Man . . . 196 G3
Carr Cross Lancs . . . 193 E11
Carreglefn Anglesey . . 178 D5
Carreg-wen Pembs 92 C4
Carreg y Garth
  Gwyn 163 B9
Carr Gate W Yorks . . 197 C10
Carr Green Gtr Man . . 184 D2
Carr Hill T&W 243 E7
Carrhouse Devon 26 F3
Carr Houses Mers . . 193 G10
Carrick Argyll 275 E10
  Dumfries 237 D7
  Fife 287 E8
Carrick Castle
  Argyll 276 C3
Carrick Ho Orkney . . 314 C5
Carriden Falk 279 E10
Carrington Gtr Man . . 184 C2
  Lincs 174 E4
  Midloth 270 C6
  Nottingham 171 G9
Carroch Dumfries . . . 246 E5
Carrog Conwy 164 F3
  Denb 165 G10
Carroglen Perth 285 E11
Carrol Highld 311 J2
Carron Falk 279 E7
  Moray 302 E2
Carronbridge
  Dumfries 247 D9
Carron Bridge
  Stirling 278 E4
Carronshore Falk . . . 279 E7
Carrot Angus 287 C8
Carroway Head
  Staffs 134 D3
Carrow Hill Mon 78 G6
Carrshield Northumb . 232 B2
Carrutherstown
  Dumfries 238 C4
Carr Vale Derbys . . . 171 B7
Carrville Durham . . . 234 C2
Carry Argyll 275 G10
Carsaig Argyll 275 E8
  Argyll 289 G7
Carscreugh
  Dumfries 236 D4
Carsegowan
  Dumfries 236 D6
Carse Gray Angus . . . 287 B8
Carse Ho Argyll 275 G8
Carseriggan
  Dumfries 236 D5
Carsethorn
  Dumfries 237 D11
Carshalton London . . . 67 G9
Carshalton Beeches
  London 67 G9
Carshalton on the Hill
  London 67 G9
Carsington Derbys . . 170 E3
Carskiey Argyll 255 G7
Carsluith Dumfries . . 236 D6
Carsphairn Dumfries . 246 E3
Carstairs S Lanark . . 269 F8
Carstairs Junction
  S Lanark 269 F9
Carswell Marsh Oxon . 82 F4
Cartbridge Sur 50 B4
Carterhaugh
  Borders 261 D10
Carter Knowle
  S Yorks 186 E4
Carter's Clay Hants . . 32 C4
Carter's Green Essex . 87 C8
Carter's Hill
  Wokingham 65 F9
Carterspiece Glos 79 C9
Carterton Oxon 82 D3
Carterway Heads
  Northumb 242 G2
Carthamartha Corn . . 12 F3
Carthew Corn 2 B5
  Corn 5 D10
Carthorpe N Yorks . . 214 C6
Cartington
  Northumb 252 C2
Cartland S Lanark . . . 269 F7
Cartledge Derbys . . . 186 F4
Cartmel Cumb 211 D7
Cartmel Fell Cumb . . 211 D8
Cartsdyke Invclyd . . . 276 F5
Cartworth W Yorks . . 196 F6
Carty Port Dumfries . 236 C6
Carway Carms 75 D7
Carwinley Cumb . . . 239 C10
Carwynnen Corn 2 B5
Cary Fitzpaine Som . . 29 B9

Carzantic Corn 12 E3
Carzield Dumfries . . 247 G11
Carzise Corn 2 C3
Cascob Powys 114 D4
Cashes Green Glos . . . 80 D4
Cashlie Perth 285 C8
Cashmoor Dorset 31 E7
Cas Mael = Puncheston
  Pembs 91 F10
Cassey Compton
  Glos 81 C9
Cassington Oxon 83 C7
Cassop Durham 234 D2
Castallack Corn 1 D5
Castell Conwy 164 B3
  Denb 165 B10
Castellau Rhondda . . . 58 B5
Castell-Howell
  Ceredig 93 B8
Castell nedd = Neath
  Neath 57 B7
Castell Newydd Emlyn =
  Newcastle Emlyn
  Carms 92 C6
Castell-y-bwch Torf . . 78 G3
Castell-y-rhingyll
  Carms 75 C9
Casterton Cumb 212 D2
Castle Devon 28 G4
  Som 27 B9
Castle Acre Norf 158 F6
Castle Ashby
  N Nhants 121 F7
Castle Bolton
  N Yorks 223 G8
Castle Bromwich
  W Mid 134 F2
Castle Bytham Lincs . 155 F8
Castlebythe Pembs . . . 91 F10
Castle Caereinion
  Powys 130 B3
Castle Camps
  Cambs 106 C2
Castle Carlton Lincs . 190 E5
Castle Carrock
  Cumb 240 F2
Castlecary N Lanark . 278 F5
Castle Cary Som 44 G6
Castle Combe Wilts . . 61 D10
Castlecraig Highld . . 301 C8
Castle Craig
  Borders 270 G2
Castlecroft Staffs . . . 133 D7
Castle Donington
  Leics 153 D8
Castle Douglas
  Dumfries 237 C9
Castle Eaton
  Swindon 81 F10
Castle Eden Durham . 234 D4
Castle End Pboro . . . 138 B2
Castlefairn Dumfries . 246 F6
Castlefields Halton . . 183 E8
Castle Fields
  Shrops 149 G10
Castle Forbes
  Aberds 293 B8
Castleford W Yorks . . 198 B2
Castle Frome
  Hereford 98 B3
Castle Gate Corn 1 C5
Castlegreen Shrops . . 130 F6
Castle Green London . 68 C3
  Sur 66 G3
  S Yorks 197 G8
Castle Gresley
  Derbys 152 F5
Castlehead Renfs . . . 267 C9
Castle Heaton
  Northumb 273 G8
Castle Hedingham
  Essex 106 D5
Castlehill Argyll 254 B4
  Borders 260 B6
  Highld 310 C5
  S Ayrs 257 E9
  W Dunb 277 F7
Castle Hill E Sus 37 B9
  Gtr Man 184 C6
  Kent 53 E7
  Suff 108 B3
  Worcs 116 F5
Castle Huntly Perth . . 287 E7
Castle Kennedy
  Dumfries 236 D3
Castlemaddy
  Dumfries 246 F3
Castlemartin Pembs . . 72 F6
Castlemilk Dumfries . 238 B5
  Glasgow 268 D2
Castlemorris Pembs . . 91 E8
Castlemorton Worcs . . 98 D5
Castle O'er Dumfries . 248 E6
Castlerigg Cumb . . . 229 G11
Castle Rising Norf . . 158 E3
Castleside Durham . . 233 B7
Castle Street
  W Yorks 196 C3
Castle Stuart Highld . 301 E7
Castlethorpe
  M Keynes 102 C6
  N Lincs 200 F3
Castleton Angus 287 C7
  Argyll 275 G9
  Derbys 185 E11
  Gtr Man 195 E11
  Moray 301 G11
  Newport 59 C9
  N Yorks 226 D3
Castleton Village
  Highld 300 E6
Castle Toward
  Argyll 266 B2
Castletown Ches W . . 166 E6
  Cumb 230 E6
  Dorset 17 G9
  Highld 301 E7
  Highld 310 C5
  IoM 192 F3
  Staffs 151 E8
  T&W 243 F9

Castletump Glos 98 F4
Castle-upon-Alun
  V Glam 58 E2
Castle Vale W Mid . . 134 E2
Castleweary
  Borders 249 C10
Castlewigg Dumfries . 236 E6
Castley N Yorks 205 D11
Castling's Heath
  Suff 107 C9
Caston Norf 141 D9
Castor Pboro 138 D2
Caswell Swansea 56 D5
Catacol N Ayrs 255 C10
Cat Bank Cumb 220 F6
Catbrain S Glos 60 C5
Catbrook Mon 79 E8
Catch Flint 182 G2
Catchall Corn 1 D4
Catchems Corner
  W Mid 118 B4
Catchems End
  Worcs 116 B5
Catchgate Durham . . 242 G5
Catchory Highld 310 D6
Catcleugh Northumb . 250 C6
Catcliffe S Yorks . . . 186 D6
Catcott Som 43 F11
Caterham Sur 51 B10
Catfield Norf 161 E7
Catfirth Shetland . . . 313 H6
Catford London 67 E11
Catforth Lancs 202 F5
Cathays Cardiff 59 D7
Cathays Park Cardiff . 59 D7
Cathcart Glasgow . . . 267 C11
Cathedine Powys 96 F2
Catherine-de-Barnes
  W Mid 134 G3
Catherine Slack
  W Yorks 196 B5
Catherington Hants . . 33 E11
Catherton Shrops . . . 116 B3
Cat Hill S Yorks 197 F8
Cathiron Warks 119 B9
Catholes Cumb 222 G3
Cathpair Borders . . . 271 F9
Catisfield Hants 33 F8
Catley Lane Head
  Gtr Man 195 D11
Catley Southfield
  Hereford 98 C3
Catlodge Highld 291 D8
Catlowdy Cumb 239 B11
Catmere End Essex . . 105 D9
Catmore W Berks 64 C3
Caton Devon 13 G11
  Lancs 211 G10
Caton Green Lancs . . 211 F10
Catrine E Ayrs 258 D2
Cat's Ash Newport . . . 78 G5
Cat's Common Norf . . 160 E6
Cats Edge Staffs 169 E7
Catsfield E Sus 38 E2
Catsfield Stream
  E Sus 38 E2
Catsgore Som 29 B8
Catshaw S Yorks 197 G8
Catshill W Mid 133 B11
  Worcs 117 C9
Cat's Hill Cross
  Staffs 150 C6
Catslackburn
  Borders 261 D8
Catslip Oxon 65 B8
Catstree Shrops 132 D4
Cattadale Argyll 274 G4
Cattal N Yorks 206 C4
Cattawade Suff 108 E2
Cattedown Plym 7 E9
Catterall Lancs 202 E5
Catterick N Yorks . . . 224 F4
Catterick Bridge
  N Yorks 224 F4
Catterick Garrison
  N Yorks 224 F3
Catterlen Cumb 230 E5
Catterline Aberds . . . 293 F10
Catterton N Yorks . . 206 D6
Catteshall Sur 50 E3
Catthorpe Leics 119 B11
Cattistock Dorset 17 B7
Cattle End
  W Nhants 102 C3
Catton Northumb . . . 241 F9
  N Yorks 215 D7
Catwick E Yorks 209 D8
Catworth Cambs . . . 121 C11
Caudle Green Glos . . 80 C6
Caudlesprings Norf . . 141 C8
Caulcott C Beds 103 C9
  Oxon 101 G10
Cauld Borders 261 G11
Cauldcoats Holdings
  Falk 279 F10
Cauldcots Angus 287 C10
Cauldhame Stirling . . 278 C2
Cauldmill Borders . . . 262 G2
Cauldon Staffs 169 F9
Cauldon Lowe
  Staffs 169 F9
Cauldwells Aberds . . 303 D7
Caulkerbush
  Dumfries 237 D11
Caulside Dumfries . . 249 G10
Caundle Marsh
  Dorset 29 E11
Caunsall Worcs 132 G6
Caunton Notts 172 D2
Causeway Hants 33 E11
  Hants 34 C2
  Mon 60 B2
Causewayend
  S Lanark 260 B2
Causeway End
  Cumb 210 C6
  Cumb 211 B9
  Dumfries 236 C6
  Essex 87 B11
  Wilts 62 C4

Causeway Foot
  W Yorks 197 E7
  W Yorks 205 G7
Causeway Green
  W Mid 133 F9
Causewayhead
  Cumb 238 G4
  Stirling 278 B6
Causewaywood
  Shrops 131 D10
Causey Durham 242 F6
Causeyend Aberds . . 293 B11
Causey Park Bridge
  Northumb 252 E5
Causeyton Aberds . . 293 B8
Caute Devon 24 E6
Cautley Cumb 222 G3
Cavendish Suff 106 B6
Cavendish Bridge
  Leics 153 D8
Cavenham Suff 124 D5
Cavers Carre
  Borders 262 D3
Caversfield Oxon . . . 101 F11
Caversham Reading . . 65 E8
Caversham Heights
  Reading 65 D8
Caverswall Staffs . . . 169 G7
Cavil E Yorks 207 G11
Cawdor Highld 301 D8
Cawkeld E Yorks . . . 208 C5
Cawkwell Lincs 190 F3
Cawood N Yorks 207 F7
Cawsand Corn 7 E8
Cawston Norf 160 E2
  Warks 119 C9
Cawthorne N Yorks . . 216 B5
  S Yorks 197 F9
Cawton N Yorks 216 D2
Caxton Cambs 122 F6
Caynham Shrops . . . 115 C11
Caythorpe Lincs 172 F6
  Notts 171 F11
Cayton N Yorks 217 C11
Ceallan W Isles 296 F4
Ceann a Bhaigh
  W Isles 296 F3
Ceann a Bhàigh
  W Isles 305 J4
Ceannacroc Lodge
  Highld 290 B4
Ceann a Deas Loch
  Baghasdail
  W Isles 297 K3
Ceann Shiphoirt
  W Isles 305 G4
Ceann Tarabhaigh
  W Isles 305 G4
Cearsiadair W Isles . . 304 F5
Ceathramh Meadhanach
  W Isles 296 E4
Cefn Newport 59 B9
Cefn Berain Conwy . . 165 B7
Cefn-brith Conwy . . . 164 E6
Cefn-bryn-brain
  Carms 76 C2
Cefn-bychan
  Swansea 56 B4
  Wrex 166 G3
Cefncaeau Carms 56 B4
Cefn Canol Powys . . 148 C4
Cefn-coch Conwy . . . 164 B5
Cefn Coch Powys . . . 129 C10
  Powys 148 D2
Cefn-coed-y-cymmer
  M Tydf 77 D9f
Cefn Cribwr
  Bridgend 57 E11
Cefn Cross Bridgend . 57 E11
Cefn-ddwysarn
  Gwyn 147 B9
Cefn Einion Shrops . . 130 F5
Cefneithin Carms 75 C9
Cefn-eurgain Flint . . 166 B2
Cefn Fforest Caerph . 77 F11
Cefn Glas Bridgend . . 57 E11
Cefn Golau
  Bl Gwent 77 D10
Cefn-gorwydd
  Powys 95 B8
Cefn Hengoed
  Caerph 77 F10
Cefn-hengoed
  Swansea 57 B7
Cefn Llwyd Ceredig . 128 G2
Cefn-mawr Wrex . . . 166 G3
Cefnpennar Rhondda . 77 E8
Cefn Rhigos Rhondda . 76 D6
Cefn-y-bedd Flint . . . 166 D4
Cefn-y-Crib Torf 78 F2
Cefn-y-Garth
  Swansea 76 E2
Cefn-y-pant Carms . . 92 F3
Cegidfa = Guilsfield
  Powys 148 G4
Cei-bach Ceredig . . . 111 F8
Ceinewydd = New Quay
  Ceredig 111 F7
Ceint Anglesey 179 F7
Ceinws Powys 128 B5
Cellan Ceredig 94 B2
Cellarhead Staffs . . . 169 F7
Cemaes Anglesey . . . 178 C5
Cemmaes Powys 128 B6
Cemmaes Road =
  Glantwymyn Powys . 128 C5
Cenarth Carms 92 C5
Cenin Gwyn 163 F7
Central Invclyd 276 F5
Central Milton Keynes
  M Keynes 102 D6
Ceos W Isles 304 F5
Ceres Fife 287 F8
Ceri = Kerry Powys . . 130 F2
Cerne Abbas Dorset . . 29 G11
Cerney Wick Glos 81 F9
Cerrigceinwen
  Anglesey 178 G6

Cerrig Llwydion
  Neath 57 C9
Cerrig-mân
  Anglesey 179 C7
Cerrigydrudion
  Conwy 165 F7
Cess Norf 161 F8
Cessford Borders . . . 262 E6
Ceunant Gwyn 163 C8
Chaceley Glos 99 E7
Chaceley Hole Glos . . 98 E6
Chaceley Stock Glos . 99 F7
Chacewater Corn 4 G4
Chackmore Bucks . . . 102 D3
Chacombe
  W Nhants 101 C9
Chadbury Worcs 99 B10
Chadderton
  Gtr Man 196 F2
Chadderton Fold
  Gtr Man 195 F11
Chaddesden Derbys . 153 B7
Chaddesley Corbett
  Worcs 117 C7
Chaddlehanger
  Devon 12 F5
Chaddlewood Plym . . 7 D11
Chaddleworth
  W Berks 64 D2
Chadkirk Gtr Man . . 184 D6
Chadlington Oxon . . 100 G6
Chadshunt Warks . . . 118 G6
Chadsmoor Staffs . . . 151 G9
Chadstone
  W Nhants 121 F7
Chadwell Leics 154 E5
  Shrops 150 F5
Chadwell End
  Bedford 121 D11
Chadwell Heath
  London 68 B3
Chadwell St Mary
  Thurrock 68 D6
Chadwick Worcs . . . 116 D6
Chadwick End
  W Mid 118 C4
Chadwick Green
  Mers 183 B8
Chaffcombe Som 28 E5
Chafford Hundred
  Thurrock 68 D5
Chagford Devon 13 D10
Chailey E Sus 36 D5
Chainbridge Cambs . 139 C8
Chain Bridge Lincs . . 174 G4
Chainhurst Kent 53 D8
Chalbury Dorset 31 F8
Chalbury Common
  Dorset 31 F8
Chaldon Sur 51 B10
Chaldon Herring or East
  Chaldon Dorset 17 E11
Chale IoW 20 F5
Chale Green IoW 20 F5
Chalfont Common
  Bucks 85 G8
Chalfont Grove Bucks . 85 G7
Chalfont St Giles
  Bucks 85 G7
Chalfont St Peter
  Bucks 85 G8
Chalford Glos 80 E5
  Oxon 84 E2
  Wilts 45 C11
Chalford Hill Glos . . 80 E5
Chalgrave C Beds . . . 103 F10
Chalgrove Oxon 83 F10
Chalk Kent 69 E7
Chalk End Essex 87 C10
Chalkfoot Cumb 230 B2
Chalkhill Norf 141 C7
Chalkhouse Green
  Oxon 65 D8
Chalksole Kent 55 E9
Chalkway Som 28 F5
Chalkwell Kent 69 G11
  Southend 69 B11
Challaborough
  Devon 8 G3
Challacombe Devon . . 41 E7
  Devon 24 E2
Challister Shetland . . 312 F7
Challoch Dumfries . . 236 C5
Challock Kent 54 C4
Chalmington Dorset . 29 G9
Chalton C Beds 103 F10
  Hants 34 D2
Chalvedon Essex 69 B8
Chalvey Slough 66 D3
Chalvington E Sus . . 23 D8
Chambercombe
  Devon 40 D4
Chamber's Green
  Kent 54 E2
Champson Devon 26 B4
Chance Inn Fife 287 F7
Chancery = Rhydgaled
  Ceredig 111 B11
Chance's Pitch
  Hereford 98 C4
Chandler's Cross
  Herts 85 F9
  Worcs 98 D5
Chandler's Ford
  Hants 32 C6
Chandlers Green
  Hants 49 B8
Channel's End
  Bedford 122 F2
Channel Tunnel Kent . 55 F7
Channerwick
  Shetland 313 L6
Chantry Devon 25 C9
  Som 45 D8
  Suff 108 C2

Chapel Brampton
  W Nhants 120 D4
Chapel Chorlton
  Staffs 150 B6
Chapel Cleeve Som . . 42 E4
Chapel Cross E Sus . . 37 C10
Chapel End
  Bedford 103 B11
  Bedford 122 F2
  Cambs 138 G3
  C Beds 103 C11
  Essex 105 G11
  N Nhants 138 F2
  Warks 134 E6
Chapel Field
  Gtr Man 195 F9
  Norf 161 E7
Chapel Fields
  W Mid 118 B6
  London 68 D3
  Northumb 251 F8
Chapelgate Lincs . . . 157 E8
Chapel Green Herts . 104 D5
  Warks 119 C9
  Warks 134 F5
Chapel Haddlesey
  N Yorks 198 B5
Chapelhall N Lanark . 268 C5
Chapel Head Cambs . 138 G6
Chapelhill Dumfries . 248 B5
  Highld 301 B8
  N Ayrs 266 C5
  Perth 286 D4
  Perth 286 E3
  Perth 286 E6
Chapel Hill Aberds . . 303 F10
  Glos 79 E10
  Lincs 174 E2
  Mon 79 F8
  N Yorks 206 D2
Chapel House Aberds . 194 F3
Chapel Knapp Wilts . 61 F11
Chapelknowe
  Dumfries 239 C8
Chapel Lawn Shrops . 114 B6
Chapel-le-Dale
  N Yorks 212 D4
Chapel Leigh Som . . 27 B10
Chapel Mains
  Borders 271 G11
Chapel Milton
  Derbys 185 E9
Chapel of Garioch
  Aberds 303 G7
Chapel of Stoneywood
  Aberdeen 293 B10
Chapel on Leader
  Borders 271 G11
Chapel Outon
  Dumfries 236 E6
Chapel Plaister
  Wilts 61 F10
Chapel Row Essex . . 88 E3
  E Sus 23 C10
  W Berks 64 F5
Chapels Blackburn . . 195 C7
  Cumb 210 C4
Chapel St Leonards
  Lincs 191 G9
Chapel Stile Cumb . . 220 D6
Chapelthorpe
  W Yorks 197 D10
Chapelton Angus . . . 287 C10
  Devon 25 B9
  Highld 291 B11
  S Lanark 268 F3
Chapelton Row
  Dumfries 237 E8
Chapeltown
  Blackburn 195 D8
  Moray 302 G2
  S Yorks 186 B5
  W Yorks 206 F2
Chapel Town Corn . . 5 D7
Chapman's Hill
  Worcs 117 B9
Chapmanslade
  Wilts 45 D11
Chapman's Town
  E Sus 23 C10
Chapmans Well
  Devon 12 C2
Chapmore End Herts . 86 B4
Chappel Essex 107 F7
Charaton Cross Corn . 6 B6
Charcott Kent 52 D4
Chard Som 28 E4
Chard Junction
  Dorset 28 G4
Chardleigh Green
  Som 28 E4
Chardstock Devon . . . 28 G4
Charfield S Glos 80 G2
Charfield Green
  S Glos 80 G2
Charfield Hill S Glos . 80 G2
Charford Worcs 117 D9
Chargrove Glos 80 B6
Charing Kent 54 D3
Charing Cross
  Dorset 31 E10
Charing Heath Kent . 54 D2
Charing Hill Kent . . . 54 C3
Charingworth Glos . . 100 D2
Charlbury Oxon 82 B5
Charlcombe Bath 61 F8
Charlcutt Wilts 62 D3
Charlecote Warks . . . 118 F5
Charlemont W Mid . . 133 E10
Charles Devon 41 G7
Charles Bottom
  Devon 41 G7
Charlesfield
  Borders 262 D3
  Dumfries 238 D5
Charleshill Sur 49 E11
Charleston Angus . . . 287 C7
  Renfs 267 C9
Charlestown
  Aberdeen 293 C11

Charlestown continued
  Corn 5 E10
  Derbys 185 C8
  Dorset 17 F9
  Fife 279 E11
  Gtr Man 195 G10
  Gtr Man 195 G11
  Highld 299 B8
  Highld 300 E6
  W Yorks 196 B5
  W Yorks 205 G8
Charlestown of Aberlour
  Moray 302 E2
Charles Tye Suff 125 G10
Charlesworth
  Derbys 185 C8
Charlton Devon 8 G5
  Hants 47 D11
  Herts 104 F3
  London 68 D2
  Northumb 251 F8
  Oxon 64 B2
  Redcar 226 B3
  Som 28 B3
  Som 44 B6
  Som 45 C7
  Sur 66 F5
  Telford 149 G11
  Wilts 30 C6
  Wilts 46 B6
  Wilts 62 B3
  W Nhants 101 D10
  Worcs 99 B10
  Worcs 116 C6
  W Sus 34 E5
Charlton Abbots
  Glos 99 G10
Charlton Adam Som . 29 B8
Charlton-All-Saints
  Wilts 31 C11
Charltonbrook
  S Yorks 186 B4
Charlton Down
  Dorset 17 C9
Charlton Horethorne
  Som 29 C11
Charlton Kings Glos . 99 G9
Charlton Mackrell
  Som 29 B8
Charlton Marshall
  Dorset 30 G5
Charlton Musgrove
  Som 30 B2
Charlton on Otmoor
  Oxon 83 B9
Charlton on the Hill
  Dorset 30 G5
Charlton Park Glos . . 99 G9
Charlton St Peter
  Wilts 46 B6
Charlwood E Sus . . . 51 G11
  Hants 49 G7
  Sur 51 E8
Charlynch Som 43 F8
Charminster BCP . . . 19 C8
  Dorset 17 C9
Charmouth Dorset . . . 16 C3
Charnage Wilts 45 G10
Charndon Bucks 102 G3
Charnes Staffs 150 C5
Charney Bassett
  Oxon 82 G5
Charnock Green
  Lancs 194 D5
Charnock Hall
  S Yorks 186 E5
Charnock Richard
  Lancs 194 D5
Charsfield Suff 126 F5
Chart Corner Kent . . 53 C9
Charter Alley Hants . 48 B5
Charterhouse Som . . 44 B3
Chartershall Stirling . 278 C6
Charterville Allotments
  Oxon 82 C4
Chartham Kent 54 C6
Chartham Hatch Kent . 54 B6
Chart Hill Kent 53 D9
Chartridge Bucks . . . 84 E6
Chart Sutton Kent . . 53 D10
Charvil Wokingham . . 65 D9
Charwelton
  W Nhants 119 F10
Chase Cross London . 87 G8
Chase End Street
  Worcs 98 D5
Chase Hill S Glos . . . 61 B8
Chase Terrace
  Staffs 133 B10
Chasetown Staffs . . . 133 B10
Chastleton Oxon . . . 100 F4
Chasty Devon 24 G4
Chatburn Lancs 203 E11
Chatcull Staffs 150 C5
Chatham Caerph 59 B7
  Medway 69 F9
Chatham Green
  Essex 88 B2
Chathill Northumb . . 264 D5
Chat Hill W Yorks . . 205 G8
Chatley Worcs 117 E7
Chattenden Medway . 69 E9
Chatter End Essex . . 105 F9
Chatteris Cambs 139 F7
Chatterley Staffs . . . 168 E4
Chatterton Lancs . . . 195 D9
Chattern Hill Sur . . . 66 E5
Chatton Northumb . . 264 D3
Chaulden Herts 85 D9
Chaul End C Beds . . 103 G11
Chavel Shrops 149 G8
Chavenage Green
  Glos 80 F5
Chavey Down Brack . 65 F11
Chawleigh Devon . . . 26 E2
Chawley Oxon 83 E7

Chawson Worcs 117 E7
Chawston Bedford . . 122 F3
Chawton Hants 49 F8
Chaxhill Glos 80 C2
Chazey Heath Oxon . 65 D7
Cheadle Gtr Man . . . 184 D5
  Staffs 169 G8
Cheadle Heath
  Gtr Man 184 D5
Cheadle Hulme
  Gtr Man 184 D5
Cheadle Park Staffs . 169 G8
Cheam London 67 G8
Cheapside Herts 105 E8
  Sur 50 B4
  Windsor 66 F2
Chearsley Bucks 84 C2
Chebsey Staffs 151 D7
Checkendon Oxon . . . 65 D7
Checkley Ches E 168 F2
  Hereford 97 D11
  Staffs 151 B11
Checkley Green
  Ches E 168 F2
Chedburgh Suff 124 F5
Cheddar Som 44 C3
Cheddington Bucks . . 84 C6
Cheddleton Staffs . . . 169 E7
Cheddleton Heath
  Staffs 169 E8
Cheddon Fitzpaine
  Som 28 B2
Chedglow Wilts 80 G6
Chedgrave Norf 143 D7
Chedington Dorset . . 29 F7
Chediston Suff 127 B7
Chediston Green
  Suff 127 B7
Chedworth Glos 81 C8
Chedworth Laines
  Glos 81 C8
Chedzoy Som 43 F10
Cheeklaw Borders . . . 272 E5
Cheeseman's Green
  Kent 54 F4
Cheetham Hill
  Gtr Man 195 G10
Cheglinch Devon . . . 40 E4
Chegworth Kent 53 C10
Cheldon Devon 26 E2
Chelfham Devon 40 F6
Chelford Ches E 184 G4
Chellaston Derby . . . 153 C7
Chell Heath Stoke . . 168 E5
Chellington Bedford . 121 F9
Chells Herts 104 F5
Chelmarsh Shrops . . 132 F4
Chelmer Village
  Essex 88 D2
Chelmick Shrops . . . 131 E9
Chelmondiston Suff . 108 D4
Chelmorton Derbys . 169 B10
Chelmsford Essex . . . 88 D2
Chelmsine Som 27 D11
Chelmsley Wood
  W Mid 134 F3
Chelsea London 67 D9
Chelsfield London . . . 68 G3
Chelsham Sur 51 B11
Chelston Som 27 C11
  Torbay 9 C7
Chelston Heathfield
  Som 27 C11
Chelsworth Suff 107 C9
Chelsworth Common
  Suff 107 B9
Cheltenham Glos . . . 99 G8
Chelveston
  N Nhants 121 D9
Chelvey N Som 60 F3
Chelvey Batch N Som . 60 F3
Chelwood Bath 60 G6
Chelwood Common
  E Sus 36 G6
Chelwood Gate
  E Sus 36 G6
Chelworth Wilts 81 G7
Chelworth Lower Green
  Wilts 81 G8
Chelworth Upper Green
  Wilts 81 G8
Chelynch Som 45 E7
Chemistry Shrops . . . 167 G8
Cheney Longville
  Shrops 131 G8
Chenhalls Corn 2 B3
Chenies Bucks 85 F8
Cheny Longville
  Shrops 131 G8
Chepstow Mon 79 G8
Chequerbent
  Gtr Man 195 F7
Chequerfield
  W Yorks 198 C3
Chequers Corner
  Norf 139 B9
Chequertree Kent . . . 54 F4
Cherhill Wilts 62 E4
Cherington Glos 80 F6
  Warks 100 D5
Cheristow Devon . . . 24 B3
Cheriton Devon 41 D8
  Hants 33 B9
  Kent 55 F7
  Swansea 56 C3
Cheriton Bishop
  Devon 13 C11
Cheriton Cross
  Devon 13 C10
Cheriton Fitzpaine
  Devon 26 F5
Cheriton or Stackpole
  Elidor Pembs 73 F7
Cherrington Telford . 150 E3
Cherrybank Perth . . . 286 E5
Cherry Burton
  E Yorks 208 E5
Cherry Green
  Essex 105 F11
  Herts 105 F7
Cherry Hinton
  Cambs 123 F9

Cherry Orchard
Shrops 149 G9
Worcs 117 G7
Cherry Tree
Blackburn 195 B7
Gtr Man 185 C7
Cherrytree Hill
Derby 153 B7
Cherry Willingham
Lincs 189 G8
Chertsey Sur 66 F4
Chertsey Meads Sur 66 F5
Cheselbourne
Dorset 17 B11
Chesham Bucks 85 E7
Gtr Man 195 E10
Chesham Bois Bucks 85 F7
Cheshunt Herts 86 E5
Chesley Kent 69 G11
Cheslyn Hay Staffs 133 B9
Chessetts Wood
Warks 118 C3
Chessington London 67 G7
Chessmount Bucks 85 E7
Chestall Staffs 151 G11
Chester Ches W 166 B6
Chesterblade Som 45 E7
Chesterfield Derbys 186 G5
Staffs 134 B2
Chesterhill Midloth 271 B7
Chesterhope
Northumb 251 F9
Chesterknowes
Borders 262 D2
Chester-le-Street
Durham 243 G7
Chester Moor
Durham 233 B11
Chesters Borders 262 E4
Borders 262 G4
Chesterton Cambs 123 E9
Cambs 138 D2
Glos 81 E8
Oxon 101 G11
Shrops 132 D5
Staffs 168 F4
Warks 118 F6
Chesterton Green
Warks 118 F6
Chesterwood
Northumb 241 D8
Chestfield Kent 70 F6
Chestnut Hill
Cumb 229 G11
Chestnut Street
Kent 69 G11
Cheston Devon 8 D3
Cheswardine
Shrops 150 D4
Cheswell Telford 150 F4
Cheswick Northumb 273 F10
Cheswick Buildings
Northumb 273 F10
Cheswick Green
W Mid 118 B2
Chetnole Dorset 29 F10
Chettiscombe Devon 27 E7
Chettisham Cambs 139 G10
Chettle Dorset 31 E7
Chetton Shrops 132 E3
Chetwode Bucks 102 F2
Chetwynd Aston
Telford 150 F5
Cheveley Cambs 124 E3
Chevening Kent 52 B3
Cheverell's Green
Herts 85 B9
Chevin End W Yorks 205 E9
Chevington Suff 124 F5
Chevithorne Devon 27 D7
Chew Magna Bath 60 G5
Chew Moor Gtr Man 195 F7
Chew Stoke Bath 60 G5
Chewton Keynsham
Bath 61 F7
Chewton Mendip
Som 44 C5
Cheylesmore
W Mid 118 B6
Chichacott Devon 13 B8
Chicheley M Keynes 103 B8
Chichester W Sus 22 C5
Chickenley W Yorks 197 C9
Chickerell Dorset 17 E8
Chicklade Wilts 46 G2
Chickney Essex 105 F11
Chicksands C Beds 104 D2
Chicksgrove Wilts 46 G3
Chickward Hereford 114 G5
Chidden Hants 33 D11
Chiddingfold Sur 50 F3
Chiddingly E Sus 23 C8
Chiddingstone Kent 52 D3
Chiddingstone
Causeway Kent 52 D4
Chiddingstone Hoath
Kent 52 E3
Chideock Dorset 16 C4
Chidgley Som 42 F4
Chidham W Sus 22 C3
Chidswell W Yorks 197 C9
Chieveley W Berks 64 E3
Chignall St James
Essex 87 D11
Chignall Smealy
Essex 87 C11
Chigwell Essex 86 G6
Chigwell Row Essex 87 G7
Chilbolton Hants 47 F11
Chilbolton Down
Hants 48 F2
Chilbridge Dorset 31 G7
Chilcomb Hants 33 B8
Chilcombe Dorset 16 C6
Som 42 F6
Chilcompton Som 44 C6
Chilcote Leics 152 G5
Childerditch Essex 68 B6
Childerley Gate
Cambs 123 F7
Childer Thornton
Ches W 182 F5
Child Okeford Dorset 30 E4
Childrey Oxon 63 B11
Childsbridge Kent 52 B5
Child's Ercall Shrops 150 E3
Child's Hill London 67 B8
Childswickham
Worcs 99 D11
Childwall Mers 182 D6
Childwick Bury
Herts 85 C10
Childwick Green
Herts 85 C10
Chilfrome Dorset 17 B7
Chilgrove W Sus 34 E4
Chilham Kent 54 C5
Chilhampton Wilts 46 G5
Chilla Devon 24 G6
Chillaton Devon 12 E4
Chillenden Kent 55 C9
Chillerton IoW 20 E5
Chillesford Suff 127 G7
Chillingham
Northumb 264 D3
Chillington Devon 8 G5
Som 28 E5
Chillmill Kent 53 E7
Chilmark Wilts 46 G3
Chilmington Green
Kent 54 E3
Chilsham E Sus 23 C10
Chilson Oxon 82 B4
Som 28 G4
Chilson Common
Som 28 G4
Chilsworthy Corn 12 G4
Devon 24 F4
Chiltern Green C
Beds 85 B10
Chilthorne Domer
Som 29 D8
Chiltington E Sus 36 D5
Chilton Bucks 83 C11
Durham 233 F11
Kent 71 G11
Oxon 64 B3
Suff 107 C7
Chilton Candover
Hants 48 E5
Chilton Cantelo Som 29 C9
Chilton Foliat Wilts 63 E10
Chilton Lane
Durham 234 E2
Chilton Moor T&W 234 B2
Chilton Polden Som 43 F11
Chilton Street Suff 106 B5
Chilton Trinity Som 43 F9
Chilvers Coton
Warks 135 E7
Chilwell Notts 153 B10
Chilworth Hants 32 D6
Sur 50 D4
Chilworth Old Village
Hants 32 D6
Chimney Oxon 82 E5
Chimney-end Oxon 82 B4
Chimney Street Suff 106 B4
Chineham Hants 49 C7
Chingford London 86 G5
Chingford Green
London 86 G5
Chingford Hatch
London 86 G5
Chinley Derbys 185 E8
Chinley Head
Derbys 185 E9
Chinnor Oxon 84 E3
Chipley Som 27 C10
Chipmans Platt Glos 80 D3
Chipnall Shrops 150 C4
Chippenhall Green
Suff 126 B5
Chippenham Cambs 124 D3
Wilts 62 E2
Chipperfield Herts 85 E8
Chipping Herts 105 E7
Lancs 203 E8
Chipping Barnet
London 86 F2
Chipping Campden
Glos 100 D3
Chipping Hill Essex 88 B4
Chipping Norton
Oxon 100 F6
Chipping Ongar
Essex 87 E8
Chipping Sodbury
S Glos 61 C8
Chipping Warden
W Nhants 101 B9
Chipstable Som 27 B8
Chipstead Kent 52 B3
Sur 51 B9
Chirbury Shrops 130 D5
Chirk = Y Waun
Wrex 148 B5
Chirk Bank Shrops 148 B5
Chirk Green Wrex 148 B5
Chirmorrie S Ayrs 236 B4
Chirnside Borders 273 D7
Chirnsidebridge
Borders 273 D7
Chirton T&W 243 D8
Wilts 46 B5
Chisbridge Cross
Bucks 65 B10
Chisbury Wilts 63 F9
Chiselborough Som 29 E7
Chiseldon Swindon 63 D7
Chiserley W Yorks 196 B4
Chislehampton Oxon 83 F9
Chislehurst London 68 E2
Chislehurst West
London 68 E2
Chislet Kent 71 G8
Chislet Forstal Kent 71 G8
Chiswell Dorset 17 G9
Chiswell Green
Herts 85 E10
Chiswick London 67 D8
Chiswick End
Cambs 105 B7
Chisworth Derbys 185 C7
Chitcombe E Sus 38 C4
Chithurst W Sus 34 C4
Chittering Cambs 123 C9
Chitterley Devon 26 G6
Chitterne Wilts 46 E3
Chittlehamholt
Devon 25 C11
Chittlehampton
Devon 25 B10
Chittoe Wilts 62 F3
Chitts Hills Essex 107 F9
Chitty Kent 71 G8
Chivelstone Devon 9 G10
Chivenor Devon 40 G4
Chivery Bucks 84 D6
Chobham Sur 66 G3
Choicelee Borders 272 E4
Cholderton Wilts 47 E8
Cholesbury Bucks 84 D6
Chollerford
Northumb 241 C10
Chollerton
Northumb 241 C10
Cholmondeston
Ches E 167 C10
Cholsey Oxon 64 B5
Cholstrey Hereford 115 F9
Cholwell Bath 44 B6
Chop Gate N Yorks 225 F11
Choppington
Northumb 253 G7
Chopwell T&W 242 F4
Chorley Ches E 167 E9
Lancs 194 D5
Shrops 132 G3
Staffs 151 G11
Chorley Common
W Sus 34 B4
Chorleywood Herts 85 F8
Chorleywood Bottom
Herts 85 F8
Chorleywood West
Herts 85 F8
Chorlton Ches E 168 E2
Chorlton-cum-Hardy
Gtr Man 184 C4
Chorlton Lane
Ches W 167 F7
Choulton Shrops 131 F7
Chowdene T&W 243 F7
Chowley Ches W 167 D7
Chownes Mead
W Sus 36 C4
Chreagain Highld 289 C10
Chrishall Essex 105 D8
Christchurch BCP 19 C9
Cambs 139 D9
Glos 79 C9
Newport 59 B10
Christian Malford
Wilts 62 D3
Christleton Ches W 166 B6
Christmas Common
Oxon 84 G2
Christon N Som 43 B11
Christon Bank
Northumb 264 E6
Christow Devon 14 D2
Chryston N Lanark 278 G3
Chub Tor Devon 7 B10
Chuck Hatch E Sus 52 G3
Chudleigh Devon 14 F3
Chudleigh Knighton
Devon 14 F2
Chulmleigh Devon 25 E11
Chunal Derbys 185 C8
Church Lancs 195 B8
Churcham Glos 80 B3
Church Aston
Telford 150 F4
Churchbank Shrops 114 B6
Church Brampton
W Nhants 120 D4
Churchbridge Corn 6 D4
Staffs 133 B9
Church Brough
Cumb 222 C5
Church Broughton
Derbys 152 C4
Church Charwelton
W Nhants 119 F10
Church Clough
Lancs 204 F3
Church Common
Hants 34 B2
Church Coombe Corn 4 G3
Church Cove Corn 2 G6
Church Crookham
Hants 49 C10
Churchdown Glos 80 B5
Church Eaton Staffs 150 F6
Churchend Essex 89 G8
Essex 106 G2
Glos 80 D3
Reading 65 E7
S Glos 80 G2
Church End Bedford 122 F2
Bucks 84 B6
Bucks 84 D2
Cambs 121 C11
Cambs 123 C7
Cambs 123 D7
Cambs 138 G4
Cambs 139 B7
C Beds 85 B8
C Beds 103 E9
C Beds 103 G9
C Beds 104 D3
C Beds 122 G3
Essex 88 B2
Essex 105 C11
Essex 105 F11
Essex 106 F4
E Yorks 209 C7
Glos 80 D2
Glos 99 D7
Hants 49 B7
Herts 85 C10
Herts 85 F8
Herts 104 E5
Herts 105 G8
Lincs 156 C4
Church End *continued*
Lincs 190 B6
London 67 C8
London 86 G2
Norf 157 F10
Oxon 82 D5
Oxon 100 E6
Suff 108 D4
Sur 50 B5
Warks 134 E4
Warks 134 E5
Wilts 62 D4
W Mid 119 B7
Worcs 98 C6
Church Enstone
Oxon 101 G7
Churches Green
E Sus 23 B10
Church Fenton
N Yorks 206 F6
Churchfield Hereford 98 B4
W Mid 133 E10
Churchfields Wilts 31 B10
Churchgate Herts 86 E4
Churchgate Street
Essex 87 C7
Church Green Devon 15 B9
Norf 141 E11
Church Gresley
Derbys 152 F5
Church Hanborough
Oxon 82 C6
Church Hill
Ches W 167 C10
Pembs 73 C7
Staffs 151 G10
W Mid 133 D9
Worcs 117 D11
Church Hougham
Kent 55 E9
Church Houses
N Yorks 226 F3
Churchill Devon 28 G4
Devon 40 E5
N Som 44 B2
Oxon 100 G5
Worcs 117 B7
Worcs 117 G8
Churchill Green
N Som 60 G2
Churchinford Som 28 E2
Church Knowle
Dorset 18 E4
Church Laneham
Notts 188 F4
Church Langton
Leics 136 E4
Church Lawford
Warks 119 B8
Church Lawton
Ches E 168 D4
Church Leigh
Staffs 151 B10
Church Lench
Worcs 117 G10
Church Mayfield
Staffs 169 G11
Church Minshull
Ches E 167 C11
Churchmoor Rough
Shrops 131 F8
Church Norton
W Sus 22 D5
Church Oakley Hants 48 C5
Churchover Warks 135 G10
Church Preen
Shrops 131 D10
Church Pulverbatch
Shrops 131 C8
Churchstanton Som 27 E11
Churchstoke Powys 130 E5
Churchstow Devon 8 F4
Church Stowe
W Nhants 120 F2
Church Street
Essex 106 C5
Kent 69 E8
Church Stretton
Shrops 131 E9
Churchton Pembs 73 D10
Churchtown Corn 11 F7
Cumb 230 C3
Derbys 170 C3
Devon 24 G3
Devon 41 E7
IoM 192 C5
Lancs 202 E5
Mers 193 D11
Shrops 130 F5
Som 42 F3
Church Town Corn 4 G3
Leics 153 F7
N Lincs 199 F9
Sur 51 C11
Church Village
Rhondda 58 B5
Church Warsop
Notts 171 B9
Church Westcote
Glos 100 G4
Church Whitfield
Kent 55 D10
Church Wilne
Derbys 153 C8
Churchwood W Sus 35 D8
Churnet Grange
Staffs 169 E7
Churnsike Lodge
Northumb 240 B5
Churscombe Torbay 9 C7
Churston Ferrers
Torbay 9 D8
Churt Sur 49 F11
Churton Ches W 166 D6
Churwell W Yorks 197 B9
Chute Cadley Wilts 47 C10
Chute Standen
Wilts 47 C10
Chwefford Conwy 180 G4
Chwilog Gwyn 145 B8
Chwitffordd = *Whitford*
Flint 181 F10
Chyandour Corn 1 C5
Chyanvounder Corn 2 E5
Chycoose Corn 3 B8
Chynhale Corn 2 C4
Chynoweth Corn 2 C2
Chyvarloe Corn 2 E5
Cicelyford Mon 79 E8
Cilan Uchaf Gwyn 144 E5
Cilau Pembs 91 D8
Cilcain Flint 165 B11
Cilcennin Ceredig 111 E10
Cilcewydd Powys 130 C4
Cilfor Gwyn 146 B2
Cilfrew Neath 76 E3
Cilfynydd Rhondda 77 G9
Cilgerran Pembs 92 C3
Cilgwyn Carms 94 F4
Ceredig 92 C6
Gwyn 163 E7
Pembs 91 D11
Ciliau Aeron Ceredig 111 F9
Cill Amhlaidh
W Isles 297 G3
Cill Donnain
W Isles 297 J3
Cille Bhrighde
W Isles 297 K3
Cill Eireabhagh
W Isles 297 G4
Cille Pheadair
W Isles 297 K3
Cilmaengwyn Neath 76 D2
Cilmery Powys 113 G10
Cilsan Carms 93 G11
Ciltalgarth Gwyn 164 G5
Ciltwrch Powys 96 C3
Cilybebyll Neath 76 E2
Cil y coed = *Caldicot*
Mon 60 B3
Cilycwm Carms 94 D5
Cimla Neath 57 B9
Cinderford Glos 79 C11
Cinderhill Derbys 170 F5
Nottingham 171 G8
Cinder Hill Gtr Man 195 F9
Kent 52 D4
W Mid 133 E8
W Sus 36 B5
Cinnamon Brow
Warr 183 C10
Cippenham Slough 66 C2
Cippyn Pembs 92 B2
Circebost W Isles 304 E3
Cirencester Glos 81 E8
Ciribhig W Isles 304 D3
City London 67 C10
Powys 130 F4
V Glam 58 D3
City Dulas Anglesey 179 D7
Clabhach Argyll 288 D3
Clachaig Argyll 276 E2
Highld 292 B2
N Ayrs 255 E10
Clachan Argyll 255 B8
Argyll 275 B8
Argyll 284 F5
Argyll 289 E10
Highld 295 B7
Highld 298 C4
Highld 307 L6
W Isles 297 G3
Clachaneasy
Dumfries 236 B5
Clachanmore
Dumfries 236 E2
Clachan na Luib
W Isles 296 E4
Clachan of Campsie
E Dunb 278 F2
Clachan of Glendaruel
Argyll 275 E10
Clachan-Seil Argyll 275 B8
Clachan Strachur
Argyll 284 G4
Clachbreck Argyll 275 F8
Clachnabrain Angus 292 G5
Clachtoll Highld 307 G5
Clackmannan Clack 279 C8
Clackmarras Moray 302 D2
Clacton-on-Sea
Essex 89 B11
Cladach N Ayrs 256 B2
Cladach Chairinis
W Isles 296 F4
Cladach Chireboist
W Isles 296 E3
Claddach Argyll 254 B2
Claddach-knockline
W Isles 296 E3
Cladich Argyll 284 E4
Cladich Steading
Argyll 284 E4
Cladswell Worcs 117 F10
Claggan Highld 289 E8
Highld 290 F3
Perth 285 D11
Claigan Highld 298 D2
Claines Worcs 117 F7
Clandown Bath 45 B7
Clanfield Hants 33 D11
Oxon 82 E3
Clanking Bucks 84 D4
Clanville Hants 47 D10
Som 44 G6
Wilts 62 D2
Claonaig Argyll 255 B9
Claonel Highld 309 J5
Clapgate Dorset 31 G8
Herts 105 G8
Clapham Bedford 121 G10
Devon 14 D3
London 67 D9
N Yorks 212 F4
W Sus 35 F9
Clapham Green
Bedford 121 G10
N Yorks 205 B10
Clapham Hill Kent 70 G6
Clapham Park London 67 E9
Clap Hill Kent 54 F5
Clapper Corn 10 G6
Clapper Hill Kent 53 F10
Clappers Borders 273 D8
Clappersgate Cumb 221 E7
Clapphoull Shetland 313 L6
Clapton Som 28 F6
Som 44 C6
W Berks 63 E11
Clapton in Gordano
N Som 60 E3
Clapton-on-the-Hill
Glos 81 B11
Clapton Park London 67 B11
Clapworthy Devon 25 C11
Clarach Ceredig 128 G2
Clarack Aberds 292 D6
Clara Vale T&W 242 E4
Clarbeston Pembs 91 G10
Clarbeston Road
Pembs 91 G10
Clarborough Notts 188 E2
Clardon Highld 310 C5
Clare Oxon 83 F11
Suff 106 B5
Clarebrand Dumfries 237 C9
Claregate W Mid 133 C7
Claremont Park Sur 66 G6
Claremount
W Yorks 196 B5
Clarencefield
Dumfries 238 D3
Clarence Park
N Som 59 G10
Clarendon Park
Leicester 135 C11
Clareston Pembs 73 C7
Clarilaw Borders 262 D3
Borders 262 F2
Clarken Green Hants 48 C5
Clark Green Ches E 184 F6
Clarksfield Gtr Man 196 G2
Clark's Green Sur 51 F7
Clark's Hill Lincs 157 E7
Clarkston E Renf 267 D11
N Lanark 268 B5
Clase Swansea 57 B7
Clashandorran
Highld 300 E5
Clashcoig Highld 309 K6
Clasheddy Highld 308 C6
Clashgour Argyll 284 C6
Clashindarroch
Aberds 302 F4
Clashmore Highld 306 F5
Highld 309 L7
Clashnessie Highld 306 F5
Clashnoir Moray 302 G2
Clate Shetland 313 G7
Clatford Wilts 63 F7
Clatford Oakcuts
Hants 47 F10
Clathy Perth 286 F3
Clatt Aberds 302 G5
Clatter Powys 129 E9
Clatterford IoW 20 D5
Clatterford End
Essex 87 C10
Essex 87 D9
Essex 87 E8
Clatterin Bridge
Aberds 293 F8
Clatto Fife 287 F8
Clatworthy Som 42 G5
Clauchlands N Ayrs 256 C2
Claughton Lancs 202 E6
Lancs 211 F11
Mers 182 D4
Clavelshay Som 43 G9
Claverdon Warks 118 E3
Claverham N Som 60 F2
Claverhambury Essex 86 E6
Clavering Essex 105 E9
Claverley Shrops 132 E5
Claverton Bath 61 G9
Claverton Down Bath 61 G9
Clawdd-côch
V Glam 58 D5
Clawdd-newydd
Denb 165 E9
Clawdd Poncen
Denb 165 G9
Clawthorpe Cumb 211 D10
Clawton Devon 12 B3
Claxby Lincs 189 C10
Lincs 191 G7
Claxby St Andrew
Lincs 191 G7
Claxton Norf 142 C6
N Yorks 216 G3
Claybokie Aberds 292 D2
Claybrooke Magna
Leics 135 F9
Claybrooke Parva
Leics 135 F9
Clay Common Suff 143 G9
Clay Coton
W Nhants 119 B11
Clay Cross Derbys 170 C5
Claydon Glos 99 E8
Oxon 119 G9
Suff 126 G2
Clay End Herts 104 F6
Claygate Dumfries 239 B9
Kent 52 C6
Kent 53 E8
Sur 67 G7
Claygate Cross Kent 52 B6
Clayhall Hants 21 B8
London 86 G6
Clayhanger Devon 27 C8
Som 28 E4
W Mid 133 C10
Clayhidon Devon 27 D11
Clayhill E Sus 38 C4
Hants 32 F4
Clay Hill Bristol 60 E6
London 86 F4
W Berks 64 E5
Clayhithe Cambs 123 E10
Clayholes Angus 287 D9
Clay Lake Lincs 156 E5
Clayland Stirling 277 D11
Clay Mills Derbys 152 D5
Clayock Highld 310 D5
Claypit Hill Cambs 123 G7
Claypits Devon 27 B7
Glos 80 D3
Kent 55 B9
Suff 140 G4
Claypole Lincs 172 F5
Clays End Bath 61 G8
Claythorpe Lincs 190 F6
Clayton Gtr Man 184 B5
Staffs 168 G5
S Yorks 198 F3
W Sus 36 E3
W Yorks 205 G8
Clayton Brook
Lancs 194 C5
Clayton Green
Lancs 194 C5
Clayton Heights
W Yorks 205 G8
Clayton-le-Dale
Lancs 203 G9
Clayton-le-Moors
Lancs 203 G10
Clayton-le-Woods
Lancs 194 C5
Clayton West
W Yorks 197 E9
Clayworth Notts 188 D2
Cleadale Highld 294 G6
Cleadon T&W 243 E9
Cleadon Park T&W 243 E9
Clearbrook Devon 7 B10
Clearwell Glos 79 D9
Newport 59 B9
Clearwood Wilts 45 D10
Cleasby N Yorks 224 C5
Cleat Orkney 314 B4
Orkney 314 H4
Cleatlam Durham 224 B2
Cleator Cumb 219 C10
Cleator Moor
Cumb 219 B10
Cleave Devon 28 G2
Clebrig Highld 308 F5
Cleckheaton
W Yorks 197 B7
Cleddon Mon 79 E8
Cleedownton
Shrops 131 G11
Cleehill Shrops 115 B11
Cleekhimin
N Lanark 268 D5
Cleemarsh Shrops 131 G11
Clee St Margaret
Shrops 131 G11
Cleestanton Shrops 115 B11
Cleethorpes
NE Lincs 201 F10
Cleeton St Mary
Shrops 116 B2
Cleeve Glos 80 C2
N Som 60 F3
Oxon 64 C6
Cleeve Hill Glos 99 F9
Cleeve Prior Worcs 99 B11
Cleghorn S Lanark 269 F8
Clegyrnant Powys 129 B8
Clehonger Hereford 97 D9
Cleirwy = *Clyro*
Powys 96 C4
Cleish Perth 279 B11
Cleland N Lanark 268 D5
Clements End Glos 79 D9
Clement's End
C Beds 85 B8
Clement Street Kent 68 E4
Clench Wilts 63 G7
Clench Common
Wilts 63 F7
Clencher's Mill
Hereford 98 D4
Clenchwarton Norf 157 E11
Clennell Northumb 251 B10
Clent Worcs 117 B8
Cleobury Mortimer
Shrops 116 B3
Cleobury North
Shrops 132 F2
Cleongart Argyll 255 D7
Clephanton Highld 301 D8
Clerkenwater Corn 5 B11
Clerkenwell London 67 C10
Clerk Green
W Yorks 197 C8
Clerklands Borders 262 E2
Clermiston Edin 280 G3
Clestrain Orkney 314 F3
Cleuch Head
Borders 262 G3
Cleughbrae
Dumfries 238 C3
Clevancy Wilts 62 D5
Clevans Renfs 267 B7
Clevedon N Som 60 E2
Cleveley Oxon 101 G7
Cleveleys Lancs 202 E2
Cleverton Wilts 62 B3
Clevis Bridgend 57 F10
Clewer Som 44 C2
Clewer Green
Windsor 66 D2
Clewer New Town
Windsor 66 D3
Clewer Village
Windsor 66 D3
Cley next the Sea
Norf 177 E8
Cliaid W Isles 297 L2
Cliasmol W Isles 305 H2
Cliburn Cumb 231 G7
Click Mill Orkney 314 D3
Cliddesden Hants 48 D6
Cliff Derbys 185 D8
Warks 134 D4
Cliffburn Angus 287 C10
Cliffe Lancs 203 G10
Medway 69 D8
N Yorks 207 G9
N Yorks 224 B4
Cliff End E Sus 38 E5
W Yorks 196 D6
Cliffe Woods Medway 69 E8
Clifford Devon 24 C4
Hereford 96 B4
W Yorks 206 E4
Clifford Chambers
Warks 118 G3
Clifford's Mesne Glos 98 G4
Cliffs End Kent 71 G10
Clifftown Southend 69 B11
Clifton Bristol 60 E5
C Beds 104 D3
Ches W 183 F8
Cumb 230 F6
Derbys 169 G11
Devon 40 E5
Gtr Man 195 G9
Lancs 202 G5
Northumb 252 G6
Nottingham 153 C11
N Yorks 205 D9
Oxon 101 E9
Stirling 285 D7
S Yorks 186 C6
S Yorks 187 B8
Worcs 98 B6
W Yorks 197 C7
York 207 C7
Clifton Campville
Staffs 152 G5
Cliftoncote Borders 263 E8
Clifton Green
Gtr Man 195 G9
Clifton Hampden
Oxon 83 F8
Clifton Junction
Gtr Man 195 G9
Clifton Manor
C Beds 104 D3
Clifton Maybank
Dorset 29 E9
Clifton Moor York 207 B7
Clifton Reynes
M Keynes 121 G8
Clifton upon Dunsmore
Warks 119 B10
Clifton upon Teme
Worcs 116 E4
Cliftonville Kent 71 E11
N Lanark 268 B4
Norf 160 B6
Climping W Sus 35 G8
Climpy S Lanark 269 D8
Clink Som 45 D9
Clinkham Wood
Mers 183 B8
Clint N Yorks 205 B11
Clint Green Norf 159 G10
Clintmains Borders 262 C4
Clints N Yorks 224 E2
Cliobh W Isles 304 E2
Clipiau Gwyn 146 G6
Clippesby Norf 161 G8
Clippings Green
Norf 159 G10
Clipsham Rutland 155 F9
Clipston Notts 154 C2
W Nhants 136 G4
Clipstone C Beds 103 F8
Clitheroe Lancs 203 E10
Cliuthar W Isles 305 J3
Clive Ches W 167 B11
Shrops 149 E10
Clive Green
Ches W 167 C11
Clive Vale E Sus 38 E4
Clivocast Shetland 312 C8
Clixby Lincs 200 G6
Cloatley Wilts 81 G7
Cloatley End Wilts 81 G7
Clocaenog Denb 165 E9
Clochan Aberds 303 E9
Moray 302 C4
Clock Face Mers 183 C8
Clock House London 67 G9
Clockmill Borders 272 E5
Clock Mills Hereford 96 B5
Cloddiau Powys 130 B4
Cloddymoss Moray 301 D9
Clodock Hereford 96 F6
Cloford Som 45 E8
Cloford Common
Som 45 E8
Cloigyn Carms 74 C6
Clola Aberds 303 E10
Clophill C Beds 103 D11
Clopton N Nhants 137 G11
Suff 126 G4
Clopton Corner Suff 126 G4
Clopton Green Suff 124 G5
Suff 125 E9
Closeburn Dumfries 247 E9
Close Clark IoM 192 E3
Close House
Durham 233 F10
Closworth Som 29 E9
Clothall Herts 104 E5
Clothall Common
Herts 104 E5
Clotton Ches W 167 C8
Clotton Common
Ches W 167 C8
Cloudesley Bush
Warks 135 F9
Clouds Hereford 97 D11
Cloud Side Staffs 168 C6
Clough Gtr Man 196 D2
Gtr Man 196 F2
W Yorks 196 E5
Clough Dene
Durham 242 F5
Cloughfold Lancs 195 C10
Clough Foot
W Yorks 196 C2
Clough Hall Staffs 168 E4
Clough Head
W Yorks 196 C5
Cloughton N Yorks 227 G10
Cloughton Newlands
N Yorks 227 F10
Clounlaid Highld 289 D9

Clousta Shetland 313 H5
Clouston Orkney 314 E2
Clova Aberds 302 G4
Angus 292 F5
Clovelly Devon 24 C4
Clove Lodge Durham .223 B8
Clovenfords
Borders 261 B10
Clovenstone Aberds .293 B9
Cloves Moray 301 C11
Clovullin Highld. . . . 290 C4
Clowance Wood Corn . . 2 C4
Clow Bridge Lancs .195 B10
Clowne Derbys. . . . 187 F7
Clows Top Worcs 116 C4
Cloy Wrex 166 G5
Cluanie Inn Highld . . 290 B2
Cluanie Lodge
Highld 290 B3
Clubmoor Mers. . . . 182 C5
Clubworthy Corn . . 11 C11
Cluddley Telford 150 G2
Clun Shrops 130 G6
Clunbury Shrops 131 G7
Clunderwen Carms . . 73 B10
Clune Highld 301 D9
Highld 301 G11
Clunes Highld. . . . 290 E4
Clungunford Shrops. .115 B7
Clunie Aberds 302 D6
Perth 286 C5
Clunton Shrops 130 G6
Cluny Fife 280 B4
Cluny Castle Aberds. .293 B8
Highld 291 D10
Clutton Bath. . . . 44 B6
Ches W. 167 E7
Clutton Hill Bath. . . . 44 B6
Clwt-grugoer
Conwy 165 C7
Clwt-y-bont Gwyn. .163 C9
Clwydyfagwyr
M Tydf 77 D8
Clydach Mon 78 C2
Swansea 75 E11
Clydach Terrace
Powys 77 C11
Clydach Vale
Rhondda 77 G7
Clydebank W Dunb . .277 G10
Clyffe Pypard Wilts . .62 D5
Clynder Argyll 276 E4
Clyne Neath 76 E4
Clynelish Highld 311 J2
Clynnog-fawr Gwyn. .162 F6
Clyro = Cleirwy
Powys 96 C4
Clyst Honiton Devon . .14 C5
Clyst Hydon Devon . . 27 G8
Clyst St George
Devon 14 D5
Clyst St Lawrence
Devon 27 G8
Clyst St Mary Devon . .14 C5
Cnip W Isles 304 E2
Cnoc Amhlaigh
W Isles 304 E7
Cnoc an t-Solais
W Isles 304 D6
Cnocbreac Argyll . .274 F5
Cnoc Fhionn
Highld 295 D10
Cnoc Màiri W Isles . .304 E6
Cnoc Rolum
W Isles 296 F3
Cnwch-coch
Ceredig 112 B3
Coachford Aberds. .302 E4
Coad's Green Corn. . . 11 F11
Coal Aston Derbys . .186 F5
Coalbank Darl 234 G3
Coalbrookdale
Telford 132 C3
Coalbrookvale
Bl Gwent 77 D11
Coalburn S Lanark. .259 C8
Coalburns T&W. . . .242 E4
Coalcleugh
Northumb 232 B2
Coaley Glos 80 E3
Coaley Peak Glos 80 E3
Coalford Aberds . .293 D10
Coalhall E Ayrs. 257 F10
Coalmoor Telford . .132 B3
Coalpit Field Warks .135 F7
Coalpit Heath S Glos . .61 C7
Coalpit Hill Staffs. . .168 E4
Coal Pool W Mid . . . 133 C10
Coalport Telford 132 C3
Coalsnaughton
Clack 279 B8
Coaltown of Balgonie
Fife 280 B5
Coaltown of Wemyss
Fife 280 B6
Coalville Leics 153 G8
Coalway Glos 79 C9
Coanwood Northumb .240 F5
Coarsewell Devon. . . . 8 E4
Coat Som 29 C7
Coatbridge
N Lanark 268 C4
Coatdyke N Lanark . .268 C5
Coate Swindon 63 C7
Wilts 62 G4
Coates Cambs 138 D6
Glos 81 E7
Lancs 204 D3
Lincs 188 E6
Midloth 270 C4
Notts 188 E4
W Sus 35 D7
Coatham Redcar 235 F7
Coatham Mundeville
Darl 233 G11
Coatsgate Dumfries .248 B3
Cobairdy Aberds . .302 E5
Cobbaton Devon . .25 B10

Cobbler's Corner
Worcs 116 F5
Cobbler's Green
Norf 142 E5
Cobbler's Plain Mon . .79 E7
Cobbs Warr 183 D10
Cobb's Cross Glos . . 98 E5
Cobby Syke N Yorks . .205 B9
Coberley Glos 81 B7
Cobhall Common
Hereford 97 D7
Cobham Kent. . . . 69 F7
Sur. . . . 66 G6
Cobleland Stirling . .277 B10
Cobler's Green
Essex 87 B11
Cobley Dorset 31 C8
Cobley Hill Worcs . .117 C10
Cobnash Hereford. . . .115 E9
Cobridge Stoke 168 F5
Cobscot Shrops 150 B3
Coburty Aberds 303 C9
Cockadilly Glos 80 E4
Cock Alley Derbys. . .186 G6
Cock and End Suff . . 124 G4
Cockayne N Yorks . .226 F3
Cockayne Hatley
C Beds 104 B5
Cock Bank Wrex. . . .166 F5
Cock Bevington
Warks 117 G11
Cock Bridge Aberds. .292 C4
Cockburnspath
Borders 282 G5
Cock Clarks Essex. . . .88 E4
Cockden Lancs 204 G3
Cockenzie and Port
Seton E Loth 281 F8
Cocker Bar Lancs . .194 C4
Cockerham Lancs. . .202 C5
Cockermouth Cumb. .229 E8
Cockernhoe Herts . .104 G2
Cockernhoe Green
Herts 104 G2
Cockersdale
W Yorks 197 B8
Cockerton Darl 224 B5
Cockett Swansea 56 C5
Cocketty Aberds 293 F9
Cockfield Durham . .233 G8
Suff 125 G8
Cockfosters London . .86 F3
Cock Gate Hereford . .115 D9
Cock Green Essex. . . .87 B11
Cockhill Som 44 G6
Cock Hill N Yorks . .206 B6
Cocking W Sus 34 D5
Cocking Causeway
W Sus 34 D5
Cockington Torbay. . . .9 C7
Cocklake Som 44 D2
Cocklaw Northumb . 241 C10
Cockleford Glos 81 C7
Cockley Beck Cumb . .220 E4
Cockley Cley Norf. . .140 C5
Cockley Hill
W Yorks 197 D7
Cock Marling W Sus . .38 D5
Cocknowle Dorset . .18 E4
Cockpole Green
Wokingham 65 C9
Cocks Corn 4 E5
Cocks Green Suff . .125 F7
Cockshead Ceredig. .112 F2
Cockshoot Hereford. .97 D11
Cockshutford
Shrops 131 F11
Cockshutt Shrops . . .149 D8
Cock Street Kent 53 C9
Suff 107 D7
Cockthorpe Norf. . . .177 E7
Cockwells Corn. 2 C2
Cockwood Devon . .14 E5
Som 43 E8
Cockyard Derbys. . . .185 F8
Hereford 97 E8
Codda Corn 11 F9
Coddenham Suff. . . .126 G2
Coddenham Green
Suff 126 F2
Coddington
Ches W. 167 D7
Hereford 98 C4
Notts 172 E4
Codford St Mary
Wilts 46 F3
Codford St Peter
Wilts 46 F3
Codicote Herts 86 B2
Codicote Bottom
Herts 86 B2
Codmore Bucks. 85 E7
Codmore Hill W Sus. . .35 C9
Codnor Derbys. 170 F6
Codnor Breach
Derbys. . . . 170 F6
Codnor Gate Derbys. .170 F6
Codnor Park Derbys. .170 E6
Codrington S Glos. . .61 D8
Codsall Staffs 133 C7
Codsall Wood Staffs .132 B6
Codsend Som 41 F11
Coed Bl Gwent 77 D11
Torf 78 D3
Coed Cwnnir Mon 78 F6
Coedely Rhondda. . . .58 B4
Coed Eva Torf 78 G3
Coedkernew
Newport 59 C9
Coed Llai = Leeswood
Flint 166 D3
Coed Mawr Gwyn . .179 G9
Coed Morgan Mon. . . .78 C5
Coedpoeth Wrex. . . .166 E3
Coed-Talon Flint 166 E3
Coedway Powys 148 G6
Coed-y-bryn Ceredig. . .93 C7
Coed-y-caerau
Newport 78 G5
Coed-y-fedw Mon 78 D6

Coed y Garth
Ceredig 128 E3
Coed y go Shrops . .148 D5
Coed-y-paen Mon. . . .78 F4
Coed-y-parc Gwyn. .163 B10
Coed-yr-ynys Powys. . .96 G3
Coed Ystumgwern
Gwyn 145 E11
Coed-y-wlad Powys .130 B4
Coelbren Powys 76 C4
Coelbrook Devon 27 F8
Coelbrooke Devon . .13 B11
Coelburn Moray 302 D2
Coelby Lincs 173 C7
Coel Fen Essex 105 D11
Coldeast Devon 14 G2
Coldeaton Derbys. . .169 D10
Cold Elm Glos 98 E6
Colden W Yorks 196 B3
Colden Common
Hants. . . . 33 C7
Coldfair Green Suff. .127 E8
Coldham Cambs 139 C8
Coldham's Common
Cambs 123 F9
Cold Hanworth
Lincs 189 E8
Coldharbour Corn . . .4 F5
Devon 27 G9
Dorset 17 E9
Glos 79 E9
Kent 52 C5
London 68 D4
Sur. . . . 50 E6
Cold Harbour Dorset. .18 D4
Herts 85 B10
Kent 69 G11
Lincs 155 C9
Oxon 64 D6
Wilts 45 B11
Wilts 45 D11
Windsor 65 C10
Cold Hatton Telford . .150 E2
Cold Hatton Heath
Telford 150 E2
Cold Hesledon
Durham 234 B4
Cold Hiendley
W Yorks 197 E11
Cold Higham
W Nhants. . . . 120 G3
Coldingham Borders .273 B8
Cold Inn Pembs 73 D10
Cold Kirby N Yorks . .215 C10
Coldmeece Staffs. . .151 C7
Cold Moss Heath
Ches E 168 C3
Cold Newton Leics . .136 B4
Cold Northcott Corn .11 D10
Cold Norton Essex. . .88 E4
Coldoch Stirling 278 B3
Colan Overton Leics. .136 G4
Coldra Newport 59 B11
Coldrain Perth 286 G4
Coldred Kent 55 D9
Coldridge Devon 25 F11
Cold Row Lancs 202 E3
Coldstream Angus . .287 D7
Borders 263 B8

Colne Engaine
Essex 107 E7
Colnefields Cambs . .123 B7
Colney Norf 142 B3
Colney Hatch London. .86 G3
Colney Heath Herts. . .86 D2
Colney Street Herts. . .85 E11
Coln Rogers Glos 81 D9
Coln St Aldwyns
Glos. . . . 81 D10
Coln St Dennis Glos. . .81 D9
Cologin Argyll 289 G10
Colpitts Grange
Northumb 241 F11
Colpy Aberds 302 F6
Colquhar Borders . .270 G6
Colscott Devon 24 E5
Colshaw Staffs. 169 B8
Colsterdale N Yorks .214 C2
Colsterworth Lincs. .155 E8
Colston S Dunb. 268 C2
Colston Bassett
Notts 154 C3
Colstrope Bucks. . . .65 B9
Coltfield Moray 301 C11
Colt Hill Hants 49 C8
Colthouse Cumb 221 F7
Coltishall Norf. 160 F5
Coltness N Lanark . .268 D6
Colton Cumb 210 B6
Norf 142 B2
N Yorks 206 E6
Staffs 151 E11
Suff 125 D7
W Yorks 206 G3
Colton Hills Staffs. . .133 D8
Colt Park Cumb 210 E5
Colt's Green S Glos. . .61 C9
Colt's Hill Kent 52 E6
Col Uarach W Isles . .304 E6
Columbia T&W. 243 F8
Columbjohn Devon. . .14 B5
Colva Powys 114 G4
Colvend Dumfries . .237 D10
Colvister Shetland . .312 D7
Colwall Hereford. . . .98 C4
Colwall Green
Hereford 98 C4
Colwall Stone
Hereford 98 C5
Colwell IoW 20 D2
Northumb 241 B11
Colwich Staffs. 151 E10
Colwick Notts 171 G10
Colwinston
V Glam. . . . 58 D2
Colworth W Sus 22 C6
Colwyn Bay = Bae Colwyn
Conwy 180 F4
Colyford Devon 15 C10
Colyton Devon 15 C10
Combe Devon 7 E10
Devon 8 B4
Devon 9 G9
Hereford 114 E6
Oxon 82 B6
Som 28 B6
W Berks 63 G11
Combe Almer Dorset. .18 B5
Combebow Devon . . .12 D5
Combe Common Sur. .50 F3
Combe Down Bath . . .61 G9
Combe Fishacre
Devon 8 C6
Combe Florey Som. . .43 G7
Combe Hay Bath 45 B8
Combeinteignhead
Devon 14 G4
Combe Martin Devon. .40 D5
Combe Moor
Hereford 115 E7
Combe Pafford Torbay. .9 B8
Combe Raleigh
Devon 27 G11
Comberbach
Ches W 183 F10
Comberford Staffs. . .134 B3
Comberton Cambs. . .123 F7
Hereford 115 D9
Combe St Nicholas
Som 28 E4
Combe Throop Som. . .30 C2
Combpyne Devon . . .15 C11
Combrew Devon 40 G4
Combridge Staffs. . .151 B11
Combrook Warks . . .118 G6
Combs Derbys 185 F8
Suff 125 F10
W Yorks 197 D8
Combs Ford Suff. . . .125 F11
Combwich Som. 43 E9
Come-to-Good Corn. . .4 G6
Cometytrowe Som. . . .28 C2
Comford Corn 2 B6
Comfort Corn. 2 D6
Comhampton
Worcs 116 D6
Comins Coch
Ceredig 128 G2
Comiston Edin. 270 B4
Comley Shrops 131 D9
Commercial End
Cambs 123 E11
Commins Denb 165 G10
Commins Capel Betws
Ceredig 112 F2
Commins Coch
Powys 128 C5
Common Cefn-llwyn
Mon. . . . 78 G4
Commondale
N Yorks 226 D3
Common Edge
Blackpool. . . . 202 G2
Common End Cumb. .228 G5
Colne Bridge
W Yorks 197 C7
Colne Edge Lancs . .204 E3

Common Hill
Hereford 97 E11
Commonmoor Corn. . .6 B4
Common Moor Corn . .6 B4
Common Platt Wilts . .62 B6
Commonside
Ches W. 183 G8
Derbys. . . . 170 G4
Notts 171 D7
Common Side
Ches W. 167 B8
Derbys. . . . 170 G6
Derbys. . . . 186 F4
Lancs 195 C10
Shrops 149 D9
Commonwood Herts. . .85 E9
Wrex 166 E5
Common-y-coed
Mon 60 B2
Comp Kent 52 B6
Compass Som 43 G9
Compstall Gtr Man . .185 C7
Compton Derbys . .169 F11
Devon 9 C7
Hants. . . . 32 B4
Hants. . . . 33 B7
Plym 7 D9
Staffs 132 G6
Sur. . . . 49 D11
Sur. . . . 50 D3
W Berks 64 D4
W Mid 133 D7
W Sus 34 E3
W Yorks 206 E3
Compton Abbas
Dorset 30 D5
Compton Abdale
Glos 81 B9
Compton Bassett
Wilts 62 E4
Compton Beauchamp
Oxon 63 B10
Compton Bishop
Som 43 B11
Compton Chamberlayne
Wilts 31 B8
Compton Common
Bath. . . . 60 G6
Compton Dando
Bath. . . . 60 G6
Compton Dundon
Som 44 G3
Compton Durville
Som 28 D6
Compton End Hants. . .33 B7
Compton Green Glos. .98 F4
Compton Greenfield
S Glos. . . . 60 C5
Compton Martin Bath 44 B4
Compton Pauncefoot
Som 29 B10
Compton Valence
Dorset 17 C7
Comrie Fife 279 D10
Highld 300 D4
Perth 285 E11
Perth 285 E11
Comrue Dumfries . .248 F3
Conaglen House
Highld 290 G2
Conanby S Yorks . .187 B7
Conchra Argyll. 275 E11
Highld 295 C10
Concord T&W. 243 F8
Concraig Perth 286 F2
Concraigie Perth . . .286 C5
Conder Green Lancs .202 B5
Conderton Worcs . . .99 D9
Condicote Glos 100 F3
Condorrat N Lanark . .278 G4
Condover Shrops . . .131 B9
Coney Hall London. . .67 G11
Coney Hill Glos 80 B5
Coneyhurst W Sus . . .35 C10
Coneysthorpe
N Yorks 216 E4
Coneythorpe
N Yorks 206 B3
Coney Weston Suff . .125 B9
Conford Hants 49 G10
Congash Highld. 301 G10
Congdon's Shop
Corn. . . . 11 F11
Congeith Dumfries . .237 C10
Congelow Kent 53 D7
Congerstone Leics. . .135 B7
Congham Norf. 158 E4
Congleton Ches E. . . .168 C5
Congleton Edge
Ches E 168 C5
Congl-y-wal Gwyn. .164 G2
Congresbury N Som. . .60 G2
Congreve Staffs 151 G8
Conham Bristol 60 E6
Conicavel Moray 301 D9
Coningsby Lincs 174 D2
Conington Cambs . . .122 D6
Cambs 138 F3
Conisbrough
S Yorks. . . . 187 B8
Conisby Argyll 274 G3
Conisholme Lincs . .190 B6
Coniston Cumb 220 F6
E Yorks. . . . 209 F8
Coniston Cold
N Yorks 204 B4
Conistone N Yorks . .213 F9
Conkwell Wilts 61 G9
Connah's Quay Flint. .166 B3
Connel Argyll 289 F11
Connel Park E Ayrs . .258 G4
Connista Highld. 298 A4
Connel Corn 6 C3
Connor Downs Corn . . 2 B5
Conock Wilts 46 B5
Conon Bridge
Highld 300 D5
Conon House Highld .300 D5
Cononish Stirling. . . .285 E7

Cononley N Yorks . . .204 D5
Cononley Woodside
N Yorks 204 D5
Cononsyth Angus . . .287 C9
Conordan Highld. 295 B7
Conquermoor Heath
Telford. . . . 150 F3
Consall Staffs. 169 F7
Consett Durham. 242 G4
Constable Burton
N Yorks 224 G3
Constable Lee
Gtr Man 195 C10
Constantine Corn 2 D6
Constantine Bay
Corn. . . . 10 G3
Contin Highld 300 D4
Contlaw Aberdeen. . .293 C10
Conwy Conwy 180 F3
Conyer Kent 70 G3
Conyers Green Suff. .125 D7
Cooden E Sus 38 F2
Cooil IoM 192 E4
Corn. . . . 11 C11
Shrops 149 G9
Sur. . . . 51 F10
Cookbury Devon 24 F6
Cookbury Wick
Devon 24 F5
Cookham Windsor . . .65 B11
Cookham Dean
Windsor. . . . 65 C11
Cookham Rise
Windsor. . . . 65 C11
Cookhill Worcs 117 F11
Cookley Suff 126 B6
Worcs 132 G6
Cookley Green
Oxon 83 G11
Cookney Aberds . . .293 D10
Cookridge
W Yorks 205 E11
Cooksbridge E Sus . . .36 E6
Cooksey Corner
Worcs 117 D8
Cooksey Green
Worcs 117 D8
Cook's Green Essex. .89 C11
Suff 125 G9
Cookshill Staffs. 168 G6
Cooksland Corn 5 B11
Cooksmill Green
Essex 87 D10
Cooksongreen
Ches W 183 G9
Coolham W Sus 35 C10
Cooling Medway 69 D9
Coolinge Kent 55 F8
Cooling Street
Medway. . . . 69 E8
Coombe Bucks. 84 D4
Corn. . . . 4 G2
Corn. . . . 4 G5
Corn. . . . 4 G6
Corn. . . . 5 E9
Corn. . . . 6 C4
Devon 14 G4
Devon 23 B9
Glos 80 G3
Hants. . . . 33 C11
Kent. . . . 55 B9
London 67 E8
Som 28 F6
Som 28 F6
Wilts 30 C5
Wilts 47 C7
Coombe Bissett
Wilts 31 B10
Coombe Dingle
Bristol 60 D5
Coombe Hill Glos 99 F7
Coombe Keynes
Dorset. . . . 18 E2
Coombes W Sus 35 F11
Coombesdale Staffs .150 B6
Coombeswood
W Mid 133 F9
Coomb Hill Kent 69 G8
Coombs End S Glos. . .61 C9
Coombses Som 28 F4
Coopersale Common
Essex 87 E7
Coopersale Street
Essex 87 E7
Cooper's Corner
Kent. . . . 52 D3
Cooper's Green
E Sus 37 C7
Herts 85 D11
Cooper's Hill
C Beds 103 D10
Sur. . . . 66 E3
Cooper Street Kent .55 B10
Cooper Turning
Gtr Man 194 F6
Cootham W Sus 35 E9
Copcut Worcs 117 E7
Copdock Suff. 108 C2
Coped Hall Wilts. . . .62 C5
Copenhagen Denb . .165 B8
Copford Essex 107 G8
Copford Green
Essex 107 G8
Copgrove N Yorks . .214 G6
Copister Shetland . .312 F6
Cople Bedford 104 B2
Copley Durham 233 F7
Gtr Man 185 B7
W Yorks 196 C5
Copley Hill W Yorks .197 B8
Coplow Dale
Derbys. . . . 185 F11
Copmanthorpe York 207 D7
Copmere End Staffs. .150 D6
Copnor Ptsmth. 33 G11
Copp Lancs 202 F4
Coppathorne Corn. . .24 G2
Coppenhall Ches E. . .167 D11
Staffs. . . . 151 F8
Coppenhall Moss
Ches E 168 D2
Copperhouse Corn . . . 2 B5
Coppice Gtr Man . . .196 G2

Coppingford Cambs. .138 G3
Coppins Corner Kent. .54 D2
Coppleham Som 42 G2
Copplestone Devon . .26 G3
Coppull Lancs. 194 E5
Coppull Moor Lancs. .194 E5
Copsale W Sus 35 C11
Copse Hill London . . .67 F7
Copster Green
Lancs. . . . 203 G9
Copster Hill
Gtr Man 196 G2
Copston Magna
Warks. . . . 135 F7
Cop Street Kent. 55 B9
Copt Green Warks . .118 C3
Copthall Green Essex .86 E6
Copt Heath W Mid. . .118 C3
Copt Hewick
N Yorks 214 E6
Copthill Durham. . . .232 C3
Copthorne Ches E . .167 G11
Corn. . . . 11 C11
Shrops 149 G9
Sur. . . . 51 F10
Coptiviney Shrops. . .149 B8
Copt Oak Leics 153 G9
Copton Kent 54 B4
Copy's Green Norf . .159 B8
Copythorne Hants . . .32 E5
Corbets Tey London . .68 C5
Corbridge
Northumb 241 E11
Corbriggs Derbys . . .170 B6
Corby N Nhants. 137 F7
Corby Glen Lincs. . . .155 E9
Corby Hill Cumb . . .239 F11
Cordon N Ayrs 256 C2
Cordwell Norf 142 E3
Coreley Shrops 116 C2
Cores End Bucks. 66 B2
Corfe Som. . . . 28 D2
Corfe Castle Dorset . .18 E5
Corfe Mullen Dorset. .18 B5
Corfton Shrops 131 F9
Corfton Bache
Shrops 131 F9
Corgarff Aberds 292 C4
Corgee Corn. . . . 5 C10
Corhampton Hants. . .33 C10
Corlae Dumfries. 246 D5
Corlannau Neath. 57 C9
Corley Warks 134 F6
Corley Ash Warks . . .134 F5
Corley Moor Warks . .134 F5
Cornaa IoM 192 D5
Cornabus Argyll. 254 C4
Cornaigbeg Argyll . .288 E2
Cornaigmore Argyll . .288 E1
Argyll. . . . 288 E1
Cornard Tye Suff . . .107 C8
Cornbank Midloth . .270 C4
Cornbrook Shrops . .116 C2
Corncatterach
Aberds. . . . 302 F5
Cornel Conwy. 164 C2
Corner Row Lancs . .202 F4
Cornett Hereford. . . .97 E11
Corney Cumb 220 G2
Cornforth Durham. . .234 D2
Cornharrow
Dumfries 246 E4
Cornhill Aberds 302 D5
Powys 96 C2
Stoke 168 E5
Cornhill-on-Tweed
Northumb 263 B9
Cornholme W Yorks . .196 B3
Cornish Hall End
Essex 106 D3
Cornquoy Orkney . . .314 G5
Cornriggs Durham . .232 C2
Cornsay Durham . . .233 C8
Cornsay Colliery
Durham. . . . 233 C9
Cornton Stirling 278 B5
Corntown Highld. . . .300 D5
V Glam 58 D2
Cornwall Oxon. 100 C5
Cornwood Devon 8 D2
Cornworthy Devon . . .8 D6
Corpach Highld 290 F2
Corpusty Norf 160 C3
Corran Highld. 290 G2
Highld 295 E10
Corran a Chan
Uachdaraich
Highld 295 C7
Corranbuie Argyll . .275 G9
Corrany IoM. . . . 192 D5
Corrichoich Highld. . .311 G4
Corrie N Ayrs 255 C11
Corrie Common
Dumfries 248 F6
Corriecravie
N Ayrs 255 E10
Corriecravie Moor
N Ayrs 255 E10
Corriedoo Dumfries .246 G5
Corriegarth Lodge
Highld 291 B7
Corriemoillie Highld .300 C3
Corriemulzie Lodge
Highld 309 K3
Corrievarkie Lodge
Perth 291 F7
Corrievorrie Highld . .301 G7
Corrigall Orkney 314 E3
Corrimony Highld . . .300 F3
Corringham Lincs. . .188 C5
Thurrock. . . . 69 C8
Corris Gwyn. . . . 128 B5
Corris Uchaf Gwyn . .128 B4
Corrour Shooting Lodge
Highld 290 G6
Corrow Argyll. 284 G5
Corry Highld 295 C8
Corrybrough Highld . .301 G8
Corrydon Perth 292 G3
Corryghoil Argyll. . . .284 E5
Corrykinloch Highld. .309 G4

Corrylach Argyll ... 255 D8
Corrymuckloch Perth ... 286 D2
Corrynachenchy Argyll ... 289 E8
Corsback Highld ... 310 B6
Corscombe Dorset ... 29 F8
Corse Aberds ... 302 E6
Glos ... 98 F5
Corse Lawn Worcs ... 98 E5
Corse of Kinnoir Aberds ... 302 E5
Corsewall Dumfries ... 236 C2
Corsham Wilts ... 61 E11
Corsindae Aberds ... 293 C8
Corsley Wilts ... 45 D10
Corsley Heath Wilts ... 45 D10
Corsock Dumfries ... 237 B9
Corston Bath ... 61 F7
Orkney ... 314 E3
Wilts ... 62 C2
Corstorphine Edin ... 280 G3
Cors-y-Gedol Gwyn ... 145 E11
Cortachy Angus ... 287 B7
Corton Suff ... 143 D10
Wilts ... 46 E2
Corton Denham Som ... 29 C10
Cortworth S Yorks ... 186 B6
Coruanan Lodge Highld ... 290 G2
Corunna W Isles ... 296 E4
Corvast Highld ... 309 K5
Corwen Denb ... 165 G9
Cory Devon ... 24 D5
Coryates Dorset ... 17 D8
Coryton Cardiff ... 58 C6
Devon ... 12 E5
Thurrock ... 69 C8
Còsag Highld ... 295 D10
Cosby Leics ... 135 E10
Coscote Oxon ... 64 B4
Coseley W Mid ... 133 E8
Cosford Warks ... 119 B9
Cosgrove W Nhants ... 102 C5
Cosham Ptsmth ... 33 F11
Cosheston Pembs ... 73 E8
Cosmeston V Glam ... 59 F7
Cosmore Dorset ... 29 E11
Cossall Notts ... 171 G7
Cossall Marsh Notts ... 171 G7
Cosses S Ayrs ... 244 G4
Cossington Leics ... 154 G2
Som ... 43 E11
Costa Orkney ... 314 D3
Costessey Norf ... 160 G3
Costessey Park Norf ... 160 G3
Costhorpe Notts ... 187 D9
Costislost Corn ... 10 G6
Costock Notts ... 153 D11
Coston Leics ... 154 E4
Norf ... 141 B11
Coswinsawsin Corn ... 2 B4
Cote Oxon ... 82 E4
Som ... 43 E10
W Sus ... 35 F10
Cotebrook Ches W ... 167 B9
Cotehill Cumb ... 239 G11
Cotes Cumb ... 211 B9
Leics ... 153 E11
Staffs ... 150 C6
Cotesbach Leics ... 135 G10
Cotes Heath Staffs ... 150 C6
Cotes Park Derbys ... 170 E6
Cotford St Lukes Som ... 27 B11
Cotgrave Notts ... 154 B2
Cothall Aberds ... 293 B10
Cotham Bristol ... 60 E5
Notts ... 172 F3
Cothelstone Som ... 43 G7
Cotheridge Worcs ... 116 G5
Cotherstone Durham ... 223 B10
Cothill Oxon ... 83 F7
Cotland Mon ... 79 E8
Cotleigh Devon ... 28 G2
Cotmanhay Derbys ... 171 G7
Cotmarsh Wilts ... 62 D5
Cotmaton Devon ... 15 D11
Coton Cambs ... 123 F8
Shrops ... 149 C10
Staffs ... 134 B3
Staffs ... 150 E6
Staffs ... 151 C9
W Nhants ... 120 C3
Coton Clanford Staffs ... 151 E7
Coton Hayes Staffs ... 151 C9
Coton Hill Shrops ... 149 G9
Staffs ... 151 C9
Coton in the Clay Staffs ... 152 D3
Coton in the Elms Derbys ... 152 F4
Coton Park Derbys ... 152 F5
Cotonwood Shrops ... 149 B10
Staffs ... 150 E6
Cotswold Community Wilts ... 81 F8
Cott Devon ... 8 C5
Cottam E Yorks ... 217 F9
Lancs ... 202 G6
Notts ... 188 F4
Cottartown Highld ... 301 F10
Cottenham Cambs ... 123 D8
Cottenham Park London ... 67 F8
Cotterdale N Yorks ... 222 G6
Cottered Herts ... 104 F6
Cotterhill Woods S Yorks ... 187 D9
Cotteridge W Mid ... 117 B10
Cotterstock N Nhants ... 137 E10
Cottesbrooke W Nhants ... 120 C4
Cottesmore Rutland ... 155 G8

Cotteylands Devon ... 26 E6
Cottingham E Yorks ... 208 G6
N Nhants ... 136 E6
Cottingley W Yorks ... 205 F8
Cottisford Oxon ... 101 E11
Cotton Staffs ... 169 F9
Suff ... 125 D11
Cotton End Bedford ... 103 B11
W Nhants ... 120 F5
Cotton Stones W Yorks ... 196 C4
Cotton Tree Lancs ... 204 F4
Cottown Aberds ... 293 B9
Aberds ... 302 G5
Aberds ... 303 E8
Cotts Devon ... 7 B8
Cottwood Devon ... 25 E10
Cotwalton Staffs ... 151 B8
Coubister Orkney ... 314 E3
Couch Green Hants ... 48 G4
Couch's Mill Corn ... 6 D2
Coughton Hereford ... 97 G11
Warks ... 117 E11
Coughton Fields Warks ... 117 F11
Cougie Highld ... 300 G2
Coulaghailtro Argyll ... 275 G8
Coulags Highld ... 299 E9
Coulby Newham Mbro ... 225 B10
Coulderton Cumb ... 219 D9
Couldoran Highld ... 299 E8
Coulgartan Stirling ... 285 G8
Coulin Highld ... 299 D10
Coulin Lodge Highld ... 299 D10
Coull Aberds ... 293 C7
Argyll ... 274 G3
Coulmony Ho Highld ... 301 E9
Coulport Argyll ... 276 D4
Coulshill Perth ... 286 G3
Coulston Wilts ... 46 C3
Coulter S Lanark ... 260 C2
Coultings Som ... 43 E8
Coulton N Yorks ... 216 E2
Coultra Fife ... 287 E7
Cound Shrops ... 131 C11
Coundlane Shrops ... 131 C11
Coundmoor Shrops ... 131 C11
Coundon Durham ... 233 F10
W Mid ... 134 G6
Coundongate Durham ... 233 F10
Coundon Grange Durham ... 233 F10
Counters End Herts ... 85 D8
Countersett N Yorks ... 213 B8
Countess Wilts ... 47 E7
Countess Cross Essex ... 107 E7
Countess Wear Devon ... 14 D4
Countesthorpe Leics ... 135 D11
Countisbury Devon ... 41 D8
Coupar Angus Perth ... 286 C6
Coup Green Lancs ... 194 B5
Coupland Cumb ... 222 B4
Northumb ... 263 C10
Cour Argyll ... 255 C9
Courance Dumfries ... 248 E3
Court-at-Street Kent ... 54 F5
Court Barton Devon ... 14 D2
Court Colman Bridgend ... 57 E11
Court Corner Hants ... 48 B6
Courteenhall W Nhants ... 120 G5
Court Henry Carms ... 93 G11
Courthill Perth ... 286 C5
Court House Green W Mid ... 135 G2
Courtsend Essex ... 89 G8
Courtway Som ... 43 G8
Cousland Midloth ... 271 B7
Cousley Wood E Sus ... 53 G7
Couston Shetland ... 275 F11
Cova Shetland ... 313 J5
Cove Argyll ... 276 E4
Borders ... 282 G5
Devon ... 27 D7
Hants ... 49 B11
Highld ... 307 K3
W Sus ... 36 B2
Cove Bay Aberdeen ... 293 C11
Cove Bottom Suff ... 127 B9
Covehithe Suff ... 143 G10
Coven Staffs ... 133 B8
Covender Hereford ... 98 C2
Coveney Cambs ... 139 G2
Covenham St Bartholomew Lincs ... 190 C4
Covenham St Mary Lincs ... 190 C4
Coven Heath Staffs ... 133 C8
Coven Lawn Staffs ... 133 B8
Coventry W Mid ... 118 B6
Coverack Corn ... 3 F7
Coverack Bridges Corn ... 2 C5
Coverham N Yorks ... 214 B2
Covesea Moray ... 301 B11
Covingham Swindon ... 63 C7
Covington Cambs ... 121 C11
S Lanark ... 259 B11
Cowan Bridge Lancs ... 212 D2
Cow Ark Lancs ... 203 D9
Cowbar Redcar ... 226 B5
Cowbeech E Sus ... 23 C10
Cowbeech Hill E Sus ... 23 C10
Cowbit Lincs ... 156 F5
Cowbog Aberds ... 303 D8
Cowbridge Lincs ... 174 F4
Som ... 42 E3

Cowbridge = Y Bont-Faen V Glam ... 58 E3
Cowdale Derbys ... 185 G9
Cowden Kent ... 52 E3
Cowdenbeath Fife ... 280 C3
Cowdenburn Borders ... 270 E4
Cowdale Derbys ... 185 G9
Cowers Lane Derbys ... 170 F4
Cowes IoW ... 20 B5
Cowesby N Yorks ... 215 B9
Cowesfield Green Wilts ... 32 C3
Cowfold W Sus ... 36 C2
Cowgill Cumb ... 212 B5
Cowhill Derbys ... 170 F5
Glos ... 79 G10
Cow Hill Lancs ... 203 G7
Cowhorn Hill S Glos ... 61 E7
Cowie Aberds ... 293 E10
Stirling ... 278 D6
Cowleaze Corner Oxon ... 82 E4
Cowley Derbys ... 186 F4
Devon ... 14 B4
Glos ... 81 C7
London ... 66 C5
Oxon ... 83 E8
Cowleymoor Devon ... 27 E7
Cowling Lancs ... 194 D5
N Yorks ... 204 E5
N Yorks ... 214 B4
Cowlinge Suff ... 124 G4
Cowlow Derbys ... 185 G9
Cowmes W Yorks ... 197 D7
Cowpe Lancs ... 195 C10
Cowpen Northumb ... 253 G7
Cowpen Bewley Stockton ... 234 G5
Cowplain Hants ... 33 E11
Cow Roast Herts ... 85 C7
Cowshill Durham ... 232 C3
Cowslip Green N Som ... 60 G3
Cowstrandburn Fife ... 279 C10
Cowthorpe N Yorks ... 206 C4
Coxall Hereford ... 115 C7
Coxbank Ches E ... 167 G11
Coxbench Derbys ... 170 G5
Coxbridge Som ... 44 F4
Cox Common Suff ... 143 G8
Coxford Corn ... 11 B9
Norf ... 158 D6
Soton ... 32 D5
Coxgreen Staffs ... 132 F6
Cox Green Gtr Man ... 195 E8
Sur ... 50 G5
Windsor ... 65 D11
Coxheath Kent ... 53 C8
Coxhill Kent ... 55 D8
Cox Hill Corn ... 4 G4
Coxhoe Durham ... 234 D2
Coxley Som ... 44 E4
Coxley Wick Som ... 44 E4
Cox Moor Notts ... 171 D8
Coxpark Corn ... 12 G4
Coxtie Green Essex ... 87 F9
Coxwold N Yorks ... 215 D10
Coychurch Bridgend ... 58 D2
Coylton S Ayrs ... 257 E10
Coylumbridge Highld ... 291 B11
Coynach Aberds ... 292 C6
Coynachie Aberds ... 302 F4
Coytrahen Bridgend ... 57 D11
CoytrahÛn Bridgend ... 57 D11
Crabadon Devon ... 8 E5
Crabbet Park W Sus ... 51 F10
Crabble Kent ... 55 E9
Crabbs Cross Worcs ... 117 E10
Crabbs Green Herts ... 105 F9
Crabgate Norf ... 159 D11
Crab Orchard Dorset ... 31 F9
Crabtree Plym ... 7 D10
W Sus ... 36 B2
Crabtree Green Wrex ... 166 G4
Crackaig Argyll ... 274 G6
Crackenedge W Yorks ... 197 C8
Crackenthorpe Cumb ... 231 G9
Crackington Haven Corn ... 11 B8
Crackley Staffs ... 168 E4
Warks ... 118 C5
Crackleybank Shrops ... 150 G5
Crackpot N Yorks ... 223 F9
Crackthorn Corner Suff ... 125 B10
Cracoe N Yorks ... 213 G9
Cracow Moss Ches E ... 168 F2
Staffs ... 168 F3
Craddock Devon ... 27 E9
Cradhlastadh W Isles ... 304 E2
Cradle Edge W Yorks ... 205 F7
Cradle End Herts ... 105 G9
Cradley Hereford ... 98 B4
W Mid ... 133 G8
Cradley Heath W Mid ... 133 F8
Cradoc Powys ... 95 E10
Craflwlt Corn ... 7 E7
Crafton Bucks ... 84 B5
Crag Bank Lancs ... 211 E9
Crag Foot Lancs ... 211 E9
Craggan Highld ... 301 G10
Moray ... 301 F11

Craggan continued Stirling ... 285 E9
Cragganvallie Highld ... 300 F5
Craggenmore Moray ... 301 F11
Craggie Highld ... 301 F7
Highld ... 311 H2
Craggiemore Highld ... 309 J7
Cragg Hill W Yorks ... 205 F10
Cragg Vale W Yorks ... 196 C4
Craghead Durham ... 242 G6
Crahan Corn ... 2 C5
Crai Powys ... 95 G7
Craibstone Moray ... 302 D4
Craichie Angus ... 287 C9
Craig Dumfries ... 237 B8
Dumfries ... 237 C8
Highld ... 299 E10
Craiganor Lodge Perth ... 285 B10
Craig Berthlwyd M Tydf ... 77 F9
Craig Castle Aberds ... 302 G4
Craig-cefn-parc Swansea ... 75 E11
Craigdallie Perth ... 286 E6
Craigdam Aberds ... 303 F8
Craigdarroch Dumfries ... 246 E6
Highld ... 300 D4
Craigdhu Highld ... 300 E4
Craigearn Aberds ... 293 B9
Craigellachie Moray ... 302 E2
Craigencallie Ho Dumfries ... 237 B7
Craigencross Dumfries ... 236 C2
Craigend Borders ... 271 F9
Glasgow ... 268 B3
Perth ... 286 E3
Perth ... 286 E5
Stirling ... 278 D5
Craigendive Argyll ... 275 E11
Craigendoran Argyll ... 276 E6
Craigends Renfs ... 267 B8
Craigens Argyll ... 274 G3
E Ayrs ... 258 F3
Craigentinny Edin ... 280 G5
Craigerne Borders ... 261 B7
Craighall Perth ... 286 C5
Craighat Stirling ... 277 E9
Craighead Fife ... 287 G10
Highld ... 301 C7
Craighill Aberds ... 303 E7
Craighlaw Mains Dumfries ... 236 C5
Craighouse Argyll ... 274 G6
Craigie Aberds ... 293 B11
Dundee ... 287 D8
Perth ... 286 C5
Perth ... 286 E5
S Ayrs ... 257 C10
S Ayrs ... 257 E8
Craigiefield Orkney ... 314 E4
Craigiehall Edin ... 280 F3
Craigielaw E Loth ... 281 F9
Craigierig Borders ... 260 E6
Craigleith Edin ... 280 G4
Craig Llangiwg Neath ... 76 D2
Craig-llwyn Shrops ... 148 D4
Craiglockhart Edin ... 280 G4
Craig Lodge Argyll ... 275 G10
Craigmalloch E Ayrs ... 245 E11
Craigmaud Aberds ... 303 D8
Craigmill Stirling ... 278 B6
Craigmillar Edin ... 280 G5
Craigmore Argyll ... 266 B2
Craig-moston Aberds ... 293 F8
Craignant Shrops ... 148 B5
Craignell Dumfries ... 237 B7
Craigneuk N Lanark ... 268 C5
N Lanark ... 268 C5
Craignish Castle Argyll ... 275 C8
Craignure Argyll ... 289 F9
Craigo Angus ... 293 G8
Craigow Perth ... 286 G4
Craig Penllyn V Glam ... 58 D3
Craigrory Highld ... 300 E6
Craigrothie Fife ... 287 F7
Craigroy Moray ... 301 D11
Craigruie Stirling ... 285 E8
Craig's End Essex ... 106 D4
Craigsford Mains Borders ... 262 B3
Craigshall Dumfries ... 237 D10
Craigshill W Loth ... 269 B11
Craigside Durham ... 233 D8
Craigston Castle Aberds ... 303 D7
Craigton Aberdeen ... 293 C10
Angus ... 287 B7
Angus ... 287 D9
Glasgow ... 267 C10
Highld ... 300 E6
Highld ... 309 H6
Highld ... 309 K6
Craiguaineach Lodge Highld ... 290 G5
Craig-y-don Conwy ... 180 E3
Craig-y-Duke Swansea ... 76 E2
Craig-y-nos Powys ... 76 B4
Craig-y-penrhyn Ceredig ... 128 E3
Craig-y-Rhacca Caerph ... 59 B7
Crai Borders ... 249 B8
Craik Fife ... 287 G10
Crail Fife ... 287 G10
Crailing Borders ... 262 E5
Crailinghall Borders ... 262 E5
Crakaig Highld ... 311 H3
Crakehill N Yorks ... 215 D8
Crakemarsh Staffs ... 151 B11

Crambe N Yorks ... 216 G4
Crambeck N Yorks ... 216 F4
Cramhurst Sur ... 50 E2
Cramlington Northumb ... 243 B7
Cramond Edin ... 280 F3
Cramond Bridge Edin ... 280 F3
Crampmoor Hants ... 32 C5
Cranage Ches E ... 168 B3
Cranberry Staffs ... 150 B6
Cranbourne Brack ... 66 E2
Cranbrook Devon ... 14 B6
Kent ... 53 F9
London ... 68 B2
Cranbrook Common Kent ... 53 F9
Crane Moor S Yorks ... 197 G10
Crane's Corner Norf ... 159 G8
Cranfield C Beds ... 103 C9
Cranford Devon ... 24 C4
London ... 66 D6
Cranford St Andrew N Nhants ... 121 B8
Cranford St John N Nhants ... 121 B8
Cranham Glos ... 80 C5
London ... 68 B5
Cranhill Glasgow ... 268 B2
Warks ... 118 G2
Crank Mers ... 183 B8
Crank Wood Gtr Man ... 194 G6
Cranleigh Sur ... 50 F5
Cranley Suff ... 126 C3
Cranley Gardens London ... 67 B9
Cranmer Green Suff ... 125 C10
Cranmore IoW ... 20 D3
Som ... 45 E7
Cranna Aberds ... 302 D6
Crannich Argyll ... 289 E7
Crannoch Moray ... 302 D4
Cranoe Leics ... 136 D5
Cransford Suff ... 126 E6
Cranstal IoM ... 192 B5
Cranswick E Yorks ... 208 C6
Crantock Corn ... 4 C5
Cranwell Lincs ... 173 F8
Cranwich Norf ... 140 E5
Cranworth Norf ... 141 C9
Craobh Haven Argyll ... 275 C8
Crapstone Devon ... 7 B10
Crarae Argyll ... 275 D10
Crask Highld ... 308 C7
Crask Inn Highld ... 309 G5
Craskins Aberds ... 293 C7
Crask of Aigas Highld ... 300 E4
Craster Northumb ... 265 F7
Craswall Hereford ... 96 D5
Crateford Shrops ... 132 F4
Staffs ... 133 B8
Cratfield Suff ... 126 B6
Crathes Aberds ... 293 D9
Crathie Aberds ... 292 D4
Highld ... 291 D7
Crathorne N Yorks ... 225 D8
Craven Arms Shrops ... 131 G8
Crawcrook T&W ... 242 E4
Crawford Lancs ... 194 G3
S Lanark ... 259 E11
Crawforddyke S Lanark ... 269 F7
Crawfordjohn S Lanark ... 259 E9
Crawick Dumfries ... 259 G7
Crawley Devon ... 28 F2
Hants ... 48 G2
Oxon ... 82 C4
W Sus ... 51 F9
Crawley Down W Sus ... 51 F10
Crawley End Essex ... 105 C8
Crawley Hill Sur ... 65 G11
Crawleyside Durham ... 232 C5
Crawshaw W Yorks ... 197 E8
Crawshawbooth Lancs ... 195 B10
Crawton Aberds ... 293 F10
Cray N Yorks ... 213 D8
Perth ... 292 G3
Crayford London ... 68 E4
Crayke N Yorks ... 215 E11
Craymere Beck Norf ... 159 C11
Crays Hill Essex ... 88 G2
Cray's Pond Oxon ... 64 C6
Crazies Hill Wokingham ... 65 C9
Creacombe Devon ... 26 D4
Creagan Argyll ... 289 E11
Creagan Sithe Argyll ... 284 G6
Creag Aoil Highld ... 290 F3
Creagastrom W Isles ... 297 G4
Creag Ghoraidh W Isles ... 297 G3
Creaguaineach Lodge Highld ... 290 G5
Creaksea Essex ... 88 F6
Creamore Bank Shrops ... 149 C10
Crean Corn ... 1 E3
Creaton W Nhants ... 120 C4
Creca Dumfries ... 238 C6
Credenhill Hereford ... 97 C9
Crediton Devon ... 26 G4
Creebridge Dumfries ... 236 C6
Creech Dorset ... 18 E4
Creech Bottom Dorset ... 18 E4
Creech Heathfield Som ... 28 B3

Creech St Michael Som ... 28 B3
Creed Corn ... 5 F8
Creediknowe Shetland ... 312 G2
Creegbrawse Corn ... 4 G4
Creekmoor BCP ... 18 C6
Creekmouth London ... 68 C3
Creeksea Essex ... 88 F6
Creeting Bottoms Suff ... 126 F2
Creeting St Mary Suff ... 125 F11
Creeton Lincs ... 155 E10
Creetown Dumfries ... 236 D6
Creggans Argyll ... 284 G4
Cregneash IoM ... 192 F1
Creg-ny-Baa IoM ... 192 D4
Cregrina Powys ... 114 G2
Creich Fife ... 287 E7
Creigau Mon ... 79 F7
Creighton Staffs ... 151 B11
Creigiau Cardiff ... 58 C5
Cremyll Corn ... 7 E9
Crendell Dorset ... 31 E9
Crepkill Highld ... 298 E4
Cressage Shrops ... 131 C11
Cressbrook Derbys ... 185 G11
Cresselly Pembs ... 73 D9
Cressex Bucks ... 84 G4
Cress Green Glos ... 80 E3
Cressing Essex ... 106 G5
Cresswell Northumb ... 253 E7
Staffs ... 151 B9
Cresswell Quay Pembs ... 73 D9
Creswell Derbys ... 187 G8
Staffs ... 151 D7
Staffs ... 151 D8
Creswell Green Staffs ... 151 G11
Cretingham Suff ... 126 E4
Cretshengan Argyll ... 275 G8
Creunant = Crynant Neath ... 76 E3
Crewe Ches E ... 168 D2
Ches W ... 166 E6
Crewe-by-Farndon Ches W ... 166 E6
Crewgarth Cumb ... 231 E8
Crewgreen Powys ... 148 F6
Crewkerne Som ... 28 F6
Crews Hill London ... 86 F4
Crew's Hole Bristol ... 60 E6
Crewton Derby ... 153 C7
Crianlarich Stirling ... 285 E7
Cribbs Causeway S Glos ... 60 C5
Cribden Side Lancs ... 195 C9
Cribyn Ceredig ... 111 G10
Criccieth Gwyn ... 145 B9
Crich Derbys ... 170 E5
Crich Carr Derbys ... 170 E4
Crichie Aberds ... 303 E9
Crichton Midloth ... 271 C7
Crick Mon ... 79 G7
W Nhants ... 119 C10
Crickadarn Powys ... 95 C11
Cricket Hill Hants ... 65 G10
Cricket Malherbie Som ... 28 E5
Cricket St Thomas Som ... 28 F5
Crickham Som ... 44 D2
Crickheath Shrops ... 148 E5
Crickheath Wharf Shrops ... 148 E5
Crickhowell Powys ... 78 B2
Cricklade Wilts ... 81 G10
Cricklewood London ... 67 B8
Crickmery Shrops ... 150 D3
Crick's Green Hereford ... 116 G2
Criddlestyle Hants ... 31 E11
Cridling Stubbs N Yorks ... 198 C4
Cridmore IoW ... 20 E5
Crieff Perth ... 286 E2
Criggan Corn ... 5 C10
Criggion Powys ... 148 F5
Crigglestone W Yorks ... 197 D10
Crimble Gtr Man ... 195 E11
Crimchard Som ... 28 F4
Crimdon Park Durham ... 234 D5
Crimond Aberds ... 303 D10
Crimonmogate Aberds ... 303 D10
Crimp Corn ... 24 D3
Crimplesham Norf ... 140 C2
Crimscote Warks ... 100 B4
Crinan Argyll ... 275 D8
Crinan Ferry Argyll ... 275 D8
Crindau Newport ... 59 B10
Crindledyke N Lanark ... 268 D6
Cringleford Norf ... 142 B3
Cringles W Yorks ... 204 D6
Cringletie Borders ... 270 G4
Crinow Pembs ... 73 C10
Cripple Corner Essex ... 107 E7
Cripplesease Corn ... 2 B2
Cripplestyle Dorset ... 31 E9
Cripp's Corner E Sus ... 38 C3
Crispie Argyll ... 275 F10
Crist Derbys ... 185 E8
Critchell's Green Hants ... 32 B5
Critchill Som ... 45 D9
Critchmere Sur ... 49 G11
Crit Hall Kent ... 53 G9
Crizeley Hereford ... 97 E8
Croanford Corn ... 10 G5
Croasdale Cumb ... 219 B11
Crobeag W Isles ... 304 F5
Crockenhill Kent ... 68 F4
Crocker End Oxon ... 65 B8
Crockerhill Hants ... 33 F9

Crockerhill continued W Sus ... 22 B6
Crockernwell Devon ... 13 C11
Crockers Devon ... 40 F5
Crocker's Ash Hereford ... 79 B8
Crockerton Wilts ... 45 E11
Crockerton Green Wilts ... 45 E11
Crocketford or Ninemile Bar Dumfries ... 237 B10
Crockey Hill York ... 207 D8
Crockham Heath W Berks ... 64 G2
Crockham Hill Kent ... 52 C2
Crockhurst Street Kent ... 52 E6
Crockleford Heath Essex ... 107 F10
Crockleford Hill Essex ... 107 F10
Crockness Orkney ... 314 G3
Crock Street Som ... 28 E4
Croesau Bach Shrops ... 148 D4
Croeserw Neath ... 57 B11
Croes-goch Pembs ... 87 E11
Croes-Hywel Mon ... 78 C4
Croes-lan Ceredig ... 93 C7
Croes Llanfair Mon ... 78 D4
Croesor Gwyn ... 163 G10
Croesau Bach Shrops ... 148 D4
Croes-wian Flint ... 181 G10
Croesyceiliog Carms ... 74 B6
Torf ... 78 F4
Croes-y-mwyalch Torf ... 78 G4
Croes y pant Mon ... 78 E4
Croesyceiliog Gwyn ... 163 D8
Croft Hereford ... 115 D9
Leics ... 135 D10
Lincs ... 175 C8
Pembs ... 92 C3
Warr ... 183 C10
Croftamie Stirling ... 277 D9
Croftfoot S Lanark ... 268 C2
Crofthandy Corn ... 4 G4
Croftlands Cumb ... 210 D5
Croftmalloch W Loth ... 269 C8
Croft Mitchell Corn ... 2 B5
Croftmoraig Perth ... 285 C11
Croft of Tillymaud Aberds ... 303 F11
Crofton Cumb ... 239 G8
Wilts ... 63 G9
W Yorks ... 197 D11
Croft-on-Tees N Yorks ... 224 D5
Crofts Dumfries ... 237 B9
Crofts Bank Gtr Man ... 184 B3
Crofts of Benachielt Highld ... 310 F5
Crofts of Haddo Aberds ... 303 F8
Crofts of Inverthernie Aberds ... 303 E7
Crofts of Meikle Ardo Aberds ... 303 E8
Crofty Swansea ... 56 B4
Croggan Argyll ... 289 G9
Croglin Cumb ... 231 B7
Croich Highld ... 309 K4
Croick Highld ... 310 D2
Croig Argyll ... 288 D5
Crois Dughaill W Isles ... 297 J3
Cromarty Highld ... 301 C7
Cromasaig Highld ... 299 C10
Crombie Fife ... 279 D10
Crombie Castle Aberds ... 302 D5
Cromblet Aberds ... 303 F7
Cromdale Highld ... 301 G10
Cromer Herts ... 104 F5
Norf ... 160 A4
Cromer-Hyde Herts ... 86 C2
Cromford Derbys ... 170 D3
Cromhall S Glos ... 79 G11
Cromhall Common S Glos ... 61 B7
Cromor W Isles ... 304 F6
Crompton Fold Gtr Man ... 196 F2
Cromra Highld ... 291 D7
Cromwell Notts ... 172 C3
Cromwell Bottom W Yorks ... 196 C6
Cronberry E Ayrs ... 258 E4
Crondall Hants ... 49 D9
Cronk-y-Voddy IoM ... 192 D4
Cronton Mers ... 183 D7
Crook Cumb ... 221 G9
Devon ... 27 G11
Durham ... 233 D9
Crookdake Cumb ... 229 C9
Crooke Gtr Man ... 194 F5
Crookedholm E Ayrs ... 257 B11
Crooked Soley Wilts ... 63 E10
Crooked Withies Dorset ... 31 F9
Crookes S Yorks ... 186 D4
Crookfur E Renf ... 267 D10
Crookgate Bank Durham ... 242 F5
Crookhall Durham ... 242 G4
Crookham Northumb ... 263 B10
W Berks ... 64 G4
Crookham Village Hants ... 49 C9
Crookhaugh Borders ... 260 D4

Crookhill T&W ... 242 E5
Crookhouse Borders ... 263 D7
Crooklands Cumb ... 211 C10
Crook of Devon Perth ... 286 G4
Crookston Glasgow ... 267 C10
Cropredy Oxon ... 101 B9
Cropston Leics ... 153 G11
Cropthorne Worcs ... 99 C9
Cropton N Yorks ... 216 B5
Cropwell Bishop Notts ... 154 B3
Cropwell Butler Notts ... 154 B3
Cros W Isles ... 304 B7
Crosben Highld ... 289 D9
Crosbost W Isles ... 304 F5
Crosby Cumb ... 229 D7
IoM ... 192 E4
Mers ... 182 B4
N Lincs ... 199 E11
Crosby Court N Yorks ... 225 G7
Crosby Garrett Cumb ... 222 D4
Crosby-on-Eden Cumb ... 239 F11
Crosby Ravensworth Cumb ... 222 C2
Crosby Villa Cumb ... 229 D7
Croscombe Som ... 44 E5
Crosemere Shrops ... 149 D8
Crosland Edge W Yorks ... 196 E6
Crosland Hill W Yorks ... 196 E6
Crosland Moor W Yorks ... 196 D6
Croslands Park Cumb ... 210 E4
Cross Devon ... 40 F3
Devon ... 40 G6
Shrops ... 149 B7
Som ... 44 C2
Crossaig Argyll ... 255 B9
Crossal Highld ... 294 B6
Crossapol Argyll ... 288 E1
Cross Ash Mon ... 78 C5
Cross-at-Hand Kent ... 53 D9
Cross Bank Worcs ... 116 C4
Crossbrae Aberds ... 302 D6
Crossburn Falk ... 279 G7
Crossbush W Sus ... 35 F8
Crosscanonby Cumb ... 229 D7
Crosscrake Cumb ... 211 B10
Crossdale Street Norf ... 160 B4
Cross End Bedford ... 121 F11
Essex ... 107 E7
M Keynes ... 103 D8
Crossens Mers ... 193 D11
Crossflatts W Yorks ... 205 E8
Crossford Fife ... 279 D11
S Lanark ... 268 F6
Crossgate Lincs ... 156 D4
Orkney ... 314 E4
Staffs ... 151 B8
Cross Gate W Sus ... 35 E8
Crossgatehall E Loth ... 271 B7
Crossgates Fife ... 280 D2
N Yorks ... 217 C10
Powys ... 113 E11
Cross Gates W Yorks ... 205 F7
Crossgill Cumb ... 231 C10
Lancs ... 211 G11
Cross Green Devon ... 12 D3
Staffs ... 133 B8
Suff ... 124 G6
Suff ... 125 F7
Suff ... 125 G9
Telford ... 150 G2
Warks ... 119 F7
W Yorks ... 206 G2
Crosshands Carms ... 92 G3
Cross Hands Carms ... 75 C9
Cross-hands Carms ... 92 G3
Cross Hands Pembs ... 73 C9
Cross Heath Staffs ... 168 F4
Crosshill E Ayrs ... 257 E11
Fife ... 280 B3
S Ayrs ... 245 B8
Cross Hill Corn ... 10 G6
Derbys ... 170 F6
Glos ... 79 F9
Cross Hills N Yorks ... 204 E6
Cross Holme N Yorks ... 225 F11
Crosshouse E Ayrs ... 257 B9
Cross Houses Shrops ... 131 B10
Shrops ... 132 E3
Crossings Cumb ... 240 B2
Cross in Hand E Sus ... 37 C9
Leics ... 135 G10
Cross Inn Carms ... 74 C3
Ceredig ... 111 E10
Ceredig ... 111 F7
Rhondda ... 58 C5
Crosskeys Caerph ... 78 G2
Cross Keys Kent ... 52 C4
Wilts ... 61 E11
Crosskirk Highld ... 310 B4
Crosslands Cumb ... 210 B6
Cross Lane Head Shrops ... 132 D4
Crosslanes Shrops ... 148 F6
Cross Lanes Corn ... 2 E5
Dorset ... 30 G3
N Yorks ... 215 F10
Oxon ... 65 D7
Wrex ... 166 F5
Crosslee Borders ... 261 F8

Crosslee continued
Renfs 267 B8
Crossley Hall
W Yorks 205 G8
Cross Llyde Hereford . 97 F8
Crossmichael
Dumfries 237 C9
Crossmill E Renf . . . 267 D10
Crossmoor Lancs . . 202 F4
Crossmount Perth . . 285 B11
Cross Oak Powys 96 G2
Cross of Jackston
Aberds 303 F7
Cross o' th' hands
Derbys 170 F3
Cross o' th' Hill
Ches E 167 F7
Crosspost W Sus 36 C3
Crossroads Aberds . . 293 D9
E Ayrs 257 C11
Fife 281 B7
Cross Roads Devon . . . 12 D5
W Yorks 204 F6
Cross Stone Aberds . 303 G9
Cross Street Suff . . 126 B3
Crosston Angus 287 B9
Crosstown Corn 24 D2
V Glam 58 F4
Cross Town Ches E . . 184 F3
Crosswater Sur 49 F11
Crossway Hereford . . 98 E2
Mon 78 B6
Powys 113 F11
Crossway Green
Mon 79 G8
Worcs 116 D6
Crossways Dorset . . . 17 D11
Kent 68 D5
Mon 96 G6
S Glos 79 G11
Sur 49 F11
Crosswell = Ffynnongroes
Pembs 92 D2
Crosswood Ceredig . 112 C3
Crosthwaite Cumb . 221 G8
Croston Lancs 194 D3
Crostwick Norf 160 F5
Crostwight Norf 160 D6
Crothair W Isles . . . 304 E3
Crouch Kent 52 B6
Kent 54 B5
Crouch End London . . 67 B9
Crouchers W Sus 22 C4
Croucheston Wilts . . . 31 B9
Crouch Hill Dorset . . 30 E2
Crouch House Green
Kent 52 D2
Croughly Moray 301 G11
Croughton
W Nhants 101 E10
Crovie Aberds 303 C8
Crow Hants 31 G11
Crowan Corn 2 C4
Crowborough E Sus . . 52 G4
Staffs 168 E3
Crowborough Warren
E Sus 52 G4
Crowcombe Som 42 F6
Crowcroft Worcs . . . 116 G5
Crowden Derbys . . . 185 B9
Devon 12 B5
Crowder Park Devon . . 8 D4
Crowdhill Hants 33 C7
Crowdicote Derbys . 169 B10
Crowdleham Kent . . . 52 B5
Crowdon N Yorks . . . 227 F9
Crow Edge S Yorks . 197 G7
Crowell Oxon 84 F2
Crowell Hill Oxon . . 84 F3
Crowfield Suff 126 F2
W Nhants 102 C2
Crowgate Street
Norf 160 E6
Crowgreaves
Shrops 132 D4
Crow Green Essex . . 87 F9
Crowhill Gtr Man . . . 184 B6
M Keynes 102 D6
Crow Hill Hereford . . 98 F2
Crowhole Derbys . . 186 F4
Crowhurst E Sus . . . 38 E2
Sur 51 D11
Crowhurst Lane End
Sur 51 D11
Crowland Lincs . . . 156 G4
Crowlas Corn 2 C2
Crowle N Lincs 199 E9
Worcs 117 F8
Crowle Green
Worcs 117 F8
Crowle Hill N Lincs . 199 E9
Crowle Park
N Lincs 199 E9
Crowmarsh Gifford
Oxon 64 B6
Crown Corner Suff . . 126 C5
Crown East Worcs . 116 G6
Crow Nest W Yorks . 205 F8
Crownfield Bucks . . . 84 F4
Crownhill Plym 7 D9
Crown Hills
Leicester 136 C2
Crownland Suff . . . 125 D10
Crownpits Sur 50 E3
Crowntown Corn 2 C4
Crown Wood Brack . . 65 F11
Crows-an-wra Corn . . 1 D3
Crow's Green Essex . 106 F3
Crowshill Norf 141 B8
Crowsnest Shrops . . 131 C7
Crow's Nest Corn 6 B5
Crowther's Pool
Powys 96 B4
Crowthorne Brack . . 65 G10
Crowton Ches W . . . 183 G10
Crow Wood Halton . 183 D8
Croxall Staffs 152 G3

Croxby Lincs 189 B11
Croxby Top Lincs . . 189 B11
Croxdale Durham . . 233 D11
Croxden Staffs 151 B11
Croxley Green Herts . . 85 F9
Croxton Cambs 122 E4
N Lincs 200 E5
Norf 141 F7
Norf 159 C9
Staffs 150 C5
Croxtonbank Staffs . 150 C5
Croxton Green
Ches E 167 E8
Croxton Kerrial
Leics 154 D6
Croy Highld 301 E7
N Lanark 278 F4
Croyde Devon 40 F2
Croyde Bay Devon . . 40 F2
Croydon Cambs . . . 104 B6
London 67 F10
Crozen Hereford . . . 97 B11
Crubenbeg Highld . . 291 D8
Crubenmore Lodge
Highld 291 D8
Cruckmeole Shrops . 131 B8
Cruckton Shrops . . . 149 G8
Cruden Bay Aberds . 303 F10
Crudgington Telford . 150 F2
Crudie Aberds 303 D7
Crudwell Wilts 81 G7
Crug Powys 114 C3
Crugmeer Corn 10 F4
Crugybar Carms 94 D3
Cruise Hill Worcs . . 117 E10
Crulabhig W Isles . . 304 E3
Crumlin Caerph 78 F2
Crumplehorn Corn . . . 6 E4
Crumpsall Gtr Man . 195 G10
Crumpsbrook
Shrops 116 B2
Crumpton Hill Worcs . 98 B5
Crundale Kent 54 D5
Pembs 73 B7
Cruwys Morchard
Devon 26 E5
Crux Easton Hants . . 48 B2
Cruxton Dorset 17 B8
Crwbin Carms 75 C7
Crya Orkney 314 F3
Cryers Hill Bucks . . . 84 F5
Crymlyn Gwyn 179 G10
Crymych Pembs 92 E3
Crynant = Creunant
Neath 76 E3
Crynfryn Ceredig . . . 111 E11
Cuaich Highld 291 E8
Cuaig Highld 299 D7
Cuan Argyll 275 B8
Cubbington Warks . . 118 D6
Cubeck N Yorks 213 B9
Cubert Corn 4 D5
Cubitt Town London . 67 D11
Cubley S Yorks 197 G8
Cubley Common
Derbys 152 B3
Cublington Bucks . . 102 G6
Hereford 97 D8
Cuckfield W Sus 36 B4
Cucklington Som . . . 30 B3
Cuckney Notts 187 G9
Cuckold's Green
Suff 143 G9
Wilts 46 B3
Cuckoo Green Suff . 143 D10
Cuckoo Hill Notts . . 188 C2
Cuckoo's Corner
Hants 49 E8
Wilts 46 B4
Cuckoo's Knob Wilts . 63 F7
Cuckoo Tye Suff . . . 107 C7
Cuckron Shetland . . 313 H6
Cucumber Corner
Norf 143 B7
Cuddesdon Oxon . . . 83 E10
Cuddington Bucks . . 84 C2
Ches W 183 G10
Cuddington Heath
Ches W 167 F7
Cuddy Hill Lancs . . 202 F5
Cudham London 52 B2
Cudlipptown Devon . 12 F6
Cudliptown Devon . . 12 F6
Cudworth Som 28 E5
Sur 51 E8
S Yorks 197 F11
Cudworth Common
S Yorks 197 F11
Cuerden Green
Lancs 194 C5
Cuerdley Cross
Warr 183 D8
Cufaude Hants 48 B6
Cuffern Pembs 91 G7
Cuffley Herts 86 E4
Cuiashader W Isles . 304 C7
Cuidhir W Isles 297 L2
Cuidhtinis W Isles . . 296 C6
Cuiken Midloth 270 C4
Cuilcheanna Ho
Highld 290 G2
Cuin Argyll 288 D6
Culbo Highld 300 C6
Culbokie Highld 300 D6
Culburnie Highld . . . 300 E4
Culcabock Highld . . 300 E6
Culcairn Highld 300 C6
Culcharry Highld . . . 301 D8
Culcheth Warr 183 B11
Culdrain Aberds . . . 302 F5
Culduie Highld 299 E7
Culeave Highld 309 K5
Culford Suff 124 D6
Culfordheath Suff . . 125 C7
Culfosie Aberds . . . 293 C9
Culgaith Cumb 231 F8
Culham Oxon 83 F8
Culkein Highld 306 F5

Culkein Drumbeg
Highld 306 F6
Culkerton Glos 80 F6
Cullachie Highld . . . 301 G9
Cullen Moray 302 C5
Cullercoats T&W . . . 243 C9
Cullicudden Highld . . 300 C6
Cullingworth
W Yorks 205 F7
Cullipool Argyll 275 B8
Cullivoe Shetland . . . 312 C7
Culloden Highld . . . 301 E7
Cullompton Devon . . . 27 F8
Cullmaily Highld . . . 311 K2
Cullmaze Dumfries . 236 D5
Cutler's Green Som . . 44 C5
Cutmadoc Corn 5 C11
Cutmere Corn 6 C6
Cutnall Green
Worcs 117 D7
Cutsdean Glos 99 E11
Cutsyke W Yorks . . . 198 C2
Cutteslowe Oxon . . . 83 C8
Cutthorpe Derbys . . 186 G4
Cuttiford's Door Som . 28 E4
Cutts Shetland 313 K6
Cuttybridge Pembs . . 72 B6
Cuttyhill Aberds . . . 303 D10
Cuxham Oxon 83 F11
Cuxton Medway 69 F8
Cuxwold Lincs 201 G7
Cwm Bl Gwent 77 D11
Denb 181 F9
Neath 57 C10
Cwmafan Neath 57 C9
Cwmaman Rhondda . . 77 F8
Cwmann Carms 93 B11
Cwmavon Torf 78 D3
Cwmbach Carms 75 E7
Carms 92 F5
Powys 96 D3
Rhondda 77 E8
Cwmbâch Rhondda . . 77 E8
Cwmbach Llechrhyd
Powys 113 G10
Cwmbelan Powys . . . 129 G8
Cwmbran Torf 78 G3
Cwmbrwyno
Ceredig 128 G4
Cwm-byr Carms 94 E2
Cwm Capel Carms . . 75 E7
Cwmcarn Caerph 78 G2
Cwmcarvan Mon 79 D7
Cwm-celyn Bl Gwent . 78 D2
Cwm-Cewydd Gwyn . 147 G7
Cwmcoednerth
Ceredig 92 B6
Cwm-cou Ceredig . . . 92 C5
Cwmcrawnon Powys . 77 B10
Cwmcych Carms 92 D5
Cwmdare Rhondda . . 77 E7
Cwm Dows Caerph . . 78 F2
Cwmdu Carms 94 E2
Powys 96 G3
Swansea 56 C6
Cwmduad Carms 93 E7
Cwm-Dulais
Swansea 75 E10
Cwmdwr Carms 94 E4
Cwmerfyn Ceredig . . 128 G3
Cwmfelin Bridgend . . 57 D11
M Tydf 77 E7
Cwmfelin Boeth
Carms 73 B11
Cwm felin fach
Caerph 77 G11
Cwmfelin Mynach
Carms 92 G4
Cwmffrwd Carms . . . 74 B4
Cwm Ffrwd-oer Torf . 78 E3
Cwm-Fields Torf 78 E3
Cwm Gelli Caerph . . 77 F11
Cwmgiedd Powys . . . 76 C3
Cwmgors Neath 76 C2
Cwmgwili Carms 75 C9
Cwmgwrach Neath . . 76 E5
Cwm Gwyn Swansea . . 56 C6
Cwm-hesgen Gwyn . 146 D5
Cwmhiraeth Carms . . 92 D6
Cwm-hwnt Rhondda . 76 D6
Cwmifor Carms 94 F3
Cwm Irfon Powys . . . 95 B7
Cwmisfael Carms . . . 75 B7
Cwm-Llinau Powys . 128 B6
Cwmllynfell Neath . . 76 C2
Cwm-mawr Carms . . 75 C8
Cwm-miles Carms . . 92 G3
Cwm Nant-gam
Bl Gwent 78 C2
Cwmnantyrodyn
Caerph 77 F11
Cwmorgan Pembs . . 92 E5
Cwmparc Rhondda . . 77 F7
Cwm-parc Rhondda . . 77 F7
Cwmpengraig Carms . 92 D6
Cwm Penmachno
Conwy 164 F3
Cwmpennar Rhondda . 77 E8
Cwmrhos Powys 96 G3
Cwmrhydyceirw
Swansea 57 B7
Cwmsychpant
Ceredig 93 B9
Cwmsyfiog Caerph . . 77 E11
Cwmsymlog Ceredig . 128 G4
Cwmtillery Bl Gwent . 78 D2
Cwm-twrch Isaf
Powys 76 C3
Cwm-twrch Uchaf
Powys 76 C3
Cwmwdig Water
Pembs 90 E6
Cwmwysg Powys . . . 95 F7
Cwm-y-glo Carms . . 75 C9
Gwyn 163 C8
Cwmyoy Mon 96 G5
Cwmystwyth
Ceredig 112 C3
W Nhants 120 E4

Custom House
London 68 C2
Cusveorth Coombe
Corn 4 G5
Cutcombe Som 42 F2
Cutgate Gtr Man . . . 195 E11
Cuthill E Loth 281 G7
Cutiau Gwyn 146 F2
Cutlers Green
Essex 105 E11
Cwrt Gwyn 128 C3
Cwrt-newydd Ceredig . 93 B9
Cwrt-y-cadno Carms . 94 C4
Cwrt-y-gollen Powys . 78 B2
Cydweli = Kidwelly
Carms 74 D6
Cyffordd Llandudno =
Llandudno Junction
Conwy 180 F3
Cyffylliog Denb 165 D9
Cyfronydd Powys . . . 130 B2
Cymau Flint 166 D3
Cymdda Bridgend . . . 58 C2
Cymer Neath 57 B11
Cymmer Rhondda . . . 77 G8
Cyncoed Cardiff 59 C7
Cynghordy Carms . . . 94 C6
Cynheidre Carms . . . 75 D7
Cynonville Neath . . . 57 B10
Cyntwell Cardiff 58 D6
Cynwyd Denb 165 G9
Cynwyl Elfed Carms . . 93 F7
Cywarch Gwyn 147 F7

D

Daccombe Devon 9 B8
Dacre Cumb 230 F5
N Yorks 214 G3
Dacre Banks
N Yorks 214 G3
Daddry Shield
Durham 232 D3
Dadford Bucks 102 D3
Dadlington Leics . . . 135 D8
Dafarn Faig Gwyn . . 163 F7
Dafen Carms 75 E8
Daffy Green Norf . . 141 B9
Dagdale Staffs 151 C11
Dagenham London . . 68 C3
Daggons Dorset 31 E10
Daglingworth Glos . . 81 D7
Dagnall Bucks 85 B7
Dagtail End Worcs . 117 E10
Dagworth Suff 125 E10
Dail Beag W Isles . . 304 D4
Dail bho Dheas
W Isles 304 B6
Dail bho Thuath
W Isles 304 B6
Daill Argyll 274 G4
Dailly S Ayrs 245 C7
Dail Mor W Isles . . . 304 D4
Dainton Devon 9 B7
Dairsie or Osnaburgh
Fife 287 F8
Daisy Green Suff . . 125 D10
Suff 125 D11
Daisy Hill Gtr Man . 195 G7
W Yorks 197 B9
W Yorks 205 F9
Daisy Nook Gtr Man . 196 G2
Dalabrog W Isles . . . 297 J3
Dalavich Argyll 275 C9
Dalbeattie
Dumfries 237 C10
Dalblair E Ayrs 258 F4
Dalbog Angus 293 F7
Dalbrack Stirling . . . 285 G11
Dalbury Derbys 152 C5
Dalby IoM 192 E3
Lincs 190 G6
N Yorks 216 E2
Dalchalloch Perth . . 291 G9
Dalchalm Highld . . . 311 J3
Dalchenna Argyll . . . 284 G4
Dalchirach Moray . . 301 F11
Dalchonzie Perth . . . 285 E11
Dalchork Highld . . . 309 H5
Dalchreichart
Highld 290 B4
Dalchruin Perth . . . 285 F11
Dalderby Lincs 174 B2
Dale Cumb 230 C6
Gtr Man 196 F3
Pembs 72 D4
Shetland 312 G6
Dale Abbey Derbys . 153 B8
Dalebank Derbys . . . 170 C3
Dale Bottom Cumb . 229 G11
Dale Brow Ches E . . 184 F6
Dale End Derbys . . . 170 C2
N Yorks 204 D5
Dale Head Cumb . . . 221 B8
Dale Hill E Sus 53 G7
E Sus 53 G8
Dalelia Highld 289 C9
Dale Moor Derbys . . 153 B8
Dale of Walls
Shetland 313 H3
Dales Brow
Gtr Man 195 G9
Dales Green Staffs . 168 D5
Daless Highld 301 F8
Dalestie Moray 292 B3
Dalestorth Notts . . . 171 C8
Daifaber Highld . . . 291 B11
Dalfoil Stirling 277 D11
Dalganachan Highld . 310 E4
Dalgarven N Ayrs . . 266 F5
Dalgety Bay Fife . . . 280 E3
Dalginross Perth . . . 285 E11
Dalguise Perth 286 C3
Dalhalvaig Highld . . 310 D2
Dalham Suff 124 E4
Dalhastnie Angus . . 293 F7
Dalhenzean Perth . . 292 G3
Dalinlongart Argyll . 276 E2
Dalkeith Midloth . . . 270 B6
Dallam Warr 183 C9
Dallas Moray 301 D11
Dallas Lodge
Moray 301 D11
Dalleagles E Ayrs . . 258 G3
Dallicott Shrops . . . 132 E5
Dallimores IoW 20 C6
Dallinghoo Suff . . . 126 G5
Dallington E Sus . . . 23 B11
W Nhants 120 E4

Dallow N Yorks 214 E3
Dalmadilly Aberds . . 293 B9
Dalmally Argyll 284 E5
Dalmarnock
Glasgow 268 C2
Perth 286 C3
Dalmary Stirling . . . 277 B10
Dalmellington
E Ayrs 245 B11
Dalmeny Edin 280 F2
Dalmigavie Highld . . 291 B9
Dalmigavie Lodge
Highld 301 G8
Dalmilling S Ayrs . . 257 E9
Dalmore Highld . . . 300 C6
Highld 301 G8
Dalmuir W Dunb . . . 277 G9
Dalnabreck Highld . . 289 C8
Dalnacardoch Lodge
Perth 291 F9
Dalnacroich Highld . 300 D3
Dalnaglar Castle
Perth 292 G3
Dalnahaitnach
Highld 301 G8
Dalnamein Lodge
Perth 291 G9
Dalnarrow Argyll . . . 289 F9
Dalnaspidal Lodge
Perth 291 F8
Dalnavie Highld 300 B6
Dalnaw Dumfries . . . 236 B5
Dalnawillan Lodge
Highld 310 E4
Dalness Highld 284 B5
Dalnessie Highld . . . 309 H6
Dalphaid Highld . . . 309 H3
Dalqueich Perth . . . 286 G4
Dalreavoch Highld . . 309 J7
Dalriach Highld 301 F10
Dalrigh Stirling 285 E7
Dalry Edin 280 G4
N Ayrs 266 F5
Dalrymple E Ayrs . . 257 G9
Dalscote W Nhants . 120 G3
Dalserf S Lanark . . . 268 E6
Dalshannon
N Lanark 278 G4
Dalston Cumb 239 G9
London 67 C10
Dalswinton
Dumfries 247 F11
Dalton Cumb 211 D10
Dumfries 238 C4
Lancs 194 F3
Northumb 241 F10
Northumb 242 C4
N Yorks 215 D8
N Yorks 224 D2
S Lanark 268 D3
S Yorks 187 C7
W Yorks 197 D7
Dalton-in-Furness
Cumb 210 E4
Dalton-le-Dale
Durham 234 B4
Dalton Magna
S Yorks 187 C7
Dalton-on-Tees
N Yorks 224 D5
Dalton Parva
S Yorks 187 C7
Dalton Piercy Hrtlpl . 234 E5
Dalveallan Highld . . 300 F6
Dalveich Stirling . . . 285 E10
Dalvina Lo Highld . . 308 E6
Dalwey Telford 132 B3
Dalwhinnie Highld . . 291 E8
Dalwood Devon 28 G3
Dalwyne S Ayrs 245 D8
Damask Green
Herts 104 F5
Damems W Yorks . . 204 F6
Damerham Hants . . . 31 D10
Damery Glos 80 G2
Damgate Norf 143 B8
Norf 161 F9
Dam Green Norf . . . 141 F11
Damhead Moray . . . 301 C10
Damhead Holdings
Midloth 270 B5
Damnaglaur
Dumfries 236 F3
Dam of Quoiggs
Perth 286 G2
Damside Borders . . . 270 F3
Dam Side Lancs . . . 202 D4
Danaway Kent 69 G11
Danbury Essex 88 E3
Danbury Common
Essex 88 E3
Danby N Yorks 226 D4
Danby Wiske
N Yorks 224 F6
Dan Caerlan Rhondda . 58 C5
Dancers Hill Herts . . 86 F2
Dancing Green
Hereford 98 G2
Dandaleith Moray . . 302 E2
Dandy Corner Suff . 125 D11
Danebank Ches E . . 185 E7
Danebridge Ches E . 169 C7
Dane End Herts . . . 104 G6
Danegate E Sus 52 G5
Danehill E Sus 36 B6
Dane in Shaw
Ches E 168 C5
Danemoor Green
Norf 141 B11
Danesfield Bucks . . . 65 C10
Danesford Shrops . . 132 E4
Daneshill Hants 49 C7
Danesmoor Derbys . . 170 C6
Danes Moss Ches E . . 184 F6
Dane Street Kent . . . 54 C5
Danna na Cloiche
Argyll 275 F7
Dannonchapel Corn . . 10 E6
Danskine E Loth . . . 271 B11
Danthorpe E Yorks . 209 G10
Danygraig Caerph . . 78 G2
Danzey Green
Warks 118 D2
Dapple Heath
Staffs 151 D10
Darby End W Mid . . 133 F9
Darby Green Hants . . 65 G10
Darbys Green Worcs . 116 F4
Darby's Hill W Mid . 133 F9
Darcy Lever
Gtr Man 195 F8
Dardy Powys 78 B2
Darenth Kent 68 E5
Daresbury Halton . . 183 E9
Daresbury Delph
Halton 183 E9
Darfield S Yorks . . . 198 G2
Darfoulds Notts . . . 187 F9
Dargate Kent 70 G5
Dargate Common
Kent 70 G5
Dargavel Village
Renfs 277 G8
Darite Corn 6 B5
Darkland Moray 302 C2
Darland Wrex 166 D5
Darlaston S Mid . . . 133 D9
Darlaston Green
W Mid 133 D9
Darley N Yorks 205 B10
Darley Abbey Derby . 153 B7
Darley Bridge
Derbys 170 C3
Darley Dale Derbys . 170 C3
Darley Green Warks . 118 C3
Darleyhall Herts . . . 104 G2
Darley Head
N Yorks 205 B9
Darley Hillside
Derbys 170 C3
Darlingscott Warks . 100 C4
Darlington Darl 224 C5
Darliston Shrops . . . 149 C11
Darlton Notts 188 G3
Darnall S Yorks 186 D5
Darnaway Castle
Moray 301 D9
Darnford Staffs 134 B2
Aberds 293 D9
Darnhall Ches W . . . 167 C10
Darnhall Mains
Borders 270 F4
Darn Hill Gtr Man . . 195 E10
Darnick Borders . . . 262 C2
Darowen Powys . . . 128 C6
Darra Aberds 303 E7
Darracott Devon . . . 24 D2
Devon 40 F3
Darras Hall
Northumb 242 C5
Darrington W Yorks . 198 D3
Darrow Green Norf . 142 F5
Darsham Suff 127 D8
Dartford Kent 68 E4
Dartford Crossing
Kent 68 D5
Dartington Devon . . . 8 C5
Dartmeet Devon . . . 13 G9
Dartmouth Devon . . . 9 E7
Dartmouth Park
London 67 B9
Darton S Yorks 197 F10
Darvel E Ayrs 258 B3
Darvillshill Bucks . . 84 F4
Darwell Hole E Sus . 23 B11
Darwen Blackburn . . 195 C7
Dassels Herts 105 F7
Datchet Windsor . . . 66 D3
Datchworth Herts . . 86 B3
Datchworth Green
Herts 86 B3
Daubhill Gtr Man . . 195 F8
Daugh of Kinermony
Moray 302 E2
Dauntsey Wilts 62 C3
Dauntsey Lock Wilts . 62 C3
Dava Moray 301 F10
Davenham Ches W . 183 G11
Davenport
Gtr Man 184 D6
Davenport Green
Ches E 184 F4
Gtr Man 184 D4
Daventry W Nhants . 119 E11
Davidson's Mains
Edin 280 F4
Davidston Highld . . 301 C7
Davidstow Corn 11 D9
David Street Kent . . . 68 G6
David's Well Powys . 113 B11
Davington Dumfries . 248 C6
Kent 70 G4
Daviot Aberds 303 G7
Highld 301 F7
Davis's Town E Sus . . 23 B8
Davoch of Grange
Moray 302 D4
Davo Mains Aberds . 293 F9
Davyhulme Gtr Man . 184 B3
Daw Cross N Yorks . 205 C11
Daw End W Mid . . . 133 C10
Dawesgreen Sur . . . 51 D8
Dawker Hill N Yorks . 207 F7
Dawley Telford 132 B3
Dawley Bank
Telford 132 B3
Dawlish Devon 14 F5

Dawlish Warren
Devon 14 F5
Dawn Conwy 180 G5
Daw's Cross Essex . 107 E7
Daw's Green Som . . . 27 C11
Daws Heath Essex . . 69 G8
Dawshill Worcs 116 G6
Daw's House Corn . . 12 E2
Dawsmere Lincs . . . 157 C8
Daybrook Notts . . . 171 F9
Dayhills Staffs 151 C9
Dayhouse Bank
Worcs 117 B9
Daylesford Glos . . . 100 F4
Ddol Flint 181 G10
Ddol Cownwy
Powys 147 F10
Ddrydwy Anglesey . . 178 G5
Deacons Hill Herts . . 85 F11
Deadman's Cross
C Beds 104 C2
Deadman's Green
Staffs 151 B11
Deadwater Hants . . . 49 F10
Northumb 250 D4
Deaf Hill Durham . . 234 D3
Deal Kent 55 C11
Deal Hall Essex . . . 89 F8
Dean Cumb 229 F7
Devon 8 C4
Devon 40 E6
Devon 40 E4
Devon 41 D8
Dorset 31 D7
Edin 280 G4
Hants 33 D9
Hants 48 C5
Lancs 195 B11
Oxon 100 G6
Som 45 E7
Dean Bank Durham . 233 E11
Deanburnhaugh
Borders 261 G9
Dean Court Oxon . . . 83 D7
Dean Cross Devon . . 40 E4
Deane Gtr Man 195 F7
Hants 48 C4
Deanend Dorset 31 D7
Dean Head S Yorks . 197 G9
Deanich Lodge
Highld 309 L3
Deanland Dorset . . . 31 D7
Deanlane End W Sus . 34 E2
Dean Lane Head
W Yorks 205 G7
Dean Park Renfs . . . 267 B10
Dean Prior Devon . . . 8 C4
Dean Row Ches E . . . 184 E5
Deans W Loth 269 B10
Deans Bottom Kent . 69 G11
Deanscales Cumb . . 229 F7
Deansgreen
Ches E 183 D11
Dean's Green Warks . 118 C2
Deanshanger
W Nhants 102 D5
Deans Hill Kent 69 G11
Deanston Stirling . . 285 G11
Dean Street Kent . . . 53 C8
Dearham Cumb 229 D7
Dearnley Gtr Man . . 196 D2
Debach Suff 126 G4
Debdale Gtr Man . . . 184 B5
Debden Essex 86 F6
Essex 105 E11
Debden Cross
Essex 105 E11
Debden Green Essex . 86 F6
Essex 105 E11
De Beauvoir Town
London 67 C10
Debenham Suff 126 E3
Deblin's Green Worcs . 98 B6
Dechmont W Loth . . 279 G10
Deckham T&W 243 E7
Deddington Oxon . . . 101 E9
Dedham Essex 107 E11
Dedham Heath
Essex 107 E11
Dedridge W Loth . . . 269 B11
Dedworth Windsor . . 66 D2
Deebank Aberds . . . 293 D8
Deecastle Aberds . . 292 D6
Deene N Nhants 137 E7
Deenethorpe
N Nhants 137 F7
Deepcar S Yorks . . . 186 B3
Deepclough Derbys . 185 B9
Deepcut Sur 50 B2
Deepdale C Beds . . . 104 C4
Cumb 212 C4
N Yorks 213 D7
Deepdene Sur 51 D7
Deepfields W Mid . . 133 E8
Deeping Gate Lincs . 138 B2
Deeping St James
Lincs 138 B3
Deeping St Nicholas
Lincs 156 F4
Deepthwaite Cumb . 211 C10
Deepweir Mon 60 B3
Deerhill Moray 302 D4
Deerhurst Glos 99 F7
Deerhurst Walton
Glos 99 F7
Deerland Pembs 73 C7
Deerness Orkney . . . 314 F5
Deer's Green Essex . 105 E9
Deerstones N Yorks . 205 C7
Deerton Street Kent . 70 G3
Defford Worcs 99 C8
Defynnog Powys 95 F8
Deganwy Conwy . . . 180 F3
Degar V Glam 58 D4
Degibna Corn 2 D5
Deighton N Yorks . . 225 D7
W Yorks 197 D7
York 207 D8
Deiniolen Gwyn 163 C9
Deishar Highld 291 B11

Delabole Corn 11 E7
Delamere Ches W 167 B9
Delfour Highld 291 C10
Delfrigs Aberds 303 G9
Delliefure Highld 301 F10
Dell Lodge Highld 292 B2
Dell Quay W Sus 22 C4
Delly End Oxon 82 C5
Delnabo Moray 292 B3
Delnadamph Aberds 292 C4
Delnamer Angus 292 G3
Delph Gtr Man 196 F3
Delves Durham 233 B8
Delvine Perth 286 C5
Delvin End Essex 106 D5
Dembleby Lincs 155 B10
Demelza Corn 5 C9
Denaby Main
S Yorks 187 B7
Denbeath Fife 281 B7
Denbigh Denb 165 B9
Denbury Devon 8 B6
Denby Derbys 170 F5
Denby Bottles
Derbys 170 F5
Denby Common
Derbys 170 F6
Denby Dale
W Yorks 197 F8
Denchworth Oxon 82 G5
Dendron Cumb 210 E4
Denel End C Beds 103 D10
Denend Aberds 302 F6
Dene Park Kent 52 C5
Deneside Durham 234 B4
Denford N Nhants 121 B9
Staffs 169 E7
Dengie Essex 89 E7
Denham Bucks 66 B4
Bucks 102 G5
Suff 124 E5
Suff 126 C3
Denham Corner
Suff 126 C3
Denham End Suff 124 E5
Denham Green Bucks 66 B4
Denham Street Suff 126 C3
Denhead Aberds 303 D9
Fife 287 F8
Denhead of Arbilot
Angus 287 C9
Denhead of Gray
Dundee 287 D7
Denholm Borders 262 F3
Denholme W Yorks 205 G7
Denholme Clough
W Yorks 205 G7
Denholme Edge
W Yorks 205 G7
Denholme Gate
W Yorks 205 G7
Denholmhill Borders 262 F3
Denio Gwyn 145 B7
Denmead Hants 33 E11
Denmore Aberdeen 293 B11
Denmoss Aberds 302 E6
Dennington Suff 126 D5
Dennington Corner
Suff 126 D5
Dennington Hall
Suff 126 D5
Denny Falk 278 E6
Denny Bottom Kent 52 F5
Denny End Cambs 123 D9
Dennyloanhead
Falk 278 E6
Denny Lodge Hants 32 F4
Dennystown
W Dunb 277 F7
Denshaw Gtr Man 196 E3
Denside Aberds 293 D10
Densole Kent 55 E8
Denston Suff 124 G5
Denstone Staffs 169 G9
Denstroude Kent 70 G6
Dent Cumb 212 B4
Dent Bank Durham 232 F4
Denton Cambs 138 F2
Darl 224 B4
E Sus 23 E7
Gtr Man 184 B6
Kent 55 D8
Kent 69 E7
Lincs 155 C7
Norf 142 F5
N Yorks 205 D8
Oxon 83 E9
W Nhants 120 F6
Denton Burn T&W 242 D5
Denton Holme
Cumb 239 G10
Denton's Green
Mers 183 B7
Denver Norf 140 C2
Denvilles Hants 22 B2
Denwick Northumb 264 G6
Deopham Norf 141 C11
Deopham Green
Norf 141 D10
Deopham Stalland
Norf 141 D10
Depden Suff 124 F5
Depden Green Suff 124 F5
Deppers Bridge
Warks 119 F7
Deptford London 67 D11
T&W 243 F9
Wilts 46 F4
Derby Derbys 153 B7
Devon 40 G5
Derbyhaven IoM 192 F3
Derbyshire Hill
Mers 183 C8
Dereham Norf 159 G9
Dergoals Dumfries 236 D4
Deri Caerph 77 E10
Derriford Plym 7 D9
Derril Devon 24 G4
Derringstone Kent 55 D8
Derrington Shrops 132 E2
Staffs 151 E7
Derriton Devon 24 G4
Derry Stirling 285 E10
Derrydaroch Stirling 285 E7
Derry Downs London 68 F3
Derry Fields Wilts 81 G8
Derryguaig Argyll 288 F6
Derry Hill Wilts 62 E3
Derry Lodge Aberds 292 D2
Derrythorpe
N Lincs 199 F10
Dersingham Norf 158 C3
Dertfords Wilts 45 D10
Dervaig Argyll 288 D6
Derwen Bridgend 58 C2
Denb 165 E9
Derwenlas Powys 128 D4
Derwydd Carms 75 B10
Desborough
N Nhants 136 G6
Desford Leics 135 C9
Deskryshiel Aberds 292 B6
Detchant Northumb 264 B3
Detling Kent 53 B9
Deuchar Angus 292 G6
Deuddwr Powys 148 F4
Deuxhill Shrops 132 F3
Devauden Mon 79 F7
Deveral Corn 2 B3
Devil's Bridge = *Pontarfynach*
Ceredig 112 B4
Devitts Green
Warks 134 E5
Devizes Wilts 62 G4
Devol Invclyd 276 G6
Devonport Plym 7 E9
Devonside Clack 279 B8
Devon Village Clack 279 B8
Devoran Corn 3 B7
Dewar Borders 270 F6
Dewartown Midloth 271 C7
Dewes Green Essex 105 E9
Dewlands Common
Dorset 31 F9
Dewlish Dorset 17 B11
Dewsbury W Yorks 197 C8
Dewsbury Moor
W Yorks 197 C8
Dewshall Court
Hereford 97 E9
Dhoon IoM 192 D5
Dhoor IoM 192 C5
Dhowin IoM 192 B5
Dhustone Shrops 115 B11
Dial Green W Sus 34 B6
Dial Post W Sus 35 D11
Dibberford Dorset 29 G7
Dibden Hants 32 F6
Dibden Purlieu Hants 32 F6
Dickens Heath
W Mid 118 B2
Dickleburgh Norf 142 G3
Dickleburgh Moor
Norf 142 G3
Dickon Hills Lincs 174 D6
Didbrook Glos 99 E11
Didcot Oxon 64 B4
Diddington Cambs 122 D3
Diddlebury Shrops 131 F10
Diddywell Devon 25 B7
Didley Hereford 97 E9
Didling W Sus 34 D4
Didlington Norf 140 D5
Didmarton Glos 61 B10
Didsbury Gtr Man 184 C4
Didworthy Devon 8 C3
Diebidale Highld 309 L4
Digbeth W Mid 133 F11
Digby Lincs 173 E9
Digg Highld 298 C4
Diggle Gtr Man 196 F4
Diglis Worcs 116 G6
Digmoor Lancs 194 F3
Digswell Herts 86 B3
Digswell Park Herts 86 C2
Digswell Water Herts 86 C3
Dihewyd Ceredig 111 F9
Dilham Norf 160 D6
Dilhorne Staffs 169 G7
Dillarburn S Lanark 268 G6
Dill Hall Lancs 195 B8
Dillington Cambs 122 D2
Som 28 D5
Dilston Northumb 241 E11
Dilton Marsh Wilts 45 D11
Dilwyn Hereford 115 G8
Dimlands V Glam 58 F3
Dimmer Som 44 G6
Dimple Derbys 170 C3
Gtr Man 195 D8
Dimsdale Staffs 168 F4
Dimson Corn 12 G4
Dinas Carms 92 E5
Corn 10 G4
Gwyn 144 B5
Gwyn 163 D7
Dinas Cross Pembs 91 D10
Dinas Dinlle Gwyn 162 D6
Dinas-Mawddwy
Gwyn 147 G7
Dinas Mawr Conwy 164 E4
Dinas Powys V Glam 59 E7
Dinbych = *Denbigh* Denb 165 B9
Dinbych y Pysgod = *Tenby* Pembs 73 E10
Dinckley Lancs 203 F9
Dinder Som 44 E5
Dinedor Hereford 97 D10
Dinedor Cross
Hereford 97 D10
Dines Green Worcs 116 F6
Dingestow Mon 79 C7
Dinghurst N Som 44 B2
Dingle Mers 182 D5
Dingleden Kent 53 G10
Dingleton Borders 262 C2
Dingley N Nhants 136 F5
Dingwall Highld 300 D5
Dinlabyre Borders 250 E2
Dinmael Conwy 165 G8
Dinnet Aberds 292 D6
Dinnington Som 28 E6
S Yorks 187 D8
T&W 242 C6
Dinorwic Gwyn 163 C9
Dinton Bucks 84 C3
Wilts 46 G4
Dinwoodie Mains
Dumfries 248 E4
Dinworthy Devon 24 D4
Dipford Som 28 C2
Dipley Hants 49 B8
Dippenhall Sur 49 D10
Dippertown Devon 12 E4
Dippin N Ayrs 256 E2
Dipple Devon 24 D4
Moray 302 D3
S Ayrs 244 C6
Diptford Devon 8 D4
Dipton Durham 242 G5
Diptonmill
Northumb 241 E10
Dirdhu Highld 301 G10
Direcleit W Isles 305 J3
Dirleton E Loth 281 E10
Dirt Pot Northumb 232 B3
Discoed Powys 114 E5
Discove Som 45 G7
Diseworth Leics 153 E9
Dishes Orkney 314 D6
Dishforth N Yorks 215 E7
Dishley Leics 153 E10
Disley Ches E 185 E7
Diss Norf 126 B2
Disserth Powys 113 F10
Distington Cumb 228 G6
Ditchampton Wilts 46 G5
Ditcheat Som 44 F6
Ditchfield Bucks 84 G4
Ditchford Hill
Worcs 100 D4
Ditchingham Norf 142 E6
Ditchling E Sus 36 D4
Ditherington
Shrops 149 G10
Ditteridge Wilts 61 F10
Dittisham Devon 9 E7
Ditton Halton 183 D7
Kent 53 B8
Ditton Green Cambs 124 F3
Ditton Priors Shrops 132 F2
Dittons E Sus 23 E10
Divach Highld 300 G4
Divlyn Carms 94 D5
Dixton Glos 99 E9
Mon 79 C8
Dizzard Corn 11 B9
Dobcross Gtr Man 196 F3
Dobs Hill Flint 166 C4
Dobson's Bridge
Shrops 149 C9
Dobwalls Corn 6 C4
Doccombe Devon 13 D11
Dochfour Ho Highld 300 F6
Dochgarroch Highld 300 E6
Dockeney Norf 143 E7
Dockenfield Sur 49 E10
Docker Lancs 211 E11
Docking Norf 158 B5
Docklow Hereford 115 F11
Dockray Cumb 230 G3
Dockroyd W Yorks 204 F6
Doc Penfro = *Pembroke Dock* Pembs 73 E7
Docton Devon 24 C2
Dodbrooke Devon 8 G4
Dodburn Borders 249 B11
Doddenham Worcs 116 F5
Doddinghurst Essex 87 F9
Doddington Cambs 139 E7
Kent 54 B2
Lincs 188 G6
Northumb 263 C11
Shrops 116 B2
Doddiscombsleigh
Devon 14 D3
Doddshill Norf 158 C3
Doddycross Corn 6 C6
Dodford W Nhants 120 E2
Worcs 117 C8
Dodington S Glos 61 C9
Som 43 E7
Dodleston Ches W 166 C5
Dodmarsh Hereford 97 C11
Dodscott Devon 25 D8
Dods Leigh Staffs 151 C10
Dodworth S Yorks 197 F10
Dodworth Bottom
S Yorks 197 G10
Dodworth Green
S Yorks 197 G10
Doe Bank W Mid 134 D2
Doe Green Warr 183 D9
Doehole Derbys 170 D5
Doe Lea Derbys 171 B7
Doffcocker Gtr Man 195 E7
Dogdyke Lincs 174 D2
Dog & Gun Mers 182 B5
Dog Hill Gtr Man 196 F3
Dogingtree Estate
Staffs 151 G9
Dogley Lane
W Yorks 197 E7
Dogmersfield Hants 49 C9
Dogridge Wilts 62 B5
Dogsthorpe Pboro 138 C3
Dog Village Devon 14 B5
Doirlinn Highld 289 D8
Dolanog Powys 147 G11
Dolau Powys 114 D2
Rhondda 58 C3
Dolbenmaen Gwyn 163 G8
Dole Ceredig 128 F2
Dolemeads Bath 61 G9
Doley Staffs 150 D4
Dolfach Powys 129 C8
Dol-ffanog Gwyn 146 G4
Dolfor Powys 130 F2
Dol-fôr Powys 128 B6
Dolgarrog Conwy 164 B3
Dolgellau Gwyn 146 F4
Dolgerdd Ceredig 111 G8
Dolgoch Gwyn 128 C3
Dolgran Carms 93 E8
Dolhelfa Powys 113 C8
Dolhendre Gwyn 147 C7
Doll Highld 311 J2
Dollar Clack 279 B9
Dolley Green Powys 114 D5
Dollis Hill London 67 B8
Dollwen Ceredig 128 G3
Dolphin Flint 181 G11
Dolphingstone
E Loth 281 G7
Dolphinholme
Lancs 202 C6
Dolphinston Borders 262 F5
Dolphinton S Lanark 270 F2
Dolton Devon 25 E9
Dolwen Conwy 180 G5
Powys 129 B9
Dolwyd Conwy 180 F4
Dolwyddelan Conwy 164 E2
Dôl-y-Bont Ceredig 128 F2
Dol-y-cannau Powys 96 B3
Dolydd Gwyn 163 D7
Dolyhir Powys 114 F4
Dolymelinau
Powys 129 D11
Dolywern Wrex 148 B4
Domewood Sur 51 E10
Domgay Powys 148 F5
Dommett Som 28 E3
Doncaster S Yorks 198 G5
Doncaster Common
S Yorks 198 G6
Dones Green
Ches W 183 F10
Donhead St Andrew
Wilts 30 C6
Donhead St Mary
Wilts 30 C6
Donibristle Fife 280 D3
Doniford Som 42 E5
Donington Lincs 156 B4
Shrops 132 C6
Donington Eaudike
Lincs 156 B4
Donington le Heath
Leics 153 G8
Donington on Bain
Lincs 190 E2
Donington South Ing
Lincs 156 C4
Donisthorpe Leics 152 G6
Don Johns Essex 106 F6
Donkey Street Kent 54 G6
Donkey Town Sur 66 G2
Donna Nook Lincs 190 B6
Donnington Glos 100 F3
Hereford 98 E4
Shrops 131 B11
Telford 150 G4
W Berks 64 F3
W Sus 22 C5
Donnington Wood
Telford 150 G4
Donwell T&W 243 F7
Donyatt Som 28 E4
Doomsday Green
W Sus 35 B11
Doonfoot S Ayrs 257 F8
Dora's Green Hants 49 D10
Dorback Lodge
Highld 292 B2
Dorcan Swindon 63 C7
Dorchester Dorset 17 C9
Oxon 83 G9
Dordale Worcs 117 C8
Dordon Warks 134 C5
Dore S Yorks 186 E4
Dores Highld 300 F5
Dorking Sur 51 D7
Dorking Tye Suff 107 D8
Dorley's Corner
Suff 127 D7
Dormansland Sur 52 E2
Dormans Park Sur 51 E11
Dormanstown
Redcar 235 G7
Dormer's Wells
London 66 C6
Dormington
Hereford 97 C11
Dormston Worcs 117 F9
Dorn Glos 100 E4
Dornal S Ayrs 236 B4
Dorney Bucks 66 D2
Dorney Reach Bucks 66 D2
Dorn Hill Worcs 100 E3
Dornie Highld 295 C10
Dornoch Highld 309 L7
Dornock Dumfries 238 D6
Dorrery Highld 310 D4
Dorridge W Mid 118 B3
Dorrington Lincs 173 E9
Shrops 131 C9
Dorsington Warks 100 B2
Dorstone Hereford 96 C6
Dorton Bucks 83 C11
Dorusduain Highld 295 C11
Doseley Telford 132 B3
Dosmuckeran
Highld 300 C2
Dosthill Staffs 134 C4
Staffs 134 D4
Dothan Anglesey 178 G5
Dothill Telford 150 G2
Dottery Dorset 16 B5
Doublebois Corn 6 C3
Double Hill Bath 45 B8
Dougarie N Ayrs 255 D9
Doughton Glos 80 G5
Norf 159 D7
Douglas IoM 192 E4
S Lanark 259 C8
Douglas & Angus
Dundee 287 D8
Douglastown Angus 287 C8
Douglas Water
S Lanark 259 B9
Douglas West
S Lanark 259 C8
Doulting Som 44 E6
Dounby Orkney 314 D2
Doune Highld 291 C10
Highld 309 J4
Stirling 285 G11
Doune Park Aberds 303 C7
Douneside Aberds 292 C6
Dounie Argyll 275 D8
Highld 309 K5
Highld 309 L6
Dounreay Highld 310 C3
Doura N Ayrs 266 G6
Dousland Devon 7 B10
Dovaston Shrops 149 E7
Dovecot Mers 182 C6
Dovecothall
Glasgow 267 D10
Dove Green Notts 171 E7
Dove Holes Derbys 185 F9
Dovenby Cumb 229 E7
Dovendale Lincs 190 E4
Dove Point Mers 182 C2
Dover Gtr Man 194 G6
Kent 55 E10
Dovercourt Essex 108 E5
Doverdale Worcs 117 D7
Doverhay Som 41 D11
Doveridge Derbys 152 C2
Doversgreen Sur 51 D9
Dowally Perth 286 C4
Dowanhill Glasgow 267 B11
Dowbridge Lancs 202 G4
Dowdeswell Glos 81 B7
Dowe Hill Norf 161 F10
Dowlais M Tydf 77 D10
Dowlais Top M Tydf 77 D9
Dowland Devon 25 E9
Dowles Worcs 116 B5
Dowlesgreen
Wokingham 65 F10
Dowlish Ford Som 28 E5
Dowlish Wake Som 28 E5
Downall Green
Gtr Man 194 G5
Down Ampney Glos 81 F10
Downan Moray 301 F11
S Ayrs 244 G3
Downcraig Ferry
N Ayrs 266 D3
Downderry Corn 6 E6
Downe London 68 G2
Downend Glos 80 F4
IoW 20 D6
S Glos 60 D6
W Berks 64 D3
Down End Som 43 E10
Downfield Dundee 287 D7
Down Field Cambs 124 C2
Downgate Corn 11 G11
Corn 12 G3
Down Hall Cumb 239 G7
Downham Essex 88 F2
Lancs 203 E11
London 67 E11
Northumb 263 C9
Downham Market
Norf 140 C2
Down Hatherley Glos 99 G7
Downhead Som 29 B9
Som 45 D7
Downhead Park
M Keynes 103 C7
Downhill Corn 5 B7
Perth 286 D4
T&W 243 F9
Downholland Cross
Lancs 193 F11
Downholme
N Yorks 224 F2
Downicary Devon 12 C3
Downies Aberds 293 D11
Downinney Corn 11 C10
Downley Bucks 84 G4
Down Park W Sus 51 F10
Downs V Glam 58 E6
Down St Mary Devon 26 G2
Downside C Beds 103 G10
E Sus 23 E9
N Som 60 F3
Som 44 D6
Sur 50 B6
Sur 51 B7
Down Street E Sus 36 C6
Down Thomas Devon 7 E10
Downton Hants 19 C11
Powys 114 E4
Shrops 149 G10
Wilts 31 C11
Downton on the Rock
Hereford 115 C8
Dowsby Lincs 156 D2
Dowsdale Lincs 156 G5
Dowslands Som 28 C2
Dowthwaitehead
Cumb 230 G3
Doxey Staffs 151 E8
Doxford Park T&W 243 G9
Doynton S Glos 61 E8
Drabblegate Norf 160 D4
Draethen Newport 59 B8
Draffan S Lanark 268 F5
Dragley Beck Cumb 210 D5
Dragonby N Lincs 200 E2
Dragons Green
W Sus 35 C10
Drakehouse S Yorks 186 E6
Drakeland Corner
Devon 7 D11
Drakelow Worcs 132 G6
Drakemyre Aberds 303 F9
N Ayrs 266 E5
Drake's Broughton
Worcs 99 B8
Drakes Cross
Worcs 117 B11
Drakestone Green
Suff 107 B9
Drakewalls Corn 12 G4
Draughton N Yorks 204 C6
W Nhants 120 B5
Drawbridge Corn 6 B3
Drax N Yorks 199 B7
Draycot Oxon 83 D10
Draycot Cerne Wilts 62 D2
Draycote Warks 119 C8
Draycot Fitz Payne
Wilts 62 G6
Draycot Foliat
Swindon 63 D7
Draycott Derbys 153 C8
Glos 80 E2
Glos 100 D3
Shrops 132 E6
Som 29 C8
Som 44 C3
Worcs 99 B7
Draycott in the Clay
Staffs 152 D3
Draycott in the Moors
Staffs 169 G7
Drayford Devon 26 E3
Drayton Leics 136 E6
Lincs 156 B4
Norf 160 G3
Oxon 83 G7
Oxon 101 C8
Ptsmth 33 F11
Som 28 C6
Som 29 D7
Warks 118 F3
W Nhants 119 E11
Worcs 117 B8
Drayton Bassett
Staffs 134 C3
Drayton Beauchamp
Bucks 84 C6
Drayton Parslow
Bucks 102 F6
Drayton St Leonard
Oxon 83 F10
Drebley N Yorks 205 B7
Dreemskerry IoM 192 C5
Dreenhill Pembs 72 C6
Drefach Carms 75 C8
Carms 92 G5
Carms 93 D7
Dre-fach Carms 75 B11
Ceredig 93 B10
Drefelin Carms 93 D7
Dreggie Highld 301 G10
Dreghorn Edin 270 B4
N Ayrs 257 B9
Dre-gôch Denb 165 B10
Drellingore Kent 55 E8
Drem E Loth 281 F10
Dresden Stoke 168 G6
Dreumasdal
W Isles 297 H3
Drewsteignton
Devon 13 C10
Driby Lincs 190 G5
Driffield E Yorks 208 B6
Glos 81 F9
Drift Corn 1 D4
Drigg Cumb 219 F11
Drighlington
W Yorks 197 B8
Drimnin Highld 289 D7
Drimnin Ho Highld 289 D7
Drimpton Dorset 28 F6
Drimsynie Argyll 284 G5
Dringhoe E Yorks 209 C9
Dringhouses York 207 D7
Drinisiadar W Isles 305 J3
Drinkstone Suff 125 E9
Drinkstone Green
Suff 125 E9
Drishaig Argyll 284 F5
Drissaig Argyll 275 B10
Drive End Dorset 29 F9
Driver's End Herts 86 B2
Drochedlie Aberds 302 C5
Drochil Borders 270 G3
Drointon Staffs 151 D10
Droitwich Spa
Worcs 117 E7
Droman Highld 306 D6
Dromore Dumfries 237 C7
Dron Perth 286 F5
Dronfield Derbys 186 F5
Dronfield Woodhouse
Derbys 186 F4
Drongan E Ayrs 257 F10
Dronley Angus 287 D7
Droop Dorset 30 F3
Drope Cardiff 58 D6
Dropping Well
S Yorks 186 C5
Droughduil
Dumfries 236 D3
Droxford Hants 33 D10
Droylsden Gtr Man 184 B6
Drub W Yorks 197 B7
Druggers End Worcs 98 D5
Druid Denb 165 G8
Druidston Pembs 72 B5
Druim Highld 301 D9
Druimarbin Highld 290 F2
Druimavuic Argyll 284 C4
Druimdrishaig
Argyll 275 F8
Druimindarroch
Highld 295 G8
Druimkinnerras
Highld 300 F4
Druimnacroish
Argyll 288 E6
Druimsornaig Argyll 289 F9
Druimyeon More
Argyll 255 B7
Drum Argyll 275 F10
Edin 270 B6
Perth 286 G4
Drumardoch
Stirling 285 F10
Drumbeg Highld 306 F6
Drumblade Aberds 302 E5
Drumblair Aberds 302 E6
Drumbuie Dumfries 246 G3
Highld 295 B9
Drumburgh Cumb 239 F7
Drumburn
Dumfries 237 C11
Drumchapel
Glasgow 277 G10
Drumchardine
Highld 300 E5
Drumchork Highld 307 L3
Drumclog S Lanark 258 B4
Drumdelgie Aberds 302 E4
Drumderfit Highld 300 D6
Drumdollo Aberds 302 F6
Drumeldrie Fife 287 G8
Drumelzier Borders 260 C4
Drumfearn Highld 295 D8
Drumgask Highld 291 D8
Drumgelloch
N Lanark 268 B5
Drumgley Angus 287 B8
Drumgreen Angus 292 F6
Drumguish Highld 291 D9
Drumhead Aberds 293 B11
Drumin Moray 301 F11
Drumindorsair
Highld 300 E4
Drumlasie Aberds 293 C8
Drumlean Stirling 285 G8
Drumlemble Argyll 255 F7
Drumliah Highld 309 K6
Drumligair Aberds 293 B11
Drumlithie Aberds 293 E9
Drumloist Stirling 285 G10
Drummersdale
Lancs 193 E11
Drummick Perth 286 E3
Drummoddie
Dumfries 236 E5
Drummond Highld 300 C6
Drummore Dumfries 236 F3
Drummuir Moray 302 E3
Drummuir Castle
Moray 302 E3
Drumnadrochit
Highld 300 G5
Drumnagorrach
Moray 302 D5
Drumness Perth 286 F2
Drumoak Aberds 293 D9
Drumore Argyll 255 E8
Drumpark Dumfries 247 G9
Drumpellier
N Lanark 268 B4
Drumphail Dumfries 236 C4
Drumrash Dumfries 237 B8
Drumrunie Highld 307 J6
Drumry W Dunb 277 G10
Drums Aberds 303 G9
Drumsallie Highld 289 B11
Drumsmittal Highld 300 E6
Drumstinchall
Dumfries 237 D10
Drumsturdy Angus 287 D8
Drumtochty Castle
Aberds 293 F8
Drumtroddan
Dumfries 236 E5
Drumuie Highld 298 E4
Drumuillie Highld 301 G9
Drumvaich Stirling 285 G10
Drumwalt Dumfries 236 D5
Drumwhindle
Aberds 303 F9
Drunkendub Angus 287 C10
Drury Flint 166 C3
Drurylane Norf 141 C8
Drury Lane Wrex 167 G7
Drury Square Norf 159 F8
Drybeck Cumb 222 B3
Drybridge Moray 302 C4
N Ayrs 257 B9
Drybrook Glos 79 B10
Dryburgh Borders 262 C3
Dryden Borders 261 E11
Dry Doddington
Lincs 172 F4
Dry Drayton Cambs 123 E7
Dryhill Kent 52 B3
Dry Hill Hants 49 F7
Dryhope Borders 261 E7
Drylaw Edin 280 F4
Drym Corn 2 C4
Drymen Stirling 277 D9
Drymere Norf 140 B5
Drymuir Aberds 303 E9
Drynachan Lodge
Highld 301 F8
Drynain Argyll 276 D3
Drynham Wilts 45 B11
Drynie Park Highld 300 D5
Drynoch Highld 294 B6
Dry Sandford Oxon 83 E7
Dryslwyn Carms 93 G11
Dry Street Essex 69 B7
Dryton Shrops 131 B11
Drywells Aberds 302 D6
Duag Bridge Highld 309 K3
Duartbeg Highld 306 F6
Duartmore Bridge
Highld 306 F6
Dubbs Cross Devon 12 C3
Dubford Aberds 303 C8
Dubhchladach
Argyll 275 G9
Dublin Suff 126 D3
Dubton Angus 287 B9
Dubwath Cumb 229 E9
Duchally Highld 309 H3
Duchlage Argyll 276 D6
Duchrae Dumfries 246 G5
Duck Corner Suff 109 C7
Duck End Bedford 103 C11
Bedford 121 G9
Bucks 102 F5
Cambs 122 E4
Essex 105 G10
Essex 106 E3
Essex 106 F3
Duckend Green
Essex 106 G4
Duckhole S Glos 79 G10
Duckington Ches W 167 E7
Ducklington Oxon 82 D5
Duckmanton Derbys 186 G6
Duck's Cross
Bedford 122 F2
Ducks Island London 86 F2
Duckswich Worcs 98 D6
Dudbridge Glos 80 E4
Dudden Hill London 67 B8
Duddenhoe End
Essex 105 D9
Duddingston Edin 280 G5
Duddington
N Nhants 137 C9
Duddlestone Som 28 C2
Duddleswell E Sus 37 B7
Duddlewick Shrops 132 G3
Duddo Northumb 273 G8
Duddon Ches W 167 C8
Duddon Bridge
Cumb 210 B3
Duddon Common
Ches W 167 B8
Dudleston Shrops 148 B6
Dudleston Grove
Shrops 149 B7
Dudleston Heath (Criftins) Shrops 149 B7
Dudley T&W 243 C7
W Mid 133 E8
Dudley Hill W Yorks 205 G9
Dudley Port W Mid 133 E9
Dudley's Fields
W Mid 133 C9
Dudley Wood
W Mid 133 F8
Dudlows Green
Warr 183 E10
Dudsbury Dorset 19 B7
Dudswell Herts 85 D7
Dudwells Pembs 91 G8
Duerdon Devon 24 D4
Duffield Derbys 170 G4
Duffieldbank
Derbys 170 G5
Duffryn Neath 57 B10
Newport 59 B9
Shrops 130 G4
Dufftown Moray 302 F3
Duffus Moray 301 C11
Dufton Cumb 231 F9
Duggleby N Yorks 217 F7
Duich Argyll 254 B4
Duiletter Argyll 284 D5
Duinish Perth 291 G8
Duirinish Highld 295 B9
Duisdalebeg Highld 295 D8
Duisdalemore
Highld 295 D9
Duisky Highld 290 F2
Duke End Warks 134 F4
Dukesfield
Northumb 241 F10
Dukestown
Bl Gwent 77 C10
Dukinfield Gtr Man 184 B6
Dulas Anglesey 179 D7
Dulcote Som 44 E5
Dulford Devon 27 F9
Dull Perth 286 C2
Dullatur N Lanark 278 F4
Dullingham Cambs 124 F2
Dullingham Ley
Cambs 124 F2
Dulnain Bridge
Highld 301 G9
Duloch Fife 280 D2
Duloe Bedford 122 E3
Corn 6 D4
Dulsie Highld 301 E9
Dulverton Som 26 B6
Dulwich London 67 E10
Dulwich Village
London 67 E10
Dumbarton W Dunb 277 F7
Dumbleton Glos 99 D10
Dumcrieff Dumfries 248 C4
Dumfries Dumfries 237 B11
Dumgoyne Stirling 277 E10
Dummer Hants 48 D5
Dumpford W Sus 34 C4
Dumpinghill Devon 24 F6
Dumpling Green
Norf 159 G10
Dumplington
Gtr Man 184 B3
Dumpton Kent 71 F11
Dun Angus 287 B10
Dunach Argyll 289 G10
Dunadd Argyll 275 D9
Dunain Ho Highld 300 E6
Dunalastair Perth 285 B11
Dunan Highld 295 C7
Dunans Argyll 275 D9
Argyll 275 D11
Dunball Som 43 E10
Dunbar E Loth 282 F3
Dunbeath Highld 311 G5
Dunbeg Argyll 289 F10
Dunblane Stirling 285 G11
Dunbog Fife 286 F6
Dunbridge Hants 32 B4
Duncansclett
Shetland 313 K5
Duncanston Highld 300 D5
Duncanstone
Aberds 302 G5
Dun Charlabhaigh
W Isles 304 D3
Dunchideock Devon 14 D3
Dunchurch Warks 119 C9
Duncombe Lancs 202 F6
Duncote W Nhants 120 G3
Duncow Dumfries 247 G11
Duncraggan Stirling 285 G9
Duncrievie Perth 286 G5
Duncroisk Stirling 285 D9
Duncton W Sus 35 D7
Dundas Ho Orkney 314 H4
Dundee Dundee 287 D8
Dundeugh Dumfries 246 F3
Dundon Som 44 G3
Dundonald Fife 280 C4
S Ayrs 257 C9
Dundon Hayes Som 44 G3
Dundonnell Highld 307 L5
Dundonnell Hotel
Highld 307 L5
Dundonnell House
Highld 307 L6

Dundraw Cumb 229 B10
Dundreggan Highld . . 290 B5
Dundreggan Lodge
  Highld 290 B5
Dundrennan
  Dumfries 237 E9
Dundridge Hants 33 D9
Dundry N Som 60 F5
Dundurn Perth 285 E11
Dundyvan N Lanark . . 268 C4
Dunecht Aberds 293 C9
Dunfermline Fife . . 279 D11
Dunfield Glos 81 F10
Dunford Bridge
  S Yorks 197 G7
Dungate Kent 54 B2
Dunge Wilts 45 C11
Dungeness Kent 39 D3
Dungworth S Yorks . . 186 D3
Dunham Notts 188 B5
Dunham-on-the-Hill
  Ches W 183 G6
Dunham on Trent
  Notts 188 G4
Dunhampstead
  Worcs 117 E8
Dunhampton Worcs . 116 D6
Dunham Town
  Gtr Man 184 D2
Dunham Woodhouses
  Gtr Man 184 D2
Dunholme Lincs . . . 189 F8
Dunino Fife 287 F9
Dunipace Falk 278 C6
Dunira Perth 285 E11
Dunkeld Perth 286 C4
Dunkerton Bath 45 B8
Dunkeswell Devon . . . 27 F10
Dunkeswick
  N Yorks 206 D2
Dunkirk Cambs 139 F10
  Ches W 182 G5
  Kent 54 B5
  Norf 160 D4
  Nottingham 153 B11
  S Glos 61 B9
  Staffs 168 E4
  Wilts 62 G3
Dunk's Green Kent . . 52 C6
Dunlappie Angus . . . 293 G2
Dunley Hants 48 C3
  Worcs 116 D5
Dunlichity Lodge
  Highld 300 F6
Dunlop E Ayrs 267 F8
Dunmaglass Lodge
  Highld 300 G5
Dunmere Corn 5 B10
Dunmore Argyll 275 G8
  Falk 279 D7
  Highld 300 E5
Dunnerholme Cumb . 210 D4
Dunnet Highld 310 B6
Dunnichen Angus . . . 287 C9
Dunnikier Fife 280 C5
Dunninald Angus . . . 287 B11
Dunning Perth 286 F4
Dunnington E Yorks . 209 C9
  Warks 117 G11
  York 207 C9
Dunningwell Cumb . . 210 C3
Dunnockshaw
  Lancs 195 B10
Dunnose IoW 21 F7
Dunnsheath Shrops . 149 F9
Dunn Street Kent . . . 54 D3
  Kent 69 G9
Dunollie Argyll . . . 289 F10
Dunoon Argyll 276 F3
Dunragit Dumfries . . 236 D3
Dunrobin Mains
  Highld 311 J2
Dunrostan Argyll . . 275 E8
Duns Borders 272 E5
Dunsa Derbys 186 G2
Dunsby Lincs 156 D2
Dunscar Gtr Man . . . 195 E8
Dunscore Dumfries . . 247 G9
Dunscroft S Yorks . . 199 F7
Dunsdale Redcar . . . 226 B2
Dunsden Green Oxon . 65 D8
Dunsfold Sur 50 F4
Dunsfold Common
  Sur 50 F4
Dunsfold Green Sur . 50 F4
Dunsford Devon 14 D2
  Sur 50 F4
Dunshalt Fife 286 F6
Dunshillock Aberds . 303 E9
Dunsill Notts 171 C7
Dunsinnan Perth . . . 286 D5
Dunskey Ho
  Dumfries 236 D2
Dunslea Corn 11 G11
Dunsley N Yorks . . . 227 C7
  Staffs 133 G7
Dunsmore Bucks 84 D5
  Warks 119 B10
Dunsop Bridge
  Lancs 203 C9
Dunstable C Beds . . 103 G10
Dunstal Staffs . . . 151 D11
Dunstall Staffs . . . 152 E3
Dunstall Common
  Worcs 99 C7
Dunstall Green Suff . 124 E4
Dunstall Hill W Mid . 133 C8
Dunstan Northumb . . 265 F7
Dunstan Steads
  Northumb 264 E6
Dunster Som 42 E3
Duns Tew Oxon 101 F9
Dunston Derbys 186 G5
  Lincs 173 C9
  Norf 142 C4
  Staffs 151 F8
  T&W 242 E6
Dunstone Devon 7 E11
  Devon 8 G5

Dunston Heath
  Staffs 151 F8
Dunston Hill T&W . . 242 E6
Dunsville S Yorks . . 198 F6
Dunswell E Yorks . . 209 F7
Dunsyre S Lanark . . 269 F11
Dunterton Devon . . . 12 F3
Duntisbourne Abbots
  Glos 81 D7
Duntisbourne Leer
  Glos 81 D7
Duntisbourne Rouse
  Glos 81 D7
Duntish Dorset 29 F11
Duntocher W Dunb . . 277 G9
Dunton Bucks 102 G6
  C Beds 104 C4
  Norf 159 C7
Dunton Bassett
  Leics 135 E10
Dunton Green Kent . . 52 B4
Dunton Patch Norf . . 159 C7
Dunton Wayletts
  Essex 87 G11
Duntrune Castle
  Argyll 275 D8
Duntulm Highld 298 B4
Dunure S Ayrs 257 F7
Dunvant = Dynfant
  Swansea 56 C5
Dunvegan Highld . . . 298 E3
Dunveth Corn 10 G5
Dunwear Som 43 F10
Dunwich Suff 127 C9
Dunwood Staffs 168 D6
Dupplin Castle
  Perth 286 F4
Durdar Cumb 239 G10
Durgan Corn 3 D7
Durgates E Sus 52 G6
Durham Durham . . . 233 C11
Durisdeer
  Dumfries 247 C9
Durisdeermill
  Dumfries 247 C9
Durkar W Yorks . . . 197 D10
Durleigh Som 43 F9
Durleighmarsh
  W Sus 34 C3
Durley Hants 33 D8
  Wilts 63 G8
Durley Street Hants . 33 D8
Durlock Kent 55 B9
Durlow Common
  Hereford 98 D2
Durn Durham 196 D2
Durnamuck Highld . . 307 K5
Durness Highld 308 C4
Durnfield Som 29 C7
Durno Aberds 303 G7
Durns Town Hants . . . 19 B11
Duror Highld 289 D10
Durran Argyll 275 C10
  Highld 310 C5
Durrant Green
  Kent 53 F11
Durrants Hants 22 B2
Durrington Wilts . . . 47 E7
  W Sus 35 F10
Durrisdale Orkney . . 314 D3
Dursley Glos 80 F3
  Wilts 45 C11
Dursley Cross Glos . 98 G3
Durston Som 28 B3
Durweston Dorset . . . 30 F5
Dury Shetland 313 G6
Duryard Devon 14 C4
Duston W Nhants . . . 120 E4
Duthil Highld 301 G9
Dutlas Powys 114 B4
Duton Hill Essex . . 106 F2
Dutson Corn 12 D2
Dutton Ches W 183 F9
Duxford Cambs 105 B9
  Oxon 82 F5
Duxmoor Shrops . . . 115 B8
Dwygyfylchi
  Conwy 180 F2
Dwyran Anglesey . . . 162 B6
Dwyrhiw Powys . . . 129 C11
Dyce Aberdeen 293 B10
Dyche Som 43 E7
Dye House
  Northumb 241 F10
Dyer's Common
  S Glos 60 C5
Dyer's Green
  Cambs 105 B7
Dyffryn Bridgend . . . 57 C11
  Carms 92 G6
  Ceredig 110 G5
  Pembs 91 D8
Dyffryn Ardudwy
  Gwyn 145 E11
Dyffryn-bern
  Ceredig 110 G5
Dyffryn Castell
  Ceredig 128 G5
Dyffryn Ceidrych
  Carms 94 F4
Dyffryn Cellwen
  Neath 76 D5
Dyke Lincs 156 E2
  Moray 301 D9
Dykehead Angus . . . 292 G5
  N Lanark 269 D7
  Stirling 277 B11
Dykelands Aberds . . 293 G9
Dykends Angus 286 B6
Dykeside Aberds . . . 303 E7
Dykesmains
  N Ayrs 266 G5
Dylife Powys 129 D6
Dymchurch Kent . . . 39 B9
Dymock Glos 98 E4
Dynfant = Dunvant
  Swansea 56 C5
Dyrham S Glos 61 D8
Dysart Fife 280 C6
Dyserth Denb 181 F9

E

Eabost Highld 294 B5
Eabost West Highld . 298 E3
Each End Kent 55 B10
Eachway Worcs 117 B9
Eachwick Northumb . 242 C4
Eadar Dha Fhadhail
  W Isles 304 E2
Eagland Hill Lancs . 202 D4
Eagle Lincs 172 B5
Eagle Barnsdale
  Lincs 172 B5
Eagle Moor Lincs . . 172 B5
Eaglesfield Cumb . . 229 F7
  Dumfries 238 C5
Eaglesham E Renf . . 267 E11
Eaglestone
  M Keynes 103 D7
Eaglethorpe
  N Nhants 137 E11
Eagle Tor Derbys . . 170 C2
Eagley Gtr Man . . . 195 E8
Eairy IoM 192 E3
Eakley Lanes
  M Keynes 120 G6
Eakring Notts 171 C11
Ealand N Lincs . . . 199 E9
Ealing London 67 C7
Eals Northumb 240 F5
Eamont Bridge
  Cumb 230 F6
Earby Lancs 204 D3
Earcroft Blackburn . 195 C7
Eardington Shrops . . 132 E4
Eardisland Hereford . 115 F8
Eardisley Hereford . 96 B6
Eardiston Shrops . . 149 D7
  Worcs 116 D3
Earith Cambs 123 C7
Earle Northumb . . . 263 D11
Earlestown Mers . . . 183 B9
Earley Wokingham . . 65 E9
Earlham Norf 142 B4
Earlish Highld . . . 298 C3
Earls Barton
  N Nhants 121 E7
Earls Colne Essex . . 107 F7
Earl's Common
  Worcs 117 F9
Earl's Court London . 67 D9
Earl's Croome Worcs . 99 C7
Earlsdon W Mid . . . 118 B6
Earl's Down E Sus . . 23 B10
Earlsferry Fife . . . 281 B9
Earlsfield Lincs . . 155 B8
  London 67 D9
Earlsford Aberds . . 303 F8
Earl's Green Suff . . 125 D10
Earl Soham Suff . . . 126 E4
Earl Sterndale
  Derbys 169 B9
Earlston Borders . . 262 B3
  E Ayrs 257 B10
Earlswood Mon 79 F7
  Sur 51 D9
  Warks 118 C2
Earlstone Common
  Hants 64 G3
Earl Stoneham Suff . 126 F2
Earl Stonham Suff . . 126 F2
Earlstoun Dumfries . 246 G4
Earlsheaton
  W Yorks 197 C9
Earl Shilton Leics . 135 D9
Earlsmill Moray . . . 301 D9
Earl Soham Suff . . . 126 E4
Earl's Down E Sus . . 23 B10
Earnley W Sus 22 D4
Earnock S Lanark . . 268 E3
Earnshaw Bridge
  Lancs 194 C4
Earsairidh W Isles . 297 M3
Earsdon T&W 243 C8
Earsham Norf 142 F6
Earsham Street Suff . 126 B4
Earswick York 207 B8
Eartham W Sus 22 B6
Earthcott Green
  S Glos 61 B7
Easby N Yorks 224 E3
  N Yorks 225 D11
Easdale Argyll 275 B8
Easebourne W Sus . . 34 C5
Easenhall Warks . . . 119 B9
Eashing Sur 50 E2
Easington Bucks . . . 83 C11
  Durham 234 C4
  E Yorks 201 D11
  Lancs 203 C10
  Northumb 264 C10
  Oxon 83 F11
  Oxon 101 D9
  Redcar 226 B4
Easington Colliery
  Durham 234 C4
Easington Lane
  T&W 234 B3
Easingwold
  N Yorks 215 F10
Easole Street Kent . 55 C9
Eason's Green E Sus . 23 B8
Eassie Angus 287 C7
East Aberthaw
  V Glam 58 F4
Eastacombe Devon . . 25 B8
  Devon 25 C7
Eastacott Devon . . . 25 C10
East Acton London . . 67 C8
East Adderbury
  Oxon 101 D9
East Allington Devon . 8 F5
East Amat Highld . . 309 K4
East Anstey Devon . . 26 B5
East Anton Hants . . . 47 D11
East Appleton
  N Yorks 224 F4
East Ardsley
  W Yorks 197 B10
East Ashling W Sus . 22 B4
East Aston Hants . . . 48 D2
East Auchronie
  Aberds 293 C10

East Ayton N Yorks . 217 B9
East Bank Bl Gwent . 78 D2
East Barkwith
  Lincs 189 E11
East Barming Kent . . 53 C8
East Barnby
  N Yorks 226 C6
East Barnet London . 86 F3
East Barns E Loth . . 282 F4
East Barsham Norf . . 159 C8
East Barton Suff . . 125 D8
East Beach W Sus . . 22 E5
East Beckham Norf . 177 E11
East Bedfont London . 66 E5
East Bergholt Suff . 107 D11
East Bierley
  W Yorks 197 B7
East Bilney Norf . . 159 F9
East Blackdene
  Durham 232 D3
East Blatchington
  E Sus 23 E7
East Bloxworth
  Dorset 18 C3
East Boldon T&W . . 243 E9
East Boldre Hants . . 32 G5
East Bonhard Perth . 286 E5
Eastbourne Darl . . . 224 C6
  E Sus 23 F10
East Bower Som . . . 43 F10
East Brent Som 43 C11
Eastbridge Suff . . . 127 D9
East Bridgford
  Notts 171 G11
East Briscoe
  Durham 223 B9
Eastbrook Som 28 C2
  V Glam 59 E7
East Buckland Devon . 41 G7
East Budleigh Devon . 15 C7
Eastburn E Yorks . . 208 B5
  W Yorks 204 E6
East Burnham Bucks . 66 C3
East Burrafirth
  Shetland 313 H5
East Burton Dorset . 18 D2
Eastbury London . . . 85 G9
  W Berks 63 D10
East Butsfield
  Durham 233 B8
East Butterleigh
  Devon 27 F7
East Butterwick
  N Lincs 199 F10
Eastby N Yorks . . . 204 C6
East Cairnbeg
  Aberds 293 F9
East Calder W Loth . 269 B11
East Carleton Norf . 142 C3
East Carlton
  N Nhants 136 F6
  W Yorks 205 E10
East Chaldon or Chaldon
  Herring Dorset . . . 17 E11
East Challow Oxon . . 63 B11
East Charleton Devon . 8 G5
East Chelborough
  Dorset 29 F9
East Chiltington
  E Sus 36 D5
East Chinnock Som . . 29 E7
East Chisenbury
  Wilts 46 C6
East Cholderton
  Hants 47 D9
Eastchurch Kent . . . 70 E3
East Clandon Sur . . 50 C5
East Claydon Bucks . 102 F4
East Clevedon N Som . 60 E2
East Clyne Highld . . 311 J3
East Clyth Highld . . 310 F7
East Coker Som 29 E8
Eastcombe Glos 80 E5
East Combe Som . . . 43 G7
East Common
  N Yorks 207 G8
East Compton Dorset . 30 D5
  Som 44 E6
East Cornworthy
  Devon 8 D6
Eastcote London . . . 66 B6
  W Mid 118 B3
  W Nhants 120 G3
Eastcott Corn 24 D3
  Wilts 46 B4
East Cottingwith
  E Yorks 207 E10
Eastcotts Bedford . . 103 B11
Eastcourt Wilts . . . 63 G8
  Wilts 81 G7
East Cowes IoW . . . 20 B6
East Cowick
  E Yorks 199 C7
East Cowton
  N Yorks 224 E6
East Cramlington
  Northumb 243 B7
East Cranmore Som . . 45 E7
East Creech Dorset . 18 E4
East Croachy Highld . 300 G6
Eastcroft Highld . . 291 B11
East Curthwaite
  Cumb 230 B2
East Dean E Sus . . . 23 F9
  Glos 98 G3
  Hants 32 B3
  W Sus 34 E6
East Dene S Yorks . . 186 C6
East Denton T&W . . 242 D6
East Didsbury
  Gtr Man 184 C5
Eastdon Devon 14 F5
Eastdown Devon 8 F6
East Down Devon . . . 40 E6
East Drayton Notts . 188 F3
East Dulwich London . 67 E10

East Dundry N Som . . 60 F5
East Ella Hull 200 B5
Eastend Essex 86 C6
  Oxon 100 G6
East End Bedford . . 122 F2
  Bucks 84 B4
  C Beds 103 C9
  Dorset 18 B5
  E Yorks 201 B9
  E Yorks 209 B9
  E Yorks 209 G9
  Glos 81 C11
  Hants 20 B3
  Hants 33 C11
  Hants 64 G2
  Herts 105 F9
  Kent 53 F11
  Kent 53 F10
  Kent 70 E3
  M Keynes 103 C8
  N Som 60 E3
  Oxon 82 C5
  Oxon 101 D9
  Oxon 101 E7
  S Glos 61 B9
  Som 44 C5
  Suff 108 E2
East End Green Herts . 86 C3
Easter Aberchalder
  Highld 291 B10
Easter Ardross
  Highld 300 B6
Easter Balgedie
  Perth 286 G5
Easter Balmoral
  Aberds 292 D4
Easter Boleskine
  Highld 300 G5
Easter Brackland
  Stirling 285 G10
Easter Brae Highld . 300 C6
Easter Cardno
  Aberds 303 C9
Easter Compton
  S Glos 60 C5
Easter Cringate
  Stirling 278 D4
Easter Culfosie
  Aberds 293 C9
Easter Davoch
  Aberds 292 C6
Easter Earshaig
  Dumfries 248 C2
Easter Ellister Argyll . 254 B3
Easter Fearn Highld . 309 L6
Easter Galcantray
  Highld 301 E8
Eastergate W Sus . . 22 B6
Easterhouse
  Glasgow 268 B3
Easter Housebyres
  Borders 262 B2
Easter Howgate
  Midloth 270 C4
Easter Howlaws
  Borders 272 G4
Easter Kinkell
  Highld 300 D5
Easter Knox Angus . . 287 D9
Easter Langlee
  Borders 262 B2
Easter Lednathie
  Angus 292 G5
Easter Milton Highld . 301 D9
Easter Moniack
  Highld 300 E5
Eastern Green
  W Mid 134 G5
Easter Ord
  Aberdeen 293 C10
Easter Quarff
  Shetland 313 K6
Easter Rhynd Perth . 286 F5
Easter Row Stirling . 278 B5
Easterside Mbro . . . 225 B10
Easter Silverford
  Aberds 303 C7
Easter Skeld
  Shetland 313 J5
Easter Softlaw
  Borders 263 C7
Easterton Wilts . . . 46 C4
Easterton of Lenabo
  Aberds 303 E10
Easterton Sands
  Wilts 46 B4
Easter Tulloch
  Aberds 293 A10
Easter Whyntie
  Aberds 302 C6
East Everleigh Wilts . 47 C8
East Ewell Sur 67 G8
East Farleigh Kent . 53 C8
East Farndon
  W Nhants 136 F4
East Fen Common
  Cambs 124 C2
East Ferry Lincs . . 188 B4
Eastfield Borders . . 262 D2
  Bristol 60 D5
  N Lanark 269 C7
  N Lanark 278 G4
  Northumb 217 C10
  S Lanark 268 C2
  W Yorks 197 G9
Eastfield Hall
  Northumb 252 B6
East Fields W Berks . 64 F3
East Finchley London . 67 B9
East Firsby Lincs . . 189 D7
East Fleet Dorset . . 17 E8

East Fortune
  E Loth 281 F10
East Garforth
  W Yorks 206 G4
East Garston
  W Berks 63 D11
Eastgate Durham . . . 232 D5
  Norf 160 E2
  Pboro 138 D4
East Gateshead
  T&W 243 E7
East Ginge Oxon . . . 64 B2
East Gores Essex . . 107 G2
East Goscote Leics . 154 G2
East Grafton Wilts . 63 G9
East Grange Moray . . 301 C10
East Green Hants . . 49 E9
  Suff 124 C3
  Suff 127 D8
East Grimstead Wilts . 32 B2
East Grinstead
  W Sus 51 F11
East Guldeford E Sus . 38 C6
East Haddon
  W Nhants 120 D3
East Hagbourne Oxon . 64 B4
East Hall Herts . . . 104 G3
East Halton N Lincs . 200 D6
Eastham Mers 182 E5
  Worcs 116 D3
East Ham London . . . 68 C2
Eastham Ferry Mers . 182 E5
East Hampnett
  W Sus 22 B6
Easthampstead
  Brack 65 F11
Easthampton
  Hereford 115 E8
East Hanney Oxon . . 82 G6
East Hanningfield
  Essex 88 E3
East Hardwick
  W Yorks 198 D3
East Harling Norf . . 141 F9
East Harlsey
  N Yorks 225 F8
East Harnham Wilts . 31 B10
East Harptree Bath . 44 B5
East Hartford
  Northumb 243 B7
East Harting W Sus . 34 D3
East Hatch Wilts . . 30 B6
East Hatley Cambs . . 122 G5
Easthaugh Norf 159 F11
East Hauxwell
  N Yorks 224 G3
East Haven Angus . . 287 D9
Eastheath
  Wokingham 65 F10
East Heckington
  Lincs 173 G11
East Hedleyhope
  Durham 233 C9
East Helmsdale
  Highld 311 H4
East Hendred Oxon . . 64 B3
East Herringthorpe
  S Yorks 187 C7
East Herrington
  T&W 243 G9
East Heslerton
  N Yorks 217 D8
East Hewish N Som . . 59 G11
East Hill Kent 68 G5
  Devon 15 B11
East Hoathly E Sus . 23 B8
East Hogaland
  Shetland 313 K5
East Holme Dorset . . 18 D3
East Holton Dorset . 18 C5
East Holywell
  Northumb 243 C8
Easthope Shrops . . . 131 D11
Easthopewood
  Shrops 131 D11
East Horndon Essex . 68 B6
Easthorpe Essex . . . 107 G8
  Leics 154 B6
  Notts 172 E2
East Horrington Som . 44 D5
East Horsley Sur . . 50 C5
East Horton
  Northumb 264 C2
Easthouse Shetland . 313 J5
Easthouses Midloth . 270 B6
East Howdon T&W . . 243 D8
East Howe BCP 19 B7
East Huntspill Som . 43 E10
East Hyde C Beds . . 85 B10
East Ilkerton Devon . 41 D8
East Ilsley W Berks . 64 C3
Easting Orkney 314 A7
Eastington Devon . . 26 F2
  Glos 80 D3
  Glos 81 C10
East Keal Lincs . . . 174 C5
East Kennett Wilts . 62 F6
East Keswick
  W Yorks 206 E3
East Kilbride
  S Lanark 268 E2
East Kimber Devon . . 12 B5
East Kingston W Sus . 35 G9
East Kirkby Lincs . . 174 C4
East Knapton
  N Yorks 217 D7
East Knighton Dorset . 18 D2
East Knowstone
  Devon 26 C4
East Knoyle Wilts . . 45 G11
East Kyle Northumb . 264 B3
East Kyo Durham . . . 242 G5
East Lambrook Som . 28 D6
East Lamington
  Highld 301 B7
East Langdon Kent . . 55 D10
East Langton Leics . 136 E4
East Langwell
  Highld 309 J7
East Lavant W Sus . . 22 B5
East Lavington
  W Sus 34 D6

East Law Northumb . 242 G3
East Layton N Yorks . 224 D3
Eastleach Martin
  Glos 82 D2
Eastleach Turville
  Glos 81 D11
East Leake Notts . . 153 D11
East Learmouth
  Northumb 263 B9
Eastleigh Devon . . . 25 C7
  Hants 32 D6
East Leigh Devon . . 8 E3
  Devon 25 C11
East Lexham Norf . . 159 F7
East Lilburn
  Northumb 264 D2
East Liss Hants . . . 34 B3
East Lockinge Oxon . 64 B2
East Loftus Redcar . 226 B4
East Looe Corn 6 E5
East Lound N Lincs . 188 B3
East Lulworth Dorset . 18 E3
East Lutton N Yorks . 217 F8
East Lydeard Som . . 27 B11
East Lydford Som . . 44 G5
East Lyng Som 28 B4
East Mains Aberds . . 293 D8
  Borders 271 F11
East Malling Kent . . 53 B8
East Malling Heath
  Kent 53 B7
East March Angus . . 287 D8
East Marden W Sus . 34 E4
East Markham Notts . 188 F3
East Marsh NE Lincs . 201 E9
East Martin Hants . . 31 D9
East Marton
  N Yorks 204 C4
East Melbury Dorset . 30 C5
East Meon Hants . . . 33 C11
East Mere Devon . . . 27 D7
East Mersea Essex . . 89 C9
East Mey Highld . . . 310 B7
East Molesey Sur . . 67 F7
Eastmoor Derbys . . . 186 G4
  Norf 140 C4
East Moor
  W Yorks 197 C10
East Morden Dorset . 18 B4
East Morton
  W Yorks 205 E7
East Moulsecoomb
  Brighton 36 F4
East Ness N Yorks . . 216 D3
East Newton
  E Yorks 209 F11
  N Yorks 216 D2
Eastney Ptsmth . . . 21 B9
Eastnor Hereford . . 98 D4
East Norton Leics . . 136 C5
East Nynehead Som . 27 C11
East Oakley Hants . . 48 C5
Eastoft N Lincs . . . 199 D10
East Ogwell Devon . . 14 G2
Eastoke Hants 21 B10
Easton Bristol 60 E6
  Cambs 122 C2
  Cumb 239 C10
  Cumb 239 F7
  Devon 13 D10
  Dorset 17 G9
  Hants 48 G4
  IoW 20 D2
  Lincs 155 D8
  Norf 160 G2
  Som 44 D4
  Suff 126 F5
  W Berks 64 E2
Easton Grey Wilts . . 61 B11
Easton-in-Gordano
  N Som 60 D4
Easton Maudit
  N Nhants 121 F7
Easton on the Hill
  N Nhants 137 C10
Easton Royal Wilts . 63 G8
Easton Town Wilts . 61 B11
East Orchard Dorset . 30 D4
East Ord Northumb . 273 E9
Eastover Som 43 F10
East Panson Devon . . 12 C3
East Parley BCP . . . 19 B8
Eastpark Dumfries . . 238 D2
East Peckham Kent . 53 D7
East Pennard Som . . 44 F5
East Perry Cambs . . 122 C3
East Portholland Corn . 5 G9
East Portlemouth
  Devon 9 G9
East Prawle Devon . . 9 G10
East Preston W Sus . 35 G9
East Pulham Dorset . 30 F2
East Putford Devon . 24 D5
East Quantoxhead
  Som 42 E6
East Rainton T&W . . 234 B2
East Ravendale
  NE Lincs 201 G7
East Raynham Norf . 159 D7
Eastrea Cambs 138 D5
East Rhidorroch Lodge
  Highld 307 K7
Eastriggs Dumfries . 238 D6
East Rigton
  W Yorks 206 E3
Eastrington E Yorks . 199 B9
Eastrip Wilts 61 E10
East Rolstone
  N Som 59 G11
East Rounton
  N Yorks 225 E8
East Row N Yorks . . 227 C7
East Rudham Norf . . 158 D6

East Runton Norf . . 177 E11
East Ruston Norf . . 160 D6
Eastry Kent 55 C10
East Saltoun E Loth . 271 B9
East Sheen London . . 67 D8
East Sherford Devon . 7 F11
East Skelston
  Dumfries 247 F8
East Sleekburn
  Northumb 253 G6
East Somerton Norf . 161 F9
East Stanley
  Durham 242 G5
East Stockwith
  Lincs 188 C3
East Stoke Dorset . . 18 D3
  Notts 172 F3
  Som 29 D7
East Stour Dorset . . 30 C4
East Stour Common
  Dorset 30 C4
East Stourmouth
  Kent 71 G9
East Stowford
  Devon 25 B10
East Stratton Hants . 48 F4
East Street Kent . . . 55 C10
  Som 44 F4
East Studdal Kent . . 55 D10
East Suisnish Highld . 295 B7
East-the-Water
  Devon 25 B7
East Third Borders . 262 B4
East Thirston
  Northumb 252 D5
East Tilbury Thurrock . 69 D7
East Tisted Hants . . 49 G8
East Torrington
  Lincs 189 E10
East Town Som 42 G4
  Som 44 E6
  Wilts 45 B11
East Trewent Pembs . 73 F8
East Tuddenham
  Norf 159 G11
East Tuelmenna Corn . 6 B4
East Tytherley Hants . 32 B3
East Tytherton Wilts . 62 E3
East Village Devon . 26 F4
  V Glam 58 E3
Eastville Bristol . . 60 E6
  Lincs 174 D6
East Wall Shrops . . 131 E11
East Walton Norf . . 158 F4
East Water Som . . . 44 C4
East Week Devon . . . 13 C9
Eastwell Leics 154 E5
East Wellow Hants . . 32 C4
Eastwell Park Kent . 54 E4
East Wemyss Fife . . 280 B6
East Whitburn
  W Loth 269 B8
East Wick Herts . . . 86 C6
East Wickham
  London 68 D3
East Williamston
  Pembs 73 E9
East Winch Norf . . . 158 F3
East Winterslow
  Wilts 47 G8
East Wittering
  W Sus 21 B11
East Witton N Yorks . 214 B2
Eastwood Hereford . . 98 C2
  Notts 171 F7
  Southend 69 B10
  S Yorks 186 C6
  W Yorks 196 B3
East Woodburn
  Northumb 251 F10
Eastwood End
  Cambs 139 E8
Eastwood Hall Notts . 171 F7
East Woodhay Hants . 64 G2
East Woodlands Som . 45 E9
East Worldham Hants . 49 F8
East Worlington
  Devon 26 E3
East Worthing
  W Sus 35 G11
East Wretham Norf . 141 E8
East Youlstone
  Devon 24 D3
Eathorpe Warks . . . 119 D7
Eaton Ches E 168 B5
  Ches W 167 C9
  Hereford 115 F10
  Leics 154 E5
  Norf 142 B4
  Notts 188 F2
  Oxon 82 E6
  Shrops 131 F7
  Shrops 131 F10
Eaton Bishop
  Hereford 97 D8
Eaton Bray C Beds . . 103 G9
Eaton Constantine
  Shrops 131 B11
Eaton Ford Cambs . . 122 E3
Eaton Green
  C Beds 103 G9
Eaton Hastings Oxon . 82 F3
Eaton Mascott
  Shrops 131 B10
Eaton on Tern
  Shrops 150 E3
Eaton Socon Cambs . 122 F3
Eaton upon Tern
  Shrops 150 E3
Eau Brink Norf 157 F11
Eau Withington
  Hereford 97 C10
Eaves Green W Mid . 134 G5
Eavestone N Yorks . . 214 F4
Ebberston N Yorks . . 217 C7
Ebbesbourne Wake
  Wilts 31 C7
Ebblake Hants 31 F10
Ebbw Vale Bl Gwent . 77 D11

Ebchester Durham 242 F4
Ebdon N Som 59 G11
Ebernoe W Sus 35 B7
Ebford Devon 14 D5
Ebley Glos 80 E4
Ebnal Ches W 167 F5
Ebnall Hereford 115 F9
Ebreywood Shrops 149 F10
Ebrington Glos 100 C3
Ecchinswell Hants 48 B4
Ecclaw Borders 272 B5
Ecclefechan Dumfries 238 C5
Eccle Riggs Cumb 210 B4
Eccles Borders 272 G5
  Gtr Man 184 B3
  Kent 69 G8
Ecclesall S Yorks 186 E4
Ecclesfield S Yorks 186 G5
Ecclesgreig Aberds 293 G9
Eccleshall Staffs 150 D6
Eccleshill W Yorks 205 F9
Ecclesmachan W Loth 279 G11
Eccles on Sea Norf 161 D9
Eccleston Ches W 166 C6
  Lancs 194 D4
  Mers 183 B7
Eccleston Park Mers 183 C7
Eccliffe Dorset 30 B3
Eccup W Yorks 205 E11
Echt Aberds 293 C9
Eckford Borders 262 D6
Eckfordmoss Borders 262 D6
Eckington Derbys 186 F6
  Worcs 99 C8
Eckington Corner E Sus 23 B8
Ecklands S Yorks 197 G8
Eckworthy Devon 24 C1
Ecton N Nhants 120 E6
  Staffs 169 D9
Ecton Brook N Nhants 120 E6
Edale Derbys 185 D10
Edale End Derbys 185 D11
Edbrook Som 43 E8
Edburton W Sus 36 E2
Edderside Cumb 229 B7
Edderton Highld 309 L7
Eddington Kent 71 F7
  W Berks 63 F10
Eddistone Devon 24 C3
Eddleston Borders 270 F4
Eddlewood S Lanark 268 E4
Edenbridge Kent 52 D2
Edenfield Lancs 195 D9
Edenhall Cumb 231 E7
Edenham Lincs 155 E11
Eden Mount Cumb 211 D8
Eden Park London 67 F11
Edensor Derbys 170 B2
Edentaggart Argyll 276 C6
Edenthorpe S Yorks 198 F6
Edentown Cumb 239 F9
Eden Vale Durham 234 D4
  Wilts 45 C11
Ederline Argyll 275 C9
Edern Gwyn 144 B5
Edford Som 45 D7
Edgarley Som 44 F4
Edgbaston W Mid 133 G11
Edgcote W Nhants 101 B10
Edgcott Bucks 102 G3
  Som 41 F10
Edgcumbe Corn 2 C5
Edge Glos 80 D4
  Shrops 131 B7
Edgebolton Shrops 149 E11
Edge End Glos 79 C9
  Lancs 203 G10
Edgefield Norf 159 C11
Edgefield Street Norf 159 C11
Edge Fold Blackburn 195 D8
  Gtr Man 195 F8
Edge Green Ches W 167 E7
  Gtr Man 183 B9
  Norf 141 F10
Edgehill Warks 101 B7
Edge Hill Mers 182 C5
  Warks 134 D4
Edge Mount S Yorks 186 C3
Edgerley Shrops 148 F6
Edgerston Borders 262 G5
Edgerton W Yorks 196 D6
Edgeside Lancs 195 C10
Edginswell Devon 9 B7
Edgiock Worcs 117 E10
Edgmond Telford 150 F4
Edgmond Marsh Telford 150 E4
Edgton Shrops 131 F7
Edgware London 85 G11
Edgwick W Mid 134 G6
Edgworth Blackburn 195 D8
Edham Borders 262 B6
Edial Staffs 133 B11
Edinample Stirling 285 E9
Edinbane Highld 298 D3
Edinburgh Edin 280 G5
Edingale Staffs 152 F4
Edingight Ho Moray 302 D5
Edinglassie Ho Aberds 292 B5
Edingley Notts 171 D11
Edingthorpe Norf 160 C6
Edingthorpe Green Norf 160 C6
Edington Som 43 G11
  Wilts 46 C2
Edingworth Som 43 C11
Edintore Moray 302 E4
Edistone Devon 24 C2
Edithmead Som 43 D10

Edith Weston Rutland 137 B8
Edlaston Derbys 169 G11
Edlesborough Bucks 85 B7
Edlingham Northumb 252 B4
Edlington Lincs 190 G2
  S Yorks 198 G5
Edmondsham Dorset 31 E9
Edmondsley Durham 233 B10
Edmondstown Rhondda 77 G8
Edmondthorpe Leics 155 F7
Edmonston S Lanark 269 G11
Edmonton Orkney 314 C6
  London 86 G4
Edmundbyers Durham 242 G2
Ednaston Derbys 170 G2
Edney Common Essex 87 E11
Ednam Borders 262 B6
Edrom Borders 272 D6
Edstaston Shrops 149 C10
Edstone Warks 118 E3
Edvin Loach Hereford 116 F3
Edwalton Notts 153 B11
Edwardstone Suff 107 C8
Edwardsville M Tydf 77 F9
Edwinsford Carms 94 E2
Edwinstowe Notts 171 B10
Edworth C Beds 104 C4
Edwyn Ralph Hereford 116 F2
Edzell Angus 293 G7
Efail-fôch Neath 57 B9
Efail Isaf Rhondda 58 C5
Efailnewydd Gwyn 145 B7
Efailwen Carms 92 F2
Efenechtyd Denb 165 D10
Effingham Sur 50 C6
Effirth Shetland 313 H5
Effledge Borders 262 F3
Efflinch Staffs 152 F3
Efford Devon 26 G5
  Plym 7 D10
Egbury Hants 48 C2
Egdon Worcs 117 G8
Egerton Gtr Man 195 E8
  Kent 54 D2
Egerton Forstal Kent 53 D11
Egerton Green Ches E 167 E8
Egford Som 45 D9
Eggbeare Corn 12 D2
Eggborough N Yorks 198 C5
Eggbuckland Plym 7 D10
Eggesford Station Devon 25 E11
Eggington C Beds 103 F9
Egginton Derbys 152 D5
Egginton Common Derbys 152 D5
Egglescliffe Stockton 225 C8
Eggleston Durham 232 G5
Egham Sur 66 E4
Egham Hythe Sur 66 E4
Egham Wick Sur 66 E3
Egleton Rutland 137 B7
Eglingham Northumb 264 F4
Egloshayle Corn 10 G5
Egloskerry Corn 11 D11
Eglwysbach Conwy 180 G4
Eglwys-Brewis V Glam 58 F4
Eglwys Cross Wrex 167 G7
Eglwys Fach Ceredig 128 D3
Eglwyswen Pembs 92 D3
Eglwyswrw Pembs 92 D2
Egmanton Notts 172 B2
Egmere Norf 159 B8
Egremont Cumb 219 C10
  Mers 182 C4
Egton N Yorks 226 D6
Egton Bridge N Yorks 226 D6
Egypt Bucks 66 B3
  Hants 48 E3
  W Berks 64 D2
  W Sus 205 G7
Eiden Highld 309 J7
Eight Ash Green Essex 107 F8
Eighton Banks T&W 243 F7
Eignaig Highld 289 E9
Eign Hill Hereford 97 D10
Eil Highld 291 B10
Eilanreach Highld 295 D10
Eildon Borders 262 C3
Eilean Anabaich W Isles 305 H4
Eilean Darach Highld 307 L6
Eilean Shona Ho Highld 289 B8
Einacleite W Isles 304 F3
Einsiob = Evenjobb
Eisgean W Isles 305 G5
Eisingrug Gwyn 146 C2
Eland Green Northumb 242 C5
Elan Village Powys 113 D8
Elberton S Glos 60 B6
Elborough N Som 43 B11
Elbridge Shrops 149 E7
  W Sus 22 C6
Elburton Plym 7 E10
Elcho Perth 286 E6

Elcombe Glos 80 F3
  Swindon 62 C6
Elcot W Berks 63 F11
Eldene Swindon 63 C7
Eldernell Cambs 138 D6
Eldersfield Worcs 98 E6
Elderslie Renfs 267 C8
Elder Street Essex 105 E11
Eldon Durham 233 F10
Eldon Lane Durham 233 F10
Eldrick S Ayrs 245 G7
Eldroth N Yorks 212 F5
Eldwick W Yorks 205 E8
Elemore Vale T&W 234 B3
Elerch = Bont-goch Ceredig 128 F3
Elford Northumb 264 C5
  Staffs 152 G3
Elford Closes Cambs 123 C10
Elgin Moray 302 C2
Elgol Highld 295 D7
Elham Kent 55 E7
Elim Anglesey 178 D5
Eling Hants 32 E5
  W Berks 64 D4
Elishader Highld 298 C5
Elishaw Northumb 251 D9
Elizafield Dumfries 238 C2
Elkesley Notts 187 F11
Elkington N Nhants 120 B3
Elkins Green Essex 87 E10
Elkstone Glos 81 C7
Ellacombe Torbay 9 C8
Ellan Highld 301 G8
Elland W Yorks 196 C6
Elland Lower Edge W Yorks 196 C6
Elland Upper Edge W Yorks 196 C6
Ellary Argyll 275 F8
Ellastone Staffs 169 G10
Ellel Lancs 202 B5
Ellemford Borders 272 C4
Ellenbrook Herts 86 D2
  IoM 192 E4
Ellenglaze Corn 4 D1
Ellenhall Staffs 150 D6
Ellen's Green Sur 50 F5
Ellerbeck N Yorks 225 F8
Ellerburn N Yorks 216 C6
Ellerby N Yorks 226 C5
Ellerdine Telford 150 E2
Ellerdine Heath Telford 150 E2
Ellerhayes Devon 27 G7
Elleric Argyll 284 C4
Ellerker E Yorks 200 B2
Ellerton E Yorks 207 F10
  N Yorks 224 F5
  Shrops 150 D4
Ellesborough Bucks 84 D4
Ellesmere Shrops 149 C8
Ellesmere Park Gtr Man 184 B3
Ellesmere Port Ches W 182 F6
Ellicombe Som 42 E3
Ellingham Hants 31 F10
  Norf 143 E7
  Northumb 264 D5
Ellingstring N Yorks 214 C3
Ellington Cambs 122 C3
  Northumb 253 E7
Ellington Thorpe Cambs 122 C3
Elliot Angus 287 D10
Elliots Green Som 45 D9
Elliot's Town Caerph 77 E10
Ellisfield Hants 48 D6
Elliston Borders 262 D3
Ellistown Leics 153 G8
Ellon Aberds 303 F9
Ellonby Cumb 230 D4
Ellough Suff 143 F8
Elloughton E Yorks 200 B2
Ellwood Glos 79 D9
Elm Cambs 139 B9
Elm Corner Sur 50 C5
Elm Cross Wilts 62 D6
Elmdon Essex 105 D9
  W Mid 134 G3
Elmdon Heath W Mid 134 G3
Elmer W Sus 35 G7
Elmers End London 67 F11
Elmer's Green Lancs 194 F3
Elmers Marsh W Sus 34 B5
Elmesthorpe Leics 135 D9
Elmfield IoW 21 C8
Elm Hill Dorset 30 B4
Elmhurst Bucks 84 B4
  Staffs 152 F2
Elmley Castle Worcs 99 C9
Elmley Lovett Worcs 117 D7
Elmore Glos 80 B3
Elmore Back Glos 80 B3
Elm Park London 68 B4
Elmscott Devon 24 C2
Elmsett Suff 107 B11
Elms Green Hereford 115 D10
  Worcs 116 D4
Elmslack Lancs 211 D9
Elmstead Essex 107 F11
  London 68 E2
Elmstead Heath Essex 107 G11
Elmstead Market Essex 107 G11
Elmsted Kent 54 E6
Elmsthorpe Leics 135 D9
Elmstone Kent 71 G9
Elmstone Hardwicke Glos 99 F8

Elmswell E Yorks 208 B5
  Suff 125 E9
Elmton Derbys 187 G8
Elness Orkney 314 C6
Elphin Highld 307 H7
Elphinstone E Loth 281 G7
Elrick Aberds 293 C10
Elrig Dumfries 236 E5
Elrington Northumb 241 E9
Elscar S Yorks 197 G11
Elsdon Hereford 114 G6
  Northumb 251 E10
Elsecar S Yorks 186 B5
  S Yorks 197 G11
Elsenham Essex 105 F10
Elsenham Sta Essex 105 F10
Elsfield Oxon 83 C8
Elsham N Lincs 200 E4
Elsing Norf 159 F11
Elslack N Yorks 204 D4
Elson Hants 33 G10
  Shrops 149 B7
Elsrickle S Lanark 269 G11
Elstead Sur 50 E2
Elsted W Sus 34 D4
Elsthorpe Lincs 155 E11
Elstob Durham 234 G2
Elston Devon 26 G3
  Notts 172 F3
  Wilts 46 E5
Elstone Devon 25 D11
Elstow Bedford 103 B11
Elstree Herts 85 F11
Elstronwick E Yorks 209 G10
Elswick Lancs 202 F4
  T&W 242 E6
Elswick Leys Lancs 202 F4
Elsworth Cambs 122 E6
Elterwater Cumb 220 E6
Eltham London 68 E2
Eltisley Cambs 122 F5
Elton Cambs 137 E11
  Ches W 183 F7
  Derbys 170 C2
  Glos 80 C2
  Gtr Man 195 E9
  Hereford 115 C9
  Notts 154 B5
  Stockton 225 B8
Elton Green Ches W 183 G7
Elton's Marsh Hereford 97 C9
Eltringham Northumb 242 E3
Elvanfoot S Lanark 259 F11
Elvaston Derbys 153 C8
Elveden Suff 124 B6
Elvet Hill Durham 233 C11
Elvingston E Loth 281 G9
Elvington Kent 55 C9
  York 207 D9
Elwell Devon 8 E2
  Dorset 17 E9
Elwick Hrtlpl 234 E5
  Northumb 264 B4
Elworth Ches E 168 C2
Elworthy Som 42 G5
Ely Cambs 139 G10
  Cardiff 59 D7
Emberton M Keynes 103 B7
Embleton Cumb 229 E9
  Durham 234 F4
  Northumb 264 E6
Embo Highld 311 K2
Emborough Som 44 C6
Embo Street Highld 311 K2
Embsay N Yorks 204 C6
Emersons Green S Glos 61 D7
Emery Down Hants 32 F3
Emley W Yorks 197 E8
Emmbrook Wokingham 65 F9
Emmer Green Reading 65 D8
Emmett Carr Derbys 187 F7
Emmington Oxon 84 E2
Emneth Norf 139 B9
Emneth Hungate Norf 139 B10
Emorsgate Norf 157 E10
Empingham Rutland 137 B8
Empshott Hants 49 G8
Empshott Green Hants 49 G8
Emstrey Shrops 149 G10
Emsworth Hants 22 B2
Enborne W Berks 64 F2
Enborne Row W Berks 64 G2
Enchmarsh Shrops 131 D10
Enderby Leics 135 D10
Endmoor Cumb 211 C10
Endon Staffs 168 E6
Endon Bank Staffs 168 E6
Energlyn Caerph 58 B6
Enfield London 86 F5
  Worcs 117 D10
Enfield Highway London 86 F5
Enfield Lock London 86 F5
Enfield Town London 86 F4
Enfield Wash London 86 F5
Enford Wilts 46 C6
Engamoor Shetland 313 H4
Engedi Anglesey 178 F5
Engine Common S Glos 61 C7
Englefield W Berks 64 E6
Englefield Green Sur 66 E3
Englesea-brook Ches E 168 E3
English Bicknor Glos 79 B9
Englishcombe Bath 61 G8

English Frankton Shrops 149 D9
Engollan Corn 10 G3
Enham Alamein Hants 47 D11
Enis Devon 25 B9
Enmore Som 43 G8
Enmore Field Hereford 115 E9
Enmore Green Dorset 30 C5
Ennerdale Bridge Cumb 219 B11
Enniscaven Corn 5 D9
Enoch Dumfries 247 C9
Enochdhu Perth 292 G2
Ensay Argyll 288 E5
Ensbury BCP 19 B7
Ensbury Park BCP 19 C7
Ensdon Shrops 149 F8
Ensis Devon 25 B9
Enslow Oxon 83 B7
Enstone Oxon 101 G7
Enterkinfoot Dumfries 247 C9
Enterpen N Yorks 225 D9
Enton Green Sur 50 E3
Enville Staffs 132 F6
Eolaigearraidh W Isles 297 L3
Eorabus Argyll 288 G5
Eòropaidh W Isles 304 B7
Epney Glos 80 D3
Epperstone Notts 171 F11
Epping Essex 87 E7
Epping Green Essex 86 D6
  Herts 86 D3
Epping Upland Essex 86 E6
Eppleby N Yorks 224 C3
Eppleworth E Yorks 208 G6
Epsom Sur 67 G8
Epwell Oxon 101 C7
Epworth N Lincs 199 G9
Epworth Turbary N Lincs 199 G9
Erbistock Wrex 166 G5
Erbusaig Highld 295 C9
Erchless Castle Highld 300 E4
Erdington W Mid 134 E2
Eredine Argyll 275 C10
Eriboll Highld 308 D4
Ericstane Dumfries 260 G3
Eridge Green E Sus 52 F5
Erines Argyll 275 F9
Eriswell Suff 124 B4
Erith London 68 D4
Erlestoke Wilts 46 C3
Ermine Lincs 189 G7
Ermington Devon 8 E2
Ernesettle Plym 7 D8
Erpingham Norf 160 C3
Erriottwood Kent 54 B2
Errogie Highld 300 G5
Errol Perth 286 E6
Errol Station Perth 286 E6
Erskine Renfs 277 G9
Erskine Bridge Renfs 277 G9
Ervie Dumfries 236 C2
Erwarton Suff 108 E4
Erwood Powys 95 C11
Eryholme N Yorks 224 D6
Eryrys Denb 166 D2
Escomb Durham 233 E9
Escott Som 42 F5
Escrick N Yorks 207 E8
Esgairdawe Carms 94 C2
Esgairgeiliog Powys 128 B5
Esgyryn Conwy 180 F4
Esh Durham 233 C9
Esher Sur 66 G6
Eshiels Borders 261 B7
Esholt W Yorks 205 E9
Eshott Northumb 252 E6
Eshton N Yorks 204 B4
Esh Winning Durham 233 C9
Eskadale Highld 300 F4
Eskbank Midloth 270 B6
Eskdale Green Cumb 220 E2
Eskdalemuir Dumfries 249 D7
Eske E Yorks 209 E7
Eskham Lincs 190 B5
Eskholme S Yorks 198 D6
Esknish Argyll 274 G4
Esk Valley N Yorks 226 E6
Eslington Park Northumb 264 G2
Esperley Lane Ends Durham 233 G8
Esprick Lancs 202 F4
Essendine Rutland 155 G10
Essendon Herts 86 D3
Essich Highld 300 F6
Essington Staffs 133 C9
Esslemont Aberds 303 G9
Eston Redcar 225 B11
Estover Plym 7 D10
Eswick Shetland 313 H6
Etal Northumb 263 B10
Etchilhampton Wilts 62 G4
Etchingham E Sus 38 B2
Etchinghill Kent 55 F7
  Staffs 151 F11
Etchingwood E Sus 37 C8
Etherley Dene Durham 233 F9
Ethie Castle Angus 287 C10
Ethie Mains Angus 287 C10
Etling Green Norf 159 G10
Etloe Glos 79 D11
Eton Windsor 66 D3
Eton Wick Windsor 66 D2
Etruria Stoke 168 F5
Etsell Shrops 131 C7
Etterby Cumb 239 F9
Etteridge Highld 291 D8
Ettersgill Durham 232 F4

Ettiley Heath Ches E 168 C2
Ettingshall W Mid 133 D8
Ettingshall Park W Mid 133 D8
Ettington Warks 100 B5
Etton E Yorks 208 E5
  Pboro 138 B2
Ettrick Borders 261 G7
Ettrickbridge Borders 261 E9
Ettrickdale Argyll 275 G11
Ettrickhill Borders 261 G7
Etwall Derbys 152 C5
Etwall Common Derbys 152 C5
Eudon Burnell Shrops 132 F3
Eudon George Shrops 132 F3
Euston Suff 125 B7
Euximoor Drove Cambs 139 D9
Euxton Lancs 194 D5
Evanstown Bridgend 58 B3
Evanton Highld 300 C6
Evedon Lincs 173 F9
Eve Hill W Mid 133 E8
Evelix Highld 309 K7
Evendine Hereford 98 C5
Evenjobb = Einsiob Powys 114 F5
Evenley N Whants 101 E11
Evenlode Glos 100 F4
Even Pits Hereford 97 D11
Even Swindon Swindon 62 B6
Evenwood Durham 233 G9
Evenwood Gate Durham 233 G9
Everbay Orkney 314 C6
Evercreech Som 44 F6
Everdon W Nhants 119 F11
Everingham E Yorks 208 E2
Everland Shetland 312 D8
Everleigh Wilts 47 C8
Everley N Yorks 217 B9
Eversholt C Beds 103 E9
Evershot Dorset 29 G9
Eversley Hants 65 G9
Eversley Centre Hants 65 G9
Eversley Cross Hants 65 G9
Everthorpe E Yorks 208 G4
Everton C Beds 122 G4
  Hants 19 C11
  Mers 182 C5
  Notts 187 C11
Evertown Dumfries 239 B9
Evesbatch Hereford 98 B3
Evesham Worcs 99 C10
Evington Kent 54 D6
  Leicester 136 C2
Ewanrigg Cumb 228 D6
Ewden Village S Yorks 186 B3
Ewell Sur 67 G8
Ewell Minnis Kent 55 E9
Ewelme Oxon 83 G10
Ewen Glos 81 F8
Ewenny V Glam 58 D2
Ewerby Lincs 173 F10
Ewerby Thorpe Lincs 173 F10
Ewes Dumfries 249 E9
Ewesley Northumb 252 E3
Ewhurst Sur 50 E5
Ewhurst Green E Sus 38 C3
  Sur 50 F5
Ewloe Flint 166 B4
Ewloe Green Flint 166 B3
Ewood Blackburn 195 B7
Ewood Bridge Lancs 195 C9
Eworthy Devon 12 C5
Ewshot Hants 49 D10
Ewyas Harold Hereford 97 F7
Exbourne Devon 25 G10
Exbury Hants 20 B4
Exceat E Sus 23 F8
Exebridge Devon 26 C4
Exelby N Yorks 214 B5
Exeter Devon 14 C4
Exford Som 41 F11
Exfords Green Shrops 131 B9
Exhall Warks 118 F2
  Warks 135 F7
Exlade Street Oxon 65 C7
Exley W Yorks 196 C5
Exley Head W Yorks 204 F6
Exminster Devon 14 D4
Exmouth Devon 14 E6
Exnaboe Shetland 313 M5
Exning Suff 124 D2
Exton Devon 14 D5
  Hants 33 C10
  Rutland 155 G8
  Som 42 G2
Exwick Devon 14 C4
Eyam Derbys 186 F2
Eydon W Nhants 119 G10
Eye Hereford 115 E9
  Pboro 138 C4
  Suff 126 C2
Eye Green Pboro 138 C4
Eyemouth Borders 273 C8
Eyeworth C Beds 104 B4
Eyhorne Street Kent 53 C10
Eyke Suff 126 G6
Eynesbury Cambs 122 F3
Eynort Highld 294 C5
Eynsford Kent 68 F4
Eynsham Oxon 82 D6
Eype Dorset 16 C5
Eyre Highld 295 B7
  Highld 298 D4
Eyres Monsell Leicester 135 D11
Eythorne Kent 55 D9
Eyton Hereford 115 E9
  Shrops 131 F7
  Shrops 149 G5
  Wrex 166 G4
Eyton on Severn Shrops 131 C11
Eyton upon the Weald Moors Telford 150 G3

F

Faberstown Wilts 47 C9
Faccombe Hants 47 B11
Faceby N Yorks 225 D9
Fachell Gwyn 163 B8
Fachwen Gwyn 163 C9
Facit Lancs 195 D11
Fackley Notts 171 C7
Faddiley Ches E 167 E9
Fadmoor N Yorks 216 B3
Faerdre Swansea 75 E11
Fagley W Yorks 205 G9
Fagwyr Swansea 75 E11
Faichem Highld 290 C4
Faifley W Dunb 277 G10
Failand N Som 60 E4
Failford S Ayrs 257 D11
Failsworth Gtr Man 195 G11
Fain Highld 299 B11
Faindouran Lodge Moray 292 C2
Fairbourne Gwyn 146 G2
Fairbourne Heath Kent 53 C11
Fairburn N Yorks 198 B3
Fairfield Clack 279 C7
  Derbys 185 G9
  Gtr Man 184 B6
  Gtr Man 195 G10
  Kent 39 B7
  Mers 182 C5
  Stockton 225 B8
  Worcs 99 C10
  Worcs 117 B8
Fairfield Park Bath 61 F9
Fairfields Glos 98 E4
Fairford Glos 81 E11
Fair Green Norf 158 F3
Fairhaven Lancs 193 B10
Fairhill S Lanark 268 E4
Fair Hill Cumb 230 E6
Fairlands Sur 50 C3
Fairlee IoW 20 C6
Fairlie N Ayrs 266 D4
Fairlight E Sus 38 E5
Fairlight Cove E Sus 38 E5
Fairmile BCP 19 C9
  Devon 15 B7
  Sur 66 G6
Fairmilehead Edin 270 B4
Fair Moor Northumb 252 F5
Fairoak Caerph 77 F11
Fair Oak Devon 27 E7
  Hants 33 D7
  Hants 64 G5
  Hants 65 G5
Fair Oak Green Hants 65 G7
Fairseat Kent 68 G6
Fairstead Essex 88 B3
  Norf 158 F2
Fairwarp E Sus 37 B7
Fairwater Cardiff 58 D6
Fairwood Wilts 45 C10
Fairy Cottage IoM 192 D5
Fairy Cross Devon 24 C6
Fakenham Norf 159 D8
Fakenham Magna Suff 125 B8
Fala Midloth 271 C8
Fala Dam Midloth 271 C8
Falahill Borders 271 D7
Falcon Hereford 98 E2
Falcon Lodge W Mid 134 D2
Falconwood London 68 D3
Falcutt W Nhants 101 C11
Faldingworth Lincs 189 E9
Faldonside Borders 262 C2
Falfield Fife 287 G8
  S Glos 79 G11
Falkenham Suff 108 D5
Falkenham Sink Suff 108 D5
Falkirk Falk 279 F7
Falkland Fife 286 G6
Falla Borders 262 G6
Fallgate Derbys 170 C5
Fallin Stirling 278 C6
Fallinge Derbys 170 B3
Fallings Heath W Mid 133 D9
Fallowfield Gtr Man 184 C4
Fallside N Lanark 268 C4
Falmer E Sus 36 F5
Falmouth Corn 3 C8
Falnash Borders 249 C10
Falsgrave N Yorks 217 B10
Falside W Loth 269 B9
Falstone Northumb 250 F6
Fanagmore Highld 306 E6
Fancott C Beds 103 F10
Fangdale Beck N Yorks 225 F10
Fangfoss E Yorks 207 C11
Fanich Highld 311 J2
Fankerton Falk 278 E5
Fanmore Argyll 288 E6
Fanner's Green Essex 87 C11

Fannich Lodge Highld 300 C2
Fans Borders 272 G2
Fanshowe Ches E 184 G5
Fant Kent 53 B8
Faoilean Highld 295 C7
Far Arnside Cumb 211 D8
Far Bank S Yorks 198 E6
Far Banks Lancs 194 C2
Far Bletchley M Keynes 103 E7
Farcet Cambs 138 E4
Far Coton Leics 135 C7
Far Cotton N Nhants 120 F4
Farden Shrops 115 B11
Fareham Hants 33 F9
Far End Cumb 220 F6
Farewell Staffs 151 G11
Far Forest Worcs 116 C4
Farforth Lincs 190 F4
Far Green Glos 80 E3
Farhill Derbys 170 C5
Far Hoarcross Staffs 152 E2
Faringdon Oxon 82 F3
Farington Lancs 194 B4
Farington Moss Lancs 194 C4
Farlam Cumb 240 F3
Farlands Booth Derbys 185 D9
Farlary Highld 309 J7
Far Laund Derbys 170 F5
Farleigh N Som 60 F3
  Sur 67 G11
Farleigh Court Sur 67 G11
Farleigh Green Kent 53 C8
Farleigh Hungerford Som 45 B10
Farleigh Wallop Hants 48 D6
Farleigh Wick Wilts 45 G10
Farlesthorpe Lincs 191 G7
Farleton Cumb 211 C10
  Lancs 211 F11
Farley Bristol 60 E2
  Derbys 170 C3
  Shrops 131 B7
  Shrops 132 C2
  Staffs 169 G9
  Wilts 32 B2
Far Ley Staffs 132 D5
Farley Green Suff 124 G4
  Sur 50 D5
Farley Hill Luton 103 G11
  Wokingham 65 G8
Farleys End Glos 80 B3
Farlington N Yorks 216 F2
  Ptsmth 33 F11
Farlow Shrops 132 G2
Farmborough Bath 61 G7
Farmbridge End Essex 87 C10
Farmcote Glos 99 F11
  Shrops 132 E5
Farmington Glos 81 B10
Farmoor Oxon 82 D6
Far Moor Gtr Man 194 G4
Farms Common Corn 2 C5
Farmtown Moray 302 D5
Farnah Green Derbys 170 F4
Farnborough Hants 49 C11
  London 68 G2
  Warks 101 B8
  W Berks 64 C3
Farnborough Green Hants 49 B11
Farnborough Park Hants 49 B11
Farnborough Street Hants 49 B11
Farncombe Sur 50 E3
Farndish Bedford 121 E8
Farndon Ches W 166 E6
  Notts 172 E3
Farnell Angus 287 B10
Farnham Dorset 31 D7
  Essex 105 F9
  N Yorks 215 G7
  Suff 127 E7
  Sur 49 D10
Farnham Common Bucks 66 C3
Farnham Green Essex 105 F9
Farnham Park Bucks 66 C3
Farnham Royal Bucks 66 C3
Farnhill N Yorks 204 D6
Farningham Kent 68 F4
Farnley N Yorks 205 E10
  W Yorks 205 G11
Farnley Bank W Yorks 197 E7
Farnley Tyas W Yorks 197 E7
Farnsfield Notts 171 D10
Farnworth Gtr Man 195 F8
  Halton 183 D8
Far Oakridge Glos 80 E6
Farr Highld 291 C10
  Highld 300 F6
  Highld 308 C7
Farraline Highld 300 F6
Farr House Highld 300 F6
Farringdon Devon 14 C6
  T&W 243 G9
Farrington Dorset 30 D4
Farrington Gurney Bath 44 B6
Far Royds W Yorks 205 G11
Far Sawrey Cumb 221 F7
Farsley W Yorks 205 F10
Farsley Beck Bottom W Yorks 205 F10
Farther Howegreen Essex 88 E4

Farthing Corner
Medway 69 G10
Farthing Green
Kent 53 D10
Farthinghoe
W Nhants 101 G10
Farthingloe Kent 55 E9
Farthingstone
W Nhants 120 F2
Far Thrupp Glos 80 E5
Fartown W Yorks . . .196 F6
Farway Devon 15 B9
Farway Marsh Devon .28 G4
Fasach Highld 297 G7
Fasag Highld 299 D8
Fascadale Highld . . .289 B7
Faslane Port Argyll . .276 D4
Fasnacloich Argyll . .284 C4
Fasnakyle Ho Highld .300 G3
Fassfern Highld 290 F2
Fatfield T&W 243 G8
Fattahead Aberds . . .302 D6
Faucheldean
W Loth 279 G11
Faugh Cumb 240 G2
Faughill Borders . . .262 C2
Fauldhouse W Loth . .269 C8
Fauldiehill Angus . . .287 D9
Fauldshope
Borders 261 D10
Faulkbourne Essex . . .88 B3
Faulkland Som 45 C8
Fauls Shrops 149 C11
Faverdale Darl. 224 B5
Faversham Kent 70 G4
Favillar Moray 302 F2
Fawdington N Yorks . 215 E8
Fawdon Northumb . . .264 F2
T&W 242 D6
Fawfieldhead Staffs. 169 C9
Fawkham Green Kent .68 F5
Fawler Oxon 63 B10
Oxon 82 B5
Fawley Bucks 65 B9
Hants 33 G7
W Berks 63 C11
Fawley Bottom Bucks .65 B8
Fawley Chapel
Hereford 97 F11
Faxfleet E Yorks . . .199 C11
Faygate W Sus 51 G8
Fazakerley Mers 182 B5
Fazeley Staffs 134 C4
Feagour Highld 291 D7
Fearby N Yorks 214 C3
Fearn Highld 301 B8
Fearnan Perth 285 C11
Fearnbeg Highld . . .299 D7
Fearnhead Warr 183 C10
Fearn Lodge Highld . .309 L6
Fearnmore Highld. . .299 C7
Fearn Station Highld .301 B8
Fearnville W Yorks . .206 F2
Featherstone Staffs. .133 B8
W Yorks 198 C2
Featherwood
Northumb 251 C8
Feckenham Worcs . .117 E10
Fedw Fawr
Anglesey 179 E10
Feering Essex 107 G7
Feetham N Yorks . . .223 F9
Fegg Hayes Stoke . . .168 E5
Feith Mhor Highld . .301 G8
Feizor N Yorks 212 F5
Felbridge Sur 51 F11
Felbrigg Norf 160 B4
Felcourt Sur. 51 E11
Felden Herts 85 E8
Felderland Kent 55 B10
Feldy Ches E. 183 F11
Felhampton Shrops . .131 F8
Felin-Crai Powys 95 G7
Felindre Carms 75 C7
Carms 93 D7
Carms 93 G11
Carms 94 E3
Carms 94 F4
Ceredig 111 F10
Powys 96 D3
Powys 96 G3
Powys 130 C3
Powys 130 G3
Rhondda 58 C3
Swansea 75 E10
Felindre Farchog
Pembs 92 D2
Felinfach Ceredig . .111 F10
Powys 95 E11
Felinfoel Carms. 75 E8
Felingwmisaf Carms .93 G10
Felingwmuchaf
Carms 93 G10
Felin Newydd Carms .94 D3
Felin-newydd Powys .96 D2
Felin Newydd = New Mills
Powys 129 C11
Felin Puleston Wrex .166 F4
Felin-Wnda Ceredig .92 B6
Felinwynt Ceredig . .110 G4
Felixkirk N Yorks . . .215 C9
Felixstowe Suff 108 E5
Felixstowe Ferry
Suff 108 D6
Felkington
Northumb 273 G8
Felkirk W Yorks 197 E11
Felldyke Cumb 219 B11
Fell End Cumb 222 F4
Fellgate T&W 243 E8
Felling T&W 243 E7
Felling Shore T&W. . .243 E7
Fell Lane W Yorks . . .204 E6
Fellside T&W 242 E6
Fell Side Cumb. 230 D2
Felmersham Bedford 121 F9
Felmingham Norf . . .160 D5
Felmore Essex. 69 B8

Felpham W Sus 35 H7
Felsham Suff 125 F8
Felsted Essex 106 G3
Feltham London. 66 E6
Som 28 D2
Felthamhill London. . .66 E5
Felthorpe Norf 160 F3
Felton Hereford 97 B11
Northumb 252 C5
N Som 60 F4
Felton Butler Shrops .149 F7
Feltwell Norf 140 E4
Fenay Bridge
W Yorks 197 D7
Fence Lancs 204 F3
Fence Houses T&W . .243 G8
Fencott Oxon 83 B9
Fen Ditton Cambs . . .123 E9
Fen Drayton Cambs . 122 D6
Fen End Lincs. 156 E4
W Mid 118 B4
Fengate Norf 160 E3
Pboro. 138 D4
Fenham Northumb . .273 G11
T&W 242 D6
Fenhouses Lincs . . .174 G3
Feniscliffe Blackburn .195 B7
Feniscowles
Blackburn 194 B6
Feniton Devon 15 B8
Fenlake Bedford 103 B11
Fenn Green Shrops. . 132 G5
Fennington Som 27 B11
Fenn's Bank Wrex . .149 B10
Fenn Street Medway . .69 D9
Fenny Bentley
Derbys. 169 E11
Fenny Bridges Devon .15 B8
Fenny Castle Som. . . .44 E4
Fenny Compton
Warks 119 G8
Fenny Drayton
Leics 134 D6
Fenny Stratford
M Keynes 103 E7
Fenrother Northumb .252 E5
Fen Side Lincs 174 D4
Fenstanton Cambs . .122 D6
Fenstead End Suff . . 124 G6
Fen Street Norf 141 G11
Suff 125 B8
Suff 125 B11
Fenton Cambs 122 B6
Cumb. 240 F2
Lincs 172 E5
Lincs 188 F4
Northumb 263 C11
Stoke. 168 G5
Fenton Barns
E Loth. 281 E10
Fenton Low Stoke. . .168 F5
Fenton Pits Corn 5 C11
Fenton Town
Northumb 263 C11
Fenwick E Ayrs 267 G9
Northumb 242 F5
Northumb 273 G11
S Yorks 198 D5
Feochaig Argyll 255 F8
Feock Corn 3 B8
Feolin Ferry Argyll . .274 G5
Ferguslie Park
Renfs 267 C9
Ferindonald Highld. .295 E8
Feriniquarrie Highld .296 F7
Ferlochan Argyll . . .289 E11
Fern Angus 292 G6
Bucks 65 B11
Fern Bank Gtr Man . .185 B7
Ferndale Kent 52 E5
Rhondda 77 F7
Ferndown Dorset 31 G9
Ferne Wilts 30 C6
Ferness Highld 301 E10
Ferney Green Cumb. .221 F8
Fernham Oxon 82 G3
Fernhill Gtr Man 195 E10
Rhondda 77 F8
W Sus 51 E10
Fern Hill Suff 106 B6
Fernhill Gate
Gtr Man 195 F7
Fernhill Heath
Worcs 117 F7
Fernhurst W Sus 34 B5
Fernie Fife 287 F7
Ferniebrae Aberds . .303 D9
Fernilea Highld 294 B5
Fernilee Derbys. 185 F8
Fernsplatt Corn. 4 G5
Ferrensby N Yorks . .215 G7
Ferring W Sus 35 G9
Ferrybridge
W Yorks 198 C3
Ferryden Angus 287 B11
Ferryhill Aberdeen . .293 C11
Durham 233 E11
Ferry Hill Cambs . . .139 G7
Ferryhill Station
Durham 234 E2
Ferry Point Highld . .309 L7
Ferryside = Glan-y-Ffer
Carms 74 C5
Ferryton Highld 300 C6
Fersfield Norf 141 G11
Fersit Highld 290 F5
Feshiebridge
Highld 291 C10
Fetcham Sur 50 B6
Fetterangus Aberds .303 D9
Fettercairn Aberds . .293 F8
Fetterdale Fife 287 E8
Fettes Highld 300 D5
Fewcott Oxon. 101 F10
Fewston N Yorks 205 C9
Fewston Bents
N Yorks 205 C9
Ffairfach Carms 94 G2
Ffair-Rhos Ceredig. .112 D4

Ffaldybrenin Carms . .94 C2
Ffarmers Carms 94 C3
Ffawyddog Powys. . . .78 B2
Ffodun = Forden
Powys. 130 C4
Ffont y gari = Font y gary
V Glam 58 F5
Fforddlas Powys 96 A4
Ffordd-las Denb 165 C10
Fford-y-Gyfraith
Bridgend 57 E11
Fforest Carms 75 E9
Fforest Goch Neath . .76 E2
Ffostrasol Ceredig . . .93 B7
Ffos-y-ffin Ceredig .111 E8
Ffos-y-go Wrex 166 E4
Ffridd Powys 130 D3
Ffrith Wrex. 166 D3
Ffrwd Gwyn 163 D7
Ffwl y mwn = Fonmon
V Glam 58 F4
Ffynnon Carms 74 B5
Ffynnon ddrain
Carms 93 G8
Ffynnongroes
= Crosswell Pembs . .92 D2
Ffynnon Gron Pembs .91 F8
Ffynnongroyw
Flint 181 E10
Ffynnon Gynydd
Powys 96 C3
Ffynnon-oer
Ceredig 111 G10
Fickleshole Sur 67 G11
Fidden Argyll 288 G5
Fiddes Aberds 293 E10
Fiddington Glos 99 E8
Som 43 E8
Fiddington Sands
Wilts 46 C4
Fiddleford Dorset. . . .30 E4
Fiddler's Green
Norf 141 D10
Fiddler's Ferry
Mers 193 C11
Warr 183 D9
Fiddler's Green Glos .99 G8
Hereford 97 D11
Fiddlers Hamlet
Essex 87 E7
Field Hereford 114 G6
Staffs 151 C10
Field Assarts Oxon . . .82 C4
Field Broughton
Cumb 211 C7
Field Common Sur . . .66 F6
Field Dalling Norf . . .159 B10
Field Green Kent. 38 B3
Field Head Leics 135 B9
Fields End Herts 85 D8
Field's Place
Hereford 115 G8
Fifehead Magdalen
Dorset 30 C3
Fifehead Neville
Dorset 30 E3
Fifehead St Quintin
Dorset 30 E3
Fife Keith Moray 302 D4
Fifield Oxon 82 B2
Wilts 46 C6
Windsor 66 D2
Fifield Bavant Wilts . .31 B8
Figheldean Wilts 47 D7
Filands Wilts 62 B2
Filby Norf 161 G8
Filby Heath Norf 161 G9
Filey N Yorks 218 C2
Filgrave M Keynes . .103 B7
Filham Devon 8 D2
Filkins Oxon 82 E2
Filleigh Devon 25 B11
Devon 26 E2
Fillingham Lincs 188 D6
Fillongley Warks. . . .134 F5
Filmore Hill Hants . . .33 B11
Filton E Yorks 209 G11
Filwood Park Bristol . .60 F5
Fimber E Yorks 217 G2
Finavon Angus. 287 B8
Fincastle Ho Perth . .291 G10
Finchairn Argyll. . . .275 C10
Fincham Mers 182 C6
Norf 140 B3
Finchampstead
Wokingham 65 G9
Finchdean Hants. 34 E2
Finchingfield Essex .106 E3
Finchley London 86 G3
Findern Derbys 152 C6
Findhorn Moray. . . .301 C10
Findhorn Bridge
Highld 301 G8
Findochty Moray. . . .302 C4
Findo Gask Perth . . .286 E2
Findon Aberds 293 D11
W Sus 35 F10
Findon Mains
Highld 300 C6
Findon Valley
W Sus 35 F10
Findrack Ho Aberds .293 C8
Finedon N Nhants . . .121 C8
Fineglen Argyll 275 B10
Fine Street Hereford. .96 D6
Fingal Street Suff . . .126 D4
Fingask Aberds 303 G7
Fingerpost Worcs. . .116 C4
Fingest Bucks. 84 G3
Finghall N Yorks. . . .214 B3
Fingland Cumb 239 F7
Dumfries 246 E6
Fingle Street Dorset . .17 B9
Finglesham Kent 55 C10
Fingringhoe Essex . .107 G10
Finham W Mid 118 B6
Finkle Street
S Yorks 186 B4
Finlarig Stirling 285 D9

Finmere Oxon 102 E2
Finnart Perth 285 B9
Finney Green
Ches E 184 E5
Staffs. 168 F3
Finningham Suff. . . .125 D11
Finningley S Yorks . .187 B11
Finnygaud Aberds . .302 D5
Finsbury London 67 C10
Finsbury Park
London. 67 B10
Finstall Worcs 117 D9
Finsthwaite Cumb. . .211 B7
Finstock Oxon 82 B5
Finstown Orkney . . .314 E3
Fintry Aberds 303 D7
Dundee 287 D8
Stirling. 278 D2
Finwood Warks 118 D3
Finzean Aberds 293 D8
Finzean Ho Aberds . .293 D8
Fionnphort Argyll . .288 G5
Fionnsbhagh
W Isles 296 C6
Firbank Cumb. 222 G2
Firbeck S Yorks 187 D9
Firby N Yorks 214 B5
N Yorks. 216 F4
Firemore Highld 307 L3
Firgrove Gtr Man . . .196 E2
Firkin Argyll 285 G7
Firle E Sus 23 D7
Firsby Lincs 175 C7
Firsdown Wilts 47 G8
Firs Lane Gtr Man . . .194 G6
First Coast Highld . .307 K4
Firswood Gtr Man . .184 B4
Firth Borders 262 E2
Firth Park S Yorks . .186 C5
Firth Moor Darl. 224 C6
Fir Toll Kent 54 E2
Fir Tree Durham 233 E8
Fir Vale S Yorks 186 C5
Firwood Fold
Gtr Man 195 E8
Fishbourne IoW 21 C7
W Sus 22 C4
Fishburn Durham . . .234 E3
Fishcross Clack 279 B7
Fisherford Aberds . .302 F6
Fishermead
M Keynes 103 D7
Fisher Place Cumb. .220 B6
Fisherrow E Loth . . .280 G6
Fishersgate Brighton . .36 F3
Fishers Green Herts. .104 F4
Fisher's Pond Hants . .33 C7
Fisherstreet W Sus . . .50 G3
Fisherton Highld . . .301 D7
S Ayrs. 257 F7
Fisherton de la Mere
Wilts 46 F4
Fisherwick Staffs . . .134 B3
Fishery Windsor. 65 C11
Fishguard = Abergwaun
Pembs 91 D9
Fishlake S Yorks. . . .199 E7
Fishleigh Devon. 25 F8
Fishleigh Barton
Devon 25 C9
Fishleigh Castle
Devon 25 F8
Fishley Norf 161 G8
W Mid 133 C10
Fishmere End Lincs .156 B5
Fishponds Bristol. . . .60 D6
Fishpool Glos 98 F3
Gtr Man 195 F10
Worcs 114 D3
Fishpools Powys 114 D3
Fishtoft Lincs 174 G5
Fishtoft Drove Lincs. .174 F4
Fishtown of Usan
Angus 287 B11
Fishwick Borders . . .273 E8
Lancs 194 B5
Fiskavaig Highld . . .294 B5
Fiskerton Lincs 189 G8
Notts 172 E2
Fitling E Yorks 209 G11
Fittleton Wilts 46 D6
Fittleworth W Sus 35 D8
Fitton End Cambs . . .157 G8
Fitton Hill Gtr Man . .196 G2
Fitz Shrops 149 F8
Fitzhead Som 27 B10
Fitzwilliam W Yorks .198 D2
Fiunary Highld 289 E8
Five Acres Glos 79 C9
Five Ash Down E Sus .37 C7
Five Ashes E Sus 37 C9
Five Bells Som 42 E5
Five Bridges Hereford .98 B3
Fivecrosses Ches W. .183 F8
Fivehead Som 28 C5
Five Houses IoW 20 D4
Five Lane Ends
Lancs 202 C6
Fivelanes Corn. 11 E10
Five Lanes Mon 78 G6
Five Oaks W Sus 35 B9
Five Oak Green Kent. .52 E6
Five Roads Carms . . .75 D7
Five Ways Warks . . .118 D4
Five Wents Kent 53 C10
Fixby W Yorks 196 C6
Flackley Ash S Sus . . .38 C5
Flack's Green Essex. . .88 B3
Flackwell Heath
Bucks. 65 B11
Fladbury Cross
Worcs 99 B9
Fladda Shetland 312 C6
Fladdabister
Shetland 313 K6
Flagg Derbys. 169 B11
Flamborough
E Yorks. 218 E4
Flamstead Herts. 85 C9

Flamstead End Herts. .86 E4
Flansham W Sus 35 G7
Flanshaw W Yorks . .197 C10
Flappit Spring
W Yorks 205 F7
Flasby N Yorks 204 B4
Flash Staffs. 169 B8
Flashader Highld . . .298 D3
Flask Inn N Yorks . . .227 E8
Flathurst W Sus 35 C7
Flaunden Herts 85 E8
Flawborough Notts . .172 G3
Flawith N Yorks 215 F9
Flax Bourton N Som . .60 F4
Flaxby N Yorks. 206 B3
Flaxholme Derbys. . .170 G4
Flaxlands Norf. 142 E2
Flaxley Glos. 79 B11
Flax Moss Lancs . . .195 C9
Flaxpool Som 42 F6
Flaxton N Yorks 216 G3
Fleckney Leics. 136 E2
Flecknoe Warks 119 E10
Fledborough Notts. . .188 G4
Fleet Dorset 17 E8
Hants. 22 C2
Hants. 49 C10
Lincs 157 E7
Fleet Downs Kent. . . .68 E5
Fleetend Hants 33 F8
Fleet Hargate Lincs . .157 E7
Fleetlands Hants 33 G9
Fleets N Yorks 213 G9
Fleetville Herts 85 D11
Fleetwood Lancs. . . .202 D2
Fleggburgh = Burgh
St Margaret Norf . .161 G8
Fleming Field
Durham 234 C3
Flemings N Yorks . . .219 B9
Flemingston V Glam . .58 E4
Flemington
S Lanark 268 D3
S Lanark 268 G4
Flempton Suff 124 D6
Fleoideabhagh
W Isles 296 C6
Fletchersbridge Corn . .6 B2
Fletcher's Green
Kent 52 C4
Fletchertown
Cumb 229 C10
Fletching E Sus 36 C6
Fletching Common
E Sus 36 C6
Fleuchary Highld. . .309 K7
Fleuchlang Dumfries 237 D8
Fleur-de-lis Caerph. . .77 F11
Flexbury Corn 24 F2
Flexford Sur. 50 D2
Flimby Cumb 228 E6
Flimwell E Sus 53 G8
Flint Flint. 182 G2
Flint Cross Cambs . .105 C8
Flintham Notts 172 F2
Flint Hill Durham . . .242 G5
Flint Mountain
= Mynydd Fflint Flint .182 G2
Flinton E Yorks. 209 F10
Flint's Green W Mid . .134 G3
Flintsham Hereford. .114 F6
Flishinghurst Kent. . . .53 F9
Flitcham Norf 158 D4
Flitholme Cumb. 222 B5
Flitton C Beds 103 D11
Flitwick C Beds 103 D10
Flixborough
N Lincs 199 D11
Flixborough Stather
N Lincs. 199 E11
Flixton Gtr Man 184 C2
N Yorks. 217 D10
Suff 142 F6
Flockton W Yorks. . .197 E8
Flockton Green
W Yorks 197 D8
Flockton Moor
W Yorks. 197 E8
Flodaigh W Isles . . .296 F4
Flodden Northumb . .263 B10
Flodigarry Highld . . .298 B4
Floodgates Hereford .114 F5
Flood's Ferry Cambs .139 E7
Flood Street Hants. . . .31 D10
Flookburgh Cumb. . .211 D7
Flordon Norf 142 D3
Flore W Nhants 120 E2
Florence Stoke 168 G6
Flotterton
Northumb 251 C11
Flowers Bottom
Bucks. 84 F4
Flowers Green
E Sus 23 C10
Flowery Field
Gtr Man 184 B6
Flowton Suff 107 B11
Flush House
W Yorks 196 F6
Flushdyke W Yorks . .197 C9
Flushing Aberds 303 E10
Corn. 3 C8
Corn. 3 D7
Flyford Flavell
Worcs 117 G9
Foals Green Suff 126 C5
Fobbing Thurrock 69 C8
Fochabers Moray . . .302 D3
Fochriw Caerph. 77 D10
Fockerby N Lincs . . .199 D10
Fodderletter
Moray 301 G11
Fodderstone Gap
Norf. 140 B3
Foddington Som 29 B9
Foel Powys 147 G9
Foel-gastell Carms . .75 C8
Foffarty Angus 287 C8

Foggathorpe
E Yorks. 207 F11
Foggbrook Gtr Man . .184 D6
Fogo Borders 272 F5
Fogorig Borders 272 F5
Fogwatt Moray 302 D2
Foindle Highld 306 E6
Folda Argyll 292 G3
Fold Head Lancs 195 D11
Fold Hill Lincs 175 E7
Foldrings S Yorks . . .186 C3
Fole Staffs 151 B10
Foleshill W Mid 135 G7
Foley Park Worcs . . .116 B6
Folke Dorset 29 E11
Folkestone Kent 55 F8
Folkingham Lincs . . .155 C11
Folkington E Sus 23 E9
Folksworth Cambs . .138 F2
Folkton N Yorks 217 D11
Folla Rule Aberds . . .303 F7
Folley Shrops 132 D5
Follifoot N Yorks . . .206 C2
Follingsby T&W 243 E8
Folly Dorset 30 G2
Pembs 91 G8
Folly Cross Devon . . .25 F7
Folly Gate Devon 13 B7
Folly Green Essex . . .106 F6
Fonmon = Ffwl-y-mwn
V Glam 58 F4
Fonston Corn 11 C10
Fonthill Bishop Wilts. .46 G2
Fonthill Gifford Wilts .46 G2
Fontmell Magna
Dorset 30 D5
Fontmell Parva
Dorset 30 E4
Fontwell W Sus 35 F7
Font-y-gary = Ffont-y-gari
V Glam 58 F5
Foodieash Fife 287 F7
Foolow Derbys. 185 F11
Footbridge Glos 99 F10
Footherley Staffs . . .134 C2
Footrid Worcs. 116 C3
Foots Cray London . . .68 E3
Forbestown Aberds . .292 B5
Force Forge Cumb . .220 G6
Force Green Kent. 52 B2
Force Mills Cumb . . .220 G6
Forcett N Yorks 224 C3
Ford Argyll 275 C9
Bucks. 84 D3
Derbys. 186 B6
Devon 8 E2
Devon 24 C6
Devon 28 G2
Glos 99 F11
Hereford 115 F10
Kent 71 F8
Mers 182 B4
Northumb 263 B10
Plym 7 D9
Shrops 149 G8
Som 27 B9
Som 44 C5
Staffs 169 E9
Wilts 47 G7
Wilts 61 E10
W Sus 35 G7
Forda Devon. 12 C6
Devon 40 F3
Fordbridge W Mid. . .134 F3
Fordcombe Kent. 52 E4
Fordell Fife. 280 D3
Forden = Ffodun
Powys 130 C4
Ford End Essex 87 B11
Essex 105 E9
Forder Corn 7 D8
Lancs 202 C5
Shrops 149 F8
Staffs 150 E5
Forder Green Devon . . .8 B5
Ford Forge
Northumb 263 B10
Fordgate Som 43 G10
Ford Green Lancs . . .202 D5
Stoke 168 E5
Fordham Cambs 124 C2
Essex 107 F8
Norf 140 D2
Fordham Heath
Essex 107 F8
Ford Heath Shrops . .149 G8
Ford Hill Northumb .263 B11
Fordhouses W Mid . .133 C8
Fordingbridge
Hants. 31 E10
Fordington E Yorks . .208 C6
Fordley T&W 243 C7
Fordon E Yorks 217 D10
Fordoun Aberds 293 F9
Ford's Green E Sus . . .36 B6
Suff 125 D11
Fordstreet Essex. . . .107 F8
Ford Street Som 27 D11
Fordton Devon. 14 B2
Fordwater Devon. . . .28 G2
Fordwells Oxon. 82 C4
Fordwich Kent 55 B7
Fordyce Aberds 302 C5
Forebridge Staffs . . .151 E8
Foredale N Yorks . . .212 F6
Forehill S Ayrs 257 E8
Foreland Fields IoW . .21 D9
Foreland Ho Argyll . .274 G3
Foremark Derbys . . .152 D6
Forest Becks
Lancs 203 D11
Forestburn Gate
Northumb 252 D3
Forest Coal Pit Mon . .96 G5
Forestdale London . . .67 G11
Foresterseat
Moray 301 D11
Forest Gate Hants . . .33 E10
London. 68 C2
Forest Green Glos . . .80 E4
Sur. 50 E6
Forest Hall Cumb . . .221 E10

Forest Hall *continued*
T&W 243 D7
Forest Head Cumb . .240 F3
Forest Hill London. . . .67 E11
Oxon 83 D9
Wilts 63 F8
Forest Holme
Lancs 195 B10
Forest-in-Teesdale
Durham 232 F3
Forest Lane Head
N Yorks 206 B2
Forest Lodge Argyll .284 C6
Highld 292 B2
Perth 291 F11
Forest Mill Clack . . .279 C9
Forest Moor
N Yorks 206 B2
Forest Row E Sus 52 G2
Forestside W Sus 34 E3
Forest Side IoW 20 D5
Forest Town Notts . .171 C9
Forewoods Common
Wilts 61 G10
Forfar Angus 287 B8
Forgandenny Perth . .286 F4
Forge Corn 4 E7
Powys 128 D5
Forge Hammer Torf. . .78 F3
Forge Side Torf. 78 D2
Forgewood
N Lanark 268 D4
Forgie Moray 302 D3
Forglen Ho Aberds . .302 D6
Forhill Worcs. 117 B11
Formby Mers 193 F10
Forncett End Norf . . .142 E2
Forncett St Mary
Norf. 142 E3
Forncett St Peter
Norf. 142 E3
Forneth Perth 286 C4
Fornham All Saints
Suff 124 D6
Fornham St Genevieve
Suff 124 D6
Fornham St Martin
Suff 125 D7
Fornighty Highld . . .301 D9
Forrabury Corn. 11 C7
Forres Moray 301 D10
Forrest Lodge
Dumfries 246 F3
Forry's Green Essex. .106 E5
Forsbrook Staffs . . .169 G7
Forse Highld 310 F6
Forse Ho Highld. . . .310 F6
Forshaw Heath
Warks 117 C11
Forsinain Highld . . .310 E3
Forsinard Highld . . .310 E2
Forsinard Station
Highld 310 E2
Forstal Kent 53 B8
Forston Dorset 17 B9
Fort Augustus
Highld 290 C5
Forteviot Perth 286 F4
Fort George Highld. .301 D7
Forth S Lanark 269 E8
Forthampton Glos . . .99 E7
Forthay Glos. 80 F2
Forth Road Bridge
Edin 280 F2
Fortis Green London. . .67 B9
Fort Matilda Invclyd. .276 F5
Forton Hants 48 D2
Lancs 202 C5
Shrops 149 F8
Som 28 E4
Staffs 150 D5
Forton Heath
Shrops 149 F8
Fortrie Aberds 302 E6
Aberds 303 D7
Fortrose Highld 301 D7
Fortuneswell Dorset . .17 G9
Fort William 290 F3
Forty Green Bucks . . .84 G3
Bucks. 84 G6
Forty Hill London 86 F4
Forward Green
Suff 125 F11
Forwood Glos 80 E5
Fosbury Wilts. 47 B10
Foscot Oxon 100 G4
Foscote Bucks 102 D4
Wilts 61 D11
W Nhants 102 B3
Fosdyke Lincs 156 C6
Fosdyke Bridge
Lincs 156 C6
Foss Perth 285 B11
Foss Cross Glos. 81 D9
Fossebridge Glos. . . .81 C9
Foster Street Essex. . .87 D7
Foston Derbys 152 C3
Leics 136 D2
Lincs 172 G5
N Yorks. 216 F3
Foston on the Wolds
E Yorks. 209 B8
Fotherby Lincs 190 C4
Fothergill Cumb 228 E6
Fotheringhay
N Nhants 137 E11
Foubister Orkney . . .314 F5
Foul Anchor Cambs .157 F9

Foulbridge Cumb . . .230 B4
Foulby W Yorks 197 D11
Foulden Borders 273 D8
Norf 140 D5
Foul End Warks 134 E4
Foulford Hants 31 F11
Foulis Castle Highld. .300 C5
Foul Mile E Sus 23 C10
Foulride Green
E Sus 23 D9
Foulridge Lancs 204 E3
Foulsham Norf 159 E10
Foundry Corn. 2 B5
Fountain Bridgend. . .57 E11
Fountainhall
Borders 271 F7
Four Ashes Bucks . . .84 F5
Staffs. 132 F6
Staffs. 133 B8
Suff 125 C10
W Mid 118 B3
Four Crosses
Powys 129 B11
Powys 148 F5
Staffs 133 B9
Wrex 166 E3
Four Elms Devon. 28 F3
Kent 52 D3
Four Foot Som. 44 G5
Four Forks Som 43 F8
Four Gates Gtr Man . .194 F6
Four Gotes Cambs . .157 F9
Four Houses Corner
W Berks 64 F6
Four Lane End
S Yorks 197 G10
Fourlane Ends
Derbys 170 D5
Four Lane Ends
Blackburn 195 B8
Ches W. 167 C9
Gtr Man 195 F9
W Yorks 205 G8
Four Lanes Corn 2 B5
Fourlanes End
Ches E 168 D4
Four Marks Hants. . . .49 G7
Four Mile Bridge
Anglesey 178 G3
Four Mile Elm Glos . .80 C4
Four Oaks E Sus 38 C5
Glos 98 F3
Kent 70 G3
W Mid 134 D2
W Mid 134 G4
Four Oaks Park
W Mid 134 D2
Fourpenny Highld . .311 L2
Four Points W Berks. .64 D5
Four Pools Worcs . . .99 C10
Four Roads Carms . . .74 D6
IoM 192 F3
Fourstones
Northumb 241 D10
Four Throws Kent. . . .38 B3
Four Wantz Essex. . . .87 C10
Four Wents Kent. 53 F9
Fovant Wilts. 31 B8
Foveran Aberds 303 G9
Fowey Corn 6 E2
Fowler's Plot Som . . .43 F10
Fowley Common
Warr 183 B11
Fowlis Angus 287 D7
Fowlis Wester Perth .286 E3
Fowlmere Cambs . . .105 B8
Fownhope Hereford . .97 E11
Foxash Estate
Essex 107 E11
Foxbar Renfs 267 C9
Foxbury London 68 E2
Foxcombe Hill Oxon . .83 E7
Fox Corner C Beds . .103 F8
Sur. 50 C3
Foxcote Glos 81 B8
Som 45 B8
Foxcotte Hants 47 D10
Foxdale IoM. 192 E3
Foxdown Hants 48 C4
Foxearth Essex 106 C6
Foxendown Kent 69 F7
Foxfield Cumb 210 B4
Foxford W Mid 135 G7
Foxham Wilts. 62 D3
Fox Hatch Essex 87 F9
Fox Hill Bath 61 G9
Hereford 98 B3
Foxhills Hants 32 E4
Foxhole Corn 5 E9
Norf 142 D4
Swansea 57 C7
Fox Hole Swansea . . .56 D5
Foxholes N Yorks . . .217 E10
Fox Holes Wilts 45 E11
Foxhunt Green E Sus .23 B8
Fox Lane Hants 49 B11
Foxley Hereford 97 B8
Norf 159 E10
Staffs 168 E3
Wilts 61 B11
Foxlydiate Worcs . . .117 D10
Fox Royd W Yorks . .197 D8
Fox Street Essex . . .107 F10
Foxt Staffs. 169 F8
Foxton Cambs 105 B8
Durham 234 F3
Leics 136 E4
N Yorks. 225 G8
Foxup N Yorks 213 D7
Foxwist Green
Ches W. 167 B10
Foxwood Shrops . . .116 B2
Foy Hereford 97 F11
Foyers Highld 300 G4
Foynesfield Highld . .301 D8
Fraddam Corn 2 C3
Fraddon Corn. 5 D8
Fradley Staffs. 152 G3
Fradley Junction
Staffs. 152 G2
Fradswell Staffs 151 C9

Fraisthorpe E Yorks 218 G3
Framfield E Sus 37 C7
Framingham Earl
Norf 142 C5
Framingham Pigot
Norf 142 C5
Framlingham Suff 126 E5
Frampton Dorset 17 B8
Lincs 156 B6
Frampton Cotterell
S Glos 61 C7
Frampton Court
Glos 99 E10
Frampton End S Glos 61 C7
Frampton Mansell
Glos 80 E6
Frampton on Severn
Glos 80 D2
Frampton West End
Lincs 174 G3
Framsden Suff 126 F3
Framwellgate Moor
Durham 233 C11
France Lynch Glos 80 E6
Franche Worcs 116 B6
Frandley Ches W 183 F10
Frankby Mers 182 D2
Frankfort Norf 160 E6
Franklands Gate
Hereford 97 B10
Frankley Worcs 133 G9
Frankley Green
Worcs 133 G9
Frankley Hill Worcs 117 B9
Frank's Bridge
Powys 114 F2
Frankton Warks 119 C8
Frankwell Shrops 149 G9
Frans Green Norf 160 G2
Frant E Sus 52 F5
Fraserburgh Aberds 303 C9
Frating Essex 107 G11
Frating Green
Essex 107 G11
Fratton Ptsmth 21 B9
Freasley Warks 134 D4
Freathy Corn 7 E8
Frecheville S Yorks 186 E5
Freckenham Suff 124 C3
Freckleton Lancs 194 B2
Fredley Sur 51 C7
Freebirch Derbys 186 G4
Freeby Leics 154 E6
Freefolk Hants 48 D3
Freehay Staffs 169 G8
Freeland Oxon 82 C6
Renfs 267 B9
Freeland Corner
Norf 160 F3
Freemantle Soton 32 E6
Freester Shetland 313 H6
Freethorpe Norf 143 B8
Free Town
Gtr Man 195 E10
Freezy Water London 86 F5
Freiston Lincs 174 G5
Freiston Shore
Lincs 174 G5
Fremington Devon 40 G4
N Yorks 223 F10
Frenchay S Glos 60 D6
Frenchbeer Devon 13 D9
Frenches Green
Essex 106 G4
Frenchmoor Hants 32 B3
French Street Kent 52 C3
Frenchwood Lancs 194 B4
Frenich Stirling 285 G8
Frensham Sur 49 E10
Frenze Norf 142 G2
Fresgoe Highld 310 C3
Freshbrook Swindon 62 C6
Freshfield Mers 193 F9
Freshford Bath 61 G9
Freshwater IoW 20 D2
Freshwater Bay IoW 20 D2
Freshwater East
Pembs 73 F8
Fressingfield Suff 126 B5
Freston Suff 108 D3
Freswick Highld 310 C7
Fretherne Glos 80 D2
Frettenham Norf 160 F4
Freuchie Fife 286 G6
Freuchies Angus 292 G4
Freystrop Pembs 73 C7
Friarn Som 43 F7
Friar Park W Mid 133 E10
Friars Cliff BCP 19 C9
Friar's Gate E Sus 52 G3
Friar's Hill E Sus 38 E5
Friarton Perth 286 E5
Friday Bridge
Cambs 139 C9
Friday Hill London 86 G5
Friday Street E Sus 23 E10
Suff 126 G6
Suff 127 E7
Sur 50 D6
Fridaythorpe
E Yorks 208 B3
Friendly W Yorks 196 C5
Friern Barnet
London 86 G3
Friesland Argyll 288 D3
Friesthorpe Lincs 189 E9
Frieston Lincs 172 F6
Frieth Bucks 84 G3
Frieze Hill Som 28 B2
Friezeland Notts 171 E7
Frilford Oxon 82 F6
Frilford Heath Oxon 82 F6
Frilsham W Berks 64 E4
Frimley Sur 49 B11
Frimley Green Sur 49 B11
Frimley Ridge Sur 49 B11
Frindsbury Medway 69 E8
Fring Norf 158 C4
Fringford Oxon 102 F2
Friningham Kent 53 B10
Frinkle Green Essex 106 C4
Frinsted Kent 53 B11
Frinton-on-Sea
Essex 108 G4
Friockheim Angus 287 C9
Friog Gwyn 146 G2
Frisby Leics 136 C4
Frisby on the Wreake
Leics 154 F3
Friskney Lincs 175 D7
Friskney Eaudyke
Lincs 175 D7
Friskney Tofts Lincs 175 E7
Friston E Sus 23 F8
Suff 127 E8
Fritchley Derbys 170 E5
Frith Kent 54 B2
Fritham Hants 32 E2
Frith Bank Lincs 174 F4
Frith Common
Worcs 116 D3
Frithelstock Devon 25 D7
Frithelstock Stone
Devon 25 D7
Frithend Hants 49 F10
Frith-hill Bucks 84 E6
Frith Hill Sur 50 E3
Frithsden Herts 85 D8
Frithville Lincs 174 E4
Frittenden Kent 53 E10
Frittiscombe Devon 8 G6
Fritton Norf 142 E4
Norf 143 C9
Norf 161 F8
Fritwell Oxon 101 F10
Frizinghall W Yorks 205 F8
Frizington Cumb 219 B10
Frizzeler's Green
Suff 124 E5
Frobost W Isles 297 J3
Frocester Glos 80 E3
Frochas Powys 148 G5
Frodesley Shrops 131 C10
Frodingham
N Lincs 199 E11
Frodsham Ches W 183 F8
Frogden Borders 263 D7
Frog End Cambs 123 F10
Cambs 123 G8
Froggatt Derbys 186 F2
Froghall Staffs 169 F8
Frogham Hants 31 E11
Kent 55 C9
Froghole Kent 52 C2
Frogholt Kent 55 F7
Frogland Cross
S Glos 60 C6
Frog Moor Swansea 56 C3
Frogmore Devon 8 G5
Hants 33 C11
Hants 49 B10
Herts 85 E11
Frognal S Ayrs 257 D8
Frognall Lincs 156 G3
Frogpool Corn 4 G5
Frog Pool Worcs 116 D5
Frogs' Green
Essex 105 D11
Frogshail Norf 160 B5
Frogwell Corn 6 B6
Frolesworth Leics 135 E10
Frome Som 45 D9
Fromebridge Glos 80 D3
Fromefield Som 45 D9
Frome St Quintin
Dorset 29 G9
Fromes Hill Hereford 98 B3
Fromington
Hereford 97 B10
Fron Denb 165 B9
Gwyn 145 B7
Gwyn 163 D8
Powys 113 D11
Powys 129 C8
Powys 130 C4
Powys 130 D3
Shrops 148 B5
Fron-Bache Denb 166 G2
Froncysyllte Wrex 166 G3
Fron-dêg Wrex 166 F3
Frongoch Gwyn 147 B8
Fron Isaf Wrex 166 G3
Frost Devon 26 F3
Frostenden Suff 143 G9
Frostenden Corner
Suff 143 G9
Frosterley Durham 232 D6
Frost Hill N Som 60 G2
Frostlane Hants 32 F6
Frost Row Norf 141 C10
Frotoft Orkney 314 D4
Froxfield C Beds 103 E9
Wilts 63 F9
Froxfield Green
Hants 34 B2
Froyle Hants 49 E9
Fryern Hill Hants 32 C6
Fryerning Essex 87 E10
Fryerns Essex 69 B8
Fryton N Yorks 216 E3
Fugglestone St Peter
Wilts 46 G6
Fulbeck Lincs 172 E6
Northumb 252 F5
Fulbourn Cambs 123 F10
Fulbrook Oxon 82 C3
Fulflood Hants 33 B7
Fulford Som 28 B2
Staffs 151 B9
York 207 D8
Fulham London 67 D8
Fulking W Sus 36 E2
Fullabrook Devon 40 E4
Fullarton Glasgow 268 C2
N Ayrs 257 B8
Fuller's End Essex 105 F10
Fuller's Moor
Ches W 167 E7
Fuller Street Essex 88 B2
Fullerton Hants 47 F11
Fulletby Lincs 190 G3
Fullshaw S Yorks 197 G8
Full Sutton
E Yorks 207 B10
Fullwell Cross
London 86 G6
Fullwood E Ayrs 267 E8
Gtr Man 196 F2
Fulmer Bucks 66 B3
Fulmodestone Norf 159 C9
Fulneck W Yorks 205 G10
Fulnetby Lincs 189 F9
Fulney Lincs 156 E5
Fulready Warks 100 B5
Fulshaw Park
Ches E 184 E4
Fulstone W Yorks 197 F7
Fulstow Lincs 190 B4
Fulthorpe Stockton 234 G4
Fulwell Oxon 101 G7
T&W 243 F9
Fulwood Lancs 202 G6
Som 28 C2
S Yorks 186 D4
Fundenhall Norf 142 D3
Fundenhall Street
Norf 142 D2
Funtington W Sus 22 B3
Funtley Hants 33 F9
Funtullich Perth 285 E11
Funzie Shetland 312 D8
Furley Devon 28 G3
Furnace Argyll 284 G4
Carms 74 E6
Carms 75 E8
Ceredig 128 D3
Highld 299 B9
Furnace End Warks 134 E4
Furnace Green
W Sus 51 F9
Furnace Wood
W Sus 51 F11
Furneaux Pelham
Herts 105 F8
Furner's Green E Sus 36 B6
Furness Vale Derbys 185 E8
Furneux Pelham
Herts 105 F8
Furnham Som 28 F4
Further Ford End
Essex 105 E9
Further Quarter
Kent 53 F11
Furtho W Nhants 102 C5
Furze Devon 25 B10
Furzebrook Dorset 18 E4
Furzedown Hants 32 B5
London 67 E9
Furzehill Devon 41 D8
Dorset 31 G8
Furze Hill Hants 31 E11
Furzeley Corner
Hants 33 E11
Furze Platt Windsor 65 C11
Furzey Lodge Hants 32 G5
Furzley Hants 32 D3
Furzton M Keynes 102 D6
Fyfett Som 28 E2
Fyfield Essex 87 D9
Glos 82 E2
Hants 47 D9
Oxon 82 F6
Wilts 63 F7
Wilts 63 G7
Fylingthorpe
N Yorks 227 D8
Fyning W Sus 34 C4
Fyvie Aberds 303 F7

G

Gabalfa Cardiff 59 D7
Gabhsann bho Dheas
W Isles 304 C6
Gabhsann bho Thuath
W Isles 304 C6
Gable Head Hants 21 B10
Gablon Highld 309 K7
Gabroc Hill E Ayrs 267 E9
Gadbrook Sur 51 D8
Gaddesby Leics 154 G3
Gadebridge Herts 85 D8
Gadfa Anglesey 179 D7
Gadfield Elm Worcs 98 E5
Gadlas Shrops 149 B7
Gadlys Rhondda 77 E7
Gadshill Kent 69 E8
Gaer Newport 59 B9
Powys 96 G3
Gaer-fawr Mon 78 F6
Gaerllwyd Mon 78 F6
Gaerwen Anglesey 179 G7
Gagingwell Oxon 101 F8
Gaick Lodge Highld 291 E9
Gailey Staffs 151 G8
Gailey Wharf Staffs 151 G8
Gainfield Oxon 82 F4
Gainford Durham 224 B3
Gain Hill Kent 53 D8
Gainsborough Lincs 188 C4
Suff 108 C3
Gainsford End
Essex 106 D4
Gairletter Argyll 276 E3
Gairloch Highld 299 B8
Gairlochy Highld 290 E3
Gairney Bank Perth 280 B2
Gairnshiel Lodge
Aberds 292 C4
Gaisgill Cumb 222 D2
Gaitsgill Cumb 230 B3
Galadean Borders 271 G11
Galashiels Borders 261 B11
Galdlys Flint 182 G2
Gale Gtr Man 196 D2
Galgate Lancs 202 B5
Galhampton Som 29 B10
Gallaberry
Dumfries 247 G11
Gallachoille Argyll 275 E8
Gallanach Argyll 288 C4
Argyll 289 G10
Highld 294 G6
Gallantry Bank
Ches E 167 E8
Gallatown Fife 280 C5
Galley Common
Warks 134 E6
Galleyend Essex 88 E2
Galley Hill Cambs 122 D6
Lincs 190 F6
Galleywood Essex 88 E2
Galligill Cumb 231 B11
Gallin Perth 285 C9
Gallovie Highld 291 E7
Gallowfauld Angus 287 C8
Gallowhill Glasgow 267 D11
Renfs 267 B9
Gallowhills Aberds 303 D10
Gallows Corner
London 87 G8
Gallowsgreen Torf 78 D3
Gallows Green
Essex 106 F2
Essex 107 F8
Staffs 169 G9
Worcs 117 E8
Gallows Inn Derbys 171 G7
Gallowstree Common
Oxon 65 C7
Galltair Highld 295 C10
Galltegfa Denb 165 D10
Gallt Melyd = *Meliden*
Denb 181 E9
Gallt-y-foel Gwyn 163 C9
Gallypot Street E Sus 52 F3
Galmington Som 28 C2
Galmisdale Highld 294 G6
Galmpton Devon 8 G3
Torbay 9 D7
Galon Uchaf M Tydf 77 D9
Galphay N Yorks 214 E5
Galston E Ayrs 258 B2
Galtrigill Highld 296 F7
Gam Corn 11 F7
Gamble Hill
W Yorks 205 G11
Gamblesby Cumb 231 D8
Gamble's Green
Essex 88 C3
Gamelsby Cumb 239 G7
Gamesley Derbys 185 C8
Gamlingay Cambs 122 G4
Gamlingay Cinques
Cambs 122 G4
Gamlingay Great Heath
Cambs 122 G4
Gammaton Devon 25 B7
Gammaton Moor
Devon 25 C7
Gammersgill
N Yorks 213 C11
Gamston Notts 154 B2
Notts 188 F2
Ganarew Hereford 79 B8
Ganavan Argyll 289 F10
Ganders Green Glos 98 G4
Gang Corn 6 B6
Ganllwyd Gwyn 146 E4
Gannetts Dorset 30 D3
Gannochy Angus 293 F7
Perth 286 E5
Gansclet Highld 310 E7
Ganstead E Yorks 209 G9
Ganthorpe N Yorks 216 E3
Ganton N Yorks 217 D9
Gants Hill London 68 B2
Ganwick Corner
Herts 86 F3
Gaodhail Argyll 289 F8
Gappah Devon 14 F3
Garafad Highld 298 C4
Garamor Highld 295 F8
Garbat Highld 300 C4
Garbhallt Argyll 275 D11
Garboldisham
Norf 141 G10
Garbole Highld 301 G7
Garden City
Bl Gwent 77 D11
Flint 166 B4
Gardeners Green
Wokingham 65 F10
Gardenstown
Aberds 303 C7
Garden Village
Swansea 56 B5
S Yorks 186 B3
Wrex 166 E4
W Yorks 206 G4
Garderhouse
Shetland 313 J5
Gardham E Yorks 208 E5
Gardie Shetland 312 D7
Gardin Shetland 312 G6
Gare Hill Som 45 E9
Garelochhead Argyll 276 C4
Garford Oxon 82 F6
Garforth W Yorks 206 G4
Gargrave N Yorks 204 C4
Gargunnock Stirling 278 C4
Garizim Conwy 179 F11
Garker Corn 5 E10
Garlandhayes Devon 27 D11
Garlands Cumb 239 G10
Garleffin S Ayrs 244 G3
Garlic Street Norf 142 G4
Garlieston Dumfries 236 E6
Garliford Devon 26 B3
Garlinge Kent 71 F10
Garlinge Green Kent 54 C6
Garlogie Aberds 293 C9
Garmelow Staffs 150 D5
Garmond Aberds 303 D8
Garmondsway
Durham 234 E2
Garmony Argyll 289 E8
Garmouth Moray 302 C3
Garmston Shrops 132 B2
Garn Powys 130 G2
Garnant Carms 75 C11
Garndiffaith Torf 78 E3
Garndolbenmaen
Gwyn 163 G7
Garnedd Conwy 164 E2
Garnett Bridge
Cumb 221 F10
Garnetts Essex 87 B10
Garnfadryn Gwyn 144 C5
Garnkirk N Lanark 268 B3
Garnlydan Bl Gwent 77 C11
Garnsgate Lincs 157 E8
Garnswllt Swansea 75 D10
Garn-swllt Swansea 75 D10
Garn-yr-erw Torf 78 C2
Garrabost W Isles 304 E7
Garrachra Argyll 275 E11
Garra Eallabus
Argyll 274 F3
Garralburn Moray 302 D4
Garraron Argyll 275 C9
Garras Corn 2 E6
Garreg Flint 181 F10
Gwyn 163 G10
Garrets Green
W Mid 134 F2
Garrick Perth 286 F2
Garrigill Cumb 231 C10
Garrison Stirling 285 G7
Garriston N Yorks 224 G3
Garroch Dumfries 246 G3
Garrogie Lodge
Highld 291 B7
Garros Highld 298 C4
Garrow Perth 286 C2
Garrowhill Glasgow 268 C3
Garrygualach Highld 290 C3
Garryhorn Dumfries 246 E2
Garsdale Cumb 212 B4
Garsdale Head
Cumb 222 G5
Garsdon Wilts 62 B3
Garshall Green
Staffs 151 C9
Garsington Oxon 83 E9
Garstang Lancs 202 D5
Garston Herts 85 F10
Mers 182 E6
Garswood Mers 183 B9
Gartachoil Stirling 277 C10
Gartbreck Argyll 254 B3
Gartcosh N Lanark 268 B3
Garth Bridgend 57 C11
Ceredig 128 G2
Flint 181 E10
Gwyn 179 G9
Newport 59 B9
Newport 78 G4
Perth 285 B11
Powys 95 B9
Powys 114 C5
Shetland 313 H4
Shetland 313 H6
Wrex 166 G3
Garthamlock
Glasgow 268 B3
Garthbeg Highld 291 B7
Garthbrengy Powys 95 E10
Garthdee Aberdeen 293 C11
Gartheli Ceredig 111 F11
Garthmyl Powys 130 D3
Garthorpe Leics 154 E6
N Lincs 199 D11
Garth Owen Powys 130 E2
Garth Row Cumb 221 F10
Garth Trevor Wrex 166 G3
Gartlea N Lanark 268 C5
Gartloch Glasgow 268 B3
Gartly Aberds 302 F5
Gartmore Stirling 277 B10
Gartmore Ho
Stirling 277 B10
Gartnagrenach
Argyll 255 B8
Gartness N Lanark 268 C5
Stirling 277 D10
Gartocharn W Dunb 277 D8
Garton E Yorks 209 F11
Garton-on-the-Wolds
E Yorks 208 B5
Gartsherrie
N Lanark 268 B4
Gartur Stirling 277 B11
Gartymore Highld 311 H4
Garvald E Loth 281 G11
Garvamore Highld 291 D7
Garvard Argyll 274 D4
Garvault Hotel
Highld 308 F7
Garve Highld 300 C3
Garvestone Norf 141 B10
Garvock Aberds 293 F9
Invclyd 276 G5
Garvock Hill Fife 280 D2
Garway Hereford 97 G9
Garway Hill Hereford 97 F8
Gaskan Highld 289 B9
Gasper Wilts 45 G9
Gastard Wilts 61 F11
Gasthorpe Norf 141 G9
Gaston Green Essex 87 B7
Gatacre Park Shrops 132 F5
Gatcombe IoW 20 D5
Gateacre Mers 182 D6
Gatebeck Cumb 211 B10
Gate Burton Lincs 188 E4
Gateford Notts 187 E9
Gateford Common
Notts 187 E9
Gateforth N Yorks 198 B5
Gatehead E Ayrs 257 B9
Gate Helmsley
N Yorks 207 B9
Gatehouse Northumb 251 F7
Gatehouse of Fleet
Dumfries 237 D8
Gatelawbridge
Dumfries 247 D10
Gateley Norf 159 E9
Gatenby N Yorks 214 B6
Gatesgarth Cumb 220 B3
Gateshead T&W 243 E7
Gatesheath Ches W 167 C7
Gateside Aberds 293 B8
Angus 287 C8
Dumfries 248 E4
E Renf 267 D9
Fife 286 G5
N Ayrs 267 E7
Gateside *continued*
Shetland 312 F4
Gatewen Wrex 166 E4
Gatherley Devon 12 E3
Gathurst Gtr Man 194 F4
Gatlas Newport 78 G4
Gatley End Cambs 104 C5
Gtr Man 184 D4
Gatton Sur 51 C9
Gattonside Borders 262 B2
Gatwick Glos 80 C2
Gatwick Airport
W Sus 51 E9
Gaufron Powys 113 D9
Gaulby Leics 136 C3
Gauldry Fife 287 E7
Gauntons Bank
Ches E 167 F9
Gaunt's Common
Dorset 31 F8
Gaunt's Earthcott
S Glos 60 C6
Gaunt's End Essex 105 F10
Gautby Lincs 189 G11
Gavinton Borders 272 E5
Gawber S Yorks 197 F10
Gawcott Bucks 102 E3
Gawsworth Ches E 168 B5
Gawthorpe W Yorks 197 C9
W Yorks 197 D7
Gawthrop Cumb 212 B3
Gawthwaite Cumb 210 C5
Gay Bowers Essex 88 E3
Gaydon Warks 119 G7
Gayfield Orkney 314 A4
Gayhurst M Keynes 103 B7
Gayle N Yorks 213 B7
Gayles N Yorks 224 D2
Gay Street W Sus 35 C9
Gayton Mers 182 E3
Norf 158 F4
Staffs 151 D9
W Nhants 120 G4
Gayton Engine
Lincs 191 D7
Gayton le Marsh
Lincs 190 E6
Gayton le Wold
Lincs 190 D2
Gayton Thorpe Norf 158 F4
Gaywood Norf 158 E2
Gaza Shetland 312 F5
Gazeley Suff 124 E4
Geanies House
Highld 301 B8
Gearraidh Bhailteas
W Isles 297 J3
Gearraidh Bhaird
W Isles 304 F5
Gearraidh Dubh
W Isles 296 F4
Gearraidh na h-Aibhne
W Isles 304 E4
Gearraidh na Monadh
W Isles 297 K3
Geàrraidh Sheilidh
W Isles 297 J3
Geary Highld 298 C2
Geat Wolford Warks 100 E4
Geddes House
Highld 301 D8
Gedding Suff 125 F9
Geddington
N Nhants 137 G7
Gedgrave Hall Suff 109 B8
Gedintailor Highld 295 B7
Gedling Notts 171 G10
Gedney Lincs 157 E8
Gedney Broadgate
Lincs 157 E8
Gedney Drove End
Lincs 157 D9
Gedney Dyke Lincs 157 D8
Gedney Hill Lincs 156 G6
Gee Cross Gtr Man 185 C7
Geeston Rutland 137 C9
Gegin Wrex 166 E3
Geilston Argyll 276 F6
Geinas Denb 165 B9
Geirinis W Isles 297 G3
Geise Highld 310 C5
Geisiadar W Isles 304 E3
Geldeston Norf 143 E7
Gell Conwy 164 B5
Gelli Pembs 73 B9
Rhondda 77 G7
Gellideg M Tydf 77 D8
Gellifor Denb 165 C10
Gelligaer Caerph 77 F10
Gelli-gaer Neath 57 C9
Gelligroes Caerph 77 G11
Gelli-hôf Caerph 77 F11
Gellilydan Gwyn 146 B3
Gellinud Neath 76 E2
Gellinudd Neath 76 E2
Gellyburn Perth 286 D4
Gellygron Neath 76 E2
Gellywen Carms 92 G5
Gelsmoor Leics 153 F8
Gelston Dumfries 237 D9
Lincs 172 G6
Gembling E Yorks 209 B8
Gemini Warr 183 C9
Gendros Swansea 56 B6
Genesis Green Suff 124 F4
Gentleshaw Staffs 151 G11
Geocrab W Isles 305 J3
Georgefield
Dumfries 249 E7
George Green Bucks 66 C4
Georgeham Devon 40 F3
George Nympton
Devon 26 C2
Georgetown
Bl Gwent 77 D10
Georgia Corn 1 B5
Gergask Highld 291 D8
Gerlan Gwyn 163 B10
Germansweek Devon 12 C4
Germiston Glasgow 268 B2
Germoe Corn 2 D3
Gernon Bushes Essex 87 E7
Gerrans Corn 3 B9
Gerrard's Bromley
Staffs 150 C5
Gerrards Cross Bucks 66 B4
Gerrick Redcar 226 C4
Geseilfa Powys 129 E8
Gestingthorpe
Essex 106 D6
Gesto Ho Highld 294 B5
Geuffordd Powys 148 G4
Geufron Denb 166 G2
Gibbet Hill Warks 135 G10
W Mid 118 C6
Gibb Hill Ches W 183 F10
Gibbshill Dumfries 237 B9
Gib Heath W Mid 133 F11
Gibraltar Bedford 103 B10
Bucks 84 C3
Kent 55 F8
Gibralter Oxon 83 B7
Gibshill Invclyd 276 G6
Gibsmere Notts 172 F2
Giddeahall Wilts 61 E11
Giddy Green Dorset 18 D2
Gidea Park London 68 B4
Gidleigh Devon 13 D9
Giffard Park
M Keynes 103 C7
Giffnock E Renf 267 D11
Gifford E Loth 271 B10
Giffordland N Ayrs 266 F5
Giffordtown Fife 286 F6
Gigg Gtr Man 195 F10
Giggetty Staffs 133 E7
Giggleswick
N Yorks 212 G6
Giggshill Sur 67 F7
Gignog Pembs 91 G7
Gilberdyke E Yorks 199 B10
Gilbert's Coombe Corn 4 G3
Gilbert's End Worcs 98 C6
Gilbert's Green
Warks 118 C2
Gilbertstone W Mid 134 G2
Gilbert Street Hants 49 G7
Gilchriston E Loth 271 B9
Gilcrux Cumb 229 D8
Gildersome
W Yorks 197 B8
Gildersome Street
W Yorks 197 B8
Gildingwells
S Yorks 187 D9
Gilesgate Durham 233 C11
Gilesgate Moor
Durham 233 C11
Gileston V Glam 58 F4
Gilfach Caerph 77 F11
Hereford 96 E6
Gilfach Goch Rhondda 58 B3
Gilfachrheda
Ceredig 111 F8
Gilgarran Cumb 228 G6
Gill N Yorks 204 E5
Gillamoor N Yorks 216 B3
Gillan Corn 3 E7
Gillar's Green Mers 183 B7
Gillbank Cumb 221 F7
Gillbent Gtr Man 184 E5
Gillen Highld 298 D2
Gillesbie Dumfries 248 E5
Gilling East N Yorks 216 D2
Gillingham Dorset 30 B4
Medway 69 F9
Norf 143 E8
Gilling West
N Yorks 224 D3
Gillmoss Mers 182 B6
Gillock Highld 310 D6
Gillow Heath Staffs 168 D5
Gills Highld 310 B7
Gill's Green Kent 53 G9
Gillway Staffs 134 C4
Gilmanscleuch
Borders 261 E8
Gilmerton Edin 270 B5
Perth 286 E2
Gilmonby Durham 223 C9
Gilmorton Leics 135 F11
Gilmourton
S Lanark 268 G3
Gilnow Gtr Man 195 F8
Gilroyd S Yorks 197 G10
Gilsland Northumb 240 D4
Gilsland Spa Cumb 240 D4
Gilson Warks 134 E3
Gilstead W Yorks 205 F8
Gilston Borders 271 D8
Herts 86 C6
Gilston Park Herts 86 C6
Giltbrook Notts 171 F7
Gilver's Lane Worcs 98 C6
Gilwell Park Essex 86 F5
Gilwern Mon 78 C2
Gimingham Norf 160 B5
Ginclough Ches E 185 F7
Ginger's Green
E Sus 23 C10
Giosla W Isles 304 F3
Gipping Suff 125 E11
Gipsey Bridge Lincs 174 F3
Gipsy Row Suff 107 D11
Gipsyville Hull 200 B5
Gipton W Yorks 206 F2
Gipton Wood
W Yorks 206 F2
Girdle Toll N Ayrs 266 G6
Girlington W Yorks 205 G8
Girlsta Shetland 313 H6
Girsby Lincs 190 D2
N Yorks 225 D7
Girt Som 29 C10
Girtford C Beds 104 B3
C Beds 122 G3
Girthon Dumfries 237 D8
Girton Cambs 123 E8
Notts 172 B4
Girvan S Ayrs 244 D5
Gisburn Lancs 204 D2
Gisleham Suff 143 F10
Gislingham Suff 125 C11
Gissing Norf 142 F2
Gittisham Devon 15 B8
Givons Grove Sur 51 C7
Glachavoil Argyll 275 F11
Glackmore Highld 300 D6
Glack of Midthird
Moray 302 E3
Gladestry Powys 114 F4
Gladsmuir E Loth 281 G9
Glaichbea Highld 300 F5
Glais Swansea 76 E2
Glaisdale N Yorks 226 D5
Glame Highld 298 E5
Glamis Angus 287 C7
Glan Adda Gwyn 179 G9
Glanafon Pembs 73 B7
Glanaman Carms 75 C11
Glan-Conwy Conwy 164 E4
Glandford Norf 177 E8
Glan-Duar Carms 93 C10
Glandwr Caerph 78 E2
Pembs 92 F3
Glan-Dwyfach
Gwyn 163 G7
Glandy Cross Carms 92 F2
Glandyfi Ceredig 128 D3
Glan Gors Anglesey 179 F7
Glangrwyney Powys 78 B2
Glanhanog Powys 129 D8
Glanmule Powys 130 E3
Glanrafon Ceredig 128 G2
Glanrhyd Gwyn 144 B5
Pembs 92 C2
Glan-rhyd Gwyn 163 D7
Powys 76 D3
Glantlees Northumb 252 B4
Glanton Northumb 264 G3
Glanton Pike
Northumb 264 G3
Glan-traeth
Anglesey 178 F3
Glantwymyn = *Cemmaes*
Road Powys 128 C6
Glanvilles Wootton
Dorset 29 F11
Glanwern Ceredig 128 F2
Glanwydden Conwy 180 E4
Glan-y-don Flint 181 F11
Glan y Ffer = *Ferryside*
Carms 74 C5
Glan-y-llyn Rhondda 58 C6
Glan-y-môr Carms 74 C4
Glan-y-nant Caerph 77 F10
Powys 129 G8
Glan-yr-afon
Anglesey 179 E10
Flint 181 E10
Gwyn 164 G6
Gwyn 165 G8
Shrops 148 E4
Glan-y-wern Gwyn 146 C2
Glapthorn
N Nhants 137 E10
Glapwell Derbys 171 B7
Glas-allt Shiel
Aberds 292 E4
Glasbury Powys 96 D3
Glaschoil Highld 301 F10
Glascoed Denb 181 G7
Mon 78 E4
Powys 129 F11
Powys 148 G2
Wrex 166 E3
Glascorrie Aberds 292 D5
Perth 286 E2
Glascote Staffs 134 C4
Glascwm Powys 114 G3
Glasdir Flint 181 E10
Glasdrum Argyll 284 C4
Glasfryn Conwy 164 E6
Glasgoed Ceredig 92 B6
Glasgoforest
Aberds 293 B10
Glasgow Glasgow 267 B11
Glashvin Highld 298 C4
Glasinfryn Gwyn 163 B9
Glasllwch Newport 59 B9
Glasnacardoch
Highld 295 F8
Glasnakille Highld 295 D7
Glasphein Highld 297 G7
Glaspwll Powys 128 D4
Glassburn Highld 300 F3
Glassenbury Kent 53 F8
Glasserton Dumfries 236 F6
Glassford S Lanark 268 F4
Glassgreen Moray 302 C2
Glasshoughton
W Yorks 198 C2
Glasshouse Glos 98 G4
Glasshouse Hill Glos 98 G4
Glasshouses
N Yorks 214 G3
Glasslie Fife 286 G6
Glasson Cumb 228 D6
Cumb 239 E7
Lancs 202 B4
Glassonby Cumb 231 D7
Glasterlaw Angus 287 B9
Glaston Rutland 137 C7
Glastonbury Som 44 F4
Glatton Cambs 138 F3
Glazebrook Warr 183 C11
Glazebury Warr 183 B11
Glazeley Shrops 132 F4
Gleadless S Yorks 186 E5
Gleadless Valley
S Yorks 186 E5
Gleadmoss Ches E 168 B4
Gleadsmoss Ches E 168 B4
Gleanhead
Dumfries 245 G10
Gleann Tholàstaidh
W Isles 304 D7
Gleaston Cumb 210 E5
Glebe Hants 33 D9
Shetland 313 J6
T&W 243 F8
Glecknabae Argyll 275 G11
Gledhow W Yorks 206 F2

Gledrid Shrops.....148 B5
Gleiniant Powys...129 E9
Glemsford Suff.....106 B6
Glen Dumfries.......237 B10
  Dumfries.......237 D7
Glenallachie Moray .302 E2
Glenalmond College
  Perth...........286 E3
Glenalmond Ho
  Perth...........286 E3
Glenamachrie
  Argyll...........289 D11
Glenample Stirling ..285 E9
Glenancross Highld ..295 F8
Glenapp Castle
  S Ayrs 244 G3
Glenaros Ho Argyll ..289 E7
Glen Auldyn IoM...192 C5
Glenbarr Argyll 255 D7
Glenbeg Highld......289 C7
  Highld...........301 G10
Glen Bernisdale
  Highld...........298 C4
Glenbervie Aberds ..293 E9
Glenboig N Lanark....268 B4
Glenborrodale
  Highld...........289 C8
Glenbranter Argyll..276 B2
Glenbreck Borders ..260 D3
Glenbrein Lodge
  Highld...........290 B6
Glenbrittle House
  Highld...........294 C6
Glenbrook Edin.....270 B2
Glenbuchat Castle
  Aberds...........292 B5
Glenbuchat Lodge
  Aberds...........292 B5
Glenbuck E Ayrs 259 D7
Glenburn Renfs......267 C9
Glenbyre Argyll 289 G7
Glencalvie Lodge
  Highld...........309 L4
Glencanisp Lodge
  Highld...........307 G6
Glencaple Dumfries 237 C11
Glencarron Lodge
  Highld...........299 D10
Glencarse Perth.....286 E5
Glencassley Castle
  Highld...........309 J4
Glencat Aberds 293 D7
Glenceitlein Highld..284 C5
Glencoe Highld......284 B4
Glencraig Fife......280 B3
Glencripesdale
  Highld...........289 D8
Glencrosh Dumfries .247 F7
Glendavan Ho
  Aberds...........292 C6
Glendearg Borders ..262 B2
Glendevon Perth....286 G3
Glendoebeg Highld..290 C6
Glendoe Lodge
  Highld...........290 C6
Glendoick Perth....286 E6
Glendoll Lodge
  Angus...........292 F4
Glendoune S Ayrs ...244 D5
Glenduckie Fife.....286 F6
Glendye Lodge
  Aberds...........293 E8
Gleneagles Hotel
  Perth...........286 F3
Gleneagles House
  Perth...........286 F3
Glenearn Perth 286 F5
Glenegedale Argyll...254 B4
Glenelg Highld......295 D10
Glenernie Moray...301 E10
Glenfarg Perth.....286 F5
Glenfarquhar Lodge
  Aberds...........293 E9
Glenferness House
  Highld...........301 E9
Glenfeshie Lodge
  Highld...........291 D10
Glenfiddich Lodge
  Moray...........302 F3
Glenfield Leics.....135 B10
Glenfinnan Highld..295 D10
Glenfinnan Lodge
  Highld...........295 G11
Glenfintaig Ho
  Highld...........290 E4
Glenfoot Perth.....286 F5
Glenfyne Lodge
  Argyll...........284 F6
Glengap Dumfries ...237 D8
Glengarnock N Ayrs...266 E6
Glengolly Highld....310 C5
Glengorm Castle
  Argyll...........288 D6
Glengoulandie
  Perth...........285 B11
Glengrasco Highld..298 E4
Glenhead Farm
  Angus...........292 G4
Glen Ho Borders 261 C10
Glenholt Plym......7 C10
Glenhoul Dumfries..246 F4
Glenhurich Highld..289 C10
Glenkerry Borders ..261 G2
Glenkiln Dumfries...237 B10
Glenkindie Aberds ..292 B9
Glenlair Dumfries...237 B9
Glenlatterach
  Moray...........301 D11
Glenlee Dumfries ...246 G4
Glenleigh Park E Sus...38 E2
Glenleraig Highld...306 F6
Glenlichorn Perth...285 F11
Glenlicht Ho Highld..290 B2
Glenlivet Moray...301 G11
Glenlochar Dumfries .237 C9
Glenlochsie Lodge
  Perth...........292 F2
Glenlocksie Lodge
  Perth...........292 F2
Glenloig N Ayrs 255 D10

Glenlomond Perth ..286 G5
Glenluce Dumfries ..236 D4
Glenlussa Ho Argyll...255 E8
Glenmallan Argyll....276 B5
Glenmarkie Lodge
  Angus...........292 G4
Glenmarksie Highld .300 D3
Glenmavis N Lanark ..268 B4
  W Loth..........269 B9
Glenmaye IoM......192 D3
Glenmayne
  Borders 261 C11
Glenmeanie Highld ..300 D2
Glenmidge Dumfries .247 F9
Glenmoidart Ho
  Highld...........289 B9
Glen Mona IoM....192 D5
Glen Mor Highld....295 B10
Glenmore Argyll....275 B9
  Highld...........298 E4
Glenmore Lodge
  Highld...........291 C11
Glenmoy Angus....292 G6
Glen Nevis House
  Highld...........290 F3
Glennoe Argyll.....284 D4
Glen of Newmill
  Moray...........302 D4
Glenogil Angus....292 G6
Glenowen Pembs...73 D7
Glen Parva Leics...135 D11
Glenprosen Lodge
  Angus...........292 G4
Glenprosen Village
  Angus...........292 G5
Glenquaich Lodge
  Perth...........286 D2
Glenquiech Angus ..292 G6
Glenquithlie Aberds ..303 C8
Glenrazie Dumfries..236 C5
Glenreasdell Mains
  Argyll...........255 B9
Glenree N Ayrs.....255 E10
Glenridding Cumb...221 B7
Glenrossal Highld...309 J4
Glenrothes Fife.....286 G6
Glensanda Highld ..289 E10
Glensaugh Aberds ..293 F8
Glensburgh Falk....279 E8
Glenshero Lodge
  Highld...........291 D10
Glenshoe Lodge
  Perth...........292 G3
Glen Sluain Argyll...275 D11
Glenstockadale
  Dumfries.........236 C2
Glenstriven Argyll...275 F11
Glentaggart
  S Lanark.........259 D8
Glen Tanar House
  Aberds...........292 D6
Glentarkie Perth....286 F5
Glenternie Borders ..260 B6
Glentham Lincs....189 C8
Glentirranmuir
  Stirling..........278 C3
Glenton Aberds....302 G6
Glentress Borders...261 B9
Glentromie Lodge
  Highld...........291 D9
Glen Trool Lodge
  Dumfries.........245 G10
Glentrool Village
  Dumfries.........236 B5
Glentruan IoM.....192 B5
Glentruim House
  Highld...........291 D8
Glentworth Lincs...188 D6
Glenuig Highld.....289 B8
Glenure Argyll.....284 C4
Glenurquhart Highld .301 C7
Glen Vic Askill
  Highld...........298 E3
Glenview Argyll.....284 E5
Glen Village Falk....279 B8
Glen Vine IoM.....192 E4
Glespin S Lanark....259 D8
Gletness Shetland...313 H6
Glewstone Hereford .97 G11
Glinton Pboro......121 G11
Globe Town London..67 C11
Glodwick Gtr Man ..196 G2
Glogue Pembs.....92 E4
Glooston Leics......136 D4
Glororum Northumb ..264 C5
Glossop Derbys....185 C8
Gloster Hill
  Northumb........253 C7
Gloucester Glos....80 B4
Gloup Shetland....312 C7
Gloweth Corn......4 G5
Glusburn N Yorks...204 E6
Glutt Lodge Highld..310 F3
Glutton Bridge
  Staffs...........169 B9
Gluvian Corn......5 C8
Glympton Oxon...101 G8
Glyn Mon........129 F8
  Powys...........129 F8
Glynarthen Ceredig...92 B6
Glynbrochan Powys 129 G8
Glyn Castle Neath...76 E4
Glyn-Ceiriog Wrex..148 B4
Glyncoch Rhondda...77 G9
Glyncoed Bl Gwent ..77 C11
Glyncorrwg Neath...57 B11
Glyn-Cywarch Gwyn .146 C2
Glynde E Sus.......23 D7
Glyndebourne E Sus .23 C7
Glyndyfrdwy Denb...165 G10
Glynedd = Glyn neath
  Neath...........76 D5
Glyne Gap E Sus....38 F3
Glyn Etwy Bl Gwent ..77 D11
Glynhafren Powys...129 G7
Glynllan Bridgend...58 B2

Glynmorlas Shrops..148 B6
Glyn-neath = Glynedd
  Neath...........76 D5
Glynogwr Bridgend..58 B3
Glyntaff Rhondda...58 B5
Glyntawe Powys....76 B4
Gnosall Staffs......150 E6
Gnosall Heath Staffs..150 E6
Goadby Leics......136 D4
Goadby Marwood
  Leics............154 D5
Goatacre Wilts......62 D4
Goathill Dorset.....29 D11
Goathland N Yorks..226 E6
Goathurst Som.....43 G9
Goathurst Common
  Kent............52 C3
Goat Lees Kent.....54 D4
Gobernuisgach Lodge
  Highld...........308 E4
Gobernuisgeach
  Highld...........310 F3
Gobhaig W Isles....305 H2
Gobley Hole Hants...48 D6
Gobowen Shrops...148 C6
Godalming Sur....50 E3
Goddards Bucks....84 D3
Goddard's Corner
  Suff............126 D5
Goddard's Green
  Kent............53 G10
  W Berks.........65 F7
Goddards' Green
  W Sus...........36 C3
Godden Green Kent..52 B5
Goddington London..68 F3
Godford Cross Devon .27 G10
Godleybrook Staffs..169 G7
Godley Hill Gtr Man ..185 C7
Godleys Green E Sus..36 D5
Godmanchester
  Cambs..........122 C4
Godmanstone Dorset .17 B9
Godmersham Kent..54 C5
Godney Som.......44 E3
Godolphin Cross Corn .2 C4
Godre'r-graig Neath ..76 D3
God's Blessing Green
  Dorset...........31 G8
Godshill Hants......31 E11
  IoW............20 E6
Godstone Sur......51 C10
Godswinscroft Hants..19 B9
Godwell Devon.....8 D2
Godwinscroft Hants..19 B9
Goetre Mon.......78 D4
Goferydd Anglesey ..178 E2
Goff's Oak Herts....86 E4
Gogar Edin........280 G3
Goginan Ceredig...128 G3
Goirtean a'Chladaich
  Highld...........290 F2
Golan Gwyn.......163 G8
Golant Corn.......6 E2
Golberdon Corn....12 G2
Golborne Gtr Man ..183 B10
Golcar W Yorks....196 D6
Golch Flint........181 F11
Goldcliff Newport...59 C11
Golden Balls Oxon..83 F9
Golden Cross E Sus..23 C8
  E Sus...........23 C10
Golden Green Kent..52 D6
Golden Grove Carms .75 B9
Goldenhill Stoke....168 E5
Golden Hill Bristol...60 D5
Golden Pot Hants...49 E8
Golden Valley
  Derbys..........170 E6
  Glos............99 G8
  Hereford.........98 B3
Golden Village Falk..279 B8
Golder Field
  Hereford.........115 E11
Golders Green
  London..........67 B9
Goldfinch Bottom
  W Berks.........64 G4
Goldhanger Essex...88 D6
Gold Hill Dorset....30 E4
  Norf............139 E10
Golding Shrops....131 C10
Goldington
  Bedford..........121 G11
Goldsborough
  N Yorks..........206 B3
  N Yorks..........226 C6
Gold's Cross Bath...60 G5
Golds Green W Mid..133 E9
Goldsithney Corn....2 C2
Goldstone Shrops...150 D4
Goldthorn Park
  W Mid...........133 D8
Goldthorpe S Yorks..198 G3
Goldworthy Devon ..24 C5
Golford Kent......53 F9
Golftyn Flint......182 G3
Golgotha Kent......55 D9
Gollanfield Highld...301 D10
Gollawater Corn....4 E5
Gollinglith Foot
  N Yorks..........214 C3
Golly Wrex.......166 D4
Golsoncott Som....42 F4
Golspie Highld.....311 J2
Golval Highld......310 C2
Golynos Torf......78 E3
Gomeldon Wilts....47 F7
Gomersal W Yorks...197 B8
Gometra Ho Argyll..288 E5
Gomshall Sur......50 D5
Gonalston Notts....171 F11
Gonamena Corn....11 G11
Gonerby Hill Foot
  Lincs............155 B8
Gonfirth Shetland...313 G5

Good Easter Essex...87 C10
Gooderstone Norf...140 C5
Goodleigh Devon ...40 G6
Goodley Stock Kent..52 C2
Goodmanham
  E Yorks..........208 E3
Goodmayes London..68 B3
Goodnestone Kent...55 C9
  Kent............70 G4
Goodrich Hereford..79 B9
Goodrington Torbay...9 C7
Good's Green
  Worcs...........132 G5
Goodshaw Lancs...195 B10
Goodshaw Chapel
  Lancs...........195 B10
Goodshaw Fold
  Lancs...........195 B10
Goodstone Devon...13 G11
Goodwick = Wdig
  Pembs..........91 D8
Goodworth Clatford
  Hants...........47 E11
Goodyers End
  Warks...........134 F6
Goodyhills Cumb...229 B8
Goole E Yorks......199 C8
Goom's Hill Worcs...117 G10
Goonabarn Corn....5 E9
Goonbell Corn.....4 F4
Goon Gumpas Corn..4 G4
Goonhavern Corn...4 E5
Goonhusband Corn..2 D5
Goonlaze Corn.....2 B6
Goonown Corn.....4 E4
Goonpiper Corn....3 B8
Goonvrea Corn.....4 F4
Gooseberry Green
  Essex...........87 F11
Goose Eye W Yorks ..204 E6
Gooseford Devon...13 C9
Goose Green
  Cumb...........211 C10
  Essex...........108 F2
  Gtr Man.........194 G5
  Hants...........32 F4
  Herts...........86 D5
  Kent............52 C6
  Kent............53 F10
  Lancs...........194 C3
  Norf............142 F2
  S Glos...........61 C8
  W Sus...........34 C3
  W Sus...........35 D10
Gooseham Mill
  Devon...........24 D3
Goosehill Green
  Worcs...........117 E8
Goosemoor Staffs...150 F6
Goosemoor Green
  Staffs...........151 G11
Goose Pool Hereford .97 D9
Goosewell Devon...40 D5
Goosey Oxon.......82 G5
Goosnargh Lancs...203 F7
Goostrey Ches E....184 G3
Gorbals Glasgow....267 C11
Gorcott Hill Warks..117 D11
Gord Shetland......313 L6
Gorddinog Conwy...179 G11
Gordon Borders....272 G2
Gordonbush Highld ..311 J2
Gordonsburgh
  Moray...........302 C4
Gordonstoun
  Moray...........301 C11
Gordonstown
  Aberds..........302 D5
  Aberds..........303 F7
Gore Dorset.......29 D9
  Kent............55 B10
Gorebridge Midloth ..270 C6
Gore Cross Wilts....46 C4
Gore End Hants....64 G2
Gorefield Cambs....157 G8
Gorehill W Sus......35 C7
Gore Pit Essex.....88 B5
Gore Street Kent....71 F9
Gorgie Edin........280 G4
Gorhambury Herts..85 D10
Goring Oxon.......64 C6
Goring-by-Sea
  W Sus...........35 G10
Goring Heath Oxon..65 D7
Gorleston-on-Sea
  Norf............143 C10
Gornalwood W Mid..133 E8
Gorrachie Aberds...303 D7
Gorran Churchtown
  Corn............5 G9
Gorran Haven Corn..5 G10
Gorran High Lanes
  Corn............5 G9
Gorrenberry
  Borders.........249 D11
Gorrig Ceredig.....93 C8
Gorse Covert Warr..183 C11
Gorsedd Flint......181 F11
Gorse Hill Gtr Man..184 B4
  Swindon.........63 B7
Gorseinon Swansea..56 B5
Gorseness Orkney...314 E4
Gorsethorpe Notts..171 B9
Gorseybank Derbys ..170 E3
Gorsgoch Ceredig...111 G9
Gorslas Carms.....75 C9
Gorsley Glos.......98 F3
Gorsley Common
  Hereford.........98 F3
Gorsley Ley Staffs..133 B11
Gorstage Ches W....183 G10
Gorstan Highld.....300 C3
Gorstanvorran
  Highld...........289 B10
Gorstella Ches W....166 C5
Gorsty Common
  Hereford.........97 D9
Gorsteyhill Ches E...168 E2
Gorst Hill Worcs....116 C4
Gorstyhill Staffs....168 E2
Gorsty Hill Staffs...151 D11

Gortan Argyll......274 G3
Gortantaoid Argyll...274 F4
Gortenacullish
  Highld...........295 G8
Gorteneorn Highld..289 C8
Gortenfern Highld...289 C8
Gortinanane Argyll...255 C8
Gorton Gtr Man....184 B5
Gortonallister
  N Ayrs..........256 D2
Gosbeck Suff......126 F3
Gosberton Lincs....156 C4
Gosberton Cheal
  Lincs............156 D4
Gosberton Clough
  Lincs............156 D3
Goscote W Mid....133 C10
Gosfield Essex.....106 F5
Gosford Hereford..115 D10
  Oxon...........83 C7
Gosford Green
  W Mid...........118 B6
Gosforth Cumb....219 E11
  T&W............242 D6
Gosforth Valley
  Derbys..........186 F4
Gosland Green Suff..124 G5
Gosling Green Suff...107 C9
Gosmere Kent......54 B4
Gosmore Herts.....104 F3
Gospel Ash Staffs...132 E6
Gospel End Village
  Staffs...........133 E7
Gospel Green W Sus..50 G2
Gospel Oak London..67 B9
Gosport Hants......21 B8
  Hants...........32 C5
Gossabrough
  Shetland.........312 E7
Gossard's Green
  C Beds..........103 C8
Gossington Glos....80 E2
Gossops Green
  W Sus...........51 F9
Goswick Northumb ..273 F11
Gotham Dorset.....31 E9
  Notts...........153 C10
Gothelney Green
  Som............43 F9
Gotherington Glos...99 F9
Gothers Corn......5 D9
Gott Argyll........288 E2
  Shetland.........313 J6
Gotton Som.......28 B2
Goudhurst Kent....53 F10
Goukstone Moray ..302 D4
Goulceby Lincs....190 F3
Goulton N Yorks....225 E9
Gourdas Aberds....303 E7
Gourdon Aberds....293 F10
Gourock Inclyd....276 F4
Govan Glasgow.....267 B11
Govanhill Glasgow ..267 C11
Goveton Devon.....8 F5
Govilon Mon.......78 C3
Gowanhill Aberds...303 C10
Gowanwell Aberds ..303 E8
Gowdall E Yorks....198 C6
Gowerton = Tre-Gwyr
  Swansea.........56 B5
Gowhole Derbys....185 E8
Gowkhall Fife......279 D11
Gowkthrapple
  N Lanark........268 E5
Gowthorpe
  E Yorks..........207 C11
Goxhill E Yorks.....209 D9
  N Lincs.........200 C6
Goxhill Haven
  N Lincs.........200 B6
Goybre Neath......57 D9
Goytre Neath......57 D9
Gozzard's Ford Oxon..83 F7
Grabhair W Isles....305 G5
Graby Lincs.......155 D11
Gracca Corn.......5 D9
Gracemount Edin...270 B5
Grade Corn........2 F6
Graffham W Sus....34 D6
Grafham Cambs....122 D3
  Sur............50 E4
Grafton Hereford...97 D9
  N Yorks..........215 G8
  Oxon...........82 E3
  Shrops..........149 F8
  Worcs...........99 D9
  Worcs...........117 F9
Grafton Flyford
  Worcs...........117 F9
Grafton Regis
  W Nhants........102 B5
Grafton Underwood
  N Nhants........137 G8
Grafty Green Kent...53 D11
Grahamston Falk...279 E7
Graianrhyd Denb...166 D2
Graig Carms.......74 E6
  Conwy..........180 G4
  Denb...........181 G9
Graig-Fawr Swansea 75 E10
Graig-fechan Denb ..165 E10
Grain Medway......69 D11
Grains Bar Gtr Man ..196 F3
Grainsby Lincs.....190 B3
Grainthorpe Lincs...190 B5
Grainthorpe Fen
  Lincs............190 B5
Graiselound N Lincs..188 B3
Grampound Corn...5 F8
Grampound Road Corn 5 E8

Gramsdal W Isles...296 F4
Granborough Bucks..102 F5
Granby Notts......154 B5
Grandborough
  Warks...........119 D9
Grandpont Oxon....83 D8
Grandtully Perth....286 B3
Grange Cumb......220 B5
  Dorset..........31 G8
  E Ayrs..........257 B10
  Halton..........183 E8
  Lancs...........203 G7
  Medway.........69 F9
  Mers...........182 D2
  NE Lincs........201 F9
  N Yorks..........223 B6
  Perth...........286 E6
  Warr...........183 D10
Grange Crossroads
  Moray...........302 D4
Grange Estate
  Dorset..........31 G10
Grange Hall Moray..301 C10
Grange Hill
  Durham.........233 F10
  Essex...........86 G6
Grangemill Derbys..170 D2
Grange Moor
  W Yorks.........197 D8
Grangemouth Falk ..279 E8
Grangemuir Fife....287 G9
Grange of Cree
  Dumfries.........236 D6
Grange of Lindores
  Fife............286 F6
Grange-over-Sands
  Cumb...........211 D8
Grangepans Falk....279 E10
Grange Park London..86 F4
Grange Villa
  Durham.........242 G6
Granish Highld.....291 B11
Gransmoor E Yorks ..209 B8
Gransmore Green
  Essex...........106 G3
Granston = Treopert
  Pembs..........91 E7
Grantchester Cambs..123 F8
Grantham Lincs....155 B8
Grantley N Yorks....214 F4
Grantley Hall
  N Yorks..........214 F4
Granton Dumfries...248 B3
  Edin............280 F4
Grantown Aberds...302 D5
Grantown-on-Spey
  Highld...........301 G10
Grantsfield
  Hereford.........115 E10
Grantshouse
  Borders.........272 B6
Grappenhall Warr ..183 D10
Grasby Lincs......200 G5
Grasmere Cumb....220 D6
Grasscroft Gtr Man ..196 G3
Grassendale Mers ..182 D5
Grassgarth Cumb...221 F8
Grassholme Durham 232 G4
Grassington
  N Yorks..........213 G10
Grassmoor Derbys ..170 B6
Grassthorpe Notts...172 B3
Grasswell T&W.....243 G8
Grateley Hants.....47 E9
Gratton Devon.....24 E5
  Staffs...........169 D7
Gratwich Staffs....151 C10
Gravel Ches W......167 B11
Gravel Castle Kent...55 C8
Gravelly Bank Staffs .151 C7
Graveley Cambs....122 E4
  Herts...........104 F4
Gravelhill Shrops...149 G9
Gravel Hill Bucks....85 G8
Gravel Hole
  Gtr Man.........196 F2
Gravelly Hill W Mid..134 E2
Gravels Shrops.....130 C6
Gravelsbank Shrops..130 C6
Graven Shetland....312 F6
Graveney Kent.....70 G5
Gravenhurst Moss
  Shrops..........168 G2
Gravesend Herts....105 F8
  Kent............68 E6
Grayingham Lincs...188 B6
Grayrigg Cumb.....221 F11
Grays Thurrock....68 D6
Grayshott Hants....49 F11
Grayson Green
  Cumb...........228 F5
Graythorp Hrtlpl....234 F6
Grazeley Wokingham..65 F7
Grazeley Green
  W Berks.........65 F7
Greadhubh Lodge
  Highld...........291 D8
Greamchary Highld..310 F2
Greasbrough
  S Yorks..........186 B6
Greasby Mers......182 D3
Greasley Notts.....171 F7
Great Abington
  Cambs..........105 B10
Great Addington
  N Nhants........121 B9
Great Alne Warks...118 F2
Great Altcar Lancs...193 F10

Great Amwell Herts..86 C5
Great Asby Cumb....222 C3
Great Ashfield Suff..125 D9
Great Ashley Wilts...61 G10
Great Ayton
  N Yorks..........225 C11
Great Baddow Essex..88 E2
Great Bardfield Essex 106 E3
Great Barford
  Bedford..........122 G2
Great Barrington
  Glos............82 C2
Great Barrow Ches W..167 B7
Great Barton Suff...125 D7
Great Barugh
  N Yorks..........216 D4
Great Bavington
  Northumb........251 G11
Great Bealings Suff..108 B4
Great Bedwyn Wilts..63 G9
Great Bentley Essex..108 G2
Great Berry Essex...69 B7
Great Billing
  W Nhants........120 E6
Great Bircham Norf..158 C5
Great Blakenham
  Suff............125 B11
Great Blencow
  Cumb...........230 E5
Great Bolas Telford..150 E2
Great Bookham Sur..50 C6
Great Bosullow Corn..1 C4
Great Bourton Oxon..101 B9
Great Bowden Leics..136 F4
Great Bower Kent....54 C4
Great Bradley Suff...124 G3
Great Braxted Essex..88 C5
Great Bricett Suff...125 G10
Great Brickhill
  Bucks...........103 E8
Great Bridge W Mid..133 E9
Great Bridgeford
  Staffs...........151 D7
Great Brington
  W Nhants........120 D3
Great Bromley Essex 107 F11
Great Broughton
  Cumb...........229 E7
  N Yorks..........225 D10
Great Buckland Kent..69 G7
Great Budworth
  Ches W..........183 F11
Great Burdon Darl ..224 B6
Great Burgh Sur....51 B8
Great Burstead
  Essex...........87 G11
Great Busby
  N Yorks..........225 D10
Great Canfield Essex..87 C9
Great Carlton Lincs..190 D6
Great Casterton
  Rutland.........137 B9
Great Cellws
  Powys...........113 E11
Great Chalfield
  Wilts...........61 G11
Great Chart Kent....54 E3
Great Chatwell
  Staffs...........150 G5
Great Chell Stoke...168 E5
Great Chesterford
  Essex...........105 C10
Great Cheverell Wilts .46 C4
Great Chilton
  Durham.........233 F11
Great Chishill
  Cambs..........105 D8
Great Clacton Essex..89 B11
Great Claydons Essex 88 E3
Great Cliff
  W Yorks.........197 D10
Great Clifton Cumb..228 F6
Great Coates
  NE Lincs........201 F7
Great Comberton
  Worcs...........99 C9
Great Common Suff..143 F7
Great Corby Cumb ..239 G11
Great Cornard Suff..107 C7
Great Cowden
  E Yorks..........209 D10
Great Coxwell Oxon..82 G3
Great Crakehall
  N Yorks..........224 G4
Great Cransley
  N Nhants........120 B6
Great Cressingham
  Norf............141 C7
Great Crosby Mers..182 B4
Great Crosthwaite
  Cumb...........229 G11
Great Cubley Derbys .152 B3
Great Dalby Leics...154 G4
Great Denham
  Bedford..........103 B10
Great Doddington
  N Nhants........121 E7
Great Doward
  Hereford.........79 B9
Great Dunham Norf..159 G7
Great Dunmow
  Essex...........106 G2
Great Durnford Wilts .46 F6
Great Easton Essex..106 F2
  Leics............136 E6
Great Eccleston
  Lancs...........202 E4
Great Edstone
  N Yorks..........216 C4
Great Ellingham
  Norf............141 D10
Great Elm Som.....45 D8
Great Eppleton
  T&W............234 B3
Greater Doward
  Hereford.........79 B9

Great Eversden
  Cambs..........123 G7
Great Fencote
  N Yorks..........224 F5
Greatfield Wilts....62 B5
Great Finborough
  Suff............125 F10
Greatford Lincs....155 G11
Great Fransham
  Norf............159 G9
Great Gaddesden
  Herts...........85 C8
Greatgap Bucks....84 B3
Great Gidding
  Cambs..........138 G2
Great Givendale
  E Yorks..........208 C2
Great Glemham
  Suff............126 E6
Great Glen Leics....135 D11
Great Gonerby Lincs..155 B7
Great Gransden
  Cambs..........122 F5
Great Green Cambs..104 C5
  Norf............142 F5
  Suff............125 B11
  Suff............125 F8
  Suff............126 B3
Great Habton
  N Yorks..........216 D5
Great Hale Lincs....173 G10
Great Hallingbury
  Essex...........87 B7
Greatham Hants....49 G9
  Hrtlpl...........234 F5
  W Sus...........35 D8
Great Hampden
  Bucks...........84 E4
Great Harrowden
  N Nhants........121 C7
Great Harwood
  Lancs...........203 G10
Great Haseley Oxon..83 E11
Great Hatfield
  E Yorks..........209 E9
Great Haywood
  Staffs...........151 E11
Great Heath W Mid..134 G6
Great Heck N Yorks..198 C5
Great Henny Essex..107 D7
Great Hinton Wilts...46 B2
Great Hivings Bucks..85 E7
Great Hockham
  Norf............141 E9
Great Holcombe
  Oxon...........83 G11
Great Holland Essex .89 B12
Great Hollands
  Brack...........65 F11
Great Holm
  M Keynes........102 D6
Great Honeyborough
  Pembs..........73 D7
Great Horkesley
  Essex...........107 E9
Great Hormead
  Herts...........105 E7
Great Horton
  W Yorks.........205 G8
Great Horwood
  Bucks...........102 E5
Great Houghton
  S Yorks..........198 F2
  W Nhants........120 F5
Great Howarth
  Gtr Man.........196 D2
Great Hucklow
  Derbys..........185 F11
Great Job's Cross
  Kent............38 B4
Great Kelk E Yorks ..209 B8
Great Kendale
  E Yorks..........217 G10
Great Kimble Bucks..84 D4
Great Kingshill Bucks .84 F5
Great Langton
  N Yorks..........224 F5
Great Lea Common
  Reading.........65 F8
Great Leighs Essex..88 B2
Great Lever Gtr Man..195 F8
Great Limber Lincs...200 F6
Great Linford
  M Keynes........103 C7
Great Livermere
  Suff............125 C7
Great Longstone
  Derbys..........186 G2
Great Lumley
  Durham.........233 B11
Great Lyth Shrops...131 B9
Great Malgraves
  Thurrock.........69 C7
Great Malvern Worcs .98 B5
Great Maplestead
  Essex...........106 E6
Great Marton
  Blackpool........202 F2
Great Marton Moss
  Blackpool........202 G2
Great Massingham
  Norf............158 E5
Great Melton Norf..142 B2
Great Milton Oxon..83 E10
Great Missenden
  Bucks...........84 E5
Great Mitton Lancs..203 F10
Great Mongeham
  Kent............55 C10
Greatmoor Bucks...102 G4
Great Moor
  Gtr Man.........184 D6
  Staffs...........132 D6
Great Moulton Norf..142 E3
Great Munden
  Herts...........105 G7
Great Musgrave
  Cumb...........222 C5
Greatness Kent.....52 B4

Great Ness Shrops . . .149 F7
Great Notley Essex . .106 G4
Great Oak Mon 78 D5
Great Oakley Essex . .108 F3
N Nhants 137 F7
Great Offley Herts . .104 F2
Great Ormside
Cumb 222 B4
Great Orton Cumb . .239 G8
Great Ouseburn
N Yorks 215 G8
Great Oxendon
W Nhants 136 G4
Great Oxney Green
Essex 87 D11
Great Palgrave Norf 158 G6
Great Parndon Essex . .86 D6
Great Pattenden
Kent 53 E8
Great Paxton Cambs .122 E4
Great Plumpton
Lancs 202 G3
Great Plumstead
Norf 160 G6
Great Ponton Lincs .155 C8
Great Preston
W Yorks 198 B2
Great Purston
W Nhants 101 D10
Great Raveley
Cambs 138 G5
Great Rissington
Glos 81 B11
Great Rollright
Oxon 100 E6
Great Ryburgh Norf .159 D9
Great Ryle Northumb 264 G2
Great Ryton Shrops .131 C9
Great Saling Essex . .106 F4
Great Salkeld Cumb .231 D7
Great Sampford
Essex 106 D2
Great Sankey Warr .183 D9
Great Saredon
Staffs 133 B9
Great Saxham Suff .124 E5
Great Shefford
W Berks 63 E11
Great Shelford
Cambs 123 G9
Great Shoddesden
Hants 47 D9
Great Smeaton
N Yorks 224 E6
Great Snoring Norf .159 C8
Great Somerford
Wilts 62 C2
Great Stainton Darl .234 G2
Great Stambridge
Essex 88 G5
Great Staughton
Cambs 122 E2
Great Steeping
Lincs 174 C6
Great Stoke S Glos . .60 C6
Great Stonar Kent . .55 B10
Greatstone-on-Sea
Kent 39 C9
Great Stretton Leics .136 C4
Great Strickland
Cumb 231 G7
Great Stukeley
Cambs 122 C4
Great Sturton Lincs .190 F2
Great Sutton
Ches W 182 F5
Shrops 131 G10
Great Swinburne
Northumb 241 B10
Great Tew Oxon 101 F7
Great Tey Essex 107 F7
Great Thirkleby
N Yorks 215 D9
Great Thurlow Suff .124 G3
Great Torrington
Devon 25 D7
Great Tosson
Northumb 252 C2
Great Totham Essex . .88 C5
Great Tows Lincs . . .190 C2
Great Tree Corn 6 D5
Great Urswick Cumb .210 E5
Great Wakering
Essex 70 B2
Great Waldingfield
Suff 107 C8
Great Walsingham
Norf 159 B8
Great Waltham
Essex 87 C11
Great Warley Essex . .87 G9
Great Washbourne
Glos 99 E9
Great Weeke Devon . .13 D10
Great Weldon
N Nhants 137 F8
Great Welnetham
Suff 125 F7
Great Wenham
Suff 107 D11
Great Whittington
Northumb 242 C2
Great Wigborough
Essex 89 C7
Great Wilbraham
Cambs 123 F10
Great Wilne Derbys .153 C8
Great Wishford Wilts. .46 F5
Great Witchingham
Norf 160 E2
Great Witcombe Glos .80 C6
Great Witley Worcs .116 D5
Great Wolford
Warks 100 E4
Greatworth
W Nhants 101 C11
Great Wratting Suff .106 B3
Great Wymondley
Herts 104 F4
Great Wyrley Staffs .133 B9
Great Wytheford
Shrops 149 F11

Great Yarmouth
Norf 143 B10
Great Yeldham
Essex 106 D5
Greave Gtr Man 184 C6
Lancs 195 C11
Grebby Lincs 174 B6
Greeba IoM 192 D4
Green Denb 165 B9
Pembs 73 E7
Powys 130 E5
Greenacres Gtr Man .196 F2
Greenan Argyll 275 G11
Greenbank
Ches W 183 G10
Falk 279 F7
Shetland 312 C7
Green Bank Cumb . .211 C7
Green Bottom Corn . . .4 F5
Glos 79 B11
Greenburn W Loth . .269 C8
Green Close
N Yorks 212 F4
Green Clough
N Yorks 204 F5
Greencroft Durham .242 G5
Green Cross Sur 49 F11
Greendale Ches E . . .184 F5
Greendikes
Northumb 264 D3
Greendown Som 44 C5
Green Down Devon . .28 G3
Greendykes
Northumb 264 D3
Green End Bedford .103 B10
Bedford 121 E11
Bedford 122 E2
Bedford 122 G2
Bucks 84 F4
Bucks 103 B8
Cambs 122 C4
Cambs 123 F7
C Beds 103 D11
Herts 85 D8
Herts 104 E5
Herts 104 E6
Herts 104 G6
Herts 105 F7
N Yorks 204 D4
N Yorks 226 E6
Warks 134 F5
Greenfaulds
N Lanark 278 G5
Greenfield C Beds . .103 E11
Glasgow 268 C2
Gtr Man 196 G3
Highld 289 D11
Highld 290 C4
Oxon 84 G2
Greenfield = Maes-Glas
Flint 181 F11
Greenfoot N Lanark .268 B4
Greenford London . . .66 C6
Greengairs
N Lanark 278 G5
Greengarth Hall
Cumb 219 E11
Greengate Gtr Man .196 D2
Green Gate Devon . . .27 D8
Greengates
W Yorks 205 F9
Greengill Cumb 229 D8
Green Hailey Bucks . .84 E4
Greenhalgh Lancs . .202 F4
Greenhall S Lanark .268 D3
Greenham Dorset . . .28 G6
Som 27 C9
W Berks 64 F3
Green Hammerton
N Yorks 206 B5
Greenhaugh
Northumb 251 F7
Green Haworth
Lancs 195 B9
Greenhead
Borders 261 D11
Dumfries 247 D9
N Lanark 268 E6
Northumb 240 D5
Staffs 169 F7
Green Head Cumb . .230 B3
Green Heath Staffs .151 G9
Greenheys Gtr Man .195 G8
Greenhill Dumfries .238 B4
Durham 234 B3
Falk 278 F6
Hereford 98 B4
Kent 71 F7
Leics 153 G8
London 67 B7
S Yorks 186 E4
Worcs 116 B6
Green Hill Kent 53 C9
Lincs 155 B8
Wilts 62 B5
Greenhill Bank
Shrops 149 B7
Greenhillocks
Derbys 170 F6
Greenhills N Ayrs . .267 E7
S Lanark 268 E2
Greenhithe Kent 68 E5
Greenholm E Ayrs . .258 G2
Greenholme Cumb . .221 D11
Greenhouse Borders .262 E3
Greenhow N Yorks . .214 G2
Greenigoe Orkney . .314 F4
Greenland Highld . .310 C6
Greenland Mains
Highld 310 C6
Greenlands Bucks . . .65 B9
Worcs 117 D11

Green Lane Devon . . .13 F11
Hereford 98 B2
Powys 130 D3
Warks 117 E11
Warks 118 B6
Greenlaw Aberds . . .302 D6
Borders 272 F4
Greenlaw Mains
Midloth 270 C4
Greenlea Dumfries . .238 B2
Greenley M Keynes . .102 D6
Greenloaning Perth .286 G2
Greenlooms
Ches W 167 C7
Greenman's Lane
Wilts 62 C3
Greenmeadow
Swindon 62 B6
Torf 78 F3
Greenmount
Gtr Man 195 E9
Greenmow Shetland .313 L6
Greenoak E Yorks . .199 B10
Green Ore Som 44 C5
Green Parlour Bath . .45 C8
Green Quarter
Cumb 221 D9
Greenrigg W Loth . .269 C8
Greenrow Cumb 238 G4
Greens Borders 249 F11
Green St Green
London 68 G3
Greensforge Staffs . .133 F7
Greensgate Norf . . .160 F2
Greenside Cumb . . .222 E4
Derbys 186 F5
Gtr Man 184 B6
T&W 242 E4
W Yorks 197 D7
W Yorks 205 G11
Green Side W Yorks .197 E7
Greensidehill
Northumb 263 F11
Greens Norton
W Nhants 102 B3
Greensplat Corn 5 D9
Greenstead Essex . .107 F10
Greenstead Green
Essex 106 F6
Greensted Essex 87 E8
Greensted Green
Essex 87 E8
Green Street Essex . .87 F10
E Sus 38 E3
Glos 80 B5
Glos 80 E3
Herts 85 F11
Herts 105 G9
Worcs 99 B7
Worcs 99 C7
W Sus 35 C10
Green Street Green
Kent 68 E5
London 68 G3
Green Tye Herts 86 B6
Greenway Hereford . .98 E4
Pembs 91 E11
Som 27 B11
V Glam 58 E5
York 207 C8
Greenwich Common
Corn 4 G5
Greenwoods Essex . .87 F11
Greenwray Orkney . .314 D2
Greep Highld 298 E2
Greet Glos 99 E10
Greete Shrops 115 C11
Greetham Lincs 190 G4
Rutland 155 G8
Greetland W Yorks . .196 C5
Greetland Wall Nook
W Yorks 196 C5
Greetwell N Lincs . .200 D4
Gregg Hall Cumb . . .221 G9
Gregson Lane Lancs .194 B5
Gregynog Powys . . .129 D11
Grèin W Isles 297 L2
Greinetobht
W Isles 296 D4
Greinton Som 44 F2
Gremista Shetland . .313 J6
Grenaby IoM 192 E3
Grendon N Nhants . .121 E7
Warks 134 C5
Grendon Bishop
Hereford 115 F11
Grendon Common
Warks 134 D5
Grendon Green
Hereford 115 F11
Grendon Underwood
Bucks 102 G3
Grenofen Devon 12 G5
Grenoside S Yorks . .186 C4
Greosabhagh
W Isles 305 J3
Gresford Wrex 166 E5
Gresham Norf 160 B3
Greshornish Highld .298 D3
Gressenhall Norf . . .159 F9
Gressingham Lancs .211 F11
Gresty Green
Ches E 168 G2
Greta Bridge
Durham 223 C11
Gretna Dumfries . . .239 D8
Gretna Green
Dumfries 239 D8
Gretton Glos 99 E10

Gretton continued
N Nhants 137 E7
Shrops 131 D10
Gretton Fields Glos . .99 E10
Grewelthorpe
N Yorks 214 D4
Greyfield Bath 44 B6
Greygarth N Yorks . .214 E3
Grey Green N Lincs . .199 F9
Greylake Som 43 G11
Greylake Fosse Som . .44 F2
Greynor Carms 75 D9
Greynor-isaf Carms . .75 D9
Greyrigg Dumfries . .248 F3
Greys Green Oxon . . .65 B8
Greysouthen Corn . .229 F7
Greystead Northumb .250 F4
Greystoke Cumb . . .230 E4
Greystoke Gill Cumb .230 F4
Greystone Aberds . . .292 D6
Aberds 302 F6
Angus 287 C9
Cumb 211 D10
Oxon 82 G6
Pembs 73 E7
Greystonegill
N Yorks 212 F3
Greystones S Yorks . .186 D4
Warks 99 B11
Warks 134 D3
Greytree Hereford . . .97 F11
Greywell Hants 49 C8
Griais W Isles 304 D6
Grianan W Isles 304 E6
Gribb Dorset 28 G5
Gribthorpe E Yorks .207 F11
Gridley Corner Devon .12 C3
Griff Warks 135 F7
Griffin's Hill W Mid .133 G10
Griffithstown Torf . . .78 F3
Griffydam Leics 153 F8
Grigg Kent 53 E11
Griggs Green Hants . .49 G10
Grillis Corn 2 B5
Grilstone Devon 26 C2
Grimbister Orkney . .314 E3
Grimblethorpe
Lincs 190 D2
Grimeford Village
Lancs 194 E6
Grimes Hill Worcs . .117 B11
Grimesthorpe
S Yorks 186 C5
Grimethorpe
S Yorks 198 F2
Griminis W Isles . . .296 D3
W Isles 296 F3
Grimister Shetland . .312 D6
Grimley Worcs 116 E6
Grimness Orkney . . .314 G4
Grimoldby Lincs 190 D5
Grimpo Shrops 149 D7
Grimsargh Lancs . . .203 G7
Grimsbury Oxon 101 C9
Grimsby NE Lincs . .201 E9
Grimscote
W Nhants 120 G3
Grimscott Corn 24 F3
Grimshaw Blackburn .195 C8
Grimshaw Green
Lancs 194 E3
Grimsthorpe
Lincs 155 E10
Grimston E Yorks . .209 F11
Leics 154 E3
Norf 158 E4
York 207 C8
Grimstone Dorset . . .17 C8
Grimstone End Suff .125 D8
Grinacombe Moor
Devon 12 C4
Grindale E Yorks . . .218 E2
Grindigar Orkney . . .314 F5
Grindiscol Shetland .313 K6
Grindle Shrops 132 C5
Grindleford Derbys .186 F2
Grindleton Lancs . . .203 D11
Grindley Staffs 151 D11
Grindley Brook
Shrops 167 G8
Grindlow Derbys . . .185 F11
Grindon Northumb . .273 G8
Staffs 169 E9
Stockton 234 F3
T&W 243 D8
Grindonmoor Gate
Staffs 169 E9
Grindsbrook Booth
Derbys 185 E10
Gringley on the Hill
Notts 188 C2
Grinsdale Cumb 239 F9
Grinshill Shrops 149 E10
Grinton N Yorks 223 F10
Griomasaigh
W Isles 297 G4
Griomsidar W Isles . .304 F5
Grisdale Cumb 222 G5
Grishipoll Argyll . . .288 D3
Grisling Common
E Sus 36 C6
Gristhorpe
N Yorks 217 C11
Griston Norf 141 D8
Gritley Orkney 314 F5
Grittenham Wilts . . .62 C4
Grittleton Wilts 61 C11
Grizebeck Cumb 210 C4
Grizedale Cumb 220 G6
Groam Highld 300 E5
Grobister Orkney . . .314 D6
Grobsness Shetland .313 G5
Groby Leics 135 B10
Groes Conwy 165 C8
Neath 57 D9
Groes Efa Denb 165 B10
Groes-faen Rhondda . .58 C5
Groes-fawr Denb . . .165 B10
Groesffordd Gwyn . .144 B5
Powys 95 F11
Groesffordd Marli
Denb 181 G8
Gretton Glos 99 E10
Groeslon Gwyn 163 C8

Groeslon continued
Gwyn 163 D7
Groes-lwyd Mon 96 G6
Powys 148 G4
Groespluan Powys . .130 B4
Groes-wen Caerph . . .58 B6
Grogport Argyll 255 C7
Gromford Suff 127 F7
Gronant Flint 181 E9
Gronwen Shrops 148 D5
Grosmont Mon 97 G8
N Yorks 226 D6
Gross Green Warks . .119 F7
Grotaig Highld 300 G4
Groton Suff 107 C9
Grotton Gtr Man 196 G3
Groucott Falk 279 F10
Grove Bucks 103 G8
Dorset 17 G10
Hereford 98 C2
Kent 71 G8
Notts 188 F2
Oxon 82 G6
Pembs 73 E7
Grove End Kent 69 G11
Warks 100 D6
Warks 134 D3
Grove Green Kent . . .53 B9
Grovehill E Yorks . .208 F6
Herts 85 D9
Grove Hill E Sus 23 C10
Kent 71 G8
Grove Park London . .67 D8
London 68 E2
Groves Kent 55 B9
Grovesend Swansea . .75 E9
Grove Town
N Yorks 198 C3
Grove Vale W Mid . .133 E10
Grubb Street Kent . . .68 F5
Grub Street Staffs . .150 D5
Grudie Highld 300 C3
Gruids Highld 309 J5
Gruinard House
Highld 307 K4
Gruinards Highld . . .309 K5
Grula Highld 294 C5
Gruline Argyll 289 E7
Gruline Ho Argyll . .289 E7
Grumbeg Highld . . .308 F6
Grumbla Corn 1 D4
Grunasound
Shetland 313 K5
Grundisburgh Suff . .126 G3
Grunsagill Lancs . . .203 C11
Gruting Shetland . . .313 J4
Grutness Shetland . .313 N6
Gryn Goch Gwyn . . .162 F6
Gualachulain Highld .284 C5
Gualin Ho Highld . .308 D3
Guardbridge Fife . . .287 F8
Guard House
W Yorks 204 E6
Guarlford Worcs 98 B6
Guay Perth 286 C4
Gubbion's Green
Essex 88 B2
Gubblecote Herts . . .84 C6
Guesachan Highld . .289 B10
Guestling Green
E Sus 38 E4
Guestling Thorn
E Sus 38 D4
Guestwick Norf 159 D11
Guestwick Green
Norf 159 D11
Guide Blackburn . . .195 B8
Guide Bridge
Gtr Man 184 B6
Guide Post
Northumb 253 F7
Guilden Morden
Cambs 104 C5
Guilden Sutton
Ches W 166 B6
Guildford Sur 50 D3
Guildford Park Sur . .50 D3
Guildiehaugh
W Loth 269 B9
Guildtown Perth 286 D5
Guilsborough
W Nhants 120 C3
Guilsfield = Cegidfa
Powys 148 G4
Guilthwaite S Yorks .187 D7
Guilton Kent 55 B9
Guineaford Devon . . .40 F5
Guisachan Highld . .300 G3
Guisborough Redcar .226 B2
Guiseley W Yorks . .205 E9
Guist Norf 159 D9
Guith Orkney 314 C5
Guiting Power Glos . .99 G11
Gulberwick Shetland .313 K6
Gullane E Loth 281 E9
Guller's End Worcs . .99 D7
Gulling Green Suff . .124 F6
Gullom Holme Cumb .231 F9
Gulval Corn 1 C5
Gulworthy Devon . . .12 G4
Gumfreston Pembs . .73 E10
Gumley Leics 136 E3
Gummow's Shop Corn . .5 D7
Gunby E Yorks 207 F10
Lincs 155 E8
Lincs 175 B7
Gundenham Som 27 C10
Gundleton Hants 48 G6
Gun Green Kent 53 G9
Gun Hill E Sus 23 C9
Gunn Devon 40 G6
Gunnersbury London .67 D7
Gunnerside N Yorks .223 F9
Gunnerton
Northumb 241 C10
Gunness N Lincs . . .199 E10
Gunnislake Corn 12 G4
Gunnista Shetland . .313 J7
Gunstone Staffs 133 C7
Gunter's Bridge
W Sus 35 C7
Gunthorpe Lincs . . .188 B5
Norf 159 C10
Notts 171 G11
Pboro. 138 C3
Rutland 137 B7
Gunton Suff 143 D10
Gunville IoW 20 D5
Gunwalloe Corn 2 E5
Gunwalloe Fishing Cove
Corn. 2 E5
Gupworthy Som 42 F3
Gurnard IoW 20 B5
Gurnett Ches E 184 G6
Gurney Slade Som . . .44 D6
Gurnos M Tydf 77 D8
Gushmere Kent 54 B4
Gussage All Saints
Dorset 31 E8
Gussage St Andrew
Dorset 31 E7
Gussage St Michael
Dorset 31 E7
Gustard Wood Herts .85 B11
Guston Kent 55 E10
Gutcher Shetland . . .312 D7
Guthram Gowt Lincs .156 E3
Guthrie Angus 287 B9
Guyhirn Cambs 139 C7
Guyhirn Gull Cambs .139 C7
Guy's Cliffe Warks . .118 D5
Guy's Head Lincs . . .157 D9
Guy's Marsh Dorset . .30 C4
Guyzance Northumb .252 C6
Gwaelod-y-garth
Cardiff 58 C6
Gwaenysgor Flint . .181 E9
Gwalchmai Anglesey .178 F5
Gwalchmai Uchaf
Anglesey 178 F5
Gwallon Corn 2 C1
Gwastad Pembs 91 G10
Gwastadgoed
Gwyn 145 G11
Gwastadnant
Gwyn 163 D10
Gwaun-Cae-Gurwen
Neath. 76 C2
Gwaun-Leision
Neath. 76 C2
Gwavas Corn 2 D5
Corn. 2 G6
Gwbert Ceredig 92 B3
Gwedna Corn 2 C4
Gweek Corn 2 D6
Gwehelog Mon 78 E5
Gwenddwr Powys . . .95 C11
Gwennap Corn 2 B6
Gwennap Pit Corn . . .2 B6
Gwenter Corn 2 F6
Gwernaffield-y-Waun
Flint 166 C2
Gwernafon Powys . .129 E8
Gwerneirin Powys . .129 F10
Powys 130 G3
Gwernesney Mon . . .78 E6
Gwernogle Carms . . .93 E10
Gwernol Denb 166 C2
Gwern y brenin
Shrops 148 D6
Gwernymynydd
Flint 166 C2
Gwern-y-Steeple
V Glam 58 D5
Gwersyllt Wrex 166 E4
Gwespyr Flint 181 E10
Gwills Corn 4 D6
Gwinear Corn 2 B3
Gwinear Downs Corn . .2 A3
Gwithian Corn 2 A3
Gwredog Anglesey . .178 D6
Gwrhay Caerph 77 F11
Gwyddelwern Denb .165 F9
Gwyddgrug Carms . .93 D9
Gwynfryn Wrex 166 E3
Gwystre Powys 113 D11
Gwytherin Conwy . .164 C5
Gyfelia Wrex 166 F4
Gyffin Conwy 180 F3
Gylen Park Argyll . .289 G10
Gyre Orkney 314 F3
Gyrn Denb 165 D11
Gyrn-goch Gwyn . . .162 F6

H

Habberley Shrops . . .131 C7
Worcs 116 B6
Habergham Lancs . .204 G2
Habertoft Lincs 175 B8
Habin W Sus 34 C4
Habrough NE Lincs . .200 E6
Haccombe Devon . . .14 G3
Haceby Lincs 155 B10
Hacheston Suff 126 F6
Hackbridge London . .67 F9
Hackenthorpe
S Yorks 186 E6
Hackford Norf 141 C11
Hackforth N Yorks . .224 G4
Hack Green
Ches E 167 F10
Hackland Orkney . . .314 D3
Hackleton W Nhants .120 F6
Hacklinge Kent 55 C10
Hackman's Gate
Worcs 117 B7
Hackness N Yorks . .227 G9
Orkney 314 G3
Hackney London 67 C10
Hackney Wick
London 67 C11
Hackthorn Lincs 189 E7
Hackthorpe Cumb . .230 G6
Haclait W Isles 297 G4
Haconby Lincs 156 D2
Hacton London 68 B4

Gre-Hal 387

Hales Green continued
Norf 143 D7
Halesowen W Mid . .133 G9
Hales Park Worcs . .116 B5
Hales Street Norf . . .142 F3
Hales Wood Hereford . .98 D3
Halesworth Suff . . .127 C7
Hale Street Kent 53 D7
Halewood Mers 183 D7
Half Moon Village
Devon 14 B3
Halford Shrops 131 G8
Warks 100 B5
Halfpenny Cumb . . .211 B10
Halfpenny Furze
Carms 74 C3
Halfpenny Green
Staffs 132 E6
Halfway Carms 75 C8
Carms 94 E2
Carms 94 E6
S Yorks 186 E6
W Berks 64 F3
Wilts 45 D11
Halfway Bridge
W Sus 34 C6
Halfway House
Shrops 148 G6
Halfway Houses
Gtr Man 195 F9
Kent 70 E2
Halfway Street Kent . .55 E9
Halgabron Corn 11 D7
Halifax W Yorks . . .196 B5
Halkburn Borders . .271 G9
Halket E Ayrs 267 E8
Halkirk Highld 310 D5
Halkyn = Helygain
Flint 182 G2
Halkyn Mountain
Flint 182 G2
Hallam Fields
Derbys 153 B9
Halland E Sus 23 B8
Hallaton Leics 136 D5
Hallatrow Bath 44 B6
Hallbankgate Cumb .240 F3
Hall Bower W Yorks .196 E6
Hall Broom S Yorks .186 D3
Hall Cross Lancs . . .202 G4
Hall Dunnerdale
Cumb 220 F4
Halleaths Dumfries . .248 G3
Hallen S Glos 60 C5
Hallend Warks 118 D2
Hall End Bedford . . .103 B10
C Beds 103 D11
Lincs 174 E6
S Glos 61 B8
Warks 134 C5
Hallew Corn 5 D10
Hallfield Gate
Derbys 170 D5
Hall Flat Worcs 117 C9
Hallgarth Durham . .234 C2
Hall Garth York 207 C9
Hallglen Falk 279 F7
Hall Green Ches E . .168 D4
Essex 106 D5
Lancs 194 C3
Lancs 194 F4
W Mid 133 G10
W Mid 134 G2
Wrex 167 G7
W Yorks 197 D10
Hall Grove Herts 89 C8
Halliburton
Borders 261 B11
Borders 272 F3
Hallin Highld 298 D2
Halling Medway 69 G8
Hallingbury Street
Essex 87 B8
Hallington Lincs . . .190 D4
Northumb 241 B11
Hall i' th' Wood
Gtr Man 195 E8
Halliwell Gtr Man . .195 E8
Hall of Clestrain
Orkney 314 F2
Hall of Tankerness
Orkney 314 F5
Hall of the Forest
Shrops 130 G4
Hallon Shrops 132 D5
Hallonsford Shrops . .132 D5
Halloughton Notts . .171 E11
Hallow Worcs 116 F6
Hallowes Derbys . . .186 F5
Hallow Heath Worcs .116 F6
Hallowsgate
Ches W 167 B8
Hallrule Borders . . .262 G3
Halls E Loth 282 G3
Hallsands Devon 9 G11
Hall Santon Cumb . .220 E2
Hall's Cross E Sus . . .23 D11
Hallsford Bridge
Essex 87 E9
Halls Green Essex . . .86 D6
Hall's Green Herts . . .104 F5
Kent 52 D4
Hallspill Devon 25 C7
Hallthwaites Cumb. .210 B3
Hall Waberthwaite
Cumb 220 F2
Hallwood Green
Glos 98 E3
Hallworthy Corn 11 D9
Hallyards Borders . .260 B6
Hallyburton House
Perth 286 D6
Hallyne Borders . . .270 G3
Halmer End Staffs . .168 F3
Halmond's Frome
Hereford 98 B3
Halmore Glos 79 E11

Halmyre Mains
Borders 270 F3
Halnaker W Sus . . . 22 B6
Halsall Lancs . . .193 E11
Halse Som. 27 B10
W Nhants 101 C11
Halsetown Corn 2 B2
Halsfordwood Devon.14 C3
Halsham E Yorks . .201 B9
Halsinger Devon . . .40 F4
Halstead Essex . . .106 E6
Kent. 68 G3
Leics 136 B4
Halstock Dorset. . .29 F8
Halsway Som 42 F6
Haltcliff Bridge
Cumb 230 D3
Halterworth Hants. .32 C5
Haltham Lincs 174 C2
Haltoft End Lincs. .174 F5
Halton Bucks 84 C5
Halton 183 E8
Lancs 211 G10
Northumb 241 D11
Wrex 148 B6
W Yorks 206 G2
Halton Barton Corn . 7 B8
Halton Brook Halton .183 E8
Halton East N Yorks .204 C6
Halton Fenside
Lincs 174 C6
Halton Gill N Yorks . 213 D7
Halton Green
Lancs. 211 F10
Halton Holegate
Lincs 174 B6
Halton Lea Gate
Northumb 240 F5
Halton Moor
W Yorks 206 G2
Halton Shields
Northumb 242 D2
Halton View Halton . 183 D8
Halton West
N Yorks 204 C2
Haltwhistle
Northumb 240 E6
Halvergate Norf . . .143 B8
Halvosso Corn 2 C6
Halwell Devon 8 E5
Halwill Devon 12 B4
Halwill Junction
Devon. 24 G6
Halwin Corn 2 C5
Ham Devon 28 G2
Glos 79 F11
Glos 99 G9
Highld 310 B6
Kent. 55 C10
London. 67 E7
Plym 7 D9
Shetland 313 K1
Som 27 C11
Som 28 B3
Som 28 E3
Som 45 D7
Wilts 63 G10
Hamar Shetland . .312 F5
Hamarhill Orkney . .314 G5
Hamars Shetland . .313 G6
Hambleden Bucks. . .65 B9
Hambledon Hants . .33 E10
Sur. 50 F3
Hamble-le-Rice
Hants. 33 F7
Hambleton Lancs . .202 E3
N Yorks. 205 C7
N Yorks. 205 C7
Hambleton Moss Side
Lancs. 202 E3
Hambridge Som . . .28 C5
Hambrook S Glos . . .60 D5
W Sus 22 B3
Ham Common Dorset .30 B4
Hameringham Lincs. .174 B4
Hamerton Cambs . .122 B2
Hametoun Shetland .313 K1
Ham Green Bucks. . .83 B11
Hants. 48 G2
Hereford 98 C4
Kent. 38 B5
Kent. 69 F10
N Som 60 D4
Wilts 61 G11
Worcs 117 E10
Ham Hill Kent. 69 G8
Hamilton S Lanark. .268 D3
Hamister Shetland. .313 G7
Hamlet Dorset 29 F9
Hammer W Sus 49 G11
Hammer Bottom
Hants. 49 G11
Hammerfield Herts. .85 D8
Hammerpot W Sus . .35 F9
Hammersmith
Derbys. 170 E5
London. 67 D8
Hammerwich
Staffs. 133 B11
Hammerwood E Sus. .52 F2
Hammill Kent. 55 B9
Hammond Street
Herts. 86 E4
Hammoon Dorset . .30 E4
Ham Moor Sur. 66 G5
Hamnavoe
Shetland 312 E4
Shetland 312 E6
Shetland 312 F6
Shetland 313 K5
Hamnish Clifford
Hereford 115 F10
Hamp Som 43 F10
Hampden Park
E Sus 23 E10
Hampen Glos 81 B9
Hamperden End
Essex 105 E11
Hamperley Shrops . .131 F8

Hampers Green
W Sus 35 C7
Hampeth Northumb. .252 B5
Hampnett Glos 81 B10
Hampole S Yorks . .198 E4
Hampreston Dorset . .19 B7
Hampsfield Cumb . .211 C8
Hampson Green
Lancs. 202 C5
Hampstead London. .67 B9
Hampstead Garden
Suburb London . . .67 B9
Hampstead Norreys
W Berks 64 D4
Hampsthwaite
N Yorks 205 B11
Hampton Kent. 71 F7
London. 66 F6
Shrops. 132 F4
Swindon. 81 G11
Worcs 99 C10
Hampton Bank
Shrops. 149 C9
Hampton Beech
Shrops. 130 B6
Hampton Bishop
Hereford 97 D11
Hampton Fields Glos. .80 F5
Hampton Gay Oxon. .83 B7
Hampton Green
Ches W. 167 F8
Glos 80 E5
Hampton Hargate
Pboro. 138 E3
Hampton Heath
Ches W. 167 F7
Hampton Hill London. .66 F6
Hampton in Arden
W Mid 134 G4
Hampton Loade
Shrops. 132 F5
Hampton Lovett
Worcs 117 D7
Hampton Lucy
Warks 118 F5
Hampton Magna
Warks 118 D5
Hampton on the Hill
Warks 118 D5
Hampton Park
Hereford 97 D10
Soton. 32 D6
Hampton Poyle Oxon. .83 B8
Hamptons Kent. . . .52 C6
Hampton Wick
London. 67 F7
Hamptworth Wilts. .32 D2
Hamrow Norf 159 E8
Hamsey E Sus 36 E6
Hamsey Green
London. 51 B10
Hamshill Glos 80 D3
Hamstall Ridware
Staffs. 152 F2
Hamstead IoW 20 C4
W Mid 133 E10
Hamstead Marshall
W Berks 64 F2
Hamsterley Durham. .233 E8
Durham. 242 F4
Hamstreet Kent. . . .54 G4
Ham Street Som . . .44 G5
Hamworthy BCP . . .18 C5
Hanbury Staffs . . .152 D3
Worcs 117 E9
Hanbury Woodend
Staffs. 152 D3
Hanby Lincs 155 C10
Hanchett Village
Suff 106 B3
Hanchurch Staffs . .168 G4
Handbridge Ches W. .166 B6
Handcross W Sus . . .36 B3
Handforth Ches E . .184 E5
Hand Green
Ches W. 167 C8
Handless Shrops . .131 E7
Handley Ches W. . . .167 D7
Derbys. 170 C5
Handley Green
Essex 87 E11
Handsacre Staffs . .151 F11
Handside Herts. . . .86 C2
Handsworth
S Yorks 186 D6
W Mid 133 E10
Handsworth Wood
W Mid 133 E11
Handy Cross Bucks. .84 G5
Devon. 24 B6
Som 42 G6
Hanford Dorset . . .30 E4
Stoke. 168 G5
Hangersley Hants. .31 F11
Hanging Bank Kent. .52 C3
Hanging Heaton
W Yorks 197 C9
Hanging Houghton
N Nhants. 120 C5
Hanging Langford
Wilts 46 F4
Hangingshaw
Borders 261 C9
Dumfries 248 F4
Hangleton Brighton . .36 F3
W Sus 35 G9
Hangsman Hill
S Yorks 199 E7
Hanham S Glos. . . .60 E6
Hanham Green
S Glos. 60 E6
Hankelow Ches E. . .167 F11
Hankerton Wilts . . .81 G7
Hankham E Sus 23 D10
Hanley Stoke 168 F5
Hanley Castle Worcs. .98 C6
Hanley Child Worcs. .116 E3
Hanley Swan Worcs. .98 C6
Hanley William
Worcs 116 D3
Hanlith N Yorks . . .213 G8
Hanmer Wrex 149 B9

Hannaford Devon . .25 B10
Hannacroft Corn . . . 6 E5
Hannah Lincs 191 F8
Hanningfields Green
Suff 125 G7
Hannington Hants . .48 B4
Swindon. 81 G11
W Nhants 120 C6
Hannington Wick
Swindon. 81 F11
Hanscombe End
C Beds 104 E2
Devon. 8 F6
Hansel Village
S Ayrs 257 C9
Hansley Cross
Staffs. 169 D7
Hanslope M Keynes. .102 B6
Hanthorpe Lincs . .155 E11
Hanwell London. . . .67 C7
Oxon 101 C8
Hanwood Shrops. . .131 B8
Hanwood Bank
Shrops. 149 G8
Norf. 66 E6
Norf. 160 B3
Happendon
S Lanark. 259 C9
Happisburgh Norf . .161 C7
Happisburgh Common
Norf. 161 D7
Hapsford Ches W . .183 G7
Som 45 D9
Hapton Lancs 203 G11
Norf 142 D3
Harberton Devon . . . 8 E5
Harbertonford Devon . 8 D5
Harbledown Kent. . .54 B6
Harborne W Mid . .133 G10
Harborough Magna
Warks 119 B9
Harborough Parva
Warks 119 B9
Harbottle
Northumb 251 C10
Harbour Heights
E Sus 36 G6
Harbourland Kent. . .53 B9
Harbourneford Devon. 8 C4
Harbours Hill
Worcs 117 D9
Harbour Village
Pembs 91 D8
Harbridge Hants . . .31 E11
Harbridge Green
Hants. 31 E10
Harburn W Loth . .269 C10
Harbury Warks . . .119 F7
Harby Leics 154 C4
Notts 188 G5
Harcombe Devon . .14 E3
Devon. 15 C9
Harcourt Corn 3 B8
Harcourt Hill Oxon. .83 E7
Hardbreck Orkney . .314 F4
Hardeicke Glos 80 C4
Harden S Yorks . . .197 G7
W Yorks 205 F7
Hardendale Cumb. .221 C11
Harden Park Ches E .184 F4
Hardgate Aberds . .293 C9
Dumfries 237 C10
N Yorks 214 G5
W Dunb 277 G10
Hardham W Sus . . .35 D8
Hardhorn Lancs. . . .202 F3
Hardingham Norf . .141 C10
Hardings Booth
Staffs. 169 C8
Hardingstone
W Nhants. 120 F5
Hardings Wood
Staffs. 168 E4
Hardington Som . . .45 C8
Hardington Mandeville
Som 29 E8
Hardington Marsh
Som 29 F8
Hardington Moor
Som 29 E8
Hardiston Perth. . .279 B11
Hardisworthy Devon. .24 C2
Hardley Hants 32 G6
Hardley Street Norf. .143 C7
Hardmead
M Keynes. 103 B8
Hardrow N Yorks . .223 G7
Hardstoft Derbys. . .170 C6
Hardstoft Common
Derbys. 170 C6
Hardway Hants 33 G10
Som 45 G8
Hardwick Bucks . . .84 B4
Cambs 122 D3
Cambs 123 F7
N Nhants 121 D7
Norf. 142 F4
Norf. 158 E2
Oxon 82 D5
Oxon 101 C8
Shrops. 131 E7
Stockton 234 G4
S Yorks 187 D7
W Mid 133 D11
Hardwicke Glos . . .80 C3
Glos 99 F8
Hereford 96 C5
Hardwick Green
Worcs 98 E6
Hardwick Village
Notts 187 F10
Hardy's Green
Essex 107 G8
Hare Som 28 D3
Hare Appletree
Lancs 202 B6

Hareby Lincs. 174 B4
Harecroft W Yorks. .205 F7
Hareden Lancs. . . .203 C8
Hare Edge Derbys. .186 G4
Harefield London. . .85 G9
Soton. 33 E7
Harefield Grove
London. 85 G9
Haregate Staffs . . .169 D7
Hare Green Essex . .107 G11
Hare Hatch
Wokingham 65 D10
Harehill Derbys . . .152 B3
Harehills W Yorks . .206 G2
Harehope Borders . .270 G4
Northumb 264 E3
Harelaw Durham . .242 G5
Hareleeshill
S Lanark. 268 E5
Hareplain Kent 53 F10
Haresceugh Cumb . .231 C8
Harescombe Glos . . .80 C4
Haresfield Glos 80 C4
Swindon. 82 G2
Haresfinch Mers. . .183 B8
Hareshaw N Lanark. .268 C6
Hareshaw Head
Northumb 251 F9
Harestanes E Dunb . .278 G3
Harestock Hants . . .48 G3
Hare Street Essex. . .86 D6
Herts. 104 F6
Herts. 105 F7
Harewood W Yorks . .206 D2
Harewood End
Hereford 97 F10
Harewood Hill
W Yorks 204 F6
Harford Carms. 94 C2
Devon. 8 D2
Devon. 40 G6
Hargate Norf 142 E2
Hargate Hill Derbys. .185 C8
Hargatewall
Derbys. 185 F10
Hargrave Ches W . .167 C7
N Nhants 121 C10
Suff 124 F5
Harker Cumb 239 E9
Harker Marsh Cumb. .229 E7
Harkland Shetland. .312 E6
Harknett's Gate
Essex 86 D6
Harkstead Suff . . .108 E3
Harlaston Staffs . .134 G4
Harlaw Ho Aberds . .303 G7
Harlaxton Lincs. . .155 C7
Harlech Gwyn . . .145 C11
Harlequin Notts. . .154 B3
Harlescott Shrops. .149 F10
Harlesden London. . .67 C8
Harlesthorpe Derbys .187 F7
Harleston Devon . . . 8 F5
Norf. 142 G4
Suff 125 F10
Harlestone
W Nhants. 120 E4
Harle Syke Lancs. . .204 F3
Harley Shrops 131 C11
S Yorks 186 B5
Harleyholm
S Lanark. 259 E10
Harley Shute E Sus . .38 F3
Harleywood Glos . . .80 F4
Harling Road Norf . .141 F9
Harlington C Beds. .103 E11
London. 66 D5
S Yorks 198 G3
Harlosh Highld. . . .298 E2
Harlow Essex. 86 C6
Harlow Carr
N Yorks 205 C11
Harlow Green T&W. .243 F7
Harlow Hill
Northumb 242 D3
N Yorks 205 C11
Harlthorpe E Yorks .207 F10
Harlton Cambs. . . .123 G7
Harlyn Corn 10 F3
Harman's Corner
Kent. 69 G11
Harman's Cross
Dorset 18 E5
Harmans Water
Brack. 65 F11
Harmby N Yorks . . .214 B2
Harmer Green Herts. .86 B3
Harmer Hill Shrops. .149 E9
Harmondsworth
London. 66 D5
Harmston Lincs . . .173 C7
Harnage Shrops. . .131 C11
Harnham Northumb. .242 B3
Wilts 31 B10
Wilts 31 B11
Harnhill Glos 81 E9
Harold Hill London. .87 G8
Harold Park London. .87 G9
Haroldston West
Pembs 72 B5
Haroldswick
Shetland 312 B8
Harold Wood London. .87 G8
Harome N Yorks . . .216 C2
Harpenden Herts . . .85 C10
Harpenden Common
Herts. 85 C10
Harper Green
Gtr Man 195 F8
Harperley Durham. .242 G5
Harper's Gate Staffs .169 D7
Harper's Green Norf. .159 E8
Harpford Devon . . .15 C7
Harpham E Yorks . .217 G11
Harpley Norf 158 D5
Worcs 116 E3
Harpole W Nhants. .120 E3
Harpsdale Highld . .310 D5
Harpsden Oxon 65 D9
Harpsden Bottom
Oxon 65 C9
Harpswell Lincs. . .188 D6

Harpton Powys 114 F4
Harpurhey
Gtr Man 195 G11
Harpur Hill Derbys. .185 G9
Harraby Cumb 239 G10
Harracott Devon . . .25 B9
Harrapool Highld. . .295 C8
Harras Cumb 219 B9
Harratton T&W . . .243 G7
Harrier Shetland . .313 J1
Harrietfield Perth. .286 E3
Harrietsham Kent. . .53 C11
Harringay London . .67 B10
Harrington Cumb . .228 F5
Lincs 190 G5
N Nhants 136 G5
Harringworth
N Nhants 137 D8
Harris Highld 294 F5
Harriseahead Staffs. .168 D5
Harriston Cumb . . .229 C9
Harrogate N Yorks. .206 C2
Harrold Bedford . .121 F8
Harrop Dale
Gtr Man 196 F4
Harrow Highld 310 B6
London. 67 B7
Harrowbarrow Corn. .7 B10
Harrowbeer Devon. . .7 B10
Harrowby Lincs . . .155 B8
Harrowden Bedford .103 B11
Harrow Green
Suff. 125 G7
Harrow Hill Lincs. .190 B10
Harrowgate Hill
Darl 224 B5
Harrowgate Village
Darl 224 B5
Harrow Green Suff. .125 G7
Harrow on the Hill
London. 67 B7
Harrow Street Suff. .107 D9
Harrow Weald
London. 85 G11
Harry Stoke S Glos. .60 D6
Harston Cambs . . .123 G8
Leics 154 C6
Harswell E Yorks . .208 E2
Hart Hrtlpl. 234 E5
Hartburn Northumb. .252 F3
Stockton 225 B8
Hartcliffe Bristol . .60 F5
Hart Common
Gtr Man 194 F6
Hartest Suff 124 G6
Hartfield E Sus. . . .52 F3
Highld 299 E7
Hartford Cambs . . .122 C5
Ches W. 183 G10
Som 27 B7
Hartfordbeach
Ches W 183 G10
Hartfordbridge Hants .49 B9
Hartford End Essex. .87 B11
Hartforth N Yorks . .224 D3
Hartgrove Dorset . .30 D4
Hartham Herts. 86 C4
Harthill Ches W . . .167 D8
N Lanark 269 C8
S Yorks 187 E7
Hart Hill Luton . . .104 G2
Hartington Derbys. .169 C10
Hartland Devon . . .24 C3
Hartle Worcs 117 B8
Hartlebury Shrops . .132 D4
Worcs 116 C6
Hartlepool Hrtlpl. .234 E6
Hartley Cumb 222 D5
Kent. 53 G9
Kent. 68 F6
Northumb 243 B8
Plym 7 D9
Hartley Green Kent. .68 F6
Staffs. 151 D9
Hartley Mauditt
Hants. 49 F8
Hartley Westpall
Hants. 49 B7
Hartley Wintney
Hants. 49 B9
Hartlington
N Yorks 213 G10
Hartlip Kent. 69 G10
Hartmoor Dorset. . .30 C3
Hartmount Highld. .301 B7
Harton N Yorks . . .216 G4
Shrops. 131 F9
T&W 243 E9
Hartpury Glos 98 F5
Hart's Green Suff . .125 G7
Hartshead Green
Gtr Man 196 G3
Hartshead Moor Side
W Yorks 197 C7
Hartshead Moor Top
W Yorks 197 B7
Hartshead Pike
Gtr Man 196 G3
Hartshill Stoke. . . .168 F5
Warks 134 E6
Hartshorne Derbys. .152 E6
Hartsop Cumb 221 C8
Hart Station Hrtlpl. .234 D5
Hartswell Som 27 B9
Hartwell Staffs . . .151 B8
W Nhants 120 G5
Hartwith N Yorks . .214 G4
Hartwood Lancs . .194 D5
N Lanark 268 D6
Hartwoodburn
Borders 261 D11
Harvel Kent. 68 G6
Harvest Hill W Mid. .134 G5
Harvieston Stirling .277 D11

Harvills Hawthorn
W Mid 133 E8
Harvington Worcs . .99 B11
Worcs 117 C7
Harvington Cross
Worcs 99 B11
Harvington Hill
Worcs 99 B10
Harwell Notts 187 C11
Oxon 64 B3
Harwich Essex 108 E5
Harwood Durham . .232 E2
Gtr Man 195 E8
Harwood Dale
N Yorks 227 F9
Harwood Lee
Gtr Man 195 E8
Harwood on Teviot
Borders 249 B10
Harworth Notts . . .187 C10
Hasbury W Mid . . .133 G9
Hascombe Sur. 50 E3
Haselbech
W Nhants. 120 B4
Haselbury Plucknett
Som 29 E7
Haseley Warks . . .118 D4
Haseley Green
Warks 118 D4
Haseley Knob
Warks 118 C4
Haselor Warks 118 F2
Hasfield Glos 98 F6
Hasguard Pembs. . .72 D5
Haskayne Lancs. . .193 F11
Hasketon Suff 126 G4
Hasland Derbys . . .170 B5
Haslemere Sur 50 G2
Haslingbourne
W Sus 35 C7
Haslingden Lancs. .195 C9
Haslingfield Cambs. .123 G8
Haslington Ches E. .168 D2
Hassall Ches E . . .168 D3
Hassall Green
Ches E 168 D3
Hassall Street Kent. .54 D5
Hassendean Borders .262 E2
Hassingham Norf . .143 B7
Hassocks W Sus . . .36 D3
Hassop Derbys . . .186 G2
Haster Highld 310 D7
Hastigrow Highld . .310 C6
Hasting Hill T&W . .243 G9
Hastingleigh Kent. . .54 E5
Hastings E Sus 38 F4
Som 28 D4
Hastingwood Essex. .87 D7
Hastoe Herts 84 D6
Haston Shrops 149 E10
Haswell Durham . .234 C2
Haswell Moor
Durham 234 C2
Haswell Plough
Durham 234 C2
Haswellsykes
Borders 260 B6
Hatch C Beds. 104 B3
Devon. 8 F4
Hants. 49 C7
Wilts 30 B6
Hatch Beauchamp
Som 28 C4
Hatch Bottom Hants. .33 E7
Hatch End Bedford. .121 E11
London. 85 G11
Hatchet Gate Hants. .32 G5
Hatchet Green
Hants. 31 D11
Hatch Farm Hill
W Sus 34 B6
Hatch Green Som. . .28 D4
Hatching Green
Herts. 85 C10
Hatchmere Ches W. .183 G9
Hatch Warren Hants. .48 D6
Hatcliffe NE Lincs. .201 G8
Hateley Heath
W Mid 133 E10
Hatfield Hereford . .115 F11
Herts. 86 D2
S Yorks 199 F7
Worcs 117 F7
Hatfield Broad Oak
Essex 87 B8
Hatfield Chase
S Yorks 199 E8
Hatfield Garden Village
Herts. 86 D2
Hatfield Heath Essex. .87 B8
Hatfield Hyde Herts. .86 C2
Hatfield Peverel
Essex 88 C3
Hatfield Woodhouse
S Yorks 199 F7
Hatford Oxon 82 G4
Hatherden Hants . .47 C10
Hatherleigh Devon. .25 G8
Hatherley Glos 99 G8
Hathern Leics. 153 E9
Hatherop Glos 81 D10
Hathersage Derbys. .186 E2
Hathersage Booths
Derbys. 186 E2
Hathershaw
Gtr Man 196 G2
Hatherton Ches E . .167 F11
Staffs. 151 G9
Hatley St George
Cambs 122 G5
Hatston Orkney . . .314 E4
Hatt Corn 7 C7
Hattersley Gtr Man .185 C7
Hatt Hill Hants 32 B4
Hatton Aberds 303 F10
Angus 287 D9
Derbys. 152 D4

Hatton *continued*
Lincs 189 F11
London. 66 D5
Moray 301 C11
Shrops. 131 E9
Warks 118 D4
Warr 183 E9
Hatton Castle
Aberds. 303 E7
Hattoncrook Aberds. 303 G8
Hatton Grange
Shrops. 132 C5
Hatton Heath
Ches W 167 C7
Hatton Hill Sur. . . .66 G5
Hattonknowe
Borders 270 F4
Hatton of Fintray
Aberds. 293 B10
Hatton Park
N Nhants 121 D7
Haugh E Ayrs 257 D11
Gtr Man 196 E2
Lincs 190 E4
Haugham Lincs . . .190 E4
Haugh-head
Borders 261 B8
Haugh Head
Northumb 264 D2
Haughland Orkney. .314 E6
Haughley Suff 125 D10
Haughley Green
Suff 125 D10
Haughley New Street
Suff 125 D10
Haugh of Glass
Moray 302 F4
Haugh of Kilmaichlie
Moray 301 G11
Haugh of Urr
Dumfries 237 C10
Haughs of Clinterty
Aberdeen. 293 B10
Haughton Ches E . .167 D9
Notts 187 G11
Powys 148 F6
Shrops. 132 B4
Shrops. 132 D4
Shrops. 149 E7
Shrops. 149 F11
Staffs. 151 E7
Haughton Castle
Northumb 241 C10
Haughton Green
Gtr Man 184 C6
Haughton Le Skerne
Darl 224 B6
Haughurst Hill
W Berks 64 G5
Haulkerton Aberds. .293 F9
Haultwick Herts . .104 G6
Haunn Argyll. 288 E5
W Isles 297 K3
Haunton Staffs . . .152 G4
Hauxton Cambs . .123 G8
Havannah Ches E . .168 C5
Havant Hants 22 B2
Haven Hereford . . .97 B11
Hereford 115 G8
Haven Bank Lincs. .174 D2
Haven Side Lincs. .201 B7
Havenstreet IoW . .21 C7
Havercroft
W Yorks 197 E11
Haverfordwest = Hwlffordd
Pembs 73 B7
Haverhill Suff. . . .106 B3
Haverigg Cumb . . .210 D2
Havering-atte-Bower
London. 87 G8
Haveringland Norf. .160 E3
Haversham
M Keynes. 102 C6
Haverthwaite Cumb. .210 C6
Haverton Hill
Stockton 234 G4
Haviker Street Kent. .53 D8
Havyatt Som 44 F4
Havyatt Green
N Som 60 G3
Hawarden = Penarlâg
Flint 166 B4
Hawbridge Worcs. . .99 B8
Hawbush Green
Essex 106 G5
Hawcoat Cumb . . .210 E4
Hawcross Glos 98 E5
Hawddamor Gwyn .146 F3
Hawen Ceredig. . . .92 B6
Hawes N Yorks . . .213 B7
Hawes' Green Norf .142 D4
Hawes Side
Blackpool 202 G2
Haw Green
Ches E 167 E11
Hawford Worcs . . .116 E6
Hawgreen Shrops . .150 D2
Hawick Borders . .262 F2
Hawkchurch Devon. .28 G4
Hawkcombe Som. . .41 D11
Hawkedon Suff . . .124 G5
Hawkenbury Kent. . .52 F5
Kent. 53 E10
Hawkeridge Wilts. . .45 C11
Hawkerland Devon. .15 D7
Hawkersland Cross
Hereford 97 B10
Hawkesbury S Glos. .61 B9
Warks 135 G7
Hawkesbury Upton
S Glos. 61 B9
Hawkes End W Mid. .134 G6
Hawkesley W Mid. .117 B10
Hawk Green
Gtr Man 185 D7
Hawkhill Northumb. .264 G6
Hawkhope Northumb. .250 F6
Hawkhurst Kent. . .53 F9
Hawkhurst Common
E Sus 23 C8
Hawkinge Kent. . . .55 F8
Hawkin's Hill Essex. .106 E3

Hawkley Gtr Man . .194 G5
Hants. 34 B2
Hawkridge Som . . .41 G11
Hawksdale Cumb . .230 B3
Hawks Green Staffs. .151 G10
Hawkshaw
Blackburn 195 D11
Hawkshead Cumb . .221 F7
Hawkshead Hill
Cumb. 220 F6
Hawks Hill Bucks. . .66 B2
Hawk's Hill Sur 51 B7
Hawksland S Lanark .259 B8
Hawkspur Green
Essex 106 E3
Hawks Stones
W Yorks 196 B2
Hawkswick N Yorks .213 E9
Hawksworth Notts. .172 G3
W Yorks 205 E9
W Yorks 205 F11
Hawkwell Essex . . .88 G4
Northumb 242 D3
Hawley Hants. 49 B11
Kent. 68 E4
Hawley Bottom
Devon. 28 G2
Hawley Lane Hants. .49 B11
Hawling Glos 99 G11
Hawn Orkney 314 G4
Hawnby N Yorks . .215 B10
Hawne W Mid 133 G9
Haworth W Yorks. .204 F6
Haws Bank Cumb . .220 F6
Hawstead Suff 125 F7
Hawstead Green
Suff 125 F7
Hawthorn Durham. .234 B4
Hants. 49 G7
Rhondda. 58 B6
Wilts 61 F11
Hawthorn Corner
Kent. 71 F7
Hawthorn Hill Brack. .65 E11
Lincs 174 D2
Hawthorns Staffs . .168 F4
Hawthorpe Lincs. .155 D10
Hawton Notts 172 E3
Haxby York 207 B8
Haxey N Lincs 188 B3
N Lincs 199 G9
Haxey Carr N Lincs. .199 G9
Haxted Sur 52 D2
Haxton Wilts 46 D6
Hay Corn 10 G5
Som 44 D4
Telford 150 G3
Haybridge Shrops. .116 C2
Som 44 D4
Haydock Mers 183 B9
Haydon Bath 45 C7
Dorset 29 D11
Som 28 C3
Som 44 D5
Swindon. 62 B6
Haydon Bridge
Northumb 241 E8
Haydon Wick Swindon .62 B6
Haye Corn 7 B7
Hayes London 66 C6
London. 68 F2
Staffs. 169 C9
Hayes End London. .66 C5
Hayes Knoll Wilts . .81 G10
Hayes Town London. .66 C6
Hayfield Derbys. . .185 D8
Fife 280 C5
Hay Field S Yorks. .187 B10
Hayfield Green
S Yorks. 187 B11
Haygate Telford . .150 G2
Haygrass Som 28 C2
Hay Green Essex . . .87 E10
Herts. 104 D6
Norf. 157 F10
Hayhill E Ayrs 257 F11
Hayhillock Angus . .287 C10
Haylands IoW 21 C7
Hayle Corn 2 B3
Hayley Green
W Mid 133 G8
Hay Mills W Mid. . .134 G2
Haymoor End Som. .28 B4
Haymoor Green
Ches E 167 E11
Hayne Devon 26 F5
Haynes C Beds . . .103 C11
Haynes Church End
C Beds 103 C11
Haynes West End
C Beds 103 C11
Hay-on-Wye Powys. .96 C4
Hayscastle Pembs. .91 F7
Hayscastle Cross
Pembs 91 G8
Haysford Pembs . . .91 G8
Hayshead Angus . .287 C10
Hayston E Dunb . . .278 G2
Haystoun Borders. .261 B7
Hay Street Herts . .105 F7
Haythorne Dorset . .31 F8
Hayton Aberdeen . .293 C11
Cumb 229 C8
Cumb 240 F2
E Yorks 208 D2
Notts 188 E2
Hayton's Bent
Shrops. 131 G10
Haytor Vale Devon . .13 F11
Haytown Devon . . .24 E5
Haywards Heath
W Sus 36 C4
Haywood S Lanark. .269 D8
S Yorks 198 E5
Haywood Oaks
Notts 171 D10
Hazard's Green
E Sus 23 C11
Hazelbank S Lanark. .268 F6
Hazelbeach Pembs. .72 E6
Hazelbury Bryan
Dorset 30 F2

Hazeleigh Essex 88 E4
Hazel End Essex 105 G9
Hazeley Hants 49 B8
Hazeley Bottom
Hants 49 B9
Hazeley Heath Hants 49 B9
Hazeley Lea Hants 49 B8
Hazelgrove Notts 171 F8
Hazel Grove
Gtr Man 184 D6
Hazelhurst Gtr Man 195 D9
Gtr Man 195 G9
Gtr Man 196 G3
Hazelslack Cumb 211 D9
Hazelslade Staffs 151 G10
Hazel Street Kent 53 B11
Kent 53 F7
Hazel Stub Suff 106 C3
Hazelton Glos 81 B9
Hazelton Walls Fife 287 E7
Hazelwood Derbys 170 F4
Devon 8 E4
London 68 G2
Hazlehead S Yorks 197 G7
Hazlemere Bucks 84 F5
Hazler Shrops 131 E9
Hazlerigg T&W 242 C6
Hazles Staffs 169 F8
Hazlescross Staffs 169 F8
Hazleton Glos 81 B9
Hazlewood N Yorks 205 C7
Hazon Northumb 252 C5
Heacham Norf 158 B3
Headbourne Worthy
Hants 48 G3
Headbrook Hereford 114 F6
Headcorn Kent 53 E10
Headingley
W Yorks 205 F11
Headington Oxon 83 D8
Headington Hill Oxon 83 D8
Headlam Durham 224 B3
Headless Cross
Cumb 211 D7
Worcs 117 D10
Headley Hants 49 F10
Hants 64 G4
Sur 51 C8
Headley Down
Hants 49 F10
Headley Heath
Worcs 117 B11
Headley Park Bristol 60 F5
Head of Muir Falk 278 E6
Headon Devon 24 G5
Notts 188 F2
Heads S Lanark 268 F4
Headshaw Borders 261 E11
Heads Nook Cumb 239 F11
Headstone London 66 B6
Headwell Fife 279 D11
Heady Hill Gtr Man 195 E10
Heage Derbys 170 E5
Healaugh N Yorks 206 D5
N Yorks 223 F10
Heald Green
Gtr Man 184 D4
Healds Green
Gtr Man 195 F11
Heale Devon 40 D6
Som 28 B5
Som 28 D2
Som 45 E7
Healey Gtr Man 195 D11
Northumb 242 F2
N Yorks 214 C3
W Yorks 197 C8
W Yorks 197 D9
Healey Cote
Northumb 252 C4
Healeyfield Durham 233 B7
Healey Hall
Northumb 242 F2
Healing NE Lincs 201 E8
Heamoor Corn 1 C5
Heaning Cumb 221 F8
Heanish Argyll 288 E2
Heanor Derbys 170 F6
Heanor Gate Derbys 170 F6
Heanton Punchardon
Devon 40 F4
Heap Bridge
Gtr Man 195 E10
Heapham Lincs 188 D5
Hearn Hants 49 F10
Hearnden Green
Kent 53 D10
Hearthstane
Borders 260 D4
Hearthstone Derbys 170 D4
Hearts Delight Kent 69 G11
Heasley Mill Devon 41 G8
Heast Highld 295 D8
Heath Cardiff 59 D7
Derbys 170 B6
Halton 183 E8
Heath and Reach
C Beds 103 F8
Heath Charnock
Lancs 194 E5
Heath Common
W Sus 35 E10
W Yorks 197 D11
Heathcot Aberds 293 C10
Heathcote Derbys 169 C10
Shrops 150 D3
Warks 118 E6
Heath Cross Devon 13 B10
Devon 14 C2
Heath End Bucks 84 F5
Bucks 85 D7
Derbys 153 E7
Hants 64 G2
Hants 64 G5
S Glos 61 B7
Sur 49 D10
Warks 118 E4
W Mid 133 C10
W Sus 35 D7
Heather Leics 153 G7
Heathercombe
Devon 13 E10
Heatherfield Highld 298 E4
Heather Row Hants 49 C8
Heatherside Sur 50 B2
Heatherwood Park
Highld 311 K2
Heatherybanks
Aberds 303 E7
Heathfield Cambs 105 B9
Devon 14 F2
E Sus 37 C9
Glos 80 F2
Hants 33 F9
Lincs 189 C10
N Yorks 214 F2
S Ayrs 257 E9
Som 27 B11
Som 43 G7
Heathfield Village
Oxon 83 B8
Heath Green Hants 48 F6
Worcs 117 C11
Heathhall Dumfries 237 B11
Heath Hayes Staffs 151 G10
Heath Hill Shrops 150 G5
Heath House Som 44 D2
Heathlands
Wokingham 65 F10
Heath Lanes Telford 150 E2
Heath Park London 68 B4
Heathrow Airport
London 66 D5
Heath Side Kent 68 E4
Heathstock Devon 28 G2
Heathton Shrops 132 E6
Heathtop Derbys 152 C4
Heath Town W Mid 133 D8
Heathwaite Cumb 221 F8
N Yorks 225 E9
Heatley Staffs 151 D11
Warr 184 D2
Heaton Gtr Man 195 F7
Lancs 211 G8
Staffs 169 C7
T&W 243 D7
W Yorks 205 G8
Heaton Chapel
Gtr Man 184 C5
Heaton Mersey
Gtr Man 184 C5
Heaton Moor
Gtr Man 184 C5
Heaton Norris
Gtr Man 184 C5
Heaton Royds
W Yorks 205 F8
Heaton's Bridge
Lancs 194 E2
Heaton Shay
W Yorks 205 F8
Heaven's Door Som 29 C10
Heaverham Kent 52 B5
Heaviley Gtr Man 184 D6
Heavitree Devon 14 C4
Hebburn T&W 243 E8
Hebburn Colliery
T&W 243 D8
Hebburn New Town
T&W 243 E8
Hebden N Yorks 213 G10
Hebden Bridge
W Yorks 196 B3
Hebden Green
Ches W 167 B10
Hebing End Herts 104 G6
Hebron Anglesey 179 E7
Carms 92 F3
Northumb 252 F5
Heck Dumfries 248 G3
Heckdyke N Lincs 188 B3
Heckfield Hants 65 G8
Heckfield Green
Suff 126 B3
Heckfordbridge
Essex 107 G8
Heckingham Norf 143 D7
Heckington Lincs 173 G10
Heckmondwike
W Yorks 197 C8
Heddington Wilts 62 F3
Heddington Wick
Wilts 62 F3
Heddle Orkney 314 E3
Heddon Devon 25 B11
Heddon-on-the-Wall
Northumb 242 D4
Hedenham Norf 142 E6
Hedge End Dorset 30 F4
Hants 33 E7
Hedgehog Bridge
Lincs 174 F3
Hedgerley Bucks 66 B3
Hedgerley Green
Bucks 66 B3
Hedgerley Hill Bucks 66 B3
Hedging Som 28 B4
Hedley Hill Durham 233 C9
Hedley on the Hill
Northumb 242 F3
Hednesford Staffs 151 G9
Hedon E Yorks 201 B7
Hedsor Bucks 66 B2
Hedworth T&W 243 E8
Heelands M Keynes 102 D6
Heeley S Yorks 186 E5
Hegdon Hill
Hereford 115 G11
Heggerscales Cumb 222 C6
Heggle Lane Cumb 230 D3
Heglibister Shetland 313 H5
Heighington Darl 233 G11
Lincs 173 B8
Heighley Staffs 168 F3
Height End Lancs 195 C9
Heightington Worcs 116 C5
Heights Gtr Man 196 F3
Heights of Brae
Highld 300 C5
Heights of Kinlochewe
Highld 299 C10
Heilam Highld 308 C4
Heiton Borders 262 C6
Helbeck Cumb 222 B5
Hele Devon 12 C2
Devon 13 G10
Devon 27 G7
Devon 40 D4
Som 27 C11
Torbay 9 B8
Helebridge Corn 24 G2
Helensburgh Argyll 276 E5
Helford Corn 3 D7
Helford Passage Corn 3 D7
Helham Green Herts 86 B5
Helhoughton Norf 159 D7
Helions Bumpstead
Essex 106 C3
Hellaby S Yorks 187 C8
Helland Corn 11 G7
Som 28 C4
Hellandbridge Corn 11 G7
Hell Corner
W Berks 63 G11
Hellesdon Norf 160 G4
Hellesveor Corn 2 A2
Hellidon W Nhants 119 F10
Hellifield N Yorks 204 B3
Hellifield Green
N Yorks 204 B3
Hellingly E Sus 23 C9
Hellington Norf 142 C6
Hellister Shetland 313 J5
Hellman's Cross
Essex 87 B9
Helm Northumb 252 D5
N Yorks 223 G8
Helmburn Borders 261 E9
Helmdon
W Nhants 101 C11
Helme W Yorks 196 E5
Helmingham Suff 126 F3
Helmington Row
Durham 233 D9
Helmsdale Highld 311 H4
Helmshore Lancs 195 C9
Helmside Cumb 212 B3
Helmsley N Yorks 216 C2
Helperby N Yorks 215 F8
Helperthorpe
N Yorks 217 E9
Helpringham Lincs 173 G10
Helpston Pboro 138 B2
Helsby Ches W 183 F7
Helscott Corn 24 G2
Helsey Lincs 191 G8
Helston Corn 2 D5
Helstone Corn 11 E7
Helston Water Corn 4 G5
Helton Cumb 230 G6
Helwith Bridge
N Yorks 212 F6
Helygain = *Halkyn*
Flint 182 G2
Hemblington Norf 160 G6
Hemblington Corner
Norf 160 G6
Hembridge Som 44 F5
Hemel Hempstead
Herts 85 D9
Hemerdon Devon 7 D11
Hemford Shrops 130 C6
Hem Heath Stoke 168 G5
Hemingbrough
N Yorks 207 G9
Hemingby Lincs 190 G2
Hemingfield
S Yorks 197 G11
Hemingford Abbots
Cambs 122 C5
Hemingford Grey
Cambs 122 C5
Hemingstone Suff 126 G3
Hemington Leics 153 D9
N Nhants 137 F11
Som 45 C8
Hemley Suff 108 C5
Hemlington Mbro 225 C10
Hemp Green Suff 127 D7
Hempholme
E Yorks 209 C7
Hempnall Norf 142 E4
Hempnall Green
Norf 142 E4
Hempriggs House
Highld 310 E7
Hemp's Green Essex 107 F8
Hempshill Vale
Notts 171 G8
Hempstead Essex 106 D2
Medway 69 G9
Norf 160 B2
Norf 161 D8
Hempsted Glos 80 B4
Hempton Norf 159 D8
Oxon 101 E8
Hempton Wainhill
Oxon 84 E3
Hemsby Norf 161 F9
Hemsted Kent 54 E6
Hemswell Lincs 188 C6
Hemswell Cliff
Lincs 188 D6
Hemsworth Dorset 31 F7
S Yorks 186 E5
W Yorks 198 E2
Hemyock Devon 27 E10
Henaford Devon 24 D2
Hen Bentref Llandegfan
Anglesey 179 G9
Henbrook Worcs 117 D8
Henbury Bristol 60 D5
Ches E 184 G5
Dorset 18 B5
Hendomen Powys 130 D4
Hendon London 67 B8
T&W 243 F10
Hendra Corn 2 B6
Corn 2 C5
Corn 2 D3
Corn 2 F6
Corn 5 C9
Corn 5 D9
Corn 11 E7
Hendrabridge Corn 6 B5
Hendraburnick Corn 11 D8
Hendra Croft Corn 4 D5
Hendre Flint 165 B11
Gwyn 110 B2
Powys 129 D9
Hendre-ddu Conwy 164 B5
Hendredenny Park
Caerph 58 B6
Hendreforgan
Rhondda 58 B3
Hendrerwydd
Denb 165 C10
Hendrewen
Swansea 75 D10
Hendy Carms 75 E9
Hendy-Gwyn Carms 74 B2
Hendy Gwyn = *Whitland*
Carms 73 B11
Hên-efail Denb 165 C9
Heneglwys Anglesey 178 F6
Hen-feddau fawr
Pembs 92 E4
Henfield S Glos 61 D7
W Sus 36 D2
Henford Devon 12 C3
Henfords Marsh
Wilts 45 E11
Henghurst Kent 54 F3
Hengoed Caerph 77 F10
Denb 165 D9
Powys 114 G4
Shrops 148 C5
Hengrave Norf 160 F2
Suff 124 D6
Hengrove Bristol 60 F6
Hengrove Park
Bristol 60 F5
Henham Essex 105 F10
Heniarth Powys 130 B2
Henlade Som 28 C3
Henleaze Bristol 60 D5
Henley Dorset 29 G11
Glos 80 B6
Shrops 115 B10
Shrops 131 F9
Som 44 G2
Suff 126 G3
Wilts 47 B10
Wilts 61 F10
W Sus 34 B5
Henley Common
W Sus 34 B5
Henley Green
W Mid 135 G7
Henley-in-Arden
Warks 118 D3
Henley-on-Thames
Oxon 65 C9
Henley's Down E Sus 38 E2
Henley Street Kent 69 F7
Henllan Ceredig 93 C7
Denb 165 B8
Henllan Amgoed
Carms 92 G3
Henlle Shrops 148 C6
Henllys Torf 78 G3
Henllys Vale Torf 78 G3
Henlow C Beds 104 D3
Hennock Devon 14 E2
Henny Street Essex 107 D7
Henryd Conwy 180 G3
Henry's Moat Pembs 91 F10
Hensall N Yorks 198 C5
Henshaw Northumb 241 E7
W Yorks 205 E10
Hensingham Cumb 219 B9
Hensington Oxon 83 B7
Henstead Suff 143 F9
Hensting Hants 33 C7
Henstridge Devon 40 E5
Som 30 D2
Henstridge Ash Som 30 C2
Henstridge Bowden
Som 29 C11
Henstridge Marsh
Som 30 C2
Henton Oxon 84 E3
Som 44 D3
Henwood Corn 11 G11
Oxon 83 E7
Henwood Green Kent 52 E6
Heogan Shetland 313 J6
Heol-ddu Carms 75 E7
Swansea 56 B6
Heolgerrig M Tydf 77 D8
Heol-laethog
Bridgend 58 C2
Heol-las Bridgend 58 C2
Swansea 57 B7
Heol Senni Powys 95 G8
Heol-y-gaer Powys 96 D3
Heol-y-mynydd
V Glam 57 G11
Hepburn Northumb 264 E3
Hepple Northumb 251 C11
Hepscott Northumb 252 G6
Hepthorne Lane
Derbys 170 C6
Heptonstall
W Yorks 196 B3
Hepworth Suff 125 C9
W Yorks 197 F7
Herbrandston Pembs 72 D5
Hereford Hereford 97 C10
Heribusta Highld 298 B4
Heriot Borders 271 E7
Hermiston Edin 280 G3
Hermitage Borders 250 D2
Dorset 29 F10
W Berks 64 E4
W Sus 22 B3
Hermitage Green
Mers 183 C10
Hermit Hill
S Yorks 197 G10
Hermit Hole
W Yorks 205 F7
Hermon Anglesey 162 B5
Carms 93 E7
Carms 94 F3
Pembs 92 E4
Herne Kent 71 F7
Herne Bay Kent 71 F7
Herne Common Kent 71 F7
Herne Hill London 67 E10
Herne Pound Kent 53 C7
Herner Devon 25 B9
Hernhill Kent 70 G5
Herniss Corn 2 C6
Herodsfoot Corn 6 C4
Heron Cross Stoke 168 G5
Heronden Kent 55 C9
Herongate Essex 87 G10
Heronsford S Ayrs 244 G4
Heronsgate Herts 85 G8
Heron's Ghyll E Sus 37 B7
Herons Green Bath 44 B5
Heronston Bridgend 58 D2
Herra Shetland 312 D8
Herriard Hants 49 D7
Herringfleet Suff 143 D9
Herring's Green
Bedford 103 C11
Herringswell Suff 124 C4
Herringthorpe
S Yorks 186 C6
Hersden Kent 71 G8
Hersham Corn 24 F3
Sur 66 G6
Herstmonceux
E Sus 23 C10
Herston Dorset 18 F6
Orkney 314 G4
Hertford Herts 86 C4
Hertford Heath
Herts 86 C4
Hertingfordbury
Herts 86 C4
Hesketh Bank Lancs 194 C2
Hesketh Lane Lancs 203 E8
Hesketh Moss Lancs 194 C2
Hesket Newmarket
Cumb 230 D2
Heskin Green Lancs 194 D4
Hesleden Durham 234 D4
Hesleyside
Northumb 251 G8
Heslington York 207 C8
Hessay York 206 C6
Hessenford Corn 6 D6
Hessett Suff 125 E8
Hessle E Yorks 200 B4
W Yorks 198 D2
Hest Bank Lancs 211 F9
Hester's Way Glos 99 G8
Hestinsetter
Shetland 313 J4
Heston London 66 D6
Hestwall Orkney 314 E2
Heswall Mers 182 E3
Hethe Oxon 101 F11
Hethel Norf 142 C3
Hethelpit Cross Glos 98 F5
Hethersett Norf 142 C3
Hethersgill Cumb 239 D11
Hetherside Cumb 239 D10
Hetherson Green
Ches W 167 F8
Hethpool Northumb 263 D9
Hett Durham 233 D11
Hetton N Yorks 204 B5
Hetton Downs T&W 234 B3
Hetton-le-Hill T&W 234 B3
Hetton-le-Hole
T&W 234 B3
Hetton Steads
Northumb 264 B2
Heugh Northumb 242 C3
Heugh-head Aberds 292 B5
Heveningham Suff 126 C6
Hever Kent 52 E3
Heversham Cumb 211 C9
Hevingham Norf 160 E3
Hewas Water Corn 5 F9
Hewelsfield Glos 79 E9
Hewelsfield Common
Glos 79 E8
Hewer Hill Cumb 230 D3
Hew Green
N Yorks 205 B10
Hewish N Som 60 G2
Som 28 F6
Hewood Dorset 28 G5
Heworth T&W 243 E7
York 207 C8
Hexham Northumb 241 E10
Hextable Kent 68 E4
Hexthorpe S Yorks 198 G5
Hexton Herts 104 E2
Hexworthy Devon 13 G9
Hey Lancs 204 E3
Heybridge Essex 87 F10
Essex 88 D5
Heybridge Basin
Essex 88 D5
Heybrook Bay Devon 7 F10
Heydon Cambs 105 C8
Norf 160 D2
Heydour Lincs 155 B10
Heyford Park Oxon 101 F10
Hey Green W Yorks 196 E4
Heyheads Gtr Man 196 G3
Hey Houses Lancs 193 B10
Heylipol Argyll 288 E1
Heylor Shetland 312 E4
Heyope Powys 114 C4
Heyrod Gtr Man 185 B7
Heysham Lancs 211 G8
Heyshaw N Yorks 214 G3
Heyshott W Sus 34 D5
Heyshott Green
W Sus 34 D5
Heyside Gtr Man 196 F2
Heytesbury Wilts 46 E2
Heythrop Oxon 101 F7
Heywood Gtr Man 195 E11
Wilts 45 C11
Hibaldstow N Lincs 200 G3
Hibb's Green Suff 125 G7
Hickford Hill Essex 106 C5
Hickleton S Yorks 198 F3
Hickling Norf 161 E8
Notts 154 D3
Hickling Green Norf 161 E8
Hickling Heath Norf 161 E8
Hickling Pastures
Notts 154 D3
Hickmans Green
Kent 54 B5
Hicks Forstal Kent 71 G7
Hicks Gate Bath 60 F6
Hick's Mill Corn 4 G5
Hickstead W Sus 36 C3
Hidcote Bartrim
Glos 100 C3
Hidcote Boyce Glos 100 C3
Hifnal Shrops 132 D4
Higginshaw
Gtr Man 196 F2
High Ackworth
W Yorks 198 D2
Higham Derbys 170 D5
Fife 286 F6
Kent 69 E8
Lancs 204 F2
Suff 107 D10
Suff 124 E4
S Yorks 197 F10
Higham Common
S Yorks 197 F10
Higham Dykes
Northumb 242 B4
Higham Ferrers
N Nhants 121 D9
Higham Gobion
C Beds 104 E2
Higham Hill London 86 G5
Higham on the Hill
Leics 135 D7
Highampton Devon 25 G7
Highams Park
London 86 G5
Higham Wood Kent 52 D5
High Angerton
Northumb 252 F3
High Bankhill Cumb 231 C7
High Banton
N Lanark 278 E4
High Barn Lincs 174 C5
High Barnes T&W 243 F9
High Barnet London 86 F2
High Beach Essex 86 F6
High Bentham
N Yorks 212 F3
High Bickington
Devon 25 C10
High Biggins Cumb 212 D2
High Birkwith
N Yorks 212 D5
High Birstwith
N Yorks 205 B10
High Blantyre
S Lanark 268 D3
High Bonnybridge
Falk 278 F6
High Bradfield
S Yorks 186 C3
High Bradley
N Yorks 204 D6
High Bray Devon 41 G7
Highbridge Cumb 230 C3
Hants 33 C7
Highld 290 E3
Som 43 D10
W Mid 133 C10
Highbrook W Sus 51 G11
High Brooms Kent 52 E5
High Brotheridge
Glos 80 C5
High Bullen Devon 25 C8
Highburton
W Yorks 197 E7
Highbury London 67 B10
Ptsmth 33 G11
Som 45 D7
Highbury Vale
Nottingham 171 G8
High Buston
Northumb 252 B6
High Callerton
Northumb 242 C5
High Cark Cumb 211 C7
High Casterton
Cumb 212 D2
High Catton
E Yorks 207 C10
High Church
Northumb 252 F5
Highclere Hants 64 G2
Highcliffe BCP 19 C10
Derbys 186 F2
High Cogges Oxon 82 D5
High Common Norf 141 B9
High Coniscliffe
Darl 224 B4
High Crompton
Gtr Man 196 F2
High Cross Cambs 123 F8
Corn 2 D6
E Sus 37 B9
Hants 34 B2
Herts 85 F10
Herts 86 B5
Newport 59 B9
Warks 118 D3
W Sus 36 D2
High Crosshill
S Lanark 268 C2
High Cunsey Cumb 221 G7
High Dubmire T&W 234 B2
High Dyke Durham 232 F5
High Easter Essex 87 C10
High Eggborough
N Yorks 198 C5
High Eldrig
Dumfries 236 C4
High Ellington
N Yorks 214 C3
Higher Alham Som 45 E7
Higher Ansty Dorset 30 G3
Higher Ashton Devon 14 E3
Higher Audley
Blackburn 195 B7
Higher Bal Corn 4 E4
Higher Ballam
Lancs 202 G3
Higher Bartle Lancs 202 G6
Higher Bebington
Mers 182 D4
Higher Berry End
C Beds 103 E9
Higher Blackley
Gtr Man 195 G10
Higher Boarshaw
Gtr Man 195 F11
Higher Bockhampton
Dorset 17 C10
Higher Bojewyan Corn 1 C3
Higher Boscaswell
Corn 1 C3
Higher Brixham
Torbay 9 D8
Higher Broughton
Gtr Man 195 G10
Higher Burrow Som 28 C6
Higher Burwardsley
Ches W 167 D8
High Ercall Telford 149 F11
Higher Chalmington
Dorset 29 G9
Higher Cheriton
Devon 27 G10
Higher Chillington
Som 28 E5
Higher Chisworth
Derbys 185 C7
Highercliff Corn 6 D4
Higher Clovelly
Devon 24 C4
Higher Condurrow
Corn 2 B5
Higher Crackington
Corn 11 B9
Higher Cransworth
Corn 5 B9
Higher Croft
Blackburn 195 B7
Higher Denham
Bucks 66 B4
Higher Dinting
Derbys 185 C8
Higher Disley
Ches E 185 E7
Higher Downs Corn 2 C3
Higher Durston Som 28 B3
Higher End Gtr Man 194 G4
Higher Folds
Gtr Man 195 G7
Higherford Lancs 204 E3
Higher Gabwell Torbay 9 B8
Higher Green
Gtr Man 195 G8
Higher Halstock Leigh
Dorset 29 F8
Higher Heysham
Lancs 211 G8
Higher Hogshead
Lancs 195 C11
Higher Holton Som 29 B11
Higher Hurdsfield
Ches E 184 G6
Higher Kingcombe
Dorset 16 B6
Higher Kinnerton
Flint 166 C4
Higher Land Corn 12 G3
Higher Marsh Som 30 C2
Higher Melcombe
Dorset 30 G2
Higher Menadew
Corn 5 D10
Higher Molland
Devon 41 G8
Higher Muddiford
Devon 40 F5
Higher Nyland Dorset 30 C2
Higher Penwortham
Lancs 194 B4
Higher Pertwood
Wilts 45 F11
Higher Porthpean
Corn 5 E10
Higher Poynton
Ches E 184 E6
Higher Prestacott
Devon 12 B3
Higher Rads End
C Beds 103 E9
Higher Ridge
Shrops 149 C7
Higher Rocombe Barton
Devon 9 B8
Higher Row Dorset 31 G8
Higher Runcorn
Halton 183 E8
Higher Sandford
Dorset 29 C10
Higher Shotton Flint 166 B4
Higher Shurlach
Ches W 183 G11
Higher Slade Devon 40 D4
Higher Street Som 42 E6
Higher Tale Devon 27 G9
Higher Tolcarne Corn 5 B7
Higher Totnell
Dorset 29 F10
Highertown Corn 4 G6
Corn 11 E8
Higher Town Corn 5 C10
Scilly 1 F4
Som 42 D3
Higher Tremarcoombe
Corn 6 B5
Higher Vexford Som 42 F6
Higher Walreddon
Devon 12 G5
Higher Walton
Lancs 194 B5
Warr 183 D9
Higher Wambrook
Som 28 F3
Higher Warcombe
Devon 40 D3
Higher Weaver
Devon 27 G9
Higher Whatcombe
Dorset 30 G4
Higher Wheelton
Lancs 194 C6
Higher Whitley
Ches W 183 E10
Higher Wincham
Ches W 183 F11
Higher Woodsford
Dorset 17 D11
Higher Wraxall
Dorset 29 G9
Higher Wych
Ches W 167 G7
High Etherley
Durham 233 F9
High Ferry Lincs 174 F5
Highfield E Yorks 207 F10
Glos 79 E10
Gtr Man 194 G5
Gtr Man 195 F8
Herts 85 D9
N Ayrs 266 E6
Oxon 101 G11
Soton 32 E6
S Yorks 186 D5
T&W 242 F4
High Field Lancs 203 C10
Highfields Cambs 123 F7
Derbys 170 B6
Essex 88 B5
Glos 80 F3
Leicester 136 C2
Northumb 273 E9
Staffs 151 E8
S Yorks 198 F4
High Flatts W Yorks 197 F8
High Forge Durham 242 G6
High Friarside
Durham 242 F5
High Gallowhill
E Dunb 278 G2
High Garrett Essex 106 F5
Highgate E Sus 52 G2
Kent 53 G9
London 67 B9
Powys 130 D2
S Yorks 198 G3
W Mid 133 F11
High Grange
Durham 233 E9
High Grantley
N Yorks 214 F4
High Green Cumb 221 E8
Norf 141 B8
Norf 142 B2
Norf 159 G8
Shrops 132 G4
Suff 125 E7
S Yorks 186 B4
Worcs 99 B7
W Yorks 197 E7
High Halden Kent 53 F11
High Halstow
Medway 69 D9
High Ham Som 44 G2
High Handenhold
Durham 242 G6
High Harrington
Cumb 228 F6
High Harrogate
N Yorks 206 B2
High Haswell
Durham 234 C3
High Hatton Shrops 150 E2
High Hauxley
Northumb 253 C7
High Hawsker
N Yorks 227 D8
High Heath Shrops 150 D3
W Mid 133 C10
High Hesket Cumb 230 C5
High Hesleden
Durham 234 D5
High Hill Cumb 229 G11
High Houses Essex 87 C11
High Hoyland
S Yorks 197 E9
High Hunsley
E Yorks 208 F4
High Hurstwood
E Sus 37 B7
High Hutton
N Yorks 216 F5
High Ireby Cumb 229 D10
High Kelling Norf 177 E10
High Kilburn
N Yorks 215 D10
High Lands Durham 233 F8
Highlane Ches E 168 B5
Derbys 186 E6
High Lane Gtr Man 185 D7
Worcs 116 E3
Highlanes Corn 10 G4
Staffs 150 C5
High Lanes Corn 2 B3
High Laver Essex 87 D8
Highlaws Cumb 229 B8
Highleadon Glos 98 G5
High Legh Ches E 184 E2
Highleigh W Sus 22 D4
High Leven Stockton 225 C8
Highley Shrops 132 G4
High Littleton Bath 44 B6
High Longthwaite
Cumb 229 B11
High Lorton Cumb 229 F9
High Marishes
N Yorks 216 D6
High Marnham
Notts 188 G4
High Melton
S Yorks 198 G4
High Mickley
Northumb 242 E3
High Mindork
Dumfries 236 D5
Highmoor Cumb 229 B11
Oxon 65 B8
High Moor Derbys 187 E7
Lancs 194 E4
Highmoor Cross
Oxon 65 C8

Highmoor Hill Mon ...60 B3
High Moorsley T&W .234 B2
Highnam Glos. ...80 B3
Highnam Green Glos. .98 G5
High Nash Glos. ...79 C9
High Newton Cumb. .211 C8
High Newton-by-the-
Sea Northumb. ...264 D6
High Nibthwaite
Cumb. ...210 B5
Highoak Norf. ...141 C11
High Oaks Cumb. ...222 G2
High Offley Staffs. .150 D5
High Ongar Essex ...87 E9
High Onn Staffs. ...150 F6
High Onn Wharf
Staffs. ...150 F6
High Park Cumb. ...221 G10
Mers. ...193 D11
Highridge Bristol ...60 F5
High Risby N Lincs. ..200 E2
Highroad Well Moor
W Yorks. ...196 B5
High Roding Essex ...87 B10
High Rougham Suff. .125 E8
High Row Cumb. ...230 D3
Cumb. ...230 G3
High Salvington
W Sus. ...35 F10
High Scales Cumb. ..229 B9
High Sellafield
Cumb. ...219 G10
High Shaw N Yorks. .223 G7
High Shields T&W ..243 D9
High Shincliffe
Durham ...233 C11
High Side Cumb. ..229 E10
High Southwick
T&W ...243 F9
High Spen T&W ...242 F4
High Stakesby
N Yorks. ...227 C7
Highstead Kent ...71 F8
Highsted Kent ...70 G2
High Stoop Durham ..233 C8
Highstreet Kent. ...70 G5
High Street Corn. ...5 E9
Kent ...53 G8
Pembs ...73 B11
Suff ...107 B7
Suff ...127 C8
Suff ...127 F8
Suff ...143 G7
Highstreet Green
Essex ...106 E5
Sur. ...50 F3
High Street Green
Suff ...125 F10
High Sunderland
Borders ...261 C11
Hightae Dumfries ..238 B3
Highter's Heath
W Mid ...117 B11
High Throston
Hrtlpl. ...234 E5
High Tirfergus
Argyll. ...255 F7
Hightown Ches E. ..168 C5
Hants. ...31 G11
Mers. ...193 G10
Soton. ...33 E7
Wrex. ...166 F4
W Yorks. ...197 C7
High Town Luton. ..103 G11
Shrops. ...132 E4
Staffs. ...151 G9
Hightown Green
Suff ...125 F9
Hightown Heights
W Yorks. ...197 C7
High Toynton Lincs. .174 B3
High Trewhitt
Northumb. ...252 B2
High Urpeth
Durham ...242 G6
High Valleyfield
Fife ...279 D10
High Walton Cumb. .219 C9
High Warden
Northumb. ...241 D10
High Water Head
Cumb. ...220 F4
Highway Corn. ...4 G4
Hereford ...97 B9
Som. ...29 C7
Wilts. ...62 E4
Windsor. ...65 C11
Highweek Devon. ...14 G2
High Westwood
Durham ...242 F4
High Whinnow
Cumb. ...239 G8
Highwood Devon. ...27 F10
Dorset. ...18 D3
Essex. ...87 E10
Hants. ...31 F11
Worcs. ...116 D3
Highwood Hill
London. ...86 G2
High Woolaston Glos. .79 F9
High Worsall
N Yorks. ...225 D7
Highworth Swindon ..82 G2
Highworthy Devon. ..24 F6
High Wray Cumb. ..221 F7
High Wych Herts. ...87 C7
High Wycombe
Bucks. ...84 G5
Hilborough Norf. ...140 C6
Hilborough Ho Norf. .140 C6
Hilcot Glos. ...81 B7
Hilcote Derbys. ...171 D7
Hilcot End Glos. ...81 E9
Hilcott Wilts. ...46 B6
Hildenborough Kent .52 E5
Hilden Park Kent ...52 D5
Hildersham Cambs. .105 B10
Hildersley Hereford ..98 G2
Hilderstone Staffs. ..151 C8

Hilderthorpe
E Yorks. ...218 F3
Hilfield Dorset. ...29 F10
Hilgay Norf. ...140 D2
Hill S Glos. ...79 G10
Warks ...119 D9
W Mid ...134 D2
Hillam N Yorks. ...198 B4
Hillbeck Cumb. ...222 B5
Hillblock Pembs. ...73 B8
Hillborough Kent ...71 F8
Hillbourne BCP. ...18 C6
Hillbrae Aberds. ...302 E6
Aberds. ...303 G7
Hill Brow W Sus. ...34 B3
Hillbutts Dorset. ...31 G7
Hill Chorlton Staffs. .150 B5
Hillcliffe Warr. ...183 D10
Hillclifflane Derbys. .170 F3
Hillcommon Som. ...27 B11
Hill Common Norf. ..161 E8
Hill Corner Som. ...45 D10
Hill Croome Worcs. ..99 C7
Hillcross Derbys. ...152 C6
Hill Dale Lancs. ...194 E3
Hill Deverill Wilts. ..45 E11
Hilldyke Lincs. ...174 F4
Hill Dyke Lincs. ...174 F4
Hillend Fife ...280 E2
N Lanark ...268 B6
N Som. ...43 B11
Shrops. ...132 E6
Swansea ...56 C2
Hill End Durham ...232 D6
Fife ...279 D10
Glos. ...99 D8
London. ...85 G8
N Yorks. ...205 C7
Som. ...29 E8
Worcs. ...117 B8
Hillend Green Glos. ..98 F4
Hillersland Glos. ...79 C9
Hillerton Devon. ...13 B10
Hillesden Bucks. ...102 F3
Hillesden Hamlet
Bucks. ...102 E3
Hillesley Glos. ...61 B9
Hillfarance Som. ...27 C11
Hillfarrance Som. ...27 C11
Hillfield Devon. ...8 E6
W Mid ...118 B2
Hillfields S Glos. ...60 D6
W Mid ...118 B6
Hillfoot Aberds. ...303 D9
W Yorks. ...205 G10
Hillfoot End C Beds. .104 E2
Hill Furze Worcs. ...99 B9
Hill Gate Hereford ...97 F9
Hillgreen W Berks. ..64 D3
Hill Green Essex ...105 E9
Kent ...69 G10
Hillgrove W Sus. ...34 B6
Hillhampton
Hereford ...97 B11
Hillhead Aberds. ...302 F5
Aberds. ...303 E8
Corn. ...5 C11
Devon. ...9 E8
E Ayrs. ...257 B10
S Ayrs. ...257 F10
Hill Head Hants. ...33 G8
Northumb. ...241 D9
Hillhead of Auchentumb
Aberds. ...303 D9
Hillhead of Blairy
Aberds. ...302 D6
Hillhead of Cocklaw
Aberds. ...303 E10
Hill Hoath Kent ...52 E3
Hill Head W Mid. ...134 C2
Hillhouse Borders. ..271 D10
Hill Houses Shrops. .116 B2
Hilliard's Cross
Staffs. ...152 G3
Hilliclay Highld. ...310 C5
Hillingdon London. ..66 C5
Hillingdon Heath
London. ...66 C5
Hillington Glasgow. .267 C10
Norf. ...158 D4
Hillis Corner IoW ...20 C5
Hillmoor Devon. ...27 E10
Hillmorton Warks. ..119 C10
Hill Mountain Pembs. .73 D7
Hillockhead Aberds. .292 B6
Aberds. ...292 C5
Hillock Vale Lancs. ..195 B9
Hill of Beath Fife. ..280 C3
Hill of Drip Stirling. .278 B5
Hill of Fearn Highld. .301 B8
Hill of Keillor Angus. .286 C6
Hill of Mountblairy
Aberds. ...302 D6
Hill of Overbrae
Aberds. ...303 C8
Hill Park Hants. ...33 F9
Kent ...52 B2
Hillpool Worcs. ...117 B7
Hillpound Hants. ...33 D9
Hill Ridware Staffs. .151 F11
Hillsborough
S Yorks. ...186 C4
Hillside Aberds. ...293 D11
Angus ...293 G9
Devon. ...8 C4
Devon. ...27 F11
Hants. ...49 C9
Mers. ...193 E10
Orkney. ...314 G4
Orkney. ...314 G4
Shetland ...313 G6
Shrops. ...131 F11
Wilts. ...81 G9
Hill Side Hants. ...34 B3
S Yorks. ...197 G8
Worcs. ...116 E5
W Yorks. ...197 D7
Hill Somersal
Derbys. ...152 C2
Hills Town Derbys. .171 B7
Hillstreet Hants. ...32 D5

Hill Street Kent ...54 D6
Hillswick Shetland. .312 F4
Hilltop Bl Gwent ...77 D11
Bucks. ...85 E7
Derbys. ...170 C4
Hill Top Derbys ...186 F5
Durham ...232 G5
Durham ...233 C10
Durham ...242 G5
Gtr Man ...195 G8
Hants. ...32 G6
Notts. ...171 F7
N Yorks. ...214 G3
N Yorks. ...214 G5
Staffs. ...133 B7
S Yorks. ...186 C5
S Yorks. ...186 D3
S Yorks. ...187 B7
S Yorks. ...197 F9
W Mid ...134 E5
Warks ...135 F7
W Mid ...133 E9
W Sus. ...34 C5
W Yorks. ...196 E5
W Yorks. ...197 D16
W Yorks. ...205 G11
Hillview T&W... 243 G9
Hill View Dorset. ...18 B5
Hillway IoW ...21 D8
Hillwell Shetland. ...313 M5
Hill Wood W Mid ...134 C2
Hill Wootton Warks. .118 D6
Hillyfields Hants. ...32 D5
Hilmarton Wilts. ...62 D4
Hilperton Wilts. ...45 B11
Hilperton Marsh
Wilts. ...45 B11
Hilsea Ptsmth. ...33 G11
Hilston E Yorks. ...209 G11
Hiltingbury Hants. ...32 C6
Hilton Aberds. ...303 F9
Borders ...273 E7
Cambs. ...122 D5
Cumb. ...231 G11
Derbys. ...152 C4
Dorset. ...30 G3
Durham ...233 G9
Highld. ...309 L7
Highld. ...311 L3
Shrops. ...132 D5
Staffs. ...133 B11
Stockton ...225 C9
Hilton House
Gtr Man ...194 F6
Hilton Lodge Highld .300 G2
Hilton of Cadboll
Highld. ...301 B8
Hilton Park
Gtr Man ...195 G10
Himbleton Worcs. ..117 F8
Himley Staffs. ...133 E7
Hincaster Cumb. ...211 C10
Hinchley Wood Sur. .67 F7
Hinchliffe Mill
W Yorks. ...196 F6
Hinchwick Glos. ...100 E3
Hinckley Leics. ...135 E8
Hinderclay Suff. ...125 B10
Hinderton Ches W. ..182 F4
Hinderwell N Yorks. .226 B5
Hindford Shrops. ...148 C6
Hindhead Sur. ...49 F11
Hindle Fold Lancs. ..203 G10
Hindley Gtr Man. ...194 G6
Northumb. ...242 F2
Hindley Green
Gtr Man ...194 G6
Hindlip Worcs. ...117 F7
Hindolveston Norf. .159 D10
Hindon Wilts. ...46 G2
Hindpool Cumb. ...210 F3
Hindringham Norf. .159 B9
Hindsford Gtr Man. .195 G7
Hingham Norf. ...141 C10
Hinstock Shrops. ...150 D3
Hintlesham Suff. ...107 C11
Hinton Glos. ...79 E11
Hants. ...19 B10
Hereford ...96 D6
S Glos. ...61 D8
Shrops. ...131 B8
Som. ...29 C9
W Nhants. ...119 G10
Hinton Ampner Hants .33 B9
Hinton Blewett Bath. .44 B5
Hinton Charterhouse
Bath. ...45 B9
Hinton Cross Worcs. .99 C10
Hinton-in-the-Hedges
W Nhants. ...101 D11
Hinton Martell Dorset .31 F8
Hinton on the Green
Worcs. ...99 C10
Hinton Parva Dorset .31 G7
Swindon ...63 C8
Hinton St George
Som. ...28 E6
Hinton St Mary
Dorset. ...30 D3
Hinton Waldrist Oxon .82 F5
Hints Shrops. ...116 C2
Staffs. ...134 C3
Hinwick Bedford ...121 E8
Hinwood Shrops. ...131 B7
Hinxhill Kent ...54 E5
Hinxton Cambs. ...105 B9
Hinxworth Herts. ...104 C4
Hipperholme
W Yorks. ...196 B6
Hipplecote Worcs. ..116 F4
Hipsburn Northumb. .264 G6
Hipswell N Yorks. ...224 F3
Hirael Gwyn ...179 G9
Hiraeth Carms. ...92 G3
Hirn Aberds. ...293 C9
Hirnant Powys. ...147 E11
Hirst N Lanark. ...269 C7
Northumb. ...253 F7
Hirst Courtney
N Yorks. ...198 C6
Hirwaen Denb. ...165 C10

Hirwaun Rhondda ...77 D7
Hirwaun Common
Bridgend ...58 C2
Hiscott Devon. ...25 B8
Hislop Borders. ...249 C9
Hisomley Wilts. ...45 D11
Histon Cambs. ...123 E8
Hitcham Suff. ...125 E9
Hitchill Dumfries ...238 D4
Hitchin Herts. ...104 F3
Hitchin Hill Herts. ..104 F3
Hitcombe Bottom
Wilts. ...45 E10
Hither Green London .67 E11
Hittisleigh Devon. ...13 C10
Hittisleigh Barton
Devon. ...13 B10
Hive E Yorks. ...208 G2
Hixon Staffs. ...151 D10
Hoaden Kent ...55 B9
Hoar Cross Staffs. ..152 E2
Hoarwithy Hereford ..97 F10
Hoath Kent ...71 G8
Hoath Corner Kent ..52 E3
Hobarris Shrops. ...114 B6
Hobbister Orkney. ..314 F3
Hobble End Staffs. ..133 B10
Hobbles Green Suff. .124 G4
Hobbs Cross Essex. ..87 C7
Essex ...87 F7
Hobbs Wall Bath. ...61 G7
Hob Hill Ches W. ...167 G7
Hobkirk Borders. ...262 G3
Hobroyd Derbys. ...185 C8
Hobson Durham. ...242 F5
Hoby Leics. ...154 F3
Hoccombe Som. ...27 B10
Hockenden London. ..68 F3
Hockerill Herts. ...105 G9
Hockering Norf. ...159 G11
Hockering Heath
Norf. ...159 G11
Hockerton Notts. ...172 D2
Hockholler Som. ...27 C11
Hockholler Green
Som. ...27 C11
Hockley Ches E. ...184 E6
Essex ...88 G4
Kent ...54 E4
Staffs. ...134 C4
W Mid ...118 B5
Hockley Heath
W Mid ...118 C4
Hockliffe C Beds. ...103 F9
Hockwold cum Wilton
Norf. ...140 F4
Hockworthy Devon. ..27 D8
Hocombe Hants. ...32 C6
Hoddesdon Herts. ...86 D5
Hoddlesden
Blackburn ...195 C8
Hoddomcross
Dumfries ...238 C5
Hoddom Mains
Dumfries ...238 C5
Hoden Worcs. ...99 B11
Hodgefield Staffs. ..168 E6
Hodgehill Ches E. ..168 B4
W Mid ...134 F2
Hodgeston Pembs. ...73 F8
Hodley Powys. ...130 E3
Hodnet Shrops. ...150 D2
Hodnetheath
Shrops. ...150 D2
Hodsock Notts. ...187 D10
Hodsoll Street Kent. .68 G6
Hodson Swindon ...63 C7
Hodthorpe Derbys. ..187 F8
Hoe Hants. ...33 D9
Norf. ...159 F9
Sur. ...50 D5
Hoe Benham
W Berks. ...64 F2
Hoe Gate Hants. ...33 E10
Hoff Cumb. ...222 B3
Hoffleet Stow Lincs. .156 B4
Hogaland Shetland. ..312 F5
Hogben's Hill Kent. ..54 B4
Hogganfield
Glasgow ...268 B2
Hoggard's Green
Suff. ...125 F7
Hoggeston Bucks. ...102 G6
Hoggington Wilts. ...45 B10
Hoggrill's End
Warks. ...134 E4
Hogha Gearraidh
W Isles ...296 D3
Hog Hatch Sur. ...49 D10
Hoghton Lancs. ...194 B6
Hoghton Bottoms
Lancs. ...194 B6
Hogley Green
W Yorks. ...196 F6
Hognaston Derbys. ..170 E2
Hogpits Bottom
Herts. ...85 E8
Hogsthorpe Lincs. ..191 G8
Hogstock Dorset. ...31 F7
Holbeach Lincs. ...157 E7
Holbeach Bank
Lincs. ...157 D7
Holbeach Clough
Lincs. ...156 D6
Holbeach Drove
Lincs. ...156 G6
Holbeache Worcs. ..116 B5
Holbeach Hurn
Lincs. ...157 D7
Holbeach St Johns
Lincs. ...156 F6
Holbeach St Marks
Lincs. ...157 C7
Holbeach St Matthew
Lincs. ...157 C8
Holbeck Notts. ...187 F8
W Yorks. ...205 G11
Holbeck Woodhouse
Notts. ...187 G8
Holberrow Green
Worcs. ...117 F10
Holbeton Devon. ...8 E2

Holborn London. ...67 C10
Holborough Kent. ...69 G8
Holbrook Derbys. ...170 G5
Suff ...108 D3
S Yorks. ...186 E6
Holbrook Common
S Glos. ...61 E7
Holbrook Moor
Derbys. ...170 F5
Holbrooks W Mid. ..134 G6
Holburn Northumb. ..264 B2
Holbury Hants. ...32 G6
Holcombe Devon. ...14 G6
Gtr Man ...195 D9
Som. ...45 D7
Holcombe Brook
Gtr Man ...195 E9
Holcombe Rogus
Devon. ...27 D9
Holcot W Nhants. ..120 D5
Holdbrook London. ..86 F5
Holden Lancs. ...203 D11
Holdenby W Nhants. .120 D3
Holden Fold
Gtr Man ...196 F2
Holdenhurst BCP. ...19 B8
Holder's Green
Essex ...106 F2
Holders Hill London. .86 G2
Holdfast Worcs. ...99 D7
Holdgate Shrops. ...131 F11
Holdingham Lincs. ..173 F9
Holditch Devon. ...28 G4
Holdsworth
W Yorks. ...196 B5
Holdworth S Yorks. .186 C3
Hole Devon. ...24 D4
W Yorks. ...204 F6
Hole Bottom
W Yorks. ...196 C2
Holefield Borders. ..263 C8
Holehills N Lanark. ..268 B5
Holehouse Derbys. ..185 C8
Holehouses Ches E. .184 F2
Hole-in-the-Wall
Hereford ...98 F2
Holemill Aberdeen ..293 C10
Holemoor Devon. ...24 F6
Hole's Hole Devon. ..7 B8
Holestane Dumfries .247 D9
Holestone Derbys. ..170 C4
Hole Street W Sus. ..35 E10
Holewater Devon. ...41 F8
Holgate York ...207 C7
Holker Cumb. ...211 D7
Holkham Norf. ...176 E5
Hollacombe Devon. ..24 G5
Devon. ...26 G4
Hollacombe Hill
Devon. ...7 E10
Holland Orkney. ...314 A4
Orkney ...314 D6
Sur. ...52 C2
Holland Fen Lincs. ..174 F2
Holland Lees Lancs. .194 F4
Holland-on-Sea
Essex ...89 B12
Hollands Som. ...29 D9
Hollandstoun
Orkney ...314 A7
Holme on the Wolds
E Yorks. ...208 D5
Hollee Dumfries ...239 D7
Hollesley Suff. ...109 C7
Hollicombe Torbay. ..9 C7
Hollies Common
Staffs. ...150 E6
Hollinfare Warr. ...183 C11
Hollingbourne Kent. .53 B10
Hollingbury Brighton .36 F4
Hollingdean Brighton .36 F4
Hollingdon Bucks. ..103 F7
Hollingrove E Sus. ..37 C11
Hollington Derbys. ..152 B4
E Sus. ...38 E3
Hants. ...48 B2
Staffs. ...151 B11
Hollington Cross
Hants. ...48 B2
Hollington Grove
Derbys. ...152 B4
Hollingwood Derbys .186 G6
Hollingworth
Gtr Man ...185 B8
Hollin Hall Lancs. ...204 F4
Hollin Park W Yorks. .206 F2
Hollins Cumb. ...222 G3
Derbys. ...186 G4
Gtr Man ...195 F8
Gtr Man ...195 F11
Staffs. ...168 D6
Staffs. ...168 E4
Staffs. ...169 F7
Hollinsclough Staffs. .169 B9
Hollins End S Yorks. .186 E5
Hollinsgreen
Ches E. ...168 C2
Hollins Green
Warr. ...183 C11
Hollins Lane Lancs. ..202 C5
Shrops. ...149 B10
Hollinswood Telford. .132 B4
Hollinthorpe
W Yorks. ...206 G3
Hollinwood
Gtr Man ...196 G2
Shrops. ...149 B10
Hollis Green Devon. ..27 F9
Hollis Head Devon. ..27 G7
Hollocombe Devon. ..25 E10
Hollocombe Town
Devon. ...25 E10
Holloway Derbys. ...170 D4
Wilts. ...45 G11
Windsor. ...65 C10
Holloway Hill Sur. ..50 E3
Hollow Brook Bath. ..60 G5
Hollowell W Nhants. .120 C3
Hollow Meadows
S Yorks. ...186 D2

Hollowmoor Heath
Ches W. ...167 B7
Hollow Oak Dorset. ..18 C2
Hollows Dumfries ...239 B9
Hollow Street Kent. ..71 G8
Holly Bank W Mid. ..133 C11
Hollyberry End
W Mid ...134 G5
Holly Brook Som. ...44 B4
Holly Bush Caerph. ..77 E11
E Ayrs. ...257 G9
Stoke ...168 G5
Torf. ...78 G3
Worcs. ...98 D5
Holly Bush Wrex. ...166 G6
Hollybush Corner
Bucks. ...66 B3
Suff ...125 F8
Hollybushes Kent. ...54 B2
Hollybush Hill Bucks. .66 B3
Essex ...89 B10
Hollycroft Leics. ...135 E8
Holly Cross Windsor. .65 C10
Holly End Norf. ...139 B9
Holly Green Bucks. ..84 E3
Worcs. ...99 C7
Holly Hill N Yorks. ..224 E3
Hollyhurst Shrops. ..131 D9
Warks. ...135 F7
Hollym E Yorks. ...201 B10
Hollywaste Shrops. ..116 B2
Holy City Devon. ...28 G3
Hollywater Hants. ...49 G10
Hollywood Worcs. ..117 B11
Holmacott Devon. ...25 B8
Holman Clavel Som. .28 D2
Holmbridge
W Yorks. ...196 F6
Holmbury St Mary
Sur. ...50 E6
Holmbush Corn. ...5 E10
Dorset. ...28 G5
Holmcroft Staffs. ...151 D8
Holme Cambs. ...138 F3
C Beds. ...104 C3
Cumb. ...211 D10
N Lincs. ...200 F2
Notts. ...172 D4
N Yorks. ...215 C7
W Yorks. ...196 F6
W Yorks. ...205 G9
Holmebridge Dorset. .18 D3
Holme Chapel
Lancs. ...195 B11
Holme Green
C Beds. ...104 C3
N Yorks. ...207 E7
Northumb. ...243 C8
Som. ...29 E8
Warks. ...118 D3
Holme Hale Norf. ...141 B7
Holme Hill NE Lincs. .201 F9
Holme Lacy
Hereford ...97 D11
Holme Lane Notts. ..154 B2
Holme Marsh
Hereford ...114 G6
Holme Mills Cumb. .211 D10
Holme next the Sea
Norf. ...176 E2
Holme-on-Spalding-
Moor E Yorks. ...208 F2
Holme on the Wolds
E Yorks. ...208 D5
Holme Pierrepont
Notts. ...154 B2
Holmer Hereford ...97 C10
Holmer Green Bucks. .84 F6
Holmes Lancs. ...194 D3
Holme St Cuthbert
Cumb. ...229 B8
Holmes Chapel
Ches E. ...168 B3
Holmesdale Derbys. .186 F4
Holmesfield Derbys. .186 F4
Holme Slack Lancs. ..203 G7
Holmes's Hill E Sus. .23 C8
Holmethorpe Sur. ...51 C9
Holmewood Derbys. .170 B6
Holme Wood
W Yorks. ...205 G9
Holmfield W Yorks. ..196 B5
Holmfirth W Yorks. ..196 F6
Holmhead Angus. ...293 F7
Dumfries. ...246 F4
E Ayrs. ...258 E3
Holmhill Highld. ...297 G7
Holmisdale Highld. ..297 G7
Holmley Common
Derbys. ...186 F5
Holmpton E Yorks. ..201 C11
Holmrook Cumb. ...219 F11
Holmsgarth Shetland .313 J6
Holmside Durham. ..233 B10
Holmston S Ayrs. ...257 E9
Holmwood Corner
Sur. ...51 E7
Holmwrangle Cumb. .230 B6
Holne Devon. ...8 B4
Holnest Dorset. ...29 E11
Holnicote Som. ...42 D2
Holsworthy Devon. ..24 G4
Holsworthy Beacon
Devon. ...24 F5
Holt Dorset. ...31 G8
Hants. ...49 D8
Norf. ...159 B11
Wilts. ...61 G11
Worcs. ...116 E6
Wrex. ...166 E6
Holtby York. ...207 C9
Holt End Hants. ...49 F7
Worcs. ...117 D11
Holt Fleet Worcs. ...116 E6
Holt Green Lancs. ...193 G11
Holt Head W Yorks. .196 F5
Holt Heath Dorset. ..31 G9
Worcs. ...116 E6
Holt Hill Kent. ...53 B8
Holton Oxon. ...83 D10

Holton continued
Som. ...29 B11
Suff ...127 B7
Holton cum Beckering
Lincs. ...189 E10
Holton Heath Dorset. .18 C4
Holton le Clay Lincs. .201 G9
Holton le Moor
Lincs. ...189 B9
Holton St Mary
Suff ...107 D11
Holt Park W Yorks. ..205 E11
Holt Pound Hants. ...49 E10
Holts Gtr Man. ...196 G3
Holtspur Bucks. ...84 G6
Holt Wood Dorset. ..31 F8
Holtye E Sus. ...52 F3
Holway Dorset. ...29 C10
Flint ...181 F11
Som. ...28 C2
Holwell Dorset. ...30 E2
Herts. ...104 E3
Leics. ...154 E4
Oxon. ...82 D2
Som. ...45 D8
Holwellbury C Beds. .104 E3
Holwick Durham ...232 F4
Holworth Dorset. ...17 E11
Holybourne Hants. ..49 E8
Holy Cross Worcs. ...98 G3
Holy Cross T&W ...243 D6
Worcs. ...117 B8
Holyfield Essex. ...86 E5
Holyhead = Caergybi
Anglesey ...178 G2
Holy Island
Northumb. ...273 B11
Holylee Borders. ...261 B9
Holymoorside
Derbys. ...170 B4
Holyport Windsor. ...65 D11
Holystone
Northumb. ...251 C11
Holytown N Lanark. .268 C5
Holywell Cambs. ...122 C6
C Beds. ...85 B8
Corn. ...4 D5
Dorset. ...29 G9
E Sus. ...23 F9
Glos. ...80 G3
Hereford ...97 C7
Herts. ...85 F9
Northumb. ...243 C8
Som. ...29 E8
Warks. ...118 D3
Holywell = Treffynnon
Flint ...181 F11
Holywell Green
W Yorks. ...196 D5
Holywell Lake Som. .27 C10
Holywell Row Suff. ..124 B4
Holywood Dumfries .247 G10
Homedowns Glos. ...99 E8
Homer Shrops. ...132 C2
Homer Green
Mers. ...193 G10
Homersfield Suff. ...142 F5
Homerton London. ...67 B11
Hom Green Hereford ..97 G11
Homington Wilts. ...31 B10
Honeybourne
Worcs. ...100 C2
Honeychurch Devon. .25 G10
Honeydon Bedford ..122 F2
Honey Hall N Som. ..60 G2
Honeyhill
Wokingham ...65 F10
Honey Hill Kent. ...70 G6
Honeystreet Wilts. ..62 G6
Honey Street Wilts. ..62 G6
Honey Tye Suff. ...107 D9
Honeywick C Beds. ..103 G9
Honicknowle Plym. ...7 D9
Honiley Warks. ...118 C4
Honing Norf. ...160 D6
Honingham Norf. ...160 G2
Honington Lincs. ...172 G6
Suff ...125 C8
Warks. ...100 C5
Honiton Devon. ...27 G11
Honkley Wrex. ...166 D4
Honley W Yorks. ...196 E6
Honley Moor
W Yorks. ...196 E6
Honnington Telford. ..150 F4
Honor Oak London. ..67 E11
Honor Oak Park
London. ...67 E11
Honresfield Gtr Man. .196 E2
Hoo Kent. ...71 G9
Hoober S Yorks. ...186 B6
Hoobrook Worcs. ...116 C6
Hood Green
S Yorks. ...197 G10
Hood Hill S Yorks. ..186 B5
Hood Manor Warr. ..183 D9
Hooe E Sus. ...23 D11
Plym. ...7 E10
Hooe Common
E Sus. ...23 C11
Hoofield Ches W. ...167 C8
Hoohill Blackpool. ..202 F2
Hoo Hole W Yorks. ..196 B6
Hook Cambs. ...139 E8
Devon. ...28 F4
E Yorks. ...199 B9
Hants. ...33 F8
Hants. ...49 C8
London. ...67 G7
Pembs. ...73 C7
Wilts. ...62 C5
Hook-a-gate Shrops. .131 B9
Hook Bank Worcs. ...98 C6
Hooke Dorset. ...16 B6
Hook End Essex. ...87 F9
Oxon. ...65 C7
W Mid ...134 G4
Hooker Gate T&W ...242 F4

Hookgate Staffs. ...150 B4
Hook Green Kent ...53 F7
Kent ...68 F6
Hook Heath Sur. ...50 B3
Hook Norton Oxon. ..101 E7
Hook Park Hants. ...33 G7
Hook's Cross Herts. ..104 G5
Hook Street Glos. ...79 F11
Wilts. ...62 C5
Hooksway W Sus. ...34 A4
Hookway Devon. ...14 B3
Hookwood Sur. ...51 E9
Hoole Ches W. ...166 B6
Hoole Bank Ches W. ..166 B6
Hooley Sur. ...51 B9
Hooley Bridge
Gtr Man. ...195 E10
Hooley Brow
Gtr Man. ...195 E11
Hooley Hill Gtr Man. .184 B6
Hoo Meavy Devon. ...7 B10
Hoop Mon. ...79 D8
Hoopers Pool Wilts. ..45 C10
Hoops Devon. ...24 C5
Hoo St Werburgh
Medway ...69 E9
Hooton Ches W. ...182 F5
Hooton Levitt
S Yorks. ...187 C8
Hooton Pagnell
S Yorks. ...198 F3
Hooton Roberts
S Yorks. ...187 B7
Hopcroft's Holt
Oxon. ...101 F9
Hope Derbys. ...185 E11
Devon. ...9 G8
Highld ...308 D4
Powys ...130 B3
Powys ...130 C6
S Yorks. ...196 F5
Staffs. ...169 G8
Hope = Yr Hôb Flint. .166 D4
Hope Bagot Shrops. .115 C11
Hopebeck Cumb. ...229 G9
Hope Bowdler
Shrops. ...131 E9
Hopedale Staffs. ...169 D10
Hope End Green
Essex. ...105 G11
Hope Green Ches E. ..184 F6
Hopeman Moray. ...301 C11
Hope Mansell
Hereford ...79 B10
Hope Park Shrops. ..130 C6
Hopesay Shrops. ...131 G7
Hopesgate Shrops. ..130 C6
Hope's Green Essex. .69 B9
Hope's Rough
Hereford ...98 B2
Hopetown
W Yorks. ...197 C11
Hope under Dinmore
Hereford ...115 G10
Hopgoods Green
W Berks. ...64 F4
Hopkinstown
Rhondda ...77 G9
Hopley's Green
Hereford ...114 G6
Hopperton N Yorks. ..206 B3
Hop Pole Lincs. ...156 G3
Hopsford Warks. ...135 G8
Hopstone Shrops. ...132 E5
Hopton Derbys. ...170 E3
Shrops. ...149 D11
Shrops. ...149 E7
Staffs. ...151 D8
Suff ...125 B9
Hoptonbank Shrops. .116 B2
Hopton Cangeford
Shrops. ...131 G10
Hopton Castle
Shrops. ...115 B7
Hoptongate Shrops. .131 G10
Hoptonheath Shrops. .115 B7
Hopton Heath
Staffs. ...151 D9
Hopton on Sea
Norf. ...143 D10
Hopton Wafers
Shrops. ...116 B2
Hopwas Staffs. ...134 B3
Hopwood Gtr Man. ..195 F11
Worcs. ...117 B10
Hopworthy Devon. ...24 G4
Horam E Sus. ...23 B9
Horbling Lincs. ...156 B2
Horbury W Yorks. ..197 D9
Horbury Bridge
W Yorks. ...197 D9
Horbury Junction
W Yorks. ...197 D10
Horcott Glos. ...81 E11
Horden Durham. ...234 C4
Horderley Shrops. ..131 F8
Hordle Hants. ...19 B11
Hordley Shrops. ...149 C7
Horeb Carms. ...75 D7
Carms. ...93 F10
Ceredig. ...93 C7
Flint ...166 D3
Horfield Bristol ...60 D5
Horgabost W Isles ..305 J2
Horham Suff. ...126 C4
Horkesley Heath
Essex. ...107 F9
Horkstow N Lincs. ..200 D3
Horkstow Wolds
N Lincs. ...200 D3
Horley Oxon. ...101 C8
Sur. ...51 E9
Horn Ash Dorset. ...28 G5
Hornblotton Som. ...44 G5
Hornblotton Green
Som. ...44 G5
Hornby Lancs. ...211 F11
N Yorks. ...224 G4
N Yorks. ...225 D7
Horncastle Lincs. ...174 B3
Reading ...65 E8
Hornchurch London. ..68 B4
Horncliffe Northumb. .273 F8

Horndean Borders ..273 F7
Hants. 34 E2
Horndon Devon 69 C7
Horndon on the Hill
Thurrock 69 C7
Horne Sur. 51 E10
Horner Som 41 D11
Horner Row Essex . ..88 E3
Horner's Green Suff .107 C9
Hornestreet Essex .107 C11
Horney Common
E Sus 37 B7
Horn Hill Som 43 E8
Hornick Corn 5 E9
Horniehaugh Angus .292 G6
Horning Norf 160 F6
Horninghall Leics . 136 D6
Horninglow Staffs . 152 D4
Horningsham Wilts . .45 E10
Horningsea Cambs ..123 E9
Horningtoft Norf. ..159 E8
Horningtops Corn. ..6 C5
Hornsbury Som 28 E4
Hornsby Cumb 240 G2
Horns Corner Kent . .38 E2
Horns Cross Devon . .24 C5
E Sus 38 C4
Hornsea E Yorks .209 D10
Hornsea Bridge
E Yorks 209 D10
Hornsea Burton
E Yorks 209 D10
Hornsey London 67 B10
Hornsey Vale
London 67 B10
Horns Green Kent . .52 B3
Horn Street Kent ..55 F7
Kent 69 G7
Hornton Oxon 101 B7
Horpit Swindon 63 C8
Horrabridge Devon ..7 B10
Horringer Suff....124 E6
Horringford IoW ..20 D6
Horrocks Fold
Gtr Man 195 E8
Horrocksford
Lancs. 203 E10
Horsalls Kent.....53 C11
Horsebridge Devon . .12 G4
Hants. 47 G10
Shrops. 131 B7
Horse Bridge Staffs .169 E7
Horsebrook Devon 8 D4
Staffs. 151 G7
Horsecastle N Som . .60 F2
Horsedown Wilts ...61 D10
Horsedowns Corn. ...2 C4
Horsehay Telford . ..132 B3
Horseheath Cambs ..106 B4
Horseholm Dumfries .238 C2
Horsehouse
N Yorks 213 C10
Horseley Heath
W Mid 133 E9
Horsell Sur. 50 B3
Horsell Birch Sur. .50 B3
Horseman's Green
Wrex 166 G6
Horseman Side Essex . .87 F8
Horsemere Green
W Sus 35 G7
Horsenden Bucks ..84 E3
Horsepools Glos....80 C4
Horseway Cambs ..139 F8
Horseway Head
Hereford 114 E6
Horsey Norf 161 E9
Som 43 F10
Horsey Corner Norf .161 E9
Horsey Down Wilts . .81 G9
Horsford Norf.....160 F5
Horsforth W Yorks . .205 F10
Horsforth Woodside
W Yorks 205 F10
Horsham Worcs ...116 F4
W Sus 51 G7
Horsham St Faith
Norf 160 F4
Horshoe Green Kent . .52 E3
Horsington Lincs ..173 B11
Som 30 C2
Horsley Derbys 170 G5
Glos. 80 F4
Northumb 242 D3
Northumb 251 D8
Horsley Cross Essex. .108 F2
Horsleycross Street
Essex. 108 F2
Horsleyhill Borders ..262 F2
Horsley Hill T&W . ..243 D9
Horsleyhope
Durham 233 B7
Horsleys Green Bucks .84 F3
Horsley Woodhouse
Derbys. 170 G5
Horsmonden Kent ...53 E7
Horspath Oxon.....83 E9
Horstead Norf 160 F5
Horsted Green E Sus . .23 B7
Horsted Keynes
W Sus 36 B5
Horton Bucks 84 B6
Dorset 31 F8
Kent 54 B6
Lancs. 204 C3
S Glos. 61 C9
Shrops. 149 D9
Som 28 E4
Staffs. 168 D6
Swansea 56 D3
Telford. 150 G3
Wilts 62 G5
Windsor 66 D4
W Hants. 120 G6
Horton Common
Dorset 31 F9
Horton Cross Som ..28 D4
Horton-cum-Studley
Oxon 83 C9
Horton Green
Ches W 167 F7
Horton Heath Dorset . .31 F9

Horton Heath continued
Hants. 33 D7
Horton in Ribblesdale
N Yorks 212 E6
Horton Kirby Kent ..68 F5
Hortonlane Shrops. .149 G8
Horton Wharf Bucks . .84 B6
Hortonwood Telford. .150 G3
Horwich Gtr Man 194 E6
Horwich End Derbys .185 E8
Horwood Devon. ...25 B8
Horwood Riding
S Glos. 61 B8
Hose Leics. 154 D4
Hoselaw Borders ...263 C8
Hoses Cumb 220 G4
Hosey Hill Kent ...52 C3
Hosh Perth 286 E2
Hosta W Isles 296 D3
Hoswick Shetland . .313 L6
Hotham E Yorks ...208 G3
Hothfield Kent.....54 D3
Hoton Leics. 153 E11
Hotwells Bristol. ...60 E5
Houbans Shetland. .312 F5
Houbie Shetland ..312 D8
Houdston S Ayrs ..244 D5
Hough Argyll.....288 E1
Ches E 168 E2
Ches E 184 F5
Hougham Lincs ...172 G5
Hough Green Halton 183 D7
Hough-on-the-Hill
Lincs 172 F6
Hough Side
W Yorks 205 G10
Houghton Cambs ..122 C5
Cumb 239 F10
Hants. 47 G10
Northumb 242 D4
Pembs 73 D7
W Sus 35 F8
Houghton Bank
Darl 233 G10
Houghton Conquest
C Beds 103 C10
Houghton Green
E Sus 38 C4
Warr 183 C10
Houghton-le-Side
Darl 233 G10
Houghton-le-Spring
T&W 234 B2
Houghton on the Hill
Leics 136 C3
Houghton Regis
C Beds 103 G10
Houghton St Giles
Norf 159 B8
Houghwood Mers. ..194 G4
Houlsyke N Yorks ..226 D4
Houlton Warwicks. .119 C11
Hound Hants 33 F7
Hound Green Hants . .49 B8
Hound Hill Dorset. ..31 G7
Houndmills Hants. . .48 C6
Houndscroft Glos....80 E5
Houndslow Borders .272 F2
Houndsmoor Som ...28 B10
Houndwood Borders .272 C6
Hounsdown Hants. ..32 E5
Hounslow London ...66 D6
Hounslow Green
Essex. 87 B11
Hounslow West
London 66 D6
Houns-a-cuff Gtr Man .197 D7
Houston Renfs.....267 B8
Houstry Highld....310 F5
Houton Orkney....314 F3
Hove Brighton.....36 G3
Hove Edge W Yorks. .196 C6
Hoveringham
Notts. 171 F11
Hoveton Norf 160 F6
Hovingham N Yorks . .216 D3
How Cumb........240 F2
Howbeck Bank
Ches E 167 F11
Howbrook S Yorks. .186 B4
How Caple Hereford. .98 E2
Howden Borders ...262 E5
E Yorks 199 B8
W Loth 269 B11
Howden Clough
W Yorks 197 B8
Howden-le-Wear
Durham 233 E9
Howdon T&W 243 D8
Howdon Pans T&W. .243 D8
Howe Highld.....310 C7
Norf 142 C5
N Yorks 214 C6
How Bridge
Gtr Man 195 G7
Howegreen Essex. ..88 E4
Howe Green Essex. ..87 B11
Essex. 88 E2
Warks 134 F6
Howell Lincs......173 F10

How End C Beds 103 C10
Howe of Teuchar
Aberds. 303 E7
Howe Street Essex. .87 C11
Essex. 106 E3
Howey Powys 113 F11
Howford Borders ..261 B8
Borders 261 E9
Howgate Cumb 228 G5
Midloth 270 D4
Howgill Cumb 222 F2
Lancs. 204 D2
N Yorks 205 B7
Howick Kent......52 D3
Mon. 79 F8
Northumb 265 F7
Howick Cross Lancs .194 B4
Howle Durham 233 F7
Telford. 150 E3
Howleigh Som.....28 D2
Howley Glos.......80 G2
Som 28 F3
Warr 183 D10
Hownam Borders ..263 F7
Hownam Mains
Borders 263 E7
Howpasley Borders .249 B8
Howsham N Lincs ..200 G4
N Yorks 216 G4
Howslack Dumfries .248 B3
Howtel Northumb. .263 C9
Howton Hereford. ..97 F8
Howtown Cumb....221 B8
Howwood Renfs....267 C7
How Wood Herts ..85 E10
Hoxne Suff 126 B3
Hoxton London.....67 C10
Hoy Orkney......314 F2
Hoylake Mers. ...182 D2
Hoyland S Yorks ..197 G11
Hoyland Common
S Yorks 197 G11
Hoylandswaine
S Yorks 197 G9
Hoyle W Sus 34 D6
Hoyle Mill S Yorks .197 F11
Hubbard's Hill Kent .52 C4
Hubberholme
N Yorks 213 D8
Hubberston Pembs. .72 D5
Hubbersty Head
Cumb 221 G8
Hubberton Green
W Yorks 196 C4
Hubbert's Bridge
Lincs 174 G3
Huby N Yorks 205 D11
N Yorks 215 F11
Hucclecote Glos....80 B5
Hucking Kent......53 B10
Hucknall Notts. ...171 F8
Huddersfield
W Yorks 196 D6
Huddington Worcs. .117 F8
Huddlesford Staffs. .134 B3
Hud Hey Lancs....195 C9
Hudnall Herts 85 C8
Hudnalls Glos......79 E8
Hudswell N Yorks ..224 E3
Wilts 61 F11
Huggate E Yorks ..208 B3
Hugglepit Devon. ...24 C4
Hugglescote Leics. .153 G8
Hughenden Valley
Bucks. 84 F5
Hughley Shrops. ..131 D11
Hugh Mill Lancs. . .195 C10
Hugh Town Scilly ...1 G4
Hugus Corn........4 G5
Huish Devon 25 B7
Devon 25 E8
Wilts 62 G6
Huish Champflower
Som 27 B9
Huish Episcopi Som. .28 B6
Huisinis W Isles ..305 G1
Hulcote C Beds 103 D8
N Whants. 102 B4
Hulcott Bucks. 84 B5
Hulland Derbys....170 F2
Hulland Moss
Derbys. 170 F3
Hulland Ward
Derbys. 170 F3
Hullavington Wilts. .61 C11
Hullbridge Essex. ..88 G4
Hull End Derbys....185 E9
Hulme Gtr Man 184 B4
Staffs. 168 F6
Warr 183 C10
Hulme End Staffs. .169 D10
Hulme Walfield
Ches E 168 B4
Hulseheath Ches E. .184 E2
Hulverstone IoW. ..20 E3
Hulver Street Suff. .143 F9
Humber Devon. 14 G3
Hereford 115 F10
Humber Bridge
N Lincs 200 C4
Humberston
NE Lincs 201 F10
Humberstone
Leicester 136 B2
Humberston Fitties
NE Lincs 201 F10
Humbie E Loth....271 C9
Humbledon T&W. ..243 F9
Humble Green Suff. .107 B8
Humbleton
E Yorks 209 G10
Northumb 263 D11
Humby Lincs......155 C10
Hume Borders 272 G4
Hummersknott Darl .224 C5
Humshaugh
Northumb 241 C10

Huna Highld......310 B7
Huncoat Lancs. ...203 G11
Huncote Leics 135 D10
Hundalee Borders. .262 F4
Hundall Derbys....186 F5
Hunderthwaite
Durham 232 G5
Hunderton Hereford. .97 D9
Hundleby Lincs....174 B5
Hundle Houses
Lincs 174 E3
Hundleshope
Borders 260 B6
Hundleton Pembs. ..73 E7
Hundon Suff......106 B4
Hundred Acres Hants .33 E9
Hundred End Lancs .194 C2
Hundred House
Powys 114 G2
Hungarton Leics. ..136 B3
Hungate N Yorks. .197 B11
Hungerford Hants. .31 E11
Shrops. 131 F10
Som 42 E4
W Berks 63 F10
Windsor 65 E10
Hungerford Green
W Berks 64 D5
Hungerford Newtown
W Berks 63 E11
Hunger Hill Gtr Man .194 E4
Lancs. 194 E4
Hungershall Park
Kent 52 F5
Hungerstone
Hereford 97 D8
Hungerton Lincs. ..155 D7
Hungladder Highld. .298 B3
Hungreyhatton
Shrops. 150 D3
Hunmanby
N Yorks 217 D11
Hunmanby Moor
N Yorks 218 D2
Hunningham Warks. 119 D7
Hunningham Hill
Warks 119 D7
Hunnington Worcs. .133 G9
Hunny Hill IoW 20 D5
Hunsdon Herts 86 C6
Hunsdonbury Herts. .86 C6
Hunsingore N Yorks .206 C4
Hunslet W Yorks ..206 G2
Hunslet Carr
W Yorks 206 G2
Hunsonby Cumb ..231 D7
Hunspow Highld. .310 B6
Hunstanton Norf. .175 G11
Hunstanworth
Durham 232 B5
Hunsterson Ches E .167 F11
Hunston Suff......125 D9
W Sus 22 C5
Hunston Green Suff. .125 D9
Hunstrete Bath....60 G6
Hunsworth W Yorks .197 B7
Hunt End Worcs ..117 E10
Huntenhull Green
Wilts 45 D10
Huntercombe End
Oxon 65 B7
Hunters Forstal Kent. .71 F7
Hunter's Quay Argyll .276 F3
Huntham Som 28 B4
Hunthill Lodge
Angus 292 F6
Huntingdon Cambs. .122 C4
Huntingfield Suff. ..126 C6
Huntingford Dorset. .45 G10
S Glos. 80 G2
Huntington Ches W. .166 C6
E Loth 281 F9
Hereford 97 C9
Hereford 114 G5
Staffs. 151 G9
Telford. 132 B3
York. 207 B8
Huntington Green
Hereford 97 C9
Huntingtower
Perth 286 E4
Huntley Glos......80 B2
Staffs. 169 G8
Huntly Aberds. ...302 F5
Huntlywood Borders .272 F2
Hunton Hants. 48 F3
Kent 53 D8
N Yorks 224 G3
Hunton Bridge
Herts 85 E9
Hunt's Corner Norf. .141 F12
Huntscott Som....42 E2
Hunt's Cross Mers. .182 D6
Hunts Green Warks .134 D3
Hunt's Green Bucks. .84 E5
W Berks 64 E2
Huntsham Devon. ..27 C8
Huntshaw Devon. ..25 C8
Huntshaw Water
Devon 25 C8
Hunt's Hill Bucks. ..84 F4
Hunt's Lane Leics. .135 C9
Huntspill Som.....43 D10
Huntstile Som.....43 G9
Huntworth Som....43 G10
Hunwick Durham. .233 E9
Hunworth Norf. ..159 B11
Hurcott Som......29 B8
Som 29 E10
Worcs 117 B7
Hurdcott Wilts.....47 G7
Hurdley Powys....130 D5
Hurdsfield Ches E. .184 G6
Hurgill N Yorks ...224 E3
Hurlet Glasgow ...267 C10
Hurley Warks 134 D4
Windsor 65 C10
Hurley Bottom
Windsor 65 C10
Hurley Common
Warks 134 D4
Hurlford S Ayrs ..257 B11
Hurliness Orkney ..314 H2
Hurlston Lancs....194 E2

Hurlston Green
Lancs. 193 E11
Hurn BCP 19 B8
E Yorks 208 E6
Hurn's End Lincs ..174 F6
Hursey Dorset 28 G6
Hursley Hants 32 B6
Hurst Cumb.......230 C4
Dorset 17 C1
Gtr Man 196 G2
N Yorks 223 E10
Som 29 D7
Wokingham 65 E9
Hurstbourne Priors
Hants. 48 D2
Hurstbourne Tarrant
Hants. 47 C11
Hurstead Gtr Man. .196 D1
Hurst Green Essex. .89 B9
E Sus 38 B2
Lancs. 203 F9
Sur. 51 C11
W Mid 133 F10
Hurst Hill W Mid. .133 E8
Hurstley Hereford. ..97 B7
Hurst Park Sur....66 F6
Hurstpierpoint
W Sus 36 D3
Hurst Wickham
W Sus 36 D3
Hurstwood Lancs. .204 G3
Hurtmore Sur.....50 D3
Hurworth-on-Tees
Darl 224 C6
Hurworth Place
Darl 224 D5
Hury Durham 223 B9
Husabost Highld. ..298 D2
Husbands Bosworth
Leics 136 G2
Husbandtown
Angus 287 D8
Husborne Crawley
C Beds 103 D9
Husthwaite
N Yorks 215 D10
Hutcherleigh Devon. ...8 E5
Hutchesontown
Glasgow 267 C11
Hutchwns Bridgend. .57 F10
Hut Green N Yorks. .198 C5
Huthwaite Notts. ..171 D7
Hutlerburn Borders .261 D10
Huttock Top Lancs. 195 C11
Huttoft Lincs......191 F8
Hutton Borders ...273 E7
Cumb 230 F4
Essex. 87 F10
E Yorks 208 C6
Lancs. 194 B3
N Som 43 B11
Hutton Bonville
N Yorks 224 E6
Hutton Buscel
N Yorks 217 C9
Hutton Conyers
N Yorks 214 E6
Hutton Cranswick
E Yorks 208 C6
Hutton End Cumb. .230 D4
Hutton Gate
Redcar 225 B11
Hutton Hang
N Yorks 214 B3
Hutton Henry
Durham 234 D4
Hutton-le-Hole
N Yorks 226 G4
Hutton Magna
Durham 224 C2
Hutton Mount
Essex. 87 G10
Hutton Roof Cumb .211 D11
Cumb 230 E3
Hutton Rudby
N Yorks 225 D9
Huttons Ambo
N Yorks 216 F5
Hutton Sessay
N Yorks 215 D9
Hutton Village
Redcar 225 C11
Hutton Wandesley
N Yorks 206 C6
Huxham Devon. 14 B4
Huxham Green Som. .44 F5
Huxley Ches W 167 C8
Huxter Shetland ..313 G7
Shetland 313 H5
Shetland 313 H6
Huxton Borders ...273 B7
Huyton Mers. 182 C6
Huyton Park Mers. .182 C6
Huyton Quarry Mers .183 C7
Hwlffordd = Haverfordwest
Pembs. 73 B7
Hycemoor Cumb. .210 B1
Hyde Glos.........80 E5
Glos. 99 F11
Gtr Man 184 B6
Hants. 31 E11
Hants. 48 G3
Hyde Chase Essex. ..88 E4
Hyde End W Berks. ..64 G5
Hyde Heath Bucks. ..84 E6
Hyde Lea Staffs. ..151 E8
Hyde Park S Yorks. .198 G5
Hydestile Sur.....50 E3
Hylton Castle T&W. .243 F9
Hylton Red House
T&W 243 F9
Hyltons Crossways
Norf 160 D4
Hyndburn Bridge
Lancs. 203 G10
Hyndford Bridge
S Lanark. 269 G8
Hyndhope Borders .261 E9
Hynish Argyll.....288 F1
Hyssington Powys. .130 E6
Hystfield Glos.....79 F11

Hythe Hants 32 F6
Kent 55 G7
Sur. 44 C2
Hythe End Windsor. .66 E4
Hythie Aberds. ...303 D10
Hyton Cumb......210 B1

I

Iarsiadar W Isles ..304 E3
Ibberton Dorset. ...30 F3
Ible Derbys 170 D2
Ibsley Hants 31 F11
Ibstock Leics 153 G8
Ibstone Bucks. 84 G3
Ibthorpe Hants. ...47 C11
Ibworth Hants 48 C5
Icelton N Som 59 F11
Ichrachan Argyll. ..284 D4
Ickburgh Norf 140 E6
Ickenham London. ..66 B5
Ickenthwaite Cumb. .210 B6
Ickford Bucks.....83 D11
Ickham Kent......55 B8
Ickleford Herts....104 E3
Icklesham E Sus ...38 D5
Ickleton Cambs ...105 C9
Icklingham Suff...124 C5
Ickornshaw N Yorks .204 E5
Ickwell Beds......104 B3
Ickwell Green
C Beds 104 B3
Icomb Glos.......100 G4
Icy Park Devon. 8 F3
Idbury Oxon 82 B2
Iddesleigh Devon ..25 F9
Ide Devon 14 C3
Ideford Devon 14 F3
Ide Hill Kent......52 C3
Iden E Sus 38 C6
Iden Green Kent. ..53 F8
Kent 53 G10
Idle W Yorks 205 F9
Idle Moor W Yorks. .205 F9
Idless Corn........4 F6
Idlicote Warks....100 C5
Idmiston Wilts. ...47 F7
Idole Carms 74 B6
Idridgehay Derbys. .170 F3
Idridgehay Green
Derbys. 170 F3
Idrigill Highld. ...298 C3
Idstone Oxon 63 C9
Idvies Angus 287 C9
Ief-y-bwlch Carms. .92 F3
Iffley Oxon 83 E8
Ifield W Sus 51 F9
Ifield Green W Sus. .51 F9
Ifieldwood W Sus. ..51 F9
Ifold W Sus 50 G4
Iford BCP 19 C8
E Sus 36 F6
Ifton Heath Shrops. .148 B5
Ightfield Shrops. .149 B11
Ightfield Heath
Shrops. 149 B11
Igtham Common
Kent 52 B5
Iken Suff 127 F8
Ilam Staffs.......169 E10
Ilchester Som 29 C8
Ilchester Mead Som. .29 C8
Ilderton Northumb. .264 E2
Ileden Kent 55 C8
Ilford London 68 B2
Som 28 D5
Ilfracombe Devon. ..40 D4
Ilkeston Derbys ..171 G7
Ilketshall St Andrew
Suff 143 F7
Ilketshall St Lawrence
Suff 143 F7
Ilketshall St Margaret
Suff 142 F7
Ilkley W Yorks ...205 D8
Illand Corn 11 F1
Illey W Mid. 133 G9
Illidge Green
Ches E 168 C3
Illington Norf 141 F8
Illingworth W Yorks .196 B5
Illogan Corn........4 G3
Illogan Highway Corn. .4 G3
Illshaw Heath
W Mid 118 C2
Illston on the Hill
Leics 136 D4
Ilmer Bucks. 84 D3
Ilmington Warks. .100 C4
Ilminster Som.....28 E5
Ilsington Devon....13 F11
Swansea 56 C5
Ilton N Yorks 214 D3
Som 28 D5
Imachar N Ayrs ..255 C9
Imber Wilts.......46 D3
Imeraval Argyll ...254 C4
Immervoulin Stirling .285 F9
Immingham
NE Lincs 201 E7
Impington Cambs. .123 E8
Ince Ches W 183 F7
Ince Blundell Mers. 193 G10
Ince in Makerfield
Gtr Man 194 G5
Inchbae Lodge
Highld 300 C4
Inchbare Angus. ..293 G8
Inchberry Moray. .302 D3
Inchbraoch Angus. .287 B11
Inchbrook Glos....80 E4
Inchcape Highld. .309 J6
Incheril Highld. ..299 C10
Inchgrundle Angus. .292 F6
Inchina Highld....307 K4
Inchinnan Renfs. .267 B9
Inchkinloch Highld. .308 E5
Inchlaggan Highld. .290 C4
Inchlumpie Highld. .300 B5

Inchmore Highld. .300 E3
Highld 300 E5
Inchnacardoch Hotel
Highld 290 B5
Inchnadamph
Highld 307 G7
Inchock Argyll 287 C10
Inch of Arnhall
Aberds. 293 F8
Inchree Highld....290 G2
Inchrory Moray...292 C3
Indian Queens Corn. ..5 D8
Inerval Argyll 254 C4
Ingatestone Essex. ..87 F11
Ingbirchworth
S Yorks 197 F8
Ingerthorpe N Yorks .214 F5
Ingham Lincs.....188 E6
Norf 161 D7
Suff 125 C7
Ingham Corner Norf .161 D7
Ingleborough Norf. .157 F9
Ingleby Derbys. ..152 D6
Lincs 188 F5
Ingleby Arncliffe
N Yorks 225 D8
Ingleby Barwick
Stockton 225 C9
Ingleby Cross
N Yorks 225 D8
Ingleby Greenhow
N Yorks 225 D11
Ingleigh Green
Devon 25 F10
Inglemire Hull ...209 G7
Inglesbatch Bath ..61 G8
Inglesham Swindon. .82 F2
Ingleton Durham. .233 G9
N Yorks 212 E3
Inglewhite Lancs. .202 E6
Ingmanthorpe
N Yorks 206 C4
Ingoe Northumb. .242 C2
Ingol Lancs 202 G6
Ingoldisthorpe Norf. 158 C3
Ingoldmells Lincs. .175 B9
Ingoldsby Lincs ..155 C10
Ingon Warks 118 F4
Ingram Northumb. .264 F2
Ingrams Green
W Sus 34 C4
Ingrave Essex. 87 G10
Ingrow W Yorks ..205 F7
Ings Cumb 221 F8
Ingst S Glos. 60 B5
Ingthorpe Rutland. .137 B9
Ingworth Norf. ...160 D3
Inham's End Cambs .138 D5
Inhurst Hants. 64 G5
Inkberrow Worcs. .117 F10
Inkersall Derbys. .186 G6
Inkersall Green
Derbys. 186 G6
Inkford Worcs ...117 C11
Inkpen W Berks ...63 G11
Inkpen Common
W Berks 63 G11
Inkstack Highld. .310 B6
Inlands W Sus.....22 B3
Inmarsh Wilts.....62 G2
Innellan Argyll ...276 G3
Inner Hope Devon. ..9 G8
Innerleithen
Borders 261 B8
Innerleven Fife ...287 G7
Innermessan
Dumfries 236 C2
Innerwick E Loth. .282 G4
Perth 285 C9
Innie Argyll 275 B9
Inninbeg Highld. .289 E8
Innis Chonain Argyll .284 E5
Innistrynich Argyll. .284 E5
Innox Hill Som 45 D9
Innsworth Glos....99 G7
Insch Aberds. 302 G6
Insh Highld......291 C10
Inshegra Highld. .306 D7
Inshore Highld....308 C3
Inskip Lancs.....202 F5
Inskip Moss Side
Lancs. 202 F5
Instoneville S Yorks .198 E5
Instow Devon.....40 G4
Insworke Corn......7 E8
Intack Blackburn ..195 B8
Intake S Yorks. ..186 E5
S Yorks 198 G5
Interfield Worcs. ..98 B5
Intwood Norf 142 C3
Inver Aberds. 292 D4
Highld 311 L2
Perth 286 C4
Inverailort Highld. .295 C9
Inveraldie Angus. .287 D8
Inveralivaig Highld. .298 E4
Inverallochy
Aberds. 303 C10
Inveran Highld....309 K5
Stirling 285 F7
Inveraray Argyll. .284 G4
Inverarish Highld. .295 B7
Inverarity Angus. .287 C8
Inverarnan Stirling. .285 F7
Inverasdale Highld. .307 L3
Inverawe Ho Argyll. .284 D4
Inverbeg Argyll ..276 B6
Inverbervie Aberds. .293 F10
Inverboyndie
Aberds. 302 C6
Invercassley Highld. .309 J4

Invercauld House
Aberds. 292 D3
Inverchaolain
Argyll 275 F11
Invercharnan Highld. .284 C5
Inverchoran Highld. .300 D2
Invercreran Argyll. .284 C4
Inverdruie Highld. .291 B11
Inverebrie Aberds. .303 F9
Invereck Argyll ...276 E2
Inverernan Ho
Aberds. 292 B5
Invereshie House
Highld 291 C10
Inveresk E Loth. ..280 G6
Inverey Aberds. ..292 E3
Inverfarigaig Highld. .300 G5
Invergarry Highld. .290 C5
Invergelder Aberds. .292 D4
Invergeldie Perth. .285 E11
Invergordon Highld. .301 C7
Invergowrie Perth. .287 D7
Inverguseran Highld. .295 D9
Inverhadden Perth. .285 B10
Inverhaggernie
Stirling 285 E7
Inverharroch Moray. .302 F3
Inverherive Stirling. .285 E7
Inverie Highld. ...295 E9
Inverinan Argyll. .275 D10
Inverinate Highld. .295 C11
Inverkeilor Angus. .287 C10
Inverkeithing Fife. .280 E2
Inverkeithny Aberds. .302 E6
Inverkip Invclyd. ..276 G4
Inverkirkaig Highld. .307 H5
Inverlael Highld. .307 L6
Inverleith Edin. ..280 F4
Inverliever Lodge
Argyll 275 C9
Inverliver Argyll. .284 D4
Inverlochlarig
Stirling 285 F8
Inverlochy Argyll. .284 E5
Highld 290 F3
Moray 301 G12
Inverlounin Argyll. .276 B4
Inverlussa Argyll. .275 E7
Inver Mallie Highld. .290 E3
Invermark Lodge
Angus 292 E6
Invermoidart Highld. .289 B8
Highld 290 B6
Invernaver Highld. .308 C7
Inverneill Argyll. .275 E9
Inverness Highld. .300 E6
Invernettie Aberds. .303 E11
Invernoaden Argyll. .276 B2
Inveronich Argyll. .284 G6
Inveroran Hotel
Argyll 284 C6
Inverpolly Lodge
Highld 307 H5
Inverquharity Angus .287 B8
Inverquhomery
Aberds. 303 E10
Inverroy Highld. ..290 E4
Inversanda Highld. .289 D11
Invershiel Highld. .295 D11
Invershin Highld. .309 K5
Inversnaid Hotel
Stirling 285 G7
Invertrossachs
Stirling 285 G9
Inverugie Aberds. .303 E11
Inveruglas Argyll. .285 G7
Inveruglass Highld. .291 C10
Inverurie Aberds. .303 G8
Invervar Perth ...285 C10
Inverythan Aberds. .303 E7
Inwardleigh Devon. .13 B7
Inwood Shrops. ..131 D9
Inworth Essex.....88 B5
Iochdar W Isles ..297 G3
Iping W Sus.......34 C5
Ipplepen Devon.....8 B6
Ipsden Oxon 64 B6
Ipsley Worcs.....117 D11
Ipstones Staffs. ..169 F8
Ipswich Suff.....108 C3
Irby Mers. 182 E3
Irby in the Marsh
Lincs 175 C7
Irby upon Humber
NE Lincs 201 G7
Irchester N Nhants .121 D8
Ireby Cumb......229 D10
Lancs. 212 D3
Ireland C Beds....104 C2
Orkney 314 F3
Shetland 313 L5
Wilts 45 C10
Ireland's Cross
Shrops. 168 G2
Ireland Wood
W Yorks 205 F11
Ireleth Cumb.....210 D4
Ireshopeburn
Durham 232 D3
Ireton Wood Derbys. .170 F3
Irlam Gtr Man 184 C2
Irlams o' th' Height
Gtr Man 195 G9
Irnham Lincs.....155 D10
Iron Acton S Glos. ..61 C7
Ironbridge Telford. .132 C3
Iron Cross Warks. .117 G11
Irongray Dumfries. .237 B11
Iron Lo Highld. ..299 G10
Ironmacannie
Dumfries 237 B8
Irons Bottom Sur. ..51 D10
Ironside Aberds. ..303 D8
Ironville Derbys. ..170 E6
Irstead Norf. 161 E7
Irstead Street Norf. .161 F7

Irthington Cumb....239 E11
Irthlingborough
  N Nhants........121 C8
Irton N Yorks....217 C10
Irwell Vale Lancs..195 C9
Irvine N Ayrs....257 F8
Isallt Bach Anglesey..178 F3
Isauld Highld....310 C3
Isbister Orkney....314 D2
  Orkney........314 E3
  Shetland......312 D5
  Shetland......313 G7
Isel Cumb........229 E9
Isfield E Sus.....36 G6
Isham N Nhants...121 C7
Ishriff Argyll....289 F8
Isington Hants....49 E9
Island Carr N Lincs..200 F3
Islands Common
  Cambs........122 E3
Islay Ho Argyll...274 G4
Isle Abbotts Som...28 C5
Isle Brewers Som..28 C5
Isleham Cambs....124 C2
Isle of Axholme
  N Lincs........199 F9
Isle of Dogs London..67 D11
Isle of Man Dumfries.238 B2
Isle of Whithorn
  Dumfries......236 F6
Isleornsay Highld..295 D9
Islesburgh Shetland.312 G5
Islesteps Dumfries..237 B11
Isleworth London...67 D7
Isley Walton Leics..153 D8
Islibhig W Isles...304 F11
Islington London...67 C10
  Telford........150 E4
Islip N Nhants....121 B9
  Oxon.........83 C8
Isombridge Telford..150 G2
Istead Rise Kent...68 F6
Isycoed Wrex.....166 E6
Itchen Soton......32 E6
Itchen Abbas Hants..48 G4
Itchen Stoke Hants..48 G5
Itchingfield W Sus..35 B10
Itchington S Glos...61 B7
Itteringham Norf...160 C2
Itteringham Common
  Norf..........160 D3
Itton Devon.......13 B9
  Mon.........79 F7
Itton Common Mon..79 F7
Ivegill Cumb......230 C4
Ivelet N Yorks.....223 F8
Iver Bucks........66 C4
Iver Heath Bucks...66 C4
Iverley Staffs......133 G2
Iveston Durham....242 G4
Ivinghoe Bucks....84 B6
Ivinghoe Aston
  Bucks.........85 B7
Ivington Hereford..115 F9
Ivington Green
  Hereford......115 F9
Ivybridge Devon....8 D2
Ivy Chimneys Essex..86 E6
Ivychurch Kent....39 B8
Ivy Cross Dorset...30 C5
Ivy Hatch Kent....52 C5
Ivy Todd Norf.....141 B7
Iwade Kent........69 F11
Iwerne Courtney or
  Shroton Dorset...30 E5
Iwerne Minster
  Dorset........30 E5
Iwood N Som......60 G3
Ixworth Suff......125 C8
Ixworth Thorpe Suff.125 C8

J
Jackfield Telford...132 C3
Jack Green Lancs...194 B5
Jack Hayes Staffs...168 F6
Jack Hill N Yorks..205 C10
Jack in the Green
  Devon.........14 B6
Jacksdale Notts...170 E6
Jack's Green
  Essex.........105 G11
  Glos..........80 D5
Jack's Hatch Essex..86 D6
Jackson Bridge
  W Yorks.......197 F7
Jackstown Aberds..303 F7
Jacobstow Corn....11 B9
Jacobstowe Devon..25 G9
Jacobs Well Sur....50 C3
Jagger Green
  W Yorks.......196 D5
Jameston Pembs....73 F9
Jamestown
  Dumfries......249 D8
  Highld........300 D4
  W Dunb.......277 E7
Jamphlars Fife....280 B4
Janetstown Highld..310 C4
Janke's Green Essex.107 F8
Jarrow T&W......243 D8
Jarvis Brook E Sus..37 B8
Jasper's Green
  Essex.........106 F4
Java Argyll.......289 F9
Jawcraig Falk.....278 F6
Jaw Hill W Yorks...197 C9
Jaywick Essex.....89 C11
Jealott's Hill Brack..65 E11
Jeaniefield
  Borders........271 G10
Jedburgh Borders..262 E2
Jedurgh Borders...262 F5
Jeffreyston Pembs...73 D9
Jellyhill E Dunb...278 G2
Jemimaville Highld..301 C7

Jennetts Hill
  W Berks........64 E5
Jennyfield N Yorks..205 B11
Jericho Gtr Man....195 E10
Jersey Farm Herts...85 D11
Jersey Marine Neath..57 C8
Jerviswood
  S Lanark.......269 F7
Jesmond T&W.....243 D7
Jevington E Sus....23 E9
Jewell's Cross Corn..24 G3
Jingle Street Mon...79 C7
Jockey End Herts...85 C8
Jodrell Bank
  Ches E.........184 G3
Johnby Cumb......230 E4
John O'Gaunt Leics.136 B4
John O'Gaunts
  W Yorks........197 B11
John o'Groats
  Highld.........310 B7
John's Cross E Sus..38 C2
Johnshaven Aberds..293 G9
Johnson Fold
  Gtr Man.......195 E7
Johnson's Hillock
  Lancs.........194 C5
Johnson Street Norf.161 F7
Johnston Pembs....72 C6
Johnstone Renfs....267 C8
Johnstonebridge
  Dumfries.......248 E3
Johnstone Mains
  Aberds.........293 F9
Johnstown Carms...74 B6
  Wrex.........166 F4
Jolly's Bottom Corn..4 F5
Joppa Corn........2 B3
  Edin..........280 G6
  S Ayrs........257 F10
Jordan Green Norf..159 E11
Jordanhill Glasgow..267 B10
Jordans Bucks.....85 G7
Jordanston Pembs...91 E8
Jordanthorpe
  S Yorks........186 E5
Jordon S Yorks.....186 C6
Joyford Glos.......79 C9
Joy's Green Glos...79 B10
Jubilee Gtr Man....196 E2
  Notts.........170 E6
Jugbank Staffs.....150 B5
Jump S Yorks.......197 G11
Jumpers Common
  BCP...........19 C8
Jumpers Green BCP..19 C8
Jumper's Town
  E Sus.........52 G3
Junction N Yorks...204 D6
Juniper Northumb..241 F10
Juniper Green Edin..270 B3
Jurby East IoM....192 C4
Jurby West IoM....192 C4
Jurston Devon.....13 E9
Jury's Gap E Sus...39 D7

K
Kaber Cumb.......222 C5
Kaimend S Lanark..269 F9
Kaimes Edin.......270 B5
Kaimrig End
  Borders........269 G11
Kalemouth Borders..262 D6
Kame Fife........287 G7
Kames Argyll......275 B9
  Argyll..........275 F10
  E Ayrs.........258 D5
Kates Hill W Mid...133 E9
Kea Corn..........4 G6
Keadby N Lincs....199 E10
Keal Cotes Lincs...174 C5
Kearby Town End
  N Yorks........206 D2
Kearnsey Kent.....55 E9
Kearsley Gtr Man...195 F9
Kearstwick Cumb...212 C2
Kearton N Yorks....223 F9
Kearvaig Highld....306 B7
Keasden N Yorks...212 F4
Kebroyd W Yorks...196 C4
Keckwick Halton...183 E9
Keddington Lincs...190 D4
Keddington Corner
  Lincs.........190 D5
Kedington Suff....106 B4
Kedleston Derbys...170 G4
Kedslie Borders....271 G11
Keekle Cumb......219 B10
Keelars Tye Essex...107 G11
Keele Staffs.......168 F4
Keeley Green
  Bedford........103 B10
Keelham W Yorks...205 G7
Keenley Northumb..241 F7
Keenthorne Som....43 F8
Keeres Green Essex..87 C9
Keeston Pembs.....72 B6
Keevil Wilts.......46 B2
Kegworth Leics....153 D9
Kehelland Corn.....4 G2
Keig Aberds.......293 B8
Keighley W Yorks...205 E7
Keil Highld........289 D11
Keilarsbrae Clack..279 C7
Keilhill Aberds.....303 D7
Keillmore Argyll....275 E7
Keillor Perth......286 C6
Keillour Perth.....286 E4
Keills Argyll......274 G5
Keils Argyll.......274 G6
Keinton Mandeville
  Som..........44 G4
Keir Mill Dumfries..247 E9
Keisby Lincs.......155 D10
Keiss Highld.......310 C7
Keistle Highld.....298 D4
Keith Moray.......302 D4
Keith Hall Aberds..303 G7
Keith Inch Aberds..303 E11

Keithock Angus....293 G8
Kelbrook Lancs....204 E4
Kelby Lincs........173 G8
Kelcliffe W Yorks...205 E9
Keld Cumb........221 C11
  N Yorks........223 F7
Keldholme N Yorks..216 B4
Kelfield N Lincs....199 G10
  N Yorks........207 F7
Kelham Notts......172 D3
Kellacott Devon....12 D4
Kellamergh Lancs..194 B2
Kellan Argyll......289 E7
Kellas Angus......287 D8
  Moray.........301 D11
Kellaton Devon.....9 G11
Kelleth Cumb......222 D3
Kelleythorpe
  E Yorks........208 B5
  E Yorks........208 B6
Kelling Norf.......177 E9
Kellingley N Yorks..198 C4
Kellington N Yorks..198 C5
Kelloe Durham.....234 D2
Kelloholm Dumfries.258 G6
Kells Cumb........219 B9
Kelly Corn........10 G6
  Devon.........12 E3
Kelly Bray Corn....12 G3
Kelmarsh N Nhants.120 B4
Kelmscott Oxon....82 F3
Kelsale Suff.......127 D7
Kelsall Ches W.....167 B8
Kelsall Hill Ches W..167 B8
Kelsay Argyll......254 B2
Kelshall Herts.....104 D6
Kelsick Cumb......238 G5
Kelso Borders......262 C6
Kelstedge Derbys...170 C4
Kelstern Lincs.....190 C3
Kelsterton Flint....182 G3
Kelston Bath......61 F8
Keltneyburn Perth..285 C11
Kelton Dumfries....237 B11
  Durham........232 G4
Kelty Fife.........280 C2
Keltybridge Fife...280 B2
Kelvedon Essex....88 B5
Kelvedon Hatch
  Essex.........87 F9
Kelvin S Lanark....268 E2
Kelvindale Glasgow..267 B11
Kelvinside Glasgow..267 B11
Kelynack Corn......1 D3
Kemacott Devon....41 D7
Kemback Fife......287 F8
Kemberton Shrops..132 C4
Kemble Glos.......81 F7
Kemble Wick Glos...81 F7
Kemerton Worcs....99 D8
Kemeys Commander
  Mon..........78 E4
Kemincham Ches E..168 B4
Kemnay Aberds....293 B9
Kempe's Corner Kent.54 D4
Kempie Highld.....308 D4
Kempley Glos......98 F3
Kempley Green Glos..98 F3
Kempsey Worcs....99 B7
Kempsford Glos....81 F11
Kemps Green
  Warks.........118 C2
Kempshott Hants...48 C6
Kempston Bedford..103 B10
Kempston Church End
  Bedford........103 B10
Kempston Hardwick
  Bedford........103 B10
Kempston West End
  Bedford........103 B9
Kempton Shrops....131 G7
Kemp Town Brighton.36 G4
Kemsing Kent......52 B4
Kemsley Kent......70 F2
Kemsley Street
  Kent..........69 G10
Kenardington Kent..54 G3
Kenchester Hereford.97 C8
Kencot Oxon.......82 E3
Kendal Cumb......221 G10
Kendal End Worcs..117 C10
Kendleshire S Glos..61 D7
Kendon Caerph....77 F11
Kendoon Dumfries..246 F4
Kendray S Yorks....197 F11
Kenfig Bridgend....57 E10
Kenfig Hill Bridgend.57 E10
Kengharair Argyll..288 E6
Kenilworth Warks..118 C5
Kenknock Stirling..285 D8
Kenley London.....51 B10
  Shrops.........131 C11
Kenmore Argyll....284 G4
  Highld........299 D7
  Perth.........285 C11
Kenn Devon........14 D4
  N Som.........60 F2
Kennacley W Isles..305 J3
Kennacraig Argyll..275 G9
Kennards House
  Corn..........11 E11
Kenneggy Corn.....2 D3
Kenneggy Downs
  Corn..........2 D3
Kennerleigh Devon..26 F4
Kennet Clack......279 C8
Kennet End Suff...124 D4
Kennethmont
  Aberds........302 G5
Kennett Cambs....124 D3
Kennford Devon....14 D4
Kenninghall Norf..141 F10
Kenninghall Heath
  Norf..........141 G10
Kennington Kent...54 E4
  London........67 D10
  Oxon.........83 E8

Kenn Moor Gate
  N Som.........60 F2
Kennoway Fife.....287 G7
Kenny Som........28 D4
Kenny Hill Suff....124 B3
Kennythorpe
  N Yorks........216 F5
Kensaleyre Highld..298 D4
Kensal Green London.67 C8
Kensal Rise London..67 C8
Kensal Town London.67 C8
Kensary Highld.....310 E6
Kensington London..67 D9
  Mers..........182 C5
Kensworth C Beds...85 B8
Kentallen Highld....284 B4
Kentchurch Hereford.97 F8
Kentford Suff......124 D4
Kentisbeare Devon..27 F9
Kentisbury Devon...40 E6
Kentisbury Ford
  Devon.........40 E6
Kentish Town London.67 C9
Kentmere Cumb....221 E9
Kenton Devon......14 E5
  London........67 B7
  Suff..........126 D3
  T&W..........242 D6
Kenton Bankfoot
  T&W..........242 D6
Kenton Bar T&W...242 D6
Kenton Corner Suff..126 D4
Kenton Green Glos..80 C3
Kentra Highld......289 C8
Kentrigg Cumb.....221 G10
Kents Bank Cumb...211 D7
Kent's Green Glos...98 G4
Kents Hill M Keynes..103 D8
Kent's Oak Hants...32 C4
Kent Street E Sus...38 D3
  Kent..........53 C7
  W Sus.........36 C2
Kenwick Shrops....149 C8
Kenwick Park
  Shrops.........149 D8
Kenwyn Corn......4 F6
Kenyon Warr......183 B10
Keoldale Highld....308 C3
Keonchulish Ho
  Highld.........307 K6
Kepdowrie Stirling..277 C11
Kepnal Wilts.......63 G7
Keppanach Highld..290 G2
Keppoch Highld....295 C11
Keprigan Argyll....255 F7
Kepwick N Yorks....225 G9
Kerchesters Borders.263 B7
Kerdiston Norf.....159 E11
Keresforth Hill
  S Yorks........197 F10
Keresley W Mid....134 G6
Keresley Newlands
  Warks.........134 G6
Kerfield Borders....270 G5
Kerley Downs Corn..4 G5
Kernborough Devon..8 G5
Kerne Bridge
  Hereford.......79 B9
Kernsary Highld....299 B8
Kerridge Ches E....184 F6
Kerridge-end
  Ches E.........184 F6
Kerris Corn........1 D4
Kerry = Ceri Powys..130 F2
Kerrycroy Argyll...266 C2
Kerry Hill Staffs....168 F6
Kerrysdale Highld..299 B8
Kerry's Gate Hereford.97 E7
Kersal Gtr Man.....195 G10
Kersall Notts.......172 C2
Kersbrook Cross
  Corn..........12 F2
Kerscott Devon.....25 B10
Kersey Suff.......107 C10
Kersey Tye Suff....107 C9
Kersey Upland Suff..107 C9
Kershopefoot
  Cumb.........249 G11
Kersoe Worcs......99 D9
Kerswell Devon.....27 F9
Kerswell Green
  Worcs........99 B7
Kerthen Wood Corn..2 C3
Kesgrave Suff......108 B4
Kessingland Suff...143 F10
Kessingland Beach
  Suff..........143 F10
Kessington E Dunb..277 G11
Kestle Corn........5 F9
Kestle Mill Corn....5 D7
Keston London.....68 G2
Keswick Cumb......229 G11
  Norf..........142 C4
  Norf..........161 C7
Kete Pembs.......72 E4
Ketford Glos.......98 E4
Ketley Telford.....150 G3
Ketley Bank Telford.150 G3
Ketsby Lincs.......190 F5
Kettering N Nhants.121 B7
Ketteringham Norf..142 C3
Kettins Perth......286 D6
Kettlebaston Suff...125 G9
Kettlebridge Fife...287 G7
Kettlebrook Staffs..134 C4
Kettleburgh Suff...126 E5
Kettle Corner Kent..53 C8
Kettle Green Herts..86 B6
Kettlehill Fife......287 G7
Kettleholm Dumfries.238 B4
Kettleness N Yorks..226 B6
Kettleshulme
  Ches E.........185 F7
Kettlesing N Yorks..205 B10
Kettlesing Bottom
  N Yorks........205 B10
Kettlesing Head
  N Yorks........205 B10

Kettlestone Norf...159 C9
Kettlethorpe Lincs..188 F4
Kettletoft Orkney...314 C6
Kettlewell N Yorks..213 E9
Ketton Rutland....137 C9
Kevingston London..68 D3
Kew London.......67 D7
Kew Bridge London..67 D7
Kewstoke N Som...59 G10
Kexbrough S Yorks..197 F9
Kexby Lincs........188 D5
  York..........207 C10
Keybridge Corn.....11 G7
Keycol Kent........69 G11
Keyford Som.......45 D9
Key Green Ches E...168 C5
  N Yorks........226 E6
Keyham Leics......136 B3
Keyhaven Hants....20 C2
Keyingham E Yorks..201 B8
Keymer W Sus......36 D4
Keynsham Bath....61 F7
Keysers Estate Essex.86 D5
Key's Green Kent...53 F7
Keysoe Bedford....121 E11
Keysoe Row
  Bedford........121 E11
Keyston Cambs....121 B10
Key Street Kent....69 G11
Keyworth Notts....154 C2
Khantore Aberds....292 D4
Kibbear Som.......28 C2
Kibblesworth T&W..242 F6
Kibworth Beauchamp
  Leics.........136 E3
Kibworth Harcourt
  Leics.........136 E3
Kidbrooke London..68 D2
Kidburngill Cumb...229 G7
Kiddal Lane End
  W Yorks........206 F4
Kiddemore Green
  Staffs.........133 B7
Kidderminster
  Worcs........116 B6
Kiddington Oxon...101 G8
Kidd's Moor Norf...142 C2
Kidlington Oxon....83 C7
Kidmore End Oxon..65 D7
Kidnal Ches W.....167 F7
Kidsdale Dumfries..236 F6
Kidsgrove Staffs....168 E4
Kidstones N Yorks..213 C9
Kidwelly = Cydweli
  Carms.........74 D6
Kiel Crofts Argyll..289 F11
Kielder Northumb..250 E4
Kierfiold Ho Orkney.314 E2
Kiff Green W Berks..64 F5
Kilbagie Fife......279 D8
Kilbarchan Renfs...267 C8
Kilbeg Highld......295 E8
Kilberry Argyll.....275 G8
Kilbirnie N Ayrs....266 E6
Kilbowie W Dunb...277 G10
Kilbraur Highld.....311 H2
Kilbride Argyll.....254 C4
  Argyll..........275 D9
  Argyll..........289 G10
  Argyll..........289 G11
Kilbridemore
  Argyll..........275 D11
Kilburn Angus.....292 G5
  Derbys........170 F5
  London........67 C9
  N Yorks........215 D10
Kilby Leics........136 D2
Kilby Bridge Leics..136 D2
Kilchamaig Argyll..275 G9
Kilchattan Argyll...274 D4
Kilchattan Bay
  Argyll..........266 E2
Kilchenzie Argyll...255 E7
Kilcheran Argyll...289 F10
Kilchiaran Argyll...274 G3
Kilchoan Argyll....289 E7
  Highld........288 C6
Kilchoman Argyll...274 G3
Kilchrenan Argyll..284 E4
Kilconquhar Fife...287 G8
Kilcot Glos........98 F3
Kilcoy Highld......300 D5
Kilcreggan Argyll..276 E4
Kildale N Yorks....226 D2
Kildalloig Argyll....255 F8
Kildary Highld.....301 B7
Kildaton Ho Argyll..254 C5
Kildavanan Argyll..275 G11
Kildermorie Lodge
  Highld.........300 B5
Kildonan Dumfries..236 D2
  Highld........298 D3
  N Ayrs.........256 E2
Kildonan Lodge
  Highld.........311 G3
Kildonnan Highld..294 G6
Kildrum N Lanark..278 F5
Kildrummy Aberds..292 B6
Kildwick N Yorks...204 D6
Kilfinan Argyll.....275 F10
Kilfinnan Highld....290 D4
Kilgetty Pembs.....73 D10
Kilgour Fife.......286 G6
Kilgrammie S Ayrs..245 C7
Kilgwrrwg Common
  Mon..........79 F7
Kilhallon Corn.....5 E11
Kilham E Yorks....217 G11
  Northumb......263 C9
Kilkeddan Argyll...255 E8
Kilkenneth Argyll..288 E1
Kilkenny Glos......81 B8
Kilkenzie Argyll....255 E7
Kilkerran Argyll....255 F8
Kilkhampton Corn..24 E3
Killamarsh Derbys..187 E7
Killaworgey Corn...5 C8
Killay Swansea.....56 C6

Killbeg Argyll......289 E8
Killean Argyll......255 C7
Killearn Stirling....277 D10
Killegruer Argyll...255 D7
Killen Highld.......300 D6
Killerby Darl......224 B3
Killichonan Perth..285 B9
Killiechoinich
  Argyll..........289 G10
Killiechronan Argyll.289 E7
Killiecrankie Perth..291 G11
Killiemor Argyll....288 F6
Killiemore House
  Argyll..........288 G6
Killilan Highld.....295 B11
Killimster Highld...310 D7
Killin Stirling......285 D9
Killinallan Argyll...274 F4
Killinghall N Yorks..205 B11
Killingbeck
  W Yorks........206 G2
Killingholme N Lincs.201 E7
Killington Cumb...212 B2
  Devon.........41 D7
Killingworth T&W..243 C7
Killingworth Moor
  T&W..........243 C7
Killingworth Village
  T&W..........243 C7
Killin Lodge Highld..291 C7
Killivose Corn......2 B4
Killmahumaig Argyll.275 D8
Killochyett Borders..271 F9
Killocraw Argyll....255 D7
Killundine Highld..289 E7
Killylung Dumfries..247 G11
Kilmacolm Inverclyd.267 B7
Kilmaha Argyll.....275 C10
Kilmahog Stirling..285 G10
Kilmalieu Highld...289 D10
Kilmaluag Highld..298 A4
Kilmany Fife.......287 E7
Kilmarie Highld....295 D7
Kilmarnock E Ayrs..257 B10
Kilmaron Castle
  Fife..........287 F7
Kilmartin Argyll....275 D9
Kilmaurs E Ayrs....267 G8
Kilmelford Argyll...275 B9
Kilmeny Argyll.....274 G4
Kilmersdon Som....45 C7
Kilmeston Hants...33 B9
Kilmichael Argyll...255 E7
Kilmichael Glassary
  Argyll..........275 D9
Kilmichael of Inverlussa
  Argyll..........275 E8
Kilmington Devon..15 B11
  Wilts.........45 F9
Kilmington Common
  Wilts.........45 F9
Kilmoluaig Argyll..288 E1
Kilmonivaig Highld..290 E3
Kilmorack Highld..300 E4
Kilmore Argyll.....289 G10
  Highld.........295 E8
Kilmory Argyll.....275 F8
  Argyll..........289 B7
  Argyll..........294 B3
  N Ayrs.........255 E10
Kilmory Lodge
  Argyll..........275 C8
Kilmote Highld.....311 H3
Kilmuir Highld.....298 B3
  Highld.........298 E4
  Highld.........300 D6
  Highld.........301 B7
Kilmun Argyll......275 B10
  Argyll..........276 E3
Kilnave Argyll......274 F3
Kilncadzow
  S Lanark.......269 F7
Kilndown Kent.....53 G8
Kiln Green Hereford.79 B10
  Wokingham.....65 D10
Kilnhill Cumb......229 E10
Kilnhurst S Yorks...187 B7
Kilninian Argyll....288 E5
Kilninver Argyll....289 G10
Kiln Pit Hill
  Northumb......242 G2
Kilnsea E Yorks....201 D12
Kilnsey N Yorks....213 F9
Kilnwick E Yorks...208 D5
Kilnwick Percy
  E Yorks........208 C2
Kilnwood Vale
  W Sus.........51 G8
Kiloran Argyll......274 D4
Kilpatrick N Ayrs..255 E10
Kilpeck Hereford...97 E8
Kilphedir Highld...311 H3
Kilpin E Yorks.....199 B9
Kilpin Pike E Yorks..199 B9
Kilrenny Fife.......287 G9
Kilsby W Nhants...119 C11
Kilspindie Perth....286 E6
Kilsyth N Lanark...278 F4
Kiltarlity Highld....300 E5
Kilton Notts.......187 F9
  Redcar........226 B4
  Som..........43 E7
Kilton Thorpe
  Redcar........226 B3
Kilvaxter Highld....298 C3
Kilve Som.........43 E7
Kilvington Notts...172 G3
Kilwinning N Ayrs..266 G6
Kimberley Norf....141 C11
  Notts.........171 G8
Kimberworth
  S Yorks........186 C6
Kimberworth Park
  S Yorks........186 C6
Kimblesworth
  Durham........233 D11
Kimble Wick Bucks..84 D4
Kimbolton Cambs..121 D11
  Hereford......115 E10
Kimbridge Hants...32 B4

Kimcote Leics......135 F11
Kimmeridge Dorset..18 F4
Kimmerston
  Northumb......263 B11
Kimpton Hants.....47 D9
  Herts.........85 B11
Kimworthy Devon..24 E4
Kinabus Argyll.....254 C3
Kinbeachie Highld..300 C6
Kinbrace Highld....310 F2
Kinbuck Stirling....285 G11
Kincaldrum Angus..287 C8
Kincaple Fife......287 F8
Kincardine Fife....279 D8
  Highld.........309 L6
Kincardine Bridge
  Falk..........279 D8
Kincardine O'Neil
  Aberds........293 D7
Kinclaven Perth....286 D5
Kincorth Aberdeen..293 C11
Kincorth Ho Moray..301 C10
Kincraig Highld....291 C10
Kincraigie Perth...286 C3
Kindallachan Perth..286 C3
Kine Moor S Yorks..197 G9
Kineton Glos......99 F11
  Warks.........118 G6
Kineton Green
  W Mid........134 G2
Kinfauns Perth.....286 E5
Kingairloch Highld..289 D10
Kingarth Argyll....255 B11
Kingates IoW......20 F6
Kingbeare Corn....11 G11
Kingcoed Mon.....78 D6
Kingdom N Som...60 G4
King Edward Aberds.303 D7
Kingerby Lincs.....189 C9
Kingfield Sur......50 B4
Kingford Devon....24 F3
Kingham Oxon.....100 G5
Kinghay Wilts......30 B5
Kinghorn Fife......280 D5
Kingie Highld......290 C3
Kinglassie Fife.....280 B4
Kingledores Borders.260 D4
Kingoodie Perth...287 E7
King's Acre Hereford.97 C9
Kingsand Corn.....7 E8
Kingsash Bucks....84 D5
Kingsbarns Fife....287 F9
Kingsbridge Devon..8 G4
  Som..........42 F3
King's Bromley
  Staffs.........152 F2
Kingsbrook
  Oxfordshire....84 C4
Kingsburgh Highld..298 D3
Kingsbury London..67 B8
  Warks.........134 D4
Kingsbury Episcopi
  Som..........28 C6
Kingsbury Regis
  Som..........29 D11
King's Caple
  Hereford......97 F11
Kingscauseway
  Highld.........301 B7
Kingscavil W Loth..279 F10
Kingsclere Hants...48 B4
Kingsclere Woodlands
  Hants.........64 G4
King's Cliffe
  N Nhants.......137 D10
Kings Clipstone
  Notts.........171 C10
Kingscote Glos.....80 F4
Kingscott Devon....25 D8
King's Coughton
  Warks.........117 F11
Kingscourt Glos....80 E4
Kingscross N Ayrs..256 D2
Kingsditch Glos....99 G8
Kingsdon Som.....29 B8
Kingsdown Kent...54 B2
  Kent..........55 D11
  Swindon.......61 F10
  Wilts.........61 F10
Kingsdown Gorse
  Wilts.........61 F10
Kings Dyke Cambs..138 D1
King's End Worcs...116 G6
Kingseat Fife......280 C2
Kingseathill Fife...280 D2
King's End Worcs...116 G6
Kingsett Devon....12 E6
Kingsey Bucks.....84 D2
Kingsfield Hereford..97 B10
Kingsfold Lancs....194 B4
  W Sus.........51 F7
Kingsford Aberds...293 B7
  E Ayrs.........267 F8
  Worcs........132 G6
Kingsforth N Lincs..200 D4
Kings Furlong Hants.48 C6
King's Green Glos..98 E5
Kingsgate Kent....71 E11
Kingsheanton Devon.40 F5
King's Heath
  W Mid........133 G11
  W Nhants......120 E4
Kings Hedges
  Cambs........123 E9
Kingshill Glos......80 F3
  Swindon.......62 C6
King's Hill Kent....53 C7
  W Mid........133 D9
Kingsholm Glos....80 B4
Kingshouse Hotel
  Highld.........284 B6
Kingshurst W Mid..134 F3
Kingside Hill Cumb..238 G5
Kingskerswell Devon..9 B7
Kingskettle Fife....287 G7

Kingsland Anglesey..178 E2
  Hereford......115 E8
  London........67 C10
  Shrops.........149 G9
Kings Langley Herts..85 E9
Kingsley Ches W....183 G9
  Hants.........49 F9
  Staffs.........169 F8
Kingsley Green
  W Sus.........49 G11
Kingsley Holt Staffs..169 F8
Kingsley Moor
  Staffs.........169 F8
Kingsley Park
  W Nhants.......120 E5
Kingslow Shrops...132 D5
Kings Lynn Norf...158 E2
King's Meaburn
  Cumb.........231 G8
Kingsmead Hants...33 E9
Kingsmere Oxon...101 G3
King's Mills Derbys..153 D8
  Wrex.........166 F4
Kingsmoor Essex...86 D6
Kings Moss Mers...194 G4
Kingsmuir Angus...287 C8
  Fife..........287 G9
Kings Muir Borders..261 B7
King's Newnham
  Warks.........119 B9
King's Newton
  Derbys........153 D7
Kingsnordley Shrops.132 F5
Kingsnorth Kent....54 F4
King's Norton Leics..136 C3
  W Mid........117 B11
King's Nympton
  Devon.........25 D11
King's Pyon
  Hereford......115 G8
Kings Ripton Cambs..122 B3
King's Somborne
  Hants.........47 G11
King's Stag Dorset..30 E2
King's Stanley Glos..80 E4
King's Sutton
  W Nhants......101 D9
King's Tamerton Plym..7 D7
Kingstanding
  W Mid........133 E11
Kingsteignton Devon..14 G3
King's Thorn
  Hereford......97 E10
Kingsthorpe
  W Nhants.......120 E5
Kingsthorpe Hollow
  W Nhants.......120 E5
Kingston Cambs....122 F6
  Devon.........8 F2
  Devon.........9 G8
  Dorset........18 F5
  Dorset........30 F3
  E Loth........281 E10
  Gtr Man.......184 B6
  Hants.........31 G11
  IoW..........20 E5
  Kent..........55 C9
  M Keynes......103 D8
  Moray........302 C3
  Ptsmth........33 G11
  Suff..........108 C5
Kingston Bagpuize
  Oxon.........82 F6
Kingston Blount
  Oxon.........84 F2
Kingston by Sea
  W Sus.........36 G2
Kingston Deverill
  Wilts.........45 F10
Kingstone Hereford..97 D8
  Som..........28 E5
  Staffs.........151 D11
  S Yorks........197 F10
Kingstone Winslow
  Oxon.........63 D9
Kingston Gorse
  W Sus.........35 G9
Kingston Lisle Oxon..63 D10
Kingston Maurward
  Dorset........17 C10
Kingston near Lewes
  E Sus.........36 F5
Kingston on Soar
  Notts.........153 D10
Kingston Park T&W..242 D6
Kingston Russell
  Dorset........17 C7
Kingston St Mary
  Som..........28 B2
Kingston Seymour
  N Som.........60 F2
Kingston Stert Oxon..84 E2
Kingston upon Hull
  Hull..........200 B5
Kingston upon Thames
  London........67 F7
Kingston Vale London.67 E8
Kingstown Cumb...239 G10
King Street Essex...87 E9
King's Walden
  Herts.........104 G3
Kingsway Bath.....61 G8
  Halton........183 D8
Kingswear Devon...9 E7
Kingswells
  Aberdeen......293 C10
Kingswinford
  W Mid........133 F7
Kingswood Bucks...83 B11
  Essex.........69 B8
  Glos..........80 G2
  Hereford......114 G5
  Herts.........85 E10
  Kent..........53 C10
  Powys........130 C4
  S Glos........60 E6
  Som..........42 F4
  Sur..........51 B8

Kingswood *continued*
Warks 118 C3
Warr 183 C9
Kingswood Brook
Warks 118 C3
Kingswood Common
Staffs 132 C6
Worcs 116 D4
Kings Worthy Hants 48 G3
Kingthorpe Lincs 189 F10
Kington Hereford 114 F5
S Glos 79 G10
Worcs 117 F9
Kington Langley
Wilts 62 D2
Kington Magna
Dorset 30 C3
Kington St Michael
Wilts 62 D2
Kingussie Highld 291 C9
Kingweston Som 44 G4
Kinhrive Highld 301 B7
Kininvie Ho Moray 302 E3
Kinkell Bridge Perth 286 F3
Kinknockie Aberds 303 E10
Aberds 303 G9
Kinkry Hill Cumb 240 B2
Kinlet Shrops 132 G4
Kinloch Fife 286 F6
Highld 289 D8
Highld 294 F5
Highld 295 D8
Highld 308 F3
Perth 286 C5
Perth 286 C6
Kinlochan Highld 289 C10
Kinlochard Stirling 285 G8
Kinlochbeoraid
Highld 295 G10
Kinlochbervie
Highld 306 D7
Kinloch Damph
Highld 299 E8
Kinlocheil Highld 289 B11
Kinlochewe Highld 299 C10
Kinloch Hourn
Highld 295 E11
Kinloch Laggan
Highld 291 E7
Kinlochleven Highld 290 G3
Kinloch Lodge
Highld 308 D5
Kinlochmoidart
Highld 289 B9
Kinlochmorar
Highld 295 F10
Kinlochmore Highld 290 G3
Kinloch Rannoch
Perth 285 B10
Kinlochspelve
Argyll 289 G8
Kinloid Highld 295 G8
Kinloss Moray 301 C10
Kinmel Bay *= Bae Cinmel*
Conwy 181 E7
Kinmuck Aberds 293 B10
Kinmundy Aberds 293 B10
Kinnadie Aberds 303 E9
Kinnaird Perth 286 B3
Perth 286 E6
Kinnaird Castle
Angus 287 B10
Kinnauld Highld 309 J7
Kinneff Aberds 293 F10
Kinneil Falk 279 E9
Kinnelhead
Dumfries 248 C2
Kinnell Angus 287 B10
Kinnerley Shrops 148 E6
Kinnersley Hereford 96 B6
Worcs 99 C7
Kinnerton Powys 114 E4
Kinnerton Green
Flint 166 C4
Kinnesswood Perth 286 G5
Kinninvie Durham 233 G7
Kinnordy Angus 287 B7
Kinoulton Notts 154 C3
Kinross Perth 286 G5
Kinrossie Perth 286 D5
Kinsbourne Green
Herts 85 B10
Kinsey Heath
Ches E 167 G11
Kinsham Hereford 115 E7
Worcs 99 D8
Kinsley W Yorks 198 E2
Kinson BCP 19 B7
Kintallan Argyll 275 E8
Kintbury W Berks 63 F11
Kintessack Moray 301 C9
Kintillo Perth 286 F5
Kintocher Aberds 293 C7
Kinton Hereford 115 C8
Shrops 149 F7
Kintore Aberds 293 B9
Kintour Argyll 254 B5
Kintra Argyll 254 C4
Argyll 288 G5
Kintradwell Highld 311 J3
Kintraw Argyll 275 C9
Kinuachdrachd
Argyll 275 D8
Kinveachy Highld 291 B11
Kinver Staffs 132 G6
Kinwalsey Warks 134 F5
Kip Hill Durham 242 G6
Kiplin N Yorks 224 F5
Kippax W Yorks 206 G4
Kippen Stirling 278 C3
Kippford or Scaur
Dumfries 237 D10
Kippilaw Borders 262 D2
Kippilaw Mains
Borders 262 D2
Kipping's Cross Kent 52 F6
Kippington Kent 52 C4
Kirbister Orkney 314 D6
Orkney 314 E2
Orkney 314 F3
Kirbuster Orkney 314 D2
Kirby Bedon Norf 142 B5
Kirby Bellars Leics 154 F4
Kirby Cane Norf 143 E7
Kirby Corner W Mid 118 B5
Kirby Cross Essex 108 G4
Kirby Fields Leics 135 C10
Kirby Green Norf 143 E7
Kirby Grindalythe
N Yorks 217 F8
Kirby Hill N Yorks 215 F7
N Yorks 224 D2
Kirby Knowle
N Yorks 215 B9
Kirby-le-Soken
Essex 108 G4
Kirby Misperton
N Yorks 216 D5
Kirby Moor Cumb 240 E2
Kirby Muxloe Leics 135 C10
Kirby Row Norf 143 E7
Kirby Sigston
N Yorks 225 G8
Kirby Underdale
E Yorks 208 B2
Kirby Wiske
N Yorks 215 C7
Kirdford W Sus 35 B8
Kirk Highld 310 D6
Kirkabister Shetland 312 G6
Shetland 313 K6
Kirkandrews
Dumfries 237 E8
Kirkandrews-on-Eden
Cumb 239 F9
Kirkapol Argyll 288 E2
Kirkbampton Cumb 239 F8
Kirkbean Dumfries 237 D11
Kirkborough Cumb 229 D7
Kirkbrae Orkney 314 B4
Kirk Bramwith
S Yorks 198 E6
Kirkbride Cumb 238 F6
Kirkbridge N Yorks 224 G5
Kirkbuddo Angus 287 C9
Kirkburn Borders 261 B7
E Yorks 208 B5
Kirkburton W Yorks 197 E7
Kirkby Lincs 189 C9
Mers 182 B6
N Yorks 225 D10
Kirkby Fenside
Lincs 174 C4
Kirkby Fleetham
N Yorks 224 G5
Kirkby Green Lincs 173 D9
Kirkby Hill N Yorks 215 F7
Kirkby in Ashfield
Notts 171 D8
Kirkby-in-Furness
Cumb 210 C4
Kirkby la Thorpe
Lincs 173 F10
Kirkby Lonsdale
Cumb 212 D2
Kirkby Malham
N Yorks 213 G7
Kirkby Mallory Leics 135 C9
Kirkby Malzeard
N Yorks 214 E4
Kirkby Mills
N Yorks 216 B4
Kirkbymoorside
N Yorks 216 B3
Kirkby on Bain
Lincs 174 C2
Kirkby Overblow
N Yorks 206 D2
Kirkby Stephen
Cumb 222 D5
Kirkby Thore Cumb 231 F8
Kirkby Underwood
Lincs 155 D11
Kirkby Wharfe
N Yorks 206 E6
Kirkby Woodhouse
Notts 171 E7
Kirkcaldy Fife 280 C5
Kirkcambeck Cumb 240 D2
Kirkcarswell
Dumfries 237 E9
Kirkcolm Dumfries 236 C2
Kirkconnel Dumfries 258 G6
Kirkconnell
Dumfries 237 C11
Kirkcowan Dumfries 236 C5
Kirkcudbright
Dumfries 237 D8
Kirkdale Mers 182 C4
Kirk Deighton
N Yorks 206 C3
Kirk Ella E Yorks 200 B4
Kirkfieldbank
S Lanark 269 G7
Kirkforthar Feus
Fife 286 G6
Kirkgunzeon
Dumfries 237 C10
Kirk Hallam Derbys 171 G7
Kirkham Lancs 202 G4
N Yorks 216 F4
Kirkhamgate
W Yorks 197 C9
Kirk Hammerton
N Yorks 206 B5
Kirkhams Gtr Man 195 F10
Kirkharle Northumb 252 G2
Kirkheaton
Northumb 242 B2
W Yorks 197 D7
Kirkhill Angus 293 G8
E Renf 267 D11
Highld 300 E5
Midloth 270 C4
Moray 302 F2
W Loth 279 G11
Kirkholt Gtr Man 195 E11
Kirkhope Borders 261 E9
Kirkhouse Borders 261 C8
Cumb 240 F3
Kirkiboll Highld 308 D5
Kirkibost Highld 295 D7
Kirkinch Angus 287 C7
Kirkinner Dumfries 236 D6
Kirkintilloch
E Dunb 278 G3
Kirk Ireton Derbys 170 E3
Kirkland Cumb 219 B11
Cumb 229 B11
Cumb 231 E8
Dumfries 247 E8
Dumfries 258 G6
S Ayrs 244 E6
Kirkland Guards
Cumb 229 C9
Kirk Langley Derbys 152 B5
Kirkleatham Redcar 235 G7
Kirklees Gtr Man 195 E9
Kirklevington
Stockton 225 D8
Kirkley Suff 143 E10
Kirklington Notts 171 D11
N Yorks 214 C6
Kirklinton Cumb 239 D10
Kirkliston Edin 280 G2
Kirkmaiden
Dumfries 236 F3
Kirk Merrington
Durham 233 E11
Kirkmichael Perth 286 B4
S Ayrs 245 B8
Kirk Michael IoM 192 C4
Kirkmichael Mains
Dumfries 248 F2
Kirkmuirhill
S Lanark 268 G5
Kirknewton
Northumb 263 C10
W Loth 270 B2
Kirkney Aberds 302 F5
Kirk of Shotts
N Lanark 268 C6
Kirkoswald Cumb 231 C7
S Ayrs 244 B6
Kirkpatrick
Dumfries 247 E10
Kirkpatrick Durham
Dumfries 237 B9
Kirkpatrick-Fleming
Dumfries 239 C7
Kirk Sandall
S Yorks 198 F6
Kirksanton Cumb 210 C2
Kirkshaw N Lanark 268 C4
Kirk Smeaton
N Yorks 198 D4
Kirkstall W Yorks 205 F11
Kirkstead Borders 261 E7
Lincs 173 C11
Kirkstile Aberds 302 F5
Kirkstyle Highld 310 B7
Kirkthorpe
W Yorks 197 C11
Kirkton
Aberds 302 E6
Aberds 302 G6
Angus 286 C6
Angus 287 C8
Angus 287 D8
Argyll 275 C8
Borders 262 G2
Dumfries 247 G11
Fife 280 D4
Fife 287 E7
Highld 295 C10
Highld 299 E9
Highld 301 D7
Highld 309 K7
Perth 286 F3
S Lanark 259 E10
Stirling 285 G9
W Loth 269 B10
Kirktonhill Borders 271 E9
W Dunb 277 G7
Kirkton Manor
Borders 260 B6
Kirkton of Airlie
Angus 287 B7
Kirkton of Auchterhouse
Angus 287 D7
Kirkton of Auchterless
Aberds 303 E7
Kirkton of Barevan
Highld 301 E8
Kirkton of Bourtie
Aberds 303 G8
Kirkton of Collace
Perth 286 D5
Kirkton of Craig
Angus 287 B11
Kirkton of Culsalmond
Aberds 302 F6
Kirkton of Durris
Aberds 293 D9
Kirkton of Glenbuchat
Aberds 292 B5
Kirkton of Glenisla
Angus 292 G4
Kirkton of Kingoldrum
Angus 287 B7
Kirkton of Largo
Fife 287 G8
Kirkton of Lethendy
Perth 286 C5
Kirkton of Logie Buchan
Aberds 303 G9
Kirkton of Maryculter
Aberds 293 D10
Kirkton of Menmuir
Angus 293 G7
Kirkton of Monikie
Angus 287 D9
Kirkton of Oyne
Aberds 302 G6
Kirkton of Rayne
Aberds 302 G6
Kirkton of Skene
Aberds 293 C10
Kirkton of Tough
Aberds 293 B8
Kirktoun E Ayrs 267 G8
Kirktown Aberds 303 D10
Kirktown of Alvah
Aberds 302 C6
Kirktown of Deskford
Moray 302 C5
Kirktown of Fetteresso
Aberds 293 E10
Kirktown of Mortlach
Moray 302 F3
Kirktown of Slains
Aberds 303 G10
Kirkurd Borders 270 G2
Kirkwall Orkney 314 E4
Kirkwhelpington
Northumb 251 G11
Kirkwood Dumfries 238 B4
N Lanark 268 C4
Kirk Yetholm
Borders 263 D8
Kirmington N Lincs 200 E6
Kirmond le Mire
Lincs 189 C11
Kirn Argyll 276 F3
Kirriemuir Angus 287 B7
Kirstead Green Norf 142 D5
Kirtlebridge
Dumfries 238 C6
Kirtleton Dumfries 249 G7
Kirtling Cambs 124 F3
Kirtling Green
Cambs 124 F3
Kirtlington Oxon 83 B7
Kirtomy Highld 308 C7
Kirton Lincs 156 B6
Notts 171 B11
Suff 108 D5
Kirton Campus
W Loth 269 B10
Kirton End Lincs 174 G3
Kirton Holme Lincs 174 G3
Kirton in Lindsey
N Lincs 188 B6
Kiskin Cumb 210 B1
Kislingbury
W Nhants 120 F3
Kitbridge Devon 28 G4
Kitchenroyd
W Yorks 197 F8
Kitebrook Warks 100 E4
Kite Green Warks 118 D3
Kite Hill IoW 21 C7
Kites Hardwick
Warks 119 D9
Kit Hill Dorset 30 D4
Kitlye Glos 80 E5
Kit's Coty Kent 69 G8
Kitt Green Gtr Man 194 F5
Kittisford Som 27 C9
Kittle Swansea 56 D5
Kitts End Herts 86 F2
Kitt's Green W Mid 134 F3
Kitt's Moss Gtr Man 184 E5
Kittwhistle Dorset 28 G5
Kittybrewster
Aberdeen 293 C11
Kitwell W Mid 133 G9
Kitwood Hants 49 G7
Kivernoll Hereford 97 E9
Kiveton Park
S Yorks 187 E7
Knaith Lincs 188 E4
Knaith Park Lincs 188 D4
Knaphill Sur 50 B3
Knapp Hants 32 C6
Perth 286 D6
Som 28 B4
Wilts 31 B8
Knapp Hill Wilts 30 B5
Knapthorpe Notts 172 D2
Knaptoft Leics 136 F2
Knapton Norf 160 C6
York 207 C7
Knapton Green
Hereford 115 G8
Knapwell Cambs 122 E6
Knaresborough
N Yorks 206 B3
Knarsdale Northumb 240 G5
Knatts Valley Kent 68 G5
Knauchland Moray 302 D5
Knaven Aberds 303 E8
Knave's Ash Kent 71 G7
Knaves Green Suff 126 D2
Knavesmire York 207 D7
Knayton N Yorks 215 B8
Knebworth Herts 104 G5
Knedlington
E Yorks 199 B8
Kneesall Notts 172 C2
Kneesworth Cambs 104 C6
Kneeton Notts 172 F2
Knelston Swansea 56 D3
Knenhall Staffs 151 B8
Knettishall Suff 141 G9
Knightacott Devon 41 F7
Knightcote Warks 119 G7
Knightcott N Som 43 B11
Knightley Staffs 150 D6
Knightley Dale
Staffs 150 E6
Knighton
BCP 18 B6
Devon 7 F10
Dorset 29 E10
Leicester 135 C11
Oxon 63 B9
Som 43 E7
Staffs 150 D4
Staffs 168 G2
Wilts 63 E9
Worcs 117 F10
Knighton *= Tref-y-Clawdd*
Powys 114 C5
Knighton Fields
Leicester 135 C11
Knighton on Teme
Worcs 116 C2
Knightor Corn 5 D10
Knightsbridge Glos 99 F7
London 67 D9
Knight's End Cambs 139 E8
Knights Enham
Hants 47 D11
Knight's Hill London 67 E10
Knightsmill Corn 11 E7
Knightsridge
W Loth 269 B10
Knightswood
Glasgow 267 B10
Knightwick Worcs 116 F4
Knill Hereford 114 E5
Knipe Fold Cumb 220 F6
Knipoch Argyll 289 G10
Knipton Leics 154 C6
Knitsley Durham 233 B8
Kniveton Derbys 170 E2
Knocharthur Highld 309 J7
Knock Argyll 289 F7
Cumb 231 F9
Moray 302 D5
Knockally Highld 311 G5
Knockan Highld 307 H7
Knockandhu Moray 302 G2
Knockando Moray 301 E11
Knockando Ho
Moray 302 E2
Knockandoo Highld 301 G7
Knockbain Highld 300 D6
Knockbreck Highld 298 C2
Knockbrex Dumfries 237 E7
Knockcarrach
Highld 290 B6
Knockdee Highld 310 C5
Knockdolian S Ayrs 244 F4
Knockdow Argyll 276 G2
Knockdown Glos 61 B10
Knockenbaird
Aberds 302 G6
Knockenkelly
N Ayrs 256 D2
Knockentiber
E Ayrs 257 B9
Knockerdown
Derbys 170 E2
Knockespock Ho
Aberds 302 G5
Knockfarrel Highld 300 D5
Knockglass
Dumfries 236 D2
Knockhall Kent 68 E5
Knockhall Castle
Aberds 303 G9
Knockholt Kent 52 B3
Knockholt Pound
Kent 52 B3
Knockie Lodge
Highld 290 B6
Knockin Shrops 148 E6
Knockin Heath
Shrops 149 E7
Knockinlaw E Ayrs 257 B10
Knockinnon Highld 310 F5
Knocklaw Northumb 252 C3
Knocklearn
Dumfries 237 B9
Knocklearoch Argyll 274 G4
Knockmill Kent 68 G5
Knocknaha Argyll 255 F7
Knocknain Dumfries 236 C1
Knockothie Aberds 303 F9
Knockrome Argyll 274 F6
Knocksharry IoM 192 D3
Knockstapplemore
Argyll 255 F7
Knockvologan
Argyll 274 B4
Knodishall Suff 127 E8
Knokan Argyll 288 G6
Knole Som 29 B7
Knollbury Mon 60 B2
Knoll Green Som 43 F8
Knolls Green
Ches E 184 F4
Knoll Top N Yorks 214 F3
Knolton Wrex 149 B7
Knolton Bryn Wrex 149 B7
Knook Wilts 46 E2
Knossington Leics 136 B6
Knotbury Staffs 169 B8
Knott End-on-Sea
Lancs 202 D3
Knotting Bedford 121 E10
Knotting Green
Bedford 121 E10
Knottingley
W Yorks 198 C4
Knott Lanes
Gtr Man 196 G2
Knott Oak Som 28 E5
Knotts Cumb 230 G4
Lancs 203 C11
Knotty Ash Mers 182 C6
Knotty Corner Devon 24 B6
Knotty Green Bucks 84 G6
Knowbury Shrops 115 C11
Knowe Dumfries 236 B5
Shetland 313 G5
Knowefield Cumb 239 F10
Knowehead Aberds 293 C7
Aberds 302 D5
Dumfries 246 E4
Knowes E Loth 282 F2
Knowesgate
Northumb 251 F11
Knowes of Elrick
Aberds 302 D6
Knoweton N Lanark 268 D5
Knowetop N Lanark 268 D5
Knowhead Aberds 303 D9
Knowl Bank Staffs 168 F3
Knowle
Bristol 60 E6
Devon 15 E7
Devon 26 G3
Devon 27 F8
Devon 40 F3
Hants 33 F9
Shrops 115 C11
Som 43 F10
Wilts 63 G7
W Mid 118 B3
Knowle Fields
Worcs 117 F10
Knowlegate Shrops 115 C11
Knowle Green Lancs 203 F8
Sur 66 E4
Knowle Grove
W Mid 118 B3
Knowle Hill Sur 66 F3
Knowle Park
W Yorks 205 E7
Knowle St Giles Som 28 E4
Knowlesands
Shrops 132 E4
Knowles Hill Devon 14 G3
Knowl Green Essex 106 C5
Knowl Hill Windsor 65 D10
Knowlton Dorset 31 E8
Kent 55 C9
Knowl Wall Staffs 151 B7
Knowl Wood
W Yorks 196 C2
Knowsley Mers 182 B6
Knowsthorpe
W Yorks 206 G2
Knowstone Devon 26 C4
Knox Bridge Kent 53 E9
Knucklas Powys 114 C5
Knuston N Nhants 121 D8
Knutsford Ches E 184 F3
Knutton Staffs 168 F4
Knuzden Brook
Lancs 195 B8
Knypersley Staffs 168 D5
Kraiknish Highld 294 C5
Krumlin W Yorks 196 D5
Kuggar Corn 2 F6
Kyleakin Highld 295 C9
Kyle of Lochalsh
Highld 295 C9
Kylepark N Lanark 268 C3
Kylerhea Highld 295 C9
Kylesknoydart
Highld 295 F10
Kylesku Highld 306 F7
Kylesmorar Highld 295 F10
Kylestrome Highld 306 F7
Kyllachy House
Highld 301 G7
Kymin Hereford 97 B11
Mon 79 C8
Kynaston Hereford 97 F10
Shrops 149 E7
Kynnersley Telford 150 F3
Kyre Worcs 116 E2
Kyre Green Worcs 116 E2
Kyre Magna Worcs 116 E2
Kyre Park Worcs 116 E2
Kyrewood Worcs 116 D2

L

Labost W Isles 304 D4
Lacasaidh W Isles 304 F5
Lacasdal W Isles 304 E6
Laceby NE Lincs 201 F8
Laceby Acres
NE Lincs 201 F8
Lacey Green Bucks 84 F4
Ches E 184 E4
Lach Dennis
Ches W 184 G2
Lache Ches W 166 C5
Lackenby Redcar 225 B11
Lackford Suff 124 C5
Lacock Wilts 62 F2
Ladbroke Warks 119 F8
Laddenvean Corn 3 E7
Laddingford Kent 53 D7
Lade Kent 39 C9
Lade Bank Lincs 174 E5
Ladies Riggs
N Yorks 214 F2
Ladmanlow Derbys 185 G8
Ladock Corn 5 E7
Ladwell Hants 32 C6
Lady Orkney 314 B6
Ladybank Fife 287 F7
Ladybrook Notts 171 C8
Ladyburn Invclyd 276 F6
Ladycross Corn 12 D2
Ladyes Hill Warks 118 C5
Lady Green Mers 193 G10
Lady Hall Cumb 210 B3
Lady Halton Shrops 115 B9
Lady House Gtr Man 196 E2
Ladykirk Borders 273 F7
Ladyoak Shrops 131 C7
Lady Park T&W 242 F6
Ladyridge Hereford 97 E11
Ladysford Aberds 303 C9
Lady's Green Suff 124 F5
Ladywell London 67 E11
Shrops 149 C9
W Loth 269 B10
Ladywood Telford 132 C3
W Mid 133 F11
Worcs 117 E7
Lady Wood W Yorks 206 F2
Laffak Mers 183 B8
Laga Highld 289 C8
Lagafater Lodge
Dumfries 236 B3
Lagalochan Argyll 275 B9
Lagavulin Argyll 254 C5
Lagg Argyll 274 F6
N Ayrs 255 E10
Laggan Argyll 254 B3
Highld 289 B9
Highld 290 D4
Highld 291 D8
S Ayrs 245 G7
Lagganlia Highld 291 C10
Laggan Lodge
Argyll 289 G8
Lagganmullan
Dumfries 237 D7
Lagganulva Argyll 288 E6
Lagness W Sus 22 C5
Laide Highld 307 K3
Laig Highld 294 G6
Laigh Carnduff
S Lanark 268 F3
Laigh Fenwick
E Ayrs 267 G9
Laigh Glengall
S Ayrs 257 F8
Laighmuir E Ayrs 267 F9
Laighstonehall
S Lanark 268 E4
Laindon Essex 69 B7
Lair Highld 299 E10
Perth 292 G3
Laira Plym 7 D10
Lairg Highld 309 J5
Lairg Lodge Highld 309 J5
Lairgmore Highld 300 F5
Lairg Muir Highld 309 J5
Laisterdyke
W Yorks 205 G9
Laithes Cumb 230 E5
Laithkirk Durham 232 G5
Laity Moor Corn 4 F3
Lake
BCP 18 C5
Devon 12 D6
Devon 24 F6
Devon 40 G5
IoW 21 E7
Wilts 46 F6
Lake End Bucks 66 D2
Lakenham Norf 142 B4
Lakenheath Suff 140 G4
Laker's Green Sur 50 F4
Lakesend Norf 139 D10
Lakeside Cumb 211 B7
Thurrock 68 D5
Worcs 117 D11
Laleham Sur 66 F5
Laleston *= Trelales*
Bridgend 57 F11
Lamanva Corn 3 C7
Lamarsh Essex 107 D7
Lamas Norf 160 E4
Lamb Corner Essex 107 E10
Lambden Borders 272 G4
Lamberden Kent 38 B4
Lamberhead Green
Gtr Man 194 G4
Lamberhurst Kent 53 F7
Lamberhurst Quarter
Kent 53 F7
Lamberton Borders 273 D9
Lambert's End
W Mid 133 E9
Lambeth London 67 D10
Lambfair Green
Suff 124 G4
Lambfoot Cumb 229 E9
Lambhill Glasgow 267 B11
Lambley Northumb 240 F5
Notts 171 F10
Lambourn W Berks 63 D10
Lambourne Corn 4 E5
Essex 87 F7
Lambourne End
Essex 87 G7
Lambourn Woodlands
W Berks 63 D10
Lambridge Bath 61 F9
Lamb's Cross Kent 53 D9
Lambs Green W Sus 51 F8
Lambs' Green Dorset 18 B5
Lambston Pembs 72 B6
Lambton T&W 243 G7
Lamellion Corn 6 C4
Lamerton Devon 12 F5
Lamesley T&W 243 F7
Laminess Orkney 314 C6
Lamington Highld 301 B7
S Lanark 259 C11
Lamlash N Ayrs 256 C2
Lamledra Corn 5 G10
Lamloch Dumfries 246 D2
Lammack Blackburn 195 B7
Lamonby Cumb 230 D4
Lamorick Corn 5 C10
Lamorna Corn 1 E4
Lamorran Corn 5 G7
Lampardbrook Suff 126 E5
Lampeter *= Llanbedr Pont Steffan* Ceredig 93 B11
Lampeter Velfrey
Pembs 73 C11
Lamphey Pembs 73 E8
Lamplugh Cumb 229 G7
Lamport W Nhants 120 C5
Lampton London 66 D6
Lamyatt Som 45 F7
Lana Devon 12 B2
Devon 24 F4
Lanark S Lanark 269 G7
Lancaster Lancs 211 G9
Lanchester Durham 233 B9
Lancing W Sus 35 G11
Landbeach Cambs 123 D9
Landcross Devon 25 C7
Landerberry Aberds 293 C9
Landewednack Corn 2 G6
Landford Wilts 32 D3
Landford Manor
Wilts 32 C3
Landfordwood Wilts 32 C3
Land Gate Gtr Man 194 G5
Landguard Manor
IoW 21 E7
Landhill Devon 12 B4
Landican Mers 182 D3
Landimore Swansea 56 C3
Landkey Devon 40 G5
Landkey Newland
Devon 40 G5
Landore Swansea 57 B7
Landport E Sus 36 E6
Ptsmth 33 G10
Landrake Corn 7 C7
Landscove Devon 8 B5
Landshipping Pembs 73 C8
Landshipping Quay
Pembs 73 C8
Landslow Green
Gtr Man 185 B7
Landulph Corn 7 C8
Landwade Suff 124 D2
Landywood Staffs 133 B9
Lane Corn 4 C6
Laneast Corn 11 E10
Lane Bottom Lancs 204 F3
W Yorks 205 F7
Lane End Bucks 84 G4
Lane-end Corn 5 B10
Lane End Cumb 220 G2
Lane End *continued*
Derbys 170 C6
Devon 24 G6
Dorset 18 C3
Flint 166 C3
Glos 79 B10
Hants 33 B9
Hants 33 B11
IoW 21 D9
Kent 68 E5
Lancs 204 D3
Sur 49 E10
S Yorks 186 B5
Wilts 45 D10
W Yorks 204 F6
Lane Ends Ches E 168 D2
Ches E 185 E7
Cumb 210 C6
Derbys 152 C4
Gtr Man 185 C7
Lancs 194 D6
Lancs 203 C11
Lancs 203 G11
N Yorks 204 E5
Stoke 168 E5
W Yorks 205 F10
Lane Green Staffs 133 C7
Laneham Notts 188 F4
Lanehead Durham 232 C2
Northumb 251 F7
Lane Head Derbys 185 F11
Durham 224 C2
Gtr Man 183 B10
Pembs 73 E8
W Mid 133 C9
W Yorks 197 F7
Lane Heads Lancs 202 F4
Lanehouse Dorset 17 F9
Lanercost Cumb 240 E3
Lanescot Corn 5 D11
Lanesend Pembs 73 D9
Lanes End Bucks 84 D6
Lane's End Shrops 132 G2
Lanesfield W Mid 133 D8
Laneshaw Bridge
Lancs 204 E4
Lane Side Lancs 195 C9
Laney Green Staffs 133 B9
Lanfach Caerph 78 F2
Langaford Devon 12 B4
Langage Devon 7 E11
Langal Highld 289 C9
Langaller Som 28 B3
Langar Notts 154 C4
Langbank Renfs 277 G7
Langbar N Yorks 205 C7
Langbaurgh
N Yorks 225 C11
Langburnshiels
Borders 250 C2
Langcliffe N Yorks 212 G6
Langdale Highld 308 E6
Langdale End
N Yorks 227 G8
Langdon Corn 12 D2
Langdon Beck
Durham 232 E3
Langdon Hills Essex 69 B7
Langdown Hants 32 F6
Langdyke Dumfries 238 C3
Fife 287 G7
Langenhoe Essex 89 B8
Langford C Beds 104 C3
Devon 14 B4
Devon 27 G8
Essex 88 D4
Notts 172 D4
Oxon 82 E2
Som 28 B2
Langford Budville
Som 27 C10
Langford Green
Devon 27 G8
N Som 44 B3
Langham Dorset 30 B3
Essex 107 E10
Norf 177 E8
Rutland 154 G6
Som 28 E4
Suff 125 C9
Langhaugh Borders 260 C6
Langho Lancs 203 G10
Langholm Dumfries 249 G9
Langholme N Lincs 188 B3
Langhope Borders 261 E10
Langland Swansea 56 D6
Langlee Borders 262 B2
Langleeford
Northumb 263 E10
Langlee Mains
Borders 262 B2
Langlees Falk 279 E7
Langley Ches E 184 G6
Derbys 170 F6
Essex 105 D8
Glos 99 F10
Gtr Man 195 F11
Hants 32 G6
Herts 104 G4
Kent 53 C10
Northumb 241 E8
Oxon 82 B4
Slough 66 D4
Som 27 B9
Warks 118 E3
W Mid 133 F9
W Sus 34 B4
Langley Burrell Wilts 62 D2
Langleybury Herts 85 E9
Langley Common
Derbys 152 B5
Wokingham 65 F9
Langley Corner
Bucks 66 C4
Langley Green
Derbys 152 B5
Essex 107 G7
Warks 118 E3
W Mid 133 F9

Langley Green continued
W Sus 51 F9
Langley Heath Kent . .53 C10
Langley Marsh Som . . .27 B9
Langley Mill Derbys .170 F6
Langley Moor
Durham 233 C11
Langley Park
Durham 233 C10
Langley Street Norf .143 C7
Langley Vale Sur 51 B8
Langloan N Lanark . . .268 C4
Langney E Sus 23 E10
Langold Notts 187 D9
Langore Corn 12 D2
Langport Som 28 B6
Langrick Lincs 174 F3
Langrick Bridge
Lincs 174 F3
Langridge Bath 61 F8
Langridge Ford
Devon 25 C9
Langrigg Cumb 222 C5
Cumb 229 B9
Langrish Hants 34 C2
Langsett S Yorks 197 G8
Langshaw Borders . .262 B2
Langside Glasgow . .267 C11
Perth 285 F11
Langskaill Orkney . .314 B4
Langstone Devon 13 E10
Hants 22 C2
Newport 78 G5
Langthorne N Yorks .224 G5
Langthorpe N Yorks .215 F7
Langthwaite
N Yorks 223 E10
Langtoft E Yorks 217 F10
Lincs 156 G2
Lincs 174 B2
N Yorks 216 F5
Langton by Wragby
Lincs 189 F11
Langton Green Kent . .52 F4
Suff 126 C2
Langton Herring
Dorset 17 E8
Langton Long Blandford
Dorset 30 F5
Langton Matravers
Dorset 18 F6
Langtree Devon 25 D7
Langtree Week
Devon 25 D7
Langwathby Cumb . .231 E7
Langwell Ho Highld . .311 G5
Langwell Lodge
Highld 307 J6
Langwith Derbys 171 B8
Langwith Junction
Derbys 171 B8
Langworth Lincs 189 F9
Lanham Green
Essex 106 G5
Lanivet Corn 5 C10
Lanjeth Corn 5 E9
Lanjew Corn 5 D11
Lank Corn 11 F7
Lanlivery Corn 5 D11
Lanner Corn 2 B6
Lanreath Corn 6 D3
Lanrick Stirling 285 G10
Lansallos Corn 6 E3
Lansbury Park
Caerph 59 B7
Lansdown Bath 61 F8
Glos 99 G8
Lanstephan Corn 12 D2
Lanteglos Corn 11 E7
Lanteglos Highway
Corn 6 E3
Lanton Borders 262 E4
Northumb 263 C10
Lantuel Corn 5 B9
Lantyan Corn 6 D2
Lapal W Mid 133 G9
Lapford Devon 26 F2
Lapford Cross Devon . .26 F2
Laphroaig Argyll 254 C4
Lapley Staffs 151 G7
Lapworth Warks 118 C3
Larachbeg Highld . . .289 E8
Larbert Falk 279 E7
Larbreck Lancs 202 E4
Larches Lancs 202 G6
Larden Green
Ches E 167 E9
Larg Highld 292 B2
Largie Aberds 302 F6
Largiebaan Argyll . . .255 F7
Largiemore Argyll . . .275 E10
Largoward Fife 287 G8
Largs N Ayrs 266 D4
Largue Aberds 302 E6
Largybeg N Ayrs 256 E3
Largymeanoch
N Ayrs 256 E2
Largymore N Ayrs . . .256 E2
Larkfield Invclyd . . .276 F4
Kent 53 B8
W Yorks 205 F10
Larkhall Bath 61 F9
S Lanark 268 E5
Larkhill Wilts 46 E6
Lark Hill Gtr Man . . .195 G4
Larklands Derbys . . .171 G7
Larks' Hill Suff 108 B3
Larling Norf 141 F9
Larport Hereford 97 D11
Larrick Corn 12 F2
Larriston Borders . . .250 E2
Lartington Durham . .223 B10
Lary Aberds 292 C5
Lasborough Glos 80 G4
Lasham Hants 49 E7
Lashenden Kent 53 E10
Lask Edge Staffs 168 D6

Lassington Glos 98 G5
Lassodie Fife 280 C2
Lastingham N Yorks .226 G4
Latcham Som 44 D2
Latchbrook Corn 7 D8
Latchford Herts 105 G7
Oxon 83 E11
Warr 183 D10
Latchingdon Essex . . .88 E5
Latchley Corn 12 G4
Latchmere Green
Hants 64 G6
Latchmore Bank
Essex 87 B7
Lately Common
Warr 183 B11
Lathallan Mill Fife . .287 G8
Lathbury M Keynes . .103 B7
Latheron Highld 310 F5
Latheronwheel
Highld 310 F5
Latheronwheel Ho
Highld 310 F5
Lathom Lancs 194 E3
Lathones Fife 287 G8
Latimer Bucks 85 F8
Latteridge S Glos 61 C7
Lattiford Som 29 B11
Lattinford Hill Suff . .107 D11
Latton Wilts 81 F9
Latton Bush Essex . . .87 D7
Lauchintilly Aberds .293 B9
Laudale Ho Highld . .289 D9
Lauder Borders 271 F10
Lauder Barns
Borders 271 F10
Laugharne = Talacharn
Carms 74 C4
Laughern Hill Worcs .116 F5
Laughterton Lincs . . .188 F4
Laughton E Sus 23 C8
Leics 136 F3
Lincs 155 C11
Lincs 188 B4
Laughton Common
E Sus 23 C7
S Yorks 187 D8
Laughton en le Morthen
S Yorks 187 D8
Launcells Corn 24 F3
Launcells Cross Corn .24 F3
Launceston Corn 12 D2
Launcherley Som 44 E4
Laund Lancs 195 C10
Launton Oxon 102 G2
Laurencekirk
Aberds 293 F9
Laurieston Dumfries .237 C8
Falk 279 F8
Lavendon M Keynes . .121 G8
Lavenham Suff 107 B8
Laverackloch
Moray 301 C11
Laverhay Dumfries . . .248 D4
Laverlaw Borders 261 B7
Laverley Som 44 F5
Lavernock V Glam 59 F7
Laversdale Cumb 239 E11
Laverstock Wilts 47 G7
Laverstoke Hants 48 D3
Laverton Glos 99 D11
N Yorks 214 E4
Som 45 C9
Lavington Sands
Wilts 46 B4
Lavister Wrex 166 D5
Lavrean Corn 5 D10
Lawers Perth 285 D11
Perth 285 E11
Lawford Essex 107 E11
Som 42 F6
Lawford Heath
Warks 119 C9
Lawhill Perth 286 F3
Law Hill S Lanark . . .268 E6
Lawhitton Corn 12 E3
Lawkland N Yorks . . .212 F5
Lawkland Green
N Yorks 212 F5
Lawley Telford 132 B3
Lawnhead Staffs 150 E6
Lawns W Yorks 197 C10
Lawnswood
W Yorks 205 F11
Lawnt Denb 165 B8
Lawrence Hill
Newport 59 B10
Lawrence Weston
Bristol 60 D4
Lawrenny Pembs 73 D8
Lawrenny Quay
Pembs 73 D8
Lawshall Suff 125 G7
Lawshall Green Suff .125 G7
Lawton Hereford 115 F8
Shrops 131 G10
Lawton-gate
Ches E 168 D4
Lawton Heath End
Ches E 168 D3
Laxey IoM 192 D5
Laxfield Suff 126 C5
Laxfirth Shetland 313 H6
Shetland 313 J6
Laxford Bridge
Highld 306 E7
Laxo Shetland 313 G6
Laxobigging
Shetland 312 F6
Laxton E Yorks 199 B9
N Nhants 137 D8
Notts 172 B2
Laycock W Yorks 204 E6
Layer Breton Essex . . .88 B6
Layer de la Haye
Essex 88 B6
Layer Marney Essex . .88 B6
Layerthorpe York 207 C8
Layham Suff 107 C10
Laymore Dorset 28 G5
Layters Green Bucks . .85 G7

Laytham E Yorks 207 F10
Layton Blackpool 202 F2
Lazenby Redcar 225 B11
Lazonby Cumb 230 D6
Lea Derbys 170 D4
Hereford 98 G3
Lancs 202 G5
Lincs 188 D4
Shrops 131 B8
Shrops 131 F7
Wilts 62 B3
Lea Bridge London . . .67 B11
Leabrooks Derbys . . .170 E6
Lea by Backford
Ches W 182 G5
Leacainn W Isles 305 H3
Leac a Li W Isles 305 J3
Leachkin Highld 300 E5
Leacnasaide Highld . .299 B7
Leadburn Midloth 270 D4
Leadendale Staffs . . .151 B8
Leadenham Lincs 173 E7
Leaden Roding Essex .87 C9
Leadgate Cumb 231 C10
Durham 242 G4
Durham 242 G4
Leadhills S Lanark . .259 G9
Leadingcross Green
Kent 53 C11
Leadmill Derbys 186 E2
Flint 166 C2
Lea End Worcs 117 B10
Leafield Oxon 82 B4
Wilts 61 F11
Lea Forge Ches E 168 F2
Leagrave Luton 103 G10
Leagreen Hants 19 C11
Lea Green Mers 183 C8
Lea Hall W Mid 134 F2
Lea Heath Staffs 151 D10
Leake Lincs 174 F6
N Yorks 225 G8
Leake Commonside
Lincs 174 E5
Leake Fold Hill
Lincs 174 E6
Lealholm N Yorks . . .226 D5
Lealholm Side
N Yorks 226 D5
Lea Line Hereford 98 G3
Lealt Argyll 275 D7
Highld 298 C5
Leam Derbys 186 F2
Lea Marston Warks . .134 E4
Leamington Hastings
Warks 119 D8
Leamoor Common
Shrops 131 F8
Leamore W Mid 133 C9
Leamside Durham 234 B2
Leanach Argyll 275 D11
Leananach Highld 290 F4
Leanaig Highld 300 D5
Leapgate Worcs 116 C6
Leargybreck Argyll . . .274 F6
Lease Rigg N Yorks . .226 E6
Leasey Bridge Herts .85 C11
Leasgill Cumb 211 C9
Leasingham Lincs 173 F9
Leasingthorne
Durham 233 F11
Leason Swansea 56 C3
Leasowe Mers 182 C3
Leatherhead Sur 51 B7
Leatherhead Common
Sur 51 B7
Leathern Bottle Glos . .80 E2
Leathley N Yorks 205 D10
Leaths Dumfries 237 C9
Leaton Shrops 149 F9
Telford 150 G2
Leaton Heath
Shrops 149 F9
Lea Town Lancs 202 G5
Lea Valley Herts 85 B11
Leaveland Kent 54 C4
Leavenheath Suff 107 D9
Leavening N Yorks . . .216 G5
Leaves Green London . .68 G2
Lea Yeat Cumb 212 B5
Leazes Durham 242 F5
Lebberston
N Yorks 217 C11
Leburnick Corn 12 E3
Lechlade-on-Thames
Glos 82 F2
Leck Lancs 212 D2
Leckford Hants 47 F11
Leckfurin Highld 308 D7
Leckgruinart Argyll . .274 G3
Leckhampstead
Bucks 102 D4
W Berks 64 D2
Leckhampstead Thicket
W Berks 64 D2
Leckhampton Glos 80 B6
Leckie Highld 299 C10
Leckmelm Highld 307 K6
Leckuary Argyll 275 D8
Leckwith V Glam 59 E7
Leconfield E Yorks . . .208 E6
Ledaig Argyll 289 F11
Ledburn Bucks 103 G8
Ledbury Hereford 98 D4
Ledcharrie Stirling . .285 E9
Leddington Glos 98 E3
Ledgemoor
Hereford 115 G8
Ledgowan Highld 299 D11
Ledicot Hereford 115 E8
Ledmore Angus 293 G2
Highld 307 H7
Lednagullin Highld . . .308 C7
Ledsham Ches W 182 G5
W Yorks 198 B2
Ledston W Yorks 198 B2
Ledstone Devon 8 F4
Ledston Luck
W Yorks 206 G4
Ledwell Oxon 101 F8

Lee Argyll 288 G6
Devon 40 D3
Devon 40 D5
Hants 32 D5
Lancs 203 B7
London 67 E11
Northumb 241 F10
Shrops 149 C8
Leeans Shetland 313 J5
Lee Bank W Mid 133 F11
Leebotten Shetland . .313 L6
Leebotwood Shrops . .131 D9
Lee Brockhurst
Shrops 149 D10
Lee Chapel Essex 69 B7
Leechpool Mon 60 B4
Lee Clump Bucks 84 E6
Lee Common Bucks . . .84 E6
Leeds Kent 53 C10
W Yorks 205 G11
Leedstown Corn 2 C5
Leeford Devon 41 D9
Lee Gate Bucks 84 D5
Leegomery Telford . . .150 G3
Lee Ground Hants 33 F8
Lee Head Derbys 185 C8
Leeholme Durham 233 E10
Leek Staffs 169 D7
Leekbrook Staffs 169 E7
Leek Wootton
Warks 118 D5
Lee Mill Devon 8 D2
Leeming N Yorks 214 B5
W Yorks 204 G6
Leeming Bar
N Yorks 224 G5
Leemings Lancs 203 D10
Lee Moor Devon 7 C11
W Yorks 197 B10
Lee-on-the-Solent
Hants 33 G9
Lee-over-Sands
Essex 89 C10
Lees Derbys 152 B5
Gtr Man 196 G3
W Yorks 204 F6
Leesthorpe Leics 154 G5
Leeswood = Coed-Llai
Flint 166 D3
Leftwich Ches W 183 G11
Legar Powys 78 B2
Legbourne Lincs 190 E5
Legburthwaite
Cumb 220 B6
Legerwood
Borders 271 G11
Leggatt Hill W Sus . . .34 C6
Legsby Lincs 189 D10
Leicester Leicester . . .135 C11
Leicester Forest East
Leics 135 C10
Leicester Grange
Warks 135 E8
Leigh Devon 26 E2
Dorset 18 B6
Dorset 29 E10
Dorset 30 F3
Glos 99 F7
Gtr Man 195 G7
Kent 52 D4
Shrops 130 C6
Sur 51 D8
Wilts 81 G9
Worcs 116 G5
Leigham Plym 7 D10
Leigh Beck Essex 69 C10
Leigh Common Som . .30 B2
Leigh Delamere
Wilts 61 D11
Leigh Green Kent 54 G2
Leighland Chapel
Som 42 F4
Leigh-on-Sea
Southend 69 B10
Highld 301 F10
Moray 302 F3
Perth 291 G11
Leighswood
W Mid 133 C10
Leighterton Glos 80 G4
Leighton N Yorks 214 D3
Shrops 132 B2
Leighton = Tre'r Llai
Powys 130 B4
Leighton Bromswold
Cambs 122 B2
Leighton Buzzard
C Beds 103 F8
Leigh upon Mendip
Som 45 D7
Leigh Woods N Som . . .60 E5
Leinthall Earls
Hereford 115 D8
Leinthall Starkes
Hereford 115 D8
Leintwardine
Hereford 115 C8
Leire Leics 135 E10
Leirinmore Highld . . .308 C4
Leiston Suff 127 E8
Leitfie Perth 286 C6
Leith Edin 280 F5
Leithenhall
Dumfries 248 D4
Leitholm Borders 272 G5
Lelant Corn 2 B2
Lelant Downs Corn 2 B2
Lelley E Yorks 209 G10
Lem Hill Worcs 116 C4
Lemington T&W 242 E5
Lemmington Hall
Northumb 264 G4
Lempitlaw Borders . . .263 C7
Lemsford Herts 86 C2
Lenacre Cumb 212 B3
Lenborough Bucks . . .102 D3
Lenchwick Worcs 99 B10
Lendalfoot S Ayrs 244 F4
Lendrick Lodge
Stirling 285 G9

Lenham Kent 53 C11
Lenham Forstal Kent . .54 C2
Lenham Heath Kent . . .54 D2
Lennel Borders 273 G7
Lennoxtown E Dunb . .278 F2
Lent Bucks 66 C2
Lenten Pool Denb 165 B8
Lenton Lincs 155 C10
Nottingham 153 B10
Lenton Abbey
Nottingham 153 B10
Lentran Highld 300 E5
Lenwade Norf 159 F11
Leny Ho Stirling 285 G10
Lenzie E Dunb 278 G3
Lenziemill N Lanark . .278 G5
Leoch Aberds 293 B7
Leochel-Cushnie
Aberds 293 B7
Leominster Hereford . .115 F9
Leomonsley Staffs . . .134 B3
Leonard Stanley Glos .80 E4
Leonardston Pembs . .72 D6
Leorin Argyll 254 C4
Lepe Hants 20 B5
Lephin Highld 297 G7
Lephinchapel
Argyll 275 D10
Lephinmore Argyll . . .275 D10
Leppington N Yorks . .216 G5
Lepton W Yorks 197 D8
Lepton Edge
W Yorks 197 D8
Lerigoligan Argyll . . .275 C9
Lerrocks Stirling 285 G11
Lerryn Corn 6 D2
Lerwick Shetland 313 J6
Lesbury Northumb . . .264 G6
Leschangie Aberds . . .293 B9
Le Skerne Haughton
Darl 224 B6
Leslie Aberds 302 G5
Fife 286 G6
Lesmahagow
S Lanark 259 B8
Lesnewth Corn 11 C8
Lessendrum Aberds . .302 E5
Lessingham Norf 161 D7
Lessness Heath
London 68 D3
Lessonhall Cumb 238 G6
Leswalt Dumfries 236 C2
Letchmore Heath
Herts 85 F11
Letchworth Herts 104 E4
Letcombe Bassett
Oxon 63 B11
Letcombe Regis
Oxon 63 B11
Letham Angus 287 C9
Falk 279 D7
Fife 287 F7
Perth 286 E4
Letham Grange
Angus 287 C10
Lethem Borders 250 B5
Lethen Ho Highld 301 D9
Lethenty Aberds 303 E8
Aberds 303 G7
Letheringham Suff . . .126 F5
Letheringsett Norf . . .159 B11
Lettaford Devon 13 E10
Lettan Orkney 314 B7
Letter Aberds 293 B9
Letterewe Highld 299 C9
Letterfearn Highld . . .295 C10
Letterfinlay Highld . . .290 D4
Lettermay Argyll 284 G5
Lettermorar Highld . .295 G9
Lettermore Argyll 288 E6
Letters Highld 307 L6
Letterston = Treletert
Pembs 91 F8
Lettoch Highld 292 B2
Highld 301 F10
Moray 302 F3
Perth 291 G11
Letton Hereford 96 B6
Hereford 115 C7
Letton Green Norf 141 B9
Lett's Green Kent 52 B3
Letty Brongu
Bridgend 57 D11
Letty Green Herts 86 C3
Letwell S Yorks 187 D9
Leuchars Fife 287 E8
Leuchars Ho Moray . .302 C2
Leumrabhagh
W Isles 305 G5
Levalsa Meor Corn 5 F10
Levan Invclyd 276 F4
Levaneap Shetland . . .313 G6
Levedale Staffs 151 F7
Level of Mendalgief
Newport 59 B10
Level's Green Essex . .105 G9
Leven E Yorks 209 D8
Fife 287 G7
Levencorroch
N Ayrs 256 E2
Levenhall E Loth 281 G7
Levens Cumb 211 B9
Levens Green Herts . .105 G7
Levenshulme
Gtr Man 184 C5
Leventhorpe
W Yorks 205 G8
Levenwick Shetland . .313 L6
Lever-Edge Gtr Man . .195 F8
Leverington Cambs . .157 G7
Leverington Common
Cambs 157 G7
Leverstock Green
Herts 85 D9
Leverton Lincs 174 F6
W Berks 63 E10
Leverton Highgate
Lincs 174 F6
Leverton Lucasgate
Lincs 174 F6

Leverton Outgate
Lincs 174 F6
Levington Suff 108 D4
Levisham N Yorks . . .226 G6
Levishie Highld 290 B6
Lew Oxon 82 D4
Lewannick Corn 11 E11
Lewcombe Dorset 29 F9
Lewdown Devon 12 D4
Lewes E Sus 36 E6
Leweston Pembs 91 G8
Lewisham London 67 D11
Lewiston Highld 300 G5
Lewistown Bridgend . .58 B2
Lewknor Oxon 84 F2
Leworthy Devon 24 G4
Devon 41 F7
Lewson Street Kent . . .70 G3
Lewth Lancs 202 F5
Lewthorn Cross
Devon 13 F11
Lewtrenchard Devon . .12 D4
Lexden Essex 107 G9
Ley Aberds 293 B7
Corn 6 B3
Som 41 F10
Leybourne Kent 53 B7
Leyburn N Yorks 224 G2
Leycett Staffs 168 F3
Leyfields Staffs 134 B4
Ley Green Herts 104 G3
Ley Hey Park
Gtr Man 185 D7
Leyhill Bucks 85 E7
Ley Hill W Mid 134 D2
Leyland Lancs 194 C4
Leylodge Aberds 293 B9
Leymoor W Yorks 196 D6
Leys Aberds 292 C6
Aberds 303 D10
Cumb 219 B11
Perth 286 D6
Staffs 169 F8
Leys Castle Highld . . .300 E6
Leysdown-on-Sea
Kent 70 E4
Leys Hill Hereford 79 B9
Leysmill Angus 287 C10
Leys of Cossans
Angus 287 C7
Leysters Hereford 115 E11
Leysters Pole
Hereford 115 E11
Leyton London 67 B11
Leytonstone London . .67 B11
Lezant Corn 12 F2
Lezerea Corn 2 C5
Leziate Norf 158 F3
Lhanbryde Moray 302 C2
Liatrie Highld 300 F2
Libanus Powys 95 F9
Libberton S Lanark . . .269 G9
Libbery Worcs 117 F9
Liberton Edin 270 B5
Liceasto W Isles 305 J3
Lichfield Staffs 134 B2
Lick Perth 286 B2
Lickey Worcs 117 B9
Lickey End Worcs 117 B9
Lickfold W Sus 34 B6
Lickhill Worcs 116 C6
Licklehead Castle
Aberds 302 G6
Liddaton Devon 12 E5
Liddel Orkney 314 H4
Liddesdale Highld . . .289 D9
Liddeston Pembs 72 D5
Liddington Swindon . .63 C8
Liden Swindon 63 C7
Lidgate Suff 124 F4
Lidget S Yorks 199 G5
Lidget Green
W Yorks 205 G8
Lidgett Notts 171 B10
Lidgett Park
W Yorks 206 F2
Lidham Hill E Sus 38 D4
Lidlington C Beds 103 D9
Lidsey W Sus 22 C6
Lidsing Kent 69 G9
Lidstone Oxon 101 G7
Lieurary Highld 310 C4
Liff Angus 287 D7
Lifford W Mid 117 B11
Lifton Devon 12 D3
Liftondown Devon 12 D3
Lightcliffe W Yorks . . .196 B6
Lightfoot Green
Lancs 202 G6
Lighthorne Warks 118 F6
Lighthorne Heath
Warks 119 F7
Lighthorne Rough
Warks 118 F6
Lightmoor Telford 132 B3
Light Oaks Staffs 168 E6
Lightpill Glos 80 E4
Lightwater Sur 66 G2
Lightwood
Shrops 132 C2
Shrops 150 D3
Staffs 169 G6
Stoke 168 G6
S Yorks 186 F5
Lightwood Green
Ches E 167 G10
Wrex 166 G5
Lilbourne N Nhants . . .119 B11
Lilburn Tower
Northumb 264 E2
Lilleshall Telford 150 F4
Lilley Herts 104 F2
W Berks 64 D2
Lilliesleaf Borders . . .262 E2
Lillingstone Dayrell
Bucks 102 D4

Lillingstone Lovell
Bucks 102 C4
Lillington Dorset 29 E10
Warks 118 D6
Lilliput BCP 18 C6
Lilstock Som 43 E7
Lilybank Invclyd 276 G6
Lilyhurst Shrops 150 G4
Lilyvale Kent 54 F5
Limbrick Lancs 194 D6
Limbury Luton 103 G11
Limebrook Hereford . .115 D7
Limebrook Hereford . .115 D7
Limefield Gtr Man 195 E10
Limehouse London . . .67 C11
Limehurst Gtr Man . . .196 G2
Limekilnburn
S Lanark 268 E4
Limekiln Field
Derbys 187 G7
Limekilns Fife 279 E11
Limerigg Falk 279 G7
Limerstone IoW 20 E4
Lime Side Gtr Man . . .196 G2
Limestone Brae
Northumb 231 B11
Lime Street Worcs 98 E5
Lime Tree Park
W Mid 118 B5
Limington Som 29 C8
Limpenhoe Norf 143 C7
Limpenhoe Hill
Norf 143 C8
Limpers Hill Wilts 45 G10
Limpley Stoke Wilts . .61 G9
Limpsfield Sur 52 C2
Limpsfield Chart Sur . .52 C2
Limpsfield Common
Sur 52 C2
Linbriggs Northumb . .251 B9
Linburn W Loth 270 B2
Linby Notts 171 E8
Linchmere W Sus 49 G11
Lincluden Dumfries . .237 B11
Lincoln Lincs 189 G7
Lincomb Worcs 116 D6
Lincombe Devon 8 C4
Devon 40 D5
Lindale Cumb 211 C8
Lindal in Furness
Cumb 210 D5
Lindean Borders 261 C11
Linden Glos 80 B4
Lindfield W Sus 36 B4
Lindford Hants 49 F10
Lindifferon Fife 287 F7
Lindley N Yorks 205 D10
W Yorks 196 D6
Lindley Green
N Yorks 205 D10
Lindores Fife 286 F6
Lindow End Ches E . . .184 F4
Lindrick Dale
S Yorks 187 E8
Lindridge Worcs 116 D3
Lindsell Essex 106 F2
Lindsey Suff 107 C9
Lindsey Tye Suff 107 B9
Lindwell W Yorks 196 C5
Lineholt Worcs 116 D6
Lineholt Common
Worcs 116 D6
Liney Som 43 F11
Linfitts Gtr Man 196 F3
Linford Hants 31 F11
Thurrock 69 D7
Lingague IoM 192 E3
Lingards Wood
W Yorks 196 E5
Lingbob W Yorks 205 F7
Lingdale Redcar 226 B3
Lingen Hereford 115 D7
Lingfield Darl 224 C6
Sur 51 E11
Lingfield Common
Sur 51 E11
Lingley Green Warr . .183 D9
Lingley Mere Warr . . .183 D10
Lingreabhagh
W Isles 296 C6
Lingwood Norf 143 B7
Linhope Borders 249 C10
Northumb 241 B11
Linicro Highld 298 C3
Link N Som 44 B3
Linkend Worcs 98 E6
Linkenholt Hants 47 B11
Linkhill Kent 38 B4
Linkinhorne Corn 12 G2
Linklater Orkney 314 H4
Linklet Orkney 314 A7
Linksness Orkney 314 F2
Orkney 314 F2
Linktown Fife 280 C5
Linley Shrops 131 E7
Shrops 132 D3
Linley Brook Shrops . .132 D3
Linleygreen Shrops . . .132 D3
Linley Green
Hereford 116 G3
Linlithgow W Loth . . .279 F10
Linlithgow Bridge
W Loth 279 F9
Linndhu Ho Argyll . . .289 D7
Linns Angus 292 F3
Linnyshaw Gtr Man . .195 G8
Linshiels Northumb . .251 B9
Linsiadar W Isles 304 E4
Linsidemore Highld . .309 K5
Linslade C Beds 103 F8
Linstead Parva Suff . .126 B6
Linstock Cumb 239 F10
Linthorpe Mbro 225 B9
Linthurst Worcs 117 C9
Linthwaite W Yorks . .196 E6
Lintlaw Borders 272 D6
Lintmill Moray 302 C5
Linton Borders 263 D7
Cambs 105 B11
Derbys 152 F5
Hereford 98 F3

Linton continued
Kent 53 D7
Northumb 253 E7
N Yorks 213 G9
W Yorks 206 F3
Linton Heath Derbys .152 F5
Linton Hill Hereford . .98 F3
Linton-on-Ouse
N Yorks 215 G9
Lintridge Glos 98 E5
Lintz Durham 242 F5
Lintzford T&W 242 F4
Lintzgarth Durham . . .232 C4
Linwood Hants 31 F11
Lincs 189 D10
Renfs 267 C8
Lionacleit W Isles 297 G3
Lional W Isles 304 B7
Lions Green E Sus 23 C9
Liphook Hants 49 G10
Lipley Shrops 150 C4
Lippitts Hill Essex 86 F5
Liquo or Bowhousebog
N Lanark 269 D7
Liscard Mers 182 C4
Liscombe Som 41 G11
Liskeard Corn 6 C5
Liss Hants 34 B3
Lissett E Yorks 209 B8
Liss Forest Hants 34 B3
Lissington Lincs 189 E10
Lisson Grove London . .67 C9
Listerdale S Yorks . . .187 C7
Listock Som 28 C4
Listoft Lincs 191 G8
Liston Essex 107 C7
Liston Garden Essex .106 B6
Lisvane Cardiff 59 C7
Liswerry Newport 59 B10
Litcham Norf 159 F7
Litchard Bridgend 58 C2
Litchborough
W Nhants 120 G2
Litchfield Hants 48 C3
Litchurch Derbys 153 B7
Litherland Mers 182 B4
Litlington Cambs 104 C6
E Sus 23 E8
Litmarsh Hereford . . .97 B10
Little Abington
Cambs 105 B10
Little Addington
N Nhants 121 C9
Little Airmyn
E Yorks 199 B8
Little Almshoe
Herts 104 F3
Little Alne Warks 118 E2
Little Altcar Mers 193 F10
Little Ann Hants 47 E10
Little Arowry Wrex . . .167 G2
Little Asby Cumb 222 D3
Little Ashley Wilts 61 G10
Little Assynt Highld . .307 G6
Little Aston Staffs . . .133 C11
Little Atherfield IoW . .20 F5
Little Ayre Orkney 314 G3
Little-ayre Shetland . .313 G6
Little Ayton
N Yorks 225 C11
Little Baddow Essex . .88 D3
Little Badminton
S Glos 61 C10
Little Ballinluig
Perth 286 B3
Little Bampton
Cumb 239 F7
Little Bardfield
Essex 106 E3
Little Barford
Bedford 122 F3
Little Barningham
Norf 160 C2
Little Barrington
Glos 82 C2
Little Barrow
Ches W 183 G7
Little Barugh
N Yorks 216 D5
Little Bavington
Northumb 241 B11
Little Bayham E Sus . .52 F6
Little Bealings Suff . .108 B4
Littlebeck N Yorks . . .227 D7
Little Beckford Glos . .99 E9
Little Bedwyn Wilts . . .63 F9
Little Bentley Essex . .108 F2
Little Berkhamsted
Herts 86 D3
Little Billing
W Nhants 120 E6
Little Billington
C Beds 103 G8
Little Birch Hereford . .97 E10
Little Bispham
Blackpool 202 E2
Little Blakenham
Suff 108 B2
Little Blencow
Cumb 230 E5
Little Bloxwich
W Mid 133 C10
Little Bognor W Sus . .35 C8
Little Bolehill
Derbys 170 E3
Little Bollington
Ches E 184 D2
Little Bolton
Gtr Man 184 C5
Little Bookham Sur . . .50 C6
Littleborough Devon . .26 E4
Gtr Man 196 D2
Notts 188 D4
Little Bosullow Corn . .1 C4
Little Bourton Oxon . .101 C9
Little Bowden Leics . .136 F4
Little Boys Heath
Bucks 84 F6
Little Bradley Suff . . .124 G3
Little Braithwaite
Cumb 229 G10

Little Brampton
Shrops. 131 G7
Little Braxted Essex. . .88 C4
Little Bray Devon. . . .41 F7
Littlebredy Dorset. . .17 D7
Little Brechin Angus 293 G7
Little Brickhill
M Keynes. 103 E8
Little Bridgeford
Staffs. 151 D7
Little Brington
W Nhants. 120 E3
Little Bristol S Glos. . .80 G2
Little Britain Warks. 118 G2
Little Bromley
Essex. 107 F11
Little Bromwich
W Mid. 134 F2
Little Broughton
Cumb. 229 E7
Little Budworth
Ches W. 167 B9
Little Burstead
Essex. 87 G11
Littlebury Essex. . . .105 D10
Littlebury Green
Essex. 105 D9
Little Bytham Lincs. .155 F10
Little Cambridge
Essex. 106 F2
Little Canfield
Essex. 105 G11
Little Canford BCP . . .18 B6
Little Carleton
Lancs. 202 F2
Little Carlton Lincs. .190 D5
Notts. 172 D3
Little Casterton
Rutland. 137 B10
Little Catwick
E Yorks. 209 E8
Little Catworth
Cambs. 122 C2
Little Cawthorpe
Lincs. 190 E5
Little Chalfield
Wilts. 61 G11
Little Chalfont Bucks. .85 F7
Little Chart Kent. . . .54 D2
Little Chart Forstal
Kent. 54 D3
Little Chell Stoke. . .168 E5
Little Chester Derby. .153 B7
Little Chesterford
Essex. 105 C10
Little Chesterton
Oxon. 101 G11
Little Cheverell Wilts. .46 C3
Little Chishill
Cambs. 105 D8
Little Clacton Essex. .89 B11
Little Clanfield Oxon. .82 E3
Little Clegg Gtr Man. .196 E2
Little Clifton Cumb. .229 F7
Little Coates
NE Lincs. 201 F8
Little Colp Aberds. . .303 E7
Little Comberton
Worcs. 99 C9
Little Comfort Corn . . .12 E2
Little Common E Sus. .38 F2
Lincs. 156 D6
Shrops. 115 B7
W Sus. 34 C6
Little Compton
Warks. 100 E5
Little Corby Cumb. . .239 F11
Little Cornard Suff. .107 D7
Littlecote Bucks. . . .102 G6
Littlecott Wilts. 46 C6
Little Cowarne
Hereford. 116 G2
Little Coxwell Oxon. .82 G3
Little Crakehall
N Yorks. 224 G4
Little Cransley
N Nhants. 120 B6
Little Crawley
M Keynes. 103 B8
Little Creaton
W Nhants. 120 C4
Little Creich Highld .309 L6
Little Cressingham
Norf. 141 D7
Little Crosby Mers . 193 G10
Little Cubley Derbys. .152 B3
Little Dalby Leics. . .154 G5
Little Dawley
Telford. 132 B2
Littledean Glos. 79 C11
Littledean Hill Glos . .79 C11
Little Dens Aberds. . .303 E10
Little Dewchurch
Hereford. 97 E10
Little Ditton Cambs. .124 F3
Little Doward
Hereford. 79 B8
Littledown BCP 19 C8
Hants. 47 B10
Little Downham
Cambs. 139 G10
Little Drayton
Shrops. 150 C3
Little Driffield
E Yorks. 208 B6
Little Drybrook Glos. .79 D9
Little Dunham Norf . 159 G7
Little Dunkeld Perth .286 C4
Little Dunmow
Essex. 106 G3
Little Durnford Wilts. .46 G6
Little Eastbury
Worcs. 116 F6
Little Easton Essex. .106 G2
Little Eaton Derbys. .170 G5
Little Eccleston
Lancs. 202 E4
Little Ellingham
Norf. 141 D10
Little End Cambs. . . .122 F3
Essex. 87 E8
E Yorks. 208 F2

Little Everdon
W Nhants. 119 F11
Little Eversden
Cambs. 123 G7
Little Faringdon
Oxon. 82 E2
Little Fencote
N Yorks. 224 G5
Little Fenton
N Yorks. 206 F6
Littleferry Highld. . .311 K2
Littlefield NE Lincs. .201 F9
Littlefield Common
Sur. 50 C3
Littlefield Green
Windsor. 65 D11
Little Finborough
Suff. 125 G10
Little Fransham
Norf. 159 G8
Little Frith Kent. 54 B2
Little Gaddesden
Herts. 85 C7
Littlegain Shrops. . .132 D5
Little Gidding
Cambs. 138 G2
Little Gight Aberds. .303 F8
Little Glemham Suff. .126 F6
Little Glenshee
Perth. 286 D3
Little Gorsley Glos. . .98 F3
Little Gransden
Cambs. 122 F5
Little Green
Cambs. 104 B5
Notts. 172 G2
Som. 45 D8
Suff. 125 C11
Wrex. 167 G7
Little Grimsby Lincs .190 C4
Little Gringley Notts .188 E2
Little Gruinard
Highld. 307 L4
Little Habton
N Yorks. 216 D4
Little Hadham Herts 105 G8
Little Hale Lincs. . . .173 G10
Little Hallam Derbys 171 G7
Little Hallingbury
Essex. 87 B7
Littleham Devon. 14 E6
Devon. 24 C6
Little Hampden
Bucks. 84 E5
Littlehampton W Sus. .35 G8
Little Haresfield Glos. .80 D4
Little Harrowden
N Nhants. 121 C7
Little Harwood
Blackburn. 195 B7
Little Haseley Oxon. .83 E10
Little Hatfield
E Yorks. 209 D8
Little Hautbois Norf. .160 E5
Little Haven Pembs. .72 C5
W Sus. 51 G7
Little Hay Staffs. . . .134 C2
Little Hayfield
Derbys. 185 D8
Little Haywood
Staffs. 151 E10
Little Heath
Ches E. 167 G11
Ches W. 166 B6
Herts. 85 B8
Herts. 86 E3
London. 68 B3
Staffs. 151 F8
Sur. 66 G6
W Berks. 65 E7
W Mid. 134 G6
Little Heck N Yorks. .198 C5
Littlehempston Devon. .8 C6
Little Henham
Essex. 105 E10
Little Henny Essex. .107 D7
Little Herbert's Glos. .81 B7
Little Hereford
Hereford. 115 D11
Little Hill Hereford. . .97 F9
Som. 28 E3
Little Holbury Hants. .32 G6
Little Honeyborough
Pembs. 73 D7
Little Hoole Moss
Houses Lancs. 194 C3
Little Horkesley
Essex. 107 E9
Little Hormead
Herts. 105 F8
Little Horsted E Sus. .23 B7
Little Horton Wilts. . .62 G4
W Yorks. 205 G9
Little Horwood
Bucks. 102 E5
Littlehoughton
Northumb. 264 F6
Little Houghton
S Yorks. 198 G2
W Nhants. 120 F6
Little Hucklow
Derbys. 185 F11
Little Hulton
Gtr Man. 195 G8
Little Humber
E Yorks. 201 C8
Little Hungerford
W Berks. 64 E4
Little Ilford London. .68 B2
Little Ingestre Staffs .151 E9
Little Inkberrow
Worcs. 117 F10
Little Irchester
N Nhants. 121 D8
Little Keyford Som. . .45 D9
Little Kimble Bucks. .84 D4
Little Kineton
Warks. 118 G6
Little Kingshill Bucks. .84 F5
Little Knowles Green
Suff. 124 F5

Little Langdale
Cumb. 220 E6
Little Langford Wilts. .46 F4
Little Laver Essex. . . .87 D8
Little Lawford
Warks. 119 B9
Little Layton
Blackpool. 202 F2
Little Leigh
Ches W. 183 F10
Little Leighs Essex. . .88 B2
Little Lepton
W Yorks. 197 E8
Little Leven E Yorks. .209 D8
Little Lever Gtr Man. .195 F9
Little Limber Lincs. .200 E6
Little Linford
M Keynes. 102 C6
Little London
Bucks. 83 C10
Bucks. 84 D5
Cambs. 139 D8
Essex. 105 F9
Essex. 106 D3
E Sus. 23 B9
Glos. 80 B2
Hants. 47 D11
Hants. 48 B6
Lincs. 156 E4
Lincs. 157 E8
Lincs. 189 D10
Norf. 140 D5
Norf. 160 C2
Norf. 160 C5
Norf. 160 E3
Oxon. 83 E8
Powys. 129 F10
Shrops. 131 F10
Som. 44 D6
Suff. 125 F10
Worcs. 116 C2
W Yorks. 205 F10
Little Longstone
Derbys. 185 G11
Little Lynturk
Aberds. 293 B7
Little Lyth Shrops. . .131 B9
Little Madeley
Staffs. 168 F3
Little Malvern Worcs. .98 C5
Little Mancot Flint. .166 B4
Little Maplestead
Essex. 106 E6
Little Marcle
Hereford. 98 D3
Little Marlow Bucks. .65 B11
Little Marsden
Lancs. 204 F3
Little Marsh Bucks. .102 G3
Norf. 159 B10
Wilts. 45 B11
Little Marton
Blackpool. 202 G2
Little Mascalls Essex. .88 E2
Little Massingham
Norf. 158 E5
Little Melton Norf. . .142 B3
Little Merthyr
Hereford. 96 B5
Little Milford Pembs. .73 C7
Littlemill Aberds. . . .292 D5
E Ayrs. 257 F11
Highld. 301 D9
Northumb. 264 F6
Little Mill Kent. 53 D7
Mon. 78 E4
Little Milton
Newport. 59 B11
Oxon. 83 E10
Little Minster Oxon. .82 C4
Little Missenden
Bucks. 84 F6
Little Mongeham
Kent. 55 C10
Littlemoor Derbys. . .170 C5
Dorset. 17 D8
Little Moor Gtr Man. .184 D6
Lancs. 203 D10
Little Moor End
Lancs. 195 B8
Little Musgrave
Cumb. 222 C5
Little Ness Shrops. . .149 F8
Little Neston
Ches W. 182 F3
Little Newcastle
Pembs. 91 F9
Little Newsham
Durham. 224 B4
Little Norlington
E Sus. 23 C7
Little Norton Som. . .29 D7
Little Oakley Essex. .108 F4
N Nhants. 137 F7
Little Odell Bedford . 121 F9
Little Offley Herts. . .104 F2
Little Onn Staffs. . . .150 F6
Little Ormside Cumb. .222 B4
Little Orton Cumb. . .239 F9
Leics. 134 B6
Little Ouse Norf. . . .140 F2
Little Ouseburn
N Yorks. 215 G8
Littleover Derby. . . .152 C6
Little Overton Wrex. .166 G5
Little Oxney Green
Essex. 87 D11
Little Packington
Warks. 134 G4
Little Parndon Essex. .86 C6
Little Paxton Cambs. .122 E3
Little Petherick Corn. .10 G4
Little Pitlurg Moray .302 E4
Little Plumpton
Lancs. 202 G3

Little Plumstead
Norf. 160 G6
Little Ponton Lincs. .155 C8
Littleport Cambs. . . .139 F11
Little Posbrook
Hants. 33 G8
Little Poulton Lancs. .202 F3
Little Preston Kent. . .53 B8
W Yorks. 206 G3
Littler Ches W. 167 B10
Little Raveley
Cambs. 122 B5
Little Reedness
E Yorks. 199 C10
Little Reynoldston
Swansea. 56 D3
Little Ribston
N Yorks. 206 C3
Little Rissington
Glos. 81 B11
Little Rogart Highld . .309 J7
Little Rollright Oxon. .100 E5
Little Ryburgh Norf. .159 D9
Little Ryle Northumb. .264 G2
Little Ryton Shrops. .131 C9
Little Salisbury Wilts. .63 G7
Little Salkeld Cumb. .231 D7
Little Sampford
Essex. 106 E2
Little Sandhurst
Brack. 65 G11
Little Saredon
Staffs. 133 B8
Little Saxham Suff. .124 E5
Little Scatwell
Highld. 300 D3
Little Scotland
Gtr Man. 194 E6
Little Sessay
N Yorks. 215 D8
Little Shelford
Cambs. 123 G9
Little Shoddesden
Hants. 47 D9
Little Shrewley
Warks. 118 D4
Little Shurdington
Glos. 80 B6
Little Silver Devon . . .26 E3
Devon. 40 E4
Little Singleton
Lancs. 202 F3
Little Skillymarno
Aberds. 303 D9
Little Skipwith
N Yorks. 207 F9
Little Smeaton
N Yorks. 198 D4
N Yorks. 224 E6
Little Snoring Norf. .159 C9
Little Sodbury S Glos. .61 C9
Little Sodbury End
S Glos. 61 C8
Little Somborne
Hants. 47 G11
Little Somerford
Wilts. 62 C3
Little Soudley
Shrops. 150 D4
Little Stainforth
N Yorks. 212 F6
Little Stainton Darl. .234 G2
Little Stanmore
London. 85 G11
Little Stanney
Ches W. 182 G6
Little Staughton
Bedford. 122 E2
Littlestead Green
Oxon. 65 D8
Little Steeping
Lincs. 174 C6
Littlester Shetland. . .312 E7
Little Stoke S Glos. . .60 C6
Little Stonham Suff. .126 E2
Little Stretton Leics. .136 C3
Shrops. 131 E8
Little Strickland
Cumb. 221 B11
Little Studley
N Yorks. 214 E6
Little Stukeley
Cambs. 122 B4
Little Sugnall Staffs. .150 C6
Little Sutton
Ches W. 182 F5
Lincs. 157 E9
Shrops. 131 G10
Little Swinburne
Northumb. 241 B10
Little Tarrington
Hereford. 98 C2
Little Tew Oxon. . . .101 F7
Little Tey Essex. . . .107 G7
Little Thetford
Cambs. 123 B10
Little Thirkleby
N Yorks. 215 D9
Little Thornage
Norf. 159 B11
Little Thornton
Lancs. 202 E3
Little Thorpe
Durham. 234 C4
W Yorks. 197 C2
Little Thurlow Suff. .124 G3
Little Thurlow Green
Suff. 124 G3
Little Thurrock
Thurrock. 68 D6
Littleton Bath. 60 G5
Ches W. 166 B6
Dorset. 30 G5
Hants. 48 G3
Perth. 286 D6
Som. 44 G3
Sur. 50 D3
Sur. 66 F5

Littleton continued
Wilts. 62 G2
Littleton Common
Sur. 66 E5
Littleton Drew Wilts. .61 C10
Littleton-on-Severn
S Glos. 60 B5
Littleton Panell Wilts. .46 C4
Littleton-upon-Severn
S Glos. 79 G9
Little Torboll Highld. .309 K7
Little Torrington
Devon. 25 D7
Little Totham Essex. .88 C5
Little Toux Aberds. . .302 D5
Littletown Durham. .234 C2
IoW. 20 C6
Little Town Cumb. . .220 B4
Lancs. 203 F9
Warr. 183 C10
Little Tring Herts. . . .84 C6
Little Twycross
Leics. 134 B6
Little Urswick Cumb. .210 E5
Little Vantage
W Loth. 270 C2
Little Wakering Essex 70 E2
Little Walden
Essex. 105 C10
Little Waldingfield
Suff. 107 B8
Little Walsingham
Norf. 159 B8
Little Waltham Essex. .88 C2
Little Warley Essex. . .87 G10
Little Warton Warks. .134 C5
Little Washbourne
Glos. 99 E9
Little Weighton
E Yorks. 208 G5
Little Weldon
N Nhants. 137 F8
Little Welland Worcs. .98 D5
Little Welnetham
Suff. 125 E7
Little Welton Lincs. .190 D4
Little Wenham
Suff. 107 D11
Little Wenlock
Telford. 132 B2
Little Weston Som. . .29 B10
Little Whitehouse
IoW. 20 C5
Little Whittingham
Green Suff. 126 B5
Littlewick Green
Windsor. 65 D10
Little Wigborough
Essex. 89 B7
Little Wilbraham
Cambs. 123 F10
Littlewindsor Dorset . .28 G6
Little Wisbeach
Lincs. 156 C2
Little Wishford Wilts. .46 F5
Little Witcombe Glos. .80 B6
Little Witley Worcs. .116 E5
Little Wittenham
Oxon. 83 G9
Little Wolford
Warks. 100 D5
Littleworth Staffs. . .133 B9
Bucks. 84 E6
Little Wood Corner
Bucks. 84 C6
Littlewood Staffs. . .133 B9
Little Woodcote
London. 67 G9
Littlewood Green
Warks. 117 E11
Little Woolgarston
Dorset. 18 E5
Littleworth
Bedford. 103 C11
Glos. 80 E4
Glos. 100 D2
Oxon. 82 F4
Oxon. 83 D9
Oxon. 83 G10
Staffs. 151 E8
Staffs. 151 G10
S Yorks. 187 B10
Warks. 118 E4
Wilts. 63 G7
Worcs. 117 E9
Worcs. 117 F7
W Sus. 35 C11
Littleworth Common
Bucks. 66 B2
Little Worthen
Shrops. 130 B6
Littleworth End
Warks. 134 D3
Little Wratting Suff. .106 B3
Little Wymington
Bedford. 121 D9
Little Wymondley
Herts. 104 F4
Little Wyrley Staffs. .133 B10
Little Wytheford
Shrops. 149 F11
Little Yeldham
Essex. 106 D5
Littley Green Essex. .87 B11
Litton Derbys. 185 F11
N Yorks. 213 E8
Som. 44 C5
Litton Cheney Dorset. .17 C7
Litton Mill Derbys. .185 G11
Liurbost W Isles. . . .304 F5
Livermead Torbay. . . .9 C8
Liverpool Mers. 182 C4
Liverpool Airport
Mers. 182 D6
Liversedge W Yorks. .197 C8
Liverton Devon. 14 F2
Redcar. 226 B4
Liverton Mines
Redcar. 226 B4
Livesey Street Kent. .53 C11
Livingshayes Devon . .27 G7

Livingston W Loth. . .269 B11
Livingston Village
W Loth. 269 B10
Lix Toll Stirling. 285 D9
Lixwm Flint. 181 G11
Lizard Corn. 2 G6
Llaingoch Anglesey. .178 E2
Llaithddu Powys. . . .129 G11
Llampha V Glam. 58 E2
Llan Powys. 129 C7
Llanaber Gwyn. 146 F2
Llanaelhaearn
Gwyn. 162 G5
Llanafan Ceredig. . . .112 C3
Llanafan-fawr
Powys. 113 F9
Llanallgo Anglesey . .179 D6
Llananno Powys. . . .113 C11
Llanarmon Gwyn. . .145 B8
Llanarmon Dyffryn
Ceiriog Wrex. 148 C3
Llanarmon Mynydd-
mawr Powys. 148 D2
Llanarmon-yn-Ial
Denb. 165 D11
Llanarth Ceredig. . . .111 F8
Mon. 78 C5
Llanarthne Carms. . .93 G10
Llanasa Flint. 181 E10
Llanbabo Anglesey . .178 D5
Llanbad Rhondda. . . .58 C3
Llanbadarn Fawr
Ceredig. 128 G2
Llanbadarn Fynydd
Powys. 114 D2
Llanbadarn-y-Garreg
Powys. 96 C3
Llanbadoc Mon. 78 E5
Llanbadrig Anglesey .178 C5
Llanbeder Newport. . .78 G5
Llanbedr Gwyn. 145 D11
Powys. 96 B2
Powys. 96 G4
Llanbedr-Dyffryn-Clwyd
Denb. 165 D10
Llanbedrgoch
Anglesey. 179 E8
Llanbedrog Gwyn. . .144 C6
Llanbedr Pont Steffan
= Lampeter Ceredig .93 B11
Llanbedr-y-cennin
Conwy. 164 B3
Llanberis Gwyn. 163 C9
Llanbethery V Glam. .58 F4
Llanbister Powys. . . .114 D2
Llanblethian = Llanfleiddan
V Glam. 58 E3
Llanboidy Carms. . . .92 G4
Llanbradach Caerph. .77 G10
Llanbrynmair
Powys. 129 C7
Llancadle = Llancatal
V Glam. 58 F4
Llancaiach Caerph. . .77 F10
Llancarfan V Glam. . .58 E5
Llancatal = Llancadle
V Glam. 58 F4
Llancayo Mon. 78 E5
Llancloudy Hereford. .97 G9
Llancowrid Powys. . .130 E3
Llancynfelyn
Ceredig. 128 E2
Llan-dafal Bl Gwent . .77 E11
Llandaff Cardiff. 59 D7
Llandaff North
Cardiff. 59 D7
Llandanwg Gwyn. . .145 D11
Llandarcy Neath. 57 B8
Llandawke Carms. . . .74 C3
Llanddaniel Fab
Anglesey. 179 G7
Llanddarog Carms. . .75 B8
Llanddeiniol
Ceredig. 111 C11
Llanddeiniolen
Gwyn. 163 B8
Llandderfel Gwyn. . .147 B9
Llanddeusant
Anglesey. 178 D4
Carms. 94 G5
Llanddew Powys. . . .95 E11
Llanddewi Swansea. .56 D3
Llanddewi-Brefi
Ceredig. 112 F3
Llanddewi Fach Mon. .78 F4
Llanddewi'r Cwm
Powys. 95 B10
Llanddewi Rhydderch
Mon. 78 C5
Llanddewi Skirrid
Mon. 78 B4
Llanddewi Velfrey
Pembs. 73 B10
Llanddewi Ystradenni
Powys. 114 D2
Llanddoged Conwy. .164 C4
Llanddona Anglesey .179 F7
Llanddowror Carms. .74 C3
Llanddulas Conwy. . .180 F6
Llanddwywe Gwyn. .145 E11
Llanddyfynan
Anglesey. 179 F7
Llandecwyn Gwyn. . .146 B2
Llandefaelog Powys. .95 E10
Llandefaelog Fach
Powys. 95 E10
Llandefaelog-tre'r-graig
Powys. 96 F2
Llandefalle Powys. . . .96 D2
Llandegai Gwyn. . . .179 G9
Llandegfan Anglesey 179 G9
Llandegla Denb. 165 D11
Llandegley Powys. . .114 E2
Llandegveth Mon. . . .78 F4
Llandegwning Gwyn. .144 C5
Llandeilo Carms. 94 G2
Llandeilo Graban
Powys. 95 C11
Llandeilo'r Fan
Powys. 95 E7
Llandeloy Pembs. . . .91 F7
Llandenny Mon. 78 E6

Llandenny Walks
Mon. 78 E5
Llandevaud Newport. .78 G6
Llandevenny Mon. . . .60 D2
Llandewi Ystradenny
Powys. 114 D2
Llandinabo Hereford. .97 F10
Llandinam Powys. . .129 E10
Llandissilio Pembs. . .92 G2
Llandogo Mon. 79 E9
Llandough V Glam. . .58 E3
V Glam. 59 E7
Llandovery = Llanymddyfri
Carms. 94 E5
Llandow = Llandw
V Glam. 58 E2
Llandre Carms. 94 C3
Ceredig. 128 F2
Llandrillo Denb. 147 B10
Llandrillo-yn-Rhôs
Conwy. 180 E4
Llandrindod Wells
Powys. 113 E11
Llandrinio Powys. . .148 F5
Llandruidion Pembs. .90 G5
Llandudno Conwy. . .180 E3
Llandudno Junction =
Cyffordd Llandudno
Conwy. 180 F3
Llandudoch = St Dogmaels
Pembs. 92 B3
Llandw = Llandow
V Glam. 58 E2
Llandwrog Gwyn. . . .163 D7
Llandybie Carms. . . .75 B10
Llandyfaelog Carms. .74 C6
Llandyfan Carms. . . .75 B10
Llandyfriog Ceredig. .92 C5
Llandyfrydog
Anglesey. 178 D6
Llandygwydd Ceredig .92 C4
Llandynan Denb. . . .165 F11
Llandyrnog Denb. . .165 B10
Llandysilio Powys. . .148 F5
Llandyssil Powys. . . .130 D3
Llandysul Ceredig. . .93 C8
Llanedeyrn Cardiff. . .59 C8
Llanedi Carms. 75 D9
Llanedwen Anglesey .163 B8
Llanegryn Gwyn. . . .110 B2
Llanegwad Carms. . . .93 G10
Llaneilian Anglesey . .179 C7
Llanelian yn-Rhôs
Conwy. 180 F5
Llanelidan Denb. . . .165 E10
Llanelieu Powys. 96 E3
Llanellen Mon. 78 C4
Llanelli Carms. 56 B4
Llanelltyd Gwyn. . . .146 F4
Llanelly Mon. 78 C2
Llanelly Hill Mon. . . .78 C2
Llanelwedd Powys. . .113 F10
Llanelwy = St Asaph
Denb. 181 G8
Llanenddwyn Gwyn .145 E11
Llanengan Gwyn. . . .144 D5
Llanerch Emrys
Powys. 148 E4
Llanerchymedd
Anglesey. 178 E6
Llanerfyl Powys. 129 B10
Llaneuddog
Anglesey. 179 D7
Llan eurgain = Northop
Flint. 166 B2
Llanfabon Caerph. . . .77 G10
Llanfachraeth
Anglesey. 178 E4
Llanfachreth Gwyn. .146 E5
Llanfaelog Anglesey .178 F4
Llanfaelrhys Gwyn. .144 D4
Llanfaenor Mon. 78 B6
Llanfaes Anglesey. . .179 F10
Powys. 95 F10
Llanfaethlu
Anglesey. 178 D4
Llanfaglan Gwyn. . . .163 C7
Llanfair Gwyn. 145 D11
Llanfair Caereinion
Powys. 130 B2
Llanfair Clydogau
Ceredig. 112 G2
Llanfair-Dyffryn-Clwyd
Denb. 165 D10
Llanfairfechan
Conwy. 179 F11
Llanfair Kilgeddin
Mon. 78 C5
Llanfair Kilgheddin
Mon. 78 C5
Llanfair-Nant-Gwyn
Pembs. 92 D3
Llanfairpwll-gwyngyll
Anglesey. 179 G8
Llanfair Talhaiarn
Conwy. 180 G6
Llanfair Waterdine
Shrops. 114 B4
Llanfairyneubwll
Anglesey. 178 F3
Llanfairynghornwy
Anglesey. 178 C4
Llanfallteg Carms. . . .73 B11
Llanfallteg West
Carms. 73 B10
Llanfaredd Powys. . .113 G11
Llanfarian Ceredig. . .111 C11
Llanfechain Powys. . .148 E3
Llanfechan Powys. . .113 G9
Llanfechell
Anglesey. 178 C5
Llanferres Denb. . . .165 C11
Llan Ffestiniog
Gwyn. 164 G2
Llanfflewyn
Anglesey. 178 D5
Llanfigael Anglesey .178 E4

Llanfihangel-ar-arth
Carms. 93 D9
Llanfihangel-Crucorney
Mon. 96 G6
Llanfihangel Glyn Myfyr
Conwy. 165 F7
Llanfihangel-helygen
Powys. 113 E10
Llanfihangel Nant Bran
Powys. 95 E8
Llanfihangel-nant-
Melan Powys. 114 F3
Llanfihangel Rhydithon
Powys. 114 D3
Llanfihangel Rogiet
Mon. 60 B2
Llanfihangel Tal-y-llyn
Powys. 96 F2
Llanfihangel Tor y
Mynydd Mon. 79 E7
Llanfihangel-uwch-
Gwili Carms. 93 G9
Llanfihangel-y-
Creuddyn Ceredig. .112 B3
Llanfihangel-yng-
Ngwynfa Powys. . . .147 F11
Llanfihangel yn Nhowyn
Anglesey. 178 F4
Llanfihangel-y-
pennant
Gwyn. 128 B3
Gwyn. 163 F8
Llanfilo Powys. 96 E2
Llanfleiddan = Llanblethian
V Glam. 58 E3
Llanfoist Mon. 78 C3
Llanfor Gwyn. 147 B8
Llanfrechfa Torf. 78 G4
Llanfrothen Gwyn. . .163 G10
Llanfrynach Powys. . .95 F11
Llanfwrog Anglesey . .178 E4
Denb. 165 D10
Llanfyllin Powys. . . .148 F2
Llanfynydd Carms. . .93 F11
Flint. 166 D3
Llanfyrnach Pembs. . .92 E4
Llangadfan Powys. . .147 G10
Llangadog Carms. . . .74 G6
Carms. 94 F4
Llangadwaladr
Anglesey. 162 B5
Powys. 148 C3
Llangaffo Anglesey . .162 B6
Llangain Carms. 74 B5
Llangammarch Wells
Powys. 95 B8
Llangan V Glam. 58 D3
Llangarron Hereford. .97 G10
Llangasty Talyllyn
Powys. 96 F2
Llangathen Carms. . .93 G11
Llangattock Powys. . .78 B2
Llangattock Lingoed
Mon. 97 G7
Llangattock nigh Usk
Mon. 78 D4
Llangattock-Vibon-Avel
Mon. 79 B7
Llangedwyn Powys. .148 E3
Llangefni Anglesey . .179 F7
Llangeinor Bridgend. .58 B2
Llangeitho Ceredig. . .112 F2
Llangeler Carms. 93 D7
Llangendeirne Carms .75 C7
Llangennech Carms. .75 E9
Llangennith Swansea. .56 C2
Llangenny Powys. . . .78 B2
Llangernyw Conwy. .164 B5
Llangeview Mon. 78 E5
Llangewydd Court
Bridgend. 57 E11
Llangian Gwyn. 144 D5
Llangloffan Pembs. . .91 E8
Llanglydwen Carms. .92 F3
Llangoed Anglesey . .179 F10
Llangoedmor Ceredig. .92 B3
Llangollen Denb. . . .166 G2
Llangolman Pembs. . .92 F2
Llangors Powys. 96 F2
Llangorwen Ceredig. .128 G2
Llangovan Mon. 79 D7
Llangower Gwyn. . . .147 C8
Llangrannog
Ceredig. 110 G6
Llangristiolus
Anglesey. 178 G6
Llangrove Hereford. .79 B8
Llangua Mon. 97 F7
Llangunllo Powys. . .114 C4
Llangunnor Carms. . .74 B6
Llangurig Powys. . . .113 B8
Llangwm Conwy. . . .165 G7
Mon. 78 E6
Pembs. 73 D7
Llangwnnadl Carms. .144 C4
Llangwyfan Denb. . .165 B10
Llangwyfan-isaf
Anglesey. 162 B4
Llangwyllog
Anglesey. 178 F6
Llangwyryfon
Ceredig. 111 C11
Llangybi Ceredig. . . .112 G2
Gwyn. 162 G6
Mon. 78 F5
Llangyfelach
Swansea. 56 B6
Llangyndeyrn Carms .75 C8
Llangynhafal Denb. .165 C10
Llangynidr Powys. . . .77 B11
Llangyniew Powys. . .130 B2
Llangynin Carms. . . .74 B2
Llangynog Carms. . . .74 B4
Powys. 147 D11
Llangynwyd
Bridgend. 57 D11
Llanhamlach Powys. .95 F11
Llanharan Rhondda. .58 C4
Llanharry Rhondda. .58 C4

Llanhennock Mon 78 G5
Llanhilleth Bl Gwent . . 78 E2
Llanhowel Pembs . . . 90 F6
Llanidloes Powys 129 G9
Llaniestyn Gwyn 144 C5
Llanifyny Powys 129 C7
Llanigon Powys 96 D4
Llanilar Ceredig . . . 112 C2
Llanilid Rhondda 58 C3
Llanilltud Fawr =
Llantwit Major V Glam . 58 F3
Llanio Ceredig 112 F2
Llanion Pembs 73 E7
Llanishen Cardiff . . . 59 C7
Mon 79 E7
Llanllawddog
Carms 93 F9
Llanllechid Gwyn . 163 B10
Llanllowell Mon 78 F5
Llanllugan Powys . . 129 C11
Llanllwch Carms 74 B5
Llanllwchaiarn
Powys 130 E2
Llanllwni Carms 93 D9
Llanllwyd Shrops . . 130 G3
Llanllyfni Gwyn . . . 163 E7
Llanmadoc Swansea . 56 C2
Llanmaes Cardiff . . . 58 D6
V Glam 58 F3
Llanmartin Newport . 59 B11
Llanmerwig Powys . . 130 E3
Llanmihangel
V Glam 58 E3
Llan-mill Pembs . . 73 C10
Llanmiloe Carms . . . 74 D3
Llanmorlais Swansea . 56 C4
Llannefydd Conwy . . 181 G7
Llannerch-y-môr
Flint 181 F11
Llannon Carms 75 D8
Llan-non = Llanon
Ceredig 111 D10
Llannor Gwyn 145 B7
Llanon Pembs 90 E6
Llanon = Llan-non
Ceredig 111 D10
Llanover Mon 78 D4
Llanpumsaint Carms . 93 F8
Llanreath Pembs . . . 73 E7
Llanreithan Pembs . . 91 F7
Llanrhaeadr Denb . . 165 C9
Llanrhaeadr-ym-
Mochnant Powys . 148 D2
Llanrhian Pembs . . . 90 E6
Llanrhidian Swansea . 56 C3
Llanrhos Conwy . . . 180 E3
Llanrhyddlad
Anglesey 178 D4
Llanrhystud
Ceredig 111 D10
Llanrosser Hereford . 96 D5
Llanrothal Hereford . . 79 B7
Llanrug Gwyn 163 C8
Llanrumney Cardiff . 59 C8
Llanrwst Conwy . . . 164 C4
Llansadurnen Carms . 74 D5
Llansadwrn
Anglesey 179 F9
Carms 94 E3
Llansaint Carms 74 D5
Llansamlet Swansea . 57 B7
Llansanffraid Glan
Conwy Conwy . . . 180 F4
Llansannan Conwy . 164 B6
Llansannor V Glam . 58 D3
Llansantffraed
Ceredig 111 D10
Powys 96 G2
Llansantffraed
Cwmdeuddwr
Powys 113 D9
Llansantffraed-in-Elwel
Powys 113 G11
Llansantffraid-ym-
Mechain Powys . . . 148 E4
Llansawel Carms . . . 94 D2
Llansawel = Briton Ferry
Neath 57 C8
Llansilin Powys . . . 148 D4
Llansoy Mon 78 E6
Llanspyddid Powys . 95 F10
Llanstadwell Pembs . . 72 D6
Llansteffan Carms . . 74 C5
Llanstephan Powys . . 96 C2
Llantarnam Torf 78 G4
Llanteems Mon 96 G6
Llanteg Pembs 73 C11
Llanthony Mon 96 F5
Llantilio Crossenny
Mon 78 C5
Llantilio Pertholey
Mon 78 B4
Llantood Pembs 92 C3
Llantrisant
Anglesey 178 E5
Mon 78 F5
Rhondda 58 C4
Llantrithyd V Glam . 58 E4
Llantwit Neath 57 C10
Llantwit Fardre
Rhondda 58 B5
Llantwit Major =
Llanilltud Fawr V Glam 58 F3
Llanussyllt = Saundersfoot
Pembs 73 E10
Llanuwchllyn Gwyn . 147 C2
Llanvaches Newport . . 78 G6
Llanvair Discoed
Mon 78 G6
Llanvapley Mon 78 C5
Llanvetherine Mon . . 78 B5
Llanveynoe Hereford . 96 E6
Llanvihangel Crucorney
Mon 96 G6
Llanvihangel Gobion
Mon 78 D4
Llanvihangel-Ystern-
Llewern Mon 78 C6
Llanwarne Hereford . . 97 F10

Llanwddyn Powys . . . 147 F10
Llanwenarth Mon 78 C3
Llanwenog Ceredig . . . 93 B9
Llanwern Newport . . . 59 B11
Llanwinio Carms 92 F5
Llanwnda Gwyn 163 D7
Pembs 91 D8
Llanwnnen Ceredig . . . 93 B10
Llanwnog Powys . . . 129 C10
Llanwrda Carms 94 E4
Llanwrin Powys 128 C5
Llanwrthwl Powys . . 113 E9
Llanwrtud = Llanwrtyd
Wells Powys 95 B7
Llanwrtyd Wells
= Llanwrtud Powys . . 95 B7
Llanwyddelan
Powys 129 C11
Llanyblodwel
Shrops 148 E4
Llanybri Carms 74 C4
Llanybydder Carms . . 93 C10
Llanycefn Pembs 91 G11
Llanychaer Pembs 91 D9
Llanycil Gwyn 147 C8
Llanycrwys Carms . . . 94 B2
Llanymawddwy
Gwyn 147 F8
Llanymddyfri
= Llandovery Carms . 94 E5
Llanymynech Powys . 148 E5
Llanynghenedl
Anglesey 178 D4
Llanynys Denb 165 C10
Llan-y-pwll Wrex . . 166 E5
Llanyrafon Torf 78 G4
Llanyre Powys 113 E10
Llanystumdwy Gwyn 145 B9
Llanywern Powys 96 F2
Llawhaden Pembs . . . 73 B9
Llawndy Flint 181 F11
Llawnt Shrops 148 C5
Llawr Dref Bellaf
Gwyn 144 D5
Llawr-y-glyn Powys . 129 E8
Llay Wrex 166 D4
Llechcynfarwy
Anglesey 178 E5
Llecheiddior Gwyn . 163 G7
Llechfaen Powys 95 F11
Llechfraith Gwyn . . . 146 F3
Llechryd Caerph 77 D10
Ceredig 92 C4
Llechrydau Powys . . 148 C4
Llechwedd Conwy . . 180 F3
Lledrod Ceredig 112 C2
Llenmerewig Powys . 130 E3
Llethrid Swansea . . . 56 C4
Llettyrychen Carms . . 75 E7
Llidiad Nenog
Carms 93 D10
Llidiardau Gwyn . . . 147 B7
Llidiart-y-parc
Denb 165 G10
Llithfaen Gwyn 162 G5
Lloc Flint 181 F10
Llong Flint 166 C3
Llowes Powys 96 C3
Lloyney Powys 114 B4
Llugwy Powys 128 D4
Llundain-fach
Ceredig 111 F11
Llwydarth Bridgend . . 57 C11
Llwydcoed Rhondda . . 77 E7
Llwyn Denb 165 C9
Shrops 130 G5
Llwyncelyn Ceredig . 111 F8
Llwyndafydd Ceredig 111 F7
Llwynderw Powys . . 130 C4
Llwyn-derw Powys . . 129 G8
Llwyndrain Pembs . . . 95 E5
Llwyn-du Mon 78 B3
Llwynduris Ceredig . . 92 C4
Llwyndyrys Gwyn . . 162 G5
Llwyneinion Wrex . . 166 F3
Llwyngwril Gwyn . . 110 B2
Llwynhendy Carms . . 56 B4
Llwyn-hendy Carms . 56 B4
Llwynmawr Wrex . . . 148 B4
Llwyn-on Village
M Tydf 77 C8
Llwyn-Têg Carms . . 75 D9
Llwyn-y-brain
Carms 73 C11
Llwyn-y-go Shrops . . 148 E6
Llwynygog Powys . . 129 E7
Llwyn-y-groes
Ceredig 111 F11
Llwynypia Rhondda . . 77 G7
Llwyn-yr-hwrdd
Pembs 92 E4
Llynclys Shrops 148 E5
Llynfaes Anglesey . . 178 F6
Llysfaen Conwy . . . 180 F5
Llyswen Powys 96 D2
Llysworney V Glam . 58 E3
Llys-y-frân Pembs . . 91 G11
Llywel Powys 95 E7
Llywernog Ceredig . . 128 G4
Load Brook S Yorks . 186 D3
Loan Falk 279 F9
Loandhu Highld . . . 301 B8
Loanend Northumb . 241 E10
Loanhead Aberds . . 302 D6
Midloth 270 B5
Perth 286 D5
Loanreoch Highld . . 300 B6
Loans S Ayrs 257 C8
Loansdean
Northumb 252 G5
Loans of Tullich
Highld 301 B8
Lobb Devon 40 F3
Lobhillcross Devon . . 12 D5
Lobley Hill T&W . . . 242 E6
Loch a Charnain
W Isles 297 G4
Loch a' Ghainmhich
W Isles 304 F4
Lochailort Highld . . 295 G9
Lochaline Highld . . 289 E8
Lochanhully Highld . 301 G9

Lochans Dumfries . . 236 D2
Locharbriggs
Dumfries 247 G11
Lochassynt Lodge
Highld 307 G6
Lochavich Ho
Argyll 275 B10
Lochawe Argyll . . . 284 E5
Loch Baghasdail
W Isles 297 K3
Lochboisdale Argyll . 289 G8
Lochbuie Argyll . . . 289 G8
Lochbuie Ho Argyll . 289 G8
Lochcallater Lodge
Aberds 292 E3
Lochcarron Highld . 295 B10
Loch Choire Lodge
Highld 308 F6
Lochdhu Highld . . . 310 E4
Lochdochart House
Stirling 285 E8
Lochdon Argyll . . . 289 F9
Lochdrum Highld . . 300 B2
Lochead Argyll . . . 275 E11
Argyll 275 F8
Lochearnhead
Stirling 285 E9
Lochee Dundee . . . 287 D7
Loch Eil Highld . . . 290 F2
Lochend Edin 280 G5
Highld 300 F5
Highld 310 C6
Lochend Ho
Stirling 277 B11
Locherben
Dumfries 247 D11
Lochetive Ho Highld . 284 C5
Loch Euphoirt
W Isles 296 E4
Lochfoot Dumfries . 237 B10
Lochgair Argyll . . . 275 D10
Lochgarthside
Highld 291 B7
Lochgelly Fife 280 C4
Lochgilphead Argyll . 275 E9
Lochgoilhead Argyll . 284 G6
Loch Head Dumfries . 236 E5
Dumfries 245 E11
Lochhill Moray 302 C2
Lochhussie Highld . . 300 D4
Lochinch Castle
Dumfries 236 C3
Lochindorb Lodge
Highld 301 F9
Lochinver Highld . . 307 G5
Lochlane Perth . . . 286 E2
Lochletter Highld . . 300 F4
Loch Loyal Lodge
Highld 308 E6
Lochluichart Highld . 300 D4
Lochmaben
Dumfries 248 G3
Lochmore Cottage
Highld 310 E4
Lochmore Lodge
Highld 306 G7
Loch nam Madadh
W Isles 296 E5
Lochnell Ho Argyll . 289 F10
Lochore Fife 280 B3
Lochorodale Argyll . 255 F7
Lochportain
W Isles 296 D5
Lochran Perth 280 B2
Lochranza N Ayrs . . 255 B10
Lochs Crofts Moray . 302 C3
Loch Sgioport
W Isles 297 H4
Lochside Aberds . . . 293 G9
Highld 301 D8
Highld 308 D4
Highld 310 F2
S Ayrs 257 E8
Lochslin Highld . . . 311 L2
Lochstack Lodge
Highld 306 E7
Lochton Aberds . . . 293 D9
Lochty Angus 293 G7
Fife 287 G9
Perth 286 E4
Lochuisge Highld . . 289 D9
Lochurr Dumfries . . 247 F7
Lochwinnoch Renfs . 267 D7
Lochwood Dumfries . 248 D3
Glasgow 268 B3
Lochyside Highld . . 290 F3
Lockengate Corn . . 5 C10
Lockerbie Dumfries . 248 G4
Lockeridge Wilts . . 62 F6
Lockeridge Dene
Wilts 62 F6
Lockerley Hants . . . 32 B3
Lockhills Cumb . . . 230 B6
Locking N Som . . . 43 B11
Lockinge Oxon . . . 64 B2
Locking Stumps
Warr 183 C10
Lockington E Yorks . 208 D5
Leics 153 D9
Lockleaze Bristol . . 60 D6
Locksbottom London . 68 F2
Locksgreen IoW . . . 20 C4
Locks Heath Hants . 33 F8
Lockton N Yorks . . 226 G6
Lockwood W Yorks . 196 D6
Loddington Leics . . 136 C5
N Nhants 136 B6
Loddiswell Devon . . 8 F4
Loddon Norf 143 D7
Loddon Ingloss
Norf 142 D6
Lode Cambs 123 E10
Lode Heath W Mid . 134 G3
Loders Dorset 16 C5
Lodgebank Shrops . 149 D11
Lodge Green
N Yorks 223 F9
W Mid 134 G5
Lodge Hill Corn . . . 6 C4
Glos 98 G6
Kent 52 B4

Lodge Hill continued
W Yorks 197 C9
Lodge Lees Kent . . . 55 D8
Lodge Moor
S Yorks 186 D3
Lodge Park Worcs . 117 D10
Lodsworth W Sus . . 34 C6
Lodsworth Common
W Sus 34 C6
Lodway Bristol 60 D4
Lofthouse N Yorks . 214 E2
W Yorks 197 B10
Lofthouse Gate
W Yorks 197 C10
Loftus Redcar 226 B4
Logan Dumfries . . . 236 E2
E Ayrs 258 E3
Loganlea W Loth . . 269 C9
Logan Mains
Dumfries 236 E2
Loggerheads Denb . 165 C11
Staffs 150 B4
Logie Angus 293 G8
Fife 287 E8
Moray 301 D10
Logiealmond Lodge
Perth 286 D3
Logie Coldstone
Aberds 292 C6
Logie Hill Highld . . 301 B7
Logie Newton
Aberds 302 F6
Logie Pert Angus . . 293 G8
Logierait Perth . . . 286 B3
Login Carms 92 G3
Logmore Green Sur . 50 D6
Long John's Hill
Norf 142 B4
Lolworth Cambs . . . 123 E7
Lomeshaye Lancs . . 204 F3
Lôn Gwyn 147 C7
Lonbain Highld . . . 298 D6
Londesborough
E Yorks 208 D3
London Apprentice
Corn 5 E10
London Beach Kent . 53 F11
London Colney
Herts 85 E11
Londonderry
N Yorks 214 B6
W Mid 133 F10
London End Cambs . 121 D11
London Fields
W Mid 133 E8
London Minstead
Hants 32 E3
Londonthorpe Lincs . 155 B9
Londubh Highld . . . 307 L3
Lonemore Highld . . 299 B7
Highld 309 L7
Long Ashton N Som . 60 E5
Long Bank Worcs . . 116 C5
Longbar N Ayrs . . . 266 E5
Longbenton T&W . . 243 D7
Longborough Glos . 100 F3
Long Bredy Dorset . 17 C7
Longbridge Plym . . 7 D10
Warks 118 E5
W Mid 117 B10
Longbridge Deverill
Wilts 45 E11
Longbridge Hayes
Stoke 168 F5
Longbridgemuir
Dumfries 238 D3
Long Buckby
W Nhants 120 D2
Long Buckby Wharf
W Nhants 120 D2
Longburgh Cumb . . 239 F8
Longburton Dorset . 29 E11
Longcause Devon . . 8 C5
Long Clawson Leics . 154 D4
Longcliffe Derbys . . 170 D2
Long Common Hants . 33 E8
Long Compton
Staffs 151 E7
Warks 100 E5
Longcot Oxon 82 G3
Long Crendon
Bucks 83 D11
Longcroft Cumb . . 238 F6
Falk 278 F5
Longcross Devon . . 12 F4
Sur 66 F3
Long Cross Wilts . . 45 G9
Longdale Cumb . . . 222 D2
Longdales N Yorks . 230 C6
Long Dean Wilts . . 61 D11
Longden Shrops . . 131 B8
Longden Common
Shrops 131 C8
Long Ditton Sur . . . 67 F7
Longdon Staffs . . . 151 G11
Worcs 98 D6
Longdon Green
Staffs 151 G11
Longdon Heath
Worcs 98 D6
Longdon Hill End
Worcs 98 D6
Longdon on Tern
Telford 150 F2
Longdown Devon . . 14 C3
Longdowns Corn . . . 2 C6
Long Drax N Yorks . 199 B7
Longdrum Angus . . 292 G4
Long Duckmanton
Derbys 186 G6
Long Eaton Derbys . 153 C9
Longfield Kent 68 F6
Shetland 313 M5
Wilts 45 B11
Longfield Hill Kent . 68 F6
Longfleet BCP 18 C6
Longford Derbys . . 152 B4
Glos 98 G6
Kent 52 B4

Longford continued
London 66 D4
Shrops 150 C2
Telford 150 F4
W Mid 135 G7
Longfordlane
Derbys 152 B4
Longforgan Perth . 287 E7
Longformacus
Borders 272 D3
Longframlington
Northumb 252 C4
Long Green
Ches W 183 G7
Suff 125 B11
Worcs 98 E6
Longham Dorset . . 19 B7
Norf 159 F8
Long Hanborough
Oxon 82 C6
Longhaven Aberds . 303 F11
Longhedge Wilts . . 45 E10
Longhill Aberds . . 303 D9
Longhirst Northumb . 252 F6
Longhope Glos . . . 79 B11
Orkney 314 G3
Longhorsley
Northumb 252 E4
Longhoughton
Northumb 264 G6
Longhouse Bath . . . 61 G8
Long Itchington
Warks 119 D8
Long Lawford
Warks 119 B9
Long Lee W Yorks . 205 E7
Longlevens Glos . . 99 G7
Longley W Yorks . . 196 C5
W Yorks 196 F6
Longley Estate
S Yorks 186 C5
Longley Green
Worcs 116 G4
Longleys Perth . . . 286 C6
Long Load Som . . . 29 C7
Longmanhill Aberds . 303 C7
Long Marston Herts . 84 B5
N Yorks 206 C6
Warks 100 B3
Long Marton Cumb . 231 G9
Long Meadow
Cambs 123 E10
Long Meadowend
Shrops 131 G8
Long Melford Suff . 107 B7
Longmoor Camp
Hants 49 G9
Longmorn Moray . . 302 D2
Longmoss Ches E . 184 G5
Long Newnton Glos . 80 G6
Longnewton
Borders 262 D3
Stockton 225 B7
Long Newton
E Loth 271 C10
Longney Glos 80 C3
Longniddry E Loth . 281 F8
Longnor Shrops . . 131 C9
Staffs 151 G7
Staffs 169 C9
Longnor Park
Shrops 131 C9
Long Oak Shrops . . 149 E7
Longparish Hants . . 48 E2
Longpark Cumb . . . 239 E10
E Ayrs 257 B10
Long Park Hants . . 48 G2
Longport Stoke . . . 168 F5
Long Preston
N Yorks 204 B2
Longridge Glos . . . 80 D5
Lancs 203 F7
Staffs 151 F8
W Loth 269 C9
Longridge End Glos . 98 G6
Long Riston E Yorks . 209 E8
Longrock Corn . . . 1 C5
Long Sandall
S Yorks 198 F6
Longscales
N Yorks 205 B10
Longsdon Staffs . . 169 E7
Longshaw Gtr Man . 194 G4
Staffs 169 F9
Longside Aberds . . 303 E10
Longsight Gtr Man . 184 B5
Long Sight Gtr Man . 196 F2
Longslow Shrops . . 150 B3
Longsowerby Cumb . 239 G9
Longstanton Cambs . 123 D7
Longstock Hants . . 47 F11
Longstone Corn . . . 2 B2
Corn 11 G7
Edin 280 G4
Som 28 B5
Long Stratton Norf . 142 E3
Longstreet Wilts . . 46 D6
Long Street
M Keynes 102 B5
Long Sutton Hants . 49 D8
Lincs 157 E8
Som 29 C7
Longthorpe Pboro . 138 D3
Long Thurlow Suff . 125 D10
Longthwaite Cumb . 230 G4
Longton Lancs . . . 194 B3
Stoke 168 G6
Longtown Cumb . . 239 D9

Longtown continued
Hereford 96 F6
Longtownmail
Orkney 314 F4
Longview Mers . . . 182 C6
Longville in the Dale
Shrops 131 E10
Longway Bank
Derbys 170 E4
Longwell Green
S Glos 61 E7
Long Whatton Leics . 153 E9
Longwick Bucks . . 84 D3
Long Wittenham
Oxon 83 G8
Longwitton
Northumb 252 F3
Longwood Shrops . 132 B2
W Yorks 196 D6
Longwood Edge
W Yorks 196 D6
Longworth Oxon . . 82 F5
Longyester E Loth . 271 B10
Lon-las Swansea . . 57 B8
Lonmay Aberds . . . 303 D10
Lonmore Highld . . 298 E2
Looe Corn 6 E5
Looe Mills Corn . . . 6 C4
Loose Kent 53 C9
Loosebeare Devon . 13 G10
Loosegate Lincs . . 156 D6
Loose Hill Kent . . . 53 C9
Loosley Row Bucks . 84 E4
Lopcombe Corner
Wilts 47 F9
Lopen Som 28 E6
Lopen Head Som . . 28 E6
Loppergarth Cumb . 210 D5
Loppington Shrops . 149 D9
Lopwell Devon . . . 7 C9
Lorbottle Northumb . 252 B6
Lorbottle Hall
Northumb 252 B2
Lordsbridge Norf . . 157 G11
Lord's Hill Soton . . 32 D5
Lordshill Common
Sur 50 E4
Lordswood Soton . . 32 D6
Lords Wood Medway . 69 G9
Lornty Perth 286 C5
Loscoe Derbys . . . 170 F6
W Yorks 198 C2
Loscombe Dorset . . 16 B6
Losgaintir W Isles . 305 J2
Lossiemouth Moray . 302 B2
Lossit Argyll 254 B2
Lossit Lodge Argyll . 274 G5
Lostford Shrops . . . 150 C2
Lostock Gtr Man . . 195 F7
Lostock Gralam
Ches W 183 F11
Lostock Green
Ches W 183 G11
Lostock Hall Lancs . 194 B4
Lostock Junction
Gtr Man 195 F7
Lostwithiel Corn . . 6 D2
Loth Orkney 314 C6
Lothbeg Highld . . . 311 H3
Lothersdale
N Yorks 204 D5
Lothianbridge
Midloth 270 C6
Lothmore Highld . . 311 H3
Lottisham Som . . . 44 G5
Loudwater Bucks . . 84 G6
Herts 85 F9
Loughborough
Leics 153 F10
Loughor Swansea . . 56 B5
Loughton Essex . . . 86 F6
M Keynes 102 D6
Shrops 132 G2
Lound Lincs 155 F11
Notts 187 D11
Suff 143 D10
Loundsley Green
Derbys 186 G5
Lount Leics 153 F7
Lour Angus 287 C8
Louth Lincs 190 D4
Lovat Highld 300 E5
Lovaton Devon . . . 7 B10
Love Clough Lancs . 195 B10
Love Green Bucks . . 66 C4
Lovedean Hants . . 33 E11
Lover Wilts 32 C2
Loversall S Yorks . . 187 B9
Loves Green Essex . 87 E10
Lovesome Hill
N Yorks 225 F7
Loveston Pembs . . 73 D9
Lovington Som . . . 44 G5
Low Ackworth
W Yorks 198 D3
Low Alwinton
Northumb 251 B10
Low Angerton
Northumb 252 G3
Low Ardwell
Dumfries 236 E2
Low Ballochdowan
S Ayrs 236 B2
Low Barlings Lincs . 189 G9
Low Barugh
S Yorks 197 F10
Low Bentham
N Yorks 212 F2
Low Biggins Cumb . 212 D2
Low Blantyre
S Lanark 268 D3
Low Borrowbridge
Cumb 222 E2
Low Bradfield
S Yorks 186 C3
Low Bradley
N Yorks 204 D6
Low Braithwaite
Cumb 230 C4
Low Bridge Wilts . . 62 G3
Low Brunton
Northumb 241 C10
Low Burnham
N Lincs 199 G9

Low Burton N Yorks . 214 C4
Low Buston
Northumb 252 B6
Lowca Cumb 228 G5
Low Catton
E Yorks 207 C10
Low Clanyard
Dumfries 236 F3
Low Common Norf . 142 E2
Low Compton
Gtr Man 196 F2
Low Coniscliffe
Darl 224 C5
Low Coylton
S Ayrs 257 F10
Low Crosby Cumb . 239 F10
Lowcross Hill
Ches W 167 E4
Low Dalby N Yorks . 217 B7
Lowdham Notts . . . 171 F11
Low Dinsdale Darl . 224 C6
Lowe Shrops 149 C10
Lowedges S Yorks . 186 E4
Lowe Hill Staffs . . 169 E7
Low Eighton T&W . 243 F7
Low Ellington
N Yorks 214 C4
Loose Lincs 156 D6
Low Barugh
S Yorks 197 F10
Low Etherley Durham . 233 F9
Low Fell T&W . . . 243 F7
Lowfield Heath
W Sus 51 E9
Low Fold
W Yorks 197 B9
Low Fulney Lincs . . 156 E5
Low Gate
N Yorks 214 B2
Northumb 241 D10
Lowgill Cumb . . . 222 F3
Lancs 212 F3

Lower Cator Devon . . 13 F9
Lower Caversham
Reading 65 E8
Lower Chapel
Powys 95 D10
Lower Chedworth
Glos 81 C9
Lower Cheriton
Devon 27 G11
Lower Chicksgrove
Wilts 46 G3
Lower Chute Wilts . 47 C10
Lower Clapton
London 67 B11
Lower Clent Worcs . 117 B8
Lower Coylton
S Ayrs 257 F10
Lower Clicker Corn . 6 C5
Lower Clopton
Warks 118 F3
Lower Common
Hants 48 F6
Hants 65 G9
Mon 78 B2
Shrops 131 F9
Lower Copthurst
Lancs 194 C5
Lower Cotburn
Aberds 303 D7
Lower Cotham
Lower Cousley Wood
E Sus 53 F6
Lower Cox Street
Kent 69 G10
Lower Cragabus
Argyll 254 C4
Lower Creedy Devon . 26 F4
Lower Croan Corn . 10 G5
Lower Crossings
Derbys 185 E8
Lower Cumberworth
W Yorks 197 F8
Lower Daggons
Hants 31 E10
Lower Darwen
Blackburn 195 B7
Lower Dean
Bedford 121 D10
Devon 8 C4
Lower Dell Highld . 292 B4
Lower Denby
W Yorks 197 F8
Lower Denzell Corn . 5 B7
Lower Deuchries
Aberds 302 D6
Lower Diabaig
Highld 299 C7
Lower Dicker E Sus . 23 C9
Lower Dinchope
Shrops 131 G9
Lower Dowdeswell
Glos 81 B8
Lower Down Shrops . 130 G6
Lower Drift Corn . . 1 D4
Lower Dunsforth
N Yorks 215 G8
Lower Durston Som . 28 B3
Lower Earley
Wokingham 65 E9
Lower East Carleton
Norf 142 C3
Lower Eastern Green
W Mid 118 B5
Lower Edmonton
London 86 G4
Lower Egleton
Hereford 98 B2
Lower Elkstone
Staffs 169 D9
Lower Ellastone
Staffs 169 G10
Lower End Bucks . . 83 C11
Bucks 102 E4
C Beds 103 D8
C Beds 103 G9
Glos 81 E7
N Nhants 121 E7
Oxon 82 B4
W Nhants 120 F6
W Nhants 120 G5
Lower Everleigh
Wilts 47 C7
Lower Eythorne Kent . 55 D9
Lower Failand N Som . 60 E4
Lower Faintree
Shrops 132 F3
Lower Falkenham
Suff 108 D3
Lower Farringdon
Hants 49 F8
Lower Feltham
London 66 E5
Lower Fittleworth
W Sus 35 D8
Lowerford Lancs . . 204 F3
Lower Forge Shrops . 132 F4
Lower Foxdale IoM . 192 E3
Lower Frankton
Shrops 149 C7
Lower Freystrop
Pembs 73 C7
Lower Froyle Hants . 49 E9
Lower Gabwell Devon . 9 B8
Lower Gledfield
Highld 309 K5
Lower Godney Som . 44 E3
Lower Goldstone
Kent 71 G9
Lower Gornal
W Mid 133 E8
Lower Grange
W Yorks 205 G8
Lower Gravenhurst
C Beds 104 D2
Lower Green Essex . 88 G2
Essex 105 E6
Essex 106 E4
Gtr Man 184 B2
Herts 104 E3
Kent 52 E5
Kent 52 E6
Norf 159 B9
Staffs 133 B8
Suff 124 D4

Lower Green *continued*
...Argyll 66 F6
Warks 119 D10
W Berks 63 G11
Lower Grove Common
Hereford 97 F11
Lower Hacheston
Suff 126 F6
Lower Halistra
Highld 298 D2
Lower Halliford Sur . .66 F5
Lower Halstock Leigh
Dorset 29 F8
Lower Halstow Kent .69 F11
Lower Hamswell
S Glos 61 E8
Lower Hamworthy
BCP 18 C6
Lower Hardres Kent . .55 C7
Lower Hardwick
Hereford 115 F8
Lower Harpton
Powys 114 E5
Lower Hartlip Kent . .69 G10
Lower Hartshay
Derbys 170 E5
Lower Hartwell
Bucks 84 C3
Lower Hatton Staffs . 150 B6
Lower Hawthwaite
Cumb 210 B4
Lower Haysden Kent . .52 D5
Lower Hayton
Shrops 131 G10
Lower Hazel S Glos . . .60 B6
Lower Heath
Ches E 168 C5
Lower Hempriggs
Moray 301 C11
Lower Heppington
Kent 54 C6
Lower Hergest
Hereford 114 F5
Lower Herne Kent . . .71 F7
Lower Heyford
Oxon 101 G9
Lower Heysham
Lancs 211 G8
Lower Higham Kent . .69 E8
Lower Highmoor
Oxon 65 B8
Lower Holbrook
Suff 108 E3
Lower Holditch
Dorset 28 G4
Lower Holloway
London 67 B10
Lower Holwell Dorset 31 E9
Lower Hook Worcs . . .98 C6
Lower Hookner
Devon 13 E10
Lower Hopton
Shrops 149 E7
W Yorks 197 D7
Lower Hordley
Shrops 149 D7
Lower Horncroft
W Sus 35 D8
Lower Horsebridge
E Sus 23 C9
Lowerhouse Ches E . . 184 F6
Lancs 204 G2
Lower House Halton. 183 D8
Lower Houses
W Yorks 197 D7
Lower Howsell Worcs 98 B5
Lower Illey Worcs . . . 133 G9
Lower Island Kent . . .70 F6
Lower Kersal
Gtr Man 195 G10
Lower Kilburn
Derbys 170 F5
Lower Kilcott Glos . . .61 B9
Lower Killeyan
Argyll 254 C3
Lower Kingcombe
Dorset 17 B9
Lower Kingswood
Sur 51 C8
Lower Kinnerton
Ches W 166 C4
Lower Kinsham
Hereford 115 E7
Lower Knapp Som 28 B4
Lower Knightley
Staffs 150 E6
Lower Knowle Bristol .60 E5
Lower Langford
N Som 60 G3
Lower Largo Fife . . . 287 G8
Lower Layham
Suff 107 C10
Lower Ledwyche
Shrops 115 C10
Lower Leigh Staffs . . 151 B10
Lower Lemington
Glos 100 E4
Lower Lenie Highld . . 300 G5
Lower Lode Glos 99 E7
Lower Lovacott
Devon 25 B8
Lower Loxhore Devon . 40 F6
Lower Lydbrook Glos . 79 B9
Lower Lye Hereford . . 115 D8
Lower Machen
Newport 59 B8
Lower Maes-coed
Hereford 96 E6
Lower Mains Clack . . . 279 B9
Lower Mannington
Dorset 31 F9
Lower Marsh Som . . .30 C2
Lower Marston Som . .45 E9
Lower Meend Glos . . .79 E9
Lower Menadue Corn .5 D10
Lower Merridge Som .43 G8
Lower Mickletown
W Yorks 198 B4
Lower Middleton Cheney
W Nhants 101 C10
Lower Midway
Derbys 152 E6

Lower Mill Corn 3 B10
Lower Milovaig
Highld 296 F7
Lower Milton Som . . .44 D4
Lower Moor Wilts . . .81 G6
Worcs 99 B9
Lower Morton
S Glos 79 G10
Lower Mountain
Flint 166 D4
Lower Nazeing Essex .86 D5
Lower Netchwood
Shrops 132 E2
Lower Netherton
Devon 14 G3
Lower New Inn Torf . .78 F4
Lower Ninnes Corn . . .1 C5
Lower Nobut
Staffs 151 C10
Lower North Dean
Bucks 84 F4
Lower Norton
Warks 118 E4
Lower Nyland Dorset . .30 C2
Lower Ochrwyth
Caerph 59 B8
Lower Oddington
Glos 100 F4
Lower Odcombe Som .29 D8
Lower Ollach Highld. . 295 B7
Lower Padworth
W Berks 64 F6
Lower Penarth
V Glam 59 F7
Lower Penn Staffs . . . 133 D7
Lower Pennington
Hants 20 C2
Lower Penwortham
Lancs 194 B4
Lower Peover
Ches W 184 G2
Lower Pexhill
Ches E 184 G5
Lower Pilsley
Derbys 170 C6
Lower Pitkerrie
Highld 311 L2
Lower Place
Gtr Man 196 E2
London 67 C8
Lower Pollicot Bucks . .84 C2
Lower Porthkerry
V Glam 58 F5
Lower Porthpean
Corn 5 E10
Lower Quinton
Warks 100 B3
Lower Rabber
Hereford 114 G5
Lower Race Torf 78 E3
Lower Radley Oxon . .83 F8
Lower Rainham
Medway 69 F10
Lower Ratley Hants . .32 C4
Lower Raydon Suff. 107 D10
Lower Rea Glos 80 B4
Lower Ridge Devon . .28 G2
Shrops 148 C3
Lower Roadwater
Som 42 F4
Lower Rochford
Worcs 116 D2
Lower Rose Corn . . .4 E5
Lower Row Dorset . . .31 G8
Lower Sapey Worcs . . 116 E3
Lower Seagry Wilts . .62 C3
Lower Sheering
Essex 87 C7
Lower Shelton
C Beds 103 C9
Lower Shiplake Oxon .65 D9
Lower Shuckburgh
Warks 119 E9
Lower Sketty
Swansea 56 C6
Lower Slackstead
Hants 32 B5
Lower Slade Devon . .40 D4
Lower Slaughter
Glos 100 G3
Lower Solva Pembs . . .87 G11
Lower Soothill
W Yorks 197 C9
Lower Soudley Glos . . .79 D11
Lower Southfield
Hereford 98 C3
Lower Stanton St
Quintin Wilts 62 C2
Lower Stoke
Medway 69 D10
W Mid 119 B7
Lower Stondon
C Beds 104 D3
Lower Stone
S Glos 79 G11
Lower Stonnall
Staffs 133 C11
Lowesby Leics 136 B4
Lowestoft Suff 143 E10
Loweswater Cumb . . 229 G8
Low Etherley
Durham 233 F9
Lower Street E Sus . . .38 E2
Norf 160 B5
Norf 160 C3
Norf 160 F6
Suff 108 E3
Suff 124 G5
Lower Strensham
Worcs 99 C8
Lower Stretton
Warr 183 E10
Lower Studley Wilts . 45 B11
Lower Sundon
C Beds 103 F10
Lower Swainswick
Bath 61 F9
Lower Swanwick
Hants 33 F7
Lower Swell Glos . . . 100 F3
Lower Sydenham
London 67 E10
Lower Tadmarton
Oxon 101 D8

Lower Tale Devon . . .27 G9
Lower Tasburgh
Norf 142 D3
Lower Tean Staffs . . 151 B10
Lower Thorpe
W Nhants 101 B10
Lower Threapwood
Wrex 166 G6
Lower Thurlton
Norf 143 D8
Lower Thurnham
Lancs 202 C5
Lower Thurvaston
Derbys 152 B4
Lower Todding
Hereford 115 B8
Lower Tote Highld . . . 298 C5
Lowertown Corn 2 D5
Corn 5 C11
Devon 12 E5
Lower Town
Devon 27 E8
Hereford 98 C2
Pembs 91 D9
Worcs 117 F7
W Yorks 204 G6
Lower Trebullett
Corn 12 F2
Lower Tregunnon
Corn 11 E10
Lower Treworrick
Corn 6 B4
Lower Tuffley Glos . . .80 C4
Lower Turmer Hants 31 F10
Lower Twitchen
Devon 24 D5
Lower Twydall
Medway 69 F10
Lower Tysoe Warks . 100 B6
Lower Upham Hants . .33 D8
Lower Upnor Medway .69 E9
Lower Vexford Som . . .42 F6
Lower Wainhill Oxon. .84 E3
Lower Walton
Warr 183 D10
Lower Wanborough
Swindon 63 C8
Lower Weacombe
Som 42 E6
Lower Weald
M Keynes 102 D5
Lower Wear Devon . . .14 D4
Lower Weare Som . . .44 C2
Lower Weedon
W Nhants 120 F2
Lower Welson
Hereford 114 G5
Lower Westholme
Som 44 E5
Lower Westhouse
N Yorks 212 E3
Lower Westmancote
Worcs 99 D8
Lower Weston Bath . .61 F8
Lower Whatcombe
Dorset 30 G4
Lower Whatley Som . .45 D8
Lower Whitley
Ches W 183 F10
Lower Wick Glos 80 F2
Worcs 116 G6
Lower Wield Hants . . .48 E6
Lower Willingdon
E Sus 23 E9
Lower Winchendon or
Nether Winchendon
Bucks 84 C2
Lower Withington
Ches E 168 B4
Lower Wolverton
Worcs 117 G8
Lower Woodend
Aberds 293 B8
Bucks 65 B10
Lower Woodford
Wilts 46 G6
Lower Woodley Corn. 5 B10
Lower Woodside
Herts 86 D2
Lower Woolston
Som 29 B11
Lower Woon Corn 5 C10
Lower Wraxall
Dorset 29 G9
Som 44 F6
Wilts 61 G10
Lower Wych
Ches W 167 G9
Lower Wyche Worcs . .98 C5
Lower Wyke
W Yorks 197 B7
Lower Yelland Devon . 40 G3
Lower Zeals Wilts 45 G9
Lowes Barn
Durham 233 C11

Low Habberley
Worcs 116 B6
Low Ham Som 28 B6
Low Hauxley
Northumb 253 C7
Low Hawsker
N Yorks 227 D8
Low Hesket Cumb . . 230 B5
Low Hesleyhurst
Northumb 252 D3
Low Hill W Mid 133 C8
Low Hutton N Yorks . 216 F5
Lowick Cumb 210 B5
N Nhants 137 G9
Northumb 264 B2
Lowick Bridge
Cumb 210 B5
Lowick Green Cumb. . 210 B5
Low Knipe Cumb . . . 230 G6
Low Laithe N Yorks . 214 G3
Low Laithes
S Yorks 197 G11
Lowlands Torf 78 F3
Low Leighton
Derbys 185 D8
Low Lorton Cumb . . 229 F9
Low Marishes
N Yorks 216 D6
Low Marnham Notts . 132 B4
Low Mill N Yorks . . . 226 F3
Low Moor Lancs . . . 203 E10
N Yorks 197 B7
Lowmoor Row Cumb. . 231 F8
Low Moorsley T&W . . 234 B2
Low Moresby Cumb . . 228 G5
Lowna N Yorks 226 G3
Low Newton Cumb . . 211 C8
Low Newton-by-the-Sea
Northumb 264 E6
Lownie Moor Angus. . 287 C8
Lowood Borders 262 B2
Low Prudhoe
Northumb 242 E4
Low Risby N Lincs . . 200 E2
Low Row Cumb 229 C9
Cumb 240 E3
N Yorks 223 F9
Low Salchrie
Dumfries 236 C2
Low Smerby Argyll . . 255 E8
Low Snaygill
N Yorks 204 D5
Lowsonford Warks . . 118 D3
Low Street Norf . . . 141 B10
Thurrock 69 D7
Low Tharston Norf . . 142 D3
Lowther Cumb 230 G6
Lowthertown
Dumfries 238 D6
Lowtherville IoW 21 F7
Low Thornley T&W . . 242 E5
Lowthorpe E Yorks . 217 G11
Lowton Gtr Man . . . 183 B10
Som 27 D11
Lowton Common
Gtr Man 183 B10
Lowton Heath
Gtr Man 183 B10
Lowton St Mary's
Gtr Man 183 B10
Low Torry Fife 279 D10
Low Town Shrops . . . 132 E4
Low Toynton Lincs . . 190 G3
Low Valley S Yorks . 198 G2
Low Valleyfield
Fife 279 D10
Low Walton Cumb . . 219 C9
Low Waters
S Lanark 268 E4
Low Westwood
Durham 242 F4
Low Whinnow
Cumb 239 G8
Low Whita N Yorks . 223 F10
Low Wood Cumb . . . 210 C6
Low Worsall
N Yorks 225 C7
Low Wray Cumb . . . 221 E7
Loxbeare Devon 26 D6
Loxford London 68 B2
Loxhill Sur 50 F4
Loxhore Devon 40 F6
Loxhore Cott Devon . 40 F6
Loxley S Yorks 186 D4
Warks 118 G5
Loxley Green
Staffs 151 C11
Loxter Hereford 98 C4
Loxton N Som 43 B11
Loxwood W Sus 50 G4
Loyter's Green Essex .87 C7
Loyterton Kent 70 G3
Lozells W Mid 133 F11
Lubachlaggan
Highld 300 B3
Lubachoinnich
Highld 309 K4
Lubberland Shrops . . 116 B2
Lubcroy Highld 309 J3
Lubenham Leics 136 F4
Lubinvullin Highld . . 308 C5
Lucas End Herts 86 E4
Lucas Green Lancs . . 194 C3
Sur 50 B2
Luccombe Som 42 E2
Luccombe Village
IoW 21 F7
Lucker Northumb . . . 264 C5
Luckett Corn 12 G3
Lucking Street
Essex 106 E6
Luckington Wilts 61 C10
Lucklawhill Fife . . . 287 E8
Luckwell Bridge Som . 42 F2
Lucton Hereford . . . 115 E8
Ludag W Isles 297 K3
Ludborough Lincs . . . 190 B3
Ludbrook Devon 8 E3
Ludchurch Pembs . . .73 C10
Luddenden W Yorks . 196 B4
Luddenden Foot
W Yorks 196 C4

Ludderburn Cumb . . 221 G8
Luddesdown Kent . . .69 F7
Luddington
N Lincs 199 D10
Warks 118 G3
Luddington in the Brook
N Nhants 138 G2
Lude House Perth . . 291 G10
Ludford Lincs 190 D2
Shrops 115 C10
Ludgershall Bucks . . .83 B11
Wilts 47 C9
Ludgvan Corn 2 C2
Ludham Norf 161 F7
Ludlow Shrops 115 C10
Ludney Lincs 190 B5
Som 28 E5
Ludstock Hereford . . .98 D3
Ludstone Shrops . . . 132 E6
Ludwell Wilts 30 C6
Ludworth Durham . . 234 C3
Luffenhall Herts . . . 104 F5
Luffincott Devon 12 C2
Lufton Som 29 D8
Lugar E Ayrs 258 E3
Lugate Borders 271 G11
Lugg Green
Hereford 115 E9
Luggiebank
N Lanark 278 G5
Lugsdale Halton . . . 183 D8
Lugton E Ayrs 267 E8
Lugwardine
Hereford 97 C11
Luib Highld 295 C7
Luibeilt Highld 290 G4
Lulham Hereford 97 C8
Lullenden Sur 52 E2
Lullington Derbys . . 152 G5
Som 45 C9
Lulsgate Bottom
N Som 60 F4
Lulsley Worcs 116 F4
Lulworth Camp
Dorset 18 E2
Lumb Lancs 195 C10
Lancs 195 D9
W Yorks 196 C4
W Yorks 197 E7
Lumb Foot W Yorks. . 204 F6
Lumburn Devon 12 G5
Lumbutts W Yorks . . 196 C3
Lumby N Yorks 206 G5
Lumley W Sus 22 B3
Lumley Thicks
Durham 243 G8
Lumloch E Dunb . . . 268 B2
Lumphanan Aberds . . 293 C7
Lumphinnans Fife . . 280 C3
Lumsdaine Borders . . 273 F7
Lumsden Aberds . . . 302 G4
Lunan Angus 287 B10
Lunanhead Angus . . 287 B8
Luncarty Perth 286 E4
Lund E Yorks 208 D5
N Yorks 207 G9
Shetland 312 C7
Lundal W Isles 304 E3
Lundavra Highld . . . 290 G2
Lunderton Aberds . . 303 E11
Lundie Angus 286 D6
Highld 290 B3
Lundin Links Fife . . 287 G8
Lundwood S Yorks . 197 F11
Lundy Green Norf . . 142 E5
Lunga Argyll 275 C8
Lunna Shetland 312 G6
Lunning Shetland . . 312 G7
Lunnister Shetland . . 312 E5
Lunnon Swansea . . . 56 D4
Lunsford Kent 53 B7
Lunsford's Cross
E Sus 38 E2
Lunt Mers 193 G10
Luntley Hereford . . . 115 F7
Lunts Heath Halton. . 183 D8
Lupin Staffs 152 F2
Luppitt Devon 27 F11
Lupridge Devon 8 E4
Lupset W Yorks . . . 197 D10
Lupton Cumb 211 C11
Lurg Aberds 293 C8
Lurgashall W Sus . . .34 B6
Lurignich Argyll . . . 289 D11
Lurley Devon 26 E6
Lusby Lincs 174 B4
Luscombe Devon 8 E6
Lushcott Shrops . . . 131 D11
Luson Devon 8 F2
Luss Argyll 277 C7
Lussagiven Argyll . . 275 E7
Lusta Highld 298 D2
Lustleigh Devon 13 E11
Lustleigh Cleave
Devon 13 E11
Luston Hereford . . . 115 E9
Lusty Som 45 G7
Luthermuir Aberds . . 293 G8
Luthrie Fife 287 F7
Lutley W Mid 133 G8
Luton Devon 27 G9
Devon 14 F4
Luton 103 G11
Medway 69 F9
Lutsford Devon 24 D3
Lutterworth Leics . . 135 G8
Lutton Devon 7 D11
Devon 8 D2
Lincs 157 D8
N Nhants 138 G2
Lutton Gowts Lincs . . 157 E8
Lutworthy Devon . . . 26 D3
Luxborough Som . . . 42 F3
Luxley Glos 98 G3
Luxted London 68 G2
Luxton Devon 28 E2
Luxulyan Corn 5 D11
Luzley Gtr Man 196 G3
Luzley Brook
Gtr Man 196 F2
Lyatts Som 29 E8

Lybster Highld 310 F6
Lydbury North
Shrops 131 F7
Lydcott Devon 41 F7
Lydd Kent 39 C8
Lydden Kent 55 D9
Kent 71 F11
Lyddington Rutland . 137 D7
Lydd on Sea Kent . . .39 D9
Lyde Orkney 314 E3
Lydeard St Lawrence
Som 42 G6
Lyde Cross Hereford. . 97 C10
Lyde Green Hants . . .49 B8
S Glos 61 D7
Lydford Devon 12 E6
Lydford Fair Place
Som 44 G5
Lydford-on-Fosse
Som 44 G5
Lydgate Derbys 186 F4
Gtr Man 196 G3
W Yorks 196 B2
Lydham Shrops 130 E6
Lydiard Green
Wilts 62 B5
Lydiard Millicent
Wilts 62 B5
Lydiard Plain Wilts. . 62 B5
Lydiard Tregoze
Swindon 62 C6
Lydiate Mers 193 G11
Lydiate Ash Worcs . . 117 B9
Lydlinch Dorset 30 E2
Lydmarsh Som 28 F5
Lydney Glos 79 E10
Lydstep Pembs 73 F9
Lye W Mid 133 G8
Lye Cross N Som 60 G3
Lye Green
Bucks 85 E7
E Sus 52 G4
Warks 118 D3
Wilts 45 B10
Lye Head Worcs 116 C5
Lye Hole N Som 60 G4
Lyewood Common
E Sus 52 F4
Lyford Oxon 82 G5
Lymbridge Green
Kent 54 E6
Lyme Green Ches E. . 184 G6
Lyme Regis Dorset . . .16 C2
Lyminge Kent 55 E7
Lymington Hants . . . 20 B2
Lyminster W Sus 35 G8
Lymm Warr 183 D11
Lymore Hants 19 C11
Lympne Kent 54 F6
Lympsham Som 43 C10
Lympstone Devon . . .14 E5
Lynbridge Devon 41 D8
Lynch Hants 48 D4
Som 42 D2
Lynchat Highld 291 C9
Lynchgate Shrops . . 131 F7
Lynch Hill Hants 48 D3
Slough 66 C2
Lyndale Ho Highld. . 298 D3
Lyndhurst Hants . . . 32 F4
Lyndon Rutland 137 C8
Lyndon Green
W Mid 134 F2
Lyne
Borders 270 G4
Sur 66 F4
Lyneal Shrops 149 C8
Lyneal Mill Shrops . . 149 C9
Lyneal Wood Shrops . 149 C9
Lyne Down Hereford. . 98 E2
Lyneham
Oxon 100 G5
Wilts 62 D4
Lynemore Highld . . . 301 G10
Lynemouth
Northumb 253 E7
Lyne of Gorthleck
Highld 300 G5
Lyne of Skene
Aberds 293 B9
Lyness Orkney 314 G3
Lyne Station
Borders 260 B6
Lyng Norf 159 F11
Som 28 B4
Lyngate Norf 160 C5
Lyngford Som 28 B2
Lynmore Highld . . . 301 F10
Lynmouth Devon . . . 41 D8
Lynn
Staffs 133 C11
Telford 150 F7
Lynnwood Borders . 261 G11
Lynsore Bottom Kent .55 D7
Lynsted Kent 70 G2
Lynstone Corn 24 F2
Lynton Devon 41 D8
Lynwilg Highld 291 B10
Lynworth Glos 99 G9
Lyons T&W 234 B3
Lyon's Gate Dorset . . 29 F11
Lyon's Green Norf . . 159 G8
Lyonshall Hereford . . 114 F6
Lyons Hall Essex . . . 88 B2
Lypiatt Glos 80 D6
Lyrabus Argyll 274 G3
Lytchett Matravers
Dorset 18 B4
Lytchett Minster
Dorset 18 C5
Lyth Highld 310 C6
Lytham Lancs 193 B11
Lytham St Anne's
Lancs 193 B10
Lythbank Shrops . . . 131 B9
Lythe N Yorks 226 C5
Lythes Orkney 314 H4
Lythmore Highld . . . 310 C4

Maam Argyll 284 F5
Mabe Burnthouse
Corn 3 C7
Mabie Dumfries 237 B11
Mabledon Kent 52 E5
Mablethorpe Lincs . . 191 D8
Macclesfield
Ches E 184 G6
Macclesfield Forest
Ches E 185 G7
Macduff Aberds 303 C7
Mace Green Suff . . . 108 C2
Machan S Lanark . . . 268 E5
Macharioch Argyll . . 255 G8
Machen Caerph 59 B8
Machrie N Ayrs 255 D9
Machrie Hotel
Argyll 254 C4
Machrihanish Argyll. . 255 F7
Machroes Gwyn 144 D6
Machynlleth Powys . . 128 C4
Machynys Carms 56 B4
Mackerel's Common
W Sus 35 B8
Mackerye End Herts . 85 B11
Mackham Devon 27 F11
Mackney Oxon 64 B5
Mackside Borders . . . 262 G4
Mackworth Derbys . . 152 B6
Macmerry E Loth . . . 281 G8
Madderty Perth 286 E3
Maddington Wilts . . .46 E5
Maddiston Falk 279 F8
Maddox Moor Pembs. . 73 C7
Madehurst W Sus . . .35 E7
Madeley Staffs 168 G3
Telford 132 C3
Madeley Heath
Staffs 168 F3
Worcs 117 B9
Madeley Park Staffs. 168 G3
Madeleywood
Telford 132 C3
Maders Corn 12 G2
Madford Devon 27 E10
Madingley Cambs . . 123 E7
Madjeston Dorset . . . 30 B4
Madley Hereford 97 D8
Madresfield Worcs . . .98 B6
Madron Corn 1 C5
Maenaddwyn
Anglesey 179 E7
Maenclochog Pembs 91 F11
Maendy V Glam 58 D4
Maenporth Corn 3 D7
Maentwrog Gwyn . . . 163 G11
Maen-y-groes
Ceredig 111 F7
Maer Corn 24 F2
Staffs 150 B5
Maerdy Carms 94 G2
Conwy 165 G8
Rhondda 77 F7
Maes-bangor
Ceredig 128 G3
Maesbrook Shrops . . 148 E5
Maesbury Shrops . . . 148 D6
Maesbury Marsh
Shrops 148 D6
Maesgeirchen
Gwyn 179 G9
Maes-glas Newport . . 59 B9
Maes Glas = *Greenfield*
Flint 181 F11
Maesgwyn-Isaf
Powys 148 G3
Maeshafn Denb 166 C2
Maesllyn Ceredig . . .93 C7
Maes llyn Ceredig . . .93 C7
Maesmynis Powys . . 95 B10
Maes Pennant Flint 181 F11
Maesteg Bridgend . . .57 C10
Maes-Treylow
Powys 114 C5
Maesybont Carms . . .75 B9
Maescoed Rhondda . . 58 B5
Maescrugiau Carms. . 93 C9
Maescwmmer
Caerph 77 G11
Maes-y-dre Flint . . . 166 C2
Maesygwartha Mon. . 78 C2
Maesymeillion
Ceredig 93 B8
Maesypandy Powys . 129 D9
Maesyrhandir
Powys 129 E11
Magdalen Laver
Essex 87 D8
Maggieknockater
Moray 302 E3
Maggots End Essex . 105 D9
Magham Down
E Sus 23 C10
Maghull Mers 193 G11
Magor Mon 60 B2
Magpie Green Suff. 125 B11
Mahaar Dumfries . . . 236 B2
Maida Vale London . . 67 C9
Maidenbower W Sus . 51 F9
Maiden Bradley
Wilts 45 E10
Maidenhall Suff . . . 108 C3
Maidenhead
Windsor 65 C11
Maiden Head N Som. . 60 F5
Maidenhead Court
Windsor 66 C2
Maiden Law Durham . 233 D7
Maiden Newton
Dorset 17 B7
Maidenpark Falk . . . 279 E9
Maidens S Ayrs 244 B6
Maidensgrave Suff . . 108 B5
Maiden's Green
Brack 65 E11
Maiden's Hall
Northumb 252 D6

Maidenwell Corn . . .11 G8
Lincs 190 F4
Maiden Wells Pembs. . 73 F7
Maidford W Nhants. . 120 G2
Maids Moreton
Bucks 102 D4
Maidstone Kent 53 B9
Maidwell W Nhants. . 120 B4
Mail Shetland 313 L6
Mailand Shetland . . . 312 C8
Mailingsland
Borders 270 G4
Main Powys 148 F3
Maindee Newport . . .59 B10
Maindy Cardiff 59 D7
Mainholm S Ayrs . . . 257 E9
Mains Cumb 229 G7
Mainsforth Durham. . 234 E2
Mains of Airies
Dumfries 236 C1
Mains of Allardice
Aberds 293 F10
Mains of Annochie
Aberds 303 E9
Mains of Ardestie
Angus 287 D9
Mains of Arnage
Aberds 303 F9
Mains of Auchoynanie
Moray 302 E4
Mains of Baldoon
Dumfries 236 D6
Mains of Balhall
Angus 293 G7
Mains of Ballindarg
Angus 287 B8
Mains of Balnakettle
Aberds 293 F8
Mains of Birness
Aberds 303 F9
Mains of Blackhall
Aberds 303 G7
Mains of Burgie
Moray 301 D10
Mains of Cairnbrogie
Aberds 303 F9
Mains of Cairnty
Moray 302 D3
Mains of Clunas
Highld 301 E8
Mains of Crichie
Aberds 303 E9
Mains of Daltulich
Highld 301 F10
Mains of Dalvey
Highld 301 F11
Mains of Dellavaird
Aberds 293 E9
Mains of Drum
Aberds 293 D10
Mains of Edingight
Moray 302 D5
Mains of Fedderate
Aberds 303 E8
Mains of Flichity
Highld 300 G6
Mains of Hatton
Aberds 303 D9
Aberds 303 E7
Mains of Inkhorn
Aberds 303 F9
Mains of Innerpeffray
Perth 286 F2
Mains of Kirktonhill
Aberds 293 G8
Mains of Laithers
Aberds 302 E6
Mains of Mayen
Moray 302 E5
Mains of Melgund
Angus 287 B9
Mains of Taymouth
Perth 285 C11
Mains of Thornton
Aberds 293 F8
Mains of Towie
Aberds 303 E7
Mains of Ulbster
Highld 310 F7
Mains of Watten
Highld 310 D6
Mainsriddle
Dumfries 237 D11
Mainstone Shrops . . 130 F5
Maisemore Glos 98 G6
Maitland Park London .67 C9
Major's Green
W Mid 118 B2
Makeney Derbys . . . 170 G5
Malacleit W Isles . . . 296 D3
Malborough Devon . . .9 G9
Malcoff Derbys 185 E10
Malden Rushett
London 67 G7
Maldon Essex 88 D4
Malehurst Shrops . . 131 B7
Maligar Highld 298 C4
Malinbridge
S Yorks 186 D4
Malinslee Telford . . . 132 B3
Malkin's Bank
Ches E 168 C3
Mallaig Highld 295 F8
Mallaig Bheag
Highld 295 F8
Malleny Mills Edin. . 270 B3
Malling Stirling 285 G9
Mallows Green
Essex 105 F9
Malltraeth Anglesey. 162 B6
Mallwyd Gwyn 147 G2
Malmesbury Wilts . . .62 B2
Malmsmead Devon . . 41 D9
Malpas Ches W 167 F7
Corn 4 G6
Newport 78 G4
W Berks 64 E6
Malswick Glos 98 F4

Maltby Lincs 190 E4
  Stockton 225 C9
  S Yorks 187 C8
Maltby le Marsh
  Lincs 191 E7
Malting End Suff 124 G4
Malting Green
  Essex 107 G9
Maltings Angus 293 G9
Maltman's Hill Kent 54 E2
Malton N Yorks 216 E5
Malvern Common
  Worcs 98 C5
Malvern Link Worcs 98 B5
Malvern Wells Worcs 98 C5
Mambeg Argyll 276 D4
Mamble Worcs 116 C3
Mamhilad Mon 78 E4
Manaccan Corn 3 E7
Manadon Plym 7 D9
Manafon Powys 130 C2
Manais W Isles 296 C7
Manar Ho Aberds 303 G7
Manaton Devon 13 E11
Manby Lincs 190 D5
Mancetter Warks 134 D6
Manchester
  Gtr Man 184 B4
Manchester Airport
  Gtr Man 184 D4
Mancot Flint 166 B4
Mancot Royal Flint 166 B4
Mandally Highld 290 C4
Manea Cambs 139 F9
Maney W Mid 134 D2
Manfield N Yorks 224 C4
Mangaster Shetland 312 F5
Mangotsfield S Glos 61 D7
Mangrove Green
  Herts 104 G2
Mangurstadh
  W Isles 304 E2
Manhay Corn 2 C5
Manian-fawr Pembs 92 B3
Mankinholes
  W Yorks 196 C3
Manley Ches W 183 G8
  Devon 27 E7
Manley Common
  Ches W 183 G8
Manmoel Caerph 77 E11
Man-moel Caerph 77 E11
Mannal Argyll 288 E1
Mannamead Plym 7 D9
Mannerston
  W Loth 279 F10
Manningford Abbots
  Wilts 46 B6
Manningford Bohune
  Wilts 46 B6
Manningford Bruce
  Wilts 46 B6
Manningham
  W Yorks 205 G9
Mannings Heath
  W Sus 36 B2
Mannington Dorset 31 F9
Manningtree Essex 107 E11
Mannofield
  Aberdeen 293 C11
Manor London 68 B2
Manorbier Pembs 73 F9
Manorbier Newton
  Pembs 73 F8
Manor Bourne Devon 7 F9
Manordeilo Carms 94 F3
Manor Estate
  S Yorks 186 D5
Manorhill Borders 262 C5
Manor Hill Corner
  Lincs 157 F8
Manor House
  W Mid 135 G7
Manorowen Pembs 91 D8
Manor Park Bucks 84 C4
  Ches W 167 B11
  E Sus 37 C7
  London 68 B2
  Notts 153 C11
  Slough 66 C3
  S Yorks 186 D5
  W Yorks 205 D9
Manor Parsley Corn 4 F4
Manor Royal W Sus 51 F9
Man's Cross Essex 106 D5
Mansegate Dumfries 247 G9
Manselfield Swansea 56 D5
Mansel Lacy Hereford 97 B8
Mansell Gamage
  Hereford 97 C7
Manselton Swansea 57 B7
Mansergh Cumb 212 C2
Mansewood
  Glasgow 267 C11
Mansfield E Ayrs 258 G4
  Notts 171 C8
Mansfield Woodhouse
  Notts 171 C8
Manson Green
  Norf 141 C10
Mansriggs Cumb 210 C5
Manston Dorset 30 D4
  Kent 71 F10
  W Yorks 206 F3
Manswood Dorset 31 F7
Manthorpe Lincs 155 B8
  Lincs 155 F11
Mantles Green Bucks 85 F7
Manton N Lincs 200 G2
  Notts 187 F9
  Rutland 137 C7
  Wilts 63 F7
Manton Warren
  N Lincs 200 F2
Manuden Essex 105 F9
Manwood Green
  Essex 87 C8
Manywells Height
  W Yorks 205 F7
Maperton Som 29 B11
Maplebeck Notts 172 C2
Maple Cross Herts 85 G8
Mapledurham Oxon 65 D7
Mapledurwell Hants 49 C7
Maple End Essex 105 D11
Maplehurst W Sus 35 C11
Maplescombe Kent 68 G5
Mapleton Derbys 169 F11
Mapperley Derbys 170 G6
  Nottingham 171 G9
Mapperley Park
  Nottingham 171 G9
Mapperton Dorset 16 B6
  Dorset 18 B4
Mappleborough Green
  Warks 117 D11
Mappleton E Yorks 209 E10
Mapplewell
  S Yorks 197 F10
Mappowder Dorset 30 F2
Maraig W Isles 305 H3
Marazanvose Corn 4 E6
Marazion Corn 2 C2
Marbhig W Isles 305 G6
Marbrack Dumfries 246 E3
Marbury Ches E 167 F9
March Cambs 139 D8
  S Lanark 259 G11
Marcham Oxon 83 F7
Marchamley
  Shrops 149 D11
Marchamley Wood
  Shrops 149 C11
Marchington Staffs 152 C2
Marchington Woodlands
  Staffs 152 D2
Marchroes Gwyn 144 D6
Marchwiel Wrex 166 F5
Marchwood Hants 32 E5
Marcross V Glam 58 F2
Marden Hereford 97 B10
  Kent 53 E8
  T&W 243 C9
  Wilts 46 B5
Marden Ash Essex 87 E9
Marden Beech Kent 53 E8
Marden's Hill E Sus 52 G3
Marden Thorn Kent 53 E9
Mardleybury Herts 86 B3
Mardu Shrops 130 G5
Mardy Mon 78 B4
  Shrops 148 C5
Marefield Leics 136 B4
Mareham le Fen
  Lincs 174 C3
Mareham on the Hill
  Lincs 174 B3
Marehay Derbys 170 F5
Marehill W Sus 35 D9
Maresfield E Sus 37 C7
Maresfield Park
  E Sus 37 C7
Marfleet Hull 200 B6
Marford Wrex 166 D5
Margam Neath 57 D9
Margaret Marsh
  Dorset 30 D4
Margaret Roding
  Essex 87 C9
Margaretting Essex 87 E11
Margaretting Tye
  Essex 87 E11
Margate Kent 71 E11
Margery Sur 51 C9
Margnaheglish
  N Ayrs 256 C2
Margreig Dumfries 237 B10
Margrove Park
  Redcar 226 B3
Marham Norf 158 G4
Marhamchurch Corn 24 G2
Marholm Pboro 138 C2
Marian Flint 181 F9
Marian Cwm Denb 181 F9
Mariandyrys
  Anglesey 179 E10
Marianglas Anglesey 179 E8
Marian-glas
  Anglesey 179 E8
Mariansleigh Devon 26 C2
Marian y de = South Beach
  Gwyn 145 C7
Marian y mor = West End
  Gwyn 145 C7
Marine Town Kent 70 E2
Marionburgh
  Aberds 293 C9
Marishader Highld 298 C4
Marjoriebanks
  Dumfries 248 G3
Mark
  Dumfries 236 D3
  Dumfries 237 C7
  S Ayrs 236 B2
  Som 43 D11
Markbeech Kent 52 E3
Markby Lincs 191 F7
Mark Causeway
  Som 43 D11
Mark Cross E Sus 23 C7
  E Sus 52 G5
Markeaton Derbys 152 B6
Market Bosworth
  Leics 135 C8
Market Deeping
  Lincs 138 B2
Market Drayton
  Shrops 150 C3
Market Harborough
  Leics 136 F4
Markethill Perth 286 D6
Market Lavington
  Wilts 46 C4
Market Overton
  Rutland 155 F7
Market Rasen
  Lincs 189 D10
Market Stainton
  Lincs 190 F2
Market Warsop
  Notts 171 B9
Market Weighton
  E Yorks 208 E3
Market Weston Suff 125 B9
Markfield Leics 153 G9
Mark Hall North
  Essex 87 C7
Mark Hall South
  Essex 87 C7
Markham Caerph 77 E11
Markham Moor
  Notts 188 G2
Markinch Fife 286 G6
Markington N Yorks 214 F5
Markland Hill
  Gtr Man 195 F7
Markle E Loth 281 F11
Marksbury Bath 61 G7
Mark's Corner IoW 20 C5
Marks Gate London 87 G7
Marks Tey Essex 107 G8
Markyate Herts 85 B9
Marland Gtr Man 195 E11
Marlas Hereford 97 F8
Marl Bank Worcs 98 C5
Marlborough Wilts 63 F7
Marlbrook
  Hereford 115 G10
  Worcs 117 C9
Marlcliff Warks 117 G11
Marldon Devon 9 C7
Marle Green E Sus 23 B9
Marle Hill Glos 99 G9
Marlesford Suff 126 F6
Marley Kent 55 C7
  Kent 55 C10
Marley Green
  Ches E 167 F9
Marley Heights
  W Sus 49 G11
Marley Hill T&W 242 F6
Marley Pots T&W 243 F9
Marlingford Norf 142 B2
Mar Lodge Aberds 292 D2
Marloes Pembs 72 D3
Marlow Bucks 65 B10
  Hereford 115 B8
Marlow Bottom
  Bucks 65 B11
Marlow Common
  Bucks 65 B10
Marlpit Hill Kent 52 D2
Marlpits E Sus 38 E2
Marlpool Derbys 170 F6
Marnhull Dorset 30 D3
Marnoch Aberds 302 D5
Marnock N Lanark 268 B4
Marple Gtr Man 185 D7
Marple Bridge
  Gtr Man 185 D7
Marpleridge
  Gtr Man 185 D7
Marr S Yorks 198 F4
Marrel Highld 311 H4
Marr Green Wilts 63 G8
Marrick N Yorks 223 F11
Marrister Shetland 313 G7
Marros Carms 74 D2
Marsden T&W 243 E9
  W Yorks 196 E4
Marsden Height
  Lancs 204 F3
Marsett N Yorks 213 B8
Marsh Bucks 84 D4
  Devon 28 E3
  W Yorks 196 D6
  W Yorks 204 F6
Marshall Meadows
  Northumb 273 D9
Marshall's Cross
  Mers 183 C8
Marshall's Elm Som 44 G3
Marshall's Heath
  Herts 85 B11
Marshalsea Dorset 28 G5
Marshalswick Herts 85 D11
Marsham Norf 160 E3
Marshaw Lancs 203 C7
Marsh Baldon Oxon 83 F9
Marsh Benham
  W Berks 64 F2
Marshborough Kent 55 B10
Marshbrook Shrops 131 F8
Marshchapel Lincs 190 B5
Marsh Common
  S Glos 60 C5
Marsh End Worcs 98 D6
Marshfield Newport 59 C9
  S Glos 61 E9
Marshfield Bank
  Ches E 167 D11
Marshgate Corn 11 C9
Marsh Gate
  W Berks 63 F10
Marsh Gibbon
  Bucks 102 G2
Marsh Green
  Ches W 183 F8
  Devon 14 C6
  Gtr Man 194 F5
  Kent 52 E2
  Staffs 168 D5
  Telford 150 G2
Marsh Houses
  Lancs 202 C5
Marshland St James
  Norf 139 B10
Marsh Lane Derbys 186 F6
  Glos 79 D9
Marsh Mills Som 43 F7
Marshmoor Herts 86 D2
Marshside Kent 71 F8
  Mers 193 D11
Marsh Side Norf 176 E3
Marsh Street Som 42 E3
Marshwood Dorset 16 B3
Marske N Yorks 224 E2
Marske-by-the-Sea
  Redcar 235 G8
Marston Ches W 183 F11
  Hereford 115 F7
  Lincs 172 G5
  Oxon 83 D8
Marston *continued*
  Staffs 150 G6
  Staffs 151 D8
  Warks 119 B8
  Warks 134 E4
  Wilts 46 B3
Marston Bigot Som 45 E9
Marston Doles
  Warks 119 F9
Marston Gate Som 45 D9
Marston Green
  W Mid 134 F3
Marston Hill Glos 81 F10
Marston Jabbett
  Warks 135 F7
Marston Magna Som 29 C9
Marston Meysey
  Wilts 81 F10
Marston Montgomery
  Derbys 152 B2
Marston Moretaine
  C Beds 103 C9
Marston on Dove
  Derbys 152 D4
Marston St Lawrence
  W Nhants 101 C10
Marston Stannett
  Hereford 115 F11
Marston Trussell
  W Nhants 136 F3
Marstow Hereford 79 B9
Marsworth Bucks 84 C6
Marten Wilts 47 B9
Marthall Ches E 184 F4
Martham Norf 161 F9
Marthwaite Cumb 222 G2
Martin Hants 31 D9
  Kent 55 D10
  Lincs 173 D10
  Lincs 174 B2
Martindale Cumb 221 B8
Martin Dales Lincs 173 C11
Martin Drove End
  Hants 31 C9
Martinhoe Devon 41 D7
Martinhoe Cross
  Devon 41 D7
Martin Hussingtree
  Worcs 117 E7
Martin Mill Kent 55 D10
Martin Moor Lincs 174 C2
Martinscroft Warr 183 D11
Martin's Moss
  Ches E 168 C4
Martinstown Dorset 17 D8
Martinstown or Winterbourne St Martin Dorset 17 D8
Martlesham Suff 108 B4
Martlesham Heath
  Suff 108 B4
Martletwy Pembs 73 C8
Martley Worcs 116 E5
Martock Som 29 D7
Marton Ches E 168 B5
  Ches W 167 B10
  Cumb 210 D4
  E Yorks 209 F9
  Lincs 188 E4
  Mbro 225 B10
  N Yorks 215 G8
  N Yorks 216 C4
  Shrops 130 C5
  Shrops 149 E8
  Warks 119 D8
Marton Green
  Ches W 167 B10
Marton Grove Mbro 225 B9
Marton-in-the-Forest
  N Yorks 215 F11
Marton-le-Moor
  N Yorks 215 E7
Marton Moor Warks 119 D8
Marton Moss Side
  Blackpool 202 G2
Martyr's Green Sur 50 B5
Martyr Worthy Hants 48 G4
Marwick Orkney 314 D2
Marwood Devon 40 F4
Marybank Highld 300 D4
  Highld 301 B7
Maryburgh Highld 300 D5
Maryfield Aberds 293 D7
  Corn 7 D8
Maryhill Glasgow 267 B11
Marykirk Aberds 293 G8
Maryland Mon 79 D8
Marylebone
  Gtr Man 194 F5
Marypark Moray 301 F11
Maryport Cumb 228 D6
  Dumfries 236 F3
Mary Tavy Devon 12 F6
Maryton Angus 287 B7
  Angus 287 B10
Marywell Aberds 293 D7
  Aberds 293 D11
  Angus 287 C10
Masbrough S Yorks 186 C6
Mascle Bridge Pembs 73 D7
Masham N Yorks 214 C4
Mashbury Essex 87 C11
Masongill N Yorks 212 D3
Masonhill S Ayrs 257 E9
Mastin Moor Derbys 187 F7
Mastrick Aberdeen 293 C10
Matchborough
  Worcs 117 D11
Matching Essex 87 C8
Matching Green
  Essex 87 C8
Matching Tye Essex 87 C8
Matfen Northumb 242 C2
Matfield Kent 53 E7
Mathern Mon 79 G8
Mathon Hereford 98 B4
Mathry Pembs 91 E7
Matlaske Norf 160 C3
Matley Gtr Man 185 B7
Matlock Derbys 170 C3
Matlock Bank
  Derbys 170 C3
Matlock Bath
  Derbys 170 D3
Matlock Bridge
  Derbys 170 D3
Matlock Cliff
  Derbys 170 D4
Matlock Dale
  Derbys 170 D3
Matshead Lancs 202 E6
Matson Glos 80 B4
Matterdale End
  Cumb 230 G3
Mattersey Notts 187 D11
Mattersey Thorpe
  Notts 187 D11
Matthewsgreen
  Wokingham 65 F10
Mattingley Hants 49 B8
Mattishall Norf 159 G11
Mattishall Burgh
  Norf 159 G11
Mauchline E Ayrs 257 D11
Maud Aberds 303 E9
Maudlin Corn 5 C11
  Dorset 28 F5
  W Sus 22 B5
Maudlin Cross Dorset 28 F5
Maugersbury Glos 100 F4
Maughold IoM 192 C5
Mauld Highld 300 F4
Maulden C Beds 103 D11
Maulds Meaburn
  Cumb 222 B2
Maunby N Yorks 215 B7
Maund Bryan
  Hereford 115 G11
Maundown Som 27 B9
Mauricewood
  Midloth 270 C4
Mautby Norf 161 G9
Mavesyn Ridware
  Staffs 151 F11
Mavis Enderby Lincs 174 B5
Maviston Highld 301 D9
Mawbray Cumb 229 B7
Mawdesley Lancs 194 E3
Mawdlam Bridgend 57 E10
Mawgan Corn 2 D6
Mawgan Porth Corn 5 B7
Maw Green Ches E 168 D2
Mawla Corn 4 F4
Mawnan Corn 3 D7
Mawnan Smith Corn 3 D7
Mawsley N Nhants 120 B6
Mawson Green
  S Yorks 198 D6
Mawthorpe Lincs 191 G7
Maxey Pboro 138 B2
Maxstoke Warks 134 F4
Maxted Street Kent 54 E6
Maxton Borders 262 C4
  Kent 55 E10
Maxwellheugh
  Borders 262 C6
Maxwelltown
  Dumfries 237 B11
Maxworthy Corn 11 C11
Mayals Swansea 56 C6
May Bank Staffs 168 F5
Maybole S Ayrs 257 G8
Maybury Sur 50 B4
Maybush Soton 32 E5
Mayer's Green
  W Mid 133 E10
Mayes Green Sur 50 F6
Mayeston Pembs 73 E8
Mayfair London 67 C9
Mayfield
  E Sus 37 B9
  Midloth 271 C7
  Northumb 243 B7
  Staffs 169 F11
  W Loth 269 B8
Mayford Sur 50 B3
Mayhill Swansea 56 C6
May Hill Mon 79 C8
May Hill Village Glos 98 G4
Mayland Essex 88 E6
Maylandsea Essex 88 E6
Maynard's Green
  E Sus 23 B9
Mayne Ho Moray 302 C2
Mayon Corn 1 D3
Maypole Kent 68 E4
  Kent 71 G7
  London 68 G3
  Mon 79 B7
  Scilly 1 G4
Maypole Green
  Essex 107 G9
  Norf 143 D8
  Suff 125 F8
  Suff 126 D5
Mays Green Oxon 65 C8
May's Green N Som 59 G11
  Sur 50 B5
Mayshill S Glos 61 C7
Maythorn S Yorks 197 F7
Maythorne Notts 171 D11
Maywick Shetland 313 L5
Mead Devon 13 G11
  Devon 24 D2
Mead End Hants 19 B11
  Hants 33 E11
  Wilts 31 C8
Meadgate Bath 45 B7
Meadle Bucks 84 D4
Meadowbank
  Ches W 167 B11
  Edin 280 G5
Meadowend Essex 106 C4
Meadowfield
  Durham 233 D10
Meadowfoot N Ayrs 266 F4
Meadow Green
  Hereford 116 F4
Meadow Hall
  S Yorks 186 C5
Meadow Head
  S Yorks 186 E4
Meadowley Shrops 132 E3
Meadowmill E Loth 281 G8
Meadows
  Nottingham 153 B11
Meadowtown
  Shrops 130 C6
Meads E Sus 23 F10
Meadside Oxon 83 G9
Mead Vale Sur 51 D9
Meadwell Devon 12 E4
Meaford Staffs 151 B7
Meagill N Yorks 205 B9
Mealabost W Isles 304 E6
Mealabost Bhuirgh
  W Isles 304 C6
Mealasta W Isles 304 F1
Meal Bank Cumb 221 F10
Meal Hill W Yorks 197 F7
Mealrigg Cumb 229 B8
Mealsgate Cumb 229 C10
Meanwood
  W Yorks 205 F11
Mearbeck N Yorks 212 G6
Meare Som 44 E3
Meare Green Som 28 B4
  Som 28 C3
Mearns Bath 45 B7
  E Renf 267 D10
Mears Ashby
  N Nhants 120 D6
Measborough Dike
  S Yorks 197 F11
Measham Leics 152 G6
Meath Green Sur 51 E9
Meathop Cumb 211 C8
Meaux E Yorks 209 F7
Meaver Corn 2 F5
Meavy Devon 7 B10
Medbourne Leics 136 E5
  M Keynes 102 D6
Medburn Northumb 242 C4
Meddon Devon 24 D3
Meden Vale Notts 171 B9
Medhurst Row Kent 52 D3
Medlam Lincs 174 D4
Medlar Lancs 202 F4
Medlicott Shrops 131 E8
Medlyn Corn 2 C6
Medmenham Bucks 65 C10
Medomsley Durham 242 G4
Medstead Hants 49 F7
Meerbrook Staffs 169 C7
Meer Common
  Hereford 115 G7
Meer End W Mid 118 C4
Meerhay Dorset 29 G7
Meers Bridge Lincs 191 D7
Meersbrook S Yorks 186 E5
Meesden Herts 105 E8
Meeson Telford 150 E3
Meeson Heath
  Telford 150 E3
Meeth Devon 25 F8
Meethe Devon 25 C11
Meeting Green Suff 124 F4
Meeting House Hill
  Norf 160 D6
Meggernie Castle
  Perth 285 C9
Meggethead
  Borders 260 E5
Meidrim Carms 92 G5
Meifod Denb 165 D8
  Powys 148 G3
Meigle N Ayrs 266 B3
  Perth 286 C6
Meikle Earnock
  S Lanark 268 E4
Meikle Ferry Highld 309 L7
Meikle Forter
  Angus 292 G3
Meikle Gluich
  Highld 309 L6
Meikle Obney Perth 286 D4
Meikleour Perth 286 D5
Meikle Pinkerton
  E Loth 282 F4
Meikle Strath
  Aberds 293 F8
Meikle Tarty Aberds 303 G9
Meikle Wartle
  Aberds 303 F7
Meinciau Carms 75 C7
Meir Stoke 168 G6
Meir Heath Staffs 168 G6
Melbourn Cambs 105 C7
Melbourne Derbys 153 D7
  E Yorks 207 E11
  S Lanark 269 G11
Melbury Abbas
  Dorset 30 D5
Melbury Bubb Dorset 29 F9
Melbury Osmond
  Dorset 29 F9
Melbury Sampford
  Dorset 29 F9
Melby Shetland 313 H3
Melchbourne
  Bedford 121 D10
Melcombe Som 43 G9
Melcombe Bingham
  Dorset 30 G3
Melcombe Regis
  Dorset 17 E9
Meldon Devon 13 C7
  Northumb 252 G4
Meldreth Cambs 105 B7
Meldrum Ho Aberds 303 G8
Melfort Argyll 275 B9
Melgarve Highld 290 D6
Meliden = *Gallt Melyd*
  Denb 181 E9
Melinbyrhedyn
  Powys 128 D6
Melin Caiach Caerph 77 F10
Melincourt Neath 76 E4
Melincryddan Neath 57 B8
Melinsey Corn 3 B10
Melin-y-coed
  Conwy 164 C4
Melin-y-ddôl
  Powys 129 B11
Melin-y-grug
  Powys 129 B11
Melin-y-Wig Denb 165 F8
Melkington
  Northumb 273 G7
Melkinthorpe Cumb 231 F7
Melkridge Northumb 240 E6
Melksham Wilts 62 G2
Melksham Forest
  Wilts 62 G2
Mellangaun Highld 307 L3
Mellangoose Corn 2 D5
Melldalloch Argyll 275 F10
Mell Green W Berks 64 D3
Mellguards Cumb 230 B4
Melling Lancs 211 E11
  Mers 193 G11
Mellingey Corn 10 G4
Melling Mount
  Mers 194 G2
Mellis Suff 126 C2
Mellis Green Suff 125 C11
Mellon Charles
  Highld 307 K3
Mellon Udrigle
  Highld 307 K3
Mellor Gtr Man 185 D7
  Lancs 203 G9
Mellor Brook Lancs 203 G8
Mells
  Som 45 D8
  Suff 127 B8
Mells Green Som 45 D8
Melmerby Cumb 231 D8
  N Yorks 213 B11
  N Yorks 214 D6
Melon Green Suff 124 F6
Melplash Dorset 16 B5
Melrose Borders 262 C2
Melsetter Orkney 314 H2
Melsonby N Yorks 224 D3
Meltham W Yorks 196 E6
Meltham Mills
  W Yorks 196 E6
Melton E Yorks 200 B3
  Suff 126 G5
Meltonby E Yorks 207 C11
Melton Constable
  Norf 159 C10
Melton Mowbray
  Leics 154 F5
Melton Ross
  N Lincs 200 E5
Melvaig Highld 307 L2
Melverley Shrops 148 F6
Melverley Green
  Shrops 148 F6
Melvich Highld 310 C2
Membland Devon 7 F11
Membury Devon 28 G3
Memsie Aberds 303 C9
Memus Angus 287 B8
Mena Corn 5 C10
Menabilly Corn 5 E11
Menadarva Corn 4 G2
Menagissey Corn 4 F4
Menai Bridge = *Porthaethwy*
  Anglesey 179 G9
Mendham Suff 142 G5
Mendlesham Suff 126 D2
Mendlesham Green
  Suff 125 E11
Menethorpe
  N Yorks 216 F5
Mengham Hants 21 B10
Menheniot Corn 6 C5
Menherion Corn 2 B6
Menithwood Worcs 116 D4
Menna Corn 5 E8
Mennock Dumfries 247 B8
Menston W Yorks 205 E9
Menstrie Clack 278 B6
Mentmore Bucks 84 B6
Menzion Borders 260 E3
Meoble Highld 295 G9
Meole Brace Shrops 149 G9
Meols Mers 182 C2
Meon Hants 33 G8
Meonstoke Hants 33 D10
Meopham Kent 68 F6
Meopham Green
  Kent 68 F6
Meopham Station
  Kent 68 F6
Mepal Cambs 139 G8
Meppershall
  C Beds 104 D2
Merbach Hereford 96 B6
Mercaton Derbys 170 G3
Merchant Fields
  W Yorks 197 B7
Merchiston Edin 280 G4
Mere Ches E 184 E2
  Wilts 45 G10
Mere Brow Lancs 194 D2
Mereclough Lancs 204 G3
Mere Green W Mid 134 D2
  Worcs 117 E9
Merehead Wrex 149 B9
Mere Heath
  Ches W 183 G11
Meresborough
  Medway 69 G10
Mereside Blackpool 202 G2
Meretown Staffs 150 E5
Mereworth Kent 53 C7
Mergie Aberds 293 E9
Meriden Herts 85 F10
  W Mid 134 G4
Merkadale Highld 294 B5
Merkland Dumfries 237 B9
  N Ayrs 256 B2
  S Ayrs 244 E6
Merkland Lodge
  Highld 309 G4
Merle Common Sur 52 D2
Merley BCP 18 B6
Merlin's Bridge
  Pembs 72 C6
Merlin's Cross Pembs 73 E7
Merridale W Mid 133 D7
Merridge Som 43 G8
Merrie Gardens IoW 21 E7
Merrifield Devon 8 F6
Merrifield *continued*
  Devon 24 G3
Merrington Shrops 149 E9
Merrion Pembs 72 F6
Merriott Dorset 16 B6
  Som 28 E6
Merriottsford Som 28 E6
Merritown BCP 19 B8
Merrivale Devon 12 F6
  Hereford 98 G2
Merrow Sur 50 C4
Merrybent Darl 224 C4
Merry Field Hill
  Dorset 31 G8
Merry Hill Herts 85 G10
  W Mid 133 D7
Merryhill Green
  Wokingham 65 E9
Merrylee E Renf 267 D11
Merry Lees Leics 135 B9
Merrymeet Corn 6 B5
Merry Meeting Corn 11 G7
Merry Oak Soton 32 E6
Mersham Kent 54 F5
Merstham Sur 51 C9
Merston W Sus 22 C5
Merstone IoW 20 E6
Merther Corn 5 G7
Merther Lane Corn 5 G7
Merthyr Carms 93 G7
Merthyr Cynog
  Powys 95 D9
Merthyr-Dyfan
  V Glam 58 F6
Merthyr Mawr
  Bridgend 57 F11
Merthyr Tydfil
  M Tydf 77 D8
Merthyr Vale M Tydf 77 F9
Merton Devon 25 E8
  London 67 E9
  Norf 141 D8
  Oxon 83 B9
Merton Park London 67 F9
Mervinslaw Borders 262 G5
Meshaw Devon 26 D3
Messing Essex 88 B5
Messingham
  N Lincs 199 G11
Mesty Croft W Mid 133 E9
Mesur-y-dorth
  Pembs 87 E11
Metal Bridge
  Durham 233 E11
Metfield Suff 142 G5
Metherell Corn 7 B8
Metheringham
  Lincs 173 C9
Methersgate Suff 108 B5
Methil Fife 281 B7
Methilhill Fife 281 B7
Methlem Gwyn 144 C3
Methley W Yorks 197 B11
Methley Junction
  W Yorks 197 B11
Methley Lanes
  W Yorks 197 B11
Methlick Aberds 303 F8
Methven Perth 286 E4
Methwold Norf 140 E4
Methwold Hythe
  Norf 140 E4
Mettingham Suff 143 F7
Metton Norf 160 B3
Mevagissey Corn 5 G10
Mewith Head
  N Yorks 212 F4
Mexborough
  S Yorks 187 B7
Mey Highld 310 B6
Meyrick Park BCP 19 C7
Meysey Hampton
  Glos 81 F10
Miabhag W Isles 305 H2
  W Isles 305 J3
Miabhig W Isles 304 E2
Mial Highld 299 B7
Michaelchurch
  Hereford 97 F10
Michaelchurch Escley
  Hereford 96 E6
Michaelchurch on Arrow
  Powys 114 G4
Michaelston-le-Pit
  V Glam 59 E7
Michaelston-y-Fedw
  Newport 59 C8
Michaelstow Corn 11 F7
Michealston-super-Ely
  Cardiff 58 D6
Michelcombe Devon 8 B3
Micheldever Hants 48 F4
Michelmersh Hants 32 B4
Mickfield Suff 126 E2
Micklebring
  S Yorks 187 C8
Mickleby N Yorks 226 C6
Micklefield Bucks 84 G5
  W Yorks 206 G4
Micklefield Green
  Herts 85 F8
Mickleham Sur 51 C7
Micklehurst
  Gtr Man 196 G3
Mickleover Derby 152 C6
Micklethwaite
  Cumb 239 G7
  W Yorks 205 E8
Mickleton Durham 232 G5
  Glos 100 C3
Mickletown
  W Yorks 197 B11
Mickle Trafford
  Ches W 166 B6
Mickley Derbys 186 F4
  N Yorks 214 D5
  Shrops 150 C2
Mickley Green Suff 124 F6
Mickley Square
  Northumb 242 E3
Midanbury Hants 33 E7
Mid Ardlaw Aberds 303 C9

Mid Auchinleck
  Invclyd. 276 G6
Midbea Orkney. 314 B4
Mid Beltie Aberds. 293 C8
Mid Calder W Loth. . . .269 B11
Middle Assendon
  Oxon 65 B8
Middle Aston Oxon. . . .101 F9
Middle Balnald
  Perth 286 B4
Middle Barton Oxon. . .101 F9
Middle Bickenhill
  W Mid 134 G4
Middlebie Dumfries. . .238 B6
Middle Bockhampton
  BCP 19 B9
Middle Bourne Sur . .49 E10
Middle Bridge
  N Som 60 D3
Middle Burnham
  Som 43 D10
Middle Cairncake
  Aberds. 303 E8
Middlecave N Yorks . .216 E5
Middle Chinnock
  Som 29 E7
Middle Claydon
  Bucks. 102 F4
Middle Cliff Staffs . .169 E8
Middlecliffe S Yorks . .198 F2
Middlecott Devon. 13 C10
  Devon 24 F6
  Devon 26 F3
Middle Crackington
  Corn. 11 B9
Middlecroft Derbys . .186 G6
Middle Drums
  Angus 287 B9
Middle Duntisbourne
  Glos. 81 D7
Middlefield Falk 279 E7
Middleforth Green
  Lancs 194 B4
Middle Green Bucks .66 C4
  Som 27 D10
  Suff 124 D4
Middleham N Yorks . .214 B2
Middle Handley
  Derbys. 186 F6
Middle Harling Norf .141 F9
Middle Herrington
  T&W 243 G9
Middlehill Corn. 6 B5
  Wilts 61 F10
Middle Hill Pembs . .73 C7
  Staffs 133 B9
Middlehope Shrops . .131 F9
Middle Kames
  Argyll. 275 E10
Middle Littleton
  Worcs 99 B11
Middle Luxton Devon. 28 E2
Middle Madeley
  Staffs 168 F3
Middle Maes-coed
  Hereford 96 E6
Middlemarsh Dorset. 29 F11
Middle Marwood
  Devon 40 F4
Middle Mayfield
  Staffs 169 G10
Middle Mill Pembs . .87 F11
Middlemoor Devon . . .12 G5
Middlemuir Aberds . .303 D9
  Aberds. 303 E8
  Aberds. 303 G9
Middleport Stoke . . .168 F5
Middle Quarter Kent. 53 F11
Middle Rainton
  T&W 234 B2
Middle Rasen Lincs .189 D9
Middlerig Falk. 279 F8
Middle Rigg Perth . .286 G4
Middle Rocombe
  Devon 9 B8
Middlesbrough
  Mbro 234 G5
Middlesceugh Cumb .230 C4
Middleshaw Cumb . .211 B11
Middle Side Durham. .232 F4
Middlesmoor
  N Yorks 213 G11
Middle Stoford Som. .27 C11
Middle Stoke Devon. . .13 G8
  Medway. 69 D10
  W Mid 119 B7
Middlestone
  Durham 233 E11
Middlestone Moor
  Durham 233 E10
Middle Stoughton
  Som 44 D2
Middlestown
  W Yorks 197 D9
Middle Strath
  W Loth 279 G8
Middle Street Glos. . . .80 E3
Middle Taphouse Corn. 6 C3
Middlethird Borders .272 G3
Middlethorpe York. . .207 D7
Middleton Aberds. . .293 B10
  Argyll. 288 E1
  Cumb. 212 B3
  Derbys. 169 C11
  Derbys. 170 D3
  Essex. 107 D7
  Gtr Man 195 F11
  Hants. 48 E4
  Hereford 115 D10
  Hrtlpl. 234 E6
  IoW 20 D2
  Lancs 202 B4
  Midloth 271 D7
  N Nhants 136 H1
  Norf 158 F3
  Northumb 252 H1
  Northumb 264 B4
  N Yorks. 204 E5
  N Yorks. 205 D8

Middleton continued
  N Yorks. 216 B5
  Perth 286 C5
  Perth 286 F2
  Perth 286 G5
  Shrops. 115 B10
  Shrops. 130 D5
  Shrops. 148 B6
  Suff 127 D8
  Swansea 56 D2
  Warks 134 D3
  W Yorks 197 B10
Middleton Baggot
  Shrops. 132 E2
Middleton Cheney
  W Nhants 101 C9
Middleton Green
  Staffs 151 B9
Middleton Hall
  Northumb 263 D11
Middleton-in-Teesdale
  Durham 232 F4
Middleton Junction
  Gtr Man 195 G11
Middleton Moor
  Suff 127 D8
Middleton of Rora
  Aberds. 303 E10
Middleton One Row
  Darl 225 C7
Middleton-on-Leven
  N Yorks. 225 D9
Middleton-on-Sea
  W Sus 35 G7
Middleton on the Hill
  Hereford 115 D10
Middleton-on-the-
  Wolds E Yorks 208 D4
Middleton Place
  Cumb 219 G11
Middleton Priors
  Shrops. 132 E2
Middleton Quernhow
  N Yorks. 214 D6
Middleton St George
  Darl 224 C6
Middleton Scriven
  Shrops. 132 F3
Middleton Stoney
  Oxon 101 G10
Middleton Tyas
  N Yorks. 224 D4
Middletown Cumb . .219 D9
  N Som 60 B4
  Powys 148 G6
  Warks 117 E11
Middle Town Scilly . . .1 F4
Middle Tysoe Warks .100 C6
Middle Wallop Hants. .47 F9
Middle Weald
  M Keynes 102 D5
Middlewich
  Ches E. 167 B11
Middlewick Wilts 61 E11
Middle Wick Glos. 80 F2
Middle Winterslow
  Wilts 47 G8
Middlewood Ches E .184 E6
  Corn. 11 F1
  S Yorks 186 C4
Middle Woodford
  Wilts 46 F6
Middlewood Green
  Suff 125 E11
Middleyard Glos. 80 E4
Middlezoy Som. 43 G11
Middridge Durham .233 F11
Midelney Som. 28 C6
Midfield Highld 308 C5
Midford Bath 61 G9
Midgard Borders . . .262 F3
Mid Garrary
  Dumfries 237 B7
Midge Hall Lancs . . .194 C4
Midgeholme W Yorks .196 B3
Midgeholme Cumb . .240 F4
Midgham W Berks. . . .64 F5
Midgham Green
  W Berks 64 F5
Midgley W Yorks 196 B4
  W Yorks 197 D9
Mid Holmwood Sur . .51 D7
Midhopestones
  S Yorks 186 B2
Midhurst W Sus 34 C5
Mid Lambrook Som . .28 D6
Midland Orkney. 314 F3
Mid Lavant W Sus 22 B5
Midlem Borders 262 D2
Mill Farm Aberds. . . .303 C8
Midlock S Lanark . . .259 E11
Mid Main Highld . . .300 F4
Midmar Aberds. 293 C8
Midmuir Argyll. 289 G11
Mid Murthat
  Dumfries 248 D3
Midpark Argyll. 255 B11
Midplaugh Aberds . .302 E5
Midsomer Norton
  Bath 45 C7
Midton Invclyd. 276 F4
Midtown Highld 307 L3
  Highld 308 C5
Midtown of Buchromb
  Moray 302 E2
Midtown of Glass
  Aberds. 302 E4
Mid Urchany Highld .301 E8
Midville Lincs. 174 D5
Mid Walls Shetland. .313 H4
Midway Ches E. 184 E6
  Som. 45 D7
Mid Yell Shetland. . .312 D7
Miekle Toux Aberds. .302 D5
Migdale Highld 309 K6
Migvie Aberds. 292 C6
Milarrochy Stirling. .277 C8
Milber Devon 14 G3
Milbourne Northumb .242 B4
  Wilts 62 B2
Milburn Aberds. 302 E5
  Aberds. 302 F6
  Cumb. 231 F9
Milbury Heath
  S Glos. 79 G11
Milby N Yorks 215 F8
Milch Hill Essex. . . .106 G4
  Oxon 101 E8
Milcombe Corn 6 D4
Milden Suff. 107 B9
Mildenhall Suff. 124 C4
  Wilts 63 F8
Mile Cross Norf. 160 G4
Mile Elm Wilts 62 F3
Mile End Cambs. . . .140 G2
  Devon 14 G2
  Essex. 107 F9
  Glos 79 C9
  London. 67 C11
  Suff 124 G6
Mileham Norf 159 F8
Mile Oak Brighton . . .36 F2
  Kent. 53 E7
  Shrops. 148 D6
  Staffs 134 C3
Miles Green Staffs . .168 F4
  Sur. 50 B3
Miles Hill W Yorks . .205 F11
Milesmark Fife 279 D11
Miles Platting
  Gtr Man 184 B5
Miles's Green
  W Berks 64 F4
Mile Town Kent. 70 E2
Milfield Northumb . .263 C10
Milford Derbys. 170 F5
  Devon 24 C2
  Powys 129 E11
  Shrops. 149 E8
  Staffs 151 E9
  Sur. 50 E2
  Wilts 31 B1
Milford Haven Pembs .72 D6
Milford on Sea
  Hants. 19 C11
Milkhouse Water
  Wilts 63 G7
Milkieston Borders . .270 F4
Milkwall Glos. 79 D9
Milkwell Wilts 30 C6
Milland W Sus 34 B4
Millarston Renfs . . .267 C9
Millbank Aberds . . .303 E11
  Highld 310 C5
  Kent. 71 F8
Mill Bank W Yorks . .196 C4
Millbeck Cumb. 229 F11
Millbounds Orkney. .314 C5
Millbreck Aberds. . .303 E10
Millbridge Sur. 49 E10
Millbrook C Beds . . .103 D10
  Corn. 7 E8
  Devon 41 G9
  Gtr Man 185 B7
  Soton. 32 E5
Millburn S Ayrs 257 D10
Millcombe Devon 8 F6
Mill Common Norf . .142 C6
  Suff 143 G8
Mill Corner E Sus . . .38 C4
Mill Dam N Yorks . . .212 F3
Millden Lodge
  Angus 293 F7
Milldens Angus 287 B9
Millend Glos. 80 D3
  Glos 80 F3
Mill End Bucks. 65 C9
  Cambs 124 F3
  Glos 81 C10
  Herts 85 G8
  Herts 104 E6
Mill End Green
  Essex. 106 F2
Millendreath Corn 6 E5
Millerhill Midloth . .270 B6
Miller's Dale
  Derbys. 185 G10
Miller's Green
  Derbys. 170 E3
  Essex. 87 D9
Millersneuk E Dunb .278 G3
Millerston Glasgow. .268 B2
Mill Green Aberds. . .303 C8
  Cambs 123 E9
  Cumb. 211 C10
  Cumb. 240 E3
  Derbys. 152 D6
  Dumfries 236 D4
  Dumfries 237 B10
  Dumfries 247 G8
  Essex. 87 E10
  Hants. 64 G4
  Herts 86 D2
  Norf 142 G2
  Shrops. 150 D3
  Suff 107 C9
  Suff 125 F9
  Suff 126 E3
  W Mid 133 C11
Millhalf Hereford. . . .96 B5
Millhall Kent. 53 B8
Mill Hall Dumfries . .237 E8
Millhayes Devon 27 E10
  Devon 28 G2
Millhead Lancs 211 E9
Millheugh S Lanark .268 E5
Millhill Devon. 12 G5
Mill Hill Blackburn . .195 B7
  Essex. 88 G4
  E Sus 23 D10
  Glos 79 D10
  Gtr Man 195 F4
  Kent. 55 C11
  Lincs 175 D8
  London. 86 G2
  Suff 125 G7
Mill Hills Suff. 108 B5

Mill Hirst N Yorks. . . .214 G3
Millholme Cumb. . . .221 G11
Millhouse Argyll. . . .275 F10
  Cumb. 230 D3
Millhousebridge
  Dumfries 248 F4
Millhouse Green
  S Yorks 197 G8
Millhouses S Yorks . .186 E4
  S Yorks 198 G2
Millikenpark Renfs . .267 C8
Millin Cross Pembs . .73 C7
Millington E Yorks. . .208 C2
Millington Green
  Derbys. 170 F3
Mill Lane Hants. 49 C9
Mill Meads London . .67 C11
Mill Side Cumb 211 C8
Mile Street Kent. 53 B7
  Norf 159 F11
  Suff 107 D9
Mill of Brydock
  Aberds. 302 D6
Mill of Chon Stirling .285 G8
Mill of Haldane
  W Dunb 277 E8
Mill of Kingoodie
  Aberds. 303 G8
Mill of Lynebain
  Aberds. 302 F4
Mill of Muiresk
  Aberds. 302 E6
Mill of Rango
  Orkney 314 E2
Mill of Sterin
  Aberds. 292 D5
Mill of Uras Aberds. .293 E10
Millom Cumb 210 C3
Millook Corn 11 B9
Millow C Beds. 104 C4
Mill Place N Lincs . .200 F3
Millpool Corn. 2 C3
  Corn. 11 G8
Mill Shaw W Yorks . .205 G11
Mill Side Cumb 211 C8
Mill Street Kent. 53 B7
  Norf 159 F11
  Suff 107 D9
Milltack Aberds. 303 D7
Millthorpe Derbys . .186 F4
  Lincs 156 C2
Mill Throop BCP 19 B8
Millthrop Cumb 222 F3
Milltimber
  Aberdeen. 293 C10
Milltown Aberds 292 C4
  Corn. 6 B2
  Corn. 6 D2
  Derbys. 170 C5
  Devon 40 F5
  Highld 301 D7
  Highld 301 E9
Milltown of Aberdalgie
  Perth 286 E4
Milltown of Auchindoun
  Moray 302 E2
Milltown of Craigston
  Aberds. 303 D7
Milltown of Edinvillie
  Moray 302 E2
Milltown of Kildrummy
  Aberds. 292 B6
Milltown of Rothiemay
  Moray 302 E5
Milltown of Towie
  Aberds. 292 B6
Millwall London 67 D11
Millnafort Perth. . . .286 G5
Milner's Heath
  Ches W 167 C7
Milngavie E Dunb . .277 G11
Millnquarter Falk. . .278 F6
Milnrow Gtr Man . . .196 E2
Milnsbridge
  W Yorks 196 D6
Milnshaw Lancs 195 B9
Milnthorpe Cumb . . .211 C9
  W Yorks 197 D10
Milo S Ayrs. 75 B9
Milson Shrops 116 C2
Milstead Kent. 54 B2
Milston Wilts 47 D7
Milton Angus 287 C7
  Angus 292 E6
  Cambs 123 E9
  Cumb. 211 C10
  Cumb. 240 E3
  Derbys. 152 D6
  Dumfries 236 D4
  Dumfries 237 B10
  Dumfries 247 G8
  Fife 287 E8
  Glasgow 267 B11
  Highld 299 E7
  Highld 300 D3
  Highld 300 E5
  Highld 300 F4
  Highld 301 B7
  Highld 301 D7
  Highld 310 D7
  Kent. 69 E7
  Moray 292 B3
  Moray 302 C5
  Notts 188 G4
  N Som 59 G10
  Oxon 83 G7
  Oxon 101 E8
  Pembs 73 D8
  Perth 286 F3
  Ptsmth. 21 B9
  Som. 29 C7
  Stirling 285 G9
  Stoke 168 E6
  S Yorks 197 G11
  W Dunb 277 G8
  Wilts 45 G11

Milton Abbas Dorset. .30 G4
Millbrook BCP 19 C7
Milton Bridge
  Midloth 270 C4
Milton Bryan
  C Beds. 103 E9
Milton Clevedon Som. 45 F7
Milton Coldwells
  Aberds. 303 F9
Milton Combe Devon . .7 B9
Milton Coombe Devon. .7 B9
Milton Damerel
  Devon 24 E5
  Derbys. 170 F3
Miltonduff Moray . . .301 C11
Milton End Glos. 80 C2
  Glos 81 E10
Milton Ernest
  Bedford 121 F10
Milton Green
  Ches W. 167 D7
  Devon 8 D2
Milton Heights Oxon. .83 G7
Miltonhill Moray . . .301 C10
Milton Hill Devon . . .14 F4
  Oxon 83 G7
Milton Keynes
  M Keynes. 103 D7
Milton Keynes Village
  M Keynes. 103 D7
Milton Lilbourne
  Wilts 63 G7
Milton Malsor
  W Nhants 120 F4
Milton Morenish
  Perth 285 D10
Milton of Auchinhove
  Aberds. 293 C7
Milton of Balgonie
  Fife 287 G7
Milton of Buchanan
  Stirling 277 C8
Milton of Campfield
  Aberds. 293 C7
Milton of Campsie
  E Dunb 278 F3
Milton of Corsindae
  Aberds. 293 C8
Milton of Cullerlie
  Aberds. 293 C9
Milton of Cultoquhey
  Perth 286 E2
Milton of Cushnie
  Aberds. 293 B7
Milton of Dalcapon
  Perth 286 B2
Milton of Drimmie
  Perth 286 B5
Milton of Edradour
  Perth 286 B3
Milton of Gollanfield
  Highld 301 D7
Milton of Lesmore
  Aberds. 302 G4
Milton of Logie
  Aberds. 292 C6
Milton of Machany
  Perth 286 F3
Milton of Mathers
  Aberds. 293 G9
Milton of Murtle
  Aberdeen. 293 C10
Milton of Noth
  Aberds. 302 G5
Milton of Tullich
  Aberds. 292 D5
Milton on Stour
  Dorset 30 B3
Milton Regis Kent. . . .70 F2
Milton Street E Sus. . .23 E8
Milton under Wychwood
  Oxon 82 B3
Milverton Som. 27 B10
  Warks 118 D6
Milwich Staffs 151 C9
Milwr Flint 181 G11
Mimbridge Sur. 66 G3
Minard Argyll 275 D10
Minard Castle
  Argyll. 275 D10
Minchington Dorset. .31 E7
Minchinhampton
  Glos 80 E5
Mindrum Northumb. .263 C8
Minehead Som 42 D3
Mineshope Corn 11 B9
Minety Wilts 81 G8
Minffordd Gwyn . . .145 B11
  Gwyn 146 G4
  Gwyn 179 G9
Mingarrypark
  Highld 289 C8
Mingoose Corn 4 F4
Miningsby Lincs 174 C4
Minions Corn 11 G11
Minishant S Ayrs . . .257 G8
Minllyn Gwyn. 147 G7
Minnes Aberds 303 G9
Minngearraidh
  W Isles 297 J3
Minnigaff Dumfries. .236 C6
Minnonie Aberds. . . .303 C7
Minnow End Essex. . .88 C2
Minnygap Dumfries. .248 D2
Minshull Vernon
  Ches E. 167 C11
Minskip N Yorks 215 G7
Minstead Hants. 32 E3
Minsted W Sus. 34 C5
Minster Kent 70 E3
  Kent. 71 G10
Minsterley Shrops. . .131 C7
Minster Lovell Oxon. .82 C4
Minsterworth Glos. . .80 B3
Minterne Magna
  Dorset 29 G11
Minterne Parva
  Dorset 29 G11
Minting Lincs 189 G11
Mintlaw Aberds. 303 E10

Minto Borders 262 E3
Minto Kames
  Borders 262 E3
Minton Shrops 131 E8
Mintsfeet Cumb. 221 G10
Minwear Pembs. 73 C8
Minworth W Mid 134 E3
Mirbister Orkney. . . .314 E2
Mirehouse Cumb. . . .219 B9
Mireland Highld. 310 C7
Mirfield W Yorks 197 D8
Miserden Glos. 80 D6
Misery Corner Norf . .142 F5
Miskin Rhondda 58 C4
  Rhondda 77 F8
Misselfore Wilts 31 C8
Misson Notts 187 C11
Misterton Leics 135 G11
  Notts 188 B3
  Som 29 F7
Misterton Soss
  Notts 188 B3
Mistley Essex 108 E2
Mistley Heath Essex. .108 E2
Mitcham London 67 F9
Mitcheldean Glos. . . .79 B11
Mitchell Corn 5 E7
Mitchell Hill
  Borders 260 C3
Mitchellslacks
  Dumfries 247 D11
Mitchelston Borders .271 F9
Mitchel Troy Mon . . .79 C7
Mitcheltroy Common
  Mon 79 D7
Mite Houses Cumb . .219 F11
Mitford Northumb . .252 F5
Mithian Corn 4 E4
Mithian Downs Corn. . .4 F4
Mitton Staffs 151 F7
  Worcs 99 E8
Mixbury Oxon. 102 E2
Mixenden W Yorks . .196 B5
Mixtow Corn. 6 E2
Moat Cumb 239 C10
Moats Tye Suff 125 F10
Mobberley Ches E . .184 F3
  Staffs 169 G8
Moblake Ches E. . . .167 G11
Mobwell Bucks. 84 E5
Moccas Hereford. . . .97 C7
Mochdre Conwy 180 F4
  Powys 129 F11
Mochrum Dumfries. .236 E5
Mockbeggar Hants . .31 F11
  Kent. 54 E6
  Medway. 69 E8
Mockerkin Cumb. . . .229 G7
Moclett Orkney. 314 B4
Modbury Devon. 8 E3
Moddershall Staffs. .151 B8
Model Village
  Derbys. 187 G8
  Warks 119 E8
Modest Corner Kent. .52 E5
Moelfre Anglesey. . .179 D8
  Conwy 181 G7
  Powys 147 E11
Moel Tryfan Gwyn . .163 D8
Moel-y-crio Flint . . .165 B11
Moffat Dumfries. . . .248 B3
Moffat Mills
  N Lanark 268 C5
Mogador Sur. 51 C8
Moggerhanger
  C Beds. 104 B2
Mogworthy Devon . . .26 D5
Moira Leics. 152 F6
Moity Powys 96 C3
Molash Kent. 54 C4
Mol-chlach Highld . .294 D6
Mold Flint 166 C2
Moldgreen W Yorks. .197 D7
Molehill Green
  Essex. 105 G11
  Essex. 106 G4
Molescroft E Yorks . .208 E6
Molesden Northumb. .252 G4
Molesworth Cambs. .121 B11
Molinnis Corn. 5 D10
Moll Highld 295 B7
Molland Devon. 26 B4
Mollington Ches W. .182 G5
  Oxon 101 B8
Mollinsburn
  N Lanark 278 G4
Monachty Ceredig. .111 E10
Monachylemore
  Stirling 285 F8
Monar Lodge Highld. .300 D1
Monaughty Powys . .114 D4
Monboddo House
  Aberds. 293 F9
Mondaytown Shrops .130 B6
Mondynes Aberds . . .293 F9
Monemore Stirling . .285 D9
Monevechadan
  Argyll. 284 G5
Monewden Suff. 126 F4
Moneyacres E Ayrs. .267 E8
Moneydie Perth. 286 E4
Moneyhill Herts 85 G8
Money Hill Leics . . .153 F7
Moneyrow Green
  Windsor. 65 D11
Moneystone Staffs . .169 F9
Mongleath Corn 3 C7
Moniaive Dumfries. .247 E7
Monifieth Angus 287 D8
Monikie Angus. 287 D8
Monimail Fife 286 F6
Monington Pembs . . .92 C2
Monk Bretton
  S Yorks 197 F11
Monken Hadley
  London. 86 F3
Monkerton Devon . . .14 C5
Monk Fryston
  N Yorks 198 B4
Monk Hesleden
  Durham 234 D5

Monkhide Hereford . .98 C2
Monkhill Cumb 239 F8
  W Yorks 198 C3
Monkhopton Shrops .132 E2
Monkland Hereford . .115 F9
Monkleigh Devon. . . .25 C7
Monkmoor Shrops .149 G10
Monknash V Glam. . . .58 E2
Monkokehampton
  Devon 25 F9
Monkscross Corn . . .12 G3
Monkseaton T&W . . .243 C8
Monks Eleigh Suff . .107 B9
Monk's Gate W Sus . .36 G2
Monks Heath
  Ches E. 184 G4
Monk Sherborne
  Hants. 48 B6
Monkshill Aberds . . .303 E7
Monks Hill Kent. 53 E11
Monksilver Som 42 F5
Monks Kirby Warks .135 G9
Monk Soham Suff. . .126 D4
Monks Orchard
  London. 67 F11
Monk's Park Wilts . . .61 E11
Monkspath W Mid. .118 B2
Monks Risborough
  Bucks. 84 E4
Monkthorpe Lincs . .174 B6
Monkston Park
  M Keynes 103 D7
Monk Street Essex . .106 F2
Monkswood Mon. . .270 C6
Monk Street Essex. . .106 F2
Monkton Devon. 27 G11
  Kent. 71 G9
  Pembs 73 E7
  S Ayrs 257 D9
  T&W 243 E8
  V Glam 58 E2
Monkton Combe
  Bath 61 G9
Monkton Deverill
  Wilts 45 F11
Monkton Farleigh
  Wilts 61 F10
Monktonhall E Loth . .280 G6
Monkton Heathfield
  Som 28 B3
Monkton Up Wimborne
  Dorset 31 E8
Monkwearmouth
  T&W 243 F9
Monkwood Hants 49 G7
Monkwood Green
  Worcs 116 E6
Monmarsh Hereford. .97 B10
Monmore Green
  W Mid 133 D8
Monmouth = Trefynwy
  Mon. 79 C9
Monmouth Cap Mon .97 F7
Monnington on Wye
  Hereford 97 C7
Monreith Dumfries. .236 E5
Monreith Mains
  Dumfries 236 E5
Montacute Som. 29 D7
Montcliffe Gtr Man . .195 E7
Montcoffer Ho
  Aberds. 302 C6
Montford Argyll. . . .266 C2
  Shrops. 149 G8
Montford Bridge
  Shrops. 149 F8
Montgarrie Aberds . .293 B7
Montgomery Powys .130 D4
Montgomery Lines
  Hants. 49 C11
Monton Gtr Man 184 B3
Montpelier Bristol . . .60 E5
Montrose Angus 287 B11
Montsale Essex. 89 F8
Monwode Lea
  Warks 134 E5
Monxton Hants 47 E10
Monyash Derbys 169 B11
Monymusk Aberds . .293 B8
Monzie Perth 286 E2
Monzie Castle Perth .286 E2
Moodiesburn
  N Lanark 278 G3
Moolham Som. 28 E5
Moon's Green Kent . .38 B5
Moon's Moat
  Worcs 117 D11
Moonzie Fife 287 F7
Moor Som. 28 D6
Mooradale Shetland. .312 F6
Moor Allerton
  W Yorks 205 F11
Mooray Wilts 46 G3
Moorby Lincs. 174 C3
Moorclose Cumb. . . .228 F5
  Gtr Man 195 F11
Moor Common Bucks .84 G4
Moorcot Hereford. . .115 F7
Moor Crichel Dorset. .31 F7
Moor Cross Devon . . .8 D2
Moordown BCP. 19 C7
Moore Halton 183 E9
Moorend Cumb 239 G8
  Derbys. 170 D2
  Dumfries 239 C7
  Glos 80 C5
  Glos 80 D2
  Glos 81 D7
  S Glos. 61 D7
  W Yorks 205 G8
Moor End Bucks. 84 G4
  Cambs 105 B7
  C Beds. 103 G9
  Durham 234 C2
  E Yorks. 208 F2
  Glos 99 G9
  Lancs 202 E5
  N Yorks. 207 F7
  N Yorks. 215 G7
  S Yorks 197 G9

Moor End continued
  Worcs 117 F8
  W Yorks 196 B5
  W Yorks 206 D4
  York 207 B9
Moorends
  Hereford 98 B4
Moorend Cross
  Hereford 98 B4
Moor End Field
  N Yorks 215 F8
Moorends S Yorks . . .199 D7
Moorfield Derbys . . .185 C8
Moorgate Norf. 160 C3
  S Yorks 186 C6
Moorgreen Hants. 33 E7
  Notts 171 F7
Moor Green Herts . . .104 F6
  Staffs 169 G7
  Wilts 61 F11
  W Mid 133 G11
Moorhaigh Notts . . .171 C8
Moorhall Derbys. . . .186 G4
Moor Hall W Mid . . .134 D2
Moorhampton
  Hereford 97 B7
Moorhaven Village
  Devon 8 D3
Moorhayne Devon . . .28 F2
Moorhead W Yorks . .205 F8
Moor Head W Yorks . .197 B8
  W Yorks 197 E8
Moorhey Gtr Man . . .196 G2
Moorhole S Yorks . . .186 E6
Moorhouse Cumb. . .239 F8
  Cumb. 239 G7
  Notts 172 B3
  S Yorks 198 E3
Moorhouse Bank Sur .52 C2
Moorhouses Lincs . .174 D3
Moorland or Northmoor
  Green Som. 43 G10
Moorledge Bath 60 G5
Moorlinch Som 43 F11
Moor Monkton
  N Yorks 206 B6
Moor Monkton Moor
  N Yorks 206 B6
Moor of Balvack
  Aberds. 293 B8
Moor of Granary
  Moray 301 D10
Moor of Ravenstone
  Dumfries 236 E5
Moor Park Cumb. . . .229 D7
  Hereford 97 C9
  Herts 85 G9
  Sur. 49 D11
Moor Row Cumb . . .219 C10
  Cumb. 229 B10
Moorsholm Redcar. .226 C3
Moorside Ches W . . .182 F3
  Dorset 30 D3
  Durham 233 B7
  Gtr Man 195 G9
  Gtr Man 196 F3
  W Yorks 197 B8
  W Yorks 205 F10
Moor Side Lancs. . . .202 F5
  Lancs 202 G4
  Lincs 174 D2
  W Yorks 197 B7
  W Yorks 204 F6
Moorstock Kent 54 F6
Moor Street Kent 69 F10
Moorswater Corn 6 C4
Moorthorpe
  S Yorks 198 E3
Moor Top W Yorks. . .197 C7
Moortown Devon 12 B2
  Devon 12 G6
  Devon 25 C8
  Hants. 31 G11
  IoW 20 E4
  Lincs 189 B9
  Telford 150 F2
  W Yorks 206 F2
Morangie Highld . . .309 L7
Morar Highld 295 C8
Moravian Settlement
  Derbys. 153 B8
Morawelon
  Anglesey 178 E3
Morayhill Highld . . .301 E7
Morborne Cambs . . .138 E2
Morchard Bishop
  Devon 26 G4
Morchard Road
  Devon 26 G3
Morcombelake
  Dorset 16 C4
Morcott Rutland 137 C8
Morda Shrops. 148 D5
Morden Dorset 18 B4
  London. 67 F9
Morden Green
  Cambs 104 C5
Morden Park London. .67 F8
Mordiford Hereford. .97 D11
Mordington Holdings
  Borders 273 D8
Mordon Durham 234 F2
More Shrops. 130 E6
Morebath Devon. 27 C7
Morebattle Borders. .263 E7
Morecambe Lancs . .211 G8
More Crichel Dorset. .31 F7
Moredon Swindon. . . .62 B6
Moredun Edin 270 B5
Morefield Highld . . .307 K6
Morehall Kent. 55 F7
Moreleggan Argyll . .284 G4
Moreleigh Devon 8 E5
Morenish Perth 285 D9
Moresby Cumb. 228 G5
Moresby Parks
  Cumb. 219 B9
Morestead Hants 33 B8
Moreton Dorset. 18 D2
  Essex. 87 D8
  Hereford 115 E10

Moreton *continued*
Mers 182 C3
Oxon 82 E6
Oxon 83 E11
Staffs 150 F5
Staffs 152 D2
Moreton Corbet
Shrops 149 E11
Moretonhampstead
Devon 13 D11
Moreton-in-Marsh
Glos 100 E4
Moreton Jeffries
Hereford 98 B2
Moreton Morrell
Warks 118 F6
Moreton on Lugg
Hereford 97 B10
Moreton Paddox
Warks 118 G6
Moreton Pinkney
W Nhants 101 B11
Moreton Say Shrops 150 C2
Moreton Valence
Glos 80 D3
Moretonwood
Shrops 150 C2
Morfa Carms 56 B4
Carms 75 C9
Ceredig 110 G6
Gwyn 144 C3
Morfa Bach Carms 74 C5
Morfa Bychan
Gwyn 145 B10
Morfa Dinlle Gwyn 162 D6
Morfa Glas Neath 76 D5
Morfa Nefyn Gwyn 162 G3
Morfydd Denb 165 F10
Morganstown Cardiff 58 C6
Morgan's Vale Wilts 31 C11
Moriah Ceredig 112 B2
Mork Glos 79 D9
Morland Cumb 231 G7
Morley Ches E 184 E4
Derbys 170 G5
Durham 233 F8
W Yorks 197 B9
Morley Green
Ches E 184 E4
Morleymoor Derbys 170 G5
Morley Park Derbys 170 F5
Morley St Botolph
Norf 141 D11
Morley Smithy
Derbys 170 G5
Mornick Corn 12 G2
Morningside Edin 280 G3
N Lanark 268 D6
Morningthorpe Norf 142 E4
Morpeth Northumb 252 F6
Morphie Aberds 293 G9
Morrey Staffs 152 F2
Morridge Side
Staffs 169 E8
Morrilow Heath
Staffs 151 B9
Morris Green Essex 106 E4
Morriston = *Treforys*
Swansea 57 B7
Morristown V Glam 59 E7
Morston Norf 177 E8
Mortehoe Devon 40 D3
Morthen S Yorks 187 D7
Mortimer W Berks 65 G7
Mortimer's Cross
Hereford 115 E8
Mortimer West End
Hants 64 G6
Mortlake London 67 D8
Mortomley S Yorks 186 B4
Morton Cumb 230 D4
Cumb 239 G9
Derbys 170 C6
IoW 21 D8
Lincs 155 E11
Lincs 172 C5
Lincs 188 C4
Norf 160 F2
Notts 172 E2
S Glos 79 G10
Shrops 148 E5
Morton Bagot
Warks 118 E2
Morton Common
Shrops 148 E5
Morton Mains
Dumfries 247 D9
Morton Mill Shrops 149 E11
Morton-on-Swale
N Yorks 224 G6
Morton Spirt
Warks 117 G10
Morton Tinmouth
Durham 233 G9
Morton Underhill
Worcs 117 F10
Morvah Corn 1 B4
Morval Corn 6 D5
Morven Lodge
Aberds 292 C5
Morvich Highld 295 C11
Highld 309 J7
Morville Shrops 132 E3
Morville Heath
Shrops 132 E3
Morwellham Quay
Devon 7 B8
Morwenstow Corn 24 E2
Mosborough
S Yorks 186 E6
Moscow E Ayrs 267 G9
Mose Shrops 132 E5
Mosedale Cumb 230 E3
Moseley W Mid 133 D8
W Mid 133 G11
Worcs 116 F6
Moses Gate Gtr Man 195 F8
Mosley Common
Gtr Man 195 G8
Moss Argyll 288 E1
Highld 289 C8
S Yorks 198 E5
Wrex 166 E4
Mossat Aberds 292 B6
Mossbank Shetland 312 F6
Moss Bank Halton 183 D8
Mers 183 B8
Mossbay Cumb 228 F5
Mossblown S Ayrs 257 E10
Mossbrow Gtr Man 184 D2
Mossburnford
Borders 262 F5
Mossdale Dumfries 237 B8
Mossedge Cumb 239 D11
Moss Edge Lancs 202 D4
Lancs 202 E4
Mossend N Lanark 268 C4
Moss End Brack 65 E11
Ches E 183 F11
Mosser Mains Cumb 229 F8
Mossfield Highld 300 B6
Mossgate Staffs 151 B8
Mossgiel E Ayrs 257 D11
Mosshouses Borders 262 B2
Moss Houses
Ches E 184 G5
Mosside Angus 287 B8
Moss Lane Ches E 184 G6
Mossley Ches E 168 C5
Gtr Man 196 G3
Mossley Brow
Gtr Man 196 G3
Mossley Hill Mers 182 D5
Moss Nook Gtr Man 184 D4
Mers 183 C8
Moss of Barmuckity
Moray 302 C2
Moss of Meft Moray 302 C2
Mosspark Glasgow 267 C10
Moss Pit Staffs 151 E8
Moss Side Cumb 238 G5
Gtr Man 184 B4
Moss-side Highld 301 D8
Moss Side
Lancs 193 G11
Lancs 194 C4
Lancs 202 G3
Mers 182 B6
Moss-side Moray 302 D5
Mosstodloch Moray 302 D3
Mosston Angus 287 C9
Mosstown Aberds 303 C10
Mossy Lea Lancs 194 E4
Mosterton Dorset 29 F7
Moston Ches E 168 C2
Ches W 182 G6
Gtr Man 195 G11
Shrops 149 D11
Moston Green
Ches E 168 C2
Mostyn Flint 181 E11
Mostyn Quay Flint 181 E11
Motcombe Dorset 30 B5
Mothecombe Devon 8 F2
Motherby Cumb 230 F4
Motherwell
N Lanark 268 D5
Motspur Park London 67 F8
Mottingham London 68 E2
Mottisfont Hants 32 B4
Mottistone IoW 20 E4
Mottram in Longdendale
Gtr Man 185 B7
Mottram Rise
Gtr Man 185 B7
Mottram St Andrew
Ches E 184 F5
Mott's Green Essex 87 B8
Mott's Mill E Sus 52 F4
Mouldsworth
Ches W 183 G8
Moulin Perth 286 B3
Moulsecoomb
Brighton 36 F4
Moulsford Oxon 64 C5
Moulsham Essex 88 D2
Moulsoe M Keynes 103 C8
Moultavie Highld 300 B6
Moulton
Ches W 167 B11
Lincs 156 E6
N Yorks 224 E4
Suff 124 E3
V Glam 58 E5
W Nhants 120 D5
Moulton Chapel
Lincs 156 F5
Moulton Eaugate
Lincs 156 F6
Moulton Park
W Nhants 120 E5
Moulton St Mary
Norf 143 B7
Moulton Seas End
Lincs 156 D6
Moulzie Angus 292 F4
Mounie Castle
Aberds 303 G7
Mount Corn 4 D5
Corn 6 B2
Highld 301 E9
W Yorks 196 D5
Mountain Anglesey 178 E2
W Yorks 205 G7
Mountain Air
Bl Gwent 77 D11
Mountain Ash = *Aberpennar*
Rhondda 77 F8
Mountain Bower
Wilts 61 D10
Mountain Cross
Borders 270 F2
Mountain Street
Kent 54 C5
Mountain Water
Pembs 91 G8
Mount Ambrose Corn 4 G4
Mount Ballan Mon 60 B3
Mount Batten Plym 7 E9
Mountbenger
Borders 261 D8
Mountbengerburn
Borders 261 D8
Mountblow W Dunb 277 G9
Mount Bovers Essex 88 G4
Mount Bures Essex 107 E8
Mount Canisp
Highld 301 B7
Mount Charles Corn 5 B10
Corn 5 E10
Mount Cowdown
Wilts 47 C9
Mount End Essex 87 E7
Mount Ephraim
E Sus 23 B7
Mounters Dorset 30 D3
Mountfield E Sus 38 C2
Mountgerald Highld 300 C5
Mount Gould Plym 7 D9
Mount Hawke Corn 4 F4
Mount Hermon Corn 2 F6
Sur 50 B4
Mount Hill S Glos 61 E7
Mountjoy Corn 5 C7
Mount Lane Devon 12 B3
Mountnessing Essex 87 F10
Mounton Mon 79 G8
Mount Pleasant
Bucks 102 E3
Ches E 168 D4
Corn 5 C10
Derbys 152 D6
Derbys 152 F5
Derbys 170 F4
Devon 27 G11
Durham 233 E11
E Sus 23 E7
E Sus 36 D6
Flint 182 G2
Hants 19 B11
Kent 71 F10
London 85 G8
M Tydf 77 F9
Neath 57 B9
Norf 141 E9
Pembs 73 D8
Shrops 149 G9
Stockton 234 G4
Stoke 168 G5
Suff 106 B4
T&W 243 E7
Warks 135 F7
Worcs 99 D10
Worcs 117 E10
W Yorks 197 C8
Mount Sion Wrex 166 E3
Mount Skippett Oxon 82 B5
Mountsolie Aberds 303 D9
Mountsorrel Leics 153 F11
Mount Sorrel Wilts 31 C8
Mount Tabor
W Yorks 196 B5
Mount Vernon
Glasgow 268 C3
Mount Wise Corn 7 E9
Mousehill Sur 50 E2
Mousehole Corn 1 D5
Mousen Northumb 264 C4
Mousley End Warks 118 D4
Mouswald Dumfries 238 C3
Mouth Mill Devon 24 B3
Mowbreck Lancs 202 G4
Mow Cop Ches E 168 D5
Mowden Darl 224 B5
Essex 88 C3
Mowhaugh Borders 263 E8
Mowmacre Hill
Leicester 135 B11
Mowshurst Kent 52 D3
Mowsley Leics 136 F2
Moxby N Yorks 215 F11
Moxley W Mid 133 D9
Moy Argyll 255 E8
Highld 290 E6
Highld 301 F7
Moy Hall Highld 301 F7
Moy Ho Moray 301 C10
Moyles Court Hants 31 F11
Moylgrove = *Trewyddel*
Pembs 92 C2
Moy Lodge Highld 290 E6
Muasdale Argyll 255 C7
Muchalls Aberds 293 D11
Much Birch Hereford 97 E10
Much Cowardne
Hereford 98 B2
Much Cowarne
Hereford 98 B2
Much Dewchurch
Hereford 97 E9
Muchelney Som 28 C6
Muchelney Ham Som 28 C6
Much Hadham Herts 86 B5
Much Hoole Lancs 194 C3
Much Hoole Moss
Houses Lancs 194 C3
Much Hoole Town
Lancs 194 C3
Muchlarnick Corn 6 D4
Much Marcle
Hereford 98 E3
Muchrachd Highld 300 F2
Much Wenlock
Shrops 132 C2
Muckairn Argyll 289 F11
Muckernich Highld 300 D5
Mucking Thurrock 69 C7
Muckle Breck
Shetland 312 G7
Muckleford Dorset 17 C8
Mucklestone Staffs 150 B4
Muckleton Norf 158 B6
Shrops 149 E11
Muckletown Aberds 302 G5
Muckley Shrops 132 D2
Muckley Corner
Staffs 133 B11
Muckley Cross
Shrops 132 D2
Muckton Lincs 190 E5
Muckton Bottom
Lincs 190 E5
Mudale Highld 308 F5
Mudd Gtr Man 185 C7
Muddiford Devon 40 F5
Muddlebridge Devon 40 G4
Muddles Green
E Sus 23 C8
Mudeford BCP 19 C9
Mudford Som 29 D9
Mudford Sock Som 29 D9
Mudgley Som 44 D2
Mugdock Stirling 277 F11
Mugeary Highld 294 B6
Mugginton Derbys 170 G3
Muggintonlane End
Derbys 170 G3
Muggleswick
Durham 232 B6
Mugswell Sur 51 C9
Muie Highld 309 J6
Muir Aberds 292 E2
Muircleugh
Borders 271 F10
Muirden Aberds 303 D7
Muirdrum Angus 287 D9
Muiredge Fife 281 B7
Muirend Glasgow 267 C11
Muirhead Angus 287 D7
Fife 286 G6
Fife 287 F8
N Lanark 268 B3
S Ayrs 257 C8
Muirhouse Edin 280 F4
N Lanark 268 D5
Muirhouselaw
Borders 262 D4
Muirhouses Falk 279 E10
Muirkirk E Ayrs 258 D5
Muirmill Stirling 278 E4
Muir of Alford
Aberds 293 B7
Muir of Fairburn
Highld 300 D4
Muir of Fowlis
Aberds 293 B7
Muir of Kinellar
Aberds 293 B10
Muir of Miltonduff
Moray 301 D11
Muir of Ord Highld 300 D5
Muir of Pert Angus 287 D8
Muirshearlich
Highld 290 E3
Muirskie Aberds 293 D10
Muirtack Aberds 303 F9
Muirton Aberds 303 D7
Highld 301 C7
Perth 286 E5
Perth 286 F3
Muirton Mains
Highld 300 D4
Muirton of Ardblair
Perth 286 C5
Muirton of Ballochy
Angus 293 G8
Muiryfold Aberds 303 D7
Muker N Yorks 223 F8
Mulbarton Norf 142 C3
Mulben Moray 302 D3
Mulberry Corn 5 B10
Mulfra Corn 1 C5
Mulindry Argyll 254 B4
Mulla Shetland 313 G6
Mullardoch House
Highld 300 F2
Mullenspond Hants 47 D9
Mullion Corn 2 F5
Mullion Cove Corn 2 F5
Mumbles Hill
Swansea 56 D6
Mumby Lincs 191 G8
Mumps Gtr Man 196 F2
Mundale Moray 301 D10
Munderfield Row
Hereford 116 G2
Munderfield Stocks
Hereford 116 G2
Mundesley Norf 160 B6
Mundford Norf 140 E6
Mundham Norf 142 D6
Mundon Essex 88 E5
Mundurno
Aberdeen 293 B11
Mundy Bois Kent 54 D2
Munerigie Highld 290 C4
Muness Shetland 312 C8
Mungasdale Highld 307 K4
Mungrisdale Cumb 230 E3
Munlochy Highld 300 D6
Munsary Cottage
Highld 310 E6
Munsley Hereford 98 C3
Munslow Shrops 131 F10
Munstone Hereford 97 C10
Murch V Glam 59 E7
Murchington Devon 13 D9
Murcot Worcs 99 C11
Murcott Oxon 83 B9
Wilts 81 G7
Murdieston Stirling 278 B3
Murdishaw Halton 183 E9
Murieston W Loth 269 C11
Murkle Highld 310 C5
Murlaggan Highld 290 D2
Highld 290 E5
Murra Orkney 314 F2
Murrayfield Edin 280 G4
Murrayshall Perth 286 E5
Murraythwaite
Dumfries 238 C4
Murrell Green Hants 49 B8
Murrell's End Glos 98 E4
Glos 98 G5
Murrion Shetland 312 F4
Murrow Cambs 139 B7
Mursley Bucks 102 F6
Murston Kent 70 G2
Murthill Angus 287 B8
Murthly Perth 286 D4
Murton Cumb 231 G10
Durham 234 B3
Northumb 273 F9
Swansea 56 D5
T&W 243 C8
Murton *continued*
York 207 C8
Murton Grange
N Yorks 215 B10
Murtwell Devon 8 D5
Musbury Devon 15 C11
Muscliff BCP 19 B7
Muscoates N Yorks 216 C3
Muscott W Nhants 120 E2
Musdale Argyll 289 G11
Mushroom Green
W Mid 133 F8
Musselburgh E Loth 280 G6
Musselwick Pembs 72 D4
Mustard Hyrn Norf 161 F8
Muston Leics 154 B6
N Yorks 217 D11
Mustow Green
Worcs 117 C7
Muswell Hill London 86 G3
Mutehill Dumfries 237 E8
Mutford Suff 143 F9
Muthill Perth 286 F2
Mutley Plym 7 D9
Mutterton Devon 27 G8
Mutton Hall E Sus 37 C9
Muxton Telford 150 G4
Mwdwl-eithin Flint 181 F11
Mwynbwll Flint 165 B11
Mybster Highld 310 D5
Myddfai Carms 94 F5
Myddle Shrops 149 E9
Myddlewood Shrops 149 E9
Myddyn-fych Carms 75 C10
Mydroilyn Ceredig 111 F9
Myerscough Lancs 202 F5
Myerscough Smithy
Lancs 203 G8
Mylor Bridge Corn 3 B8
Mylor Churchtown
Corn 3 B8
Mynachdy Cardiff 59 D7
Rhondda 77 F8
Mynachlog-ddu
Pembs 92 E2
Mynd Shrops 115 C7
Myndd Llandegai
Gwyn 163 B10
Myndtown Shrops 131 F7
Mynydd Bach
Ceredig 112 B4
Mynydd-bach Mon 79 G7
Swansea 57 B7
Mynydd-bach-y-glo
Swansea 56 B6
Mynydd Bodafon
Anglesey 179 D7
Mynydd Fflint = *Flint*
Mountain Flint 182 G2
Mynydd Gilan Gwyn 144 E5
Mynydd-isa Flint 166 C3
Mynyddislwyn
Caerph 77 G11
Mynydd-llan Flint 181 G11
Mynydd Marian
Conwy 180 F5
Mynydd Mechell
Anglesey 178 D5
Mynyddygarreg
Carms 74 D6
Mynytho Gwyn 144 C6
Myrebird Aberds 293 D9
Myrelandhorn
Highld 310 D6
Myreside Perth 286 E6
Myrtle Hill Carms 94 E5
Mytchett Sur 49 B11
Mytchett Place Sur 49 C11
Mytholm W Yorks 196 B3
Mytholmes W Yorks 204 F6
Mytholmroyd
W Yorks 196 B4
Mythop Lancs 202 G3
Mytice Aberds 302 F4
Myton Warks 118 E6
Myton Hall N Yorks 215 F8
Myton-on-Swale
N Yorks 215 F8
Mytton Shrops 149 F8

N

Naast Highld 307 L3
Nab Hill W Yorks 197 D7
Nab's Head Lancs 194 B6
Naburn York 207 D7
Nab Wood W Yorks 205 F8
Naccolt Kent 54 E4
Nackington Kent 55 C7
Nacton Suff 108 C4
Nadderwater Devon 14 C3
Nafferton E Yorks 209 B7
Na Gearrannan
W Isles 304 D3
Nag's Head Glos 80 F5
Naid-y-march
Flint 181 F11
Nailbridge Glos 79 B10
Nailsbourne Som 28 B2
Nailsea N Som 60 D3
Nailstone Leics 135 B8
Nailsworth Glos 80 F5
Nailwell Bath 61 G8
Nairn Highld 301 D8
Nalderswood Sur 51 D8
Nance Corn 4 G3
Nanceddan Corn 2 C2
Nancegollan Corn 2 C4
Nancemellin Corn 4 G2
Nancenoy Corn 2 D6
Nancledra Corn 1 B5
Nangreaves Lancs 195 D10
Nanhoron Gwyn 144 C5
Nanhyfer = *Nevern*
Pembs 91 D11
Nannau Gwyn 146 E4
Nannerch Flint 165 B11
Nanpantan Leics 153 F10
Nanpean Corn 5 D9
Nanquidno Corn 1 D3
Nanstallon Corn 5 B10
Nant Carms 74 B6
Denb 165 D11
Nant Alyn Flint 165 B11
Nant-ddu Powys 77 B8
Nanternis Ceredig 111 F7
Nantgaredig Carms 93 G9
Nantgarw Rhondda 58 B6
Nant-glas Powys 113 E9
Nantglyn Denb 165 C8
Nantgwyn Powys 113 B9
Nantithet Corn 2 E5
Nantlle Gwyn 163 E8
Nantmawr Shrops 148 E5
Nant Mawr Flint 166 C3
Nantmel Powys 113 D10
Nantmor Gwyn 163 F10
Nant Peris = *Old Llanberis*
Gwyn 163 D10
Nantserth Powys 113 C9
Nant Uchaf Denb 165 D8
Nantwich Ches E 167 E11
Nant-y-Bai Carms 94 C5
Nant-y-Bwch
Bl Gwent 77 C10
Nant-y-cafn Neath 76 D4
Nantycaws Carms 75 B7
Nant y Caws Shrops 148 D5
Nant-y-ceisiad
Caerph 59 B8
Nant-y-derry Mon 78 D4
Nant-y-felin
Conwy 179 G11
Nant-y-ffin Carms 93 E11
Nantyffyllon
Bridgend 57 C11
Nantyglo Bl Gwent 77 C11
Nant-y-gollen
Shrops 148 D4
Nant-y-moel
Bridgend 76 G6
Nant-y-pandy
Conwy 179 G11
Nant-y-Rhiw Conwy 164 D4
Nantyronen Station
Ceredig 112 B3
Napchester Kent 55 D10
Naphill Bucks 84 F4
Napleton Worcs 99 B7
Napley Staffs 150 B4
Napley Heath Staffs 150 B4
Nappa N Yorks 204 C3
Nappa Scar N Yorks 223 G9
Napton on the Hill
Warks 119 E9
Narberth = *Arberth*
Pembs 73 C10
Narberth Bridge
Pembs 73 C10
Narborough Leics 135 D10
Norf 158 G4
Narfords Som 28 F3
Narkurs Corn 6 D6
Narracott Devon 24 D5
Narrowgate Corner
Norf 161 F8
Nasareth Gwyn 163 E7
Naseby W Nhants 120 B3
Nash Bucks 102 E5
Hereford 114 E6
Kent 55 B9
London 68 G2
Newport 59 C10
Shrops 116 C2
Som 29 E8
Nashend Glos 80 D5
Nash End Worcs 132 G5
Nashes Green Hants 49 D7
Nash Lee Bucks 84 D4
Nash Mills Herts 85 E9
Nash Street E Sus 23 C8
Kent 68 F6
Nassington
N Nhants 137 D11
Nastend Glos 80 D3
Nast Hyde Herts 86 D2
Nasty Herts 105 G7
Natcott Devon 24 C3
Nateby Cumb 222 D5
Lancs 202 E5
Nately Scures Hants 49 C8
Natland Cumb 211 B10
Natton Glos 99 E8
Naughton Suff 107 B10
Naunton Glos 100 G2
Worcs 99 D7
Naunton Beauchamp
Worcs 117 G9
Navant Hill W Sus 34 B6
Navenby Lincs 173 D7
Navestock Heath
Essex 87 F8
Navestock Side Essex 87 F9
Navidale Highld 311 H4
Navity Highld 301 C7
Nawton N Yorks 216 C3
Nayland Suff 107 E9
Nazeing Essex 86 D6
Nazeing Gate Essex 86 D6
Nazeing Long Green
Essex 86 E6
Nazeing Mead Essex 86 D5
Neacroft Hants 19 B9
Nealhouse Cumb 239 G8
Neal's Green Warks 134 G6
Neames Forstal Kent 54 B5
Neap Shetland 313 H7
Near Hardcastle
N Yorks 214 F2
Near Sawrey Cumb 221 F7
Nearton End Bucks 102 F6
Neasden London 67 B8
Neasham Darl 224 C6
Neat Enstone Oxon 101 G7
Neath = *Castell-nedd*
Neath 57 B8
Neath Abbey Neath 57 B8
Neatham Hants 49 E8
Neath Hill M Keynes 103 C7
Neatishead Norf 160 E6
Neat Marsh E Yorks 209 G9
Neaton Norf 141 C8
Nebo Anglesey 179 C7
Nebo *continued*
Ceredig 111 D10
Conwy 164 D4
Gwyn 163 E7
Nebsworth Warks 100 C3
Nechells W Mid 133 F11
Necton Norf 141 B7
Nedd Highld 306 F6
Nedderton
Northumb 252 G6
Nedge Hill Som 44 C5
Telford 132 B4
Nedging Suff 107 B9
Nedging Tye Suff 107 B10
Needham Norf 142 G4
Needham Green
Essex 87 B9
Needham Market
Suff 125 G11
Needham Street
Suff 124 D4
Needingworth
Cambs 122 C6
Needwood Staffs 152 E3
Neen Savage Shrops 116 B3
Neen Sollars Shrops 116 C3
Neenton Shrops 132 F2
Nefod Shrops 148 B6
Nefyn Gwyn 162 G4
Neighbourne Som 44 D6
Neight Hill Worcs 117 F8
Neilston E Renf 267 D9
Neinthirion Powys 129 B9
Neithrop Oxon 101 C8
Nelly Andrews Green
Powys 130 B5
Nelson Caerph 77 F10
Lancs 204 F3
Nelson Village
Northumb 243 B7
Nemphlar S Lanark 269 G7
Nempnett Thrubwell
N Som 60 G4
Nene Terrace Lincs 138 B5
Nenthall Cumb 231 B11
Nenthead Cumb 231 C11
Nenthorn Borders 262 B5
Neopardy Devon 13 B11
Nepcote W Sus 35 F10
Nepgill Cumb 229 F7
Nep Town W Sus 36 D2
Nerabus Argyll 254 B3
Nercwys Flint 166 C2
Nerston S Lanark 268 D2
Nesbit Northumb 263 C11
Ness Ches W 182 F4
Orkney 314 C4
Nesscliffe Shrops 149 F7
Nessholt Ches W 182 F4
Nesstoun Orkney 314 A7
Neston Ches W 182 F3
Wilts 61 F11
Netchells Green
W Mid 133 F11
Netham Bristol 60 E6
Nethanfoot
S Lanark 268 F6
Nether Alderley
Ches E 184 F4
Netheravon Wilts 46 D6
Nether Blainslie
Borders 271 G10
Nether Booth
Derbys 185 D10
Netherbrae Aberds 303 D7
Netherbrough
Orkney 314 E3
Nether Broughton
Leics 154 D3
Netherburn
S Lanark 268 F6
Nether Burrow
Lancs 212 D2
Nether Burrows
Derbys 152 B5
Netherbury Dorset 16 B5
Netherby Cumb 239 C9
N Yorks 206 D2
Nether Cassock
Dumfries 248 C6
Nether Cerne Dorset 17 B9
Nether Chanderhill
Derbys 186 G4
Netherclay Som 28 C3
Nether Compton
Dorset 29 D9
Nethercote Oxon 101 C9
Warks 119 E10
Nethercott Devon 12 B3
Devon 40 F3
Oxon 101 G9
Som 42 G6
Nether Crimond
Aberds 303 G8
Netherdale Shetland 313 H3
Nether Dalgliesh
Borders 249 B7
Nether Dallachy
Moray 302 C3
Nether Edge
S Yorks 186 E4
Netherend Glos 79 E9
Nether End Derbys 186 G3
Leics 154 G4
W Yorks 197 F8
Nether Exe Devon 26 G6
Netherfield E Sus 38 D2
M Keynes 103 D7
Notts 171 G10
Nethergate Norf 159 D11
Nether Glasslaw
Aberds 303 D8
Nether Hall
Leicester 136 B2
Netherhampton
Wilts 31 B10
Nether Handley
Derbys 186 F6
Nether Handwick
Angus 287 C7
Nether Haugh
S Yorks 186 B6
Nether Headon
Notts 188 F2
Nether Heage
Derbys 170 E5
Nether Heyford
W Nhants 120 F3
Nether Hindhope
Borders 263 G7
Nether Horsburgh
Borders 261 B8
Nether Howecleuch
S Lanark 260 G2
Nether Kellet
Lancs 211 F10
Nether Kidston
Borders 270 G4
Nether Kinmundy
Aberds 303 E10
Nether Kirton
E Renf 267 D9
Netherland Green
Staffs 152 C2
Nether Langwith
Notts 187 G8
Netherlaw Dumfries 237 E9
Netherlay Dorset 28 F6
Nether Leask
Aberds 303 F10
Netherlee E Renf 267 D11
Nether Lenshie
Aberds 302 E6
Netherley Aberds 293 D10
Mers 182 D6
W Yorks 196 E4
Nether Loads
Derbys 170 B4
Nethermill Dumfries 248 F2
Nethermills Moray 302 D5
Nether Monynut
Borders 272 C4
Nether Moor Derbys 170 B5
Nethermuir Aberds 303 E9
Netherne on-the-Hill
Sur 51 B9
Netheroyd Hill
W Yorks 196 D6
Nether Padley
Derbys 186 F3
Nether Park
Aberds 303 D10
Netherplace
E Renf 267 D10
Nether Poppleton
York 207 B7
Netherraw Borders 262 E3
Nether Row Cumb 230 D2
Nether Savock
Aberds 303 E10
Netherseal Derbys 152 G5
Nether Shiels
Borders 271 F8
Nether Silton
N Yorks 225 G9
Nether Skyborry
Shrops 114 C5
Nether St Suff 125 E8
Netherstoke Dorset 29 F8
Nether Stowe Staffs 152 G2
Nether Stowey Som 43 F7
Nether Street Essex 87 C9
Herts 86 B6
Netherthird E Ayrs 258 F3
Netherthong
W Yorks 196 F6
Netherthorpe
Derbys 186 G6
S Yorks 187 E8
Netherton Aberds 303 E8
Angus 287 B9
Ches W 183 F8
Corn 11 G11
Cumb 228 D6
Devon 14 G3
Glos 81 E11
Hants 47 B11
Hereford 97 F10
Mers 193 G11
N Lanark 268 E5
Northumb 251 B11
Oxon 82 F6
Perth 286 B5
Shrops 132 G4
Stirling 277 F11
W Mid 133 F8
Worcs 99 C9
W Yorks 196 E6
W Yorks 197 D9
Netherton of Lonmay
Aberds 303 C10
Nethertown Cumb 219 D9
Highld 310 B7
Lancs 203 F10
Staffs 152 F2
Nether Urquhart
Fife 286 G5
Nether Wallop
Hants 47 F10
Nether Warden
Northumb 241 D10
Nether Wasdale
Cumb 220 E2
Nether Welton
Cumb 230 B3
Nether Westcote
Glos 100 G4
Nether Whitacre
Warks 134 E4
Nether Winchendon or
Lower Winchendon
Bucks 84 C2
Netherwitton
Northumb 252 E4
Netherwood E Ayrs 258 D5
Nether Worton
Oxon 101 E8
Nether Yeadon
W Yorks 205 E10
Nethy Bridge
Highld 301 G10
Netley Hants 33 F7
Netley Hill Soton 33 E7
Netley Marsh Hants 32 E4

Nettacott Devon 14 B4
Netteswell Essex 87 C7
Nettlebed Oxon 65 B8
Nettlebridge Som 44 D6
Nettlecombe Dorset 16 B6
IoW 20 F6
Nettleden Herts 85 C8
Nettleham Lincs 189 F8
Nettlestead Kent 53 C7
Suff 107 B11
Nettlestead Green Kent 53 C7
Nettlestone IoW 21 C8
Nettlesworth Durham 233 B11
Nettleton Glos 80 C6
Lincs 200 G6
Wilts 61 D10
Nettleton Green Wilts 61 D10
Nettleton Hill W Yorks 196 D5
Nettleton Shrub Wilts 61 D10
Nettleton Top Lincs 189 B10
Netton Wilts 46 F6
Neuadd Carms 94 G3
Nevendon Essex 88 G2
Nevern = *Nanhyfer* Pembs 91 D11
Nevilles Cross Durham 233 C11
New Abbey Dumfries 237 C11
New Aberdour Aberds 303 C8
New Addington London 67 G11
Newall W Yorks 205 D10
Newall Green Gtr Man 184 D4
New Alresford Hants 48 G5
New Alyth Perth 286 C6
Newark Orkney 314 B7
Pboro 138 C4
Newark-on-Trent Notts 172 E3
New Arley Warks 134 F5
New Arram E Yorks 208 E6
Newarthill N Lanark 268 D5
New Ash Green Kent 68 F6
New Balderton Notts 172 E4
Newball Lincs 189 F9
Newbarn Kent 55 F7
New Barn Kent 68 F6
New Barnet London 86 F3
New Barnetby N Lincs 200 E5
Newbarns Cumb 210 E4
New Barton N Nhants 121 E7
New Basford Nottingham 171 G9
Newbattle Midloth 270 B6
New Beaupre V Glam 58 E4
New Beckenham London 67 E11
New Bewick Northumb 264 E3
Newbie Dumfries 238 D5
Newbiggin Cumb 210 F5
Cumb 211 D11
Cumb 219 G11
Cumb 230 F5
Cumb 231 B7
Cumb 231 F8
Durham 232 B5
Durham 232 F4
Durham 233 B8
N Yorks 213 B9
N Yorks 223 G9
Newbiggin-by-the-Sea Northumb 253 F8
Newbigging Aberds 303 G7
Angus 287 D8
Borders 262 F6
Edin 280 F2
S Lanark 269 F10
New-bigging Angus 286 C6
Newbiggings Orkney 314 B6
Newbiggin Hall Estate T&W 242 D6
Newbiggin-on-Lune Cumb 222 D4
New Bilton Warks 119 B9
Newbold Derbys 186 G5
Gtr Man 196 E2
Leics 136 B5
Leics 153 F8
Newbold Heath Leics 135 B8
Newbold on Avon Warks 119 B9
Newbold on Stour Warks 100 B4
Newbold Pacey Warks 118 F5
Newbolds W Mid 133 C8
Newbold Verdon Leics 135 C8
New Bolingbroke Lincs 174 D4
New Bolsover Derbys 187 G7
Newborough Pboro 138 B4
Staffs 152 D2
New Boston Mers 183 B9
New Botley Oxon 83 D7
Newbottle T&W 243 G8
W Nhants 101 D10
New Boultham Lincs 189 G7
Newbourne Suff 108 C5
New Bradwell M Keynes 102 C6
New Brancepeth Durham 233 C10
Newbridge Bath 61 F8
Caerph 78 F2
Ceredig 111 F10
Newbridge *continued*
Corn 1 C4
Corn 4 G5
Corn 7 B7
Dumfries 237 B11
Edin 280 G2
E Sus 52 G3
Hants 32 D3
IoW 20 D4
Lancs 204 F3
N Yorks 216 B6
Oxon 82 E6
Pembs 91 E8
Shrops 148 D6
W Mid 133 D7
Wrex 166 G3
New Bridge Wrex 166 G3
Newbridge Green Worcs 98 D6
Newbridge-on-Usk Mon 78 G5
Newbridge-on-Wye Powys 113 F10
New Brighton Flint 166 B3
Mers 182 C4
Wrex 166 E3
W Sus 22 B3
W Yorks 197 B9
W Yorks 205 F8
New Brimington Derbys 186 G6
New Brinsley Notts 171 E7
New Brotton Redcar 235 G9
Newbrough Northumb 241 D9
New Broughton Wrex 166 E4
New Buckenham Norf 141 E11
Newbuildings Devon 26 G3
New Buildings Bath 45 B7
Dorset 18 E5
Newburgh Aberds 303 D9
Aberds 303 G9
Borders 261 F8
Fife 286 F6
Lancs 194 E3
Newburn T&W 242 D5
Newbury Kent 54 B2
W Berks 64 F3
Wilts 45 E10
New Bury Gtr Man 195 F8
Newbury Park London 68 B2
Newby Cumb 231 G7
Lancs 204 D2
N Yorks 205 D11
N Yorks 212 E4
N Yorks 215 F7
N Yorks 225 C10
N Yorks 227 G10
Newby Bridge Cumb 211 B7
Newby Cote N Yorks 212 E4
Newby East Cumb 239 F11
Newby Head Cumb 231 G7
New Byth Aberds 303 D8
Newby West Cumb 239 G9
Newby Wiske N Yorks 215 B7
Newcastle Bridgend 58 D2
Mon 78 B6
Shrops 130 G4
Newcastle Emlyn = *Castell Newydd Emlyn* Carms 92 C6
Newcastleton or Copshaw Holm Borders 249 F11
Newcastle-under-Lyme Staffs 168 F4
Newcastle upon Tyne T&W 242 E6
New Catton Norf 160 G4
Newchapel Powys 129 G9
Staffs 168 E5
Sur 51 E11
Newchapel = *Capel Newydd* Pembs 92 D4
New Charlton London 68 D2
New Cheltenham S Glos 61 E7
New Cheriton Hants 33 B9
Newchurch Bl Gwent 77 C11
Carms 93 G7
Hereford 115 G7
IoW 21 D7
Kent 54 G5
Lancs 195 C10
Mon 79 F7
Powys 114 G4
Staffs 152 E2
Newchurch in Pendle Lancs 204 F2
New Clipstone Notts 171 C9
New Costessey Norf 160 G3
Newcott Devon 28 F2
New Coundon Durham 233 E10
New Cowper Cumb 229 B8
Newcraighall Edin 280 G6
New Crofton W Yorks 197 D11
New Cross Ceredig 112 B2
London 67 D11
Oxon 65 D9
Som 28 D6
New Cross Gate London 67 D11
New Cumnock E Ayrs 258 G4
New Deer Aberds 303 E8
New Delaval Northumb 243 B7
New Delph Gtr Man 196 F3
New Denham Bucks 66 C4
Newdigate Sur 51 E7
New Downs Corn 1 C3
Corn 4 E4
New Duston W Nhants 120 E4
New Earswick York 207 B8
New Eastwood Notts 171 F7
New Edlington S Yorks 187 B8
New Elgin Moray 302 C2
New Ellerby E Yorks 209 F9
Newell Green Brack 65 E11
New Eltham London 68 E2
New End Lincs 190 G2
Warks 118 E2
Worcs 117 F11
Newenden Kent 38 B4
New England Essex 106 C4
Lincs 175 D8
Pboro 138 C3
Som 28 E4
Newent Glos 98 F4
Newerne Glos 79 E10
New Farnley W Yorks 205 G10
New Ferry Mers 182 D4
Newfield Durham 233 E10
Durham 242 G6
Highld 301 B7
Stoke 168 E6
New Fletton Pboro 138 D3
Newford Scilly 1 G4
Newfound Hants 48 C5
New Fryston W Yorks 198 B3
Newgale Pembs 90 G6
New Galloway Dumfries 237 B8
Newgarth Orkney 314 E2
Newgate Lancs 194 F4
Norf 177 E9
Newgate Corner Norf 161 G8
Newgate Street Herts 86 D4
New Gilston Fife 287 G8
New Greens Herts 85 D10
New Grimsby Scilly 1 F3
New Ground Herts 85 C7
Newgrounds Hants 31 E11
Newhailes Edin 280 G6
New Hainford Norf 160 F4
Newhall Ches E 167 F10
Derbys 152 E5
Newhall Green Warks 134 F5
New Hall Hey Lancs 195 C10
Newhall House Highld 300 C6
Newhall Point Highld 301 C7
Newham Lincs 174 E3
Northumb 264 D5
New Hartley Northumb 243 B8
Newhaven Derbys 169 C11
Devon 24 C5
Edin 280 F5
E Sus 36 G6
New Haw Sur 66 G5
Newhay N Yorks 207 G9
New Headington Oxon 83 D9
New Heaton Northumb 273 G7
New Hedges Pembs 73 E10
New Herrington T&W 243 G8
Newhey Gtr Man 196 E2
Newhill Fife 286 F6
Perth 286 G5
S Yorks 186 B6
Newhills Aberdeen 293 C10
New Hinksey Oxon 83 E8
New Ho Durham 232 D3
New Holkham Norf 159 B7
New Holland N Lincs 200 C5
W Yorks 205 F7
Newholm N Yorks 227 C7
New Horwich Derbys 185 E8
New Houghton Derbys 171 B7
Norf 158 D5
Newhouse Borders 262 E2
N Lanark 268 C5
Shetland 313 G6
New House Kent 68 E6
Newhouses Borders 271 G10
New Houses Gtr Man 194 G5
N Yorks 212 E6
New Humberstone Leicester 136 B2
New Hunwick Durham 233 E9
New Hutton Cumb 221 G11
New Hythe Kent 53 B8
Newick E Sus 36 C6
Newingreen Kent 54 F6
Newington Edin 280 G5
Kent 55 F7
Kent 69 G11
Kent 71 F11
London 67 D10
Notts 187 C11
Oxon 83 F10
Shrops 131 G8
Newington Bagpath Glos 80 G4
New Inn Carms 93 D9
Devon 24 F6
Mon 79 E7
Pembs 91 E11
Torf 78 F4
New Invention Shrops 114 B5
W Mid 133 C9
New Kelso Highld 299 E9
New Kingston Notts 153 D10
New Kyo Durham 242 G5
New Ladykirk Borders 273 F7
New Lanark S Lanark 269 G7
Newland Cumb 210 D6
E Yorks 199 B10
Glos 79 D9
Hull 209 G7
N Yorks 199 C7
Oxon 82 C5
Worcs 98 B5
Newland Bottom Cumb 210 C5
Newland Common Worcs 117 E8
Newland Green Kent 54 D2
Newlandrig Midloth 271 C7
Newlands Borders 250 E2
Borders 262 E2
Cumb 229 G10
Cumb 230 D2
Derbys 170 F6
Dumfries 247 F11
Glasgow 267 C11
Highld 301 E7
Moray 302 D3
Northumb 242 F3
Notts 171 C9
Staffs 151 E11
Newlands Corner Sur 50 D4
Newlandsmuir S Lanark 268 E2
Newlands of Geise Highld 310 C4
Newlands of Tynet Moray 302 C3
Newlands Park Anglesey 178 E3
New Lane Lancs 194 E2
New Lane End Warr 183 B10
New Langholm Dumfries 249 G9
New Leake Lincs 174 D6
New Leeds Aberds 303 D9
Newliston Edin 280 G2
Fife 280 C5
New Lodge S Yorks 197 F10
New Longton Lancs 194 B4
Newlot Orkney 314 E5
New Lubbesthorpe Leics 135 C10
New Luce Dumfries 236 C3
Newlyn Corn 1 D5
Newmachar Aberds 293 B10
Newmains N Lanark 268 D6
New Malden London 67 F8
Newman's End Essex 87 C8
Newman's Green Suff 107 C7
Newman's Place Hereford 96 B5
Newmarket Glos 80 F4
Suff 124 E2
W Isles 304 E6
New Marske Redcar 235 G8
New Marston Oxon 83 D8
New Marton Shrops 148 C6
New Micklefield W Yorks 206 G4
Newmill Borders 261 G11
Corn 1 C5
Moray 302 D4
New Mill Aberds 293 E9
Borders 262 G2
Corn 1 C5
Corn 4 F6
Cumb 219 E11
Herts 84 C6
Wilts 63 G7
W Yorks 197 F7
Newmillerdam W Yorks 197 D10
Newmill of Inshewan Angus 292 G6
Newmills Corn 11 D11
Fife 279 D10
Highld 300 C6
New Mills Borders 271 F10
Ches E 184 E3
Corn 5 E7
Derbys 185 D7
Glos 79 E10
Hereford 98 D4
New Mills = *Felin Newydd* Powys 129 C11
Newmills of Boyne Aberds 302 D5
Newmiln Perth 286 D5
Newmilns E Ayrs 258 B2
New Milton Hants 19 B10
New Mistley Essex 108 E2
New Moat Pembs 91 F11
Newmore Highld 300 B6
Highld 300 D5
New Moston Gtr Man 195 G11
Newnes Shrops 149 C7
Newney Green Essex 87 D11
Newnham Cambs 123 F8
Glos 79 C11
Hants 49 C8
Herts 104 D4
Kent 54 B3
Warks 118 E3
W Nhants 119 F11
Newnham Bridge Worcs 116 D2
New Ollerton Notts 171 B11
New Oscott W Mid 133 E11
New Pale Ches W 183 G8
Newpark Fife 287 F8
New Park N Yorks 205 B11
New Parks Leicester 135 B11
New Passage S Glos 60 B4
New Pitsligo Aberds 303 D8
New Polzeath Corn 10 F4
Newpool Staffs 168 D5
Newport Corn 12 D2
Devon 40 G5
Dorset 18 C3
Essex 105 E10
E Yorks 208 G3
Glos 79 F11
Highld 311 G5
IoW 20 D6
Newport 59 B10
Norf 161 F10
Som 28 C4
Telford 150 F4
Newport = *Trefdraeth* Pembs 91 D11
Newport-on-Tay Fife 287 E8
Newport Pagnell M Keynes 103 C7
Newpound Common W Sus 35 B9
Newquay Corn 4 C6
New Quay = *Ceinewydd* Ceredig 111 F7
New Rackheath Norf 160 G5
New Radnor Powys 114 E4
New Rent Cumb 230 D5
New Ridley Northumb 242 F3
New Road Side N Yorks 204 E5
W Yorks 197 B7
New Romney Kent 39 C9
New Rossington S Yorks 187 B10
New Row Ceredig 112 C4
Lancs 203 F8
N Yorks 226 C2
Newsam Green W Yorks 206 G3
New Sarum Wilts 46 G6
New Sawley Derbys 153 C9
Newsbank Ches E 168 B4
New Scarbro W Yorks 205 G10
Newseat Aberds 303 E10
Aberds 303 F7
Newsells Herts 105 D7
Newsham Lancs 202 F6
Northumb 243 B8
N Yorks 215 C7
N Yorks 224 C2
New Sharlston W Yorks 197 C11
Newsholme E Yorks 199 B8
Lancs 204 C2
W Yorks 204 F6
New Silksworth T&W 243 G9
New Skelton Redcar 226 B3
New Smithy Derbys 185 E9
Newsome W Yorks 196 E6
New Southgate London 86 G3
New Springs Gtr Man 194 F6
New Sprowston Norf 160 G4
New Stanton Derbys 153 B9
Newstead Borders 262 C3
Northumb 264 D5
Notts 171 E8
Staffs 168 G5
W Yorks 197 E11
New Stevenston N Lanark 268 D5
New Street Kent 68 G6
Staffs 169 E9
Newstreet Lane Shrops 150 B2
New Swanage Dorset 18 E6
New Swannington Leics 153 F8
Newtake Devon 14 G3
New Thirsk N Yorks 215 C8
Newthorpe Notts 171 F7
N Yorks 206 G5
Newthorpe Common Notts 171 F7
New Thundersley Essex 69 B9
Newtoft Lincs 189 D8
Newton Argyll 275 D11
Borders 262 E3
Borders 262 F2
Bridgend 57 F10
Cambs 105 B8
Cambs 157 G8
Cardiff 59 D8
C Beds 104 C4
Ches W 166 B6
Ches W 167 D8
Ches W 183 F8
Corn 5 C11
Cumb 210 E4
Derbys 170 D6
Dorset 30 E3
Dumfries 239 C7
Dumfries 248 E4
Gtr Man 185 B7
Hereford 96 C5
Hereford 96 E6
Hereford 115 D7
Hereford 115 G10
Highld 301 C7
Highld 301 E7
Highld 306 F7
Highld 310 E7
Lancs 202 F2
Lancs 202 G4
Lancs 203 C9
Lancs 211 E11
Lincs 155 B10
Mers 182 D2
Moray 301 C11
N Nhants 137 G7
Norf 158 F6
Northumb 242 E2
Notts 171 G11
Perth 286 D2
S Glos 79 G10
Newton *continued*
Shetland 312 E5
Shetland 313 K5
Shrops 132 D4
Shrops 149 C8
S Lanark 259 C10
S Lanark 268 C3
Som 42 F6
Staffs 151 D10
Suff 107 C8
Swansea 56 D6
S Yorks 198 G5
Warks 119 B10
Wilts 32 C2
W Loth 279 F11
W Mid 133 E10
Newton Abbot Devon 14 G3
Newtonairds Dumfries 247 G9
Newton Arlosh Cumb 238 F5
Newton Aycliffe Durham 233 G11
Newton Bewley Hrtlpl 234 F5
Newton Blossomville M Keynes 121 G8
Newton Bromswold N Nhants 121 D9
Newton Burgoland Leics 135 B7
Newton by Toft Lincs 189 D9
Newton Cross Pembs 91 F7
Newton Ferrers Devon 7 F10
Newton Flotman Norf 142 D4
Newtongrange Midloth 270 C6
Newton Green Mon 79 G8
Newton Hall Durham 233 B11
Northumb 242 D2
Newton Harcourt Leics 136 D2
Newton Heath Gtr Man 195 G11
Newtonhill Aberds 293 D11
Highld 300 E5
Newton Hill W Yorks 197 C10
Newton Ho Aberds 302 G6
Newton Hurst Staffs 151 D11
Newtonia Ches E 167 B11
Newton Ketton Darl 234 G2
Newton Kyme N Yorks 206 E5
Newton-le-Willows Mers 183 B9
N Yorks 214 B4
Newton Leys Milton Keynes 103 E7
Newton Longville Bucks 102 E6
Newton Mearns E Renf 267 D10
Newtonmill Angus 293 G8
Newtonmore Highld 291 D9
Newton Morrell N Yorks 224 D4
Oxon 102 F2
Newton Mulgrave N Yorks 226 B5
Newton of Ardtoe Highld 289 B8
Newton of Balcanquhal Perth 286 F5
Newton of Balcormo Fife 287 G9
Newton of Falkland Fife 286 G6
Newton of Mountblairy Aberds 302 D6
Newton of Pitcairns Perth 286 F4
Newton on Ayr S Ayrs 257 E8
Newton on Ouse N Yorks 206 B6
Newton-on-Rawcliffe N Yorks 226 G6
Newton on the Hill Shrops 149 E9
Newton on the Moor Northumb 252 B5
Newton on Trent Lincs 188 G4
Newton Park Argyll 266 B2
Mers 183 C9
Newton Peveril Dorset 18 B4
Newton Poppleford Devon 15 D7
Newton Purcell Oxon 102 E2
Newton Regis Warks 134 B5
Newton Reigny Cumb 230 E5
Newton Rigg Cumb 230 E5
Newton St Boswells Borders 262 C3
Newton St Cyres Devon 14 B3
Newton St Faith Norf 160 F4
Newton St Loe Bath 61 G8
Newton St Petrock Devon 24 E6
Newton Solney Derbys 152 D5
Newton Stacey Hants 48 E2
Newton Stewart Dumfries 236 C6
Newton Tony Wilts 47 E8
Newton Tracey Devon 25 B8
Newton under Roseberry Redcar 225 C11
Newton Underwood Northumb 252 F4
Newton upon Derwent E Yorks 207 D10
Newton Valence Hants 49 G8
Newton with Scales Lancs 202 G4
Newton Wood Gtr Man 184 B6
New Totley S Yorks 186 F4
Newtown Argyll 284 G4
BCP 18 C6
Bl Gwent 77 C11
Bucks 85 E7
Caerph 78 G2
Cambs 121 D11
Ches E 184 E6
Ches W 183 F8
Corn 2 D3
Corn 11 F11
Cumb 229 B7
Cumb 239 F9
Cumb 240 E2
Derbys 185 E7
Devon 26 B3
Dorset 29 G7
Falk 279 E9
Glos 79 E11
Glos 80 D3
Glos 99 E8
Gtr Man 194 F5
Gtr Man 195 G9
Hants 21 B8
Hants 32 C4
Hants 32 E3
Hants 33 D8
Hants 33 E10
Hants 33 F7
Hants 49 F8
Hants 49 G10
Hants 64 G3
Hereford 97 E10
Hereford 98 C2
Highld 290 C5
IoM 192 E4
IoW 20 C4
Mers 183 B7
Norf 143 B10
Northumb 252 C2
Northumb 263 C11
Northumb 264 D2
Oxon 65 C9
Powys 130 E2
Rhondda 77 F9
Shrops 132 C2
Shrops 149 C9
Shrops 149 E8
Som 28 E3
Som 43 F9
Staffs 133 C9
Staffs 168 C6
Staffs 169 C9
Wilts 30 B6
Wilts 63 G10
W Mid 133 F11
Worcs 116 F5
Worcs 117 E7
New Town Bath 45 B9
Bath 60 G5
Dorset 30 C3
Dorset 30 D6
Dorset 31 D7
Dorset 31 F7
Edin 280 G4
Edin 280 G5
E Loth 281 G8
E Sus 37 C7
Glos 99 E10
Kent 53 B7
Kent 68 E4
Lancs 203 F8
Luton 103 G11
Medway 69 G8
Oxon 100 F5
Reading 65 E8
Shetland 312 E6
Som 29 D9
Som 29 D11
Som 44 D3
Soton 33 E7
Swindon 63 C7
T&W 234 B2
T&W 243 E8
W Berks 64 D6
Wilts 46 C6
Wilts 63 E9
W Mid 133 B11
W Mid 133 E9
W Sus 35 B11
W Yorks 198 C3
Newtown-in-St Martin Corn 2 E6
Newtown Linford Leics 135 B10
Newtown St Boswells Borders 262 C3
Newtown Unthank Leics 135 C9
New Tredegar Caerph 77 E10
New Trows S Lanark 259 B8
Newtyle Angus 286 C6
New Ulva Argyll 275 E8
New Village E Yorks 209 G7
S Yorks 198 F5
New Walsoken Cambs 139 B9
New Waltham NE Lincs 201 G9
New Well Powys 113 B11
New Wells Powys 130 D3
New Whittington Derbys 186 F5
New Wimpole Cambs 104 B6
New Winton E Loth 281 G8
New Woodhouses Shrops 167 G9
New Works Telford 132 B3
New Wortley W Yorks 205 G11
New Yatt Oxon 82 C5
Newyears Green London 66 B5
New York Lincs 174 D2
N Yorks 214 G3
T&W 243 C8
New Zealand Wilts 62 D4
Nextend Hereford 114 F6
Neyland Pembs 73 D7
Niarbyl IoM 192 E3
Nib Heath Shrops 149 F8
Nibley Glos 79 D11
S Glos 61 C7
Nibley Green Glos 80 F2
Nibon Shetland 312 F5
Nicholashayne Devon 27 D10
Nicholaston Swansea 56 D4
Nidd N Yorks 214 G6
Niddrie Edin 280 G5
Nigg Aberdeen 293 C11
Highld 301 B8
Nigg Ferry Highld 301 C7
Nightcott Som 26 B5
Nilig Denb 165 D8
Nimble Nook Gtr Man 196 G2
Nimlet S Glos 61 E8
Nimmer Som 28 E4
Nine Ashes Essex 87 E9
Ninebanks Northumb 241 G7
Nine Elms London 67 D9
Swindon 62 B6
Nine Maidens Downs Corn 2 B5
Nine Mile Burn Midloth 270 D3
Nineveh Worcs 116 C3
Worcs 116 E2
Ninewells Glos 79 C9
Nine Wells Pembs 90 G5
Ninfield E Sus 38 E2
Ningwood IoW 20 D3
Ningwood Common IoW 20 D3
Ninnes Bridge Corn 2 B2
Nisbet Borders 262 D5
Nisthouse Orkney 314 E3
Shetland 313 G7
Nithbank Dumfries 247 D9
Niton IoW 20 F6
Nitshill Glasgow 267 C10
Noah's Arks Kent 52 B5
Noah's Green Worcs 117 E10
Noak Bridge Essex 87 G11
Noak Hill Essex 87 G11
London 87 G8
Nob End Gtr Man 195 F9
Nobland Green Herts 86 B5
Noblethorpe S Yorks 197 F9
Nobold Shrops 149 G9
Nobottle W Nhants 120 E3
Nob's Crook Hants 33 C7
Nocton Lincs 173 C9
Noctorum Mers 182 D3
Nodmore W Berks 64 D2
Noel Park London 86 G4
Nogdam End Norf 143 C7
Nog Tow Lancs 202 G6
Noke Oxon 83 C8
Noke Street Medway 69 E8
Nolton Pembs 72 B5
Nolton Haven Pembs 72 B5
No Man's Heath Ches W 167 F8
Warks 134 B5
Nomansland Devon 26 E4
Herts 85 C11
Wilts 32 D3
No Man's Land Corn 6 D5
Hants 33 B8
Noneley Shrops 149 D9
Noness Shetland 313 L6
Nonikiln Highld 300 B6
Nonington Kent 55 C9
Nook Cumb 211 C10
Noon Nick W Yorks 205 F8
Noonsbrough Shetland 313 H4
Noonsun Ches E 184 F4
Noonvares Corn 2 C3
Noranside Angus 292 G6
Norbiton London 67 F7
Norbreck Blackpool 202 E2
Norbridge Hereford 98 C4
Norbury Ches E 167 F9
Derbys 169 G10
London 67 F10
Shrops 131 E7
Staffs 150 E5
Norbury Common Ches E 167 F9
Norbury Junction Staffs 150 E5
Norbury Moor Gtr Man 184 D6
Norby N Yorks 215 C8
Shetland 313 H3
Norchard Worcs 116 D6
Norcote Glos 81 E8
Norcott Brook Ches W 183 E10
Norcross Blackpool 202 E2
Nordelph Norf 139 C11
Nordelph Corner Norf 141 C10
Norden Dorset 18 E4
Gtr Man 195 E11
Norden Heath Dorset 18 E4
Nordley Shrops 132 D3
Norham Northumb 273 F8
Norham West Mains Northumb 273 F8
Nork Sur 51 B8

Norland Town
  W Yorks 196 C5
Norleaze Wilts. 45 C11
Norley Ches W 183 G9
  Devon 25 G8
Norley Common Sur . .50 E4
Norleywood Hants . .20 B3
Norlington E Sus 36 E6
Normacot Stoke 168 G6
Normanby N Lincs . . .199 D11
  N Yorks 216 C4
  Redcar 226 C4
Normanby-by-Spital
  Lincs 189 D7
Normanby by Stow
  Lincs 188 E5
Normanby le Wold
  Lincs 189 B10
Norman Cross
  Cambs 138 E3
Normandy Sur 50 C2
Norman Hill Glos . . .80 F3
Norman's Bay E Sus . .23 D11
Norman's Green
  Devon 27 G9
Normanston Suff . . .143 E10
Normanton Derby . . .152 C6
  Leics 172 G4
  Lincs 172 F6
  Notts 172 E2
  Rutland 137 B8
  Wilts 46 E6
  W Yorks 197 C11
Normanton le Heath
  Leics 153 G7
Normanton on Soar
  Notts 153 E10
Normanton-on-the-
  Wolds Notts. 154 C2
Normanton on Trent
  Notts 172 B3
Normanton Spring
  S Yorks 186 E6
Normanton Turville
  Leics 135 D9
Normoss Lancs 202 F2
Norney Sur 50 E2
Norr W Yorks 205 F7
Norrington Common
  Wilts 61 G11
Norris Green Corn . . .7 B8
  Mers 182 C5
Norris Hill Leics. 152 F6
Norristhorpe
  W Yorks 197 C8
Norseman Orkney . . .314 E3
Northacre Norf 141 D9
North Acton London . .67 C8
Northall Bucks 103 G9
Northallerton
  N Yorks 225 G7
Northall Green Norf. .159 G9
Northam Devon 24 B6
  Soton 32 E6
Northampton
  W Nhants 120 E5
North Anston
  S Yorks 187 E8
North Ascot Brack . . .66 F2
North Aston Oxon . . .101 F9
Northaw Herts 86 E3
Northay Devon 28 G5
  Som 28 E3
North Ayre Shetland . .312 F6
North Baddesley
  Hants 32 D5
North Ballachulish
  Highld 290 G2
North Barrow Som . . .29 B10
North Barsham Norf . .159 C6
North Batsom Som . . .41 G10
Northbeck Lincs 173 G9
North Beer Corn 12 C2
North Benfleet Essex. .69 B9
North Bersted W Sus . .22 C6
North Berwick
  E Loth 281 D11
North Bitchburn
  Durham 233 E9
North Blyth
  Northumb 253 G8
North Boarhunt
  Hants 33 E10
North Bockhampton
  BCP 19 B9
Northborough
  Pboro 138 B3
Northbourne BCP 19 B7
  Kent 55 C10
North Bovey Devon . .13 E10
North Bradley Wilts . .45 C11
North Brentor Devon . .12 E5
North Brewham Som . .45 F8
Northbridge Street
  E Sus 38 C2
Northbrook Dorset . .17 C11
  Hants 33 D9
  Hants 48 F4
  Oxon 101 G9
  Wilts 46 C4
North Brook End
  Cambs 104 C5
North Broomage
  Falk 279 E7
North Buckland
  Devon 40 E3
North Burlingham
  Norf 161 G7
North Cadbury Som . .29 B10
North Cairn
  Dumfries 236 B1
North Camp Hants . . .49 C11
North Carlton Lincs . .188 F6
  Notts 187 E9
North Carrine Argyll . .255 G7
North Cave E Yorks . . .208 G3
North Cerney Glos . . .81 D8
North Chailey E Sus . .36 C5
Northchapel W Sus . .35 B7

North Charford
  Wilts 31 D11
North Charlton
  Northumb 264 E5
North Cheam London . .67 F8
North Cheriton Som . .29 B11
Northchurch Herts. . .85 D7
North Cliff E Yorks . . .209 D10
North Cliffe E Yorks . .208 F3
North Clifton Notts . .188 G4
North Close
  Durham 233 E11
North Cockerington
  Lincs 190 C5
North Coker Som 29 E8
North Collafirth
  Shetland 312 E5
North Common
  S Glos 61 E7
  Suff 125 B9
North Connel
  Argyll 289 F11
North Cornelly
  Bridgend 57 E10
North Corner Corn . . .3 F7
  Aberds. 303 D11
North Corriegills
  N Ayrs 256 C2
North Corry Highld . .289 D10
Northcote Devon 27 G11
North Cotes Lincs . . .201 G11
Northcott Corn 24 F2
  Devon 12 C2
  Devon 27 E9
  Devon 27 F10
North Country Corn . .4 G3
Northcourt Oxon 83 F8
North Court Som 41 F11
North Cove Suff 143 F9
North Cowton
  N Yorks 224 E5
North Craigo Angus . .293 G8
North Crawley
  M Keynes 103 C8
North Cray London . .68 E3
North Creake Norf . . .159 B7
North Curry Som. . . .28 B4
North Dalton
  E Yorks 208 C4
North Darley Lincs . . .11 G11
North Dawn Orkney . .314 F4
North Deighton
  N Yorks 206 C3
North Denes Norf . . .161 G10
Northdown Kent 71 E11
North Dronley
  Angus 287 D7
North Drumachter
  Lodge Highld. 291 F8
North Duffield
  N Yorks 207 F9
Northdyke Orkney . . .314 D2
North Dykes Cumb . .230 D6
North Eastling Kent . .54 B3
Northedge Derbys . . .170 B5
North Elham Kent. . . .55 E7
North Elkington
  Lincs 190 C3
North Elmham Norf . .159 E9
North Elmsall
  W Yorks 198 E3
North Elmshall
  W Yorks 198 E3
North Elphinestone
  E Loth 281 G7
Northend Bath 61 F9
  Bucks 84 G2
  Essex 89 E7
  Essex 106 D5
  Warks 119 G7
North End
  Bath 60 G6
  Bedford 103 B9
  Bedford 121 C7
  Bucks 102 F4
  Bucks 102 F6
  Cumb 27 D10
  Devon 30 B4
  Dorset 233 C11
  Essex 87 B11
  Essex 106 D5
  E Yorks 209 C9
  E Yorks 209 G11
  Hants 31 D10
  Hants 33 B9
  Hants 64 G2
  Leics 153 F11
  Lincs 174 G2
  Lincs 189 B8
  Lincs 190 C5
  Lincs 190 D6
  Lincs 191 D7
  Lincs 201 G10
  London 67 B9
  London 68 D4
  N Lincs 200 C6
  Norf 141 E10
  Northumb 252 C4
  N Som 60 F2
  Ptsmth 33 G11
  Som 28 B3
  Wilts 81 G8
  W Sus 35 G10
  W Sus 51 F11
Northenden
  Gtr Man 184 C4
Northern Moor
  Gtr Man 184 C4
North Erradale
  Highld 307 L2
North Evington
  Leicester 136 C2
North Ewster
  N Lincs 199 G10
North Fambridge
  Essex 88 F5
North Fearns Highld. .295 B7
North Featherstone
  W Yorks 198 C2

North Feltham
  London 66 E6
North Feorline
  N Ayrs 255 E10
North Ferriby
  E Yorks 200 B3
Northfield
  Aberdeen 293 C11
  Borders 262 D3
  Borders 273 B8
  Edin 280 G5
  E Yorks 200 B4
  Highld 301 B7
  M Keynes 103 C7
  N Nhants 137 E7
  Som 43 F9
  W Mid 117 B10
Northfields Hants. . . .33 B7
  Lincs 137 B10
North Finchley
  London 86 G3
Northfleet Kent 68 E6
Northfleet Green
  Kent 68 E6
North Flobbets
  Aberds 303 F7
North Frodingham
  E Yorks 209 C8
Northgate Lincs 156 D3
  Som 27 B9
  W Sus 51 F9
North Gluss Shetland . .312 F5
North Gorley Hants . .31 E11
North Green Norf . . .141 B10
  Norf 142 F4
  Suff 126 B6
  Suff 126 E6
  Suff 127 D7
North Greetwell
  Lincs 189 G8
North Grimston
  N Yorks 216 F6
North Halley Orkney . .314 F5
North Halling
  Medway 69 F8
North Harrow London . .66 B6
North Hayling Hants . .22 C2
North Hazelrigg
  Northumb 264 C3
North Heasley Devon . .41 G8
North Heath W Berks . .64 E4
  W Sus 35 C9
North Hill Corn 11 F11
North Hillingdon
  London 66 C5
North Hinksey Oxon. .83 D7
North Hinksey Village
  Oxon 83 D7
North Ho Shetland. . .313 J5
North Holmwood Sur . .51 D7
North Houghton
  Hants 47 G10
Northhouse
  Borders 249 B10
North Howden
  E Yorks 207 G11
North Huish Devon . .8 D4
North Hyde London . .66 D6
North Hykeham
  Lincs 172 B6
North Hylton T&W . . .243 F8
Northiam E Sus 38 B4
Northill C Beds 104 B2
Northington Glos 80 D2
  Hants 48 F5
North Kelsey Lincs . . .200 G4
North Kelsey Moor
  Lincs 200 G5
North Kensington
  London 67 C8
North Kessock
  Highld 300 E6
North Killingholme
  N Lincs 200 D6
North Kilvington
  N Yorks 215 B8
North Kilworth
  Leics 136 G2
North Kingston
  Hants 31 G11
North Kirkton
  Aberds 303 D11
North Kiscadale
  N Ayrs 256 D2
North Kyme Lincs . . .173 E11
North Laggan
  Highld 290 D4
North Lancing
  W Sus 35 F11
North Landing
  E Yorks 218 E4
Northlands Lincs 174 E4
Northlea Durham . . .243 G10
Northleach Glos 81 C10
North Lee Bucks 84 D4
North Lees N Yorks . .214 E6
Northleigh Devon . . .15 B9
  Devon 40 G6
North Leigh Kent 54 D6
  Oxon 82 B6
North Leverton with
  Habblesthorpe
  Notts 188 E3
Northlew Devon 12 B6
North Littleton
  Worcs 99 B11
North Looe Sur 67 G8
North Lopham
  Norf 141 G10
North Luffenham
  Rutland 137 C8
North Marden W Sus . .34 D4
North Marston
  Bucks 102 F4
North Middleton
  Midloth 271 D7
  Northumb 264 E2
North Millbrex
  Aberds 303 E8
North Molton Devon . .26 B2
Northmoor Devon . . .24 D4
  Oxon 82 E6

Northmoor Corner
  Som 43 G10
Northmoor Green or
  Moorland Som 43 G10
North Moreton Oxon . .64 B5
North Mosstown
  Aberds. 303 D10
North Motherwell
  N Lanark 268 D4
North Moulsecoomb
  Brighton 36 F4
North Mundham
  W Sus 22 C5
North Muskham
  Notts 172 D3
North Newbald
  E Yorks 208 F4
North Newington
  Oxon 101 D8
North Newnton Wilts . .46 B6
North Newton Som . .43 G9
Northney Hants 22 C2
North Nibley Glos. . . .80 F3
North Oakley Hants . .48 C4
North Ockendon
  London 68 C5
Northolt London 66 C6
Northop = Llan-eurgain
  Flint 166 B2
Northop Hall Flint . . .166 B3
North Ormesby
  Mbro 234 G6
North Ormsby Lincs . .190 C3
Northorpe Lincs 155 F11
  Lincs 156 B4
  Lincs 188 B5
  W Yorks 197 C8
North Otterington
  N Yorks 215 B7
Northover Som 29 C8
  Som 44 F3
North Owersby
  Lincs 189 C9
Northowram
  W Yorks 196 B6
Northpark Argyll 275 G11
North Perrott Som . . .28 E6
North Petherton Som . .43 G9
North Petherwin
  Corn 11 D11
North Pickenham
  Norf 141 B7
North Piddle Worcs . .117 G9
North Poorton Dorset . .16 B6
Northport Dorset 18 D4
North Port Argyll. . . .284 E4
North Poulner Hants . .31 F11
Northpunds Shetland . .313 L6
North Queensferry
  Fife 280 E2
North Radworthy
  Devon 41 G9
North Rauceby
  Lincs 173 F8
North Reddish
  Gtr Man 184 C5
Northrepps Norf. . . .160 B4
North Reston Lincs. . .190 E5
North Rigton
  N Yorks 205 D11
North Ripley Hants . .19 B9
North Rode Ches E . .168 B5
North Roe Shetland . .312 E5
North Row Cumb 229 E10
North Runcton Norf. .158 F2
North Sandwick
  Shetland 312 D7
North Scale Cumb . . .210 F3
North Scarle Lincs . . .172 B5
North Seaton
  Northumb 253 F7
North Seaton Colliery
  Northumb 253 F7
North Sheen London . .67 D7
North Shian Argyll . . .289 E11
North Shields T&W . . .243 D9
North Shoebury
  Southend 70 B2
North Shore
  Blackpool 202 F2
Northside Aberds 303 D8
  Orkney 314 G2
North Side Cumb 228 F6
  Pboro 138 D5
North Skelmanae
  Aberds 303 D9
North Skelton
  Redcar 226 B3
North Somercotes
  Lincs 190 B6
North Stainley
  N Yorks 214 D5
North Stainmore
  Cumb 222 F6
North Stifford
  Thurrock 68 C6
North Stoke Bath 61 F8
  Oxon 64 B6
  W Sus 35 E8
North Stoneham
  Hants 32 D6
Northstowe Cambs . .123 D8
North Street Hants . . .31 D11
  Hants 48 G6
  Kent 54 B4
  Medway 69 E10
  W Berks 64 E6
  Norf 159 D11
North Sunderland
  Northumb 264 C6
North Synton
  Borders 261 E11
North Tamerton Corn . .12 B2
North Tawton
  Devon 25 G10
North Thoresby
  Lincs 190 B3
North Tidworth Wilts . .47 D8
North Togston
  Northumb 252 C6
North Town Devon . .24 D4
  Hants 49 C11
  Shetland 313 J4

Northtown continued
  Shetland 313 M5
North Town Devon . . .25 F8
  Hants 49 C11
  Som 29 B10
  Windsor 65 C11
North Tuddenham
  Norf 159 G10
North Walbottle
  T&W 242 D5
North Walney Cumb. .210 F3
North Walsham
  Norf 160 C5
North Waltham
  Hants 48 D5
North Warnborough
  Hants 49 C8
North Water Bridge
  Angus 293 G8
North Waterhayne
  Devon 28 F3
North Watford Herts . .85 F10
North Watten
  Highld 310 D6
Northway Devon 24 C5
  Glos 99 E8
  Som 27 B10
  Swansea 56 D5
North Weald Bassett
  Essex 87 E7
North Weirs Hants . . .32 G3
North Wembley
  London 67 B7
North Weston
  N Som 60 D3
  Oxon 83 D11
North Wheatley
  Notts 188 D3
North Whilborough
  Devon 9 B7
North Whiteley
  Moray 302 E4
Northwich Ches W . . .183 G11
Northwick S Glos 60 B5
  Som 43 D11
  Worcs 116 F6
North Wick Bath 60 F5
North Widcombe
  Bath 44 B5
North Willingham
  Lincs 189 D11
North Wingfield
  Derbys. 170 B6
North Witham Lincs . .155 E8
Northwold Norf 140 D5
Northwood Derbys . . .170 C3
  IoW 20 C5
  Kent 71 F11
  London 85 G9
  Mers 182 B6
  Shrops 149 C9
  Staffs 168 G5
  Stoke 168 F5
Northwood Green
  Glos 80 B2
Northwood Hills
  London 85 G9
North Woolwich
  London 68 D2
North Wootton
  Dorset 29 E11
  Norf 158 E2
  Som 44 E5
North Wraxall Wilts . .61 D10
North Wroughton
  Swindon 63 C7
Norton
  Devon 9 E7
  Devon 24 B3
  E Sus 23 E7
  Glos 99 G9
  Halton 183 E9
  Herts 104 E4
  IoW 20 D2
  Mon 78 B6
  Notts 187 G9
  N Som 59 G10
  Powys 114 D6
  Shrops 131 B11
  Shrops 131 G9
  Shrops 132 C4
  Stockton 234 G4
  Suff 125 D9
  Swansea 56 D3
  Swansea 56 D6
  S Yorks 186 E5
  S Yorks 198 D4
  Wilts 61 C11
  W Mid 133 G7
  W Nhants 120 E2
  Worcs 99 B10
  Worcs 117 G7
  W Sus 22 B6
  W Sus 22 D5
Norton Ash Kent 70 G3
Norton Bavant Wilts . .46 E2
Norton Bridge
  Staffs 151 C7
Norton Canes
  Staffs 133 B10
Norton Canon
  Hereford 97 B7
Norton Corner
  Norf 159 D11
Norton Disney Lincs . .172 D5
Norton East Staffs . . .133 B10
Norton Ferris Wilts . . .45 F9
Norton Fitzwarren
  Som 27 B11
Norton Green Herts . .104 G4
  IoW 20 D2
  Staffs 168 E6
  W Mid 118 C5
Norton Hawkfield
  Bath 60 G5
Norton Heath Essex . .87 E10
Norton in Hales
  Shrops 150 B4

Norton-in-the-Moors
  Stoke 168 E5
Norton-Juxta-Twycross
  Leics 134 C6
Norton-le-Clay
  N Yorks 215 E8
Norton Lindsey
  Warks 118 E3
Norton Little Green
  Suff 125 D9
Norton Malreward
  Bath 60 F6
Norton Mandeville
  Essex 87 E9
Norton-on-Derwent
  N Yorks 216 E4
Norton St Philip Som. .45 B9
Norton Subcourse
  Norf 143 D8
Norton sub Hamdon
  Som 29 D7
Norton's Wood
  N Som 60 E2
Norton Woodseats
  S Yorks 186 E5
Norwell Lincs 172 C3
Norwell Woodhouse
  Notts 172 C3
Norwich Norf 142 B4
Norwick Shetland . . .312 B8
Norwood Derbys 187 E7
  Dorset 29 E8
Norwood End Essex . .87 D9
Norwood Green
  London 66 D6
  W Yorks 196 B6
Norwood Hill Sur 51 E8
Norwood New Town
  London 67 E10
Norwoodside
  Cambs 139 D8
Noseley Leics 136 D4
Noss Highld 310 D7
  Shetland 313 M5
Noss Mayo Devon . . .7 F11
Nosterfield N Yorks . . .214 C5
Nosterfield End
  Cambs 106 C2
Nostie Highld 295 C10
Notgrove Glos 100 G2
Nottage Bridgend 57 F10
Notter Corn 7 C7
Nottingham
  Nottingham 153 B11
Notting Hill London . .67 C8
Nottington Dorset . . .17 E9
Notton Wilts 62 F2
  W Yorks 197 E10
Noutard's Green
  Worcs 116 D5
Novar House
  Highld 300 C6
Nova Scotia
  Ches W 167 B10
  Fife 279 D10
Novers Park Bristol . .60 F5
Noverton Glos 99 G9
Nowton Suff 125 E7
Nox Shrops 149 G8
Noyadd Trefawr
  Ceredig 92 B5
Noyadd Wilym
  Ceredig 92 C4
Nuffield Oxon 65 B7
Nun Appleton
  N Yorks 207 F7
Nunburnholme
  E Yorks 208 D3
Nuncargate Notts . . .171 E8
Nunclose Cumb 230 B5
Nuneaton Warks 135 E7
Nuneham Courtenay
  Oxon 83 F9
Nuney Green Oxon . . .65 D7
Nunhead London 67 D11
Nun Hills Lancs 195 C11
Nun Monkton
  N Yorks 206 B6
Nunney Som 45 D8
Nunney Catch Som . . .45 E8
Nunnington
  N Yorks 216 D3
Nunnykirk Northumb . .252 E3
Nunsthorpe
  NE Lincs 201 F9
Nunthorpe Mbro 225 C10
  York 207 C8
Nunton Wilts 31 B11
Nunwick N Yorks 214 E6
  Northumb 241 D10
Nupdown S Glos 79 F10
Nupend Glos 80 D3
  Glos 80 G4
Nup End Bucks 84 B5
  Herts 86 B2
Nuppend Glos 79 E10
Nuptown Brack 65 E11
Nursling Hants 32 D5
Nursted Hants 34 C3
Nursteed Wilts 62 G4
Nurston V Glam 58 F5
Nurton Staffs 132 D6
Nurton Hill Staffs . . .132 D6
Nutbourne W Sus . . .22 B3
  W Sus 35 C9
Nutbourne Common
  W Sus 35 C9
Nutburn Hants 32 C5
Nutcombe Sur 49 G11
Nutfield Sur 51 C10
Nut Grove Mers 183 C7
Nuthall Notts 171 G8
Nuthampstead
  Herts 105 D8
Nuthurst Warks 118 C3
  W Sus 35 B11
Nutley E Sus 36 C5
  Hants 48 E6
Nuttall Gtr Man. 195 D9
Nutwell S Yorks 198 G6
Nybster Highld 310 C7
Nye N Som 60 G2
Nyetimber W Sus 22 D5

Nyewood W Sus. 34 C4
Nyland Som 44 C3
Nymet Rowland
  Devon 26 F2
Nymet Tracey Devon . .26 G2
Nympsfield Glos 80 E4
Nynehead Som 27 C10
Nythe Som 44 G2
Nyton W Sus 22 B6

O

Oadby Leics 136 C2
Oad Street Kent 69 G11
Oakall Green Worcs . .116 E6
Oakamoor Staffs 169 G9
Oakbank W Loth 269 B11
  Oak Bank Gtr Man . . .195 F10
Oak Cross Devon 12 B5
Oakdale BCP 18 C6
  Caerph 77 F11
Oake Som 27 B11
Oake Green Som 27 B11
Oaken Staffs 133 C7
Oakenclough Lancs . .202 D6
Oakengates Telford . .150 G4
Oakenholt Flint 182 G3
Oakenshaw
  Durham 233 D11
  Lancs 203 G10
  W Yorks 197 B7
Oakerthorpe Derbys . .170 E5
Oakes W Yorks 196 D6
Oakfield Herts 104 F3
  IoW 21 C7
  Torf 78 G4
Oakford Ceredig 111 F9
  Devon 26 C6
Oakfordbridge Devon . .26 C6
Oakgrove Ches E 168 B6
Oakham Rutland 137 B7
Oakhanger Ches E . . .168 E3
  Hants 49 F9
Oakhill Som 44 D6
  W Sus 51 F6
Oakhurst Kent 52 C4
Oakington Cambs . . .123 D8
Oaklands Carms 74 B6
  Herts 86 B2
  Powys 113 G10
Oakle Street Glos 80 B3
Oakley BCP 18 B6
  Bedford 121 G10
  Bucks 83 C10
  Glos 99 G9
  Hants 48 C5
  Oxon 84 E3
  Suff 126 B3
Oakley Court Oxon . . .64 B6
Oakley Green
  Windsor 66 D2
Oakley Park Powys . . .129 F9
  Suff 126 B3
Oakley Wood Oxon . . .64 B6
Oakmere Ches W 167 B9
Oakridge Glos 80 E6
  Hants 48 C6
Oakridge Lynch Glos. .80 E6
Oaks Shrops 131 C8
Oaksey Wilts 81 G7
Oaks Green Derbys . . .152 C3
Oaks in Charnwood
  Leics 153 F9
Oakthorpe Leics 152 G6
Oak Tree Darl 225 C7
Oakwell W Yorks 197 B8
Oakwood Derby 153 B7
  London 86 F3
  Northumb 241 D10
  Warr 183 C11
  W Yorks 206 F2
Oakwoodhill Sur 50 F6
Oakworth W Yorks . . .204 F6
Oape Highld 309 J4
Oare Kent 70 G4
  Som 41 D10
  W Berks 64 D5
  Wilts 63 G7
Oareford Som 41 D10
Oasby Lincs 155 B10
Oath Som 28 B5
Oathill Dorset 28 F6
Oathlaw Angus 287 B8
Oatlands Glasgow . . .267 C11
  N Yorks 205 C11
Oatlands Park Sur . . .66 G5
Oban Argyll 289 G10
  Highld 295 G10
  W Isles 305 H3
Obley Shrops 114 B6
Oborne Dorset 29 D11
Obthorpe Lincs 155 F11
Obthorpe Lodge
  Lincs 156 F2
Occlestone Green
  Ches W 167 C11
Occold Suff 126 C3
Ocean Village Soton . .32 E6
Ochiltree E Ayrs 258 E2
Ochr-y-foel Denb. . . .181 F9
Ochtermuthill Perth . .286 F2
Ochtertyre Perth 286 E2
Ochtow Highld 309 J4
Ockbrook Derbys 153 B8
Ocker Hill W Mid 133 E9
Ockeridge Worcs 116 E5
Ockford Ridge Sur . . .50 E3
Ockham Sur 50 B5

Ockle Highld 289 B7
Ockley Sur 50 F6
Ocle Pychard
  Hereford 97 B11
Octon E Yorks 217 F10
Octon Cross Roads
  E Yorks 217 F10
Odam Barton Devon . .26 E4
Odcombe Som 29 D8
Odd Down Bath 61 G8
Oddendale Cumb 221 C11
Odder Lincs 188 G6
Oddingley Worcs 117 F8
Oddington Glos 100 F4
  Oxon 83 C9
Odell Bedford 121 F9
Odham Devon 25 G7
Odie Orkney 314 D6
Odiham Hants 49 C8
Odsal W Yorks 197 B7
Odsey Cambs 104 D5
Odstock Wilts 31 B10
Odstone Leics 135 B7
Offchurch Warks 119 D7
Offenham Worcs 99 B11
Offenham Cross
  Worcs 99 B11
Offerton Gtr Man 184 D6
  T&W 243 F8
Offerton Green
  Gtr Man 184 D6
Offham E Sus 36 E5
  Kent 53 B7
  W Sus 35 F8
Offleyhay Staffs 150 D5
Offleymarsh Staffs . . .150 D5
Offleyrock Staffs 150 D5
Offord Cluny Cambs . .122 D4
Offord D'Arcy
  Cambs 122 D4
Offton Suff 107 C11
Offwell Devon 15 B9
Ogbourne Maizey
  Wilts 63 D7
Ogbourne St Andrew
  Wilts 63 D7
Ogbourne St George
  Wilts 63 E8
Ogden Gtr Man 205 G2
Ogdens Hants 31 E11
Ogil Angus 292 G6
Ogle Northumb 242 B4
Ogmore V Glam 57 F11
Ogmore-by-
  Sea = Aberogwr V Glam .57
  F11
Ogmore Vale
  Bridgend 76 G5
Okeford Fitzpaine
  Dorset 30 E4
Okehampton Devon . .13 B7
Okehampton Camp
  Devon 13 C7
Oker Ches W 170 C3
Okewood Hill Sur 50 F6
Okle Green Glos 98 F5
Okraquoy Shetland . . .313 K6
Okus Swindon 62 C6
Olchard Devon 14 F3
Old W Nhants 120 C5
Old Aberdeen
  Aberdeen 293 C11
Old Alresford Hants . .48 G5
Oldany Highld 306 F6
Old Arley Warks 134 E5
Old Balornock
  Glasgow 268 B2
Old Basford
  Nottingham 171 G8
Old Basing Hants 49 C7
Old Belses Borders . . .262 E3
Oldberrow Warks 118 D2
Old Bewick
  Northumb 264 E5
Old Bexley London . . .68 E3
Old Blair Perth 291 G10
Old Bolingbroke
  Lincs 174 B4
Old Boston Mers 183 B9
Old Bramhope
  W Yorks 205 E10
Old Brampton
  Derbys. 186 G4
Old Bridge of Tilt
  Perth 291 G10
Old Bridge of Urr
  Dumfries 237 D10
Oldbrook M Keynes . .103 D7
Old Buckenham
  Norf 141 E10
Old Burdon T&W 243 G9
Old Burghclere Hants . .48 B3
Oldbury Kent 52 B5
  Shrops 132 E4
  Warks 134 E6
  W Mid 133 F9
Oldbury Naite
  S Glos 79 G10
Oldbury-on-Severn
  S Glos 79 G10
Oldbury on the Hill
  Glos 61 B10
Old Byland
  N Yorks 215 B11
Old Cambus Borders . .272 B6
Old Cardinham Castle
  Corn 6 B2
Old Carlisle Cumb . . .229 B11
Old Cassop Durham . .234 D2
Oldcastle Mon 96 G6
Oldcastle Heath
  Ches W 167 F7
Old Castleton
  Borders 250 E2
Old Catton Norf 160 G4
Old Chalford Oxon . . .100 F6
Old Church Stoke
  Powys 130 E5
Old Clee NE Lincs . . .201 F9
Old Cleeve Som 42 E4
Old Colwyn Conwy . .180 F5

Old–Pas 403

Old Coppice Shrops 131 B9
Old Corry Highld 295 C8
Oldcotes Notts 187 D9
Old Coulsdon London 51 B10
Old Country Hereford 98 C4
Old Craig Aberds 303 G9
Angus 292 G4
Oldcroft Glos 79 D10
Old Crombie Aberds 302 D5
Old Cryals Kent 53 E7
Old Cullen Moray 302 C5
Old Dailly S Ayrs 244 D6
Old Dalby Leics 154 E3
Old Dam Derbys 185 F10
Old Deer Aberds 303 E9
Old Denaby S Yorks 187 B7
Old Ditch Som 44 D4
Old Dolphin W Yorks 205 G8
Old Down S Glos 60 B6
Old Duffus Moray 301 C11
Old Edlington S Yorks 187 B8
Old Eldon Durham 233 F10
Old Ellerby E Yorks 209 F9
Oldend Glos 80 D3
Old Fallings W Mid 133 C8
Oldfallow Staffs 151 G9
Old Farm Park M Keynes 103 D8
Old Felixstowe Suff 108 D6
Oldfield Cumb 229 F7
Shrops 132 F3
Worcs 116 E6
W Yorks 196 E6
W Yorks 204 F6
Old Field Shrops 115 B9
Oldfield Brow Gtr Man 184 D3
Oldfield Park Bath 61 G8
Old Fletton Pboro 138 D3
Old Fold T&W 243 E7
Oldford Som 45 C9
Old Ford London 67 C11
Old Forge Hereford 79 B9
Oldfurnace Staffs 169 G8
Old Furnace Torf 78 E3
Old Gate Lincs 157 E8
Old Glossop Derbys 185 C8
Old Goginan Ceredig 128 G3
Old Goole E Yorks 199 C8
Old Gore Hereford 98 F2
Old Graitney Dumfries 239 D8
Old Grimsby Scilly 1 F3
Oldhall Renfs 267 C10
Old Hall Powys 129 G8
Oldhall Green Suff 125 F7
Old Hall Green Herts 105 G7
Oldhall Ho Highld 310 D6
Old Hall Street Norf 160 C6
Oldham Gtr Man 196 F2
Oldham Edge Gtr Man 196 F2
Oldhamstocks E Loth 282 G4
Old Harlow Essex 87 C7
Old Hatfield Herts 86 D2
Old Heath Essex 107 G10
Old Heathfield E Sus 37 C9
Old Hill W Mid 133 F9
Old Hills Worcs 98 B6
Old Hunstanton Norf 175 G11
Oldhurst Cambs 122 B6
Old Hurst Cambs 122 B5
Old Hutton Cumb 211 B11
Oldington Shrops 132 D4
Old Johnstone Dumfries 248 D6
Old Kea Corn 4 G6
Old Kilpatrick W Dunb 277 G9
Old Kinnernie Aberds 293 C9
Old Knebworth Herts 104 G4
Oldland S Glos 61 E7
Oldland Common S Glos 61 E7
Old Langho Lancs 203 F10
Old Laxey IoM 192 D5
Old Leake Lincs 174 E6
Old Leckie Stirling 278 C3
Old Lindley W Yorks 196 D5
Old Linslade C Beds 103 F8
Old Llanberis = *Nant Peris* Gwyn 163 D10
Old Malden London 67 F8
Old Malton N Yorks 216 E5
Old Marton Shrops 148 C6
Old Mead Essex 105 F10
Oldmeldrum Aberds 303 G8
Old Micklefield W Yorks 206 G4
Old Mill Corn 12 G3
Old Milton Hants 19 C10
Old Milverton Warks 118 D5
Oldmixon N Som 43 B10
Old Monkland N Lanark 268 C4
Old Nenthorn Borders 262 B5
Old Netley Hants 33 F7
Old Neuadd Powys 129 F11
Old Newton Suff 125 E11
Old Oak Common London 67 C8
Old Park Corn 6 B4
Telford 132 B3
Old Passage S Glos 60 B5
Old Perton Staffs 133 D7
Old Philpstoun W Loth 279 F11
Old Polmont Falk 279 F8
Old Portsmouth Ptsmth 21 B8
Old Quarrington Durham 234 D2
Old Radnor Powys 114 F5
Old Rattray Aberds 303 D10
Old Rayne Aberds 302 G6
Old Romney Kent 39 B8
Old Shirley Soton 32 E5
Oldshore Beg Highld 306 D6
Old Shoreham W Sus 36 F2
Oldshoremore Highld 306 D7
Old Snydale W Yorks 198 C2
Old Sodbury S Glos 61 C9
Old Somerby Lincs 155 C9
Oldstead N Yorks 215 C10
Old Stillington Stockton 234 G3
Old Storridge Common Worcs 116 G4
Old Stratford W Nhants 102 C5
Old Struan Perth 291 G10
Old Swan Mers 182 C5
Old Swarland Northumb 252 C5
Old Swinford W Mid 133 G8
Old Tame Gtr Man 196 F3
Old Tebay Cumb 222 D2
Old Thirsk N Yorks 215 C8
Old Tinnis Borders 261 D9
Old Toll S Ayrs 257 E9
Oldtown Aberds 293 C7
Aberds 302 G5
Highld 309 L5
Old Town Cumb 211 C11
Cumb 230 C5
Edin 280 G5
E Sus 23 F9
E Sus 38 F2
E Sus 38 F4
E Yorks 218 F3
Herts 104 F4
Scilly 1 G4
Swindon 63 C7
W Yorks 196 B3
Oldtown of Ord Aberds 302 D6
Old Trafford Gtr Man 184 B4
Old Tree Kent 71 G8
Old Tupton Derbys 170 B5
Oldwalls Swansea 56 C3
Old Warden C Beds 104 C2
Old Warren Flint 166 C4
Oldway Swansea 56 D5
Torbay 9 C7
Old Way Som 28 D5
Oldways End Devon 26 B5
Old Weston Cambs 121 B11
Old Wharf Hereford 98 D4
Oldwhat Aberds 303 D8
Old Whittington Derbys 186 G5
Oldwich Lane W Mid 118 C4
Old Wick Highld 310 D7
Old Wimpole Cambs 122 G6
Old Windsor Windsor 66 E3
Old Wingate Durham 234 D3
Old Wives Lees Kent 54 C5
Old Woking Sur 50 B4
Old Wolverton M Keynes 102 C6
Oldwood Worcs 115 D11
Old Woodhall Lincs 174 B2
Old Woodhouses Shrops 167 G9
Old Woodstock Oxon 82 B6
Olgrinmore Highld 310 D4
Olive Green Staffs 152 F2
Oliver's Battery Hants 33 B7
Ollaberry Shetland 312 E5
Ollag W Isles 297 G3
Ollerbrook Booth Derbys 185 D10
Ollerton Ches E 184 F3
Notts 171 B11
Shrops 150 D2
Ollerton Fold Lancs 194 C6
Ollerton Lane Shrops 150 D3
Olmarch Ceredig 112 F2
Olmstead Green Essex 106 C2
Olney M Keynes 121 G7
Olrig Ho Highld 310 C5
Olton W Mid 134 G2
Olveston S Glos 60 B6
Olwen Ceredig 93 B11
Ombersley Worcs 116 E6
Ompton Notts 171 B11
Omunsgarth Shetland 313 J5
Onchan IoM 192 E4
Onecote Staffs 169 D9
Onehouse Suff 125 F10
Onen Mon 78 C6
Onesacre S Yorks 186 C3
Ongar Hill Norf 157 E11
Ongar Street Hereford 115 D7
Onibury Shrops 115 B9
Onich Highld 290 G2
Onllwyn Neath 76 C4
Onneley Staffs 168 G3
Onslow Village Sur 50 D3
Onthank E Ayrs 267 G8
Onziebust Orkney 314 D4
Openshaw Gtr Man 184 B5
Openwoodgate Derbys 170 F5
Opinan Highld 299 B7
Highld 307 K3
Orange Lane Borders 272 G5
Orange Row Norf 157 E10
Orasaigh W Isles 305 G5
Orbiston N Lanark 268 D4
Orbliston Moray 302 D3
Orbost Highld 298 E2
Orby Lincs 175 B7
Orchard Hill Devon 24 B6
Orchard Leigh Bucks 85 E7
Orchard Portman Som 28 C2
Orcheston Wilts 46 D5
Orcop Hereford 97 F9
Orcop Hill Hereford 97 F9
Ord Highld 295 D8
Ordale Shetland 312 C8
Ordhead Aberds 293 B8
Ordie Aberds 292 C6
Ordiequish Moray 302 D3
Ordiqhill Aberds 302 D5
Ordley Northumb 241 F10
Ordsall Gtr Man 184 B4
Notts 187 E11
Ore E Sus 38 E4
Oreston Plym 7 E10
Oreton Shrops 132 G3
Orford Suff 109 B8
Warr 183 C10
Organford Dorset 18 C4
Orgreave Staffs 152 F3
S Yorks 186 D6
Oridge Street Glos 98 F5
Orlandon Pembs 72 D4
Orlestone Kent 54 G3
Orleton Hereford 115 D9
Worcs 116 D3
Orleton Common Hereford 115 D9
Orlingbury N Nhants 121 C7
Ormacleit W Isles 297 H3
Ormathwaite Cumb 229 F11
Ormesby Redcar 225 B10
Ormesby St Margaret Norf 161 G9
Ormesby St Michael Norf 161 G9
Ormiclate Castle W Isles 297 H3
Ormidale Lodge Argyll 275 F11
Ormiscaig Highld 307 K3
Ormiston Borders 262 G2
E Loth 271 B8
Ormsaigbeg Highld 288 C6
Ormsaigmore Highld 288 C6
Ormsary Argyll 275 F8
Ormsgill Cumb 210 E3
Ormskirk Lancs 194 F2
Ornsby Hill Durham 233 B9
Orpington London 68 F3
Orrell Gtr Man 194 F4
Mers 182 B4
Orrell Post Gtr Man 194 G4
Orrisdale IoM 192 C4
Orrock Fife 280 D4
Orroland Dumfries 237 E9
Orsett Thurrock 68 C6
Orsett Heath Thurrock 68 D6
Orslow Staffs 150 F6
Orston Notts 172 G3
Orthwaite Cumb 229 E11
Ortner Lancs 202 C6
Orton Cumb 222 D2
N Nhants 120 B6
Staffs 133 D7
Orton Brimbles Pboro 138 D3
Orton Goldhay Pboro 138 D3
Orton Longueville Pboro 138 D3
Orton Malborne Pboro 138 D3
Orton-on-the-Hill Leics 134 C6
Orton Rigg Cumb 239 G8
Orton Southgate Pboro 138 E2
Orton Waterville Pboro 138 D3
Orton Wistow Pboro 138 D2
Orwell Cambs 123 G7
Osbaldeston Lancs 203 G8
Osbaldeston Green Lancs 203 G8
Osbaldwick York 207 C8
Osbaston Leics 135 C8
Shrops 148 E6
Telford 149 F11
Osbaston Hollow Leics 135 B8
Osbournby Lincs 155 B11
Oscroft Ches W 167 B8
Ose Highld 298 E3
Osea Island Essex 88 D6
Osehill Green Dorset 29 F11
Osgathorpe Leics 153 F8
Osgodby Lincs 189 C9
N Yorks 207 G8
N Yorks 217 C11
Osgodby Common N Yorks 207 F8
Osidge London 86 G3
Oskaig Highld 295 B7
Oskamull Argyll 288 E6
Osleston Derbys 152 B4
Osmaston Derby 153 C7
Derbys 170 G2
Osmington Dorset 17 E10
Osmington Mills Dorset 17 E10
Osmondthorpe W Yorks 206 G2
Osmotherley N Yorks 225 F9
Osney Oxon 83 D8
Ospisdale Highld 309 L7
Ospringe Kent 70 G4
Ossaborough Devon 40 E3
Ossemsley Hants 19 B10
Osset Spa W Yorks 197 D9
Ossett W Yorks 197 C9
Ossett Street Side W Yorks 197 C9
Ossington Notts 172 C3
Ostend Essex 88 F6
Norf 161 C7
Osterley London 66 D6
Oswaldkirk N Yorks 216 D2
Oswaldtwistle Lancs 195 B8
Oswestry Shrops 148 D5
Otby Lincs 189 C10
Oteley Shrops 149 C8
Otford Kent 52 B4
Otham Kent 53 C9
Otham Hole Kent 53 C10
Otherton Staffs 151 G8
Othery Som 43 G11
Otley Suff 126 F4
W Yorks 205 D10
Otterbourne Hants 33 C7
Otterburn Northumb 251 E9
N Yorks 204 B3
Otterburn Camp Northumb 251 D9
Otterden Place Kent 54 C2
Otter Ferry Argyll 275 E10
Otterford Som 28 E2
Otterham Corn 11 C9
Otterhampton Som 43 E8
Otterham Quay Kent 69 F10
Otterham Station Corn 11 D9
Otter Ho Argyll 275 F10
Ottershaw Sur 66 G4
Otterspool Mers 182 D5
Otterswick Shetland 312 E7
Otterton Devon 15 D7
Otterwood Hants 32 G6
Ottery St Mary Devon 15 B8
Ottinge Kent 55 E7
Ottringham E Yorks 201 C9
Oughterby Cumb 239 F7
Oughtershaw N Yorks 213 C7
Oughterside Cumb 229 C8
Oughtibridge S Yorks 186 C4
Oughtrington Warr 183 D11
Oulston N Yorks 215 E10
Oulton Cumb 238 G6
Norf 160 D2
Staffs 150 E5
Staffs 151 B8
Suff 143 D10
W Yorks 197 B11
Oulton Broad Suff 143 E10
Oultoncross Staffs 151 C8
Oulton Grange Staffs 151 B8
Oulton Heath Staffs 151 B8
Oulton Street Norf 160 D3
Oundle N Nhants 137 F10
Ounsdale Staffs 133 E7
Ousby Cumb 231 E8
Ousdale Highld 311 G4
Ousden Suff 124 F4
Ousefleet E Yorks 199 C10
Ousel Hole W Yorks 205 E8
Ouston Durham 243 G7
Northumb 241 G7
Northumb 242 C3
Outcast Cumb 210 D6
Out Elmstead Kent 55 C8
Outer Hope Devon 8 G3
Outertown Orkney 314 E2
Outgate Cumb 221 F7
Outhgill Cumb 222 E5
Outhill Warks 118 D2
Outhills Aberds 303 D10
Outlands Staffs 150 C5
Outlane W Yorks 196 D5
Outlane Moor W Yorks 196 D5
Outlet Village Ches W 182 G6
Outmarsh Wilts 61 G11
Out Newton E Yorks 201 C11
Out Rawcliffe Lancs 202 E4
Outwell Norf 139 C10
Outwick Hants 31 D10
Outwood Gtr Man 195 F9
Som 28 B4
Sur 51 D10
W Yorks 197 C10
Outwoods Leics 153 F8
Staffs 150 F5
Staffs 152 E4
Warks 134 G4
Ouzlewell Green W Yorks 197 B10
Ovenden W Yorks 196 B5
Ovenscloss Borders 261 C11
Over Cambs 123 C7
Ches W 167 B10
Glos 80 B4
S Glos 60 C5
Overa Farm Stud Norf 141 F9
Overbister Orkney 314 B6
Over Burrow Lancs 212 D2
Over Burrows Derbys 152 B5
Overbury Worcs 99 D9
Overcombe Dorset 17 E9
Over Compton Dorset 29 D9
Overend W Mid 133 G9
Over End Cambs 137 E11
Derbys 186 G3
Overgreen Derbys 186 G4
Over Green W Mid 134 E3
Over Haddon Derbys 170 B2
Over Hulton Gtr Man 195 F7
Over Kellet Lancs 211 E10
Over Kiddington Oxon 101 G8
Over Knutsford Ches E 184 F3
Over Langshaw Borders 271 G10
Overleigh Som 44 F3
Overley Staffs 152 F3
Overley Green Warks 117 F11
Over Monnow Mon 79 C8
Overmoor Staffs 169 F7
Over Norton Oxon 100 F6
Over Peover Ches E 184 G3
Overpool Ches W 182 F5
Overs Shrops 131 D7
Overscaig Hotel Highld 309 G4
Overseal Derbys 152 F5
Over Silton N Yorks 225 G9
Overslade Warks 119 C9
Oversland Kent 54 B5
Oversley Green Warks 117 F11
Overstone W Nhants 120 D6
Over Stowey Som 43 F7
Overstrand Norf 160 A4
Over Stratton Som 28 D6
Over Tabley Ches E 184 E2
Overthorpe W Nhants 101 C9
W Yorks 197 D8
Overton Aberdeen 293 B10
Aberds 293 B9
Ches W 183 F8
Dumfries 237 C11
Glos 80 C2
Hants 48 D4
Invclyd 276 G5
Lancs 202 B4
N Yorks 207 B7
Shrops 115 C10
Staffs 151 B10
Swansea 56 D3
W Yorks 197 D9
Overton = *Owrtyn* Wrex 166 G5
Overton Bridge Wrex 166 G5
Overtown Lancs 212 D2
N Lanark 268 E6
Swindon 63 D7
W Yorks 197 D11
Over Town Lancs 195 B11
Over Wallop Hants 47 F9
Over Whitacre Warks 134 E5
Over Worton Oxon 101 F8
Oving Bucks 102 G5
W Sus 22 C6
Ovingdean Brighton 36 G5
Ovingham Northumb 242 E3
Ovington Durham 224 C2
Essex 106 C5
Hants 48 G5
Norf 141 C8
Northumb 242 E3
Owen's Bank Staffs 152 D4
Ower Hants 32 D4
Owermoigne Dorset 17 D11
Owlbury Shrops 130 E6
Owlcotes Derbys 170 B6
Owl End Cambs 122 B4
Owler Bar Derbys 186 F3
Owlerton S Yorks 186 D4
Owlet W Yorks 205 F9
Owlpen Glos 80 F4
Owl's Green Suff 126 D5
Owlsmoor Brack 65 G11
Owlswick Bucks 84 D3
Owlthorpe S Yorks 186 E6
Owmby Lincs 200 G5
Owmby-by-Spital Lincs 189 D8
Ownham W Berks 64 E2
Owrtyn = *Overton* Wrex 166 G5
Owslebury Hants 33 C8
Owston Leics 136 B5
S Yorks 198 E5
Owston Ferry N Lincs 199 G10
Owstwick E Yorks 209 G11
Owthorne E Yorks 201 B10
Owthorpe Notts 154 C3
Owton Manor Hrtlpl 234 F5
Oxborough Norf 140 C4
Oxclose S Yorks 186 E6
T&W 243 F7
Oxcombe Lincs 190 F4
Oxcroft Derbys 187 G7
Oxcroft Estate Derbys 187 G7
Oxen End Essex 106 F3
Oxenhall Glos 98 F4
Oxenholme Cumb 211 B10
Oxenhope W Yorks 204 F6
Oxen Park Cumb 210 B6
Oxenpill Som 44 E2
Oxenton Glos 99 E9
Oxenwood Wilts 47 B10
Oxford Oxon 83 D8
Stoke 168 E5
Oxgang E Dunb 278 G3
Oxgangs Edin 270 B4
Oxhey Herts 85 F10
Oxhill Durham 242 G5
Warks 100 B6
Oxlease Herts 86 D2
Oxley W Mid 133 C8
Oxley Green Essex 88 C6
Oxley's Green E Sus 37 C11
Oxlode Cambs 139 F9
Oxnam Borders 262 F5
Oxnead Norf 160 E4
Oxshott Sur 66 G6
Oxspring S Yorks 197 G9
Oxted Sur 51 C11
Oxton Borders 271 E9
Mers 182 D3
Notts 171 E10
N Yorks 206 E6
Oxton Rakes Derbys 186 G4
Oxwich Swansea 56 D3
Oxwich Green Swansea 56 D3
Oxwick Norf 159 D8
Oykel Bridge Highld 309 J3
Oyne Aberds 302 G6
Oystermouth Swansea 56 D6
Ozleworth Glos 80 G3

P

Pabail Iarach W Isles 304 E7
Pabail Uarach W Isles 304 E7
Pabo Conwy 180 F4
Pace Gate N Yorks 205 C8
Pachesham Park Sur 51 B7
Packers Hill Dorset 30 E2
Packington Leics 153 G7
Packmoor Staffs 168 E5
Packmores Warks 118 D5
Packwood W Mid 118 C3
Packwood Gullet W Mid 118 C3
Padanaram Angus 287 B8
Padbury Bucks 102 E4
Paddington London 67 C9
Warr 183 D10
Paddlesworth Kent 55 F7
Kent 69 G7
Paddock Kent 54 C3
W Yorks 196 D6
Paddockhaugh Moray 302 D2
Paddockhill Ches E 184 F4
Paddockhole Dumfries 248 G6
Paddock Wood Kent 53 E7
Paddolgreen Shrops 149 C10
Padfield Derbys 185 B8
Padgate Warr 183 D10
Padham's Green Essex 87 F10
Padiham Lancs 203 G11
Padney Cambs 123 C10
Padog Conwy 164 E4
Padside N Yorks 205 B9
Padside Green N Yorks 205 B9
Padson Devon 13 B7
Padstow Corn 10 F4
Padworth W Berks 64 F6
Padworth Common Hants 64 G6
Paganhill Glos 80 D4
Page Bank Durham 233 D10
Page Moss Mers 182 C6
Page's Green Suff 126 D2
Pagham W Sus 22 D5
Paglesham Churchend Essex 88 G6
Paglesham Eastend Essex 88 G6
Paibeil W Isles 296 E3
Paible W Isles 305 J2
Paignton Torbay 9 C7
Pailton Warks 135 G9
Painleyhill Staffs 151 C10
Painscastle Powys 96 B3
Painshawfield Northumb 242 E3
Pains Hill Sur 52 C2
Painsthorpe E Yorks 208 B2
Painswick Glos 80 D5
Painter's Forstal Kent 54 B3
Painters Green Wrex 167 G8
Painter's Green Herts 86 B3
Painthorpe W Yorks 197 D10
Paintmoor Som 28 F4
Pairc Shiaboist W Isles 304 D4
Paisley Renfs 267 C9
Pakefield Suff 143 E10
Pakenham Suff 125 D8
Pale Gwyn 147 B9
Pale Green Essex 106 C3
Palehouse Common E Sus 23 B7
Palestine Hants 47 E9
Paley Street Windsor 65 D11
Palfrey W Mid 133 D10
Palgowan Dumfries 245 G9
Palgrave Suff 126 B2
Pallaflat Cumb 219 C9
Pallington Dorset 17 C11
Pallion T&W 243 F9
Pallister Mbro 225 B10
Palmarsh Kent 54 G6
Palmer Moor Derbys 152 C2
Palmersbridge Corn 11 F9
Palmers Cross Staffs 133 C7
Sur 50 E4
Palmer's Flat Glos 79 D9
Palmers Green London 86 G4
Palmer's Green Kent 53 E7
Palmerstown V Glam 58 F6
Palmersville T&W 243 C7
Palmstead Kent 55 D7
Palnackie Dumfries 237 D10
Palnure Dumfries 236 C6
Palterton Derbys 171 B7
Pamber End Hants 48 B6
Pamber Green Hants 48 B6
Pamber Heath Hants 64 G6
Pamington Glos 99 E8
Pamphill Dorset 31 G7
Pampisford Cambs 105 B9
Pan IoW 20 D6
Orkney 314 G3
Panborough Som 44 D3
Panbride Angus 287 D9
Pancakehill Glos 81 C9
Pancrasweek Devon 24 F3
Pancross V Glam 58 F4
Pandy Gwyn 128 C2
Gwyn 146 F4
Gwyn 147 D7
Mon 96 G6
Powys 129 C8
Wrex 148 B3
Wrex 166 G6
Pandy'r Capel Denb 165 E9
Pandy Tudur Conwy 164 C5
Panfield Essex 106 F4
Pangbourne W Berks 64 D6
Panhall Fife 280 C6
Panks Bridge Hereford 98 B2
Pannal N Yorks 206 C2
Pannal Ash N Yorks 205 C11
Pannel's Ash Essex 106 C5
Panpunton Powys 114 C5
Panshanger Herts 86 C3
Pant Denb 166 E2
Flint 181 G10
Gwyn 144 C4
M Tydf 77 D9
Powys 129 C11
Shrops 148 E5
Wrex 166 D5
Wrex 166 F3
Pantasaph Flint 181 F11
Pantdu Neath 57 C9
Panteg Ceredig 111 E9
Torf 78 F4
Pantersbridge Corn 6 B3
Pant-glas Gwyn 163 F7
Pant-glâs Powys 128 D5
Pant-glas Shrops 148 C5
Pantgwyn Carms 93 F11
Ceredig 92 B4
Pant-lasau Swansea 57 B7
Pantmawr Cardiff 58 C6
Pant Mawr Powys 129 G7
Panton Lincs 189 F11
Pant-pastynog Denb 165 C8
Pantperthog Gwyn 128 C4
Pantside Caerph 78 F2
Pant-teg Carms 93 F9
Pant-y-Caws Carms 92 F3
Pant-y-crûg Ceredig 112 B3
Pant-y-dwr Powys 113 B9
Powys 113 C9
Pant-y-ffridd Powys 130 C3
Pantyffynnon Carms 75 C10
Pantygasseg Torf 78 F3
Pantymwyn Flint 165 C11
Pant-y-pyllau Bridgend 58 C2
Pant-yr-awel Bridgend 58 B2
Pant-y-Wacco Flint 181 F10
Panxworth Norf 161 G7
Papcastle Cumb 229 E8
Papermill Bank Shrops 149 D11
Papigoe Highld 310 D7
Papil Shetland 313 K5
Papley N Nhants 138 F2
Orkney 314 G4
Papple E Loth 281 G11
Papplewick Notts 171 E8
Papworth Everard Cambs 122 E5
Papworth St Agnes Cambs 122 E5
Papworth Village Settlement Cambs 122 E5
Par Corn 5 E11
Paradise Glos 80 C5
Paradise Green Hereford 97 B10
Paramoor Corn 5 F9
Paramour Street Kent 71 G9
Parbold Lancs 194 E3
Parbrook Som 44 F5
W Sus 35 B9
Parc Gwyn 147 C7
Parc Erissey Corn 4 G3
Parc-hendy Swansea 56 B4
Parchey Som 43 F10
Parciau Anglesey 179 E7
Parcllyn Ceredig 110 G4
Parc Mawr Caerph 77 G10
Parc-Seymour Newport 78 G6
Parc-y-rhôs Carms 93 B11
Pardown Hants 48 D5
Pardshaw Cumb 229 G7
Pardshaw Hall Cumb 229 F8
Parham Suff 126 E6
Park Corn 10 G6
Devon 14 B2
Dumfries 247 E10
Som 44 G3
Swindon 63 C7
Park Barn Sur 50 C3
Park Bottom Corn 4 G3
Park Bridge Gtr Man 196 G2
Park Broom Cumb 239 F10
Park Close Lancs 204 E3
Park Corner Bath 45 B9
E Sus 23 C8
E Sus 52 F4
Oxon 65 B7
Windsor 65 C11
Parkend Glos 79 D10
Glos 80 C3
Park End Bedford 121 G9
Cambs 123 E11
Mbro 225 B10
Northumb 241 B9
Som 43 G7
Staffs 168 E3
Worcs 116 C5
Parkengear Corn 5 F8
Parker's Corner W Berks 64 E6
Parker's Green Herts 104 F6
Kent 52 D6
Parkeston Essex 108 E4
Parkfield Corn 6 B6
S Glos 61 D7
W Mid 133 D8
Parkfoot Falk 278 F6
Parkgate Ches E 184 G3
Ches W 182 F3
Cumb 229 B10
Dumfries 248 F2
Essex 87 B11
Kent 53 G11
Sur 51 E8
S Yorks 186 B6
Park Gate Dorset 30 F2
Hants 33 F8
Kent 55 D7
Suff 124 F4
Worcs 117 C8
W Yorks 197 E8
Park Green Essex 105 F9
Parkhall W Dunb 277 G9
Park Hall Shrops 148 C6
Parkham Devon 24 C5
Parkham Ash Devon 24 C5
Parkhead Cumb 230 C2
Glasgow 268 C2
S Yorks 186 E4
Park Head Cumb 231 C7
Derbys 170 E5
W Yorks 197 F7
Parkhill Aberds 303 E10
Invclyd 277 G7
Park Hill Glos 79 F9
Kent 54 G3
Mers 194 G3
Notts 171 E11
N Yorks 214 F6
S Yorks 186 D5
Parkhill Ho Aberds 293 B10
Parkhouse Mon 79 E7
Parkhouse Green Derbys 170 C6
Parkhurst IoW 20 C5
Parklands W Yorks 206 F3
Park Lane Staffs 133 B7
Wrex 149 B8
Park Langley London 67 F11
Park Mains Renfs 277 G9
Parkmill Swansea 56 D4
Park Mill W Yorks 197 E9
Parkneuk Aberds 293 F9
Fife 279 D11
Park Royal London 67 C7
Parkside C Beds 103 G10
Cumb 219 B10
Durham 234 B4
N Lanark 268 D6
Staffs 151 D8
Wrex 166 D5
Parkstone BCP 18 C6
Park Street Herts 85 E10
W Sus 50 G6
Park Town Luton 103 G11
Oxon 83 D8
Park Village Northumb 240 E5
W Mid 133 C8
Park Villas W Yorks 206 F2
Parkway Hereford 98 D4
Som 29 C9
Park Wood Kent 53 C9
Medway 69 G10
Parkwood Springs S Yorks 186 D4
Parley Cross Dorset 19 B7
Parley Green BCP 19 B7
Parliament Heath Suff 107 C9
Parlington W Yorks 206 F4
Parmoor Bucks 65 B9
Parnacott Devon 24 F4
Parney Heath Essex 107 E10
Parr Mers 183 C8
Parracombe Devon 41 E7
Parr Brow Gtr Man 195 G8
Parrog Pembs 91 D10
Parsley Hay Derbys 169 C10
Parslow's Hillock Bucks 84 E4
Parsonage Green Essex 88 D2
Parsonby Cumb 229 D8
Parson Cross S Yorks 186 C5
Parson Drove Cambs 139 B7
Parsons Green London 67 D9
Parson's Heath Essex 107 F10
Partick Glasgow 267 B11
Partington Gtr Man 184 C2
Partney Lincs 174 B6
Parton Cumb 228 G5
Cumb 239 G7
Dumfries 237 B8
Glos 99 G7
Hereford 96 B6
Partridge Green W Sus 35 D11
Partrishow Powys 96 G5
Parwich Derbys 169 E11
Pasford Staffs 132 D6
Passenham W Nhants 102 D5
Passfield Hants 49 G10
Passingford Bridge Essex 87 F8
Passmores Essex 86 D6
Paston Norf 160 C6
Pboro 138 C3
Paston Green Norf 160 C6
Pasturefields Staffs 151 D9

Patchacott Devon . . . 12 B5
Patcham Brighton . . 36 F4
Patchetts Green
Herts 85 F10
Patching W Sus 35 F9
Patchole Devon 40 E6
Patchway S Glos 60 C6
Pategill Cumb 230 F6
Pateley Bridge
N Yorks 214 F3
Paternoster Heath
Essex 88 C6
Pathe Som 43 G11
Pather N Lanark . . .268 E5
Pathfinder Village
Devon 14 C2
Pathhead Aberds . . .293 G6
E Ayrs 258 G4
Fife 280 C5
Midloth 271 C7
Path Head T&W. . . .242 E5
Pathlow Warks 118 F3
Path of Condie
Perth 286 F4
Pathstruie Perth . . .286 F4
Patient End Herts . . .105 F8
Patmore Heath
Herts 105 F8
Patna E Ayrs 257 G10
Patney Wilts 46 B5
Patrick IoM 192 D3
Patrick Brompton
N Yorks 224 G4
Patricroft Gtr Man . .184 B3
Patrington E Yorks . 201 C10
Patrington Haven
E Yorks 201 C10
Patrixbourne Kent . . .55 B7
Patsford Devon 40 F4
Patterdale Cumb . . .221 B7
Pattiesmuir Fife . . .279 E11
Pattingham Staffs . .132 D6
Pattishall W Nhants. .120 G3
Pattiswick Essex . . .106 G6
Patton Shrops 131 E11
Patton Bridge
Cumb 221 F11
Paul Corn 1 D5
Paulerspury
W Nhants. 102 B4
Paull E Yorks 201 B7
Paul's Green Corn 2 C4
Paulsgrove Ptsmth . .33 F10
Paulton Bath 45 B7
Paulville W Loth. . . .269 B9
Pave Lane Telford . .150 F5
Pavenham Bedford . .121 F9
Pawlett Som 43 E10
Pawlett Hill Som 43 E10
Pawston Northumb . .263 C9
Paxford Glos 100 D3
Paxton Borders 273 E8
Payden Street Kent . .54 C2
Payhembury Devon . .27 G9
Paynes Green Sur 50 F6
Paynter's Cross Corn . .7 C7
Paynter's Lane End
Corn. 4 G3
Paythorne Lancs . . .204 C2
Payton Som 27 C10
Peacehaven E Sus. . .36 G6
Peacehaven Heights
E Sus 36 G6
Peacemarsh Dorset . .30 B4
Peak Dale Derbys . .185 F9
Peak Forest Derbys .185 F10
Peak Hill Lincs 156 F5
Peakirk Pboro 138 B3
Pean Hill Kent 70 G6
Pear Ash Som 45 G9
Pearsie Angus 287 B7
Pearson's Green Kent .53 E7
Peartree Herts. 86 C2
Pear Tree Derby 153 C7
Peartree Green
Essex 87 F9
Hereford 97 E11
Soton. 32 E6
Sur. 50 F3
Peas Acre W Yorks . .205 E8
Peasedown St John
Bath. 45 B8
Peasehill Derbys . . .170 F6
Peaseland Green
Norf. 159 F11
Peasemore W Berks . .64 D3
Peasenhall Suff. . . .127 E7
Pease Pottage
W Sus 51 G9
Peas Hill Cambs. . . .139 D8
Peaslake Sur 50 E5
Peasley Cross Mers .183 C8
Peasmarsh
E Sus. 38 C5
Som 28 E4
Sur. 50 D3
Peaston E Loth 271 B8
Peastonbank E Loth .271 B8
Peathill Aberds 303 C9
Peat Inn Fife. 287 G8
Peatling Magna
Leics 135 E11
Peatling Parva
Leics 135 F11
Peaton Shrops 131 G10
Peatonstrand
Shrops. 131 G10
Peats Corner Suff. . .126 E3
Pebmarsh Essex . . .107 E7
Pebsham E Sus 38 E3
Pebworth Worcs . . .100 B2
Pecket Well
W Yorks 196 B3
Peckforton Ches E . .167 D8
Peckham London. . . .67 D10
Peckham Bush Kent . .53 D7
Peckingell Wilts 62 E2
Pecking Mill Som. . . .44 F6
Peckleton Leics. . . .135 C9

Pedair-ffordd
Powys 148 E2
Pedham Norf 160 G6
Pedlars End Essex . . .87 D8
Pedlar's Rest
Shrops 131 G3
Pedlinge Kent 54 F6
Pedmore W Mid 133 G8
Pednor Bottom Bucks 84 E6
Pedwell Som 44 F2
Peebles Borders . . .261 B10
Peel Borders. 261 B10
IoM 192 D3
Lancs 202 G3
Peel Common Hants . .33 G9
Peel Green Gtr Man .184 B2
Peel Hall Gtr Man . .184 D3
Peel Hill Lancs 202 G3
Peel Park S Lanark . .268 C2
Peene Kent. 55 F7
Peening Quarter
Kent. 38 B5
Peggs Green Leics . .153 F8
Pegsdon C Beds. . . .104 E2
Pegswood Northumb .252 F6
Pegwell Kent. 71 G11
Peinaha Highld 298 D4
Peinchorran Highld .295 B7
Peingown Highld. . . .298 B4
Peinlich Highld 298 E4
Peinmore Highld. . . .298 E4
Pelaw T&W. 243 E7
Pelcomb Pembs 72 B6
Pelcomb Bridge
Pembs 72 B6
Pelcomb Cross
Pembs 72 B6
Peldon Essex 89 B7
Pelhamfield IoW 21 C7
Pell Green E Sus 52 G6
Pellon W Yorks 196 B5
Pelsall W Mid 133 C10
Pelsall Wood
W Mid 133 C10
Pelton Durham. 243 G7
Pelton Fell Durham. .243 G7
Pelutho Cumb 229 B8
Pelynt Corn. 6 D4
Pemberton Carms . . .75 E8
Gtr Man 194 G5
Pembles Cross Kent .53 D11
Pembre = Pembrey
Pembrey
Carms 74 E6
Pembridge Hereford .115 F7
Pembroke = Penfro
Pembs 73 E7
Pembroke Dock =
Doc Penfro Pembs. .73 E7
Pembroke Ferry
Pembs 73 E7
Pembury Kent 52 E6
Pempwell Corn 12 F3
Penallt Mon 79 C8
Pen-allt Hereford . . .97 F11
Penally = Penalun
Pembs 73 F10
Penalt Hereford 97 F11
Penalun = Penally
Pembs 73 F10
Penare Corn. 5 G9
Penarlâg = Hawarden
Flint. 166 B4
Penarron Powys 130 F2
Penarth V Glam 59 E7
Penarth Moors
Cardiff. 59 E7
Penbeagle Corn 2 B2
Penbedw Flint 165 B11
Pen-bedw Pembs 92 D4
Penberth Corn. 1 E4
Penbidwal Mon 96 G6
Penbodlas Gwyn. . . .144 C5
Pen-bont Rhydybeddau
Ceredig 128 G3
Penboyr Carms 93 D7
Penbryn Ceredig . . .110 G5
Pencader Carms 93 D8
Pencaenewydd
Gwyn 162 G6
Pencaerau Neath 57 B8
Pen-caer-fenny
Swansea 56 B4
Pencaitland E Loth . .271 B8
Pencarnisiog
Anglesey 178 G5
Pencarreg Carms . . .93 B10
Pencarrow Corn 11 E8
Penceiliogi Carms . . .75 E8
Pencelli Powys 95 F11
Pen-clawdd Swansea .56 B4
Pencoed Bridgend. . .58 C3
Pencombe
Hereford 115 G11
Pen-common Powys . .76 D6
Pencoyd Hereford . . .97 F10
Pencoys Corn 2 B5
Pencraig Anglesey . .179 F7
Hereford 97 G11
Powys 147 D10
Pencroesoped Mon . . .78 D4
Pencuke Corn 11 C9
Pendas Fields
W Yorks 206 F3
Pendeen Corn 1 C3
Pendeford W Mid . . .133 C7
Pendine = Pentywn
Carms 74 D2
Pendlebury
Gtr Man 195 G9
Pendleton Gtr Man . .184 B4
Lancs 203 F11
Pendock Worcs 98 E5
Pendoggett Corn 10 F6
Pendomer Som 29 E8
Pendoylan V Glam. . .58 D5
Pendre Bridgend 58 C2
Gwyn 110 C2

Pendre continued
Powys 95 F10
Pendrift Corn. 11 G8
Penegoes Powys. . . .128 C5
Penelewey Corn 4 G6
Penenden Heath
Kent. 53 B9
Penffordd Pembs 91 G11
Penffordd Lâs = Staylittle
Powys. 129 E7
Penfro = Pembroke
Pembs. 73 E7
Pengam Caerph 77 F11
Penge London. 67 E11
Pengegon Corn 2 B5
Pengelly Corn 11 E7
Pengenffordd Powys . .96 E3
Pengersick Corn 2 D3
Pen-gilfach Gwyn . . .163 C9
Pengold Corn 11 C8
Pengorffwysfa
Anglesey 179 C7
Pengover Green Corn . 6 B5
Penguithal Hereford. .97 G10
Pengwern Denb 181 F8
Penhale Corn. 2 F5
. . . . .5 D8
Penhale Jakes Corn. . .2 D4
Penhallick Corn 3 F7
. . . . .4 G3
Penhallow Corn 4 E5
Penhalurick Corn 2 B6
Penhalvean Corn 2 B6
Penhelig Gwyn 128 D2
Penhill Devon 40 G4
Swindon. 63 B7
Penhow Newport. . . .78 G6
Penhurst E Sus 23 B11
Peniarth Gwyn. 128 B2
Penicuik Midloth . . .270 C4
Peniel Carms 93 G8
Penifiler Highld. 298 E4
Peninver Argyll 255 F8
Penisa'r Waun
Gwyn. 163 C9
Penistone S Yorks . .197 G8
Penjerrick Corn 3 C7
Penketh Warr 183 D9
Penkhull Stoke 168 G5
Penkill S Ayrs. 244 D6
Penknap Wilts 45 D11
Penkridge Staffs. . . .151 G8
Pen-lan Swansea 56 B6
Pen-Lan-mabws
Pembs 91 F7
Penleigh Wilts. 45 C11
Penley Wrex. 149 B8
Penllech Gwyn. 144 C4
Penllergaer Swansea. .56 B6
Penllwyn Caerph. . . .77 F11
Ceredig 128 G3
Penllyn V Glam 58 D3
Pen-llyn Anglesey . .178 E4
Pen-lôn Anglesey . . .162 B6
Penmachno Conwy. .164 E3
Penmaen Caerph 77 F11
Swansea 56 D4
Penmaenan Conwy. .180 F2
Penmaenmawr
Conwy 180 F2
Penmaenpool Gwyn .146 F3
Penmaen Rhôs
Conwy 180 F5
Penmark V Glam 58 F5
Penmarth Corn 2 B6
Penmayne Corn 10 F4
Pen Mill Som 29 D9
Penmon Anglesey . . .179 E10
Penmore Mill Argyll. .288 D6
Penmorfa Ceredig. . .110 G6
Gwyn 163 G9
Penmynydd
Anglesey 179 G8
W Mid 133 D7
Pennal Gwyn 128 C4
Pennan Aberds 303 C8
Pennance Corn 4 G4
Pennant Ceredig 111 E10
Conwy 164 D5
Denb 165 E8
Powys 129 D7
Pennant Melangell
Powys 147 D10
Pennar Pembs 73 E7
Pennard Swansea. . . .56 D5
Pennar Park Pembs . .72 E6
Penn Bottom Bucks . .84 G6
Pennerley Shrops. . .131 D7
Pennington Cumb. . .210 D5
Gtr Man 183 B11
Hants 20 C2
Pennington Green
Gtr Man 194 F6
Pennorth Powys 96 F2
Penn Street Bucks . .84 F6
Pennsylvania Devon. .14 C4
S Glos. 61 B8
Penny Bridge Cumb .210 C6
Pennycross Argyll. . .289 G7
Plym 7 D9
Pennygate Norf. . . .160 E6
Pennygown Argyll . .289 G7
Penny Green Derbys .187 F8
Penny Hill Lincs . . .157 D7
W Yorks 196 D5
Pennylands Lancs . .194 F3
Pennymoor Devon . . .26 E5
Pennypot Kent. 54 G6
Penny's Green Norf . 142 D3
Pennytinney Corn. . . .11 F7
Pennywell T&W 243 F9
Pen-onn V Glam 58 F5
Penparc Ceredig 92 B4
Pembs 91 E7
Penparcau Ceredig. .111 B11
Penpedairheol
Caerph. 77 F10

Penpedairheol continued
Mon 78 E4
Penpergym Mon 78 E4
Penperlleni Mon 78 E4
Penpethy Corn. 11 D7
Penpillick Corn 5 D11
Penplas Carms. 74 B5
Penpol Corn 6 E2
Penpoll Corn 6 E2
Penponds Corn 2 B4
Penpont Corn 11 G7
Dumfries 247 E8
Powys 95 F9
Penprysg Bridgend . .58 C3
Penquit Devon 8 E2
Penrallt Gwyn 145 B7
Powys 129 F9
Penrherber Carms . . .92 D5
Penrhiw Caerph. 78 G2
Penrhiwceiber
Rhondda 77 F8
Pen-Rhiw-fawr
Neath. 76 C2
Penrhiwgarreg
Bl Gwent 78 E2
Penrhiw-llan Ceredig .93 C7
Penrhiw-pal Ceredig .92 B6
Penrhiwtyn Neath. . . .57 B8
Penrhôs Anglesey . .178 E3
Gwyn 144 C6
Hereford 114 F6
Penrhôs Mon 78 C6
Penrhos Mon 78 C6
Powys 76 C3
Pen-rhos Wrex 166 E3
Penrhosfeilw
Anglesey 178 E2
Penrhos Garnedd
Gwyn 179 G9
Penrhyd Lastra
Anglesey 178 C6
Penrhyn Bay = Bae-Penrhyn
Conwy 180 E4
Penrhyn Castle
Pembs 92 B2
Penrhyn-coch
Ceredig 128 G2
Penrhyndeudraeth
Gwyn 146 B2
Penrhynside Conwy. .180 E4
Penrhys Rhondda. . . .77 F8
Penrice Swansea. . . .56 D3
Penrith Cumb. 230 E6
Penrose Corn. 10 G3
Penruddock Cumb . .230 F4
Penryn Corn 3 C7
Pensarn Carms 74 B6
Conwy 181 F7
Pen-sarn Gwyn 145 D11
Gwyn 162 G6
Pensax Worcs 116 D4
Pensby Mers 182 E3
Penselwood Som 45 G9
Pensford Bath 60 G6
Pensham Worcs 99 C8
Penshaw T&W. 243 G8
Penshurst Kent 52 E4
Pensilva Corn 6 B5
Pensnett W Mid 133 F8
Penston E Loth 281 G8
Penstone Devon 26 G3
Penstraze Corn 4 F5
Pentewan Corn 5 F10
Pentiken Shrops 130 G4
Pentir Gwyn 163 B9
Pentire Corn. 4 C5
Pentirvin Shrops . . .130 C5
Pentlepoir Pembs. . . .73 D10
Pentlow Essex 106 B4
Pentlow Street
Essex 106 B4
Pentney Norf 158 G4
Penton Corner
Hants. 47 D10
Penton Grafton
Hants. 47 D10
Penton Mewsey
Hants. 47 D10
Pentonville London. .67 C10
Pentowin Carms 74 B3
Pentraeth Anglesey . .179 F8
Pentre-bach Powys . .77 E11
Pentre
Carms 75 C8
Denb 165 D10
Denb 165 C11
Flint. 181 F11
Flint. 165 C11
Flint. 166 B4
Flint. 166 C2
Flint. 166 C2
Powys 129 F11
Powys 130 B4
Powys 130 E5
Powys 147 D11
Powys 148 G3
Rhondda 77 F7
Shrops 148 D4
Shrops 149 F7
Wrex 148 B2
Wrex 166 G3
Pentrebach Carms. . .94 E6
M Tydf 77 E9
Rhondda 58 B5
Swansea 75 D10
Pentre-bâch
Ceredig 93 B11
Pentre-bach Powys . .95 D9
Pentrebane Cardiff. . .58 D6
Pentrebeirdd Powys 148 G3
Pentre Berw
Anglesey 179 G6
Pentre-bont Conwy. .164 E2
Pentre Broughton
Wrex 166 E4
Pentre Bychan
Wrex 166 F4
Pentrecagal Carms. . .92 C6
Pentre-cefn Shrops . .148 E5
Pentre-celyn Denb . .165 E11
Powys 129 B7

Pentre-chwyth
Swansea 57 B7
Pentre Cilgwyn
Wrex 148 B4
Pentre-clawdd
Shrops 148 C5
Pentre-coed Shrops .149 B7
Pentre-cwrt Carms . .93 D7
Pentre Dolau-Honddu
Powys 95 C9
Pentredwr Denb 165 F11
Pentre-dwr Swansea .57 B7
Pentrefelin
Anglesey 178 C6
Carms 93 G11
Ceredig 94 B2
Conwy 180 G4
Denb 166 G2
Gwyn 145 B10
Pentre-Ffwrndan
Flint 182 G3
Pentrefoelas Conwy .164 E5
Pentref-y-groes
Caerph. 77 F11
Pentre-galar Pembs . .92 E3
Pentregat Ceredig. . .111 G7
Pentre-Gwenlais
Carms 75 B10
Pentre Gwynfryn
Gwyn 145 D11
Pentre Halkyn Flint . 182 G2
Pentreheyling
Shrops 130 E4
Pentre Hodre
Shrops 114 B6
Pentre Isaf Conwy. .164 B5
Pentre Llanrhaeadr
Denb 165 C9
Pentre Llifior Powys 130 D2
Pentrellwyn Ceredig. .93 C8
Pentre-llwyn-llwyd
Powys 113 G9
Pentre-llyn Ceredig .112 C2
Pentre-llyn cymmer
Conwy 165 E7
Pentre Maelor Wrex .166 F5
Pentre Meyrick
V Glam 58 D3
Pentre-newydd
Shrops 148 B5
Pentre-Piod Torf 78 E3
Pentre-Poeth Carms . .75 E8
Newport. 59 B9
Pentre'r beirdd
Powys 148 G3
Pentre'r Felin
Conwy 164 B4
Pentre'r-felin
Denb 165 B10
Powys 95 E8
Pentre-rhew
Ceredig 112 G3
Pentre-tafarn-y-fedw
Conwy 164 C4
Pentre-ty-gwyn
Carms 94 D6
Pentreuchaf Gwyn . .145 B7
Pentre-uchaf Conwy .180 F5
Pentrich Derbys 170 E5
Pentridge Dorset 31 D8
Pentrisil Pembs 91 E11
Pentwyn Caerph 77 E10
Cardiff. 59 C8
Pen-twyn Caerph 78 E2
Pentwyn = Pendine
Carms 74 D2
Pen-twyn Carms. 75 C9
Mon 79 D8
Torf 78 E3
Pentwyn Berthlwyd
Caerph. 77 E10
Pentwyn-mawr
Caerph. 77 F11
Pentyrch Cardiff. . . .58 C6
Penuchadre V Glam .57 G11
Pen-Uchar Plwyf
Flint 181 G11
Penuwch Ceredig . . .111 E11
Penwartha Corn 4 E5
Penwartha Coombe
Corn. 4 E5
Penweathers Corn . . .4 G6
Penwithick Corn 5 D10
Penwood Hants. 64 G2
Penwortham Lane
Lancs 194 B4
Penwyllt Powys. 76 B5
Pen-y-Ball Top
Flint 181 F11
Penybanc Carms. 75 C10
Pen-y-banc Carms . . .93 G8
Carms 94 G2
Pen-y-bank Carms . . .77 E10
Penybedd Carms. . . .74 E6
Penybont Ceredig . . .128 F2
Powys 114 E2
Pen-y-Bont
Bl Gwent 78 D2
Carms 92 F6
Gwyn 128 C4
Gwyn 146 D2
Powys 148 G3
Shrops 148 B6
Wrex 166 G3
Pen y Bont ar ogwr
= Bridgend Bridgend .58 C2
Penybontfawr
Powys 147 E11
Penybryn Caerph. . . .77 F10
Pen-y-Bryn Gwyn . .145 B9
Gwyn 146 F3
Pembs 92 C3
Powys 130 C3
Shrops 148 B6
Pen-y-cae
Bridgend 58 C2
Neath. 57 D7
Powys 76 C3
Pen-y-cae-mawr
Mon 78 F6
Penycaerau Gwyn. . .144 D3
Pen-y-cefn Flint. . . .181 F10

Pen-y-clawdd Mon . .79 D7
Pen-y-coed Shrops . .148 E5
Pen-y-coedcae
Rhondda 58 B5
Penycwm Pembs. 90 G6
Pen-y-Darren
M Tydf 77 D9
Pendyre Swansea . . .75 E11
Pen-y-fai Bridgend. . .57 E11
Carms 75 E7
Pen-y-fan Carms 56 B4
Mon 79 D8
Penyfeidr Pembs 91 F7
Pen-y-felin Flint 165 B11
Penyffordd Flint 166 C4
Flint 181 F8
Pen-y-ffordd Denb . .181 F8
Flint 181 F10
Penyffridd Gwyn . . .163 D8
Pen y Foel Shrops . .148 E5
Penygarn Torf 78 E3
Pen-y-garn Carms . . .93 E11
Ceredig 128 F2
Penygarnedd Powys .148 E2
Pen-y-garnedd
Anglesey 179 F8
Penygelli Powys 130 E2
Pen-y-gop Conwy . .164 G6
Penygraig Rhondda. . .77 G7
Pen-y-graig Gwyn. . .144 C3
Penygraigwen
Anglesey 178 D6
Penygroes Gwyn. . . .163 E7
Pen-y-groes Carms . .75 C9
Pen-y-groeslon
Gwyn 144 C4
Pen-y-Gwryd Hotel
Gwyn 163 D11
Pen-y-lan Cardiff. . . .59 D7
Newport. 59 B9
V Glam 58 D3
Pen-y-maes Flint . . .181 F11
Penymynydd Flint. . .166 C4
Pen-y-Park Hereford .96 C5
Penyraber Pembs 91 D9
Pen-yr-englyn
Rhondda 76 F6
Penyrheol Caerph. . .58 B6
Swansea 56 B5
Torf 78 F3
Pen-yr-heol Bridgend 58 C2
Mon 78 C6
Pen-yr-Heolgerrig
M Tydf 77 D8
Pen-y-rhiw Rhondda . .58 B5
Penysarn Anglesey . .179 C7
Pen-y-stryt Denb . . .165 E11
Penywaun Rhondda . .77 E7
Pen-y-wern Shrops . .114 B6
Penzance Corn 1 C5
Peopleton Worcs . . .117 G8
Peover Heath
Ches E 184 G3
Peper Harow Sur 50 E2
Peppercombe Devon. .24 C5
Pepper Hill Som 43 F7
Pepper's Green
Essex 87 C10
Pepperstock C Beds . .85 B9
Perceton N Ayrs . . .267 G7
Percie Aberds 293 D7
Percuil Corn. 3 C9
Percyhorner Aberds. .303 C9
Percy Main T&W. . . .243 D8
Perham Down Wilts. . .47 D9
Periton Som 42 D3
Perivale London. 67 C7
Perkhill Aberds 293 C7
Perkinsville Durham. .243 G7
Perlethorpe Notts . . .187 G11
Perranarworthal Corn . 3 B7
Perrancoombe Corn . .4 E5
Perran Downs Corn . . .2 C3
Perranporth Corn 4 E5
Perranuthnoe Corn . . .2 D2
Perranwell Corn 3 B7
Corn. 4 E5
Perranwell Station
Corn. 3 B7
Perran Wharf Corn . . .3 B7
Perranzabuloe Corn . .4 E5
Perrott's Brook Glos. .81 D8
Perry Devon 26 F5
Kent. 55 B9
W Mid 133 E11
Perry Barr W Mid. . .133 E11
Perry Beeches
W Mid 133 E11
Perry Common
W Mid 133 E11
Perry Crofts Staffs . .134 C4
Perryfields Worcs. . .117 C8
Perryfoot Derbys. . .185 E10
Perry Green Essex . .106 G6
Herts 86 B6
Som 43 F9
Wilts 62 B3
Perrymead Bath 61 G9
Perrystone Hill
Hereford 98 F2
Perry Street Kent . . .68 E6
Som 28 F4
Perrywood Kent 54 B4
Pershall Staffs. 150 C5
Pershore Worcs 99 B8
Pert Angus 293 G8
Perthcelyn Rhondda. .77 F9
Perthy Shrops 149 C7
Perton Hereford. 97 C11
Staffs. 133 D7
Pertwood Wilts 45 F11
Pested Kent 54 C4
Peterborough
Pboro. 138 D3

Peterburn Highld . . .307 L2
Peterchurch Hereford .96 D6
Peterculter
Aberdeen. 293 C10
Peterhead Aberds. . .303 E11
Peterlee Durham. . . .234 C4
Petersburn
N Lanark 268 C5
Petersfield Hants 34 C2
Peter's Finger Devon. .12 D3
Peter's Green Herts . .85 B10
Petersham London . . .67 E7
Peterstone Wentlooge
Newport. 59 C9
Peterston-super-Ely
V Glam 58 D5
Peterstow Hereford . .97 G11
Peter Tavy Devon . . .12 F6
Petertown Orkney. . .314 F3
Petham Kent 54 C6
Petherwin Gate
Corn. 11 D11
Petrockstow Devon . .25 F8
Petsoe End
M Keynes 103 B7
Pett E Sus 38 E5
Pettaugh Suff 126 F3
Pett Bottom Kent 54 E6
Kent. 55 C7
Petteridge Kent 53 E7
Pettinain S Lanark . .269 G9
Pettings Kent. 68 G6
Pettistree Suff. 126 G5
Petton Devon 27 C8
Shrops 149 D8
Petts Wood London . .68 F2
Petty Aberds 303 F7
Pettycur Fife 280 D5
Petty France S Glos . .61 B9
Pettymuick Aberds. .303 G9
Pettywell Norf. 159 E11
Petworth W Sus. 35 C7
Pevensey E Sus. 23 E11
Pevensey Bay E Sus .23 E11
Peverell Plym. 7 D9
Pewsey Wilts 63 G7
Pewsey Wharf Wilts .63 G7
Pewterspear Warr . .183 E10
Phantassie E Loth . .281 F11
Pharisee Green
Essex 106 G2
Pheasants Bucks. . . .65 B9
Pheasant's Hill Bucks .65 B9
Pheasey W Mid 133 C11
Phepson Worcs. 117 F8
Philadelphia T&W. . .243 G8
Philham Devon 24 C3
Philiphaugh
Borders 261 D10
Phillack Corn 2 B3
Philleigh Corn 3 B9
Phillip's Town
Caerph. 77 E10
Philpot End Essex. . . .87 B10
Philpstoun W Loth . .279 F10
Phocle Green
Hereford 98 F2
Phoenix Green Hants .49 B9
Phoenix Row
Durham. 233 F9
Phorp Moray 301 D10
Pibsbury Som 28 B6
Pibwrlwyd Carms . . .74 B6
Pica Cumb 228 G2
Piccadilly S Yorks . .187 B7
Warks 134 D4
Piccadilly Corner
Norf 142 F5
Piccotts End Herts . . .85 D9
Pickburn S Yorks . . .198 F4
Picken End Worcs . . .98 C6
Pickering N Yorks . .216 C5
Pickering Nook
Durham. 242 F5
Picket Hill Hants. . . .31 F11
Picket Piece Hants . .47 D11
Picket Post Hants . . .31 F11
Pickford W Mid 134 G5
Pickford Green
W Mid 134 G5
Pickhill N Yorks 214 C6
Picklenash Glos 98 F4
Picklescott Shrops . .131 D8
Pickles Hill W Yorks .204 F6
Pickletillem Fife . . .287 E8
Pickley Green
Gtr Man 195 G7
Pickmere Ches E . . .183 F11
Pickney S Yorks 27 B11
Pickstock Telford. . .150 E4
Pickup Bank
Blackburn 195 C8
Pickwell Devon 40 E3
Leics 154 G5
Pickwick Wilts. 61 E11
Pickwood Scar
W Yorks 196 C5
Pickworth Lincs 155 C10
Rutland 155 G9
Picton Ches W 182 G6
Flint 181 E10
N Yorks. 225 D8
Pict's Hill Som. 28 B6
Piddinghoe E Sus . . .36 G6
Piddington Bucks . . .84 G4
Oxon 83 B10
W Nhants 120 G6
Piddletrenthide
Dorset. 17 B10
Pidley Cambs 122 B6
Pidney Dorset 30 F2
Piece Corn 2 B5
Piercebridge Darl . .224 B4
Piercing Hill Essex . .86 F6
Pierowall Orkney. . .314 A4
Piff's Elm Glos 99 F8

Pigdon Northumb. . .252 F5
Pightley Som 43 F8
Pig Oak Dorset. 31 G8
Pigstye Green Essex .87 D10
Pike End W Yorks . .196 D5
Pikehall Derbys 169 D11
Pike Hill Lancs 204 G3
Pike Law W Yorks . .196 D4
Pikeshill Hants 32 F3
Pikestye Hereford . . .97 B10
Pilford Dorset 31 G8
Pilgrims Hatch Essex .87 F9
Pilham Lincs. 188 C5
Pilhough Derbys . . .170 C3
Pill N Som 60 D4
Pembs 72 D6
Pillaton Corn 7 C7
Staffs. 151 G8
Pillerton Hersey
Warks 100 B5
Pillerton Priors
Warks 100 B5
Pilleth Powys 114 D5
Pilley Glos 81 B7
Hants. 20 B2
S Yorks. 197 G10
Pilley Bailey Hants. . .20 B2
Pillgwenlly Newport. .59 B10
Pilling Lancs 202 D4
Pilling Lane Lancs . .202 D3
Pillmouth Devon 25 C7
Pillowell Glos 79 D10
Pillows Green Glos . . .98 F5
Pillwell Dorset 30 D2
Pilmuir Borders 261 G11
Pilning S Glos. 60 B5
Pilrig Edin 280 F5
Pilsbury Derbys 169 C10
Pilsdon Dorset. 16 B4
Pilsgate Pboro 137 B11
Pilsley Derbys 170 C4
Derbys. 186 G2
Pilsley Green
Derbys. 170 C6
Pilson Green Norf . .161 G7
Piltdown E Sus. 36 C6
Pilton Devon. 40 G4
Edin 280 F4
N Nhants 137 G10
Rutland 137 C8
Som 44 F5
Pilton Green
Swansea 56 D2
Piltown Som. 44 F5
Pimhole Gtr Man . . .195 E10
Pimlico Herts. 85 E9
Lancs 203 E10
London. 67 D9
N Nhants. 102 C2
Pimperne Dorset 29 F9
Dorset. 30 F6
Pinchbeck Lincs 156 D4
Pinchbeck Bars
Lincs 156 D3
Pinchbeck West
Lincs 156 D4
Pincheon Green
S Yorks. 199 D7
Pinckney Green
Wilts 61 G10
Pincock Lancs 194 D5
Pineham Kent 55 D10
M Keynes 103 C7
Pinehurst Swindon . . .63 B7
Pinfarthings Glos 80 E5
Pinfold Lancs 193 E11
Pinfold Hill S Yorks .197 G9
Pinfoldpond C Beds . .103 E8
Pinford End Suff. . . .124 F6
Pinged Carms 74 E6
Pingewood W Berks . .65 F7
Pin Green Herts 104 F4
Pinhoe Devon. 14 C5
Pinkett's Booth
W Mid 134 G5
Pink Green Worcs. . .117 D11
Pinkie Braes E Loth. .281 G7
Pinkney Wilts. 61 B11
Pinkneys Green
Windsor. 65 C11
Pinksmoor Som 27 D10
Pinley W Mid. 119 B7
Pinley Green Warks. .118 D4
Pin Mill Suff 108 D4
Pinminnoch
Dumfries 236 D2
S Ayrs. 244 E6
Pinmore S Ayrs 244 E6
Pinmore Mains
S Ayrs. 244 E6
Pinnacles Essex 86 D6
Pinner London 66 B6
Pinner Green
London. 66 B6
Pinnerwood Park
London. 85 G10
Pin's Green Worcs . . .98 B6
Pinsley Green
Ches E 167 F9
Pinstones Shrops . . .131 F9
Pinvin Worcs 99 B9
Pinwall Leics 134 C6
Pinwherry S Ayrs. . .244 F5
Pinxton Derbys 171 E7
Pipe and Lyde
Hereford 97 C10
Pipe Aston Hereford. .115 C9
Pipe Gate Shrops . . .168 G2
Pipehill Staffs 133 B11
Pipehouse Bath. 45 B9
Piperhall Argyll 266 D2
Piperhill Highld 301 D10
Pipe Ridware
Staffs. 151 F11
Piper's Ash Ches W. .166 B6
Piper's End Worcs . . .98 E6
Piper's Hill Worcs . .117 D9
Piper's Pool Corn . . .11 E11
Pipewell N Nhants. .136 F6
Pippacott Devon 40 F4
Pippin Street Lancs .194 C5
Pipps Hill Essex. 69 B7

Pipsden Kent 53 G9
Pipton Powys 96 D3
Pirbright Sur 50 B2
Pirbright Camp Sur 50 B2
Pirnmill N Ayrs 255 C9
Pirton Herts 104 E2
Worcs 99 B7
Pisgah Ceredig 112 B3
Stirling 285 G11
Pishill Oxon 65 B8
Pishill Bank Oxon 84 G2
Pismire Hill S Yorks 186 C5
Pistyll Gwyn 162 G4
Pit Mon 78 D5
Pitagowan Perth 291 G10
Pitblae Aberds 303 C9
Pitcairngreen Perth 286 E4
Pitcalnie Highld 301 B8
Pitcaple Aberds 303 G7
Pitchcombe Glos 80 D5
Pitchcott Bucks 102 G5
Pitcher's Green Suff 125 F8
Pitchford Shrops 131 C10
Pitch Green Bucks 84 E3
Pitch Place Sur 49 F11
Sur 50 C3
Pitcombe Som 45 G7
Pitcorthie Fife 280 D2
Fife 287 G9
Pitcot Som 45 D7
V Glam 57 G11
Pitcox E Loth 282 F2
Pitcur Perth 286 D6
Pitfancy Aberds 302 E5
Pitfichie Aberds 293 B8
Pitforthie Aberds 293 F10
Pitgair Aberds 303 D7
Pitgrudy Highld 309 K7
Pithmaduthy Highld 301 B7
Pitkennedy Angus 287 B9
Pitkevy Fife 286 G6
Pitkierie Fife 287 G9
Pitlessie Fife 287 G7
Pitlochry Perth 286 B3
Pitmachie Aberds 302 G6
Pitmain Highld 291 C9
Pitmedden Aberds 303 G8
Pitminster Som 28 D2
Pitmuies Angus 287 C9
Pitmunie Aberds 293 B8
Pitney Som 29 B7
Pitrocknie Perth 286 C6
Pitscottie Fife 287 F8
Pitsea Essex 69 B8
Pitses Gtr Man 196 G2
Pitsford W Nhants 120 D5
Pitsford Hill Som 42 G6
Pitsmoor S Yorks 186 D5
Pitstone Bucks 84 B6
Pitstone Green Bucks 84 B6
Pitstone Hill Bucks 85 C7
Pitt Hants 33 B7
Pittachar Perth 286 E2
Pitt Court Glos 80 F3
Pittendreich
Moray 301 C11
Pittentrail Highld 309 J7
Pittenweem Fife 287 G9
Pitteuchar Fife 280 B5
Pittington Durham 234 C2
Pittodrie Aberds 302 G6
Pitton Swansea 56 D2
Wilts 47 G8
Pitts Hill Stoke 168 E5
Pittswood Kent 52 D6
Pittulie Aberds 303 C9
Pittville Glos 99 G9
Pityme Corn 10 F5
Pity Me Durham 233 B11
Pityoulish Highld 291 B11
Pixey Green Suff 126 B4
Pixham Sur 51 C7
Worcs 98 B6
Pixley Hereford 98 D3
Shrops 150 D3
Pizien Well Kent 53 C7
Place Newton
N Yorks 217 E7
Plaidy Aberds 303 D7
Corn 6 E5
Plain-an-Gwarry Corn 4 G3
Plain Dealings Pembs 73 B9
Plains N Lanark 268 B5
Plainsfield Som 43 F7
Plain Spot Notts 171 E7
Plain Street Corn 10 F5
Plaish Shrops 131 D10
Plaistow London 68 C2
London 68 E2
W Sus 50 G4
Plaistow Green
Essex 106 F6
Plaitford Wilts 32 D3
Plaitford Green
Hants 32 C3
Plank Lane Gtr Man 194 G6
Plans Dumfries 238 D3
Plantation Bridge
Cumb 221 F9
Plantationfoot
Dumfries 248 E4
Plardiwick Staffs 150 E6
Plasau Shrops 149 E7
Plâs Berwyn Denb 165 G11
Plas-canol Gwyn 145 F11
Plas Coch Wrex 166 E4
Plas Dinam Powys 129 F10
Plas Gogerddan
Ceredig 128 G2
Plashet London 68 C2
Plashett Carms 74 D3
Plasiolyn Powys 129 C11
Plas Llwyngwern
Powys 128 C5
Plas Meredydd
Powys 130 D3
Plas Nantyr Wrex 148 B3
Plasnewydd Powys 129 D9
Plaster's Green Bath 60 G4
Plastow Green Hants 64 G4
Plas-yn-Cefn Denb 181 G8
Platt Kent 52 B6
Platt Bridge
Gtr Man 194 G6
Platt Lane Shrops 149 B10
Platts Common
S Yorks 197 G11
Platt's Heath Kent 53 C11
Plawsworth
Durham 233 B11
Plaxtol Kent 52 C6
Playden E Sus 38 C6
Playford Suff 108 B4
Play Hatch Oxon 65 D8
Playing Place Corn 4 G6
Playley Green Glos 98 E5
Plealey Shrops 131 B8
Pleamore Cross
Som 27 D10
Plean Stirling 278 D6
Pleasant Valley
Pembs 73 D10
Pleasington
Blackburn 194 B6
Pleasley Derbys 171 C8
Pleasleyhill Notts 171 C8
Pleck Dorset 30 D3
Dorset 30 E2
W Mid 133 D9
Pleckgate Blackburn 203 G9
Pleck or Little Ansty
Dorset 30 G3
Pledgdon Green
Essex 105 F11
Pledwick W Yorks 197 D10
Plemstall Ches W 183 G7
Plenmeller
Northumb 240 E6
Pleshey Essex 87 C11
Plockton Highld 295 B10
Plocrapol W Isles 305 J3
Plot Gate Som 44 G4
Plot Street Som 44 F5
Ploughfield Hereford 97 C7
Plough Hill Warks 134 E6
Plowden Shrops 131 F7
Ploxgreen Shrops 131 C7
Pluckley Kent 54 D2
Pluckley Thorne Kent 54 E2
Plucks Gutter Kent 71 G9
Plumbland Cumb 229 D9
Plumbley S Yorks 186 E6
Plumford Kent 54 B4
Plumley Ches E 184 F2
Plump Hill Glos 79 B11
Plumpton Cumb 230 D5
E Sus 36 E5
W Nhants 101 B11
Plumpton End
W Nhants 102 B4
Plumpton Foot
Cumb 230 D5
Plumpton Green
E Sus 36 D5
Plumpton Head
Cumb 230 E6
Plumstead London 68 D3
Norf 160 C2
Plumstead Common
London 68 D3
Plumstead Green
Norf 160 C2
Plumtree Notts 154 C2
Plumtree Green
Kent 53 D10
Plumtree Park
Notts 154 C2
Plungar Leics 154 C5
Plush Dorset 30 G2
Plusha Corn 11 E11
Plushabridge Corn 12 G2
Plusterwine Glos 79 F9
Plwmp Ceredig 111 G7
Plymouth Plym 7 E9
Plympton Plym 7 D10
Plymstock Plym 7 E10
Plymtree Devon 27 G9
Pobgreen Gtr Man 196 F4
Pochin Houses
Caerph 77 E11
Pocket Nook
Gtr Man 183 B10
Pockley N Yorks 216 B2
Pocklington
E Yorks 208 D2
Pockthorpe Norf 141 D8
Norf 158 D6
Norf 159 E10
Norf 159 F11
Pode Hole Lincs 156 E4
Podimore Som 29 C8
Podington Bedford 121 E8
Podmoor Worcs 117 C7
Podmore Norf 159 G9
Staffs 150 B5
Podsmead Glos 80 B4
Poffley End Oxon 82 C5
Pogmoor S Yorks 197 F10
Point Corn 3 B8
Point Clear Essex 89 C9
Pointon Lincs 156 C2
Pokesdown BCP 19 C8
Pol a Charra
W Isles 297 K3
Polbae Dumfries 236 B4
Polbain Highld 307 H4
Polbathic Corn 7 D7
Polbeth W Loth 269 C10
Polborder Corn 7 C7
Polbrock Corn 5 B10
Polchar Highld 291 C10
Polebrook
N Nhants 137 F11
Pole Elm Worcs 98 B6
Polegate E Sus 23 D9
Pole Moor W Yorks 196 D5
Poles Highld 309 K7
Polesden Lacey Sur 50 C6
Poleshill Som 27 C9
Pole's Hole Wilts 45 C10
Polesworth Warks 134 C5
Polgear Corn 2 B5
Polgigga Corn 1 E3
Polglass Highld 307 J5
Polgooth Corn 5 E9
Poling W Sus 35 G8
Poling Corner W Sus 35 F8
Polkerris Corn 5 E11
Polla Highld 308 D3
Polladras Corn 2 C4
Pollard Street Norf 160 C6
Pollhill Kent 53 C11
Poll Hill Mers 182 E3
Pollie Highld 309 H7
Pollington E Yorks 198 D6
Polliwilline Argyll 255 G8
Polloch Highld 289 C9
Pollok Glasgow 267 C10
Pollokshields
Glasgow 267 C11
Polmadie Glasgow 267 C11
Polmarth Corn 2 B6
Polmassick Corn 5 F9
Polmear Corn 5 E11
Polmont Falk 279 F8
Polmorla Corn 10 G5
Polnessan E Ayrs 257 G10
Polnish Highld 295 G9
Polopit N Nhants 121 B10
Polpenwith Corn 2 D6
Polpeor Corn 2 B2
Polperro Corn 6 E4
Polruan Corn 6 E2
Polsham Som 44 E4
Polsloe Devon 14 C4
Polstead Suff 107 D9
Polstead Heath Suff 107 C9
Poltalloch Argyll 275 D9
Poltesco Corn 2 F6
Poltimore Devon 14 B5
Polton Midloth 270 C5
Polwarth Borders 272 E4
Polwheveral Corn 2 D6
Polyphant Corn 11 E11
Polzeath Corn 10 F4
Pomeroy Derbys 169 B10
Pomphlett Plym 7 E10
Ponciau Wrex 166 F3
Pond Close Som 27 B10
Ponde Powys 96 D2
Pondersbridge
Cambs 138 E5
Ponders End London 86 F5
Pond Park Bucks 85 E7
Pond Street Essex 105 D9
Pondtail Hants 49 C10
Pondwell IoW 21 C8
Poniou Corn 1 B4
Ponjeravah Corn 2 D6
Ponsanooth Corn 3 B7
Ponsford Devon 27 F8
Ponsonby Cumb 219 D11
Ponsongath Corn 3 F7
Ponsworthy Devon 13 G10
Pont Corn 6 E2
Pont Aber Carms 94 G4
Pont Aber-Geirw
Gwyn 146 D5
Pontamman Carms 75 C10
Pontantwn Carms 74 C6
Pontardawe Neath 76 E2
Pontarddulais
Swansea 75 E9
Pontarfynach = *Devils*
Bridge Ceredig 112 B4
Pont-ar-gothi
Carms 93 G10
Pont ar Hydfer
Powys 95 F7
Pont-ar-llechau
Carms 94 G4
Pontarsais Carms 93 F8
Pontblyddyn Flint 166 C3
Pontbren Araeth
Carms 94 G3
Pontbren Llwyd
Rhondda 76 D6
Pontcanna Cardiff 59 D7
Pont Cyfyng Conwy 164 D2
Pont Cysyllte Wrex 166 G3
Pontdolgoch
Powys 129 E10
Pont Dolydd Prysor
Gwyn 146 B4
Pontefract W Yorks 198 C3
Ponteland Northumb 242 C5
Ponterwyd Ceredig 128 G4
Pontesbury Shrops 131 B7
Pontesbury Hill
Shrops 131 B7
Pontesford Shrops 131 B8
Pontfadog Wrex 148 B4
Pontfaen Pembs 91 E10
Pont-faen Powys 95 E9
Shrops 148 B5
Pont Fronwydd
Gwyn 146 E6
Pont-gareg Pembs 92 C2
Pontgarreg Ceredig 110 G6
Ponthen Shrops 148 F6
Pont-Henri Carms 75 D7
Ponthir Torf 78 G4
Ponthirwaun Ceredig 92 B5
Pont Hwfa Anglesey 178 E2
Pontiago Pembs 91 D8
Pont iets = *Pontyates*
Carms 75 D7
Pontithel Powys 96 D3
Pontllanfraith
Caerph 77 F11
Pontlliw Swansea 75 E10
Pont-Llogel Powys 147 F10
Pontllyfni Gwyn 162 E6
Pontlottyn Caerph 77 D10
Pontneddfechan
Powys 76 D6
Pontnewydd Torf 78 F3
Pont-newydd Carms 74 D6
Flint 165 B11
Pontnewynydd Torf 78 E3
Pont Pen-y-benglog
Gwyn 163 C10
Pontrhydfendigaid
Ceredig 112 D4
Pont Rhydgaled
Powys 128 G6
Pont Rhyd-goch
Conwy 163 C11
Pont-Rhyd-sarn
Gwyn 147 D7
Pont Rhyd-y-berry
Powys 95 D9
Pont Rhyd-y-cyff
Bridgend 57 D11
Pontrhydyfen Neath 57 C9
Pont-rhyd-y-groes
Ceredig 112 C4
Pontrhydyrun Torf 78 F3
Pont-Rhythallt
Gwyn 163 C8
Pontrilas Hereford 97 F7
Pontrobert Powys 148 G2
Pont-rug Gwyn 163 C8
Pont Senni = *Sennybridge*
Powys 95 F8
Ponts Green E Sus 23 B11
Pontshill Hereford 98 G2
Pont-siôn Ceredig 93 B8
Pont Siôn Norton
Rhondda 77 G9
Pontsticill M Tydf 77 C9
Pont-Walby Neath 76 D5
Pontwgan Conwy 180 G3
Pontyates = *Pont-iets*
Carms 75 D7
Pontyberem Carms 75 C8
Pont-y-blew Shrops 148 B6
Pontyclun Rhondda 58 C4
Pontycymer Bridgend 76 G6
Pontyglasier Pembs 92 D2
Pont-y-gwaith
Rhondda 77 G8
Pontymister Caerph 78 G2
Pontymoel Torf 78 E3
Pont-y-pant Conwy 164 E3
Pont y Pennant
Gwyn 147 E8
Pontypool Torf 78 E3
Pontypridd Rhondda 58 B5
Pont yr Afon-Gam
Gwyn 164 G2
Pont-yr-hafod
Pembs 91 F8
Pont-y-rhyl Bridgend 58 B2
Pont-Ystrad Denb 165 C9
Pont-y-wal Powys 96 D2
Pontywaun Caerph 78 G2
Pooksgreen Hants 32 E5
Pool Corn 4 G3
W Yorks 205 D10
Poolbrook Worcs 98 C5
Poole BCP 18 C6
N Yorks 198 B3
Som 27 C10
Poole Keynes Glos 81 F8
Poolend Staffs 169 D7
Poolestown Dorset 30 D2
Poolewe Highld 307 L3
Pooley Bridge
Cumb 230 G5
Pooley Street Norf 141 G11
Poolfold Staffs 168 D5
Poolhead Shrops 149 C9
Pool Head
Hereford 115 G11
Pool Hey Lancs 193 D11
Poolhill Glos 98 F4
Poolmill Hereford 97 G11
Pool o' Muckhart
Clack 286 G4
Pool Quay Powys 148 G5
Poolsbrook Derbys 186 G6
Poolside Moray 302 E4
Poolstock Gtr Man 194 G5
Pooltown Som 42 F3
Pootings Kent 52 D3
Pope Hill Pembs 72 C6
Pope's Hill Glos 79 C11
Popeswood Brack 65 F10
Popham Devon 41 G8
Hants 48 E5
Poplar London 67 C11
Poplar Grove Lincs 190 B6
Poplars Herts 104 G5
Popley Hants 48 C6
Porchester
Nottingham 171 G9
Porchfield IoW 20 C4
Porin Highld 300 D3
Poringland Norf 142 C5
Porkellis Corn 2 C5
Porlock Som 41 D11
Porlockford Som 41 D11
Porlock Weir Som 41 D11
Portachoillan Argyll 255 B8
Port Allen Perth 286 E6
Port Ann Argyll 275 E10
Port Appin Argyll 289 E11
Port Arthur Shetland 313 K5
Portash Wilts 46 G3
Port Askaig Argyll 274 G5
Portavadie Argyll 275 G10
Port Bannatyne
Argyll 275 G11
Port Brae Fife 280 C5
Port Bridge Devon 9 D7
Portbury N Som 60 D4
Port Carlisle Cumb 238 E6
Port Charlotte
Argyll 254 B3
Portchester Hants 33 F10
Portclair Highld 290 B6
Port Clarence
Stockton 234 G5
Port Dinorwic = *Y Felinheli*
Gwyn 163 B8
Port Driseach
Argyll 275 F10
Port Dundas
Glasgow 267 B11
Porteath Corn 10 F5
Port Edgar Edin 280 F2
Port Ellen Argyll 254 C4
Port Elphinstone
Aberds 293 B9
Portencalzie
Dumfries 236 B2
Portencross N Ayrs 266 F3
Porterfield Renfs 267 B9
Port Erin IoM 192 F2
Port Erroll Aberds 303 F10
Porter's End Herts 85 B11
Portesham Dorset 17 D8
Portessie Moray 302 C4
Port e Vullen IoM 192 C5
Port-Eynon Swansea 56 D3
Portfield Argyll 289 G9
Som 28 B6
W Sus 22 B5
Portfield Gate Pembs 72 B6
Portgate Devon 12 D4
Port Gaverne Corn 10 E6
Port Glasgow
Invclyd 276 G6
Portgordon Moray 302 C3
Portgower Highld 311 H4
Porth Corn 4 C6
Rhondda 77 G8
Porthallow Corn 3 E7
Corn 6 E4
Porthcawl Bridgend 57 F10
Porth Colmon Gwyn 144 C3
Porthcothan Corn 10 G3
Porthcurno Corn 1 E3
Portheiddy Pembs 90 E6
Port Henderson
Highld 299 B7
Porthgain Pembs 90 E6
Porthgwarra Corn 1 E3
Porthhallow Corn 3 E7
Porthill Shrops 149 G9
Staffs 168 F5
Port Hill Oxon 65 B7
Porthilly Corn 10 F4
Porth Kea Corn 4 G6
Porthkerry V Glam 58 F5
Porthleven Corn 2 D4
Porthllechog = *Bull Bay*
Anglesey 178 C6
Porthloo Scilly 1 G4
Porthmadog Gwyn 145 B11
Porthmeor Corn 1 B4
Porth Navas Corn 3 D7
Porthoustock Corn 3 E8
Porthpean Corn 5 E10
Porthtowan Corn 4 F3
Porth Tywyn = *Burry Port*
Carms 74 E6
Porth-y-felin
Anglesey 178 E2
Porthyrhyd Carms 75 B8
Carms 94 D4
Porth-y-waen
Shrops 148 E5
Portico Mers 183 C7
Portincaple Argyll 276 C4
Portington Devon 12 F4
E Yorks 207 G11
Portinnisherrich
Argyll 275 B10
Portinscale Cumb 229 G11
Port Isaac Corn 10 E5
Portishead N Som 60 D3
Portkil Argyll 276 E5
Portknockie Moray 302 C4
Port Lamont Argyll 275 F11
Portland Som 44 F3
Portlethen Aberds 293 D11
Portlethen Village
Aberds 293 D11
Portlevorchy Highld 306 D7
Portling Dumfries 237 D10
Port Lion Pembs 73 D7
Portloe Corn 3 B10
Port Logan Dumfries 236 E2
Portlooe Corn 6 E4
Portmahomack
Highld 311 L3
Port Mead Swansea 56 B6
Portmeirion Gwyn 145 B11
Portmellon Corn 5 G10
Port Mholair
W Isles 304 E7
Port Mor Highld 288 B6
Portmore Hants 20 B2
Port Mulgrave
N Yorks 226 B5
Portnacroish Argyll 289 E11
Portnahaven Argyll 254 B2
Portnalong Highld 294 B5
Portnaluchaig
Highld 295 G8
Portnancon Highld 308 C4
Port Nan Giùran
W Isles 304 E7
Port nan Long
W Isles 296 D4
Portnellan Stirling 285 E8
Stirling 285 F8
Port Nis W Isles 304 B7
Portobello Edin 280 G6
T&W 243 F7
W Mid 133 D9
W Yorks 197 D10
Port of Menteith
Stirling 285 G9
Porton Wilts 47 F7
Portpatrick
Dumfries 236 D2
Port Quin Corn 10 E5
Portrack Stockton 225 B9
Port Ramsay Argyll 289 E10
Portreath Corn 4 F3
Portree Highld 298 E4
Port St Mary IoM 192 F3
Portscatho Corn 3 B9
Portsea Ptsmth 33 G10
Portsea Island
Ptsmth 33 G11
Portskerra Highld 310 C2
Portskewett Mon 60 B4
Portslade Brighton 36 F3
Portslade-by-Sea
Brighton 36 G3
Portslade Village
Brighton 36 F3
Portsmouth Ptsmth 21 B9
W Yorks 196 B2
Port Solent Ptsmth 33 F10
Portsonachan Argyll 284 E4
Portsoy Aberds 302 C5
Port Sunlight Mers 182 E4
Port Sutton Bridge
Lincs 157 E9
Portswood Soton 32 E6
Port Talbot Neath 57 D9
Porttanachy Moray 302 C3
Port Tennant
Swansea 57 C7
Portuairk Highld 288 C6
Portvasgo Highld 308 C5
Portway
Dorset 18 D2
Glos 98 E5
Hereford 97 B9
Hereford 97 D9
Som 28 B6
Som 44 F3
W Mid 133 F9
Worcs 117 C11
Port Wemyss Argyll 254 B2
Port William
Dumfries 236 E5
Portwood Gtr Man 184 C6
Portwrinkle Corn 7 E7
Posenhall Shrops 132 C3
Poslingford Suff 106 B5
Posso Borders 260 C6
Postbridge Devon 13 F9
Postcombe Oxon 84 F2
Post Green Dorset 18 C5
Postling Kent 54 F6
Postlip Glos 99 F10
Post Mawr = *Synod Inn*
Ceredig 111 G8
Postwick Norf 142 B5
Potarch Aberds 293 D8
Potash Suff 108 D2
Potbridge Hants 49 C8
Pot Common Sur 50 E2
Potholm Dumfries 249 F9
Potmaily Highld 300 F4
Potman's Heath Kent 38 B5
Potsgrove C Beds 103 F9
Potten End Herts 85 D8
Potten Street Kent 71 F9
Potter Brompton
N Yorks 217 D9
Pottergate Street
Norf 142 E3
Potterhanworth
Lincs 173 B9
Potterhanworth Booths
Lincs 173 B9
Potter Heigham
Norf 161 F8
Potter Hill Leics 154 E4
S Yorks 186 B4
Potterne Wilts 46 B3
Potterne Wick Wilts 46 B4
Potternewton
W Yorks 206 F2
Potters Bar Herts 86 E3
Potters Brook Lancs 202 C5
Potters Corner Kent 54 E3
Potter's Cross
Staffs 132 G6
Potters Crouch
Herts 85 D10
Potter's Forstal
Kent 53 D11
Potter's Green E Sus 37 C8
W Mid 135 G7
Pottersheath Herts 86 B2
Potters Hill N Som 60 F4
Potters Marston
Leics 135 D9
Potter Somersal
Derbys 152 B2
Potterspury
W Nhants 102 C5
Potter Street Essex 87 D7
Potterton Aberds 293 B11
W Yorks 206 F4
Pottery Field
W Yorks 206 G2
Potthorpe Norf 159 E8
Pottington Devon 40 G5
Potto N Yorks 225 E9
Potton C Beds 104 B4
Pott Row Norf 158 E4
Pott Shrigley
Ches E 184 F6
Pouchen End Herts 85 D8
Poughill Corn 24 F2
Devon 26 F5
Poulner Hants 31 F11
Poulshot Wilts 46 B3
Poulton Ches W 166 D5
Glos 81 E10
Mers 182 C4
Mers 182 E4
Poulton-le-Fylde
Lancs 202 F2
Pound Som 28 D6
Pound Bank Worcs 98 B5
Worcs 116 C4
Poundbury Dorset 17 C9
Poundffald Swansea 56 C5
Poundfield E Sus 52 G4
Poundford E Sus 37 C9
Poundgate E Sus 37 B7
Poundgreen
Wokingham 65 F7
Pound Green E Sus 37 C8
Hants 48 B5
IoW 20 D2
Suff 124 G4
Worcs 116 B5
Pound Hill W Sus 51 F9
Poundland S Ayrs 244 F5
Poundon Bucks 102 F2
Poundsbridge Kent 52 E4
Poundsgate Devon 13 G10
Poundstock Corn 11 B10
Pound Street Hants 64 G3
Pounsley E Sus 37 C8
Poverest London 68 F3
Povey Cross Sur 51 E9
Powburn Northumb 264 F3
Powderham Devon 14 E5
Powder Mills Kent 52 D5
Powers Hall End
Essex 88 B4
Powerstock Dorset 16 B6
Powfoot Dumfries 238 D4
Pow Green Hereford 98 C4
Powhill Cumb 238 F6
Powick Worcs 116 G6
Powler's Piece Devon 24 D5
Powmill Perth 279 B10
Pownall Park
Ches E 184 E4
Powntley Copse
Hants 49 E8
Poxwell Dorset 17 E10
Poyle Slough 66 D4
Poynings W Sus 36 E3
Poyntington Dorset 29 D11
Poynton Ches E 184 E6
Telford 149 F11
Poynton Green
Telford 149 F11
Poyntzfield Highld 301 C7
Poyston Pembs 73 B7
Poyston Cross Pembs 73 B7
Poystreet Green
Suff 125 F9
Praa Sands Corn 2 D3
Pratling Street Kent 53 B8
Pratt's Bottom
London 68 G3
Praze Corn 2 B3
Praze-an-Beeble Corn 2 B4
Predannack Wollas
Corn 2 F5
Prees Shrops 149 C11
Preesall Lancs 202 D3
Preesall Park Lancs 202 D3
Prees Green
Shrops 149 C11
Preesgweene
Shrops 148 B5
Prees Heath
Shrops 149 B11
Preeshenlle Shrops 148 C6
Prees Higher Heath
Shrops 149 B11
Prees Lower Heath
Shrops 149 C11
Prees Wood
Shrops 149 C11
Prenbrigog Flint 166 C3
Prendergast Pembs 73 B7
Pembs 90 G6
Prenderguest
Borders 273 D8
Prendwick
Northumb 264 G2
Pren-gwyn Ceredig 93 C8
Prenteg Gwyn 163 G9
Prenton Mers 182 D4
Prescot Mers 183 C7
Prescott Devon 27 E9
Glos 99 F9
Shrops 132 G3
Shrops 149 E8
Presdales Herts 86 C5
Preshome Moray 302 C4
Press Derbys 170 B5
Pressen Northumb 263 B8
Prestatyn Denb 181 E9
Prestbury Ches E 184 F6
Glos 99 G9
Presteigne Powys 114 E6
Presthope Shrops 131 D11
Prestleigh Som 44 E6
Prestolee Gtr Man 195 F9
Preston Borders 272 D5
Brighton 36 F4
Devon 14 G3
Dorset 17 E10
E Loth 281 F11
E Loth 281 G7
E Yorks 209 G9
Glos 81 E8
Glos 98 E3
Herts 104 G3
Kent 70 G4
Kent 71 G8
Lancs 194 B4
London 67 B7
Northumb 264 D5
Rutland 137 C7
Shrops 149 G10
Torbay 9 C7
T&W 243 D8
Wilts 62 D4
Wilts 63 E9
Preston Bagot
Warks 118 D3
Preston Bissett
Bucks 102 F3
Preston Bowyer
Som 27 B10
Preston Brockhurst
Shrops 149 E10
Preston Brook
Halton 183 E9
Preston Candover
Hants 48 E6
Preston Capes
W Nhants 119 G11
Preston Crowmarsh
Oxon 83 G10
Preston Deanery
W Nhants 120 F5
Prestonfield Edin 280 G5
Preston Fields
Warks 118 D3
Preston Grange
T&W 243 C8
Preston Green
Warks 118 D3
Preston Gubbals
Shrops 149 F9
Preston-le-Skerne
Durham 234 G2
Preston Marsh
Hereford 97 B11
Prestonmill
Dumfries 237 D11
Preston Montford
Shrops 149 G8
Preston on Stour
Warks 118 G4
Preston-on-Tees
Stockton 225 B8
Preston on the Hill
Halton 183 E9
Preston on Wye
Hereford 97 C7
Prestonpans E Loth 281 G7
Preston Pastures
Worcs 100 B3
Preston Plucknett
Som 29 D8
Preston St Mary
Suff 125 G8
Preston-under-Scar
N Yorks 223 G11
Preston upon the Weald
Moors Telford 150 F3
Preston Wynne
Hereford 97 B11
Prestwich Gtr Man 195 G10
Prestwick Northumb 242 C5
S Ayrs 257 D9
Prestwold Leics 153 E11
Prestwood Bucks 84 E5
Staffs 133 F7
Staffs 169 G10
Prey Heath Sur 50 B3
Price Town Bridgend 76 G6
Prickwillow Cambs 139 G11
Priddy Som 44 C4
Pride Park Derbys 153 B7
Priestacott Devon 24 F6
Priestcliffe Derbys 185 G10
Priestcliffe Ditch
Derbys 185 G10
Priest Down Bath 60 G6
Priestfield W Mid 133 D8
Worcs 98 C6
Priesthaugh
Borders 249 C11
Priesthill Glasgow 267 C10
Priesthorpe
W Yorks 205 F10
Priest Hutton
Lancs 211 E10
Priestley Green
W Yorks 196 B6
Prieston Borders 262 D2
Priestside Dumfries 238 D4
Priestthorpe
W Yorks 205 F8
Priest Weston
Shrops 130 D5
Priestwood Brack 65 F11
Kent 69 G7
Priestwood Green
Kent 69 G7
Primethorpe Leics 135 E10
Primrose T&W 243 E8
Primrose Corner
Norf 160 G6
Primrose Green
Norf 159 F11
Primrosehill Herts 85 E9
Primrose Hill Bath 61 F8
Lancs 193 F11
London 67 C9
W Mid 133 F8
Primrose Valley
N Yorks 218 D2
Primsland Worcs 117 E8
Prince Hill Ches E 168 G2
Prince Royd
W Yorks 196 D6
Princes End W Mid 133 E9
Princes Gate Pembs 73 C10
Prince's Marsh Hants 34 B3
Princes Park Mers 182 D5
Princes Risborough
Bucks 84 E4
Princethorpe Warks 119 C8
Princetown Caerph 77 C10
Devon 13 G7
Prinsted W Sus 22 B3
Printstile Kent 52 E5
Prion Denb 165 C9
Prior Muir Fife 287 F9
Prior Park Northumb 273 E9
Prior Rigg Cumb 239 D11
Priors Frome
Hereford 97 D11
Priors Halton
Shrops 115 B9
Priors Hardwick
Warks 119 F9
Priorslee Telford 150 G4
Priors Marston
Warks 119 F9
Prior's Norton Glos 99 G7
Priors Park Glos 99 E7
Priorswood Som 28 B2
Priory Pembs 72 D6
Priory Green Suff 107 C8
Priory Heath Suff 108 C3
Priory Wood Hereford 96 B5
Prisk V Glam 58 D4
Pristacott Devon 25 B8
Priston Bath 61 G7
Pristow Green Norf 142 F2
Prittlewell Southend 69 B11
Privett Hants 21 B7
Hants 33 B11
Prixford Devon 40 F4
Probus Corn 5 F7
Proncy Highld 309 K7
Prospect Cumb 229 C8
Prospect Village
Staffs 151 G10
Prospidnick Corn 2 C4
Provanmill Glasgow 268 B2
Prowse Devon 26 F4
Prudhoe Northumb 242 E3
Prussia Cove Corn 2 D3
Ptarmigan Lodge
Stirling 285 G7
Pubil Perth 285 C8
Publow Bath 60 G6

Puckeridge Herts . . . 105 G7
Puckington Som 28 D5
Pucklechurch S Glos . . 61 D7
Pucknall Hants 32 B5
Puckrup Glos 99 D7
Puckshole Glos 80 D4
Puddaven Devon 8 C5
Puddinglake
  Ches W 168 B2
Pudding Pie Nook
  Lancs 202 F6
Puddington
  Ches W 182 G4
  Devon 26 E4
Puddle Corn 5 D11
Puddlebridge Som 28 E4
Puddledock Kent 52 C3
  Kent 68 E4
  Norf 141 E11
Puddletown Dorset . . 17 C11
Pudleigh Som 28 E4
Pudleston Hereford . . 115 F11
Pudsey W Yorks 196 B2
  W Yorks 205 G4
Pulborough W Sus . . . 35 D8
Pulcree Dumfries . . . 237 D7
Pule Hill W Yorks . . . 196 B5
Puleston Telford 150 E4
Pulford Ches W 166 D5
Pulham Dorset 30 F2
Pulham Market Norf 142 F3
Pulham St Mary
  Norf 142 F4
Pullens Green
  S Glos 79 G10
Pulley Shrops 131 B9
Pullington Kent 53 G10
Pulloxhill C Beds . . . 103 E11
Pulverbatch Shrops . . 131 C8
Pumpherston
  W Loth 269 B11
Pumsaint Carms 94 C3
Puncheston = Cas-Mael
  Pembs 91 F10
Puncknowle Dorset . . 16 D6
Punnett's Town
  E Sus 37 C10
Purbrook Hants 33 F11
Purewell BCP 19 C9
Purfleet Thurrock . . . 68 D5
Puriton Som 43 E10
Purleigh Essex 88 E4
Purley London 67 G10
Purley on Thames
  W Berks 65 D7
Purlogue Shrops 114 B5
Purlpit Wilts 61 F11
Purls Bridge Cambs 139 F9
Purn N Som 43 B10
Purse Caundle
  Dorset 29 D11
Purslow Shrops 131 G7
Purston Jaglin
  W Yorks 198 D2
Purtington Som 28 F5
Purton Glos 79 E11
  W Berks 64 D3
  Wilts 62 B5
Purton Common
  Wilts 62 B5
Purton Stoke Wilts . . 81 G9
Purwell Herts 104 F4
Pury End W Nhants . . 102 B4
Pusey Oxon 82 F5
Putley Hereford 98 D2
Putley Common
  Hereford 98 D2
Putley Green
  Hereford 98 D3
Putloe Glos 80 D3
Putney London 67 D8
Putney Heath London . 67 E8
Putney Vale London . . 67 E8
Putnoe Bedford 121 G11
Putsborough Devon . . 40 E3
Putson Hereford 97 D10
Puttenham Herts 84 C5
  Sur 50 D2
Puttock End Essex . . 106 C6
Puttock's End Essex . . 87 B9
Putton Dorset 17 E9
Puxey Dorset 30 E3
Puxley W Nhants 102 C5
Puxton N Som 60 G2
Pwll Carms 75 E7
  Powys 130 C3
Pwll-clai Flint 181 G11
Pwllcrochan Pembs . . 72 E6
Pwll-glas Denb 165 E10
Pwllgloyw Powys 95 E10
Pwllheli Gwyn 145 B7
Pwll-Mawr Cardiff . . 59 D8
Pwll-melyn Flint 181 G11
Pwllmeyric Mon 79 G8
Pwll-trap Carms 74 B3
Pwll-y-glaw Neath . . 57 C9
Pwllypant Caerph . . . 59 B7
Pye Bridge Derbys . . 170 E6
Pyecombe W Sus 36 E3
Pye Corner Devon . . . 14 B4
  Kent 53 D11
  Newport 59 B9
  S Glos 60 D6
Pye Green Staffs 151 G9
Pye Hill Notts 170 E6
Pyewipe NE Lincs . . . 201 E9
Pyle IoW 20 F5
  Swansea 56 D4
Pyle = Y Pîl
  Bridgend 57 E10
Pylehill Hants 33 D7
Pyle Hill Sur 50 B3
Pyleigh Som 42 G6
Pylle Som 44 F6
Pymore or Pymoor
  Cambs 139 F9
Pype Hayes W Mid . . 134 E2
Pyrford Sur 50 B4
Pyrford Green Sur . . . 50 B4
Pyrford Village Sur . . 50 B4

Pyrland Som 28 B2
Pyrton Oxon 83 F11
Pytchley N Nhants . . 121 C7
Pyworthy Devon 24 G4

Q

Quabbs Shrops 130 G4
Quabrook E Sus 52 G2
Quadring Lincs 156 C4
Quadring Eaudike
  Lincs 156 C4
Quags Corner W Sus . 34 C5
Quainton Bucks 84 B2
Quaker's Yard M Tydf . 77 F9
Quaking Houses
  Durham 242 G5
Quality Corner
  Cumb 219 B9
Quarhouse Glos 80 E5
Quarley Hants 47 E9
Quarmby W Yorks . . 196 D6
Quarndon Derbys . . . 170 G4
Quarndon Common
  Derbys 170 G4
Quarrelton Renfs . . . 267 C8
Quarrendon Bucks . . 84 B4
Quarr Hill IoW 21 C7
Quarriers Village
  Invclyd 267 B7
Quarrington Lincs . . 173 B9
Quarrington Hill
  Durham 234 D2
Quarrybank Ches W . 167 B8
Quarry Bank W Mid . 133 F8
Quarryford E Loth . . 271 B11
Quarryhead Aberds . 303 C9
Quarry Heath Staffs . 151 B8
Quarryhill Highld . . . 309 L7
Quarry Hill Staffs . . 134 C4
Quarrywood Moray 301 C11
Quarter S Lanark . . . 268 E4
Quartley Devon 27 B7
Quatford Shrops 132 E4
Quatquoy Orkney . . . 314 E3
Quatt Shrops 132 F5
Quebec Durham 233 C9
  W Sus 34 C3
Quedgeley Glos 80 C4
Queen Adelaide
  Cambs 139 G11
Queenborough Kent . 70 E2
Queen Camel Som . . 29 C9
Queen Charlton Bath . 60 F6
Queenhill Worcs 99 D7
Queen Oak Dorset . . 45 G9
Queen's Bower IoW . 21 E7
Queensbury London . . 67 B7
  W Yorks 205 B8
Queen's Corner
  W Sus 34 B5
Queensferry Edin . . 280 F2
  Flint 166 B4
Queen's Head
  Shrops 148 D6
Queenslie Glasgow . . 268 B3
Queen's Park
  Bedford 103 B10
  Blackburn 195 B7
  Ches W 166 B6
  Essex 87 F11
  W Nhants 120 E5
Queenstown
  Blackpool 202 F2
Queen Street Kent . . 53 D7
  Wilts 62 B5
Queensville Staffs . . 151 E8
Queenzieburn
  N Lanark 278 F3
Quemerford Wilts . . 62 F4
Quendale Shetland . . 313 M5
Quendon Essex 105 E10
Queniborough Leics 154 G2
Quenington Glos 81 E10
Quernmore Lancs . . 202 B6
Queslett W Mid 133 E11
Quethiock Corn 6 C6
Quholm Orkney 314 E2
Quick Gtr Man 196 G3
Quick Edge
  Gtr Man 196 G3
Quicks Green
  W Berks 64 D5
Quidenham Norf . . . 141 H10
Quidhampton Hants . 48 C4
  Wilts 46 G6
Quilquox Aberds . . . 303 F9
Quina Brook
  Shrops 149 C10
Quinbury End
  W Nhants 120 G2
Quindry Orkney 314 G4
Quinton W Mid 133 G9
  W Nhants 120 G5
Quintrell Downs Corn . 5 C7
Quixhill Staffs 169 G10
Quoditch Devon 12 B4
Quoig Perth 286 E2
Quoisley Ches E 167 F8
Quoit Corn 5 C8
Quorndon or Quorn
  Leics 153 F11
Quothquan
  S Lanark 259 B11
Quoyloo Orkney 314 D2
Quoynee Highld 310 D6
Quoyness Orkney . . . 314 F2
Quoys Shetland 312 B8
  Shetland 313 G6

R

Raasay Ho Highld . . . 295 B7
Rabbit's Cross Kent . 53 D9
Rableyheath Herts . . 86 B2
Raby Cumb 238 G5
  Mers 182 F4
Racecourse Suff 108 C3

Racedown Hants 47 E9
Rachan Mill Borders . 260 C4
Rachub Gwyn 163 B10
Rack End Oxon 82 E6
Rackenford Devon . . 26 D5
Rackham W Sus 35 D9
Rackheath Norf 160 G5
Rackley Som 43 C11
Racks Dumfries 238 C2
Rackwick Orkney . . . 314 B4
  Orkney 314 G2
Radbourne Derbys . . 152 B5
Radcliffe Gtr Man . . 195 F9
Radcliffe on Trent
  Notts 154 B2
Radclive Bucks 102 E3
Radcot Oxon 82 F3
Raddery Highld 301 D7
Raddington Som . . . 27 B8
Raddon Devon 26 G6
Radernie Fife 287 G8
Radfall Kent 70 G6
Radfield Kent 70 G2
Radford Bath 45 B7
  Nottingham 171 G9
  Oxon 101 G8
  W Mid 134 G6
  Worcs 117 F10
Radfordbridge
  Oxon 101 G8
Radford Semele
  Warks 118 E6
Radipole Dorset 17 E9
Radlet Som 43 F8
Radlett Herts 85 F11
Radley Oxon 83 F8
Radley Green Essex . . 87 D10
Radley Park Oxon . . 83 F8
Radlith Shrops 131 B8
Radmanthwaite
  Notts 171 C8
Radmoor Shrops . . . 150 E2
Radmore Green
  Ches E 167 D9
Radmore Wood
  Staffs 151 D11
Radnage Bucks 84 F3
Radnor Corn 4 G4
Radnor Park
  W Dunb 277 G9
Radstock Bath 45 B7
Radstone
  W Nhants 101 C11
Radway Warks 101 B7
Radway Green
  Ches E 168 E3
Radwell Bedford . . . 121 F10
  Herts 104 D4
Radwinter Essex . . . 106 D2
Radwinter End
  Essex 106 D2
Radyr Cardiff 58 C6
Raera Argyll 289 G10
Rafborough Hants . . 49 B11
Rafford Moray 301 D10
Raga Shetland 312 D6
Ragdale Leics 154 F3
Ragdon Shrops 131 E9
Raggalds W Yorks . . 205 G7
Ragged Appleshaw
  Hants 47 D10
Raginnis Corn 1 D5
Raglan Mon 78 D6
Ragmere Norf 141 E11
Ragnal Kent 63 G10
Ragnall Notts 188 G4
Rahane Argyll 276 D4
Rahoy Highld 289 D8
Raigbeg Highld 301 G8
Rails S Yorks 186 D3
Rainbow Hill Worcs . 117 F7
Rainford Mers 194 G3
Rainford Junction
  Mers 194 G3
Rainham London . . . 68 C4
  Medway 69 F10
Rainhill Mers 183 C7
Rainhill Stoops
  Mers 183 D8
Rainow Ches E 185 F7
Rainowlow Ches E . . 185 F7
Rain Shore
  Gtr Man 195 D11
Rainsough
  Gtr Man 195 G10
Rainton Dumfries . . . 237 D8
  N Yorks 215 D7
Rainton Bridge
  T&W 234 B2
Rainton Gate
  Durham 234 B2
Rainworth Notts . . . 171 D9
Raisbeck Cumb 222 D2
Raise Cumb 231 B10
Rait Perth 286 E6
Raithby Lincs 190 E4
Raithby by Spilsby
  Lincs 174 B5
Rake W Sus 34 B4
Rake Common W Sus . 34 B3
Rake End Staffs 151 F11
Rake Head Lancs . . . 195 C10
Rakes Dale Staffs . . 169 G9
Rakeway Staffs 169 G8
Rakewood Gtr Man . . 196 E2
Raleigh Devon 40 G5
Ralia Lodge Highld . 291 D9
Rallt Swansea 56 C4
Ram Carms 93 B11
Ram Alley Wilts 63 G8
Ramasaig Highld . . . 297 G7
Rame Corn 2 C6
  Corn 7 F8
Rameldry Mill Bank
  Fife 287 G7
Ram Hill S Glos 61 D7
Ram Lane Kent 54 D3
Ramnageo Shetland . 312 C8
Rampisham Dorset . . 29 G9
Rampside Cumb 210 F4

Rampton Cambs . . . 123 D8
  Notts 188 F3
Ramsbottom
  Gtr Man 195 D9
Ramsburn Moray . . . 302 D5
Ramsbury Wilts 63 E9
Ramscraigs Highld . 311 G5
Ramsdean Hants . . . 34 C2
Ramsdell Hants 48 B5
Ramsden London . . . 68 F3
  Oxon 82 B5
  Worcs 99 B8
Ramsden Bellhouse
  Essex 88 G2
Ramsden Heath
  Essex 88 F2
Ramsden Wood
  W Yorks 196 C5
Ramsey Cambs 138 F5
  Essex 108 E4
  IoM 192 C5
Ramsey Forty Foot
  Cambs 138 F6
Ramsey Heights
  Cambs 138 F5
Ramsey Island Essex . 89 D7
Ramsey Mereside
  Cambs 138 F5
Ramsey St Mary's
  Cambs 138 F5
Ramsgate Kent 71 G11
Ramsgill N Yorks . . . 214 E2
Ramshaw Durham . . 232 B5
  Durham 233 F8
Ramsholt Suff 108 C6
Ramshorn Staffs . . . 169 F9
Ramsley Devon 13 C8
Ramslye Kent 52 F5
Ramsnest Common
  Sur 50 G2
Ranais W Isles 304 F6
Ranby Lincs 190 F2
  Notts 187 E11
Rand Lincs 189 F10
Randwick Glos 80 D4
Ranfurly Renfs 267 C7
Rangag Highld 310 E5
Rangemore Staffs . . 152 E3
Rangeworthy S Glos . 61 B7
Rankinston E Ayrs . 257 G11
Rank's Green Essex . 88 B3
Ranmoor S Yorks . . . 186 D4
Ranmore Common
  Sur 50 C6
Rannerdale Cumb . . 220 B3
Rannoch Lodge
  Perth 285 B9
Rannoch Station
  Perth 285 B8
Ranochan Highld . . 295 G10
Ranskill Notts 187 D11
Ranton Staffs 151 E7
Ranton Green Staffs . 150 E6
Ranworth Norf 161 G7
Rapkyns W Sus 50 G6
Raploch Stirling . . . 278 C5
Rapness Orkney 314 B5
Rapps Som 28 D4
Rascal Moor
  E Yorks 208 F2
Rascarrel Dumfries . 237 E9
Rashielee Renfs . . . 277 G9
Rashiereive Aberds . 303 G9
Rashwood Worcs . . . 117 D8
Raskelf N Yorks 215 E9
Rassal Highld 299 E8
Rassau Bl Gwent 77 C11
Rastrick W Yorks . . . 196 C6
Ratagan Highld 295 D11
Ratby Leics 135 B10
Ratcliffe Culey
  Leics 134 D6
Ratcliffe on Soar
  Leics 153 D9
Ratcliffe on the Wreake
  Leics 154 G2
Ratford Wilts 62 E3
Ratfyn Wilts 47 E7
Rathen Aberds 303 C10
Rathillet Fife 287 E7
Rathmell N Yorks . . 204 B2
Ratho Edin 280 G2
Ratho Station Edin . . 280 G2
Rathven Moray 302 C4
Ratlake Hants 32 C6
Ratley Hants 47 E7
  Warks 101 B7
Ratling Kent 55 C8
Ratlinghope Shrops . 131 D8
Ratsloe Devon 14 B5
Rattar Highld 310 B6
Ratten Row Cumb . . 230 B3
  Cumb 230 C2
  Lancs 202 E4
  Norf 157 G10
Rattery Devon 8 C4
Rattlesden Suff 125 F7
Rattray Perth 286 C5
Raughton Cumb . . . 230 B3
Raughton Head
  Cumb 230 B3
Raunds N Nhants . . 121 C9
Ravelston Edin 280 G4
Ravenglass Cumb . . 219 F11
Ravenhall Essex . . . 106 G5
Ravenhead Mers . . . 183 C8
Ravenhills Green
  Worcs 116 G4
Raveningham Norf . . 143 E7
Ravenscar N Yorks . 227 E9
Ravenscliffe Stoke . 168 E4
  W Yorks 205 F9
Ravenscraig Invclyd . 276 F5
Ravensdale IoM 192 C4
Ravensden Bedford 121 G11
Ravenseat N Yorks . 223 E7
Raven's Green
  Essex 108 G2
Ravenshall Staffs . . 168 E3
Ravenshead Notts . . 171 D9

Ravensmoor
  Ches E 167 E10
Ravensthorpe Pboro 138 C3
  Leics 135 D10
  W Nhants 120 C3
  W Yorks 197 C8
Ravenstone Leics . . 153 G8
  M Keynes 120 G6
Ravenstonedale
  Cumb 222 E4
Ravenstown Cumb . 211 D7
Ravenstruther
  S Lanark 269 F8
Ravenswood Village
  Settlement
  Wokingham 65 G10
Ravensworth
  N Yorks 224 D2
Raw N Yorks 227 D8
Rawcliffe E Yorks . . 199 C7
  York 207 C7
Rawcliffe Bridge
  E Yorks 199 C7
Rawdon W Yorks . . . 205 F10
Rawdon Carrs
  W Yorks 205 F10
Rawfolds W Yorks . . 197 C8
Rawgreen
  Northumb 241 F10
Raw Green S Yorks . 197 F9
Rawmarsh S Yorks . 186 B6
Rawnsley Staffs . . . 151 G10
Rawreth Essex 88 G3
Rawreth Shot Essex . 88 G3
Rawridge Devon 28 F2
Rawson Green
  Derbys 170 F5
Rawtenstall Lancs . . 195 C10
Rawthorpe W Yorks . 197 D7
Rawyards N Lanark . 268 B5
Raxton Aberds 303 F8
Raydon Suff 107 D11
Raygill N Yorks 204 D4
Raylees Northumb . . 251 D10
Rayleigh Essex 88 G4
Rayne Essex 106 G4
Rayners Lane London . 66 B6
Raynes Park London . 67 F8
Read Lancs 203 G11
Reader's Corner
  Essex 88 E2
Reading Reading . . . 65 E8
Readings Glos 79 D9
Reading Street Kent . 54 G2
  Kent 71 F11
Readymoney Corn . . . 6 E2
Ready Token Glos . . . 81 E10
Reagill Cumb 222 B2
Rearquhar Highld . . 309 K7
Rearsby Leics 154 G3
Reasby Lincs 189 F9
Rease Heath
  Ches E 167 E10
Reaster Highld 310 C6
Reawla Corn 2 B4
Reay Highld 310 C3
Rechullin Highld . . . 299 D8
Reculver Kent 71 F8
Red Ball Devon 27 D9
Redberth Pembs . . . 73 E9
Redbourn Herts 85 C10
Redbournbury Herts 85 C10
Redbourne N Lincs . 189 B7
Redbridge Dorset . . 17 D11
  London 68 B2
  Soton 32 E5
Red Bridge Lancs . . 211 D9
Redbrook Mon 79 C8
  Wrex 167 G8
Red Bull Ches E . . . 168 D4
  Staffs 150 B4
Redburn Highld . . . 300 C5
  Highld 301 E9
  Northumb 241 E7
Redcar Redcar 235 G4
Redcastle Angus . . . 287 B10
  Highld 300 E5
Redcliff Bay N Som . 60 D2
Redcroft Dumfries . . 237 B9
Redcross Corn 117 C7
Red Dial Cumb 229 B11
Reddicap Heath
  W Mid 134 D2
Redding Falk 279 F8
Reddingmuirhead
  Falk 279 F8
Reddish Gtr Man . . 184 C5
Redditch Worcs . . . 117 D10
Rede Suff 124 F6
Redenhall Norf 142 G5
Redenham Hants . . . 47 D10
Redesdale Camp
  Northumb 251 D8
Redesmouth
  Northumb 251 G9
Redford Aberds . . . 293 F9
  Angus 287 C9
  Dorset 29 F10
  Durham 233 E7
  W Sus 34 B5
Redfordgreen
  Borders 261 F9
Redgorton Perth . . . 286 E4
Redgrave Suff 125 B10
Redheugh Angus . . . 292 G6
Redhill Aberds 293 C9
  Aberds 302 F6
  Herts 104 E6
  Notts 171 F9
  N Som 60 G4
  Shrops 131 B9
  Shrops 150 G4
  Staffs 150 D6
  Sur 51 C9
  Telford 150 G4
Red Hill BCP 19 B7
  Hants 34 E2

Red Hill continued
  Hereford 97 D10
  Kent 53 C7
  Pembs 72 B6
  Warks 118 F2
  Worcs 117 G7
  W Yorks 198 B2
Ravenstone Leics . . 153 G8
Redhouse Argyll . . . 275 G9
Redhouses Argyll . . 274 G4
Redisham Suff 143 G8
Red Lake Telford . . . 150 G3
Redland Bristol 60 D5
  Orkney 314 D3
Redland End Bucks . 84 E4
Redlands Dorset . . . 17 E9
  Som 44 G3
  Swindon 81 G11
Redlane Som 28 E2
Redlingfield Suff . . . 126 C3
Red Lodge Suff 124 C3
Red Lumb Gtr Man . 195 D10
Redlynch Som 45 G8
  Wilts 32 C2
Redmain Cumb 229 E8
Redmarley D'Abitot
  Glos 98 E5
Redmarshall
  Stockton 234 G3
Redmile Leics 154 B5
Redmire N Yorks . . . 223 G10
Redmonsford Devon 24 D4
Redmoor Corn 5 C11
Rednal Shrops 149 D7
  W Mid 117 B10
Redpath Borders . . . 262 B3
Red Pits Norf 159 D11
Redpoint Highld . . . 299 C7
Red Post Corn 24 F3
Red Rail Hereford . . 97 F10
Red Rice Hants 47 E10
Red Rock Gtr Man . . 194 F5
Red Roses Carms . . 74 C2
Red Row Northumb . 253 D7
Redruth Corn 4 G3
Red Scar Lancs 203 G7
Redscarhead
  Borders 270 G4
Redstocks Wilts 62 G2
Red Street Staffs . . . 168 E4
  Flint 181 G11
Redtye Corn 5 C10
Redvales Gtr Man . . 195 F10
Red Wharf Bay
  Anglesey 179 E8
Redwick Newport . . 60 C2
  S Glos 60 B4
Redwith Shrops . . . 148 E6
Redworth Darl 233 G10
Reed Herts 105 D7
Reed End Herts 104 D6
Reedham Lincs 174 D2
  Norf 143 C8
Reedley Lancs 204 F2
Reedness E Yorks . . 199 C9
Reed Point Lincs . . . 174 E2
Reeds Beck Lincs . . 174 B2
Reedsford Northumb 263 C9
Reeds Holme
  Lancs 195 C10
Reeds Green
  W Mid 118 B5
Reemshill Aberds . . 303 E7
Rees Green
  W Mid 118 G6
Reeth N Yorks 223 F10
Reeves Green
  W Mid 118 B5
Refail Powys 130 C3
Regaby IoM 192 C5
Regil Bath 60 G4
Regoul Highld 301 D8
Reiff Highld 307 H4
Reigate Sur 51 C9
Reigate Heath Sur . . 51 C8
Reighton N Yorks . . 218 D2
Reighton Gap
  N Yorks 218 D2
Reinigeadal
  W Isles 305 H4
Reisque Aberds 293 B10
Reiss Highld 310 D7
Rejerrah Corn 4 D5
Releath Corn 2 C5
Relubbus Corn 2 C3
Relugas Moray 301 E10
Remenham
  Wokingham 65 C9
Remenham Hill
  Wokingham 65 C9
Remony Perth 285 C11
Rempstone Notts . . . 153 E11
Remusaig Highld . . . 309 J7
Rendcomb Glos 81 D8
Rendham Suff 126 E6
Rendlesham Suff . . . 126 G6
Renfrew Renfs 267 B10
Renhold Bedford . . 121 G11
Renishaw Derbys . . 186 F6
Rennington
  Northumb 264 F6
Renton W Dunb 277 F7
Renwick Cumb 231 C7
Repps Norf 161 F8
Repton Derbys 152 D6
Reraig Highld 295 C10
Reraig Cot Highld . . 295 B10
Rerwick Shetland . . 313 M5
Rescassa Corn 5 G9
Rescobie Angus . . . 287 B9
Rescorla Corn 5 D10
  Corn 5 E9
Reskadinnick Corn . . 4 G2
Resipole Highld . . . 289 C9
Resolfen = Resolven
  Neath 76 E4
Resolis Highld 300 C6

Resolven = Resolfen
  Neath 76 E4
Restalrig Edin 280 G5
Reston Borders 273 C7
  Cumb 221 F9
Restronguet Passage
  Corn 3 B8
Restrop Wilts 62 B5
Resugga Green Corn . 5 D10
Reswallie Angus . . . 287 B9
Retallack Corn 5 B8
Retew Corn 5 D8
Retford Notts 188 E2
Retire Corn 5 C10
Rettendon Essex . . . 88 F3
Rettendon Place
  Essex 88 F3
Revesby Lincs 174 C3
Revesby Bridge
  Lincs 174 C4
Revidge Blackburn . 195 B7
Rew Devon 9 G9
  Devon 13 G11
  Dorset 29 F11
Rewe Devon 14 B4
Rew Street IoW 20 C5
Rexon Devon 12 D4
Rexon Cross Devon . 12 D4
Reybridge Wilts 62 F2
Reydon Suff 127 B9
Reydon Smear Suff . 127 B9
Reymerston Norf . . 141 B10
Reynalton Pembs . . . 73 D9
Reynoldston Swansea 56 C3
Rezare Corn 12 F3
Rhadyr Mon 78 E5
Rhaeadr Gwy = Rhayader
  Powys 113 D9
Rhandir Conwy 180 G4
Rhandirmwyn Carms 94 C5
Rhayader = Rhaeadr Gwy
  Powys 113 D9
Rhedyn Gwyn 144 C5
Rhemore Highld . . . 289 D7
Rhenetra Highld . . . 298 D4
Rhes-y-cae Flint . . . 181 G11
Rhewl Denb 165 C10
  Denb 165 F11
  Shrops 148 C6
  Wrex 148 B7
Rhewl-fawr Flint . . 181 E10
Rhewl-Mostyn
  Flint 181 E11
Rhian Highld 309 H5
Rhicarn Highld 307 G5
Rhiconich Highld . . 306 D7
Rhicullen Highld . . . 300 B6
Rhidorroch Ho
  Highld 307 K6
Rhiews Shrops 150 B2
Rhifail Highld 308 E7
Rhigolter Highld . . . 308 D3
Rhigos Rhondda 76 D6
Rhilochan Highld . . 309 J7
Rhippinllwyd Ceredig 92 C5
  Ceredig 110 G6
Rhiroy Highld 307 L6
Rhitongue Highld . . 308 D6
Rhivichie Highld . . . 306 D7
Rhiw Gwyn 144 D4
Rhiwabon = Ruabon
  Wrex 166 G4
Rhiwbebyll Denb . . 165 B10
Rhiwbina Cardiff . . . 59 C7
Rhiwbryfdir Gwyn . . 163 F11
Rhiwceiliog Bridgend 58 C3
Rhiwderin Newport . 59 B9
Rhiwen Gwyn 163 C9
Rhiwfawr Neath 76 C2
Rhiwinder Rhondda . 58 B4
Rhiwlas Gwyn 147 B8
  Gwyn 163 B9
  Powys 148 C3
Rhode Som 43 G9
Rhode Common
  Kent 54 B5
Rhodes Gtr Man . . . 195 F11
Rhodesia Notts 187 F9
Rhodes Minnis Kent . 55 E7
Rhodiad Pembs 90 F5
Rhonadale Argyll . . 255 D8
Rhondda Rhondda . . 77 F7
Rhonehouse or Kelton
  Hill Dumfries 237 D9
Rhoose V Glam 58 F5
Rhos Carms 93 D7
Rhôs Denb 165 C10
  Neath 76 E2
Rhos Powys 148 F5
Rhosaman Carms . . 76 C2
Rhosbeirio Anglesey 178 C5
Rhoscefnhir
  Anglesey 179 F8
Rhoscolyn Anglesey 178 F3
Rhôs Common
  Powys 148 F5
Rhoscrowther Pembs 72 E6
Rhosddu Gwyn 166 E4
Rhos-ddû Gwyn . . . 144 B5
Rhosdylluan Gwyn . 147 D7
Rhosesmor Flint . . . 166 B2
Rhosfach Pembs . . . 92 F2
Rhos-fawr Gwyn . . . 145 B7
Rhosgadfan Gwyn . . 163 D8
Rhosgoch Anglesey . 178 C6
  Powys 96 B3
Rhos-goch Powys . . 96 B3
Rhosgyll Gwyn 163 G7
Rhos Haminiog
  Ceredig 111 E10
Rhos-hill Pembs . . . 92 C3
Rhoshirwaun Gwyn . 144 D3
Rhos Isaf Gwyn . . . 163 D7
Rhoslan Gwyn 163 G7
Rhoslefain Gwyn . . 110 B2
Rhosllanerchrugog
  Wrex 166 F3
Rhôs Lligwy
  Anglesey 179 D7
Rhosmaen Carms . . 94 G2

Rhosmeirch
  Anglesey 179 F7
Rhosneigr Anglesey 178 G4
Rhosnesni Wrex . . . 166 E5
Rhôs-on-Sea
  Conwy 180 E4
Rhosrobin Wrex . . . 166 E4
Rhossili Swansea . . 56 D2
Rhosson Pembs 90 F4
Rhostrehwfa
  Anglesey 178 G6
Rhostryfan Gwyn . . 163 D7
Rhostyllen Wrex . . . 166 F4
Rhoswiel Shrops . . . 148 B5
Rhosybol Anglesey . 178 D6
Rhos-y-brithdir
  Powys 148 E2
Rhosycaerau Pembs . 91 D8
Rhosygadair Newydd
  Ceredig 92 C3
Rhosygadfa Shrops . 148 C6
Rhos-y-garth
  Ceredig 112 C2
Rhosygilwen Pembs . 92 C4
Rhos-y-gwaliau
  Gwyn 147 C8
Rhos-y-llan Gwyn . 144 B4
Rhos-y-Madoc
  Wrex 166 G4
Rhosymedre Wrex . . 166 G3
Rhos-y-meirch
  Powys 114 D5
Rhosyn-coch Carms . 92 G5
Rhu Argyll 276 D5
  Argyll 276 E5
Rhuallt Denb 181 F9
Rhubodach Argyll . . 275 F11
Rhuddall Heath
  Ches W 167 C9
Rhuddlan Ceredig . . 93 C9
  Denb 181 F8
Rhue Highld 307 K5
Rhulen Powys 96 C3
Rhunahaorine
  Argyll 255 D7
Rhyd Ceredig 92 C5
  Gwyn 163 G10
  Powys 129 C9
Rhydaman = Ammanford
  Carms 75 C10
Rhydargaeau Carms . 93 F8
Rhydcymerau
  Carms 93 D11
Rhydd Worcs 98 B6
Rhyd-Ddu Gwyn . . 163 E9
Rhydd Green Worcs . 98 B6
Rhydfudr Ceredig . . 111 D10
Rhydgaled Conwy . . 165 C10
Rhydgaled = Chancery
  Ceredig 111 B11
Rhydlewis Ceredig . . 92 B6
Rhydlios Gwyn 144 C3
Rhydlydan Conwy . . 164 E5
  Powys 129 C11
Rhydmoelddu
  Powys 113 B9
Rhydness Powys . . . 96 C2
Rhydowen Carms . . 92 F3
  Ceredig 93 B8
Rhyd-Rosser
  Ceredig 111 D11
Rhydspence Hereford 96 B4
Rhydtalog Flint . . . 166 D2
Rhyd-uchaf Gwyn . . 147 B8
Rhydwen Gwyn 146 F4
Rhydwyn Anglesey . 178 D4
Rhyd-y-Brown
  Pembs 91 G11
Rhyd-y-clafdy Gwyn 144 B6
Rhydycroesau
  Shrops 148 C5
Rhyd-y-cwm
  Shrops 130 G3
Rhydyfelin Carms . . 92 C3
  Ceredig 111 B11
  Powys 129 E11
  Rhondda 58 B5
Rhyd-y-foel Conwy . 180 F6
Rhyd-y-fro Neath . . 76 D2
Rhydgele Pembs . . . 91 G7
Rhyd-y-gwin
  Swansea 75 C11
Rhyd-y-gwystl
  Gwyn 145 B7
Rhydymain Gwyn . . 146 E6
Rhyd-y-meirch Mon . 78 D4
Rhyd-y-meudwy
  Denb 165 G10
Rhydymwyn Flint . . 166 B2
Rhyd-y-pandy
  Swansea 75 E11
Rhyd-yr-onen Gwyn 128 C2
Rhyd-y-sarn Gwyn . 163 G11
Rhydywrach Carms . 73 B11
Rhyl Denb 181 E8
Rhymney Caerph . . 77 D10
Rhyn Wrex 148 B6
Rhynd Fife 287 E8
  Perth 286 E5
Rhynie Aberds 302 G4
  Highld 301 B8
Ribbesford Worcs . . 116 C5
Ribblehead N Yorks . 212 D5
Ribble Head
  N Yorks 212 D5
Ribbleton Lancs . . . 203 G7
Ribby Lancs 202 G4
Ribchester Lancs . . 203 F8
Riber Derbys 170 D4
Ribigill Highld 308 D5
Riby Lincs 201 F7
Riby Cross Roads
  Lincs 201 F7
Riccall N Yorks 207 F8
Riccarton E Ayrs . . 257 B10
Richards Castle
  Hereford 115 D9
Richborough Port
  Kent 71 G10
Richings Park Bucks . 66 D4
Richmond London . . 67 E7

Richmond *continued*
N Yorks. 224 E3
S Yorks. 186 D6
Richmond Hill
W Yorks. 206 G2
Richmond's Green
Essex 106 F2
Rich's Holford Som 42 G6
Rickard's Down
Devon 24 B6
Rickarton Aberds 293 E10
Rickerby Cumb 239 F10
Rickerscote Staffs 151 E8
Rickford N Som 44 B3
Rickinghall Suff 125 B10
Rickleton T&W 243 G7
Rickling Essex 105 E9
Rickling Green
Essex 105 F10
Rickmansworth
Herts 85 G9
Rickney E Sus 23 D10
Riddell Borders 262 E2
Riddings Derbys 170 E6
Riddlecombe Devon 25 E10
Riddlesden W Yorks 205 E7
Riddrie Glasgow 268 B2
Ridgacre W Mid 133 G10
Ridge Bath 44 B5
Dorset 18 D4
Hants 32 D4
Herts 86 E2
Lancs 211 G9
Som 28 F3
Wilts 46 G3
Ridgebourne
Powys 113 E11
Ridge Common
Hants 34 C2
Ridge Green Sur 51 D10
Ridgehill N Som 60 G4
Ridge Hill Gtr Man 185 B7
Ridge Lane Warks 134 E5
Ridgemarsh Herts 85 G8
Ridge Row Kent 55 E8
Ridgeway Bristol 60 D6
Derbys 170 E5
Derbys 186 E6
Kent 54 E5
Newport 59 B9
Pembs 73 D10
Som 45 D8
Staffs 168 E5
Ridgeway Cross
Hereford 98 B4
Ridgeway Moor
Derbys 186 E6
Ridgewell Essex 106 C4
Ridgewood E Sus 23 B7
Ridgmont C Beds 103 D9
Ridgway Shrops 131 F7
Sur 50 B4
Riding Gate Som 30 B2
Riding Mill
Northumb 242 E2
Ridley Kent 68 G6
Northumb 241 E7
Ridley Stokoe
Northumb 250 F6
Ridleywood Wrex 166 E6
Ridlington Norf 160 C6
Rutland 136 C6
Ridlington Street
Norf 160 C6
Ridsdale Northumb 251 G10
Riechip Perth 286 C4
Riemore Perth 286 C4
Rienachait Highld 306 F5
Rievaulx N Yorks 215 B11
Riff Orkney 314 E4
Riffin Aberds 303 E7
Rifle Green Torf 78 D3
Rift House Hrtlpl 234 E5
Rigg Dumfries 239 D7
Riggend N Lanark 278 G5
Rigsby Lincs 190 F6
Rigside S Lanark 259 B9
Riley Green Lancs 194 B6
Rileyhill Staffs 152 F2
Rilla Mill Corn 11 G11
Rillaton Corn 11 G11
Rillington N Yorks 217 E7
Rimac Lincs 191 C7
Rimington Lancs 204 D2
Rimpton Som 29 C10
Rimswell E Yorks 201 B10
Rimswell Valley
E Yorks 201 B10
Rinaston Pembs 91 F9
Rindleford Shrops 132 D4
Ringasta Shetland 313 M5
Ringford Dumfries 237 D8
Ringing Hill Leics 153 F9
Ringinglow S Yorks 186 E3
Ringland Newport 59 B11
Norf 160 G2
Ringles Cross E Sus 37 C7
Ringlestone Kent 53 B9
Kent 53 B11
Ringley Gtr Man 195 F9
Ringmer E Sus 36 E6
Ringmore Devon 8 F3
Ring o' Bells Lancs 194 E3
Ringorm Moray 302 E2
Ring's End Cambs 139 C7
Ringsfield Suff 143 F8
Ringsfield Corner
Suff 143 F8
Ringshall Herts 85 C7
Suff 125 G10
Ringshall Stocks
Suff 125 G10
Ringstead N Nhants 121 B9
Norf 176 E2
Ringtail Green
Essex 87 B11
Ringwood Hants 31 F11
Ringwould Kent 55 D11
Rinmore Aberds 292 B6
Rinnigill Orkney 314 G3
Rinsey Corn 2 D3
Rinsey Croft Corn 2 D4
Riof W Isles 304 E3
Ripe E Sus 23 C8
Ripley Derbys 170 E5
Hants 19 B9
N Yorks 214 G5
Sur 50 B5
Riplingham E Yorks 208 G5
Ripon N Yorks 214 E6
Ripper's Cross Kent 54 E3
Rippingale Lincs 155 D11
Ripple Kent 55 D10
Worcs 99 D7
Ripponden W Yorks 196 D4
Rireavach Highld 307 K5
Risabus Argyll 254 C4
Risbury Hereford 115 G10
Risby E Yorks 208 G6
Lincs 189 C10
Suff 124 D5
Risca Caerph 78 G2
Rise E Yorks 209 E9
Rise Carr Darl 224 B5
Riseden E Sus 52 G6
Kent 53 F8
Rise End Derbys 170 D3
Risegate Lincs 156 D4
Riseholme Lincs 189 F7
Risehow Cumb 228 E6
Riseley Bedford 121 E10
Wokingham 65 G8
Rise Park London 87 G8
Nottingham 171 F9
Rishangles Suff 126 D3
Rishton Lancs 203 G10
Rishworth W Yorks 196 D4
Rising Bridge Lancs 195 B9
Risingbrook Staffs 151 E8
Risinghurst Oxon 83 D9
Rising Sun Corn 12 G3
Risley Derbys 153 B9
Warr 183 C10
Risplith N Yorks 214 F4
Rispond Highld 308 C4
Rivar Wilts 63 G10
Rivenhall Essex 88 B4
Rivenhall End Essex 88 B4
River Kent 55 E9
W Sus 34 C6
River Bank Cambs 123 D10
Riverhead Kent 52 B4
Rivers' Corner Dorset 30 E3
Riverside Cardiff 59 D7
Plym 7 D8
Stirling 278 C6
Worcs 117 D10
Riverside Docklands
Lancs 194 B4
Riverton Devon 40 G6
Riverview Park Kent 69 E7
Rivington Lancs 194 E6
Rixon Dorset 30 E3
Rixton Warr 183 C11
Roach Bridge Lancs 194 B5
Roaches Gtr Man 196 G3
Roachill Devon 26 C4
Roade W Nhants 120 G5
Road Green Norf 142 E5
Roadhead Cumb 240 C2
Roadmeetings
S Lanark 269 F7
Roadside Highld 310 C5
Roadside of Catterline
Aberds 293 F10
Roadside of Kinneff
Aberds 293 F10
Roadwater Som 42 F4
Road Weedon
W Nhants 120 F2
Roag Highld 298 E2
Roa Island Cumb 210 G4
Roast Green Essex 105 E9
Roath Cardiff 59 D7
Roath Park Cardiff 59 D7
Roberton Borders 261 G10
S Lanark 259 D10
Robertsbridge E Sus 38 C2
Robertstown Moray 302 E2
Rhondda 77 E8
Roberttown
W Yorks 197 C7
Robeston Back
Pembs 73 B9
Robeston Cross
Pembs 72 D5
Robeston Wathen
Pembs 73 B9
Robeston West
Pembs 72 D5
Robhurst Kent 54 G2
Robin Hill Staffs 168 D6
Robin Hood Derbys 186 G3
Lancs 194 E4
W Yorks 197 B10
Robinhood End
Essex 106 D4
Robin Hood's Bay
N Yorks 227 D9
Robins W Sus 34 B4
Robinson's End
Warks 134 E6
Roborough Devon 7 C10
Devon 25 D9
Rob Roy's House
Argyll 284 F5
Robroyston Glasgow 268 B2
Roby Mers 182 C6
Roby Mill Lancs 194 F4
Rocester Staffs 152 B2
Roch Pembs 91 G7
Rochdale Gtr Man 195 E11
Roche Corn 5 C9
Roche Grange
Staffs 169 C7
Rochester Medway 69 F8
Northumb 251 D8
Rochford Essex 88 G5
Worcs 116 D2
Roch Gate Pembs 91 G7
Rock Caerph 77 F11
Corn 10 G4
Devon 28 G3
Neath 57 C9
Rock *continued*
Northumb 264 E6
Som 28 C4
Worcs 116 C4
W Sus 35 E10
Rockbeare Devon 14 C6
Rockbourne Hants 31 D10
Rockcliffe Cumb 239 E9
Dumfries 237 D10
Flint 182 G3
Lancs 195 C11
Rockcliffe Cross
Cumb 239 E8
Rock End Staffs 168 D5
Rock Ferry Mers 182 D4
Rockfield Highld 311 L3
Mon 79 C7
Rockford Devon 41 D9
Hants 31 F11
Rockgreen Shrops 115 B10
Rockhampton
S Glos 79 G11
Rockhead Corn 11 E7
Rockhill Shrops 114 B5
Rockingham
N Nhants 137 E7
Rockland All Saints
Norf 141 D9
Rockland St Mary
Norf 142 C6
Rockland St Peter
Norf 141 D9
Rockley Notts 188 G2
Wilts 63 E7
Rockley Ford Som 45 C8
Rockness Glos 80 F4
Rockrobin E Sus 52 G6
Rocksavage Halton 183 E8
Rocks Park E Sus 37 C7
Rockstowes Glos 80 F3
Rockville Argyll 276 C4
Rockwell End Bucks 65 B9
Rockwell Green
Som 27 C10
Rocky Hill Scilly 1 G4
Rodbaston Staffs 151 G8
Rodborough Glos 80 E4
Rodbourne Swindon 62 C6
Wilts 62 C2
Rodbourne Bottom
Wilts 62 C2
Rodbourne Cheney
Swindon 62 B6
Rodbridge Corner
Essex 107 C7
Rodd Hereford 114 E6
Roddam Northumb 264 E2
Rodden Dorset 17 E8
Rodd Hurst Hereford 114 E6
Roddymoor Durham 233 D9
Rode Som 45 C10
Rodeheath Ches E 168 B5
Rode Heath Ches E 168 D3
Rode Hill Som 45 C10
Roden Telford 149 F11
Rodford S Glos 61 C7
Rodgrove Som 30 C2
Rodhuish Som 42 F4
Rodington Telford 149 G11
Rodington Heath
Telford 149 G11
Rodley Glos 80 C2
W Yorks 205 F10
Rodmarton Glos 80 F6
Rodmell E Sus 36 F6
Rodmer Clough
W Yorks 196 B3
Rodmersham Kent 70 G2
Rodmersham Green
Kent 70 G2
Rodney Stoke Som 44 C3
Rodsley Derbys 170 G2
Rodway Som 43 F9
Telford 150 F3
Rodwell Dorset 17 F9
Roebuck Low
Gtr Man 196 F3
Roecliffe N Yorks 215 F7
Roe Cross Gtr Man 185 B7
Roedean Brighton 36 G4
Roe End Herts 85 B8
Roe Green Gtr Man 195 G9
Herts 86 D2
Herts 104 E6
Roehampton London 67 E8
Roe Lee Blackburn 203 G9
Roesound Shetland 312 G5
Roestock Herts 86 D2
Roffey W Sus 51 G7
Rogart Highld 309 J7
Rogart Station
Highld 309 J7
Rogate W Sus 34 C4
Roger Ground Cumb 221 F7
Rogerstone Newport 59 B9
Rogerton S Lanark 268 D2
Roghadal W Isles 296 C6
Rogiet Mon 60 B3
Rogue's Alley Cambs 139 B7
Roke Oxon 83 G10
Rokemarsh Oxon 83 G10
Roker T&W 243 F10
Rollesby Norf 161 F8
Rolleston Leics 136 C4
Notts 172 E2
Rollestone S Yorks 186 E5
Wilts 46 E5
Rollestone Camp
Wilts 46 E5
Rolleston-on-Dove
Staffs 152 D4
Rolls Mill Dorset 30 E3
Rolston E Yorks 209 D10
Rolstone N Som 59 G11
Rolvenden Kent 53 G10
Rolvenden Layne
Kent 53 G11
Romaldkirk Durham 232 G5
Romanby N Yorks 225 G7
Roman Hill Suff 143 E10
Romannobridge
Borders 270 F3
Romansleigh Devon 26 C2
Rome Angus 293 G7
Romesdal Highld 298 D4
Romford Dorset 31 F9
Kent 52 E6
London 68 B4
Romiley Gtr Man 184 C6
Romney Street Kent 68 G4
Rompa Shetland 313 L6
Romsey Hants 32 C5
Romsey Town
Cambs 123 F9
Romsley Shrops 132 G5
Worcs 117 B9
Romsley Hill Worcs 117 B9
Ronachan Ho Argyll 255 B8
Ronague IoM 192 E3
Rondlay Telford 132 B4
Ronkswood Worcs 117 G7
Rood End W Mid 133 F10
Rookby Cumb 222 C6
Rook End Essex 105 E11
Rookhope Durham 232 C4
Rooking Cumb 221 B8
Rookley IoW 20 E6
Rookley Green IoW 20 E6
Rooks Bridge Som 43 C11
Rooksey Green Suff 125 G8
Rooks Hill Kent 52 C5
Rooksmoor Glos 80 E4
Rook's Nest Som 42 G5
Rook Street Wilts 45 G10
Rookwith N Yorks 214 B4
Rookwood W Sus 21 B11
Roos E Yorks 209 G11
Roose Cumb 210 F4
Roosebeck Cumb 210 F5
Roosecote Cumb 210 F4
Roost End Essex 106 C4
Rootham's Green
Bedford 122 F2
Rooting Street Kent 54 D3
Rootpark S Lanark 269 E9
Ropley Hants 48 G6
Ropley Dean Hants 48 G6
Ropley Soke Hants 49 G7
Ropsley Lincs 155 C9
Rora Aberds 303 D10
Rorandle Aberds 293 B8
Rorrington Shrops 130 C5
Rosarie Moray 302 E3
Roscroggan Corn 4 G3
Rose Corn 4 E5
Roseacre Kent 53 B9
Lancs 202 F4
Rose-an-Grouse Corn 2 B2
Rose Ash Devon 26 C3
Rosebank E Dunb 278 G3
S Lanark 268 F6
Rosebery Midloth 270 D6
Rosebrae Moray 301 C11
Rosebrough
Northumb 264 D4
Rosebush Pembs 91 F11
Rosecare Corn 11 B9
Rosedale Herts 86 E4
Rosedale Abbey
N Yorks 226 F4
Roseden Northumb 264 E2
Rosedinnick Corn 5 B8
Rosedown Devon 24 C3
Rosefield Highld 301 D8
Rose Green Essex 107 F8
Suff 107 C9
Suff 107 D8
W Sus 22 D6
Rose Grove Lancs 204 G2
Rosehall Highld 309 J4
N Lanark 268 C4
Rosehaugh Mains
Highld 300 D6
Rosehearty Aberds 303 C9
Rosehill Blackburn 195 C8
Corn 4 E5
Corn 5 C10
Gtr Man 184 D3
London 67 F9
Pembs 72 B5
Shrops 150 C3
T&W 243 D8
Rose Hill Bucks 66 C2
Derbys 153 B7
E Sus 23 B7
Gtr Man 195 F8
Lancs 204 G2
Oxon 83 E8
Suff 108 C3
Sur 51 D7
Roseisle Moray 301 C11
Roseland Corn 6 C5
Roselands E Sus 23 E10
Rosemarket Pembs 73 D7
Rosemarkie Highld 301 D7
Rosemary Lane
Devon 27 E11
Rosemelling Corn 5 D10
Rosemergy Corn 1 B4
Rosemount Perth 286 C5
Rosenannon Corn 5 B9
Rosenithon Corn 3 E8
Roser's Cross E Sus 37 C9
Rose Valley Pembs 73 E8
Rosevean Corn 5 D10
Rosevear Corn 2 E5
Roseville W Mid 133 E8
Rosevine Corn 3 B9
Rosewarne Corn 2 B4
Corn 4 G2
Rosewell Midloth 270 C5
Roseworth Stockton 234 G4
Roseworthy Corn 2 B4
Corn 4 F5
Roseworthy Barton
Corn 2 B4
Rosgill Cumb 221 B10
Rosherville Kent 68 E6
Roshven Highld 289 B9
Roskear Croft Corn 4 G3
Roskhill Highld 298 E2
Roskill House
Highld 300 D6
Roskorwell Corn 3 E7
Rosley Cumb 230 B2
Roslin Midloth 270 C5
Rosliston Derbys 152 F4
Rosneath Argyll 276 E5
Ross Borders 273 C9
Dumfries 237 E8
Northumb 264 B4
Perth 285 E11
Rossett Wrex 166 D5
Rossett Green
N Yorks 206 C2
Ross Green Worcs 116 E5
Rossie Ochill Perth 286 F4
Rossie Priory Perth 286 D6
Rossington
S Yorks 187 B10
Rosskeen Highld 300 C6
Rossland Renfs 277 G8
Rossmore BCP 19 C7
Ross-on-Wye
Hereford 98 G2
Roster Highld 310 F6
Rostherne Ches E 184 E2
Rostholme S Yorks 198 F5
Rosthwaite Cumb 220 C5
Cumb 220 G4
Roston Derbys 169 G10
Rosudgeon Corn 2 D3
Rosyth Fife 280 E2
Rotchfords Essex 107 E8
Rotcombe Bath 44 B6
Rothbury Northumb 252 C3
Rotherbridge W Sus 35 C7
Rotherby Leics 154 F3
Rotherfield E Sus 37 B9
Rotherfield Greys
Oxon 65 C8
Rotherfield Peppard
Oxon 65 C8
Rotherham S Yorks 186 C6
Rotherhithe London 67 D11
Rothersthorpe
W Nhants 120 F4
Rotherwas Hereford 97 D10
Rotherwick Hants 49 B8
Rothes Moray 302 E2
Rothesay Argyll 275 G11
Rothiebrisbane
Aberds 303 F7
Rothiemay Crossroads
Moray 302 E5
Rothiemurchus Lodge
Highld 291 C11
Rothienorman
Aberds 303 F7
Rothiesholm Orkney 314 D6
Rothley Leics 153 G11
Northumb 252 F2
Rothley Plain Leics 153 G11
Rothley Shield East
Northumb 252 E2
Rothmaise Aberds 302 F6
Rothwell Lincs 189 B11
N Nhants 136 G6
W Yorks 197 B10
Rothwell Haigh
W Yorks 197 B10
Rotsea E Yorks 209 C7
Rottal Angus 292 G5
Rotten End Essex 106 F4
Suff 127 D7
Rotten Green Hants 49 B9
Rotten Row W Berks 64 E5
W Mid 118 B3
Rottingdean Brighton 36 G5
Rottington Cumb 219 C9
Rotton Park
W Mid 133 F10
Roud IoW 20 E6
Rougham Norf 158 E6
Suff 125 E8
Rougham Green
Suff 125 E8
Rough Bank
Gtr Man 196 E2
Roughbirchworth
S Yorks 197 G9
Roughburn Highld 290 E5
Rough Close Staffs 151 B8
Rough Common Kent 54 B6
Roughcote Staffs 168 G6
Rough Haugh Highld 308 E7
Rough Hay Staffs 152 E4
Roughlee Lancs 204 E2
Roughley W Mid 134 D2
Roughmoor Som 28 B2
Swindon 62 B6
Roughrigg N Lanark 278 G6
Roughsike Cumb 240 B2
Roughton Lincs 174 C2
Norf 160 B4
Shrops 132 E5
Roughton Moor
Lincs 174 C2
Roughway Kent 52 C6
Roundbush Essex 88 E5
Round Bush Herts 85 F10
Roundbush Green
Essex 87 C9
Round Green
Luton 103 G11
Roundham Som 28 F6
Roundhay W Yorks 206 F2
Round Maple Suff 107 C9
Round Oak Shrops 131 G7
W Mid 133 F8
Round's Green
W Mid 133 F9
Roundshaw London 67 G10
Round Spinney
W Nhants 120 D5
Roundstonefoot
Dumfries 248 B4
Round Street Kent 69 F7
Roundstreet Common
W Sus 35 B9
Roundswell Devon 40 G4
Roundthorn
Gtr Man 184 D4
Roundthwaite Cumb 222 E2
Roundway Wilts 62 G4
Roundyhill Angus 287 B7
Rousdon Devon 15 C11
Rousham Oxon 101 G9
Rous Lench Worcs 117 G10
Routenburn N Ayrs 266 C3
Routh E Yorks 209 E7
Rout's Green Bucks 84 F3
Row Corn 11 F7
Cumb 211 B8
Cumb 231 E8
Rowanburn
Dumfries 239 B10
Rowanfield Glos 99 G8
Rowardennan
Stirling 277 B7
Rowarth Derbys 185 D8
Row Ash Hants 33 E8
Rowbarton Som 28 B2
Rowberrow Som 44 B3
Row Brow Cumb 229 D7
Rowde Wilts 62 G3
Rowden Devon 13 B8
N Yorks 205 B11
Rowe Head Cumb 210 D5
Rowen Conwy 180 G3
Rowfoot Northumb 240 E5
Rowford Som 28 B2
Row Green Essex 106 G4
Row Heath Essex 89 B10
Rowhedge Essex 107 G10
Rowhill Sur 66 G4
Rowhook W Sus 50 G6
Rowington Warks 118 D4
Rowington Green
Warks 118 D4
Rowland Derbys 186 G2
Rowlands Castle
Hants 34 E2
Rowlands Gill T&W 242 F5
Rowland's Green
Hereford 98 D3
Rowledge Sur 49 E10
Rowlestone Hereford 97 F7
Rowley E Yorks 208 G5
Shrops 130 B6
Rowley Green London 86 F2
Rowley Hill W Yorks 197 E7
Rowley Park Staffs 151 E8
Rowley Regis
W Mid 133 F9
Rowley's Green
W Mid 134 G6
Rowling Kent 55 C9
Rowly Sur 50 E4
Rownall Staffs 169 F7
Rowner Hants 33 G9
Rowney Green
Worcs 117 C10
Rownhams Hants 32 D5
Row-of-trees
Ches E 184 F4
Rowrah Cumb 219 B11
Rowsham Bucks 84 B4
Rowsley Derbys 170 B3
Rowstock Oxon 64 B3
Rowston Lincs 173 D9
Rowthorne Derbys 171 C7
Rowton Ches W 166 C6
Shrops 149 G7
Telford 150 F2
Rowton Moor
Ches W 166 C6
Row Town Sur 66 G4
Roxburgh Borders 262 C5
Roxburgh Mains
Borders 262 D5
Roxby N Lincs 200 D2
N Yorks 226 B5
Roxeth London 66 B6
Roxton Bedford 122 G3
Roxwell Essex 87 D10
Royal British Legion
Village Kent 53 B8
Royal Leamington Spa
Warks 118 D6
Royal Oak Darl 233 G10
Lancs 194 G2
N Yorks 218 D2
Royal's Green
Ches E 167 G10
Royal Tunbridge Wells =
Tunbridge Wells
Kent 52 F5
Royal Wootton Bassett
Wilts 62 C5
Roybridge Highld 290 E4
Royd S Yorks 197 G8
Roydhouse W Yorks 197 E8
Royd Moor S Yorks 197 G8
W Yorks 198 E2
Roydon Essex 86 D6
Norf 141 G11
Norf 158 E4
Roydon Hamlet
Essex 86 D6
Royds Green
W Yorks 197 B11
Royston Glasgow 268 B2
Herts 105 C7
S Yorks 197 E11
Royston Water Som 28 E2
Royton Gtr Man 196 F2
Ruabon = *Rhiwabon*
Wrex 166 G4
Ruaig Argyll 288 E2
Ruan High Lanes
Corn 3 B10
Ruan Lanihorne Corn 5 G7
Ruan Major Corn 2 F6
Ruan Minor Corn 2 F6
Ruarach Highld 295 C11
Ruardean Glos 79 B10
Ruardean Hill Glos 79 B10
Ruardean Woodside
Glos 79 B10
Rubery Worcs 117 B9
Rubha Ghaisinis
W Isles 297 G4
Rubha Stoer Highld 306 F5
Ruchazie Glasgow 268 B3
Ruchill Glasgow 267 B11
Ruckcroft Cumb 230 C6
Ruckhall Hereford 97 D9
Ruckinge Kent 54 G4
Ruckland Lincs 190 F4
Rucklers Lane Herts 85 E9
Ruckley Shrops 131 C10
Rudbaxton Pembs 91 G9
Rudby N Yorks 225 D9
Ruddington Notts 153 C11
Ruddle Glos 79 C11
Rudford Glos 98 G5
Rudge Shrops 132 D6
Som 45 C10
Rudge Heath
Shrops 132 D5
Rudgeway S Glos 60 B6
Rudgwick W Sus 50 G5
Rudhall Hereford 98 F2
Rudheath Ches W 183 G11
Rudheath Woods
Ches W 184 G2
Rudhja Garbh
Argyll 289 E11
Rudley Green Essex 88 E4
Rudloe Wilts 61 E10
Rudry Caerph 59 B7
Rudston E Yorks 217 F11
Rudyard Staffs 169 D7
Ruewood Shrops 149 D9
Rufford Lancs 194 D3
Rufforth York 206 C6
Ruffs Notts 171 F8
Rugby Warks 119 B10
Rugeley Staffs 151 F10
Ruggin Som 27 D11
Ruglen S Ayrs 245 C7
Rugley Northumb 264 G5
Ruilick Highld 300 E5
Ruishton Som 28 C3
Ruisigearraidh
W Isles 296 C5
Ruislip London 66 B5
Ruislip Common
London 66 B5
Ruislip Gardens
London 66 B5
Ruislip Manor London 66 B6
Ruiton W Mid 133 E8
Ruloe Ches W 183 G9
Rumach Highld 295 G8
Rumbling Bridge
Perth 279 B10
Rumbow Cottages
Worcs 117 B8
Rumburgh Suff 142 G6
Rumbush W Mid 118 B2
Rumer Hill Staffs 133 B9
Rumford Corn 10 G3
Falk 279 F8
Rumney Cardiff 59 D8
Rumsam Devon 40 G5
Rumwell Som 27 C11
Runcorn Halton 183 E8
Runcton W Sus 22 C5
Runcton Holme
Norf 140 B2
Rundlestone Devon 13 G7
Runfold Sur 49 D11
Runhall Norf 141 B11
Runham Norf 143 B10
Norf 161 G9
Runham Vauxhall
Norf 143 B10
Running Hill Head
Gtr Man 196 F4
Runnington Som 27 C10
Running Waters
Durham 234 C2
Runsell Green Essex 88 D3
Runshaw Moor
Lancs 194 D4
Runswick Bay
N Yorks 226 B6
Runwell Essex 88 G2
Ruscombe Glos 80 D4
Wokingham 65 D9
Ruscote Oxon 101 C8
Rushall Hereford 98 E2
Norf 142 G3
Wilts 46 B6
W Mid 133 C10
Rushbrooke Suff 125 E7
Rushbury Shrops 131 E10
Rushcombe Bottom
BCP 18 B5
Rushden Herts 104 E6
N Nhants 121 D9
Rushenden Kent 70 E2
Rusher's Cross
E Sus 37 B10
Rushey Mead
Leicester 136 B2
Rushford Devon 12 F4
Norf 141 G8
Rushgreen Warr 183 D11
Rush Green Essex 89 B11
Herts 86 C5
Herts 104 G4
London 68 B4
Norf 141 B11
Rush-head Aberds 303 E8
Rush Hill Bath 61 G8
Rushington Hants 32 E5
Rushlake Green
E Sus 23 B10
Rushland Cross
Cumb 210 B6
Rushley Green
Essex 106 D5
Rushmere C Beds 103 F8
Suff 143 F9
Rushmere St Andrew
Suff 108 B4
Rushmere Street
Suff 108 B4
Rushmoor Sur 49 E11
Telford 150 G2
Rushmore Hants 33 E11
Rushmore Hill
London 68 G3
Rushock Hereford 114 F6
Worcs 117 C7
Rusholme Gtr Man 184 B5
Rushton Ches W 167 C9
Rushton *continued*
Dorset 18 D3
N Nhants 136 G6
N Yorks 217 C9
Shrops 132 B2
Rushton Spencer
Staffs 168 C6
Rushwick Worcs 116 G6
Rushyford Durham 233 F11
Rushy Green E Sus 23 C7
Ruskie Stirling 285 G10
Ruskington Lincs 173 E9
Rusland Cumb 210 B6
Rusling End Herts 104 G4
Rusper W Sus 51 F8
Ruspidge Glos 79 C11
Russel Highld 299 E8
Russell Hill London 67 G10
Russell's Green
E Sus 38 E2
Russell's Hall
W Mid 133 F8
Russell's Water Oxon 65 B8
Russel's Green Suff 126 C5
Russ Hill Sur 51 E8
Rusthall Kent 52 F5
Rustington W Sus 35 G9
Ruston N Yorks 217 C9
Ruston Parva
E Yorks 217 G11
Ruswarp N Yorks 227 D7
Ruthall Shrops 131 F11
Rutherford Borders 262 C4
Rutherglen
S Lanark 268 C2
Ruthernbridge Corn 5 B10
Ruthin V Glam 58 D3
Ruthin = *Rhuthun*
Denb 165 D10
Ruthrieston
Aberdeen 293 C11
Ruthun = *Ruthin*
Denb 165 D10
Ruthven Aberds 302 E5
Angus 286 C6
Highld 291 D9
Highld 301 F8
Ruthven House
Angus 287 C7
Ruthvoes Corn 5 C8
Ruthwaite Cumb 229 D10
Ruthwell Dumfries 238 D3
Ruxley London 68 E3
Ruxton Hereford 97 F11
Ruxton Green
Hereford 79 B8
Ruyton-XI-Towns
Shrops 149 E7
Ryal Northumb 242 C2
Ryal Fold Blackburn 195 C7
Ryall Dorset 16 C4
Worcs 99 C7
Ryarsh Kent 53 B7
Rychraggan Highld 300 F4
Rydal Cumb 221 D7
Ryde IoW 21 C7
Rydens Sur 66 F6
Rydeshill Sur 50 C3
Rydon Devon 14 G3
Rye E Sus 38 C6
Ryebank Shrops 149 C10
Rye Common Hants 49 C9
Ryecroft S Yorks 186 B6
W Yorks 205 F7
Ryecroft Gate Staffs 168 C6
Ryeford Glos 80 E4
Rye Foreign E Sus 38 C5
Rye Harbour E Sus 38 D6
Ryehill E Yorks 201 B8
Ryeish Green
Wokingham 65 F8
Ryelands Hereford 115 F9
Rye Park Herts 86 C5
Rye Street Worcs 98 D5
Ryeworth Glos 99 G9
Ryhall Rutland 155 G10
Ryhill W Yorks 197 E11
Ryhope T&W 243 G10
Rylah Derbys 171 B7
Rylands Notts 153 B10
Rylstone N Yorks 204 B5
Ryme Intrinseca
Dorset 29 E9
Ryther N Yorks 207 F7
Ryton Glos 98 E4
N Yorks 216 D5
Shrops 132 C5
T&W 242 E5
Warks 135 F7
Ryton-on-Dunsmore
Warks 119 C7
Ryton Woodside
T&W 242 E4

S

Sabden Lancs 203 F11
Sabine's Green Essex 87 F8
Sackers Green Suff 107 D8
Sacombe Herts 86 B4
Sacombe Green
Herts 86 B4
Sacriston Durham 233 B10
Sadberge Darl 224 B6
Saddell Argyll 255 D8
Saddell Ho Argyll 255 D8
Saddington Leics 136 E3
Saddle Bow Norf 158 F2
Saddlescombe
W Sus 36 E3
Saddle Street Dorset 28 G5
Sadgill Cumb 221 D9
Saffron's Cross
Hereford 115 G10
Saffron Walden
Essex 105 D10
Sageston Pembs 73 E9
Saham Hills Norf 141 C8

Saham Toney Norf . . .141 C8
Saighdinis W Isles . . .296 E4
Saighton Ches W 166 C6
Sain Dunwyd = St Donats
V Glam 58 F2
St Abbs Borders 273 B8
St Abb's Haven
Borders 273 B8
St Agnes Corn 4 E4
Scilly 1 H3
St Albans Herts 85 D10
St Allen Corn 4 E6
St Andrews Fife 287 F9
St Andrew's Major
V Glam 58 E6
St Andrew's Wood
Devon 27 F9
St Annes Lancs 193 B10
St Anne's Park Bristol .60 E6
St Ann's Dumfries . . .248 E3
Nottingham 171 G9
St Ann's Chapel Corn .12 G4
Devon 8 F3
St Anthony Corn 3 C9
St Anthony-in-Meneage
Corn 3 D7
St Anthony's T&W . . .243 E7
St Anthony's Hill
E Sus 23 E10
St Arvans Mon 79 F8
St Asaph = Llanelwy
Denb 181 G8
St Athan = Sain Tathon
V Glam 58 F4
Sain Tathon = St Athan
V Glam 58 F4
St Augustine's Kent . .54 C6
St Austell Corn 5 E10
St Austins Hants 20 B2
St Bees Cumb 219 C9
St Blazey Corn 5 E11
St Blazey Gate Corn . .5 E11
St Boswells Borders .262 C3
St Breock Corn 10 G5
St Breward Corn 11 F7
St Briavels Glos 79 E9
St Briavels Common
Glos 79 E8
St Bride's Pembs 72 C4
St Brides Major =
Saint-y-Brid V Glam .57 G11
St Bride's Netherwent
Mon 60 B2
St Brides-super-Ely
V Glam 58 D5
St Brides Wentlooge
Newport 59 C9
Saintbridge Glos 80 B5
St Budeaux Plym 7 D2
Saintbury Glos 100 D2
St Buryan Corn 1 D4
St Catherine Bath 61 E9
St Catherine's Argyll 284 G5
St Catherine's Hill
BCP 19 B8
St Chloe Glos 80 E4
St Clears = Sanclêr
Carms 74 B3
St Cleer Corn 6 B5
St Clement Corn 4 G6
St Clether Corn 11 E10
St Colmac Argyll 275 G11
St Columb Major Corn .5 C8
St Columb Minor Corn .4 C6
St Columb Road Corn .5 D10
St Combs Aberds 303 C10
St Cross Hants 33 B7
St Cross South Elmham
Suff 142 G5
St Cyrus Aberds 293 G9
St David's Perth 286 E3
St David's = Tyddewi
Pembs 90 F5
St Day Corn 4 G4
St Decumans Som 42 E5
St Dennis Corn 5 D9
St Denys Soton 32 E6
St Devereux Hereford .97 E8
St Dials Torf 78 G3
St Dogmaels = Llandudoch
Pembs 92 B3
St Dominick Corn 7 B8
St Donat's = Sain Dunwyd
V Glam 58 F2
St Edith's Wilts 62 G3
St Endellion Corn 10 F5
St Enoder Corn 5 D7
St Erme Corn 4 E6
St Erney Corn 7 D7
St Erth Corn 2 B3
St Erth Praze Corn 2 B3
St Ervan Corn 10 G3
St Eval Corn 5 B7
St Ewe Corn 5 F9
St Fagans Cardiff 58 D6
St Fergus Aberds 303 D10
St Fillans Perth 285 E10
St Florence Pembs . . .73 E7
St Gennys Corn 11 B8
St George Bristol 60 E6
Conwy 181 F7
St George in the East
London 67 C10
St Georges N Som . . .59 G11
St George's
Gtr Man 184 B4
Telford 150 G4
St George's Hill Sur. . .66 G5
St George's Well
Devon 27 F8
St Germans Corn 7 D7
St Giles Lincs 189 C8
London 67 C10
St Giles in the Wood
Devon 25 D10
St Giles on the Heath
Devon 12 C3
St Giles's Hill Hants . .33 B7

St Gluvias Corn 3 C7
St Godwalds Worcs . .117 D9
St Harmon Powys 113 C9
St Helena Warks 134 C5
St Helen Auckland
Durham 233 F9
St Helens Cumb 228 E6
IoW 21 D8
Mers 183 B8
St Helen's E Sus 38 E4
S Yorks 197 F11
St Helen's Wood
E Sus 38 E4
St Helier London 67 F9
St Hilary Corn 2 C3
V Glam 58 E4
St Ibbs Herts 104 F3
St Illtyd Bl Gwent 78 E2
St Ippollytts Herts . . .104 F3
St Ishmael's Pembs . .72 D4
St Issey Corn 10 G4
St Ive Corn 6 B6
St Ive Cross Corn 6 B6
St Ives Cambs 122 C6
Corn 2 A2
Dorset 31 G10
St James Dorset 30 C5
London 67 C9
Norf 160 E5
St James's End
N Whants 120 E4
St James South Elmham
Suff 142 G6
St Jidgey Corn 5 B8
St John Corn 7 E8
St Johns London 67 D11
Warks 118 C5
St John's E Sus 52 G4
IoM 192 D3
Kent 52 B4
Kent 52 E5
Sur. 50 B3
Worcs 116 G6
W Yorks 206 F4
St John's Chapel
Devon 25 B8
Durham 232 D3
St John's Fen End
Norf 157 G10
St John's Highway
Norf 157 G10
St John's Park IoW . . .21 C8
St John's Town of Dalry
Dumfries 246 G4
St John's Wells
Aberds 303 F7
St John's Wood
London 67 C9
St Judes IoM 192 C4
St Julians Herts 85 D10
Newport 59 B10
St Just Corn 1 C3
St Justinian Pembs . .90 F4
St Just in Roseland
Corn 3 B9
St Katharines Wilts . .63 G9
St Katherine's
Aberds 303 F7
St Keverne Corn 3 E7
St Kew Corn 10 F6
St Kew Highway Corn .10 F6
St Keyne Corn 6 C4
St Lawrence Corn 5 B10
Essex 89 E7
IoW 20 F6
Kent 71 F11
St Leonards Dorset . . .31 G10
Devon 15 D9
E Sus 38 F4
S Lanark. 268 E2
St Leonard's Bucks . .84 D6
St Leonard's Street
Kent 53 B7
St Levan Corn 1 E3
St Luke's Derby 152 B6
London 67 C10
St Lythans V Glam . . .58 E6
St Mabyn Corn 10 G6
St Madoes Perth 286 E5
St Margarets Herts . . .86 C5
London 67 E7
St Margaret's
Hereford 97 E7
St Margaret's at Cliffe
Kent 55 E11
St Margaret's Hope
Orkney 314 G4
St Margaret South
Elmham Suff 142 G6
St Mark's Glos 99 G8
IoM 192 E3
St Martin Corn 2 E6
Corn 6 E5
St Martins Perth 286 D5
St Martin's Shrops . . .148 B6
St Martin's Moor
Shrops 148 B6
St Mary Bourne
Hants 48 C2
St Marychurch Torbay .9 B8
St Mary Church
V Glam 58 E4
St Mary Cray London .68 F3
Salperton Glos 99 G9
St Mary Hill V Glam . . .58 D3
St Mary Hoo
Medway 69 D10
St Mary in the Marsh
Kent 39 B9
St Mary's Orkney . . .314 G4
St Mary's Bay Kent . . .39 B9
St Maughans Mon 79 B7
St Maughans Green
Mon 79 B7
St Mawes Corn 3 C8
St Mawgan Corn 5 B7
St Mellion Corn 7 B8
St Mellons Cardiff . . .59 C8
St Merryn Corn 10 G3
St Mewan Corn 5 E9
St Michael Caerhays
Corn 5 G9

St Michael Church
Som 43 G10
St Michael Penkevil
Corn 5 G7
St Michaels Kent 53 F11
Torbay 9 C7
Worcs 115 D11
St Michael's Hamlet
Mers 182 D5
St Michael's on Wyre
Lancs 202 E5
St Michael South
Elmham Suff 142 G6
St Minver Corn 10 F5
St Monans Fife 287 G9
St Neot Corn 6 B3
St Neots Cambs 122 E3
St Newlyn East Corn . .4 D6
St Nicholas Herts 104 F5
Pembs 91 D7
V Glam 58 E5
St Nicholas at Wade
Kent 71 G9
St Nicholas South
Elmham Suff 142 G6
St Nicolas Park
Warks 135 E7
St Ninians Stirling . . .278 C5
St Olaves Norf 143 D9
St Osyth Essex 89 B10
St Osyth Heath
Essex 89 B10
St Owens Cross
Hereford 97 C10
St Pancras London . . .67 C10
St Paul's Glos 80 B4
St Paul's Cray London .68 F3
St Paul's Walden
Herts 104 G3
St Peters Kent 71 F11
St Peter's Glos 99 G8
T&W 243 E7
St Peter South Elmham
Suff 142 G6
St Peter The Great
Worcs 117 G7
St Petrox Pembs 73 F7
St Pinnock Corn 6 C4
St Quivox S Ayrs 257 E9
St Ruan Corn 2 F6
Saint's Hill Kent 52 E4
St Stephen Corn 5 E8
St Stephens Corn 8 D10
Herts 85 D10
St Stephen's Corn. . . .12 D2
St Teath Corn 11 E7
St Thomas Devon 14 C4
Swansea 57 C7
Sampool Bridge
Cumb 211 B9
Samuel's Corner
Essex 70 B3
Samuelston E Loth . . .281 G9
Sanachan Highld 299 E8
Sanaigmore Argyll . . .274 F3
Sanclêr = St Clears
Carms 74 B3
Sancreed Corn 1 D4
Sancton E Yorks. 208 F4
Sand Highld 307 K4
Shetland 313 J5
Som 44 D2
Sandaig Highld 295 E9
Sandal W Yorks 197 D10
Sandale Cumb 229 C10
Sandal Magna
W Yorks 197 D10
Sandavore Highld . . .294 G6
Sandbach Ches E 168 C3
Sandbach Heath
Ches E 168 C3
Sandbank Argyll 276 E3
Sandbanks BCP 18 C6
Kent 70 G4
Sandborough Staffs. .152 F2
Sandbraes Lincs 200 G6
Sandend Aberds 302 C5
Sanderstead London .67 G10
Sandfields Glos. 99 G8
Neath 57 C8
Staffs 134 B2
Sandford Cumb 222 B4
Devon 26 G4
Dorset 18 D4
Hants 31 G11
IoW 20 E6
N Som 44 B2
Shrops 148 E6
Shrops 149 C11
S Lanark 268 G4
Worcs 99 B7
W Yorks 205 F11
Sandford Batch
N Som 44 B2
Sandfordhill
Aberds 303 E11
Sandford Hill Stoke . .168 G6
Sandford on Thames
Oxon 83 E8
Sandford Orcas
Dorset 29 C10
Sandford St Martin
Oxon 101 F8
Sandgate Kent 55 G7
Sand Gate Cumb 211 D7
Sandgreen Dumfries. .237 D7
Sandhaven Aberds . . .303 C9
Argyll 276 E3
Sandhead Dumfries . .236 E2
Sandhill Bucks 102 F4
Cambs 139 F11
S Yorks 198 F2
Sandhills Dorset 29 E11
Dorset 29 G9
Oxon 83 D9
Sur. 50 E3
Saltby Leics 155 D7
Salt Coates Cumb . . .238 G5
Saltcoates Cumb 219 F11
N Ayrs 266 G4
Saltcotes Lancs 193 B11
Saltdean Brighton . . .36 G5
Salt End E Yorks 201 B7

Salter Lancs 212 G2
Salterbeck Cumb 228 F5
Salterforth Lancs 204 D3
Salters Heath Hants . .48 B6
Saltershill Shrops 150 D2
Salter Street W Mid . .118 C2
Salterswall
Ches W 167 B10
Salterton Wilts 46 F6
Saltfleet Lincs 191 C7
Saltfleetby All Saints
Lincs 191 C7
Saltfleetby St Clement
Lincs 191 C7
Saltfleetby St Peter
Lincs 190 D6
Saltford Bath 61 F7
Salt Hill Slough 66 C3
Salthouse Cumb 210 F4
Norf 177 E9
Saltley W Mid 133 F11
Saltmarsh Newport . . .59 C11
Saltmarshe E Yorks. . .199 C9
Saltness Orkney 314 G2
Shetland 313 J4
Saltney Flint 166 B5
Salton N Yorks 216 D4
Saltrens Devon 25 C7
Saltwell T&W 243 E7
Saltwick Northumb . .242 B5
Saltwood Kent 55 F7
Salum Argyll 288 E2
Salvington W Sus 35 F10
Salwarpe Worcs 117 E7
Salwayash Dorset 16 B5
Sambourne Warks . . .117 E11
Sambrook Telford 150 E4
Samhla W Isles 296 E3
Samlesbury Lancs . . .203 G7
Samlesbury Bottoms
Lancs 194 B6
Sampford Arundel
Som 27 D10
Sampford Brett Som . .42 E5
Sampford Chapple
Devon 25 G10
Sampford Courtenay
Devon 25 G10
Sampford Moor
Som 27 D10
Sampford Peverell
Devon 27 E8
Sampford Spiney
Devon 12 G6
Sandsound Shetland. .313 J5
Sandtoft N Lincs 199 F8
Sandvoe Shetland . . .312 D5
Sandway Kent 53 C11
Sandwell W Mid 133 F10
Sandwich Kent 55 B10
Sandwich Bay Estate
Kent 55 B11
Sandwick Cumb 221 B8
Orkney 314 H4
Shetland 313 L6
Sandwith Cumb 219 C9
Sandwith Newtown
Cumb 219 C9
Sandy Carms 75 E7
C Beds 104 B3
Sandybank Orkney . . .314 C5
Sandy Bank Lincs 174 E3
Sandy Carrs Durham .234 C3
Sandycroft Flint 166 B4
Sandy Cross E Sus . . .37 C9
Sur 49 D11
Sandy Down Hants . . .20 B2
Sandyford Dumfries . .248 E6
Stoke 168 E5
Sandygate Devon 14 G3
IoM 192 C4
S Yorks 186 D4
Sandy Gate Devon . . .14 E5
Sandy Haven Pembs . .72 D5
Sandyhills
Dumfries 237 D10
Sandylake Corn 6 C2
Sandylands Lancs . . .211 G8
Som 27 C10
Sandylane Swansea . .56 D5
Sandy Lane Wilts 62 F3
Wrex 166 G5
W Yorks 205 F8
Sandypark Devon 13 D10
Sandysike Cumb 239 D9
Sandy Way IoW. 20 F5
Sangobeg Highld. . . .308 C4
Sangomore Highld . . .308 C4
Sanham Green
W Berks 63 F10
Sankey Bridges
Warr 183 D9
Sankyns Green
Worcs 116 E5
Sanna Highld 288 C6
Sanndabhaig
W Isles 297 G4
W Isles 304 E6
Sannox N Ayrs 255 C11
Sanquhar Dumfries . .247 B7
Sansaw Heath
Shrops 149 E10
Santon Cumb 220 E2
N Lincs 200 E2
Santon Bridge
Cumb 220 E2
Santon Downham
Suff 140 F6
Sapcote Leics 135 E9
Sapey Bridge Worcs . .116 F4
Sapey Common
Hereford 116 E4
Sapiston Suff 125 B8
Sapley Cambs 122 C4
Sapperton Derbys . . .152 C3
Glos 80 E6
Lincs 155 C10
Saracen's Head
Lincs 156 D6
Sarclet Highld 310 E7
Sardis Carms 75 D9
Pembs 73 D10
Sarisbury Hants. 33 F8
Sarn Bridgend. 58 C2
Sarn Carms 74 B4
Ceredig 110 G6
Gwyn 147 B9
Powys 95 G10
Powys 148 F4
Sarn Bach Gwyn 144 D6
Sarnesfield
Hereford 115 G7
Sarn Meyllteyrn
Gwyn 144 C4
Saron Carms 75 C10
Carms 93 D7
Denb 165 C8

Saron continued
Gwyn 163 B8
Gwyn 163 D7
Sarratt Herts 85 E9
Sarratt Bottom Herts. .85 F8
Sarre Kent. 71 G9
Sarsden Oxon. 100 G5
Sarsden Halt Oxon . . .100 G5
Sarsgrum Highld 308 C3
Sasaig Highld 295 E8
Sascott Shrops. 149 G8
Satley Durham 233 C8
Satmar Kent 55 F9
Satron N Yorks 223 F8
Satterleigh Devon. . . .25 C11
Satterthwaite Cumb. .220 G6
Satwell Oxon 65 C8
Sauchen Aberds 293 B8
Saucher Perth 286 D5
Sauchie Clack 279 C7
Sauchieburn Aberds .293 G8
Saughall Ches W 182 G5
Saughall Massie
Mers 182 D3
Saughton Edin. 280 G4
Saughtree Borders . . .250 D3
Saul Glos. 80 D2
Saundby Notts 188 D3
Saundersfoot = Llanussyllt
Pembs 73 D10
Saunderton Bucks . . .84 E3
Saunderton Lee
Bucks. 84 F4
Saunton Devon 40 F3
Sausthorpe Lincs 174 B5
Saval Highld 309 J5
Savary Highld 289 E8
Saveock Corn. 4 F5
Saverley Green
Staffs. 151 B9
Savile Park
W Yorks 196 C5
Savile Town
W Yorks 197 C8
Sawbridge Warks 119 D10
Sawbridgeworth
Herts 87 B7
Sawdon N Yorks 217 B8
Sawley Derbys 153 C9
Lancs 203 D11
N Yorks 214 F4
Sawood W Yorks 204 G6
Sawston Cambs 105 B9
Sawtry Cambs 138 G3
Sawyers Hill Wilts . . .81 G8
Sawyer's Hill Som 27 C11
Saxby Leics 154 F6
Lincs 189 D8
W Sus 35 G7
Saxby All Saints
N Lincs. 200 D3
Saxelbye Leics 154 E4
Saxham Street
Suff 125 E11
Saxilby Lincs 188 F5
Saxlingham Norf. 159 B10
Saxlingham Green
Norf 142 D4
Saxlingham Nethergate
Norf 142 D4
Saxlingham Thorpe
Norf 142 D4
Saxmundham Suff . . .127 E7
Saxondale Notts 154 B3
Saxon Street Cambs. .124 F3
Saxtead Suff. 126 D5
Saxtead Green Suff . .126 E5
Saxtead Little Green
Suff 126 D5
Saxthorpe Norf 160 C2
Saxton N Yorks 206 F5
Sayers Common
W Sus 36 D3
Scackleton N Yorks . .216 E2
Scadabhagh
W Isles 305 J3
Scaftworth Notts 187 C11
Scagglethorpe
N Yorks 216 E6
Scaitcliffe Lancs 195 B9
Scaladal W Isles 305 G3
Scalan Moray 292 B4
Scalasaig Argyll 274 D4
Scalby E Yorks 199 B10
N Yorks 227 G10
Scald End Bedford. . . .121 F10
Scaldwell W Nhants . .120 C5
Scale Hall Lancs 211 G9
Scale Houses Cumb . .231 B7
Scales
Cumb 210 E5
Cumb 230 F2
Cumb 231 C7
Lancs 202 G5
Scalford Leics 154 E5
Scaling Redcar 226 C4
Scaliscro W Isles 304 F3
Scallasaig Highld 295 D10
Scallastle Argyll 289 F8
Scalloway Shetland. . .313 K6
Scalpay W Isles 305 J4
Scalpay Ho Highld . . .295 C8
Scalpsie Argyll 255 E11
Scamadale Highld. . . .295 F9
Scambleby Lincs 190 F3
Scamland E Yorks 207 E11
Scamodale Highld. . . .289 G10
Scampston N Yorks . .217 D7
Scampton Lincs. 189 F7
Scaniport Highld 300 F6
Scapa Orkney 314 F4
Scapegoat Hill
W Yorks 196 D5
Scar Orkney 314 B6
Scarborough
N Yorks 217 B10
Scarcewater Corn 5 E8

Scarcliffe Derbys 171 B7
Scarcroft W Yorks . . .206 E3
Scarcroft Hill
W Yorks 206 E3
Scardroy Highld. 300 D2
Scarff Shetland. 312 E4
Scarfskerry Highld . . .310 B6
Scargill Durham. 223 C11
Scar Head Cumb 220 G5
Scarinish Argyll 288 E2
Scarisbrick Lancs . . .193 E11
Scarness Cumb 229 E10
Scarning Norf 159 G9
Scarrington Notts 172 G2
Scarth Hill Lancs 194 F2
Scarthingwell
N Yorks 206 F5
Scartho NE Lincs 201 F9
Scarvister Shetland. . .313 J5
Scarwell Orkney 314 D2
Scatness Shetland. . . .313 M5
Scatraig Highld 301 F7
Scatwell Ho Highld . . .300 D3
Scawby N Lincs 200 F3
Scawsby S Yorks 198 F5
Scawthorpe S Yorks . .198 F5
Scawton N Yorks 215 C10
Scayne's Hill W Sus . .36 C5
Scethrog Powys 96 F2
Scholar Green
Ches E 168 D4
Scholemoor
W Yorks 205 G8
Scholes Gtr Man 194 F5
S Yorks 186 B5
W Yorks 197 B7
W Yorks 197 F7
W Yorks 204 F5
W Yorks 206 F3
Scholey Hill
W Yorks 197 B11
School Aycliffe
Durham 233 G11
Schoolgreen
Wokingham 65 F9
School Green
Ches W 167 C10
Essex 106 E4
IoW 20 D2
W Yorks 205 G8
Schoolhill Aberds 293 D11
School House Dorset. .28 G5
Sciberscross Highld . .309 H7
Scilly Bank Cumb 219 B9
Scissett W Yorks 197 E8
Scleddau Pembs 91 E8
Scofton Notts 187 E10
Scole Norf 126 B2
Scole Common
Norf 142 G2
Scolpaig W Isles 296 D3
Scone Perth 286 E5
Sconser Highld 295 B7
Scoonie Fife. 287 G7
Scoor Argyll 274 B5
Scopwick Lincs 173 D9
Scoraig Highld 307 K5
Scorborough
E Yorks 208 D6
Scorrier Corn 4 G4
Scorriton Devon 8 B4
Scorton Lancs 202 D6
N Yorks. 224 E5
Sco Ruston Norf 160 E5
Scotbheinn W Isles . .296 F4
Scotby Cumb 239 G10
Scotch Corner
N Yorks. 224 F4
Scotches Derbys 170 F4
Scotforth Lancs 202 B5
Scotgate W Yorks 196 E6
Scot Hay Staffs 168 F4
Scothern Lincs 189 F8
Scotland Leics 136 D3
Lincs 155 C10
W Berks 64 F5
Scotland End Oxon . . .100 D6
Scotland Gate
Northumb 253 G7
Scotlands W Mid 133 C8
Scotland Street
Suff 107 D9
Scotlandwell Perth . . .286 G5
Scot Lane End
Gtr Man 194 F6
Scotsburn Highld 301 B7
Scotscalder Station
Highld 310 D4
Scotscraig Fife 287 E8
Scots' Gap Northumb .252 F2
Scotston Aberds 293 F9
Perth 286 C3
Scotstoun Glasgow . .267 B10
Scotstown Highld 289 C10
Scotswood T&W 242 E5
Windsor 66 F2
Scottas Highld 295 E9
Scotter Lincs 199 G11
Scotterthorpe
Lincs 199 G11
Scottlethorpe
Lincs 155 E11
Scotton Lincs 188 B5
N Yorks. 206 B2
N Yorks. 224 F3
Scottow Norf 160 E5
Scott Willoughby
Lincs 155 B11
Scoughall E Loth 282 E2
Scoulag Argyll 266 D2
Scoulton Norf 141 C9
Scounslow Green
Staffs. 151 D11
Scourie Highld 306 E6
Scourie More Highld . .306 E6
Scousburgh
Shetland 313 M5
Scout Dike S Yorks . .197 G8
Scout Green Cumb . . .221 D11
Southead Gtr Man. . .196 F2
Scowles Glos 79 C9

Scrabster Highld. 310 B4
Scraesburgh
Borders. 262 F5
Scrafield Lincs 174 B4
Scragged Oak Kent . . .69 G10
Scrainwood
Northumb 251 B10
Scrane End Lincs 174 G5
Scrapsgate Kent. 70 E2
Scraptoft Leics 136 B2
Scrapton Som 28 E3
Scratby Norf. 161 F10
Scrayingham
N Yorks. 216 A3
Scredda Corn. 5 E10
Scredington Lincs 173 G9
Screedy Som 27 B9
Screens Lincs 174 B6
Scremerston
Northumb 273 F10
Screveton Notts 172 G2
Scrivelsby Lincs 174 B3
Scriven N Yorks 206 B2
Scronkey Lancs. 202 D4
Scrooby Notts 187 C11
Scropton Derbys 152 C3
Scrub Hill Lincs 174 D2
Scruton N Yorks 224 G5
Scrwgan Powys 148 E3
Scuddaborg Highld . . .298 C3
Scuggate Cumb 239 C10
Sculcoates Hull. 209 G7
Sculthorpe Norf. 159 C7
Scunthorpe
N Lincs 199 E11
Scurlage Swansea 56 D3
Sea Som 28 E4
Seaborough Dorset . .28 F5
Seabridge Staffs 168 G4
Seabrook Kent. 55 G7
Seaburn T&W 243 F10
Seacombe Mers 182 C4
Seacox Heath Kent. . .53 G8
Seacroft Lincs 175 C9
W Yorks 206 F3
Seadyke Lincs 156 B6
Seafar N Lanark 278 G5
Seafield Highld 311 L3
Midloth 270 C5
S Ayrs 257 E8
W Loth 269 B10
Seaford E Sus 23 F7
Seaforth Mers 182 B4
Seagrave Leics 154 F2
Seagry Heath Wilts . . .62 C3
Seaham Durham 234 B4
Seahouses
Northumb 264 C6
Seal Kent 52 B4
Sealand Flint 166 B5
Seale Sur 49 D11
Seamer N Yorks 217 C10
N Yorks. 225 C9
Seamill N Ayrs 266 F4
Sea Mill Cumb 210 F5
Sea Mills Bristol 60 D5
Corn 10 G4
Sea Palling Norf 161 D8
Searby Lincs 200 F5
Seasalter Kent 70 F5
Seascale Cumb 219 C10
Seathorne Lincs 175 B9
Seathwaite Cumb 220 C4
Cumb 220 F5
Seatle Cumb 211 C7
Seatoller Cumb 220 C4
Seaton
Corn 6 E6
Cumb 228 E6
Devon 15 C10
Durham 243 G9
E Yorks 209 D9
Kent 55 B8
Northumb 243 B8
Rutland 137 D7
Seaton Burn T&W. . . .242 C6
Seaton Carew Hrtlpl .234 F6
Seaton Delaval
Northumb 243 B8
Seaton Ross
E Yorks 207 E11
Seaton Sluice
Northumb 243 B8
Seatown Aberds 302 C5
Dorset 16 C4
Seaureagh Moor
Corn 2 B6
Seave Green
N Yorks. 225 E11
Seaview IoW 21 C8
Seaville Cumb 238 G5
Seavington St Mary
Som 28 E6
Seavington St Michael
Som 28 D6
Seawick Essex. 89 C10
Sebastopol Torf 78 F3
Sebay Orkney 314 F5
Sebergham Cumb 230 C3
Sebiston Velzian
Orkney. 314 D2
Seckington Warks 134 B5
Second Coast
Highld 307 K4
Second Drove
Cambs 139 F10
Sedbergh Cumb 222 G3
Sedbury Glos 79 G8
Sedbusk N Yorks 223 G7
Seddington C Beds . .104 B3
Sedgeberrow Worcs . .99 D10
Sedgebrook Lincs. . . .155 B7
Sedgefield Durham. . .234 F3
Sedgeford Norf. 158 B4
Sedgehill Wilts 30 B5
Sedgemere W Mid . . .118 B4
Sedgley W Mid. 133 E8
Sedgley Park
Gtr Man 195 G10
Sedgwick Cumb 211 B10
Sedlescombe E Sus . .38 D3

Sedlescombe Street
E Sus 38 D3
Sedrup Bucks. 84 C2
Seed Kent 54 B2
Seed Lee Lancs 194 C5
Seedley Gtr Man 184 B4
Seend Wilts 62 G2
Seend Cleeve Wilts . . .62 G2
Seend Head Wilts 62 G2
Seer Green Bucks 85 G7
Seething Norf 142 D6
Seething Wells
London. 67 F7
Sefton Mers 193 G11
Segensworth Hants. .33 F8
Seggat Aberds 303 E7
Seghill Northumb. . . .243 C7
Seifton Shrops. 131 G9
Seighford Staffs 151 D7
Seilebost W Isles 305 J2
Seion Gwyn. 163 B8
Seisdon Staffs 132 E6
Seisiadar W Isles 304 E7
Selattyn Shrops 148 C5
Selborne Hants 49 G8
Selby N Yorks 207 G8
Selgrove Kent 54 B4
Selham W Sus 34 C6
Selhurst London. 67 F10
Selkirk Borders 261 D11
Sellack Hereford 97 F11
Sellack Boat
Hereford 97 F11
Sellafirth Shetland . .312 D7
Sellan Corn. 1 C4
Sellibister Orkney . . .314 B7
Sellick's Green Som .28 D2
Sellindge Kent. 54 F6
Selling Kent 54 B4
Sells Green Wilts 62 G2
Selly Hill N Yorks . . .227 D7
Selly Oak W Mid. . . .133 G10
Selly Park W Mid . . .133 G11
Selmeston E Sus 23 D8
Selsdon London. 67 G10
Selsey W Sus 22 E5
Selsfield Common
W Sus 51 G10
Selside Cumb 221 F10
N Yorks 212 D5
Selsley Glos 80 E4
Selson Kent 55 B10
Selsted Kent 55 E8
Selston Notts 171 E7
Selston Common
Notts 171 E7
Selston Green Notts .171 E7
Selwick Orkney 314 F2
Selworthy Som 42 D2
Semblister Shetland . 313 H5
Semer Suff 107 B9
Sem Hill Wilts 30 B5
Semington Wilts 61 G11
Semley Wilts 30 B5
Sempringham Lincs. .156 C2
Send Sur 50 B4
Send Grove Sur. 50 C4
Send Marsh Sur 50 B4
Senghenydd Caerph. .77 G10
Sennen Corn 1 D3
Sennen Cove Corn . . .1 D3
Sennybridge = Pont Senni
Powys 95 F8
Serlby Notts 187 D10
Serrington Wilts 46 F5
Sessay N Yorks 215 D9
Setchey Norf 158 G2
Setley Hants. 32 G4
Seton E Loth 281 G8
Seton Mains E Loth . .281 F8
Setter Shetland 312 E6
Shetland 313 H5
Shetland 313 J7
Shetland 313 L6
Settiscarth Orkney . .314 E3
Settle N Yorks 212 G6
Settrington N Yorks . .216 E6
Seven Ash Som 43 G7
Sevenhampton
Glos 99 G10
Swindon. 82 G2
Seven Kings London. . .68 B3
Sevenoaks Kent 52 C4
Sevenoaks Common
Kent 52 C4
Sevenoaks Weald
Kent 52 C4
Seven Sisters =
Blaendulais Neath . .76 D4
Seven Springs Glos . .81 B7
Seven Star Green
Essex 107 F8
Severn Beach S Glos . .60 B4
Severnhampton
Swindon. 82 G2
Severn Stoke Worcs . .99 C7
Sevick End Bedford. .121 G11
Sevington Kent 54 E4
Sewards End
Essex 105 D11
Sewardstone Essex . . .86 F5
Sewardstonebury
Essex 86 F5
Sewell C Beds 103 G9
Sewerby E Yorks 218 F3
Seworgan Corn 2 C6
Sewstern Leics 155 E7
Sexhow N Yorks 225 D9
Sezincote Glos 100 E3
Sgarasta Mhor
W Isles. 305 J2
Sgiogarstaigh
W Isles 304 B7
Sgiwen = Skewen
Neath. 57 B8
Shabbington Bucks .83 D11
Shab Hill Glos 80 B6
Shackerley Shrops . . .132 B6
Shackerstone Leics . .135 B7
Shacklecross
Derbys. 153 C8

Shackleford Sur 50 D2
Shackleton W Yorks .196 B3
Shacklewell London. .67 B10
Shacklford Sur 50 D2
Shade W Yorks 196 C2
Shadforth Durham . .234 C2
Shadingfield Suff . . .143 G8
Shadoxhurst Kent. . . .54 F3
Shadsworth
Blackburn. 195 B8
Shadwell Glos 80 F3
London. 67 C11
Norf 141 G8
Shaffalong Staffs . . .169 E7
Shaftenhoe End
Herts 105 D8
Shaftesbury Dorset . .30 C5
Shafton S Yorks 197 E11
Shafton Two Gates
S Yorks 197 E11
Shaggs Dorset 18 E3
Shakeford Shrops. . . .150 D3
Shakerley Gtr Man . .195 G7
Shakesfield Glos. 98 E3
Shalbourne Wilts 63 G10
Shalcombe IoW 20 D3
Shalden Hants 49 E7
Shalden Green Hants .49 E7
Shaldon Devon 14 G4
Shalfleet IoW 20 D4
Shalford Essex 106 F4
Som 45 G8
Sur. 50 D4
Shalford Green
Essex 106 F4
Shallcross Derbys . . .185 E8
Shalloch Moray 302 D3
Shallowford Devon . .25 B11
Devon 41 E8
Staffs 151 D7
Shalmsford Street
Kent. 54 C5
Shalstone Bucks 102 D2
Shamley Green Sur . .50 E4
Shandon Argyll 276 D5
Shandwick Highld . . .301 B8
Shangton Leics 136 D4
Shankhouse
Northumb 243 B7
Shanklin IoW 21 E7
Shannochie
N Ayrs 255 E10
Shannochill Stirling .277 B10
Shanquhar Aberds . .302 F5
Shanwell Fife. 287 E8
Shanzie Perth 286 B6
Shap Cumb 221 B11
Shapridge Glos 79 B11
Shapwick Dorset. 30 G6
Som 44 F2
Sharcott Wilts 46 B6
Shard End W Mid. . . .134 F3
Shardlow Derbys. . . .153 C8
Shareshill Staffs 133 B8
Sharlston W Yorks . .197 D11
Sharlston Common
W Yorks 197 D11
Sharmans Cross
W Mid 118 B2
Sharnal Street
Medway 69 E9
Sharnbrook Bedford. .121 F9
Sharneyford Lancs . .195 C11
Sharnford Leics. 135 E9
Sharnhill Green
Dorset. 30 F2
Sharoe Green Lancs. .202 G6
Sharow N Yorks 214 E6
Sharpenhoe
C Beds 103 E11
Sharperton
Northumb 251 C11
Sharpes Gtr Man 195 E8
Sharpley Heath
Staffs. 151 B9
Sharpness Glos 79 E11
Sharpsbridge E Sus . .36 C6
Sharp's Corner E Sus .23 B9
Sharpstone Bath. 45 B9
Sharp Street Norf. . . .161 E7
Sharpthorne W Sus . .51 G11
Sharptor Corn 11 G11
Sharpway Gate
Worcs 117 D9
Sharrington Norf . . .159 B10
Sharrow S Yorks 186 D4
Sharston Gtr Man . . .184 D4
Shatterford Worcs . .132 G5
Shatterling Kent. 55 B9
Shatton Derbys 185 E11
Shaugh Prior Devon. . .7 C10
Shavington Ches E . .168 E2
Shaw Gtr Man 196 F1
Swindon. 62 B6
W Berks 64 F3
Wilts 61 G11
W Yorks 204 F6
Shawbank Shrops . . .131 G9
Shawbirch Telford . .150 G2
Shawbury Shrops . . .149 E11
Shawclough
Gtr Man 195 G11
Shaw Common Glos . .98 F3
Shawdon Hall
Northumb 264 G3
Shawell Leics. 135 G10
Shawfield Gtr Man . .195 E11
Staffs. 169 C9
Shawfield Head
N Yorks 205 C11
Shawford Hants 33 C7
Som 45 C7
Shawforth Lancs 195 C11
Shaw Green Herts . .104 E5
Lancs. 194 D4
N Yorks 205 C11
Shawhead
Dumfries 237 B10
N Lanark 268 C4
Shaw Heath Ches E . .184 F3
Gtr Man 184 D5
Shawhill Dumfries . .238 D6

Shawlands
Glasgow 267 C11
Shaw Lands
S Yorks 197 F10
Shaw Mills N Yorks .214 G5
Shawsburn S Lanark. .268 E5
Shaw Side Gtr Man . .196 F2
Shawton S Lanark . .268 F3
Shawtonhill
S Lanark. 268 F3
Shay Gate W Yorks . .205 F8
Sheandow Moray . . .302 F2
Shear Cross Wilts 45 D11
Shearington
Dumfries 238 D2
Shearsby Leics 136 E2
Shearston Som 43 G9
Shebbear Devon 24 F6
Shebdon Staffs 150 D5
Shebster Highld. 310 C4
Sheddens E Renf 267 D11
Shedfield Hants 33 E9
Sheen Staffs 169 C10
Sheepbridge Derbys .186 G5
Sheepdrove
W Berks 63 D10
Sheep Hill Durham . .242 F5
Sheeplane C Beds . . .103 E8
Sheepridge Bucks . . .65 B11
W Yorks 197 D7
Sheepscar Leeds 206 G2
Sheepscombe Glos . . .80 C5
Sheepwash Devon 7 B11
Northumb 253 F7
Sheepway N Som 60 D3
Sheepy Magna
Leics 134 C6
Sheepy Parva Leics . .134 C6
Sheering Essex 87 C8
Sheerness Kent. 70 E2
Sheerwater Sur 66 G4
Sheet Hants 34 C3
Sheets Heath Sur 50 B2
Sheffield Corn 1 D5
S Yorks 186 D4
Sheffield Bottom
W Berks 65 F7
Sheffield Green
E Sus 36 C6
Sheffield Park
S Yorks 186 D5
Shefford C Beds 104 D2
Shefford Woodlands
W Berks 63 E11
Sheigra Highld. 306 C6
Sheildmuir
N Lanark 268 D5
Shelderton Shrops . .115 B8
Sheldon Derbys. 169 B11
Devon 27 F10
W Mid 134 G3
Sheldwich Kent. 54 B4
Sheldwich Lees Kent. .54 B4
Shelf Bridgend 58 C2
W Yorks 196 B6
Shelfanger Norf 142 G3
Shelfield Warks 118 E2
W Mid 133 C10
Shelfield Green
Warks 118 E2
Shelford Notts 171 G11
Warks 135 F8
Shell Worcs 117 F9
Shelland Suff 125 C10
Shellbrook Leics 152 F6
Shelley Essex 87 E9
Suff 107 D10
W Yorks 197 E8
Shelley Woodhouse
W Yorks 197 E8
Shell Green Halton . .183 D8
Shellingford Oxon . . .82 G4
Shellow Bowells
Essex 87 D10
Shellwood Cross Sur. .51 D8
Shelsley Beauchamp
Worcs 116 E4
Shelsley Walsh
Worcs 116 E4
Shelthorpe Leics. . . .153 F10
Shelton Bedford 121 D10
Norf 142 E4
Notts 172 G3
Shrops 149 G9
Stoke 168 F5
Shelton Green Norf . .142 E4
Shelton Lock Derby . .153 C7
Shelton under Harley
Staffs. 150 B6
Shelve Shrops 130 D6
Shelvin Devon 27 G11
Shelvingford Kent . . .71 F8
Shelwick Hereford . . .97 C10
Shelwick Green
Hereford 97 C10
Shenfield Essex. 87 G10
Shenington Oxon . . .101 C7
Shenley Herts 85 E11
Shenley Brook End
M Keynes 102 D6
Shenleybury Herts. . . .85 E11
Shenley Church End
M Keynes 102 D6
Shenley Fields
W Mid 133 G10
Shenley Lodge
M Keynes 102 D6
Shenley Wood
M Keynes 102 D6
Shenmore Hereford . . .97 D7
Shennanton
Dumfries 236 C5
Shennanton Ho
Dumfries 236 C5
Shenstone Staffs 134 C2
Worcs 117 C7
Shenstone Woodend
Staffs. 134 C2

Shenton Leics 135 C7
Shenval Highld. 300 G4
Moray 302 G2
Shenvault Moray. . . .301 E10
Shepeau Stow Lincs. .156 G6
Shephall Herts 104 G5
Shepherd Hill
W Yorks 197 C9
Shepherd's Bush
London. 67 C8
Shepherd's Gate
Norf. 157 F11
Shepherd's Green
Oxon 65 C8
Shepherd's Hill Sur. .50 G2
Shepherd's Patch
Glos 80 E2
Shepherd's Port
Norf. 158 C3
Shepherdswell or
Sibertswold Kent. . . .55 D9
Shepley W Yorks 197 F7
Shepperdine S Glos . .79 F10
Shepperton Sur 66 F5
Shepreth Green
Sur 66 F5
Shepreth Cambs 105 B7
Shepshed Leics. 153 F9
Shepton Beauchamp
Som 28 D6
Shepton Mallet Som . .44 E6
Shepton Montague
Som 45 G7
Shepway Kent 53 C9
Sheraton Durham . . .234 D4
Sherborne Bath 44 B5
Dorset 29 D10
Glos 81 C11
Sherborne St John
Hants. 48 B6
Sherbourne Warks. . .118 E5
Sherbourne Street
Suff 107 C9
Sherburn Durham . . .234 C2
N Yorks 217 D10
Sherburn Grange
Durham 234 C2
Sherburn Hill
Durham 234 C2
Sherburn in Elmet
N Yorks 206 G5
Shere Sur 50 D5
Shereford Norf 159 D7
Sherfield English
Hants. 32 C3
Sherfield on Loddon
Hants. 49 B7
Sherfin Lancs. 195 B9
Sherford Devon 8 G5
Dorset 18 C4
Som 28 C2
Sheriffhales Shrops. .150 G5
Sheriff Hill T&W 243 E7
Sheriff Hutton
N Yorks 216 F3
Sheriff's Lench
Worcs 99 B10
Sheringham Norf . . .177 E11
Sheringwood Norf . .177 E11
Shermanbury W Sus . .36 D2
Shernal Green
Worcs 117 E8
Shernborne Norf . . .158 C4
Sherrard's Green
Worcs 98 B5
Sherrardspark Herts. .86 C2
Sherriffhales
Shrops 150 G5
Sherrington Wilts . . .46 F3
Sherston Wilts. 61 B11
Sherwood
Nottingham 171 G9
Sherwood Green
Devon 25 C9
Sherwood Park Kent. .52 E6
Shettleston Glasgow .268 C2
Shevington Gtr Man .194 F4
Shevington Moor
Gtr Man 194 E4
Shevington Vale
Gtr Man 194 F4
Sheviock Corn 7 D7
Shewalton N Ayrs . . .257 B8
Shibden Head
W Yorks 196 B5
Shide IoW. 20 D5
Shiel Aberds 292 B4
Shiel Bridge
Highld 295 D11
Shieldaig Highld 299 B8
Highld 299 D8
Shieldhall Glasgow . .267 B10
Shieldhill Dumfries. .248 F2
Falk 279 F7
S Lanark. 269 G10
Shield Row Durham . .242 G6
Shielfoot Highld 289 C8
Shielhill Angus 287 B8
Invclyd. 276 G4
Shifford Oxon 82 E5
Shifnal Shrops 132 B4
Shilbottle Northumb. .252 B5
Shilbottle Grange
Northumb 252 B6
Shildon Durham. 233 F10
Shillford E Renf 267 D8
Shillingford Devon. . .27 C7
Oxon 83 G9
Shillingford Abbot
Devon 14 D4
Shillingford St George
Devon 14 D4
Shillingstone Dorset. .30 E4
Shillington C Beds . . .104 D2
Shillmoor Northumb. .251 B9
Shilton Oxon 82 D3
Warks 135 G8
Shilvington
Northumb 252 G5

Shimpling Norf 142 G3
Suff 125 G7
Shimpling Street
Suff 125 G7
Shincliffe Durham. . .233 C11
Shiney Row T&W . . .243 G8
Shinfield Wokingham. .65 F8
Shingay Cambs. 104 B6
Shingham Norf 140 C4
Shingle Street Suff . .109 C7
Shinner's Bridge
Devon 8 C5
Shinness Highld. 309 H5
Shipbourne Kent. 52 C5
Shipdham Norf 141 B9
Shipdham Airfield
Norf. 141 B9
Shipham Som 44 B2
Shiphay Torbay 9 B7
Shiplake Oxon 65 D9
Shiplake Bottom
Oxon 65 D9
Shiplake Row Oxon . .65 D9
Shiplate N Som 43 B11
Shiplaw Borders 270 F4
Shipley Derbys 170 G6
Northumb 264 F4
Shrops 132 D6
W Sus 35 C10
W Yorks 205 F8
Shipley Bridge Sur. . .51 E10
Shipley Common
Derbys. 171 G7
Shipley Shiels
Northumb 251 D7
Shipmeadow Suff. . .143 F7
Shippea Hill Cambs . .73 D10
Shippon Oxon 83 F7
Shipston-on-Stour
Warks 100 C5
Shipton Bucks 102 F5
Glos 81 B8
N Yorks 207 B7
Shipton Bellinger
Hants. 47 D10
Shipton Gorge
Dorset. 16 C5
Shipton Green
W Sus 22 C4
Shipton Lee Bucks . .102 G4
Shipton Moyne Glos .61 B11
Shipton Oliffe Glos . .81 B8
Shipton on Cherwell
Oxon 83 B7
Shipton Solers Glos. .81 B8
Shiptonthorpe
E Yorks 208 E3
Shipton-under-
Wychwood Oxon . . .82 B3
Shirburn Oxon 83 F11
Shirdley Hill Lancs . .193 E11
Shirebrook Derbys. . .171 B8
Shirecliffe S Yorks . .186 C5
Shiregreen S Yorks . .186 C5
Shirehampton Bristol .60 D4
Shiremoor T&W 243 C8
Shirenewton Mon. . . .78 G6
Shire Oak W Mid . . .133 C11
Shireoaks Derbys. . . .185 E9
Notts 187 E9
Shires Mill Fife 279 D10
Shirkoak Kent 54 F2
Shirland Derbys. 170 D6
Shirlett Shrops. 132 D3
Shirley Derbys 170 G2
Hants. 19 B9
London. 67 F11
Soton 32 E6
W Mid 118 B2
Shirley Heath
W Mid 118 B2
Shirley Warren Soton .32 E5
Shirl Heath Hereford. .115 F8
Shirrell Heath Hants . .33 E9
Shirwell Devon 40 F5
Shirwell Cross Devon .40 F5
Shiskine N Ayrs 255 E10
Shitterton Dorset 18 C2
Shobdon Hereford. . .115 E8
Shobley Hants 31 F11
Shobnall Staffs 152 E4
Shobrooke Devon. . . .26 G5
Shoby Leics 154 F3
Shocklach Ches W . .166 F6
Shocklach Green
Ches W 166 F6
Shoeburyness
Southend 70 C2
Sholden Kent. 55 C11
Sholing Soton 32 E6
Sholing Common
Soton 33 E7
Sholver Gtr Man 196 F3
Shootash Hants. 32 C4
Shooters Hill London. .68 D2
Shootersway Herts . .85 D7
Shoot Hill Shrops . . .149 G8
Shop Corn. 10 G3
Corn. 24 E2
Devon 24 D4
Shop Corner Suff . . .108 E4
Shopford Cumb 240 C3
Shopnoller Som 43 G7
Shopp Hill W Sus. . . .34 B6
Shopwyke W Sus. 22 B5
Shore Gtr Man 196 D2
W Yorks 196 B2
Shore Bottom Devon .28 G2
Shoreditch London. . .67 C10
Som 28 C2
Shoregill Cumb 222 E5
Shoreham Kent. 52 E6
Shoreham Beach
W Sus 36 G2
Shoreham-by-Sea
W Sus 36 F2
Shore Mill Highld . . .301 C7
Shoresdean
Northumb 273 F9
Shores Green Oxon . .82 D5

Shoreside Shetland. . .313 J4
Shoreswood
Northumb 273 F8
Shoreton Highld. 300 C6
Shorley Hants 33 B9
Shorncliffe Camp
Kent. 55 F7
Shorncote Glos 81 F8
Shorne Kent. 69 E7
Shorne Ridgeway
Kent. 69 E7
Shorne West Kent . . .69 E7
Shortacombe Devon . .12 D6
Shortacross Corn 6 D5
Shortbridge E Sus . . .37 C7
Short Cross W Mid . .133 G9
Shortfield Common
Sur. 49 G10
Shortgate E Sus 23 B7
Short Green Norf . . .141 F11
Shorthampton Oxon .100 G6
Shortheath Hants. . . .49 F9
Sur. 49 E10
Short Heath Derbys . .133 G9
W Mid 133 E11
Shorthill Shrops 131 B8
Shortlands London . . .67 F11
W Sus 35 C10
W Yorks 205 F8
Shortlanesend Corn . .4 F6
Shortlees E Ayrs 257 B10
Shortmoor Devon 28 G2
Dorset. 29 G7
Shorton Torbay 9 C7
Shortroods Renfs . . .267 B9
Shortstanding Glos . .79 C9
Shortstown
Bedford 103 B11
Shortwood Glos 80 F4
S Glos 61 D7
Glos 81 B8
Shorwell IoW 20 E5
Shoscombe Bath 45 B8
Shoscombe Vale
Bath. 45 B8
Shotatton Shrops . . .149 E7
Shotesham Norf 142 D5
Shotgate Essex 88 G3
Shotley N Nhants . . .137 D8
Shotley Suff 108 D4
Shotley Bridge
Durham 242 G3
Shotleyfield
Northumb 242 G3
Shotley Gate Suff . . .108 E4
Shottenden Kent. 54 C4
Shottermill Sur. 49 G11
Shottery Warks 118 G3
Shotteswell Warks . .101 B8
Shottisham Suff 108 C6
Shottle Derbys 170 F4
Shottlegate Derbys . .170 F4
Shotton Durham 234 D4
Durham 234 F3
Flint 166 B4
Northumb 242 B6
Northumb 263 C8
Shotton Colliery
Durham 234 C3
Shotts N Lanark 269 C7
Shotwick Ches W. . . .182 G4
Shreding Green
Bucks. 66 C4
Shrawardine Shrops .149 F8
Shrawley Worcs 116 E6
Shreding Green
Bucks. 66 C4
Shrewley Warks 118 D4
Shrewley Common
Warks 118 D4
Shrewsbury Shrops . .149 G9
Shrewton Wilts. 46 E5
Shripney W Sus 22 C6
Shrivenham Oxon 63 B8
Shropham Norf 141 E9
Shroton or Iwerne
Courtney Dorset . . .30 E5
Shrub End Essex 107 G9
Shrubs Hill Sur 66 F3
Shrutherhill
S Lanark. 268 F5
Shucknall Hereford. . .97 C11
Shudy Camps
Cambs 106 C2
Shulishadermor
Highld 298 E4
Shulista Highld 298 B4
Shuna Ho Argyll. . . .275 C9
Shurdington Glos. . . .80 B6
Shurlock Row
Windsor. 65 E10
Shurnock Worcs 117 E10
Shurrery Highld. 310 D4
Shurrery Lodge
Highld 310 D4
Shurton Som 43 E8
Shustoke Warks 134 E4
Shute Devon 15 B11
Devon 26 G5
Shute End Wilts 31 B11
Shutford Oxon 101 C7
Shut Heath Staffs . . .151 E7
Shuthonger Glos 99 D7
Shutlanger
W Nhants. 120 G4
Shutta Corn 6 E5
Shutt Green Staffs . .133 B7
Shuttington Warks. . .134 C4
Shuttlesfield Kent. . . .55 E7
Shuttlewood Derbys .187 G7
Shuttleworth
Gtr Man 195 D10
Shwt Bridgend 57 D11
Siabost bho Dheas
W Isles 304 D4
Siabost bho Thuath
W Isles 304 D4

Siadar W Isles 304 C5
Siadar Iarach
W Isles 304 C5
Siadar Uarach
W Isles 304 C5
Sibbaldbie Dumfries. .248 F4
Sibbertoft
W Nhants 136 G3
Sibdon Carwood
Shrops. 131 G8
Sibford Ferris Oxon . .101 D7
Sibford Gower
Oxon 101 D7
Sible Hedingham
Essex. 106 E5
Sibsey Lincs 174 E5
Sibsey Fen Side
Lincs 174 E4
Sibson Cambs 137 D11
Leics 135 C7
Sibster Highld 310 D7
Sibthorpe Notts 172 F3
Notts 188 G2
Sibton Suff 127 D7
Sibton Green Suff. . .127 C7
Sicklesmere Suff . . .125 E7
Sicklinghall
N Yorks 206 D3
Sid Devon 15 D8
Sidbrook Som 28 B3
Sidbury Devon 15 C8
Shrops 132 F3
Sidcot N Som 44 B2
Sidcup London 68 E3
Siddal W Yorks 196 C6
Siddick Cumb 228 E6
Siddington Ches E . .184 G4
Glos 81 F8
Siddington Heath
Ches E 184 G4
Sidemoor Worcs. . . .117 C9
Side of the Moor
Gtr Man 195 E8
Sidestrand Norf 160 B5
Sideway Stoke 168 G5
Sidford Devon 15 C8
Sidlesham W Sus 22 D5
Sidlesham Common
W Sus 22 C5
Sidley E Sus 38 F2
Sidlow Sur 51 D9
Sidmouth Devon . . .15 D8
Sidway Staffs 150 B5
Sigford Devon 13 G11
Sigglesthorne
E Yorks 209 D9
Sighthill Edin. 280 G3
Glasgow 268 B2
Signingstone = Tresigin
V Glam 58 E3
Signet Oxon 82 C2
Sigwells Som 29 C10
Silchester Hants 64 G6
Sildinis W Isles 305 G4
Sileby Leics 153 F11
Silecroft Cumb. 210 C2
Silfield Norf 142 D2
Silford Devon 24 B6
Silian Ceredig. 111 G11
Silkstead Hants 32 C6
Silkstone S Yorks . . .197 F9
Silkstone Common
S Yorks 197 G9
Silk Willoughby
Lincs 173 G9
Silloth Cumb 238 G4
Sills Northumb 251 C8
Sillyearn Moray 302 D5
Siloh Carms 94 D4
Silpho N Yorks 227 G9
Silsden W Yorks 204 D6
Silsoe C Beds 103 D11
Silton Dorset 30 B3
Silverburn Midloth. .270 C4
Silverdale Lancs 211 E9
Staffs. 168 F4
Silverdale Green
Lancs 211 E9
Silver End Essex 88 B4
W Mid 133 F9
Silvergate Norf 160 D3
Silver Green Norf . .142 E5
Silverhill E Sus 38 E4
Silverhill Park E Sus .38 E4
Silver Knap Som 29 C11
Silverknowes Edin. . .280 F4
Silverley's Green
Suff 126 B5
Silvermuir S Lanark .269 F8
Silverstone
W Nhants 102 C3
Silver Street Glos. . . .80 D4
Som 27 C11
Som 44 G4
Worcs 117 B11
Silverton Devon. 27 G7
W Dunb 277 F8
Silvertonhill
S Lanark. 268 E4
Silvertown London. . .68 D2
Silverwell Corn 4 F4
Silvington Shrops . . .116 B2
Silwick Shetland 313 J4
Sim Hill S Yorks 197 G9
Simister Gtr Man . . .195 F10
Simmondley Derbys. .185 C8
Simm's Cross
Halton 183 D8
Simm's Lane End
Mers 194 G4
Simonburn
Northumb 241 C9
Simonsbath Som 41 F9
Simonsburrow
Devon 27 D10
Simonside T&W 243 E8
Simonstone Lancs . .203 G11
N Yorks 223 G7
Simprim Borders . . .272 F6

Simpson M Keynes . .103 D7
Pembs 72 B5
Simpson Cross
Pembs 72 B5
Simpson Green
W Yorks 205 F9
Sinclair's Hill
Borders 272 E6
Sinclairston E Ayrs . .257 F11
Sinclairtown Fife . . .280 C5
Sinderby N Yorks . . .214 C6
Sinderhope
Northumb 241 G8
Sinderland Green
Gtr Man 184 C2
Sindlesham
Wokingham 65 F9
Sinfin Derby 152 C6
Sinfin Moor Derby . .153 C7
Singdean Borders. . .250 C3
Singleborough
Bucks. 102 E5
Single Hill Bath. 45 B8
Singleton Lancs 202 F3
W Sus 34 E5
Singlewell Kent 69 E7
Singret Wrex 166 D4
Sinkhurst Green
Kent. 53 E10
Sinnahard Aberds. . .292 B6
Sinnington N Yorks . .216 B4
Sinton Worcs 116 E6
Sinton Green Worcs. .116 E6
Sion Hill Bath. 61 F8
Sipson London 66 D5
Sirhowy Bl Gwent. . .77 C11
Sisland Norf 142 D6
Sissinghurst Kent. . . .53 F9
Sisterpath Borders . .272 F5
Siston S Glos. 61 D7
Sithney Corn 2 D4
Sithney Common Corn .2 D4
Sithney Green Corn . .2 D4
Sittingbourne Kent . .70 G2
Six Ashes Staffs. . . .132 F5
Six Bells Bl Gwent . . .78 E2
Sixhills Lincs 189 D11
Six Hills Leics 154 E2
Sixmile Kent. 54 E6
Six Mile Bottom
Cambs 123 F11
Sixpenny Handley
Dorset. 31 D7
Sizewell Suff 127 E9
Skaigh Devon 13 C8
Skail Highld. 308 E7
Skaill Highld. 314 C4
Orkney 314 D2
Orkney 314 F5
Skares E Ayrs 258 F2
Skateraw E Loth. . . .282 F4
Skaw Shetland 312 B8
Shetland 312 G7
Skeabost Highld 298 E4
Skeabrae Orkney . . .314 D2
Skeeby N Yorks 224 E4
Skeete Kent 54 E6
Skeffington Leics . . .136 C4
Skeffling E Yorks . . .201 D11
Skegby Notts 171 C7
Notts 188 G3
Skegness Lincs 175 C9
Skelberry Shetland . .313 G6
Shetland 313 M5
Skelbo Highld. 309 K7
Skelbo Street Highld .309 K7
Skelbrooke S Yorks . .198 E4
Skeldyke Lincs 156 B6
Skelfhill Borders . . .249 C11
Skellingthorpe
Lincs 188 G6
Skellister Shetland . .313 H6
Skellorn Green
Ches E 184 E6
Skellow S Yorks 198 E4
Skelmanthorpe
W Yorks 197 E8
Skelmersdale Lancs. .194 F3
Skelmonae Aberds. . .303 F8
Skelmorlie N Ayrs . .266 B3
Skelmuir Aberds. . . .303 E9
Skelpick Highld 308 D7
Skelton Cumb 230 D4
E Yorks 199 B9
N Yorks 223 E11
Redcar. 226 B3
York 207 B7
Skelton-on-Ure
N Yorks 215 F7
Skelwick Orkney . . .314 B4
Skelwith Bridge
Cumb. 220 E6
Skendleby Lincs 174 B6
Skendleby Psalter
Lincs 190 G6
Skene Ho Aberds. . . .293 C9
Skenfrith Mon 97 G9
Skerne E Yorks 208 B6
Skerne Park Darl . . .224 C5
Skeroblingarry
Argyll. 255 E8
Skerray Highld. 308 C6
Skerricha Highld. . . .306 D7
Skerryford Pembs . . .72 C6
Skerton Lancs 211 G9
Sketchley Leics 135 E8
Sketty Swansea 56 C6
Skewen = Sgiwen
Neath. 57 B8
Skewes Corn 5 B9
Skewsby N Yorks . . .216 E2
Skeyton Norf 160 D5
Skeyton Corner
Norf 160 D5
Skiag Bridge Highld. .307 F2
Skibo Castle Highld . .309 L7
Skidbrooke Lincs . . .190 C6
Skidbrooke North End
Lincs 190 B6

Skidby E Yorks 208 G6
Skilgate Som 27 B7
Skillington Lincs 155 D7
Skinburness Cumb . . 238 F4
Skinflats Falk 279 E8
Skinidin Highld 298 E2
Skinner's Bottom Corn. 4 F4
Skinners Green W Berks . . 64 F2
Skinnet Highld 308 C5
Skinningrove Redcar . . 226 B4
Skipness Argyll 255 B9
Skippool Lancs 202 E3
Skiprigg Cumb 230 B3
Skipsea E Yorks 209 B9
Skipsea Brough E Yorks . . 209 C9
Skipton N Yorks 204 C5
Skipton-on-Swale N Yorks . . 215 D7
Skipwith N Yorks . . . 207 F9
Skirbeck Lincs 174 G4
Skirbeck Quarter Lincs . . 174 G4
Skirethorns N Yorks . . 213 G9
Skirlaugh E Yorks . . 209 F8
Skirling Borders 260 B3
Skirmett Bucks 65 B9
Skirpenbeck E Yorks . . 207 B10
Skirwith Cumb 231 E8
Skirza Highld 310 C7
Skitby Cumb 239 D10
Skitham Lancs 202 E4
Skittle Green Bucks . . 84 E3
Skulamus Highld . . . 295 C8
Skullomie Highld . . . 308 C6
Skyborry Green Shrops . . 114 C5
Skye Green Essex . . . 107 G7
Skye of Curr Highld . 301 G6
Skyfog Pembs 90 F6
Skyreholme N Yorks . . 213 G11
Slack Derbys 170 C4
  W Yorks 196 B3
  W Yorks 196 D5
  W Yorks 196 F3
Slackcote Gtr Man. . . 196 F3
Slackhall Derbys . . . 185 E9
Slackhead Moray . . . 302 C4
Slack Head Cumb . . . 211 D9
Slackholme End Lincs . . 191 G8
Slacks of Cairnbanno Aberds . . 303 D5
Slad Glos 80 D5
Sladbrook Glos 98 F5
Slade Devon 27 F10
  Devon 40 D4
  Kent 54 C2
  Pembs 72 B6
Slade End Oxon 83 G9
Slade Green London . 68 D4
Slade Heath Staffs . . 133 B8
Slade Hooton S Yorks . . 187 D8
Sladen Green Hants . . 48 C2
Sladesbridge Corn. . 10 G6
Slades Green Worcs . . 99 E7
Slaggyford Northumb . . 240 G5
Slaidburn Lancs . . . 203 C10
Slaithwaite W Yorks . 196 E5
Slaley Derbys 170 D3
  Northumb 241 F11
Slamannan Falk 279 G7
Slape Cross Som . . . 43 F10
Slapewath Redcar . . 226 B2
Slapton Bucks 103 G8
  Devon 8 G6
  W Nhants 102 B2
Slateford Edin 280 G4
Slate Haugh Moray . . 302 C4
Slatepit Dale Derbys . 170 B4
Slattocks Gtr Man . . 195 F11
Slaugham W Sus 36 B3
Slaughterbridge Corn. . 11 D8
Slaughterford Wilts. . 61 E10
Slaughter Hill Ches E . . 168 D2
Slawston Leics 136 E5
Slay Pits S Yorks . . . 199 F7
Sleaford Hants 49 F10
  Lincs 173 F9
Sleagill Cumb 221 B11
Sleap Shrops 149 D9
Sleapford Telford . . . 150 F2
Sleapshyde Herts . . . 86 D2
Sleastary Highld . . . 309 K6
Slebech Pembs 73 B8
Sledge Green Worcs . 98 E6
Sledmere E Yorks . . 217 G8
Sleeches Cross E Sus . . 52 G5
Sleepers Hill Hants . . 33 B7
Sleetbeck Cumb 240 B2
Sleet Moor Derbys . . 170 E6
Sleight Dorset 18 B5
Sleights N Yorks . . . 227 D7
Slepe Dorset 18 C4
Sliabh na h-Airde W Isles . . 296 F3
Slickly Highld 310 C6
Sliddery N Ayrs 255 E10
Slideslow Worcs 117 C9
Sligachan Hotel Highld . . 294 C6
Sligneach Argyll . . . 288 G3
Sligrachan Argyll . . . 276 C3
Slimbridge Glos 80 E2
Slindon Staffs 150 C6
  W Sus 35 F7
Slinfold W Sus 50 G6
Sling Glos 79 D9
  Gwyn 163 B10
Slingsby N Yorks . . . 216 E3

Slioch Aberds 302 F5
Slip End C Beds 85 B9
  Herts 104 D5
Slippery Ford W Yorks . . 204 E6
Slipton N Nhants . . . 121 B9
Slitting Mill Staffs. . . 151 F10
Slochd Highld 301 G8
Slockavullin Argyll . . 275 D9
Sloley Norf 160 E5
Sloncombe Devon . . . 13 D10
Sloothby Lincs 191 G7
Slough Slough 66 D3
Slough Green Som. . . 28 C3
  W Sus 36 B3
Slough Hill Suff 125 G7
Sluggan Highld 301 G8
Sluggans Highld . . . 298 E4
Slumbay Highld . . . 295 B10
Sly Corner Kent 54 G3
Slyfield Sur 50 C3
Slyne Lancs 211 F9
Smailholm Borders . . 262 B4
Smallbridge Gtr Man . . 196 D2
Smallbrook Devon . . 14 B3
  Glos 79 E9
Smallburgh Norf . . . 160 E6
Smallburn Aberds . . 303 E10
  E Ayrs 258 D5
  Derbys 185 F9
Small Dole W Sus . . . 36 E2
Small End Lincs . . . 174 D6
Smalley Derbys 170 G6
Smalley Common Derbys . . 170 G6
Smalley Green Derbys . . 170 G6
Smallfield Sur 51 E10
Smallford Herts 85 D11
Small Heath W Mid . . 134 F2
Smallholm Borders . . 238 B4
Small Hythe Kent . . . 53 G11
Smallmarsh Devon . . 25 C10
Smallrice Staffs 151 C9
Smallridge Devon . . . 28 G4
Smallshaw Gtr Man. . 196 G2
Smallthorne Stoke . . 168 E5
Small Way Som 44 G6
Smallwood Ches E . . 168 C4
  Worcs 117 D10
Smallwood Green Suff . . 125 F8
Smallwood Hey Lancs . . 202 D3
Smallworth Norf . . . 141 G10
Smannell Hants 47 D11
Smardale Cumb 222 D4
Smarden Kent 53 E11
Smarden Bell Kent . . 53 E11
Smart's Hill Kent. . . 52 E4
Smaull Argyll 274 G3
Smeatharpe Devon. . 27 E11
Smeaton Fife 280 C5
Smeeth Kent 54 F5
Smeeton Westerby Leics . . 136 E3
Smelthouses N Yorks . . 214 G3
Smercleit W Isles . . . 297 K3
Smerral Highld 310 F5
Smestow Staffs 133 E7
Smethcott Shrops . . . 131 D9
Smethwick W Mid . . 133 F10
Smethwick Green Ches E . . 168 C4
Smirisary Highld . . . 289 B8
Smisby Derbys 152 F6
Smite Hill Worcs . . . 117 F7
Smithaleigh Devon. . 7 D11
Smithbrook W Sus . . 34 C6
Smith End Green Worcs . . 116 G5
Smithfield Cumb . . . 239 D10
Smith Green Lancs . . 202 C5
Smithies S Yorks . . . 197 F11
Smithincott Devon . . 27 E9
Smiths Green Ches E . . 184 G4
Smith's Green Ches E . . 168 G4
  Essex 105 G11
  Essex 106 C3
  Lincs 200 F5
Smithston Aberds . . 302 G5
Smithstown Highld . 299 B7
Smithton Highld . . . 301 E7
Smithwood Green Suff . . 125 G8
Smithy Bridge Gtr Man . . 196 D2
Smithy Gate Flint . . . 181 F11
Smithy Green Ches E . . 184 G2
  Gtr Man 184 D5
Smithy Houses Derbys . . 170 F5
Smithy Lane Ends Lancs . . 194 E2
Smock Alley W Sus. . 35 D9
Smockington Leics . . 135 F9
Smoky Row Bucks . . 84 D4
Smoogro Orkney . . . 314 F3
Smug Oak Herts 85 E10
Smyrton S Ayrs 244 G4
Smythe's Green Essex . . 88 B6
Snagshall E Sus. . . . 38 C3
Snaigow House Perth . . 286 C4
Snailbeach Shrops . . 131 C7
Snails Hill Som 29 E7
Snailswell Herts . . . 104 E3
Snailwell Cambs . . . 124 D2
Snainton N Yorks . . . 217 C8
Snaisgill Durham. . . 232 F5
Snaith E Yorks 198 C6
Snape N Yorks 214 C4
  Suff 127 F7

Snape Green Lancs . 193 E11
Snape Hill Derbys. . 186 F5
  S Yorks 198 G2
Snapper Devon 40 G5
Snaresbrook London. 67 B11
Snarestone Leics . . 134 B6
Snarford Lincs 189 E9
Snargate Kent 39 B7
Snave Kent 39 B8
Sneachill Worcs . . . 117 G8
Snead Powys 130 E6
Snead Common Worcs . . 116 D4
Sneads Green Worcs . . 117 D7
Sneath Common Norf . . 142 F3
Sneaton N Yorks . . . 227 D7
Sneatonthorpe N Yorks . . 227 D8
Snelland Lincs 189 E9
Snelston Derbys . . . 169 G11
Snetterton Norf 141 E9
Snettisham Norf . . . 158 C3
Sneyd Green Stoke . 168 F5
Sneyd Park Bristol . . 60 D5
Snibston Leics 153 G8
Snig's End Glos 98 F5
Snipeshill Kent 70 G2
Snitter Northumb . . . 252 C2
Snitterby Lincs 189 C7
Snitterfield Warks . . 118 F4
Snitton Shrops 115 B11
Snittongate Shrops . 115 B11
Snittlegarth Cumb . . 229 D10
Snodhill Hereford . . . 96 C6
Snodland Kent. 69 G7
Snods Edge Northumb . . 242 G3
Snowden Hill S Yorks . . 197 G9
Snowdown Kent 55 C8
Snow End Herts 105 E8
Snow Hill Ches E . . . 167 E10
  W Yorks 197 C10
Snow Lea W Yorks. . 196 D5
Snowshill Glos 99 E11
Snow Street Norf . . . 141 G11
Snydale W Yorks . . . 198 D2
Soake Hants 33 E11
Soar Anglesey 178 G5
  Carms 94 F2
  Devon 9 G9
  Gwyn 146 B2
  Powys 95 E9
Soar-y-Mynydd Ceredig . . 112 G5
Soberton Hants 33 D10
Soberton Heath Hants . . 33 E10
Sockbridge Cumb . . . 230 F6
Sockburn Darl. 224 D6
Sockety Dorset 29 F7
Sodom Denb 181 G9
  Shetland 313 G7
Sodylt Bank Shrops . 148 B6
Soham Cambs 123 C11
Soham Cotes Cambs . . 123 B11
Soho London 67 C9
  Som 45 D7
  W Mid 133 F10
Solas W Isles 296 D4
Soldon Cross Devon . 24 E4
Soldridge Hants . . . 49 G7
Sole Street Kent . . . 54 D5
  Kent 69 F7
Solfach = Solva Pembs . . 90 G5
Solihull W Mid 118 B2
Solihull Lodge W Mid . . 117 B11
Sollers Dilwyn Hereford . . 115 F8
Sollers Hope Hereford . . 98 E2
Sollom Lancs 194 D3
Solva = Solfach Pembs. 90 G5
Somerby Leics 154 G5
  Lincs 200 F5
Somercotes Derbys . 170 E6
Somerdale BCP 61 F7
Somerford BCP. 19 C9
  Ches E 168 B4
  Staffs 133 B7
Somerford Keynes Glos . . 81 G8
Somerley Flint 181 F11
Somerleyton Suff . . . 143 D9
Somersal Herbert Derbys . . 152 B2
Somersby Lincs 190 G4
Somersham Cambs . . 123 B7
  Suff 107 B11
Somers Town London . . 67 C9
  Ptsmth 21 B8
Somerton Newport . . 59 B10
  Oxon 101 F9
  Som 29 B7
  Suff 124 G6
Somerton Hill Som. . 29 B7
Somerwood Shrops . . 149 G11
Sompting W Sus . . . 35 G11
Sompting Abbotts W Sus . . 35 F11
Sonning Wokingham . 65 D9
Sonning Common Oxon . . 65 C8
Sonning Eye Oxon . . 65 D9
Sontley Wrex 166 F4
Sookholme Notts . . . 171 B8
Sopley Hants 19 B9
Sopwell Herts 85 D11

Sopworth Wilts. 61 B10
Sorbie Dumfries. . . . 236 E6
Sordale Highld 310 C5
Sorisdale Argyll. . . . 288 C4
Sorley Devon 8 F4
Sorn E Ayrs 258 D3
Sornhill E Ayrs 258 C2
Sortat Highld 310 C6
Sotby Lincs 190 F2
Sothall S Yorks 186 E6
Sots Hole Lincs 173 C10
Sotterley Suff 143 G9
Soudley Shrops 131 E9
  Shrops 150 D4
Soughton = Sychdyn Flint . . 166 B2
Soulbury Bucks 103 F7
Soulby Cumb 222 C4
  Cumb 230 F5
Souldern Oxon 101 E10
Souldrop Bedford . . . 121 E9
Sound Ches E 167 F10
  Shetland 313 H5
  Shetland 313 J6
Sound Heath Ches E . . 167 F10
Soundwell S Glos . . . 60 D6
Sourhope Borders . . 263 E8
Sourin Orkney 314 C4
Sourlie N Ayrs 266 G6
Sourton Devon. 12 C6
Soutergate Cumb . . . 210 C4
South Acre Norf 158 F5
South Acton London. . 67 D7
South Alkham Kent . . 55 E8
South Allington Devon . . 9 G10
South Alloa Falk . . . 279 C7
Southam Glos 99 F9
  Warks 119 E8
South Ambersham W Sus . . 34 C6
Southampton Soton. . 32 E6
South Anston S Yorks . . 187 E8
South Ascot Windsor . 66 F2
South Ashford Kent. . 54 E4
South Auchmachar Aberds . . 303 E9
Southay Som 28 D6
South Baddesley Hants . . 20 B3
South Ballachulish Highld . . 284 B4
South Balloch S Ayrs . . 245 D8
South Bank Redcar. . 234 G6
  York. 207 C7
South Barrow Som. . 29 B10
South Beach Northumb . . 243 B8
South Beach = Marian-y-de Gwyn . . 145 C2
South Beddington London . . 67 G9
South Benfleet Essex . 69 B9
South Bents T&W. . 243 E10
South Bersted W Sus . . 22 C6
South Blainslie Borders . . 271 G10
South Bockhampton BCP . . 19 B9
Southborough Kent. . 52 E5
  London 67 F11
  London 68 F2
Southbourne BCP . . 19 C8
  W Sus 22 B3
South Bramwith S Yorks . . 198 E6
South Brent Devon . . 8 D3
South Brewham Som . 45 F8
South Bromley London . . 67 C11
Southbrook Wilts . . . 45 G10
South Broomage Falk . . 279 E7
South Broomhill Northumb . . 252 D6
Southburgh Norf . . . 141 C9
South Burlingham Norf . . 143 B7
Southburn E Yorks. . 208 C5
South Cadbury Som. . 29 B10
South Cairn Dumfries . . 236 C1
South Carlton Lincs . 189 F7
  Notts 187 E9
South Carne Corn. . 11 G10
South Cave E Yorks . 208 G4
South Cerney Glos. . 81 F8
South Chailey E Sus . 36 D5
South Chard Som . . 28 F4
South Charlton Northumb . . 264 E5
South Cheriton Som . 29 C11
Southchurch Southend . . 70 B2
South Church Durham . . 233 F10
South Cliffe E Yorks . 208 F3
South Clifton Notts . 188 G4
South Clunes Highld. 300 E5
South Cockerington Lincs . . 190 D5
South Common Devon . . 28 G4
Southcoombe Oxon. . 100 F6
South Cornelly Bridgend . . 57 E10
South Corriegills N Ayrs . . 256 C2
South Corrielaw Dumfries . . 248 G5

Southcourt Bucks 84 C4
South Cove Suff 143 G9
South Creagan Argyll . . 289 D11
South Creake Norf . . 159 B7
Southcrest Worcs . . 117 D10
South Crosland W Yorks . . 196 E6
South Croxton Leics . 154 G3
South Croydon London . . 67 G10
South Cuil Highld . . 298 C3
South Dalton E Yorks . . 208 D5
South Darenth Kent. . 68 F5
Southdean Borders . 250 B4
Southdene Mers. . . . 182 B6
South Denes Norf . . 143 C10
Southdown Bath. . . . 61 G8
  Corn. 7 E8
South Down Hants . . 33 C7
South Duffield N Yorks . . 207 G9
South Dunn Highld . 310 D5
South Earlswood Sur . 51 E9
Southease E Sus. . . . 36 F6
South Elkington Lincs . . 190 D3
South Elmsall W Yorks . . 198 E3
South Elphinstone E Loth . . 281 G7
Southend Argyll . . . 255 G7
  Bucks 65 B9
  Glos 80 F2
  London 67 E11
  Oxon 83 E9
  W Berks 64 D2
  W Berks 65 F4
  Wilts 63 E7
South End Bedford . 103 B10
  Bucks 103 F7
  Cumb 210 G4
  E Yorks 209 E9
  Hants 31 D10
  N Lincs 200 C6
  Norf 141 E9
Southend-on-Sea Southend . . 69 B11
Southerhouse Shetland . . 313 K5
Southerly Devon . . . 12 D6
Southern Cross Brighton . . 36 F3
Southernden Kent . . 53 D11
Southerndown V Glam . . 57 G11
Southerness Dumfries . 237 D11
Southerton Devon . . 15 C10
South Erradale Highld . . 299 B7
Southey Green Essex . . 106 E5
South Fambridge Essex . . 88 G5
South Farnborough Hants . . 49 C11
South Fawley W Berks . . 63 C11
South Ferriby N Lincs . . 200 C3
Southfield Northumb . 243 B7
South Field E Yorks . . 200 B4
  Windsor 66 D3
Southfields London . . 67 E9
Southfleet Kent 68 E6
South Flobbets Aberds . . 303 F7
Southford IoW 20 F6
South Garth Shetland . . 312 D7
South Garvan Highld . 289 B11
Southgate Ceredig . 111 A11
  London 86 G3
  Norf 159 C7
  Norf 160 E2
  Swansea 56 D5
  W Sus 51 F9
South Glendale W Isles . . 297 K3
South Gluss Shetland . . 312 F5
South Godstone Sur . 51 D11
South Gorley Hants . 31 E11
South Gosforth T&W . 242 D6
South Green Essex . . 87 G11
  Essex 89 B8
  Kent 69 G11
  Norf 157 F10
  Norf 159 G11
  Suff 126 B3
South Gyle Edin . . . 280 G3
South-haa Shetland . 312 E5
South Hackney London . . 67 C11
South Ham Hants . . . 48 C6
South Hampstead London . . 67 C9
South Hanningfield Essex . . 88 F2
South Harefield London . . 66 B5
South Harrow London . 66 B6
South Harting W Sus . 34 D3
South Hatfield Herts . 86 D2
South Hayling Hants . 21 B10
South Hazelrigg Northumb . . 264 C3
South Heath Bucks . . 84 E6
  Essex 89 B10
South Heighton E Sus . . 23 E7

South-heog Shetland . . 312 E5
South Hetton Durham . . 234 B3
South Hiendley W Yorks . . 197 E11
South Hill Corn 12 G2
  N Som 43 B10
South Hinksey Oxon . 83 E8
South Hole Devon . . 24 C2
South Holme N Yorks . . 216 D3
South Holmwood Sur . 51 D7
South Hornchurch London . . 68 C4
South Huish Devon . . 8 G3
South Hykeham Lincs . . 172 C6
South Hylton T&W . . 243 F9
Southill C Beds 104 C3
  Dorset 17 E9
South Kelsey Lincs . . 189 B8
South Kensington London . . 67 D9
South Kessock Highld . . 300 E6
South Killingholme N Lincs . . 201 D7
South Kilvington N Yorks . . 215 C8
South Kilworth Leics . 136 G2
South Kirkby W Yorks . . 198 E2
South Kirkton Aberds . . 293 C9
South Kiscadale N Ayrs . . 256 D2
South Knighton Devon . . 14 G2
  Leicester 136 C2
South Kyme Lincs . . 173 F11
South Lambeth London . . 67 D10
South Lancing W Sus . . 35 G11
South Lane S Yorks . . 197 F9
South Leigh Oxon . . 82 D5
South Leverton Notts . . 188 E3
South Littleton Worcs . . 99 B11
South Lopham Norf . . 141 G10
South Luffenham Rutland . . 137 C8
South Malling E Sus . 36 E6
South Marston Swindon . . 63 B7
South Middleton Northumb . . 263 E11
South Milford N Yorks . . 206 G5
South Millbrex Aberds . . 303 E8
South Milton Devon . . 8 G4
South Mimms Herts . . 86 E2
Southminster Essex . . 89 F7
South Molton Devon . . 26 B2
Southmoor Oxon . . . 82 F5
South Moor Durham . . 242 G5
South Moreton Oxon . 64 B5
South Mundham W Sus . . 22 C5
South Muskham Notts . . 172 D3
South Newbald E Yorks . . 208 F4
South Newbarns Cumb . . 210 D4
South Newington Oxon . . 101 E8
South Newsham Northumb . . 243 B8
South Newton Wilts . 46 G5
South Normanton Derbys . . 170 D6
South Norwood London . . 67 F10
South Nutfield Sur. . 51 D10
South Ockendon Thurrock . . 68 C5
Southoe Cambs 122 E3
Southolt Suff 126 D3
South Ormsby Lincs . 190 F5
Southorpe Pboro . . . 137 C11
South Ossett W Yorks . . 197 D9
South Otterington N Yorks . . 215 B7
Southover Dorset . . . 17 C8
  E Sus 36 F6
  E Sus 37 B11
South Owersby Lincs . 189 D9
Southowram W Yorks . 196 C6
South Oxhey Herts . . 85 G10
South Park Sur 51 D8
South Pelaw Durham . 243 G7
South Perrott Dorset . 29 F7
South Petherton Som . 28 D6
South Petherwin Corn . 12 E2
South Pickenham Norf . . 141 C7
South Pill Corn 7 D8
South Pool Devon . . 8 G5
South Poorton Dorset . 16 B6
Southport Mers 193 D10
South Port Argyll . . . 284 E4

Southpunds Shetland . . 313 L6
South Quilquox Aberds . . 303 F8
South Radworthy Devon . . 41 G9
South Rauceby Lincs . 173 F8
South Raynham Norf . 159 E7
South Reddish Gtr Man . . 184 C4
South Reston Lincs . . 190 E6
Southrey Lincs 173 B10
Southrop Glos 81 E11
  Oxon 101 E7
Southrope Hants . . . 49 E7
South Ruislip London . 66 C6
South Runcton Norf . 140 B2
South Scarle Notts . . 172 C4
Southsea Ptsmth . . . 21 B8
  Wrex 166 E4
South Shian Argyll . . 289 E11
South Shields T&W . 243 D9
South Shore Blackpool . . 202 G2
South Side Durham . . 233 F8
  Orkney 314 D5
South Somercotes Lincs . . 190 C6
South Stainley N Yorks . . 214 G6
South Stainmore Cumb . . 222 C6
South Stanley Durham . . 242 G5
South Stifford Thurrock . . 68 D6
Southstoke Bath . . . 61 G8
South Stoke Oxon . . 64 C6
  W Sus 35 F8
South Stour Kent . . . 54 F4
South Street E Sus . . 36 D5
  Kent 54 B5
  Kent 68 G6
  Kent 69 G10
  Kent 70 F6
  London 52 B2
South Tawton Devon . 13 C9
South Tehidy Corn . . 4 G3
South Thoresby Lincs . 190 F6
South Tidworth Wilts . 47 D8
South Tottenham London . . 67 C10
Southtown Norf 143 B10
  Orkney 314 G4
  Som 28 D4
South Town Devon . . 14 E5
  Hants 49 G7
South Twerton Bath . 61 G8
South Ulverston Cumb . . 210 D6
South View Hants . . 48 C6
Southville Devon. . . . 8 G4
South Voxter Shetland . . 313 G5
South Walsham Norf . 161 G7
South Warnborough Hants . . 49 D8
Southwater W Sus . . 35 B11
Southwater Street W Sus . . 35 B11
Southway Plym 7 C9
  Som 44 E4
South Weald Essex . . 87 G9
South Weirs Hants . . 32 G3
Southwell Dorset . . . 17 G9
  Notts 172 E2
South Weston Oxon . 84 F2
South Wheatley Corn . 11 C10
  Notts 188 D3
South Whiteness Shetland . . 313 J5
Southwick Hants . . . 33 E10
  N Nhants 137 E10
  Som 43 D11
  T&W 243 F9
  Wilts 45 D10
  W Sus 36 G2
South Widcombe Bath . . 44 B5
South Wigston Leics . 135 D10
South Willesborough Kent . . 54 E4
South Willingham Lincs . . 189 E11
South Wimbledon London . . 67 E9
South Wingate Durham . . 234 D3
South Wingfield Derbys . . 170 D5
South Witham Lincs . 155 F8
Southwold Suff 127 B10
South Wonford Devon . . 24 F5
South Wonston Hants . 48 F3
Southwood Derbys . . 153 E7
  Hants 49 B10
  Norf 143 B7
  Som 44 G5
  Worcs 116 C4
South Woodford London . . 86 G5
South Woodham Ferrers Essex . . 88 F4
South Wootton Norf . 158 E2
South Wraxall Wilts. . 61 G10
South Yardley W Mid . 134 G2
South Yarrows Highld . . 310 E7
South Yeo Devon. . . . 25 G8

South Zeal Devon 13 C9
Soval Lodge W Isles . . 304 F5
Sowber Gate N Yorks . . 215 C6
Sowerby N Yorks . . . 215 C6
  W Yorks 196 C4
Sowerby Bridge W Yorks . . 196 C5
Sowerby Row Cumb . 230 D3
Sower Carr Lancs . . . 202 E3
Sowley Green Suff . . 124 G4
Sowood Green W Yorks . . 196 D5
Sowton Devon 14 C5
Sowton Barton Devon . . 14 D2
Soyal Highld 309 K5
Soyland Town W Yorks . . 196 C4
Spacey Houses N Yorks . . 206 C2
Spa Common Norf . . 160 C5
Spalding Lincs 156 E4
Spaldington E Yorks . . 207 G11
Spaldwick Cambs . . 122 C3
Spalford Notts 172 B4
Spanby Lincs 155 B11
Spango Invclyd 276 G4
Spanish Green Hants . 49 B7
Sparham Norf 159 F11
Sparhamhill Norf . . . 159 F11
Spark Bridge Cumb . 210 C6
Sparkbrook W Mid . . 133 G11
Sparkford Som 29 B10
Sparkhill W Mid . . . 133 G11
Sparkwell Devon . . . 7 D11
Sparl Shetland 312 G5
Sparnon Corn 1 E3
Sparnon Gate Corn . 4 G3
Sparrow Green Norf . 159 G9
Sparrow Hill Som . . 44 C2
Sparrowpit Derbys . . 185 E9
Sparrow's Green E Sus . . 52 G5
Sparsholt Hants . . . 48 G3
  Oxon 63 B10
Spartylea Northumb . 232 B3
Spath Staffs 151 B11
Spaunton N Yorks . . 226 C4
Spaxton Som 43 F8
Spean Bridge Highld . 290 E4
Spear Hill W Sus . . . 35 D10
Spearywell Hants . . . 32 B4
Speckington Som . . . 29 C9
Speed Gate Kent . . . 68 F5
Speedwell Bristol . . . 60 E6
Speen Bucks 84 F4
  W Berks 64 F3
Speeton N Yorks . . . 218 E2
Speke Mers 182 E6
Speldhurst Kent . . . 52 E5
Spellbrook Herts . . . 87 B7
Spelsbury Oxon. . . . 101 G7
Spelter Bridgend . . . 57 C11
Spen W Yorks 197 B7
Spencers Wood Wokingham . . 65 F8
Spen Green Ches E . . 168 C4
Spennells Worcs . . . 116 C5
Spennithorne N Yorks . . 214 B2
Spennymoor Durham . . 233 E11
Spernall Warks 117 E11
Spetchley Worcs . . . 117 G7
Spetisbury Dorset . . . 30 G6
Spexhall Suff 143 G7
Speybank Highld . . . 291 C10
Spey Bay Moray . . . 302 C3
Speybridge Highld . . 301 G10
Speyview Moray . . . 302 E2
Spillardsford Aberds . 303 D10
Spilsby Lincs 174 B6
Spindlestone Northumb . . 264 C5
Spinkhill Derbys . . . 187 F7
Spinney Hill N Nhants . . 120 E6
Spinney Hills Leicester . . 136 C2
Spinningdale Highld . 309 L6
Spion Kop Notts . . . 171 B9
Spirthill Wilts. 62 D3
Spital Mers 182 E4
  Windsor 66 D3
Spitalbrook Herts. . . 86 D5
Spitalfields London . 67 C10
Spitalhill Derbys . . . 169 F11
Spital Hill S Yorks . . 187 C10
Spital in the Street Lincs . . 189 D7
Spital Tongues T&W . 242 D6
Spithurst E Sus 36 D6
Spittal Dumfries . . . 236 D5
  E Loth 281 F9
  E Yorks 207 C10
  Highld 310 D5
  Northumb 273 D9
  Pembs 91 G9
  Stirling 277 D10
Spittalfield Perth . . . 286 C5
Spittal Houses S Yorks . . 186 B5
Spittal of Glenmuick Aberds . . 292 D4
Spittal of Glenshee Perth . . 292 F3
Spittlegate Lincs . . . 155 C8
Spixworth Norf 160 F4
Splatt Corn 11 D10
  Corn 11 E10
  Devon 25 F10
Splayne's Green E Sus . . 36 G6

Splott Cardiff 59 D7
Spofforth N Yorks 206 C3
Spondon Derby 153 B8
Spon End W Mid 118 B6
Spon Green Flint 166 C3
Spooner Row Norf 141 D11
Spooneylgate
Shrops 132 D6
Sporle Norf 158 G6
Spotland Bridge
Gtr Man 195 E11
Spott E Loth 282 F3
Spratton W Nhants 120 C4
Spreakley Sur 49 E10
Spreyton Devon 13 B9
Spriddlestone Devon 7 E10
Spridlington Lincs 189 E8
Sprig's Alley Oxon 84 F3
Springbank Glos 99 G8
Spring Bank Cumb 229 G10
Springboig Glasgow 268 C3
Springbourne BCP 19 C8
Springburn Glasgow 268 B2
Spring Cottage
Leics 152 F6
Spring End N Yorks 223 F9
Springfield Argyll 275 F11
Caerph 77 F11
Dumfries 239 D8
Essex 88 D2
Fife 287 F7
Gtr Man 194 F5
Highld 300 C6
M Keynes 103 D7
Moray 301 D10
W Mid 133 D8
W Mid 133 F9
W Mid 133 G11
Springfields Stoke 168 G5
Spring Gardens Som 45 D9
Spring Green Lancs 204 E4
Spring Grove London 67 D7
Springhead
Gtr Man 196 G3
Springhill E Renf 267 D10
IoW 20 B6
N Lanark 269 D7
Staffs 133 B11
Staffs 133 C9
Spring Hill Gtr Man 196 F2
Lancs 195 B8
W Mid 133 D7
Springholm
Dumfries 237 C10
Springkell Dumfries 239 B7
Spring Park London 67 F11
Springside N Ayrs 257 B9
Springthorpe Lincs 188 D5
Spring Vale S Yorks 197 G9
Spring Valley IoM 192 E4
Springwell Essex 105 C10
T&W 243 F7
T&W 243 F9
Springwells
Dumfries 248 E3
Sproatley E Yorks 209 G9
Sproston Green
Ches W 168 B2
Sprotbrough
S Yorks 198 G4
Sproughton Suff 108 C2
Sprouston Borders 263 B7
Sprowston Norf 160 G4
Sproxton Leics 155 E7
N Yorks 216 C2
Sprunston Cumb 230 B3
Spunhill Shrops 149 C8
Spurlands End Bucks 84 F5
Spurstow Ches E 167 D9
Spurtree Shrops 116 D2
Spynie Moray 302 C2
Spyway Dorset 16 C6
Square and Compass
Pembs 91 E7
Squires Gate
Blackpool 202 G2
Sraid Ruadh Argyll 288 E1
Srannda W Isles 296 C6
Sronphadruig Lodge
Perth 291 F9
Stableford Shrops 132 D5
Staffs 150 B6
Stacey Bank
S Yorks 186 C3
Stackhouse N Yorks 212 F6
Stackpole Pembs 73 F7
Stackpole Quay
Pembs 73 F7
Stacksford Norf 141 E11
Stacksteads Lancs 195 C10
Stackyard Green
Suff 107 B9
Staddiscombe Plym 7 E10
Staddlethorpe
E Yorks 199 B10
Staddon Devon 24 C3
Devon 24 G5
Staden Derbys 185 G9
Stadhampton Oxon 83 F10
Stadhlaigearraidh
W Isles 297 H3
Stadmorslow Staffs 168 D5
Staffield Cumb 230 C6
Staffin Highld 298 C4
Stafford Staffs 151 E8
Stafford Park
Telford 132 B4
Stafford's Corner
Essex 89 B7
Stafford's Green
Dorset 29 C10
Stagbatch Hereford 115 F9
Stagden Cross
Essex 87 C10
Stagehall Borders 271 G9
Stagsden Bedford 103 B9
Stagsden West End
Bedford 103 B9
Stag's Head Devon 25 B11
Stain Highld 310 C7
Stainburn Cumb 228 F6
N Yorks 205 D10
Stainby Lincs 155 E8
Staincliffe W Yorks 197 C8
Staincross S Yorks 197 E10
Staindrop Durham 233 G8
Staines Green Herts 86 C3
Staines-upon-Thames
Sur 66 E4
Stainfield Lincs 155 D11
Lincs 189 G10
Stainforth N Yorks 212 F6
S Yorks 198 E6
Staining Lancs 202 F3
Stainland W Yorks 196 D5
Stainsacre N Yorks 227 D8
Stainsby Derbys 170 B6
Lincs 190 G4
Stainton
Cumb 211 B10
Cumb 230 F5
Cumb 239 F9
Durham 223 B11
Mbro 225 C9
N Yorks 224 F2
S Yorks 187 C9
Stainton by Langworth
Lincs 189 F9
Staintondale
N Yorks 227 F9
Stainton le Vale
Lincs 189 C11
Stainton with Adgarley
Cumb 210 E5
Stair Cumb 229 G10
E Ayrs 257 E10
Stairfoot S Yorks 197 F11
Stairhaven Dumfries 236 D4
Staithes N Yorks 226 B5
Stakeford Northumb 253 F7
Stake Hill Gtr Man 195 F11
Stakenbridge Worcs 117 B7
Stake Pool Lancs 202 D4
Stalbridge Dorset 30 D2
Stalbridge Weston
Dorset 30 D2
Stalham Norf 161 D7
Stalham Green Norf 161 E7
Stalisfield Green
Kent 54 C3
Stallen Dorset 29 D10
Stallingborough
NE Lincs 201 E7
Stalling Busk
N Yorks 213 B8
Stallington Staffs 151 B8
Stalmine Lancs 202 D3
Stalmine Moss Side
Lancs 202 D3
Stalybridge Gtr Man 185 B7
Stambermill W Mid 133 G8
Stamborough Som 42 F4
Stambourne Essex 106 D4
Stambourne Green
Essex 106 D4
Stamford Lincs 137 B10
Stamford Bridge
Ches W 167 B7
E Yorks 207 B10
Stamfordham
Northumb 242 C3
Stamford Hill
London 67 B10
Stamperland
E Renf 267 D11
Stamshaw Ptsmth 33 G10
Stanah Cumb 220 B6
Lancs 202 E3
Stanborough Herts 86 C2
Stanbridge C Beds 103 G9
Dorset 31 G8
Stanbridgeford
C Beds 103 G9
Stanbrook Essex 106 F2
Worcs 98 B6
Stanbury W Yorks 204 F6
Stand Gtr Man 195 F9
N Lanark 268 B5
Standburn Falk 279 G8
Standeford Staffs 133 B8
Standen Kent 53 E11
Standen Hall Lancs 203 E10
Standen Street Kent 53 G10
Standerwick Som 45 C10
Standford Hants 49 G10
Standford Bridge
Telford 150 E4
Standingstone
Cumb 229 B11
Cumb 229 E7
Standish Glos 80 D4
Gtr Man 194 E5
Standish Lower Ground
Gtr Man 194 F5
Standlake Oxon 82 E5
Standon Hants 32 B6
Herts 105 G7
Staffs 150 B6
Standon Green End
Herts 86 B5
Stane N Lanark 269 D7
Stanecastle N Ayrs 257 B8
Stanfield Norf 159 E8
Stoke 168 E5
Stanford C Beds 104 C3
Kent 54 F6
Norf 141 E7
Shrops 148 G6
Stanford Bishop
Hereford 116 G3
Stanford Bridge
Worcs 116 D4
Stanford Dingley
W Berks 64 E5
Stanford End
Wokingham 65 G8
Stanford Hills
Notts 153 E10
Stanford in the Vale
Oxon 82 G4
Stanford-le-Hope
Thurrock 69 C7
Stanford on Avon
W Nhants 119 B11
Stanford on Soar
Notts 153 E10
Stanford on Teme
Worcs 116 D4
Stanford Rivers
Essex 87 E8
Stanfree Derbys 187 G7
Stanground Pboro 138 D4
Stanhill Lancs 195 B8
Stanhoe Norf 158 B6
Stanhope Borders 260 D4
Durham 232 D5
Kent 54 E3
Stanion N Nhants 137 F8
Stank Cumb 210 E4
Stanklyn Worcs 117 C7
Stanks W Yorks 206 F3
Stanley Derbys 170 G6
Durham 242 G5
Lancs 194 F3
Notts 171 C7
Perth 286 D5
Shrops 132 G3
Shrops 132 G5
Staffs 168 E6
Wilts 62 E3
W Yorks 197 C10
Stanley Common
Derbys 170 G6
Stanley Crook
Durham 233 D9
Stanley Downton
Glos 80 E4
Stanley Ferry
W Yorks 197 C11
Stanley Gate Lancs 194 G2
Stanley Green BCP 18 C6
Ches E 184 E5
Shrops 149 B10
Stanley Hill Hereford 98 C3
Stanley Moor Staffs 168 E6
Stanley Pontlarge
Glos 99 E9
Stanleytown Rhondda 77 G8
Stanlow Ches W 182 F6
Staffs 132 D5
Stanmer Brighton 36 F4
Stanmore Hants 33 B7
London 85 G11
Shrops 132 E4
W Berks 64 D3
Stanner Powys 114 F5
Stannergate Dundee 287 D8
Stannersburn
Northumb 250 F6
Stanners Hill Sur 66 G3
Stanningfield Suff 125 F7
Stanningley
W Yorks 205 G10
Stannington
Northumb 242 B6
S Yorks 186 D4
Stanpit BCP 19 C9
Stansbatch Hereford 114 E6
Stansfield Suff 124 G5
Stanshope Staffs 169 E10
Stanstead Suff 106 B6
Stanstead Abbotts
Herts 86 C5
Stansted Kent 68 G6
Stansted Airport
Essex 105 G11
Stansted Mountfitchet
Essex 105 G10
Stanthorne
Ches W 167 B11
Stanton Glos 99 E11
Mon 96 G6
Northumb 252 F4
Staffs 169 F10
Suff 125 C9
Stantonbury
M Keynes 102 C6
Stanton by Bridge
Derbys 153 D7
Stanton-by-Dale
Derbys 153 B9
Stanton Chare Suff 125 C9
Stanton Drew Bath 60 G5
Stanton Fitzwarren
Swindon 81 G11
Stanton Gate Notts 153 B9
Stanton Harcourt
Oxon 82 D6
Stanton Hill Notts 171 C7
Stanton in Peak
Derbys 170 C2
Stanton Lacy Shrops 115 B9
Stanton Lees
Derbys 170 C3
Stanton Long
Shrops 131 E11
Stanton-on-the-Wolds
Notts 154 C2
Stanton Prior Bath 61 G7
Stanton St Bernard
Wilts 62 G5
Stanton St John
Oxon 83 D9
Stanton St Quintin
Wilts 62 D2
Stanton Street Suff 125 D9
Stanton under Bardon
Leics 153 G9
Stanton upon Hine
Heath Shrops 149 E11
Stanton Wick Bath 60 G6
Stantway Glos 80 C2
Stanwardine in the
Fields Shrops 149 E8
Stanwardine in the
Wood Shrops 149 D8
Stanway Essex 107 G8
Glos 99 E11
Stanway Green
Essex 107 G9
Suff 126 C4
Stanwell Sur 66 E5
Stanwell Moor Sur 66 E4
Stanwick N Nhants 121 C9
Stanwick-St-John
N Yorks 224 C3
Stanwix Cumb 239 F10
Stanycliffe
Gtr Man 195 F11
Stanydale Shetland 313 H4
Staoinebrig
W Isles 297 H3
Stape N Yorks 226 G5
Stapehill Dorset 31 G9
Stapeley Ches E 167 F11
Stapenhill Staffs 152 E5
Staple Kent 55 B9
Som 42 E6
Staplecross E Sus 38 C3
Staple Cross Devon 27 C8
Staplefield W Sus 36 B3
Staple Fitzpaine Som 28 D3
Stapleford Cambs 123 G9
Herts 86 B4
Leics 154 F6
Lincs 172 D5
Notts 153 B9
Wilts 46 F5
Stapleford Abbotts
Essex 87 G8
Stapleford Tawney
Essex 87 F8
Staplegrove Som 28 B2
Staplehay Som 28 C2
Staple Hill S Glos 61 D7
Worcs 117 C9
Staplehurst Kent 53 E9
Staple Lawns Som 28 D3
Staplers IoW 20 D6
Staples Hill W Sus 35 B8
Staplestreet Kent 70 G5
Stapleton Bristol 60 D6
Cumb 240 C2
Hereford 114 D6
Leics 135 D8
N Yorks 198 D4
N Yorks 224 C5
Shrops 131 C9
Som 29 C7
Stapley Som 27 E11
Staploe Bedford 122 E2
Staplow Hereford 98 C3
Stapness Shetland 313 J4
Star Anglesey 179 G8
Fife 287 G7
Pembs 92 E4
Som 44 B2
Stara Orkney 314 D2
Starbeck N Yorks 206 B2
Starbotton N Yorks 213 E9
Starcross Devon 14 E5
Stareton Warks 118 C6
Stargate T&W 242 E5
Star Hill Mon 79 E7
Starkholmes Derbys 170 D4
Starling Gtr Man 195 E9
Starlings Green
Essex 105 E9
Starr's Green E Sus 38 D3
Starston Norf 142 G4
Start Devon 8 G6
Startforth Durham 223 B10
Start Hill Essex 105 G10
Startley Wilts 62 C2
Startop's End Bucks 84 C6
Starveall S Glos 61 B9
Starvecrow Kent 52 D5
Statenborough Kent 55 B10
Statford St Andrew
Suff 127 E7
Statham Warr 183 D11
Stathe Som 28 B5
Stathern Leics 154 C5
Station Hill Cumb 229 B11
Station Town
Durham 234 D4
Statland Common
Norf 141 D10
Staughton Green
Cambs 122 D2
Staughton Highway
Cambs 122 E2
Staughton Moor
Cambs 122 E2
Staunton Glos 79 C8
Glos 98 F5
Staunton in the Vale
Notts 172 G4
Staunton on Arrow
Hereford 115 E7
Staunton on Wye
Hereford 97 B7
Staupes N Yorks 205 B10
Staveley Cumb 211 B7
Cumb 221 F9
Derbys 186 G6
N Yorks 215 G7
Staveley-in-Cartmel
Cumb 211 B7
Staverton Devon 8 C5
Glos 99 G7
Wilts 61 G11
W Nhants 119 E10
Staverton Bridge
Glos 99 G7
Stawell Som 43 F11
Stawley Som 27 C9
Staxigoe Highld 310 D7
Staxton N Yorks 217 D10
Staylittle Ceredig 128 F2
Staylittle = Penffordd-Lâs
Powys 129 E7
Staynall Lancs 202 E3
Staythorpe Notts 172 E3
Stead W Yorks 205 D8
Steam Mills Glos 79 B10
Stean N Yorks 213 E11
Steanbow Som 44 F5
Stearsby N Yorks 216 E2
Steart Som 29 B9
Som 43 D9
Stebbing Essex 106 G3
Stebbing Green
Essex 106 G3
Stechford W Mid 134 F2
Stede Quarter Kent 53 F11
Stedham W Sus 34 C5
Steel Northumb 241 F10
Steel *continued*
Northumb 251 G9
Steel Bank S Yorks 186 D4
Steel Cross E Sus 52 G4
Steelend Fife 279 C10
Steele Road Borders 250 E2
Steeleroad-end
Borders 250 E2
Steel Green Cumb 210 D3
Steel Heath Shrops 149 B10
Steen's Bridge
Hereford 115 F10
Steep Hants 34 B2
Steephill IoW 21 F7
Steep Lane W Yorks 196 C4
Steeple Dorset 18 E4
Essex 88 E6
Steeple Ashton Wilts 46 B2
Steeple Aston Oxon 101 F9
Steeple Barton
Oxon 101 G8
Steeple Bumpstead
Essex 106 C3
Steeple Claydon
Bucks 102 F3
Steeple Gidding
Cambs 138 G2
Steeple Langford
Wilts 46 F4
Steeple Morden
Cambs 104 C5
Steep Marsh Hants 34 B3
Steeraway Telford 132 B3
Steeton W Yorks 204 E6
Stein Highld 298 D2
Steinmanhill Aberds 303 E7
Stella T&W 242 E5
Stelling Minnis Kent 54 D6
Stelvio Newport 59 B9
Stembridge Som 28 C6
Swansea 56 C3
Stemster Highld 310 C5
Stemster Ho Highld 310 C5
Stenalees Corn 5 D10
Stenaquoy Orkney 314 C5
Stencoose Corn 4 F4
Stenhill Devon 27 E9
Stenhouse Dumfries 247 E8
Edin 280 G4
Stenhousemuir Falk 279 E7
Stenigot Lincs 190 E3
Stennack Corn 2 B5
Stenness Shetland 312 F4
Stenscholl Highld 298 C4
Stenso Orkney 314 D3
Stenson Derbys 152 D6
Stenton E Loth 282 G2
Fife 280 B5
Stentwood Devon 27 F10
Stenwith Lincs 154 B6
Stepaside Corn 5 F9
Pembs 73 D10
Powys 129 F11
Stepping Hill
Gtr Man 184 D6
Steppingley
C Beds 103 D10
Stepps N Lanark 268 B3
Sterndale Moor
Derbys 169 B10
Sternfield Suff 127 E7
Sterridge Devon 40 D5
Stert Wilts 46 B4
Sterte BCP 18 C6
Stetchworth Cambs 124 F2
Stevenage Herts 104 G4
Steven's Crouch
E Sus 38 D2
Stevenston N Ayrs 266 G5
Stevenstone Devon 25 D8
Steventon Hants 48 D4
Oxon 83 G7
Shrops 115 C10
Steventon End
Essex 105 C11
Stevington Bedford 121 G9
Stewards Essex 87 D7
Steward's Green
Essex 87 E7
Stewartby Bedford 103 C10
Stewarton Argyll 255 F7
E Ayrs 267 F8
Stewkley Bucks 103 F7
Stewkley Dean
Bucks 102 F6
Stewley Som 28 D4
Stewton Lincs 190 D5
Steyne Cross IoW 21 D8
Steyning W Sus 35 E11
Steynton Pembs 72 D6
Stibb Corn 24 E2
Stibbard Norf 159 D9
Stibb Cross Devon 24 E6
Stibb Green Wilts 63 G8
Stibbington Cambs 137 D11
Stichill Borders 262 B6
Sticker Corn 5 E9
Stickford Lincs 174 D5
Stick Hill Kent 52 E3
Sticklepath Devon 13 C8
Devon 40 G5
Som 28 E4
Som 42 F4
Sticklinch Som 44 F5
Stickling Green
Essex 105 E9
Stickney Lincs 174 D4
Stiffkey Norf 177 E7
Stifford's Bridge
Hereford 98 B4
Stiff Street Kent 69 G11
Stileway Som 44 E3
Stillingfleet N Yorks 207 E7
Stillington N Yorks 215 F11
Stockton 234 G3
Stilton Cambs 138 F3
Stinchcombe Glos 80 F2
Stinsford Dorset 17 C10
Stiperstones Shrops 131 C7
Stirchley Telford 132 B4
W Mid 133 G11
Stirkoke Ho Highld 310 D7
Stirling Aberds 303 E11
Stirling 278 C5
Stirtloe Cambs 122 D3
Stirton N Yorks 204 C5
Stisted Essex 106 G5
Stitchcombe Wilts 63 F8
Stitchin's Hill Worcs 116 G5
Stithians Corn 2 B6
Stittenham Highld 300 B6
Stivichall W Mid 118 B6
Stixwould Lincs 173 B11
Stoak Ches W 182 G6
Stobhill Northumb 252 G6
Stobhillgate
Northumb 252 F6
Stobieside S Lanark 258 B4
Stobo Borders 260 B5
Stoborough Dorset 18 D4
Stoborough Green
Dorset 18 D4
Stobs Castle
Borders 250 B2
Stobshiel E Loth 271 C9
Stobswood
Northumb 252 E6
Stock Essex 87 F11
Lancs 204 D3
N Som 60 G3
Stockbridge Hants 47 G11
S Yorks 198 F5
W Sus 22 C5
W Yorks 205 E7
Stockbridge Village
Mers 182 C6
Stockbury Kent 69 G10
Stockcross W Berks 64 F2
Stockend Glos 80 D4
Stocker's Head Kent 54 C3
Stockerston Leics 136 D6
Stockfield W Mid 134 G2
Stock Green Worcs 117 F9
Stockheath Hants 22 B2
Stock Hill Suff 125 D9
Stockholes Turbary
N Lincs 199 F9
Stockiemuir
Stirling 277 E10
Stocking Hereford 98 E2
Stockingford Warks 134 E6
Stocking Green
Essex 105 D11
Stocking Pelham
Herts 105 F9
Stockland Devon 28 G2
Stockland Bristol
Som 43 E8
Stockland Green
Kent 52 E5
W Mid 133 E11
Stockleigh English
Devon 26 F5
Stockleigh Pomeroy
Devon 26 G5
Stockley Wilts 62 F4
Stocklinch Som 28 D5
Stockport Gtr Man 184 C5
Stocksbridge
S Yorks 186 B3
Stocksfield
Northumb 242 E3
Stocks Green Kent 52 D5
Stockstreet Essex 106 G6
Stockton Hereford 115 E10
Norf 143 E7
Shrops 130 C5
Shrops 132 D4
Telford 150 F5
Warks 119 E8
Wilts 46 F3
Stockton Brook
Staffs 168 E6
Stockton Heath
Warr 183 D10
Stockton-on-Tees
Stockton 225 B8
Stockton on Teme
Worcs 116 D4
Stockton on the Forest
York 207 B9
Stocktonwood
Shrops 130 C5
Stockwell Devon 27 G7
Glos 80 C6
London 67 D10
Stockwell End
W Mid 133 C7
Stockwell Heath
Staffs 151 E11
Stockwitch Cross
Som 29 C9
Stockwood Bristol 60 F6
Dorset 29 F9
Stock Wood Worcs 117 F10
Stockwood Vale Bath 60 F6
Stodday Lancs 202 B5
Stodmarsh Kent 71 G8
Stody Norf 159 C11
Stoer Highld 307 G5
Stoford Som 29 E9
Wilts 46 F5
Stoford Water Devon 27 F9
Stogumber Som 42 F5
Stogursey Som 43 E8
Stoke Devon 24 C2
Hants 22 C2
Hants 48 C2
Medway 69 D10
Plym 7 D9
Suff 108 C3
W Mid 119 B7
Stoke Abbott Dorset 29 G7
Stoke Albany
N Nhants 136 F6
Stoke Aldermoor
W Mid 119 B7
Stoke Ash Suff 126 C2
Stoke Bardolph
Notts 171 G10
Stoke Bishop Bristol 60 D5
Stoke Bliss Worcs 116 E3
Stoke Bruerne
W Nhants 102 B4
Stoke by Clare Suff 106 C4
Stoke-by-Nayland
Suff 107 D9
Stoke Canon Devon 14 B4
Stoke Charity Hants 48 F3
Stoke Climsland
Corn 12 G3
Stoke Common
Hants 33 C7
Stoke Cross
Hereford 116 G2
Stoke D'Abernon Sur 50 B6
Stoke Doyle
N Nhants 137 F10
Stoke Dry Rutland 137 D7
Stoke Edith Hereford 98 C2
Stoke End Warks 134 D3
Stoke Farthing Wilts 31 B9
Stoke Ferry Norf 140 D4
Stoke Fleming Devon 9 F7
Stokeford Dorset 18 D3
Stoke Gabriel Devon 8 D6
Stoke Gifford S Glos 60 D6
Stoke Golding Leics 135 D7
Stoke Goldington
M Keynes 102 B6
Stokegorse Shrops 131 G11
Stoke Green Bucks 66 C3
Stokeham Notts 188 F3
Stoke Hammond
Bucks 103 F7
Stoke Heath Shrops 150 D3
W Mid 135 G7
Worcs 117 D8
Stoke Hill Devon 14 C4
Hereford 98 B2
Stoke Holy Cross
Norf 142 C4
Stokeinteignhead
Devon 14 G4
Stoke Lacy Hereford 98 B2
Stoke Lane Hereford 116 G2
Stoke Lyne Oxon 101 F11
Stoke Mandeville
Bucks 84 C4
Stokenchurch Bucks 84 F3
Stoke Newington
London 67 B10
Stokenham Devon 8 G6
Stoke on Tern
Shrops 150 D2
Stoke-on-Trent
Stoke 168 F5
Stoke Orchard Glos 99 F8
Stoke Park Suff 108 C3
Stoke Poges Bucks 66 C3
Stoke Pound Worcs 117 D9
Stoke Prior
Hereford 115 F10
Worcs 117 D8
Stoke Rivers Devon 40 F6
Stoke Rochford
Lincs 155 D8
Stoke Row Oxon 65 C7
Stoke St Gregory
Som 28 B4
Stoke St Mary Som 28 C3
Stoke St Michael
Som 45 D7
Stoke St Milborough
Shrops 131 G11
Stokesay Shrops 131 G8
Stokesby Norf 161 G8
Stokesley N Yorks 225 D10
Stoke sub Hamdon
Som 29 D7
Stoke Talmage Oxon 83 F11
Stoke Trister Som 30 B2
Stoke Wake Dorset 30 F3
Stoke Water Dorset 29 G7
Stoke Wharf Worcs 117 D9
Stokoe Northumb 250 F6
Stolford Som 43 D8
Stondon Massey
Essex 87 E9
Stone Bucks 84 C3
Glos 79 F11
Kent 38 B6
Kent 68 E5
Som 44 G5
Staffs 151 C8
S Yorks 187 D9
Worcs 117 B7
Stonea Cambs 139 E9
Stoneacton Shrops 131 E10
Stone Allerton Som 44 C2
Ston Easton Som 44 C6
Stonebow Worcs 99 B8
Stonebridge
Essex 70 B2
London 67 C8
Norf 141 E8
N Som 43 B11
Sur 51 D7
W Mid 134 G4
Stone Bridge Corner
Pboro 138 C5
Stonebridge Green
Kent 54 D2
Stonebroom Derbys 170 D6
Stonebyres Holdings
S Lanark 268 G6
Stone Chair
W Yorks 196 B6
Stoneclough
Gtr Man 195 F9
Stonecombe Devon 40 E6
Stone Cross E Sus 23 E10
E Sus 37 B8
E Sus 52 G6
Kent 52 F4
Kent 54 F4
Kent 55 B10
W Mid 133 E10
Stonecrouch Kent 53 G7
Stone-edge Batch
N Som 60 E3
Stoneferry Hull 209 G8
Stonefield Argyll 289 F11
S Lanark 268 D3
Staffs 151 C7
Stonefield Castle Hotel
Argyll 275 F9
Stonegate E Sus 37 B11
N Yorks 226 D5
Stonegrave N Yorks 216 D3
Stonegravels
Derbys 186 G5
Stonehall Kent 55 D9
Worcs 99 B7
Stonehaugh
Northumb 241 B7
Stonehaven Aberds 293 E10
Stone Head N Yorks 204 E4
Stone Heath Staffs 151 B9
Stonehill Sur 66 G4
Stone Hill Kent 54 D2
Kent 54 F5
S Glos 60 E6
S Yorks 199 F7
Stonehills Hants 33 G7
Stonehouse Aberds 303 F8
Glos 80 D4
Northumb 240 F5
Plym 7 E9
S Lanark 268 F5
Stone House Cumb 212 B5
Stonehouses Staffs 169 G7
Stone in Oxney Kent 38 B6
Stoneleigh London 67 G8
Warks 118 C6
Stoneley Green
Ches E 167 E10
Stonely Cambs 122 D2
Stonepits Worcs 117 F10
Stonequarry W Sus 52 F2
Stone Raise Cumb 230 B4
Stoner Hill Hants 34 B2
Stonesby Leics 154 E6
Stonesfield Oxon 82 B5
Stones Green Essex 108 F3
Stone Street Kent 52 C5
Suff 107 D9
Suff 143 G7
Stonestreet Green
Kent 54 F5
Stonethwaite Cumb 220 C5
Stoneton Warks 119 G9
Stonewells Moray 302 C2
Stonewood Kent 68 E5
Stoneyard Green
Hereford 98 C4
Stoneybank E Loth 280 G6
Stoneybreck
Shetland 313 N2
Stoneyburn W Loth 269 C9
Stoneycombe Devon 9 B7
Stoneycroft Mers 182 C5
Stoney Cross Hants 32 E3
Stoneyfield
Gtr Man 195 E11
Moray 301 D11
Stoneyford Derbys 170 F6
Devon 27 F8
Stoneygate Aberds 303 F10
Leicester 136 C2
Stoney Hill Worcs 117 C9
Stoneyhills Essex 88 F6
Stoneykirk Dumfries 236 D2
Stoneylane Shrops 115 B11
Stoney Middleton
Derbys 186 F2
Stoney Royd
W Yorks 196 C5
Stoney Stanton
Leics 135 E9
Stoney Stoke Som 45 G8
Stoney Stratton Som 45 F7
Stoney Stretton
Shrops 131 B7
Stoneywood
Aberdeen 293 B10
Falk 278 E5
Stonganess Shetland 312 C7
Stonham Aspal Suff 126 F2
Stonnall Staffs 133 C11
Stonor Oxon 65 B8
Stonton Wyville
Leics 136 D4
Stony Batter Hants 32 B3
Stony Cross Devon 25 B8
Hereford 98 B4
Hereford 115 D10
Stony Dale Notts 172 G2
Stonyfield Highld 300 B6
Stonyford Hants 32 D4
Stony Gate T&W 243 G9
Stony Green Bucks 84 F5
Stony Heap Durham 242 G4
Stony Heath Hants 48 B5
Stony Houghton
Derbys 171 B7
Stony Knaps Dorset 28 G5
Stonyland Devon 25 B8
Stony Littleton Bath 45 B8
Stonymarsh Hants 32 B4
Stony Stratford
M Keynes 102 C5
Stoodleigh Devon 26 D6
Stop-and-Call
Pembs 91 D8
Stopes S Yorks 186 D3
Stopgate Devon 28 F2
Stopham W Sus 35 D8
Stopper Lane Lancs 204 D2
Stopsley Luton 104 G2
Stoptide Corn 10 F4
Stores Corner Suff 109 B7
Storeton Mers 182 E4
Storiths N Yorks 205 C7
Stormontfield Perth 286 E5
Stormore Wilts 45 D10
Stornoway W Isles 304 E6
Storridge Hereford 98 B4
Storrington W Sus 35 E9
Storrs Cumb 221 G7
S Yorks 186 D3
Storth Cumb 211 C9
Storwood E Yorks 207 E10
Stotfield Moray 302 B2

Stotfold C Beds 104 D4
Stottesdon Shrops . 132 G3
Stoughton Leics 136 C2
  Sur. 50 C3
  W Sus 34 E4
Stoughton Cross
  Som 44 D2
Stoul Highld 295 F9
Stourbridge W Mid . 133 G8
Stourpaine Dorset . . 30 F5
Stourport on Severn
  Worcs 116 C6
Stour Provost Dorset . 30 C3
Stour Row Dorset . . 30 C4
Stourton Staffs 133 F7
  Warks 100 D5
  Wilts 45 G9
  W Yorks 206 G2
Stourton Caundle
  Dorset 30 C2
Stourton Hill Warks 100 D6
Stout Som 44 G2
  Dorset 17 C9
Stove Orkney 314 C6
  Shetland 313 L6
Stoven Suff 143 G8
Stow Borders 271 G9
  Lincs 155 B11
  Lincs 188 E5
Stow Bardolph Norf. . 140 B2
Stow Bedon Norf . . . 141 D9
Stowbridge Norf. . . . 140 B2
Stow cum Quy
  Cambs 123 E10
Stowe Glos. 79 D9
  Hereford 96 B5
  Lincs 156 D5
  Shrops. 114 C6
  Staffs. 152 G2
Stowe-by-Chartley
  Staffs 151 D10
Stowe Green Glos. . . 79 D9
Stowell Glos. 81 C9
  Som 29 C11
Stowey Bath. 44 B5
Stowford Hereford . . 79 B9
Stowford Devon . . 12 B4
  Devon 12 D4
  Devon 24 E3
  Devon 25 B10
  Devon 41 E7
Stowgate Lincs 156 G3
Stowlangtoft Suff . . 125 D9
Stow Low W Mid . . . 133 D8
Stow Longa Cambs. . 122 C2
Stow Maries Essex . . 88 F4
Stowmarket Suff . . 125 F10
Stow-on-the-Wold
  Glos. 100 F3
Stow Park Newport. . 59 B10
Stowting Kent 54 E6
Stowting Common
  Kent. 54 E6
Stowting Court Kent. 54 E6
Stowupland Suff. . . 125 F11
Straad Argyll 275 G11
Strachan Aberds . . . 293 D8
Strachurmore Argyll 284 G5
Stradbroke Suff 126 C4
Stradishall Suff 124 G4
Stradsett Norf 140 C3
Stragglethorpe
  Lincs 172 E6
Straid S Ayrs 244 E4
Straight Soley Wilts . 63 E10
Straith Dumfries. . . . 247 F8
Straiton Edin 270 B5
  S Ayrs. 245 C9
Straloch Aberds . . . 303 G8
  Perth 292 G2
Stramshall Staffs . . 151 B11
Strand Glos 80 C2
  London. 67 C10
Strands Cumb 210 C3
Strang IoM 192 E4
Strangeways
  Gtr Man 184 B4
Strangford Hereford. . 97 F11
Stranghow Redcar . . 226 B3
Strangways Wilts . . 46 E6
Stranog Aberds . . . 293 D10
Stranraer Dumfries. 236 C2
Strata Florida
  Ceredig. 112 D4
Stratfield Mortimer
  W Berks 65 G7
Stratfield Saye Hants .65 G7
Stratfield Turgis
  Hants. 49 B7
Stratford C Beds . . . 104 B3
  Glos 99 D7
  London. 67 C11
Stratford Marsh
  London. 67 C11
Stratford New Town
  London. 67 C11
Stratford St Andrew
  Suff 127 E7
Stratford St Mary
  Suff 107 E10
Stratford Sub Castle
  Wilts 46 G6
Stratford Tony Wilts . 31 B9
Stratford-upon-Avon
  Warks 118 F3
Strath Highld 299 B7
  Highld 310 D6
Strathallan Castle
  Perth 286 F3
Strathan Highld . . . 295 F11
  Highld 307 G5
  Highld 308 C5
Strathan Skerray
  Highld 308 C5
Strathaven S Lanark . 268 G4
Strathavon Lo
  Moray 301 G11
Strathblane Stirling . 277 F11
Strathcanaird Highld 307 J6

Strathcarron Highld . .299 E9
Strathcoil Argyll 289 F8
Strathcoul Highld . . 310 D5
Strathdon Aberds . . .292 B5
Strathellie Aberds . . 303 C10
Strathgarve Lodge
  Highld 300 C4
Strathkinness Fife . . 287 F8
Strathmashie House
  Highld 291 D7
Strathmiglo Fife 286 F6
Strathmore Lodge
  Highld 310 E5
Strathpeffer Highld . 300 D4
Strathrannoch
  Highld 300 B3
Strathtay Perth 286 B3
Strathvaich Lodge
  Highld 300 B3
Strathwhillan
  N Ayrs 256 G2
Strathy Highld 300 B6
  Highld 310 D2
Strathyre Stirling . . .285 F9
Stratton Corn. 24 F2
  Dorset 17 C9
  Glos 81 E8
Stratton Audley
  Oxon 102 F2
Stratton Chase Bucks .85 G7
Stratton St Margaret
  Swindon. 63 B7
Stratton St Michael
  Norf. 142 E4
Stratton Strawless
  Norf. 160 E4
Stravithie Fife 287 F9
Strawberry Bank
  Cumb 211 B8
Strawberry Hill
  E Sus 52 F5
  London. 67 E7
  W Yorks 198 C2
Streat E Sus 36 D5
Streatham London . . 67 E10
Streatham Hill
  London. 67 E10
Streatham Park
  London. 67 E10
Streatham Vale
  London. 67 E10
Streatley C Beds . . . 103 F11
  W Berks 64 C5
Street Cumb 222 D2
  Lancs 202 C6
  N Yorks 226 B4
  Som 28 F5
  Som 44 F3
Street Ash Som 28 E3
Street Ashton
  Warks 135 G9
Street Dinas Shrops . 148 B6
Street End Hants. . . . 33 D9
  Kent. 54 C6
  W Sus 22 D5
Street Gate T&W. . . . 242 F6
Streethay Staffs . . . 152 G2
Streethouse
  W Yorks 197 C11
Street Houses
  N Yorks 206 D4
Streetlam N Yorks. . . 224 F6
Street Lane Derbys. . 170 F3
Streetly W Mid 133 D11
Street Lydan Wrex . . 149 B8
Streetly End Cambs . 106 C2
Street of Kincardine
  Highld 291 B11
Street on the Fosse
  Som 44 F6
Strefford Shrops . . . 131 F8
Strelley Notts. 171 G8
Strensall York 216 G2
Strensham Worcs. . . . 99 C8
Stretch Down Devon . 26 E4
Stretcholt Som 43 E9
Strete Devon. 8 G6
Stretford Gtr Man . . 184 C4
  Hereford 115 F10
Stretford Court
  Hereford 115 F8
Strethall Essex 105 D9
Stretham Cambs . . . 123 C10
Strettington W Sus. . . 22 B5
Stretton Ches W . . . 166 E6
  Derbys. 170 C5
  Rutland. 155 F8
  Staffs. 151 G7
  Staffs. 152 D5
  Warr 183 E10
Stretton en le Field
  Leics 152 G6
Stretton Grandison
  Hereford 98 C2
Stretton-on-Dunsmore
  Warks 119 C8
Stretton-on-Fosse
  Warks 100 D4
Stretton Sugwas
  Hereford 97 C9
Stretton under Fosse
  Warks 135 G8
Stretton Westwood
  Shrops 131 D11
Strichen Aberds . . . 303 D9
Strines Gtr Man . . . 185 D7
Stringston Som. 43 E7
Strixton N Nhants. . . 121 E8
Stroat Glos 79 F9
Strode N Som 60 G4
Strom Shetland 313 J6
Stromeferry Highld. 295 B10
Stromemore
  Highld 295 B10
Stromness Orkney . 314 F2
Stronaba Highld . . . 290 E4
Stronachlachar
  Stirling 285 F8
Stronachullin Lodge
  Argyll. 275 F9

Stronchreggan
  Highld 290 F2
Stronchrubie Highld 307 H7
Strone Argyll 255 F7
  Argyll. 274 G6
  Highld 276 E3
  Highld 290 E3
  Highld 291 D9
  Highld 300 G5
  Invclyd. 276 G5
Stronelairg Lodge
  Highld 291 C7
Stroneskar Argyll . . .275 C9
Stronmachair
  Stirling 285 G8
Stronmilchan Argyll. .284 E5
Stronord Dumfries . .236 C6
Stronsaul Argyll. 276 F2
Stronvar Stirling 285 E9
Strood Kent 53 G11
  Medway. 69 F8
Strood Green Sur. . . . 51 D8
  W Sus 35 C8
  W Sus 50 G6
Strothers Dale
  Northumb 241 F11
Stroud Glos 80 D4
  Hants. 34 C2
  Sur. 50 F2
Stroud Green Sur. . . . 66 F4
  W Sus 50 G6
Strouden BCP 19 C8
Stroud Green Essex . . 88 G5
  Glos 80 D4
  London. 67 B10
Stroul Argyll 276 E4
Stroupster Highld . . 310 C7
Stroxton Lincs 155 C8
Stroxworthy Devon. . 24 D4
Struan Highld 294 B5
  Perth 291 G10
Strubby Lincs 191 E7
Structon's Heath
  Worcs 116 D5
Strugg's Hill Lincs . . 156 B5
Strumpshaw Norf. . . 142 B6
Strutherhill
  S Lanark 268 F5
Struthers Fife 287 G7
Struy Highld 300 F3
Stryd Anglesey 178 E2
Stryd y Facsen
  Anglesey 178 E4
Stryt-issa Wrex. 166 F3
Stuartfield Aberds . . 303 E9
Stubb Norf 161 E8
Stubber's Green
  W Mid 22 B3
Stubbington Hants. . . 33 G9
Stubbins Lancs 195 D9
Stubble Green
  Cumb 219 F11
Stubbles W Berks . . . 64 D5
Stubbs Cross Kent . . 54 F3
Stubbs Green Norf . . 143 D7
Stubb's Green Norf . 142 D5
Stubhampton Dorset. .30 E6
Stubshaw Cross
  Gtr Man 194 G5
Stubton Lincs 172 F5
Stubwood Staffs . . . 151 B11
Stuckgowan Argyll . 285 G7
Stuckton Hants 31 E11
Studdal Kent. 55 D10
Studd Hill Kent 71 F7
Studfold N Yorks . . . 212 F6
Stud Green Ches E . . 168 C2
  Windsor. 65 D11
Studham C Beds 85 B8
Studland Dorset 18 E6
Studley Warks 117 E11
  Wilts 62 E3
Studley Green Bucks. 84 F3
Studley Roger
  N Yorks 214 E5
Studley Royal
  N Yorks 214 E5
Stump Cross Essex. 105 C10
Stumps Cross Glos. . . 99 E11
Stuntney Cambs . . . 123 B11
Stunts Green E Sus. . . 23 C10
Sturbridge Staffs . . 150 C6
Sturford Wilts 45 E10
Sturgate Lincs 188 D5
Sturmer Essex 106 C2
Sturminster Common
  Dorset 30 E2
Sturminster Marshall
  Dorset 31 G7
Sturminster Newton
  Dorset 30 E2
Sturry Kent 71 G7
Sturton N Lincs 200 G3
Sturton by Stow
  Lincs 188 E5
Sturton le Steeple
  Notts 188 E3
Stuston Suff 126 B2
Stutton N Yorks 206 E5
  Suff 108 E3
Styal Ches E 184 E4
Styants Bottom Kent. 52 B5
Stydd Lancs 203 F9
Styrrup Notts 187 C10
Suainebost W Isles. . 304 B7
Suardail W Isles . . . 304 E6
Succoth Aberds . . . 302 F4
  Argyll. 284 G6
Suckley Worcs 116 G4
Suckley Green
  Worcs 116 G4
Suckley Knowl
  Worcs 116 G4
Suckquoy Orkney . . 314 H4

Sucksted Green
  Essex 105 F11
Sudborough
  N Nhants 137 G9
Sudbourne Suff. . . . 127 G8
Sudbrook Lincs 173 G7
  Mon 60 B4
Sudbrooke Lincs. . . 189 F8
Sudbury Derbys. . . . 152 C3
  London. 67 C7
  Suff 107 C7
Sudden Gtr Man . . . 195 E11
Suddie Highld 300 D6
Sudgrove Glos. 80 D6
Suffield Norf 160 C5
  N Yorks 227 G9
Sugnall Staffs 150 C5
Sugwas Pool
  Hereford 97 C9
Suisnish Highld 295 D7
Suladale Highld 298 D3
Sulaisiadar W Isles. .304 E7
Sulby IoM 192 C4
Sulgrave T&W 243 F8
Sulham W Berks 64 D6
Sulhampstead
  W Berks 64 F6
Sulhampstead Abbots
  W Berks 64 F6
Sulhampstead Bannister
  Upper End W Berks. 64 F6
Sulhamstead
  W Berks 64 F6
Sulland Orkney 314 B5
Sullington W Sus. . . . 35 E9
Sullington Warren
  W Sus 35 E9
Sullom Shetland. . . . 312 F5
Sullom Voe Oil Terminal
  Shetland 312 F5
Sully V Glam 59 F7
Sumburgh Shetland . 313 N6
Summerbridge
  N Yorks 214 G4
Summer Bridge
  N Yorks 214 G4
Summercourt Corn . . 5 D7
Summerfield Kent . . 55 B9
  Norf. 158 B5
  Worcs 116 C6
Summerfield Park
  W Mid 133 F10
Summergangs Hull . 209 G8
Summer Heath Bucks .84 G2
Summerhill Newport . 59 B10
  Pembs 73 D11
  Staffs. 133 B11
  Telford 150 F4
  Worcs 116 B6
  Wrex 166 E4
Summer Hill E Sus. . . 23 D9
  W Mid 133 E9
Summerhouse Darl . . 224 B4
Summerlands
  Cumb 211 B10
  Som 29 D8
Summerleaze Mon. . . 60 B2
Summerley Derbys. . 186 F5
Summerscales
  N Yorks 205 C8
Summersdale W Sus . .22 B5
Summerseat
  Gtr Man 195 E9
Summerston
  Glasgow 277 G11
Summerstown
  Bucks. 102 G3
  London. 67 E9
Summertown Oxon . . 83 D8
Summit Gtr Man . . . 195 E10
  Gtr Man 196 D2
  Gtr Man 196 F2
Sunbrick Cumb 210 E5
Sunbury Common
  Sur. 66 E5
Sunbury-on-Thames
  Sur. 66 F6
Sundayshill S Glos. . . 79 G11
Sundaywell
  Dumfries 247 G8
Sunderland Argyll . . 274 G3
  Cumb 229 D9
  Lancs 202 B4
  T&W 243 F9
Sunderland Bridge
  Durham 233 D11
Sundhope Borders . 261 D8
Sundon Park Luton . 103 F11
Sundridge Kent. 52 B3
  London. 68 E2
Sun Green Gtr Man . 185 B7
Sunhill Glos 81 E10
Sunipol Argyll 288 D5
Sunken Marsh
  Essex 69 C10
Sunk Island E Sus . 201 D9
Sunningdale Windsor. 66 F3
Sunninghill Windsor. 66 F2
Sunningwell Oxon . . 83 E7
Sunniside Durham . 233 D8
  T&W 242 F6
  T&W 243 G6
Sunny Bank
  Gtr Man 195 F10
Sunny Bower
  Lancs 203 G10
Sunnybrow Durham .233 E9
Sunnylaw Stirling . . 278 B5
Sunnymead Oxon . . 83 D8
Sunnymeads Windsor .66 D4
Sunnymede Essex . . 87 G11
Sunnyside S Yorks. . 187 C7
  W Sus 51 F11
Sunset Hereford. . . . 114 F6
Sunton Wilts 47 C8
Surbiton London . . . 67 F7
Surby IoM 192 E3

Surfleet Lincs. 156 D5
Surfleet Seas End
  Lincs 156 D5
Surlingham Norf. . . . 142 B6
Surrex Essex 107 G2
Sustead Norf 160 B3
Susworth Lincs 199 G3
Sutcombe Devon. . . . 24 E4
Sutcombemill Devon . 24 E4
Sutherland Grove
  Argyll. 289 E11
Suton Norf 141 D11
Sutors of Cromarty
  Highld 301 C8
Sutterby Lincs 190 G5
Sutterton Lincs 156 B5
Sutterton Dowdyke
  Lincs 156 C5
Sutton Bucks. 66 D4
  Cambs 123 B8
  C Beds 104 B4
  Devon 8 G4
  E Sus 23 F7
  Kent. 55 D10
  Lincs 172 E5
  London. 67 G9
  Mers 183 C8
  Norf. 161 E7
  Notts 154 B5
  N Yorks 187 E11
  N Yorks 198 B3
  Oxon 82 D6
  Pboro. 137 D11
  Pembs 72 B6
  Shrops 132 F4
  Shrops 149 D7
  Shrops 149 G10
  Shrops 150 C3
  Som 44 G6
  Staffs 150 E5
  Suff 108 B6
  Sur. 50 D5
  S Yorks 198 E5
  W Sus 35 D9
Sutton Abinger Sur. . 50 D6
Sutton at Hone Kent . 68 E5
Sutton Bassett
  N Nhants 136 E5
Sutton Benger Wilts . .62 D2
Sutton Bingham Som . 29 E8
Sutton Bonington
  Notts 153 E10
Sutton Bridge Lincs . 157 E9
Sutton Cheney
  Leics 135 C8
Sutton Coldfield
  W Mid 134 D2
Sutton Corner. Lincs. 157 D8
Sutton Courtenay
  Oxon 83 G8
Sutton Crosses
  Lincs 157 E8
Sutton Cum Lound
  Notts 187 E11
Sutton End W Sus . . . 35 D7
Sutton Forest Side
  Notts 171 D8
Sutton Gault Cambs . 123 B8
Sutton Green
  Ches W. 182 F5
  Sur. 50 C4
  Wrex 166 F6
Sutton Hall Shrops . . 132 C4
Sutton Heath Mers. . 183 C8
Sutton Hill Telford . . 132 C4
Sutton Holms Dorset . 31 F9
Sutton Howgrave
  N Yorks 214 D6
Sutton in Ashfield
  Notts 171 D7
Sutton in the Elms
  Leics 135 E10
Sutton Ings Hull . . . 209 G8
Sutton-in-Craven
  N Yorks 204 E6
Sutton Lakes
  Hereford 97 B10
Sutton Lane Ends
  Ches E 184 G6
Sutton Leach Mers. . 183 C8
Sutton Maddock
  Shrops 132 C4
Sutton Mallet Som . . 43 F11
Sutton Mandeville
  Wilts 31 B7
Sutton Manor Mers. . 183 C8
Sutton Marsh
  Hereford 97 C10
Sutton Mill N Yorks. . 204 E6
Sutton Montis Som. . 29 C10
Sutton on Hull Hull . 209 G8
Sutton on Sea Lincs. 191 E8
Sutton-on-the-Forest
  N Yorks 215 G11
Sutton on the Hill
  Derbys. 152 C4
Sutton on Trent
  Notts 172 B3
Sutton Poyntz
  Dorset 17 C10
Sutton Row Wilts . . . 31 B7
Sutton St Edmund
  Lincs 157 G7
Sutton St James
  Lincs 157 F7
Sutton St Michael
  Hereford 97 B10
Sutton St Nicholas
  Hereford 97 B10
Sutton Scarsdale
  Derbys. 170 B6
Sutton Scotney Hants. 48 E3
Sutton Street Suff . . 108 C6
Sutton under Brailes
  Warks 100 D6
Sutton-under-
  Whitestonecliffe
  N Yorks 215 C10
Sutton upon Derwent
  E Yorks. 207 D10

Sutton Valence
  Kent. 53 D10
Sutton Veny Wilts . . . 45 E11
Sutton Waldron
  Dorset 30 E5
Sutton Weaver
  Ches W 183 F8
Sutton Wick Bath. . . . 44 B5
  Oxon 83 G7
Swaby Lincs 190 F5
Swadlincote Derbys. 152 F6
Swaffham Norf 140 B6
Swaffham Bulbeck
  Cambs 123 E11
Swaffham Prior
  Cambs 123 E11
Swafield Norf. 160 C5
Swain House
  W Yorks 205 F9
Swainshill Hereford . .97 C9
Swainsthorpe Norf. . 142 C4
Swainswick Bath . . . 61 F9
Swaithe S Yorks . . . 197 G11
Swalcliffe Oxon. . . . 101 D7
Swalecliffe Kent . . . 70 F6
Swallow Lincs 201 G7
Swallow Beck Lincs . 173 B7
Swallowcliffe Wilts . . 31 B7
Swallowfield
  Wokingham 65 G8
Swallownest S Yorks. 187 E7
Swallows Cross
  Essex 87 F10
Swalwell T&W 242 E6
Swampton Hants 48 C2
Swan Bottom Bucks. .84 D6
Swanbourne Bucks . 102 F6
Swanbridge V Glam . 59 F7
Swan Green
  Ches W. 184 G2
  Suff 126 C5
Swanland E Yorks . . 200 B3
Swanley Glos. 80 F2
  Kent. 68 F4
Swanley Bar Herts . . 86 E3
Swanley Village
  Kent 68 F4
Swanmore Hants . . . 33 D9
  IoW 21 C7
Swannay Orkney . . . 314 D2
Swannington Leics . 153 F8
  Norf. 160 F2
Swanpool Lincs 189 G7
Swanscombe Kent. . 68 E6
Swansea = Abertawe
  Swansea 56 C6
Swanside Mers 182 C6
Swanston Edin. 270 B4
Swan Street Essex . . 107 F7
Swanton Abbott
  Norf. 160 D5
Swanton Hill Norf. . . 160 D5
Swanton Morley
  Norf. 159 F10
Swanton Novers
  Norf. 159 C10
Swanton Street
  Kent. 53 B11
Swan Village W Mid . 133 E9
Swanwick Derbys . . 170 E6
  Hants. 33 F8
Swanwick Green
  Ches E 167 F9
Swarby Lincs 173 G8
Swarcliffe W Yorks . 206 F3
Swardeston Norf . . . 142 C4
Swarister Shetland . 312 E7
Swarkestone
  Derbys. 153 D7
Swarland Northumb . 252 C5
Swarraton Hants . . . 48 F5
Swartha W Yorks . . . 205 D7
Swarthmoor Cumb . 210 D5
Swartland Orkney . . 314 D2
Swathwick Derbys . . 170 B5
Swaton Lincs 156 B2
Swavesey Cambs. . . 123 D7
Sway Hants 19 B11
Swayfield Lincs 155 E9
Swaythling Soton . . . 32 D6
Sweet Green Worcs . 116 E2
Sweetham Devon . . . 14 B3
Sweethaws E Sus . . . 37 B8
Sweethay Som. 28 D2
Sweetholme Cumb . 221 B11
Sweethouse Corn. . . . 5 C11
Sweets Corn. 11 B9
Sweetshouse Corn. . 5 C11
Swefling Suff 126 E6
Swell Som. 28 C5
Swelling Hill Hants. . 49 G7
Swepstone Leics . . . 153 F7
Swerford Oxon 101 E7
Swettenham Ches E . 168 B4
Swetton N Yorks . . . 214 E3
Swffryd Caerph 78 F2
Swift's Green Kent . . 53 E11
Swiftsden E Sus. . . . 38 B2
Swilland Suff 126 G3
Swillbrook Lancs . . . 202 G5
Swillington
  W Yorks 206 G3
Swillington Common
  W Yorks 206 G3
Swimbridge Devon. . . 25 B10
Swimbridge Newland
  Devon 40 G6
Swinbrook Oxon. . . . 82 C3
Swincliffe N Yorks . . 205 B10
  W Yorks 197 B8
Swincombe Devon . . 41 E7
Swinden N Yorks . . . 204 C3
Swinderby Lincs . . . 172 C5

Swindon Glos 99 G8
  Staffs. 133 E7
  Swindon. 63 C7
Swine E Yorks 209 F8
Swinefleet E Yorks . 199 C9
Swineford S Glos. . . . 61 F7
Swineshead
  Bedford 121 D11
  Lincs 174 G2
Swineshead Bridge
  Lincs 174 G2
Swinethorpe Lincs . . 172 B5
Swiney Highld 310 F6
Swinford Leics 119 B11
  Oxon 82 D6
Swingate Notts 171 G8
Swingbrow Cambs. . 139 F7
Swingfield Minnis
  Kent. 55 E8
Swingfield Street
  Kent. 55 E8
Swingleton Green
  Suff 107 B9
Swinhoe Northumb . 264 D6
Swinhope Lincs 190 B2
Swining Shetland . . 312 G6
Swinister Shetland . 312 E5
  Shetland 313 L6
Swinithwaite
  N Yorks 213 B10
Swinmore Common
  Hereford 98 C3
Swinnie Borders . . . 262 F4
Swinnow Moor
  W Yorks 205 G10
Swinscoe Staffs . . . 169 F10
Swinside Cumb 229 G10
Swinside Townfoot
  Borders 262 F6
Swinstead Lincs . . . 155 E10
Swinton Borders . . . 272 F6
  Glasgow 268 C3
  Gtr Man 195 G9
  N Yorks 214 D4
  N Yorks 216 E5
  S Yorks 186 B6
Swinton Bridge
  S Yorks 187 B7
Swinton Hill Borders. 272 F6
Swintonmill Borders .272 F6
Swinton Park
  Gtr Man 195 G9
Swiss Valley Carms . . 75 E8
Swithland Leics . . . 153 G10
Swordale Highld . . . 300 C5
  Highld 309 K6
Swordland Highld . . 295 F9
Swordly Highld 308 C7
Sworton Heath
  Ches E 183 E11
Swyddffynnon
  Ceredig. 112 D3
Swynnerton Staffs . . 151 B7
Swyre Dorset 16 D6
Sycamore Devon . . . 28 F3
Sychdyn = Soughton
  Flint 166 B2
Sychtyn Powys. 129 B9
Sydallt Wrex. 166 D4
Sydenham London . . 67 E10
  Oxon 84 E2
  Som 43 F10
Sydenham Damerel
  Devon 12 F4
Syderstone Norf. . . . 158 C4
Sydling St Nicholas
  Dorset 17 B8
Sydmonton Hants. . . 48 B3
Sydney Ches E 168 D2
Syerston Notts 172 F2
Syke Gtr Man. 195 D11
Sykehouse S Yorks . 198 D6
Sykes Lancs 203 C8
Syleham Suff 126 B4
Sylen Carms 75 D8
Symbister Shetland . 313 G7
Symington Borders . 271 F8
  S Ayrs 257 C9
  S Lanark 259 B11
Symondsbury Dorset. 16 C4
Symonds Green
  Herts. 104 F4
Symonds Yat
  Hereford 79 B9
Synderford Dorset. . 28 G5
Synod Inn = Post Mawr
  Ceredig. 111 G8
Synton Borders . . . 261 E11
Synton Mains
  Borders 261 E11
Synwell Glos 80 G3
Syre Highld 308 E6
Syreford Glos. 99 G10
Syresham W Nhants . 102 C2
Syston Leics 154 G2
  Lincs 173 G8
Sytchampton Worcs 116 D6
Sytch Ho Green
  Shrops 132 E5
Sytch Lane Telford . . 150 E2
Sywell N Nhants . . . 120 D6

T

Taagan Highld 299 C10
Tabley Hill Ches E . . 184 F2
Tabor Gwyn 146 F5
Tàbost W Isles 304 B7
Tàbost W Isles 305 G5
Tachbrook Mallory
  Warks 118 E6
Tacker Street Som . . 42 F4
Tackley Oxon 101 G9
Tacleit W Isles 304 E3
Tacolneston Norf . . 142 D2
Tadcaster N Yorks . . 206 E5
Tadden Dorset 31 G7
Taddington Derbys . 185 G10
  Glos 99 E11

Taddiport Devon 25 D7
Tadhill Som 45 D7
Tadley Hants 64 G5
  Oxon 64 B4
Tadlow Cambs. 104 B5
  C Beds 104 B5
Tadmarton Oxon . . . 101 D7
Tadnoll Dorset. 17 D11
Tadwick Bath. 61 E8
Tadworth Sur 51 B8
Tafarnau-bach
  Bl Gwent 77 C10
Tafarn-y-bwlch
  Pembs 91 E11
Tafarn-y-gelyn
  Denb 165 C11
Taff Merthyr Garden
  Village M Tydf 77 F10
Taff's Well Rhondda . 58 C6
Tafolwern Powys . . 129 C7
Tai Conwy 164 C3
Taibach Neath 57 D9
Tai-bach Powys . . . 148 D3
Taigh a Ghearraidh
  W Isles 296 D3
Taigh Bhalaigh
  W Isles 296 D3
Tai-mawr Conwy. . . 165 F9
Tai-morfa Gwyn . . . 144 D5
Tain Highld 309 L7
  Highld 310 C6
Tai-nant Wrex. 166 F3
Tainlon Gwyn 162 E6
Tairbeart W Isles . . 305 H3
Tai'r-Bull Powys. . . . 95 F9
Tai'r-ysgol Swansea . 57 B7
Tai-Ucha Denb 165 D10
Takeley Essex 105 G11
Takeley Street
  Essex 105 G10
Talacharn = Laugharne
  Carms 74 C4
Talachddu Powys . . . 95 E11
Talacre Flint. 181 E10
Talardd Gwyn. 147 D2
Talaton Devon 15 B7
Talbenny Pembs 72 C4
Talbot Green
  Rhondda 58 C4
Talbot Heath BCP. . . . 19 C7
Talbot's End S Glos. . 80 G2
Talbot Village BCP. . . 19 C7
Talbot Woods BCP. . . 19 C7
Tale Devon 27 G9
Talerddig Powys. . . 129 C8
Talgarreg Ceredig. . 111 G8
Talgarth Powys. 96 E3
Talgarth's Well
  Swansea 56 D2
Talisker Highld. . . . 294 B5
Talke Staffs. 168 E4
Talke Pits Staffs . . . 168 E4
Talkin Cumb 240 F3
Talladale Highld . . . 299 C9
Talla Linnfoots
  Borders 260 E4
Tallaminnoch
  S Ayrs 245 D10
Talland Corn 6 E4
Tallarn Green Wrex . 166 G6
Tallentire Cumb. . . . 229 D8
Talley Carms. 94 E2
Tallington Lincs . . . 137 B11
Talmine Highld 308 C5
Talog Carms 92 F6
Talsarn Carms 94 F5
Tal-sarn Ceredig . . . 111 F10
Talsarnau Gwyn . . . 146 B2
Talskiddy Corn 5 B8
Talwrn Anglesey . . . 179 F7
  Wrex 166 F3
Tal-y-bont Ceredig . 128 F3
  Conwy 164 B3
  Gwyn 145 E11
  Gwyn 179 G10
Talybont-on-Usk
  Powys 96 G2
Tal-y-cafn Conwy . . 180 G3
Tal-y-coed Mon 78 B6
Talygarn Rhondda . . 58 C4
Talyllyn Powys. 96 F2
Tal-y-llyn Gwyn . . . 128 B4
Talysarn Gwyn 163 E7
Tal-y-waenydd
  Gwyn 163 F11
Talywain Torf 78 E3
Tal-y-wern Powys . . 128 C6
Tamanabhagh
  W Isles 304 F2
Tame Bridge
  N Yorks 225 D10
Tamer Lane End
  Gtr Man 194 G6
Tamerton Foliot Plym . 7 C9
Tame Water
  Gtr Man 196 F3
Tamfourhill Falk. . . . 279 E7
Tamworth Staffs. . . 134 C4
Tamworth Green
  Lincs 174 G5
Tancred N Yorks . . . 206 B5
Tandem W Yorks . . . 197 D7
Tanden Kent. 54 F2
Tandlehill Renfs . . . 267 C8
Tandridge Sur. 51 C11
Tanerdy Carms 93 G8
Tanfield Durham . . . 242 F5
Tanfield Lea
  Durham 242 G5
Tang N Yorks. 205 B10
Tangasdal W Isles . 297 M2
Tang Hall York. 207 C8
Tangiers Pembs . . . 73 B7
Tangley Hants 47 C10
Tanglwst Carms . . . 92 E6
Tangmere W Sus . . . 22 B6
Tangwick Shetland . 312 F4
Tangy Argyll 255 E7
Tan Hills Durham. . . 233 B11
Tan Hinon Powys . . 129 F7

Tanhouse Lancs 194 F3
Tanis Wilts 62 G3
Tankersley
  S Yorks 197 G10
Tankerton Kent 70 F6
Tan-lan Conwy 164 C3
  Gwyn 163 G10
Tanlan Flint 181 E10
Tanlan Banks Flint . .181 E10
Tannach Highld 310 E7
Tannachie Aberds 293 E9
Tannadice Angus 287 B8
Tanner's Green
  Worcs 117 C11
Tannington Suff 126 D4
Tannington Place
  Suff 126 D4
Tannochside
  N Lanark 268 C4
Tan Office Suff 126 E2
Tan Office Green
  Suff 124 F5
Tansley Derbys 170 D4
Tansley Hill W Mid . . .133 F9
Tansley Knoll
  Derbys 170 C4
Tansor N Nhants 137 E11
Tanterton Lancs 202 G6
Tantobie Durham 242 G5
Tanton N Yorks 225 C10
Tanwood Worcs 117 C8
Tanworth-in-Arden
  Warks 118 C2
Tan-y-bwlch
  Gwyn 163 G11
Tanyfron Wrex 166 E3
Tan-y-fron Conwy . . .165 C7
Tan-y-graig
  Anglesey 179 F8
  Gwyn 144 B6
Tangyrisiau Gwyn . . .163 F11
Tan-y-groes Ceredig . .92 B5
Tan-y-mynydd
  Gwyn 144 C6
Tan-y-pistyll
  Powys 147 D11
Tan-yr-allt Denb 181 E9
  Gwyn 163 E7
Tanyrhydiau Ceredig 112 D4
Tanysgafell Gwyn . .163 G10
Taobh a Chaolais
  W Isles 297 K3
Taobh a' Ghlinne
  W Isles 305 G5
Taobh a Thuath Loch
  Aineort W Isles 297 J3
Taobh a Tuath Loch
  Baghasdail
  W Isles 297 J3
Taobh Siar W Isles . . 305 H3
Taobh Tuath
  W Isles 296 C5
Taplow Bucks 66 C2
Tapnage Hants 33 E9
Tapton Derbys 186 G5
Tapton Hill S Yorks . .186 D4
Tarbat Ho Highld 301 B7
Tarbert Argyll 255 B7
  Argyll 275 E2
  Argyll 275 G5
Tarbet Argyll 285 G7
  Highld 295 F9
  Highld 306 E6
Tarbock Green
  Mers 183 D7
Tarbolton S Ayrs 257 D10
Tarbrax S Lanark 269 D10
Tardebigge Worcs . . .117 D10
Tardy Gate Lancs 194 B4
Tarfside Angus 292 F6
Tarland Aberds 292 C6
Tarleton Lancs 194 C3
Tarleton Moss
  Lancs 194 C2
Tarlogie Highld 309 L7
Tarlscough Lancs 194 E2
Tarlton Glos 81 F7
Tarn N Yorks 205 F9
Tarnbrook Lancs 203 B7
Tarnock Som 43 C11
Tarns Cumb 229 B8
Tarnside Cumb 221 G8
Tarporley Ches W 167 C9
Tarpots Essex 69 B9
Tarr Som 42 G6
Tarraby Cumb 239 F10
Tarrant Crawford
  Dorset 30 G6
Tarrant Gunville
  Dorset 30 E6
Tarrant Hinton
  Dorset 30 E6
Tarrant Keyneston
  Dorset 30 G6
Tarrant Launceston
  Dorset 30 F6
Tarrant Monkton
  Dorset 30 F6
Tarrant Rawston
  Dorset 30 F6
Tarrant Rushton
  Dorset 30 F6
Tarrel Highld 311 L2
Tarring Neville
  E Sus 36 G6
Tarrington Hereford . .98 C2
Tarrington Common
  Hereford 98 D2
Tarryblake Ho
  Moray 302 E5
Tarsappie Perth 286 E5
Tarskavaig Highld. . . .295 E7
Tarts Hill Shrops 149 B8
Tarves Aberds 303 F8
Tarvie Highld 300 D4
  Perth 292 G2
Tarvin Ches W 167 B7
Tarvin Sands
  Ches W 167 B7
Tasburgh Norf 142 D4
Tasley Shrops 132 E3
Taston Oxon 101 G7

Tat Bank W Mid 133 F9
Tatenhill Staffs 152 E4
Tatenhill Common
  Staffs 152 E3
Tathall End
  M Keynes 102 B6
Tatham Lancs 212 F2
Tathwell Lincs 190 E4
Tatling End Bucks 66 B4
Tatsfield Sur 52 B2
Tattenhall Ches W . . .167 D7
Tattenhoe M Keynes .102 E6
Tatterford Norf 159 D7
Tattersett Norf 158 C6
Tattershall Lincs 174 D2
Tattershall Bridge
  Lincs 173 D11
Tattershall Thorpe
  Lincs 174 D2
Tattingstone Suff 108 D2
Tattingstone White
  Horse Suff 108 D2
Tattle Bank Warks . . .118 E3
Tatton Dale Ches E . . .184 E2
Tatworth Som 28 F4
Taunton Gtr Man 196 G2
  Som 28 C2
Taverham Norf 160 G3
Taverners Green
  Essex 87 B9
Tavernspite Pembs . . .73 C11
Tavistock Devon 12 G5
Taw Green Devon 13 B9
Tawstock Devon 25 B9
Taxal Derbys 185 F8
Tayinloan Argyll 255 C7
Taymouth Castle
  Perth 285 C11
Taynish Argyll 275 E8
Taynton Glos 98 G4
  Oxon 82 C2
Taynuilt Argyll 284 D4
Tayport Fife 287 E8
Tayvallich Argyll 275 E8
Tea Green Herts 104 G2
Tealby Lincs 189 C11
Tealing Angus 287 D8
Teams T&W 242 E6
Team Valley T&W 242 E6
Teanford Staffs 169 G8
Teangue Highld 295 E8
Teanna Mhachair
  W Isles 296 F3
Teasley Mead E Sus . . .52 F4
Tebay Cumb 222 E2
Tebworth C Beds 103 F9
Tedburn St Mary
  Devon 14 C2
Teddington Glos 99 E9
  London 67 E7
Teddington Hands
  Worcs 99 E9
Tedsmore Shrops 149 D7
Tedstone Delamere
  Hereford 116 F3
Tedstone Wafer
  Hereford 116 F3
Teeton W Nhants 120 C3
Teffont Evias Wilts . . .46 G3
Teffont Magna Wilts . .46 G3
Tegryn Pembs 92 E4
Teigh Rutland 155 F7
Teigncombe Devon . . .13 D9
Teigngrace Devon 14 G2
Teignmouth Devon . . .14 G4
Teign Village Devon . .14 E2
Telford Telford 132 B3
Telham E Sus 38 E3
Tellisford Som 45 B10
Telscombe E Sus 36 G6
Telscombe Cliffs
  E Sus 36 G5
Templand Dumfries . .248 F3
Temple Corn 11 G8
  Glasgow 267 B10
  Midloth 270 D6
  Wilts 45 B10
  W Sus 65 C10
Temple Balsall
  W Mid 118 B4
Temple Bar
  Carms 75 B9
  Ceredig 111 G10
  W Sus 22 B5
Templeborough
  S Yorks 186 C6
Temple Cloud Bath . . .44 B6
Templecombe Som . . .30 C2
Temple Cowley Oxon. .83 E8
Temple End Essex . . .106 C6
  Suff 124 G3
Temple Ewell Kent . . .55 E9
Temple Fields Essex . .87 C7
Temple Grafton
  Warks 118 G2
Temple Guiting Glos 99 F11
Temple Herdewyke
  Warks 119 G7
Temple Hill Kent 68 D5
Temple Hirst
  N Yorks 198 C6
Templeman's Ash
  Dorset 28 G6
Temple Normanton
  Derbys 170 B6
Temple Sowerby
  Cumb 231 F8
Templeton Devon 26 E5
  Pembs 73 C10
  W Berks 63 F11
Templeton Bridge
  Devon 26 E5
Templetown
  Durham 242 G4
Tempsford C Beds . . .122 G3
Ten Acres W Mid 133 G11
Tenandry Perth 291 G11
Tenbury Wells
  Worcs 115 D11

Tenby = Dinbych-y-Pysgod
  Pembs 73 E10
Tencreek Corn 6 E4
Tendring Essex 108 G2
Tendring Green
  Essex 108 F2
Tendring Heath
  Essex 108 F2
Ten Mile Bank Norf . .140 D2
Tenpenny Heath
  Essex 108 G2
Ten Mile Bank Norf . .140 D2
Tenston Orkney 314 E2
Terfyn Conwy 180 F6
  Gwyn 163 C9
Terhill Som 43 G7
Terling Essex 88 B3
Ternhill Shrops 150 C2
Terras Corn 5 E8
Terregles Banks
  Dumfries 237 B11
Terrible Down E Sus . .23 B7
Terrick Bucks 84 D4
Terriers Bucks 84 G5
Terrington N Yorks . .216 E3
Terrington St Clement
  Norf 157 E10
Terrington St John
  Norf 157 G10
Terryhorn Aberds 302 F4
Terry's Green Warks .118 C2
Terwick Common
  W Sus 34 C4
Teston Kent 53 C8
Testwood Hants 32 E5
Tetbury Glos 80 G5
Tetbury Upton Glos. . .80 F5
Tetchill Shrops 149 C7
Tetcott Devon 12 B2
Tetford Lincs 190 G4
Tetley N Lincs 199 E9
Tetney Lincs 201 G10
Tetney Lock Lincs 201 G10
Tetsworth Oxon. 83 E11
Tettenhall W Mid 133 D7
Tettenhall Wood
  W Mid 133 D7
Tetworth Cambs 122 G4
Teuchan Aberds 303 F10
Teversal Notts 171 C7
Teversham Cambs . . .123 F9
Teviothead Borders .249 B10
Tewel Aberds 293 E10
Tewin Herts 86 C3
Tewin Wood Herts . . .86 B3
Tewitfield Lancs 211 E10
Tewkesbury Glos 99 E7
Teynham Kent 70 G3
Teynham Street Kent .70 G3
Thackley W Yorks 205 F9
Thackley End
  W Yorks 205 F9
Thackthwaite Cumb . .229 G8
Thainston Aberds 293 F8
Thakeham W Sus 35 D10
Thame Oxon 84 D2
Thames Ditton Sur . . .67 F7
Thames Haven
  Thurrock 69 C8
Thames Head Glos . . .81 F7
Thamesmead London. .68 C3
Thanington Kent. 54 B6
Thankerton
  S Lanark 259 B11
Tharston Norf 142 E3
Thatcham W Berks . . .64 F4
Thatto Heath Mers . . .183 C8
Thaxted Essex 106 E2
The Aird Highld 298 D4
Theakston N Yorks . .214 B6
Thealby N Lincs 199 D11
Thealby N Lincs 199 D11
The Alders Staffs 134 C3
Theale Som 44 D3
  W Berks 64 E6
The Arms Norf 141 D7
Thearne E Yorks 209 F7
The Bage Hereford . . .96 C5
The Balloch Perth . . .286 F2
The Bank Ches E 168 D4
The Banks Gtr Man . .185 D4
  Wilts 62 D4
The Barony Ches E . .167 E11
  Orkney 314 D2
The Barton Wilts 62 D5
The Batch S Glos 61 E7
The Beeches Glos 81 E8
The Bell Gtr Man 194 F4
The Bents Staffs 151 C10
Theberton Suff 127 D8
The Blythe Staffs 151 D10
The Bog Shrops 131 D7
The Borough Dorset . .30 E2
  London 67 D10
The Bourne Sur 49 E10
The Bows Stirling 285 G11
The Braes Highld 295 B7
The Brampton
  Staffs 168 F4
The Brand Leics 153 G10
The Bratch Staffs 133 E7
The Breck Orkney 314 F3
The Brents Kent 70 G4
The Bridge Dorset 30 E2
The Broad Hereford . .115 E9
The Brook Suff 125 B11
The Brushes Derbys . .186 F5
The Bryn Mon 78 D4
The Burf Worcs 116 D6
The Butts Hants 49 F8
  Som 45 D9
The Camp Glos 80 D6
  Herts 85 C11
The Cape Warks 118 D5
The Chart Kent 52 C3
The Chequer Wrex . . .167 G7
The Chuckery
  W Mid 133 D10
The City Bucks 84 F3
The Cleaver
  Hereford 97 F10

The Close W Sus 22 C5
The Colony Oxon 100 D6
The Common Bath. . . .60 G6
  Bucks 102 E5
  Dorset 30 E3
  Shrops 150 D3
  Suff 108 B2
  Swansea 56 C4
  Wilts 47 G8
  Wilts 61 G11
  W Sus 51 G7
The Corner Kent 53 E8
  Shrops 131 F8
The Cot Mon 79 F8
The Craigs Highld . . .309 K4
The Crofts E Yorks . . .218 E4
The Cronk IoM 192 C4
The Cross Hands
  Leics 134 C6
The Cwm Mon 79 G7
Theddingworth
  Leics 136 F3
Theddlethorpe All Saints
  Lincs 191 D7
Theddlethorpe St Helen
  Lincs 191 D7
The Dell Suff 143 D9
The Delves W Mid . . .133 D10
The Den N Ayrs 266 E6
The Dene Durham 242 G4
  Hants 47 C11
The Down Kent 53 F7
  Shrops 132 E3
The Downs Sur 50 F3
The Dunks Wrex 166 E4
The Eals Northum 251 F7
The Eaves Glos 79 D10
The Fall W Yorks 197 B10
The Fence Glos 79 D8
The Flat Glos 80 B3
The Flatt Cumb 240 B2
The Flourish Derbys . .153 B8
The Folly Herts 85 C11
  S Glos 61 E8
The Fording Hereford .98 F3
The Forge Hereford . .114 F6
The Forstal Kent 54 F4
The Forties Shrops . . .152 F6
The Four Alls
  Shrops 150 C3
The Fox Wilts 62 B6
The Foxholes
  Shrops 132 G2
The Frenches Hants. . .32 C4
The Frythe Herts 86 C2
The Garths Shetland . .312 B8
The Gibb Wilts 61 D10
The Glack Borders . . .260 B6
The Gore Shrops 131 G11
The Grange Norf 160 E2
  N Yorks 225 F11
The Green Cambs 122 D5
  C Beds 85 B8
  Cumb 210 C3
  Cumb 211 D7
  Essex 88 B3
  Hants 32 B3
  M Keynes 103 C7
  Norf 141 C11
  Norf 159 B11
  Oxon 101 F9
  Shrops 130 G6
  S Yorks 197 G8
  Warks 118 F4
  Wilts 45 G11
  W Nhants 102 C5
The Grove
  Dumfries 237 B11
  Durham 242 G3
  Herts 85 F9
  Shrops 131 B7
  Shrops 131 G8
  Worcs 99 C7
The Gutter Derbys . . .170 F5
The Hacket S Glos 61 B7
The Hague Derbys . . .185 C8
The Hall Shetland 312 D8
The Hallands
  N Lincs 200 C5
The Ham Wilts 45 C11
The Handfords
  Staffs 151 E7
The Harbour Kent 53 D8
The Haven W Sus 50 G5
The Headland Hrtlpl. .234 E6
The Heath Norf 159 D8
  Norf 160 E3
  Norf 160 E4
  Staffs 151 C11
  Suff 108 D2
The Hem Shrops 132 B4
The Hendre Mon 79 C7
The Herberts V Glam . .58 E3
The Hermitage
  Cambs 123 C7
The High Essex 86 C6
The Highlands E Sus . .38 F2
The Hill Cumb 210 C3
The Hobbins Shrops. .132 E4
The Hollands Staffs . .168 D6
The Hollies Notts 172 E4
The Holmes Derbys . .153 B7
The Holt Wokingham. .65 D10
The Hook Worcs 98 C6
The Hope Shrops 115 B10
The Howe Cumb 211 B9
  IoM 192 F2
The Humbers
  Telford 150 G3
The Hundred
  Hereford 115 D10
The Hyde London 67 B8
  Worcs 98 C6
The Hythe Essex 107 G10
The Inch Edin. 280 G5
The Knab Swansea . . .56 D6
The Knap V Glam 58 F5
The Knapp Hereford . .116 G4
  S Glos 79 G11
The Knowle W Mid . .133 F9

The Laches Staffs 133 B8
The Lake Dumfries . . .237 E10
  Lincs 116 B5
The Lakes Worcs. 116 C6
The Lawe T&W 243 D9
The Lawns W Sus 208 G6
Thelbridge Barton
  Devon 26 E3
The Leacon Kent. 54 G3
The Leath Shrops 131 F11
The Lee Bucks 84 E6
The Lees Kent 54 C4
The Leigh Glos 99 F7
The Leys Staffs 134 C4
The Lhen IoM 192 B4
The Ling Norf 142 D6
The Lings Norf 141 B10
  S Yorks 199 F7
The Linleys Wilts 61 F11
Thelnetham Suff 125 B10
The Lunt W Mid 133 D9
Thelveton Norf 142 G3
Thelwall Warr 183 D10
The Manor W Sus 22 C4
The Marsh Ches E 168 C4
  Hereford 115 F9
  Powys 130 D6
  Shrops 150 D3
  Staffs 150 D6
  Suff 125 B11
  Suff 126 B2
  Wilts 45 B10
Themelthorpe Norf .159 E11
The Middles
  Durham 242 G6
The Mint Hants 34 B3
The Moor Flint 166 B4
  Kent. 38 B3
The Moors Hereford . .97 G10
The Mount Hants 64 G2
  Reading 65 E8
The Mumbles = Y Mwmbwls
  Swansea 56 D6
The Murray
  S Lanark 268 E2
The Mythe Glos. 99 E7
The Nant Wrex 166 E3
The Narth Mon 79 D8
The Neuk Aberds 293 D9
Thenford
  W Nhants 101 C10
The Node Herts 104 G4
The Nook Shrops 149 C11
  Shrops 150 E3
The North Mon 79 D8
The Oval Bath 61 G8
The Park Glos 99 G8
The Parks S Yorks . . .198 F6
The Pitts Wilts 31 B9
The Platt Oxon 83 E9
The Pludds Glos 79 B10
The Point Devon 14 E5
The Pole of Itlaw
  Aberds 302 D6
The Port of Felixstowe
  Suff 108 E5
The Potteries Stoke .168 F5
The Pound Worcs 98 E4
The Quarry Glos 80 F2
  Shrops 149 G9
The Quarter Kent 53 E11
  Kent. 53 C11
The Rampings Worcs .99 F7
The Rectory Lincs 156 G2
The Reddings Glos . . .99 G8
Therfield Herts 104 D6
The Rhos Pembs 73 C8
The Rhydd Hereford . .97 E9
The Riddle Hereford .115 E9
The Ridge Wilts 61 F11
The Ridges
  Wokingham. 65 G10
The Riding
  Northumb 241 D10
The Riggs Borders . . .261 C8
The Rink Borders 261 C11
The Rise Windsor 66 F2
The Rock Telford 132 B3
The Rocks Kent. 53 B8
The Roe Denb 181 G8
The Rookery Herts . . .85 G10
  Staffs 168 D5
The Row Lancs 211 D9
The Rowe Staffs 150 B6
The Ryde Herts 86 D2
The Sands Sur 49 D11
The Scarr Glos 98 F4
The Shoe Wilts 61 E10
The Shruggs Staffs . .151 E8
The Slack Durham . . .233 F8
The Slade W Berks . . .64 F4
The Smeeth Norf 157 G10
The Smithies
  Shrops 132 D3
The Spa Wilts 62 G2
The Spring Warks 118 C5
The Square Torf 78 F3
The Stocks Kent 38 B6
  Wilts 62 G2
The Straits Hants 49 F9
  W Mid 133 E8
The Strand Wilts 46 B2
The Swillett Herts 85 F8
The Sydnall Shrops. . .150 C3
Thetford Lincs 156 F2
  Norf 141 G7
The Thrift Cambs 104 D6
The Throat
  Wokingham 65 F10
The Toft Staffs 151 E8
The Towans Corn 2 B3
The Town Scilly 1 F3
The Hythe Essex 107 G10
The Twittocks Glos . . .99 D7
The Tynings Glos 80 B6
The Vale W Mid 133 G11
The Valley Ches E 167 D11
  Kent. 54 C3
  Leics 154 F4
  Pembs 73 D10

The Vauld Hereford. . .97 B10
The Village Newport. . .78 G4
  Windsor 66 E3
  W Mid 133 F7
The Walshes Worcs. . .116 C6
The Warren Kent 54 E3
  Wilts 63 F8
The Waterwheel
  Shrops 131 C7
The Weaven
  Hereford 97 E10
The Wells Sur 67 G2
The Wern Wrex 166 E3
The Willows
  NE Lincs 201 F8
The Wood Shrops 148 E6
  Shrops 149 D9
The Woodlands
  Leics 136 D3
  Suff 107 C11
  Suff 108 B3
The Woods W Mid. . . .133 D10
The Wrangle Bath 44 B4
The Wrythe London. . .67 F9
The Wyke Shrops 132 B4
The Wymm Hereford . .97 B10
Theydon Bois Essex. . .86 F6
Theydon Garnon
  Essex 87 F7
Theydon Mount
  Essex 87 F7
The Yeld Shrops 131 G11
Thick Hollins
  W Yorks 196 E6
Thickthorn Hall
  Norf 142 B3
Thickwood Wilts. 61 E11
Thimbleby Lincs 190 G2
  N Yorks 225 F9
Thimble End W Mid . .134 E2
Thinford Durham 233 E11
Thingley Wilts 61 E11
Thingwall Mers 182 E3
Thirdpart N Ayrs 266 F5
Thirlby N Yorks 215 C9
Thirlestane
  Borders 271 F11
Thirn N Yorks 214 B4
Thirsk N Yorks 215 C8
Thirtleby E Yorks 209 G9
Thistleton Lancs 202 F4
  Rutland 155 F8
Thistley Green Essex. .88 B2
Thixendale N Yorks . .216 E6
Thockrington
  Northumb 241 B11
Tholomas Drove
  Cambs 139 B7
Tholthorpe N Yorks. .215 F9
Thomas Chapel
  Pembs 73 D10
Thomas Close Cumb .230 C4
Thomastown Aberds .302 F5
  Rhondda 58 B4
Thompson Norf 141 D8
Thomshill Moray 302 D2
Thong Kent 69 E7
Thongsbridge
  W Yorks 196 F6
Thoralby N Yorks 213 B10
Thoresby Notts 187 G10
Thoresthorpe Lincs . .191 F7
Thoresway Lincs 189 B11
Thorganby Lincs 190 B2
  N Yorks 207 E9
Thorgill N Yorks 226 F4
Thorington Suff 127 C8
Thorington Street
  Suff 107 D10
Thorlby N Yorks 204 C5
Thorley Herts 87 B7
  IoW 20 D3
Thorley Houses
  Herts 105 G9
Thorley Street Herts . .87 B7
  IoW 20 D3
Thormanby N Yorks . .215 E9
Thorn Devon 13 D9
  Powys 114 E5
Thornaby on Tees
  Stockton 225 B9
Thornage Norf 159 B11
Thornborough
  Bucks 102 E4
  N Yorks 214 D5
Thornbury Devon 24 F6
  Hereford 116 F2
  S Glos 79 G10
  W Yorks 205 G9
Thornby Cumb 239 G7
  W Nhants 120 B3
Thorncliff W Yorks . .197 E8
Thorncliffe Staffs . . .169 D8
Thorncombe Dorset . .28 G5
  Dorset 30 G5
Thorncombe Street
  Sur 50 E4
Thorncote Green
  C Beds 104 B3
Thorncross IoW 20 E4
Thorndon Suff 126 D2
Thorndon Cross
  Devon 12 C6
Thorpe Cumb 230 F5
  Derbys 169 E11
  E Yorks 208 D5
Thorne Corn 24 G2
  S Yorks 199 E7
Thorne Coffin Som. . .29 D8
Thornehillhead
  Devon 24 D6
Thorne Moor Devon . .12 D3
Thornend Wilts 62 D3
Thorner W Yorks 206 E3
Thornes Staffs 133 C11
  W Yorks 197 D10
Thorne St Margaret
  Som 27 C9
Thorney Bucks 66 D4
  Notts 188 G4
  Pboro 138 C5
  Som 28 C6
Thorney Close T&W. .243 G9

Thorney Crofts
  E Yorks 201 C8
Thorney Green
  Suff 125 E11
Thorney Hill Hants . . .19 B9
Thorney Island
  W Sus 22 C3
Thorney Toll Pboro . .138 C6
Thorneywood Notts .171 G9
Thornfalcon Som 28 C3
Thornford Dorset 29 E10
Thorngrafton
  Northumb 241 D9
Thorngrove Som. 43 G11
Thorngumbald
  E Yorks 201 B8
Thornham Norf 176 B3
Thornham Fold
  Gtr Man 195 F11
Thornham Magna
  Suff 126 C2
Thornham Parva
  Suff 126 C2
Thornhaugh Pboro. . .137 C11
Thornhill Cardiff 59 C7
  Cumb 219 D10
  Derbys 185 E11
  Dumfries 247 D9
  Soton 33 E7
  Stirling 278 B3
  Torf 78 F3
  Wilts 62 D5
  W Yorks 197 D9
Thornhill Edge
  W Yorks 197 D8
Thornhill Lees
  W Yorks 197 D8
Thornhill Park Hants. .33 E7
Thornhills W Yorks . .197 C7
Thornholme
  E Yorks 218 G2
Thornicombe Dorset . .30 G5
Thornielee Borders .261 B10
Thornley Durham 233 D8
  Durham 234 D3
Thornliebank
  E Renf 267 D10
Thornly Park Renfs . .267 C9
Thornroan Aberds . . .303 F8
Thorns N Yorks 223 E7
  Suff 124 F4
Thornseat S Yorks . . .186 C2
Thornsett Derbys 185 D8
Thorns Green
  Ches E 184 E3
Thornthwaite
  Cumb 229 F10
  N Yorks 205 B9
Thornton Angus 287 C7
  Bucks 102 D5
  E Yorks 207 D11
  Fife 280 B5
  Lancs 202 E2
  Leics 135 B9
  Lincs 174 B2
  Mbro 225 C9
  Mers 193 G10
  Northumb 273 F6
  Pembs 72 D6
  W Yorks 205 G8
Thornton Curtis
  N Lincs 200 D5
Thorntonhall
  S Lanark 267 D11
Thornton Heath
  London 67 F10
Thornton Hough
  Mers 182 E4
Thornton in Craven
  N Yorks 204 D4
Thornton in Lonsdale
  N Yorks 212 E3
Thornton-le-Beans
  N Yorks 225 G7
Thornton-le-Clay
  N Yorks 216 F3
Thornton-le-Dale
  N Yorks 216 C6
Thornton le Moor
  Lincs 189 C9
Thornton-le-Moor
  N Yorks 215 B7
Thornton-le-Moors
  Ches W 182 G6
Thornton-le-Street
  N Yorks 215 B8
Thorntonloch
  E Loth 282 G6
Thornton Park
  Northumb 273 F6
Thornton Rust
  N Yorks 213 B9
Thornton Steward
  N Yorks 214 B4
Thornton Watlass
  N Yorks 214 B4
Thornwood Common
  Essex 87 D7
Thornydykes
  Borders 272 F2
Thoroton Notts 172 G3
Thorp Gtr Man 196 F2
Thorp Arch
  W Yorks 206 D4
Thorpe Cumb 230 F5
  Derbys 169 E11
  E Yorks 208 D5
  Lincs 191 E7
  Norf 143 D8
  Notts 172 F3
  N Yorks 213 G9
  Sur 66 F4
Thorpe Abbotts
  Norf 126 B3
Thorpe Acre Leics . . .153 E10
Thorpe Arnold Leics .154 E5
Thorpe Audlin
  W Yorks 198 D3
Thorpe Bassett
  N Yorks 217 E7
Thorpe Bay Southend .70 B2

Thorpe by Water
  Rutland 137 D7
Thorpe Common
  Suff 108 D5
Thorpe Constantine
  Staffs 134 B5
Thorpe Culvert
  Lincs 175 C7
Thorpe Edge
  W Yorks 205 F9
Thorpe End Norf 160 G5
Thorpe Fendykes
  Lincs 175 C7
Thorpe Green
  Essex 108 G3
  Lancs 194 C5
  Suff 125 G8
  Sur 66 F4
Thorpe Hamlet Norf .142 B4
Thorpe Hesley
  S Yorks 186 B5
Thorpe in Balne
  S Yorks 198 E5
Thorpe in the Fallows
  Lincs 188 E6
Thorpe Langton
  Leics 136 E4
Thorpe Larches
  Durham 234 F3
Thorpe Latimer
  Lincs 156 B2
Thorpe Lea Sur 66 F4
Thorpe-le-Soken
  Essex 108 G3
Thorpe le Street
  E Yorks 208 E2
Thorpe le Vale
  Lincs 190 C2
Thorpe Malsor
  N Nhants 120 B6
Thorpe Mandeville
  W Nhants 101 B10
Thorpe Market Norf .160 B4
Thorpe Marriot Norf .160 F3
Thorpe Morieux
  Suff 125 G8
Thorpeness Suff 127 F9
Thorpe on the Hill
  Lincs 172 B6
  W Yorks 197 B10
Thorpe Row Norf 141 B9
Thorpe St Andrew
  Norf 142 B5
Thorpe St Peter
  Lincs 175 C7
Thorpe Salvin
  S Yorks 187 E8
Thorpe Satchville
  Leics 154 G4
Thorpe Street Suff . .125 B10
Thorpe Thewles
  Stockton 234 G4
Thorpe Tilney
  Lincs 173 D10
Thorpe Underwood
  N Nhants 136 G5
  N Yorks 206 B5
Thorpe Waterville
  N Nhants 137 G2
Thorpe Willoughby
  N Yorks 207 G7
Thorpe Wood
  N Yorks 207 G7
Thorpland Norf 140 B2
Thorrington Essex . . .89 B9
Thorverton Devon . . .26 G6
Thoulstone Wilts 45 D10
Thrandeston Suff 126 B2
Thrapston N Nhants .121 B9
Thrashbush
  N Lanark 268 B5
Threapland Cumb . . .229 D9
  N Yorks 213 G9
Threapwood
  Ches W 166 F6
  Staffs 169 G8
Three Ashes Hants . . .64 G6
  Hereford 97 G10
  Shrops 115 B7
  Som 45 D7
Three Bridges
  Argyll 284 F4
  Lincs 190 D6
  W Sus 51 F9
Three Burrows Corn . .4 F4
Three Chimneys
  Kent. 53 F10
Three Cocked Hat
  Norf 143 D8
Three Cocks = Aberllynfi
  Powys 96 D3
Three Crosses
  Swansea 56 C5
Three Cups Corner
  E Sus 37 C10
Three Fingers Wrex. .167 G7
Three Gates Dorset . .29 F10
Threehammer Common
  Norf 160 E6
Three Hammers
  Corn. 11 D10
Three Holes Norf 139 C10
Three Holes Cross
  Corn. 10 G6
Threekingham
  Lincs 155 B11
Three Leg Cross
  E Sus 37 C11
Three Legged Cross
  Dorset 31 F9
Threelows Staffs 169 F9
Three Maypoles
  W Mid 118 B2
Three Mile Cross
  Wokingham 65 F10
Threemilestone Corn . .4 G5
Threemiletown
  W Loth 279 F11
Three Oaks E Sus 38 E4

Threepwood
  Borders 271 G10
Three Sisters Denb . . 165 C9
Threewaters Corn . . .5 B10
Threlkeld Cumb. . . 230 F2
Threshers Bush
  Essex. 87 D7
Threshfield N Yorks. 213 G9
Thrigby Norf. 161 G9
Thringarth Durham. 232 G4
Thringstone Leics . 153 F8
Thrintoft N Yorks. . 224 G6
Thriplow Cambs . . 105 B8
Throapham S Yorks. 187 D8
Throckenholt Lincs 139 B7
Throcking Herts. . . 104 E6
Throckley T&W . . 242 D5
Throckmorton Worcs .99 B9
Throop Dorset 18 C2
Thropton Northumb. 252 C2
Throphill Northumb. 252 C2
Throsk Stirling . . . 279 C7
Througham Glos. . . .80 D6
Throughgate
  Dumfries 247 G9
Throwleigh Devon . .13 C9
Throwley Kent 54 C3
Throwley Forstal
  Kent. 54 C3
Throxenby N Yorks . 217 B10
Thrumpton Notts . 153 C10
  Notts 188 E2
Thrumster Highld . 310 E7
Thrunton Northumb . 264 G3
Thrupe Som. 44 D6
Thrupp Glos. 80 E5
  Oxon 82 F3
  Oxon 83 B7
Thruscross N Yorks . 205 B9
Thrushelton Devon. .12 D4
Thrussington Leics. . 154 F2
Thruxton Hants . . .47 D9
  Hereford 97 E8
Thrybergh S Yorks. . 187 B7
Thulston Derbys . . 153 C8
Thunder Bridge
  W Yorks 197 E7
Thundergay N Ayrs. 255 C9
Thunder Hill Norf. . 161 F8
Thunder's Hill E Sus. .23 C9
Thundersley Essex . .69 B9
Thundridge Herts. . .86 B5
Thurcaston Leics . 153 G9
Thurcroft S Yorks . 187 D7
Thurdon Corn 24 E3
Thurgarton Norf. . . 160 C3
  Notts 171 F11
Thurgoland S Yorks . 197 G9
Thurlaston Leics . . 135 D10
  Warks 119 C9
Thurlbear Som 28 C3
Thurlby Lincs . . . 156 F2
  Lincs 172 C6
  Lincs 191 F11
Thurleigh Bedford . 121 F11
Thurlestone Devon. . .8 G3
Thurloxton Som . . .43 G9
Thurlstone S Yorks . 197 G8
Thurlton Norf. . . . 143 D8
Thurlton Links Norf. 143 D8
Thurlwood Ches E . 168 D4
Thurmaston Leics . 136 B2
Thurnby Leics . . . 136 C2
Thurne Norf 161 F8
Thurnham Kent. . . .53 B10
  Lancs. 202 C5
Thurning N Nhants . 137 G11
  Norf. 159 D11
Thurnscoe S Yorks . 198 F3
Thurnscoe East
  S Yorks 198 F3
Thursby Cumb . . . 239 G8
Thursford Norf . . . 159 C9
Thursford Green
  Norf. 159 C9
Thursley Sur 50 F2
Thurso Highld . . . 310 C5
Thurso East Highld . 310 C5
Thurstaston Mers. . 182 E2
Thurston Suff. . . . 125 D8
Thurston Clough
  Gtr Man 196 F3
Thurston End Suff . 124 G5
Thurstonfield Cumb . 239 F8
Thurstonland
  W Yorks 197 E7
Thurton Norf 142 C6
Thurvaston Derbys. . 152 B2
  Derbys. 152 B4
Thuxton Norf. . . . 141 B10
Thwaite N Yorks. . . 223 F7
  Suff 126 D2
Thwaite Flat Cumb. 210 E4
Thwaite Head Cumb. 220 G6
Thwaites W Yorks . . 205 E7
Thwaite St Mary
  Norf. 142 E6
Thwaites Brow
  W Yorks 205 E7
Thwing E Yorks . . . 217 E11
Tibberton Perth. . . 286 E4
Tibberton Glos 98 G5
  Telford 150 E3
  Worcs 117 F8
Tibenham Norf . . . 142 F2
Tibshelf Derbys . . . 170 C6
Tibshelf Wharf
  Notts 171 C7
Tibthorpe E Yorks . 208 B5
Ticehurst E Sus 53 G7
Tichborne Hants . . .48 G5
Tickencote Rutland. . 137 B9
Tickenham N Som. . .60 E3
Ticket Wood Devon . .8 G4
Tickford End
  M Keynes 103 C7
Tickhill S Yorks . . . 187 C9
Tickleback Row
  Brack 65 E11

Ticklerton Shrops . 131 E9
Tickmorend Glos . . .80 F4
Ticknall Derbys . . . 153 E7
Tickton E Yorks . . . 209 E7
Tidbury Green
  W Mid 117 B11
Tidcombe Wilts. . . .47 B9
Tiddington Oxon. . .83 E11
  Warks 118 F4
Tidebrook E Sus . . .37 B10
Tideford Corn 6 D6
Tideford Cross Corn . .6 C6
Tidenham Glos 79 F9
Tidenham Chase
  Glos 79 F9
Tideswell Derbys . . 185 F11
Tidmarsh W Berks. . .64 E6
Tidmington Warks . 100 D5
Tidnor Hereford . . .97 D11
Tidpit Hants 31 D9
Tidworth Wilts. . . .47 D8
Tiers Cross Pembs . .72 C6
Tiffield W Nhants . . 120 G3
Tifty Aberds. 303 E7
Tigerton Angus . . . 293 G7
Tigh-na-Blair
  Perth. 285 F11
Tighnabruaich
  Argyll. 275 F10
Tighnacachla Argyll. 274 G3
Tighnafiline Highld. . 307 L3
Tighness Argyll . . . 284 G6
Tigley Devon 8 C5
Tilbrook Cambs . . 121 D11
Tilbury Thurrock . . .68 D6
Tilbury Green Essex. 106 C4
Tilbury Juxta Clare
  Essex. 106 C4
Tile Cross W Mid . . 134 F3
Tilegate Green Essex .87 D8
Tile Hill W Mid . . . 118 B5
Tilehouse Green
  W Mid 118 B3
Tilehurst Reading . .65 E7
Tilekiln Green
  Essex. 105 G10
Tiley Dorset 29 E11
Tilford Sur 49 E11
Tilford Common
  Sur. 49 E11
Tilford Reeds Sur . .49 E11
Tilgate W Sus 51 G9
Tilgate Forest Row
  W Sus 51 G9
Tilkey Essex 106 G6
Tilland Corn 6 C6
Tillathrowie Aberds . 302 F4
Tillers' Green Glos. . .98 E3
Tilley Shrops. . . . 149 D10
Tilley Green
  Shrops 149 D10
Tillicoultry Clack . . 279 B8
Tillietudlem
  S Lanark. 268 F6
Tillingham Essex . . .89 E7
Tillington Hereford. . .97 B9
  Staffs. 151 E8
  W Sus 35 C7
Tillington Common
  Hereford 97 B9
Tillislow Devon. . . .12 C3
Tillworth Devon. . . .28 G4
Tilly Shrops 149 D10
Tillyarblet Angus. . . 293 G8
Tillybirloch Aberds. . 293 C8
Tillycorthie Aberds. . 303 G9
Tilly Down Hants . . .47 D10
Tillydrone Aberds . 293 B11
Tillyfour Aberds. . . 293 B8
Tillyfourie Aberds. . 293 B8
Tillygarmond
  Aberds. 293 D8
Tillygreig Aberds. . 303 G8
Tillykerie Aberds. . 303 G8
Tilly Lo Aberds . . . 293 C7
Tillynaught Aberds. . 302 C5
Tilmanstone Kent. . .55 C10
Tilney All Saints
  Norf. 157 F11
Tilney cum Islington
  Norf. 157 G11
Tilney Fen End
  Norf. 157 G10
Tilney High End
  Norf. 157 F11
Tilney St Lawrence
  Norf. 157 G10
Tilsdown Glos. 80 F2
Tilshead Wilts. 46 D4
Tilsmore E Sus 37 C9
Tilsop Shrops 116 C2
Tilstock Shrops . . 149 B10
Tilston Ches W . . . 167 E7
Tilstone Bank
  Ches W 167 D9
Tilstone Fearnall
  Ches W 167 C9
Tilsworth C Beds . . 103 G9
Tilton on the Hill
  Leics 136 B4
Tilts S Yorks 198 F5
Tiltups End Glos . . .80 F4
Tilty Essex 105 F11
Timberden Bottom
  Kent. 68 G4
Timberhonger
  Worcs 117 D8
Timberland Lincs . . 173 D10
Timbersbrook
  Ches E 168 C4
Timberscombe Som . .42 E3
Timble N Yorks. . . 205 C9
Timbold Hill Kent . .54 B2
Timbrelham Corn . .12 E3
Timperley Gtr Man . 184 D3
Timsbury Bath. . . .45 B7
  Hants. 32 C4
Timsgearraidh
  W Isles 304 E2
Timworth Suff . . . 125 D7
Timworth Green
  Suff 125 D7
Tincleton Dorset . . .17 C11

Tindale Cumb. . . . 240 F4
Tindale Crescent
  Durham. 233 F9
Tindon End Essex . . 106 E2
Tingewick Bucks. . . 102 E3
Tingley W Yorks. . . 197 B9
Tingon Shetland. . . 312 D4
Tingrith C Beds . . . 103 E10
Tinhay Devon 12 E3
Tinkers End Bucks. . 102 F5
Tinshill W Yorks. . . 205 F11
Tinsley S Yorks . . . 186 C6
Tinsley Green W Sus . .51 F9
Tintagel Corn 11 D7
Tintern Parva Mon . .79 E8
Tintinhull Som. 29 D8
Tintwistle Derbys . . 185 B8
Tinwald Dumfries . . 248 G2
Tinwell Rutland . . . 137 B10
Tipner Ptsmth 33 G10
Tippacott Devon . . .41 D9
Tipperty Aberds. . . 303 C6
  Aberds. 303 G9
Tipps End Norf . . . 139 D10
Tiptoe Hants. 19 B11
Tipton W Mid 133 E8
Tipton Green
  W Mid 133 E9
Tipton St John Devon .15 C7
Tiptree Essex 88 B5
Tiptree Heath Essex. .88 B5
Tirabad Powys 95 C7
Tiraghoil Argyll . . . 288 G5
Tircanol Swansea . . .57 B7
Tirdeunaw Swansea. .57 B7
Tirinie Perth 291 G10
Tirley Glos 98 F6
Tirley Knowle Glos. . .98 F6
Tiroran Argyll 288 G6
Tirphil Caerph 77 E10
Tirril Cumb 230 F2
Tirryside Highld . . 309 H5
Tir-y-berth Caerph . .77 F11
Tir-y-dail Carms . . .75 C10
Tisbury Wilts 30 B6
Tisman's Common
  W Sus 50 G5
Tissington Derbys. . 169 E11
Titchberry Devon . . .24 B2
Titchfield Hants 33 F8
Titchfield Common
  Hants. 33 F8
Titchmarsh
  N Nhants 121 B10
Titchwell Norf . . . 176 E3
Titcomb W Berks. . .63 F11
Tithby Notts 154 B3
Tithebarn Staffs . . 169 G9
Tithe Barn Hillock
  Mers 183 B9
Titley Hereford 114 E6
Titlington Northumb. 264 F4
Titmore Green
  Herts 104 F4
Titsey Sur 52 C2
Titson Corn 24 G2
Tittenhurst Windsor. .66 F3
Tittensor Staffs . . . 151 B7
Titterhill Shrops . . 131 G10
Tittle Row Windsor. .65 C11
Tittleshall Norf . . . 159 E7
Titton Worcs 116 D6
Titty Hill W Sus 34 B5
Tiverton Ches W . . 167 C9
  Devon 27 E7
Tivetshall St Margaret
  Norf. 142 F3
Tivetshall St Mary
  Norf. 142 F3
Tividale W Mid . . . 133 E9
Tivington Som 42 D2
Tivington Knowle
  Som 42 E2
Tivoli Cumb. 228 G5
Tivy Dale S Yorks . . 197 F9
Tixall Staffs 151 E9
Tixover Rutland . . . 137 C9
Toab Orkney 314 F5
  Shetland 313 M5
Toadmoor Derbys. . 170 E4
Toad Row Suff . . . 143 F10
Tobermory Argyll . . 289 D7
Toberonochy Argyll . 275 C8
Tobha Beag
  W Isles 296 D5
Tobha Mor W Isles. . 297 H3
Tobhtarol W Isles . . 304 E3
Tobson W Isles . . . 304 E3
Toby's Hill Lincs . . 191 C7
Tocher Aberds . . . 302 F6
Tockenham Wilts. . .62 D4
Tockenham Wick
  Wilts 62 C4
Tockholes Blackburn. 195 C7
Todd's Green Herts . 104 F4
Tockwith N Yorks . . 206 C5
Todber Dorset 30 C4
Todding Hereford . . .115 B8
Toddington
  C Beds 103 F10
  Glos. 99 E10
Toddlehills Aberds. . 303 E10
Todenham Glos. . . 100 D4
Todhills Cumb . . . 239 E10
  Angus 287 D8
Todlachie Aberds . . 293 B8
Todmorden
  W Yorks 196 C2
Todpool Corn 4 G4
Todrig Borders . . . 261 D11
Todwick S Yorks . . 187 E7
Toft Cambs 123 F7
  Lincs 155 F11
  Shetland 312 F6

Toft continued
  Warks 119 C9
Toft Hill Durham . . 233 F9
  Lincs 174 C2
Toft Monks Norf . . 143 E8
Toft next Newton
  Lincs 189 D8
Toftrees Norf 159 D7
Tofts Highld 310 C7
Toftshaw W Yorks . . 197 B7
Toftwood Norf. . . . 159 G9
Togston Northumb. . 252 C6
Tokavaig Highld. . . 295 D8
Tokers Green Oxon. . .65 D8
Tokyngton London . .67 C7
Tolastadh a Chaolais
  W Isles 304 E3
Tolastadh bho Thuath
  W Isles 304 D7
Tolborough Corn . . .11 F9
Tolcarne Corn 2 B5
  Corn 2 C5
Tolcarne Wartha Corn .2 B5
Toldish Corn. 5 D8
Tolgus Mount Corn . .4 G3
Tolhurst E Sus 53 G7
Tolladine Worcs . . .117 F7
Tolland Som 42 G6
Tollard Farnham
  Dorset 30 D6
Tollard Royal Wilts . .30 D6
Toll Bar Mers 183 C7
  Rutland 137 B10
  S Yorks 198 F5
Tollbar End W Mid . 119 B7
Toll End W Mid . . . 133 E9
Tollerford Dorset . . .17 B7
Toller Fratrum
  Dorset 17 B7
Toller Porcorum
  Dorset 17 B7
Tollerton Notts . . . 154 C2
  N Yorks 215 G10
Toller Whelme
  Dorset 29 G8
Tollesbury Essex. . . .89 C7
Tollesby Mbro . . . 225 B10
Tolleshunt D'Arcy
  Essex. 88 C6
Tolleshunt Knights
  Essex. 88 C6
Tolleshunt Major
  Essex. 88 C5
Tollie Highld 300 D5
Toll of Birness
  Aberds. 303 F10
Tolm W Isles. 304 E6
Tolmers Herts 86 E4
Tolpuddle Dorset . . .17 C11
Tolskithy Corn 4 G3
Tolvaddon Downs
  Corn. 4 G3
Tolvah Highld . . . 291 D10
Tolworth London. . . .67 F7
Tomaknock Perth. . 286 E2
Tom an Fhuadain
  W Isles 305 G5
Tomatin Highld . . . 301 G8
Tombreck Highld . . 300 F6
Tombui Perth. . . . 286 B2
Tomchrasky Highld . 290 B4
Tomdoun Highld . . 290 C3
Tomich Highld. . . . 300 B6
  Highld 300 D5
Tomich House
  Highld 300 E5
Tomintoul Aberds. . 292 D3
  Moray 292 B3
Tomlow Warks . . . 119 E9
Tomnaven Moray . . 302 F4
Tomnavoulin Moray. 302 G2
Tomperrow Corn . . .4 G5
Tompkin Staffs . . . 168 E6
Tompset's Bank
  E Sus 52 G2
Tomsleibhe Argyll. . 289 F8
Tomthorn Derbys . . 185 F9
Ton Mon 78 F5
Ton Breigam V Glam. .58 D3
Tondu Bridgend . . .57 E11
Tone Som 27 C10
Tonedale Som 27 C10
Tone Green Som . . .27 C11
Tong Kent 53 D10
  Shrops 132 B5
  W Yorks 205 G9
Tonge Leics 153 E8
Tonge Corner Kent . .70 F2
Tonge Fold Gtr Man. 195 F8
Tong Moor
  Gtr Man 195 E8
Tong Forge Shrops. . 132 B5
Tong Green Kent . . .54 C3
Tongham Sur. 49 D11
Tongland Dumfries . 237 D8
Tong Norton Shrops. 132 B5
Tong Park W Yorks . 205 F9
Tong Street
  W Yorks 205 G9
Tongue Highld . . . 308 D5
Tongue End Lincs . . 156 F3
Tongwell M Keynes . 103 C7
Tongwynlais Cardiff. .58 C6
Tonmawr Neath . . .57 B10
Tonna = Tonnau Neath .57 B9
Tonnau = Tonna Neath 57 B9
Ton-Pentre Rhondda. .77 F7
Ton-teg Rhondda . . .58 B5
Tontine Lancs 194 G4
Tonwell Herts 86 B4
Tonypandy Rhondda. .77 G7
Tonyrefail Rhondda. .58 B4
Toot Baldon Oxon. . .83 E9

Toot Hill Essex 87 E8
  Staffs. 169 G8
Tooting Graveney
  London. 67 E9
Topcliffe N Yorks . . 215 D8
  W Yorks 197 B9
Topcroft Norf. . . . 142 E5
Topcroft Street
  Norf. 142 E5
Top End Bedford . . 121 E10
Top Green S Yorks . 172 F3
Topham S Yorks . . 198 D6
Topleigh W Sus 34 G6
Top Lock Gtr Man . . 194 F6
Top of Hebers
  Gtr Man 195 F11
Top o' th' Lane
  Lancs. 194 C5
Top o' th' Meadows
  Gtr Man 196 F3
Toppesfield Essex . . 106 D4
Toppings Gtr Man . . 195 E8
Toprow Norf. 142 D3
Topsham Devon . . .14 D5
Top Valley
  Nottingham . . . 171 F9
Torbeg N Ayrs . . . 255 E10
Torboll Farm Highld . 309 K7
Torbothie N Lanark . 269 D7
Torbreck Highld . . 309 J7
Torbrex Stirling . . . 278 C5
Torbryan Devon 8 B6
Torcastle Highld. . . 290 F3
Torcross Devon 8 G6
Torcroy Highld . . . 291 D9
Tore Highld 300 D6
Torfrey Corn. 6 E2
Torgyle Highld. . . . 290 B5
Torinturk Argyll. . . 275 G9
Torkington Gtr Man . 184 D6
Torksey Lincs. . . . 188 F4
Torlum W Isles . . . 296 F3
Torlundy Highld . . 290 F3
Tormarton S Glos . . .61 D9
Tormisdale Argyll . . 254 B2
Tormitchell S Ayrs . 244 E6
Tormore Highld . . . 295 C8
  N Ayrs 255 D9
Tornagrain Highld. . 301 E7
Tornahaish Aberds . 292 C4
Tornapress Aberds . 299 E8
Tornaveen Aberds . 293 C8
Torness Highld. . . . 300 G5
Toronto Durham . . 233 E9
Torpenhow Cumb. . 229 D10
Torphichen W Loth. . 279 G9
Torphin Edin 270 B4
Torphins Aberds . . 293 C8
Torpoint Corn 7 E8
Torquay Torbay 9 C8
Torquhan Borders. . 271 F11
Torr Devon 7 E11
Torra Argyll 254 B4
Torran Argyll 275 C9
  Highld 298 E5
  Highld 301 B7
Torrance E Dunb . . 278 G2
Torrans Argyll . . . 288 G6
Torre Som. 42 E4
  Torbay 9 C8
Torridon Highld. . . 299 D9
Torridon Ho Highld. 299 D8
Torries Aberds . . . 293 B8
Torrin Highld 295 C7
Torrisdale Highld . . 308 C6
Torrisdale Castle
  Argyll. 255 D8
Torrisdale-Square
  Argyll. 255 D8
Torrish Highld . . . 311 H3
Torrisholme Lancs . 211 G9
Torroble Highld . . . 309 J5
Torroy Highld . . . 309 K5
Torrpark Corn 11 D5
Torry Aberdeen . . 293 C11
Torryburn Fife. . . . 279 D10
Torsonce Borders . . 271 F11
Torsonce Mains
  Borders 271 G9
Torterston Aberds . 303 E10
Torthorwald
  Dumfries 238 B2
Tortington W Sus . . .35 F8
Torton Worcs 116 C6
Tortworth S Glos. . . .79 G11
Torvaig Highld . . . 298 E4
Torver Cumb. . . . 220 G5
Torwood Falk. . . . 278 E6
Torwoodlee Mains
  Borders 261 B11
Torworth Notts . . . 187 D11
Tosberry Devon 24 C3
Toscaig Highld. . . . 295 B9
Toseland Cambs . . 122 E4
Tosside N Yorks . . . 203 B11
Tostock Suff 125 E9
Totaig Highld 295 C10
  Highld 298 D2
Totardor Highld . . . 294 B5
Tote Highld 298 E4
Totegan Highld . . . 310 C2
Tote Hill Hants 32 C4
  W Sus 34 C5
Totford Hants 48 F5
Totham Hill Essex. . .88 C5
Totham Plains Essex. .88 C5
Tothill Lincs 190 E6
Totley S Yorks. . . . 186 F4
  Pembs 72 C4
Totley Brook
  S Yorks. 186 E4
Totley Rise S Yorks . 186 E4
Totmonslow Staffs. . 151 B9
Totnell Dorset 29 F10
Totnes Devon 8 C6
Totnor Hereford. . . .97 D11
Totronald Argyll . . 288 D3

Totscore Highld . . . 298 C3
Tottenham London . .86 G4
Tottenham Hale
  London. 67 B10
Tottenhill Norf . . . 158 G2
Tottenhill Row Norf. 158 G2
Totteridge Bucks. . . .84 E5
  London 86 G2
Totternhoe C Beds . 103 G9
Totteroak S Glos . . .61 C8
Totterton Shrops . . 131 F7
Totties W Yorks . . . 197 F7
Tottington Gtr Man . 195 E9
  Norf. 141 D7
Tottlebank Cumb . . 210 C6
Tottleworth Lancs . 203 G10
Totton Hants 32 E5
Touchen End
  Windsor. 65 D11
Toulston N Yorks . . 206 E5
Toulton Som 43 G7
Toulvaddie Highld. . .311 L2
Tournaig Highld. . . 307 L3
Toux Aberds 303 D9
Tovil Kent 53 C9
Towan Corn 10 G3
Towan Cross Corn . . .4 F4
Toward Argyll 266 B2
Towcester
  W Nhants 102 B3
Towednack Corn 1 B5
Towerage Bucks . . .84 G4
Tower End Norf . . . 158 F3
Tower Hamlets Kent. 55 E10
Towerhead N Som. . .44 B2
Tower Hill Ches E . . 184 F6
  Devon 12 C3
  Essex 108 E5
  Herts 85 E8
  Mers 194 G2
  Sur. 51 D7
  W Mid 133 E11
  W Sus 35 B11
Towersey Oxon. . . .84 D2
Tow House
  Northumb 241 E7
Towie Aberds 292 B6
  Aberds 302 G5
Towiemore Moray . . 302 E3
Tow Law Durham. . 233 D8
Town Barton Devon. .14 C2
Townend Derbys . . 185 E9
  Staffs 151 B9
  W Dunb 277 F8
Town End Bucks . . .84 F3
  Cambs 139 D8
  Cumb 211 B7
  Cumb 211 B8
  Cumb 212 C2
  Cumb 220 D6
  Cumb 221 E8
  Cumb 221 F8
Townfield Durham . 232 B5
Town Fields
  Ches W 167 B10
Towngate Cumb . . 230 B6
  Lincs 156 G2
Town Green
  Gtr Man 183 B9
  Lancs 194 F2
  Norf. 161 G7
Town Head Cumb . . 220 D6
  Cumb 221 D6
  Cumb 222 C2
  Cumb 222 C3
  Cumb 231 E8
  Cumb 231 G9
  Derbys 185 F11
  N Yorks 204 B2
  N Yorks 212 F5
  Staffs 169 F8
  W Yorks 204 D6
Townhead of Greenlaw
  Dumfries 237 C9
Townhill Fife 280 D2
  Swansea 56 C6
Townhill Park Hants . 33 E7
Town Kelloe
  Durham 234 D3
Townlake Devon. . . .12 G4
Townland Green
  Kent. 54 G2
Town Lane
  Gtr Man 183 B11
Town Littleworth
  E Sus 36 D6
Town of Lowton
  Mers 183 B10
Town Park Telford . 132 B3
Town Row E Sus . . .52 G5
Townsend Bath. . . .44 B5
  Bucks. 84 D2
  Devon 25 B10
  Herts 85 D10
  Oxon 64 B2
  Pembs 72 D4
  Som 44 B3
  Som 44 B4
Towns End Hants . . .48 B5
  Som 30 D2
Town's End Bucks . 102 G2
  Dorset 18 B3

Town's End continued
  Dorset 18 E5
  Dorset 29 F9
  Som 45 D7
Townsend Fold
  Lancs 195 C10
Townshend Corn 2 C3
Town Street Glos . . .98 F6
Townwell S Glos . . .79 G11
Town Yetholm
  Borders 263 D8
Towthorpe E Yorks . 217 G8
  York 207 B8
Towton N Yorks . . . 206 F5
Towyn Conwy . . . 181 G9
Toxteth Mers 182 D5
Toynton All Saints
  Lincs 174 C5
Toynton Fen Side
  Lincs 174 C5
Toynton St Peter
  Lincs 174 C6
Toy's Hill Kent 52 C3
Trabboch E Ayrs . . 257 E10
Traboe Corn 2 E6
Tracebridge Som . . .27 C9
Tradespark Highld . 301 D8
  Orkney 314 G4
Trafford Park
  Gtr Man 184 B3
Traigh Ho Highld . . 295 F8
Trallong Powys 95 F9
Trallwn Rhondda . . .77 G8
  Swansea 57 B7
Tramagenna Corn . . .11 E7
Tram Inn Hereford. . .97 E9
Tranch Torf 78 E3
Tranent E Loth . . . 281 G8
Tranmere Mers. . . . 182 D4
Trantlebeg Highld. . 310 D2
Trantlemore Highld . 310 D2
Tranwell Northumb. 252 G5
Trapp Carms. 75 B11
Traprain E Loth . . . 281 F11
Trap's Green Warks . 118 D2
Trapshill W Berks . . .63 G11
Traquair Borders . . 261 C8
Trash Green W Berks. .65 F7
Travellers' Rest
  Carms 74 B5
Trawden Lancs . . . 204 F4
Trawscoed Powys . . .95 E11
Trawsfynydd Gwyn. . 146 B4
Trawsnant Ceredig . 111 D11
Treadam Mon 78 B5
Treaddow Hereford . .97 G10
Treal Corn 2 F6
Trealaw Rhondda. . . .77 G8
Treales Lancs 202 G4
Trearddur Anglesey . 178 F3
Treaslane Highld . . 298 D3
Treath Corn 3 D7
Treator Corn 10 F4
Tre-Aubrey V Glam. . .58 E4
Trebanog Rhondda. . .77 G8
Trebanos Neath. . . .76 E2
Trebarber Corn 5 C7
Trebartha Corn 11 F11
Trebarwith Corn . . .11 D7
Trebarwith Strand
  Corn. 10 D6
Trebeath Corn. 11 D11
Tre-Beferad V Glam. .58 F3
Trebell Green Corn . . .5 C11
Treberfydd Powys . .96 F2
Trebetherick Corn . .10 F4
Trebilcock Corn 5 C9
Treborough Som . . .42 F4
Trebudannon Corn . . .5 C7
Trebullett Corn 12 F2
Treburgett Corn 11 F7
Treburgie Corn 6 C4
Treburley Corn 12 F3
Treburrick Corn 10 G3
Trebyan Corn 5 C11
Trecastle Powys . . .95 F7
Trecenydd Caerph . . .58 B6
Trecott Devon 25 G10
Trecwn Pembs 91 E9
Trecynon Rhondda . .77 E7
Tredannick Corn . . .10 G6
Tredaule Corn 11 E10
Tredavoe Corn 1 D5
Treddiog Pembs . . .91 F7
Tredegar Bl Gwent . .77 D10
Trederwen Powys. . 148 F4
Tre-derwen Powys. . 148 F4
Tredethy Corn 11 G7
Tredington Glos . . .99 F8
  Warks 100 C5
Tredinnick Corn 5 D9
  Corn 6 B3
  Corn 6 D4
  Corn 10 G4
  Corn 10 G6
Tredizzick Corn . . .10 F5
Tredogan V Glam. . . .58 F5
Tredomen Caerph. . . .77 G10
Tredomen Powys . . .96 E2
Tredrissi Pembs 91 D10
Tredunnock Mon . . .78 G5
Tredustan Powys . . .96 E2
Tredworth Glos. . . .80 B4
Treen Corn 1 B4
  Corn 1 E3
Treesmill Corn. 5 D11
Treeton S Yorks . . . 186 D6
Trefanny Hill Corn . . .6 D4
Trefasser Pembs . . .91 D7
Trefdraeth Anglesey. 178 G6
Trefdraeth = Newport
  Pembs. 91 D11
Trefecca Powys 96 E2
Trefechan Ceredig. . .111 A11
Trefechan M Tydf . . .77 F10
Trefeglwys Powys . . 129 D11
Trefeitha Powys 96 E2

Trefenter Ceredig . .112 D2
Treffgarne Pembs . . .91 G9
Treffynnon Pembs . .90 F6
Treffynnon = Holywell
  Flint 181 F11
Trefgarn Owen
  Pembs. 91 F7
Trefil Bl Gwent 77 C10
Trefilan Ceredig. . . .111 F11
Trefin = Trevine
  Pembs 90 E6
Treflach Shrops . . . 148 E5
Trefnant Powys . . . 148 F4
Trefnant Denb . . . 181 G9
Trefonen Shrops . . 148 D5
Trefor Anglesey . . . 178 E5
  Gwyn. 162 F5
Treforda Corn 11 E7
Treforest Rhondda . .58 B5
Treforgan Neath . . .76 D3
Tre-Forgan Neath. . .76 D3
Treforys = Morriston
  Swansea 57 B7
Trefriw Conwy . . . 164 C3
Trefrize Corn 12 F2
Tref y Clawdd = Knighton
  Powys. 114 C5
Trefynwy = Monmouth
  Mon 79 C8
Tregada Corn. 12 E2
Tregadgwith Corn . . .1 E4
Tregadillett Corn . . .12 E2
Tre-gagle Mon 79 D8
Tregaian Anglesey . . 178 F6
Tregajorran Corn 4 G3
Tregamere Corn 5 C8
Tregardock Corn . . .10 E6
Tregarland Corn 6 D5
Tregarlandbridge
  Corn. 6 D4
Tregarne Corn 3 E7
Tregaron Ceredig . . 112 F3
Tregarrick Mill Corn . .6 C4
Tregarth Gwyn . . . 163 B10
Tregaswith Corn 5 C8
Tregatillian Corn 5 C8
Tregavarah Corn 1 D4
Tregear Corn 5 D7
Tregeare Corn 11 E10
Tregeiriog Wrex. . . 148 C3
Tregele Anglesey. . . 178 C5
Tregellist Corn 10 F6
Tregeseal Ceredig. . . .1 C3
Tregew Corn 3 B8
Tre-Gibbon Rhondda. .77 E7
Tregidden Corn 3 E7
Treginnis Pembs. . . .90 G4
Treglemais Pembs . .90 F6
Tregole Corn 11 B9
Tregolls Corn 2 B6
Tregolwyn = Colwinston
  V Glam. 58 D2
Tregona Corn. 5 B7
Tregonce Corn 10 G4
Tregonetha Corn 5 C8
Tregonning Corn 5 D7
Tregony Corn 5 G8
Tregoodwell Corn . . .11 E8
Tregorden Corn 10 G6
Tregorrick Corn 5 E9
Tregoss Corn 5 C9
Tregoyd Powys 96 D4
Tregoyd Mill Powys . .96 D3
Tregreenwell Corn . .11 F7
Tregrehan Mills Corn. .5 E10
Tregroes Ceredig . . .93 C8
Tregullon Corn 5 C11
Tregunna Corn 10 G5
Tregurrian Corn 5 B7
Tregurtha Downs Corn. 2 C2
Tre Gwyr = Gowerton
  Swansea 56 B5
Tregyddulan Pembs . .91 D7
Tre-gynwr Carms . . .74 B6
Trehafod Rhondda. . .77 G8
Treharris Pembs. . . 129 G11
Trehan Corn. 7 D8
Treharris M Tydf. . . .77 F9
Trehemborne Corn . .10 G3
Treherbert Rhondda. .76 F6
Tre-hill V Glam. 58 E5
Trehunist Corn 6 C6
Tre-Ifor Rhondda. . . .77 D7
Trekeivesteps Corn . .11 G10
Trekenner Corn 12 F2
Trekenning Corn 5 C8
Treknow Corn 11 D7
Trelales = Laleston
  Bridgend 57 F11
Trelan Corn 3 F7
Tre-lan Flint 165 B11
Trelash Corn 11 C9
Trelassick Corn 5 E7
Trelawnyd Flint . . . 181 F9
Trelech Carms 92 D4
Treleddyd-fawr
  Pembs 90 F5
Treleigh Corn 4 G4
Treletert = Letterston
  Pembs. 91 F8
Trelewis M Tydf 77 F10
Treliga Corn 11 E7
Trelights Corn 10 F5
Trelill Corn 10 F6
Trelion Corn 5 E8
Trelissick Corn 3 B8
Treliver Corn. 5 B8
Trellech Mon 79 D8
Trelleck Grange Mon . 79 E7
Trelogan Flint 181 E10
Treloquithack Corn . . .2 D5
Trelowia Corn 6 D5
Trelowth Corn 5 E9
Trelystan Powys . . . 130 C5
Tremadog Gwyn . . . 163 G9
Tremail Corn 11 D9

Tremain Ceredig 92 B4
Tremaine Corn 11 D10
Tremains Bridgend 58 D2
Tremar Corn 6 B5
Trematon Corn 7 D7
Trematon Castle Corn 7 D8
Tremayne Corn 2 B4
Trembraze Corn 6 B5
Tremedda Corn 1 B5
Tremeirchion Denb 181 G9
Tremethick Cross
Corn 1 C4
Tremore Corn 5 C10
Tremorebridge Corn 5 C10
Tremorfa Cardiff 59 D8
Tre-Mostyn Flint 181 F10
Trenance Corn 4 C6
Corn 5 B7
Corn 5 C9
Corn 10 G4
Trenant Corn 6 B4
Corn 10 G5
Trenarren Corn 5 F10
Trenay Corn 6 B3
Trench Telford 150 G3
Trench Green Oxon 65 D7
Trench Wood Kent 52 D5
Trencreek Corn 4 C6
Trencrom Corn 2 B2
Trendeal Corn 5 E7
Trenear Corn 2 C5
Treneglos Corn 11 D10
Trenerth Corn 2 B4
Trenewan Corn 6 E3
Trengune Corn 11 C9
Trenhorne Corn 11 F11
Treningle Corn 5 B10
Treninnick Corn 4 C6
Trenoon Corn 2 F6
Trenoweth Corn 3 C7
Trent Dorset 29 D9
Trentham Stoke 168 G5
Trentishoe Devon 40 D6
Trentlock Derbys 153 C9
Trent Vale Stoke 168 G5
Trenwheal Corn 2 C4
Treoes V Glam 58 D2
Treopert = *Granston*
Pembs 91 E7
Treorchy = *Treorci*
Rhondda 77 F7
Treorci = *Treorchy*
Rhondda 77 F7
Treowen Caerph 78 F2
Powys 130 E2
Tre-pit V Glam 58 E2
Trequite Corn 10 F6
Tre'r-ddôl Ceredig 128 E3
Trerhyngyll V Glam 58 D4
Trerise Corn 2 F6
Trer Ilai = *Leighton*
Powys 130 B4
Trerose Corn 3 D7
Trerulefoot Corn 6 D6
Tresaith Ceredig 110 G5
Tresamble Corn 3 B7
Tresarrett Corn 11 G7
Tresavean Corn 2 B6
Tresawle Corn 5 F7
Tresawsen Corn 4 F5
Trescoll Corn 5 C10
Trescott Staffs 132 D6
Trescowe Corn 2 C3
Tresean Corn 4 D5
Tresevern Croft Corn 2 B6
Tresham Glos 80 G3
Tresigin = *Sigingstone*
V Glam 58 E3
Tresillian Corn 5 F7
Tresimwn = *Bonvilston*
V Glam 58 E5
Tresinney Corn 11 E8
Tresinwen Pembs 91 C7
Treskerby Corn 4 G4
Treskillard Corn 2 B5
Treskilling Corn 5 D10
Treskinnick Cross
Corn 11 B10
Treslothan Corn 2 B5
Tresmeer Corn 11 D10
Tresowes Green Corn 2 D3
Tresoweshill Corn 2 D4
Tresparrett Corn 11 C8
Tresparrett Posts
Corn 11 C8
Tressady Highld 309 J7
Tressait Perth 291 G10
Tresta Shetland 312 D8
Shetland 313 H5
Treswell Notts 188 F3
Treswithian Corn 4 G2
Treswithian Downs
Corn 4 G2
Tre-Taliesin Ceredig 128 E3
Trethellan Water Corn 2 B6
Trethevy Corn 11 D7
Trethewell Corn 3 B9
Trethewey Corn 1 E3
Trethillick Corn 10 F4
Trethomas Caerph 59 B7
Trethosa Corn 5 E8
Trethowel Corn 5 E10
Trethurgy Corn 5 D10
Tretio Pembs 90 F5
Tretire Hereford 97 G10
Tretower Powys 96 G3
Treuddyn Flint 166 D3
Trevadlock Corn 11 F11
Trevail Corn 4 D5
Trevalga Corn 11 D7
Trevalgan Corn 1 A5
Trevalyn Wrex 166 D5
Trevance Corn 10 G4
Trevanger Corn 10 F5
Trevanson Corn 10 G5
Trevarrack Corn 1 C5
Trevarren Corn 5 C8
Trevarrian Corn 4 B6
Trevarrick Corn 5 G9
Trevarth Corn 4 G4
Trevaughan Carms 73 B11
Carms 93 G7
Tre-vaughan Carms 93 G8
Treveal Corn 1 A5
Trevegean Corn 1 D3
Treveighan Corn 11 F7
Trevellas Corn 4 E4
Trevelmond Corn 6 C4
Trevelver Corn 10 G5
Trevemper Corn 4 D6
Treven Corn 11 D7
Trevena Corn 2 D4
Trevenen Corn 2 D5
Trevenen Bal Corn 2 D5
Trevenning Corn 11 F7
Treveor Corn 5 G9
Treverbyn Corn 5 D10
Corn 6 B4
Treverva Corn 3 C7
Trevescan Corn 1 E3
Trevethin Torf 78 E3
Trevia Corn 11 E7
Trevigro Corn 6 B6
Trevilder Corn 10 G6
Trevilla Corn 3 B8
Trevilson Corn 4 D6
Trevine Corn 10 F5
Trevine = *Trefin*
Pembs 90 E6
Treviscoe Corn 5 D8
Treviskey Corn 2 B6
Trevithal Corn 1 D5
Trevoll Corn 4 D6
Trevone Corn 10 F3
Trevor Wrex 166 G3
Trevorrick Corn 10 G4
Trevor Uchaf Denb 166 G2
Trevowah Corn 4 D5
Trevowhan Corn 1 B4
Trew Corn 2 D4
Trewalder Corn 11 E7
Trewarmett Corn 11 D7
Trewartha Corn 2 B2
Corn 3 B10
Trewassa Corn 11 D8
Treween Corn 11 E10
Trewellard Corn 1 C3
Trewen Corn 11 E7
Corn 11 E11
Mon 79 G7
Trewennack Corn 2 D5
Trewennan Corn 11 E7
Trewern Powys 148 G5
Trewetha Corn 10 E6
Trewethen Corn 10 F6
Trewethern Corn 10 F6
Trewey Corn 1 B5
Trewidland Corn 6 D5
Trewindle Corn 6 C2
Trewint Corn 6 C5
Corn 11 B9
Corn 11 E10
Trewithian Corn 3 B9
Trewithick Corn 11 D11
Trewollock Corn 5 G10
Trewoodloe Corn 12 G2
Trewoofe Corn 1 D4
Trewoon Corn 2 F5
Corn 5 E9
Treworga Corn 5 G7
Treworgan Common
Mon 78 D6
Treworlas Corn 3 B9
Treworld Corn 11 C8
Treworman Corn 10 G5
Treworrick Corn 6 B4
Treworthal Corn 3 B9
Trewyddel = *Moylgrove*
Pembs 92 C2
Trewyn Devon 24 G4
Tre-wyn Mon 96 G6
Treyarnon Corn 10 G3
Treyford W Sus 34 D4
Trezaise Corn 5 D9
Trezelah Corn 1 C5
Triangle Glos 79 E8
Staffs 133 B11
W Yorks 196 C4
Trickett's Cross
Dorset 31 G9
Triffleton Pembs 91 G9
Trillacott Corn 11 D11
Trimdon Durham 234 E3
Trimdon Colliery
Durham 234 D3
Trimdon Grange
Durham 234 D3
Trimingham Norf 160 B5
Trimley Lower Street
Suff 108 D5
Trimley St Martin
Suff 108 D5
Trimley St Mary
Suff 108 D5
Trimpley Worcs 116 B5
Trimsaran Carms 75 E7
Trims Green Herts 87 B7
Trimstone Devon 40 E3
Trinafour Perth 291 G9
Trinant Caerph 78 E2
Tring Herts 84 C6
Tringford Herts 84 C6
Tring Wharf Herts 84 C6
Trinity Angus 293 G8
Devon 27 F7
Edin 280 F4
Trinity Fields Staffs 151 D8
Trisant Ceredig 112 B4
Triscombe Som 43 F7
Trislaig Highld 290 F2
Trispen Corn 4 E6
Tritlington Northumb 252 E6
Troan Corn 5 D7
Trochry Perth 286 C3
Trodigal Argyll 255 E7
Troedrhiwgwair
Bl Gwent 77 D11
Troedrhiwdalar
Powys 113 G9
Troedrhiwffenyd
Ceredig 93 C8
Troedrhiwfuwch
Caerph 77 E10
Troedyraur Ceredig 92 B6
Troedyrhiw M Tydf 77 E9
Trofarth Conwy 180 G5
Trolliloes E Sus 23 C10
Tromode IoM 192 E4
Trondavoe Shetland 312 F5
Troon Corn 2 B5
S Ayrs 257 C8
Trooper's Inn Pembs 73 C7
Trosaraidh W Isles 297 K3
Trossachs Hotel
Stirling 285 G9
Troston Suff 125 C7
Trostre Carms 56 B4
Trostrey Common
Mon 78 E5
Troswell Corn 11 C11
Trotshill Worcs 117 F7
Trotten Marsh W Sus 34 B4
Trottiscliffe Kent 68 G6
Trotton W Sus 34 C4
Trough Gate Lancs 195 C11
Troutbeck Cumb 221 E8
Cumb 230 F3
Troutbeck Bridge
Cumb 221 F8
Troway Derbys 186 F5
Trowbridge Cardiff 59 C8
Wilts 45 B11
Trowell Notts 153 B9
Trow Green Glos 79 D9
Trowle Common
Wilts 45 B10
Trowley Bottom
Herts 85 C9
Trows Borders 262 C5
Trowse Newton
Norf 142 B4
Troydale W Yorks 205 G10
Troy Town Kent 52 D2
Kent 54 E5
Medway 69 F8
Truas Corn 11 D7
Trub Gtr Man 195 F11
Trudoxhill Som 45 E8
Trueman's Heath
Worcs 117 B11
True Street Devon 8 C6
Trull Som 28 C2
Trumaisgearraidh
W Isles 296 D4
Trumfleet S Yorks 198 E6
Trumpan Highld 298 C2
Trumpet Hereford 98 D3
Trumpington Cambs 123 F8
Trumpsgreen Sur 66 F3
Trunch Norf 160 C5
Trunnah Lancs 202 E2
Truro Corn 4 G6
Truscott Corn 12 D2
Trusham Devon 14 E3
Trusley Derbys 152 B5
Trussall Corn 2 D5
Trussell Corn 11 D10
Trusthorpe Lincs 191 E8
Truthan Corn 4 E6
Truthwall Corn 2 C2
Trwstllewelyn
Powys 130 D3
Tryfil Anglesey 178 E6
Trysull Staffs 133 E7
Trythogga Corn 1 C5
Tubbs Mill Corn 5 G9
Tubney Oxon 82 F6
Tubslake Kent 53 G9
Tuckenhay Devon 8 D6
Tuckermarsh Devon 7 B8
Tuckerton Som 28 B3
Tuckhill Shrops 132 F5
Tuckingmill Corn 4 G3
Corn 11 F7
Wilts 30 B6
Tucking Mill Bath 61 G9
Tuckton BCP 19 C8
Tuddenham Suff 108 B3
Suff 124 C4
Tuddenham St Martin
Suff 108 B3
Tudeley Kent 52 D6
Tudeley Hale Kent 52 D6
Tudhay Devon 28 G4
Tudhoe Durham 233 D11
Tudhoe Grange
Durham 233 E11
Tudor Hill W Mid 134 D2
Tudorville Hereford 97 G11
Tudweiliog Gwyn 144 B4
Tuebrook Mers 182 C5
Tuesley Sur 50 E3
Tuesnoad Kent 54 E2
Tuffley Glos 80 C4
Tufnell Park London 67 B9
Tufton Hants 48 D3
Pembs 91 F10
Tugby Leics 136 C5
Tugford Shrops 131 F11
Tughall Northumb 264 D6
Tulchan Lodge
Angus 292 F3
Tullecombe W Sus 34 B4
Tullibardine Perth 286 F3
Tullibody Clack 279 B7
Tullich Argyll 284 F4
Highld 299 E9
Highld 300 G6
Tullich Muir Highld 301 B7
Tulliemet Perth 286 B3
Tulloch Aberds 303 F8
Highld 290 E5
Perth 286 E4
Tulloch Castle
Highld 300 C5
Tullochgorm
Argyll 275 D10
Tulloch-gribban
Highld 301 G9
Tullochroisk Perth 285 B11
Tullochvenus
Aberds 293 C7
Tulloes Angus 287 C9
Tullybannocher
Perth 285 E11
Tullybelton Perth 286 D4
Tullycross Stirling 277 D9
Tullyfergus Perth 286 C6
Tullymurdoch Perth 286 B5
Tullynessle Aberds 293 B7
Tulse Hill London 67 E10
Tumble = *Y Tymbl*
Carms 75 C8
Tumbler's Green
Essex 106 F6
Tumby Lincs 174 D2
Tumby Woodside
Lincs 174 D3
Tummel Bridge
Perth 285 B11
Tumpy Green Glos 80 E2
Tumpy Lakes
Hereford 97 B10
Tunbridge Hill
Medway 69 E10
Tunbridge Wells =
Royal Tunbridge Wells
Kent 52 F5
Tunga W Isles 304 E6
Tungate Norf 160 D5
Tunley Bath 45 B7
Glos 80 E6
Tunnel Hill Worcs 98 C6
Tunnel Pits N Lincs 199 G8
Tunshill Gtr Man 196 E2
Tunstall E Yorks 209 G12
Kent 69 G11
Lancs 212 E2
Norf 143 B8
N Yorks 224 F4
Staffs 150 D5
Stoke 168 E5
Suff 127 G7
T&W 243 G9
Tunstead Derbys 185 G10
Gtr Man 196 G4
Norf 160 E5
Tunworth Hants 49 D7
Tupsley Hereford 97 C10
Tupton Derbys 170 B5
Turbary Common
BCP 19 C7
Turfdown Corn 5 B11
Turf Hill Gtr Man 196 E2
Turfholm S Lanark 259 B8
Turfmoor Devon 28 G3
Shrops 149 F7
Turgis Green Hants 49 B7
Turin Angus 287 B9
Turkdean Glos 81 B10
Turkey Island Hants 33 E9
W Sus 34 D3
Turkey Tump
Hereford 97 F10
Tur Langton Leics 136 E4
Turleigh Wilts 61 G10
Turleygreen Shrops 132 F5
Turlin Moor BCP 18 C5
Turmer Hants 31 F10
Turn Lancs 195 D10
Turnalt Argyll 275 C9
Turnastone Hereford 97 D7
Turnberry S Ayrs 244 B6
Turnchapel Plym 7 E9
Turnditch Derbys 170 F3
Turner Green Lancs 203 G8
Turner's Green
E Sus 23 B10
E Sus 52 G6
Warks 118 D3
W Berks 64 F4
Turners Hill W Sus 51 F10
Turners Puddle
Dorset 18 C2
Turnerwood
S Yorks 187 E8
Turnford Herts 86 E5
Turnhouse Edin 280 G3
Turnhurst Stoke 168 E5
Turnstead Milton
Derbys 185 E8
Turnworth Dorset 30 F4
Turrerich Perth 286 D2
Turriff Aberds 303 D7
Tursdale Durham 234 D2
Turton Bottoms
Blackburn 195 D8
Turves Cambs 138 D6
Turves Green
W Mid 117 B10
Turvey Bedford 121 G8
Turville Bucks 84 G3
Turville Heath Bucks 84 G2
Turweston Bucks 102 D2
Tushielaw Borders 261 F8
Tutbury Staffs 152 D4
Tutnall Worcs 117 C9
Tutnalls Glos 79 E10
Tutshill Glos 79 G8
Tutt Hill Kent 54 D3
Tuttington Norf 160 D4
Tutts Clump W Berks 64 E5
Tutwell Corn 12 F3
Tuxford Notts 188 G2
Twatt Orkney 314 D2
Shetland 313 H5
Twechar E Dunb 278 F4
Tweedale Telford 132 C4
Tweeddaleburn
Borders 270 E5
Tweedmouth
Northumb 273 E9
Tweedsmuir
Borders 260 E3
Twelve Heads Corn 4 G5
Twelve Oaks E Sus 37 C11
Twelvewoods Corn 6 B4
Twemlow Green
Ches E 168 B3
Twenties Kent 71 F10
Twenty Lincs 156 E3
Twerton Bath 61 G8
Twickenham London 67 E7
Twigworth Glos 98 G6
Twineham W Sus 36 D3
Twineham Green
W Sus 36 C3
Twinhoe Bath 45 B8
Twinstead Essex 107 D7
Twinstead Green
Essex 106 D6
Twiss Green Warr 183 B11
Twist Devon 28 G3
Twiston Lancs 204 E2
Twitchen Devon 41 G9
Shrops 115 B7
Twitchen Mill Devon 41 G9
Twitham Kent 55 B9
Twitton Kent 52 B4
Two Bridges Devon 13 G8
Glos 79 D11
Two Burrows Corn 4 F4
Two Dales Derbys 170 C3
Two Gates Staffs 134 C4
Two Mile Ash
M Keynes 102 D6
W Sus 35 B10
Two Mile Hill Bristol 60 E6
Two Mile Oak Cross
Devon 8 B6
Two Mills Ches W 182 G5
Two Pots Devon 40 E4
Two Waters Herts 85 D9
Twr Anglesey 178 E2
Twycross Leics 134 C6
Twydall Medway 69 F9
Twyford Bucks 102 F3
Derbys 152 D6
Dorset 30 D5
Hants 33 C7
Leics 154 G4
Lincs 155 E8
Norf 159 E10
Oxon 101 D9
Shrops 148 D6
Wokingham 65 D9
Worcs 99 B10
Twyford Common
Hereford 97 D10
Twyn-Allws Mon 78 C3
Twynholm Dumfries 237 D8
Twyning Glos 99 D7
Twyning Green Glos 99 D8
Twynllanan Carms 94 G5
Twynmynydd Carms 75 C11
Twyn Shôn-Ifan
Caerph 77 G11
Twynyrodyn M Tydf 77 D9
Twyn-yr-odyn
V Glam 58 E6
Twyn-y-Sheriff Mon 78 D6
Twywell N Nhants 121 B9
Tyberton Hereford 97 D7
Tyburn W Mid 134 E2
Tyby Norf 159 D11
Ty-coch Swansea 56 C6
Tycroes Carms 75 C10
Tycrwyn Powys 148 F2
Tyddewi = *St Davids*
Pembs 90 F5
Tydd Gote Lincs 157 F9
Tydd St Giles Cambs 157 F8
Tydd St Mary Lincs 157 F8
Tyddyn Powys 129 F9
Tyddyn Angharad
Denb 165 F9
Tyddyn Dai Anglesey 178 C6
Tyddyn-mawr Gwyn 163 G9
Ty-draw Conwy 164 D5
Swansea 57 C7
Tye Hants 22 C2
Tye Common Essex 87 G11
Tyegate Green Norf 161 G7
Tye Green Essex 87 C10
Essex 87 D7
Essex 87 F11
Essex 105 D11
Essex 105 G10
Essex 106 G5
Tyersal W Yorks 205 G9
Ty-fry Mon 78 F6
Tyganol V Glam 58 E4
Ty-hen Carms 92 G6
Gwyn 144 C3
Ty-isaf Carms 56 B4
Tyla Mon 78 C2
Tylagwyn Bridgend 58 B2
Tyldesley Gtr Man 195 G7
Tyle Carms 94 F3
Tyle-garw Rhondda 58 C4
Tyler Hill Kent 70 G6
Tylers Causeway
Herts 86 D3
Tylers Green Bucks 84 G6
Tyler's Green Essex 87 D8
Sur 51 C11
Tyler's Hill Bucks 85 E7
Ty Llwyn Bl Gwent 77 D11
Tylorstown Rhondda 77 F8
Tylwch Powys 129 G9
Ty-mawr Anglesey 179 D7
Ty Mawr Carms 93 C10
Ty-mawr Conwy 181 F7
Ty Mawr Cwm
Conwy 164 F6
Tynant Rhondda 58 B5
Ty-nant Conwy 165 G7
Gwyn 147 D8
Tyncelyn Ceredig 112 E2
Tyndrum Stirling 285 D7
Tyne Dock T&W 243 D9
Tyneham Dorset 18 E3
Tynehead Midloth 271 D7
Tynemouth T&W 243 D9
Tyne Tunnel T&W 243 D8
Tynewydd Ceredig 92 B4
Neath 76 D4
Rhondda 76 F6
Ty-Newydd
Ceredig 111 D10
Tyning Bath 45 B7
Tyninghame E Loth 282 F2
Tyn-Ion Gwyn 163 D7
Tynron Dumfries 247 E8
Tyntesfield N Som 60 E4
Tyntetown Rhondda 77 F9
Ty'n-y-bryn Rhondda 58 B4
Tyn-y-celyn Wrex 148 B3
Tyn-y-coed Shrops 148 D4
Ty'n-y-coedcae
Caerph 59 B7
Tyn-y-cwm
Swansea 75 E10
Tynyfedw Conwy 165 B7
Tyn-y-fedwen
Powys 148 C2
Ty'n-y-ffordd Denb 181 G8
Tyn-y-ffridd Powys 148 C2
Ty'n-y-garn
Bridgend 57 E11
Tynygongl Anglesey 179 E8
Tynygraig Ceredig 112 D3
Tyn-y-graig Powys 113 G10
Ty'n-y-groes Conwy 180 G3
Ty'n-y-maes Gwyn 163 C10
Tyn-y-pwll Anglesey 178 D6
Ty'n-yr-eithin
Ceredig 112 E3
Tynyrwtra Powys 129 F7
Tyrells End C Beds 103 E9
Tyrell's Wood Sur 51 B7
Ty'r-felin-isaf
Conwy 164 C5
Ty Rhiw Rhondda 58 C6
Tyrie Aberds 303 C9
Tyringham
M Keynes 103 B7
Tyseley W Mid 134 G2
Ty-Sign Caerph 78 G2
Tythecott Devon 24 D6
Tythegston Bridgend 57 F11
Tytherington
Ches E 184 F6
S Glos 61 B7
Som 45 D9
Wilts 46 E2
Tytherleigh Devon 28 G4
Tytherton Lucas
Wilts 62 E2
Tyttenhanger Herts 85 D11
Ty-uchaf Powys 147 E10
Tywardreath Corn 5 E11
Tywardreath Highway
Corn 5 D11
Tywyn Conwy 180 F3
Gwyn 110 C2

U

Uachdar W Isles 296 F3
Uags Highld 295 B9
Ubberley Stoke 168 F6
Ubbeston Green
Suff 126 C6
Ubley Bath 44 B4
Uckerby N Yorks 224 E4
Uckfield E Sus 37 C7
Uckinghall Worcs 99 D7
Uckington Glos 99 G8
Shrops 131 B11
Uddingston
S Lanark 268 C3
Uddington S Lanark 259 C9
Udimore E Sus 38 D5
Udley N Som 60 G3
Udny Green Aberds 303 G8
Udny Station
Aberds 303 G9
Udston S Lanark 268 D3
Udstonhead
S Lanark 268 F4
Uffcott Wilts 62 D6
Uffculme Devon 27 E9
Uffington
Lincs 137 B11
Oxon 63 B10
Shrops 149 G10
Ufford Pboro 137 C11
Suff 126 G5
Ufton Warks 119 E7
Ufton Green W Berks 64 F6
Ufton Nervet
W Berks 64 F6
Ugadale Argyll 255 E8
Ugborough Devon 8 D3
Ugford Wilts 46 G5
Uggeshall Suff 143 G8
Ugglebarnby
N Yorks 227 D7
Ughill S Yorks 186 C3
Ugley Essex 105 F10
Ugley Green Essex 105 F10
Ugthorpe N Yorks 226 C5
Uidh W Isles 297 M2
Uig Argyll 276 E2
Argyll 288 D3
Highld 296 F7
Highld 298 C3
Uigen W Isles 304 E2
Uigshader Highld 298 E4
Uisken Argyll 274 B4
Ulaw Aberds 303 G9
Ulbster Highld 310 E7
Ulcat Row Cumb 230 G4
Ulceby Lincs 190 G6
N Lincs 200 E6
Ulceby Skitter
N Lincs 200 E6
Ulcombe Kent 53 D10
Uldale Cumb 229 D10
Uley Glos 80 F3
Ulgham Northumb 252 E6
Ullapool Highld 307 K6
Ullcombe Devon 28 F2
Ullenhall Warks 118 D2
Ullenwood Glos 80 B6
Ulleskelf N Yorks 206 E6
Ullesthorpe Leics 135 F10
Ulley S Yorks 187 D7
Ullingswick Hereford 97 B11
Ullington Worcs 100 B2
Ullinish Highld 294 B5
Ullock Cumb 229 G7
Cumb 229 G10
Ulnes Walton Lancs 194 D4
Ulpha Cumb 220 G3
Ulrome E Yorks 209 B9
Ulshaw N Yorks 214 B2
Ulsta Shetland 312 E6
Ulva House Argyll 288 F6
Ulverley Green
W Mid 134 G2
Ulverston Cumb 210 D5
Ulwell Dorset 18 E6
Umberleigh Devon 25 C10
Unapool Highld 306 F7
Unasary W Isles 297 J3
Under Bank
W Yorks 196 F6
Underbarrow Cumb 221 G9
Undercliffe
W Yorks 205 G9
Underdale Shrops 149 G10
Underdown Devon 14 D3
Underhill London 86 F3
Wilts 45 G11
Underhoull Shetland 312 C7
Underling Green
Kent 53 D9
Underriver Kent 52 C5
Underriver Ho Kent 52 C5
Under the Wood Kent 71 F8
Under Tofts S Yorks 186 D4
Underton Shrops 132 E3
Underwood Newport 59 B11
Notts 171 E7
Pembs 73 C7
Plym 7 D10
Undley Suff 140 G3
Undy Mon 60 B2
Ungisiadar W Isles 304 F3
Unifirth Shetland 313 H4
Union Cottage
Aberds 293 D10
Union Mills IoM 192 E4
Union Street E Sus 53 G8
United Downs Corn 4 G4
Unstone Derbys 186 F5
Unstone Green
Derbys 186 F5
Unsworth Gtr Man 195 F10
Unthank Cumb 230 B3
Cumb 230 D5
Cumb 231 C8
Derbys 186 F4
Unthank End Cumb 230 D5
Upavon Wilts 46 C6
Up Cerne Dorset 29 G11
Upchurch Kent 69 F10
Upcott Devon 24 D2
Devon 25 F9
Devon 25 F11
Devon 40 F3
Hereford 114 G6
Som 27 C11
Upend Cambs 124 F3
Up End M Keynes 103 B8
Up Exe Devon 26 G6
Upgate Norf 160 F2
Upgate Street Norf 141 E11
Norf 142 E5
Up Green Hants 65 G9
Uphall Dorset 29 G9
W Loth 279 G11
Uphall Station
W Loth 279 G11
Upham Devon 26 F5
Hants 33 C8
Uphampton
Hereford 115 E7
Worcs 116 E6
Up Hatherley Glos 99 G8
Uphempston Devon 8 C6
Uphill N Som 43 B10
Uphill Manor N Som 43 B10
Up Holland Lancs 194 F4
Uplands Glos 80 D5
Swansea 56 C6
Uplawmoor E Renf 267 D8
Upleadon Glos 98 F5
Upleadon Court Glos 98 F5
Upleatham Redcar 226 B2
Uplees Kent 70 G3
Uploders Dorset 16 C6
Uplowman Devon 27 D8
Uplyme Devon 16 C2
Up Marden W Sus 34 E3
Upminster London 68 B5
Up Mudford Som 29 D9
Up Nately Hants 49 C7
Upnor Medway 69 E9
Upottery Devon 28 F2
Upacott Devon 25 B9
Uppat Highld 311 J2
Uppend Essex 105 F9
Upper Affcot Shrops 131 F8
Upper Ardchronie
Highld 309 L6
Upper Ardgrain
Aberds 303 F9
Upper Ardroscadale
Argyll 275 G11
Upper Arley Worcs 132 G5
Upper Armley
W Yorks 205 G11
Upper Arncott Oxon 83 B10
Upper Astley
Shrops 149 F10
Upper Aston Shrops 132 E6
Upper Astrop
W Nhants 101 D10
Upper Badcall
Highld 306 E6
Upper Bangor Gwyn 179 G9
Upper Basildon
W Berks 64 D5
Upper Batley
W Yorks 197 B8
Upper Battlefield
Shrops 149 F10
Upper Beeding
W Sus 35 E11
Upper Benefield
N Nhants 137 F9
Upper Bentley
Worcs 117 D9
Upper Bighouse
Highld 310 D2
Upper Birchwood
Derbys 170 E6
Upper Blainslie
Borders 271 G10
Upper Boat
Rhondda 58 B6
Upper Boddam
Aberds 302 F6
Upper Boddington
W Nhants 119 G9
Upper Bogrow
Highld 309 L7
Upper Bogside
Moray 302 D2
Upper Bonchurch
IoW 21 F7
Upper Booth
Derbys 185 D10
Upper Borth Ceredig 128 F2
Upper Boyndlie
Aberds 303 C9
Upper Brailes
Warks 100 D6
Upper Brandon Parva
Norf 141 B10
Upper Breakish
Highld 295 C8
Upper Breinton
Hereford 97 C9
Upper Broadheath
Worcs 116 F6
Upper Brockholes
W Yorks 196 B5
Upper Broughton
Notts 154 D3
Upper Broxwood
Hereford 115 G7
Upper Bruntingthorpe
Leics 136 F2
Upper Brynamman
Carms 76 C2
Upper Buckenhill
Hereford 97 E11
Upper Bucklebury
W Berks 64 F4
Upper Bullington
Hants 48 E3
Upper Burgate
Hants 31 D11
Upper Burnhaugh
Aberds 293 D10
Upper Bush Medway 69 F7
Upperby Cumb 239 G10
Upper Caldecote
C Beds 104 B3
Upper Cam Glos 80 F3
Upper Canada
N Som 43 B11
Upper Canterton
Hants 32 E3
Upper Catesby
W Nhants 119 F10
Upper Catshill
Worcs 117 C9
Upper Chapel
Powys 95 C10
Upper Cheddon Som 28 B2
Upper Chicksgrove
Wilts 31 B7
Upper Church Village
Rhondda 58 B5
Upper Chute Wilts 47 C9
Upper Clapton
London 67 B10
Upper Clatford
Hants 47 E11
Upper Coberley Glos 81 B7
Upper College
Shrops 149 C11
Upper Colwall
Hereford 98 C5
Upper Common
Hants 48 D6
Upper Cotburn
Aberds 303 D7
Upper Cotton Staffs 169 F9
Upper Coullie
Aberds 293 B9
Upper Cound
Shrops 131 C11
Upper Coxley Som 44 E4
Upper Cudworth
S Yorks 197 F11
Upper Culphin
Aberds 302 D6
Upper Cumberworth
W Yorks 197 F8
Upper Cwmbran Torf 78 F3
Upperdale Derbys 185 G11
Upper Dallachy
Moray 302 C3
Upper Deal Kent 55 C11
Upper Dean
Bedford 121 D10
Devon 8 C4
Upper Denby
W Yorks 197 D8
W Yorks 197 F8
Upper Denton Cumb 240 D4
Upper Derraid
Highld 301 F10
Upper Diabaig
Highld 299 C8
Upper Dicker E Sus 23 D9
Upper Dinchope
Shrops 131 G9
Upper Dormington
Hereford 97 D11
Upper Dounreay
Highld 310 C4
Upper Dovercourt
Essex 108 E4
Upper Dowdeswell
Glos 81 B8
Upper Druimfin
Argyll 289 D7
Upper Dunsforth
N Yorks 215 G8
Upper Dunsley Herts 84 C6
Upper Eashing Sur 50 E3
Upper Eastern Green
W Mid 134 G5
Upper Eathie Highld 301 C7

Upper Edmonton
London 86 G4
Upper Egleton
Hereford 98 C2
Upper Elkstone
Staffs 169 D9
Upper Ellastone
Staffs 169 G10
Upper Elmers End
London 67 F11
Upper End Derbys . .185 F9
Glos 81 C10
Glos 81 D8
Leics 154 G4
Upper Enham Hants .47 C10
Upper Farmcote
Shrops 132 E5
Upper Farringdon
Hants 49 F8
Upper Feorlig
Highld 298 D2
Upper Fivehead Som . .28 C4
Upper Forge Shrops . .132 F4
Upper Framilode
Glos 80 C3
Upper Froyle Hants . .49 E9
Upper Gambolds
Worcs 117 D9
Upper Gills Highld . .310 B7
Upper Glenfintaig
Highld 290 E4
Upper Godney Som . .44 E3
Upper Goldstone
Kent 71 G9
Upper Gornal
W Mid 133 E8
Upper Gravenhurst
C Beds 104 D2
Upper Green Essex .105 E8
Mon 78 B5
Suff 124 E4
W Berks 63 G11
W Yorks 197 B9
Upper Grove Common
Hereford 97 F11
Upper Guist Norf . .159 D10
Upper Hackney
Derbys 170 C3
Upper Hale Sur 49 D10
Upper Halistra
Highld 298 D2
Upper Halliford Sur . .66 F5
Upper Halling
Medway 69 G7
Upper Ham Worcs . . .99 D7
Upper Hambleton
Rutland 137 B8
Upper Hamnish
Hereford 115 F10
Upper Harbledown
Kent 54 B6
Upper Hardres Court
Kent 55 C7
Upper Hardwick
Hereford 115 F8
Upper Hartfield
E Sus 52 G3
Upper Hartshay
Derbys 170 E5
Upper Haselor
Worcs 99 C10
Upper Hatton Staffs .150 B6
Upper Haugh
S Yorks 186 B6
Upper Hawkhillock
Aberds 303 F10
Upper Hayesden
Kent 52 E5
Upper Hayton
Shrops 131 G10
Upper Heath
Shrops 131 F11
Upper Heaton
W Yorks 197 D7
Upper Hellesdon
Norf 160 G4
Upper Helmsley
N Yorks 207 B9
Upper Hengoed
Shrops 148 C5
Upper Hergest
Hereford 114 G5
Upper Heyford Oxon .101 F9
W Nhants 120 F11
Upper Hill Glos . . .79 F11
Hereford 115 G9
Upper Hindhope
Borders 251 B7
Upper Holloway
London 67 B9
Soton 32 E6
Upper Holton Suff .127 B8
Upper Hopton
W Yorks 197 D7
Upper Horsebridge
E Sus 23 C9
Upper Howsell Worcs .98 B5
Upper Hoyland
S Yorks 197 G11
Upper Hulme Staffs .169 C8
Upper Hyde IoW . . .21 E7
Upper Ifold Sur 50 G4
Upper Inglesham
Swindon 82 F2
Upper Inverbrough
Highld 301 F8
Upper Kergord
Shetland 313 H6
Upper Kidston
Borders 270 G4
Upper Kilcott Glos . .61 B9
Upper Killay Swansea .56 C5
Upper Killeyan
Argyll 254 C3
Upper Kinsham
Hereford 115 D7
Upper Knockando
Moray 301 E11
Upper Lambourn
W Berks 63 C10

Upper Landywood
Staffs 133 B9
Upper Langford
N Som 44 B3
Upper Langwith
Derbys 171 B8
Upper Layham
Suff 107 C10
Upper Leigh Staffs .151 B10
Upper Lenie Highld . .300 G5
Upper Littleton
N Som 60 G5
Upper Loads Derbys . .170 B4
Upper Lochton
Aberds 293 D8
Upper Lode Worcs . .99 E7
Upper Longdon
Staffs 151 G11
Upper Longwood
Shrops 132 B2
Upper Ludstone
Shrops 132 D6
Upper Lybster
Highld 310 F6
Upper Lydbrook
Glos 79 B10
Upper Lye Hereford . .97 C9
Upper Lyde Hereford .115 D7
Upper Maes-coed
Hereford 96 D6
Upper Marsh
W Yorks 204 F6
Upper Midhope
S Yorks 186 B2
Upper Midway
Derbys 152 E5
Upper Milland Gtr Man .196 F3
Upper Milovaig
Highld 297 G7
Upper Milton Oxon . .82 B3
Som 44 D4
Upper Minety Wilts . .81 G8
Upper Mitton Worcs .116 C6
Upper Moor Worcs . .99 B9
Upper Moor Side
W Yorks 205 G10
Upper Morton
S Glos 79 G11
Upper Nash
Pembs 73 E8
Upper Netchwood
Shrops 132 E2
Upper Newbold
Derbys 186 G5
Upper Nobut Staffs .151 B10
Upper North Dean
Bucks 84 F4
Upper Norwood
London 67 F10
W Sus 34 D6
Upper Obney Perth . .286 D4
Upper Ochrwyth
Caerph 59 B8
Upper Oddington
Glos 100 F4
Upper Ollach Highld. .295 B7
Upper Padley
Derbys 186 F2
Upper Pickwick
Wilts 61 E11
Upper Pollicott
Bucks 84 C2
Upper Poppleton
York 207 C7
Upper Port Highld. .301 G10
Upper Postern Kent . .52 D6
Upper Quinton
Warks 100 B3
Upper Race Torf . . .78 F3
Upper Ratley Hants . .32 C4
Upper Ridinghill
Aberds 303 D10
Upper Rissington
Glos 82 B2
Upper Rochford
Worcs 116 D2
Upper Rodmersham
Kent 70 G2
Upper Sandaig
Highld 295 D9
Upper Sanday
Orkney 314 F5
Upper Sapey
Hereford 116 E3
Upper Saxondale
Notts 154 B3
Upper Seagry Wilts . .62 C2
Upper Shelton
C Beds 103 C9
Upper Sheringham
Norf 177 E10
Upper Shirley
London 67 G11
Soton 32 E6
Upper Siddington
Glos 81 F8
Upper Skelmorlie
N Ayrs 266 B4
Upper Slackstead
Hants 32 B5
Upper Slaughter
Glos 100 G3
Upper Solva Pembs . .90 G5
Upper Soudley Glos . .79 C11
Uppersound
Shetland 313 J6
Upper Stanton Drew
Bath 60 G6
Upper Staploe
Bedford 122 F2
Upper Stoke Norf . .142 C5
W Mid 135 G7
Upper Stondon
C Beds 104 D2
Upper Stowe
W Nhants 120 F2
Upper Stratton
Swindon 63 B7
Upper Street Hants .31 D11
Norf 142 G3
Norf 160 B5
Norf 160 E6
Norf 160 F5

Upper Street continued
Norf 161 F7
Suff 108 E2
Suff 124 G5
Suff 126 G2
Upper Strensham
Worcs 99 D8
Upper Studley Wilts. .45 B10
Upper Sundon
C Beds 103 F10
Upper Swainswick
Bath 61 F9
Upper Swanmore
Hants 33 D9
Upper Swell Glos . . .100 F3
Upper Sydenham
London 67 E10
Upper Tankersley
S Yorks 186 B4
Upper Tean Staffs . .151 B10
Upperthong
W Yorks 196 F6
Upperthorpe Derbys .187 E7
N Lincs 199 G9
Upper Threapwood
Ches W 166 F6
Upper Thurnham
Lancs 202 C5
Upper Tillyrie Perth .286 G5
Upperton E Sus 23 E10
Oxon 83 G11
W Sus 35 C7
Upper Tooting
London 67 E9
Upper Tote Highld . .298 D5
Uppertown Derbys . .170 C4
Highld 300 F4
Highld 310 B7
Northumb 241 C9
Orkney 314 G4
Upper Town Derbys .170 D3
Derbys 170 E2
Durham 233 D7
Hereford 97 B11
N Som 60 F4
Suff 125 D8
Wilts 62 D3
W Yorks 204 G6
Upper Treverward
Shrops 114 B5
Upper Tysoe Warks . .100 C6
Upper Up Glos 81 F8
Upper Upham Wilts . .63 D8
Upper Upnor Medway .69 E9
Upper Vobster Som . .45 D8
Upper Walthamstow
London 67 B11
Upper Wardington
Oxon 101 B9
Upper Wardley
W Sus 34 B4
Upper Weald
M Keynes 102 D5
Upper Weedon
W Nhants 120 F1
Upper Welland
Worcs 98 C5
Upper Wellingham
E Sus 36 E4
Upper Welson
Hereford 114 G5
Upper Westholme
Som 44 E5
Upper Weston Bath . .61 F8
Upper Weybread
Suff 126 B4
Upper Whiston
S Yorks 187 D7
Upper Wick Glos. . . .80 F2
Worcs 116 G6
Upper Wield Hants . .48 F6
Upper Wigginton
Shrops 148 B6
Upper Winchendon
Bucks 84 C2
Upper Witton
W Mid 133 E11
Upper Wolvercote
Oxon 83 D7
Upper Wolverton
Worcs 117 G9
Upperwood Derbys . .170 D3
Upper Woodend
Aberds 293 B8
Upper Woodford
Wilts 46 F6
Upper Woolhampton
W Berks 64 F5
Upper Wootton
Hants 48 C5
Upper Wraxall Wilts .61 E10
Upper Wyche
Hereford 98 C5
Uppincott Devon . . .26 G5
Uppington Rutland . .137 D7
Dorset 31 F8
Shrops 132 B2
Upsall N Yorks . . .215 B9
Upshire Essex 86 E6
Up Somborne Hants .47 G11
Upstreet Kent 71 G8
Up Sydling Dorset. . .29 G10
Upthorpe Glos 80 E3
Suff 125 C9
Upton Bucks 84 C3
Cambs 122 B3
Ches W 166 B6
Corn 11 G11
Corn 24 G2
Cumb 230 D2
Devon 8 G4
Devon 27 G9
Dorset 17 E10
Dorset 18 C5
E Yorks 209 C8
Hants 32 D5
Hants 47 B11
IoW 21 C7
Leics 135 D7
Lincs 188 D5

Upton continued
London 68 C2
Mers 182 D3
Mers 183 D7
Norf 161 G7
Notts 172 D2
Notts 188 F2
Oxon 64 B4
Oxon 82 C2
Pboro 138 C2
Slough 66 D3
Som 27 B7
Som 29 B7
Warks 118 F2
Wilts 45 G11
W Nhants 120 E4
W Yorks 198 E3
Upton Bishop
Hereford 98 F2
Upton Cheyney
S Glos 61 F7
Upton Cressett
Shrops 132 E3
Upton Crews
Hereford 98 F2
Upton Cross Corn . .11 G11
Upton End C Beds . .104 E2
Upton Field Notts . .172 E2
Upton Green Norf. . .161 G7
Upton Grey Hants . .49 D7
Upton Heath
Ches W 166 B6
Upton Hellions
Devon 26 G4
Upton Lea Bucks . . .66 C3
Upton Lovell Wilts . .46 E2
Upton Magna
Shrops 149 G11
Upton Noble Som . .45 F8
Upton Park London . .68 C2
Upton Pyne Devon . .14 B4
Upton Rocks Halton .183 D8
Upton St Leonards
Glos 80 C5
Upton Scudamore
Wilts 45 D11
Upton Snodsbury
Worcs 117 G8
Upton upon Severn
Worcs 99 C7
Upton Warren
Worcs 117 D8
Upwaltham W Sus . .34 E6
Upware Cambs 123 C10
Upwell Norf 139 C9
Upwey Dorset. 17 E9
Upwick Green Herts .105 G9
Upwood Cambs 138 G5
Uradale Shetland . . .313 K6
Urafirth Shetland . . .312 F5
Uragaig Argyll 274 D4
Urchfont Wilts. 46 B4
Urdimarsh Hereford . .97 B10
Ure Shetland 312 F4
Ure Bank N Yorks. . .214 E6
Urgashay Som 29 C9
Urgha W Isles 305 J3
Urgha Beag
W Isles 305 H3
Urishay Common
Hereford 96 D6
Urlar Perth 286 C2
Urlay Nook Stockton. .225 C7
Urmston Gtr Man. . .184 C3
Urpeth Durham 242 G6
Urquhart Highld . . .300 D5
Moray 302 C2
Urra N Yorks 225 E11
Urray Highld 300 D5
Ushaw Moor
Durham 233 C10
Usk Mon. 78 E5
Usselby Lincs 189 C9
Usworth T&W 243 F8
Utkinton Ches W . . .167 B8
Utley W Yorks 204 E6
Utterby Lincs 190 C4
Uton Devon 14 B2
Uttoxeter Staffs. . . .151 C11
Uwchmynydd Gwyn . .144 D3
Uxbridge London . . .66 C5
Uxbridge Moor
London 66 C5
Uyea Shetland 312 D5
Uyeasound Shetland. .312 C7
Uzmaston Pembs 73 C7

V

Vachelich Pembs 90 F5
Vadlure Shetland . . .313 J4
Vagg Som 29 D8
Vaila Hall Shetland . .313 J4
Vaivoe Shetland 312 G7
Vale W Yorks 196 B2
Vale Down Devon . . .12 D6
Vale of Health
London 67 B9
Valeswood Shrops . .149 E7
Valley = Y Fali
Anglesey 178 F3
Valleyfield Dumfries .237 D8
Valley Park Hants . . .32 C6
Valley Truckle Corn . .11 E7
Valsgarth Shetland . .312 B8
Valtos Highld 298 C5
Van Caerph 59 B7
Vange Essex 69 B8
Vanlop Shetland. . . .313 M5
Varchoel Powys. 148 G4
Varfell Corn 2 C2
Varteg Torf 78 D3
Vassa Shetland 313 H6
Vastern Wilts 62 C5
Vatsetter Shetland . .312 E7
Vatten Highld 298 E2
Vaul Argyll 288 E2
Vauxhall London 67 D10
Mers 182 C4

Vauxhall continued
W Mid 133 F11
Vaynol Hall Gwyn . .163 B8
Vaynor M Tydf 77 C8
Veensgarth Shetland .313 J6
Velator Devon 40 F3
Veldo Hereford. 97 C11
Velindre Powys 96 D3
Vellanoweth Corn . . .2 C2
Vellow Som 42 F5
Velly Devon 24 C3
Veness Orkney 314 D5
Venn Devon 8 F4
Venngreen Devon . . .24 E5
Venn Green Devon . .24 E5
Vennington Shrops. . .130 B6
Venn Ottery Devon . .15 C7
Venn's Green
Hereford 97 B10
Venny Tedburn
Devon 14 B2
Venterdon Corn 12 G3
Vention Devon 40 E3
Ventnor IoW 21 F7
Venton Devon 7 D11
Ventongimps Corn . . .4 E5
Ventonleague Corn . . .2 B3
Venus Hill Herts 85 E8
Veraby Devon 26 B5
Vermentry Shetland . .313 H5
Vernham Bank
Hants 47 B10
Vernham Dean
Hants 47 B10
Vernham Row Hants .47 B10
Vernham Street
Hants 47 B11
Vernolds Common
Shrops 131 G9
Verwood Dorset 31 F9
Veryan Corn 3 B10
Veryan Green Corn. . .5 G8
Vicarage Devon 15 D7
Vicarscross Ches W . .166 B6
Vickerstown Cumb. . .210 F3
Victoria Corn 5 C9
S Yorks 197 F7
Victoria Dock Village
Hull 200 B6
Victoria Park Bucks . .84 C4
Victory Gardens
Renfs 267 B10
Vidlin Shetland 312 G6
Viewpark N Lanark. . .268 C4
Vigo W Mid 133 C10
Vigo Village Kent . . .68 G6
Vinegar Hill Mon. . . .60 B2
Vinehall Street
E Sus 38 C3
Vines Cross E Sus . .23 B9
Viney Hill Glos 79 D11
Vinney Green S Glos. . .61 D7
Virginia Water Sur . .66 F3
Virginstow Devon . . .12 C3
Viscar Corn 2 C6
Vobster Som 45 D8
Voe Shetland 312 E5
Shetland 313 G6
Vogue Corn 4 G4
Vole Som 43 D11
Vowchurch Hereford. .97 D7
Vowchurch Common
Hereford 97 D7
Voxmoor Som 27 D10
Voxter Shetland 312 F5
Voy Orkney 314 E2
Vron Gate Shrops . . .130 B6
Vulcan Village Mers .183 C9

W

Waberthwaite Cumb .220 G2
Wackerfield Durham .233 G9
Wacton Hereford. . . .116 F2
Norf 142 E3
Wacton Common
Norf 142 F3
Wadbister Shetland . .313 J6
Wadborough Worcs. . .99 B8
Wadbrook Devon 28 G4
Waddesdon Bucks . . .84 B2
Waddeton Devon 9 D7
Waddicar Mers 182 B5
Waddicombe Devon. . .26 B5
Waddingham Lincs . .189 B7
Waddington Lancs. . .203 E10
Lincs 173 C7
Waddingworth
Lincs 189 G11
Waddon Devon 14 F3
London 67 G10
Wadebridge Corn. . . .10 G5
Wadeford Som 28 E4
Wade Hall Lancs . . .194 C4
Wadenhoe
N Nhants 137 G10
Wades Green
Ches E 167 C11
Wadesmill Herts 86 B5
Wadhurst E Sus 52 G6
Wadshelf Derbys . . .186 G4
Wadsley S Yorks . . .186 C4
Wadsley Bridge
S Yorks 186 C4
Wadswick Wilts 61 F10
Wadwick Hants 48 C2
Wadworth S Yorks. . .187 B9
Waen Denb 165 B10
Denb 165 C7
Flint 181 G11
Powys 129 E9
Waen Aberwheeler
Denb 165 B9
Waen-fâch Powys . . .148 G4
Waen-pentir Gwyn . .163 B9
Waen-wen Gwyn . . .163 B9
Wag Highld 311 G4
Wagbeach Shrops. . . .131 C7
Wagg Som 28 B6

Waggersley Staffs . .151 B7
Waggs Plot Devon . . .28 G4
Wainfelin Torf 78 E3
Wainfleet All Saints
Lincs 175 D7
Wainfleet Bank
Lincs 175 D7
Wainfleet St Mary
Lincs 175 D7
Wainfleet Tofts
Lincs 175 D7
Wainford Norf 142 E6
Waingroves Derbys . .170 F6
Wainhouse Corner
Corn 11 B9
Wain Lee Staffs 168 D5
Wainscott Medway . . .69 E8
Wainstalls W Yorks. .196 B6
Waitby Cumb 222 D5
Waithe Lincs 201 G9
Wakefield W Mid . .197 C10
Wake Green
W Mid 133 G11
Wake Hill N Yorks . .214 E3
Wake Lady Green
N Yorks 226 F3
Wakeley Herts 104 F6
Wakerley N Nhants . .137 D9
Wakes Colne Essex . .107 F7
Wakes Colne Green
Essex 107 E7
Walberswick Suff. . . .127 C9
Walberton W Sus . . .35 F7
Walbottle T&W 242 D5
Walby Cumb 239 E10
Walcombe Som 44 D5
Walcot
Bath 61 F9
Lincs 155 B11
N Lincs 199 C11
Oxon 82 B4
Shrops 130 F6
Swindon 63 C7
Telford 149 G11
Worcs 99 B8
Walcote Leics 135 G11
Warks 118 F2
Walcot Green Norf. . .142 G2
Walcott Lincs 173 D10
Norf 161 C7
Walden N Yorks 213 C10
Walden Head
N Yorks 213 C9
Walden Stubbs
N Yorks 198 D5
Waldersey Cambs . . .139 C8
Waldershaigh
S Yorks 186 B3
Walderslade Medway. .69 G9
Walderton W Sus . . .34 E3
Walditch Dorset 16 C5
Waldley Derbys 152 B2
Waldridge Durham . .243 G7
Waldringfield Suff . .108 C5
Waldringfield Heath
Suff 108 B5
Waldron E Sus 23 B8
Waldron Down E Sus .37 C8
Wales Som 29 C9
S Yorks 187 E7
Wales Bar S Yorks . .187 E7
Walesby Lincs 189 C10
Notts 187 G11
Walesby Grange
Lincs 189 C10
Wales End Suff 106 B5
Waleswood S Yorks . .187 E7
Walford Hereford 97 G11
Hereford 115 C7
Shrops 149 E8
Som 28 B3
Staffs 150 C6
Walford Heath
Shrops 149 F8
Walgherton
Ches E 167 F11
Walgrave W Nhants . .120 C6
Walham Glos 98 G6
Walham Green
London 67 D9
Walhampton Hants . .20 B2
Walkden Gtr Man. . . .195 G8
Walker T&W 243 E7
Walker Barn Ches E .185 G7
Walkerburn Borders .261 B9
Walker Fold Lancs . .203 E9
Walkeringham
Notts 188 C3
Walkerith Lincs 188 C3
Walkern Herts 104 F5
Walker's Green
Hereford 97 B10
Walker's Heath
W Mid 117 B11
Walkerville N Yorks .224 F4
Walkford BCP 19 C10
Walkhampton Devon. . .7 B10
Walkington E Yorks .208 F5
Walkley S Yorks . . .186 D4
Walkmill Shrops 131 E7
Walkmills Shrops . . .131 D9
Wall Corn 2 B4
Northumb 241 D10
Staffs 134 B2
Wallacestone Falk . .279 F8
Wallaceton Dumfries .247 F8
Wallacetown
N Som 60 E2
S Ayrs 245 C7
S Ayrs 257 E8
Shetland 313 H5
Wallands Park E Sus. .36 E6
Wallasey Mers 182 C4
Wallbank Lancs 195 D11
Wall Bank Shrops . . .131 E10
Wallbrook W Mid . . .133 E8
Wallcrouch E Sus . . .53 G7
Wallend London 68 C2
Wall End Cumb 210 C4
Kent 71 G8
Waller's Green
Hereford 98 D3

Walley's Green
Ches E 167 C11
Wall Heath W Mid . .133 F7
Wall Hill Gtr Man . . .196 F3
Wallingford Oxon . . .64 B6
Wallington Hants 33 F9
Herts 104 E5
London 67 G9
Wallington Heath
W Mid 133 C10
Wallingwells Notts. . .187 E9
Wallis Pembs 91 F10
Wallisdown BCP 19 C7
Walliswood Sur 50 F5
Wall Mead Bath 45 B7
Wall Nook Durham . .233 B10
Wallow Green Glos . . .80 F4
Walls Shetland 313 J4
Wallsend T&W 243 D7
Wallsuches Gtr Man .195 E7
Wallsworth Glos 98 G6
Wall under Heywood
Shrops 131 E10
Wallyford E Loth . . .281 G7
Walmer Kent 55 C11
Walmer Bridge
Lancs 194 C3
Walmersley
Gtr Man 195 E10
Walmgate Stray
York 207 C8
Walmley W Mid 134 E2
Walmsgate Lincs . . .190 F5
Walnut Grove Perth. .286 E5
Walnut Tree
M Keynes 103 D7
Walnuttree Green
Herts 105 G9
Walpole Som 43 D10
Suff 127 C7
Walpole Cross Keys
Norf 157 F10
Walpole Highway
Norf 157 G10
Walpole Marsh Norf .157 F9
Walpole St Andrew
Norf 157 F10
Walpole St Peter
Norf 157 F9
Walrow Som 43 D10
Walsal End W Mid . .118 B4
Walsall W Mid 133 D10
Walsall Wood
W Mid 133 C10
Walsden W Yorks . . .196 C2
Walsgrave on Sowe
W Mid 135 G7
Walsham le Willows
Suff 125 C9
Walshaw Gtr Man . . .195 E9
Walshford N Yorks . .206 C4
Walsoken Norf 157 G9
Walson Mon 97 G8
Walston S Lanark . . .269 F11
Walsworth Herts 104 E4
Walters Ash Bucks . .84 F4
Walter's Green Kent . .52 E4
Walterston V Glam . . .58 E5
Walterstone Hereford . .96 F6
Waltham Kent 54 D6
NE Lincs 201 G9
Waltham Abbey
Essex 86 E6
Waltham Chase
Hants 33 D9
Waltham Cross Herts .86 E5
Waltham on the Wolds
Leics 154 E6
Waltham St Lawrence
Windsor 65 D10
Waltham's Cross
Essex 106 E3
Walthamstow
London 67 B11
Walton
Bucks 84 C4
Cumb 240 E2
Derbys 170 B5
Leics 135 F11
Mers 182 C5
M Keynes 103 D7
Pboro 138 C3
Powys 114 F5
Shrops 115 B9
Som 44 F3
Staffs 151 C7
Staffs 151 D7
Suff 108 D5
Telford 149 F11
Warks 118 F5
W Yorks 197 D11
W Yorks 206 D4
Walton Cardiff Glos . .99 E8
Walton Court Bucks. . .84 C4
Walton East Pembs . .91 G10
Walton Elm Dorset . . .30 D3
Walton Grounds
W Nhants 101 D10
Walton Heath Hants. .33 F10
Walton Highway
Norf 157 G9
Walton in Gordano
N Som 60 E2
Walton-le-Dale
Lancs 194 B5
Walton Manor Oxon. .83 D8
Walton-on-Thames
Sur 66 F6
Walton on the Hill
Staffs 151 E9
Sur 51 B8
Walton on the Wolds
Leics 153 F11
Walton-on-Trent
Derbys 152 F4
Walton Pool Worcs. . .117 B8
Walton St Mary
N Som 60 E2

Walton Summit
Lancs 194 B5
Walton Warren Norf .158 G4
Walton West Pembs . .72 C5
Walwen Flint 181 F10
Flint 181 F10
Flint 182 F2
Walwick Northumb . .241 C10
Darl 224 B4
London 67 D10
Walworth Gate
Darl 233 G10
Walwyn's Castle
Pembs 72 C5
Wambrook Som 28 F3
Wampool Cumb 238 G6
Wanborough Sur 50 D2
Swindon 63 C8
Wandel Dyke
S Lanark 259 D11
Wandle Park London .67 F10
Wandon End Herts. . .104 G2
Wandsworth London . .67 E9
Wangford Suff 127 B9
Wanlip Leics 154 G2
Wanlockhead
Dumfries 259 G9
Wannock E Sus 23 E9
Wansford E Yorks . . .209 B7
Pboro 137 D11
Wanshurst Green
Kent 53 D9
Wanson Corn 24 G1
Wanstead London . . .68 B2
Wanstrow Som 45 E8
Wanswell Glos 79 E11
Wantage Oxon 63 B11
Wants Green Worcs. .116 F5
Wapley S Glos 61 D8
Wappenbury Warks. .119 D7
Wappenham
W Nhants 102 B2
Wapping London 67 C10
Warbleton E Sus 23 B10
Warblington Hants . . .22 B2
Warborough Oxon . . .83 G9
Warboys Cambs. 138 G5
Warbreck Blackpool . .202 F2
Warbstow Corn 11 C10
Warbstow Cross
Corn 11 C10
Warburton Gtr Man. .184 C2
Warburton Green
Gtr Man 184 C1
Warcop Cumb 222 B4
Warden Kent 70 E4
Northumb 241 D10
Powys 114 B6
Ward End W Mid . . .134 F2
Warden Hill Glos 99 G8
Warden Point IoW . . .20 D2
Warden Street
C Beds 104 C2
Ward Green Suff. . . .125 E10
S Yorks 197 G8
Ward Green Cross
Lancs 203 F8
Wardhedges
C Beds 103 D11
Wardhill Orkney 314 D6
Wardington Oxon . . .101 B9
Wardlaw Borders . . .261 G11
Wardle Ches E 167 D10
Gtr Man 196 D2
Wardle Bank
Ches E 167 D10
Wardley
Gtr Man 195 G9
Rutland 136 C6
T&W 243 E7
W Sus 34 B4
Wardlow Derbys 185 G11
Mordour Wilts 30 B6
Wardpark N Lanark . .278 F5
Wardrobes Bucks 84 E4
Wardsend Ches E . . .184 E6
Wardy Hill Cambs . . .139 G9
Ware Herts 86 C5
Kent 71 G9
Wareham Dorset. 18 D4
Warehorne Kent 54 G3
Warenford
Northumb 264 C4
Waren Mill
Northumb 264 C4
Warenton Northumb. .264 C4
Wareside Herts 86 B5
Waresley Cambs 122 G4
Worcs 116 C6
Ware Street Kent . . .53 B9
Warfield Brack. 65 E11
Warfleet Devon 9 E7
Wargate Lincs 156 C4
Wargrave Mers 183 C9
Wokingham 65 D9
Warham Hereford 97 D9
Norf 176 E6
Warhill Gtr Man 185 B7
Waring's Green
W Mid 118 C2
Wark Northumb 241 C9
Northumb 263 B8
Wark Common
Northumb 263 B8
Warkleigh Devon 25 C10
Warkton N Nhants . .121 G7
Warkworth
Northumb 252 B6
Nhants 101 C9
Warlaby N Yorks 224 G6
Warland W Yorks . . .196 C2
Warleggan Corn 6 B3
Warleigh Bath 61 G9
Warley Essex 87 G2
Warley Town
W Yorks 196 B5
Warley Woods
W Mid 133 F10
Warlingham Sur 51 B11
Warmbrook Derbys . .170 E3
Warmfield
W Yorks 197 C11

Warmingham
Ches E 168 C2
Warminghurst
W Sus 35 D10
Warmington
N Nhants 137 E11
Warks 101 B8
Warminster Wilts 45 D11
Warminster Common
Wilts 45 E11
Warmlake Kent 53 C10
Warmley S Glos 61 E7
Warmley Hill S Glos 61 E7
Warmley Tower
S Glos 61 E7
Warmonds Hill
N Nhants 121 D9
Warmsworth
S Yorks 198 G4
Warmwell Dorset 17 D11
Warnborough Green
Hants 49 C8
Warndon Worcs 117 F7
Warners End Herts 85 D8
Warnford Hants 33 C10
Warnham W Sus 51 G7
Warningcamp W Sus 35 F8
Warninglid W Sus 36 B2
Warpsgrove Oxon 83 F10
Warren Ches E 184 G5
Dorset 18 C3
Pembs 72 F6
S Yorks 186 B5
Warrenby Redcar 235 F7
Warren Corner Hants 34 B2
Hants 49 D10
Warren Heath Suff 108 C4
Warren Row
Windsor 65 C10
Warren's Green
Herts 104 F5
Warren Street Kent 54 C2
Warrington
M Keynes 121 G7
Warr 183 D10
Warriston Edin 280 F5
Warsash Hants 33 F7
Warsill N Yorks 214 F4
Warslow Staffs 169 D9
Warsop Vale Notts 171 B8
Warstock W Mid 117 B11
Warstone Staffs 133 B9
Warter E Yorks 208 C3
Warthermarske
N Yorks 214 D4
Warthill N Yorks 207 B9
Wartle Aberds 293 C7
Wartling E Sus 23 D11
Wartnaby Leics 154 E4
Warton Lancs 194 B2
Lancs 211 E9
Northumb 252 C2
Warks 134 C5
Warton Bank Lancs 194 B2
Warwick Warks 118 E5
Warwick Bridge
Cumb 239 F11
Warwick on Eden
Cumb 239 F11
Warwicksland
Cumb 239 B10
Warwick Wold Sur 51 C10
Wasbister Orkney 314 C3
Wasdale Head
Cumb 220 D3
Wash Derbys 185 E9
Washall Green
Herts 105 E8
Washaway Corn 5 B10
Washbourne Devon 8 E5
Washbrook Som 44 C2
Suff 108 C2
Washbrook Street
Suff 108 C2
Wash Common
W Berks 64 G3
Wash Dyke Norf 157 F10
Washerwall Staffs 168 F6
Washfield Devon 26 D6
Washfold N Yorks 223 E11
Washford Som 42 E5
Worcs 117 D11
Washford Pyne
Devon 26 E4
Washingborough
Lincs 189 G8
Washingley Cambs 138 F2
Washington T&W 243 F8
W Sus 35 E10
Washington Village
T&W 243 F8
Washmere Green
Suff 107 B8
Washpit W Yorks 196 F6
Wash Water W Berks 64 G3
Washwood Heath
W Mid 134 F2
Wasing W Berks 64 G5
Waskerley Durham 233 B7
Wasperton Warks 118 F5
Wasp Green Sur 51 D10
Wasps Nest Lincs 173 C9
Wass N Yorks 215 D11
Waste Green Warks 118 D4
Wastor Devon 8 F2
Watchet Som 42 E5
Watchfield Oxon 63 B8
Som 43 D10
Watchgate Cumb 221 F10
Watchhill Cumb 229 C9
Watch House Green
Essex 106 G3
Watchill Dumfries 238 D6
Dumfries 248 G3
Watcombe Torbay 9 B8
Watendlath Cumb 220 B5
Water Devon 13 E11
Lancs 195 B10
Waterbeach Cambs 123 D9
W Sus 22 B5
Waterbeck Dumfries 238 B6
Waterdale Herts 85 E10
Waterden Norf 159 B7
Waterditch Hants 19 B9
Water Eaton
M Keynes 103 E7
Oxon 83 C8
Waterend Bucks 84 F3
Cumb 229 G8
Glos 80 C3
Herts 86 C2
Water End Bedford 104 B2
C Beds 103 D11
C Beds 104 B5
Essex 105 C11
E Yorks 207 F11
Hants 49 C7
Herts 85 C8
Herts 86 E2
Waterfall Staffs 169 E9
Waterfoot Argyll 255 D9
Cumb 230 G5
E Renf 267 D11
Lancs 195 C10
Waterford Hants 20 B2
Herts 86 C4
Water Fryston
W Yorks 198 B3
Water Garth Nook
Cumb 210 F3
Watergate Corn 6 E4
Corn 11 E8
Watergore Som 28 D6
Waterhales Essex 87 F8
Waterham Kent 70 G5
Waterhay Wilts 81 G9
Waterhead Angus 292 F6
Cumb 221 E7
Devon 8 F3
Dumfries 248 E5
Waterhead on Minnoch
S Ayrs 245 E9
Waterheads Borders 270 E4
Waterheath Norf 143 E8
Waterhouses
Durham 233 C9
Staffs 169 E9
Water Houses
N Yorks 213 F7
Wateringbury Kent 53 C7
Waterlane Glos 80 E6
Waterlip Som 45 E7
Waterloo BCP 18 C6
Blackburn 195 B7
Corn 11 G8
Derbys 170 C6
Gtr Man 196 G2
Highld 295 C8
Mers 182 B4
N Lanark 268 E6
Norf 126 B2
Norf 143 E8
Norf 160 F4
Pembs 73 E7
Perth 286 D4
Shrops 149 C9
Waterloo Park Mers 182 B4
Waterloo Port Gwyn 163 C7
Waterlooville Hants 33 F11
Waterman Quarter
Kent 53 E10
Watermead Glos 80 B5
Watermeetings
S Lanark 259 G11
Watermill E Sus 38 E2
Watermillock Cumb 230 G4
Watermoor Glos 81 E8
Water Newton
Cambs 138 D2
Water Orton Warks 134 E3
Waterperry Oxon 83 D10
Waterrow Som 27 B9
Watersfield W Sus 35 D8
Watersheddings
Gtr Man 196 F2
Waterside Aberds 292 B5
Aberds 303 G10
Blackburn 195 C8
Bucks 85 E7
Cumb 229 B10
Derbys 185 E8
E Ayrs 245 B10
E Ayrs 267 G9
E Dunb 278 G3
E Renf 267 D10
Sur 51 D11
S Yorks 199 E7
Telford 150 F2
Waterslack Lancs 211 D9
Water's Nook
Gtr Man 195 F7
Waterstein Highld 297 G7
Waterstock Oxon 83 D10
Waterston Pembs 72 D6
Water Stratford
Bucks 102 E3
Waters Upton
Telford 150 F2
Waterthorpe
S Yorks 186 E6
Waterton Aberds 303 F9
Bridgend 58 D2
Water Yeat Cumb 210 B5
Watford Herts 85 F10
W Nhants 120 D2
Watford Gap Staffs 134 C2
Watford Heath
Herts 85 G10
Watford Park Caerph 58 B6
Wath Cumb 222 D3
N Yorks 214 D6
N Yorks 214 F2
N Yorks 216 D3
Wath Brow Cumb 219 C10
Watherston Borders 271 F8
Wath upon Dearne
S Yorks 198 G2
Watledge Glos 80 E4
Watley's End S Glos 61 C7
Watlington Norf 158 G2
Oxon 83 G11
Watnall Notts 171 F8
Watsness Shetland 313 H3
Watten Highld 310 D6
Wattisfield Suff 125 C10
Wattisham Suff 125 G10
Wattisham Stone
Suff 125 G10
Wattlefield Norf 142 D2
Wattlesborough Heath
Shrops 149 G7
Watton E Yorks 208 C6
Norf 141 C8
Watton at Stone
Herts 86 B4
Watton Green Norf 141 C8
Watton's Green Essex 87 F8
Wattston N Lanark 268 B5
Wattstown Rhondda 77 G8
Wattsville Caerph 78 G2
Wauchan Highld 295 G11
Waulkmill Lodge
Orkney 314 F3
Waun Gwyn 163 C9
Powys 148 F4
Waunarlwydd
Swansea 56 B6
Waun Beddau Pembs 90 F5
Waunclunda Carms 94 E3
Waunfawr Gwyn 163 D8
Waun Fawr Ceredig 128 G2
Waungilwen Carms 92 D6
Waungron Swansea 75 E9
Waunlwyd Bl Gwent 77 D11
Waun-Lwyd
Bl Gwent 77 D11
Waun-y-clyn Carms 75 E7
Waun y Gilfach
Bridgend 57 D10
Wavendon
M Keynes 103 D8
Wavendon Gate
M Keynes 103 D8
Waverbridge Cumb 229 B10
Waverley S Yorks 186 D6
Waverton Ches W 167 C7
Cumb 229 B10
Wavertree Mers 182 D5
Wawcott W Berks 63 F11
Wawne E Yorks 209 F7
Waxham Norf 161 D8
Waxholme E Yorks 201 B10
Way Kent 71 F10
Waye Devon 13 G11
Wayend Street
Hereford 98 D4
Wayfield Medway 69 F9
Wayford Som 28 F6
Waymills Shrops 167 G9
Wayne Green Mon 78 B6
Way's Green
Ches W 167 B10
Waytown Devon 24 C5
Devon 40 G5
Way Village Devon 26 E5
Way Wick N Som 59 G11
Wdig = *Goodwick*
Pembs 91 D8
Weachyburn Aberds 302 D6
Weacombe Som 42 E6
Weald Oxon 82 E4
Wealdstone London 67 B7
Wearde Corn 7 D8
Weardley W Yorks 205 E11
Weare Som 44 C2
Weare Giffard Devon 25 C7
Wearhead Durham 232 D3
Wearne Som 28 B6
Weasdale Cumb 222 E3
Weasenham All Saints
Norf 158 E6
Weasenham St Peter
Norf 159 E7
Weaste Gtr Man 184 B4
Weatherhill Sur 51 E10
Weatheroak Hill
Worcs 117 C11
Weaverham
Ches W 183 G10
Weavering Street
Kent 53 B9
Weaverslake Staffs 152 F2
Weaverthorpe
N Yorks 217 E9
Webbington Som 43 B11
Webheath Worcs 117 D10
Webscott Shrops 149 E9
Wecock Hants 33 E11
Wedderlairs Aberds 303 F8
Wedderlie Borders 272 E2
Weddington Kent 55 B9
Warks 135 E7
Wedhampton Wilts 46 B5
Wedmore Som 44 D2
Wednesbury W Mid 133 D9
Wednesbury Oak
W Mid 133 E9
Wednesfield W Mid 133 C8
Weecar Notts 172 B4
Weedon Bucks 84 B4
Weedon Bec
W Nhants 120 F2
Weedon Lois
W Nhants 102 B2
Weeford Staffs 134 C2
Week Devon 8 C5
Devon 12 E5
Devon 25 B9
Devon 26 D2
Weeke Devon 26 F3
Hants 48 G3
Week Green Corn 11 B10
Weekley N Nhants 137 G7
Weekmoor Som 27 B10
Weeks IoW 21 C7
Week St Mary Corn 11 B10
Weel E Yorks 209 F7
Weeley Essex 108 G2
Weeley Heath Essex 108 G3
Weelsby NE Lincs 201 F9
Weem Perth 286 C2
Weeping Cross
Staffs 151 E8
Weethley Warks 117 F11
Weethley Bank
Warks 117 G11
Weethley Gate
Warks 117 G11
Weeting Norf 140 F5
Weeton E Yorks 201 C11
Lancs 202 G3
N Yorks 205 D11
Weetwood
W Yorks 205 F11
Weetwood Common
Ches W 167 B8
Weetwood Hall
Northumb 264 D2
Weir Essex 69 B10
Lancs 195 B11
Weirbrook Shrops 148 E6
Weir Quay Devon 7 C8
Welborne Norf 159 G11
Welborne Common
Norf 141 B11
Welbourn Lincs 173 E7
Welburn N Yorks 216 C3
N Yorks 216 F4
Welbury N Yorks 225 E7
Welby Lincs 155 B9
Welches Dam
Cambs 139 F9
Welcombe Devon 24 D2
Weld Bank Lancs 194 D5
Weldon N Nhants 137 F8
Northumb 252 D4
Welford W Berks 64 E2
W Nhants 136 G2
Welford-on-Avon
Warks 118 G3
Welham Leics 136 E5
Notts 188 E2
Som 45 G7
Welhambridge
E Yorks 207 G11
Welham Green Herts 86 D2
Well Hants 49 D9
Lincs 190 G6
N Yorks 214 C5
Welland Worcs 98 C5
Welland Stone
Worcs 98 D6
Wellbank Angus 287 D8
Well Bottom Dorset 30 D6
Wellbrook E Sus 37 B9
Welldale Dumfries 238 D5
Well End Bucks 65 B11
Herts 86 F2
Weller's Town Kent 52 E4
Wellesbourne
Warks 118 F5
Well Green Gtr Man 184 D3
Wellheads Aberds 302 F4
Well Heads
W Yorks 205 G7
Well Hill Kent 68 G3
Wellhouse W Berks 64 E4
W Yorks 196 E5
Welling London 68 D3
Wellingborough
N Nhants 121 D7
Wellingham Norf 159 E7
Wellingore Lincs 173 D7
Wellington Cumb 219 E11
Hereford 97 B9
Som 27 C10
Telford 150 G3
Wellington Heath
Hereford 98 C4
Wellington Hill
W Yorks 206 F2
Wellisford Som 27 C9
Wellow Bath 45 B8
IoW 20 D3
NE Lincs 201 F9
Notts 171 B11
Wellow Wood Hants 32 C3
Well Place Oxon 65 B7
Wellpond Green
Herts 105 G8
Wellroyd W Yorks 205 F10
Wells Som 44 D5
Wellsborough Leics 135 C7
Wells Green
Ches E 167 E11
Wells-next-the-Sea
Norf 176 E6
Wellsprings Som 28 B2
Well Street Kent 53 B7
Wellstye Green
Essex 87 B10
Wellswood Torbay 9 C8
Welltown Corn 6 B2
Well Town Devon 26 F6
Wellwood Fife 279 D11
Welney Norf 139 E10
Welsford Devon 24 C3
Welshampton
Shrops 149 B8
Welsh Bicknor
Hereford 79 B9
Welsh End Shrops 149 B10
Welsh Frankton
Shrops 149 C7
Welsh Harp London 67 B8
Welsh Hook Pembs 91 F8
Welsh Newton
Hereford 79 B7
Welsh Newton Common
Hereford 79 B8
Welshpool Powys 130 B4
Welsh St Donats
V Glam 58 D4
Welshwood Park
Essex 107 F10
Welstor Devon 13 G10
Welton Bath 45 C7
Cumb 230 C3
E Ayrs 258 D2
E Yorks 200 B3
Lincs 189 F8
W Nhants 119 D11
Welton Hill Lincs 189 E8
Welton le Marsh
Lincs 175 B7
Welton le Wold
Lincs 190 D3
Welwick E Yorks 201 C10
Welwyn Herts 86 B2
Welwyn Garden City
Herts 86 C2
Wem Shrops 149 D10
Wembdon Som 43 F9
Wembley London 67 B7
Wembley Park
London 67 B7
Wembury Devon 7 F10
Wembworthy Devon 25 F11
Wemyss Bay Invclyd 266 B3
Wenallt Ceredig 112 C3
Gwyn 146 F4
Gwyn 165 G7
Wendens Ambo
Essex 105 D10
Wendlebury Oxon 83 B9
Wendling Norf 159 G8
Wendover Bucks 84 D5
Wendover Dean
Bucks 84 E5
Wendron Corn 2 C5
Wendy Cambs 104 B6
Wenfordbridge Corn 11 F7
Wenhaston Suff 127 B8
Wenhaston Black Heath
Suff 127 C8
Wennington
Cambs 122 B4
Lancs 212 E2
London 68 C4
Wensley Derbys 170 C3
N Yorks 213 B11
Wentbridge
W Yorks 198 D3
Wentnor Shrops 131 E7
Wentworth Cambs 123 B9
S Yorks 186 B5
Wenvoe V Glam 58 E6
Weobley Hereford 115 G8
Weobley Marsh
Hereford 115 G8
Weoley Castle
W Mid 133 G10
Wepham W Sus 35 F8
Wepre Flint 166 B3
Wereham Norf 140 C3
Wereham Row Norf 140 C3
Wereton Staffs 168 E3
Wergs W Mid 133 C7
Wern Gwyn 145 B10
Powys 77 B10
Powys 147 G9
Powys 148 E5
Powys 148 G5
Shrops 148 C5
Swansea 56 C4
Wern ddu Shrops 148 D4
Werneth Gtr Man 196 G2
Werneth Low
Gtr Man 185 C7
Wernffrwd Swansea 56 C4
Wern-Gifford Mon 96 G6
Wernlas Shrops 148 E6
Wern-olau Swansea 56 B5
Wernrheolydd Mon 78 C5
Wern Tarw Bridgend 58 C3
Wern-y-cwrt Mon 78 D5
Wern-y-gaer Flint 166 B2
Wernyrheolydd Mon 78 C5
Werrington Corn 12 D2
Pboro 138 C3
Staffs 168 F6
Wervin Ches W 182 G6
Wescoe Hill
N Yorks 205 D11
Wesham Lancs 202 G4
Wessington Derbys 170 D5
West Aberthaw
V Glam 58 F4
Westacott Devon 40 G5
West Acre Norf 158 F5
West Acton London 67 C7
West Adderbury
Oxon 101 D9
West Allerdean
Northumb 273 F9
West Allotment
T&W 243 C8
West Alvington Devon 8 G4
West Amesbury Wilts 46 E6
West Anstey Devon 26 B5
West Appleton
N Yorks 224 G4
West Ardhu Argyll 288 D6
West Ardsley
W Yorks 197 B9
West Ardwell
Dumfries 236 E2
West Arthurlie
E Renf 267 D9
West Ashby Lincs 190 G3
West Ashford Devon 40 F4
West Ashling W Sus 22 B4
West Ashton Wilts 45 B11
West Auckland
Durham 233 F9
West Ayton N Yorks 217 C9
West Bagborough
Som 43 G7
West Bank Bl Gwent 78 D2
Halton 183 E8
West Barkwith
Lincs 189 E11
West Barnby
N Yorks 226 C6
West Barnes London 67 F8
West Barns E Loth 282 F3
West Barsham Norf 159 C8
West Bay Dorset 16 C5
West Beckham Norf 160 B2
West Bedfont Sur 66 E5
West Benhar
N Lanark 269 C7
Westbere Kent 71 G7
West Bergholt
Essex 107 F9
West Bexington
Dorset 16 D6
West Bilney Norf 158 F4
West Blackdene
Durham 232 D3
West Blackdown
Devon 12 E5
West Blatchington
Brighton 36 F3
West Bold Borders 261 B9
West Boldon T&W 243 E9
Westborough Lincs 172 G5
Westbourne BCP 19 C7
Suff 108 B2
W Sus 22 B3
Westbourne Green
London 67 C9
West Bourton Dorset 30 B3
West Bowling
W Yorks 205 G9
West Bradford
Lancs 203 E10
West Bradley Som 44 F5
West Bretton
W Yorks 197 E9
West Bridgford
Notts 153 B11
West Brompton
London 67 D9
West Bromwich
W Mid 133 E10
Westbrook Hereford 96 C5
Kent 71 E10
Sur 50 E3
Warr 183 C9
W Berks 64 E2
Wilts 62 F3
Westbrook Green
Norf 142 G2
Westbrook Hay Herts 85 D8
West Broughton
Derbys 152 C2
West Buckland
Devon 41 G7
Som 27 C11
Westburn S Lanark 268 C3
West Burnside
Aberds 293 F8
West Burrafirth
Shetland 313 H4
West Burton
N Yorks 213 B10
W Sus 35 E7
Westbury Bucks 102 D2
Shrops 131 B7
Wilts 45 C11
Westbury Leigh
Wilts 45 C11
Westbury-on-Severn
Glos 80 C2
Westbury on Trym
Bristol 60 D5
Westbury Park
Bristol 60 D5
Westbury-sub-Mendip
Som 44 D4
West Butsfield
Durham 233 C8
West Butterwick
N Lincs 199 F10
Westby Lancs 202 G3
Lincs 155 D9
West Byfleet Sur 66 G4
West Caister Norf 161 G10
West Calder
W Loth 269 C10
West Camel Som 29 C9
West Carlton
W Yorks 205 E10
West Carr Hull 209 G7
N Lincs 199 F8
West Chadsmoor
Staffs 151 G9
West Challow Oxon 63 B11
West Charleton Devon 8 G5
West Chelborough
Dorset 29 F8
West Chevington
Northumb 252 D6
West Chiltington
W Sus 35 D9
West Chiltington
Common W Sus 35 D9
West Chinnock Som 29 E7
West Chirton T&W 243 D8
West Chisenbury
Wilts 46 C6
West Clandon Sur 50 C4
West Cliff BCP 19 C7
N Yorks 227 C7
West Cliffe Kent 55 E10
Westcliff-on-Sea
Southend 69 B11
West Clyne Highld 311 J2
Highld 311 J2
West Clyth Highld 310 F6
Highld 310 F6
West Coker Som 29 E8
Westcombe Som 29 B7
Som 45 F7
West Common Hants 32 G6
West Compton
Dorset 17 C7
Som 44 E5
West Cornforth
Durham 234 E2
Westcot Oxon 63 B10
Westcote Glos 100 G4
Westcotes
Leicester 135 C11
Westcott Bucks 84 B2
Devon 27 G8
Shrops 131 C8
Sur 50 D6
Westcott Barton
Oxon 101 F8
Westcourt Wilts 63 G8
West Cowick
E Yorks 199 C7
West Cranmore Som 45 E7
Westcroft M Keynes 102 E6
W Mid 133 C8
West Cross Kent 53 G10
Swansea 56 D6
West Crudwell Wilts 80 G6
West Cullery Aberds 293 C9
West Curry Corn 11 C11
West Curthwaite
Cumb 230 B2
West Darlochan
Argyll 255 E7
Westdean E Sus 23 F8
West Dean Wilts 32 B3
W Sus 34 E5
West Deeping Lincs 138 B2
West Denant Pembs 72 C6
Westdene Brighton 36 F3
West Denton T&W 242 D5
West Derby Mers 182 C5
West Dereham Norf 140 C3
West Didsbury
Gtr Man 184 C4
West Down Devon 40 E4
Herts 47 F11
Westdown Camp
Wilts 46 D4
Westdowns Corn 11 E7
West Downs Corn 5 C10
West Drayton London 66 D5
Notts 188 G2
West Dulwich
London 67 E10
West Ealing London 67 C7
West Edge Derbys 170 C4
West Ella E Yorks 200 B4
Westend Oxon 100 G6
S Glos 79 G10
West End Bedford 121 E11
Bedford 121 G9
Brack 65 E11
Brack 66 G2
Caerph 78 F2
Cumb 239 F8
Dorset 30 G6
E Yorks 201 B9
E Yorks 208 G4
E Yorks 209 B9
E Yorks 209 G9
E Yorks 217 G11
Glos 80 F5
Hants 33 E7
Hants 33 F9
Hants 48 F6
Herts 86 D3
Kent 54 B2
Kent 71 F7
Lancs 195 B8
Lancs 211 G8
Leics 153 F8
Lincs 174 F5
Lincs 190 B5
Mon 78 F6
Norf 141 B8
Norf 161 G10
N Som 60 F3
N Yorks 205 B8
N Yorks 206 E6
N Yorks 207 F7
Oxon 64 B5
Oxon 82 E6
S Glos 61 B8
S Lanark 269 F9
Som 44 C5
Som 45 G7
Suff 143 G9
Sur 49 E10
Sur 66 G6
S Yorks 199 F7
Wilts 30 C6
Wilts 31 C7
Wilts 62 D3
Windsor 65 D10
Worcs 99 D11
W Sus 36 D2
W Yorks 197 B7
W Yorks 205 F10
West End = *Marian-y-mor*
Gwyn 145 C7
West End Green
Hants 65 G7
Westend Town
Northumb 241 D7
West-end Town
V Glam 58 F3
Westenhanger Kent 54 F6
Wester Aberchalder
Highld 300 G5
Wester Arboll
Highld 311 L2
Wester Auchinloch
N Lanark 278 G3
Wester Auchnagallin
Highld 301 F10
Wester Balgedie
Perth 286 G5
Wester Brae Highld 300 C6
Wester Broomhouse
E Loth 282 F3
Wester Craiglands
Highld 301 D7
Wester Culbeuchly
Aberds 302 C6
Westerdale Highld 310 D5
N Yorks 226 D3
Wester Dalvoult
Highld 291 B11
Wester Dechmont
W Loth 269 B10
Wester Deloraine
Borders 261 E8
Wester Denoon
Angus 287 C7
Wester Ellister
Argyll 254 B2
Wester Essendy
Perth 286 C5
Wester Essenside
Borders 261 E10
Wester Feddal
Perth 286 G2
Westerfield
Shetland 313 H5
Suff 108 B3
Wester Fintray
Aberds 293 B10
Westerfolds Moray 301 C11
Wester Galgantray
Highld 301 E8
Westergate W Sus 22 C6
Wester Gospetry
Fife 286 G5
Wester Gruinards
Highld 309 K5
Wester Hailes Edin 270 B4
Westerham Kent 52 C2
Westerhope T&W 242 D5
Wester Housebyres
Borders 262 B2
Wester Kershope
Borders 261 D9
Wester Lealty
Highld 300 B6
Westerleigh S Glos 61 D8
Westerleigh Hill
S Glos 61 D8
Wester Lix Stirling 285 E9
Wester Milton
Highld 301 D9
Wester Mosshead
Aberds 302 F5
Western Bank
Cumb 229 B10
Western Downs
Staffs 151 E8
Western Newburn
Fife 287 G8
Western Heights
Kent 55 E10
Western Hill
Durham 233 C11
Western Park
Leicester 135 C11
Wester Ord Aberds 293 C10
Wester Parkgate
Dumfries 248 F2
Wester Quarff
Shetland 313 K6
Wester Skeld
Shetland 313 J4
Wester Strath
Highld 300 D6
Westerton Aberds 293 B9
Aberds 302 E5
Angus 287 B10
Durham 233 E10
Moray 302 D3
W Sus 22 B5
Westertown Aberds 303 F7
Wester Watten
Highld 310 D6
Westerwick Shetland 313 J4
West Ewell Sur 67 G8
West Farleigh Kent 53 C8
West Farndon
W Nhants 119 G10
West Felton Shrops 148 D6
West Fenton E Loth 281 E9
West Ferry Dundee 287 D8
Westfield Bath 45 C7
Cumb 228 F5
E Sus 38 D4
Hants 21 B10
Hereford 98 B4
Highld 310 C4
N Lanark 278 G4
Norf 141 B9
Redcar 235 G7
Sur 50 B4
S Yorks 186 E6
W Loth 279 G8
W Yorks 197 C8
W Yorks 205 E9
West Field N Lincs 200 D6
York 207 C7
Westfields Dorset 30 F2
Hereford 97 C9
West Fields W Berks 64 F3
Westfields of Rattray
Perth 286 C5
Westfield Sole Kent 69 G9
West Firle E Sus 23 D7
West Fleetham
Northumb 264 D5
West Flodden
Northumb 263 C10
Westford Som 27 C10
West Garforth
W Yorks 206 G3
Westgate Durham 232 D4
N Lincs 199 F9
Norf 176 E4
Norf 177 E7
Westgate Hill
W Yorks 197 B8
Westgate on Sea
Kent 71 E10
Westgate Street
Norf 160 E3
West Ginge Oxon 64 B2
West Gorton
Gtr Man 184 B5
West Grafton Wilts 63 G8
West Green Hants 49 B8
London 67 B10
S Yorks 197 F11
W Sus 51 F9
West Greenskares
Aberds 303 C7
West Grimstead
Wilts 32 B2
West Grinstead
W Sus 35 C11
West Haddlesey
N Yorks 198 B5
West Haddon
W Nhants 120 C2
West Hagbourne
Oxon 64 B4
West Hagley Worcs 133 G8
Westhall Aberds 302 G6
Suff 143 G8
West Hall Cumb 240 D3
West Hallam Derbys 170 G6
Westhall Hill Oxon 82 C3
West Halton
N Lincs 200 C2
Westham Dorset 17 F9
E Sus 23 E10

Westham continued
Som.....44 D2
West Ham Hants...48 C6
London.....68 C2
Westhampnett
W Sus.....22 B5
West Hampstead
London.....67 B9
West Handley
Derbys.....186 F5
West Hanney Oxon..82 G6
West Hanningfield
Essex.....88 F2
West Hardwick
W Yorks.....198 D2
West Harling Norf..141 G9
West Harlsey
N Yorks.....225 F8
West Harnham
Wilts.....31 B10
West Harptree Bath..44 B5
West Harrow London..66 B6
West Harting W Sus....34 C3
West Harton T&W..243 E9
West Hatch Som....28 C3
Wilts.....30 B6
Westhay Som.....44 F2
Westhead Lancs..194 F2
West Head Norf...139 B11
West Heath Ches E..168 C4
Hants.....48 B5
Hants.....49 B11
London.....68 D3
W Mid.....117 B10
West Helmsdale
Highld.....311 H4
West Hendon London..67 B8
West Hendred Oxon..64 B2
West Herrington
T&W.....243 G8
West Heslerton
N Yorks.....217 D8
West Hewish
N Som.....59 G11
Westhide Hereford..97 C11
Westhill Aberds..293 C10
E Yorks.....209 F10
Highld.....301 E7
West Hill Devon...15 C7
E Sus.....38 E4
E Yorks.....218 F3
London.....67 E8
N Som.....60 D3
Som.....30 B2
Staffs.....151 G9
Wilts.....61 F11
W Sus.....51 G10
West Hoathly
W Sus.....51 G11
West Holme Dorset..18 D3
West Holywell T&W..243 C8
Westhope Hereford..115 G9
Shrops.....131 F9
West Horndon Essex..68 B6
Westhorp
W Nhants.....119 G10
Westhorpe Lincs....156 C4
Notts.....171 E11
Suff.....125 D10
West Horrington
Som.....44 D5
West Horsley Sur....50 C5
West Horton
Northumb.....264 C2
West Hougham Kent..55 E9
Westhoughton
Gtr Man.....195 F7
West Houlland
Shetland.....313 H4
Westhouse N Yorks..212 E3
Westhouses Derbys..170 D6
West Houses Lincs..174 E4
West Howe BCP....19 B7
West Howetown Som..42 G2
Westhumble Sur....51 C7
West Huntington
York.....207 B8
West Huntspill Som..43 E10
West Hurn BCP....19 B8
West Hyde Herts....85 G8
West Hynish Argyll..288 F1
West Hythe Kent....54 G6
West Ilkerton Devon..41 D8
West Ilsley W Berks..64 C3
Westing Shetland..312 C7
Westington Glos....100 D2
West Itchenor W Sus..22 C3
West Jesmond
T&W.....243 D7
West Keal Lincs....174 C5
West Kennett Wilts..62 F6
West Kensington
London.....67 D8
West Kilbride
N Ayrs.....266 F4
West Kilburn London..67 C8
West Kingsdown
Kent.....68 G5
West Kingston
W Sus.....35 G9
West Kington Wilts..61 D10
West Kington Wick
Wilts.....61 D10
West Kinharrachie
Aberds.....303 F9
West Kirby Mers..182 D2
West Kirkby Mers..182 D2
West Knapton
N Yorks.....217 D7
West Knighton
Dorset.....17 D10
West Knoyle Wilts..45 G11
West Kyloe
Northumb.....273 G11
West Kyo Durham..242 G5
Westlake Devon....8 E2
West Lambrook
Som.....28 D6
Westland Argyll....275 G11

Westland Green
Herts.....105 G8
Westlands Staffs..168 G4
Worcs.....117 E7
West Langdon Kent..55 D10
West Langwell
Highld.....309 J6
West Lavington Wilts..46 C4
W Sus.....34 C5
West Layton
N Yorks.....224 D2
West Lea Durham..234 B4
West Leake Notts..153 D10
West Learmouth
Northumb.....263 B9
Westleigh Devon....25 B7
Devon.....27 D9
Gtr Man.....194 G6
West Leigh Devon..25 F11
Hants.....22 B2
Som.....42 G6
Westleton Suff....127 D8
West Lexham Norf..158 F6
Westley Shrops....131 B7
Suff.....124 E6
Westley Heights
Essex.....69 B7
Westley Waterless
Cambs.....124 F2
West Lilling N Yorks..216 F2
Westlington Bucks..84 C3
Westlinton Cumb..239 E9
West Linton Borders..270 C2
West Liss Hants....34 B3
West Littleton S Glos..61 D10
West Lockinge Oxon..64 B2
West Looe Corn.....6 E5
West Luccombe
Som.....41 D11
West Lulworth Dorset 18 E2
West Lutton
N Yorks.....217 F8
West Lydford Som..44 G5
West Lydiatt
Hereford.....97 C11
West Lyn Devon....41 D8
West Lyng Som....28 B4
West Lynn Norf....158 E2
West Mains
Borders.....271 F11
S Lanark.....268 G2
West Malling Kent..53 B7
West Malvern Worcs..98 B5
Westmancote Worcs..99 D8
West Marden W Sus..34 E3
West Marina E Sus..38 F3
West Markham
Notts.....188 G2
Westmarsh Kent....71 G9
West Marsh
NE Lincs.....201 E9
West Marton
N Yorks.....204 C3
West Mathers
Aberds.....293 G9
West Melbury Dorset..30 C5
West Melton
S Yorks.....198 G2
West Meon Hants..33 C10
West Meon Woodlands
Hants.....33 B10
West Merkland
Highld.....308 F3
West Mersea Essex..89 C8
Westmeston E Sus..36 E4
Westmill Herts....104 C3
Herts.....105 F7
West Milton Dorset..16 B6
Westminster London..67 D10
West Minster Kent..70 E2
West Molesey Sur..66 F6
West Monkseaton
T&W.....243 C8
West Monkton Som..28 B3
West Moor T&W....243 C7
Westmoor End
Cumb.....229 D8
West Moors Dorset..31 G9
West Morden Dorset..18 B4
West Morriston
Borders.....272 G2
West Morton
W Yorks.....205 E7
West Mudford Som..29 C9
Westmuir Angus..287 B7
West Muir Angus..293 G7
West Myreriggs
Perth.....286 C6
Westness Orkney..314 D3
West Ness N Yorks..216 D3
West Newham
Northumb.....242 B3
Westnewton Cumb..229 C8
Northumb.....263 C10
West Newton
E Yorks.....209 F9
Norf.....158 D3
Som.....28 B3

Weston continued
Shrops.....149 D11
S Lanark.....269 F10
Soton.....32 E6
Staffs.....151 D9
Suff.....143 F8
W Berks.....63 E11
W Nhants.....101 B11
Weston Bampfylde
Som.....29 C10
Weston Beggard
Hereford.....97 C11
Westonbirt Glos....61 B11
Weston by Welland
N Nhants.....136 E5
Weston Colley Hants..48 F4
Weston Colville
Cambs.....124 G2
Westoncommon
Shrops.....149 D8
Weston Common
Soton.....33 E7
Weston Corbett
Hants.....49 D7
Weston Coyney
Stoke.....168 G6
Weston Ditch Suff..124 B3
Weston Favell
W Nhants.....120 E5
Weston Green
Cambs.....124 G2
Norf.....160 G2
Sur.....67 F7
Weston Heath
Shrops.....150 G5
Weston Hills Lincs..156 E5
Weston in Arden
Warks.....135 F7
Westoning C Beds..103 E10
Weston-in-Gordano
N Som.....60 E2
Weston Jones
Staffs.....150 E5
Weston Longville
Norf.....160 F2
Weston Lullingfields
Shrops.....149 E8
Weston Manor IoW..20 D2
Weston Mill Plym....7 D9
Weston-on-Avon
Warks.....118 G3
Weston-on-the-Green
Oxon.....83 B8
Weston-on-Trent
Derbys.....153 D8
Weston Park Bath..61 F8
Weston Patrick
Hants.....49 D7
Weston Point
Halton.....183 E7
Weston Rhyn Shrops..148 B5
Weston-sub-Edge
Glos.....100 C2
Weston-super-Mare
N Som.....59 G10
Weston Town Som..45 E8
Weston Turville
Bucks.....84 C5
Weston under Lizard
Staffs.....150 G6
Weston under Penyard
Hereford.....98 G2
Weston under Wetherley
Warks.....119 D7
Weston Underwood
Derbys.....170 G3
M Keynes.....121 G7
Westonwharf
Shrops.....149 D8
Westonzoyland
Som.....43 G11
West Orchard Dorset..30 D4
West Overton Wilts..62 F6
Westow N Yorks....216 F5
Westowe Som....42 G6
Westown Devon....27 E10
Perth.....286 E6
West Panson Devon..12 C2
West Park Hrtlpl....234 E5
Hull.....200 B5
Mers.....183 B7
T&W.....243 D9
W Yorks.....205 F11
West Parley Dorset..19 B7
West Pasture
Durham.....232 G4
West Peckham Kent..52 C6
West Pelton
Durham.....242 G6
West Pennard Som..44 F4
West Pentire Corn....4 C5
West Perry Cambs..122 D2
West Pontnewydd
Torf.....78 F3
West Poringland
Norf.....142 C5
West Porlock Som..41 D11
West Portholland
Corn.....5 G9
West Porton Renfs..277 G8
West Pulham Dorset..30 F2
West Putford Devon..24 D5
West Quantoxhead
Som.....42 G6
Westra V Glam....58 E6
West Rainton
Durham.....234 B2
West Rasen Lincs..189 D9
West Ravendale
NE Lincs.....190 B3
West Raynham Norf..159 D7
West Retford Notts..187 E11
Westridge Green
W Berks.....64 D5
Westrigg W Loth..269 B8
Westrip Glos.....80 D4
Westrop Wilts.....61 G11
Westrop Green
W Berks.....64 E3

West Rounton
N Yorks.....225 E8
West Row Suff....124 B3
West Royd W Yorks..205 F9
West Rudham Norf..158 D6
West Ruislip London..66 B5
Westrum N Lincs..200 F4
West Runton Norf...177 E11
Westruther Borders..272 F2
Westry Cambs.....139 D7
West Saltoun
E Loth.....271 B9
West Sandford
Devon.....26 G4
West Sandwick
Shetland.....312 E6
West Scholes
W Yorks.....205 G7
West Scrafton
N Yorks.....213 C11
West Shepton Som..44 E6
West Sherford Devon..9 G7
West Side Bl Gwent..77 D11
Orkney.....314 C5
West Skelston
Dumfries.....247 F8
West Sleekburn
Northumb.....253 G7
West Somerton
Norf.....161 F9
West Southbourne
BCP.....19 C8
West Stafford
Dorset.....17 D10
West Stockwith
Notts.....188 C3
West Stoke Devon....13 G9
Som.....29 D7
W Sus.....22 B4
West Stonesdale
N Yorks.....223 E7
West Stoughton Som..44 D2
West Stour Dorset..30 C3
West Stourmouth
Kent.....71 G9
West Stow Suff....124 C6
West Stowell Wilts..62 G6
West Strathan
Highld.....308 C5
West Stratton Hants..48 E4
West Street Kent....54 C2
Kent.....55 C10
Medway.....69 D8
Suff.....125 C9
West Tanfield
N Yorks.....214 D5
West Taphouse Corn..6 C3
West Tarbert Argyll..275 G9
West Tarring
W Sus.....35 G10
West Third Borders..262 B4
West Thirston
Northumb.....252 D5
West Thorney W Sus..22 C3
Westthorpe Derbys..187 F7
West Thurrock
Thurrock.....68 D5
West Tilbury
Thurrock.....69 D7
West Tisted Hants..33 B11
West Tofts Norf....140 E6
Perth.....286 D5
West Tolgus Corn....4 G3
West Torrington
Lincs.....189 E10
West Town Bath....60 G4
Cambs.....104 B6
Devon.....14 B3
Devon.....24 C4
Hants.....21 B10
Hereford.....115 E8
N Som.....60 F3
Som.....44 F4
W Sus.....36 B4
West Tytherley Hants..32 B3
West Tytherton Wilts..62 E2
Westvale Mers.....182 B6
West Vale W Yorks..196 C5
West View Hrtlpl....234 D5
West Village V Glam..58 E3
Westville Devon....8 G4
Notts.....171 F8
West Walton Norf..157 G9
West Walton Highway
Norf.....157 G9
Westward Cumb..229 C11
Westward Ho! Devon..24 B6
West Watergate Corn..6 E4
West Watford Herts..85 F10
Westweekmoor
Devon.....12 C4
Westwell Kent....54 D3
Oxon.....82 D2
Westwell Leacon
Kent.....54 D3
West Wellow Hants..32 D3
Westwells Wilts....61 F11
West Wemyss Fife..280 C6
Westwick Cambs..123 D8
Durham.....223 B11
Norf.....160 D5
West Wick N Som..59 G11
West Wickham
Cambs.....106 B2
London.....67 F11
Westwick Row Herts..85 D9
West Williamston
Pembs.....73 D8
West Willoughby
Lincs.....173 G7
West Winch Norf..158 F2
West Winterslow
Wilts.....47 G8
West Wittering
W Sus.....21 B11
West Witton
N Yorks.....213 B11
Westwood Devon..14 B6
Devon.....14 G5
Kent.....55 D7
Kent.....71 F11
Notts.....171 E7
Pboro.....138 D3

Westwood continued
S Lanark.....268 E2
Wilts.....45 B10
Wilts.....46 G6
West Woodburn
Northumb.....251 F9
West Woodhay
W Berks.....63 G11
Westwood Heath
W Mid.....118 B5
West Woodlands
Som.....45 E9
Westwood Park
Essex.....107 E9
Gtr Man.....184 B3
Westwoodside
N Lincs.....188 B3
West Worldham
Hants.....49 F8
West Worlington
Devon.....26 E3
West Worthing
W Sus.....35 G10
West Wratting
Cambs.....124 G2
West Wycombe
Bucks.....84 G4
West Wylam
Northumb.....242 E4
Westy Warr.....183 D10
West Yatton Wilts..61 E11
West Yell Shetland..312 E6
West Yeo Som.....43 G10
West Yoke Kent....68 F5
West Youlstone Corn..24 D3
Wetham Green Kent..69 E10
Wetheral Cumb..239 G11
Wetheral Plain
Cumb.....239 G11
Wetherby W Yorks..206 D4
Wetherden Suff....125 D10
Wetherden Upper Town
Suff.....125 D10
Wetheringsett Suff..126 D2
Wethersfield Essex..106 E4
Wethersta Shetland..312 G5
Wetherup Street
Suff.....126 E2
Wetley Rocks Staffs..169 F7
Wetmore Staffs....152 E5
Wettenhall Ches E..167 C10
Wettenhall Green
Ches E.....167 C10
Wettles Shrops....131 F8
Wetton Staffs.....169 D10
Wetwang E Yorks..208 B4
Wetwood Staffs....150 C5
Wexcombe Wilts....47 B9
Wexham Street
Bucks.....66 C3
Weybourne Norf..177 E10
Sur.....49 D11
Weybread Suff....142 G4
Weybridge Sur....66 G5
Weycroft Devon....16 B2
Weydale Highld...310 C5
Weyhill Hants.....47 D10
Weymouth Dorset..17 F9
Weythel Powys....114 F4
Whaddon Bucks..102 E6
Cambs.....104 B6
Glos.....80 C4
Glos.....99 G9
Wilts.....31 B11
Wilts.....61 G11
Whaddon Gap
Cambs.....104 B6
Whale Cumb.....230 G6
Whaley Derbys....187 G8
Whaley Bridge
Derbys.....185 E8
Whaley Thorns
Derbys.....187 G8
Whaligoe Highld..310 E7
Whalley Lancs....203 F10
Whalley Banks
Lancs.....203 F10
Whalley Range
Gtr Man.....184 C4
Whalleys Lancs....194 F3
Whalton Northumb..252 G4
Wham N Yorks....212 G5
Whaplode Lincs....156 E6
Whaplode Drove
Lincs.....156 G6
Whaplode St Catherine
Lincs.....156 G6
Wharf Warks.....119 G8
Wharfe N Yorks....212 F5
Wharles Lancs....202 F4
Wharley End
C Beds.....103 C8
Wharmley Northumb..241 D9
Wharncliffe Side
S Yorks.....186 C3
Wharram le Street
N Yorks.....217 F7
Wharram Percy
N Yorks.....217 G7
Wharton Ches W..167 B11
Hereford.....115 F10
Wharton Green
Ches W.....167 B11
Whashton N Yorks..224 D3
Whasset Cumb....211 C10
Whatcombe Dorset..30 G4
Whatcote Warks..100 C6
Whatcroft Ches W..167 B11
Whateley Staffs....134 D4
Whatfield Suff....107 B10
Whatley Som.....28 F5
Som.....45 D9
Whatlington E Sus..38 D3
Whatmore Shrops..116 D2
Whatsole Street Kent..54 E6
Whatstandwell
Derbys.....170 E4
Whatton Notts....154 B4
Whauphill Dumfries..236 E6
Whaw N Yorks....223 E9
Wheal Alfred Corn....2 B3

Wheal Baddon Corn....4 G5
Wheal Busy Corn....4 G4
Wheal Frances Corn..4 E5
Wheal Kitty Corn....4 E4
Wheal Rose Corn....4 G4
Wheatacre Norf....143 E9
Wheatcroft Derbys..170 D5
Wheathampstead
Herts.....85 C11
Wheathill Shrops..132 G2
Som.....44 G5
Wheat Hold Hants..64 G5
Wheatley Devon....14 C4
Hants.....49 E9
Oxon.....83 D9
Wheatley Hill
Durham.....234 D3
Wheatley Hills
S Yorks.....198 G6
Wheatley Lane
Lancs.....204 F2
Wheatley Park
S Yorks.....198 F5
Wheaton Aston
Staffs.....151 G7
Wheddon Cross Som..42 F2
Wheedlemont
Aberds.....302 G4
Wheelbarrow Town
Kent.....55 D7
Wheeler End Bucks..84 G4
Wheelerstreet Sur..50 E2
Wheelock Ches E..168 D3
Wheelock Heath
Ches E.....168 D2
Wheelton Lancs....194 C6
Lancs.....194 C6
Lancs.....194 D6
Wheen Angus.....292 F5
Wheldale W Yorks..198 B3
Wheldrake York....207 D9
Whelford Glos....81 F11
Whelley Gtr Man..194 F5
Whelp Street Suff..107 B8
Whelston Flint....182 F2
Whempstead Herts..104 G6
Whenby N Yorks..216 F2
Whepstead Suff....124 F6
Wherry Town Corn....1 D5
Wherstead Suff....108 B3
Wherwell Hants....47 E11
Wheston Derbys..185 F10
Whetley Cross Dorset..29 G7
Whetsted Kent....53 D7
Whetstone Leics..135 D11
London.....86 G3
Whettleton Shrops..131 G8
Whicham Cumb..210 C2
Whichford Warks..100 E6
Whickham T&W..242 E6
Whiddon Devon....40 F5
Whiddon Down
Devon.....13 C9
Whifflet N Lanark..268 C4
Whigstreet Angus..287 C8
Whilton W Nhants..120 E2
Whilton Locks
W Nhants.....120 E2
Whimble Devon....24 G5
Whim Farm Borders..270 E4
Whimple Devon....14 B6
Whimpwell Green
Norf.....161 D7
Whinburgh Norf....141 B10
Whinfield Darl....224 B6
Whinhall N Lanark..268 B5
Whin Lane End
Lancs.....202 E3
Whinmoor W Yorks..206 F3
Whinney Hill
Stockton.....225 B7
S Yorks.....187 C7
Whinnieliggate
Dumfries.....237 D9
Whinnyfold Aberds..303 F10
Whinny Heights
Blackburn.....195 B7
Whins of Milton
Stirling.....278 C5
Whins Wood
W Yorks.....205 F7
Whipcott Devon....27 D9
Whippendell Botton
Herts.....85 E9
Whippingham IoW..20 C6
Whipsiderry Corn....4 C6
Whipsnade C Beds..85 B8
Whipton Devon....14 C5
Whirley Grove
Ches E.....184 F5
Whirlow S Yorks..186 E4
Whisby Lincs....172 B6
Whissendine
Rutland.....154 G6
Whissonsett Norf..159 E8
Whisterfield Ches E..184 G4
Whistlefield Argyll..276 C2
Argyll.....276 C4
Whistley Green
Wokingham.....65 E9
Whistlow Oxon....101 F9
Whiston Mers....183 C7
Staffs.....151 G7
Staffs.....169 E7
S Yorks.....186 D6
W Nhants.....120 E6
Whiston Cross
Mers.....183 C7
Shrops.....132 C5
Whitacre Heath
Warks.....134 E4
Whitbarrow Village
Cumb.....230 F4
Whitbeck Cumb..210 C2

Whitbourne
Hereford.....116 F4
Whitbourne Moor
Wilts.....45 D10
Whitburn T&W..243 E10
W Loth.....269 C8
Whitburn Colliery
T&W.....243 E10
Whitby Ches W..182 F5
Whitby N Yorks....227 C7
Whitbyheath
Ches W.....182 F5
Whitchurch Bath..60 F6
Bucks.....102 G5
Cardiff.....59 C7
Devon.....12 G5
Hants.....48 D3
Hereford.....79 B9
Pembs.....90 F5
Shrops.....167 G8
Som.....30 C2
Whitchurch
Canonicorum
Dorset.....16 B3
Whitchurch Hill Oxon..64 D6
Whitchurch-on-Thames
Oxon.....64 D6
Whitcombe Dorset..17 D10
Whitcot Shrops....131 E7
Whitcott Keysett
Shrops.....130 G6
Whiteacre Moray..302 E2
Kent.....54 D6
Whiteacre Heath
Warks.....134 E4
Whiteash Green
Essex.....106 E5
White Ball Som....27 D9
Whitebirk Blackburn..195 B8
Whitebog Highld..301 C7
Whitebridge Highld..290 B6
Whitebrook Mon....79 D8
Whitebushes Sur....51 D11
Whitecairn Dumfries..236 D4
Whitecairns Aberds..303 B11
Whitecastle
S Lanark.....269 G10
Whitechapel Lancs..203 E7
London.....67 C10
Whitechurch Maund
Hereford.....97 B11
Whitecleat Orkney..314 F5
Whitecliff Glos....79 C9
Whiteclosegate
Cumb.....239 F10
Whitecote W Yorks..205 F10
White Colne Essex..107 F7
White Coppice
Lancs.....194 D6
Whitecote W Yorks..205 F10
Whitecraig E Loth..281 G7
Whitecraigs
E Renf.....267 D11
Whitecroft Glos....79 D10
Whitecrook
W Dunb.....267 B10
Whitecross Corn....2 C2
Corn.....6 E2
Corn.....10 G5
Falk.....279 F9
Som.....28 C6
Staffs.....151 E7
White Cross Bath....44 B5
Bath.....44 B6
Corn.....2 E5
Corn.....5 D7
Som.....43 D10
Wilts.....45 G9
White Cross Hill
Cambs.....123 B9
White End Worcs....98 E5
Whiteface Highld..309 L7
Whitefarland
N Ayrs.....255 C9
Whitefaulds S Ayrs..245 B7
Whitefield Aberds..303 C11
Dorset.....18 B5
Gtr Man.....195 F10
Perth.....286 D5
Som.....27 B9
Whitefield Lane End
Mers.....183 D7
Whiteflat E Ayrs..258 D2
Whiteford Aberds..303 G7
Whitegate Ches W..167 B10
White Gate
Gtr Man.....195 G11
Som.....28 F4
Whitehall Blackburn..195 C7
Bristol.....60 E6
Devon.....27 E10
Devon.....40 F4
Hants.....49 C8
Herts.....104 E6
W Sus.....35 C10
Whitehall Village
Orkney.....314 D6
Whitehaven Cumb..219 B9
Shrops.....148 E5
Whitehawk Brighton..36 G4
Whiteheath Gate
W Mid.....133 F9
Whitehill E Sus....37 B8
Hants.....49 G9
Kent.....54 B4
Staffs.....151 G7
Staffs.....169 F8
S Yorks.....186 D6
W Nhants.....120 E4
White Hill Bath....45 G10
Wilts.....45 G10
White Hills Herts..104 G5
W Nhants.....120 E4

Whiteholme
Blackpool.....202 F2
Whitehough Derbys..185 E8
Whitehouse Aberds..293 B8
Argyll.....275 G9
White House Suff..108 B2
Whitehouse Common
W Mid.....134 D2
Whitehouse Green
W Berks.....65 F7
White Houses Notts..188 F3
Whiteinch Glasgow..267 B10
Whitekirk E Loth..281 E11
Whiteknights Reading 65 E9
Whiteknowes
Aberds.....293 C10
Whitelackington
Som.....28 D5
White Ladies Aston
Worcs.....117 G8
Whitelaw S Lanark..268 G2
Whiteleaf Bucks....84 E4
Whiteleas T&W....243 E9
Whiteleaved Oak
Glos.....98 D5
Whitelee Borders..262 F5
Northumb.....250 B6
Whiteleys S Ayrs..257 C9
White-le-Head
Durham.....242 G5
Whiteley Bank IoW..21 E7
Whiteley Green
Ches E.....184 F6
Whiteley Village Sur..66 G5
White Lund Lancs..211 G8
Whitelye Mon.....79 E9
Whitemans Green
W Sus.....36 B4
White Mill Carms..93 G9
Whitemire Moray..301 D9
Whitemoor Corn....5 D9
Nottingham.....171 G8
Staffs.....118 C5
White Moor Derbys..170 F5
Whitemore Staffs..168 C5
Whitenap Hants....32 C5
White Ness Shetland..313 J5
White Notley Essex..88 B3
White Oak Kent....68 F4
Whiteoak Green
Oxon.....82 C4
White Ox Mead Bath..45 B8
Whiteparish Wilts..32 C2
White Pit Lincs....190 F5
Whitepits Wilts....45 G11
White Post Kent....52 E4
Notts.....171 D8
Whiterashes Aberds. 303 G9
Whiteriggs Borders..262 C3
Whiterock Bridgend..58 C2
White Rocks Hereford..97 G8
White Roding or White
Roothing Essex....87 C9
Whiterow Highld..310 E7
White's Green W Sus..34 B6
Whiteshill Glos....80 D4
S Glos.....60 D6
Whiteside Northumb..240 D6
W Loth.....269 B9
Whitesmith E Sus..23 C8
Whitespots
Dumfries.....247 F10
White Stake Lancs..194 B4
Whitestaunton Som..28 E3
Whitestone Aberds..293 D8
Devon.....14 C3
Devon.....40 B3
Warks.....135 F7
White Stone
Hereford.....97 C11
Whitestones Aberds..303 D8
Whitestreet Green
Suff.....107 D9
Whitewall Common
Mon.....60 B2
Whitewall Corner
N Yorks.....216 E5
White Waltham
Windsor.....65 D10
Whiteway Bath....61 G8
Dorset.....18 E3
Glos.....80 C6
Glos.....80 F4
Whitewell Aberds..303 C9
Corn.....11 G5
Highld.....291 C11
Lancs.....203 D9
Wrex.....167 G2
Whitewell Bottom
Lancs.....195 C10
Whiteworks Devon..13 G8
Whitfield Kent....55 D10
Northumb.....241 F7
S Glos.....79 G11
W Nhants.....102 D2
Whitfield Court Sur..50 E3
Whitfield Hall
Northumb.....241 F7
Whitford = Chwitffordd
Flint.....181 F10
Whitgift E Yorks..199 C10
Whitgreave Staffs..151 D7
Whithaugh Borders..249 F11
Whithebeir Orkney..314 C6
Whithorn Dumfries..236 E6
Whiting Bay N Ayrs..256 D2
Whitington Norf..140 D4
Whitkirk W Yorks..206 G3
Whitland = Hendy-Gwyn
Carms.....73 B11
Whitlaw Borders..271 F9
Whitleigh Plym.....7 D9
Whitletts S Ayrs..257 E9
Whitley Gtr Man..194 F5
N Yorks.....198 C5
Reading.....65 E8
S Yorks.....186 C4
Wilts.....61 F11

Whitley continued
Whitley 119 B7
Whitley Bay T&W . . .243 C9
Whitley Bridge
N Yorks 198 C5
Whitley Chapel
Northumb 241 F10
Whitley Head
W Yorks 204 E6
Whitley Heath
Staffs 150 D6
Whitley Lower
W Yorks 197 D8
Whitley Reed
Ches W 183 E10
Whitley Row Kent 52 C3
Whitley Sands T&W . .243 C9
Whitley Thorpe
N Yorks 198 C5
Whitley Wood
Reading 65 F8
Whitlock's End
W Mid 118 B2
Whitminster Glos 80 D3
Whitmoor Devon 27 E9
Whitmore Dorset 31 F9
Staffs 168 G4
Whitmore Park
W Mid 134 G6
Whitnage Devon 27 D8
Whitnash Warks 118 E6
Whitnell Som 43 F8
Whitney Bottom Som .28 E4
Whitney-on-Wye
Hereford 96 B5
Whitrigg Cumb 229 D10
Cumb 238 F6
Whitriggs Borders . .262 F3
Whitsbury Hants 31 D10
Whitslaid Borders . . .271 G11
Whitsome Borders . . .273 E7
Whitsomehill
Borders 273 F7
Whitson Newport 59 C11
Whitstable Kent 70 F6
Whitstone Corn 11 B11
Whittingham
Northumb 264 G3
Whittingslow Shrops .131 F8
Whittington Glos 99 G10
Lancs 212 D2
Norf 140 D4
Shrops 148 C6
Staffs 133 C7
Staffs 134 B3
Staffs 150 C5
Warks 134 D5
Worcs 117 C7
Whittington Moor
Derbys 186 G5
Whittlebury
N Nhants 102 C3
Whittleford Warks . . .134 E6
Whittle-le-Woods
Lancs 194 C5
Whittlesey Cambs . . .138 D5
Whittlesford Cambs . .105 B9
Whittlestone Head
Blackburn 195 D8
Whitton Borders 263 E7
Hereford 115 C8
London 66 E6
N Lincs 200 C2
Northumb 252 C3
Powys 114 D5
Shrops 115 C11
Stockton 234 G3
Suff 108 B2
Whittonditch Wilts . . .63 E9
Whittonstall
Northumb 242 F3
Whittytree Shrops . . .115 B8
Whitway Hants 48 B3
Whitwell Derbys 187 F8
Herts 104 G3
IoW 20 F6
N Yorks 224 F5
Rutland 137 B8
Whitwell-on-the-Hill
N Yorks 216 F4
Whitwell Street
Norf 160 E2
Whitwick Leics 153 F8
Whitwood W Yorks . . .198 C2
Whitworth Lancs 195 D11
Whixall Shrops 149 C10
Whixley N Yorks 206 B4
Whoberley W Mid 118 B6
Wholeflats Falk 279 E8
Whome Orkney 314 G3
Whorlton Durham 224 C2
N Yorks 225 E9
Whydown E Sus 38 F2
Whygate Northumb . .241 B7
Whyke W Sus 22 C5
Whyle Hereford 115 E11
Whyteleafe Sur 51 B10
Wibdon Glos 79 F9
Wibsey W Yorks 205 G8
Wibtoft Leics 135 F9
Wichenford Worcs . . .116 E5
Wichling Kent 54 B2
Wick
BCP 19 C8
Devon 27 G11
Highld 310 D7
S Glos 61 B8
Shetland 313 K6
Som 28 B6
Som 43 C10
Som 43 G8
V Glam 58 E2
Wilts 31 C11
Worcs 99 B9
W Sus 35 G8
Wicken Cambs 123 C11
N Nhants 102 D4
Wicken Bonhunt
Essex 105 E9
Wickenby Lincs 189 E9
Wicken Green Village
Norf 158 C6

Wick Episcopi
Worcs 116 G6
Wickersley S Yorks . .187 C7
Wicker Street Green
Suff 107 C9
Wickford Essex 88 G3
Wickham Hants 33 E9
W Berks 63 E11
Wickham Bishops
Essex 88 C4
Wickhambreaux Kent .55 B8
Wickhambrook Suff .124 G4
Wickhamford Worcs . .99 C11
Wickham Green
Suff 125 D11
W Berks 63 E11
Wickham Heath
W Berks 64 F2
Wickham Market
Suff 126 F6
Wickhampton Norf . .143 B8
Wickham St Paul
Essex 106 D6
Wickham Skeith
Suff 125 D11
Wickham Street
Suff 124 G5
Suff 125 D11
Wick Hill Brack 65 E11
Kent 53 E10
Wokingham 65 G9
Wickhurst Kent 52 D4
Wicklane Bath 45 B7
Wicklewood Norf 141 C11
Wickmere Norf 160 C3
Wickridge Street
Glos 98 F6
Wick Rocks S Glos . . .61 E8
Wick St Lawrence
N Som 59 F11
Wickstreet E Sus 23 D8
Wick Street E Sus 80 D5
Wickwar S Glos 61 B8
Widbrook Wilts 45 B10
Widcombe Bath 61 G9
Widdington Essex . . .105 E10
Widdrington
Northumb 253 D7
Widdrington Station
Northumb 252 E6
Widecombe in the Moor
Devon 13 G11
Widegates Corn 6 D5
Widemouth Bay Corn .24 G2
Wideopen T&W 242 C6
Widewall Orkney 314 G4
Widewell Plym 7 C9
Widford Essex 87 D11
Herts 86 B6
Widham Green
Cambs 124 F3
Widham Wilts 62 B5
Widley Hants 33 F11
Widmer End Bucks . . .84 F5
Widmerpool Notts . . .154 D2
Widmoor Bucks 66 B2
Widmore London 68 F2
Widnes Halton 183 D8
Wierton Kent 53 D9
Wig Powys 130 F2
Wigan Gtr Man 194 F5
Wiganthorpe
N Yorks 216 E3
Wigbeth Dorset 31 F8
Wigborough Som 28 D6
Wig Fach Bridgend . . .57 F10
Wiggaton Devon 15 C8
Wiggenhall St Germans
Norf 157 G11
Wiggenhall St Mary
Magdalen Norf 157 G11
Wiggenhall St Mary the
Virgin Norf 157 G11
Wiggenhall St Peter
Norf 158 G2
Wiggens Green
Essex 106 C3
Wigginton Staffs 134 B4
Wigginstall Staffs . . .169 C9
Wigginton Herts 84 C6
Oxon 101 E7
Shrops 148 B6
Staffs 134 B4
York 207 B7
Wigginton Bottom
Herts 84 C6
Wigginton Heath
Oxon 101 D7
Wigglesworth
N Yorks 204 B2
Wiggonby Cumb 239 G7
Wiggonholt W Sus . . .35 D9
Wighill N Yorks 206 D5
Wighton Norf 159 B8
Wightwick Manor
Staffs 133 D7
Wigley Derbys 186 G4
Hants 32 D4
Wigmore Hereford . . .115 D8
Medway 69 G10
Wigsley Notts 188 G5
Wigsthorpe
N Nhants 137 G10
Wigston Leics 136 D2
Wigston Magna
Leics 136 D2
Wigston Parva Leics .135 F9
Wigthorpe Notts 187 E9
Wigtoft Lincs 156 B5
Wigton Cumb 229 B11
Wigtown Dumfries . . .236 D6
Wigtwizzle S Yorks . .186 B2
Wike W Yorks 206 D1
Wike Well End
S Yorks 199 E7
Wilberfoss E Yorks . .207 C10

Wilberlee W Yorks . . .196 E5
Wilburton Cambs 123 C9
Wilby N Nhants 121 D7
Norf 141 F10
Suff 126 C4
Wilcot Wilts 62 G6
Wilcott Shrops 149 F7
Wilcott Marsh
Shrops 149 F7
Wilcove Corn 7 D8
Wilcrick Newport 60 B2
Wilday Green
Derbys 186 G4
Wildboarclough
Ches E 169 B7
Wilden Bedford 121 F11
Worcs 116 C6
Wildern Hants 33 E7
Wildernesse Kent 52 B4
Wilderspool Warr . . .183 D10
Wilderswood
Gtr Man 194 E6
Wilde Street Suff 124 B4
Wildhern Hants 47 C11
Wildhill Herts 86 D3
Wildmanbridge
S Lanark 268 E6
Wild Mill Bridgend . . .58 C2
Wildmoor Hants 49 B7
Oxon 83 F7
Worcs 117 B9
Wildridings Brack 65 F11
Wildsworth Lincs 188 B4
Wildwood Staffs 151 E8
Wilford Nottingham . .153 B11
Wilgate Green Kent . . .54 B3
Wilkesley Ches E 167 G10
Wilkhaven Highld 311 L3
Wilkieston W Loth . . .270 B2
Wilkinthroop Som 29 C11
Wilkin Throop Som . . .29 C11
Wilksby Lincs 174 C3
Willacy Lane End
Lancs 202 F5
Willand Devon 27 E8
Som 27 E8
Willand Moor Devon . .27 E8
Willard's Hill E Sus . . .38 C2
Willaston Ches E 167 E11
Ches W 182 F4
Shrops 149 B11
Willen M Keynes 103 C7
Willenhall W Mid 119 B7
W Mid 133 D9
Willerby E Yorks 208 G6
N Yorks 217 D10
Willersey Glos 100 D2
Willersley Hereford . . .96 B6
Willesborough Kent . . .54 E4
Willesborough Lees
Kent 54 E4
Willesden London 67 C8
Willesden Green
London 67 C8
Willesleigh Devon 40 G5
Willesley Leics 152 G6
Wilts 61 B11
Willett Som 42 G6
Willey Shrops 132 D3
Warks 135 G9
Willey Green Sur 50 C2
Willhayne Som 28 E4
Williamhope
Borders 261 C10
Williamscott Oxon . . .101 B9
William's Green
Suff 107 C9
Williamslee Borders . .270 G6
Williamstown
Rhondda 77 G8
Williamthorpe
Derbys 170 B6
Willian Herts 104 E4
Willicote Pastures
Worcs 100 B3
Willingale Essex 87 D9
Willingcott Devon 40 E3
Willingdon E Sus 23 E9
Willingham Cambs . . .123 C8
Suff 143 G8
Willingham by Stow
Lincs 188 E5
Willingham Green
Cambs 124 G2
Willington Bedford . . .104 B2
Derbys 152 D5
Durham 233 D9
Kent 53 C9
T&W 243 D8
Warks 100 D5
Willington Corner
Ches W 167 B8
Willington Quay
T&W 243 D8
Willisham Suff 125 G11
Willisham Tye Suff . . .125 G11
Willitoft E Yorks 207 F10
Williton Som 42 E5
Willoughbridge
Staffs 168 G3
Willoughby Lincs 191 G7
Warks 119 D10
Willoughby Hills
Lincs 174 F4
Willoughby-on-the-
Wolds Notts 154 D2
Willoughby Waterleys
Leics 135 E11
Willoughton Lincs . . .188 C6
Willowbank Bucks 66 B5
Willow Green
Ches W 183 F10
Worcs 116 F5
Willow Holme Cumb .239 F9
Willows Gtr Man 195 F8
Willows Green Essex . .88 B2
Willowtown
Bl Gwent 77 C11
Will Row Lincs 191 D7
Willsbridge S Glos 61 E7
Willslock Staffs 151 D11
Willstone Shrops 131 D9
Willsworthy Devon . . .12 E6

Wilmcote Warks 118 F3
Wilmington Bath 61 G7
Devon 15 B10
E Sus 23 E8
Kent 68 E5
Wilmington Green
E Sus 23 D8
Wilminstone Devon . . .12 F5
Wilmslow Ches E 184 E4
Wilmslow Park
Ches E 184 E5
Wilnecote Staffs 134 C4
Wilney Green Norf . . .141 G11
Wilpshire Lancs 203 G9
Wilsden W Yorks 205 F7
Wilsden Hill
W Yorks 205 F7
Wilsford Lincs 173 G8
Wilts 46 B6
Wilts 46 F6
Wilsham Devon 41 D9
Wilshaw W Yorks 196 F6
Wilsic S Yorks 187 B9
Wilsill N Yorks 214 G3
Wilsley Green Kent . . .53 F9
Wilsley Pound Kent . .53 F9
Wilsom Hants 49 F8
Wilson Hereford 97 G11
Leics 153 E8
Wilsontown
S Lanark 269 D9
Wilstead Bedford 103 C11
Wilsthorpe Derbys . . .153 C9
Lincs 155 G11
Wilstone Herts 84 C6
Wilstone Green
Herts 84 C6
Wilthorpe S Yorks . . .197 F10
Wilton Borders 261 G11
Cumb 219 C10
Hereford 97 G11
N Yorks 217 C7
Redcar 225 B11
Som 28 C2
Wilts 46 G5
Wilts 46 B5
Wilton Park Bucks . . .85 G7
Wiltown Devon 27 D11
Som 28 C5
Wimbish Essex 105 D11
Wimbish Green
Essex 106 D2
Wimblebury Staffs . . .151 G10
Wimbledon London . . .67 E8
Wimble Hill Hants 49 D10
Wimblington Cambs . .139 E8
Wimboldsley
Ches W 167 C11
Wimbolds Trafford
Ches W 182 G6
Wimborne Minster
Dorset 18 B6
Wimborne St Giles
Dorset 31 E8
Wimbotsham Norf . . .140 B2
Wimpole Cambs 104 B6
Wimpson Soton 32 E5
Wimpstone Warks . . .100 B4
Wincanton Som 30 B2
Winceby Lincs 174 B4
Wincham Ches W 183 F11
Winchburgh
W Loth 279 G11
Winchcombe Glos 99 F10
Winchelsea E Sus 38 D6
Winchelsea Beach
E Sus 38 D6
Winchester Hants 33 B7
Winchestown
Bl Gwent 77 C11
Winchet Hill Kent 53 E8
Winchfield Hants 49 C9
Winchfield Hurst
Hants 49 C9
Winchmore Hill
Bucks 84 G6
London 86 G4
Wincle Ches E 169 B7
Wincobank S Yorks . .186 C5
Winder Cumb 219 B10
Windermere Cumb . . .221 F8
Winderton Warks 100 C6
Windhill Highld 300 E5
Windhill W Yorks 205 F9
Wind Hill Cumb 210 E5
Pembs 73 F9
Windhouse Shetland . .312 D6
Winding Wood
W Berks 63 E11
Windle Ches W 182 F4
Windlehurst
Gtr Man 185 D7
Windlesham Sur 66 G2
Windley Derbys 170 F4
Windmill Corn 10 G3
Flint 181 G11
Flint 182 G2
Windmill Hill Bristol . .60 E5
E Sus 23 C10
Halton 183 E9
Kent 69 F10
Som 28 D4
Worcs 99 B8
W Yorks 197 D11
Windrush Glos 81 C11
Windsor N Lincs 199 E9
Windsor 66 D3
Windsoredge Glos 80 E4
Windsor Green Suff . .125 G7
Windwhistle Som 28 E5
Windy Arbor Mers . . .183 D7
Windy Arbour
Warks 118 C5
Windydoors
Borders 261 B10
Windyedge Fife 287 G7
Windyharbour
Ches E 184 G4
Windy Hill Wrex 166 E4
Windyknowe
W Loth 269 B9

Windy Nook T&W 243 E7
Windywalls Borders . .263 C7
Windy-Yett E Ayrs . . .267 E9
Wineham W Sus 36 C2
Winestead E Yorks . . .201 C10
Winewall Lancs 204 E4
Winfarthing Norf 142 F2
Winford IoW 21 E7
N Som 60 F4
Winforton Hereford . . .96 B5
Winfrith Newburgh
Dorset 18 E2
Wing Bucks 103 G7
Rutland 137 C7
Wingate Durham 234 D4
Wingates Gtr Man . . .195 F7
Northumb 252 D4
Wingerworth
Derbys 170 B5
Wingfield C Beds 103 F10
Suff 126 B4
S Yorks 186 B6
Wilts 45 B10
Wingfield Green
Suff 126 B4
Wingfield Park
Derbys 170 E5
Wingham Kent 55 B8
Wingham Green Kent .55 B8
Wingham Well Kent . . .55 B8
Wingmore Kent 55 E7
Wingrave Bucks 84 B5
Winkburn Notts 172 D2
Winkfield Brack 66 E2
Winkfield Place
Brack 66 E2
Winkfield Row
Brack 65 E11
Winkhill Staffs 169 E9
Winkhurst Green
Kent 52 D3
Winklebury Hants 48 C6
Winkleigh Devon 25 F10
Winksley N Yorks 214 E5
Winkton BCP 19 B9
Winlaton T&W 242 E5
Winlaton Mill T&W . . .242 E5
Winless Highld 310 D7
Winllan Powys 148 E4
Winmarleigh Lancs . .202 D5
Winmarleigh Moss
Lancs 202 D4
Winnal Hereford 97 E9
Winnal Common
Hereford 97 E9
Winnall Hants 33 B7
Worcs 116 C5
Winnard's Perch Corn . .5 B8
Winnersh Wokingham . .65 E9
Winnington
Ches W 183 G10
Staffs 150 B4
Winnington Green
Shrops 148 G6
Winnothdale Staffs . .169 G8
Winscales Cumb 228 F6
Winscombe N Som . . .44 B2
Winsdon Hill Luton . .103 G11
Winsford
Ches W 167 B10
Som 42 G2
Winsham Devon 40 F3
Som 28 F5
Winshill Staffs 152 E5
Winsh-wen Swansea . .57 B7
Winsick Derbys 170 B6
Winskill Cumb 231 D7
Winslade Devon 24 D5
Hants 49 D7
Winsley N Yorks 214 G4
Wilts 61 G10
Winslow Bucks 102 F5
Winslow Mill
Hereford 98 D2
Winson Glos 81 D9
Winson Green
W Mid 133 F10
Winsor Hants 32 E4
Winstanley Gtr Man . .194 G5
Winstanleys
Gtr Man 194 F5
Winster Cumb 221 G8
Derbys 170 C2
Winston Durham 224 B2
Suff 126 E3
Winstone Glos 81 D7
Winston Green Suff . .126 E3
Winswell Devon 25 E7
Winterborne Bassett
Wilts 62 E6
Winterborne Came
Dorset 17 D10
Winterborne Clenston
Dorset 30 G4
Winterborne
Herringston Dorset . .17 D9
Winterborne Houghton
Dorset 30 G4
Winterborne Kingston
Dorset 18 B3
Winterborne Monkton
Dorset 17 D9
Winterborne Muston
Dorset 18 B3
Winterborne Stickland
Dorset 30 F4
Winterborne Tomson
Dorset 18 B3
Winterborne
Whitechurch
Dorset 30 G4
Winterborne Zelston
Dorset 18 B3
Winterbourne Kent . . .54 B5
S Glos 60 C6
W Berks 64 E3
Winterbourne Abbas
Dorset 17 C8
Winterbourne Bassett
Wilts 62 E6
Winterbourne Dauntsey
Wilts 47 G7

Winterbourne Down
S Glos 61 D7
Winterbourne Earls
Wilts 47 G7
Winterbourne Gunner
Wilts 47 F7
Winterbourne Monkton
Dorset 17 D9
Winterbourne
Steepleton Dorset . .17 D8
Winterbourne Stoke
Wilts 46 E5
Winterbrook Oxon . . .64 B6
Winterburn N Yorks . .204 B4
Winterfield Bath 45 B7
Winter Gardens
Essex 69 C9
Winterhay Green
Som 28 D5
Winterhead N Som . . .44 B2
Winteringham
N Lincs 200 C2
Winterley Ches E 168 D2
Wintersett
W Yorks 197 D11
Wintershill Hants 33 D8
Winterton N Lincs . . .200 C2
Winterton-on-Sea
Norf 161 F10
Winter Well Som 28 C3
Winthorpe Lincs 175 B9
Notts 172 D4
Winton BCP 19 C7
Cumb 222 C5
E Sus 23 E8
Gtr Man 184 B3
N Yorks 225 F8
Wintringham
N Yorks 217 E7
Winwick Cambs 138 G2
Warr 183 C10
Winwick Quay
Warr 183 C10
Winyard's Gap Dorset .29 F7
Winyates Worcs 117 D11
Winyates Green
Worcs 117 D11
Wirksworth Derbys . . .170 E3
Wirksworth Moor
Derbys 170 E4
Wirswall Ches E 167 G8
Wisbech Cambs 139 B9
Wisbech St Mary
Cambs 139 B8
Wisborough Green
W Sus 35 B8
Wiseton Notts 188 D2
Wishanger Glos 80 D6
Wishaw N Lanark 268 D5
Warks 134 E3
Wisley Sur 50 B5
Wispington Lincs 190 G2
Wissenden Kent 54 E2
Wissett Suff 127 B7
Wistanstow Shrops . .131 F8
Wistanswick Shrops . .150 D3
Wistaston Ches E 167 E11
Wistaston Green
Ches E 167 E11
Wiston Pembs 73 B8
S Lanark 259 C11
W Sus 35 E10
Wiston Mains
S Lanark 259 C11
Wistow Cambs 138 G5
Leics 136 D2
N Yorks 207 F7
Wiswell Lancs 203 F10
Witcham Cambs 139 G9
Witchampton Dorset . .31 F7
Witchford Cambs 123 B10
Witcombe Som 29 C7
Witham Essex 88 C4
Witham Friary Som . . .45 E8
Witham on the Hill
Lincs 155 F11
Witham St Hughs
Lincs 172 C5
Withcall Lincs 190 E3
Withdean Brighton . . .36 F4
Witherenden Hill
E Sus 37 B10
Withergate Norf 160 D5
Witheridge Devon 26 E4
Witheridge Hill Oxon . .65 C7
Witherley Leics 134 D6
Withermarsh Green
Suff 107 D10
Withern Lincs 190 E6
Withernsea
E Yorks 201 B10
Withernwick
E Yorks 209 F9
Withersdale Street
Suff 142 G5
Withersdane Kent 54 D5
Withersfield Suff 106 B3
Witherslack Cumb . . .211 C8
Witherwack T&W 243 F9
Withial Som 44 F5
Withiel Corn 5 B9
Withiel Florey Som . . .42 G3
Withielgoose Corn 5 B10
Withielgoose Mills
Corn 5 B10
Withington Glos 81 B8
Gtr Man 184 C5
Hereford 97 C11
Shrops 149 G11
Staffs 151 B11
Withington Green
Ches E 184 G4
Withington Marsh
Hereford 97 C11
Withleigh Devon 26 E6
Withnell Lancs 194 C6
Withnell Fold Lancs . .194 C6
Withybed Green
Worcs 117 C10
Withybrook Som 45 D7

Withybrook continued
Warks 135 G8
Withybush Pembs 73 B7
Withycombe Som 41 F11
Som 42 E4
Withycombe Raleigh
Devon 14 E6
Withyditch Bath 45 B8
Withyham E Sus 52 F3
Withy Mills Bath 45 B7
Withymoor Village
W Mid 133 F8
Withypool Som 41 F10
Withystakes Staffs . . .169 E7
Withywood Bristol 60 F5
Witley Sur 50 F2
Witnells End Worcs . .132 G5
Witney Oxon 82 C5
Wittersham Kent 38 B5
Wittering Pboro 137 C11
Wittersham Kent 38 B5
Witton Angus 293 F7
Norf 142 B6
W Mid 133 E11
Worcs 117 E7
Witton Bridge Norf . .160 C6
Witton Gilbert
Durham 233 B10
Witton Hill Worcs . . .116 E5
Witton-le-Wear
Durham 233 E8
Witton Park Durham . .233 E9
Wiveliscombe Som . . .27 B9
Wivelrod Hants 49 F7
Wivelsfield E Sus 36 C4
Wivelsfield Green
E Sus 36 C5
Wivenhoe Essex 107 G10
Wivenhoe Cross
Essex 107 G10
Wiveton Norf 177 E8
Wix Essex 108 F3
Wixams Bedford 103 C10
Wixford Warks 117 G11
Wixhill Shrops 149 D11
Wixoe Suff 106 C4
Woburn C Beds 103 E8
Woburn Sands
M Keynes 103 D8
Wofferwood Common
Hereford 116 G3
Wokefield Park
W Berks 65 F7
Woking Sur 50 B4
Wokingham
Wokingham 65 F10
Wolborough Devon . . .14 G3
Woldhurst W Sus 22 C5
Woldingham Sur 51 B11
Woldingham Garden
Village Sur 51 B11
Wold Newton
E Yorks 217 E10
NE Lincs 190 B2
Wolfclyde S Lanark . .260 B2
Wolferd Green Norf . .142 D5
Wolferlow Hereford . .116 E3
Wolferton Norf 158 D3
Wolfhampcote
Warks 119 D10
Wolfhill Perth 286 D5
Wolf's Castle Pembs . .91 F9
Wolfsdale Pembs 91 G8
Wolfsdale Hill Pembs . .91 G8
Woll Borders 261 E11
Wollaston N Nhants . .121 E8
Shrops 148 G6
W Mid 133 G7
Wollaton
Nottingham 153 B10
Wollerton Shrops 150 C2
Wollerton Wood
Shrops 150 C2
Wollescote W Mid . . .133 G8
Wollrig Borders 261 E11
Wolsingham
Durham 233 D7
Wolstanton Staffs . . .168 F5
Wolstenholme
Gtr Man 195 D11
Wolston Warks 119 B8
Wolsty Cumb 238 G4
Wolterton Norf 160 C3
Wolvercote Oxon 83 D7
Wolverham Ches W . .182 F6
Wolverhampton
W Mid 133 D8
Wolverley Shrops 149 C9
Worcs 116 B6
Wolverstone Devon . . .27 G10
Wolverton Hants 48 B5
Kent 55 E9
M Keynes 102 C6
Shrops 131 F9
Warks 118 E4
Wilts 45 G9
Wolverton Common
Hants 48 B5
Wolvesnewton Mon . . .79 F7
Wolvey Warks 135 F8
Wolvey Heath
Warks 135 F8
Wolviston Stockton . .234 F5
Womaston Powys 114 E5
Wombleton N Yorks . .216 C3
Wombourne Staffs . . .133 E7
Wombridge Telford . . .150 G3
Wombwell S Yorks . . .197 G11
Womenswold Kent . . .55 C8
Womersley N Yorks . .198 D4
Wonastow Mon 79 C7
Wonderstone
N Som 43 D10
Wonersh Sur 50 D4
Wonford Devon 14 C4
Wonson Devon 13 D9
Wonston Dorset 30 F2
Hants 48 F3
Wooburn Bucks 66 B2
Wooburn Green
Bucks 66 B2

Wood Pembs 91 G7
Som 28 D4
Woodacott Cross
Devon 24 F5
Woodale N Yorks 213 D10
Woodbank Argyll 255 F7
Ches W 182 G5
Shrops 131 F11
Woodbastwick Norf . .160 F6
Woodbeck Notts 188 F3
Wood Bevington
Warks 117 G11
Woodborough
Notts 171 F10
Wilts 46 B6
Woodbridge Dorset . . .30 E2
Glos 81 C8
Northumb 253 F7
Suff 108 B5
Woodbridge Hill Sur . .50 C3
Woodbridge Walk
Suff 109 B7
Wood Burcote
N Nhants 102 B3
Woodburn Common
Bucks 66 B2
Woodburn Moor
Bucks 84 G6
Woodbury Devon 14 D6
Woodbury Salterton
Devon 14 D6
Woodchester Glos 80 E4
Woodchurch Kent 54 G2
Mers 182 D3
Woodcock Wilts 45 E11
Woodcock Heath
Staffs 151 D11
Woodcock Hill Herts . .85 G9
W Mid 133 G10
Woodcombe Som 42 D3
Woodcot Hants 33 G9
Woodcote London 67 G10
Oxon 64 C6
Sur 51 B8
Telford 150 F5
Woodcote Green
London 67 G9
Worcs 117 C8
Woodcott Hants 48 C2
Woodcroft Glos 79 F8
Woodcutts Dorset 31 D7
Wood Dalling Norf . . .159 D11
Wooddisford Cambs . .124 F3
Woodeaton Oxon 83 C8
Wood Eaton Staffs . .150 F6
Wooden Pembs 73 D10
Wooden Green Ches E .185 D7
Woodend Ches E 185 D7
Cumb 219 C10
Cumb 220 F3
Cumb 229 F10
Cumb 229 G7
Essex 87 C9
Fife 280 B4
Notts 171 C7
Staffs 152 D3
W Loth 279 F11
W Nhants 102 B2
W Sus 22 B4
Wood End Bedford . . .103 B10
Bedford 121 F11
Bucks 102 E5
C Beds 103 C9
Gtr Man 196 F2
Hereford 98 C2
Herts 104 F6
Warks 118 C2
Warks 134 D4
Warks 134 F5
Windsor 66 E2
W Mid 133 C8
W Mid 135 G7
Wood Enderby
Lincs 174 C3
Woodend Green
Essex 105 F11
W Nhants 102 B2
Wood End Green
London 66 C5
Woodend Ho
Argyll 275 G11
Woodfalls Wilts 31 C11
Woodfield Glos 80 F2
Oxon 101 G11
S Ayrs 257 E8
Wood Field Sur 51 B7
Woodford Corn 24 E2
Devon 8 E5
Glos 79 F11
Gtr Man 184 E5
London 86 G6
N Nhants 121 B9
Plym 7 D10
Som 42 E5
Som 44 E4
Woodford Bridge
London 86 G6
Woodford Green
London 86 G6
Woodford Halse
W Nhants 119 G10
Woodford Wells
London 86 G6
Woodgate Devon 27 D10
Norf 159 F10
W Mid 133 G9
Worcs 117 C8
W Sus 22 C6
Wood Gate Staffs 152 D3
Woodgate Hill
Gtr Man 195 E10
Woodgates End
Essex 105 F11
Woodgates Green
Worcs 116 C2
Woodgate Valley
W Mid 133 G10

Woodgreen Hants . . .31 D11
Oxon 82 C5
Wood Green Essex . . .86 E6
London. 86 G4
Norf. 142 E4
W Mid 133 D9
Worcs 116 D6
Woodhall Herts. 86 C2
Wood Hall Essex . . .105 E9
Woodhall Hills
W Yorks 205 F10
Woodhall Spa
Lincs 173 C11
Woodham Bucks. . . .84 B2
Durham 233 F11
Sur. 66 G4
Woodham Ferrers
Essex 88 F3
Woodham Mortimer
Essex. 88 E4
Woodham Walter
Essex 88 D4
Woodhatch Sur. 51 D9
Woodhaven Fife . . .287 E8
Wood Hayes W Mid. .133 C8
Woodhead Aberds . .303 F7
Woodheads
Borders 271 F10
Woodhey Gtr Man . .195 D9
Mers 182 D4
Woodhey Green
Ches E 167 E3
Woodhill Essex 88 E3
N Som 60 D3
Shrops. 132 G4
Som 28 B5
Woodhorn Northumb .253 F7
Woodhouse Cumb . .211 C10
Cumb. 219 B9
Hants. 47 D11
Leics 153 F10
N Lincs 199 F9
S Yorks 186 D6
W Yorks 196 C6
W Yorks 197 C11
W Yorks 205 E7
W Yorks 205 F11
Wood House Lancs. 203 C10
Woodhouse Down
S Glos. 60 B6
Woodhouse Eaves
Leics 153 G10
Woodhouse Green
Staffs. 168 C6
Woodhouselee
Midloth 270 C4
Woodhouselees
Dumfries 239 C9
Woodhouse Mill
S Yorks. 186 D6
Woodhouse Park
Gtr Man 184 D4
Woodhouses
Ches W. 183 F8
Cumb. 239 G8
Gtr Man 184 C3
Gtr Man 196 B6
Staffs. 133 B11
Staffs. 152 F3
Woodhurst Cambs . .122 B6
Woodingdean
Brighton 36 F5
Woodington Hants. . .32 C4
Woodkirk W Yorks . .197 C9
Woodlake Dorset . . .18 C3
Woodland
Cumb. 210 B4
Devon. 8 B5
Devon 8 D2
Durham 233 F7
Kent. 54 E6
Woodland Head
Devon 13 B11
Woodlands
Aberdeen 293 B10
Aberds 293 D9
Aberds. 303 G8
Dorset 31 F9
Dumfries 238 B3
Gtr Man 185 B7
Hants. 32 E4
Highld 300 C5
Kent. 68 G5
London. 67 D7
N Yorks. 206 C2
Som 43 E7
Som 44 F4
S Yorks. 198 F4
Wokingham 65 C9
W Yorks 196 B5
Woodlands Common
Dorset 31 F9
Woodlands Park
Windsor. 65 D11
Woodlands St Mary
W Berks. 63 E10
Staffs. 152 E2
Wood Lane Shrops. .149 C8
Staffs. 168 E4
Wood Lanes Ches E .184 E6
Woodleigh Devon. . . .8 F4

Woodlesford
W Yorks 197 B11
Woodley Gtr Man . . .184 C6
Hants. 32 C5
Wokingham 65 E9
Woodley Green
Wokingham 65 E9
Woodleys Oxon 82 B6
Woodlinkin Derbys. .170 F6
Woodloes Park
Warks 118 D5
Woodmancote Glos. .80 F3
Glos. 81 D8
Glos. 99 F9
Worcs 99 C8
W Sus 22 B3
W Sus 36 E2
Woodmancott Hants. .48 E5
Woodmansey
E Yorks. 209 F7
Woodmansgreen
W Sus 34 B5
Woodmans Green
E Sus 38 D3
Woodmansterne Sur. .51 B9
Woodmill Staffs. . . .152 E2
Woodminton Wilts. . .31 C8
Woodnesborough
Kent. 55 B10
Woodnewton
N Nhants 137 E10
Woodnook Lancs . . .195 B9
Lincs 155 C8
Wood Norton Norf. .159 D10
Worcs 99 B10
Woodplumpton
Lancs 202 G6
Woodram Som 28 D2
Woodrising Norf. . . .141 C9
Wood Road Gtr Man .195 E9
Woodrow Bucks 84 F6
Cumb 229 B10
Dorset 30 E3
Dorset 30 F2
Worcs 117 B7
Worcs 117 D11
Wood Row
W Yorks 197 B11
Woods Hereford. . . .96 B5
Woods Bank W Mid .133 D9
Wood's Corner
E Sus 23 B11
Woodsden Kent 53 G9
Woodseaves Derbys. .185 C7
Wood Seats S Yorks .186 B4
Woodseaves Shrops. .150 C3
Staffs. 150 D5
Woodsend Pembs . . .72 C5
Wilts 63 D8
Woods End Gtr Man .184 B2
Woodsetton W Mid. .133 E8
Woodsetts S Yorks . .187 E9
Woodsfield Worcs . . .98 B6
Woodsfold Lancs . . .202 F5
Woodsford Dorset . .17 C11
Wood's Green
E Sus 52 G6
Woodside
Aberdeen 293 C11
Aberds. 303 E10
Bedford 121 G11
Brack. 66 E2
C Beds 85 B9
Ches E 167 C10
Cumb 239 G7
Derbys. 170 G5
Derbys. 187 G7
Dumfries 238 B2
Essex. 87 E7
Fife 287 G8
Hants. 20 C2
Herts. 85 E10
Herts. 86 D3
IoW 20 C6
London. 67 F10
N Lincs 199 G8
Perth 286 D6
Shrops. 130 G6
Telford. 132 C3
W Mid 133 F8
W Yorks 196 B6
Woodside Green
Essex. 87 B8
Kent. 54 C2
Woodside of Arbeadie
Aberds. 293 D9
Woodside Park
London. 86 G3
Woods Moor
Gtr Man 184 D6
Woodspeen W Berks .64 F2
Woodspring Priory
N Som 59 F10
Wood Stanway Glos. .99 E11
Woodstock Kent 70 G2
Oxon 82 B6
Pembs 91 F10
Woodston Pboro . . .138 D3
Wood Street Norf. . .161 E7
Sur. 50 C3
Wood Street Village
Sur. 50 C3
Woodthorpe Derbys .187 G7
Leics 153 F10
Lincs 190 G6
Notts 171 G9
York 207 D7

Woodton Norf 142 E5
Woodtown Devon. . . .24 C6
Devon 25 B7
Woodvale Mers. 193 E10
Woodville Derbys. . .152 F6
Dorset 30 C4
Woodville Feus
Angus 287 C10
Woodwall Green
Staffs. 150 C5
Wood Walton
Cambs 138 G4
Woodway Oxon 64 C4
Woodway Park
W Mid 135 G7
Woodwell N Nhants .121 B9
Woodwick Orkney . .314 D3
Woodworth Green
Ches E 167 D9
Woodyates Dorset . .31 D8
Woody Bay Devon. . .41 D7
Woofferton Shrops. 115 D10
Wookey Som 44 D4
Wookey Hole Som . .44 D4
Wool Dorset 18 D2
Woolacombe Devon. .40 E3
Woolage Green Kent. .55 D8
Woolage Village
Kent. 55 C8
Woolaston Glos. 79 F9
Woolaston Common
Glos. 79 E9
Woolaston Slade
Glos. 79 E9
Woolaston Woodside
Glos. 79 E9
Woolavington Som . .43 E10
Woolbeding W Sus . .34 C5
Wooldale W Yorks. . .197 F7
Wooler Northumb . . .263 D11
Woolfall Heath
Mers 182 C6
Woolfardisworthy
Devon 26 F4
Woolfardisworthy or
Woolsery Devon. . . .24 C4
Woolfold Gtr Man . . .195 E9
Woolfords Cottages
S Lanark. 269 D10
Woolford's Water
Dorset 29 F11
Woolgarston Dorset . .18 E5
Woolgreaves
W Yorks 197 D10
Woolhampton
W Berks 64 F5
Woolhope Hereford . .98 D2
Woolhope Cockshoot
Hereford 98 D2
Woolland Dorset 30 F3
Woollard Bath 60 G6
Woollaston Staffs. . .151 F7
Woollaton Devon. . . .25 E7
Woollensbrook Herts. .86 C5
Woolley Bath 61 F8
Cambs 122 C3
Corn. 24 D3
Derbys. 170 C5
W Yorks 197 E10
Woolley Bridge
Gtr Man 185 B8
Woolley Green
Wilts 61 G10
Windsor. 65 C11
Woolmere Green
Worcs 117 E9
Woolmer Green
Herts 86 B3
Woolmer Hill Sur. . . .49 G11
Woolmersdon Som . .43 G9
Woolminstone Som . .28 F6
Woolpack Corner
Kent. 53 F11
Woolpit Suff. 125 E9
Woolpit Green Suff. .125 E9
Woolpit Heath Suff . .125 E9
Woolridge Glos. 98 G6
Woolsbridge Dorset. .31 F9
Woolscott Warks . . .119 D9
Woolsery or
Woolfardisworthy
Devon 24 C4
Woolsgrove Devon. . .26 G3
Woolsington T&W . .242 D5
Woolstanwood
Ches E 167 D11
Woolstaston Shrops. 131 D9
Woolsthorpe Lincs. .155 E8
Woolsthorpe by Belvoir
Lincs 154 C6
Woolsthorpe-by-
Colsterworth Lincs .155 E8
Woolston
Corn. 6 B5
Devon. 8 G4
Shrops. 131 F8
Shrops. 148 E6
Som 29 B10
Som 42 F5
Soton. 32 E6
Warr 183 D10
Woolstone Glos. 99 E9
M Keynes. 103 D7
Oxon 63 B9
Woolston Green Devon. 8 B5
Woolton Mers 182 D6
Woolton Hill Hants. . .64 G2

Woolvers Hill
N Som 59 G11
Woolverstone Suff. . .108 D3
Woolverton Som. 45 C9
Woolwell Devon 7 C10
Woolwich London . . .68 D2
Woolwich Ferry
London. 68 D2
Woon Corn 5 D10
Woonton Hereford . .115 E10
Hereford 115 G7
Wooperton
Northumb 264 E2
Wooplaw Borders . . .271 G9
Woore Shrops 168 G2
Wooton Shrops 115 C11
Shrops. 132 F5
Wootten Green Suff. .126 C4
Wootton Bedford . . .103 B10
Hants. 19 B10
Hereford 97 D11
Hereford 114 G6
IoW 20 C6
Kent. 55 B10
N Lincs 200 D5
Oxon 82 B6
Oxon 83 E7
Shrops. 115 B9
Shrops. 148 G6
Staffs. 150 D6
Staffs. 169 F10
W Nhants 120 F5
Wootton Bourne End
Bedford 103 B9
Wootton Bridge IoW. .20 C6
Wootton Broadmead
Bedford 103 C10
Wootton Common
IoW 20 C6
Wootton Courtenay
Som 42 E2
Wootton Fitzpaine
Dorset 16 B3
Wootton Green
C Beds 103 C9
W Mid 118 B4
Wootton Rivers Wilts .63 G7
Woottons Staffs 151 B11
Wootton St Lawrence
Hants. 48 C5
Wootton Wawen
Warks 118 E3
Worbarrow Dorset . . .18 F3
Worcester Worcs . . .117 F7
Worcester Park
London. 67 F8
Wordsley W Mid. . . .133 F7
Wordwell Suff. 124 C6
Worfield Shrops 132 D5
Worgret Dorset 18 D4
Work Orkney. 314 E4
Workhouse Common
Norf. 161 E7
Workhouse End
Bedford 122 G2
Workhouse Green
Suff 107 D8
Workhouse Hill
Essex. 107 E9
Workington Cumb . .228 F5
Worksop Notts 187 F9
Worlaby Lincs 190 F4
N Lincs 200 E4
Worlds End Hants. . . .33 E10
W Mid 134 G2
World's End
Bucks. 84 D5
London. 86 F4
Suff 125 F9
W Sus 36 D4
Worle N Som. 59 G11
Worlebury N Som . . .59 G10
Worleston Ches E . . .167 D11
Worley Glos. 80 F4
Worlingham Suff 143 F8
Worlington Devon . . .40 G3
Suff 124 C4
Worlingworth Suff. . .126 D4
Wormadale Shetland .313 J5
Wormald Green
N Yorks 214 G6
Wormbridge Hereford .97 E8
Wormbridge Common
Hereford 97 E8
Wormegay Norf. 158 G3
Wormelow Tump
Hereford 97 E9
Wormhill Derbys. . . .185 G10
Worminghall Bucks. .83 D10
Wormington Glos. . . .99 D10
Worminster Som 44 E5
Wormiston Ho Fife. .287 G10
Wormit Fife. 287 E7
Wormleighton
Warks 119 G8
Wormley Herts 86 D5
Sur. 50 F2
Wormleybury Herts. . .86 D5
Wormley West End
Herts. 86 D4
Worms Ash Worcs . .117 C8
Wormshill Kent. 53 B11
Worms Hill Kent 53 F8
Wormsley Hereford . .97 B8
Wornish Nook
Ches E 168 B4
Worplesdon Sur. 50 C3

Worrall S Yorks 186 C4
Worrall Hill Glos. . . .79 C10
Worsbrough
S Yorks. 197 G11
Worsbrough Bridge
S Yorks. 197 G11
Worsbrough Common
S Yorks. 197 F10
Worsbrough Dale
S Yorks. 197 G11
Worsham Oxon 82 C3
Worsley Gtr Man 195 G8
Worsley Hall
Gtr Man 194 F5
Worsley Mesnes
Gtr Man 194 G5
Worstead Norf. 160 D6
Worsthorne Lancs . .204 G3
Worston Devon 7 E11
Lancs 203 E11
Worswell Devon 7 F10
Worten Kent. 54 E3
Worth Kent. 55 B10
Som 44 D4
W Sus 51 F9
Worth Abbey
W Sus 51 G10
Wortham Suff 125 B11
Worthen Shrops 130 C6
Worthenbury Wrex . .166 F6
Worthing Norf. 159 F9
W Sus 35 G10
Worthington Leics . .153 E8
Worth Matravers
Dorset 18 F5
Worthy Som 41 D11
Worthybrook Mon . . .79 C7
Worting Hants 48 C6
Wortley Glos. 80 G3
S Yorks. 186 B4
W Yorks. 205 G11
Worton N Yorks 223 G9
Oxon 83 C7
Wilts 46 B3
Wortwell Norf. 142 G5
Wotherton Shrops. . .130 C5
Wothorpe Pboro 137 B10
Wotter Devon 7 C11
Wotton Glos. 80 B4
Sur. 50 D6
Wotton-under-Edge
Glos. 80 G3
Wotton Underwood
Bucks. 83 B11
Woughton on the Green
M Keynes. 103 D7
Woughton Park
M Keynes. 103 D7
Wouldham Kent 69 G8
Woundale Shrops . . .132 E5
Wrabness Essex 108 E3
Wraes Aberds. 302 F5
Wrafton Devon. 40 F3
Wragby Lincs 189 F10
W Yorks 198 D2
Wragholme Lincs . . .190 B5
Wramplingham
Norf. 142 B2
Wrangaton Devon. 8 D3
Wrangbrook
W Yorks 198 E3
Wrangham Aberds . .302 F6
Wrangle Lincs 174 E6
Wrangle Bank Lincs .174 E6
Wrangle Lowgate
Lincs 174 E6
Wrangle Low Ground
Lincs 174 E6
Wrangway Som 27 D10
Wrantage Som 28 C4
Wrawby N Lincs 200 F4
Wraxall Dorset. 29 G9
N Som 60 E3
Som 44 F6
Wray Lancs 212 G2
Wray Common Sur . .51 C9
Wraysbury Windsor . .66 E4
Wrayton Lancs 212 F2
Wrea Green Lancs . .202 G3
Wreaks End Cumb . .210 B4
Wreath Som 28 F4
Wreay Cumb. 230 B4
Cumb 230 G4
Wrecclesham Sur 49 D11
Wrekenton T&W. . . .243 F7
Wrelton N Yorks. 216 B5
Wrenbury Ches E. . . .167 F9
Wrenbury cum Frith
Ches E 167 F9
Wrench Green
N Yorks 217 B9
Wreningham Norf . . .142 D3
Wrentham Suff 143 G9
Wrenthorpe
W Yorks 197 C10
Wrentnall Shrops . . .131 C8
Wressle E Yorks 207 G10
N Lincs 200 F3
Wrestlingworth
C Beds 104 B5
Wretham Norf. 141 F8
Wretton Norf 140 D3
Wrexham Wrex 166 E4
Wreyland Devon 13 E11
Wribbenhall Worcs . .116 B5
Wrickton Shrops. . . .132 F2
Wrightington Bar
Lancs 194 E4

Wrights Green
Warr 183 E10
Wright's Green Essex .87 B8
Wrinehill Staffs. 168 F3
Wringsdown Corn . . .12 D2
Wrington N Som 60 G3
Writhlington Bath . . .45 C8
Writtle Essex 87 D11
Wrockwardine
Telford. 150 G2
Wrockwardine Wood
Telford. 150 G3
Wroot N Lincs 199 G8
Wrose W Yorks 205 F9
Wrotham Kent. 52 B6
Wrotham Heath Kent .52 B6
Wroughton Swindon. .62 C6
Wroxall IoW 21 F7
Warks 118 C4
Wroxeter Shrops. . . .131 B11
Wroxham Norf. 160 F6
Wroxton Oxon 101 C8
Wyaston Derbys 169 G11
Wyatt's Green Essex . .87 F9
Wybers Wood
NE Lincs 201 F8
Wyberton Lincs 174 G4
Wyboston Bedford . .122 F3
Wybunbury Ches E . .168 F2
Wych Cross E Sus . . .52 G2
Wychnor Staffs 152 F3
Wychnor Bridges
Staffs. 152 F3
Wyck Hants. 49 F9
Wyck Rissington
Glos. 100 G3
Wycliffe Durham 224 C2
Wycoller Lancs 204 F4
Wycomb Leics 154 E5
Wycombe Marsh
Bucks. 84 G5
Wyddial Herts. 105 E7
Wydra N Yorks 205 D10
Wye Kent. 54 E5
Wyebanks Kent. 54 C2
Wyegate Green Glos. .79 D9
Wyesham Mon. 79 C8
Wyfordby Leics 154 F5
Wyke Dorset. 30 B3
Shrops. 132 C2
Sur. 50 C2
W Yorks 197 B7
Wyke Champflower
Som 45 G7
Wykeham
Lincs 156 D5
N Yorks. 216 B6
N Yorks. 217 C9
Wyken Shrops 132 E5
W Mid 135 G7
Wyke Regis Dorset . . .17 F9
Wykey Shrops. 149 E7
Wykin Leics 135 D8
Wylam Northumb 242 E4
Wylde Hereford 115 D9
Wylde Green W Mid .134 E2
Wyllie Caerph. 77 G11
Wylye Wilts 46 F4
Wymans Brook Glos. .99 G8
Wymbush M Keynes. .102 D6
Wymering Ptsmth. . . .33 F10
Wymeswold Leics . . .154 E2
Wymington Bedford . .121 E9
Wymondham Leics . .155 F7
Norf. 142 D2
Wymondley Bury
Herts. 104 F4
Wymott Lancs 194 C4
Wyndham Bridgend . .76 G2
Wyndham Park
V Glam 58 D5
Wynds Point Hereford .98 C5
Wynford Eagle
Dorset 17 B7
Wyng Orkney. 314 G3
Wynn's Green
Hereford 98 B2
Wynyard Village
Stockton. 234 F4
Wyre Piddle Worcs . . .99 B9
Wysall Notts 154 D2
Wyson Hereford 115 D10
Wythall Worcs 117 B11
Wytham Oxon 83 D7
Wythburn Cumb 220 C6
Wythenshawe
Gtr Man 184 D4
Wythop Mill Cumb . .229 F9
Wyton Cambs 122 C5
E Yorks. 209 G9
Wyverstone Suff 125 D10
Wyverstone Green
Suff 125 D10
Wyverstone Street
Suff 125 D10
Wyville Lincs 155 D7
Wyvis Lodge Highld . .300 B4

Y

Yaddlethorpe
N Lincs 199 F11
Yafford IoW 20 E4
Yafforth N Yorks 224 G6

Yair Borders 261 C11
Yalberton Torbay 9 D7
Yalding Kent 53 C7
Yanley N Som 60 F5
Yanworth Glos. 81 C9
Yapham E Yorks 207 C11
Yapton W Sus. 35 G7
Yarberry N Som. 43 B11
Yarborough
NE Lincs 201 F9
Yarbridge IoW 21 D8
Yarburgh Lincs 190 C5
Yarcombe Devon 28 F2
Yard Som 42 F5
Yarde Som 42 F5
Yardhurst Kent 54 E3
Yardley W Mid. 134 F2
Yardley Gobion
W Nhants. 102 C5
Yardley Hastings
W Nhants. 121 F7
Yardley Wood
W Mid 118 B2
Yardro Powys. 114 F4
Yarford Som 28 B2
Yarhampton Worcs . .116 D5
Yarhampton Cross
Worcs 116 D5
Yarkhill Hereford. 98 C2
Yarlet Staffs 151 D8
Yarley Som 44 D4
Yarlington Som 29 B11
Yarlside Cumb. 210 F4
Yarm Stockton 225 C8
Yarmouth IoW 20 D3
Yarnacott Devon 40 G6
Yarnbrook Wilts 45 C11
Yarnfield Staffs 151 C7
Yarningale Common
Warks 118 D3
Yarnscombe Devon . .25 C9
Yarnton Oxon 83 C7
Yarpole Hereford. . . .115 E9
Yarrow
Borders 261 D9
Northumb 250 F6
Som 43 D11
Yarrow Feus
Borders 261 D8
Yarrowford
Borders 261 C10
Yarsop Hereford 97 B8
Yarwell N Nhants . . .137 D11
Yate S Glos. 61 C8
Yateley Hants. 65 G10
Yate Rocks S Glos. . . .61 C8
Yatesbury Wilts. 62 E5
Yattendon W Berks . .64 E5
Yatton Hereford 115 D8
N Som 60 F2
Yatton Keynell
Wilts 61 D11
Yaverland IoW 21 D8
Yawthorpe Lincs 188 C5
Yaxham Norf 159 G10
Yaxley Cambs 138 E3
Suff 126 C2
Yazor Hereford 97 B8
Y Bala = *Bala* Gwyn . .147 B8
Y Bont Faen = *Cowbridge*
V Glam. 58 E3
Y Borth = *Borth*
Ceredig. 128 E2
Yeabridge Som. 28 D6
Yeading London. 66 C6
Yeadon W Yorks. 205 E10
Yealand Conyers
Lancs 211 E10
Yealand Redmayne
Lancs 211 D10
Yealand Storrs
Lancs 211 D9
Yealmbridge Devon . . .7 E11
Yealmpton Devon. 7 E11
Yearby Redcar 235 G8
Yearngill Cumb 229 C8
Yearsley N Yorks 215 E11
Yeaton Shrops 149 F8
Yeaveley Derbys 169 G11
Yedingham N Yorks . .217 D7
Yelden Bedford 121 D10
Yeldersley Hollies
Derbys. 170 G2
Yeldon Bedford 121 D10
Yelford Oxon 82 E5
Yelland Devon 40 G3
Yelling Cambs 122 E5
Yelsted Kent. 69 G10
Yelvertoft
W Nhants. 119 B11
Yelverton Devon 7 B10
Norf. 142 C5
Yenston Som 30 C2
Yeoford Devon 13 B11
Yeolmbridge Corn . . .12 D2
Yeo Mill Devon. 26 B4
Yeo Vale Devon 24 C6
Yeovil Som 29 D9
Yeovil Marsh Som. . . .29 C9
Yeovilton Som. 29 C8
Yerbeston Pembs 73 D9
Yesnaby Orkney. 314 E2
Yetlington Northumb .252 B2
Yetminster Dorset . . .29 E9
Yett N Lanark. 268 D5
Yettington Devon 15 D7
Yetts o' Muckhart
Clack 286 G4

Yew Green Warks. . . .118 D4
Yewhedges Kent. 54 B3
Yew Tree Gtr Man . . .185 B7
W Mid 133 D10
Yewtree Cross Kent. . .55 E7
Y Fali = *Valley*
Anglesey 178 D3
Y Felinheli = *Port Dinorwic*
Gwyn. 163 B8
Y Ferwig Ceredig. 92 B3
Y Ffôr Gwyn 145 B7
Y Gors Ceredig 112 B2
Y Gribyn Powys 129 E5
Yieldshields
S Lanark. 269 E7
Yiewsley London 66 C5
Yinstay Orkney. 314 E5
Y Mwmbwls = *The Mumbles*
Swansea 56 D6
Ynus-tawelog
Swansea 75 D10
Ynys Gwyn. 145 G3
Ynysboeth Rhondda . .77 F9
Ynysddu Caerph 77 G11
Ynysforgan Swansea .57 B8
Ynysgyfflog Gwyn. . .146 G2
Ynyshir Rhondda 77 G8
Ynys-isaf Powys 76 C3
Ynyslas Ceredig. 128 E2
Ynysmaerdy Neath. . . .57 B8
Rhondda 58 C4
Ynysmeudwy Neath. .76 D2
Neath. 76 D1
Ynys Tachwedd
Ceredig. 128 E2
Ynystawe Swansea . .75 E11
Ynyswen Powys. 76 C4
Rhondda 77 F7
Ynysybwl Rhondda . . .77 G9
Ynysygwas Neath. . . .57 C9
Yockenthwaite
N Yorks 213 D9
Yockleton Shrops . . .149 G7
Yodercott Devon. 27 E7
Yokefleet E Yorks . . .199 C10
Yoker W Dunb. 267 B10
Yonder Bognie
Aberds. 302 E5
Yondertown Devon 7 D11
Yopps Green Kent . . .52 C6
York Lancs 203 G10
York 207 C7
Yorkletts Kent. 70 G5
Yorkley Glos. 79 D10
Yorkley Slade Glos. . .79 D10
York Town Sur 65 G11
Yorton Shrops 149 E10
Yorton Heath
Shrops. 149 E10
Yottenfews Cumb . . .219 D10
Youlgrave
Derbys. 170 G2
Youlstone
Devon 24 D3
Youlthorpe
E Yorks. 207 B11
Youlton N Yorks 215 G9
Youngsbury Herts . . .86 B5
Young's End Essex. . .88 B2
Young Wood Lincs . .189 G10
Yoxall Staffs. 152 F2
Yoxford Suff. 127 D7
Y Pil = *Pyle* Bridgend . .57 E10
Yr Hôb = *Hope* Flint. .166 D4
Ysbyty Cynfyn
Ceredig. 112 B5
Ysbyty Ifan Conwy. . .164 F4
Ysbyty Ystwyth
Ceredig. 112 C4
Ysceifiog Flint 181 G11
Ysgeibion Denb. 165 D9
Yspitty Carms. 56 B5
Ystalyfera Neath 76 D3
Ystrad Rhondda 77 F7
Ystrad Aeron
Ceredig. 111 F10
Ystradfellte Powys . . .76 C6
Ystradffin Carms. 94 B5
Ystradgynlais
Powys. 76 C3
Ystradmeurig
Ceredig. 112 D4
Ystrad-mynach
Caerph. 77 G10
Ystradowen Carms. . .76 C2
V Glam 58 D4
Ystrad Uchaf
Powys 129 C11
Ystumtuen Ceredig. .112 B4
Ythanbank Aberds . .303 F9
Ythanwells Aberds. .302 F6
Ythsie Aberds. 303 F8

Z

Zeal Monachorum
Devon 26 G2
Zeals Wilts 45 G9
Zelah Corn 4 E6
Zennor Corn. 1 B5
Zoar Corn 3 F7
Zouch Notts 153 E10